Lecture Notes in Artificial Intelligence 3120

Edited by J. G. Carbonell and J. Siekmann

Subseries of Lecture Notes in Computer Science

John Shawe-Taylor Yoram Singer (Eds.)

Learning Theory

17th Annual Conference on Learning Theory, COLT 2004
Banff, Canada, July 1-4, 2004
Proceedings

Series Editors

Jaime G. Carbonell, Carnegie Mellon University, Pittsburgh, PA, USA
Jörg Siekmann, University of Saarland, Saarbrücken, Germany

Volume Editors

John Shawe-Taylor
University of Southampton
ISIS Group, School of Electronics and Computer Science
Southampton SO17 1BJ, UK
E-mail: jst@ecs.soton.ac.uk

Yoram Singer
Hebrew University
School of Computer Science and Engineering
Givat-Ram campus, Jerusalem 91904, Israel
E-mail: singer@cs.huji.ac.il

Library of Congress Control Number: 2004107575

CR Subject Classification (1998): I.2.6, I.2.3, I.2, F.4.1, F.2, F.1.1

ISSN 0302-9743
ISBN 3-540-22282-0 Springer-Verlag Berlin Heidelberg New York

Springer-Verlag is a part of Springer Science+Business Media

springeronline.com

Printed in Germany

Typesetting: Camera-ready by author, data conversion by PTP-Berlin, Protago-TeX-Production GmbH
Printed on acid-free paper SPIN: 11016298 06/3142 5 4 3 2 1 0

Preface

This volume contains papers presented at the 17th Annual Conference on Learning Theory (previously known as the Conference on Computational Learning Theory) held in Banff, Canada from July 1 to 4, 2004.

The technical program contained 43 papers selected from 107 submissions, 3 open problems selected from among 6 contributed, and 3 invited lectures. The invited lectures were given by Michael Kearns on 'Game Theory, Automated Trading and Social Networks', Moses Charikar on 'Algorithmic Aspects of Finite Metric Spaces', and Stephen Boyd on 'Convex Optimization, Semidefinite Programming, and Recent Applications'. These papers were not included in this volume.

The Mark Fulk Award is presented annually for the best paper co-authored by a student. This year the Mark Fulk award was supplemented with two further awards funded by the Machine Learning Journal and the National Information Communication Technology Centre, Australia (NICTA). We were therefore able to select three student papers for prizes. The students selected were Magalie Fromont for the single-author paper "Model Selection by Bootstrap Penalization for Classification", Daniel Reidenbach for the single-author paper "On the Learnability of E-Pattern Languages over Small Alphabets", and Ran Gilad-Bachrach for the paper "Bayes and Tukey Meet at the Center Point" (co-authored with Amir Navot and Naftali Tishby).

This year saw an exceptional number of papers submitted to COLT covering a wider range of topics than has previously been the norm. This exciting expansion of learning theory analysis to new models and tasks marks an important development in the growth of the area as well as in the linking with practical applications. The large number of quality submissions placed a heavy burden on the program committee of the conference: Shai Ben-David (Cornell University), Stephane Boucheron (Université Paris-Sud), Olivier Bousquet (Max Planck Institute), Sanjoy Dasgupta (University of California, San Diego), Victor Dalmau (Universitat Pompeu Fabra), Andre Elisseeff (IBM Zurich Research Lab), Thore Graepel (Microsoft Research Labs, Cambridge), Peter Grunwald (CWI, Amsterdam), Michael Jordan (University of California, Berkeley), Adam Kalai (Toyota Technological Institute), David McAllester (Toyota Technological Institute), Manfred Opper (University of Southampton), Alon Orlitsky (University of California, San Diego), Rob Schapire (Princeton University), Matthias Seeger (University of California, Berkeley), Satinder Singh (University of Michigan), Eiji Takimoto (Tohoku University), Nicolas Vayatis (Université Paris 6), Bin Yu (University of California, Berkeley) and Thomas Zeugmann (University at Lübeck). We are extremely grateful for their careful and thorough reviewing and for the detailed discussions that ensured the very high quality of the final program. We would like to have mentioned the subreviewers who assisted the program committee in reaching their assessments, but unfortunately space constraints do not permit us to include this long list of names and we must simply ask them to accept our thanks anonymously.

We particularly thank Rob Holte and Dale Schuurmans, the conference local chairs, as well as the registration chair Kiri Wagstaff. Together they handled the conference publicity and all the local arrangements to ensure a successful event. We would also like to thank Microsoft for providing the software used in the program committee deliberations, and Ofer Dekel for maintaining this software and the conference Web site. Bob Williamson and Jyrki Kivinen assisted the organization of the conference in their role as consecutive Presidents of the Association of Computational Learning, and heads of the COLT Steering Committee. We would also like to thank the ICML organizers for ensuring a smooth co-location of the two conferences and arranging for a 'kernel day' at the overlap on July 4. The papers appearing as part of this event comprise the last set of 8 full-length papers in this volume.

Finally, we would like to thank the Machine Learning Journal, the Pacific Institute for the Mathematical Sciences (PIMS), INTEL, SUN, the Informatics Circle of Research Excellence (iCORE), and the National Information Communication Technology Centre, Australia (NICTA) for their sponsorship of the conference. This work was also supported in part by the IST Programme of the European Community, under the PASCAL Network of Excellence, IST-2002-506778.

April, 2004

John Shawe-Taylor,
Yoram Singer
Program Co-chairs, COLT 2004

Sponsored by:

Table of Contents

Economics and Game Theory

OnLine Learning

Inductive Inference

Probabilistic Models

Boolean Function Learning

Empirical Processes

MDL

Generalisation I

Generalisation II

Clustering and Distributed Learning

Boosting

Kernels and Probabilities

Towards a Characterization of Polynomial Preference Elicitation with Value Queries in Combinatorial Auctions*
(Extended Abstract)

Paolo Santi[1**], Vincent Conitzer[2], and Tuomas Sandholm[2]

[1] Istituto di Informatica e Telematica, Pisa, 56124, Italy
paolo.santi@iit.cnr.it
[2] Dept. of Computer Science, Carnegie Mellon University
5000 Forbes Avenue Pittsburgh, PA 15213
{conitzer,sandholm}@cs.cmu.edu

Abstract. Communication complexity has recently been recognized as a major obstacle in the implementation of combinatorial auctions. In this paper, we consider a setting in which the auctioneer (elicitor), instead of passively waiting for the bids presented by the bidders, elicits the bidders' preferences (or valuations) by asking value queries. It is known that in the more general case (no restrictions on the bidders' preferences) this approach requires the exchange of an exponential amount of information. However, in practical economic scenarios we might expect that bidders' valuations are somewhat structured. In this paper, we consider several such scenarios, and we show that polynomial elicitation in these cases is often sufficient. We also prove that the family of "easy to elicit" classes of valuations is closed under union. This suggests that efficient preference elicitation is possible in a scenario in which the elicitor, contrary to what it is commonly assumed in the literature on preference elicitation, does not exactly know the class to which the function to elicit belongs. Finally, we discuss what renders a certain class of valuations "easy to elicit with value queries".

1 Introduction

Combinatorial auctions (CAs) have recently emerged as a possible mechanism to improve economic efficiency when many items are on sale. In a CA, bidders can present bids on bundle of items, and thus may easily express complementarities (i.e., the bidder values two items together more than the sum of the valuations of the single items), and substitutabilities (i.e., the two items together are worth less than the sum of the valuations of the single items) between the objects

* This work is supported in part by NSF under CAREER Award IRI-9703122, Grant IIS-9800994, ITR IIS-0081246, and ITR IIS-0121678.
** This work was done when the author was visiting the Dept. of Computer Science, Carnegie Mellon University.

J. Shawe-Taylor and Y. Singer (Eds.): COLT 2004, LNAI 3120, pp. 1–16, 2004.

on sale[1]. CAs can be applied, for instance, to sell spectrum licenses, pollution permits, land lots, and so on [9].

The implementation of CAs poses several challenges, including computing the optimal allocation of the items (also known as the winner determination problem), and efficiently communicating bidders' preferences to the auctioneer.

Historically, the first problem that has been addressed in the literature is winner determination. In [16], it is shown that solving the winner determination problem is NP-hard; even worse, finding a $n^{1/2-\epsilon}$-approximation (here, n is the number of bidders) to the optimal solution is NP-hard [18]. Despite these impossibility results, recent research has shown that in many scenarios the average-case performance of both exact and approximate winner determination algorithms is very good [4,13,17,18,22]. This is mainly due to the fact that, in practice, bidders' preferences (and, thus, bids) are somewhat structured, where the bid structure is usually induced by the economic scenario considered.

The communication complexity of CAs has been addressed only more recently. In particular, *preference elicitation*, where the auctioneer is enhanced by elicitor software that incrementally elicits the bidders' preferences using queries, has recently been proposed to reduce the communication burden. Elicitation algorithms based on different type of queries (e.g., rank, order, or value queries) have been proposed [6,7,12]. Unfortunately, a recent result by Nisan and Segal [15] shows that elicitation algorithms in the worst case have no hope of considerably reducing the communication complexity, because computing the optimal allocation requires the exchange of an exponential amount of information between the elicitor and the bidders. Indeed, the authors prove an even stronger negative result: obtaining a better approximation of the optimal allocation than that generated by auctioning off all objects as a bundle requires the exchange of an exponential amount of information. Thus, the communication burden produced by *any* combinatorial auction design that aims at producing a non-trivial approximation of the optimal allocation is overwhelming, unless the bidders' valuation functions display some structure. This is a far worse scenario than that occurring in single item auctions, where a good approximation to the optimal solution can be found by exchanging a very limited amount of information [3].

For this reason, elicitation in restricted classes of valuation functions has been studied [2,8,15,21]. The goal is to identify classes of valuation functions that are general (in the sense that they allow to express super-, or sub-additivity, or both, between items) and can be elicited in polynomial time.

Preference elicitation in CAs has recently attracted significant interest from machine learning theorists in general [6,21], and at COLT in particular [2].

1.1 Full Elicitation with Value Queries

In this paper, we consider a setting in which the elicitor's goal is *full* elicitation, i.e., learning the entire valuation function of all the bidders. This definition should be contrasted with the other definition of preference elicitation, in which

[1] In this paper, we will use also the terms super- and sub-additivity to refer complementarities and substitutabilities, respectively.

the elicitor's goal is to elicit enough information from the bidders so that the optimal allocation can be computed. In this paper, we call this type of elicitation *partial* elicitation. Note that, contrary to the case of partial elicitation, in full elicitation we can restrict attention to learning the valuation of a single bidder.

One motivation for studying full elicitation is that, once the full valuation functions of all the bidders are known to the auctioneer, the VCG payments [5,11, 20] can be computed without further message exchange. Since VCG payments prevent strategic bidding behavior [14], the communication complexity of full preference elicitation is an upper bound to the communication complexity of truthful mechanisms for combinatorial auctions.

In this paper, we focus our attention on a restricted case of full preference elicitation, in which the elicitor can ask only *value queries* (what is the value of a particular bundle?) to the bidders. Our interest in value queries is due to the fact that, from the bidders' point of view, these queries are very intuitive and easy to understand. Furthermore, value queries are in general easier to answer than, for instance, demand (given certain prices for the items, which would be your preferred bundle?) or rank (which is your most valuable bundle?) queries.

Full preference elicitation with value queries has been investigated in a few recent papers. In [21], Zinkevich et al. introduce two classes of valuation functions (read-once formulas and ToolboxDNF formulas) that can be elicited with a polynomial number of value queries. Read-once formulas can express both sub- and super-additivity between objects, while ToolboxDNF formulas can only express super-additive valuations. In [8], we have introduced another class of "easy to elicit with value queries" functions, namely k-wise dependent valuations. Functions in this class can display both sub- and super-additivity, and in general are not monotone[2] (i.e., they can express costly disposal).

1.2 Our Contribution

The contributions of this paper can be summarized as follows:

• We introduce the *hypercube representation* of a valuation function, which makes the contribution of every sub-bundle to the valuation of a certain bundle S explicit. This representation is a very powerful tool in the analysis of structural properties of valuations.

• We study several classes of "easy to elicit with value queries" valuations. Besides considering the classes already introduced in the literature, we introduce several new classes of polynomially elicitable valuations.

• We show that the family of "easy to elicit" classes of valuations is closed under union. More formally, we prove that, if $\mathbf{C_1}$ and $\mathbf{C_2}$ are classes of valuations elicitable asking at most $p_1(m)$ and $p_2(m)$ queries, respectively, then any function in $\mathbf{C_1} \bigcup \mathbf{C_2}$ is elicitable asking at most $p_1(m) + p_2(m) + 1$ queries. Furthermore, we prove that this bound cannot be improved.

[2] A valuation function f is *monotone* if $f(S) \geq f(S')$, for any $S' \subseteq S$. This property is also know as *free disposal*, meaning that bidders that receive extra items incur no cost for disposing them.

• The algorithm used to elicit valuations in $\mathbf{C_1} \bigcup \mathbf{C_2}$ might have super-polynomial running time (but asks only polynomially many queries). The question of whether a general polynomial *time* elicitation algorithm exists remains open. However, we present a polynomial time elicitation algorithm which, given any valuation function f in $\mathbf{RO_{+M}} \bigcup \mathbf{Tool_{-t}} \bigcup \mathbf{Tool_t} \bigcup \mathbf{G_2} \bigcup \mathbf{INT}$ (see Section 3 for the definition of the various classes of valuations), learns f correctly. This is an improvement over existing results, in which the elicitor is assumed to know exactly the class to which the valuation function belongs.

• In the last part of the paper, we discuss what renders a certain class of valuations "easy to elicit" with value queries. We introduce the concept of *strongly non-inferable set* of a class of valuations, and we prove that if this set has super-polynomial size then efficient elicitation is not possible. On the other hand, even classes of valuations with empty strongly non-inferable set can be hard to elicit. Furthermore, we introduce the concept of non-deterministic poly-query elicitation, and we prove that a class of valuations is non-deterministically poly-query elicitable if and only if its *teaching dimension* is polynomial.

Overall, our results seem to indicate that, despite the impossibility result of [15], efficient and truthful CA mechanisms are a realistic goal in many economic scenarios. In such scenarios, elicitation can be done using only a simple and very intuitive kind of query, i.e. value query.

2 Preliminaries

Let I denotes the set of items on sale (also called the *grand bundle*), with $|I| = m$. A *valuation function* on I (*valuation* for short) is a function $f : 2^I \mapsto \mathbb{R}^+$ that assigns to any bundle $S \subseteq I$ its valuation. A valuation is *linear*, denoted f_l, if $f_l(S) = \sum_{a \in S} f(a)$. To make the notation less cumbersome, we will use $a, b, \ldots$ to denote singletons, $ab, bc, \ldots$ to denote two-item bundles, and so on.

Given any bundle S, $q(S)$ denotes the value query correspondent to S. In this paper, value queries are the only type of queries the elicitor can ask the bidder in order to learn her preferences. Unless otherwise stated, in the following by "query" we mean "value query".

Definition 1 (PQE). *A class of valuations* $\mathbf{C}$ *is said to be poly-query (fully) elicitable if there exists an elicitation algorithm which, given as input a description of* $\mathbf{C}$*, and by asking value queries only, learns any valuation* $f \in \mathbf{C}$ *asking at most* $p(m)$ *queries, for some polynomial* $p(m)$*. PQE is the set of all classes* $\mathbf{C}$ *that are poly-query elicitable.*

The definition above is concerned only with the number of queries asked (communication complexity). Below, we define a stronger notion of efficiency, accounting for the computational complexity of the elicitation algorithm.

Definition 2 (PTE). *A class of valuations* $\mathbf{C}$ *is said to be poly-time (fully) elicitable if there exists an elicitation algorithm which, given as input a description of* $\mathbf{C}$*, and by asking value queries only, learns any valuation* $f \in \mathbf{C}$ *in polynomial time. PTE is the set of all classes* $\mathbf{C}$ *that are poly-time elicitable.*

It is clear that poly-time elicitability implies poly-query elicitability.

Throughout this paper, we will make extensive use of the following representation of valuation functions. We build the undirected graph H_I introducing a node for any subset of I (including the empty set), and an edge between any two nodes S_1, S_2 such that $S_1 \subset S_2$ and $|S_1| = |S_2| + 1$ (or vice versa). It is immediate that H_I, which represents the lattice of the inclusion relationship between subsets of I, is a binary hypercube of dimension m. Nodes in H_I can be partitioned into levels according to the cardinality of the corresponding subset: level 0 contains the empty set, level 1 the m singletons, level 2 the $\frac{m(m-1)}{2}$ subsets of two items, and so on.

The valuation function f can be represented using H_I by assigning a weight to each node of H_I as follows. We assign weight 0 to the empty set[3], and weight $f(a)$ to any singleton a. Let us now consider a node at level 2, say node ab[4]. The weight of the node is $f(ab) - (f(a) + f(b))$. At the general step i, we assign to node S_1, with $|S_1| = i$, the weight $f(S_1) - \sum_{S \subset S_1} w(S)$, where $w(S)$ denotes the weight of the node corresponding to subset S. We call this representation of f the *hypercube representation* of f, denoted $H_I(f)$.

The hypercube representation of a valuation function makes it explicit the fact that, under the common assumption of no externalities[5], the bidder's valuation of a bundle S depends only on the valuation of all the singletons $a \in S$, and on the relationships between all possible sub-bundles included in S. In general, an arbitrary sub-bundle of S may show positive or negative interactions between the components, or may show no influence on the valuation of S. In the hypercube representation, the contribution of any such sub-bundle on the valuation of S is isolated, and associated as a weight to the corresponding node in H_I.

Given the hypercube representation $H_I(f)$ of f, the valuation of any bundle S can be obtained by summing up the weights of all the nodes S' in $H_I(f)$ such that $S' \subseteq S$. These are the only weights contained in the sub-hypercube of $H_I(f)$ "rooted" at S.

Proposition 1. *Any valuation function f admits a hypercube representation, and this representation is unique.*

Proof. For the proof of this proposition, as well as of all for the proofs of the other theorems presented in this work, see the full version of the paper [19].

Given Proposition 1, the problem of learning f can be equivalently restated as the problem of learning all the weights in $H_I(f)$. In this paper, we will often state the elicitation problem in terms of learning the weights in $H_I(f)$, rather than the value of bundles.

---

[3] That is, we assume that the valuation function is normalized.

[4] Slightly abusing the notation, we denote with ab both the bundle composed by the two items a and b, and the corresponding node in H_I.

[5] With no externalities, we mean here that the bidder's valuation depends only on the set of items S that she wins, and not on the identity of the bidders who get the items not in S.

Since the number of nodes in H_I is exponential in m, the hypercube representation of f is not compact, and cannot be used directly to elicit f. However, this representation is a powerful tool in the analysis of structural properties of valuation functions.

3 Classes of Valuations in PTE

In this section, we consider several classes of valuation functions that can be elicited in polynomial time using value queries.

3.1 Read-Once Formulas

The class of valuation functions that can be expressed as read-once formulas, which we denote **RO**, has been introduced in [21]. A read-once formula is a function that can be represented as a "reverse" tree, where the root is the output, the leaves are the inputs (corresponding to items), and internal nodes are gates. The leaf nodes are labeled with a real-valued multiplier. The gates can be of the following type: SUM, MAX_c, and ATLEAST_c. The SUM operator simply sums the values of its inputs; the MAX_c operator returns the sum of the c highest inputs; the ATLEAST_c operator returns the sum of its inputs if at least c of them are non-zero, otherwise returns 0. In [21], it is proved that read-once formulas are in PTE.

In general, valuation functions in **RO** can express both complementarities (through the ATLEAST_c operator) and substitutabilities (through the MAX_c operator) between items. If we restrict our attention to the class of read-once formulas that can use only SUM and MAX operators (here, MAX is a shortcut for MAX_1), then only sub-additive valuations can be expressed. This restricted class of read-once formulas is denoted $\mathbf{RO_{+M}}$ in the following.

3.2 k-wise Dependent Valuations

The class of k-wise dependent valuations, which we denote $\mathbf{G_k}$, has been defined and analyzed in [8]. k-wise dependent valuations are defined as follows:

Definition 3. *A valuation function f is k-wise dependent if the only mutual interactions between items are on sets of cardinality at most k, for some constant $k > 0$. In other words, the $\mathbf{G_k}$ class corresponds to all valuation functions f such that the weights associated to nodes at level i in $H_I(f)$ are zero whenever $i > k$.*

Note that functions in $\mathbf{G_k}$ might display both sub and super-additivity between items. Furthermore, contrary to most of the classes of valuation functions described so far, k-wise dependent valuations might display costly disposal.

In [8], it is shown that valuations in $\mathbf{G_k}$ can be elicited in polynomial time asking $O(m^k)$ value queries.

3.3 The $\mathbf{Tool_t}$ Class

The class of ToolboxDNF formulas, which we denote $\mathbf{Tool_t}$, has been introduced in [21], and is defined as follows:

Definition 4. *A function f is in $\mathbf{Tool_t}$, where t is polynomial in m, if it can be represented by a polynomial p composed of t monomials (minterms), where each monomial is positive.*

For instance, polynomial $p = 3a + 4ab + 2bc + cd$ corresponds to the function which gives value 3 to item a, 0 to item b, value 9 to the bundle abc, and so on. Note if $f \in \mathbf{Tool_t}$, the only non-zero weights in $H_I(f)$ are those associated to the minterms of f.

ToolboxDNF valuations can express only substitutability-free valuations[6], and can be elicited in polynomial time asking $O(mt)$ value queries [21].

3.4 The $\mathbf{Tool_{-t}}$ Class

This class of valuation functions is a variation of the ToolboxDNF class introduced in [21]. The class is defined as follows.

Definition 5. $\mathbf{Tool_{-t}}$ *is the class of all the valuation functions f such that exactly t of the weights in $H_I(f)$ are non-zero, where t is polynomial in m. Of these weights, only those associated to singletons can be positive. The bundles associated to non-zero weights in $H_I(f)$ are called the minterms of f.*

In other words, the $\mathbf{Tool_{-t}}$ class corresponds to all valuation functions that can be expressed using a polynomial p with t monomials (minterms), where the only monomials with positive sign are composed by one single literal. For instance, function f defined by $p = 10a + 15b + 3c - 2ab - 3bc$ gives value 10 to item a, value 23 to the bundle ab, and so on.

Theorem 1. *If $f \in \mathbf{Tool_{-t}}$, where t is polynomial in m, then it can be elicited in polynomial time by asking $O(mt)$ queries.*

3.5 Interval Valuation Functions

The class of interval valuations is inspired by the notion of interval bids [16,17], which have important economic applications. The class is defined as follows. The items on sale are ordered according to a linear order, and they can display superadditive valuations when bundled together only when the bundle corresponds to an interval in this order. We call this class of sustitutability-free valuations INTERVAL, and we denote the set of all valuations in this class as **INT**.

An example of valuation in **INT** is the following: there are three items on sale, a, b and c, and the linear order is $a < b < c$. We have $f(a) = 10$, $f(b) = 5$,

[6] A valuation function f is substitutability-free if and only if, for any $S_1, S_2 \subseteq I$, we have $f(S_1) + f(S_2) \leq f(S_1 \bigcup S_2)$.

$f(c) = 3$, $f(ab) = 17$, $f(bc) = 10$, $f(ac) = f(a) + f(c) = 13$ (because bundle ac is not an interval in the linear order), and $f(abc) = 21$.

The **INT** class displays several similarities with the $\mathbf{Tool_t}$ class: there are a number of basic bundles (minterms) with non-zero value, and the value of a set of items depends on the value of the bundles that the bidder can form with them. However, the two classes turn out to be not comparable with respect to inclusion, i.e. there exist valuation functions f, f' such that $f \in \mathbf{Tool_t} - \mathbf{INT}$ and $f' \in \mathbf{INT} - \mathbf{Tool_t}$. For instance, the valuation function corresponding to the polynomial $p = a+b+c+ab+bc+ac$ is in $\mathbf{Tool_t} - \mathbf{INT}$, since objects can be bundled "cyclically". On the other hand, the valuation function f of the example above cannot be expressed using a ToolboxDNF function. In fact, the value of the bundles a, b, c, ab, bc and ac gives the polynomial $p' = 10a + 5b + 3c + 2ab + 2bc$. In order to get the value 21 for the bundle abc, which clearly include all the sub-bundles in p', we must add the term abc in p' with *negative* weight -1. Since only positive terms are allowed in $\mathbf{Tool_t}$, it follows that $f \in \mathbf{INT} - \mathbf{Tool_t}$.

What about preference elicitation with value queries in case $f \in \mathbf{INT}$? It turns out that the efficiency of elicitation depends on what the elicitor knows about the linear ordering of the objects. We distinguish three scenarios:

a) the elicitor knows the linear ordering of the items;

b) the elicitor does not know the linear ordering of the items, but the valuation function f to be elicited is such that $f(ab) > f(a) + f(b)$ if and only if a and b are immediate neighbors in the ordering.

c) the elicitor does not know the linear ordering of the items, and the valuation function to be elicited is such that $f(ab) = f(a) + f(b)$ does not imply that a and b are not immediate neighbors in the ordering. For instance, we could have $a < b < c$, $f(ab) > f(a) + f(b)$, $f(bc) = f(b) + f(c)$, and $f(abc) > f(ab) + f(c)$ (i.e., the weight of abc in $H_I(f)$ is greater than zero).

The following theorem shows that poly-time elicitation is feasible in scenarios a) and b). Determining elicitation complexity under the scenario c) remains open.

Theorem 2. *If $f \in \mathbf{INT}$, then:*

- *Scenario a): it can be elicited in polynomial time asking $\frac{m(m+1)}{2}$ value queries;*
- *Scenario b): it can be elicited in polynomial time asking at most $m^2 - m + 1$ value queries.*

3.6 Tree Valuation Functions

A natural way to extend the **INT** class is to consider those valuation functions in which the relationships between the objects on sale have a tree structure. Unfortunately, it turns out that the valuation functions that belong to this class, which we denote **TREE**, are not poly-query elicitable even if the structure of the tree is known to the elicitor.

Theorem 3. *There exists a valuation function $f \in \mathbf{TREE}$ that can be learned correctly only asking at least $2^{m/2}$ value queries, even if the elicitor knows the structure of the tree.*

However, if we restrict the super-additive valuations to be only on subtrees of the tree T that describes the item relationships, rather than on arbitrary connected subgraphs of T, then polynomial time elicitation with value queries is possible (given that T itself can be learned in polytime using value queries).

Theorem 4. *Assume that the valuation function $f \in \mathbf{TREE}$ is such that super-additive valuations are only displayed between objects that form a subtree of T, and assume that the elicitor can learn T asking a polynomial number of value queries. Then, f can be elicited asking a polynomial number of value queries.*

4 Generalized Preference Elicitation

In the previous section we have considered several classes of valuation functions, proving that most of them are in PTE. However, the definition of PTE (and of PQE) assumes that the elicitor has access to a description of the class of the valuation to elicit; in other words, *the elicitor a priori knows the class to which the valuation function belongs.* In this section, we analyze preference elicitation under a more general framework, in which the elicitor has some uncertainty about the actual class to which the valuation to elicit belongs.

We start by showing that the family of poly-query elicitable classes of valuations is closed under union.

Theorem 5. *Let $\mathbf{C_1}$ and $\mathbf{C_2}$ be two classes of poly-query elicitable valuations, and assume that $p_1(m)$ (resp., $p_2(m)$) is a polynomial such that any valuation in $\mathbf{C_1}$ (resp., $\mathbf{C_2}$) can be elicited asking at most $p_1(m)$ (resp., $p_2(m)$) queries. Then, any valuation in $\mathbf{C_1} \bigcup \mathbf{C_2}$ can be elicited asking at most $p_1(m)+p_2(m)+1$ queries.*

In the following theorem, we prove that the bound on the number of queries needed to elicit a function in $\mathbf{C_1} \bigcup \mathbf{C_2}$ stated in Theorem 5 is tight.

Theorem 6. *There exist families of valuation functions $\mathbf{C_1}, \mathbf{C_2}$ such that either $\mathbf{C_i}$ can be elicited asking at most $m-1$ queries, but $\mathbf{C_1} \cup \mathbf{C_2}$ cannot be elicited asking less than $2m-1 = 2(m-1)+1$ queries (in the worst case).*

Theorem 5 shows that, as far as communication complexity is concerned, efficient elicitation can be implemented under a very general scenario: if the only information available to the elicitor is that $f \in \mathbf{C_1} \bigcup \cdots \bigcup \mathbf{C_{q(m)}}$, where the $\mathbf{C_i}$s are in PQE and $q(m)$ is an arbitrary polynomial, then elicitation can be done with polynomially many queries. This is a notable improvement over traditional elicitation techniques, in which it is assumed that the elicitor knows exactly the class to which the function to elicit belongs.

Although interesting, Theorem 5 leaves open the question of the *computational* complexity of the elicitation process. In fact, the general elicitation algorithm $A_{1\bigcup 2}$ used in the proof of the theorem (see the full version of the paper [19]) has running time which is super-polynomial in m. So, a natural question to ask is the following: let $\mathbf{C_1}$ and $\mathbf{C_2}$ be *poly-time* elicitable classes of valuations; Is the $\mathbf{C_1} \bigcup \mathbf{C_2}$ class elicitable in polynomial *time*?

Even if we do not know the answer to this question in general, in the following we show that, at least for many of the classes considered in this paper, the answer is *yes*. In particular, we present a polynomial time algorithm that elicits correctly any function $f \in \mathbf{RO_{+M}} \bigcup \mathbf{Tool_{-t}} \bigcup \mathbf{Tool_t} \bigcup \mathbf{G_2} \bigcup \mathbf{INT}$. The algorithm is called GenPolyLearn, and is based on a set of theorems which show that, given any $f \in \mathbf{C_1} \bigcup \mathbf{C_2}$, where $\mathbf{C_1}, \mathbf{C_2}$ are any two of the classes listed above, f can be learned correctly with a low-order polynomial bound on the runtime (see [19]).

The algorithm, which is reported in Figure 1, is very simple: initially, the hypothesis set Hp contains all the five classes. After asking the value of any singleton, GenPolyLearn asks the value of any two-item bundles and, based on the corresponding weights on $H_I(f)$, discards some of the hypotheses. When the hypotheses set contains at most two classes, the algorithm continues preference elicitation accordingly. In case Hp contains more than two classes after all the two-item bundles have been elicited, one more value query (on the grand bundle) is sufficient for the elicitor to resolve uncertainty, reducing the size of the hypotheses set to at most two. The following theorem shows the correctness of GenPolyLearn, and gives a bound on its runtime.

Theorem 7. *Algorithm* GenPolyLearn *learns correctly in polynomial time any valuation function in* $\mathbf{RO_{+M}} \bigcup \mathbf{Tool_{-t}} \bigcup \mathbf{Tool_t} \bigcup \mathbf{G_2} \bigcup \mathbf{INT}$ *asking at most* $O(m(m+t))$ *value queries.*

From the bidders' side, a positive feature of GenPolyLearn is that it asks relatively easy to answer queries: valuation of singletons, two-item bundles, and the grand bundle. (In many cases, the overall value of the market considered (e.g., all the spectrum frequencies in the US) is publicly available information.)

5 Towards Characterizing Poly-query Elicitation

In the previous sections we have presented several classes of valuation functions that can be elicited asking polynomially many queries, and we have proved that efficient elicitation can be implemeted in a quite general setting. In this section, we discuss the properties that these classes have in common, thus making a step forward in the characterization of what renders a class of valuations easy to elicit with value queries.

Let $\mathbf{C}$ be a class of valuations, f any valuation in $\mathbf{C}$, and $A_{\mathbf{C}}$ an elicitation algorithm for $\mathbf{C}$[7]. Let $\mathcal{Q}$ be an arbitrary set of value queries, representing the

[7] In the following, we assume that the elicitation algorithm is a "smart" algorithm for $\mathbf{C}$, i.e. an algorithm which is able to infer the largest amount of knowledge from the answers to the queries asked so far.

Algorithm GENPOLYLEARN:

0. Hp={$\mathbf{RO_{+M}}$,$\mathbf{G_2}$,$\mathbf{Tool_t}$,$\mathbf{Tool_{-t}}$,**INT**}
1. build the first level of $H_I(f)$ asking the value of singletons

2. build the second level of $H_I(f)$ asking the value of two-items bundles in arbitrary order
3. let $w(ab)$ the computed weight for bundle ab
4. repeat
5. if $w(ab) < 0$ then
6. remove $\mathbf{Tool_t}$ and **INT** from Hp
7. if $w(ab) \neq -\min\{f(a), f(b)\}$ then remove $\mathbf{RO_{+M}}$ from Hp
8. if $w(ab) > 0$ then
9. remove $\mathbf{RO_{+M}}$ and $\mathbf{Tool_{-t}}$ from Hp
10. if $w(ab)$ is not compatible with the linear order discovered so far then
11. remove **INT** from Hp
12. until $|\text{Hp}| \leq 2$ or all the $w(ab)$ have been considered
13. if $|\text{Hp}| \leq 2$ then continue elicitation as described in theorems 6–15 of [19].

otherwise:
14. *case 1*: all the $w(ab)$ weights are ≥ 0 and compatible with the linear order, and at least one weight is positive
15. ask the value of the grand bundle I
16. if $f(I) = \sum_{S \subseteq I, |S| \leq 2} w(S)$ then
17. remove $\mathbf{Tool_t}$ from Hp
18. continue elicitation as in the proof of Th. 9 of [19]
19. else
20. remove $\mathbf{G_2}$ from Hp
21. continue elicitation as in the proof of Th. 10 of [19]
22. *case 2*: all the $w(ab)$ weights are ≤ 0, at least one weight is negative, and $\mathbf{RO_{+M}} \in$Hp
23. ask the value of the grand bundle I
24. if $f(I) \neq \sum_{S \subseteq I, |S| \leq 2} w(S)$ then
25. remove $\mathbf{G_2}$ from Hp
26. continue elicitation as in the proof of Th. 15 of [19]
27. else
28. remove $\mathbf{Tool_{-t}}$ from Hp
29. continue elicitation as in the proof of Th. 6 of [19]
30. *case 3*: $w(ab) = 0$ for all ab
31. ask the value of the grand bundle I
32. if $f(I) < \sum_{a \in I} f(a)$ then
33. remove **INT**, $\mathbf{Tool_t}$, $\mathbf{G_2}$, $\mathbf{RO_{+M}}$ from Hp
34. $f \in \mathbf{Tool_{-t}}$; continue elicitation accordingly
35. else
36. remove $\mathbf{Tool_{-t}}$, $\mathbf{G_2}$, $\mathbf{RO_{+M}}$ from Hp
37. proceed as in the proof of Th. 10 of [19]

Fig. 1. Algorithm for learning correctly any valuation function in $\mathbf{RO_{+M}} \bigcup \mathbf{Tool_{-t}} \bigcup \mathbf{Tool_t} \bigcup \mathbf{G_2} \bigcup$ **INT** asking a polynomial number of value queries.

queries asked by $A_{\mathbf{C}}$ at a certain stage of the elicitation process. Given the answers to the queries in $\mathcal{Q}$, which we denote $\mathcal{Q}(f)$ (f is the function to be elicited), and a description of the class $\mathbf{C}$, $A_{\mathbf{C}}$ returns a set of *learned values* $V_{\mathbf{C}}(\mathcal{Q}(f))$. This set obviously contains any S such that $q(S) \in \mathcal{Q}$; furthermore, it may contain the value of other bundles (the *inferred values*), which are inferred given the description of $\mathbf{C}$ and the answers to the queries in $\mathcal{Q}$. The elicitation process ends when $V_{\mathbf{C}}(\mathcal{Q}(f)) = 2^I$.

Definition 6 (Inferability). *Let S be an arbitrary bundle, and let f be any function in $\mathbf{C}$. The f-inferability of S w.r.t. $\mathbf{C}$ is defined as:*

$$IN_{f,\mathbf{C}}(S) = \min\{|\mathcal{Q}| \text{ s.t. } (q(S) \notin \mathcal{Q}) \text{ and } (S \in V_{\mathbf{C}}(\mathcal{Q}(f)))\} \ .$$

If the value of S can be learned only by asking $q(S)$, we set $IN_{f,\mathbf{C}}(S) = 2^m - 1$. The inferability of S w.r.t. to $\mathbf{C}$ is defined as:

$$IN_{\mathbf{C}}(S) = \max_{f \in \mathbf{C}} IN_{f,\mathbf{C}}(S) \ .$$

Intuitively, the inferability[8] of a bundle measures how easy it is for an elicitation algorithm to learn the value of S without explicitly asking it.

Definition 7 (Polynomially-inferable bundle). *A bundle S is said to be poly-nomially-inferable (inferable for short) w.r.t. $\mathbf{C}$ if $IN_{\mathbf{C}}(S) = p(m)$, for some polynomial $p(m)$.*

Definition 8 (Polynomially non-inferable bundle). *A bundle S is said to be polynomially non-inferable (non-inferable for short) w.r.t. $\mathbf{C}$ if $IN_{\mathbf{C}}(S)$ is super-polynomial in m.*

Definition 9 (Strongly polynomially non-inferable bundle). *A bundle S is said to be strongly polynomially non-inferable (strongly non-inferable for short) with respect to class $\mathbf{C}$ if $\forall f \in \mathbf{C}$, $IN_{f,\mathbf{C}}(S)$ is super-polynomial in m.*

Note the difference between poly and strongly poly non-inferable bundle: in the former case, there exists a function f in $\mathbf{C}$ such that, on input f, the value of S can be learned with polynomially many queries only by asking $q(S)$; in the latter case, this property holds *for all* the valuations in $\mathbf{C}$.

Definition 10 (Non-inferable set). *Given a class of valuations $\mathbf{C}$, the non-inferable set of $\mathbf{C}$, denoted $NI_{\mathbf{C}}$, is the set of all bundles in 2^I that are non-inferable w.r.t. $\mathbf{C}$.*

Definition 11 (Strongly non-inferable set). *Given a class of valuations $\mathbf{C}$, the non-inferable set of $\mathbf{C}$, denoted $SNI_{\mathbf{C}}$, is the set of all bundles in 2^I that are strongly non-inferable w.r.t. $\mathbf{C}$.*

[8] When clear from the context, we simply speak of inferability, instead of inferability w.r.t. $\mathbf{C}$.

Clearly, we have $SNI_{\mathbf{C}} \subseteq NI_{\mathbf{C}}$. The following theorem shows that for some class of valuations **C** the inclusion is strict. Actually, the gap between the size of $SNI_{\mathbf{C}}$ and that of $NI_{\mathbf{C}}$ can be super-polynomial in m.

The theorem uses a class of valuations introduced by Angluin [1] in the related context of concept learning. The class, which we call **RDNF** (RestrictedDNF) since it is a subclass of DNF formulas, is defined as follows. There are $m = 2k$ items, for some $k > 0$. The items are arbitrarily partitioned into k pairs, which we denote S_i, with $i = 1, \ldots, k$. We also define a bundle $\bar{S}$ of cardinality k such that $\forall i, |S_i \bigcap \bar{S}| = 1$. In other words, $\bar{S}$ is an arbitrary bundle obtained by taking exactly one element from each of the pairs. We call the S_is and the bundle $\bar{S}$ the minterms of the valuation function f. The valuations in **RDNF** are defined as follows: $f(S) = 1$ if S contains one of the minterms; $f(S) = 0$ otherwise.

Theorem 8. *We have $|SNI_{\mathbf{RDNF}}| = 0$, while $|NI_{\mathbf{RDNF}}|$ is super-polynomial in m.*

Proof. We first prove that $|SNI_{\mathbf{RDNF}}| = 0$. Let f be any function in **RDNF**, and let $S_1, \ldots, S_k, \bar{S}$ be its minterms. Let S be an arbitrary bundle, and assume that S is not a minterm. Then, the value of S can be inferred given the answers to the queries $\mathcal{Q}' = \{q(S_1), \ldots, q(S_k), q(\bar{S})\}$, which are polynomially many. Thus, S is not in $SNI_{\mathbf{RDNF}}$. Since for any bundle S there exists a function f in **RDNF** such that S is not one of the minterms of f, we have that $SNI_{\mathbf{RDNF}}$ is empty. Let us now consider $NI_{\mathbf{RDNF}}$. Let S be an arbitrary bundle of cardinality k, and let f be a function in **RDNF**. If S is one of the minterms of f (i.e., $S = \bar{S}$) the only possibility for the elicitor to infer its value is by asking the value of *all* the other bundles of cardinality k (there are super-polynomially many such bundles). In fact, queries on bundles of cardinality $< k$ of $\geq k+1$ give no information on the identity of $\bar{S}$. So, $\bar{S}$ is in $NI_{\mathbf{RDNF}}$. Since for any bundle S of cardinality k there exists a function f in **RDNF** such that S is a minterm of f, we have that $NI_{\mathbf{RDNF}}$ contains super-polynomially many bundles.

The following theorem shows that whether a certain class **C** is in PQE depends to a certain extent on the size of $SNI_{\mathbf{C}}$.

Theorem 9. *Let **C** be an arbitrary class of valuations. If the size of $SNI_{\mathbf{C}}$ is super-polynomial in m, then $\mathbf{C} \notin PQE$.*

Theorem 9 states that a necessary condition for a class of valuations **C** to be easy to elicit is that its strongly non-inferable set has polynomial size. Is this condition also sufficient? The following theorem, whose proof follows immediately by the fact that the **RDNF** class is hard to elicit with value queries [1], gives a negative answer to this question, showing that even classes **C** with an empty strongly non-inferable set may be hard to elicit.

Theorem 10. *The condition $|SNI_{\mathbf{C}}| = p(m)$ for some polynomial $p(m)$ is not sufficient for making **C** easy to elicit with value queries. In particular, we have that $|SNI_{\mathbf{RDNF}}| = 0$, and $\mathbf{RDNF} \notin PQE$.*

Theorem 10 shows that the size of the strongly non-inferable set alone is not sufficient to characterize classes of valuations which are easy to elicit. Curiously, the size of the non-inferable set of **RDNF** is super-polynomial in m. Thus, the following question remains open: "Does there exist a class of valuations $\mathbf{C}$ such that $|NI_{\mathbf{C}}| = p(m)$ for some polynomial $p(m)$ and $\mathbf{C} \notin PQE$?" or, equivalently, "Is the condition $|NI_{\mathbf{C}}| = p(m)$ for some polynomial $p(m)$ sufficient for making $\mathbf{C}$ poly-query elicitable?"

Furthermore, Theorem 10 suggests the definition of another notion of poly-query elicitation, which we call "non-deterministic poly-query elicitation" and denote with NPQE. Let us consider the **RDNF** class used in the proof of Theorem 8. In a certain sense, this class seems easier to elicit than a class $\mathbf{C}$ with $|SNI_{\mathbf{C}}|$ superpolynomial in m. In case of the class $\mathbf{C}$, any set of polynomially many queries is not sufficient to learn the function (no "poly-query certificate" exists). Conversely, in case of **RDNF** such "poly-query certificate" exists for any $f \in \mathbf{RDNF}$ (it is the set $\mathcal{Q}'$ as defined in the proof of Theorem 8); what makes elicitation hard in this case is the fact that this certificate is "hard to guess". So, the **RDNF** class is easy to elicit if non-deterministic elicitation is allowed. The following definition captures this concept:

Definition 12 (NPQE). *A class of valuations* $\mathbf{C}$ *is said to be poly-query non-deterministic (fully) elicitable if there exists a nondeterministic elicitation algorithm which, given as input a description of* $\mathbf{C}$*, and by asking value queries only, learns any valuation* $f \in \mathbf{C}$ *asking at most* $p(m)$ *queries in at least one of the nondeterministic computations, for some polynomial* $p(m)$*. NPQE is the set of all classes* $\mathbf{C}$ *that are poly-query nondeterministic elicitable.*

It turns out that non-deterministic poly-query elicitation can be characterized using a notion introduced in [10], which we adapt here to the framework of preference elicitation.

Definition 13 (Teaching dimension). *Let* $\mathbf{C}$ *be a class of valuations, and let* f *be an arbitrary function in* $\mathbf{C}$*. A teaching set for* f *w.r.t.* $\mathbf{C}$ *is a set of queries* $\mathcal{Q}$ *such that* $V_{\mathbf{C}}(\mathcal{Q}(f)) = 2^I$*. The teaching dimension of* $\mathbf{C}$ *is defined as*

$$TD(\mathbf{C}) = \max_{f \in \mathbf{C}} \min \left\{ |\mathcal{Q}| \text{ s.t. } (\mathcal{Q} \subseteq 2^{2^I}) \text{ and } (\mathcal{Q} \text{ is a teaching set for } f) \right\} .$$

Theorem 11. *Let* $\mathbf{C}$ *be an arbitrary class of valuations.* $\mathbf{C} \in NPEQ$ *if and only if* $TD(\mathbf{C}) = p(m)$ *for some polynomial* $p(m)$*.*

The following results is straightforward by observing that **RDNF** is in NPQE (it has $O(m)$ teaching dimension) but not in PQE:

Proposition 2. $PQE \subset NPQE$*.*

References

1. D. Angluin, "Queries and Concept Learning", *Machine Learning*, Vol. 2, pp. 319–342, 1988.
2. A. Blum, J. Jackson, T. Sandholm, M. Zinkevic, "Preference Elicitation and Query Learning", *in Proc. Conference on Computational Learning Theory (COLT)*, 2003.
3. L. Blumrosen, N. Nisan, "Auctions with Severely Bounded Communication", *in Proc. IEEE Symposium on Foundations of Computer Science (FOCS)*, pp. 406–415, 2002.
4. A. Bonaccorsi, B. Codenotti, N. Dimitri, M. Leoncini, G. Resta, P. Santi, "Generating Realistic Data Sets for Combinatorial Auctions", *Proc. IEEE Conf. on Electronic Commerce (CEC)*, pp. 331–338, 2003.
5. E.H. Clarke, "Multipart Pricing of Public Goods", *Public Choice*, Vol. 11, pp. 17–33, 1971.
6. W. Conen, T. Sandholm, "Preference Elicitation in Combinatorial Auctions", *Proc. ACM Conference on Electronic Commerce (EC)*, pp. 256–259, 2001. A more detailed description of the algorithmic aspects appeared in the IJCAI-2001 Workshop on Economic Agents, Models, and Mechanisms, pp. 71–80.
7. W. Conen, T. Sandholm, "Partial-Revelation VCG Mechanisms for Combinatorial Auctions", *Proc. National Conference on Artificial Intelligence (AAAI)*, pp. 367–372, 2002.
8. V. Conitzer, T. Sandholm, P. Santi, "On K-wise Dependent Valuations in Combinatorial Auctions", *internet draft*.
9. S. de Vries, R. Vohra, "Combinatorial Auctions: a Survey", *INFORMS J. of Computing*, 2003.
10. S. Goldman, M.J. Kearns, "On the Complexity of Teaching", *Journal of Computer and System Sciences*, Vol. 50, n. 1, pp. 20–31, 1995.
11. T. Groves, "Incentive in Teams", *Econometrica*, Vol. 41, pp. 617–631, 1973.
12. B. Hudson, T. Sandholm, "Effectiveness of Query Types and Policies for Preference Elicitation in Combinatorial Auctions", *International Joint Conference on Autonomous Agents and Multi Agent Systems (AAMAS-04)*, 2004.
13. D. Lehmann, L. Ita O'Callaghan, Y. Shoham, "Truth Revelation in Approximately Efficient Combinatorial Auctions", *Journal of the ACM*, Vol.49, n.5, pp. 577–602, 2002.
14. J. MacKie-Mason, H.R. Varian, "Generalized Vickrey Auctions", *working paper*, Univ. of Michigan, 1994.
15. N. Nisan, I. Segal, "The Communication Requirements of Efficient Allocations and Supporting Lindhal Prices", *internet draft*, version March 2003.
16. M.H. Rothkopf, A. Pekec, R.H. Harstad, "Computationally Managable Combinatorial Auctions", *Management Science*, Vol. 44, n. 8, pp. 1131–1147, 1998.
17. T. Sandholm, S. Suri, "BOB: Improved Winner Determination in Combinatorial Auctions and Generalizations", *Artificial Intelligence*, Vol. 145, pp. 33–58, 2003.
18. T. Sandholm, "Algorithm for Optimal Winner Determination in Combinatorial Auctions", *Artificial Intelligence*, Vol. 135, pp. 1–54, 2002.
19. P. Santi, V. Conitzer, T. Sandholm, "Towardsa a Characterization of Polynomial Preference Elicitation with Value Queries in Combinatorial Auctions", *internet draft*, available at *http://www.imc.pi.cnr.it/~santi.*
20. W. Vickrey, "Counterspeculation, Auctions, and Competitive Sealed Tenders", *Journal of Finance*, Vol. 16, pp. 8–37, 1961.

21. M. Zinkevich, A. Blum, T. Sandholm, "On Polynomial-Time Preference Elicitation with Value Queries", *Proc. ACM Conference on Electronic Commerce (EC)*, pp. 176–185, 2003.
22. E. Zurel, N. Nisan, "An Efficient Approximate Allocation Algorithm for Combinatorial Auctions", *Proc. 3rd ACM Conference on Electronic Commerce (EC)*, pp. 125–136, 2001.

Graphical Economics

Sham M. Kakade, Michael Kearns, and Luis E. Ortiz

Department of Computer and Information Science
University of Pennsylvania, Philadelphia, PA 19104
{skakade,mkearns,leortiz}@linc.cis.upenn.edu

Abstract. We introduce a graph-theoretic generalization of classical Arrow-Debreu economics, in which an undirected graph specifies which consumers or economies are permitted to engage in direct trade, and the graph topology may give rise to local variations in the prices of commodities. Our main technical contributions are: (1) a general existence theorem for *graphical equilibria*, which require *local* markets to clear; (2) an improved algorithm for computing approximate equilibria in standard (non-graphical) economies, which generalizes the algorithm of Deng et al. [2002] to non-linear utility functions; (3) an algorithm for computing equilibria in the graphical setting, which runs in time polynomial in the number of consumers in the special but important case in which the graph is a tree (again permitting non-linear utility functions). We also highlight many interesting learning problems that arise in our model, and relate them to learning in standard game theory and economics, graphical games, and graphical models for probabilistic inference.

1 Introduction

Models for the exchange of goods and their prices in a large economy have a long and storied history within mathematical economics, dating back more than a century to the work of Walras [1874] and Fisher [1891], and continuing through the model of Wald [1936] (see also Brainard and Scarf [2000]). A pinnacle of this line of work came in 1954, when Arrow and Debreu provided extremely general conditions for the existence of an equilibrium in such models (in which markets clear, *i.e.* supply balances demand, and all individual consumers and firms optimize their utility subject to budget constraints). Like Nash's roughly contemporary proof of the existence of equilibria for normal-form games (Nash [1951]), Arrow and Debreu's result placed a rich class of economic models on solid mathematical ground.

These important results established the *existence* of various notions of equilibria. The *computation* of game-theoretic and economic equilibria has been a more slippery affair. Indeed, despite decades of effort, the computational complexity of computing a Nash equilibrium for a general-sum normal-form game remains unknown, with the best known algorithms requiring exponential time in the worst case. Even less is known regarding the computation of Arrow-Debreu equilibria. Only quite recently, a polynomial-time algorithm was discovered for the special but challenging case of linear utility functions (Devanur et al. [2002], Jain et al. [2003], Devanur and Vazirani [2003]). Still less is known about the *learning* of economic equilibria in a distributed, natural fashion.

J. Shawe-Taylor and Y. Singer (Eds.): COLT 2004, LNAI 3120, pp. 17–32, 2004.

One promising direction for making computational progress is to introduce alternative ways of *representing* these problems, with the hope that wide classes of "natural" problems may permit special-purpose solutions. By developing new representations that permit the expression of common types of structure in games and economies, it may be possible to design algorithms that exploit this structure to yield computational as well as modeling benefits. Researchers in machine learning and artificial intelligence have proven especially adept at devising models that balance representational power with computational tractability and learnability, so it has been natural to turn to these literatures for inspiration in strategic and economic models.

Among the most natural and common kinds of structure that arise in game-theoretic and economic settings are constraints and asymmetries in the *interactions* between the parties. By this we mean, for example, that in a large-population game, not all players may directly influence the payoffs of all others. The recently introduced formalism of *graphical games* captures this notion, representing a game by an undirected graph and a corresponding set of local game matrices (Kearns et al. [2001]). In Section 2 we briefly review the history of graphical games and similar models, and their connections with other topics in machine learning and probabilistic inference.

In the same spirit, in this paper we introduce a new model called *graphical economics* and show that it provides representational and algorithmic benefits for Arrow-Debreu economics. Each vertex i in an undirected graph represents an individual party in a large economic system. The presence of an edge between i and j means that free trade is allowed between the two parties, while the absence of this edge means there is an embargo or other restriction on direct trade. The graph could thus represent a network of individual business people, with the edges indicating who knows whom; or the global economy, with the edges representing nation pairs with trade agreements; and many other settings. Since not all parties may directly engage in trade, the graphical economics model permits (and realizes) the emergence of *local* prices — that is, *the price of the same good may vary* across the economy. Indeed, one of our motivations in introducing the model is to capture the fact that price differences for identical goods can arise due to the network structure of economic interaction.

We emphasize that the mere introduction of a network or graph structure into economic models is in itself not a new idea; while a detailed history of such models is beyond our scope, Jackson [2003] provides an excellent survey. However, to our knowledge, the great majority of these models are designed to model specific economic settings. Our model has deliberately incorporated a network model into the general Arrow-Debreu framework. Our motivation is to capture and understand network interactions in what is the most well-studied of mathematical economic models.

The graphical economics model suggests a *local* notion of clearance, directly derived from that of the Arrow-Debreu model. Rather than asking that the entire (global) market clear in each good, we can ask for the stronger "provincial" conditions that the *local* market for each good must clear. For instance, the United States is less concerned that the worldwide production of beef balances worldwide demand than it is that the production of *American* beef balances *worldwide* demand for American beef. If this latter condition holds, the American beef industry is doing a good job at matching the global demand for their product, even if other countries suffer excess supply or demand.

The primary contributions of this paper are:

- The introduction of the graphical economics model (which lies within the Arrow-Debreu framework) for capturing structured interaction between individuals, organizations or nations.
- A proof that under very general conditions (essentially analogous to Arrow and Debreu's original conditions), graphical equilibria always exist. This proof requires a non-trivial modification to that of Arrow and Debreu.
- An algorithm for computing approximate standard market equilibria in the non-graphical setting that runs in time polynomial in the number of players (fixing the number of goods) for a rather general class of non-linear utility functions. This result generalizes the algorithm of Deng et al. [2002] for linear utility functions.
- An algorithm, called **ADProp** (for *Arrow-Debreu Propagation*) for computing approximate graphical equilibria. This algorithm is a message-passing algorithm working directly on the graph, in which neighboring consumers or economies exchange information about trade imbalances between them under potential equilibria prices. In the case that the graph is a tree, the running time of the algorithm is exponential in the graph degree and number of goods k, but only polynomial in the number of vertices n (consumers or economies). It thus represents dramatic savings over treating the graphical case with a non-graphical algorithm, which results in a running time exponential in n (as well as in k).
- A discussion of the many challenging learning problems that arise in both the traditional and graphical economic models. This discussion is provided in Section 6.

2 A Brief History of Graphical Games

In this section, we review the short but active history of work in the model known as *graphical games*, and highlight connections to more longstanding topics in machine learning and graphical models.

Graphical games were introduced in Kearns et al. [2001], where a representation consisting of an undirected graph and a set of local payoff matrices was proposed for multi-player games. The interpretation is that the payoff to player i is a function of the actions of only those players in the neighborhood of vertex i in the graph. Exactly as with the graphical models for probabilistic inference that inspired them (such as Bayesian and Markov networks), graphical games provide an exponentially more succinct representation in cases where the number of players is large, but the degree of the interaction graph is relatively small.

A series of papers by several authors established the computational benefits of this model. Kearns et al. [2001] gave a provably efficient (polynomial in the model size) algorithm for computing all approximate Nash equilibria in graphical games with a tree topology; this algorithm can be formally viewed as the analogue of the junction tree algorithm for inference in tree-structured Markov networks. A related algorithm described in Littman et al. [2002] computes a single but exact Nash equilibrium.

In the same way that the junction tree and polytree algorithms for probabilistic inference were generalized to obtain the more heuristic belief propagation algorithm, Ortiz and Kearns [2003] proposed the NashProp algorithm for arbitrary graphical games, proved its convergence, and experimentally demonstrated promising performance on a wide class of graphs. Vickrey and Koller [2002] proposed and experimentally compared a wide range of natural algorithms for computing equilibria in graphical games, and quite recently Blum et al. [2003] developed an interesting new algorithm based on continuation methods.

An intriguing connection between graphical games and Markov networks was established in Kakade et al. [2003], in the context of the generalization of Nash equilibria known as *correlated equilibria.* There it was shown that if G is the underlying graph of a graphical game, then all the correlated equilibria of the game (up to payoff equivalence) can be represented as a Markov network whose underlying graph is almost identical to G — in particular, only a small number of highly localized connections need to be added. This result establishes a natural and very direct relationship between the *strategic* structure of interaction in a multi-player game, and the *probabilistic* dependency structure of any (correlated) equilibrium. In addition to allowing one to establish non-trivial independencies that must hold at equilibrium, this result is also thought-provoking from a learning perspective, since a series of recent papers has established that correlated equilibrium appears to be the natural convergence notion for a wide class of "rational" learning dynamics. We shall return to this topic when we discuss learning in Section 6.

3 Graphical Economies

The classical Arrow-Debreu (AD in the sequel) economy (without firms) consists of n consumers who trade k commodities of goods amongst themselves in an unrestricted manner. In an AD economy, each unit of commodity $h \in \{1, \ldots, k\}$ can be bought by any consumer at prices p_h. We denote the vector of prices to be $\boldsymbol{p} \in \mathcal{R}_+^k$ (where $\mathcal{R}_+ = \{x \geq 0\}$).

Each consumer i purchases a *consumption plan* $\boldsymbol{x}^i \in \mathcal{R}_+^k$, where x_h^i is the amount of commodity h that is purchased by i. We assume that each consumer i has an initial *endowment* $\boldsymbol{e}^i \in \mathcal{R}_+^k$ of the k commodities, where e_h^i is the amount of commodity h initially held by i. These commodities can be sold to other consumers and thus provide consumer i with *wealth* or cash, which can in turn be used to purchase other goods. Hence, if the initial endowment of consumer i is completely sold, then the wealth of consumer i is $\boldsymbol{p} \cdot \boldsymbol{e}^i$. A consumption plan $\boldsymbol{x}^i$ is *budget constrained* if $\boldsymbol{p} \cdot \boldsymbol{x}^i \leq \boldsymbol{p} \cdot \boldsymbol{e}^i$, which implicitly assumes the endowment is completely sold (which in fact holds at equilibrium).

Every consumer i has a *utility function* $u_i : \mathcal{R}_+^k \to \mathcal{R}_+$, where $u_i(\boldsymbol{x}^i)$ describes how much utility consumer i receives from consuming the plan $\boldsymbol{x}^i$. The utility function thus expresses the preferences a consumer has for varying bundles of the k goods.

A *graphical economy* with n players and k goods can be formalized as a standard AD economy with nk "traditional" goods, which are indexed by the pairs (i, h). The good (i, h) is interpreted as "good h sold by consumer i". The key restriction is that free trade is not permitted between consumers, so all players may not be able to purchase (i, h). It turns out that with these trade restrictions, we were not able to invoke the original existence proof used in the standard Arrow-Debreu model, and we had to use some interesting techniques to prove existence.

It is most natural to specify the trade restrictions through an undirected graph, G, over the n consumers [1]. The graph G specifies how the consumers are allowed to trade with each other — each consumer may have a limited choice of where to purchase commodities. The interpretation of G is that if (i, j) is an edge in G, then free trade exists between consumers i and j, meaning that i is allowed to buy commodities from j and vice-versa; while the lack of an edge between i and j means that no direct trade is permitted. More precisely, if we use $N(i)$ to denote the neighbor set of i (which by convention includes i itself), then consumer i is free to buy any commodity *only* from any of the consumers in $N(i)$. It will naturally turn out that rational consumers only purchase goods from a neighbor with the best available price.

Associated with each consumer i is a *local price vector* $\boldsymbol{p}^{\,i} \in \mathcal{R}_+^k$, where p_h^i is the price at which commodity h is being sold by i. We denote the set of all local price vectors by $P = \{\boldsymbol{p}^{\,i} : i = 1, \ldots, n\}$. Each consumer i purchases an amount of commodities $\boldsymbol{x}^{\,ij} \in \mathcal{R}_+^k$, where x_h^{ij} is the amount of commodity h that is purchased from consumer j by consumer i. The trade restrictions imply that $\boldsymbol{x}^{\,ij} = 0$ for $j \notin N(i)$. Here, the consumption plan is the set $X^i = \{\boldsymbol{x}^{\,ij} : j \in N(i)\}$ and an X^i is *budget constrained* if $\sum_{j \in N(i)} \boldsymbol{p}^{\,j} \cdot \boldsymbol{x}^{\,ij} \leq \boldsymbol{p}^{\,i} \cdot \boldsymbol{e}^{\,i}$ which again implicitly assumes the endowment is completely sold (which holds at equilibrium).

In the graphical setting, we assume the utility function only depends on the *total amount* of each commodity consumed, independent of whom it was purchased from. This expresses the fact that the goods are identical across the economy, and consumers seek the best prices available to them. Slightly abusing notation, we define $\boldsymbol{x}^{\,i} = \sum_{j \in N(i)} \boldsymbol{x}^{\,ij}$, which is the total vector amount of goods consumed by i under the plan X^i. The utility of consumer i is given by the function $u_i(\boldsymbol{x}^{\,i})$, which is a function from $\mathcal{R}_+^k \to \mathcal{R}_+$.

4 Graphical Equilibria

In equilibrium, there are two properties which we desire to hold — consumer rationality and market clearance. We now define these and state conditions under which an equilibrium is guaranteed.

The economic motivation for a consumer in the choice of consumption plans is to maximize utility subject to a budget constraint. We say that a consumer i uses an *optimal plan* at prices P if the plan maximizes utility over the set of all plans which are budget constrained under P. For instance, in the graphical setting, a plan X^i for i is optimal at prices P if the plan X^i maximizes the function u_i over all X'^i subject to $\sum_{j \in N(i)} \boldsymbol{p}^{\,j} \cdot \boldsymbol{x}^{\,\prime ij} \leq \boldsymbol{p}^{\,i} \cdot \boldsymbol{e}^{\,i}$.

We say the *market clears* if the supply equals the demand. In the standard setting, define the total demand vector as $\boldsymbol{d} = \sum_i \boldsymbol{x}^{\,i}$ and the total supply vector as $\boldsymbol{e} = \sum_i \boldsymbol{e}^{\,i}$ and say the market clears if $\boldsymbol{d} = \boldsymbol{e}$. In the graphical setting, the concept of clearance is applied to each "commodity h sold by i", so we have a *local* notion of clearance, in which all the goods sold by each consumer clear in the neighborhood. Define the local

[1] Throughout the paper we describe the model and results in the setting where the graph constrains exchange between individual consumers, but everything generalizes to the case in which the vertices are themselves complete AD economies, and the graph is viewed as representing trade agreements.

demand vector $\boldsymbol{d}^{\,i} \in \mathcal{R}_+^k$ on consumer i as $\boldsymbol{d}^{\,i} = \sum_{j \in N(i)} \boldsymbol{x}^{\,ji}$. The clearance condition is for each i, $\boldsymbol{d}^{\,i} = \boldsymbol{e}^{\,i}$.

A *market or graphical equilibrium* is a set of prices and plans in which all plans are optimal at the current prices and in which the market clears. We note that the notions of traditional AD and graphical equilibria coincide when the graph is fully connected.

As with the original notion of AD equilibria, it is important to establish the general existence of graphical equilibria. Also as with the original notion, in order to prove the existence of equilibria, two natural technical assumptions are required, one on the utility functions and the other on the endowments. We begin with the assumption on utilities.

Assumption I: For all consumers i, the utility function u_i satisfies the following three properties:

- *(Continuity)* u_i is a continuous function.
- *(Monotonicity)* u_i is strictly monotonically increasing with each commodity.
- *(Quasi-Concavity)* If $u_i(\boldsymbol{x}\,') > u_i(\boldsymbol{x})$ then $u_i(\alpha \boldsymbol{x}\,' + (1-\alpha)\boldsymbol{x}) > u_i(\boldsymbol{x})$ for all $0 < \alpha < 1$.

The monotonicity assumption is somewhat stronger than the original "non-satiability" assumption made by AD, but is made primarily for expository purposes. Our results can be generalized to the original assumption as well.

The following facts follow from Assumption I and the consumers' rationality:

1. At equilibrium, the budget constraint inequality for consumer i is saturated, *e.g.*, in a standard AD economy, a consumer using an equilibrium plan $\boldsymbol{x}^{\,i}$ spends all the money obtained from the sale of the endowment $\boldsymbol{e}^{\,i}$.
2. In any graphical equilibrium, a consumer only purchases a commodity at the cheapest price among the neighboring consumers. Note that the neighboring consumer with the cheapest price may not be unique.

Assumption II: (Non-Zero Endowments) For each consumer i and good h, $e_h^i > 0$.

The seminal theorem of Arrow and Debreu [1954] states that these assumptions are sufficient to ensure existence of a market equilibrium. However, this theorem does not immediately imply existence of an equilibrium in a graphical economy, due to the restricted nature of trade. Essentially, Assumption II in the AD setting implies that each consumer owns a positive amount of every good in the economy. In the graphical setting, there are effectively nk goods, but each consumer only has an endowment in k of them. To put it another way, consumer i may only obtain income from selling goods at the k *local* prices $\boldsymbol{p}^{\,i}$, and is *not* able to sell any of its endowment at prices $\boldsymbol{p}^{\,j}$ for $j \neq i$.

Nevertheless, Assumptions I and II still turn out to be sufficient to allow us to prove the following graph-theoretic equilibrium existence theorem.

Theorem 1. *(Graphical Equilibria Existence) For any graphical economy in which Assumptions I and II hold, there exists a graphical equilibrium.*

Before proving existence, let us examine these equilibria with some examples.

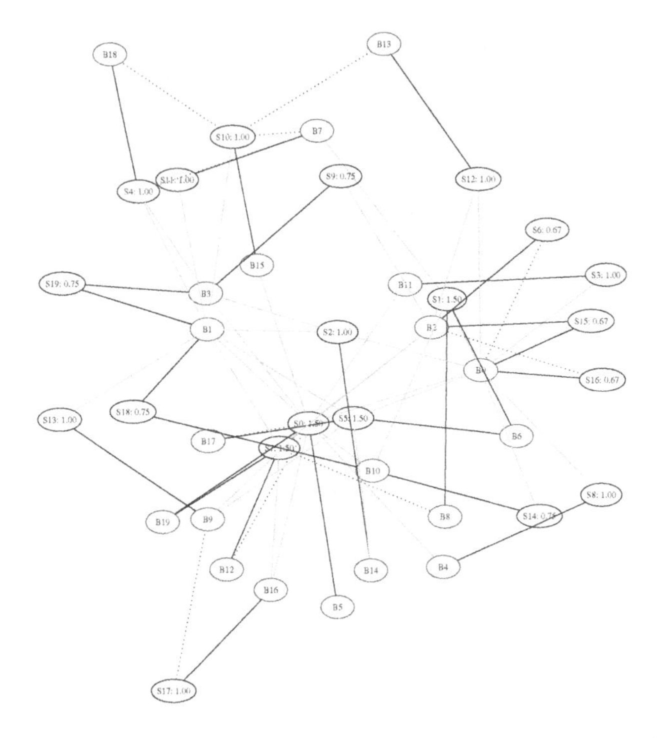

Fig. 1. Price variation and the exchange subgraph at graphical equilibrium in a preferential attachment network. See text for description.

4.1 Local Price Variation at Graphical Equilibrium

To illustrate the concept of graphical equilibrium and its difference with the traditional AD notion, we now provide an example in which local price differences occur at equilibrium. The economy consists of three consumers, c_1, c_2 and c_3, and two goods, g_1 and g_2. The graph of the economy is the line $c_1 - c_2 - c_3$.

The utility functions for all three consumers are linear. Consumer c_1 has linear utility for g_1 with coefficient 1, and zero utility for g_2. Consumer c_2 has linear utility for both g_1 and g_2, with both coefficients 1. Consumer c_3, has zero utility for g_1, and linear utility for g_2 with coefficient 1. The endowments (e_1, e_2) for g_1 and g_2 for the consumers are as follows: $(1, 2)$ for c_1, $(1, 1)$ for c_2, and $(2, 1)$ for c_3.

We claim that the following local prices (p_1, p_2) for g_1 and g_2 constitute a graphical equilibrium: prices $(2, 1)$ to purchase from c_1, $(2, 2)$ to purchase from c_2, and $(1, 2)$ to purchase from c_3. It can also be shown that there is *no* graphical equilibrium in which the prices for both goods is the same from all consumers, so price variations are essential for equilibrium. We leave the verification of these claims as an exercise for the interested reader.

Essentially, in this example, c_1 and c_3 would like to exchange goods, but the graphical structure prohibits direct trade. Consumer c_2, however, is indifferent to the two goods, and thus acts as a kind of arbitrage agent, selling each of c_1 and c_2 their desired good at a high price, while buying their undesired good at a low price.

A more elaborate and interesting equilibrium computation which also contains price variation is shown in Figure 4.1. In this graph, there are 20 buyers and 20 sellers (labeled by 'B' or 'S' respectively, followed by an index). The bipartite connectivity structure (in which edges are only between buyers and sellers) was generated according to a statistical model known as *preferential attachment* (Barabasi and Albert [1999]), which accounts for the heavy-tailed distribution of degrees often found in real social and economic networks. All buyers have a single unit of currency and utility only for an abstract good, while all sellers have a single unit of this good and utility only for currency. Each seller vertex is labeled with the price they charge at graphical equilibrium. Note that in this example, there is non-trivial price variation, with the most fortunate sellers charging 1.50 for the unit of the good, and the least fortunate 0.67.

The black edges in the figure show the *exchange subgraph* — those pairs of buyers and sellers who actually exchange currency and goods at equilibrium. Note the sparseness of this graph compared to the overall graph. The yellow edges (the most faint in a black and white version) are edges of the original graph that are unused at equilibrium because they represent inferior prices for the buyers, while the dashed edges are edges of the original graph that have competitive prices, but are unused at equilibrium due to the local market clearance conditions.

In a forthcoming paper (Kakade et al. [2004]) we report on a series of large-scale computational experiments of this kind.

4.2 Proof of Graphical Equilibrium Existence

For reasons primarily related to Assumption II, the proof uses the interesting concept of a "quasi-equilibrium", originally defined by Debreu [1962] in work a decade after his seminal existence result with Arrow. It turns out that much previous work has gone into weakening this assumption in the AD setting. If this assumption is not present, then Debreu [1962] shows that although true equilibria may not exist, "quasi-equilibrium" still exist. In a quasi-equilibrium, consumers with 0 wealth are allowed to be irrational.

Our proof proceeds by establishing the existence of a quasi-equilibria in the graphical setting, and then showing that this in fact implies existence of graphical equilibria. This last step involves a graph-theoretic argument showing that every consumer has positive wealth.

A "graphical quasi-equilibrium" is defined as follows.

Definition 1. *A* graphical quasi-equilibrium *for a graphical economy is a set of globally normalized prices P (i.e. $\sum_{i,h} p^i_h = 1$) and a set of consumption plans $\{X^i\}$, in which the local markets clear and for each consumer i, with wealth $w^i = \mathbf{p}^i \cdot \mathbf{e}^i$, the following condition holds:*

- *(Rational) If consumer i has positive wealth ($w^i > 0$), then i is rational (utility-maximizing).*
- *(Quasi-Rational) Else if has no wealth ($w^i = 0$), then the plan X^i is only budget constrained (and does not necessarily maximize utility).*

Lemma 1. *(Graphical Quasi-Equilibria Existence) In any graphical economy in which Assumption I holds, there exists a graphical quasi-equilibrium.*

The proof is straightforward and is provided in a longer version of this paper. Note that if all consumers have positive wealth at a quasi-equilibrium, then all consumers are rational. Hence, to complete the proof of Theorem 1 it suffices to prove that all consumers have positive wealth at a quasi-equilibrium. For this we provide the following lemma, which demonstrates how wealth propagates in the graph.

Lemma 2. *If the graph of a graphical economy is connected and if Assumptions I and II hold, then for any quasi-equilibrium set of prices $\{\boldsymbol{p}^{\,i}\}$, it holds that every consumer has non-zero wealth.*

Proof. Note that by price normalization, there exists at least one consumer that has one commodity with non-zero price. We now show that if for any consumer i, $\boldsymbol{p}^{\,i} \neq \mathbf{0}$, then this implies that for all $j \in N(i)$, $\boldsymbol{p}^{\,j} \neq \mathbf{0}$. This is sufficient to prove the result, since the graph is assumed to be connected and $\boldsymbol{e}^{\,i} > 0$.

Let $\{X^i\}$ and $\{\boldsymbol{p}^{\,i}\}$ be a quasi-equilibrium. Assume that in some i, $\boldsymbol{p}^{\,i} \neq \mathbf{0}$. Since every consumer has positive endowments in each commodity (Assumption II), $\boldsymbol{p}^{\,i} \cdot \boldsymbol{e}^{\,i} > 0$, and so consumer i is rational. By Fact 1, the budget constraint inequality of i must be saturated, so $\sum_{j \in N(i)} \boldsymbol{p}^{\,j} \cdot \boldsymbol{x}^{\,ij} = \boldsymbol{p}^{\,i} \cdot \boldsymbol{e}^{\,i} > 0$. Hence, there must exist a commodity h and a $j \in N(i)$ such that $x_h^{ij} > 0$ and $p_h^j \neq 0$, else the money spent would be 0. In other words, there must exist a commodity that is consumed by i from a neighbor at a non-zero price.

The rationality of i implies that consumer j has the cheapest price for the commodity h, otherwise i would buy h from a cheaper neighbor (Fact 2). More formally, $j \in \arg\min_{\ell \in N(i)} p_h^\ell$, which implies for all $\ell \in N(i)$, $p_h^\ell \geq p_h^j > 0$. Thus we have shown that for all $\ell \in N(i)$, $\boldsymbol{p}^{\,\ell} \neq \mathbf{0}$, and since by Assumption II, $\boldsymbol{e}^{\,l} > 0$, this completes the proof. □

Without graph connectivity, it is possible that all the consumers in a disconnected graph could have zero wealth at a quasi-equilibrium. Hence, to complete the proof of Theorem 1, we observe that in each connected region we have a separate graphical equilibria.

It turns out that the "propagation" argument in the previous proof, with more careful accounting, actually leads to a quantitative lower bound on consumer wealth in a graphical economy, which we now present. This lower bound is particularly useful when we turn towards computational issues in a moment.

The following definitions are needed:

$$e_+ = \max_{i,h} e_h^i\,, \quad e_- = \min_{i,h} e_h^i$$

Note that Assumption II implies that $e_- > 0$.

Lemma 3. *(Wealth Propagation) In a graphical economy, in which Assumptions I and II hold, with a connected graph of degree $m-1$, the wealth of any consumer i at* *equilibrium prices* $\{\boldsymbol{p}^{\,i}\}$ *is bounded as follows:*

$$\boldsymbol{p}^{\,i} \cdot \boldsymbol{e}^{\,i} \geq \left(\frac{e_-}{e_+ mk}\right)^{diameter(G)} \frac{e_-}{n} > 0$$

The proof is provided in the long version of this paper.

Interestingly, note that a graph that maximizes free trade (*i.e.* a fully connected graph) maximizes this lower bound on the wealth of a consumer.

5 Algorithms for Computing Economic Equilibria

All of our algorithmic results compute approximate, rather than exact, economic equilibria. We first give the requisite definitions. We use the natural definition originally presented in Deng et al. [2002]. First, two concepts are useful to define — approximate optimality and approximate clearance. A plan is *ε-optimal* at some price P if the plans are budget constrained under P and if the utility of the plan is at least $1-\varepsilon$ times the optimal utility under P. The market *ε-clears* if, in the standard setting, $(1-\varepsilon)\boldsymbol{e} \leq \boldsymbol{d} \leq \boldsymbol{e}$ and, in the graphical setting, for all i, $(1-\varepsilon)\boldsymbol{e}^{\,i} \leq \boldsymbol{d}^{\,i} \leq \boldsymbol{e}^{\,i}$. Now we say a set of plans and prices constitute an *ε-equilibrium* if the market ε-clears and if the plans are ε-optimal. [2]

The algorithms we present search for an approximate ADE on a discretized grid. Hence, we need some sort of "smoothness" condition on the utility function in order for the discretized grid to be a good approximation to the true space. More formally,
Assumption III: We assume there is exists $\gamma \geq 0$ such that for all i and for all $\boldsymbol{x}$

$$u_i(\,(1+\gamma)\boldsymbol{x}\,) \leq \exp(\gamma d) u_i(\boldsymbol{x})$$

for some constant d.

Note that for polynomials with positive weights, the constant d can be taken to be the degree of the polynomial. Essentially, the condition states that if a consumer increases his consumption plan by some multiplicative factor γ, then his utility cannot increase by the exponentially larger, multiplicative factor of $\exp(\gamma d)$. This condition is a natural one to consider, since the "growth rate" constant d is dimensionless (unlike the derivative of the utility function $\partial u_i / \partial \boldsymbol{x}$, which has units of $utility/goods$).

Naturally, for reasons of computational generality, we make a "black box" representational assumption on the utility functions.
Assumption IV: We assume that for all i, the utility function u_i is given as an oracle, which given an input $\boldsymbol{x}^{\,i}$, outputs $u_i(\boldsymbol{x}^{\,i})$ in unit time.

For the remainder of the paper, we assume that Assumptions I-IV hold.

---

[2] It turns out that any ε-approximate equilibrium in our setting with monotonically increasing utility functions can be transformed into an approximate equilibrium in which the market *exactly* clears while the plans are still ε-optimal. To see this note that the cost of the unsold goods is equal to the surplus money in the consumers' budgets. The monotonicity assumption allows us to increase the consumption plans, using the surplus money, to take up the excess supply without decreasing utilities. This transformation is in general not possible if we weaken the monotonicity assumption to a non-satiability assumption.

5.1 An Improved Algorithm for Computing AD Equilibria

We now present an algorithm for computing AD equilibria for rather general utility functions in the non-graphical setting. The algorithm is a generalization of the algorithm provided by Deng et al. [2002], which computes equilibria for the case in which the utilities are linear functions. While our primary interest in this algorithm is as a subroutine for the graphical algorithm presented in Section 5.3, it is also of independent interest.

The idea of the algorithm is as follows. For each consumer i, a binary valued "best-response" table $M_i(\boldsymbol{p}, \boldsymbol{x})$ is computed, where the indices $\boldsymbol{p}$ and $\boldsymbol{x}$ are prices and plans. The value of $M_i(\boldsymbol{p}, \boldsymbol{x})$ is set to 1 if and only if $\boldsymbol{x}$ is ε-optimal for consumer i at prices $\boldsymbol{p}$. Once these tables are computed, the "price player's" task is then to find $\boldsymbol{p}$ and $\{\boldsymbol{x}^{\,i}\}$ such that $(1-\varepsilon)\boldsymbol{e} \leq \boldsymbol{d} \leq \boldsymbol{e}$ and for all i, $M_i(\boldsymbol{p}, \boldsymbol{x}^{\,i}) = 1$.

To keep the tables of M_i of finite size, we only consider prices and plans on a grid. As in Deng et al. [2002] and Papadimitriou and Yannakakis [2000], we consider a relative grid of the form:

$$\mathcal{G}_{\text{price}} = \{p_0,\, (1+\varepsilon)p_0,\, (1+\varepsilon)^2 p_0,\, \dots, 1\}\,,$$

$$\mathcal{G}_{\text{plan}} = \{x_0,\, (1+\varepsilon)x_0,\, (1+\varepsilon)^2 x_0,\, \dots, ne_+\}$$

where the maximal grid price is 1 and maximal grid plan is ne_+ (since there is at most an amount ne_+ of any good in the market). The intuitive reason for the use of a relative grid is that demand is more sensitive to price perturbations of cheaper priced goods, since consumers have more purchasing power for these goods.

In Section 5.2, we sketch the necessary approximation scheme, which shows how to set p_0 and x_0 such that an ε-equilibrium on this grid exists. The natural method to set p_0 is to use a lower bound on the equilibrium prices. Unfortunately, under rather general conditions, only the trivial lower bound of 0 is possible. However, we can set p_0 and x_0 based on a non-trivial *wealth* bound.

Now let us sketch how we use the tables to compute an ε-equilibrium. Essentially, the task now lies in checking that the demand vector $\boldsymbol{d}$ is close to $\boldsymbol{e}$ for a set of plans and prices which are true for the M_i. As in Deng et al. [2002], a form of dynamic programming suffices. Consider a binary, "partial sum of demand" table $S_i(\boldsymbol{p}, \boldsymbol{x})$ defined as follows: $S_i(\boldsymbol{p}, \boldsymbol{d}) = 1$ if and only if there exists $\boldsymbol{x}^1, \dots, \boldsymbol{x}^i$ such that $\boldsymbol{d} = \boldsymbol{x}^1 + \boldsymbol{x}^2 + \dots + \boldsymbol{x}^i$ and $M_1(\boldsymbol{p}, \boldsymbol{x}^1) = 1, \dots, M_i(\boldsymbol{p}, \boldsymbol{x}^i) = 1$. These tables can be computed recursively as follows: if $S_{i-1}(\boldsymbol{p}, \boldsymbol{d}) = 1$ and if $M_i(\boldsymbol{p}, \boldsymbol{x}) = 1$, then we set $S_i(\boldsymbol{p}, \boldsymbol{x} + \boldsymbol{d}) = 1$. Further, we keep track of a "witness" $\boldsymbol{x}^1, \dots, \boldsymbol{x}^i$ which proves that the table entry is 1. The approximation lemmas in Section 5.2 show how to keep this table of finite "small" size (see also long version of the paper).

Once we have S_n, we just search for some index $\boldsymbol{p}$ and $\boldsymbol{d}$ such that $S_n(\boldsymbol{p}, \boldsymbol{d}) = 1$ and $\boldsymbol{d} \approx \boldsymbol{e}$. This $\boldsymbol{p}$ and the corresponding witness plans then constitute an equilibrium. The time complexity of this algorithm is polynomial in the tables sizes, which we shall see is of polynomial size for a fixed k. This gives rise to the following theorem.

Theorem 2. *For fixed k, there exists an algorithm which takes as input an AD economy and outputs an ε-equilibrium in time polynomial in n, $1/\varepsilon$, $\log(e_+/e_-)$, and d.*

The approximation details and proof are provided in the long version of this paper.

5.2 Approximate Equilibria on a Relative Grid

We now describe a relative discretization scheme for prices and consumption plans that is used by the algorithm just described for computing equilibria in classical (non-graphical) AD economies. This scheme can be generalized for the graphical setting, but is easier to understand in the standard setting.

Without loss of generality, throughout this section we assume the prices in a market are globally normalized, *i.e.* $\sum_h p_h = 1$.

A price and consumption plan can be mapped onto the relative grid in the obvious way. Define $grid(\boldsymbol{p}) \in \mathcal{R}_+^k$ to be the closest price to $\boldsymbol{p}$ such that each component of $grid(\boldsymbol{p})$ is on the price grid. Hence,

$$\frac{1}{1+\varepsilon}\boldsymbol{p} \leq grid(\boldsymbol{p}) \leq \max\{(1+\varepsilon)\boldsymbol{p}, p_0\mathbf{1}\}$$

where the max is taken component-wise and $\mathbf{1}$ is a k-length vector of all ones. Note that the value of p_0 is a threshold where all prices below p_0 get set to this threshold price. Similarly, for any consumption plan $\boldsymbol{x}^i$, let $grid(\boldsymbol{x}^i)$ be the closest plan to $\boldsymbol{x}^i$ such that $grid(\boldsymbol{x}^i)$ is componentwise on $\mathcal{G}_{\text{plan}}$.

In order for such a discretization scheme to work, we require two properties. First, the grid should certainly *contain* an approximate equilibrium of the desired accuracy. We shall refer to this property as *Approximate Completeness* (of the grid). Second, and more subtly, it should also be the case that maximizing consumer utility, while *constrained* to the grid, results in utilities close to those achieved by the *unconstrained* maximization — otherwise, our grid-restricted search for equilibria might result in highly suboptimal consumer plans. We shall refer to this property as *Approximate Soundness* (of the grid). It turns out that Approximate Soundness only holds if prices ensure a minimum level of wealth for each consumer, but conveniently we shall always be in such a situation due to Lemma 3.

The next two lemmas establish Approximate Completeness and Soundness for the grid. The Approximate Completeness Lemma also states how to set p_0 and x_0. It is straightforward to show that if we have a lower bound on the price at equilibrium, then p_0 can be set to this lower bound. Unfortunately, it turns out that under our rather general conditions we cannot provide a lower bound. Instead, as the lemmas show, it is sufficient to use a lower bound w_0 on the wealth of any consumer at equilibrium, and set p_0 and x_0 based on this wealth. Note that in the traditional AD setting e_- is a bound on the wealth, since the prices are normalized.

Lemma 4. *(Approximate Completeness) Let the grids $\mathcal{G}_{price}$ and $\mathcal{G}_{plan}$ be defined using*

$$p_0 = \frac{\varepsilon}{nke_+}w_0\ ,\ x_0 = \frac{\varepsilon}{(1+13\varepsilon)nk}w_0$$

where w_0 is a lower bound on equilibrium wealth of all consumers and let $\{\boldsymbol{x}^{*i}\}$ and $\{\boldsymbol{p}^{*i}\}$ be equilibrium prices and plans. Then the plans $\{\boldsymbol{x}^i = grid\left(\frac{1}{1+13\varepsilon}\boldsymbol{x}^{*i}\right)\}$ are $19d\varepsilon$ approximately optimal for the price $\boldsymbol{p} = grid(\boldsymbol{p}^*)$ and the market 14ε-approximately clears. Furthermore, a useful property of this approximate equilibrium is that every consumer has wealth greater than $\frac{w_0}{1+\varepsilon}$.

There are a number of important subtleties to be addressed in the proof, which we formally present in the longer version. For instance, note that the closest point on the grid to some true equilibria may not even be budget constrained.

Lemma 5. *(Approximate Soundness) Let the grid be defined as in Theorem 4 and let* $\boldsymbol{p}$ *be on the grid such that every consumer has wealth above* $\frac{w_0}{1+\varepsilon}$*. If the plans* $\{\boldsymbol{x}^{\,i}\}$ β*-approximately maximize utility over the budget constrained plans which are componentwise on the grid,* i.e. *if for all budget constrained* $\boldsymbol{x}^{\,\prime i}$ *which lie on the plan grid,*

$$u_i(\boldsymbol{x}^{\,i}) \geq (1-\beta)u_i(\boldsymbol{x}^{\,\prime i})\,.$$

then

$$u_i(\boldsymbol{x}^{\,i}) \geq (1-(\beta+4\varepsilon d))u_i^*$$

where u_i^* *is the optimal utility under* $\boldsymbol{p}$*.*

5.3 Arrow-Debreu Propagation for Graphical Equilibria

We now turn to the problem of computing equilibria in graphical economies. We present the **ADProp** algorithm, which is a dynamic programming, message-passing, algorithm for computing approximate graphical equilibria when the graph has a tree structure. Recall that in a graphical economy there are effectively nk goods, so we cannot keep the number of goods fixed as we scale the number of consumers. Hence, the algorithm described in the previous section cannot be directly applied if we wish to scale polynomially with the number of consumers.

As we will see from the description of **ADProp** below, an appealing conceptual property of the algorithm is how it achieves the computation of *global* economic equilibria in a distributed manner through the *local* exchange of economic trade and price information between just the neighbors in the graph.

We orient the graph such that "downstream" from a vertex lies the root and "upstream" lies the leaves. For any consumer j that is not the root there exists a unique downstream consumer, say ℓ. Let $UP(j)$ be the set of neighbors of j which are not downstream, *i.e.* $UP(j)$ is the set $N(j)-\{\ell\}$ so it includes j itself.

We now define a binary valued table $T_{\ell j}$, which can be viewed as the message that consumer $j \in UP(\ell)$ sends downstream to l. The table $T_{\ell j}(\boldsymbol{p}^{\,\ell}, \boldsymbol{x}^{\,\ell j}, \boldsymbol{p}^{\,j}, \boldsymbol{x}^{\,j\ell})$ is indexed by the prices for ℓ and j and the consumption that flows along the edge between ℓ and j — from ℓ to j, the consumption is $\boldsymbol{x}^{\,\ell j}$, and from j to ℓ, the consumption is $\boldsymbol{x}^{\,j\ell}$. The table entry $T_{\ell j}(\boldsymbol{p}^{\,\ell}, \boldsymbol{x}^{\,\ell j}, \boldsymbol{p}^{\,j}, \boldsymbol{x}^{\,j\ell})$ evaluates to 1 if and only if there exists a *conditional* ε-equilibria upstream from j (inclusive) in which the respective prices and plans are fixed to $\boldsymbol{p}^{\,\ell}, \boldsymbol{x}^{\,\ell j}, \boldsymbol{p}^{\,j}, \boldsymbol{x}^{\,j\ell}$. For the special case where $j=\ell$, the table entry $T_{jj}(\boldsymbol{p}^{\,\ell}, \boldsymbol{x}^{\,\ell j}, \boldsymbol{p}^{\,j}, \boldsymbol{x}^{\,j\ell})$ is set to 1 if and only if $\boldsymbol{p}^{\,\ell} = \boldsymbol{p}^{\,j}$ and $\boldsymbol{x}^{\,\ell j} = \boldsymbol{x}^{\,j\ell}$ (note that $\boldsymbol{x}^{\,jj}$ is effectively the amount of the goods that j desires not to sell).

The tables provide all the information needed to apply dynamic programming in the obvious way. In its *downstream pass*, **ADProp** computes the table $T_{\ell j}$ recursively, in the typical dynamic programming fashion. If j is an internal node in the tree, when j has received the appropriate tables from all $i \in UP(j)$, we must set $T_{\ell j}(\boldsymbol{p}^{\,\ell}, \boldsymbol{x}^{\,\ell j}, \boldsymbol{p}^{\,j}, \boldsymbol{x}^{\,j\ell}) = 1$, if: 1) a conditional upstream equilibrium exists, which we can computed from the tables passed to j, 2) the plan X^j, consistent with the upstream equilibrium, is ε-optimal for the neighborhood prices, and 3) the market ε-clear at j. Naturally, a special but similar operation occurs at the leaves and the root of the tree.

Once **ADProp** computes the message at the root consumer, it performs an *upstream pass* to obtain a single graphical equilibrium, again, in the typical dynamic programming fashion. At every node, starting with the root, **ADProp** selects price and allocation assignments consistent with the tables at the node and passes those assignments up to their upstream neighbors, until it reaches the leaves of the tree.

As presented in Section 5.2, we can control the approximation error by using appropriate sized grids. This leads to our main theorem for computing graphical equilibrium.

Theorem 3. *(ADProp) For fixed k and graph degree,* **ADProp** *takes as input a tree graphical economy in which Assumptions I-IV hold and outputs an ε-equilibrium in time polynomial in n, $1/\varepsilon$, $\log(e_+/e_-)$, and d.*

Heuristic generalizations of **ADProp** are possible to handle more complex (loopy) graph structures (*a la* **NashProp** [Ortiz and Kearns, 2003]).

6 Learning in Graphical Games and Economics

Although the work described here has focused primarily on the graphical economics representation, and algorithms for equilibrium computation, the general area of graphical models for economic and strategic settings is rich with challenging learning problems and issues. We conclude by mentioning just a few of these.

Rational Learning in Graphical Games. What happens if each player in a repeated graphical game plays according to some "rational" dynamics (like fictitious play, best response, or other variants), but using only *local* observations (the actions of neighbors)? In cases where convergence occurs, how does the graph structure influence the equilibrium chosen? Are there particular topological properties that favor certain players in the network?

No-Regret Learning in Graphical Games. It has recently been established that if all players in a repeated graphical game play a local *no internal regret* algorithm, the population empirical play will converge to the set of *correlated equilibria*. It was also noted in the introduction that all such equilibrium can be represented up to payoff equivalence on a related Markov network; under what conditions will no-regret learning dynamics actually settle on one of these *succinct* equilibria? In preliminary experiments using the algorithms of Foster and Vohra [1999] as well as those of Hart and Mas-Colell [200] and Hart and Mas-Colell [2001], one does not observe convergence to the set of payoff-equivalent Markov network correlated equilibria.

Learning in Traditional AD Economies. Even in the non-graphical Arrow-Debreu setting, little is known about reasonable distributed learning procedures. Aside from a strong (impossibility) result by Saari and Simon [1978] suggesting that general convergence results may not be possible, there is considerable open territory here. Conceptual challenges include the manner in which the "price player" should be modeled in the learning process.

Learning in Graphical Economics. Finally, problems of learning in the graphical economics model are entirely open, including the analogues to all of the questions above. Generally speaking, one would like to formulate reasonable procedures for *local* learning (adjustment of seller prices and buyer purchasing decisions), and examine how these procedures are influenced by network structure.

References

Kenneth J. Arrow and Gerard Debreu. Existence of an equilibrium for a competitive economy. *Econometrica*, 22(3):265–290, 1954.

A. Barabasi and R. Albert. Emergence of scaling in random networks. *Science*, 286:509–512, 1999.

Ben Blum, Christian R. Shelton, and Daphne Koller. A continuation method for Nash equilibria in structured games. In *Proceedings of the Eighteenth International Joint Conference on Artificial Intelligence*, 2003.

William C. Brainard and Herbert E. Scarf. How to compute equilibrium prices in 1891. *Cowles Foundation Discussion Paper 1272*, 2000.

Gerard Debreu. New concepts and techniques for equilibrium analysis. *International Economic Review*, 3(3):257–273, 1962.

Xiaotie Deng, Christos Papadimitriou, and Shmuel Safra. On the complexity of equilibria. In *Proceedings of the Thiry-fourth Annual ACM Symposium on Theory of Computing*, pages 67–71. ACM Press, 2002.

Nikhil R. Devanur, Christos H. Papadimitriou, Amin Saberi, and Vijay V. Vazirani. Market equilibrium via a primal-dual-type algorithm. In *Proceedings of the 43rd Annual IEEE Symposium on Foundations of Computer Science*, 2002.

Nikhil R. Devanur and Vijay V. Vazirani. An improved approximation scheme for computing Arrow-Debreu prices for the linear case. In *Proceedings of the 23rd Conference on Foundations of Software Technology and Theoretical Computer Science*, 2003. To appear.

Irving Fisher. PhD thesis, Yale University, 1891.

D. Foster and R. Vohra. Regret in the on-line decision problem. *Games and Economic Behavior*, pages 7 – 36, 1999.

Sergiu Hart and Andreu Mas-Colell. A simple adaptive procedure leading to correlated equilibrium. *Econometrica*, 68(5):1127 – 1150, 200.

Sergiu Hart and Andreu Mas-Colell. A reinforcement procedure leading to correlated equilibrium. In Gerard Debreu, Wilhelm Neuefeind, and Walter Trockel, editors, *Economic Essays*, pages 181 – 200. Springer, 2001.

Matthew Jackson. A survey of models of network formation: Stability and efficiency. In *Group Formation in Economics: Networks, Clubs and Coalitions*. Cambridge University Press, 2003. Forthcoming.

Kamal Jain, Mohammad Mahdian, and Amin Saberi. Approximating market equilibria. In *Proceedings of the 6th. International Workshop on Approximation Algorithms for Combinatorial Optimization Problems*, 2003.

S. Kakade, M. Kearns, J. Langford, and L. Ortiz. Correlated equilibria in graphical games. In *Proceedings of the 4th ACM Conference on Electronic Commerce*, pages 42–47, 2003.

S. Kakade, M. Kearns, L. Ortiz, R. Pemantle, and S. Suri. The economics of social networks. 2004. Preprint.

M. Kearns, M. Littman, and S. Singh. Graphical models for game theory. In *Proceedings of the Conference on Uncertainty in Artificial Intelligence*, pages 253–260, 2001.

M. Littman, M. Kearns, and S. Singh. An efficient exact algorithm for singly connected graphical games. In *Neural Information Processing Systems*, 2002.

J. F. Nash. Non-cooperative games. *Annals of Mathematics*, 54:286–295, 1951.

L. Ortiz and M. Kearns. Nash propagation for loopy graphical games. In *Neural Information Processing Systems*, 2003.

Christos H. Papadimitriou and Mihalis Yannakakis. On the approximability of trade-offs and optimal access of web sources. In *Proceedings of the 41st Annual IEEE Symposium on Foundations of Computer Science*, 2000.

D. G. Saari and C. P. Simon. Effective price mechanisms. *Econometrica*, 46, 1978.

D. Vickrey and D. Koller. Multi-agent algorithms for solving graphical games. In *Proceedings of the National Conference on Artificial Intelligence*, 2002.

Abraham Wald. Über einige Gleichungssysteme der mathematischen Ökonomie (On some systems of equations of mathematical economics). *Zeitschrift für Nationalökonomie*, 7(5):637–670, 1936. English translation by Otto Eckstein in *Econometrica*, Vol. 19, No. 4 (Oct., 1951), 368–403.

Léon Walras. *Éléments d'économie politique pure; ou, Théorie de la richesse sociale (Elements of Pure Economics, or the Theory of social wealth).* Lausanne, Paris, 1874. (1899, 4th ed.; 1926, rev ed., 1954, Engl. transl.).

Deterministic Calibration and Nash Equilibrium

Sham M. Kakade and Dean P. Foster

University of Pennsylvania, Philadelphia, PA 19104

Abstract. We provide a natural learning process in which the joint frequency of empirical play converges into the set of convex combinations of Nash equilibria. In this process, all players rationally choose their actions using a public prediction made by a deterministic, *weakly calibrated* algorithm. Furthermore, the public predictions used in any given round of play are frequently close to some Nash equilibrium of the game.

1 Introduction

Perhaps the most central question for justifying any game theoretic equilibrium as a general solution concept is: can we view the equilibrium as a convergent point of a sensible learning process? Unfortunately for Nash equilibria, there are currently no learning algorithms in the literature in which play generally converges (in some sense) to a Nash equilibrium of the one shot game, short of exhaustive search — see Foster and Young [ming] for perhaps the most general result in which players sensibly search through hypothesis. In contrast, there is a long list of special cases (*eg* zero sum games, 2x2 games, assumptions about the players' prior subjective beliefs) in which there exist learning algorithms that have been shown to converge (a representative but far from exhaustive list would be Robinson [1951], Milgrom and Roberts [1991], Kalai and Lehrer [1993], Fudenberg and Levine [1998], Freund and Schapire [1999]).

If we desire that the mixed strategies themselves converge to a Nash equilibrium, then a recent result by Hart and Mas-Colell [2003] shows that this is, in general, not possible under a certain class of learning rules [1]. Instead, one can examine the convergence of the joint frequency of the empirical play, which has the advantage of being an observable quantity. This has worked well in the case of a similar equilibrium concept, namely correlated equilibrium (Foster and Vohra [1997], Hart and Mas-Colell [2000]). However, for Nash equilibria, previous general results even for this weaker form of convergence are limited to some form of exhaustive search (though see Foster and Young [ming]).

In this paper, we provide a learning process in which the joint frequency of empirical play converges to a Nash equilibrium, if it is unique. More generally, convergence is into the set of convex combinations of Nash equilibria (where

[1] They show that, in general, there exists no continuous time dynamics which converge to a Nash equilibrium (even if the equilibrium is unique), with the natural restriction that a players mixed strategy is updated without using the knowledge of the other players' utility functions.

J. Shawe-Taylor and Y. Singer (Eds.): COLT 2004, LNAI 3120, pp. 33–48, 2004.

the empirical play could jump from one Nash equilibrium to another infinitely often). Our learning process is the most traditional one: players make predictions of their opponents and take best responses to their predictions. Central to our learning process is the use of public predictions formed by an "accurate" (*eg* calibrated) prediction algorithm.

We now outline the main contributions of this paper.

"Almost" Deterministic Calibration. Formulating sensible prediction algorithms is a notoriously difficult task in the game theoretic setting [2]. A rather minimal requirement for any prediction algorithm is that it should be *calibrated* (see Dawid [1982]). An informal explanation of calibration would go something like this. Suppose each day a weather forecaster makes some prediction, say p, of the chance that it rains the next day. Now from the subsequence of days on which the forecaster announced p, compute the empirical frequency that it actually rained the next day, and call this $\rho(p)$. Crudely speaking, calibration requires that $\rho(p)$ equal p, if the forecast p is used often.

If the weather acts adversarially, then Oakes [1985] and Dawid [1985] show that a deterministic forecasting algorithm will not be always be calibrated. However, Foster and Vohra [1998] show that calibration is almost surely guaranteed with a randomized forecasting rule, *ie* where the forecasts are chosen using private randomization and the forecasts are hidden from the weather until the weather makes its decision to rain or not. Of course, this solution makes it difficult for a weather forecaster to publicly announce a prediction.

Although stronger notions of calibration have been proposed (see Kalai *et al.* [1999]), here we actually consider a weaker notion [3]. Our contribution is to provide a *deterministic* algorithm that is always *weakly calibrated*. Rather than precisely defining weak calibration here, we continue to with our example to show how this deterministic algorithm can be used to obtain calibrated forecasts in the standard sense.

Assume the weather forecaster uses our deterministic algorithm and publicly announces forecasts to a number of observers interested in the weather. Say the following forecasts are made over some period of 5 days:

$$0.8606, 0.2387, 0.57513, 0.4005, 0.069632, \ldots$$

How can an interested observer make calibrated predictions using this announced forecast? In our setting, an observer can just *randomly round* the forecasts in order to calibrate. For example, if the observer rounds to the second digit, then on the first day, the observer will privately predict .87 with probability .06 and .86 otherwise, and, on the second day, the private predictions will be 0.24 with probability 0.87 and 0.23 otherwise. Under this scheme, the asymptotic calibration

[2] Subjective notions of probability fall prey to a host of impossibility results — crudely, Alice wants to predict Bob while Bob wants to predict Alice, which leads to a feedback loop (if Alice and Bob are both rational). See Foster and Young [2001].

[3] We use the word "weak" in the technical sense of weak convergence of measures (see Billingsley [1968]) rather than how it used by Kalai *et al.* [1999].

error of the observer will, almost surely, be small (and if the observer rounded to the third digit, this error would be yet even smaller).

Unlike previous calibrated algorithms, this deterministic algorithm provides a meaningful forecast, which can be calibrated using only randomized rounding.

Nash Convergence. The existence of a deterministic forecasting scheme leaves open the possibility that all players can rationally use some public forecast, since each player is guaranteed to form calibrated predictions (*regardless* of how the other players behave). For example, say some public forecaster provides a prediction of the *full joint distribution* of all n players. The algorithm discussed above can be generalized such that each player can use this prediction (with randomized rounding) to construct a prediction of the other players. Each player can then use their own prediction to choose a best response.

We formalize this scheme later, but point out that our (weakly) calibrated forecasting algorithm only needs to observe the history of play (and does not require any information about the players' utility functions). Furthermore, there need not be any "publicly announced" forecast provided to every player at each round — alternatively, each player could have knowledge of the deterministic forecasting algorithm and could perform the computation themselves.

Now Foster and Vohra [1997] showed that if players make predictions that satisfy the rather minimal calibration condition, then the joint frequency of the empirical play converges into the set of correlated equilibria. Hence, it is immediate that in our setting, convergence is into the set of correlated equilibria. However, we can prove the stronger condition that the joint frequency of empirical play converges into the set of convex combinations of Nash equilibria, a smaller set than that of correlated equilibria. This directly implies that the average payoff achieved by each player is at least the player's payoff under some Nash equilibrium — a stronger guarantee than achieving a (possibly smaller) correlated equilibrium payoff.

This setting deals with the coordination problem of "which Nash equilibrium to play?" in a natural manner. The setting does not arbitrarily force play to any single equilibrium and allows the possibility that players could (jointly) switch play from one Nash equilibrium to another — perhaps infinitely often. Furthermore, although play converges to the convex combinations of Nash equilibria, we have the stronger result that the public forecasts themselves are frequently close to some Nash equilibrium (*not* general combinations of them). Of course if the Nash equilibrium is unique, then the empirical play converges to it.

The convergence rate, until the empirical play is an approximate Nash equilibrium, is $O(\sqrt{T})$ (where T is the number of rounds of play), with constants that are exponential in both the number of players and actions. Hence, our setting does not lead to a polynomial time algorithm for computing an approximate Nash equilibrium (which is currently an important open problem).

2 Deterministic Calibration

We first describe the online prediction setting. There is a finite outcome space $\Omega = \{1, 2, \ldots |\Omega|\}$. Let X be an infinite sequence of outcomes, whose t-th element, X_t, indicates the outcome on time t. For convenience, we represent the outcome $X_t = (X_t[1], X_t[2], \ldots X_t[|\Omega|])$ as a binary vector in $\{0,1\}^{|\Omega|}$ that indicates which state at time t was realized — if the realized state was i, then the i-th component of X_t is 1 and all other components are 0. Hence, $\frac{1}{T}\sum_{t=1}^{T} X_t$ is the empirical frequency of the outcomes up to time T and is a valid probability distribution.

A forecasting method, F, is simply a function from a sequence of outcomes to a probability distribution over Ω. The forecast that F makes in time t is denoted by $f_t = F(X_1, X_2, \ldots, X_{t-1})$ (clearly, the t-th forecast must be made without knowledge of X_t). Here $f_t = (f_t[1], f_t[2], \ldots f_t[|\Omega|])$, where the ith component is the forecasted probability that state i will be realized in time t.

2.1 Weak Calibration

We now define a quantity to determine if F is calibrated with respect to some probability distribution p. Define $I_{p,\epsilon}(f)$ to be a "test" function indicating if the forecast f is ϵ-close to p, *ie*

$$I_{p,\epsilon}(f) = \begin{cases} 1 & \text{if } |f - p| \leq \epsilon \\ 0 & \text{else} \end{cases}$$

where $|f|$ denotes the l_1 norm, *ie* $|f| = \sum_{k \in \Omega} \left|f[k]\right|$. We define the calibration error μ_T of F with respect to $I_{p,\epsilon}$ as:

$$\mu_T(I_{p,\epsilon}, X, F) = \frac{1}{T}\sum_{t=1}^{T} I_{p,\epsilon}(f_t)(X_t - f_t)$$

Note that $X_t - f_t$ is the immediate error (which is a vector) and the above error μ_T measures this instantaneous error on those times when the forecast was ϵ-close to p.

We say that F is *calibrated* if for all sequences X and all test functions $I_{p,\epsilon}$, the calibration error tends to 0, *ie*

$$\mu_T(I_{p,\epsilon}, X, F) \to 0$$

as T tends to infinity. As discussed in the Introduction, there exist no deterministic rules F that are calibrated (Dawid [1985], Oakes [1985]). However, Foster and Vohra [1998] show that there exist randomized forecasting rules F (*ie* F is a randomized function) which are calibrated. Namely, there exists a randomized F such that for all sequences X and for all test functions $I_{p,\epsilon}$, the error $\mu_T(I_{p,\epsilon}, X, F) \to 0$ as T tends to infinity, with probability 1 (where the probability is taken with respect to the randomization used by the forecasting scheme).

We now generalize this definition of the calibration error by defining it with respect to arbitrary test functions w, where a *test function* is defined as a mapping from probability distributions into the interval $[0,1]$. We define the calibration error μ_T of F with respect to the test function w as:

$$\mu_T(w, X, F) = \frac{1}{T}\sum_{t=1}^{T} w(f_t)(X_t - f_t)$$

This is consistent with the previous definition if we set $w = I_{p,\epsilon}$.

Let W be the set of all test functions which are Lipschitz continuous functions [4]. We say that F is *weakly calibrated* if for all sequences X and all $w \in W$,

$$\mu_T(w, X, F) \to 0$$

as T tends to infinity. Also, we say that F is *uniformly, weakly calibrated* if for all $w \in W$,

$$\sup_X \mu_T(w, X, F) \to 0$$

as T tends to infinity. The latter condition is strictly stronger. Our first main result follows.

Theorem 1. *(Deterministic Calibration) There exists a deterministic forecasting rule which is uniformly, weakly calibrated.*

The proof of this theorem is constructive and is presented in section 4.

2.2 Randomized Rounding for Standard Calibration

We now show how to achieve calibration in the standard sense (with respect to the indicator functions $I_{p,\epsilon}$), using a deterministic weakly calibrated algorithm along with some randomized rounding. Essentially, the algorithm rounds any forecast to some element in a finite set, V, of forecasts. In the example in the Introduction, the set V was the set of probability distributions which are specified up to the second digit of precision.

Let Δ be the simplex in which the forecasts live ($\Delta \subset \mathcal{R}^{|\Omega|}$). Consider some triangulation of Δ. By this, we mean that Δ is partitioned into a set of simplices such that any two simplices intersect in either a common face, common vertex, or not at all. Let V be the vertex set of this triangulation. Note that any point p lies in some simplex in this triangulation, and, slightly abusing notation, let $V(p)$ be the set of corners for this simplex [5]. Informally, our rounding scheme rounds a point p to nearby points in V — p will be randomly mapped into $V(p)$ in the natural manner.

[4] The function g is Lipschitz continuous if g is continuous and if there exists a finite constant λ such that $|g(a) - g(b)| \leq \lambda |a - b|$.

[5] If this simplex is not unique, *ie* if p lies on a face, then choose any adjacent simplex

To formalize this, associate a test function $w_v(p)$ with each $v \in V$ as follows. Each distribution p can be uniquely written as a weighted average of its neighboring vertices, $V(p)$. For $v \in V(p)$, let us define the test functions $w_v(p)$ to be these linear weights, so they are uniquely defined by the linear equation:

$$p = \sum_{v \in V(p)} w_v(p) v \, .$$

For $v \notin V(p)$, we define $w_v(p) = 0$. A useful property is that

$$\sum_{v \in V(p)} w_v(p) = \sum_{v \in V} w_v(p) = 1$$

which holds since p is an average (under w_v) of the points in $V(p)$.

The functions w_v imply a natural randomized rounding function. Define the randomized rounding function $Round_V$ as follows: for some distribution p, $Round_V(p)$ chooses $v \in V(p)$ with probability $w_v(p)$. We make the following assumptions about a randomized rounding forecasting rule F_V with respect to F and triangulation V:

1. F is weakly calibrated.
2. If F makes the forecast f_t at time t, then F_V makes the random forecast $Round_V(f_t)$ at this time.
3. The (l_1) diameter of any simplex in the triangulation is less than ϵ, *ie* for any p and q in the same simplex, $|p - q| \leq \epsilon$.

An immediate corollary to the previous theorem is that F_V is ϵ-calibrated with respect to the indicator test functions.

Corollary 1. *For all X, the calibration error of F_V is asymptotically less than ϵ,* ie *the probability (taken with respect to the randomization used by $Round_V$) that*

$$|\mu_T(I_{p,\epsilon}, X, F_V)| \leq \epsilon$$

tends to 1 as T tends to infinity.

To see this, note that the instantaneous error at time t, $X_t - Round_V(f_t)$, has an expected value of $\sum_v w_v(f_t)(X_t - v)$ which is ϵ-close to $\sum_v w_v(f_t)(X_t - f_t)$. The sum of this latter quantity converges to 0 by the previous theorem. The (martingale) strong law of large numbers then suffices to prove this corollary.

This randomized scheme is "almost deterministic" in the sense that at each time t the forecast made by F_V is ϵ-close to a deterministic forecast. Interestingly, this shows that an adversarial nature cannot foil the forecaster, even if nature almost knows the forecast that will be used every round.

3 Publicly Calibrated Learning

First, some definitions are in order. Consider a game with n players. Each player i has a finite action space $\mathcal{A}_i$. The joint action space is then $\mathcal{A} = \Pi_{i=1}^{n} \mathcal{A}_i$. Associated with each player is a payoff function $u_i : \mathcal{A} \to [0, 1]$. The interpretation is that if the joint action $a \in \mathcal{A}$ is taken by all players then player i will receive payoff $u_i(a)$.

If p is a joint distribution over $\mathcal{A}_{-i} = \Pi_{j \neq i} \mathcal{A}_j$, then we define $BR_i(p)$ to be the set of all actions which are best responses for player i to p, *ie* it is the set of all $a \in \mathcal{A}_i$ which maximize the function $E_{a_{-i} \sim p}[u_i(a, a_{-i})]$. It is also useful to define $\epsilon\text{-}BR_i(p)$ as the set of all actions which are ϵ-best responses to p, *ie* if $a \in \epsilon\text{-}BR_i(p)$ then the utility $E_{a_{-i} \sim p}[u_i(a, a_{-i})]$ is ϵ-close to the maximal utility $\max_{a' \in A} E_{a_{-i} \sim p}[u_i(a', a_{-i})]$.

Given some distribution f over $\mathcal{A}$, it is convenient to denote the marginal distribution of f over $\mathcal{A}_{-i}$ as f_{-i}. We say a distribution f is a Nash equilibrium (or, respectively, ϵ-Nash equilibrium) if the following two conditions hold:

1. f is a product distribution.
2. If action $a \in \mathcal{A}_i$ has positive probability under f then a is in $BR_i(f_{-i})$ (or, respectively, in $\epsilon\text{-}BR_i(f_{-i})$).

We denote the set of all Nash equilibria (or ϵ-Nash equilibria) by NE (or NE_ϵ).

3.1 Using Public Forecasts

A standard setting for learning in games is for each player i to make some forecast p over $\mathcal{A}_{-i}$ at time t. The action taken by player i during this time would then be some action that is a best response to p.

Now consider the setting in which all players observe some forecast f_t over all n players, *ie* the forecast f_t is a full joint probability distribution over $\Omega = \mathcal{A}$. Each player is only interested in the prediction of other players, so player i can just use the marginal distribution $(f_t)_{-i}$ to form a prediction for the other players. In order to calibrate, some randomized rounding is in order.

More formally, we define the *public learning process* with respect to a forecasting rule F and vertex set V as follows: At each time t, F provides a prediction f_t and each player i:

1. makes a prediction $p = Round_V(f_t)$
2. chooses a best response to p_{-i}

We make the following assumptions.

1. F is weakly calibrated.
2. Ties for a best response are broken with a deterministic, stationary rule.
3. If p and q are in the same simplex (of the triangulation) then $|p - q| \leq \epsilon$.

It is straightforward to see that the forecasting rule of player i, which is $(Round_V(f_t))_{-i}$, is calibrated *regardless* of how the other players behave. By the previous corollary the randomized scheme $Round_V(f_t)$ will be ϵ-calibrated. Player i can then simply ignore the direction i of this forecast (by marginalizing) and hence has an ϵ-calibrated forecast over the reduced space $\mathcal{A}_{-i}$.

Thus, the rather minimal accuracy condition that players make calibrated predictions is satisfied, and, in this sense, it is rational for players to use the forecasts made by F. In fact, the setting of "publicly announced" forecasts is only one way to view the scheme. Alternatively, one could assume that each player has knowledge of the deterministic rule F and makes the computations of f_t themselves. Furthermore, F only needs the history of play as an input (and does not need any knowledge of the players' utility functions).

It is useful to make the following definitions. Let Convex(Q) be the set of all convex combinations of distributions in Q [6]. Define the distance between a distribution p and a set Q as:

$$d(p, Q) = \inf_{q \in Q} |p - q|$$

Using the result of Foster and Vohra [1997], it is immediate that the frequency of empirical play in the public learning process will (almost surely) converge into the set of 2ϵ-correlated equilibria, since the players are making ϵ-calibrated predictions, *ie*

$$d\left(\frac{1}{T}\sum_{t=1}^{T} X_t,\ CE_{2\epsilon}\right) \to 0$$

where $CE_{2\epsilon}$ is the set of 2ϵ-correlated equilibria. Our second main result shows we can further restrict the convergent set to convex combinations of Nash equilibria, a potentially much smaller set than the set of correlated equilibria.

Theorem 2. *(Nash Convergence) The joint frequency of empirical play in the public learning process converges into the set of convex combinations of* 2ϵ*-Nash equilibria,* ie *with probability* 1

$$d\left(\frac{1}{T}\sum_{t=1}^{T} X_t,\ Convex(NE_{2\epsilon})\right) \to 0$$

as T goes to infinity. Furthermore, the rule F rarely uses forecasts that are not close to a 2ϵ-Nash equilibrium — by this, we mean that with probability one

$$\frac{1}{T}\sum_{t=1}^{T} d(f_t,\ NE_{2\epsilon}) \to 0$$

as T goes to infinity.

[6] If $q_1, q_2, \ldots q_m \in Q$ then $\alpha_1 q_1 + \alpha_2 q_2 \ldots + \alpha_m q_m \in$ Convex(Q), where α_i are positive and sum to one.

Since our convergence is with respect to the *joint* empirical play, an immediate corollary is that the average payoff achieved by each player is at least the player's payoff under some 2ϵ-Nash equilibrium. Also, we have the following corollary showing convergence to NE.

Corollary 2. *If F is uniformly, weakly calibrated and if the triangulation V is made finer (*ie *if ϵ is decreased) sufficiently slowly, then the joint frequency of empirical play converges into the set of convex combinations of NE.*

As we stated in the Introduction, we argue that the above result deals with the coordination problem of "which Nash equilibrium to play?" in a sensible manner. Though the players cannot be pinned down to play any particular Nash equilibrium, they do jointly play some Nash equilibrium for long subsequences. Furthermore, it is public knowledge of which equilibrium is being played since the predictions f_t are frequently close to some Nash equilibrium (*not* general combinations of them).

Now of course if the Nash equilibrium is unique, then the empirical play converges to it. This does not contradict the (impossibility) result of Hart and Mas-Colell [2003] — crudely, our learning setting keeps track of richer statistics from the history of play (which is not permitted in their setting).

3.2 The Proof

On some round in which f is forecasted, every player acts according to a fixed randomized rule. Let $\pi(f)$ be this "play distribution" over joint actions $\mathcal{A}$ on any round with forecast f. More precisely, if f_t is the forecast at time t, then $\pi(f_t)$ is the expected value of X_t given f_t. Clearly, $\pi(f)$ is a product distribution since all players choose actions independently (since their randomization is private).

Lemma 1. *For all Lipschitz continuous test functions w, with probability 1, we have*

$$\frac{1}{\tau}\sum_{t=1}^{\tau} w(f_t)(f_t - \pi(f_t)) \to 0$$

as τ tends to infinity.

Proof. Consider the stochastic process $Y_\tau = \frac{1}{\tau}\sum_{t=1}^{\tau} w(f_t)(X_t - \pi(f_t))$. This is a martingale average (i.e. τY_τ is a martingale), since at every round, the expected value of X_t is $\pi(f_t)$. By the martingale strong law we have $Y_\tau \to 0$ as τ tends to infinity, with probability one. Also, by calibration, we have $\frac{1}{\tau}\sum_{t=1}^{\tau} w(f_t)(f_t - X_t) \to 0$ as τ tends to infinity. Combining these two leads to the result. □

We now show that fixed points of π are approximate Nash equilibria.

Lemma 2. *If $f = \pi(f)$, then f is a 2ϵ-Nash equilibrium.*

Proof. Assume that $a \in \mathcal{A}_i$ has positive probability under $\pi(f)$. By definition of the public learning process, action a must be a best response to some distribution p_{-i}, where $p \in V(f)$. Assumption 3 implies that $|p - f| \leq \epsilon$, so it follows that $|p_{-i} - f_{-i}| \leq \epsilon$. Since the utility of taking a under any distribution q_{-i} is $\sum_{a_{-i} \in \mathcal{A}_{-i}} q_{-i}[a_{-i}] u_i(a, a_{-i})$, the previous inequality and boundedness of u_i by 1 imply that a must be a 2ϵ-best response to f_{-i}. Furthermore, f is a product distribution, since $\pi(f)$ is one. The result follows. □

Taken together, these last two lemmas suggest that forecasts which are used often must be a 2ϵ-Nash equilibrium — the first lemma suggests that forecasts f which are used often must be equal to $\pi(f)$, and the second lemma states that if this occurs, then f is a 2ϵ Nash equilibrium. We now make this precise.

Define a forecast f to be *asymptotically unused* if there exists a continuous test function w such that $w(f) = 1$ and $\frac{1}{T}\sum_{t=1}^{T} w(f_t) \to 0$. In other words, a forecast is asymptotically unused if we can find some small neighborhood around it such that the limiting frequency of using a forecast in this neighborhood is 0.

Lemma 3. *If f is not a 2ϵ-Nash equilibrium, then it is asymptotically unused, with probability one.*

Proof. Consider a sequence of ever finer balls around f, and associate a continuous test function with each ball that is nonzero within the ball. Let r_1, r_2, r_3, ... be a sequence of decreasing radii such that $r_i \to 0$ as i tends to infinity. Define the open ball B_i as the set of all points p such that $|p - f| < r_i$. Associate a continuous test function w_i with the i-th ball such that: if $p \notin B_i$, $w_i(p) = 0$ and if $p \in B_i$, $w_i(p) > 0$, with $w_i(f) = 1$. Clearly, this construction is possible.

Define the radius r'_i as the maximal variation of π within the the $i - th$ ball, *ie* $r'_i = \sup_{p,q \in B_i} |\pi(p) - \pi(q)|$. Since $\pi(p)$ is continuous, then $r'_i \to 0$ as i tends to infinity.

Using the fact that $|f - \pi(f)|$ is a constant (for the following first equality),

$$\begin{aligned}
&\left(\sum_{t=1}^{T} w_i(f_t)\right) |f - \pi(f)| \\
&= \left|\sum_{t=1}^{T} w_i(f_t)(f - \pi(f))\right| \\
&= \left|\sum_{t=1}^{T} w_i(f_t)\Big((f - f_t) - (\pi(f) - \pi(f_t)) + (f_t - \pi(f_t))\Big)\right| \\
&\leq \left|\sum_{t=1}^{T} w_i(f_t)(f - f_t)\right| + \left|\sum_{t=1}^{T} w_i(f_t)(\pi(f) - \pi(f_t))\right| + \left|\sum_{t=1}^{T} w_i(f_t)(f_t - \pi(f_t))\right| \\
&\leq (r_i + r'_i)\sum_{t=1}^{T} w_i(f_t) + \left|\sum_{t=1}^{T} w_i(f_t)(f_t - \pi(f_t))\right|
\end{aligned}$$

where the last step uses the fact that $w_i(f_t)$ is zero if $|f_t - f| \geq r_i$ (*ie* if $f_t \notin B_i$) along with the definitions of r_i and r'_i.

Now to prove that f is asymptotically unused it suffices to show that there exists some i such that $\frac{1}{T}\sum_{t=1}^{T} w_i(f_t) \to 0$ as T tends to infinity. For a proof by contradiction, assume that such an i does not exist. Dividing the above equation by these sum weights, which are (asymptotically) nonzero by this assumption, we have

$$|f - \pi(f)| \leq r_i + r'_i + \frac{|\frac{1}{T}\sum_{t=1}^{T} w_i(f_t)(f_t - \pi(f_t))|}{\frac{1}{T}\sum_{t=1}^{T} w_i(f_t)}$$

Now by lemma 1, we know the numerator of the last term goes to 0. So, for all i, we have that $|f - \pi(f)| \leq r_i + r'_i$. By taking the limit as i tends to infinity, we have $|f - \pi(f)| = 0$. Thus f is a 2ϵ-Nash equilibrium by the previous lemma, which contradicts our assumption on f. □

We say a set of forecasts Q is asymptotically unused if there exists a continuous test function w such that $w(f) = 1$ for all $f \in Q$ and $\frac{1}{T}\sum_{t=1}^{T} w(f_t) \to 0$.

Lemma 4. *If Q is a compact set of forecasts such that every $f \in Q$ is not a 2ϵ-Nash equilibrium, then Q is asymptotically unused, with probability one.*

Proof. By the last lemma, we know that each $q \in Q$ is asymptotically unused. Let w_q be a test function which proves that q is asymptotically unused. Since w_q is continuous and $w_q(q) = 1$, there exists an open neighborhood around q in which w_q is strictly positive. Let $N(q)$ be this open neighborhood.

Clearly the set Q is covered by the (uncountable) union of all open neighborhoods $N(q)$, *ie* $Q \subset \cup_{q \in Q} N(q)$. Since Q is compact, every cover of Q by open sets has a finite subcover. In particular, there exists a finite sized set $C \subset Q$ such that $Q \subset \cup_{c \in C} N(c)$.

Let us define the test function $w = \frac{1}{|C|}\sum_{c \in C} w_c$. We use this function to prove that Q is asymptotically unused (we modify it later to have value 1 on Q). This function is continuous, since each w_c is continuous. Also, w is non-zero for all $q \in Q$. To see this, for every $q \in Q$ there exists some $c \in C$ such that $q \in N(c)$ since C is a cover, and this implies that $w_c(q) > 0$. Furthermore, for every $c \in C$, $\frac{1}{T}\sum_{t=1}^{T} w_c(f_t) \to 0$ with probability one and since $|C|$ is finite, we have that $\frac{1}{T}\sum_{t=1}^{T} w(f_t) \to 0$ with probability one.

Since Q is compact, w takes on its minimum value on Q. Let $\alpha = \min_{q \in Q} w(q)$, so $\alpha > 0$ since w is positive on Q. Hence, the function $w(q)/\alpha$ is at least 1 on Q. Now the function $w'(q) = \min\{w(q)/\alpha, 1\}$ is continuous, one on Q, and with probability one, $\frac{1}{T}\sum_{t=1}^{T} w'(f_t) \to 0$. Therefore, w' proves that Q is asymptotically unused. □

It is now straightforward to prove theorem 2. We start by proving that $\frac{1}{T}\sum_{t=1}^{T} d(f_t, NE_{2\epsilon}) \to 0$ with probability one. It suffices to prove that with probability one, for all $\delta > 0$ we have that

$$\frac{1}{T}\sum_{t=1}^{T} I\Big[d(NE_{2\epsilon}, f_t) \geq \delta\Big] \to 0$$

where I is the indicator function. Let Q_δ be the set of q such that $d(q, NE_{2\epsilon}) \geq \delta$. This set is compact, so each Q_δ is asymptotically unused. Let w_δ be the function which proves this. Since $w_\delta(f_t) \geq I\left[d(NE_{2\epsilon}, f_t) \geq \delta\right]$ (with equality on Q_δ), the above claim follows since $\frac{1}{T}\sum_{t=1}^{T} w_\delta(f_t) \to 0$.

Now let us prove that $d\left(\frac{1}{T}\sum_{t=1}^{T} X_t, \text{Convex}(NE_{2\epsilon})\right) \to 0$ with probability one. First, note that calibration implies $\frac{1}{T}\sum_{t=1}^{T} X_t \to \frac{1}{T}\sum_{t=1}^{T} f_t$ (just take w to be the constant test function to see this). Now the above statement directly implies that $\frac{1}{T}\sum_{t=1}^{T} f_t$ must converge into the set $Convex(NE_{2\epsilon})$.

4 A Deterministically Calibrated Algorithm

We now provide an algorithm that is uniformly, weakly calibrated for a constructive proof of theorem 1. For technical reasons, it is simpler to allow our algorithm to make forecasts which are not valid probability distributions — the forecasts lie in the expanded set $\widetilde{\Delta}$, defined as:

$$\widetilde{\Delta} = \{f : \sum_{k \in \Omega} f[k] = 1 \text{ and } f[k] \geq -\epsilon\}$$

so clearly $\Delta \subset \widetilde{\Delta}$, where Δ is the probability simplex in $\mathcal{R}^{|\Omega|}$. We later show that we can run this algorithm and simply project its forecasts back onto Δ (which does not alter our convergence results).

Similar to Subsection 2.2, consider a triangulation over this larger set $\widetilde{\Delta}$ with vertex set V, and let $V(p)$ be the corners of the simplex which contain p. It useful to make the following assumptions:

1. If p, q are in the same simplex in the triangulation, $|p - q| \leq \epsilon$.
2. Associated with each $v \in V$ we have a test function w_v which satisfies:
   a) If $v \notin V(p)$, then $w_v(p) = 0$.
   b) For all $p \in \widetilde{\Delta}$, $\sum_v w_v(p) = 1$ and $\sum_v w_v(p)v = p$.
3. For convenience, assume ϵ is small enough ($\epsilon \leq \frac{1}{4|\Omega|}$) suffices) such that for all $p, q \in \widetilde{\Delta}$, we have $|p - q| \leq 3$ (whereas for all $p, q \in \Delta$, $|p - q| \leq 2$).

In the first subsection, we present an algorithm, *Forecast the Fixed Point*, which (uniformly) drives the calibration error to 0 for those functions w_v. As advertised, the algorithm simply forecasts a fixed point of a particular function. It turns out that these fixed points can be computed efficiently (by tracking how the function changes at each timestep), but we do not discuss this here. The next subsection provides the analysis of this algorithm, which uses an "approachability" argument along with properties of the fixed point. Finally, we take $\epsilon \to 0$ which drives the calibration error to 0 (at a bounded rate) for any Lipschitz continuous test function, thus proving uniform, weak calibration.

4.1 The Algorithm: Forecast the Fixed Point

For notational convenience, we use $\mu_T(v)$ instead of $\mu_T(w_v, X, F)$, *ie*

$$\mu_T(v) = \frac{1}{T}\sum_{t=1}^{T} w_v(f_t)(X_t - f_t)$$

For $v \in V$, define a function $\rho_T(v)$ which moves v along the direction of calibration error $\mu_T(v)$, *ie*

$$\rho_T(v) = v + \mu_T(v)$$

For an arbitrary point $p \in \widetilde{\Delta}$, define $\rho_T(p)$ by interpolating on V. Since $p = \sum_{v\in V} w_v(p)v$, define $\rho_T(p)$ as:

$$\begin{aligned}\rho_T(p) &= \sum_{v\in V} w_v(p)\rho_T(v) \\ &= p + \sum_{v\in V} w_v(p)\mu_T(v)\end{aligned}$$

Clearly, this definition is consistent with the above when $p \in V$. In the following section, we show that ρ_T maps $\widetilde{\Delta}$ into $\widetilde{\Delta}$, which allows us to prove that ρ_T has a fixed point in $\widetilde{\Delta}$ (using Brouwer's fixed point theorem).

The algorithm, *Forecast the Fixed Point*, chooses a forecast $f \in \widetilde{\Delta}$ at time T which is any fixed point of the function ρ_{T-1}, *ie*:

1. At time $T = 1$, set $\mu_0(v) = 0$ for all $v \in V$.
2. At time T, compute a fixed point of ρ_{T-1}.
3. Forecast this fixed point.

4.2 The Analysis of This Algorithm

First, let us prove the algorithm exists.

Lemma 5. *(Existence) For all X and T, a fixed point of ρ_T exists in $\widetilde{\Delta}$. Furthermore, the forecast f_T at time T satisfies:*

$$\sum_{v\in V} w_v(f_T)\mu_{T-1}(v) = 0$$

Proof. We use Brouwer's fixed point theorem to prove existence, which involves proving that: 1) the mapping is into, *ie* $\rho_T : \widetilde{\Delta} \to \widetilde{\Delta}$ and 2) the mapping is continuous. First, let us show that $\rho_T(v) \in \widetilde{\Delta}$ for points $v \in V$. We know

$$\begin{aligned}\rho_T(v) &= v + \frac{1}{T}\sum_{t=1}^{T} w_v(f_t)(X_t - f_t) \\ &= \left(1 - \frac{1}{T}\sum_{t=1}^{T} w_v(f_t)\right) v + \frac{1}{T}\sum_{t=1}^{T} w_v(f_t)(X_t + v - f_t)\end{aligned}$$

It suffices to prove that X_t+v-f_t is in $\widetilde{\Delta}$ (when $w_v(f_t)>0$), since then the above would be in $\widetilde{\Delta}$ (by the convexity of $\widetilde{\Delta}$). Note that $w_v(f_t)=0$ when $|v-f_t|>\epsilon$. Now if $|v-f_t|\le\epsilon$, then $v-f_t$ perturbs each component of X_t by at most ϵ, which implies that $X_t+v-f_t\in\widetilde{\Delta}$ since $X_t\in\Delta$. For general points $p\in\widetilde{\Delta}$, the mapping $\rho_T(p)$ must also be in Δ, since the mapping is an interpolation. The mapping is also continuous since the w_v's are continuous. Hence, a fixed point exists. The last equation follows by setting $\rho_{T-1}(f_T)=f_T$. □

Now let us bound the summed l_2 error, where $||x||=\sqrt{x\cdot x}$.

Lemma 6. *(Error Bound) For any X, we have*

$$\sum_{v\in V}||\mu_T(v)||^2\le\frac{9}{T}$$

Proof. It is more convenient to work with the unnormalized quantity $r_T(v)=T\mu_T(v)=\sum_{t=1}^T w_v(f_t)(X_t-f_t)$. Note that

$$||r_T(v)||^2=||r_{T-1}(v)||^2+w_v(f_T)^2||X_T-f_T||^2+2w_v(f_T)r_{T-1}(v)\cdot(X_T-f_T)$$

Summing the last term over V, we have

$$\begin{aligned}\sum_{v\in V}w_v(f_T)r_{T-1}(v)\cdot(X_T-f_T)&=T(X_T-f_T)\cdot\sum_{v\in V}w_v(f_T)\mu_{T-1}(v)\\&=0\end{aligned}$$

where we have used the fixed point condition of the previous lemma. Summing the middle term over V and using $||X_T-f_T||\le|X_T-f_T|\le 3$, we have:

$$\begin{aligned}\sum_{v\in V}w_v(f_T)^2||X_T-f_T||^2&\le 9\sum_{v\in V}w_v(f_T)^2\\&\le 9\sum_{v\in V}w_v(f_T)\\&=9\end{aligned}$$

Using these bounds along with some recursion, we have

$$\begin{aligned}\sum_{v\in V}||r_T(v)||^2&\le\sum_{v\in V}||r_{T-1}(v)||^2+9\\&\le 9T\end{aligned}$$

The result follows by normalizing (*ie* by dividing the above by T^2). □

4.3 Completing the Proof for Uniform, Weak Calibration

Let g be an arbitrary Lipschitz function with Lipschitz parameter λ_g, *ie* $|g(a)-g(b)|\le\lambda_g|a-b|$. We can use V to create an approximation of g as follows

$$\hat{g}(p)=\sum_{v\in V}g(v)w_v(p).$$

This is a good approximation in the sense that:

$$|\hat{g}(p) - g(p)| \leq \epsilon \lambda_g$$

which follows from the Lipschitz condition and the fact that $p = \sum_{v \in V} w_v(p)v$.

Throughout this section we let F be "Forecast the Fixed Point". Using the definition of $\mu_T(g, X, F)$ along with $|X_t - f_t| \leq 3$, we have

$$|\mu_T(g, X, F)| \leq \left| \frac{1}{T} \sum_{t=1}^{T} \hat{g}(f_t)(X_t - f_t) \right| + 3\epsilon\lambda_g = |\mu_T(\hat{g}, X, F)| + 3\epsilon\lambda_g$$

Continuing and using our shorthand notation of $\mu_T(v)$,

$$\begin{aligned}
|\mu_T(\hat{g}, X, F)| &= \left| \frac{1}{T} \sum_{t=1}^{T} \sum_{v \in V} g(v) w_v(f_t)(X_t - f_t) \right| \\
&= \left| \sum_{v \in V} g(v) \mu_T(w_v, X, F) \right| \\
&\leq \sum_{v \in V} |\mu_T(v)| \\
&\leq \sqrt{|V| \sum_{v \in V} ||\mu_T(v)||^2}
\end{aligned}$$

where the first inequality follows from the fact that $g(v) \leq 1$, and the last from the Cauchy-Schwarz inequality.

Using these inequalities along with lemma 6, we have

$$|\mu_T(g, X, F)| \leq \sqrt{\frac{9|V|}{T}} + 3\epsilon\lambda_g$$

Thus, for any fixed g we can pick ϵ small enough to kill off λ_g This unfortunately implies that $|V|$ is large (since the vertex set size grow with $1/\epsilon$). But we can make T large enough to kill off this $|V|$. To get convergence to precisely zero, we follow the usual approach of slowly tightening the parameters. This will be done in phases. Each phase will half the value of the target accuracy and will be long enough to cover the burn in part of the following phase (where error accrues).

Our proof is essentially complete, except for the fact that the algorithm F described so far could sometimes forecast outside the simplex (with probabilities greater than 1 or less than zero). To avoid this, we can project a forecast in $\widetilde{\Delta}$ onto the closest point in Δ. Let $P(\cdot)$ be such a projection operator. For any $f \in \widetilde{\Delta}$, we have $|P(f) - f| \leq |\Omega|\epsilon$. Thus, for any Lipschitz weighting function w we have

$$\mu_T(w, X, P \circ F) = \sum_{v \in V} w(P(f_t))(X_t - P(f_t))$$

$$= \sum_{v \in V} w(P(f_t))(X_t - f_t) + \sum_{v \in V} w(P(f_t))(f_t - P(f_t))$$
$$\leq \mu_T(w \circ P, X, F) + |\Omega|\epsilon$$

Hence the projected version also converges to 0 as $\epsilon \to 0$ (since $w \circ P$ is also Lipschitz continuous). Theorem 1 follows.

References

Billingsley, P. (1968). *Convergence of Probability Measures.* John Wiley and sons.

Dawid, A. P. (1982). The well-calibrated bayesian. *Journal of the Am. Stat. Assoc*, **77**.

Dawid, A. P. (1985). The impossibility of inductive inference. *Journal of the Am. Stat. Assoc*, **80**.

Foster, D. and Vohra, R. (1997). Calibrated learning and correlated equilibrium. *Games and Economic Behavior.*

Foster, D. and Vohra, R. V. (1998). Asymptotic calibration. *Biometrika*, **85**.

Foster, D. P. and Young, H. P. (2001). On the impossibility of predicting the behavior of rational agents. *Proceedings of the National Academy of Sciences*, **98**.

Foster, D. P. and Young, H. P. (forthcoming). Learning, hypothesis testing, and nash equilibrium.

Freund, Y. and Schapire, R. (1999). Adaptive game playing using multiplicative weights. *Games and Economic Behavior*, **29**.

Fudenberg, D. and Levine, D. (1998). *The Theory of Learning in Games.* MIT Press.

Hart, S. and Mas-Colell, A. (2000). A simple adaptive procedure leading to correlated equilibrium. *Econometrica*, **68**.

Hart, S. and Mas-Colell, A. (2003). Uncoupled dynamics do not lead to nash equilibrium. *American Economic Review*, **93**, 1830–1836.

Kalai, E. and Lehrer, E. (1993). Rational learning leads to nash equilibrium. *Econometrica.*

Kalai, E., Lehrer, E., and Smorodinsky, R. (1999). Calibrated forecasting and merging. *Games and Economic Behavior*, **29**.

Milgrom, P. and Roberts, J. (1991). Adaptive and sophisticated learning in normal form games. *Games and Economic Behavior*, **3**, 82 – 100.

Oakes, D. (1985). Self-calibrating priors do not exist. *Journal of the Am. Stat. Assoc*, **80**.

Robinson, J. (1951). An iterative method of solving a game. *Ann. Math.*

Reinforcement Learning for Average Reward Zero-Sum Games

Shie Mannor

Laboratory for Information and Decision Systems
Massachusetts Institute of Technology, Cambridge, MA 02139
shie@mit.edu

Abstract. We consider Reinforcement Learning for average reward zero-sum stochastic games. We present and analyze two algorithms. The first is based on relative Q-learning and the second on Q-learning for stochastic shortest path games. Convergence is proved using the ODE (Ordinary Differential Equation) method. We further discuss the case where not all the actions are played by the opponent with comparable frequencies and present an algorithm that converges to the optimal Q-function, given the observed play of the opponent.

1 Introduction

Since published in [DW92], the Q-learning algorithm was implemented in many applications and was analyzed in several different setups (e.g., [BT95,ABB01, BM00]). The Q-learning algorithm for learning an optimal policy in Markov Decision Processes (MDPs) is a direct off-policy learning algorithm in which a Q-value vector is learned for every state and action. For the discounted case, the Q-value of a specific state-action pair represents the expected discounted utility if the action is chosen in the specific state and an optimal policy is then followed. In this work we deviate from the standard Q-learning scheme in two ways. First, we discuss games, rather than MDPs. Second, we consider the average reward criterion rather than discounted reward.

Reinforcement learning for average reward MDPs was suggested in [Sch93] and further studied in [Sin94,Mah96]. Some analysis appeared later in [ABB01, BT95]. The analysis for average reward is considerably more cumbersome than that of discounted reward, since the dynamic programming operator is no longer a contraction. There are several methods for average reward reinforcement learning, including Q-learning ([ABB01]), a polynomial PAC model-based learning model ([KS98]), actor critic ([KT03]), etc. Convergence proofs of Q-learning based algorithms for average reward typically rely on the ODE method and the fact that the Q-learning algorithm is essentially an asynchronous stochastic approximation algorithm.

Q-learning for zero-sum stochastic games (SGs) was suggested in [Lit94] for discounted reward. The convergence proof of this algorithm appears, in a broader context, in [LS99]. The main difficulty in applying Q-learning to games is that

J. Shawe-Taylor and Y. Singer (Eds.): COLT 2004, LNAI 3120, pp. 49–63, 2004.

Q-learning is inherently an off-policy learning algorithm. This means that the optimal policy is learned while another policy is played. Moreover, the opponent may refrain from playing certain actions (or play them only a few times) so the model parameters may never be fully revealed. Consequently, every learning algorithm is doomed to learn a potentially inferior policy. On-policy algorithms, whose performance is measured according to the reward they accumulate may, however, attain an average reward which is close to the value of the game (e.g., [BT02]). We note two major difficulties with Q-learning style algorithms. First, one needs all actions in all states to be chosen infinitely often by both players (actually comparatively often for average reward). Second, the standard analysis of Q-learning (e.g., [Tsi94,BT95]) relies on contraction properties of the dynamic programming operator which follow easily for discounted reward or shortest path problems, but do not hold for average reward. We start by addressing the second issue and present two Q-learning type algorithms for SGs. We show that if all actions in all states are played comparatively often then convergence to the true Q-value is guaranteed. We then tackle the problem of exploration and show that by slightly modifying the Q-learning algorithm we can make sure that the Q-vector converges to the Q-vector of the observed game.

The convergence analysis of the Q-learning algorithms is based on [BM00, ABB02]. The main problem is the unfortunate fact that the dynamic programming operator of interest is not a contraction operator. In Section 3 we present a version of Relative Q-learning (e.g., [BS98]) adapted to average reward SGs. We later modify the λ–SSP (Stochastic Shortest Path) formulation of [BT95, Section 7.1] to average reward SGs. The idea is to define a related SSPG (Stochastic Shortest Path Game) and show that by solving the SSPG the original average reward problem is solved as well.

The paper is organized as follows: In Section 2 we define the stochastic game (SG) model, and recall some results from the theory of stochastic games. The relative Q-learning algorithm for average reward games is presented in Section 3. The λ-SSPG algorithm is described in Section 4. Since the opponent may refrain from playing certain actions, the true Q-vector may be impossible to learn. We show how this can be corrected by concerning the observed game. This is done in Section 5. Brief concluding remarks are drawn in Section 6. The convergence proofs of both algorithms are deferred to the appendix.

2 Model and Preliminaries

In this section we formally define SGs. We then state a stability assumption which is needed in order to guarantee that our analysis holds and that the value is independent of the initial state. We finally survey some known results from the theory of SGs.

2.1 Model

We consider an average reward zero-sum finite (states and action) SG which is played ad-infinitum. We refer to the players as P1 (the decision maker in interest) and P2 (the adversary). The game is defined by the five-tuple $(\mathcal{S}, \mathcal{A}, \mathcal{B}, P, r)$, where:

1. $\mathcal{S}$ is the finite set of states of the stochastic game, $\mathcal{S} = \{1, \dots, S\}$.
2. $\mathcal{A}$ is the set of actions of P1 in each state, $\mathcal{A} = \{1, \dots, A\}$. To streamline the notations it is assumed that in all states P1 has the same available actions.
3. $\mathcal{B}$ is the set of actions of P2 in each state, $\mathcal{B} = \{1, \dots, B\}$. It is assumed that in all states P2 has the same available actions.
4. P is the conditional transition law. $P : \mathcal{S} \times \mathcal{A} \times \mathcal{B} \times \mathcal{S} \to [0, 1]$ such that $P(s'|s, a, b)$ is the probability that the next state is s' given that current state is s, P1 plays a, and P2 plays b.
5. r is P1's (random) reward function, $r : \mathcal{S} \times \mathcal{A} \times \mathcal{B} \mapsto \mathbb{R}$. The reward obtained when P1 plays a, P2 plays b, and the current state is s is distributed according to a measure $\mu(s, a, b)$ whose mean is $r(s, a, b)$. A bounded second moment is assumed.

At each time epoch n, both players observe the current state s_n, and then P1 and P2 choose actions a_n and b_n, respectively. As a result P1 receives a reward of r_n which is distributed according to $\mu(s_n, a_n, b_n)$. The next state is determined according to the transition probability $P(\cdot|s_n, a_n, b_n)$. A policy $\sigma_1 \in \Sigma_1$ for P1 is a mapping from all possible histories (including states, actions, and rewards) to the set of mixed actions $\Delta(\mathcal{A})$, where $\Delta(\mathcal{A})$ is the set of all probability measures over $\mathcal{A}$. Similarly, a policy $\sigma_2 \in \Sigma_2$ for P2 is a mapping from all possible histories to the mixed actions $\Delta(\mathcal{B})$. A policy of either player is called *stationary* if the mixed action in time n depends only on the state s_n. Let the average reward at time n be denoted by $\hat{r}_n \triangleq \sum_{\tau=1}^{n} r_\tau / n$.

2.2 A Stability Assumption

We shall make the following assumption throughout the paper. The assumption can be thought of as a stability or recurrence assumption. The state s^* is a reference state to which a return is guaranteed. Recall that a state is recurrent under a certain pair of policies of P1 and P2 if that state is visited with probability 1 in finite time when the players follow their policies.

Assumption 1 (Recurrent State). *There exists a state $s^* \in \mathcal{S}$ which is recurrent for every pair of stationary strategies played by P1 and P2.*

We say that an SG has a value v if

$$\mathrm{v} = \sup_{\sigma_1} \inf_{\sigma_2} \liminf_{n \to \infty} \mathbb{E}_{\sigma_1, \sigma_2}[\hat{r}_n] = \inf_{\sigma_2} \sup_{\sigma_1} \limsup_{n \to \infty} \mathbb{E}_{\sigma_1, \sigma_2}[\hat{r}_n] .$$

For finite games, the value exists ([MN81]). If Assumption 1 holds, then the value is independent of the initial state and can be achieved in stationary strategies (e.g., [FV96]).

2.3 Average Reward Zero-Sum Stochastic Games – Background

We now recall some known results from the theory of average reward scalar games. We assume henceforth that Assumption 1 is satisfied. For such games it is known (e.g., [FV96, Theorem 5.3.3]) that there is a value and a bias vector, that is there exists a number v and a vector $H \in \mathbb{R}^s$ such that for each $s \in \mathcal{S}$:

$$H(s) + \mathrm{v} = \operatorname*{val}_{a,b}\left[r(s,a,b) + \sum_{s' \in \mathcal{S}} P(s'|s,a,b)H(s)\right] , \tag{2.1}$$

where $\mathrm{val}_{a,b}$ is the minimax operator,which is defined for a matrix R with A rows and B columns as $\mathrm{val}_{a,b}[R] \stackrel{\triangle}{=} \inf_{v \in \Delta(A)} \sup_{u \in \Delta(B)} \sum_{a=1}^{A} \sum_{b=1}^{B} v_a u_b R_{ab}$. Furthermore, in [Pat97, page 90] it was shown that under Assumption 1 there exists a unique H such that Equation (2.1) holds for every $s \in \mathcal{S}$ and for some specific s' we have that $H(s') = 0$. We note that when the game parameters are known there are efficient methods to compute H and v; see [FV96,Pat97]. It is often convenient to use operator notations. In this case the resulting (vector) equation is:

$$\mathrm{v}e + H^* = TH^* , \tag{2.2}$$

where $e \in \mathbb{R}^s$ is the ones vector ($e = (1, \ldots, 1)$)) and $T : \mathbb{R}^S \mapsto \mathbb{R}^S$ is the dynamic programming operator defined by:

$$TH(s) \stackrel{\triangle}{=} \operatorname*{val}_{a,b}\left[\sum_{s' \in \mathcal{S}} r(s,a,b) + P(s'|s,a,b)H(s')\right] . \tag{2.3}$$

It turns out that T is not a contraction, so that Q-learning style mechanisms that rely on contraction properties may not converge. Thus, a refined scheme should be developed. Note that if H^* is a solution of (2.2) so is $H^*{+}ce$, so that one must take into account the non uniqueness of the solutions of (2.2). We propose two different schemes to overcome this non-uniqueness. The first scheme is based on the uniqueness of the solution of Equation (2.2) that satisfies $H(s^*) = 0$, and the second is based on a contraction property of a related dynamic programming operator (for an associated stochastic shortest path game).

Our goal is to find the optimal Q-vector which satisfies that: $Q^*(s,a,b) \stackrel{\triangle}{=} r(s,a,b) + \sum_{s'} P(s'|s,a,b)H^*(s')$, where H^* is a solution of the optimality equation (2.2). Note that if H^* is determined uniquely (by requiring $H^*(s^*) = 0$) then Q^* is also unique. The Q-vector is defined on $\mathbb{R}^{S \cdot A \cdot B}$, the interpretation of $Q(s,a,b)$ is the relative gain for P1 to use action a assuming P2 will use action b, when current state is s. Given the vector Q^*, the maximin policy is to play at state s a maximin (mixed) action with respect to the matrix game whose entries are $Q(s,\cdot,\cdot)$.

3 Relative Q-learning

Relative Q-learning for average reward MDPs was suggested by [Sch93], and studied later in [Sin94,Mah96]. It is the simulation counterpart of the relative value iteration algorithm (e.g., [Put94]) for solving average reward MDPs. The following algorithm is the SG (asynchronous) version of the relative Q-learning algorithm.

$$Q_{n+1}(s,a,b) = Q_n(s,a,b) + 1_{\{s_n=s,a_n=a,b_n=b\}}\gamma(N(n,s,a,b))\Big(r_n + FQ_n(s_{n+1}) - f(Q_n) - Q_n(s,a,b)\Big), \qquad (3.4)$$

where $N(n,s,a,b)$ denote the number of times that state s and actions a and b were played up to time n (i.e., $N(n,s,a,b) = \sum_{\tau=1}^{n} 1_{\{s_\tau=s,a_\tau=a,b_\tau=b\}}$), and $F : \mathbb{R}^{S\cdot A\cdot B} \mapsto \mathbb{R}^S$ is the per state value function which satisfies: $FQ(s) \triangleq \text{val}_{a,b}[Q(s,a,b)]$. The function $f(Q) : \mathbb{R}^{S\cdot A\cdot B} \to \mathbb{R}$ is required to have the following properties: 1. f is Lipschitz; 2. f is scaling invariant – $f(aQ) = af(Q)$; 3. f is translation invariant—$f(Q+er) = f(Q)+r$ where e is the vector of ones (note the abuse of notations - e is RSA dimensional here). Examples for valid f's are $f(Q) = Q(s^0,a^0,b^0)$ for some (s^0,a^0,b^0) or $f(Q) = \frac{1}{SAB}\sum_{s,a,b} Q(s,a,b)$. Intuitively, f takes care of having the Q-vector bounded. More precisely, we shall use f in the proof to ensure that the underlying ODE has a unique solution.

We require the standard stochastic approximation assumption on the learning rate γ. Namely, γ should be square summable but not summable, and "regular" in the sense that is does not vanish occasionally. More precisely:

Assumption 2 (Learning Rate). *The sequence $\gamma(n)$ satisfies:*[1]

1. *For every $0 < x < 1$, $\sup_k \gamma(\lfloor xk \rfloor)/\gamma(k) < \infty$.*
2. *$\sum_{n=1}^{\infty} \gamma(n) = \infty$ and $\sum_{n=1}^{\infty} \gamma(n)^2 < \infty$.*
3. *For every $0 < x < 1$ the limit $(\sum_{m=1}^{\lfloor yn \rfloor} \gamma(m))/(\sum_{m=1}^{n} \gamma(m)) \to 1$ uniformly in $y \in [x,1]$.*

For example, $\gamma(n) = 1/n$ and $1/n \log n$ $(n > 1)$ satisfy this assumption. The following assumption is crucial in analyzing the asynchronous stochastic approximation algorithm.

Assumption 3 (Often updates). *There exists a deterministic $\delta > 0$ such that for every $s \in \mathcal{S}, a \in \mathcal{A}, b \in \mathcal{B}$, $\liminf_{n\to\infty} \frac{N(n,s,a,b)}{n} \geq \delta$ with probability 1. That is, all component are updated comparatively often.*

The following theorem is proved in Appendix A.1.

Theorem 1. *Suppose that Assumptions 1, 2 and 3 hold. Then the asynchronous algorithm (3.4) converges with probability 1 to Q^*.*

4 λ-SSPG Q-learning

A different approach is to use the λ-SSP (Stochastic Shortest Path) formulation, suggested by Bertsekas and Tsitsiklis [BT95, Section 7.1] for average reward

[1] $\lfloor x \rfloor$ is the integer part of x.

MDPs and analyzed in [ABB01]. The key idea is to view the average reward as the ratio of the expected total reward between renewals and the expected time between renewals. We consider a similar approach for SGs, using results from [Pat97] regarding SSPGs. From the stochastic approximation point of view we maintain two time scales. We iterate the average reward estimate, λ, slowly towards the value of the game, while the Q-vector is iterated on a faster scale so that it tracks the Q-vector of the associated SSPG. The convergence follows from Borkar's two-time-scale stochastic approximation ([Bor97]). There are two equations that are iterated simultaneously, the first is related to the Q-vector, is defined as a vector in $\mathbb{R}^{S \cdot A \cdot B}$ and the second is related to λ which is a real number. The λ-SSPG Q-learning algorithm is:

$$
\begin{aligned}
Q_{n+1}(s,a,b) &= Q_n(s,a,b) + \gamma(N(n,s,a,b))\Big(r_n + FQ_n(s_{n+1})1_{\{s_{n+1} \neq s^*\}} \\
&\qquad - \lambda_n - Q_n(s,a,b))\Big)1_{\{s_n = s, a_n = a, b_n = b\}} \\
\lambda_{n+1} &= \Lambda(\lambda_n + b(n)FQ_n(s^*)),
\end{aligned} \tag{4.5}
$$

where $b(n) = o(\gamma(n))$, Λ is the projection to the interval $[-K, K]$ chosen such that $|\mathrm{v}| < K$, and $N(n,s,a,b)$ and F are as before.

An additional assumption we require is that all the elements are sampled in an evenly distributed manner. More precisely:

Assumption 4. *For every $x > 0$ let $M(n,x) = \min\{m \geq n : \sum_{k=n}^{m} \gamma(k) \geq x\}$, for every $s, s' \in \mathcal{S}$, $a, a' \in \mathcal{A}$, $b, b' \in \mathcal{B}$ the limit:*

$$
\lim_{n \to \infty} \frac{\sum_{k=N(n,s,a,b)}^{N(M(n,x),s,a,b)} \gamma(k)}{\sum_{k=N(n,s',a',b')}^{N(M(n,x),s',a',b')} \gamma(k)}
$$

exists almost surely.

The following theorem is proved in Appendix A.2.

Theorem 2. *Suppose that Assumptions 1, 2, 3, and 4 hold. Further, assume that $b(n)$ satisfies Assumption 2 and that $b(n) = o(\gamma(n))$. Then the asynchronous algorithm (4.5) converges with probability 1 so that $Q_n \to Q^*$ and $\lambda_n \to \mathrm{v}$.*

5 The Often Update Requirement

The convergence of both algorithms described in the previous sections required several assumptions. Assumption 1 is a property of the (unknown) game. Assumption 2 is controlled by P1's choice of the learning rate and can be easily satisfied. Assumption 3 (and 4 for the second algorithm) presents an additional difficulty. The often updates requirement restricts not only on P1's policy but also P2's actual play. Obviously, P1 cannot impose on P2 to perform certain actions and consequently we cannot guarantee that $Q_n \to Q^*$. In this section we consider methods to relax the often updates assumption. We will suggest a modification of the relative Q-learning algorithm to accommodate for state-action-action triplets that are not played comparatively often.

If certain state-action-action triplets are performed finitely often their Q-values cannot be learned (since even the estimation of the immediate reward is not consistent). We therefore must restrict the attention of the learning algorithm to Q-value of triplets that are played infinitely often, and make sure that the triplets that are not played often do not interfere with the estimation of the Q-value of the other triplets. The main problem is that we do not know (at any given time) if an action will be chosen finitely often (and can be ignored) or comparatively often (and should be used in the Q-learning). We therefore suggest to maintain a set of triplets that have been played often enough, and essentially learn only on this set. Let $Y_n(\delta)$ denote the set of triplets that were sampled more than δ fraction of the time up to time n, that is: $Y_n(\delta) \stackrel{\triangle}{=} \{(s,a,b) \in \mathcal{S} \times \mathcal{A} \times \mathcal{B} : \frac{N(n,s,a,b)}{n} \geq \delta\}$. The algorithm we suggest is the following modification of (3.4):

$$Q_{n+1}(s,a,b) = \begin{cases} Q_n(s,a,b) + 1_{\{s_n=s,a_n=a,b_n=b\}}\gamma(N(n,s,a,b))\Big(r_n + FQ_n(s_{n+1}) \\ \qquad -f(Q_n) - Q_n(s,a,b)\Big) & \text{if } (s,a,b) \in Y_n(\delta) \\ -M & \text{if } (s,a,b) \notin Y_n(\delta) \end{cases} \tag{5.6}$$

where M is a large positive number which is larger than $\max_{s,a,b} |Q(s,a,b)|$. Let

$$Y_\infty(\delta) = \{(s,a,b) \in \mathcal{S} \times \mathcal{A} \times \mathcal{B} : \liminf_n \frac{N(n,s,a,b)}{n} \geq \delta\}$$

denote the set of triplets that are chosen comparatively often (δ is a deterministic constant). We refer to the game which is restricted to triplets in $Y_\infty(\delta)$ as the δ-observed game. We denote the solution of Bellman's equation (2.3) where the a,b entry for all the triplets not in $Y_\infty(\delta)$ is replaced by $-M$ (and are therefore not relevant to the optimal policy) by $H^*_{Y_\infty}$ and the matching Q-vector by $Q^*_{Y_\infty}$.

Theorem 3. *Suppose that Assumptions 1 and 2 hold, and suppose that for every state-action-action triplet* (s,a,b) *we have that:*

$$\liminf_{n\to\infty} \frac{N(n,s,a,b)}{n} \geq \delta \quad \textit{or} \quad \limsup_n \frac{N(n,s,a,b)}{n} < \delta\,.$$

Then (5.6) converges with probability one so that $Q_n(s,a,b) \to Q^*_{Y_\infty}$ *for every* $(s,a,b) \in Y_\infty(\delta)$.

Proof. For every triplet (s,a,b) in $Y_\infty(\delta)$ there exists a time $\tau(s,a,b)$ such that for every $n > \tau(s,a,b)$ the triplet $(s,a,b) \in Y_n(\delta)$. By the condition in the theorem if $(s,a,b) \notin Y_\infty(\delta)$ then there exists a time $\tau'(s,a,b)$ such that for every $n > \tau'(s,a,b)$ the triplet $(s,a,b) \notin Y_n(\delta)$. Let τ be the time after which $Y_n(\delta)$ is fixed, i.e., $\tau = \max\{\max_{(s,a,b)\in Y_\infty(\delta)} \tau(s,a,b), \max_{(s,a,b)\notin Y_\infty(\delta)} \tau'(s,a,b)\}$. Suppose now that the learning algorithm begins at time τ. Since τ is finite it is easy to see that Assumptions 1-3 are satisfied restricted to $(s,a,b) \in Y_\infty(\delta)$ so that by Theorem 1 the result follows. Note that the triplets which are not in $Y_\infty(\delta)$ are updated every epoch (after τ) with the value $-M$. □

Naturally, some actions may satisfy neither the lim inf condition nor the lim sup conditions. A method that controls δ dynamically, and allows to circumvent this problem is under current study.

6 Concluding Remarks

We presented two Q-learning style algorithms for average reward zero-sum SGs. Under appropriate recurrence and often updates assumptions the convergence to the optimal policy was established. Our results generalize the discounted case that was proved in [LS99]. There are several open questions that warrants further study. First, the extension of the results presented in this paper to games with a large state space, where function approximation is needed, appears nontrivial. Second, we only partially addressed the issue of actions that are not chosen comparatively often by the Q-learning algorithm. There are several other possibilities that can be considered (using a promotion function as in [EDM01], adding bias factor as in [LR85], and optimistic initial conditions as in [BT02]) none have proved a panacea for the complications introduced by "uneven" exploration. Third, we only considered zero-sum games. Extending the algorithms presented here to general sum games appears difficult (even the extension for discounted reward is a daunting task). Finally, universal consistency in SGs (e.g., [MS03]) is a related challenging problem. In this setup P1 tries to attain an average reward which is as high as the average reward that could have been attained had P2's strategy (or some statistical measure thereof) was provided in advance. The definitions for universal consistency in SGs are involved and the strategies suggested to date are highly complex. Devising a simple algorithm in the style of Q-learning is of great interest. We note, however, that the distinctive property of universal consistency is that P2's strategy cannot be assumed stationary, so stochastic approximation algorithms which rely on stationarity may not work.

References

[ABB01] J. Abounadi, D. Bertsekas, and V. Borkar. Learning algorithms for Markov decision processes with average cost. *SIAM J. Control Optim.*, 40:681 – 698, 2001.

[ABB02] J. Abounadi, D. Bertsekas, and V. Borkar. Stochastic approximation for non-expansive maps: Application to Q-learning algorithms. *SIAM J. Control Optim.*, 41:1–22, 2002.

[BM00] V.S. Borkar and S.P Meyn. The O.D.E. method for convergence of stochastic approximation and reinforcement learning. *SIAM J. Control Optim.*, 38(2):447–469, 2000.

[Bor97] V.S. Borkar. Stochastic approximation with two time scales. *IEEE systems and Control letters*, 29:291–294, 1997.

[Bor98] V.S. Borkar. Asynchronous stochastic approximation. *SIAM J. Control Optim.*, 36:840–851, 1998.

[BS98] A.G. Barto and R.S. Sutton. *Reinforcement Learning.* MIT Press, 1998.

[BS99] V.S. Borkar and K. Soumyanath. An analog scheme for fixed point computation - part I: Theory. *IEEE Trans. On Circuits and Systems*, 44(4):7–13, April 1999.

[BT95] D.P. Bertsekas and J.N. Tsitsiklis. *Neuro-Dynamic Programming.* Athena Scientific, 1995.

[BT02] R.I. Brafman and M. Tennenholtz. R-MAX, a general polynomial time algorithm for near-optimal reinforcement learning. *Journal of Machine Learning Research*, 3:213–231, 2002.

[DW92] P. Dayan and C. Watkins. Q-learning. *Machine Learning*, 8:279–292, 1992.

[EDM01] E. Even-Dar and Y. Mansour. Convergence of optimistic and incremental Q-learning. In *NIPS*, 2001.

[FV96] J. Filar and K. Vrieze. *Competitive Markov Decision Processes.* Springer Verlag, 1996.

[KB00] V. Konda and V. Borkar. Actor-critic-type algorithms for Markov decision problems. *SIAM J. Control Optim.*, 38:94–123, 2000.

[KS98] M. Kearns and S. Singh. Near-optimal reinforcement learning in polynomial time. In *Proceedings of the 15th International Conference on Machine Learning*, pages 260–268. Morgan Kaufmann, 1998.

[KT03] V. R. Konda and J. N. Tsitsiklis. Actor-critic algorithms. *SIAM J. Control Optim.*, 42(4):1143–1166, 2003.

[KY97] H.J. Kushner and C.J. Yin. *Stochastic Approximation Algorithms and Applications.* Springer Verlag, 1997.

[Lit94] M.L. Littman. Markov games as a framework for multi-agent reinforcement learning. In *Proceedings of the 11th International Conference on Machine Learning*, pages 157–163. Morgan Kaufman, 1994.

[LR85] T.L. Lai and H. Robbins. Asymptotically efficient adaptive allocation rules. *Advances in Applied Mathematics*, 6:4–22, 1985.

[LS99] M.L. Littman and C. Szepesvári. A unified analysis of value-function-based reinforcement-learning algorithms. *Neural Computation*, 11(8):2017–2059, 1999.

[Mah96] S. Mahadevan. Average reward reinforcement learning: Foundations, algorithms, and empirical results. *Machine Learning*, 22(1):159–196, 1996.

[MN81] J.F. Mertens and A. Neyman. Stochastic games. *International Journal of Game Theory*, 10(2):53–66, 1981.

[MS03] S. Mannor and N. Shimkin. The empirical Bayes envelope and regret minimization in competitive Markov decision processes. *Mathematics of Operations Research*, 28(2):327–345, May 2003.

[Pat97] S.D. Patek. *Stochastic Shortest Path Games.* PhD thesis, LIDS, MIT, January 1997.

[Put94] M. Puterman. *Markov Decision Processes.* Wiley-Interscience, 1994.

[Sch93] A. Schwartz. A reinforcement learning method for maximizing undiscounted rewards. In *Proceedings of the Tenth International Conference on Machine Learning*, pages 298–305. Morgan Kaufmann, 1993.

[Sin94] S. Singh. Reinforcement learning algorithms for average payoff Markovian decision processes. In *Proceedings of the 12th International Conference on Machine Learning*, pages 202–207. Morgan Kaufmann, 1994.

[Tsi94] J.N. Tsitsiklis. Asynchronous stochastic approximation and Q-learning. *Machine Learning*, 16:185–202, 1994.

A Appendix

In this appendix we provide convergence proofs of the two learning algorithms presented above. We start by from the Relative Q-learning algorithm and then turn to the λ-SSPG Q-learning algorithm. In both cases we also discuss the synchronous algorithm where it is assumed that all the state-action-action triplets are sampled simultaneously in every iteration. Much of the derivation here relies on [ABB01] and [BM00].

A.1 Proof of Theorem 1

We start with defining a synchronous version of (3.4).

$$Q_{n+1}(s,a,b) = Q_n(s,a,b) + \gamma(n)\left(r_\xi(s,a,b) + FQ_n(\xi(s,a,b)) - f(Q_n) - Q_n(s,a,b)\right) \tag{A.7}$$

where $\xi(s,a,b)$ and $r_\xi(s,a,b)$ are the independently simulated random values of the next state and the immediate reward assuming $s_n = s$, $a_n = a$, and $b_n = b$, respectively. The above algorithm is the off-policy version of relative value iteration for average reward games.

Let us refer to Equation (A.7). In order to use the ODE method of [BM00] we first reformulate the synchronous Relative Q-learning iteration as a vector iterative equation:

$$Q_{n+1} = Q_n + \gamma(n)(TQ_n - f(Q_n)e - Q_n + M_{n+1}),$$

where: 1. TQ is the operator $T : R^{S\cdot A\cdot B} \mapsto R^{S\cdot A\cdot B}$ that is defined by: $TQ(s,a,b) = \sum_{s'\in\mathcal{S}} P(s'|s,a,b)(r(s,a,b) + FQ(s'))$; $f(Q)$ is a relative function as defined previously; and M_{n+1} is the "random" part of the iteration: $M_{n+1}(s,a,b) = r_\xi(s,a,b) + FQ(\xi(s,a,b)) - TQ_n(s,a,b)$. Denoting the σ-algebra until time n by $\mathcal{F}_n = \sigma(Q_m, M_m, m \leq n)$ it follows that for all n, under the assumption that all random variables are bounded: $\mathbb{E}(M_{n+1}|\mathcal{F}_n) = 0$ and $\mathbb{E}(\|M_{n+1}\|^2|\mathcal{F}_n) \leq C(1 + \|Q_n\|^2)$ for some constant C. We follow the analysis made by [ABB01] for the rest of the section.

Let us define the following operators $T' : \mathbb{R}^{S\cdot A\cdot B} \to \mathbb{R}^{S\cdot A\cdot B}$ and $\hat{T} : \mathbb{R}^{S\cdot A\cdot B} \to \mathbb{R}^{S\cdot A\cdot B}$: $\hat{T}(Q) \triangleq TQ - ve$ and $T'(Q) \triangleq TQ - f(Q)e$, where v is the value of the game. In order to apply the ODE method we need to prove that the following ODE is asymptotically stable:

$$\dot{Q}(t) = T'(Q(t)) - Q(t)\,. \tag{A.8}$$

The operator T' is not a contraction, furthermore, it is not even non-expansive. We therefore establish its stability directly by considering the following ODE:

$$\dot{Q}(t) = \hat{T}(Q(t)) - Q(t)\,. \tag{A.9}$$

The following lemmas establish the properties of the operators.

Lemma 1. *The operator T is sup norm non-expansive*

Proof. Recall that $TQ(s,a,b) = \sum_{s' \in S} P(s'|s,a,b)(r(s,a,b) + FQ(s'))$. Fix Q_1 and Q_2, the sup norm of the difference, $\|T(Q_1) - T(Q_2)\|_\infty$ is achieved by some element (s,a,b).

$$\|T(Q_1) - T(Q_2)\|_\infty = \Big| \sum_{s' \in S} P(s'|s,a,b) \Big(\max_{v \in \Delta(A)} \min_{\mu \in \Delta(B)} \sum_{a',b'} Q_1(s',a',b') v_{a'}(s') \mu_{b'}(s')) \\ - \max_{v \in \Delta(A)} \min_{\mu \in \Delta(B)} \sum_{a',b'} Q_2(s',a',b') v_{a'}(s') \mu_{b'}(s') \Big) \Big| .$$

Assume without loss of generality that the sum inside the absolute value is positive. For every s' fix $v(s')$ which is a max-min strategy and first element is maximized (the element that relates to Q_1). Similarly, fix $\mu(s')$ for the second element which is a min-max strategy of P2 for each game defined by the second element for every s'. By the min-max theorem the first element cannot decrease and the second cannot increase. Since for every element s' the difference may only increase we have that:

$$\|T(Q_1) - T(Q_2)\|_\infty \leq \Big| \sum_{s' \in S} P(s'|s,a,b) \Big(\sum_{a'} \sum_{b'} (Q_1(s',a',b') - \\ Q_2(s',a',b')) v_{a'}(s') \mu_{b'}(s') \Big) \Big| .$$

But this is a convex combination of elements of $Q_1 - Q_2$ and is certainly not more than the sup norm of the difference. □

Corollary 1. *$\hat{T}$ is sup norm non-expansive.*

Proof. $\|\hat{T}(Q_1) - \hat{T}(Q_2)\|_\infty = \|T(Q_1) - T(Q_2)\|_\infty \leq \|Q_1 - Q_2\|_\infty$ □

Let us denote the span semi-norm by $\|\cdot\|_s$. That is $\|Q\|_s \triangleq \max_{s,a,b} Q(s,a,b) - \min_{s,a,b} Q(s,a,b)$.

Lemma 2. *The operator T is span semi-norm non-expansive.*

Proof.

$$\|TQ_1 - TQ_2\|_s = \max_{s,a,b}\{TQ_1(s,a,b) - TQ_2(s,a,b)\} - \min_{s',a',b'}\{TQ_1(s',a',b') - TQ_2(s',a',b')\}.$$

There exist $(\bar{s},\bar{a},\bar{b})$ and $(\underline{s},\underline{a},\underline{b})$ that achieve the maximum and minimum of the span semi-norm, respectively. By writing the operator T explicitly and cancelling the reward elements:

$$\|TQ_1 - TQ_2\|_s = \sum_{s'} P(s'|\bar{s},\bar{a},\bar{b}) \Big(\max_{v \in \Delta(A)} \min_{\mu \in \Delta(B)} \sum_{a',b'} Q_1(s',a',b') v_{a'} \mu_{b'} - \\ \max_{v \in \Delta(A)} \min_{\mu \in \Delta(B)} \sum_{a',b'} Q_2(s',a',b') v_{a'} \mu_{b'} \Big) \\ - \sum_{s'} P(s'|\underline{s},\underline{a},\underline{b}) \Big(\max_{v \in \Delta(A)} \min_{\mu \in \Delta(B)} \sum_{a',b'} Q_1(s',a',b') v_{a'} \mu_{b'} \\ - \max_{v \in \Delta(A)} \min_{\mu \in \Delta(B)} \sum_{a',b'} Q_2(s',a',b') v_{a'} \mu_{b'} \Big) .$$

For every s there are four min-max operation in the above, lets us denote the maximizing strategy for P1's of the i-th item for state s by $v^i(s)$ and the minimizing strategy for P2's of the i-th item for state s by $\mu^i(s)$. For every s fix $v^1(s)$ as P1's strategy for the two first elements and $\mu^2(s)$ as P2's strategy for P2 strategy for the two first elements. The sum of the first two elements can only increase, as the first element cannot decrease and the second cannot increase. Similarly, for every s fix for the third and fourth elements, P1's strategy to be $v^4(s)$ and P2's strategy to be $\mu^3(s)$. The difference between the third and fourth elements can only increase, thus the total difference increases. We therefore obtain that $\|TQ_1 - TQ_2\|_s$ can be bounded by a convex combination of $Q_1 - Q_2$, which is certainly not greater than the span semi-norm. □

Corollary 2. *T' and $\hat{T}$ are span semi-norm non-expansive.*

Denote the set of equilibrium points of the ODE (A.9) by G, that is $G \triangleq \{Q : TQ = Q - \text{v}e\}$.

Lemma 3. *G is of the form $Q^* + ce$.*

Proof. First note that for every $c \in \mathbb{R}$ and $Q \in \mathbb{R}^{S \cdot A \cdot B}$ we have $T(Q + ce) = TQ + ce$ (e is now an SAB dimensional vector of ones). Also note that $F(Q+ce) = FQ+ce$ as equality in $\mathbb{R}^S$. Activate the operator F on the equation $TQ = Q - \text{v}e$, so that for $Q \in G$ we have that $FTQ = FQ - ce$. Under Assumption 1 we can apply Proposition 5.1 from [Pat97]. According to this proposition there exists a unique solution to the equation $TH = H - \text{v}e$ up to an additive constant. □

Theorem 4. *Q^* is the globally asymptotically stable equilibrium point for (A.8)*

Proof. This is proved by direct computation using the above lemmas, and the Lipschitz continuity of f. We omit the details as the proof follows [ABB01, Theorem 3.4]. □

We use the formulation of [BM00] for establishing convergence for the synchronous and the asynchronous cases. For the synchronous case we only need the stability assumption and the standard stochastic approximation assumption on the learning rate.

Theorem 5. *Under Assumptions 1 and 2 the synchronous algorithm (A.7) converges to Q^* almost surely.*

Proof. We apply Theorem 2.2 from [BM00] to show the boundedness of Q_n and to prove convergence to Q^*. As in [BM00], let $h(x) \triangleq T(Q) - Q - f(Q)e$. The ODE $\dot{x}(t) = h(x(t))$ has a globally stable solution by Theorem 4. Since $f(aQ) = af(Q)$ it follows that the limit $h_\infty \triangleq \lim_{z\to\infty} h(zx)/z$ exists and is simply the operator T with the payoffs $r(s, a, b)$ set to zero for all s, a, b. According to Theorem 4 the origin is asymptotically stable since the theorem can be applied to the game with zero payoffs. The other assumptions of Theorem 2.2 from [BM00] are satisfied by construction. □

The asynchronous algorithm converges under the appropriate assumptions.
Proof of Theorem 1: This is a corollary of Theorem 2.5 in [BM00], the condition are satisfied as proved for the synchronous case. □

A critical component in the proof is the boundedness of Q_n. We used the method of [BM00], however, one can show it directly as in [ABB01, Theorem 3.5]. By showing the boundedness directly a somewhat weaker assumption on f can be made, namely that $|f(Q)| \leq \|Q\|_\infty$ instead of $f(aQ) = af(Q)$.

A.2 Proof of Theorem 2

We associate with the average reward game an SSPG parameterized by $\lambda \in \mathbb{R}$. This SSPG has a similar state space, reward function, and conditional transition probability to the average reward game. The only difference is that s^* becomes an absorbing state with zero-reward, and the reward in all other states is reduced by λ. Let V_λ denote the value function of the associated SSPG which is given as the unique (by Proposition 4.1 from [Pat97]) solution of:

$$
\begin{aligned}
V_\lambda(s) &= \operatorname*{val}_{a,b}\left[r(s,a,b) + \sum_{s' \in \mathcal{S}} P(s'|s,a,b)V_\lambda(s') - \lambda\right], \qquad s \neq s^*, \qquad \text{(A.10)}\\
V_\lambda(s^*) &= 0.
\end{aligned}
$$

If $\lambda = \mathrm{v}$ we retrieve the Bellman equation (2.2) for average reward. Let us first consider the synchronous version of (4.5):

$$
\begin{aligned}
Q_{n+1}(s,a,b) &= Q_n(s,a,b) + \gamma(n)\big(r_\xi(s,a,b) + FQ_n((\xi_n(s,a,b))1_{\{\xi_n(s,a,b)\neq s^*\}} \\
&\qquad - \lambda_n - Q_n(s,a,b)\big), \\
\lambda_{n+1} &= \lambda_n + b(n)FQ_n(s^*), \qquad \text{(A.11)}
\end{aligned}
$$

where we require that $b(n) = o(\gamma(n))$ and ξ and r_ξ are as before. The problem with using the ODE method directly is that λ_n may be unbounded. As in [ABB01], this can be solved using the projection method (e.g., [KY97]) by replacing the iteration of λ by: $\lambda_{n+1} = \Lambda(\lambda_n + b(n)FQ(s^*))$, where $\Lambda(\cdot)$ is projection onto the interval $[-K, K]$ with K chosen so $\mathrm{v} \in [-K, K]$. The following relies on a two time scale analysis as suggested in [Bor97]. The analysis closely follows Section 4 of [ABB01]. The limiting ODE of the iteration (A.10) assuming that $b(n) = o(\gamma(n))$ is:

$$
\dot{Q}(t) = T'(Q(t), \lambda(t)) - Q(t), \qquad \dot{\lambda}(t) = 0,
$$

where $T'(Q, \lambda)$ is s $T(Q) - \lambda e$. Thus, it suffices to prove that the following equation:

$$
\dot{Q}(t) = T'(Q(t), \lambda) - Q(t) \qquad \text{(A.12)}
$$

is asymptotically stable equation for a fixed λ. The stability can be deduced from the fact that T is a weighted maximum norm contraction as the following lemma proves. Recall that a weighted maximum norm with weights norm w in

$\mathbb{R}^d$ is defined as: $\|x\|_w \triangleq \max_{1\leq i\leq d} |x_i|w_i$. A policy is called *proper* in an SSPG if its total reward is finite (almost surely for every policy of the opponent). Assumption 1 implies that all policies are proper in the associated SSPG.

Lemma 4. *Assume that all the policies are proper in an SSPG. Then the operator $T(Q)$ is a weighted maximum norm contraction*

Proof. We define a stochastic shortest path (SSP) problem where both players cooperate in trying to minimize the time of arrival to the absorbing state. Using the solution to this problem we bound the difference between Q-vectors when the players do not cooperate. Define a new single player SSP ([BT95], Section 2.3) where all the rewards are set to -1 (except for s^* which is zero reward) and the transition probabilities are unchanged. The two players are allowed to cooperate. By [BT95], there exists an optimal reward $\tilde{J}$ and stationary policies $\tilde{\mu} \in \Delta(\mathcal{A})^S$ for P1 and $\tilde{\nu} \in \Delta(\mathcal{B})^S$ for P2 such that the optimal time of arrival to the absorbing state is minimal. The vector $\tilde{Q}$ is defined as: $\tilde{Q}(s,a,b) = \sum_{s'} P(s'|s,a,b)\tilde{J}(s')$, and Bellman's equation for that SSP is: $\tilde{Q}(s,a,b) = -1 + \sum_{s'} P(s'|s,a,b) \sum_{a',b'} \tilde{\mu}_{a'}(s')\tilde{\nu}_{b'}(s')\tilde{Q}(s',a',b')$. Moreover, for any μ and ν we have ($P(s'|s,\mu,\nu)$ is the transition matrix assuming μ and ν are played), in vector notations: $\tilde{Q} \leq -1e + P(s'|s,\mu,\nu)\tilde{Q}$. that is:

$$-\sum_{s'} P(s'|s,a',b') \sum_{a',b'} \mu_{a'}(s')\nu_{b'}(s')\tilde{Q}(s',a',b') \leq -\tilde{Q}-1 \leq \tilde{Q}(s,a,b)\alpha\,, \quad \text{(A.13)}$$

where $\alpha \triangleq \max_{s,a,b}(\tilde{Q}(s,a,b)+1)/(\tilde{Q}(s,a,b))$, since $\tilde{Q} \leq -1$ we have $\alpha \in [0,1)$. We now show that α is the contraction factor for the weighted max norm which vector is $w \triangleq -\tilde{Q}$.

Resume the discussion of the original SSPG, let Q and $\bar{Q}$ be elements such that $\|Q-\bar{Q}\|_w^\infty = c$. Let $\mu \in \Delta(\mathcal{A})^S$ be a policy such that $T_\mu Q = TQ$ (maximizing policy), where:

$$T_\mu Q(s,a,b) \triangleq \sum_{s'} P(s'|s,a,b) \left(r(s,a,b) + \min_{u\in\Delta(B)} \sum_{a',b'} \mu_{a'}(s')u_{b'}(s')Q(s',a',b') \right).$$

Let $\nu \in \Delta(\mathcal{B})^S$ be a policy for P2 such that $T_\mu\bar{Q} = T_{\mu\nu}(\bar{Q})$ (minimizing policy for P2) where $T_{\mu\nu}(s,a,b) = \sum_{s'} P(s'|s,a,b)\big(r(s,a,b) + \sum_{a',b'} \mu_{a'}(s')\nu_{b'}(s')Q(s',a',b')\big)$. It follows then: $TQ - T\bar{Q} = T_\mu Q - T\bar{Q} \leq T_\mu Q - T_\mu\bar{Q} = T_\mu Q - T_{\mu\nu}\bar{Q} \leq T_{\mu\nu}Q - T_{\mu\nu}\bar{Q}$. The inequalities follow by imposing on the minimizer and the maximizer policies that might be suboptimal. We therefore have that for every s,a,b

$$\frac{TQ(s,a,b) - T\bar{Q}(s,a,b)}{cw(s,a,b)} \leq \tfrac{1}{cw(s,a,b)} \sum_{s'} \sum_{a',b'} P(s'|s,a',b')\mu_{a'}(s')\nu_{b'}(s') \\ \left(Q(s',a',b') - \bar{Q}(s',a',b')\right),$$

since $\|Q - \bar{Q}\|_w^\infty = c$ we have $Q - \bar{Q} \leq cw$ (as a vector inequality) and therefore:

$$\frac{TQ(s,a,b) - T\bar{Q}(s,a,b)}{cw(s,a,b)} \leq \frac{1}{w(s,a,b)} \sum_{s'} \sum_{a',b'} \left(P(s'|s,a',b')\mu_{a'}(s')\nu_{b'}(s')w(s',a',b')\right).$$

Plugging in w as defined above:

$$\frac{TQ(s,a,b) - T\bar{Q}(s,a,b)}{cw(s,a,b)} \leq \frac{1}{-\tilde{Q}(s,a,b)} \sum_{s'} \sum_{a',b'} P(s'|s,a',b')\mu_{a'}(s')\nu_{b'}(s')(-\tilde{Q}(s',a',b')).$$

Finally, using the previous argument regarding the minimality of $\tilde{\mu}$ and $\tilde{\nu}$ and (A.13) we have

$$\frac{TQ(s,a,b) - T\bar{Q}(s,a,b)}{cw(s,a,b)} \leq \frac{1}{-\tilde{Q}(s,a,b)}(-\tilde{Q}(s,a,b))\alpha = \alpha < 1.$$

□

Let $Q^*(\lambda)$ be the Q-vector that appears in each entry of (A.10). Adapting the arguments of [BS99] and using the fact that $T'(\cdot, \lambda)$ is a weighted maximum norm contraction we can deduce that:

Lemma 5. *The globally asymptotically stable equilibrium for (A.12) is $Q^*(\lambda)$. Furthermore, every solution of the ODE (A.12) satisfies that $\|Q(t) - Q^*(\lambda)\|_w \to 0$ monotonically.*

In order to use two time scale stochastic approximation (e.g., [Bor97]) convergence theorem we need to establish the boundedness of Q:

Lemma 6. *Q_n remains bounded almost surely for both the synchronous (A.11) and asynchronous (4.5) iterations.*

Proof. According to Lemma 4 we have: $\|T(Q)\|_w \leq \alpha\|Q\|_w + D$. Since λ is bounded by K there exists some D such that $\|T'(Q,\lambda)\|_w \leq \alpha\|Q\|_w + D + K$. If $\|Q\|_w \geq 2/(1-\alpha)(D+K)$ we have $\|TQ\|_w \leq \alpha\|Q\|_w + D + K \leq (1/2 + \alpha/2)\|Q\|_w$ and therefore for Q whose norm is large enough the iteration reduces the norm. The asynchronous case follows in a similar manner to [BT95, Section 2.3]. □

A convergence theorem can finally be proved in a similar manner to [ABB01].

Theorem 6. *Suppose that Assumptions 1 and 2 hold. Then the synchronous λ-SSPG Q-learning algorithm (A.11) satisfies that $(Q_n, \lambda_n) \to (Q^*, \mathrm{v})$ almost surely.*

Proof. The assumptions needed for Theorem 1.1 in [Bor97] are satisfied by construction. By definition λ_n is bounded. The vector Q_n is bounded by Lemma 6. Since T' is continuous w.r.t. λ and using the stability of the underlying ODE (Lemma 5) we have ensured convergence to the appropriate limit. The only difference from Theorem 4.5 in [ABB01] is that we need to make sure that the slope of the mapping $\lambda \to Q^*(\lambda)$ is finite. But this was shown by Lemma 5.1 of [Pat97]. □

For the asynchronous case the same can be proved.

Proof of Theorem 2: The analysis of [Bor98,KB00] applies since boundedness holds by Lemma 6. The only difference from Theorem 6 is that a time scaled version is used. □

Polynomial Time Prediction Strategy with Almost Optimal Mistake Probability

Nader H. Bshouty*

Department of Computer Science Technion, Haifa, Israel 32000

Abstract. We give the first *polynomial time* prediction strategy for any PAC-learnable class C that probabilistically predicts the target with mistake probability

$$\frac{poly(\log(t))}{t} = \tilde{O}\left(\frac{1}{t}\right)$$

where t is the number of trials. The lower bound for the mistake probability is [HLW94] $\Omega(1/t)$, so our algorithm is almost optimal.[1]

1 Introduction

In the Probabilistic Prediction model [HLW94] a teacher chooses a boolean function $f : X \to \{0, 1\}$ from some class of functions C and a distribution D on X. At trial t the learner receives from the teacher a point x_t chosen from X according to the distribution D and is asked to predict $f(x_t)$. The learner uses some prediction strategy S (algorithm), predicts $S(x_t)$ and sends it to the teacher. The teacher then answers "correct" if the prediction is correct, i.e. if $S(x_t) = f(x_t)$ and answers "mistake" otherwise. The goal of the learner is to run in polynomial time at each trial (polynomial in $\log t$ and some measures of the class and the target) minimize the worst case (over all $f \in C$ and D) probability of mistake in predicting $f(x_t)$.

Haussler et. al. in [HLW94] gave a double exponential time prediction strategy (exponential in the number of trials t) that achieves mistake probability $V_C/t = O(1/t)$ where V_C is the VC-dimension of the class C. They also show a lower bound of $\Omega(V_C/t)$ for the mistake probability. They then gave an exponential time algorithm (polynomial in t) that achieves mistakes probability $(V_C/t)\log(t/V_C) = O(\log t/t)$ assuming that C is PAC-learnable in polynomial time. Since learning in the probabilistic model implies learning in the PAC model, the requirement that C is efficiently PAC-learnable is necessary for efficient probabilistic prediction. The results from [BG02] gives a randomized strategy that achieves mistake probability exponentially small in the number of mistakes.

* This research was supported by the fund for promotion of research at the Technion. Research no. 120-025.

[1] The lower bound proved in [HLW94] is $\Omega(V_C/t)$ where V_C is the VC-dimension of the class C. In our case V_C is fixed and therefore is $O(1)$ with respect to t

J. Shawe-Taylor and Y. Singer (Eds.): COLT 2004, LNAI 3120, pp. 64–76, 2004.

In this paper we give an algorithm that generate a deterministic prediction strategy S. We show that if C is PAC-learnable then there is deterministic prediction strategy that runs in polynomial time and achieves mistake probability at most

$$\frac{poly(\log t)}{t} = \tilde{O}\left(\frac{1}{t}\right).$$

This is the first prediction strategy that runs in polynomial time and achieves an almost optimal mistake probability.

Our algorithm is based on building a new booster for the PAExact model [BG02]. The booster is randomized but the hypotheses it produce (that are used for the predictions) are deterministic. We believe that the same technique used in this paper (section 4) may also be used for the booster in [BG02] to achieve the same result (with much greater time complexity and randomized prediction strategy).

The first part of the paper gives a PAExact-learning algorithm that uses deterministic hypothesis for any PAC-learnable class that achieves exponentially small error in the number of equivalence queries. In the second part we show how to turn this algorithm to a deterministic prediction strategy that achieves the required mistake probability.

In section 2 and 3 we build a new deterministic booster for the PAExact-model and then in section 4 we show how to change the PAExact-learning algorithm to a prediction strategy that achieves the above bound.

2 Learning Models and Definitions

Let C be a class of functions $f : X \to \{0,1\}$. The domain X can be finite, countable infinite, or $\mathcal{R}^n$ for some $n \geq 1$. In learning, a *teacher* has a *target function* $f \in C$ and a *probability distribution* D on X. The *learner* knows C but does not know the probability distribution D nor the function f.

The *problem size* I_f that we will use in this paper depends on X, C and f and it can be different in different settings. The term "polynomial" means polynomial in the problem size I_f. For example, for Boolean functions with $X = \{0,1\}^n$, C is a set of formulas (e.g. DNF, Decision tree, etc.). The problem size is $I_f = n + size_C(f)$ where $size_C(f)$ is the minimal size of a formula in C that is equivalent to f. Then "polynomial" means $poly(I_f) = poly(n, size_C(f))$. For infinite domains X the parameter n is usually replaced by the VC-dimension of the class V_C and $I_f = V_C + size_C(f)$. Then "polynomial" in this case is $poly(V_C, size_C(f))$.

The learner can ask the teacher *queries* about the target. The teacher can be regarded as an adversary with unlimited computational power that must answer honestly but also wants to fail the learner from learning quickly. The queries we consider in this paper are:

Example Query according to D ($\mathbf{Ex}_D$) [V84] For the example query the teacher chooses $x \in X$ according to the probability distribution D and returns $(x, f(x))$ to the learner.

We say that the hypothesis h_r *ε-approximates* f with respect to distribution D if $\Pr_{D,r}[f(x) \neq h_r(x)] \leq \varepsilon$.

Equivalence Query according to D ($\mathbf{EQ}_D$) [B97] For the equivalence query according to distribution D the learner asks $\mathrm{EQ}_D(h)$ for some polynomial size circuit[2] h. The teacher chooses $y \in X_{f\Delta h}$ according to the induced distribution of D on $X_{f\Delta h}$ and returns $(y, f(y))$. If $\Pr_D[X_{f\Delta h}] = 0$, the teacher answers "YES". Equivalence queries with randomized hypothesis is defined in [BG02].

The learning models we will consider in this paper are

PAC (Probably Approximately Correct)[V84] In the PAC learning model we say that an algorithm $\mathcal{A}$ of the learner *PAC-learns* the class C if for any $f \in C$, any probability distribution D and any $\varepsilon, \delta > 0$ the algorithm $\mathcal{A}(\varepsilon, \delta)$ asks example queries according to D, Ex_D, and with probability at least $1 - \delta$, outputs a polynomial size circuit h that ε-approximates f with respect to D. That is $\Pr_D[X_{f\Delta h}] \leq \varepsilon$. We say that C is *PAC-learnable* if there is an algorithm that PAC-learns C in time $poly(1/\varepsilon, \log(1/\delta), I_f)$.

PAExact (Probably Almost Exactly Correct)[BJT02] In the PAExact learning model we say that an algorithm $\mathcal{A}$ of the learner *PAExact-learns* the class C if for any $f \in C$, any probability distribution D and any $\eta, \delta > 0$ the algorithm $\mathcal{A}(\eta, \delta)$ asks equivalence queries according to D, EQ_D, and with probability at least $1-\delta$, outputs a polynomial size circuit h that η-approximates f with respect to D. That is $\Pr_D[X_{f\Delta h}] \leq \eta$. We say that C is *PAExact-learnable* if there is an algorithm that PAExact-learns C in time $poly(\log(1/\eta), \log(1/\delta), I_f)$.

In the online learning model [L88] the teacher at each trial sends a point $x \in X$ to the learner and the learner has to predict $f(x)$. The learner returns to the teacher the prediction y. If $f(x) \neq y$ then the teacher returns "mistake" to the learner. The goal of the learner is to minimize the number of prediction mistakes.

Online [L88] In the online model we say that algorithm $\mathcal{A}$ of the learner *Online-learns* the class C if for any $f \in C$ and for any δ, algorithm $\mathcal{A}(\delta)$ with probability at least $1 - \delta$ makes bounded number of mistakes. We say that C is *Online-learnable* if the number of mistakes and the running time of the learner for each prediction is $poly(\log(1/\delta), I_f)$.

Probabilistic Prediction (PP) [HLW94] In the Probabilistic Prediction model the points sent to the learner $x_1, x_2, \cdots$ are chosen from X according to some distribution D. The goal of the prediction strategy at trial t is to predict $f(x_t)$ with minimal mistake probability. We say that C is *ϵ-PP-learnable* if the prediction strategy runs in time $poly(I_f, \log t)$ and achieve mistake probability ϵ.

[2] For infinite domains X, the definition of "circuit" depends on the setting in which the elements of C are represented. The hypothesis h must have polynomial size in this setting. E.g., if $X = \mathcal{R}^n$ we may ask of h to be a polynomial size *arithmetic* circuit

3 The New Algorithm

In this section we give our new booster for the PAExact learning model and prove its correctness. In Subsection 3.1 we show how to start from a hypothesis that approximates the target function f and refine it to get a better one. In Subsection 3.2 we give the main algorithm and prove its correctness.

3.1 Refining the Hypothesis

We will first give a booster for the PAExact-learning model that takes a hypothesis that η-approximates the target and builds a new hypothesis that $\eta/2$-approximates the target.

Let $\mathcal{A}$ be a PAC-learning algorithm that learns the class C in polynomial time from $m_{\mathcal{A}}(\varepsilon, \delta, I_f)$ examples. Let h_0 be a hypothesis such that

$$\Pr_D[f \neq h_0] \leq \eta. \tag{1}$$

Our booster learns a sequence of hypotheses $\mathcal{H} = h_1, h_2, h_3, \ldots, h_k$ and then uses this sequence to build the refined hypothesis.

We start with the following notation. Let

$$H_j^{\wedge} = \begin{cases} 1 & j = 1 \\ h_1 \wedge \cdots \wedge h_{j-1} & j > 1 \end{cases} \text{ and } H_j^{\vee} = \begin{cases} 0 & j = 1 \\ h_1 \vee \cdots \vee h_{j-1} & j > 1 \end{cases}.$$

Let $H_j = \overline{h_0} H_j^{\wedge} \vee h_0 H_j^{\vee}$ and $G_j = \overline{h_0} H_j^{\wedge} \vee h_0 \overline{H_j^{\vee}}$.

Now we show how the booster learns h_j from $h_1, h_2, \ldots, h_{j-1}$. The booster runs the procedure **Learnh**(j, ε, δ). See Figure 1. This procedure either returns a refined hypothesis h (see steps 10 and 11 in **Learnh**) or returns the next hypothesis h_j in the sequence $\mathcal{H}$ (see step 14 in **Learnh**). In the former case h_j =NULL indicating that h_{j-1} is the last function in the sequence $\mathcal{H}$ and then $\mathcal{H} = h_1, h_2, \ldots, h_k$ for $k = j-1$. In the latter case a new function h_j is generated in $\mathcal{H}$. We will show that for some $\varepsilon = 1/poly(\log(1/\eta))$ and $k = poly(\log(1/\eta))$, either h_0 or H_k or H_{k+1} (this depends where the algorithm returns in the last call for **Learnh**. In step 10, 11 or 14, respectively) is an $\eta/2$-approximation of f. For the analysis of the algorithm we define three values: For $j \leq k$

$$\begin{aligned} w_j &= \Pr_D[\overline{h_0} H_j^{\wedge} \overline{h_j} = 1, f = 1] + \Pr_D[h_0 \overline{H_j^{\vee}} h_j = 1, f = 0] \\ u_j &= \Pr_D[\overline{h_0} H_{j+1}^{\wedge} = 1, f = 0] + \Pr_D[h_0 \overline{H_{j+1}^{\vee}} = 1, f = 1] \\ v_j &= \Pr_D[\overline{h_0}\ \overline{H_{j+1}^{\wedge}} = 1, f = 1] + \Pr_D[h_0 H_{j+1}^{\vee} = 1, f = 0] \end{aligned}$$

We prove the following

Property 1. *We have (1)* $u_0 \leq 1$. *(2)* $v_j = \sum_{i=1}^{j} w_i$ *(3)* $\Pr_D[f \neq H_{j+1}] = u_j + v_j$.

```
Learnh (j, ε, δ)

1) Set m ← m_A(ε/2, δ, I_f); r_0 ← 0; r_j ← 0.
2)     For i ← 1 to m
3)         Flip a fair coin →result
4)         If result="Head" Then
5)             Repeat EQ_D(h_0) → (x_i, f(x_i)); r_0 ← r_0 + 1;
6)             Until G_j(x_i) = 1 or r_0 = 4m.
7)         Else
8)             Repeat EQ_D(H_j) → (x_i, f(x_i)); r_j ← r_j + 1;
9)             Until G_j(x_i) = 1 or r_j = 4m.
10)        If r_0 = 4m Then Return(h_j ≡NULL, h ≡ h_0)
11)        If r_j = 4m Then Return(h_j ≡NULL, h ≡ H_j)
12)        S ← S ∪ {(x_i, f(x_i))}.
13) Run A with examples S → h_j
14) Return(h_j, h ≡NULL)
```

Fig. 1. The algorithm **Learnh**(j, ε, δ) learns the jth function in the sequence $\mathcal{H}$.

Claim 3.1 *For every j, with probability at least $1-\delta$ we have $w_j \le \varepsilon\eta$ and $u_j \le \varepsilon u_{j-1}$.*

Claim 3.2 *With probability at least $1 - j\delta$ we have: For all $i \le j$, we have $w_i \le \varepsilon\eta$, $u_i \le \varepsilon^i$, $v_i \le i\varepsilon\eta$ and $\Pr_D[f \ne H_{i+1}] \le i\varepsilon\eta + \varepsilon^i$.*

Claim 3.3 *If $\Pr_D[f \ne h_0] > 2(j-1)\varepsilon\eta$ then the probability that* **Learnh**(j, ε, δ) *returns $h \equiv h_0$ is less than $j\delta$.*

Claim 3.4 *If $\Pr_D[f \ne H_j] > 2(j-1)\varepsilon\eta$ then the probability that* **Learnh**(j, ε, δ) *returns $h \equiv H_j$ is less than $j\delta$.*

The first and the second claims give bounds for w_i, u_i and v_i and show that with high probability the error of the hypothesis H_{j+1} is less than $j\varepsilon\eta + \varepsilon^j$. The other two claims show that if the algorithm stops in steps 10 or 11 then with high probability the hypothesis h_0 or H_j, respectively, achieves error at most $2(j-1)\varepsilon\eta$. In the next subsection we will choose j and ε such that those errors are less than $\eta/2$.

Proof of Property 1. We have $u_0 = \Pr_D[f = h_0] < 1$ which follows *1.* Now

$$\begin{aligned} v_j &= \Pr_D[\overline{h_0}\ \overline{H^{\wedge}_{j+1}} = 1, f = 1] + \Pr_D[h_0 H^{\vee}_{j+1} = 1, f = 0] \\ &= \sum_{i=1}^{j} (\Pr_D[\overline{h_0} H^{\wedge}_i \overline{h_i} = 1, f = 1] + \Pr[h_0 \overline{H^{\vee}_i} h_i = 1, f = 0]) = \sum_{i=1}^{j} w_i. \end{aligned}$$

This follows *2*. Finally we have

$$\begin{aligned}\Pr_D[f \neq H_{j+1}] &= \Pr_D[f \neq H_{j+1}, h_0 = 0, f = 0] + \Pr_D[f \neq H_{j+1}, h_0 = 1, f = 1] + \\ &\quad \Pr_D[f \neq H_{j+1}, h_0 = 0, f = 1] + \Pr_D[f \neq H_{j+1}, h_0 = 1, f = 0] \\ &= \Pr_D[\overline{h_0} H^{\wedge}_{j+1} = 1, f = 0] + \Pr_D[h_0 \overline{H^{\vee}_{j+1}} = 1, f = 1] + \\ &\quad \Pr_D[\overline{h_0}\ \overline{H^{\wedge}_{j+1}} = 1, f = 1] + \Pr_D[h_0 H^{\vee}_{j+1} = 1, f = 0] \\ &= u_j + v_j.\end{aligned}$$

and this follows *3*.□

Proof of Claim 3.1. When **Learnh** learns h_j it asks with probability 1/2, $\mathrm{EQ}_D(h_0)$ and with probability 1/2, $\mathrm{EQ}_D(H_j)$ and takes only points x_i that satisfies $G_j(x_i) = 1$ (see steps 5-6 and 8-9 in **Learnh**). Let D_j be the probability distribution of x_i. Since the events $f \neq h_0, G_j = 1$ and $f \neq H_j, G_j = 1$ are disjoint (take two cases $f = 0$ and $f = 1$ and use property P4) and since the algorithm takes $m_{\mathcal{A}}(\varepsilon/2, \delta, I_f)$ examples to learn h_j, with probability at least $1 - \delta$ we have

$$\begin{aligned}\frac{\varepsilon}{2} &\geq \Pr_{D_j}[f \neq h_j] \\ &= \frac{1}{2}\Pr_D[f \neq h_j | f \neq h_0, G_j = 1] + \frac{1}{2}\Pr_D[f \neq h_j | f \neq H_j, G_j = 1] \qquad (2)\end{aligned}$$

By (1) and (2) we have

$$\begin{aligned}\varepsilon \geq \Pr_D[f \neq h_j | f \neq h_0, G_j = 1] &= \frac{\Pr_D[f \neq h_j, f \neq h_0, G_j = 1]}{\Pr_D[f \neq h_0, G_j = 1]} \\ \geq \frac{\Pr_D[\overline{h_0} H^{\wedge}_j \overline{h_j} = 1, f = 1] + \Pr_D[h_0 \overline{H^{\vee}_j} h_j = 1, f = 0]}{\eta} &= \frac{w_j}{\eta}.\end{aligned}$$

Therefore $w_j \leq \varepsilon\eta$.

By (2) we have

$$\begin{aligned}\varepsilon \geq \Pr_D[f \neq h_j | f \neq H_j, G_j = 1] &= \frac{\Pr_D[f \neq h_j, f \neq H_j, G_j = 1]}{\Pr_D[f \neq H_j, G_j = 1]} \\ = \frac{\Pr_D[\overline{h_0} H^{\wedge}_{j+1} = 1, f = 0] + \Pr_D[h_0 \overline{H^{\vee}_{j+1}} = 1, f = 1]}{\Pr_D[\overline{h_0} H^{\wedge}_j = 1, f = 0] + \Pr_D[h_0 \overline{H^{\vee}_j} = 1, f = 1]} &= \frac{u_j}{u_{j-1}}.\end{aligned}$$

Therefore $u_j \leq \varepsilon u_{j-1}$. □

Now the proof of Claim 3.2 follows from Property 1 and Claim 3.1.

Proof of Claim 3.3. We have $\Pr_D[G_j = 0 | f \neq h_0]$ is equal to

$$\begin{aligned}\frac{\Pr_D[G_j = 0, f \neq h_0]}{\Pr_D[f \neq h_0]} &= \frac{\Pr_D[\overline{h_0}\ \overline{H^{\wedge}_j} = 1, f = 1] + \Pr_D[h_0 H^{\vee}_j = 1, f = 0]}{\Pr_D[f \neq h_0]} \\ &\leq \frac{v_{j-1}}{2(j-1)\varepsilon\eta}\end{aligned}$$

By Claim 3.2, with probability at least $1-(j-1)\delta$, $\Pr_D[G_j=0|f\neq h_0]\leq 1/2$.

Suppose **Learnh** calls the equivalence query $\mathrm{EQ}_D(h_0)$, $4m$ times. Let X_r be a random variable that is equal to 1 if the rth call of $\mathrm{EQ}_D(h_0)$ returns a counterexample x' such that $G_j(x')=0$ and $X_r=0$ otherwise. Then

$$E[X_r]=\Pr_D[G_j=0|f\neq h_0]\leq\frac{1}{2}.$$

If **Learnh**(j,ε,δ) outputs h_0 then since the algorithm makes at most m coin flips (see steps 2-3 in **Learnh**) we have

$$\sum_{i=1}^{4m}X_i\geq 3m.$$

Now given that $\{X_r\}_r$ are independent random variables and $E[X_r]\leq 1/2$ and using Chernoff bound we have Pr[**Learnh**(j,ε,δ) outputs h_0] is

$$\Pr\left[\sum_{i=1}^{4m}X_i>3m\right]\leq\Pr\left[\frac{\sum_{i=1}^{4m}X_i}{4m}\geq E[X_r]+\frac{1}{4}\right]\leq e^{-(m/4)}\leq\delta$$

The later inequality follows because $m\geq 4\ln(1/\delta)$. Therefore, the probability that **Learnh**(j,ε,δ) outputs h_0 is at most $j\delta$.□

Proof of Claim 3.4: We have $\Pr_D[G_j=0|f\neq H_j]$ is

$$\frac{\Pr_D[G_j=0,f\neq H_j]}{\Pr_D[f\neq H_j]}=\frac{\Pr_D[h_0H_j^{\vee}=1,f=0]+\Pr_D[\overline{h_0}\ \overline{H_j^{\wedge}}=1,f=1]}{\Pr_D[f\neq H_j]}$$
$$\leq\frac{v_{j-1}}{2(j-1)\varepsilon\eta}.$$

Then the proof is exactly the same as the proof of Claim 3.3.□

Refine $(h_0,k,\varepsilon,\delta)$

1) $j\leftarrow 0$
2) **Repeat**
3) $\quad j\leftarrow j+1$
4) $\quad$ **Learnh**$(j,\varepsilon,\delta/(3k^2))\rightarrow(h_j,h)$
5) **Until** $j=k$ or $h_j=$NULL
6) **If** $j=k$ **Then** $h\leftarrow H_{k+1}$
7) **Return**(h).

Fig. 2. A PAExact-learning algorithm that refine h_0

We now can build the procedure that refines the function h_0. In Figure 2 the procedure **Refine** runs **Learnh** at most k times. It stops running **Learnh** and output a refined hypothesis if one of the following happen:

1. The function h_j is equal to NULL and then it outputs either h_0 or H_j (depends what is h).
2. We get $j = k$ and then it outputs H_{k+1}.

We now prove

Lemma 1. *Suppose* $\Pr_D[f \neq h_0] \leq \eta$ *and* $h = \textbf{Refine}(h_0, k, \varepsilon, \delta)$. *Then with probability at least* $1 - \delta$ *we have*

$$\Pr_D[f \neq h] \leq \max(k\varepsilon\eta + \varepsilon^k, 2k\varepsilon\eta).$$

Proof. Let $\mathcal{H} = h_1, h_2, \ldots, h_t$, $t \leq k$ be the sequence of hypotheses generated by **Learnh**. Let $\delta' = \delta/(3k^2)$. We want to measure the probability that the algorithm fails to output a hypothesis h that η'-approximates f where $\eta' = \max(k\varepsilon\eta + \varepsilon^k, 2k\varepsilon\eta)$. This happen if and only if one of the following events happen:

[A_1] For some $j = t \leq k$, $\textbf{Learnh}(j, \varepsilon, \delta')$ outputs $h \equiv h_0$ and $\Pr_D[f \neq h_0] \geq \eta'$.
[A_2] For some $j = t \leq k$, $\textbf{Learnh}(j, \varepsilon, \delta')$ outputs $h \equiv H_j$ and $\Pr_D[f \neq H_j] \geq \eta'$.
[A_3] We have $t = k$ and $\Pr_D[f \neq H_{k+1}] \geq \eta'$.

Now since for $j = 1, \ldots, k$ we have $2(j-1)\varepsilon\eta \leq 2k\varepsilon\eta \leq \eta'$, by Claim 3.3

$$\begin{aligned}\Pr[A_1] &\leq \Pr[\exists\, 1 \leq j \leq k : \textbf{Learnh}(j, \varepsilon, \delta') \\ &\qquad \text{outputs } h \equiv h_0 \text{ and } \Pr_D[f \neq h_0] \geq 2(j-1)\varepsilon\eta] \\ &\leq \sum_{j=1}^{k} j\delta' \leq k^2\delta' = \frac{\delta}{3}\end{aligned}$$

In the same way one can prove $\Pr[A_2] \leq \frac{\delta}{3}$. Now since $k\varepsilon\eta + \varepsilon^k \leq \eta'$, by Claim 3.2

$$\Pr[A_3] \leq \Pr[\Pr_D[f \neq H_{k+1}] > k\varepsilon\eta + \varepsilon^k] \leq k\delta' \leq \frac{\delta}{3}.$$

Therefore, the probability that the algorithm fails to output a hypothesis that η' approximates f is less than δ.□

3.2 The Algorithm and Its Analysis

We are now ready to give the PAExact-learning algorithm. We will first give the algorithm and prove its correctness. Then we give the analysis of the algorithm's complexity.

Let $\mathcal{A}$ be a PAC-learning algorithm that learns C in polynomial time and $m_{\mathcal{A}}(\varepsilon, \delta, I_f)$ examples. In Figure 3 , the algorithm $\textbf{PAExact-Learn}(\eta, \delta)$ defines

$$\varepsilon = \frac{\log\log\frac{1}{\eta}}{16\log\frac{1}{\eta}},\quad \delta' = \frac{\delta}{6\log\frac{1}{\eta}} \text{ and } k = \left\lceil \frac{2\log\frac{1}{\eta}}{\log\log\frac{1}{\eta}} \right\rceil. \tag{3}$$

The algorithm first runs $\mathcal{A}$ to get some hypothesis h_0. Then it runs **Refine** $\lceil \log(1/\eta) \rceil$ times. From the above analysis the following Theorems follows.

PAExact-Learn (η, δ)

1) **Set** $\varepsilon \leftarrow \frac{\log\log\frac{1}{\eta}}{16\log\frac{1}{\eta}}$, $\delta' \leftarrow \frac{\delta}{6\log\frac{1}{\eta}}$, $k \leftarrow \left\lceil \frac{2\log\frac{1}{\eta}}{\log\log\frac{1}{\eta}} \right\rceil$.
2) **Run** $\mathcal{A}$ with $m_{\mathcal{A}}(\varepsilon, \delta', I_f)$ examples $\rightarrow h_0$
3) **For** $t \leftarrow 1$ **to** $\lceil \log\frac{1}{\eta} \rceil$
4) $\quad h_0 \leftarrow$ **Refine**$(h_0, k, \varepsilon, \delta')$
5) **Output**(h_0)

Fig. 3. An PAExact-learning algorithm that learns the class C with error η and confidence δ.

Theorem 1. (**Correctness**) *Algorithm* **PAExact-Learn**(η, δ) *learns with probability at least* $1-\delta$ *a hypothesis that* η*-approximates* f.

Proof or Theorem 1. Let $h_0^{(0)}, h_0^{(1)}, \ldots, h_0^{(t)}$, $t = \lceil \log(1/\eta) \rceil$ be the functions learned in line 4 of the algorithm. Here $h_0^{(0)} = h_0$ is the hypothesis that is learned in line 2 of the algorithm. We have with probability at least $1-\delta'$, $\Pr[f \neq h_0^{(0)}] \leq \varepsilon$ and by Lemma 1 with probability at least $1-\delta'$ we have

$$\Pr[f \neq h_0^{(k)}] \leq \max(k\varepsilon\eta_0 + \varepsilon^k, 2k\varepsilon\eta_0)$$

where $\Pr_D[f \neq h_0^{(k-1)}] = \eta_0$. Now since $k\varepsilon\eta_0 + \varepsilon^k \leq \eta_0 + \eta/4$ and $2k\varepsilon\eta_0 \leq \eta_0/2$ and since $\max(\eta_0 + \eta/4, \eta_0/2) \leq \max(\eta_0/2, \eta)$, we have

$$\Pr_D[f \neq h_0^{(k)}] \leq \max\left(\frac{\Pr_D[f \neq h_0^{(k-1)}]}{2}, \eta\right).$$

Therefore, with probability at least $1-\delta$ we have $\Pr_D[f \neq h_0^{\lceil \log(1/\eta) \rceil}] \leq \eta$. This completes the proof of the Theorem.□

For the analysis of the algorithm we first give a very general Theorem and then apply it to different settings.

Theorem 2. (**Efficiency**) *Algorithm* **PAExact_Learn**(η, δ) *uses*

$$\frac{16\log^2\frac{1}{\eta}}{\log\log\frac{1}{\eta}} m_{\mathcal{A}}\left(\frac{\log\log\frac{1}{\eta}}{32\log\frac{1}{\eta}}, \frac{\left(\log\log\frac{1}{\eta}\right)^2\delta}{72\log^3\frac{1}{\eta}}, I_f\right)$$

equivalence queries.

Proof of Theorem 2. We will use the notations in (3). Algorithm **PAExact_Learn**(η, δ) calls the procedure **Refine**$(h_0, k, \varepsilon, \delta')$, $\lceil \log(1/\eta) \rceil$ times. The procedure **Refine** $(h_0, k, \varepsilon, \delta')$ calls the procedure **Learnh** $(j, \varepsilon, \delta'/3k^2)$, k times and the procedure **Learnh**$(j, \varepsilon, \delta'/3k^2)$ calls the example oracle at most $8m_{\mathcal{A}}(\varepsilon/2, \delta'/(3k^2), I_f)$ times. This follows the result.□

It follows from Theorem 2

Theorem 3. *If C is PAC-learnable with error $\frac{1}{2} - \gamma$ and confidence λ with sample of size V_0, then C is PAExact-learnable with*

$$d(\delta, \eta) = O\left(w \log \frac{1}{\delta} + \frac{V_0 w}{\gamma^2} \log^2 \frac{V_0 w}{\gamma^2} \right),$$

equivalence queries where

$$w = \frac{32 \log^3 \frac{1}{\eta}}{\left(\log \log \frac{1}{\eta} \right)^2}$$

and time polynomial in d and $1/\lambda$.

Proof. Follows from Theorem 2 and Corollary 3.3 in [F95].□

Before we leave this section we give the algorithm that will be used in the next section. We will use $d(\delta, \eta)$ to denote the complexity of the algorithm **PAExact-Learn**(η, δ). Let $\eta(d)$ be a function of d such that $d = 2d(\delta, \eta(d))$. We now prove

Theorem 4. *The algorithm* **PAExact-Learn**(δ) *after the dth mistake, will be holding a hypothesis that with probability at least $1 - \delta$ has error $\eta(d)$.*

Proof. Set a constant d_0. We run PAExact-Learn$(\delta, \eta(d_0))$ twice and after $2d_0$ mistakes we run PAExact-Learn$(\delta, \eta(2d_0))$ and so on. When $d = d_0 + d_0 + 2d_0 + \cdots + 2^i d_0 = 2^{i+1} d_0$ with probability at least $1 - \delta$ the final hypothesis has error η where $2^i d_0 = d(\delta, \eta)$. This gives $d = 2d(\delta, \eta(d))$.□

4 A Prediction Strategy and Its Analysis

In this section we use the algorithm **PAExact-Learn**(δ) to give a deterministic prediction strategy. Then give an analysis of its mistake probability.

First we may assume that t is known. This is because we may run our prediction strategy assuming $t = t_0$ and get a prediction strategy with mistake probability $\epsilon(t_0)$. If $t > t_0$ then at trials $t_0 + 1, t_0 + 2, \ldots, 3t_0$ we use the prediction strategy used in trial t_0 and at the same time learn a new prediction strategy (from the last $2t_0$ examples) that has mistake probability $\epsilon(2t_0)$. It is easy to see that this doubling technique will solve the problem when t is not known.

Second we may assume that t is large enough. As long as t is polynomial in the other parameters then we can use the PAC-learning algorithm to learn a hypothesis and use this hypothesis for the prediction. This hypothesis will achieve error $\log t/t$.

We also need a bound on the VC-dimension of the class of all possible output hypotheses of **PAExact-Learn** (δ) at trial t. Obviously this cannot be more than the number of examples we use in PAExact algorithm which is $poly(\log t, \log(1/\delta), I_f)$. We denote this by $V_t^\star$.

The strategy prediction algorithm is described in Figure 4. The procedure saves the hypotheses $h_0, h_1, h_2, \ldots$ generated from **PAExact-Learn**(δ) and for

Predict $(x_t, S = ((h_0, t_0), \ldots, (h_d, t_d)))$

1) **Initial** $h_0 = 1; t_0 = 0; S = ((h_0, t_0))$.
2) **Let** $\ell = \arg\max t_i$.
3) **Find** η_0 and η_1 in
 $d = 2d(\eta_0, \eta_0)$ and
 $\frac{t}{d} = \frac{V_t^\star}{\eta_1} \log \frac{1}{\eta_1} + \frac{1}{\eta_1} \log \frac{t^2}{\eta_1}$
4) **If** $\eta_1 < \eta_0$ **Predict** $h_\ell(x_t)$ **Else Predict** $h_d(x_t)$.
5) **Receive** $f(x_t)$
6) **If** $h_d(x_t) \neq f(x_t)$ **Then**
7) **Answer** x_t to $\mathrm{EQ}_D(h_d)$ that is asked in **PAExact-Learn** (η_0) and
8) **Receive** a new hypothesis h_{d+1} when the next $\mathrm{EQ}_D(h_{d+1})$ is asked
9) **Add** $S \leftarrow (S, (h_{d+1}, 0))$.
10) **Else**
11) $t_d = t_d + 1$.
12) **Goto** 2.

Fig. 4. A deterministic prediction strategy.

each hypothesis h_i it saves t_i the number of examples x_j in which h_i predicted correctly. Notice that the algorithm in line 4 does not necessarily choose the last hypothesis h_d for the prediction. In some cases, (depends on η_0 and η_1) it chooses the hypothesis that is consistent with the longest sequence of consecutive examples (see line 2-4 in the algorithm).

The idea of the proof is very simple. If the number of mistakes d is "large" then the probability of the mistake of the final hypothesis is small. Otherwise, (if d is small) then there is a hypothesis that is consistent with t/d consecutive examples and then this hypothesis will have a small prediction error.

We prove the following Theorem

Theorem 5. *The probability of the prediction error of the strategy* **Predict** *is smaller than*

$$\frac{poly(\log(t))}{t},$$

and the running time in each trial is $poly(\log t)$.

Proof Sketch. Notice that the number of mistakes $d = poly(\log t)$ and the size of each hypothesis h_i is at most $poly(\log t)$. Therefore, the running time is $poly(\log t)$ at each trial.

If $\eta_0 \leq \eta_1$ then $d = 2d(\eta_0, \eta_0)$ and by Theorem 4 the hypothesis h_d is with probability $1 - \eta_0$ has error η_0. Therefore h_d will predict x_{t+1} with mistake probability at most $2\eta_0$.

If $\eta_1 < \eta_0$ then since h_ℓ is consistent on at least

$$\frac{t}{d} = \frac{V_t^\star}{\eta_1} \log \frac{1}{\eta_1} + \frac{1}{\eta_1} \log \frac{t^2}{\eta_1}$$

consecutive examples, and since there is at most t^2 subsequences of consecutive examples, then by OCCAM, with probability at least $1-\eta_1$ the hypothesis h_ℓ has error η_1. Therefore h_ℓ predicts $f(x_{t+1})$ with probability mistake at most $2\eta_1$. This implies that the probability of the prediction mistake at trial t is at most $\eta = 2\min(\eta_0, \eta_1)$.

Since t is fixed we can consider η_0 and η_1 as functions of d. The error η_0 is monotonically decreasing as a function of d and η_1 is monotonically increasing as a function of d. Therefore, $\eta \le 2\eta'$ where $\eta' = \eta_0 = \eta_1$. Replacing η_0 and η_1 by η' we get

$$d = O\left(\omega \log\frac{1}{\eta'} + \frac{V_C}{\gamma^2}\log^2\frac{V_C\omega}{\gamma^2}\right), \quad \omega = \frac{32\log^3\frac{1}{\eta'}}{\left(\log\log\frac{1}{\eta'}\right)^2}$$

and

$$\frac{t}{d} = \frac{V_t^\star}{\eta'}\log\frac{1}{\eta'} + \frac{1}{\eta'}\log\frac{t^2}{\eta'}.$$

Then

$$t = d\left(\frac{V_t^\star}{\eta'}\log\frac{1}{\eta'} + \frac{1}{\eta'}\log\frac{t^2}{\eta'}\right) = \frac{poly\left(\log\frac{1}{\eta'}\right)poly(\log t)}{\eta'}$$

Which implies $\eta \le 2\eta' = poly(\log t)/t.\Box$

References

[A88] D. Angluin. Queries and concept learning. *Machine Learning*, 2:319-342, 1987.

[B94] A. Blum. Separating distribution-free and mistake-bound learning models over the boolean domain, *SIAM Journal on Computing 23(5)*,pp. 990-1000,1994.

[B97] N. H. Bshouty, Exact learning of formulas in parallel. *Machine Learning, 26*,pp. 25-41,1997.

[BC+96] N. H. Bshouty, R. Cleve, R. Gavaldà, S. Kannan, C. Tamon, Oracles and Queries That Are Sufficient for Exact Learning. *Journal of Computer and System Sciences* **52**(3): pp. 421-433 (1996).

[BG02] N. H. Bshouty and D. Gavinsky, PAC=PAExact and other equivalent models in learning Proceedings of the 43rd Ann. Symp. on Foundation of Computer Science (FOCS). pp. 167-176 2002.

[BJT02] N. H. Bshouty, J. Jackson and C. Tamon, Exploring learnability between exact and PAC, Proceedings of the 15th Annual Conference on Computational Learning Theory, pp. 244-254 2002.

[F95] Y. Freund, Boosting a weak learning algorithm by majority, *Information and Computation*, **121**, 256-285 (1995).

[HLW94] D. Haussler, N. Littlestone and M. K. Warmuth, Predicting 0,1-functions on randomly drawn points, *Information and Computation, 115*,pp. 248-292,1994.

[KM96] M. Kearns and Y. Mansour, On the Boosting Ability of Top-Down Decision Tree Learning Algorithms, Proceedings of the 28th Symposium on Theory of Computing, pp. 459-468,1996.

[L88] N. Littlestone. Learning when irrelevant attributes abound: A new linear-threshold algorithm. *Machine Learning*, 2:285–318, 1988.

[MA00] Y. Mansour and D. McAllester, Boosting using Branching Programs, Proceedings of the 13th Annual Conference on Computational Learning Theory,pp. 220-224,2000.

[O03] D. Gavinsky and A. Owshanko, PExact=Exact learning, manuscript.

[S90] R. E. Schapire, The strength of weak learnability, *Machine Learning, 5(2)*pp. 197-227, 1990.

[V84] L. Valiant. A theory of the learnable. *Communications of the ACM*, 27(11):1134–1142, November 1984.

Minimizing Regret with Label Efficient Prediction*

Nicolò Cesa-Bianchi[1], Gábor Lugosi[2], and Gilles Stoltz[3]

[1] DSI, Università di Milano
via Comelico 39, 20135 Milano, Italy
cesa-bianchi@dsi.unimi.it

[2] Department of Economics, Universitat Pompeu Fabra
Ramon Trias Fargas 25-27, 08005 Barcelona, Spain
lugosi@upf.es

[3] Laboratoire de Mathématiques, Université Paris-Sud,
91405 Orsay Cedex, France
gilles.stoltz@math.u-psud.fr

Abstract. We investigate label efficient prediction, a variant of the problem of prediction with expert advice, proposed by Helmbold and Panizza, in which the forecaster does not have access to the outcomes of the sequence to be predicted unless he asks for it, which he can do for a limited number of times. We determine matching upper and lower bounds for the best possible excess error when the number of allowed queries is a constant. We also prove that a query rate of order $(\ln n)(\ln \ln n)^2/n$ is sufficient for achieving Hannan consistency, a fundamental property in game-theoretic prediction models. Finally, we apply the label efficient framework to pattern classification and prove a label efficient mistake bound for a randomized variant of Littlestone's zero-threshold Winnow algorithm.

1 Introduction

Prediction with expert advice, a framework introduced about fifteen years ago in learning theory, may be viewed as a direct generalization of the theory of repeated games, a field pioneered by Hannan in the mid-fifties. At a certain level of abstraction, the common subject of these studies is the problem of forecasting each element y_t of an unknown "target" sequence given the knowledge of the previous elements $y_1, \ldots, y_{t-1}$. The forecaster's goal is to predict the target sequence almost as well as any forecaster using the same guess all the times. We call this the sequential prediction problem. To provide a suitable parametrization of the problem, we assume that the set from which the forecaster picks its guesses is finite of size $N > 1$, while the set to which the target sequence elements belong may be of arbitrary cardinality. A real-valued bounded loss function ℓ is then used to quantify the discrepancy between each outcome y_t and the forecaster's

* The authors gratefully acknowledge partial support by the PASCAL Network of Excellence under EC grant no. 506778.

J. Shawe-Taylor and Y. Singer (Eds.): COLT 2004, LNAI 3120, pp. 77–92, 2004.

LABEL EFFICIENT PREDICTION

Parameters: number N of actions, outcome space $\mathcal{Y}$, loss function ℓ, time horizon n, budget m of queries.

For each round $t = 1, \dots, n$

(1) the environment chooses the next outcome $y_t \in \mathcal{Y}$ without revealing it;
(2) the forecaster chooses an action $I_t \in \{1, \dots, N\}$;
(3) each action i incurs loss $\ell(i, y_t)$;
(4) if less than m queries have been issued so far the forecaster may issue a new query to obtain y_t; if no query is issued then y_t remains unknown.

Fig. 1. Label efficient prediction as a game between the forecaster and the environment.

guess for y_t. Hannan's seminal result [7] showed that randomized forecasters exist whose excess cumulative loss (or regret), with respect to the loss of any constant forecaster, grows sublinearly in the length n of the target sequence, and this holds for any individual target sequence. In particular, Hannan found the optimal growth rate, $\Theta(\sqrt{n})$, of the regret as a function of the sequence length n when no other assumption other than boundedness is made on the loss ℓ. Only relatively recently, Cesa-Bianchi, Freund, Haussler, Helmbold, Schapire, and Warmuth [4] have revealed that the correct dependence on N in the minimax regret rate is $\Theta(\sqrt{n \ln N})$.

Game theorists and learning theorists, who independently studied the sequential prediction model, addressed the fundamental question of whether a sub-linear regret rate is achievable in case the past outcomes $y_1, \dots, y_{t-1}$ are not entirely accessible when computing the guess for y_t. In this work we investigate a variant of sequential prediction known as *label efficient prediction*. In this model, originally proposed by Helmbold and Panizza [8], after choosing its guess at time t the forecaster decides whether to query the outcome y_t. However, the forecaster is limited in the number of queries he can issue within a given time horizon. We prove that a query rate of order $(\ln n)(\ln \ln n)^2/n$ is sufficient for achieving Hannan consistency (i.e., regret growing sub-linearly with probability one). Moreover, we show that any forecaster issuing at most m queries must suffer a regret of at least order $n\sqrt{(\ln N)/m}$ on some outcome sequence of length n, and we show a randomized forecaster achieving this regret to within constant factors. We conclude the paper by proving a label efficient mistake bound for a randomized variant of Littlestone's zero-threshold Winnow, an algorithm based on exponential weights for binary pattern classification.

2 Sequential Prediction and the Label Efficient Model

The sequential prediction problem is parametrized by a number $N > 1$ of player actions, by a set $\mathcal{Y}$ of outcomes, and by a loss function ℓ. The loss function has domain $\{1, \ldots, N\} \times \mathcal{Y}$ and takes values in a bounded real interval, say $[0, 1]$. Given an unknown mechanism adaptively generating a sequence $y_1, y_2, \ldots$ of elements from $\mathcal{Y}$, a prediction strategy, or forecaster, chooses an action $I_t \in \{1, \ldots, N\}$ incurring a loss $\ell(I_t, y_t)$. A crucial assumption in this model is that the forecaster can choose I_t only based on information related to the past outcomes $y_1, \ldots, y_{t-1}$. That is, the forecaster's decision must not depend on any of the future outcomes. In the label efficient model, after choosing I_t the forecaster decides whether to issue a query to access y_t. If no query is issued, then y_t remains unknown. In other words, I_t does not depend on all the past outcomes $y_1, \ldots, y_{t-1}$, but only on the queried ones. The label efficient model is best described as a repeated game between the forecaster, choosing actions, and the environment, choosing outcomes (see Figure 1).

3 Regret and Hannan Consistency

The cumulative loss of the forecaster on a sequence $y_1, y_2, \ldots$ of outcomes is denoted by

$$\widehat{L}_n = \sum_{t=1}^{n} \ell(I_t, y_t) \qquad \text{for } n \geq 1.$$

As our forecasting strategies are randomized, each I_t is viewed as a random variable whose distribution over $\{1, \ldots, N\}$ must be fully determined at time t. Without further specifications, all probabilities and expectations will be understood with respect to the σ-algebra of events generated by the sequence $I_1, I_2, \ldots$ of the forecaster's random choices. We compare the forecaster's loss $\widehat{L}_n$ with the cumulative losses of the N constant forecasters, $L_{i,n} = \sum_{t=1}^{n} \ell(i, y_t)$, $i = 1, \ldots, N$.

In particular, we devise label efficient forecasting strategies whose expected regret $\mathbb{E}\,\widehat{L}_n - \min_{i=1,\ldots,N} L_{i,n}$ grows sublinearly in n for any individual sequence $y_1, y_2, \ldots$ of outcomes. Via a more refined analysis, we also prove the stronger result

$$\widehat{L}_n - \min_{i=1,\ldots,N} L_{i,n} = o(n) \qquad \text{a.s.}\ ,$$

for any sequence $y_1, y_2, \ldots$ of outcomes, almost surely with respect to the auxiliary randomization the forecaster has access to. This property, known as *Hannan consistency* in game theory, rules out the possibility that the regret is much larger than its expected value with a significant probability.

Parameters: Real numbers $\eta > 0$ and $0 \le \varepsilon \le 1$.
Initialization: $\boldsymbol{w}_1 = (1, \dots, 1)$.
For each round $t = 1, 2, \dots$

(1) draw an action from $\{1, \dots, N\}$ according to the distribution

$$p_{i,t} = \frac{w_{i,t}}{\sum_{j=1}^{N} w_{j,t}} \qquad i = 1, \dots, N$$

(2) draw a Bernoulli random variable Z_t such that $\mathbb{P}[Z_i = 1] = \varepsilon$;
(3) if $Z_t = 1$ then obtain y_t and compute

$$w_{i,t+1} = w_{i,t}\, e^{-\eta\, \ell(i,y_t)/\varepsilon} \qquad \text{for each } i = 1, \dots, N$$

else, let $\boldsymbol{w}_{t+1} = \boldsymbol{w}_t$.

Fig. 2. The label efficient exponentially weighted average forecaster.

4 A Label Efficient Forecaster

We start by introducing a simple forecaster whose expected regret is bounded by $n\sqrt{2(\ln N)/m}$, where m is the bound on the number of queries. Thus, if $m = n$ we recover the order of the optimal experts bound. It is easy to see that in order to achieve a nontrivial performance, a forecaster must use randomization in determining whether a label should be revealed or not. It turns out that a simple biased coin does the job. The strategy we propose, sketched in Figure 2, uses an i.i.d. sequence $Z_1, Z_2, \dots, Z_n$ of Bernoulli random variables such that $\mathbb{P}[Z_i = 1] = 1 - \mathbb{P}[Z_i = 0] = \varepsilon$ and asks the label y_t to be revealed whenever $Z_t = 1$. Here $\varepsilon > 0$ is a parameter of the strategy. (Typically, we take $\varepsilon \approx m/n$ so that the number of solicited labels during n rounds is about m. Note that this way the forecaster may ask the value of more than m labels but we ignore this detail as it can be dealt with by a simple adjustment.) Our label efficient forecaster uses the *estimated losses*

$$\widetilde{\ell}(i, y_t) \stackrel{\text{def}}{=} \begin{cases} \ell(i, y_t)/\varepsilon & \text{if } Z_t = 1, \\ 0 & \text{otherwise.} \end{cases}$$

Note that $\mathbb{E}[\widetilde{\ell}(i, y_t) \mid Z_1^{t-1}, I_1^{t-1}] = \ell(i, y_t)$, where $Z_1^t = (Z_1, \dots, Z_{t-1})$ and $I_1^t = (I_1, \dots, I_{t-1})$. (The conditioning on Z_1^{t-1} and I_1^{t-1} is merely needed to fix the value of y_t, which may depend on the forecaster's past actions.) Therefore, $\widetilde{\ell}(i, y_t)$ may be considered as an unbiased estimate of the true loss $\ell(i, y_t)$. The label efficient forecaster then uses the estimated losses to form an exponentially weighted average forecaster. The expected performance of this strategy may be bounded as follows.

Theorem 1. *Consider the label efficient forecaster of Figure 2 run with* $\varepsilon = m/n$ *and* $\eta = (\sqrt{2m \ln N})/n$. *Then, the expected number of revealed labels equals* m *and*

$$\mathbb{E}\,\widehat{L}_n - \min_{i=1,\dots,N} L_{i,n} \le n\sqrt{\frac{2\ln N}{m}} .$$

In the sequel we write $\boldsymbol{p}_t$ for the N-vector of components $p_{i,t}$. We also use the notation

$$\ell(\boldsymbol{p}_t, y_t) = \sum_{i=1}^{N} p_{i,t}\,\ell(i, y_t) \quad \text{and} \quad \widetilde{\ell}(\boldsymbol{p}_t, y_t) = \sum_{i=1}^{N} p_{i,t}\,\widetilde{\ell}(i, y_t) .$$

Finally, we denote for $i = 1, \dots, N$,

$$\widetilde{L}_{i,n} = \sum_{t=1}^{n} \widetilde{\ell}(i, y_t) .$$

Proof. It is enough to adapt the proof of [1, Theorem 3.1], in the following way. First, we note that we have an upper bound over the regret in terms of squares of the losses, see also [12, Theorem 1],

$$\sum_{t=1}^{n} \widetilde{\ell}(\boldsymbol{p}_t, y_t) - \min_{i=1,\dots,N} \widetilde{L}_{i,n} \le \frac{\ln N}{\eta} + \frac{\eta}{2} \sum_{t=1}^{n} \sum_{j=1}^{N} p_{j,t} \widetilde{\ell}(j, y_t)^2 .$$

Since $\widetilde{\ell}(j, y_t) \in [0, 1/\varepsilon]$ for all j and y_t, we finally get

$$\sum_{t=1}^{n} \widetilde{\ell}(\boldsymbol{p}_t, y_t) \left(1 - \frac{\eta}{2\varepsilon}\right) \le \widetilde{L}_{i,n} + \frac{\ln N}{\eta} \qquad i = 1, \dots, N . \tag{1}$$

Taking expectations on both sides and substituting the values of η and ϵ yields the desired result.

Theorem 1 guarantees that the expected per-round regret converges to zero whenever $m \to \infty$ as $n \to \infty$. The next result shows that in fact this regret is, with overwhelming probability, bounded by a quantity proportional to $n\sqrt{(\ln N)/m}$.

Theorem 2. *Let* $\delta \in (0, 1)$ *and consider the label efficient forecaster of Figure 2 run with parameters*

$$\varepsilon = \max\left\{0, \frac{m - \sqrt{2m \ln(4/\delta)}}{n}\right\} \qquad \text{and} \qquad \eta = \sqrt{\frac{2\varepsilon \ln N}{n}} .$$

Then, with probability at least $1 - \delta$ *the number of revealed labels is at most* m *and*

$$\widehat{L}_n - \min_{i=1,\dots,N} L_{i,n} \le 2n\sqrt{\frac{\ln N}{m}} + 7n\sqrt{\frac{\ln(4N/\delta)}{m}} .$$

In the full paper, we will prove a more refined bound in which the factors $n\sqrt{(\ln N)/m}$ are replaced by $(1+o(1))\sqrt{n\,L^*(\ln N)/m}$ in all cases where L^*, the cumulative loss of the best action, is $\Omega((n/m)\ln N)$. In the cases when L^* is small, then the quantity replacing the above terms is of the order of $(n/m)\ln N$. In particular, we recover the behavior already observed by Helmbold and Panizza [8] in the case $L^* = 0$ (the best expert makes no mistakes).

Even though the label efficient forecaster investigated above assumes the preliminary knowledge of the time horizon n (just note that both η and ε depend on the value of the parameters n and m), using standard adaptive techniques—such as those described in [2]—, a label efficient forecaster may be constructed without knowing n in advance. By letting the query budget m depend on n, one can then achieve Hannan consistency, as stated in the next result.

Corollary 1. *There exists a randomized label efficient forecaster that achieves Hannan consistency while issuing, for all $n > 1$, at most $O((\ln\ln n)^2 \ln n)$ queries in the first n prediction steps.*

Proof. An algorithm that achieves Hannan consistency divides time into consecutive blocks of exponentially increasing length $1, 2, 4, 8, 16, \ldots$. In the r-th block (of length 2^{r-1}) it uses the forecaster of Theorem 2 with parameters $n = 2^{r-1}$, $m = (\ln r)(\ln\ln r)$ and $\delta = 1/r^3$. Then, using the bound of Theorem 2 it is easy to see that, with probability one, for all n, the algorithm does not ask for more than $O((\ln\ln n)^2 \ln n)$ labels and the cumulative regret is $o(n)$. Details are omitted. Just note that it is sufficient to prove the statement for $n = 2^{r-1}$ for $r \geq 1$.

Before proving Theorem 2, note that if $\delta \leq 4Ne^{-m/8}$, then the right-hand side of the inequality is greater than n and therefore the statement is trivial. Thus, we may assume throughout the proof that $\delta > 4Ne^{-m/8}$. This also ensures that $\varepsilon > 0$. We need a number of preliminary lemmas. The first is obtained by a simple application of Bernstein's inequality.

Lemma 1. *The probability that the strategy asks for more than m labels is at most $\delta/4$.*

Lemma 2. *With probability at least $1 - \delta/4$,*

$$\sum_{t=1}^{n} \ell(\boldsymbol{p}_t, y_t) \leq \sum_{t=1}^{n} \widetilde{\ell}(\boldsymbol{p}_t, y_t) + 2n\sqrt{\frac{2}{m}\ln\frac{4}{\delta}} \; .$$

Furthermore, with probability at least $1 - \delta/4$, for all $i = 1, \ldots, N$,

$$\widetilde{L}_{i,n} \leq L_{i,n} + 2\sqrt{2}n\sqrt{\frac{\ln(4N/\delta)}{m}} \; .$$

Proof. The proofs of both inequalities rely on Chernoff's bounding. We therefore only prove the first one. Let $s \leq 1$ be a positive number. Define $u = 2\sqrt{\frac{n}{\varepsilon}\ln\frac{4}{\delta}}$

and observe that since $n/m \geq 1/(2\varepsilon)$ (which is implied by the above assumption on δ),

$$\begin{aligned}
&\mathbb{P}\left[\sum_{t=1}^{n} \ell(\boldsymbol{p}_t, y_t) > \sum_{t=1}^{n} \widetilde{\ell}(\boldsymbol{p}_t, y_t) + u\right] \\
&\leq \mathbb{E}\left[\exp\left(s \sum_{t=1}^{n} (\ell(\boldsymbol{p}_t, y_t) - \widetilde{\ell}(\boldsymbol{p}_t, y_t))\right)\right] e^{-su} \qquad \text{(by Markov's inequality)} \\
&= \mathbb{E}\left[\exp\left(s \sum_{t=1}^{n-1} (\ell(\boldsymbol{p}_t, y_t) - \widetilde{\ell}(\boldsymbol{p}_t, y_t))\right)\right. \\
&\qquad \left. \times \mathbb{E}\left[\exp\left(s(\ell(\boldsymbol{p}_n, y_n) - \widetilde{\ell}(\boldsymbol{p}_n, y_n))\right) \mid Z_1^{n-1}, I_1^{n-1}\right]\right] e^{-su} .
\end{aligned}$$

To bound the right-hand side, note that $\ell(\boldsymbol{p}_n, y_n) - \widetilde{\ell}(\boldsymbol{p}_n, y_n) \leq 1$ and therefore, since we assumed $s \leq 1$,

$$\begin{aligned}
&\mathbb{E}\left[\exp\left(s(\ell(\boldsymbol{p}_n, y_n) - \widetilde{\ell}(\boldsymbol{p}_n, y_n))\right) \mid Z_1^{n-1}, I_1^{n-1}\right] \\
&\leq \mathbb{E}\left[1 + s(\ell(\boldsymbol{p}_n, y_n) - \widetilde{\ell}(\boldsymbol{p}_n, y_n)) + s^2(\ell(\boldsymbol{p}_n, y_n) - \widetilde{\ell}(\boldsymbol{p}_n, y_n))^2 \mid Z_1^{n-1}, I_1^{n-1}\right] \\
&\quad \text{(since } e^x \leq 1 + x + x^2 \text{ for all } x \leq 1) \\
&= 1 + \mathbb{E}\left[s^2(\ell(\boldsymbol{p}_n, y_n) - \widetilde{\ell}(\boldsymbol{p}_n, y_n))^2 \mid Z_1^{n-1}, I_1^{n-1}\right] \\
&\quad \text{(since } \mathbb{E}[(\ell(\boldsymbol{p}_n, y_n) - \widetilde{\ell}(\boldsymbol{p}_n, y_n)) \mid Z_1^{n-1}, I_1^{n-1}] = 0) \\
&\leq 1 + \frac{s^2}{\varepsilon}
\end{aligned}$$

where the last step holds because

$$\mathbb{E}\left[(\ell(\boldsymbol{p}_n, y_n) - \widetilde{\ell}(\boldsymbol{p}_n, y_n))^2 \mid Z_1^{n-1}, I_1^{n-1}\right] \leq \mathbb{E}\left[\widetilde{\ell}(\boldsymbol{p}_n, y_n)^2 \mid Z_1^{n-1}, I_1^{n-1}\right] \leq 1/\varepsilon .$$

Therefore, using $1 + s^2/\varepsilon \leq e^{s^2/\varepsilon}$, we have

$$\begin{aligned}
&\mathbb{P}\left[\sum_{t=1}^{n} \ell(\boldsymbol{p}_t, y_t) > \sum_{t=1}^{n} \widetilde{\ell}(\boldsymbol{p}_t, y_t) + u\right] \\
&\leq \mathbb{E}\left[\exp\left(s \sum_{t=1}^{n-1} (\ell(\boldsymbol{p}_t, y_t) - \widetilde{\ell}(\boldsymbol{p}_t, y_t))\right)\right] e^{s^2/\varepsilon} e^{-su} \\
&\leq e^{ns^2/\varepsilon} e^{-su}
\end{aligned}$$

by repeating the previous argument $n-1$ times. The value of s minimizing the obtained upper bound is $s = u\varepsilon/2n$ which satisfies the condition $s \leq 1$ because $n \geq m \geq u\varepsilon/2$ due to our assumption on δ. Resubstituting this choice for s we get

$$\mathbb{P}\left[\sum_{t=1}^{n} \ell(\boldsymbol{p}_t, y_t) > \sum_{t=1}^{n} \widetilde{\ell}(\boldsymbol{p}_t, y_t) + u\right] \le e^{-u^2\varepsilon/(4n)} = \frac{\delta}{4} ,$$

and the proof is completed.

Proof (of Theorem 2). We start again from (1). It remains to show that $\widetilde{L}_{i,n}$ is close, with large probability to its expected value $L_{i,n}$ and that $\sum_{t=1}^{n} \widetilde{\ell}(\boldsymbol{p}_t, y_t)$ is close to $\sum_{t=1}^{n} \ell(\boldsymbol{p}_t, y_t) = \widehat{L}_n$.

A straightforward combination of Lemmas 1 and 2 with (1) shows that with probability at least $1 - 3\delta/4$, the strategy asks for at most m labels and has an expected cumulative loss

$$\sum_{t=1}^{n} \ell(\boldsymbol{p}_t, y_t)\left(1 - \frac{\eta}{2\varepsilon}\right) \le \min_{i=1,\dots,N} L_{i,n} + 4\sqrt{2}\, n\sqrt{\frac{1}{m}\ln\frac{4N}{\delta}} + \frac{\ln N}{\eta} ,$$

which, since $\sum_{t=1}^{n} \ell(\boldsymbol{p}_t, y_t) \le n$, implies

$$\begin{aligned}\sum_{t=1}^{n} \ell(\boldsymbol{p}_t, y_t) - \min_{i=1,\dots,n} L_{i,n} &\le \frac{n\eta}{2\varepsilon} + 4\sqrt{2}\, n\sqrt{\frac{1}{m}\ln\frac{4N}{\delta}} + \frac{\ln N}{\eta} \\ &= 2n\sqrt{\frac{\ln N}{m}} + 4\sqrt{2} n\sqrt{\frac{1}{m}\ln\frac{4N}{\delta}}\end{aligned}$$

by our choice of η and using $1/(2\varepsilon) \le n/m$ derived, once more, from our assumption $\delta > 4N\, e^{-m/8}$. The proof is finished by noting that the Hoeffding-Azuma inequality implies that, with probability at least $1 - \delta/4$,

$$\widehat{L}_n = \sum_{t=1}^{n} \ell(I_t, y_t) \le \sum_{t=1}^{n} \ell(\boldsymbol{p}_t, y_t) + \sqrt{\frac{n}{2}\ln\frac{4}{\delta}} \le \sum_{t=1}^{n} \ell(\boldsymbol{p}_t, y_t) + n\sqrt{\frac{1}{2m}\ln\frac{4N}{\delta}}$$

since $m \le n$.

5 A Lower Bound for Label Efficient Prediction

Here we show that the performance bounds proved in the previous section for the label efficient exponentially weighted average forecaster are essentially unimprovable in the strong sense that no other label efficient forecasting strategy can have a significantly better performance for all problems. Denote the set of natural numbers by $\mathbb{N} = \{1, 2, \dots\}$.

Theorem 3. *There exist an outcome space $\mathcal{Y}$, a loss function $\ell : \mathbb{N} \times \mathcal{Y} \to [0, 1]$, and a universal constant $c > 0$ such that, for all $N \ge 2$ and for all $n \ge m \ge 20\frac{e}{1+e}\ln(N-1)$, the cumulative (expected) loss of any (randomized) forecaster* *that uses actions in* $\{1, \ldots, N\}$ *and asks for at most* m *labels while predicting a sequence of* n *outcomes satisfies the inequality*

$$\sup_{y_1,\ldots,y_n \in \mathcal{Y}} \left(\mathbb{E}\left[\sum_{t=1}^{n} \ell(I_t, y_t)\right] - \min_{i=1,\ldots,N} \sum_{t=1}^{n} \ell(i, y_t) \right) \geq cn\sqrt{\frac{\ln(N-1)}{m}} .$$

In particular, we prove the theorem for $c = \dfrac{\sqrt{e}}{(1+e)\sqrt{5(1+e)}}$.

Proof. First, we define $\mathcal{Y} = [0,1]$ and ℓ. Given $y \in [0,1]$, we denote by $(y_1, y_2, \ldots)$ its dyadic expansion, that is, the unique sequence not ending with infinitely many zeros such that

$$y = \sum_{k \geq 1} y_k \, 2^{-k} .$$

Now, the loss function is defined as $\ell(k, y) = y_k$ for all $y \in \mathcal{Y}$ and $k \in \mathbb{N}$.

We construct a random outcome sequence and show that the expected value of the regret (with respect both to the random choice of the outcome sequence and to the forecaster's possibly random choices) for any possibly randomized forecaster is bounded from below by the claimed quantity.

More precisely, we denote by $U_1, \ldots, U_n$ the auxiliary randomization which the forecaster has access to. Without loss of generality, it can be taken as an i.i.d. sequence of uniformly distributed random variables over $[0,1]$. Our underlying probability space is equipped with the σ-algebra of events generated by the random outcome sequence $Y_1, \ldots, Y_n$ and by the randomization $U_1, \ldots, U_n$. The random outcome sequence is independent of the auxiliary randomization: we define N different probability distributions, $\mathbb{P}_i \otimes \mathbb{P}_A$, $i = 1, \ldots, N$, formed by the product of the auxiliary randomization (whose associated probability distribution is denoted by $\mathbb{P}_A$) and one of the N different probability distributions $\mathbb{P}_1, \ldots, \mathbb{P}_N$ over the outcome sequence defined as follows.

For $i = 1, \ldots, N$, $\mathbb{Q}_i$ is defined as the distribution (over $[0,1]$) of

$$Z^* 2^{-i} + \sum_{k=1,\ldots,N,\ k \neq i} Z_k 2^{-k} + 2^{-(N+1)} U ,$$

where U, Z^*, $Z_1, \ldots, Z_N$ are independent random variables such that U has uniform distribution, and Z^* and the Z_k have Bernoulli distribution with parameter $1/2 - \epsilon$ for Z^* and $1/2$ for the Z_k. Now, the randomization is such that under $\mathbb{P}_i$, the outcome sequence $Y_1, \ldots, Y_n$ is i.i.d. with common distribution $\mathbb{Q}_i$.

Then, under each $\mathbb{P}_i$ (for $i = 1, \ldots, N$), the losses $\ell(k, Y_t)$, $k = 1, \ldots, N$, $t = 1, \ldots, n$, are i.i.d. Bernoulli random variables. In addition, $\ell(i, Y_t) = 1$ with probability $1/2 - \varepsilon$ and $\ell(k, Y_t) = 1$ with probability $1/2$ for each $k \neq i$, where ε is a positive number specified below.

We have

$$\max_{y_1,\dots,y_n}\left(\mathbb{E}_A\widehat{L}_n - \min_{i=1,\dots,N} L_{i,n}\right) = \max_{y_1,\dots,y_n}\max_{i=1,\dots,N}\left(\mathbb{E}_A\widehat{L}_n - L_{i,n}\right)$$
$$\geq \max_{i=1,\dots,N}\mathbb{E}_i\left[\mathbb{E}_A\widehat{L}_n - L_{i,n}\right] ,$$

where $\mathbb{E}_i$ (resp. $\mathbb{E}_A$) denotes expectation with respect to $\mathbb{P}_i$ (resp. $\mathbb{P}_A$).

Now, we use the following decomposition lemma, which states that a randomized algorithm performs, on the average, just as a convex combination of deterministic algorithms. The simple but cumbersome proof is omitted from this extended abstract.

Lemma 3. *For any given randomized forecaster, there exists an integer D, a point $\alpha = (\alpha_1,\dots,\alpha_D) \in \mathbb{R}^D$ in the probability simplex, and D deterministic algorithms (indexed by a superscript $d = 1,\dots,D$) such that, for every t and every possible outcome sequence $y_1^{t-1} = (y_1,\dots,y_{t-1})$,*

$$\mathbb{P}_A\left[I_t = i \,|\, y_1^{t-1}\right] = \sum_{d=1}^{D}\alpha_d\,\mathbb{I}_{[I_t^d = i\,|\,y_1^{t-1}]} ,$$

where $\mathbb{I}_{[I_t^d = i\,|\,y_1^{t-1}]}$ is the indicator function that the d-th deterministic algorithm chooses action i when the sequence of past outcomes is formed by y_1^{t-1}.

Using this lemma, we have that there exist D, α and D deterministic subalgorithms such that

$$\max_{i=1,\dots,N}\mathbb{E}_i\Big[\mathbb{E}_A\widehat{L}_n - L_{i,n}\Big] = \max_{i=1,\dots,N}\mathbb{E}_i\left[\sum_{t=1}^{n}\sum_{d=1}^{D}\alpha_d\sum_{k=1}^{N}\mathbb{I}_{[I_t^d=k\,|\,Y_1^{t-1}]}\ell(k,Y_t) - L_{i,n}\right]$$
$$= \max_{i=1,\dots,N}\sum_{d=1}^{D}\alpha_d\,\mathbb{E}_i\left[\sum_{t=1}^{n}\sum_{k=1}^{N}\mathbb{I}_{[I_t^d=k\,|\,Y_1^{t-1}]}\ell(k,Y_t) - L_{i,n}\right]$$

Now, under $\mathbb{P}_i$ the regret grows by ε whenever an action different from i is chosen and remains the same otherwise. Hence,

$$\max_{i=1,\dots,N}\mathbb{E}_i\Big[\mathbb{E}_A\widehat{L}_n - L_{i,n}\Big] = \max_{i=1,\dots,N}\sum_{d=1}^{D}\alpha_d\,\mathbb{E}_i\left[\sum_{t=1}^{n}\sum_{k=1}^{N}\mathbb{I}_{[I_t^d=k\,|\,Y_1^{t-1}]}\ell(k,Y_t) - L_{i,n}\right]$$
$$= \varepsilon\max_{i=1,\dots,N}\sum_{d=1}^{D}\alpha_d\sum_{t=1}^{n}\mathbb{P}_i\left[I_t^d \neq i\right]$$
$$= \varepsilon\, n\left(1 - \min_{i=1,\dots,N}\sum_{d=1}^{D}\sum_{t=1}^{n}\frac{\alpha_d}{n}\mathbb{P}_i[I_t^d = i]\right) .$$

For the d-th deterministic subalgorithm, let $1 \leq T_1^d < \ldots < T_m^d \leq n$ be the times when the m queries were issued. Then $T_1^d,\dots,T_m^d$ are finite stopping times with respect to the i.i.d. process $Y_1, \ldots, Y_n$. Hence, by a well-known fact in probability theory (see, e.g., [5, Lemma 2, page 138]), the revealed outcomes $Y_{T_1^d}, \ldots, Y_{T_m^d}$ are independent and indentically distributed as Y_1.

Let R_t^d be the number of revealed outcomes at time t and note that R_t^d is measurable with respect to the random outcome sequence. Now, as the subalgorithm we consider is deterministic, R_t^d is fully determined by $Y_{T_1^d}, \ldots, Y_{T_m^d}$. Hence, I_t^d may be seen as a function of $Y_{T_1^d}, \ldots, Y_{T_m^d}$ rather than a function of $Y_{T_1^d}, \ldots, Y_{T_{R_t^d}^d}$ only. This essentially means that the knowledge of the extra values cannot hurt in the sense that it cannot lead the forecaster to choose different actions. As the joint distribution of $Y_{T_1^d}, \ldots, Y_{T_m^d}$ under $\mathbb{P}_i$ is $\mathbb{Q}_i^m$, we have proven indeed that

$$\mathbb{P}_i[I_t^d = i] = \mathbb{Q}_i^m[I_t^d = i] .$$

Consequently, our lower bound rewrites as

$$\max_{i=1,\ldots,N} \mathbb{E}_i \left[\mathbb{E}_A \widehat{L}_n - L_{i,n} \right] = \varepsilon\, n \left(1 - \min_{i=1,\ldots,N} \sum_{d=1}^{D} \sum_{t=1}^{n} \frac{\alpha_d}{n} \mathbb{Q}_i^m [I_t^d = i] \right) .$$

By the generalized Fano's lemma (see Lemma 5 in the Appendix), it is guaranteed that

$$\min_{i=1,\ldots,N} \sum_{d=1}^{D} \sum_{t=1}^{n} \frac{\alpha_d}{n} \mathbb{Q}_i^m [I_t^d = i] \le \max \left\{ \frac{e}{1+e}, \frac{\bar{K}}{\ln(N-1)} \right\} ,$$

where

$$\bar{K} = \sum_{t=1}^{n} \sum_{d=1}^{D} \sum_{i=2}^{N} \frac{\alpha_d}{n(N-1)} \mathrm{KL}(\mathbb{Q}_i^m, \mathbb{Q}_1^m) = \frac{1}{N-1} \sum_{i=2}^{N} \mathrm{KL}(\mathbb{Q}_i^m, \mathbb{Q}_1^m) ,$$

and KL is the Kullback-Leibler divergence (or relative entropy) between two probability distributions.

Moreover, $\mathbb{B}_p$ denoting the Bernoulli distribution with parameter p,

$$\begin{aligned} \mathrm{KL}(\mathbb{Q}_i^m, \mathbb{Q}_1^m) &= m\, \mathrm{KL}(\mathbb{Q}_i, \mathbb{Q}_1) \le m \left(\mathrm{KL}\left(\mathbb{B}_{1/2-\varepsilon}, \mathbb{B}_{1/2}\right) + \mathrm{KL}\left(\mathbb{B}_{1/2}, \mathbb{B}_{1/2-\varepsilon}\right) \right) \\ &= m\, \varepsilon \ln \left(1 + \frac{4\varepsilon}{1-2\varepsilon} \right) \le 5 m\, \varepsilon^2 \end{aligned}$$

for $0 \le \varepsilon \le 1/10$, where the first inequality holds by noting that the definition of the $\mathbb{Q}_i$ implies that the considered Kullback-Leibler divergence is upper bounded by the Kullback-Leibler divergence between $(Z_1, \ldots, Z^*, \ldots, Z_n, U)$, where Z^* is in the i-th position, and $(Z^*, Z_2 \ldots, Z_n, U)$. Therefore,

$$\max_{y_1,\ldots,y_n} \left(\mathbb{E}_A \widehat{L}_n - \min_{i=1,\ldots,N} L_{i,n} \right) \ge \varepsilon\, n \left(1 - \max \left\{ \frac{e}{1+e}, \frac{5 m\, \varepsilon^2}{\ln(N-1)} \right\} \right) .$$

Algorithm Label efficient zero-threshold Winnow
Parameters $\eta > 0$
Initialization $w_{i,1} = 1$ for $i = 1, \dots, N$
For $t = 1, 2 \dots$

1. get $\boldsymbol{x}_t \in \mathbb{R}^d$, define $\boldsymbol{p}_t$ by $p_{i,t} = w_{i,t}/W_t$, where $W_t = \sum_{i=1}^N w_{i,t}$, and let $q_t = \boldsymbol{p}_t \cdot \boldsymbol{x}_t$
2. predict with $\hat{y}_t = \mathrm{sgn}(q_t)$
3. draw a Bernoulli variable Z_t of parameter $(2\,|q_t|/\gamma + 1)^{-1}$.
4. if $Z_t = 1$, then
   a) get $y_t \in \{-1, 1\}$.
   b) if $\hat{y}_t \neq y_t$, then let $w_{i,t+1} = w_{i,t}\, e^{\eta\, y_t x_{i,t}}$ for all $i = 1, \dots, N$
5. else, $w_{i,t+1} = w_{i,t}$ for all $i = 1, \dots, N$.

Fig. 3. The randomized label-efficient zero-threshold Winnow.

The choice

$$\varepsilon = \sqrt{\frac{e \ln(N-1)}{5(1+e)m}}$$

yields the claimed bound.

6 A Label Efficient Algorithm for Pattern Classification

So far, we have shown that exponentially weighted average forecasters can be made label efficient without losing important properties, such as Hannan consistency. In this section we move away from the abstract sequential decision problem defined in Section 2 and show that the idea of label efficient prediction finds interesting applications in more concrete pattern classification problems. More specifically, consider the problem of predicting the binary labels of an arbitrarily chosen sequence $\boldsymbol{x}_1, \boldsymbol{x}_2, \ldots \in \mathbb{R}^d$ of instances where, for each $t = 1, 2, \ldots$, the label $y_t \in \{-1, 1\}$ of $\boldsymbol{x}_t$ satisfies $y_t\, \boldsymbol{u} \cdot \boldsymbol{x}_t > 0$. Here $\boldsymbol{u} \in \mathbb{R}^d$ is a fixed but unknown linear separator for the labeled sequence. In this framework, we show that the zero-threshold Winnow algorithm of Littlestone [10], a natural extension to pattern classification of the exponentially weighted average forecaster, can be made label efficient. In particular, for the label efficient variant of this algorithm (described in Figure 3) we prove an expected mistake bound exactly equal to the mistake bound of the original zero-threshold Winnow. In addition, unlike the algorithms shown in previous sections, in our variant the probability of querying a label is a function of the previously observed instances and previously queried labels.

Theorem 4. *Pick any sequence* $(\boldsymbol{x}_1, y_1), \ldots, (\boldsymbol{x}_n, y_n) \in \mathbb{R}^d \times \{-1, 1\}$ *such that, for all* $t = 1, \ldots, n$, $y_t \boldsymbol{u} \cdot \boldsymbol{x}_t \geq \gamma$ *for some* $\gamma > 0$ *and some vector* $\boldsymbol{u}$ *from* *the probability simplex in* $\mathbb{R}^d$. *Let* X_∞ *be any number such that* $\max_t \|\boldsymbol{x}_t\|_\infty \le X_\infty$. *Then the randomized label efficient zero-threshold Winnow algorithm of Figure 3, run with parameter* $\eta = \gamma/X_\infty^2$, *makes an expected number of mistakes bounded by* $(2\,X_\infty^2 \ln N)/\gamma^2$ *while querying an expected number of labels equal to* $\sum_{t=1}^n (2\,|q_t|/\gamma + 1)^{-1}$.

The dependence of η on γ is inherited from the original Winnow algorithm and is not caused by the label efficient framework. Note also that, while the expected mistake bound is the same as the mistake bound for the original zero-threshold Winnow, the probability of querying a label at step t attains 1 as the "margin" $|q_t|$ shrinks to 0, and attains $(2\,X_\infty/\gamma+1)^{-1}$ as $|q_t|$ grows to its maximum value X_∞. Obtaining an explicit bound on the expected number of queried labels appears hard as q_t depends in a complicated way on the structure of the labeled sequence. Hence, the result demonstrates that the label efficient framework in this case does provide an advantage (in expectation), even though the theoretical assessment of this advantage appears to be problematic.

Proof. Let M_t be the indicator function for a mistake in step t. Pick a step t such that M_t and Z_t are both 1. Then,

$$\ln \frac{W_{t+1}}{W_t} = \ln\left(\sum_{i=1}^N p_{i,t} e^{\eta\, y_t x_{i,t}}\right) \le \eta\, y_t \boldsymbol{p}_t \cdot \boldsymbol{x}_t + \frac{\eta^2}{2} X_\infty^2 = -\eta\,|q_t| + \frac{\eta^2}{2} X_\infty^2$$

where the inequality is an application of the Hoeffding inequality [9] while the last equality holds because $M_t = 1$ implies $y_t q_t \le 0$. On the other hand, if M_t or Z_t is 0 at step t, then $W_{t+1} = W_t$ and thus $\ln(W_{t+1}/W_t) = 0$. Summing for $t = 1, \ldots, n$ we get

$$\ln \frac{W_{n+1}}{W_1} \le \eta \sum_{t=1}^n \left(\frac{\eta}{2} X_\infty^2 - |q_t|\right) M_t\, Z_t \tag{2}$$

Now consider any vector $\boldsymbol{u}$ of convex coefficients such that $y_t \boldsymbol{u} \cdot \boldsymbol{x}_t \ge \gamma$ for all $t = 1, \ldots, n$. Let

$$\boldsymbol{R} = \sum_{t=1}^n (y_t\, \boldsymbol{x}_t) M_t\, Z_t\ .$$

Using the log-sum inequality [6], and recalling that $y_t \boldsymbol{u} \cdot \boldsymbol{x}_t \ge \gamma$ for all t,

$$\begin{aligned}\ln \frac{W_{n+1}}{W_1} &= -\ln N + \ln \sum_{i=1}^N e^{\eta\, R_i} \ge -\ln N + \eta\, \boldsymbol{R} \cdot \boldsymbol{u} + H(\boldsymbol{u}) \\ &\ge\ -\ln N + \eta\gamma \sum_{t=1}^n M_t\, Z_t + H(\boldsymbol{u})\ . \end{aligned} \tag{3}$$

Dropping $H(\boldsymbol{u}) \ge 0$, the entropy of $\boldsymbol{u}$, from (2) and (3) we obtain

$$-\ln N + \eta\gamma \sum_{t=1}^n M_t\, Z_t \le \eta \sum_{t=1}^n \left(\frac{\eta}{2} X_\infty^2 - |q_t|\right) M_t\, Z_t\ .$$

Dividing by $\eta > 0$ and rearranging yields

$$\sum_{t=1}^{n} \left(\gamma - \frac{\eta}{2} X_\infty^2 + |q_t|\right) M_t \, Z_t \le \frac{\ln N}{\eta} \, .$$

Replacing η with γ / X_∞^2 gets us

$$\sum_{t=1}^{n} \left(\frac{\gamma}{2} + |q_t|\right) M_t \, Z_t \le \frac{X_\infty^2 \ln N}{\gamma} \, . \tag{4}$$

Now recall that $\mathbb{E}[Z_t \mid Z_1, \ldots , Z_{t-1}] = (2 \, |q_t| / \gamma + 1)^{-1}$, where the conditioning is needed as q_t is a function of $Z_1, \ldots , Z_{t-1}$. Taking expectation on both sides of (4) yields

$$\begin{aligned} \frac{X_\infty^2 \ln N}{\gamma} &\ge \mathbb{E}\left[\sum_{t=1}^{n} \left(\frac{\gamma}{2} + |q_t|\right) M_t \, Z_t\right] \\ &= \mathbb{E}\left[\sum_{t=1}^{n} \left(\frac{\gamma}{2} + |q_t|\right) M_t \, \mathbb{E}[Z_t \mid Z_1, \ldots , Z_{t-1}]\right] \\ &= \mathbb{E}\left[\sum_{t=1}^{n} \left(\frac{\gamma}{2} + |q_t|\right) \frac{M_t}{2 \, |q_t| / \gamma + 1}\right] = \frac{\gamma}{2} \mathbb{E}\left[\sum_{t=1}^{n} M_t\right] \, . \end{aligned}$$

Multiplying both sides by $2/\gamma$ gets us the desired result.

References

1. P. Auer, N. Cesa-Bianchi, Y. Freund, and R.E. Schapire. The nonstochastic multiarmed bandit problem. *SIAM Journal on Computing*, 32(1):48–77, 2002.
2. P. Auer, N. Cesa-Bianchi, and C. Gentile. Adaptive and self-confident on-line learning algorithms. *Journal of Computer and System Sciences*, 64(1), 2002.
3. L. Birgé. A new look at an old result: Fano's lemma. Technical report, Université Paris 6. 2001.
4. N. Cesa-Bianchi, Y. Freund, D. Haussler, D.P. Helmbold, R. Schapire, and M.K. Warmuth. How to use expert advice. *Journal of the ACM*, 44(3):427–485, 1997.
5. Y.S. Chow and H. Teicher. *Probability Theory*. Springer, 1988.
6. T.M. Cover and J.A. Thomas. *Elements of Information Theory*. John Wiley and Sons, 1991.
7. J. Hannan. Approximation to Bayes risk in repeated play. *Contributions to the theory of games*, 3:97–139, 1957.
8. D.P. Helmbold and S. Panizza. Some label efficient learning results. In *Proceedings of the 10th Annual Conference on Computational Learning Theory*, pages 218–230. ACM Press, 1997.
9. W. Hoeffding. Probability inequalities for sums of bounded random variables. *Journal of the American Statistical Association*, 58:13–30, 1963.
10. N. Littlestone. *Mistake Bounds and Logarithmic Linear-threshold Learning Algorithms*. PhD thesis, University of California at Santa Cruz, 1989.

11. P. Massart. *Concentration inequalities and model selection.* Saint-Flour summer school lecture notes, 2003. To appear.
12. A. Piccolboni and C. Schindelhauer Discrete prediction games with arbitrary feedback and loss. In *Proceedings of the 14th Annual Conference on Computational Learning Theory*, pages 208-223, 2001.

A Technical Lemmas

The crucial point in the proof of the lower bound theorem is an extension of Fano's lemma to a convex combination of probability masses, which may be proved thanks to a straightforward modification of the techniques developed by Birgé [3] (see also Massart [11]). Recall first a consequence of the variational formula for entropy.

Lemma 4. *For arbitrary probability distributions* $\mathbb{P}, \mathbb{Q}$ *and for each* $\lambda > 0$,

$$\lambda\, \mathbb{P}[A] - \psi_{\mathbb{Q}[A]}(\lambda) \le \mathrm{KL}(\mathbb{P}, \mathbb{Q})$$

where $\psi_p(\lambda) = \ln\left(p\,(e^\lambda - 1) + 1\right)$.

Lemma 5 (Generalized Fano). *Let* $\{A_{s,j} : s = 1, \ldots, S,\ j = 1, \ldots, N\}$ *be a family of subsets of a set* Ω *such that* $A_{s,1}, \ldots, A_{s,N}$ *form a partition of* Ω *for each fixed* s. *Let* $\alpha_1, \ldots, \alpha_s$ *be such that* $\alpha_s \ge 0$ *for* $s = 1, \ldots, S$ *and* $\alpha_1 + \ldots + \alpha_S = 1$. *Then, for all sets* $\mathbb{P}_{s,1}, \ldots, \mathbb{P}_{s,N}$, $s = 1, \ldots, S$, *of probability distributions on* Ω,

$$\min_{j=1,\ldots,N} \sum_{s=1}^{S} \alpha_s\, \mathbb{P}_{s,j}[A_{s,j}] \le \max\left\{ \frac{e}{1+e}, \frac{\bar{K}}{\ln(N-1)} \right\} ,$$

where

$$\bar{K} = \sum_{s=1}^{S} \sum_{j=2}^{N} \frac{\alpha_s}{N-1} \mathrm{KL}(\mathbb{P}_{s,j}, \mathbb{P}_{s,1}) .$$

Proof. Using Lemma 4, we have that

$$\sum_{s=1}^{S} \sum_{j=2}^{N} \frac{\alpha_s}{N-1} \lambda\, \mathbb{P}_{s,j}[A_{s,j}] - \sum_{s=1}^{S} \sum_{j=2}^{N} \frac{\alpha_s}{N-1} \psi_{\mathbb{P}_{s,1}[A_{s,j}]}(\lambda)$$
$$\le \sum_{s=1}^{S} \sum_{j=2}^{N} \frac{\alpha_s}{N-1} \mathrm{KL}(\mathbb{P}_{s,j}, \mathbb{P}_{s,1}) = \bar{K} .$$

Now, for each fixed $\lambda > 0$, the function that maps p to $-\psi_p(\lambda)$ is convex. Hence, letting

$$p_1 = \sum_{s=1}^{S} \sum_{j=2}^{N} \frac{\alpha_s}{N-1} \mathbb{P}_{s,1}[A_{s,j}] = \frac{1}{N-1} \left(1 - \sum_{s=1}^{S} \alpha_s \mathbb{P}_{s,1}[A_{s,1}] \right) ,$$

by Jensen's inequality we get

$$\sum_{s=1}^{S}\sum_{j=2}^{N}\frac{\alpha_s}{N-1}\lambda\,\mathbb{P}_{s,j}[A_{s,j}]-\psi_{p_1}(\lambda)$$
$$\leq \sum_{s=1}^{S}\sum_{j=2}^{N}\frac{\alpha_s}{N-1}\lambda\,\mathbb{P}_{s,j}[A_{s,j}]-\sum_{s=1}^{S}\sum_{j=2}^{N}\frac{\alpha_s}{N-1}\psi_{\mathbb{P}_{s,1}[A_{s,j}]}(\lambda)\,.$$

Recalling that the right-hand side of the above inequality above is less than $\bar{K}$, and introducing the quantities

$$a_j=\sum_{s=1}^{S}\alpha_s\mathbb{P}_{s,j}[A_{s,j}]\qquad\text{for } j=1,\ldots,N,$$

we conclude

$$\lambda\min_{j=1,\ldots,N}a_j-\psi_{\frac{1-a_1}{N-1}}(\lambda)\leq\lambda\frac{1}{N-1}\sum_{j=2}^{N}a_j-\psi_{\frac{1-a_1}{N-1}}(\lambda)\leq\bar{K}\,.$$

Denote by a the minimum of the a_j's and let $p^* = (1-a)/(N-1) \geq p_1$. We only have to deal with the case when $a \geq e/(1+e)$. As for all $\lambda > 0$, the function that maps p to $-\psi_p$ is decreasing, we have

$$\bar{K}\geq\sup_{\lambda>0}(\lambda\,a-\psi_{p^*}(\lambda))\geq a\,\ln\frac{a}{e\,p^*}\geq a\,\ln\frac{a\,(N-1)}{(1-a)\,e}\geq a\,\ln(N-1)\,,$$

whenever $p^* \leq a \leq 1$ for the second inequality to hold, and by using $a \geq e/(1+e)$ for the last one. As $p^* \leq 1/(N-1) \leq e/(1+e)$ whenever $N \geq 3$, the case $a < p^*$ may only happen when $N = 2$, but then the result is trivial.

Regret Bounds for Hierarchical Classification with Linear-Threshold Functions*

Nicolò Cesa-Bianchi[1], Alex Conconi[1], and Claudio Gentile[2]

[1] Dipartimento di Scienze dell'Informazione
Università degli Studi di Milano, Italy
{cesa-bianchi,conconi}@dsi.unimi.it
[2] Dipartimento di Informatica e Comunicazione
Università dell'Insubria, Varese, Italy
gentile@dsi.unimi.it

Abstract. We study the problem of classifying data in a given taxonomy when classifications associated with multiple and/or partial paths are allowed. We introduce an incremental algorithm using a linear-threshold classifier at each node of the taxonomy. These classifiers are trained and evaluated in a hierarchical top-down fashion. We then define a hierachical and parametric data model and prove a bound on the probability that our algorithm guesses the wrong multilabel for a random instance compared to the same probability when the true model parameters are known. Our bound decreases exponentially with the number of training examples and depends in a detailed way on the interaction between the process parameters and the taxonomy structure. Preliminary experiments on real-world data provide support to our theoretical results.

1 Introduction

In this paper, we investigate the problem of classifying data based on the knowledge that the graph of dependencies between class elements is a tree forest. The trees in this forest are collectively interpreted as a taxonomy. That is, we assume that every data instance is labelled with a (possibly empty) set of class labels and, whenever an instance is labelled with a certain label i, then it is also labelled with all the labels on the path from the root of the tree where i occurs down to node i. We also allow multiple-path labellings (instances can be tagged with labels belonging to more than one path in the forest), and partial-path labellings (instances can be tagged with labels belonging to a path that does not end on a leaf).

The problem of hierarchical classification, especially of textual information, has been extensively investigated in past years (see, e.g., [5,6,7,11,12,13,17, 19] and references therein). Whereas the use of hierarchically trained linear-threshold classifiers is common to several of these previous approaches, to our

* The first and third author gratefully acknowledge partial support by the PASCAL Network of Excellence under EC grant no. 506778.

J. Shawe-Taylor and Y. Singer (Eds.): COLT 2004, LNAI 3120, pp. 93–108, 2004.

knowledge our research is the first one to provide a rigorous performance analysis of hierarchical classification problem in the presence of multiple and partial path classifications.

Following a standard approach in statistical learning theory, we assume that data are generated by a parametric and hierarchical stochastic process associated with the given taxonomy. Building on the techniques from [3], we design and analyze an algorithm for estimating the parameters of the process. Our algorithm is based on a hierarchy of regularized least-squares estimators which are incrementally updated as more data flow into the system. We prove bounds on the instantaneous regret; that is, we bound the probability that, after observing any number t of examples, our algorithm guesses the wrong multilabel on the next randomly drawn data element, while the hierarchical classifier knowing the true parameters of the process predicts the correct multilabel. Our main concern in this analysis is stressing the interaction between the taxonomy structure and the process generating the examples. This is in contrast with the standard approach in the literature about regret bounds, where a major attention is paid to studying how the regret depends on time.

To support our theoretical findings, we also briefly describe some experiments concerning a more practical variant of the algorithm we actually analyze. Though these experiments are preliminary in nature, their outcomes are fairly encouraging.

The paper is organized as follows. In Section 2 we introduce our learning model, along with the notational conventions used throughout the paper. Our hierarchical algorithm is described in Section 3 and analyzed in Section 4. In Section 5 we briefly report on the experiments. Finally, in Section 6 we summarize and mention future lines of research.

2 Learning Model and Notation

We assume data elements are encoded as real vectors $\boldsymbol{x} \in \mathbb{R}^d$ which we call *instances*. A *multilabel* for an instance $\boldsymbol{x}$ is any subset of the set $\{1, \ldots, c\}$ of all labels, including the empty set. We represent the multilabel of $\boldsymbol{x}$ with a vector $\boldsymbol{v} = (v_1, \ldots, v_c) \in \{-1, 1\}^c$, where i belongs to the multilabel of $\boldsymbol{x}$ if and only if $v_i = 1$. A *taxonomy* G is a forest whose trees are defined over the set of labels. We use $j = \text{PAR}(i)$ to denote the unique parent of i and $\text{ANC}(i)$ to denote the set of ancestors of i. The depth of a node i (number of edges on the path from the root to i) is denoted by h_i.

A multilabel $\boldsymbol{v}$ belongs to a given taxonomy if and only if it is the union of one or more paths in the forest, where each path must start from a root but need not terminate on a leaf (see Figure 1). A probability distribution f_G over the set of multilabels is associated to a taxonomy G as follows. Each node i of G is tagged with a $\{-1, 1\}$-valued random variable V_i distributed according to a conditional probability function $\mathbb{P}(V_i \mid V_{\text{PAR}(i)}, \boldsymbol{X})$ To model the dependency between the labels of nodes i and $j = \text{PAR}(i)$ we assume $\mathbb{P}\left(V_i = 1 \mid V_j = -1, \boldsymbol{X} = \boldsymbol{x}\right) = 0$

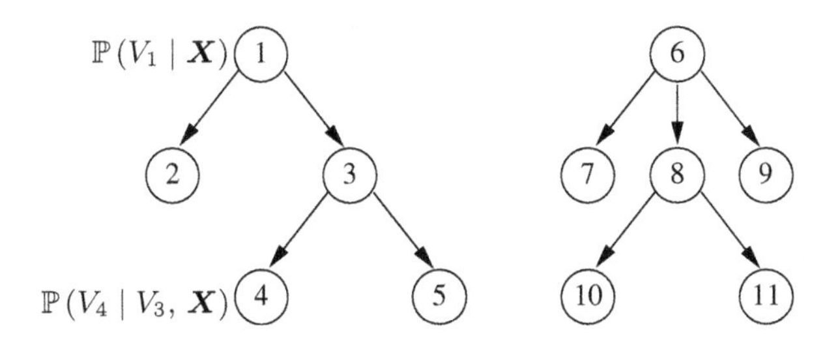

Fig. 1. A forest made up of two disjoint trees. The nodes are tagged with the name of the labels, so that in this case $c = 11$. According to our definition, the multilabel $\boldsymbol{v} = (1, 1, 1, -1, -1, 1, -1, 1, -1, 1, -1)$ belongs to this taxonomy (since it is the union of paths $1 \to 2$, $1 \to 3$ and $6 \to 8 \to 10$), while the multilabel $\boldsymbol{v} = (1, 1, -1, 1, -1, -1, -1, -1, -1, -1, -1)$ does not, since $1 \to 2 \to 4$ is not a path in the forest.

for all nonroot nodes i and all instances $\boldsymbol{x}$. For example, in the taxonomy of Figure 1 we have $\mathbb{P}(V_4 = 1 \mid V_3 = -1, \boldsymbol{X} = \boldsymbol{x}) = 0$ for all $\boldsymbol{x} \in \mathbb{R}^d$. The quantity

$$f_G(\boldsymbol{v} \mid \boldsymbol{x}) = \prod_{i=1}^{c} \mathbb{P}(V_i = v_i \mid V_j = v_j,\ j = \text{PAR}(i),\ \boldsymbol{X} = \boldsymbol{x})$$

thus defines a joint probability distribution on $V_1, \ldots, V_c$ conditioned on $\boldsymbol{x}$ being the current instance.

Through f_G we specify an i.i.d. process $\{(\boldsymbol{X}_1, \boldsymbol{V}_1), (\boldsymbol{X}_2, \boldsymbol{V}_2), \ldots\}$, where, for $t = 1, 2, \ldots$, the multilabel $\boldsymbol{V}_t$ is distributed according to the joint distribution $f_G(\cdot \mid \boldsymbol{X}_t)$ and $\boldsymbol{X}_t$ is distributed according to a fixed and unknown distribution D. We call each realization $(\boldsymbol{x}_t, \boldsymbol{v}_t)$ of $(\boldsymbol{X}_t, \boldsymbol{V}_t)$ an *example*.

We now introduce a parametric model for f_G. First, we assume that the support of D is the surface of the d-dimensional unit sphere (in other words, instances $\boldsymbol{x} \in \mathbb{R}^d$ are normalized, so that $||\boldsymbol{x}|| = 1$). With each node i in the taxonomy, we associate a unit-norm weight vector $\boldsymbol{u}_i \in \mathbb{R}^d$. Then, we define the conditional probabilities for a nonroot node i with parent j as follows:

$$\mathbb{P}(V_i = 1 \mid V_j = 1, \boldsymbol{X} = \boldsymbol{x}) = (1 + \boldsymbol{u}_i^\top \boldsymbol{x})/2 . \tag{1}$$

If i is a root node, the above simplifies to

$$\mathbb{P}(V_i = 1 \mid \boldsymbol{X} = \boldsymbol{x}) = (1 + \boldsymbol{u}_i^\top \boldsymbol{x})/2 .$$

Note that, in this model, the labels of the children of any given node are independent random variables. This is motivated by the fact that, unlike previous investigations, we are explicitely modelling labellings involving multiple paths. A more sophisticated analysis could introduce an arbitrary negative correlation between the labels of the children nodes. We did not attempt to follow this route.

In this parametric model, we would like to perform almost as well as the hierarchical predictor that knows all vectors $\boldsymbol{u}_1, \ldots, \boldsymbol{u}_c$ and labels an instance $\boldsymbol{x}$ with the multilabel $\boldsymbol{y} = (y_1, \ldots, y_c)$ computed in the following natural top-down fashion:[1]

[1] SGN denotes the usual signum function: $\text{SGN}(x) = 1$ if $x \geq 0$; -1, otherwise.

$$y_i = \begin{cases} \text{SGN}(\boldsymbol{u}_i^\top \boldsymbol{x}) & \text{if } i \text{ is a root node,} \\ \text{SGN}(\boldsymbol{u}_i^\top \boldsymbol{x}) & \text{if } i \text{ is not a root and } y_j = +1 \text{ for } j = \text{PAR}(i), \\ -1 & \text{if } i \text{ is not a root and } y_j = -1 \text{ for } j = \text{PAR}(i) . \end{cases} \tag{2}$$

In other words, if a node has been labelled $+1$ then each child is labelled according to a linear-threshold function. On the other hand, if a node happens to be labelled -1 then *all* of its descendants are labelled -1.

For our theoretical analysis, we consider the following on-line learning model. In the generic time step $t = 1, 2, \ldots$ the algorithm receives an instance $\boldsymbol{x}_t$ (a realization of $\boldsymbol{X}_t$) and outputs c binary predictions $\hat{y}_{1,t}, \hat{y}_{2,t}, \ldots, \hat{y}_{c,t} \in \{-1, +1\}$, one for each node in the taxonomy. These predictions are viewed as guesses for the true labels $v_{1,t}, v_{2,t}, \ldots, v_{c,t}$ (realizations of $V_{1,t}, V_{2,t}, \ldots, V_{c,t}$, respectively) associated with $\boldsymbol{x}_t$. After each prediction, the algorithm observes the true labels and updates its estimates of the true model parameters. Such estimates will then be used in the next time step.

In a hierarchical classification framework many reasonable accuracy measures can be defined. As an attempt to be as fair as possible,[2] we measure the accuracy of our algorithm through its global instantaneous regret on instance $\boldsymbol{X}_t$,

$$\mathbb{P}(\exists i : \hat{y}_{i,t} \neq V_{i,t}) - \mathbb{P}(\exists i : y_{i,t} \neq V_{i,t}) ,$$

being $y_{i,t}$ the i-th label output at time t by the reference predictor (2). The above probabilities are w.r.t. the random draw of $(\boldsymbol{X}_1, \boldsymbol{V}_1), \ldots, (\boldsymbol{X}_t, \boldsymbol{V}_t)$. The regret bounds we prove in Section 4 are shown to depend on the interaction between the structure of the multi-dimensional data-generating process and the structure of the taxonomy on which the process is applied.

Further notation. We denote by $\{\phi\}$ the Bernoulli random variable which is 1 if and only if predicate ϕ is true. Let ψ be another predicate. We repeatedly use simple facts such as $\{\phi \vee \psi\} = \{\phi\} + \{\psi, \neg\phi\} \leq \{\phi\} + \{\psi\}$ and $\{\phi\} = \{\phi \wedge \psi\} + \{\phi \wedge \neg\psi\} \leq \{\phi \wedge \psi\} + \{\neg\psi\}$.

3 The Learning Algorithm

We consider linear-threshold algorithms operating on each node of the taxonomy. The algorithm sitting on node i maintains and adjusts a weight vector $\boldsymbol{W}_{i,t}$ which represents an estimate at time t of the corresponding unknown vector $\boldsymbol{u}_i$.

Our hierarchical classification algorithm combines the weight vectors $\boldsymbol{W}_{i,t}$ associated to each node in much the same way as the hierarchical predictor (2). However, since $\boldsymbol{u}_i$ parameterizes a conditional distribution where the label associated with the parent of node i is 1—recall (1), it is natural to update $\boldsymbol{W}_{i,t}$ only when such a conditioning event actually occurs. The pseudocode of our algorithm is given in Figure 2.

[2] It is worth mentioning that the machinery developed in this paper could also be used to analyze loss functions more sophisticated that the 0-1 loss. However, we will not pursue this more sophisticated analysis here.

Initialization: Weight vectors $\boldsymbol{W}_{i,1} = (0, \ldots, 0)$, $i = 1, \ldots, c$.
For $t = 1, 2, \ldots$ do:

1. Observe instance $\boldsymbol{X}_t$;
2. Compute prediction values $\hat{y}_{i,t} \in \{-1, 1\}$ as follows:

$$\hat{y}_{i,t} = \begin{cases} \text{SGN}(\boldsymbol{W}_{i,t}^\top \boldsymbol{X}_t) & \text{if } i \text{ is a root node,} \\ \text{SGN}(\boldsymbol{W}_{i,t}^\top \boldsymbol{X}_t) & \text{if } i \text{ is not a root node and } \hat{y}_{j,t} = +1 \text{ for } j = \text{PAR}(i), \\ -1 & \text{if } i \text{ is not a root node and } \hat{y}_{j,t} = -1 \text{ for } j = \text{PAR}(i), \end{cases}$$

where

$$\begin{aligned} \boldsymbol{W}_{i,t} &= (I + S_{i,t-1} S_{i,t-1}^\top + \boldsymbol{X}_t \boldsymbol{X}_t^\top)^{-1} S_{i,t-1} \boldsymbol{V}_{i,t-1} \\ \boldsymbol{V}_{i,t-1} &= (V_{i,i_1}, V_{i,i_2}, \ldots, V_{i,i_{N(i,t-1)}})^\top \\ S_{i,t-1} &= [\boldsymbol{X}_{i_1}\ \boldsymbol{X}_{i_2}\ \ldots\ \boldsymbol{X}_{i_{N(i,t-1)}}], \qquad i = 1, \ldots, c\ ; \end{aligned}$$

3. Observe multilabel $\boldsymbol{V}_t$ and perform update.

Fig. 2. The hierarchical learning algorithm.

Given the i.i.d. process $\boldsymbol{X}_1, \boldsymbol{X}_2, \ldots$ generating the instances, for each node i we define the derived process $\boldsymbol{X}_{i_1}, \boldsymbol{X}_{i_2}, \ldots$ including all and only the instances $\boldsymbol{X}_s$ of the original process that satisfy $V_{\text{PAR}(i),s} = 1$. We call this derived process the *process at node* i. Note that, for each i, the process at node i is an i.i.d. process. However, its distribution might depend on i; that is, the process distribution at note i is generally different from the process distribution at node $j \neq i$.

Let $N(i,t)$ denote the number of times the *parent* of node i observes a positive label up to time t; i.e., $N(i,t) = |\{1 \le s \le t : V_{\text{PAR}(i),s} = 1\}|$. The weight vector $\boldsymbol{W}_{i,t}$ stored at time t in node i is a (conditional) regularized least squares estimator given by

$$\boldsymbol{W}_{i,t} = (I + S_{i,t-1} S_{i,t-1}^\top + \boldsymbol{X}_t \boldsymbol{X}_t^\top)^{-1} S_{i,t-1} \boldsymbol{V}_{i,t-1}\ , \tag{3}$$

where I is the $d \times d$ identity matrix, $S_{i,t-1}$ is the $d \times N(i,t-1)$ matrix whose columns are the instances $\boldsymbol{X}_{i_1}, \ldots, \boldsymbol{X}_{i_{N(i,t-1)}}$ and $\boldsymbol{V}_{i,t-1} = (V_{i,i_1}, \ldots, V_{i,i_{N(i,t-1)}})^\top$ is the $N(i,t-1)$-dimensional vector of the corresponding labels observed by node i.

This estimator is a slight variant of regularized least squares for classification [2,15] where we include the current instance $\boldsymbol{x}_t$ in the computation of $\boldsymbol{W}_{i,t}$ (see, e.g., [1,20] for analyses of similar algorithms in different contexts). Efficient incremental computations of the inverse matrix and dual variable formulations of the algorithm are extensively discussed in [2,15].

4 Analysis

In this section we state and prove our main result, a bound on the regret of our hierarchical classification algorithm. In essence, the analysis hinges on proving that for any node i, the estimated margin $\boldsymbol{W}_{i,t}^\top \boldsymbol{X}_t$ is an asymptotically unbiased estimator of the true margin $\boldsymbol{u}_i^\top \boldsymbol{X}_t$, and then on using known large deviation arguments to obtain the stated bound. For this purpose, we bound the variance of the margin estimator at each node and prove a bound on the rate at which the bias vanishes. Both bounds will crucially depend on the convergence of the smallest empirical eigenvalue of the process at each node i, and the next result is the key to keeping this convergence under control.

Lemma 1 (Shawe-Taylor et al. [18]). *Let $\boldsymbol{X} = (X_1, \ldots, X_d) \in \mathbb{R}^d$ be a random vector such that $\|\boldsymbol{X}\| = 1$ with probability 1, and let $\lambda \geq 0$ be the smallest eigenvalue of the correlation matrix $\{\mathbb{E}[X_i X_j]\}_{i,j=1}^d$. If $\boldsymbol{X}_1, \ldots, \boldsymbol{X}_s$ are i.i.d. random vectors distributed as $\boldsymbol{X}$, S is the $d \times s$ matrix whose columns are $\boldsymbol{X}_1, \ldots, \boldsymbol{X}_s$, $C = S\,S^\top$ is the associated empirical correlation matrix, and $\hat{\lambda}_s \geq 0$ is the smallest eigenvalue of C, then*

$$\mathbb{P}\left(\tfrac{\hat{\lambda}_s}{s} < \lambda/2\right) \leq 2(s+1)\, e^{-s\,\lambda^2/304} \qquad \text{provided } s \geq 96d/\lambda^2 \,. \tag{4}$$

We now state our main result.

Theorem 1. *Consider a taxonomy G with c nodes of depths $h_1, \ldots, h_c$ and fix an arbitrary choice of parameters $\boldsymbol{u}_1, \ldots, \boldsymbol{u}_c \in \mathbb{R}^d$, such that $||\boldsymbol{u}_i|| = 1$, $i = 1, \ldots, c$. Assume there exist $\gamma_1, \ldots, \gamma_c > 0$ such that distribution D satisfies $\mathbb{P}\left(|\boldsymbol{u}_i^\top \boldsymbol{X}_t| \geq \gamma_i\right) = 1$, $i = 1, \ldots, c$. Then, for all*

$$t > \max\left\{ \max_{i=1,\ldots,c} \frac{2^{h_i+1}}{\mathbb{P}(\mathcal{A}_{i,t})} \frac{8}{\lambda_i \gamma_i},\ \max_{i=1,\ldots,c} \frac{2^{h_i+1}}{\mathbb{P}(\mathcal{A}_{i,t})} \frac{96d}{\lambda_i^2} \right\}$$

the regret at time t of the algorithm described in Figure 2 satisfies

$$\begin{aligned}
&\mathbb{P}(\exists i\,:\, \hat{y}_{i,t} \neq V_{i,t}) - \mathbb{P}(\exists i\,:\, y_{i,t} \neq V_{i,t}) \\
&\leq \sum_{i=1}^{c} \mathbb{P}(\mathcal{A}_{i,t}) \Bigg[2\,e\,t\, \exp\left(-\frac{\gamma_i^2 \lambda_i (t-1)\, \mathbb{P}(\mathcal{A}_{i,t})}{16 \cdot 2^{h_i+1}} \right) \\
&\quad + e\,(t+1)^2 \exp\left(-\frac{\lambda_i^2\,(t-1)\,\mathbb{P}(\mathcal{A}_{i,t})}{304 \cdot 2^{h_i+1}} \right) + \exp\left(-\frac{(t-1)\mathbb{P}(\mathcal{A}_{i,t})}{5 \cdot 2^{h_i+1}} \right) \Bigg],
\end{aligned}$$

where $\mathcal{A}_{i,t} = \{\forall j \in \text{ANC}(i)\,:\, \boldsymbol{u}_j^\top \boldsymbol{X}_t \geq 0\}$ and λ_i is the smallest eigenvalue of the process at node i.

Remark 1. Note that the dependence of $\mathbb{P}(\mathcal{A}_{i,t})$ on t is purely formal, as evinced by the definition of $\mathcal{A}_{i,t}$. Hence, the regret vanishes exponentially in t. This unnaturally fast rate is mainly caused by our assumptions on the data and, in particular, on the existence of $\gamma_1, \ldots, \gamma_c$ constraining the support of D. As shown in [3], we would recover the standard $t^{-1/2}$ rate by assuming, instead, some reasonable bound on the tail of the distribution of the inverse squared margin $(\boldsymbol{u}_i^\top \boldsymbol{X}_t)^{-2}$, though this would make our analysis somewhat more complicated.

Remark 2. The values $\mathbb{P}(\mathcal{A}_{i,t})/2^{h_i}$ express the main interplay between the taxonomy structure and the process generating the examples. It is important to observe how our regret bound depends on such quantities. For instance, if we just focus on the probability values $\mathbb{P}(\mathcal{A}_{i,t})$, we see that the regret bound is essentially the sum over all nodes i in the taxonomy of terms of the form

$$\mathbb{P}(\mathcal{A}_{i,t}) \exp(-k_i \, \mathbb{P}(\mathcal{A}_{i,t}) \, t) \ , \tag{5}$$

where the k_i's are positive constants. Clearly, $\mathbb{P}(\mathcal{A}_{i,t})$ decreases as we descend along a path. Hence, if node i is a root then $\mathbb{P}(\mathcal{A}_{i,t})$ tends to be relatively large, whereas if i is a leaf node then $\mathbb{P}(\mathcal{A}_{i,t})$ tends to be close to zero. In both cases (5) tends to be small: when $\mathbb{P}(\mathcal{A}_{i,t})$ is close to one it does not affect the negative exponential decrease with time; on the other hand, if $\mathbb{P}(\mathcal{A}_{i,t})$ is close to zero then (5) is small anyway. In fact, this is no surprise, since it is a direct consequence of the hierarchical nature of our prediction algorithm (Figure 2). Let us consider, for the sake of clarity, two extreme cases: 1) i is a root node; 2) i is a (very deep) leaf node.

1) A root node observes all instances. The predictor at this node is required to predict through $\text{SGN}(\boldsymbol{W}_{i,t}^{\top} \boldsymbol{X}_t)$ on *all* instances $\boldsymbol{X}_t$, but the estimator $\boldsymbol{W}_{i,t}$ gets close to $\boldsymbol{u}_i$ very quickly. In this case the negative exponential convergence of the associated term (5) is fast ($\mathbb{P}(\mathcal{A}_{i,t})$ is "large").

2) A leaf node observes a possibly small subset of the instances, but it is also required to produce only a small subset of linear-threshold predictions (the associated weight vector $\boldsymbol{W}_{i,t}$ might be an unreliable estimator, but is also used less often). Therefore, in this case, (5) is small just because so is $\mathbb{P}(\mathcal{A}_{i,t})$.

In summary, $\mathbb{P}(\mathcal{A}_{i,t})$ somehow measures both the rate at which the estimator in node i gets updated and the relative importance of the accuracy of this estimator when computing the overall regret.

Remark 3. The bound of Theorem 1 becomes vacuous when $\lambda_i = 0$ for some i. However, note that whenever the smallest eigenvalue of the original process (i.e., the process at the roots) is positive, then $\lambda_i > 0$ for all nodes i, up to pathological collusions between D and the $\boldsymbol{u}_j$'s. As an example of such collusions, note that the process at node i is a filtered version of the original process, as each ancestor j of i filters out $\boldsymbol{X}_t$ with probability depending on the angle between $\boldsymbol{X}_t$ and $\boldsymbol{u}_j$. Hence, to make the process at node i have a correlation matrix with rank strictly smaller than the one at $j = \text{PAR}(i)$, the parameter $\boldsymbol{u}_j$ should be perfectly aligned with an eigenvector of the process at node j.

Remark 4. We are measuring regret against a reference predictor that is not Bayes optimal for the data model at hand. Indeed, the Bayes optimal predictor would use the maximum likelihood multilabel assignment given G and $\boldsymbol{u}_1, \dots, \boldsymbol{u}_c$ (this assignment is easily computable using a special case of the sum-product algorithm [10]). Finding a good algorithm to approximate the maximum-likelihood assignment has proven to be a difficult task.

Proof (of Theorem 1). We first observe that

$$\{\exists i\,:\,\hat{y}_{i,t}\neq V_{i,t}\}\leq\{\exists i\,:\,y_{i,t}\neq V_{i,t}\}+\{\exists i\,:\,\hat{y}_{i,t}\neq y_{i,t}\}$$
$$=\{\exists i\,:\,y_{i,t}\neq V_{i,t}\}$$
$$+\sum_{i=1}^{c}\{\hat{y}_{i,t}\neq y_{i,t},\,\hat{y}_{j,t}=y_{j,t},\ j=1,\dots,i-1\}\,. \qquad (6)$$

Without loss of generality we can assume that the nodes in the taxonomy are assigned numbers such that if node i is a child of node j then $i>j$. The regret (6) can then be upper bounded as

$$\sum_{i=1}^{c}\{\hat{y}_{i,t}\neq y_{i,t},\,\hat{y}_{j,t}=y_{j,t},\ j=1,\dots,i-1\}$$
$$\leq\sum_{i=1}^{c}\{\hat{y}_{i,t}\neq y_{i,t},\ \ \forall j\in\text{ANC}(i)\,:\,\hat{y}_{j,t}=y_{j,t}\}$$
$$=\sum_{i=1}^{c}\{\hat{y}_{i,t}\neq y_{i,t},\ \forall j\in\text{ANC}(i)\,:\,\hat{y}_{j,t}=y_{j,t}=1\}$$
(since $\hat{y}_{j,t}=y_{j,t}=-1$ for some ancestor j implies $\hat{y}_{i,t}=y_{i,t}=-1$)
$$\leq\sum_{i=1}^{c}\{\hat{y}_{i,t}\neq y_{i,t},\ \forall j\in\text{ANC}(i)\,:\,y_{j,t}=1\}\,.$$

Taking expectations we get

$$\mathbb{P}(\exists i\,:\,\hat{y}_{i,t}\neq V_{i,t})-\mathbb{P}(\exists i\,:\,y_{i,t}\neq V_{i,t})$$
$$\leq\sum_{i=1}^{c}\mathbb{P}\left(\hat{y}_{i,t}\neq y_{i,t},\ \forall j\in\text{ANC}(i)\,:\,y_{j,t}=1\right)\,.$$

We now bound from above the simpler probability terms in the right-hand side. For notational brevity, in the rest of this proof we will be using $\Delta_{i,t}$ to denote the margin variable $\boldsymbol{u}_i^\top\boldsymbol{X}_t$ and $\widehat{\Delta}_{i,t}$ to denote the algorithm's margin $\boldsymbol{W}_{i,t}^\top\boldsymbol{X}_t$. As we said earlier, our argument centers on proving that for any node i, $\widehat{\Delta}_{i,t}$ is an asymptotically unbiased estimator of $\Delta_{i,t}$, and then on using known large deviation techniques to obtain the stated bound. For this purpose, we need to study both the conditional bias and the conditional variance of $\widehat{\Delta}_{i,t}$.

Recall Figure 2. We first observe that the multilabel vectors $\boldsymbol{V}_1,\dots,\boldsymbol{V}_{t-1}$ are conditionally independent given the instance vectors $\boldsymbol{X}_1,\dots,\boldsymbol{X}_{t-1}$. More precisely, we have

$$\mathbb{P}\left(\boldsymbol{V}_1,\dots,\boldsymbol{V}_{t-1}\mid\boldsymbol{X}_1,\dots,\boldsymbol{X}_{t-1}\right)=\mathbb{P}\left(\boldsymbol{V}_1\mid\boldsymbol{X}_1\right)\times\dots\times\mathbb{P}\left(\boldsymbol{V}_{t-1}\mid\boldsymbol{X}_{t-1}\right)\,.$$

Also, for any given node i with parent j, the child's labels $V_{i,i_1},\dots,V_{i,i_{N(i,t-1)}}$ are independent when conditioned on both $\boldsymbol{X}_1,\dots,\boldsymbol{X}_{t-1}$ and the parent's labels $V_{j,1},\dots,V_{j,t-1}$. Let us denote by $\mathbb{E}_{i,t}$ the conditional expectation

$$\mathbb{E}[\,\cdot\mid(\boldsymbol{X}_1,V_{j,1}),\dots,(\boldsymbol{X}_{t-1},V_{j,t-1}),\,\boldsymbol{X}_t]\,.$$

By definition of our parametric model (1) we have $\mathbb{E}_{i,t}[\boldsymbol{V}_{i,t-1}] = S_{i,t-1}^\top \boldsymbol{u}_i$. Recalling the definition (3) of $\boldsymbol{W}_{i,t}$, this implies

$$\mathbb{E}_{i,t}[\widehat{\Delta}_{i,t}] = \boldsymbol{u}_i^\top S_{i,t-1} S_{i,t-1}^\top (I + S_{i,t-1} S_{i,t-1}^\top + \boldsymbol{X}_t \boldsymbol{X}_t^\top)^{-1} \boldsymbol{X}_t \ .$$

In the rest of the proof, we use $\hat{\lambda}_{i,t-1}$ to denote the smallest eigenvalue of the empirical correlation matrix $S_{i,t-1} S_{i,t-1}^\top$. The conditional bias is bounded in the following lemma (proven in the appendix).

Lemma 2. *With the notation introduced so far, we have: $\Delta_{i,t} = \mathbb{E}_{i,t}[\widehat{\Delta}_{i,t}] + B_{i,t}$, where the conditional bias $B_{i,t}$ satisfies $B_{i,t} \le 2/(1 + \hat{\lambda}_{i,t-1})$.*

Next, we consider the conditional variance of $\widehat{\Delta}_{i,t}$. Recalling Figure 2, we see that

$$\widehat{\Delta}_{i,t} = \sum_{k=1}^{N(i,t-1)} V_{i,i_k} Z_k$$

where $\boldsymbol{Z}^\top = (Z_1, ..., Z_{N(i,t-1)})^\top = S_{i,t-1}^\top \left(I + S_{i,t-1} S_{i,t-1}^\top + \boldsymbol{X}_t \boldsymbol{X}_t^\top \right)^{-1} \boldsymbol{X}_t$. The next lemma (proven in the appendix) handles the conditional variance $\|\boldsymbol{Z}\|^2$.

Lemma 3. *With the notation introduced so far, we have: $\|\boldsymbol{Z}\|^2 \le 1/(2 + \hat{\lambda}_{i,t-1})$.*

Armed with these two lemmas, we proceed through our large deviation argument. For the sake of brevity, denote $N(i, t-1)$ by N. Also, in order to stress the dependence of $\hat{\lambda}_{i,t-1}$, $\widehat{\Delta}_{i,t}$ and $B_{i,t}$ on $N(i, t-1)$, we denote them by $\hat{\lambda}_{i,N}$, $\widehat{\Delta}_{i,t,N}$ and $B_{i,N}$, respectively. The case when subscript N is replaced by its realization n should be intended as the random variable obtained by restricting to sample realizations such that N takes on value n. Thus, for instance, any predicate $\phi(\widehat{\Delta}_{i,t,n})$ involving $\widehat{\Delta}_{i,t,n}$ should actually be intended as a short-hand for $\phi(\widehat{\Delta}_{i,t,N}) \wedge N = n$.

Recall that $\mathcal{A}_{i,t} = \{\forall j \in \text{ANC}(i) \, : \, \boldsymbol{u}_j^\top \boldsymbol{X}_t \ge 0\} = \{\forall j \in \text{ANC}(i) \, : \, y_{j,t} = 1\}$. We have

$$\begin{aligned}
&\{\hat{y}_{i,t} \ne y_{i,t}, \ \mathcal{A}_{i,t}\} \\
&\quad \le \left\{ \widehat{\Delta}_{i,t,N}\, \Delta_{i,t} \le 0, \ \mathcal{A}_{i,t} \right\} \\
&\quad \le \left\{ |\widehat{\Delta}_{i,t,N} - \Delta_{i,t}| \ge |\Delta_{i,t}|, \ \mathcal{A}_{i,t} \right\} \\
&\quad \le \left\{ |\widehat{\Delta}_{i,t,N} + B_{i,N} - \Delta_{i,t}| \ge |\Delta_{i,t}| - |B_{i,N}|, \ \mathcal{A}_{i,t} \right\} \\
&\quad \le \left\{ |\widehat{\Delta}_{i,t,N} + B_{i,N} - \Delta_{i,t}| \ge |\Delta_{i,t}|/2, \ \mathcal{A}_{i,t} \right\} + \{|B_{i,N}| \ge |\Delta_{i,t}|/2, \ \mathcal{A}_{i,t}\} \, .
\end{aligned} \tag{7}$$

We can bound the two terms of (7) separately. Let $M < t$ be an integer constant to be specified later. For the first term we obtain

$$
\begin{aligned}
&\left\{|\widehat{\Delta}_{i,t,N} + B_{i,N} - \Delta_{i,t}| \geq |\Delta_{i,t}|/2,\ \mathcal{A}_{i,t}\right\} \\
&\quad \leq \left\{|\widehat{\Delta}_{i,t,N} + B_{i,N} - \Delta_{i,t}| \geq |\Delta_{i,t}|/2,\ \mathcal{A}_{i,t},\ N \geq M,\ \hat{\lambda}_{i,N} \geq \lambda_i N/2\right\} \\
&\qquad + \left\{\mathcal{A}_{i,t},\ N \geq M,\ \hat{\lambda}_{i,N} < \lambda_i N/2\right\} + \{\mathcal{A}_{i,t},\ N < M\} \\
&\quad \leq \sum_{n=M}^{t-1} \left\{|\widehat{\Delta}_{i,t,n} + B_{i,n} - \Delta_{i,t}| \geq |\Delta_{i,t}|/2,\ \mathcal{A}_{i,t},\ \hat{\lambda}_{i,n} \geq \lambda_i n/2\right\} \\
&\qquad + \sum_{n=M}^{t-1} \left\{\mathcal{A}_{i,t},\ \hat{\lambda}_{i,n} < \lambda_i n/2\right\} + \{\mathcal{A}_{i,t},\ N < M\} .
\end{aligned}
$$

For the second term, using Lemma 2 we get

$$
\begin{aligned}
&\left\{|B_{i,N}| \geq |\Delta_{i,t}|/2,\ \mathcal{A}_{i,t}\right\} \\
&\leq \left\{\frac{2}{1+\hat{\lambda}_{i,N}} \geq |\Delta_{i,t}|/2,\ \mathcal{A}_{i,t}\right\} \\
&\leq \left\{\frac{2}{1+\hat{\lambda}_{i,N}} \geq |\Delta_{i,t}|/2,\ \mathcal{A}_{i,t},\ N \geq M,\ \hat{\lambda}_{i,N} \geq \lambda_i N/2\right\} \\
&\quad + \left\{\mathcal{A}_{i,t},\ N \geq M,\ \hat{\lambda}_{i,N} < \lambda_i N/2\right\} + \{\mathcal{A}_{i,t},\ N < M\} .
\end{aligned}
$$

Now note that the choice $M \geq 8/(\lambda_i\, \gamma_i) \geq 8/(\lambda_i |\Delta_{i,t}|)$ makes the first term vanish. Hence, under this condition on M,

$$
\begin{aligned}
\left\{|B_{i,N}| \geq |\Delta_{i,t}|/2,\ \mathcal{A}_{i,t}\right\} &\leq \left\{\mathcal{A}_{i,t},\ N \geq M,\ \hat{\lambda}_{i,N} < \lambda_i N/2\right\} + \{\mathcal{A}_{i,t},\ N < M\} \\
&\leq \sum_{n=M}^{t-1} \left\{\mathcal{A}_{i,t},\ \hat{\lambda}_{i,n} < \lambda_i n/2\right\} + \{\mathcal{A}_{i,t},\ N < M\} .
\end{aligned}
$$

Plugging back into (7) and introducing probabilities yields

$$
\begin{aligned}
&\mathbb{P}(\hat{y}_{i,t} \neq y_{i,t},\ \mathcal{A}_{i,t}) \\
&\leq \sum_{n=M}^{t-1} \mathbb{P}\left(|\widehat{\Delta}_{i,t,n} + B_{i,n} - \Delta_{i,t}| \geq |\Delta_{i,t}|/2,\ \mathcal{A}_{i,t},\ \hat{\lambda}_{i,n} \geq \lambda_i n/2\right) && (8) \\
&\quad + 2\sum_{n=M}^{t-1} \mathbb{P}\left(\mathcal{A}_{i,t},\ \hat{\lambda}_{i,n} < \lambda_i n/2\right) && (9) \\
&\quad + 2\,\mathbb{P}(\mathcal{A}_{i,t},\ N < M) . && (10)
\end{aligned}
$$

Let $j = \text{PAR}(i)$ and $\mathbb{P}_{i,t}$ denote $\mathbb{P}\big(\cdot \mid (\boldsymbol{X}_1, V_{j,1}), \ldots, (\boldsymbol{X}_{t-1}, V_{j,t-1}),\ \boldsymbol{X}_t\big)$. Notice that $V_{i,i_1}, \ldots, V_{i,i_{N(i,t-1)}}$ are independent w.r.t. $\mathbb{P}_{i,t}$. We bound (8) by combining

Chernoff-Hoeffding inequalities [8] with Lemma 3:

$$\begin{aligned}
&\mathbb{P}_{i,t}\left(|\widehat{\Delta}_{i,t,n} + B_{i,n} - \Delta_{i,t}| \geq |\Delta_{i,t}|/2,\ \mathcal{A}_{i,t},\ \hat{\lambda}_{i,n} \geq \lambda_i n/2\right) \\
&= \{\mathcal{A}_{i,t}\} \times \left\{\hat{\lambda}_{i,n} \geq \lambda_i n/2\right\} \times \mathbb{P}_{i,t}\left(|\widehat{\Delta}_{i,t,n} + B_{i,n} - \Delta_{i,t}| \geq |\Delta_{i,t}|/2\right) \\
&\leq \{\mathcal{A}_{i,t}\} \times \left\{\hat{\lambda}_{i,n} \geq \lambda_i n/2\right\} \times 2e^{-\Delta_{i,t}^2(2+\hat{\lambda}_{i,n})/8} \\
&\leq 2\ \{\mathcal{A}_{i,t}\}\, e^{-\gamma_i^2\,\lambda_i\,n/16}\ .
\end{aligned}$$

Thus, integrating out the conditioning, we get that (8) is upper bounded by

$$2\,\mathbb{P}(\mathcal{A}_{i,t}) \sum_{n=M}^{t-1} e^{-\gamma_i^2\,\lambda_i\,n/16} \leq 2\,\mathbb{P}(\mathcal{A}_{i,t})\, t\, e^{-\gamma_i^2\,\lambda_i\,M/16}\ .$$

Since the process at each node i is i.i.d., we can bound (9) through the concentration result contained in Lemma 1. Choosing $M \geq 96d/\lambda_i^2$, we get

$$\begin{aligned}
\mathbb{P}_{i,t}\left(\mathcal{A}_{i,t},\ \hat{\lambda}_{i,n} < \lambda_i n/2\right) &= \{\mathcal{A}_{i,t}\}\ \mathbb{P}_{i,t}\left(\hat{\lambda}_{i,n} < \lambda_i n/2\right) \\
&\leq 2(n+1)\,\{\mathcal{A}_{i,t}\}\ e^{-n\lambda_i^2/304}\ .
\end{aligned}$$

Thus, integrating out the conditioning again, we get that (9) is upper bounded by

$$2\,\mathbb{P}(\mathcal{A}_{i,t}) \sum_{n=M}^{t-1} (n+1)e^{-n\lambda_i^2/304} \leq \mathbb{P}(\mathcal{A}_{i,t})\,(t+1)^2\, e^{-M\lambda_i^2/304}\ .$$

Finally, we analyze (10) as follows. Recall that $N = N(i, t-1)$ counts the number of times node j, the parent of node i, has observed $V_{j,s} = 1$ for $s = 1, \ldots, t-1$. Therefore $\mathbb{P}\left(\mathcal{A}_{i,t},\ N < M\right) = \mathbb{P}\left(\mathcal{A}_{i,t}\right)\,\mathbb{P}\left(N < M\right)$, and we can focus on the latter probability. The random variable N is binomial and we can bound its parameter μ_i as follows. Let $j(1) \rightarrow j(2) \rightarrow \ldots \rightarrow j(h_i) \rightarrow i$ be the unique path from a root down to node i (that is, $\text{ANC}(i) = \{j(1), \ldots, j(h_i)\}$ and $j(h_i) = \text{PAR}(i)$). Fix any $\boldsymbol{X} \in \mathbb{R}^d$ such that $||\boldsymbol{X}|| = 1$. Exploiting the way conditional probabilities are defined in our taxonomy (see Section 2), for a generic time step $s \leq t-1$ we can write

$$\begin{aligned}
\mathbb{P}(V_{\text{PAR}(i),s} = 1 \mid \boldsymbol{X}) &= \prod_{k=1}^{h_i} \mathbb{P}(V_{j(k),s} = 1 \mid V_{j(k-1),s} = 1, \boldsymbol{X}) \\
&= \prod_{k=1}^{h_i} \left(\frac{1 + \boldsymbol{u}_{j(k)}^\top \boldsymbol{X}}{2}\right) \qquad \text{(using (1))} \\
&\geq \prod_{k=1}^{h_i} \left(\frac{1 + \boldsymbol{u}_{j(k)}^\top \boldsymbol{X}}{2}\right) \{\mathcal{A}_{i,t}\} \geq \left(\frac{1}{2}\right)^{h_i} \{\mathcal{A}_{i,t}\}\,,
\end{aligned}$$

since $\mathcal{A}_{i,t}$ is equivalent to $\boldsymbol{u}_{j(k)}^\top \boldsymbol{X} \geq 0$ for $k = 1, \ldots, h_i$. Integrating over $\boldsymbol{X}$ we conclude that the parameter μ_i of the binomial random variable N satisfies $\mu_i = \mathbb{P}(V_{\mathrm{PAR}(i),s} = 1) \geq \left(\frac{1}{2}\right)^{h_i} \mathbb{P}(\mathcal{A}_{i,t})$. We now set M as follows:

$$M = \lfloor (t-1)\mu_i/2 \rfloor \geq \frac{(t-1)\mathbb{P}(\mathcal{A}_{i,t})}{2^{h_i+1}} - 1 \, .$$

This implies

$$\begin{aligned} \mathbb{P}\left(\mathcal{A}_{i,t},\ N < M\right) &= \mathbb{P}(\mathcal{A}_{i,t})\mathbb{P}\left(N < M\right) \\ &\leq \mathbb{P}(\mathcal{A}_{i,t})\, e^{-(t-1)\mu_i/10} \qquad (11) \\ &\leq \mathbb{P}(\mathcal{A}_{i,t}) \exp\left(-\frac{(t-1)\mathbb{P}(\mathcal{A}_{i,t})}{10 \cdot 2^{h_i}}\right), \end{aligned}$$

where we used Bernstein's inequality (see, e.g., [4, Ch. 8]) and our choice of M to prove (11).

Piecing together, overapproximating, and using in the bounds for (8) and (9) the conditions on t, along with $M \geq (t-1)\mathbb{P}(\mathcal{A}_{i,t})/2^{h_i+1} - 1$ results in

$$\begin{aligned} &\mathbb{P}(\exists i \,:\, \hat{y}_{i,t} \neq V_{i,t}) - \mathbb{P}(\exists i \,:\, y_{i,t} \neq V_{i,t}) \\ &\leq \sum_{i=1}^{c} \mathbb{P}\left(\hat{y}_{i,t} \neq y_{i,t},\, \mathcal{A}_{i,t}\right) \\ &\leq \sum_{i=1}^{c} \mathbb{P}(\mathcal{A}_{i,t}) \Bigg[2\,e\,t \exp\left(-\frac{\gamma_i^2 \lambda_i (t-1)\, \mathbb{P}(\mathcal{A}_{i,t})}{16 \cdot 2^{h_i+1}}\right) \\ &\quad + e\,(t+1)^2 \exp\left(-\frac{\lambda_i^2\,(t-1)\,\mathbb{P}(\mathcal{A}_{i,t})}{304 \cdot 2^{h_i+1}}\right) + \exp\left(-\frac{(t-1)\mathbb{P}(\mathcal{A}_{i,t})}{5 \cdot 2^{h_i+1}}\right) \Bigg], \end{aligned}$$

thereby concluding the proof. □

5 Preliminary Experimental Results

To support our theoretical results, we are testing some variants of our hierarchical classification algorithm on real-world textual data. In a preliminary series of experiments, we used the first 40,000 newswire stories from the Reuters Corpus Volume 1 (RCV1). The newswire stories in RCV1 are classified in a taxonomy of 102 nodes divided into 4 trees, where multiple-path and partial-path classifications repeatedly occur throughout the corpus. We trained our algorithm on the first 20,000 consecutive documents and tested it on the subsequent 20,000 documents (to represent documents as real vectors, we used the standard TF-IDF bag-of-words encoding — more details will be given in the full paper). To make the algorithm of Figure 2 more space-efficient, we stored in the estimator associated with each node only the examples that achieved a small margin *or* those that were incorrectly classified by the current estimator. In [3] this technique is shown to be quite effective in terms of the number of instances stored and not disruptive in terms of classification performance. This space-efficient version of our algorithm achieved a test error of 46.6% (recall that an instance is considered mistaken if *at least one* out of 102 labels is guessed wrong). For comparison, if we replace our estimator with the standard Perceptron algorithm [16,14] (without touching the rest of the algorithm) the test error goes up to 65.8%, and this performance does not change significantly if we train the Perceptron algorithm at each node with all the examples independently (rather than using only the examples that are positive for the parent). For the space-efficient variant of our algorithm, we observed that training independently each node causes a moderate increase of the test error from 46.6% to 49.6%. Besides, hierarchical training is in general much faster than independent training.

6 Conclusions and Ongoing Research

We have introduced a new hierarchical classification algorithm working with linear-threshold functions. The algorithm has complete knowledge of the taxonomy and maintains at each node a regularized least-squares estimator of the true (unknown) margin associated to the process at that node. The predictions at the nodes are combined in a top-down fashion. We analyzed this algorithm in the i.i.d. setting by providing a bound on the instantaneous regret, i.e., on the amount by which the probability of misclassification by the algorithm exceeds on a randomly drawn instance the probability of misclassification by the hierarchical algorithm knowing all model parameters. We also reported on preliminary experiments with a few variants of our basic algorithm.

Our analysis in Section 4 works under side assumptions about the distribution D generating the examples. We are currently investigating the extent to which it is possible to remove some of these assumptions with no further technical complications. A major theoretical open question is the comparison between our algorithm (or variants thereof) and the Bayes optimal predictor for our parametric model. Finally, we are planning to perform a more extensive experimental study on a variety of hierarchical datasets.

References

1. K.S. Azoury and M.K. Warmuth. Relative loss bounds for on-line density estimation with the exponential familiy of distributions. *Machine Learning*, 43(3):211–246, 2001.
2. N. Cesa-Bianchi, A. Conconi, and C. Gentile. A second-order Perceptron algorithm. In *Proc. 15th COLT*, pages 121–137. LNAI 2375, Springer, 2002.
3. N. Cesa-Bianchi, A. Conconi, and C. Gentile. Learning probabilistic linear-threshold classifiers via selective sampling. In *Proc. 16th COLT*, pages 373–386. LNAI 2777, Springer, 2003.
4. L. Devroye, L. Győrfi, and G. Lugosi. *A Probabilistic Theory of Pattern Recognition*. Springer Verlag, 1996.

5. S.T. Dumais and H. Chen. Hierarchical classification of web content. In *Proceedings of the 23rd ACM International Conference on Research and Development in Information Retrieval*, pages 256–263. ACM Press, 2000.
6. M. Granitzer. *Hierarchical Text Classification using Methods from Machine Learning.* PhD thesis, Graz University of Technology, 2003.
7. T. Hofmann, L. Cai, and M. Ciaramita. Learning with taxonomies: classifying documents and words. Nips 2003: Workshop on syntax, semantics, and statistics, 2003.
8. W. Hoeffding. Probability inequalities for sums of bounded random variables. *Journal of the American Statistical Association*, 58:13–30, 1963.
9. R.A. Horn and C.R. Johnson. *Matrix Analysis.* Cambridge University Press, 1985.
10. F.R. Kschischang, B.J. Frey, and H. Loeliger, Factor graphs and the sum-product algorithm *IEEE Trans. of Information Theory*, 47(2): 498–519, 2001.
11. D. Koller and M. Sahami. Hierarchically classifying documents using very few words. In *Proc. 14th ICML*, pages 170–178. Morgan Kaufmann Publishers, 1997.
12. A.K. McCallum, R. Rosenfeld, T.M. Mitchell, and A.Y. Ng. Improving text classification by shrinkage in a hierarchy of classes. In *Proc. 15th ICML*, pages 359–367. Morgan Kaufmann Publishers, 1998.
13. D. Mladenic. Turning yahoo into an automatic web-page classifier. In *Proc. 13th European Conference on Artificial Intelligence*, pages 473–474, 1998.
14. A.B.J. Novikov. On convergence proofs on perceptrons. *Proc. of the Symposium on the Mathematical Theory of Automata, vol. XII*, pp. 615–622, 1962.
15. R. Rifkin, G. Yeo, and T. Poggio. Regularized least squares classification. In *Advances in Learning Theory: Methods, Model and Applications. NATO Science Series III: Computer and Systems Sciences*, volume 190, pages 131–153. IOS Press, 2003.
16. F. Rosenblatt. The perceptron: A probabilistic model for information storage and organization in the brain. *Psychological Review*, 65, 386–408, 1958.
17. M.E. Ruiz and P. Srinivasan. Hierarchical text categorization using neural networks. *Information Retrieval*, 5(1):87–118, 2002.
18. J. Shawe-Taylor, C. Williams, N. Cristianini, and J.S. Kandola. On the eigenspectrum of the Gram matrix and its relationship to the operator eigenspectrum. In *Proc. 13th ALT*, pages 23–40. LNCS 2533, Springer, 2002.
19. A. Sun and E.-P. Lim. Hierarchical text classification and evaluation. In *Proc. 2001 International Conference on Data Mining*, pages 521–528. IEEE Press, 2001.
20. V. Vovk. Competitive on-line statistics. *International Statistical Review*, 69:213–248, 2001.

Appendix

This appendix contains the proofs of Lemma 2 and Lemma 3 mentioned in the main text. Recall that, given a positive definite matrix A, the spectral norm of A, denoted by $||A||$, equals the largest eigenvalue of A. As a simple consequence, $||A^{-1}||$ is the reciprocal of the smallest eigenvalue of A.

Proof of Lemma 2

Setting $A = I + S_{i,t-1}S_{i,t-1}^\top$ we get

$$\begin{aligned}\Delta_{i,t} &= \mathbb{E}_{i,t}[\widehat{\Delta}_{i,t}] + \boldsymbol{u}_i^\top (I + \boldsymbol{X}_t\boldsymbol{X}_t^\top)(A + \boldsymbol{X}_t\boldsymbol{X}_t^\top)^{-1}\boldsymbol{X}_t \\ &= \mathbb{E}_{i,t}[\widehat{\Delta}_{i,t}] + \boldsymbol{u}_i^\top (A + \boldsymbol{X}_t\boldsymbol{X}_t^\top)^{-1}\boldsymbol{X}_t + \Delta_{i,t}\,\boldsymbol{X}_t^\top (A + \boldsymbol{X}_t\boldsymbol{X}_t^\top)^{-1}\boldsymbol{X}_t . \quad (12)\end{aligned}$$

Using the Sherman-Morrison formula (e.g., [9, Ch. 1]) and the symmetry of A, we can rewrite the second term of (12) as

$$\begin{aligned}\boldsymbol{u}_i^\top (A + \boldsymbol{X}_t\boldsymbol{X}_t^\top)^{-1}\boldsymbol{X}_t &= \boldsymbol{u}_i^\top \left(A^{-1} - \frac{A^{-1}\boldsymbol{X}_t\boldsymbol{X}_t^\top A^{-1}}{1 + \boldsymbol{X}_t^\top A^{-1}\boldsymbol{X}_t}\right)\boldsymbol{X}_t \\ = \boldsymbol{u}_i^\top A^{-1}\boldsymbol{X}_t - \frac{\boldsymbol{u}_i^\top A^{-1}\boldsymbol{X}_t\,\boldsymbol{X}_t A^{-1}\boldsymbol{X}_t}{1 + \boldsymbol{X}_t^\top A^{-1}\boldsymbol{X}_t} &= \frac{\boldsymbol{u}_i^\top A^{-1}\boldsymbol{X}_t}{1 + \boldsymbol{X}_t^\top A^{-1}\boldsymbol{X}_t}\end{aligned}$$

and the third term of (12) as

$$\Delta_{i,t}\,\boldsymbol{X}_t^\top (A + \boldsymbol{X}_t\boldsymbol{X}_t^\top)^{-1}\boldsymbol{X}_t = \Delta_{i,t}\,\frac{\boldsymbol{X}_t^\top A^{-1}\boldsymbol{X}_t}{1 + \boldsymbol{X}_t^\top A^{-1}\boldsymbol{X}_t} .$$

Plugging back into (12) yields $\Delta_{i,t} = \mathbb{E}_{i,t}[\widehat{\Delta}_{i,t}] + B_{i,t}$ where the conditional bias $B_{i,t}$ satisfies

$$\begin{aligned}B_{i,t} &= \frac{\boldsymbol{u}_i^\top A^{-1}\boldsymbol{X}_t}{1 + \boldsymbol{X}_t^\top A^{-1}\boldsymbol{X}_t} + \Delta_{i,t}\,\frac{\boldsymbol{X}_t^\top A^{-1}\boldsymbol{X}_t}{1 + \boldsymbol{X}_t^\top A^{-1}\boldsymbol{X}_t} \\ &\le \frac{||\boldsymbol{u}_i||\,||A^{-1}||\,||\boldsymbol{X}_t||}{1 + \boldsymbol{X}_t^\top A^{-1}\boldsymbol{X}_t} + \frac{|\Delta_{i,t}|\,||\boldsymbol{X}_t||^2\,||A^{-1}||}{1 + \boldsymbol{X}_t^\top A^{-1}\boldsymbol{X}_t} \\ &\le \frac{||A^{-1}||}{1 + \boldsymbol{X}_t^\top A^{-1}\boldsymbol{X}_t} + \frac{||A^{-1}||}{1 + \boldsymbol{X}_t^\top A^{-1}\boldsymbol{X}_t} \le 2||A^{-1}|| .\end{aligned}$$

Here the second inequality holds because $||\boldsymbol{u}_i|| = ||\boldsymbol{X}_t|| = 1$ and $|\Delta_{i,t}| \le ||\boldsymbol{u}_i||\,||\boldsymbol{X}_t|| = 1$, and the third inequality holds because $\boldsymbol{X}_t^\top A^{-1}\boldsymbol{X}_t \ge 0$ by the positive definiteness of A^{-1}. Recalling that $||A^{-1}|| = 1/(1 + \hat{\lambda}_{i,t-1})$, where $1 + \hat{\lambda}_{i,t-1}$ is the smallest eigenvalue of A, concludes the proof. □

Proof of Lemma 3

Setting for brevity $H = S_{i,t-1}^\top A^{-1}\boldsymbol{X}_t$ and $r = \boldsymbol{X}_t^\top A^{-1}\boldsymbol{X}_t$ we can write

$$\begin{aligned}||\boldsymbol{Z}||^2 &= \boldsymbol{X}_t^\top \left(A + \boldsymbol{X}_t\boldsymbol{X}_t^\top\right)^{-1} S_{i,t-1}S_{i,t-1}^\top \left(A + \boldsymbol{X}_t\boldsymbol{X}_t^\top\right)^{-1} \boldsymbol{X}_t \\ &= \boldsymbol{X}_t^\top \left(A^{-1} - \frac{A^{-1}\boldsymbol{X}_t\boldsymbol{X}_t^\top A^{-1}}{1 + \boldsymbol{X}_t^\top A^{-1}\boldsymbol{X}_t}\right) S_{i,t-1}S_{i,t-1}^\top \left(A^{-1} - \frac{A^{-1}\boldsymbol{X}_t\boldsymbol{X}_t^\top A^{-1}}{1 + \boldsymbol{X}_t^\top A^{-1}\boldsymbol{X}_t}\right)\boldsymbol{X}_t\end{aligned}$$

(by the Sherman-Morrison formula)

$$
\begin{aligned}
&= H^\top H - \frac{r}{1+r} H^\top H - \frac{r}{1+r} H^\top H + \frac{r^2}{(1+r)^2} H^\top H \\
&= \frac{H^\top H}{(1+r)^2} = \frac{\boldsymbol{X}_t^\top A^{-1} S_{i,t-1} S_{i,t-1}^\top A^{-1} \boldsymbol{X}_t}{\left(1 + \boldsymbol{X}_t^\top A^{-1} \boldsymbol{X}_t\right)^2} \\
&\le \frac{||A^{-1/2} \boldsymbol{X}_t||\, ||A^{-1/2} S_{i,t-1} S_{i,t-1}^\top A^{-1/2}||\, ||\boldsymbol{X}_t^\top A^{-1/2}||}{\left(1 + \boldsymbol{X}_t^\top A^{-1} \boldsymbol{X}_t\right)^2} \\
&= \frac{r}{(1+r)^2} \, ||A^{-1/2} S_{i,t-1} S_{i,t-1}^\top A^{-1/2}|| \, . \qquad (13)
\end{aligned}
$$

We continue by bounding the two factors in (13). Observe that

$$
r = \boldsymbol{X}_t^\top A^{-1} \boldsymbol{X}_t \le ||A^{-1}|| = \frac{1}{1 + \hat{\lambda}_{i,t-1}} \le 1
$$

and that the function $f(x) = x/(1+x)^2$ is monotonically increasing when $x \in [0,1]$. Hence

$$
\frac{r}{(1+r)^2} = f(r) \le f\left(\frac{1}{1+\hat{\lambda}_{i,t-1}}\right) = \frac{1+\hat{\lambda}_{i,t-1}}{(2+\hat{\lambda}_{i,t-1})^2} \le \frac{1}{2+\hat{\lambda}_{i,t-1}} \, .
$$

As far as the second factor is concerned, we just note that the two matrices $A^{-1/2}$ and $S_{i,t-1} S_{i,t-1}^\top$ have the same eigenvectors. Therefore

$$
\left\| A^{-1/2} S_{i,t-1} S_{i,t-1}^\top A^{-1/2} \right\| = \frac{\hat{\lambda}}{1+\hat{\lambda}} \le 1 \, ,
$$

where $\hat{\lambda}$ is *some* eigenvalue of $S_{i,t-1} S_{i,t-1}^\top$. Substituting into (13) yields

$$
||\boldsymbol{Z}||^2 \le \frac{1}{2+\hat{\lambda}_{i,t-1}} \, ,
$$

as desired. □

Online Geometric Optimization in the Bandit Setting Against an Adaptive Adversary

H. Brendan McMahan and Avrim Blum

Carnegie Mellon University, Pittsburgh, PA, 15213,
{mcmahan,avrim}@cs.cmu.edu

Abstract. We give an algorithm for the bandit version of a very general online optimization problem considered by Kalai and Vempala [1], for the case of an adaptive adversary. In this problem we are given a bounded set $S \subseteq \mathbb{R}^n$ of feasible points. At each time step t, the online algorithm must select a point $\mathbf{x}^t \in S$ while simultaneously an adversary selects a cost vector $\mathbf{c}^t \in \mathbb{R}^n$. The algorithm then incurs cost $\mathbf{c}^t \cdot \mathbf{x}^t$. Kalai and Vempala show that even if S is exponentially large (or infinite), so long as we have an efficient algorithm for the *offline* problem (given $\mathbf{c} \in \mathbb{R}^n$, find $\mathbf{x} \in S$ to minimize $\mathbf{c} \cdot \mathbf{x}$) and so long as the cost vectors are bounded, one can efficiently solve the *online* problem of performing nearly as well as the best fixed $\mathbf{x} \in S$ in hindsight. The Kalai-Vempala algorithm assumes that the cost vectors $\mathbf{c}^t$ are given to the algorithm after each time step. In the "bandit" version of the problem, the algorithm only observes its cost, $\mathbf{c}^t \cdot \mathbf{x}^t$. Awerbuch and Kleinberg [2] give an algorithm for the bandit version for the case of an oblivious adversary, and an algorithm that works against an adaptive adversary for the special case of the shortest path problem. They leave open the problem of handling an adaptive adversary in the general case. In this paper, we solve this open problem, giving a simple online algorithm for the bandit problem in the general case in the presence of an adaptive adversary. Ignoring a (polynomial) dependence on n, we achieve a regret bound of $\mathcal{O}(T^{3/4}\sqrt{\ln(T)})$.

1 Introduction

Kalai and Vempala [1] give an elegant, efficient algorithm for a broad class of online optimization problems. In their setting, we have an arbitrary (bounded) set $S \subseteq \mathbb{R}^n$ of feasible points. At each time step t, an online algorithm $\mathcal{A}$ must select a point $\mathbf{x}^t \in S$ and simultaneously an adversary selects a cost vector $\mathbf{c}^t \in \mathbb{R}^n$ (throughout the paper we use superscripts to index iterations). The algorithm then observes $\mathbf{c}^t$ and incurs cost $\mathbf{c}^t \cdot \mathbf{x}^t$. Kalai and Vempala show that so long as we have an efficient algorithm for the *offline* problem (given $\mathbf{c} \in \mathbb{R}^n$ find $\mathbf{x} \in S$ to minimize $\mathbf{c} \cdot \mathbf{x}$) and so long as the cost vectors are bounded, we can efficiently solve the *online* problem of performing nearly as well as the best fixed $\mathbf{x} \in S$ in hindsight. This generalizes the classic "expert advice" problem, because we do not require the set S to be represented explicitly: we just need an efficient oracle for selecting the best $\mathbf{x} \in S$ in hindsight. Further, it decouples the number

J. Shawe-Taylor and Y. Singer (Eds.): COLT 2004, LNAI 3120, pp. 109–123, 2004.

of experts from the underlying dimensionality n of the decision set, under the assumption the cost of a decision is a linear function of n features of the decision. The standard experts setting can be recovered by letting $S = \{\mathbf{e}_1, \ldots, \mathbf{e}_n\}$, the columns of the $n \times n$ identity matrix.

A problem that fits naturally into this framework is an online shortest path problem where we repeatedly travel between two points a and b in some graph whose edge costs change each day (say, due to traffic). In this case, we can view the set of paths as a set S of points in a space of dimension equal to the number of edges in the graph, and $\mathbf{c}^t$ is simply the vector of edge costs on day t. Even though the number of paths in a graph can be exponential in the number of edges (i.e., the set S is of exponential size), since we can solve the shortest path problem for any *given* set of edge lengths, we can apply the Kalai-Vempala algorithm. (Note that a different algorithm for the special case of the online shortest path problem is given by Takimoto and Warmuth [3].)

A natural generalization of the above problem, considered by Awerbuch and Kleinberg [2], is to imagine that rather than being given the entire cost vector $\mathbf{c}^t$, the algorithm is simply told the cost incurred $\mathbf{c}^t \cdot \mathbf{x}^t$. For example, in the case of shortest paths, rather than being told the lengths of all edges at time t, this would correspond to just being told the total time taken to reach the destination. Thus, this is the "bandit version" of the Kalai-Vempala setting. Awerbuch and Kleinberg present two results: an algorithm for the general problem in the presence of an *oblivious* adversary, and an algorithm for the special case of the shortest path problem that works in the presence of an *adaptive* adversary. The difference between the two adversaries is that an oblivious adversary must commit to the entire sequence of cost vectors in advance, whereas an adaptive adversary may determine the next cost vector based on the online algorithm's play (and hence, the information the algorithm received) in the previous time steps. Thus, an adaptive adversary is in essence playing a repeated game. They leave open the question of achieving good regret guarantees for an adaptive adversary in the general setting.

In this paper we solve the open question of [2], giving an algorithm for the general bandit setting in the presence of an adaptive adversary. Moreover, our method is significantly simpler than the special-purpose algorithm of Awerbuch and Kleinberg for shortest paths. Our bounds are somewhat worse: we achieve regret bounds of $\mathcal{O}(T^{3/4}\sqrt{\ln T})$ compared to the $\mathcal{O}(T^{2/3})$ bounds of [2]. We believe improvement in this direction may be possible, and present some discussion of this issue at the end of the paper.

The basic idea of our approach is as follows. We begin by noticing that the only history information used by the Kalai-Vempala algorithm in determining its action at time t is the sum $\mathbf{c}^{1:t-1} = \sum_{\tau=1}^{t-1} \mathbf{c}^\tau$ of all cost vectors received so far (we use this abbreviated notation for sums over iteration indexes throughout the paper). Furthermore, the way this is used in the algorithm is by adding random noise $\boldsymbol{\mu}$ to this vector, and then calling the offline oracle to find the $\mathbf{x}^t \in S$ that minimizes $(\mathbf{c}^{1:t-1} + \boldsymbol{\mu}) \cdot \mathbf{x}^t$. So, if we can design a bandit algorithm that produces an estimate $\hat{\mathbf{c}}^{1:t-1}$ of $\mathbf{c}^{1:t-1}$, and show that with high probability even an adaptive adversary will not cause $\hat{\mathbf{c}}^{1:t-1}$ to differ too substantially from $\mathbf{c}^{1:t-1}$, we can then argue that the distribution $\hat{\mathbf{c}}^{1:t-1} + \boldsymbol{\mu}$ is close enough to $\mathbf{c}^{1:t-1} + \boldsymbol{\mu}$ for the Kalai-Vempala analysis to apply. In fact, to make our analysis a bit more general, so that we could potentially use other algorithms as subroutines, we will argue a little differently. Let $\text{OPT}(\mathbf{c}) = \min_{\mathbf{x} \in S}(\mathbf{c} \cdot \mathbf{x})$. We will show that with high probability, $\text{OPT}(\hat{\mathbf{c}}^{1:T})$ is close to $\text{OPT}(\mathbf{c}^{1:T})$ and $\hat{\mathbf{c}}^{1:T}$ satisfies conditions needed for the subroutine to achieve low regret on $\hat{\mathbf{c}}^{1:T}$. This means that our subroutine, which believes it has seen $\hat{\mathbf{c}}^{1:T}$, will achieve performance on $\hat{\mathbf{c}}^{1:T}$ close to $\text{OPT}(\mathbf{c}^{1:T})$. We then finish off by arguing that our performance on $\mathbf{c}^{1:T}$ is close to its performance on $\hat{\mathbf{c}}^{1:T}$.

The behavior of the bandit algorithm will in fact be fairly simple. We begin by choosing a basis B of (at most) n points in S to use for sampling (we address the issue of how B is chosen when we describe our algorithm in detail). Then, at each time step t, with probability γ we *explore* by playing a random basis element, and otherwise (with probability $1 - \gamma$) we *exploit* by playing according to the Kalai-Vempala algorithm. For each basis element $\mathbf{b}_j$, we use our cost incurred while exploring with that basis element, scaled by n/γ, as an estimate of $\mathbf{c}^{1:t-1} \cdot \mathbf{b}_j$. Using martingale tail inequalities, we argue that even an adaptive adversary cannot make our estimate differ too wildly from the true value of $\mathbf{c}^{1:t-1} \cdot \mathbf{b}_j$, and use this to show that after matrix inversion, our estimate $\hat{\mathbf{c}}^{1:t-1}$ is close to its correct value with high probability.

2 Problem Formalization

We can now fully formalize the problem. First, however, we establish a few notational conventions. As mentioned previously, we use superscripts to index iterations (or rounds) of our algorithm, and use the abbreviated summation notation $\mathbf{c}^{1:t}$ when summing variables over iterations. Vectors quantities are indicated in bold, and subscripts index into vectors or sets. Hats (such as $\hat{\mathbf{c}}^t$) denote estimates of the corresponding actual quantities. The variables and constants used in the paper are summarized in Table (1).

As mentioned above, we consider the setting of [1] in which we have an arbitrary (bounded) set $S \subseteq \mathbb{R}^n$ of feasible points. At each time step t, the online algorithm $\mathcal{A}$ must select a point $\mathbf{x}^t \in S$ and simultaneously an adversary selects a cost vector $\mathbf{c}^t \in \mathbb{R}^n$. The algorithm then incurs cost $\mathbf{c}^t \cdot \mathbf{x}^t$. Unlike [1], however, rather than being told $\mathbf{c}^t$, the algorithm simply learns its cost $\mathbf{c}^t \cdot \mathbf{x}^t$.

For simplicity, we assume a fixed adaptive adversary $\mathcal{V}$ and time horizon T for the duration of this paper. Since our choice of algorithm parameters depends on T, we assume[1] T is known to the algorithm. We refer to the sequence of decisions made by the algorithm so far as a decision history, which can be written $h^t = [\mathbf{x}^1, \ldots, \mathbf{x}^t]$. Let H^* be the set of all possible decision histories of length 0 through $T - 1$. Without loss of generality (e.g., see [5]), we assume our adaptive adversary is deterministic, as specified by a function $\mathcal{V} : H^* \to \mathbb{R}^n$, a mapping

[1] One can remove this requirement by guessing T, and doubling the guess each time we play longer than expected (see, for example, Theorem 6.4 from [4]).

from decision histories to cost vectors. Thus, $\mathcal{V}(h^{t-1}) = \mathbf{c}^t$ is the cost vector for timestep t.

We can view our online decision problem as a game, where on each iteration t the adversary $\mathcal{V}$ selects a new cost vector $\mathbf{c}^t$ based on h^{t-1}, and the online algorithm $\mathcal{A}$ selects a decision $\mathbf{x} \in S$ based on its past plays and observations, and possibly additional hidden state or randomness. Then, $\mathcal{A}$ pays $\mathbf{c}^t \cdot \mathbf{x}^t$ and observes this cost. For our analysis, we assume a L_1 bound on S, namely $\|\mathbf{x}\|_1 \leq D/2$ for all $\mathbf{x} \in S$, so $\|\mathbf{x} - \mathbf{y}\|_1 \leq D$ for all $\mathbf{x}, \mathbf{y} \in S$. We also assume that $|\mathbf{c} \cdot \mathbf{x}| \leq M$ for all $\mathbf{x} \in S$ and all $\mathbf{c}$ played by $\mathcal{V}$. We also assume S is full rank, if it is not we simply project to a lower-dimensional representation. Some of these assumptions can be lifted or modified, but this set of assumptions simplifies the analysis.

For a fixed decision history h^T and cost history $k^T = (\mathbf{c}^1, \ldots, \mathbf{c}^T)$, we define $\text{loss}(h^T, k^T) = \sum_{t=1}^{T}(\mathbf{c}^t \cdot \mathbf{x}^t)$. For a randomized algorithm $\mathcal{A}$ and adversary $\mathcal{V}$, we define the random variable $\text{loss}(\mathcal{A}, \mathcal{V})$ to be $\text{loss}(h^T, k^T)$, where h^T is drawn from the distribution over histories defined by $\mathcal{A}$ and $\mathcal{V}$, and $k^T = (\mathcal{V}(h^0), \ldots, \mathcal{V}(h^{T-1}))$. When it is clear from context, we will omit the dependence on $\mathcal{V}$, writing only $\text{loss}(\mathcal{A})$.

Our goal is to define an online algorithm with low regret. That is, we want a guarantee that the total loss incurred will, in expectation, not be much larger than the optimal strategy in hindsight against the cost sequence we actually faced. To formalize this, first define an oracle $\mathcal{R} : \mathbb{R}^n \to S$ that solves the offline optimization problem, $\mathcal{R}(\mathbf{c}) = \text{argmin}_{\mathbf{x} \in S}(\mathbf{c} \cdot \mathbf{x})$. We then define $\text{OPT}(k^T) = \mathbf{c}^{1:T} \cdot \mathcal{R}(\mathbf{c}^{1:T})$. Similarly, $\text{OPT}(\mathcal{V}, \mathcal{A})$ is the random variable $\text{OPT}(k^T)$ when k^T is generated by playing $\mathcal{V}$ against $\mathcal{A}$. We again drop the dependence on $\mathcal{V}$ and $\mathcal{A}$ when it is clear from context. Formally, we define expected regret as

$$E\left[\text{loss}(\mathcal{A}, \mathcal{V}) - \text{OPT}(\mathcal{A}, \mathcal{V})\right] = E[\text{loss}(\mathcal{A}, \mathcal{V})] - E\left[\min_{\mathbf{x} \in S} \sum_{t=1}^{T} (\mathbf{c}^t \cdot \mathbf{x})\right]. \quad (1)$$

Note that the $E[\text{OPT}(\mathcal{V}, \mathcal{A})]$ term corresponds to applying the min operator separately to each possible cost history to find the best fixed decision with respect to that particular cost history, and then taking the expectation with respect to these histories. In [5], an alternative weaker definition of regret is given. We discuss relationships between the definitions in Appendix B.

3 Algorithm

We introduce an algorithm we call BGA, standing for *Bandit-style Geometric decision algorithm against an Adaptive adversary*. The algorithm alternates between playing decisions from a fixed basis to get unbiased estimates of costs, and playing (hopefully) good decisions based on those estimates. In order to determine the good decisions to play, it uses some online geometric optimization algorithm for the full observation problem. We denote this algorithm by GEX (*Geometric Experts algorithm*). The implementation of GEX we analyze is based on the FPL algorithm of Kalai and Vempala [1]; we detail this implementation

```
Choose parameters γ and ϵ, where ϵ is a parameter of GEX
t = 1
Fix a basis B = {b_1, ..., b_n} ⊆ S
while playing do
  Let χ^t = 1 with probability γ and χ^t = 0 otherwise
  if χ^t = 0 then
    Select x^t from the distribution GEX(ĉ^1, ..., ĉ^{t-1})
    Incur cost z^t = c^t · x^t
    ĉ^t = 0 ∈ R^n
  else
    Draw j uniformly at random from {1, ..., n}
    x^t = b_j
    Incur cost and observe z^t = c^t · x^t
    Define ℓ̂^t by ℓ̂^t_i = 0 for i ≠ j and ℓ̂^t_j = (n/γ)z^t
    ĉ^t = (B^†)^{-1} ℓ̂^t
  end if
  ĉ^{1:t} = ĉ^{1:t-1} + ĉ^t
  t = t + 1
end while
```

Algorithm 1: BGA

and analysis in Appendix A. However, other algorithms could be used, for example the algorithm of Zinkevich [6] when S is convex. We view GEX as a function from the sequence of previous cost vectors $(\hat{\mathbf{c}}^1, \dots, \hat{\mathbf{c}}^{t-1})$ to distributions over decisions.

Pseudocode for our algorithm is given in Algorithm (1). On each timestep, we make decision $\mathbf{x}^t$. With probability $(1-\gamma)$, BGA plays a recommendation $\mathbf{x}^t = \tilde{\mathbf{x}}^t \in S$ from GEX. With probability γ, we ignore $\tilde{\mathbf{x}}^t$ and play a basis decision, $\mathbf{x}^t = \mathbf{b}_i$ uniformly at random from a sampling basis $B = \{\mathbf{b}_1, \dots, \mathbf{b}_n\}$. The indicator variable χ^t is 1 on exploration iterations and 0 otherwise.

Our sampling basis B is a $n \times n$ matrix with columns $\mathbf{b}_i \in S$, so we can write $\mathbf{x} = B\mathbf{w}$ for any $\mathbf{x} \in \mathbb{R}^n$ and weights $\mathbf{w} \in \mathbb{R}^n$. For a given cost vector $\mathbf{c}$, let $\boldsymbol{\ell} = B^\dagger \mathbf{c}$ (the superscript $\dagger$ indicates transpose). This is the vector of decision costs for the basis decisions, so $\ell^t_i = \mathbf{c}^t \cdot \mathbf{b}_i$. We define $\hat{\boldsymbol{\ell}}^t$, an estimate of $\boldsymbol{\ell}^t$, as follows: Let $\hat{\boldsymbol{\ell}}^t = 0 \in \mathbb{R}^n$ on exploitation iterations. If on an exploration iteration we play $\mathbf{b}_j$, then $\hat{\boldsymbol{\ell}}^t$ is the vector where $\hat{\ell}^t_i = 0$ for $i \neq j$ and $\hat{\ell}^t_j = \frac{n}{\gamma}(\mathbf{c}^t \cdot \mathbf{b}_j)$. Note that $\mathbf{c}^t \cdot \mathbf{b}_j$ is the observed quantity, the cost of basis decision $\mathbf{b}_j$. On each iteration, we estimate $\mathbf{c}^t$ by $\hat{\mathbf{c}}^t = (B^\dagger)^{-1}\hat{\boldsymbol{\ell}}^t$. It is straightforward to show that $\hat{\boldsymbol{\ell}}^t$ is an unbiased estimate of basis decision costs and that $\hat{\mathbf{c}}^t$ is an unbiased estimate of $\mathbf{c}^t$ on each timestep t.

The choice of the sampling basis plays an important role in the analysis of our algorithm. In particular, we use a baricentric spanner, introduced in [2]. A baricentric spanner $B = \{\mathbf{b}_1, \dots, \mathbf{b}_n\}$ is a basis for S such that $\mathbf{b}_i \in S$ and for all $\mathbf{x} \in S$ we can write $\mathbf{x} = B\mathbf{w}$ with coefficients $w_i \in [-1, 1]$. It may not be easy to find exact baricentric spanners in all cases, but [2] proves they always exist and gives an algorithm for finding 2-approximate baricentric spanners (where the weights $w_i \in [-2, 2]$), which is sufficient for our purposes.

Table 1. Summary of notation

$S \subseteq \mathbb{R}^n$	set of decisions, a compact subset of $\mathbb{R}^n$
$D \in \mathbb{R}$	L_1 bound on diameter of S, $\forall \mathbf{x}, \mathbf{y} \in S$, $\lvert \mathbf{x} - \mathbf{y} \rvert_1 \leq D$
$n \in N$	dimension of decision space
h^t	decision history , $h^t = \mathbf{x}^1, \ldots, \mathbf{x}^t$
H^*	set of possible decision histories
$\mathcal{V} : H^* \to \mathbb{R}^n$	adversary, function from decision histories to cost vectors
$\mathcal{A}$	an online optimization algorithm
G^{t-1}	history of BGA randomness for timesteps 1 through $t-1$
$\mathbf{c}^t \in \mathbb{R}^n$	cost vector on time t
$\hat{\mathbf{c}}^t \in \mathbb{R}^n$	BGA's estimate of the cost vector on time t
$M \in \mathbb{R}^+$	bound on single-iteration cost, $\lvert \mathbf{c}^t \cdot \mathbf{x}^t \rvert \leq M$
$B \subseteq S$	sampling basis $B = \{\mathbf{b}_1, \ldots, \mathbf{b}_n\}$
$\beta_\infty \in \mathbb{R}$	matrix max norm on $(B^\dagger)^{-1}$
$\boldsymbol{\ell}^t \in [-M, M]^n$	vector, $\ell_i^t = \mathbf{c}^t \cdot \mathbf{b}_i$ for $\mathbf{b}_i \in B$
$\hat{\boldsymbol{\ell}}^t \in \mathbb{R}^n$	BGA's estimate of $\boldsymbol{\ell}^t$
$T \in \mathbb{N}$	end of time, index of final iteration
$\mathbf{x}^t \in S$	BGA's decision on time t
$\tilde{\mathbf{x}}^t \in S$	decision recommended by GEX on time t
$\chi^t \in \{0, 1\}$	indicator, $\chi^t = 1$ if BGA explores on t, 0 otherwise
$\gamma \in [0, 1]$	the probability BGA explores on each timestep
$z^t \in [-M, M]$	BGA's loss on iteration t, $z^t = \mathbf{c}^t \cdot \mathbf{x}^t$,
$\hat{z}^t \in [-R, R]$	loss of GEX, $\hat{z}^t = \hat{\mathbf{c}}^t \cdot \tilde{\mathbf{x}}^t$

4 Analysis

4.1 Preliminaries

At each time step, BGA either (with probability $1-\gamma$) plays the recommendation $\tilde{\mathbf{x}}^t$ from GEX, or else (with probability γ) plays a random basis vector from B. For purposes of analysis, however, it will be convenient to imagine that we request a recommendation $\tilde{\mathbf{x}}^t$ from GEX on every iteration, and also that we randomly pick a basis to explore, $\mathbf{b}^t \in \{\mathbf{b}_1, \ldots, \mathbf{b}_n\}$, on each iteration. We then decide to play either $\tilde{\mathbf{x}}^t$ or $\mathbf{b}^t$ based on the outcome χ^t of a coin of bias γ. Thus, the complete history of the algorithm is specified by the *algorithm history* $G^{t-1} = [\chi^1, \tilde{\mathbf{x}}^1, \mathbf{b}^1, \chi^2, \tilde{\mathbf{x}}^2, \mathbf{b}^2, \ldots, \chi^{t-1}, \tilde{\mathbf{x}}^{t-1}, \mathbf{b}^{t-1}]$, which encodes all previous random choices. The sample space for all probabilities and expectations is the set of all possible algorithm histories of length T. Thus, for a given adversary $\mathcal{V}$, the various random variables and vectors we consider, such as $\mathbf{x}^t, \mathbf{c}^t, \hat{\mathbf{c}}^t, \tilde{\mathbf{x}}^t$, and others, can all be viewed as functions on the set of possible algorithm histories. Unless otherwise stated, our expectations and probabilities are with respect to the distribution over these histories.

A partial history G^{t-1} can be viewed a subset of the sample space (an event) consisting of all complete histories that have G^{t-1} as a prefix. We frequently consider conditional distributions and corresponding expectations with respect to partial algorithm histories. For instance, if we condition on a history G^{t-1}, the random variables $\mathbf{c}^1, \ldots, \mathbf{c}^t, \boldsymbol{\ell}^1, \ldots, \boldsymbol{\ell}^t, \hat{\boldsymbol{\ell}}^1, \ldots, \hat{\boldsymbol{\ell}}^{t-1}, \hat{\mathbf{c}}^1, \ldots \hat{\mathbf{c}}^{t-1}, \mathbf{x}^1, \ldots, \mathbf{x}^{t-1}$, and $\chi^1, \ldots, \chi^{t-1}$ are fully determined.

We now outline the general structure of our argument. Let $\hat{z}^t = \hat{\mathbf{c}}^t \cdot \tilde{\mathbf{x}}^t$ be the loss perceived by the GEX on iteration t. In keeping with earlier definitions, $\text{loss(BGA)} = z^{1:T}$ and $\text{loss(GEX)} = \hat{z}^{1:T}$. We also let $\text{OPT} = \text{OPT}(\text{BGA}, \mathcal{V}) = \mathbf{c}^{1:T} \cdot \mathcal{R}(\mathbf{c}^{1:T})$, the performance of the best post-hoc decision, and similarly $\widehat{\text{OPT}} = \text{OPT}(\hat{\mathbf{c}}^1, \ldots, \hat{\mathbf{c}}^T) = \hat{\mathbf{c}}^{1:t} \cdot \mathcal{R}(\hat{\mathbf{c}}^{1:t})$.

The base of our analysis is a bound on the loss of GEX with respect to the cost vectors $\hat{\mathbf{c}}^t$ of the form

$$E[\text{loss(GEX)}] \leq E[\widehat{\text{OPT}}] + (\text{terms}). \tag{2}$$

Such a result is given in Appendix A, and follows from an adaptation of the analysis from [1]. We then prove statements having the general form

$$E[\text{loss(BGA)}] \leq E[\text{loss(GEX)}] + (\text{terms}) \tag{3}$$

and

$$E[\widehat{\text{OPT}}] \leq E[\text{OPT}] + (\text{terms}). \tag{4}$$

These statements connect our real loss to the "imaginary" loss of GEX, and similarly connect the loss of the best decision in GEX's imagined world with the loss of the best decision in the real world. Combining the results corresponding to Equations (2), (3), and (4) leads to an overall bound on the regret of BGA.

4.2 High Probability Bounds on Estimates

We prove a bound on the accuracy of BGA's estimates $\hat{\boldsymbol{\ell}}^t$, and use this to show a relationship between OPT and $\widehat{\text{OPT}}$ of the form in Equation 4.

Define random variables $\mathbf{e}^0 = \mathbf{0}$ and $\mathbf{e}^t = \boldsymbol{\ell}^t - \hat{\boldsymbol{\ell}}^t$. We are really interested in the corresponding sums $\mathbf{e}^{1:t}$, where $e_i^{1:t}$ is the total error in our estimate of $\mathbf{c}^{1:t} \cdot \mathbf{b}_i$. We now bound $|e_i^{1:t}|$.

Theorem 1. *For $\lambda > 0$,*

$$\Pr\left[|e_i^{1:t}| \geq \lambda \frac{nM}{\gamma}\sqrt{t}\right] \leq 2e^{-\lambda^2/2}.$$

Proof. It is sufficient to show the sequence $\mathbf{e}^0, \mathbf{e}^1, \mathbf{e}^{1:2}, \mathbf{e}^{1:3}, \ldots, \mathbf{e}^{1:T}$ of random variables is a bounded martingale sequence with respect to the filter $G^0, G^1, \ldots, G^T$; that is, $E[e_i^{1:t} \mid G^{t-1}] = e_i^{1:t-1}$. The result then follows from Azuma's Inequality (see, for example,[7]).

First, observe that $e_i^{1:t} = \ell_i^t - \hat{\ell}_i^t + e_i^{1:t-1}$. Further, the cost vector $\mathbf{c}^t$ is determined if we know G^{t-1}, and so ℓ_i^t is also fixed. Thus, accounting for the $\frac{\gamma}{n}$ probability we explore a particular basis decision $\mathbf{b}_i$, we have

$$E\left[e_i^{1:t} \mid G^{t-1}\right] = \frac{\gamma}{n}\left[\ell_i^t - \frac{n}{\gamma}\ell_i^t + e_i^{1:t-1}\right] + \left(1 - \frac{\gamma}{n}\right)\left[\ell_i^t - 0 + e_i^{1:t-1}\right] = e_i^{1:t-1},$$

and so we conclude that the $e_i^{1:t}$ forms a martingale sequence. Notice that $|e_i^{1:t} - e_i^{1:t-1}| = |\ell_i^t - \hat{\ell}_i^t|$. If we don't sample, $\hat{\ell}_i^t = 0$ and so $|e_i^{1:t} - e_i^{1:t-1}| \leq M$. If we do sample, we have $\hat{\ell}_i^t = \frac{n}{\gamma}\ell_i^t$, and so $|e_i^{1:t} - e_i^{1:t-1}| \leq \frac{nM}{\gamma}$. This bound is worse, so it holds in both cases. The result now follows from Azuma's inequality. □

Let $\beta_\infty = \|(B^\dagger)^{-1}\|_\infty$, a matrix L_∞-norm on $(B^\dagger)^{-1}$, so that for any $\mathbf{w}$, $\|(B^\dagger)^{-1}\mathbf{w}\|_\infty \leq \beta_\infty \|\mathbf{w}\|_\infty$.

Corollary 1. *For $\delta \in (0, 1]$, and all t from 1 to T,*

$$\Pr\left[\|\hat{\mathbf{c}}^{1:t} - \mathbf{c}^{1:t}\|_\infty \geq \beta_\infty J(\delta, \gamma)\sqrt{t}\right] \leq \delta.$$

where $J(\delta, \gamma) = \frac{1}{\gamma} nM\sqrt{2\ln(2n/\delta)}$.

Proof. Solving $\delta/n = 2e^{-\lambda^2/2}$ yields $\lambda = \sqrt{2\ln(2n/\delta)}$, and then using this value in Theorem (1) gives

$$\Pr\left[|e_i^{1:t}| \geq J(\delta, \gamma)\sqrt{t}\right] \leq \delta/n.$$

for all $i \in \{1, 2, \ldots, n\}$. Then,

$$\begin{aligned}\Pr\left[\ \|\mathbf{e}^{1:t}\|_\infty \geq J(\delta, \gamma)\sqrt{t}\right] &\leq \sum_{i=1}^{n} \Pr\left[|e_i^{1:t}| \geq J(\delta, \gamma)\sqrt{t}\right] \\ &\leq \delta\end{aligned}$$

by the union bound. Now, notice that we can relate $\hat{\boldsymbol{\ell}}^{1:t}$ and $\hat{\mathbf{c}}^{1:t}$ by

$$(B^\dagger)^{-1}\hat{\boldsymbol{\ell}}^{1:t} = (B^\dagger)^{-1}\sum_{\tau=1}^{t} \boldsymbol{\ell}^\tau = \sum_{\tau=1}^{t}(B^\dagger)^{-1}\boldsymbol{\ell}^\tau = \sum_{\tau=1}^{t} \hat{\mathbf{c}}^\tau = \hat{\mathbf{c}}^{1:t}.$$

and similarly for $\boldsymbol{\ell}^{1:t}$ and $\mathbf{c}^{1:t}$. Then

$$\begin{aligned}\Pr\left[\|\hat{\mathbf{c}}^{1:t} - \mathbf{c}^{1:t}\|_\infty \geq \beta_\infty J(\delta, \gamma)\sqrt{t}\right] &= \Pr\left[\|(B^\dagger)^{-1}(\hat{\boldsymbol{\ell}}^{1:t} - \boldsymbol{\ell}^{1:t})\|_\infty \geq \beta_\infty J(\delta, \gamma)\sqrt{t}\right] \\ &\leq \Pr\left[\beta_\infty \|\mathbf{e}^{1:t}\|_\infty \geq \beta_\infty J(\delta, \gamma)\sqrt{t}\right] \\ &= \Pr\left[\|\mathbf{e}^{1:t}\|_\infty \geq J(\delta, \gamma)\sqrt{t}\right] \\ &\leq \delta.\end{aligned}$$

□

We can now prove our main result for the section, a statement of the form of Equation (4) relating OPT and $\widehat{\mathrm{OPT}}$:

Theorem 2. *If we play $\mathcal{V}$ against* BGA *for T timesteps,*

$$E[\widehat{\mathrm{OPT}}] \leq E[\mathrm{OPT}] + (1-\delta)\left(\frac{3}{2}D\beta_\infty J(\delta,\gamma)\sqrt{T}\right) + \delta MT.$$

Proof. Let $\Phi = \hat{\mathbf{c}}^{1:T} - \mathbf{c}^{1:T}$. By definition of $\mathcal{R}$, $\mathcal{R}(\hat{\mathbf{c}}^{1:T}) \cdot \hat{\mathbf{c}}^{1:T} \leq \mathcal{R}(\mathbf{c}^{1:T}) \cdot \hat{\mathbf{c}}^{1:T}$ or equivalently $\mathcal{R}(\mathbf{c}^{1:T} + \Phi) \cdot (\mathbf{c}^{1:T} + \Phi) \leq \mathcal{R}(\mathbf{c}^{1:T}) \cdot (\mathbf{c}^{1:T} + \Phi)$, and so by expanding and rearranging we have

$$\begin{aligned}\mathcal{R}(\mathbf{c}^{1:T} + \Phi) \cdot \mathbf{c}^{1:T} - \mathcal{R}(\mathbf{c}^{1:T}) \cdot \mathbf{c}^{1:T} &\leq (\mathcal{R}(\mathbf{c}^{1:T}) - \mathcal{R}(\mathbf{c}^{1:T} + \Phi)) \cdot \Phi \\ &\leq D\|\Phi\|_\infty. \end{aligned} \tag{5}$$

Then,

$$\begin{aligned}|\,\mathrm{OPT} - \widehat{\mathrm{OPT}}| &= |\mathcal{R}(\mathbf{c}^{1:T}) \cdot \mathbf{c}^{1:T} - \mathcal{R}(\mathbf{c}^{1:T} + \Phi) \cdot (\mathbf{c}^{1:T} + \Phi)| \\ &\leq |(\mathcal{R}(\mathbf{c}^{1:T}) - \mathcal{R}(\mathbf{c}^{1:T} + \Phi)) \cdot \mathbf{c}^{1:T}| + |\mathcal{R}(\mathbf{c}^{1:T} + \Phi) \cdot \Phi| \\ &\leq (D + D/2)\|\Phi\|_\infty,\end{aligned}$$

where we have used Equation (5). Recall from Section (2), we assume $\|\mathbf{x}\|_1 \leq D/2$ for all $\mathbf{x} \in S$, so $\|\mathbf{x} - \mathbf{y}\|_1 \leq D$ for all $\mathbf{x}, \mathbf{y} \in S$. The theorem follows by applying the bound on Φ given by Corollary (1), and then observing that the above relationship holds for at least a $1 - \delta$ fraction of the possible algorithm histories. For the other δ fraction, the difference might be as much as δMT. Writing the overall expectation as the sum of two expectations conditioned on whether or not the bound holds gives the result. □

4.3 Relating the Loss of BGA and Its GEX Subroutine

Now we prove a statement like Equation (3), relating loss(BGA) to loss(GEX).

Theorem 3. *If we run* BGA *with parameter γ against $\mathcal{V}$ for T timesteps,*

$$E[\mathit{loss}(\mathrm{BGA})] \leq (1-\gamma)E[\mathit{loss}(\mathrm{GEX})] + \gamma MT.$$

Proof. For a given adversary $\mathcal{V}$, G^{t-1} fully determines the sequence of cost vectors given to algorithm GEX. So, we can view GEX as a function from G^{t-1} to probability distributions over S. If we present a cost vector $\hat{\mathbf{c}}$ to GEX, then the expected cost to GEX given history G^{t-1} is $\sum_{\tilde{\mathbf{x}} \in S} \Pr(\tilde{\mathbf{x}} \mid G^{t-1})\ (\hat{\mathbf{c}} \cdot \tilde{\mathbf{x}})$. If we define $\bar{\mathbf{x}}^t = \sum_{\tilde{\mathbf{x}} \in S} \Pr(\tilde{\mathbf{x}} \mid G^{t-1})\, \tilde{\mathbf{x}}$, we can re-write the expected loss of GEX against $\hat{\mathbf{c}}$ as $\hat{\mathbf{c}} \cdot \bar{\mathbf{x}}^t$; that is, we can view GEX as incurring the cost of some convex combination of the possible decisions in expectation. Let $\hat{\boldsymbol{\ell}}^{t,j}$ be $\hat{\boldsymbol{\ell}}^t$ given that we explore by playing basis vector $\mathbf{b}_j$ on time t, and similarly let $\hat{\mathbf{c}}^{t,j} = (B^\dagger)^{-1}\hat{\boldsymbol{\ell}}^{t,j}$. Observe that $\hat{\ell}_i^{t,j} = \frac{n}{\gamma}\ell_i^t$ for $j = i$ and 0 otherwise, and so

$$\sum_{j=1}^{n} \hat{\boldsymbol{\ell}}^{t,j} = \frac{n}{\gamma}\boldsymbol{\ell}^t = \frac{n}{\gamma}B^\dagger \mathbf{c}^t. \tag{6}$$

Now, we can write

$$\begin{aligned}
E[\hat{z}^t \mid G^{t-1}] &= (1-\gamma)\,0 + \gamma \sum_{j=1}^{n} \frac{1}{n} \sum_{\tilde{\mathbf{x}}^t \in S} \Pr(\tilde{\mathbf{x}}^t \mid G^{t-1})\ (\hat{\mathbf{c}}^{t,j} \cdot \tilde{\mathbf{x}}^t) \\
&= \gamma \left[\sum_{j=1}^{n} \frac{1}{n} \hat{\mathbf{c}}^{t,j} \right] \cdot \bar{\mathbf{x}}^t \\
&= \frac{\gamma}{n}(B^\dagger)^{-1} \left[\sum_{j=1}^{n} \hat{\boldsymbol{\ell}}^{t,j} \right] \cdot \bar{\mathbf{x}}^t, \quad \text{and using Equation (6),} \\
&= \mathbf{c}^t \cdot \bar{\mathbf{x}}^t.
\end{aligned}$$

Now, we consider the conditional expectation of z^t and see that

$$\begin{aligned}
E[z^t \mid G^{t-1}] &= (1-\gamma)(\mathbf{c}^t \cdot \bar{\mathbf{x}}^t) + \gamma \sum_{i=1}^{n} \frac{1}{n}(\mathbf{c}^t \cdot \mathbf{b}_i) \\
&\le (1-\gamma)E[\hat{z}^t \mid G^{t-1}] + \gamma M,
\end{aligned} \tag{7}$$

Then we have,

$$\begin{aligned}
E[z^t] &= E\left[E[z^t \mid G^{t-1}]\right] \\
&\le E\left[(1-\gamma)E[\hat{z}^t \mid G^{t-1}] + \gamma M\right] \\
&= (1-\gamma)E\left[E[\hat{z}^t \mid G^{t-1}]\right] + \gamma M \\
&= (1-\gamma)E[\hat{z}^t] + \gamma M,
\end{aligned} \tag{8}$$

by using the inequality from Equation (7). The theorem follows by summing the inequality (8) over t from 1 to T and applying linearity of expectation. □

4.4 A Bound on the Expected Regret of BGA

Theorem 4. *If we run* BGA *with parameter* γ *using subroutine* GEX *with parameter* ϵ *(as defined in Appendix A), then for all* $\delta \in (0,1]$,

$$\begin{aligned}
&E[\mathit{loss}(\text{BGA})] \\
&\quad \le E[\text{OPT}] + \mathcal{O}\left(D\frac{1}{\gamma}nM\sqrt{2\ln(2n/\delta)}\sqrt{T} + \delta MT + \frac{\epsilon}{\gamma^2}n^3M^2T + \frac{n}{\epsilon} + \gamma MT \right)
\end{aligned}$$

Proof. In Appendix A, we show an algorithm to plug in for GEX, based on the FPL algorithm of [1] and give bounds on regret against a deterministic adaptive adversary. We first show how to apply that analysis to GEX running as a subroutine to BGA.

First, we need to bound $|\hat{\mathbf{c}}^t \cdot \mathbf{x}|$. By definition, for any $\mathbf{x} \in S$, we can write $\mathbf{x} = B\mathbf{w}$ for weights $\mathbf{w}$ with $\mathbf{w}_i \in [-1, 1]$ (or $[-2, 2]$ if it is an approximate baricentric spanner). Note that $\|\hat{\boldsymbol{\ell}}^t\|_1 \leq (\frac{n}{\gamma})M$, and for any $\mathbf{x} \in S$, we can write $\mathbf{x}$ as $B\mathbf{w}$ where $\mathbf{w}_i \in [-2, 2]$. Thus,

$$|\hat{\mathbf{c}}^t \cdot \mathbf{x}| = |(B^\dagger)^{-1}\hat{\boldsymbol{\ell}}^t \cdot B\mathbf{w}| = |(\hat{\boldsymbol{\ell}}^t)^\dagger B^{-1}B\mathbf{w}| = |\hat{\boldsymbol{\ell}}^t \cdot \mathbf{w}| \leq \|\hat{\boldsymbol{\ell}}^t\|_1 \, \|\mathbf{w}\|_\infty \leq \frac{2nM}{\gamma}.$$

Let $R = 2nM/\gamma$. Suppose at the beginning of time we fix the random decisions of BGA that are not made by GEX, that is, we fix a sequence $X = [\chi^1, \mathbf{b}^1, \ldots, \chi^T, \mathbf{b}^T]$. Fixing this randomness together with $\mathcal{V}$ determines a new deterministic adaptive adversary $\hat{\mathcal{V}}$ that GEX is effectively playing against. To see this, let $\tilde{h}^{t-1} = [\tilde{\mathbf{x}}^1, \ldots, \tilde{\mathbf{x}}^{t-1}]$. If we combine $\tilde{h}^{t-1}$ with the information in X, it fully determines a partial history G^{t-1}. If we let $h^{t-1} = [\mathbf{x}^1, \ldots, \mathbf{x}^{t-1}]$ be the partial decision history that can be recovered from G^{t-1}, then $\hat{\mathcal{V}}(\tilde{h}^{t-1}) = \chi^t \frac{d}{\gamma} \mathcal{V}(h^{t-1})$. Thus, when GEX is run as a subroutine of BGA, we can apply Lemma (2) from the Appendix and conclude

$$E[\text{loss(GEX)} \mid X] \leq E[\widehat{\text{OPT}} \mid X] + \epsilon(4n + 2)R^2T + \frac{4n}{\epsilon} \tag{9}$$

For the remainder of this proof, we use big-Oh notation to simplify the presentation. Now, taking the expectation of both sides of Equation (9),

$$E[\text{loss(GEX)}] \leq E[\widehat{\text{OPT}}] + \mathcal{O}\left(\epsilon n R^2 T + \frac{n}{\epsilon}\right)$$

Applying Theorem (3),

$$E[\text{loss(BGA)}] \leq (1 - \gamma)E[\widehat{\text{OPT}}] + \mathcal{O}\left(\epsilon n R^2 T + \frac{n}{\epsilon} + \gamma M T\right)$$

and then using Theorem (2) we have

$$\begin{aligned}
&E[\text{loss(BGA)}] \\
&\quad \leq (1 - \gamma)E[\text{OPT}] + \mathcal{O}\left(J(\delta, \gamma)D\sqrt{T} + \delta M T + \epsilon n R^2 T + \frac{n}{\epsilon} + \gamma M T\right) \\
&\quad \leq E[\text{OPT}] + \mathcal{O}\left(D\frac{1}{\gamma}nM\sqrt{2\ln(2n/\delta)}\sqrt{T} + \delta M T + \frac{\epsilon}{\gamma^2}n^3M^2T + \frac{n}{\epsilon} + \gamma M T\right)
\end{aligned}$$

For the last line, note that while $E[OPT]$ could be negative, it is still bounded by MT, and so this just adds another γMT term, which is captured in the big-Oh term. □

Ignoring the dependence on n, M, and D and simplifying, we see BGA's expected regret is bounded by

$$E[\text{regret(BGA)}] = \mathcal{O}\left(\frac{\sqrt{T}\sqrt{\ln(1/\delta)}}{\gamma} + \delta T + \frac{\epsilon T}{\gamma^2} + \frac{1}{\epsilon} + \gamma T\right).$$

Setting $\gamma = \delta = T^{-1/4}$ and $\epsilon = T^{-3/4}$, we get a bound on our loss of order $\mathcal{O}(T^{3/4}\sqrt{\ln T})$.

5 Conclusions and Open Problems

We have presented a general algorithm for online optimization over an arbitrary set of decisions $S \subseteq \mathbb{R}^n$, and proved regret bounds for our algorithm that hold against an adaptive adversary.

A number of questions are raised by this work. In the "flat" bandits problem, bounds of the form $\mathcal{O}(\sqrt{T})$ are possible against an adaptive adversary [4]. Against a oblivious adversary in the geometric case, a bound of $\mathcal{O}(T^{2/3})$ is achieved in [2]. We achieve a bound of $\mathcal{O}(T^{3/4}\sqrt{\ln T})$ for this problem against an adaptive adversary. In [4], lower bounds are given showing that the $\mathcal{O}(\sqrt{T})$ result is tight, but no such bounds are known for the geometric decision-space problem. Can the $\mathcal{O}(T^{3/4}\sqrt{\ln T})$ and possibly the $\mathcal{O}(T^{2/3})$ bounds be tightened to $\mathcal{O}(\sqrt{T})$? A related issue is the use of information received by the algorithm; our algorithm and the algorithm of [2] only use a γ fraction of the feedback they receive, which is intuitively unappealing. It seems plausible that an algorithm can be found that uses all of the feedback, possibly achieving tighter bounds.

Acknowledgments. The authors wish to thank Geoff Gordon and Bobby Kleinberg for useful conversations and correspondence. Funding provided by NSF grants CCR-0105488, NSF-ITR CCR-0122581, and NSF-ITR IIS-0312814.

References

1. Kalai, A., Vempala, S.: Efficient algorithms for on-line optimization. In: Proceedings of the The 16th Annual Conference on Learning Theory. (2003)
2. Awerbuch, B., Kleinberg, R.: Adaptive routing with end-to-end feedback: Distributed learning and geometric approaches. In: Proceedings of the 36th ACM Symposium on Theory of Computing. (2004) To appear.
3. Takimoto, E., Warmuth, M.K.: Path kernels and multiplicative updates. In: Proceedings of the 15th Annual Conference on Computational Learning Theory. Lecture Notes in Artificial Intelligence, Springer (2002)
4. Auer, P., Cesa-Bianchi, N., Freund, Y., Schapire, R.E.: The nonstochastic multiarmed bandit problem. SIAM Journal on Computing **32** (2002) 48–77
5. Auer, P., Cesa-Bianchi, N., Freund, Y., Schapire, R.E.: Gambling in a rigged casino: the adversarial multi-armed bandit problem. In: Proceedings of the 36th Annual Symposium on Foundations of Computer Science, IEEE Computer Society Press, Los Alamitos, CA (1995) 322–331

6. Zinkevich, M.: Online convex programming and generalized infinitesimal gradient ascent. In: Proceedings of the Twentieth International Conference on Machine Learning. (2003)
7. Motwani, R., Raghavan, P.: Randomized algorithms. Cambridge University Press (1995)
8. Zinkevich, M.: Online convex programming and generalized infinitesimal gradient ascent. Technical Report CMU-CS-03-110, Carnegie Mellon University (2003)

A Specification of a Geometric Experts Algorithm

In this section we point out how the FPL algorithm and analysis of [1] can be adapted to our setting to use as our GEX subroutine, and prove the corresponding bound needed for Theorem (4). In particular, we need a bound for an arbitrary $S \subseteq \mathbb{R}^n$ and arbitrary cost vectors, requiring only that on each timestep, $|\mathbf{c} \cdot \mathbf{x}| \leq R$. Further, the bound must hold against an adaptive adversary.

FPL solves the online optimization problem when the entire cost vector $\mathbf{c}^t$ is observed at each timestep. It maintains the sum $\mathbf{c}^{1:t-1}$, and on each timestep plays decision $\mathbf{x}^t = \mathcal{R}(\mathbf{c}^{1:t-1} + \boldsymbol{\mu})$, where $\boldsymbol{\mu}$ is chosen uniformly at random from $[0, 1/\epsilon]^n$, given ϵ, a parameter of the algorithm. The analysis of FPL in [1] assumes positive cost vectors $\mathbf{c}$ satisfying $\|\mathbf{c}\|_1 \leq A$, and positive decision vectors from $S \subseteq \mathbb{R}^n_+$ with $\|\mathbf{x} - \mathbf{y}\|_1 \leq D$ for all $\mathbf{x}, \mathbf{y} \in S$ and $|\mathbf{c} \cdot \mathbf{x} - \mathbf{c} \cdot \mathbf{y}| \leq R$ for all cost vectors $\mathbf{c}$ and $\mathbf{x}, \mathbf{y} \in S$. Further, the bounds proved are with respect to a fixed series of cost vectors, not an adaptive adversary. We now show how to bridge the gap from these assumptions to our assumptions.

First, we adapt an argument from [2], showing that by using our baricentric spanner basis, we can transform our problem into one where the assumptions of FPL are met. We then argue that a corresponding bound holds against an adaptive adversary.

Lemma 1. *Let $S \subseteq \mathbb{R}^n$ be a set of (not necessarily positive) decisions, and $k^t = [\mathbf{c}^1, \ldots, \mathbf{c}^T]$ a set of cost vectors on those decisions, such that $|\mathbf{c}^t \cdot \mathbf{x}| \leq R$ for all $\mathbf{x} \in S$ and $\mathbf{c}^t \in k^t$. Then, there is an algorithm $\mathcal{A}(\epsilon)$ that achieves*

$$E[\text{loss}(\mathcal{A}(\epsilon), k^t)] \leq \text{OPT}(k^t) + \epsilon(4n+2)R^2T + \frac{4n}{\epsilon}$$

Proof. This an adaptation of the arguments of Appendix A of [2]. Fix a baricentric spanner $B = \{\mathbf{b}_1, \ldots, \mathbf{b}_n\}$ for S. Then, for each $\mathbf{x} \in S$, let $\mathbf{x} = B\mathbf{w}$ and define $f(\mathbf{x}) = [-\sum_{i=1}^n \mathbf{w}_i, \mathbf{w}_1, \ldots, \mathbf{w}_n]$. Let $f(S) = S'$. For each cost vector $\mathbf{c}^t$ define $g(\mathbf{c}^t) = [R,\ R + \mathbf{c}^t \cdot \mathbf{b}_1,\ \ldots,\ R + \mathbf{c}^t \cdot \mathbf{b}_n]$. It is straightforward to verify that $\mathbf{c}^t \cdot \mathbf{x} = g(\mathbf{c}^t) \cdot f(\mathbf{x})$, and further $g(\mathbf{c}^t) \geq 0$, $\|g(\mathbf{c}^t)\|_1 \leq (2n+1)R$, and the difference in cost of any two decisions against a fixed $g(\mathbf{c}^t)$ is at most $2R$. By definition of a baricentric spanner, $\mathbf{w}_i \in [-1, 1]$ and so the L_1 diameter of S' is at most $4n$. Note the assumption of positive decision vectors in Theorem 1 of [1] can easily be lifted by additively shifting the space of decision vectors until it is positive. This changes the loss of the algorithm and of the best decision by the same amount, so additive regret bounds are unchanged. The result of this lemma then follows from the bound of Theorem 1 from [1]. □

Now, we extend the above bound to play against an adaptive adversary. While we specialize the result to the particular algorithm implied by Lemma (1), the argument is in fact more general and can be extended to all self-oblivious algorithms, that is, algorithms whose play depends only on the cost history [8].

Lemma 2. *Let $S \subseteq \mathbb{R}^n$ be a set of (not necessarily positive) decisions, and $\mathcal{V}$ be an adaptive adversary such that $|\mathbf{c}^t \cdot \mathbf{x}| \leq R$ for all $\mathbf{x} \in S$ and any $\mathbf{c}^t$ produced by the adversary. Then, if we run $\mathcal{A}(\epsilon)$ from Lemma (1) against this adversary,*

$$E[\text{loss}(\mathcal{A}(\epsilon), \mathcal{V})] \leq E[\text{OPT}(\mathcal{A}(\epsilon), \mathcal{V})] + \epsilon(4n+2)R^2T + \frac{4n}{\epsilon}.$$

Proof. Fixing $\mathcal{V}$ also determines a distribution over decision/cost histories. Our expectations for this Lemma are with respect to this distribution. Let $k^T = [\mathbf{c}^1, \ldots, \mathbf{c}^T]$, and let k^{t-1} be the first t costs in k^T. Note that $\mathcal{A}(\epsilon)$ is self-oblivious, so $\bar{\mathbf{x}}^t = \sum_{\mathbf{x} \in S} \Pr(\mathbf{x} \mid k^{t-1})\mathbf{x}$ is well defined. Adopting our earlier notation, let z^t be our loss on time t, so, $\text{loss}(\mathcal{A}(\epsilon)) = z^{1:T}$. Then,

$$E[z^{1:T} \mid k^T] = \sum_{t=1}^{T} E[z^t \mid k^T] = \sum_{t=1}^{T} \mathbf{c}^t \cdot E[\tilde{\mathbf{x}}^t \mid k^T] = \sum_{t=1}^{T} \mathbf{c}^t \cdot \bar{\mathbf{x}}^t.$$

Now, consider the oblivious adversary that plays the fixed sequence of cost vectors $k^T = [\mathbf{c}^1, \ldots, \mathbf{c}^T]$. It is easy to see the expected loss to FPL against this adversary is also $\sum_{t=1}^{T} \mathbf{c}^t \cdot \bar{\mathbf{x}}^t$, and so the performance bound from Lemma (1) applies. The result follows by writing $E[\text{loss}(\mathcal{A}(\epsilon), \mathcal{V})] = E[\, E[\text{loss}(\mathcal{A}(\epsilon), \mathcal{V}) \mid k^T]\,]$, and applying that bound to the inner expectation. □

Thus, we can use $\mathcal{A}(\epsilon)$ as our GEX subroutine for full-observation online geometric observation.

B Notions of Regret

In [5], an alternative definition of regret is given, namely,

$$E[\text{loss}_{\mathcal{V},\mathcal{A}}(h^T)] - \min_{x \in S} E\left[\sum_{t=1}^{T} \mathbf{c}^t \cdot \mathbf{x}\right]. \tag{10}$$

This definition is equivalent to ours in the case of an *oblivious* adversary, but against an adaptive adversary the "best decision" for this definition is not the best decision for a *particular* decision history, but the best decision if the decision must be chosen before a cost history is selected according to the distribution over such histories. In particular,

$$E\left[\min_{x \in S} \sum_{t=1}^{T} \mathbf{c}^t \cdot \mathbf{x}\right] \leq \min_{x \in S} E\left[\sum_{t=1}^{T} \mathbf{c}^t \cdot \mathbf{x}\right]$$

and so a bound on Equation (1) is at least as strong as a bound on Equation (10). In fact, bounds on Equation (10) can be very poor when the adversary is adaptive. There are natural examples where the stronger definition (1) gives regret $\mathcal{O}(T)$ while the weaker definition (10) indicates no regret. Adapting an example from [5], let $S = \{\mathbf{e}_1, \ldots, \mathbf{e}_n\}$ (the "flat" bandit setting) and consider the algorithm $\mathcal{A}$ that plays uniformly at random from S. The adversary $\mathcal{V}$ gives $\mathbf{c}^1 = \mathbf{0}$, and if $\mathcal{A}$ then plays $\mathbf{e}_i$ on the first iteration, thereafter the adversary plays the cost vector $\mathbf{c}^t$ where $c_i^t = 0$ and $c_j^t = 1$ for $j \neq i$. The expected loss of $\mathcal{A}$ is $\frac{n-1}{n}T$. For regret as defined by Equation (10), $\min_{\mathbf{x} \in S} E[\mathbf{c}^{1:T} \cdot \mathbf{x}] = \frac{n-1}{n}T$, indicating no regret, while $E[\min_{\mathbf{x} \in S}(\mathbf{c}^{1:T} \cdot \mathbf{x})] = 0$, and so the stronger definition indicates $\mathcal{O}(T)$ regret.

Unfortunately, this implies like the proof techniques for bounds on expected weak regret like those in [4] and [2] cannot be used to get bounds on regret as defined by Equation (1). The problem is that even if we have unbiased estimates of the costs, these cannot be used to evaluate the term $E[\min_{x \in S} \sum_{t=1}^{T} (\mathbf{c}^t \cdot \mathbf{x})]$ in (1) because min is a non-linear operator. We surmount this problem by proving high-probability bounds on our estimates of $\mathbf{c}^t$, which allows us to use a union bound to evaluate the expectation over the min operator. Note that the high probability bounds proved in [4] and [2] can be seen as corresponding to our definition of expected regret.

Learning Classes of Probabilistic Automata

François Denis and Yann Esposito

LIF-CMI, 39, rue F. Joliot Curie
13453 Marseille Cedex 13 FRANCE,
{fdenis,esposito}@cmi.univ-mrs.fr

Abstract. Probabilistic finite automata (PFA) model stochastic languages, i.e. probability distributions over strings. Inferring PFA from stochastic data is an open field of research. We show that PFA are identifiable in the limit with probability one. Multiplicity automata (MA) is another device to represent stochastic languages. We show that a MA may generate a stochastic language that cannot be generated by a PFA, but we show also that it is undecidable whether a MA generates a stochastic language. Finally, we propose a learning algorithm for a subclass of PFA, called PRFA.

1 Introduction

Probabilistic automata (PFA) are formal objects which model *stochastic languages*, i.e. probability distributions over words [1]. They are composed of a *structure* which is a finite automaton (NFA) and of *parameters* associated with states and transitions which represent the probability for a state to be initial, terminal or the probability for a transition to be chosen. Given the structure of a probabilistic automaton A and a sequence of words $u_1, \ldots, u_n$ independently distributed according to a probability distribution P, computing parameters for A which maximize the likelihood of the observation is NP-hard [2]. However in practical cases, algorithms based on the EM (*Expectation-Maximization*) method [3] can be used to compute approximate values. On the other hand, inferring a probabilistic automaton (structure and parameters) from a sequence of words is a widely open field of research. In some applications, prior knowledge may help to choose a structure (for example, the standard model for biological sequence analysis [4]). Without prior knowledge, a complete graph structure can be chosen. But it is likely that in general, inferring both the appropriate structure and parameters from data would provide better results (see for example [5]).

Several learning frameworks can be considered to study inference of PFA. They often consist in adaptations to the stochastic case of classical learning models. We consider a variant of the identification in the limit model of Gold [6], adapted to the stochastic case in [7]. Given a PFA A and a sequence of words $u_1, \ldots, u_n, \ldots$ independently drawn according to the associated distribution P_A, an inference algorithm must compute a PFA A_n from each subsequence $u_1, \ldots, u_n$ such that with probability one, the support of A_n is stationary from

J. Shawe-Taylor and Y. Singer (Eds.): COLT 2004, LNAI 3120, pp. 124–139, 2004.

some index n and P_{A_n} converges to P_A; moreover, when parameters of the target are rational numbers, it can be requested that A_n itself is stationary from some index. The set of probabilistic automata whose structure is deterministic (PDFA) is identifiable in the limit with probability one [8,9,10], the identification being exact when the parameters of the target are rational numbers. However, PDFA are far less expressive than PFA, i.e. the set of probability distributions associated with PDFA is stricly included in the set of distributions generated from general PFA. We show that PFA are identifiable in the limit, with exact identification when the parameters of the target are rational numbers (Section 3).

Multiplicity automata (MA) are devices which model functions from Σ^* to $\mathbb{R}$. It has been shown that functions that can be computed by MA are very efficiently learnable in a variant of the exact learning model of Angluin, where the learner can ask *equivalence* and *extended membership queries*[11,12,13]. As PFA are particular MA, they are learnable in this model. However, the learning is improper in the sense that the output function is not a PFA but a multiplicity automaton. We show that a MA is maybe not a very convenient representation scheme to represent a PFA if the goal is to learn it from stochastic data. This representation is not robust, i.e. there are MA which do not compute a stochastic language and which are arbitrarily close to a given PFA. Moreover, we show that it is undecidable whether a MA generates a stochastic language. That is, given a MA computed from stochastic data: it is possible that it does not compute a stochastic language and there may be no way to detect it! We also show that MA can compute stochastic languages that cannot be computable by PFA. These two results are proved in Section 4: they solve problems that were left open in [1].

Our identification in the limit algorithm of PFA is far from being efficient while algorithms that identifies PDFA in the limit can also be used in practical learning situations (ALERGIA [8], RLIPS [9], MDI [14]). Note also that we do not have a model that describes algorithms "that can be used in practical cases": identification in the limit model is clearly too weak, exact learning via queries is irrealistic, PAC-model is maybe too strong (PDFA are not PAC-learnable [15]). So, it is important to define subclasses of PFA, as rich as possible, while keeping good empirical learnability properties. We have introduced in [16,17] a new class of PFA based on the notion of *residual languages*: a *residual language* of a stochastic language P is the language $u^{-1}P$ defined by $u^{-1}P(v) = P(uv)/P(u\Sigma^*)$. It can be shown that a stochastic language can be generated by a PDFA iff it has a finite number of residual languages. We consider the class of Probabilistic Residual Finite Automata (PRFA): a PFA A is a PRFA iff each of its states generates a residual language of P_A. It can be shown that a stochastic language can be generated by a PRFA iff P_A has a finite number of *prime* residual languages $u_1^{-1}P, \ldots, u_n^{-1}P$ sufficient to express all the residual languages as a convex linear combination of $u_1^{-1}P, \ldots, u_n^{-1}P$, i.e. for every word v, there exist non negative real numbers α_i such that $v^{-1}P = \sum \alpha_i u_i^{-1}P$ ([17,16]). Clearly, the class of PRFA is much more expressive than PDFA. We introduce a first learning algorithm for PRFA, which identifies this class in the limit with probability one, and can be used in practical cases (Section 5).

2 Preliminaries

2.1 Automata and Languages

Let Σ be a finite *alphabet*, and Σ^* be the set of words on Σ. The empty word is denoted by ε and the length of a word u is denoted by $|u|$. Let $<$ denote the length-lexicographic order on Σ^*. A *language* is a subset of Σ^*. For any language L, let $\text{pref}(L) = \{u \in \Sigma^* | \exists v \in \Sigma^*, uv \in L\}$. L is *prefixial* iff $L = \text{pref}(L)$.

A *non deterministic finite automaton (NFA)* is a 5-tuple $A = \langle \Sigma, Q, Q_0, F, \delta \rangle$ where Q is a finite set of states, $Q_0 \subseteq Q$ is the set of initial states, $F \subseteq Q$ is the set of terminal states, δ is the *transition* function defined from $Q \times \Sigma$ to 2^Q. Let δ also denote the extension of the transition function defined from $2^Q \times \Sigma^*$ to 2^Q. An NFA is *deterministic (DFA)* if $|Q_0| = 1$ and if $\forall q \in Q, \forall x \in \Sigma, |\delta(q,x)| \leq 1$. An NFA is *trimmed* if for any state q, $q \in \delta(Q_0, \Sigma^*)$ and $\delta(q, \Sigma^*) \cap F \neq \emptyset$. Let $A = \langle \Sigma, Q, Q_0, F, \delta \rangle$ be an NFA. A word $u \in \Sigma^*$ is *recognized* by A if $\delta(Q_0, u) \cap F \neq \emptyset$. The language recognized by A is $L_A = \{u \in \Sigma^* | \ \delta(Q_0, u) \cap F \neq \emptyset\}$.

2.2 Multiplicity and Probabilistic Automata, Stochastic Languages

A *multiplicity automaton (MA)* is a 5-tuple $\langle \Sigma, Q, \varphi, \iota, \tau \rangle$ where Q is a finite set of states, $\varphi : Q \times \Sigma \times Q \to \mathbb{R}$ is the transition function, $\iota : Q \to \mathbb{R}$ is the initialization function and $\tau : Q \to \mathbb{R}$ is the termination function. We extend the transition function φ to $Q \times \Sigma^* \times Q$ by $\varphi(q, wx, r) = \sum_{s \in Q} \varphi(q, w, s)\varphi(s, x, r)$ where $x \in \Sigma$ and $\varphi(q, \varepsilon, r) = 1$ if $q = r$ and 0 otherwise. We extend again φ to $Q \times 2^{\Sigma^*} \times 2^Q$ by $\varphi(q, U, R) = \sum_{w \in U} \sum_{r \in R} \varphi(q, w, r)$. Let $A = \langle \Sigma, Q, \varphi, \iota, \tau \rangle$ be a MA. Let P_A be the function defined by: $P_A(u) = \sum_{q \in Q} \sum_{r \in Q} \iota(q)\varphi(q, u, r)\tau(r)$. The *support* of A is the NFA $\langle \Sigma, Q, Q_I, Q_T, \delta \rangle$ where $Q_I = \{q \in Q \mid \iota(q) \neq 0\}$, $Q_T = \{q \in Q \mid \tau(q) \neq 0\}$ and $\delta(q, x) = \{r \in Q | \ \varphi(q, x, r) \neq 0\}$ for any state q and letter x. An MA is said to be *trimmed* if its support is a trimmed NFA.

A *semi-PFA* is a MA such that ι, φ and τ take their values in $[0,1]$, $\sum_{q \in Q} \iota(q) \leq 1$ and for any state q, $\tau(q) + \varphi(q, \Sigma, Q) \leq 1$. A *Probabilistic Finite Automaton (PFA)* is a trimmed semi-PFA such that $\sum_{q \in Q} \iota(q) = 1$ and for any state q, $\tau(q) + \varphi(q, \Sigma, Q) = 1$. A *Probabilistic Deterministic Finite Automaton (PDFA)* is a PFA whose support is deterministic.

A *stochastic language* on Σ is a probability distribution over Σ^*, i.e. a function P defined from Σ^* to $[0,1]$ such that $\sum_{u \in \Sigma^*} P(u) = 1$. The function P_A associated with a PFA A is a stochastic language. Let us denote by $\mathcal{S}$ the set of stochastic languages on Σ. Let $P \in \mathcal{S}$ and let $\text{res}(P) = \{u \in \Sigma^* | P(u\Sigma^*) \neq 0\}$. Let $u \in \text{res}(P)$, the *residual language* of P associated with u is the stochastic language $u^{-1}P$ defined by $u^{-1}P(w) = P(uw)/P(u\Sigma^*)$. Let $\text{Res}(P) = \{u^{-1}P | \ u \in \text{res}(P)\}$. It can easily be shown that $\text{Res}(P)$ spans a finite dimension vector space iff P can be generated by a MA. Let $\text{MA}_{\mathcal{S}}$ be the set composed of MA which generate stochastic languages. Let us denote by $\mathcal{S}_{\text{MA}}$ (resp. $\mathcal{S}_{\text{PFA}}, \mathcal{S}_{\text{PDFA}}$) the set of stochastic languages generated by MA (resp. PFA, PDFA) on Σ. Let $R \subseteq MA$. Let us denote by $R[\mathbb{Q}]$ the set of elements of R, the parameters of which are all in $\mathbb{Q}$.

2.3 Learning Stochastic Languages

We are interested in learnable subsets of MA which generate stochastic languages. Several learning model can be used, we consider two of them.

Identification in the limit with probability 1. The identification in the limit learning model of Gold [6] can be adapted to the stochastic case ([7]).

Let $P \in \mathcal{S}$ and let S be a finite sample drawn according to P. For any $X \subseteq \Sigma^*$, let $P_S(X) = \frac{1}{\mathrm{Card}(S)} \sum_{x \in S} 1_{x \in X}$ be the empirical distribution associated with S. A *complete presentation* of P is an infinite sequence S of words generated according to P. Let S_n be the sequence composed of the n first words (not necessarily different) of S. We shall write $P_n(A)$ instead of $P_{S_n}(A)$.

Definition 1. *Let* $\mathcal{R} \subseteq \mathrm{MA}_{\mathcal{S}}$. $\mathcal{R}$ *is said to be* identifiable in the limit with probability one *if there exists a learning algorithm* $\mathcal{L}$ *such that for any* $R \in \mathcal{R}$, *with probability 1, for any complete presentation* S *of* P_R, $\mathcal{L}$ *computes for each* S_n *given as input, a hypothesis* R_n *such that the support of* R_n *is stationary from some index* n^* *and such that* $P_{R_n} \to P_R$ *as* $n \to \infty$. *Moreover,* $\mathcal{R}$ *is* strongly identifiable in the limit with probability one *if* P_{R_n} *is also stationary from some index.*

It has been shown that PDFA is identifiable in the limit with probability one [8, 9] and that PDFA[$\mathbb{Q}$] is strongly identifiable in the limit [10].

We show below that PFA is identifiable in the limit with probability one and that PFA[$\mathbb{Q}$] is strongly identifiable in the limit.

Learning using queries. The MAT model of Angluin [18], which allows to use *membership queries* (MQ) and *equivalence queries* (EQ) has been extended to functions computed by MA. Let P be the target function, let u be a word and let A be a MA. The answer to the query MQ(u) is the value $P(u)$; the answer to the query EQ(A) is YES if $P_A = P$ and NO otherwise. Functions computed by MA can be learned exactly within polynomial time provided that the learning algorithm can make extended membership queries and equivalence queries. Therefore, any stochastic language in $\mathcal{S}_{\mathrm{MA}}$ can be learned by this algorithm.

However, using MA to represent stochastic languages has some drawbacks: first, this representation is not robust, i.e. a MA may compute a stochastic language for a given set of parameters θ_0 and computes a function which is not a stochastic language for any $\theta \neq \theta_0$; moreover, it is undecidable whether a MA computes a stochastic language. That is, by using MA to represent stochastic languages, a learning algorithm using approximate data might infer a MA which does not compute a stochastic language and with no means to detect it.

3 Identifying $\mathcal{S}_{\mathrm{PFA}}$ in the Limit

We show in this Section that $\mathcal{S}_{\mathrm{PFA}}$ is identifiable in the limit with probability one. Moreover, the identification is strong when the target can be generated by a PFA whose parameters are rational numbers.

3.1 Weak Identification

Let P be a stochastic language over Σ, let $\mathcal{A} = (A_i)_{i \in I}$ be a family of subsets of Σ^*, let S be a finite sample drawn according to P, and let P_S be the empirical distribution associated with S. It can be shown [19,20] that for any confidence parameter δ, with a probability greater than $1 - \delta$, for any $i \in I$,

$$|P_S(A_i) - P(A_i)| \leq c\sqrt{\frac{\text{VC}(\mathcal{A}) - \log\frac{\delta}{4}}{Card(S)}} \quad (1)$$

where VC($\mathcal{A}$) is the dimension of Vapnik-Chervonenkis of $\mathcal{A}$ and c is an universal constant. When $\mathcal{A} = (\{w\})_{w \in \Sigma^*}$, $\text{VC}(\mathcal{A}) = 1$. Let $\Psi(\epsilon, \delta) = \frac{c^2}{\epsilon^2}(1 - \log\frac{\delta}{4})$.

Lemma 1. *Let $P \in \mathcal{S}$ and let S be a complete presentation of P. For any precision parameter ϵ, any confidence parameter δ, any $n \geq \Psi(\epsilon, \delta)$, with a probability greater than $1 - \delta$, $|P_n(w) - P(w)| \leq \epsilon$ for all $w \in \Sigma^*$.*

Proof. Use Inequality (1). □

For any integer k, let $Q_k = \{1, \ldots, k\}$ and let $\Theta_k = \{\iota_i, \tau_i, \varphi_{i,j}^x | i, j \in Q_k, x \in \Sigma\}$ be a set of variables. We consider the following set of constraints C_k on Θ_k:

$$C_k = \begin{cases} 0 \leq \iota_i, \tau_i, \varphi_{i,j}^x \leq 1 \text{ for any } i, j \in Q_k, x \in \Sigma, \\ \sum_{i \in Q_k} \iota_i \leq 1, \\ \tau_i + \sum_{j \in Q_k, x \in \Sigma} \varphi_{i,j}^x \leq 1 \text{ for any } i \in Q_k. \end{cases}$$

Any assignment θ of these variables satisfying C_k is said to be *valid*; any valid assignement θ defines a semi-PFA A_k^θ by letting $\iota(i) = \iota_i$, $\tau(i) = \tau_i$ and $\varphi(i, x, j) = \varphi_{i,j}^x$ for any states i and j and any letter x. We simply denote by P_θ the function $P_{A_k^\theta}$ associated with A_k^θ. Let V_k be the sets of valid assignments. For any $\theta \in V_k$, let θ^t be the associated trimmed assignment which set to 0 every parameter which is never effectively used to compute the probability $P_\theta(w)$ of some word w. Clearly, θ^t is valid and $P_\theta = P_{\theta^t}$.

For any w, $P_\theta(w)$ is a polynomial and is therefore a continuous function of θ. On the other hand, the series $\sum_w P_\theta(w)$ are convergent but not uniformly convergent and $P_\theta(w\Sigma^*)$ is not a continous function of θ (see Fig. 1). However, we show below that the function $(\theta, w) \to P_\theta(w)$ is uniformly continuous.

A^{θ_α} $\frac{1}{2}$ → (α) $a, 1-\alpha$ $\frac{1}{2}$ → ($\frac{1}{2}$) $a, \frac{1}{2}$ | $A^{\theta_0^t}$ 0 → (0) $a, 0$ $\frac{1}{2}$ → ($\frac{1}{2}$) $a, \frac{1}{2}$

Fig. 1. $P_{\theta_\alpha}(\varepsilon) = 1/4 + \alpha/2$; $P_{\theta_0}(\Sigma^*) = 1/2$ and $P_{\theta_\alpha}(\Sigma^*) = 1$ when $\alpha > 0$.

Proposition 1. *For any $k \in \mathbb{N}$, the function $(\theta, w) \to P_\theta(w)$ is uniformly continuous: $\forall \epsilon, \exists \alpha, \forall w \in \Sigma^*, \forall \theta, \theta' \in V_k, \|\theta - \theta'\| < \alpha \Rightarrow |P_\theta(w) - P_{\theta'}(w)| < \epsilon$.*

Proof. We prove the proposition in several steps.

1. Let $\theta_0 \in V_k$, let $A_k^{\theta_0^t} = \langle \Sigma, Q_k, \varphi_0, \iota_0, \tau_0 \rangle$ and let $\beta_0 = \max\left\{\varphi_0(q, \Sigma^k, Q_k) \middle| q \in Q_k\right\}$. For any state q s.t. $\varphi_0(q, \Sigma^k, Q_k) > 0$, there must exist a word w of length $< k$ and a state q' s.t. $\varphi_0(q, w, q') \neq 0$ and $\tau_0(q') \neq 0$. Hence, $\beta_0 < 1$.
2. For any integer n and any state q, $\varphi_0(q, \Sigma^{nk}, Q_k) \leq \beta_0^n$. Proof by induction on n: clearly true when $n = 0$ and
$\varphi_0(q, \Sigma^{nk}, Q_k) \leq \sum_{q' \in Q_k, w \in \Sigma^k} \varphi_0(q, w, q')\varphi_0(q', \Sigma^{(n-1)k}, Q_k)$
$\leq \beta_0^{n-1} \sum_{q' \in Q_k, w \in \Sigma^k} \varphi_0(q, w, q') \leq \beta_0^n$.
3. For any integer n, $P_{\theta_0^t}(\Sigma^{nk}\Sigma^*) = \sum_{q \in Q_k} \iota_0(q)\varphi_0(q, \Sigma^{nk}, Q_k) \leq \beta_0^n$.
4. For any state q, $\varphi_0(q, \Sigma^*, Q_k) = \sum_{n \in \mathbb{N}} \sum_{m=0}^{k} \varphi_0(q, \Sigma^{nk+m}, Q_k)$
$\leq \sum_{n \in \mathbb{N}} \sum_{m=0}^{k} \sum_{q' \in Q_k} \varphi_0(q, \Sigma^m, q')\varphi_0(q', \Sigma^{nk}, Q_k)$
$\leq \sum_{n \in \mathbb{N}} \sum_{m=0}^{k} \sum_{q' \in Q_k} \beta_0^n \varphi_0(q, \Sigma^m, q') \leq k/(1 - \beta_0)$.
5. Let α_0 be the minimal non null parameter in θ_0^t, let $\alpha < \alpha_0/2$, let θ be a valid assignement such that $||\theta - \theta_0|| < \alpha$ and let $A_k^{\theta^t} = \langle \Sigma, Q_k, \varphi, \iota, \tau \rangle$. Note that any non null parameter in θ_0^t corresponds to a non null parameter in θ^t but that the converse is false (see Fig. 1). Let θ' be the assignment obtained from θ^t by setting to 0 every parameter which is null in θ_0^t, let $A_k^{\theta'} = \langle \Sigma, Q_k, \varphi', \iota', \tau' \rangle$ and let $\beta' = \max\left\{\varphi'(q, \Sigma^k, Q_k) \middle| q \in Q_k\right\}$. As θ' and θ_0^t have the same set of non null parameters, there exists $\alpha_1 < \alpha_0/2$ such that $||\theta - \theta_0|| < \alpha_1$ implies $\beta' < (1 + \beta_0)/2$. Let $\beta_1 = (1 + \beta_0)/2$.
6. Let w be a word of length $\geq nk$. There are two categories of derivations of w in $A_k^{\theta^t}$:
   - those which exist in $A_k^{\theta'}$. Their contribution to $P_{\theta^t}(w)$ is not greater than β_1^n.
   - those which do not entirely exist in $A_k^{\theta'}$ and one parameter of which is $\leq \alpha_1$. Let $q_0, \ldots, q_{|w|}$ be such a derivation. Either $\iota(q) \leq \alpha_1$, either $\tau(q_{|w|}) \leq \alpha_1$, or there exists a first state q_i such that $q_0, \ldots, q_i$ is a derivation in $A_k^{\theta'}$ and $\varphi(q_i, w_i, q_{i+1}) \leq \alpha_1$, where w_i is the ith letter of w. The contribution of these derivations to $P_{\theta^t}(w)$ is bounded by

$$\sum_{q, \iota(q) \leq \alpha_1} \alpha_1 \varphi(q, w, Q) + \sum_{q, q', \iota(q') \leq \alpha_1} \iota(q)\varphi(q, w, q')\alpha_1 +$$
$$\sum_{q_0, q_i \in Q_k} \iota'(q_0)\varphi'(q_0, \Sigma^*, q_i)\alpha_1 \leq \alpha_1(k + 1 + k/(1 - \beta_1)) \ .$$

   Therefore, $P_{\theta^t}(w) \leq \beta_1^n + \alpha_1(k + 1 + k/(1 - \beta_1))$.
7. Let $\epsilon > 0$. Let $\alpha_2 = \min(\alpha_1, \epsilon/[4(k + 1 + k/(1 - \beta_1))])$ and let N be such that $\beta_1^N < \epsilon/4$. As for any fixed w, $P_\theta(w)$ is continuous, there exists $\alpha \leq \alpha_2$ such that $||\theta - \theta_0|| < \alpha$ implies that for any $w \in \Sigma^{\leq N}$, $|P_{\theta_0}(w) - P_\theta(w)| < \epsilon$. As $P_{\theta_0}(w) \leq \epsilon/2$ and $P_\theta(w) \leq \epsilon/2$ when $|w| \geq N$, we conclude that for all words w, $|P_{\theta_0}(w) - P_\theta(w)| < \epsilon$.

8. We have shown that: $\forall \epsilon, \forall \theta_0 \in V_k, \exists \alpha, \forall w \in \Sigma^*, \forall \theta \in V_k, ||\theta - \theta_0|| < \alpha \Rightarrow |P_\theta(w) - P_{\theta_0}(w)| < \epsilon$. Now, suppose that:

$$\exists \epsilon, \forall n \in \mathbb{N}, \exists w_n \in \Sigma^*, \exists \theta_n, \theta'_n \in V_k \text{ s.t.} \quad ||\theta_n - \theta'_n|| < 1/n \text{ and } \left|P_{\theta_n}(w_n) - P_{\theta'_n}(w_n)\right| \geq \epsilon$$

As valid assignments are elements of a compact set, there would exist a valid assignement θ_0 such that $\theta_{\sigma(n)} \to \theta_0$ and $\theta'_{\sigma(n)} \to \theta_0$ (for some subsequence $\sigma(n)$). We know that there exists $\alpha > 0$ such that $||\theta - \theta_0|| < \alpha$ implies that for all w, $|P_{\theta_0}(w) - P_\theta(w)| < \epsilon/2$. When $1/n < \alpha$, the hypothesis leads to a contradiction. □

Let $P \in \mathcal{S}$ and let S be a complete presentation of P. For any integers n and k and for any $\epsilon > 0$, let $I_{\Theta_k}(S_n, \epsilon)$ be the following system

$$I_{\Theta_k}(S_n, \epsilon) = C_k \cup \{|P_\theta(w) - P_n(w)| \leq \epsilon \text{ for } w \in S_n\}.$$

Lemma 2. *Let $P \in \mathcal{S}$ be a stochastic language and let S be a complete presentation of P. Suppose that there exists an integer k and a PFA $A_k^{\theta_0}$ such that $P = P_{\theta_0}$. Then, for any precision parameter ϵ, any confidence parameter δ and any $n \geq \Psi(\epsilon/2, \delta)$, with a probability greater than $1-\delta$, $I_{\Theta_k}(S_n, \epsilon)$ has a solution that can be computed.*

Proof. From Lemma 1, with a probability greater than $1-\delta$, we have $|P_{\theta_0}(w) - P_n(w)| \leq \epsilon/2$ for all $w \in S_n$. For any $w \in S_n$, $P_\theta(w)$ is a polynomial in θ whose coefficients are all equal to 1. A bound M_w of $||\frac{dP_\theta(w)}{d\theta}||$ can easily be computed. We have

$$|P_\theta(w) - P_{\theta'}(w)| \leq M_w ||\theta - \theta'||.$$

Let $\alpha = \inf\{\frac{\epsilon}{2M_w} | w \in S_n\}$. If $||\theta - \theta'|| < \alpha$, $|P_\theta(w) - P_{\theta'}(w)| \leq \epsilon/2$ for all $w \in S_n$. So, we can compute a finite number of assignments: $\theta_1^\alpha, \ldots \theta_{N_\alpha}^\alpha$ such that for all valid assignment θ, there exists $1 \leq i \leq N_\alpha$ such that $||\theta - \theta_i^\alpha|| \leq \alpha$. Let i be such that $||\theta_0 - \theta_i^\alpha|| \leq \alpha$: θ_i^α is a solution of $I_{\Theta_k}(S_n, \epsilon)$. □

The Borel-Cantelli Lemma is often used to show that a given property holds with probability 1: let $(A_n)_{n \in \mathbb{N}}$ be a sequence of events such that $\sum_{n \in \mathbb{N}} P(A_n) < \infty$; then, the probability that a finite number of A_n occur is 1.

For any integer n, let $\epsilon_n = n^{-\frac{1}{3}}$ and $\delta_n = n^{-2}$. Clearly, $\epsilon_n \to 0$ and $\sum_{n \in \mathbb{N}} \delta_n < \infty$. Moreover, there exists an integer N s.t. $\forall n > N, n \geq \psi_1(\epsilon_n/2, \delta_n)$.

Proposition 2. *Let P be a stochastic language and let S be a complete presentation of P. Suppose that there exists an integer k and a PFA $A_k^{\theta_0}$ such that $P = P_{\theta_0}$. With probability 1 there exists an integer N such that for any $n > N$, $I_{\Theta_k}(S_n, \epsilon_n)$ has a solution θ_n and $\lim_{n \to \infty} P_{\theta_n}(w) \to P(w)$ uniformly in w.*

Proof. The Borel-Cantelli Lemma proves that with probability 1 there exists an integer N s.t. for any $n > N$, $I_{\Theta_k}(S_n, \epsilon_n)$ has a solution θ_n. Now suppose that

$$\exists \epsilon, \forall N, \exists n \geq N, \exists w_n \in \Sigma^*, |P_{\theta_n}(w_n) - P(w_n)| \geq \epsilon.$$

Let $(\theta_{\sigma(n)})$ be a subsequence of (θ_n) such that for every integer n, $\sigma(n) \geq n$, $|P_{\theta_{\sigma(n)}}(w_{\sigma(n)}) - P(w_{\sigma(n)})| \geq \epsilon$ and $\theta_{\sigma(n)} \to \theta$. As each $\theta_{\sigma(n)}$ is a solution of $I_{\Theta_k}(S_{\sigma(n)}, \epsilon_{\sigma(n)})$, θ is a valid assignement such that for all w such that $P(w) \neq 0$, $P(w) = P_\theta(w)$. As P is a stochastic language, we must have $P(w) = P_\theta(w)$ for every word w, i.e. $P = P_\theta$. From Proposition 1, $P_{\theta_{\sigma(n)}}$ converges uniformy to P, which contradicts the hypothesis. □

It remains to show that when the target cannot be expressed by a PFA on k states, the system $I_{\Theta_k}(S_n, \epsilon_n)$ has no solution from some index.

Proposition 3. *Let P be a stochastic language and let S be a complete presentation of P. Let k be an integer such that there exists no θ satisfying $P = P_\theta$. Then, with probability 1, there exists an integer N such that for any $n > N$, $I_{\Theta_k}(S_n, \epsilon_n)$ has no solution.*

Proof. Suppose that $\forall N \in \mathbb{N}$, $\exists n \geq N$ such that $I_{\Theta_k}(S_n, \epsilon_n)$ has a solution. Let $(n_i)_{i \in \mathbb{N}}$ be an increasing sequence such that $I_{\Theta_k}(S_{n_i}, \epsilon_{n_i})$ has a solution θ_i and let (θ_{k_i}) be a subsequence of (θ_i) that converges to a limit value $\overline{\theta}$.

Let $w \in \Sigma^*$ be such that $P(w) \neq 0$. We have $|P_{\overline{\theta}}(w) - P(w)| \leq |P_{\overline{\theta}}(w) - P_{\theta_i}(w)| + |P_{\theta_i}(w) - P_{n_i}(w)| + |P_{n_i}(w) - P(w)|$ for any integer i.

With probability 1, the last term converges to 0 as i tends to infinity (Lemma 1). With probability 1, there exists an index i such that $w \in S_{n_i}$. From this index, the second term is less than ϵ_{n_i} which tends to 0 as i tends to infinity. Now, as $P_\theta(w)$ is a continuous function of θ, the first term tends to 0 as i tends to infinity. Therefore, $P_{\overline{\theta}}(w) = P(w)$ and $P_{\overline{\theta}} = P$, which contradicts the hypothesis. □

Theorem 1. *$\mathcal{S}_{\mathrm{PFA}}$ is identifiable in the limit with probability one.*

Proof. Consider the following algorithm $\mathcal{A}$:

```
Input: A stochastic sample S_n of length n.
for k = 1 to n do {
    compute α and θ_1^α, ... θ_{N_α}^α as in Lemma 2
    if ∃1 ≤ i ≤ N_α s.t. θ_i^α is a solution of I_{Θ_k}(S_n, ε_n) then
        {return the smallest solution (in some order) A_k^{θ_i^α}}}
return a default hypothesis if no solution has been found
```

Let P be the target and let $A_k^{\theta_0}$ be a minimal state PFA which computes P. Previous propositions prove that with probability one, from some index N, the algorithm shall output a PFA $A_k^{\theta_n}$ such that P_{θ_n} converges uniformely to P. □

3.2 Strong Identification

When the target can be computed by a PFA whose parameters are in $\mathbb{Q}$, an equivalent PFA can be identified in the limit with probability 1. In order to show a similar property for PDFA, a method based on Stern-Brocot trees was used in [10]. Here we use the representation of real numbers by continuous fractions [21].

Let $x \geq 0$. Define $x_0 = x$, $a_0 = \lfloor x_0 \rfloor$ and while $x_n \neq a_n$, $x_{n+1} = 1/(x_n - a_n)$ and $a_{n+1} = \lfloor x_n \rfloor$. The sequences (x_n) and (a_n) are finite iff $x \in \mathbb{Q}$. Suppose from now on that $x \in \mathbb{Q}$, let N be the greatest index such that $x_N \neq a_N$, and for any $n \leq N$, let the nth *convergent* of x be the fraction

$$p_n/q_n = a_0 + 1/\left(a_1 + 1/\left(\cdots(1/a_n)\cdots\right)\right)$$

where $gcd(p_n, q_n) = 1$.

Lemma 3 ([21]). *We have $x = \frac{p_N}{q_N}$ and $\forall n < N$, $\left|x - \frac{p_n}{q_n}\right| \leq \frac{1}{q_n q_{n+1}} < \frac{1}{q_n^2}$. If a and b are two integers such that $\left|\frac{a}{b} - x\right| < \frac{1}{2b^2}$, then there is an integer $n \leq N$ such that $\frac{a}{b} = \frac{p_n}{q_n}$. For any integer A, there exists only a finite number of rational numbers $\frac{p}{q}$ such that $\left|x - \frac{p}{q}\right| \leq \frac{A}{q^2}$.*

Let $x = 5/14$. We have $p_0/q_0 = 0$, $p_1/q_1 = 1/2$, $p_2/q_2 = 1/3$ and $p_3/q_3 = x$.

Lemma 4. *Let (ϵ_n) be a sequence of non negative real numbers which converges to 0, let $x \in \mathbb{Q}$, let (y_n) be a sequence of elements of $\mathbb{Q}$ such that $|x - y_n| \leq \epsilon_n$ for all but finitely many n. Let $\frac{p_m^n}{q_m^n}$ the convergents associated with y_n. Then, there exists an integer N such that, for any $n \geq N$, there is an integer m such that $x = \frac{p_m^n}{q_m^n}$. Moreover, $\frac{p_m^n}{q_m^n}$ is the unique rational number such that $\left|y_n - \frac{p_m^n}{q_m^n}\right| \leq \epsilon_n \leq \frac{1}{(q_m^n)^2}$.*

Proof. Omitted. All proofs omitted here can be found in a complete version of the paper available `http://www.cmi.univ-mrs.fr/~fdenis` .

Example 1. Let $y_n = 1/2 - 1/n$ and $\epsilon_n = 1/n$. Then $y_3 = 1/6$, $y_4 = 1/4$, $y_5 = 3/10$, $y_6 = 1/3$, $y_7 = 5/14$. The first n s.t. $\left|y_n - \frac{p_m^n}{q_m^n}\right| \leq \frac{1}{n} \leq \frac{1}{(q_m^n)^2}$ has a solution is $n = 4$. Let z_n be the first solution. We have $z_4 = 1/4$, $z_5 = 1/3$, $z_6 = 1/3$ and $z_n = 1/2$ for $n \geq 7$.

Theorem 2. *Let $\mathcal{S}_{\text{PFA}}[\mathbb{Q}]$ be the set of stochastic languages that can be generated from a PFA whose parameters are in $\mathbb{Q}$. $\mathcal{S}_{\text{PFA}}[\mathbb{Q}]$ is strongly identifiable in the limit with probability one.*

Proof. Omitted.

4 $\mathcal{S}_{\mathrm{MA}}$ and $\mathcal{S}_{\mathrm{PFA}}$

The representation of stochastic languages by MA is not robust. Fig. 2 shows two MA which depend on parameter x. They define a stochastic language when $x = 0$ but not when $x > 0$. When $x > 0$, the first one generates negative values, and the second one generates unbounded values.

Let $P \in \mathcal{S}_{\mathrm{MA}}$ and let A be the MA which generates P output by the exact learning algorithm defined in [12]. A sample S drawn according to P defines an empiric distribution P_S that could be used by some variant of this learning algorithm. In the best case, this variant is expected to output a hypothesis $\hat{A}$ having the same support as A and with approximated parameters close to those of A. But there is no guaranty that $\hat{A}$ defines a stochastic language. More seriously, we show below that it is impossible to decide whether a given MA generates a stochastic language. The conclusion is that MA representation of stochastic languages is maybe not appropriate to learn stochastic languages.

Fig. 2. Two MA generating stochastic language if $x = 0$. If $x > 0$, the first generates negative values and the second unbounded values.

4.1 Membership to $\mathcal{S}_{\mathrm{MA}}$ Is Undecidable

We reduce the decision problem to a problem about *acceptor PFA*. An MA $\langle \Sigma, Q, \varphi, \iota, \tau \rangle$ is an *acceptor PFA* if φ, ι and τ are non negative functions, $\sum_{q \in Q} \iota(q) = 1$, $\forall q \in Q, \forall x \in \Sigma, \sum_{r \in Q} \varphi(q, x, r) = 1$ and if there exists a unique terminal state t such that $\tau(t) = 1$.

Theorem 3 ([22]). *Given an acceptor PFA A whose parameters are in $\mathbb{Q}$ and $\lambda \in \mathbb{Q}$, it is undecidable whether there exists a word w such that $P_A(w) < \lambda$.*

The following lemma shows some constructions on MA.

Lemma 5. *Let A and B be two MA and let $\lambda \in \mathbb{Q}$. We can construct:*

1. *a MA I_λ such that $\forall w \in \Sigma^*, P_{I_\lambda}(w) = \lambda$,*
2. *a MA $A + B$ such that $P_{A+B} = P_A + P_B$*
3. *a MA $\lambda \cdot A$ such that $P_{\lambda \cdot A} = \lambda P_A$,*
4. *a MA $\mathrm{tr}(A)$ such that for any word w, $P_{\mathrm{tr}(A)}(w) = \frac{P_A(w)}{(|\Sigma|+1)^{|w|+1}}$*

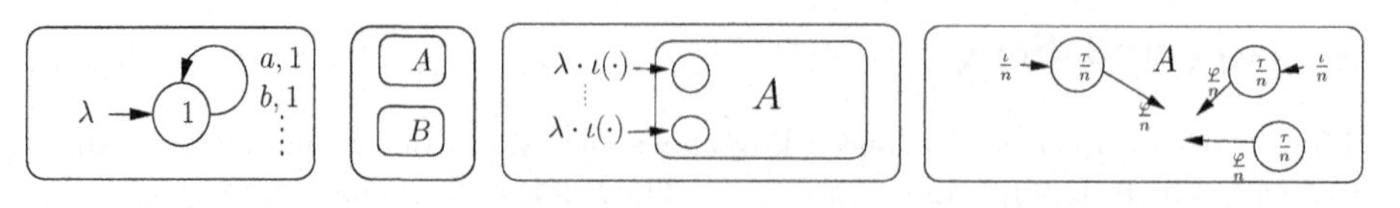

Fig. 3. How to construct I_λ, $A + B$, $\lambda \cdot A$ and $\mathrm{tr}(A)$, where $n = |\Sigma| + 1$. Note that when A is an acceptor PFA, $\mathrm{tr}(A)$ is a semi-PFA.

Proof. Proofs are omitted. See Fig. 3.

Lemma 6. *Let* $A = \langle \Sigma, Q, \varphi, \iota, \tau \rangle$ *be a semi-PFA, let* $Q^t = \{q \in Q | \varphi(Q_I, \Sigma^*, q) > 0$ *and* $\varphi(q, \Sigma^*, Q_T) > 0\}$ *and let* $A^t = \langle \Sigma, Q^t, \varphi_{|Q_t}, \iota_{|Q_t}, \tau_{|Q_t} \rangle$. *Then,* A^t *is a trimmed semi-PFA such that* $P_A = P_{A^t}$ *and which can be constructed from* A.

Proof. Straightforward.

Lemma 7. *Let* A *be a trimmed semi-PFA, we can compute* $P_A(\Sigma^*)$.

Proof. Omitted.

Proposition 4. *It is undecidable whether a MA generates a stochastic language.*

Proof. Let A be an acceptor PFA on Σ and $\lambda \in \mathbb{Q}$. For every word w, we have $P_{\mathrm{tr}(A-I_\lambda)}(w) = (|\Sigma| + 1)^{-(|w|+1)} (P_A(w) - \lambda) = P_{\mathrm{tr}(A)}(w) - \lambda(|\Sigma| + 1)^{-(|w|+1)}$ and therefore $P_{\mathrm{tr}(A-I_\lambda)}(\Sigma^*) = P_{\mathrm{tr}(A)}(\Sigma^*) - \lambda$.

- If $P_{\mathrm{tr}(A)}(\Sigma^*) = \lambda$ then either $\exists w$ s.t. $P_A(w) < \lambda$ or $\forall w, P_A(w) = \lambda$. Let B be the PFA such that $P_B(w) = 1$ if $w = \varepsilon$ and 0 otherwise. We have, $P_{B+\mathrm{tr}(A-I_\lambda)}(\Sigma^*) = 1$. Therefore, $\forall w, P_A(w) \geq \lambda$ iff $P_A(\varepsilon) \geq \lambda$ and $B + \mathrm{tr}(A - I_\lambda)$ generates a stochastic language.
- If $P_{\mathrm{tr}(A)}(\Sigma^*) \neq \lambda$, let $B = \left|P_{\mathrm{tr}(A)}(\Sigma^*) - \lambda\right|^{-1} \cdot \mathrm{tr}(A - I_\lambda)$. Check that B is computable from A, that $P_B(\Sigma^*) = 1$ and that $P_B(w) = \left|P_{\mathrm{tr}(A)}(\Sigma^*) - \lambda\right|^{-1} \left(\mathrm{Card}(\Sigma + 1)^{|w|+1}\right)^{-1} (P_A(w) - \lambda)$. So, $\exists w \in \Sigma^*, P_A(w) < \lambda$ iff B does note generate a stochastic language.

In both cases, we see that deciding whether a MA generates a stochastic language would solve the decision problem on PFA acceptors. □

Remark that in fact, we have proved a stronger result: it is undecidable whether a MA A such that $\sum_{w \in \Sigma^*} P_A(w) = 1$ generates a stochastic language. As a consequence, it can be proved that there exist stochastic languages that can be computed by MA but not by PFA.

Theorem 4. $\mathcal{S}_{\mathrm{PFA}} \subsetneq \mathcal{S}_{\mathrm{MA}}$.

Proof. Omitted.

5 Learning PRFA

The inference algorithm given in Section 3 is highly inefficient and cannot be used for real applications. It is unknown whether PFA can be efficiently learned. Here, we study a subclass of PFA, for which there exists a learning algorithm which can be efficiently implemented.

5.1 Probabilistic Residual Finite Automata

Definition 2 (Probabilistic Residual Finite Automaton). *A* PRFA *is a PFA $A = \langle \Sigma, Q, \varphi, \iota, \tau \rangle$ whose states define residual languages of P_A, i.e.such that $\forall q \in Q$, $\exists u \in \Sigma^*$, $P_{A,q} = u^{-1}P_A$, where $P_{A,q}$ denotes the stochastic language generated by $< \Sigma, Q, \varphi, \iota_q, \tau >$ where $\iota_q(q) = 1$ [16].*

Remark that PDFA are PRFA but that the converse is false. Fig. 4 represents a PRFA $\langle \Sigma, Q, \varphi, \iota, \tau \rangle$ where $\Sigma = \{a, b\}$, $Q = \{\varepsilon, a, b\}$, $\iota(\varepsilon) = 1$, $\tau(b) = \frac{2}{3}$, $\varphi(\varepsilon, a, a) = \frac{1}{2}$, $\varphi(\varepsilon, b, b) = \frac{1}{2}$, $\varphi(a, a, a) = \frac{1}{2}$, $\varphi(a, a, b) = \frac{1}{2}$ and $\varphi(b, a, b) = \frac{1}{3}$.

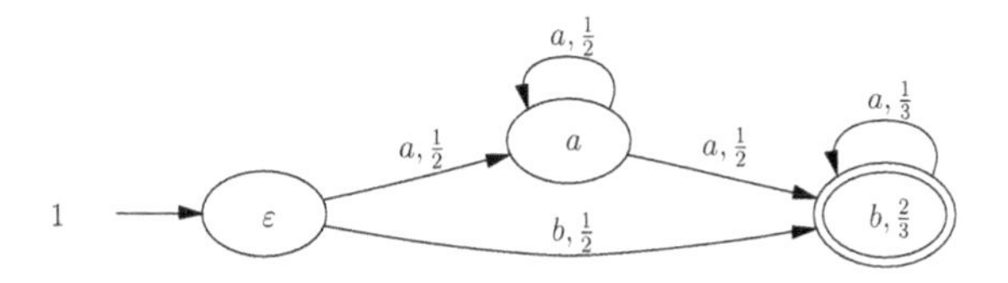

Fig. 4. A prefix PRFA.

Let $\mathcal{P}$ be a finite subset of $\mathcal{S}$. The convex closure of $\mathcal{P}$ is denoted by $\mathrm{conv}(\mathcal{P}) = \{P \in \mathcal{S} | \exists P_1, \ldots, P_n \in \mathcal{P}, \exists \lambda_1, \ldots \lambda_n \geq 0, P = \sum_{i=1}^{n} \lambda_i P_i\}$. We say that $\mathcal{P}$ is a *residual net* if for every $Q \in \mathcal{P}$ and every $u \in \mathrm{res}(Q)$, $u^{-1}Q \in \mathrm{conv}(\mathcal{P})$. A residual net $\mathcal{P}$ is a *convex generator* for $P \in \mathcal{S}$ if $P \in \mathrm{conv}(\mathcal{P})$.

It can be shown that $\mathcal{S}_{\mathrm{PDFA}} \subsetneq \mathcal{S}_{\mathrm{PRFA}} \subsetneq \mathcal{S}_{\mathrm{PFA}} \subsetneq \mathcal{S}_{\mathrm{MA}} \subsetneq \mathcal{S}$ [16]. More precisely, let $P \in \mathcal{S}$:

- $P \in \mathcal{S}_{\mathrm{PDFA}}$ iff P has a finite number of residual languages.
- $P \in \mathcal{S}_{\mathrm{PRFA}}$ iff there exists a convex generator for P composed of residual languages of P.
- $P \in \mathcal{S}_{\mathrm{PFA}}$ iff there exists a convex generator for P.
- $P \in \mathcal{S}_{\mathrm{MA}}$ iff $\mathrm{res}(P)$ spans a finite dimensional vector space.

Any $P \in \mathcal{S}_{\mathrm{PDFA}}$ can be generated by a minimal (in number of states) PDFA whose states correspond to the residual languages of P. In a similar way, it can be shown that any $P \in \mathcal{S}_{\mathrm{PRFA}}$ has a unique minimal convex generator, composed of *prime* residual languages of P which correspond to the states of a minimal (in number of states) PRFA generating P (see [17] for a complete study). Such a canonical form does not exist for PFA or MA.

A PRFA $A = \langle \Sigma, Q, \varphi, \iota, \tau \rangle$ is *prefix* if Q is a prefixial subset of Σ^*, $\iota(\varepsilon) = 1$, and $\forall (u, x, v) \in Q \times \Sigma \times Q$, $\varphi(u, x, v) \neq 0$ implies $ux = v$ or $ux \notin Q$. Transitions of the form (u, x, ux) are called *internal transitions*; the others are called *return transitions*. For example, automaton on Fig. 4, which can be built on the set $\{\varepsilon, a, b\}$, is a prefix PRFA, the transitions (ε, a, a) and (ε, b, b) are internal while (a, a, a), (a, a, b) and (b, a, b) are return transitions. Prefix PRFA are sufficient to generate all languages in $\mathcal{S}_{\text{PRFA}}$.

Let $P \in \mathcal{S}_{\text{PRFA}}$, $\text{Pm}(P)$ is the smallest prefixial subset of Σ^* such that $\forall u \in \text{Pm}(P)$, $\forall x \in \Sigma \cap \text{res}(u^{-1}P)$, $(ux)^{-1}P \in \text{conv}(\{v \in \text{Pm}(P) \mid v < ux\}) \Rightarrow ux \notin Pm(P)$. Let $U_{ux} = \{v \in \text{Pm}(P) \mid v < ux\}$ and for any word $u, v \in \text{Pm}(P)$, any $x \in \Sigma$ let $(\alpha_v^{ux})_{v \in U_{ux}}$ be positive parameters such that $(ux)^{-1}P = \sum_{v \in U_{ux}} \alpha_v^{ux} v^{-1}P$. Consider now the following PFA $A_P = \langle \Sigma, \text{Pm}(P), \varphi, \iota, \tau \rangle$ where $\iota(\epsilon) = 1$, $\varphi(u, x, v) = P(ux\Sigma^*)/P(u\Sigma^*)$ if $v = ux$ and $\varphi(u, x, v) = \alpha_v^{ux} P(ux\Sigma^*)/P(u\Sigma^*)$ if $(ux)^{-1}P = \sum_{v \in U_{ux}} \alpha_v^{ux} v^{-1}P$. It can be proved that A_P is a prefix PRFA which generates P [16]. See Fig. 4 for an example, where $\text{Pm}(P) = \{\epsilon, a, b\}$.

5.2 The Inference Algorithm

For any finite prefixial set Q, let $\Theta_Q = \left\{\iota_u, \tau_u, \varphi_{u,v}^x \middle| u, v \in Q, x \in \Sigma\right\}$ be a set of variables. We consider the following set of constraints C_Q on Θ_Q:

$$C_Q = \begin{cases} 0 \leq \iota_u, \tau_u, \varphi_{u,v}^x \leq 1 & \text{for any } u, v \in Q, x \in \Sigma, \\ \iota_\varepsilon = 1 & \\ \iota_u = 0 & \text{for any } u \in Q \setminus \{\varepsilon\}, \\ \tau_u + \sum_{v \in Q, x \in \Sigma} \varphi_{u,v}^x = 1 & \text{for any } u \in Q, \\ \varphi_{u,v}^x = 0 & \text{for any } u, v, x \text{ s.t. } ux \neq v \text{ and } ux \in Q \ . \end{cases} \tag{2}$$

Any assignment θ of these variables satisfying C_Q defines a prefix PRFA A^θ.

Let $P \in \mathcal{S}$, let S be a complete presentation of P, for any finite prefixial set Q, any $\epsilon > 0$, any integer n and any $v \in \text{res}(P)$ such that $\forall u \in Q$, $v > u$, let $I_{\Theta_Q}(v, S_n, \epsilon)$ be the following system: $I_{\Theta_Q}(v, S_n, \epsilon) = C_Q \cup C_{\text{internal}} \cup C_{\text{return}}(v)$ where $C_{\text{internal}} = \{P_{A^\theta}(w) = P_n(w) | \, w \in Q\}$ and $C_{\text{return}}(vx)$ $(x \in \Sigma)$ is the set of constraints $\left|(vx)^{-1}P_n(w\Sigma^*) - \sum_{u \in Q} \frac{\varphi_{v,u}^x}{P_n(vx\Sigma^*)} u^{-1}P_n(w\Sigma^*)\right| \leq \epsilon$ for all $w \in \text{pref}(S_n)$ successors of vx. Let $I_{\Theta_Q}(S_n, \epsilon) = C_Q \cup C_{\text{internal}} \bigcup_{vx \in \text{fr}(Q, P_n)} C_{\text{return}}(vx)$.

The constraint set C_{internal} can be solved immediatly and give parameters of the internal part of the automaton. It can be solved with $\iota(\varepsilon) = 1$, $\forall (u, x, ux) \in Q \times \Sigma \times Q$, $\varphi(u, x, ux) = P_n(ux\Sigma^*)/P_n(u\Sigma^*)$ and for all $u \in Q$, $\tau(u) = P_n(u)/P_n(u\Sigma^*)$. C_{return} is used to get parameters of return transitions. Remark $I_{\Theta_Q}(S_n, \epsilon)$ is a system composed of linear inequations.

Let DEES be the following algorithm:

Input: a stochastic sample S_n
Output: a prefix PRFA $A = \langle \Sigma, Q, \varphi, \iota, \tau \rangle$
$Q \leftarrow \{\varepsilon\}$, $F \leftarrow \Sigma \cap \text{res}(P_n)$

```
while F ≠ ∅ do {
    v = min F, F ← F \ {v}
    if I_ΘQ(v, S_n, ε_n) has no solution then{
        Q ← Q ∪ {v}, F ← F ∪ {vx ∈ res(P_n) | x ∈ Σ}}}
if I_ΘQ(S_n, ε_n) has some solution A^θ then return A^θ.
else return the prefix tree automaton of S_n.
```

DEES identifies $\mathcal{S}_{\mathrm{PRFA}}$ in the limit with probability 1.

Theorem 5. *Let $P \in \mathcal{S}_{\mathrm{PRFA}}$ and let S be a complete presentation of P, then with probability one, there exists $N \in \mathbb{N}$, such that for any $n > N$, the set of states of* DEES (S_n) *is* $\mathrm{Pm}(P)$ *and $P_{\mathrm{DEES}(S_n)}$ converges to P.*

Proof. It can be proved that, with probability one, after some rank, $I_{\Theta_Q}(S_n, \epsilon_n)$ has solutions if and only if there exists a prefix PRFA A^θ such that $P_{A^\theta} = P$. More precisely, it can be shown that $\mathrm{Pm}(P)$ is identified as the set of states from some index. Proofs are similar as the proofs of Prop. 2 and Prop. 3. □

Example. The the target be the prefix PRFA of Fig. 4. Let S_{20} be the sample such that $\mathrm{pref}(S_{20}) = \{(\varepsilon : 20), (a : 12), (b : 8), (aa : 12), (ba : 2), (aaa : 11), (baa : 1), (aaaa : 4), (aaaaa : 3), (aaaaaa : 2)\}$ where $(u : n)$ means that n occurrences of u are counted.

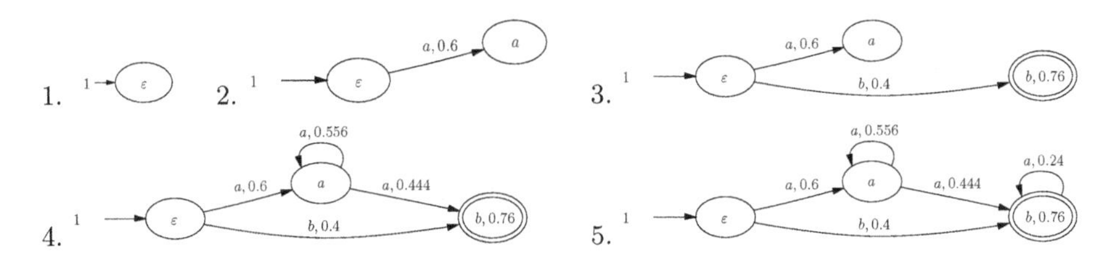

Fig. 5. DEES on S_{20}.

In the first step of the algorithm, $Q = \{\varepsilon\}$ (see Fig. 5.1).
$I_{\Theta_Q}(a, S_n, \epsilon)$ is the system:

$$\left\{\begin{array}{ll} \left|a^{-1}P_n(\Sigma^*) - \frac{\varphi^a_{\varepsilon,\varepsilon}}{P_n(a\Sigma^*)}\varepsilon^{-1}P_n(\Sigma^*)\right| & \leq \epsilon \\ \left|a^{-1}P_n(a\Sigma^*) - \frac{\varphi^a_{\varepsilon,\varepsilon}}{P_n(a\Sigma^*)}\varepsilon^{-1}P_n(a\Sigma^*)\right| & \leq \epsilon \\ & \vdots \end{array}\right. \Leftrightarrow \left\{\begin{array}{ll} \left|1 - \varphi^a_{\varepsilon,\varepsilon}\frac{20}{12} \cdot 1\right| & \leq \epsilon \\ \left|\frac{12}{12} - \varphi^a_{\varepsilon,\varepsilon}\frac{20}{12} \cdot \frac{12}{20}\right| & \leq \epsilon \\ & \vdots \end{array}\right.$$

which has no solution. Then we add the state a to Q (see Fig. 5.2). In the second step, $Q = \{\varepsilon, a\}$ and $I_{\Theta_Q}(b, S_{20}, \epsilon)$ has no solution. Then b is added to Q (see Fig. 5.3). In the third step, $Q = \{\varepsilon, a, b\}$ and as $\varphi^a_{a,\epsilon} = 0$, $\varphi^a_{a,a} = 0,556$ and $\varphi^a_{a,b} = 0,444$ is a solution of $I_{\Theta_Q}(aa, S_n, \epsilon)$, we construct the automaton with these values (see Fig. 5.4). In the last step, $Q = \{\epsilon, a, b\}$, and $\varphi^a_{b,\varepsilon} = \varphi^a_{b,a} = 0$, $\varphi^a_{b,b} = 0,24$ is a valid solution of $I_{\Theta_Q}(ba, S_n, \epsilon)$. The returned automaton is a prefix PRFA close to the target represented on Fig. 4.

6 Conclusion

We have shown that PFA are identifiable in the limit with probability one, that representing stochastic languages using Multiplicity Automata presents some serious drawbacks and we have proposed a subclass of PFA, the class of PRFA, and a learning algorithm which identifies this class and which should be implemented efficiently. In the absence of models which could precisely measure the performances of learning algorithms of PFA, we plan to compare experimentally our algorithm to other learning algorithms used in this field. We predict that we shall have better performances than algorithms that infer PDFA, since PRFA is a much more expressive class, but this has to be experimentally established. The questions remain whether richer subclasses of PFA can be efficiently inferred, and what is the level of expressivity needed in practical learning situations.

References

1. Paz, A.: Introduction to probabilistic automata. Academic Press, London (1971)
2. Abe, N., Warmuth, M.: On the computational complexity of approximating distributions by probabilistic automata. Machine Learning **9** (1992) 205–260
3. Dempster, A., Laird, N.M., Rubin, D.B.: Maximum likelyhood from incomplete data via the em algorithm. Journal of the Royal Statistical Society **39** (1977) 1–38
4. Baldi, P., Brunak, S.: Bioinformatics: The Machine Learning Approach. MIT Press (1998)
5. Freitag, D., McCallum, A.: Information extraction with HMM structures learned by stochastic optimization. In: AAAI/IAAI. (2000) 584–589
6. Gold, E.: Language identification in the limit. Inform. Control **10** (1967) 447–474
7. Angluin, D.: Identifying languages from stochastic examples. Technical Report YALEU/DCS/RR-614, Yale University, New Haven, CT (1988)
8. Carrasco, R., Oncina, J.: Learning stochastic regular grammars by means of a state merging method. In: ICGI, Heidelberg, Springer-Verlag (1994) 139–152
9. Carrasco, R.C., Oncina, J.: Learning deterministic regular grammars from stochastic samples in polynomial time. RAIRO **33** (1999) 1–20
10. de la Higuera, C., Thollard, F.: Identification in the limit with probability one of stochastic deterministic finite automata. In: Proceedings of the 5th ICGI. Volume 1891 of Lecture Notes in Artificial Intelligence. (2000) 141
11. Bergadano, F., Varricchio, S.: Learning behaviors of automata from multiplicity and equivalence queries. In: Italian Conf. on Algorithms and Complexity. (1994)
12. Beimel, A., Bergadano, F., Bshouty, N.H., Kushilevitz, E., Varricchio, S.: On the applications of multiplicity automata in learning. In: IEEE Symposium on Foundations of Computer Science. (1996) 349–358
13. Beimel, A., Bergadano, F., Bshouty, N.H., Kushilevitz, E., Varricchio, S.: Learning functions represented as multiplicity automata. Journal of the ACM **47** (2000) 506–530
14. Thollard, F., Dupont, P., de la Higuera, C. (In: Proc. 17th ICML, title =)
15. Kearns, M., Mansour, Y., Ron, D., Rubinfeld, R., Schapire, R.E., Sellie, L.: On the learnability of discrete distributions. (1994) 273–282
16. Esposito, Y., Lemay, A., Denis, F., Dupont, P.: Learning probabilistic residual finite state automata. In: ICGI'2002, 6th ICGI. LNAI, Springer Verlag (2002)

17. Denis, F., Esposito, Y.: Residual languages and probabilistic automata. In: 30th International Colloquium, ICALP 2003. Number 2719 in LNCS, SV (2003) 452–463
18. Angluin, D.: Queries and concept learning. Machine Learning **2** (1988) 319–342
19. Vapnik, V.N.: Statistical Learning Theory. John Wiley (1998)
20. Lugosi, G.: Pattern classification and learning theory. In: Principles of Nonparametric Learning. Springer (2002) 1–56
21. Hardy, G.H., Wright, E.M.: An introduction to the theory of numbers. Oxford University Press (1979)
22. Blondel, V.D., Canterini, V.: Undecidable problems for probabilistic automata of fixed dimension. Theory of Computing Systems **36** (2003) 231–245

On the Learnability of E-pattern Languages over Small Alphabets

Daniel Reidenbach*

Fachbereich Informatik, Technische Universität Kaiserslautern,
Postfach 3049, 67653 Kaiserslautern, Germany
reidenba@informatik.uni-kl.de

Abstract. This paper deals with two well discussed, but largely open problems on E-pattern languages, also known as extended or erasing pattern languages: primarily, the learnability in Gold's learning model and, secondarily, the decidability of the equivalence. As the main result, we show that the full class of E-pattern languages is not inferrable from positive data if the corresponding terminal alphabet consists of exactly three or of exactly four letters – an insight that remarkably contrasts with the recent positive finding on the learnability of the subclass of terminal-free E-pattern languages for these alphabets. As a side-effect of our reasoning thereon, we reveal some particular example patterns that disprove a conjecture of Ohlebusch and Ukkonen (*Theoretical Computer Science* 186, 1997) on the decidability of the equivalence of E-pattern languages.

1 Introduction

In the context of this paper, a pattern – a finite string that consists of variables and terminal symbols – is used as a device for the definition of a formal language. A word of its language is generated by a uniform substitution of all variables with arbitrary strings of terminal symbols. For instance, the language generated by the pattern $\alpha = x_1 x_1 \, \mathtt{a} \, \mathtt{b} \, x_2$ (with x_1, x_2 as variables and a, b as terminals) includes all words where the prefix can be split in two occurrences of the same string, followed by the string ab and concluded by an arbitrary suffix. Thus, the language of α contains, among others, the words $w_1 = \mathtt{a\,a\,a\,b\,a}$, $w_2 = \mathtt{a\,b\,a\,b\,a\,b\,a\,b}$, $w_3 = \mathtt{a\,b\,b\,b}$, whereas the following examples are not covered by α: $v_1 = \mathtt{b\,a}$, $v_2 = \mathtt{b\,b\,b\,b\,b}$, $v_3 = \mathtt{b\,a\,a\,b\,a}$. Consequently, numerous regular and nonregular languages can be described by patterns in a compact and "natural" way.

The investigation of patterns in strings – initiated by Thue in [22] – may be seen as a classical topic in the research on word monoids and combinatorics of words (cf. [19]); the definition of *pattern languages* as described above goes back to Angluin [1]. Pattern languages have been the subject of several analyses within the scope of formal language theory, e.g. by Jiang, Kinber, Salomaa, Salomaa, Yu [7], [8]) – for a survey see [19] again. These examinations reveal

* Supported by the Deutsche Forschungsgemeinschaft (DFG), Grant Wi 1638/1-2

J. Shawe-Taylor and Y. Singer (Eds.): COLT 2004, LNAI 3120, pp. 140–154, 2004.

that a definition disallowing the substitution of variables with the empty word – as given by Angluin – leads to a language with particular features being quite different from the one allowing the empty substitution (that has been applied when generating w_3 in our example). Languages of the latter type have been introduced by Shinohara in [20]; contrary to those following Angluin's definition (called *NE*-pattern languages), they are referred to as *extended*, *erasing*, or simply *E*-pattern languages.

Particularly for E-pattern languages, a number of fundamental properties is still unresolved; one of the best-known open problems among these is the decidability of the *equivalence*, i.e. the question on the existence of a total computable function that, given any pair of patterns, decides whether or not they generate the same language. This problem, that for NE-pattern languages has a trivial answer in the affirmative, has been discussed several times (cf. [7], [8], [5], and [12]), contributing a number of conjectures, conditions and positive results on subclasses, but no comprehensive answer.

When dealing with pattern languages, manifold questions arise from the problem of computing a pattern that is common to a given set of words. Therefore, pattern languages have been a focus of interest of algorithmic learning theory from the very beginning. In the elementary learning model of inductive inference – known as *learning in the limit* or *Gold style learning* (introduced by Gold in 1967, cf. [6]) – a class of languages is said to be *inferrable from positive data* if and only if a computable device (the so-called *learning strategy*) – that reads growing initial segments of texts (an arbitrary stream of words that, in the limit, fully enumerates the language) – after finitely many steps converges for every language and for every corresponding text to a distinct output exactly representing the given language. In other words, the learning strategy is expected to extract a complete description of a (potentially infinite) language from finite data. According to [6], this task is too challenging for many well-known classes of formal languages: All superfinite classes of languages – i.e. all classes that contain every finite and at least one infinite language – such as the regular, context-free and context-sensitive languages are not inferrable from positive data. Consequently, the number of rich classes of languages that are known to be learnable is rather small. Finally, it is worth mentioning that Gold's model has been complemented by several criteria on language learning (e.g. in [2]) and, moreover, that it has been transformed into a widely analysed learning model for classes of recursive functions (cf., e.g., [4], for a survey see [3]).

The current state of knowledge concerning the learnability of pattern languages considerably differs when regarding NE- or E-pattern languages, respectively. The learnability of the class of NE-pattern languages was shown by Angluin when introducing its definition in 1980 (cf. [1]). In the sequel there has been a variety of additional studies – e.g. in [9], [23], [17] and many more (for a survey see [21]) – concerning the complexity of learning algorithms, consequences of different input data, efficient strategies for subclasses, and so on. The question, however, whether or not the class of E-pattern languages is learnable – considered to be "one of the outstanding open problems in inductive inference" (cf. [11]) – remained unresolved for two decades, until it was answered in [14] in a negative way for terminal alphabets with exactly two letters. Positive results on subclasses have been presented in [20], [11], [13], and [15]. Moreover, [11] proves the full class of E-pattern languages to be learneable for infinite and unary alphabets as these alphabets significantly facilitate inferrability.

In the present paper we show that the class of E-pattern languages is not inferrable from positive data if the corresponding terminal alphabet consists of exactly three or of exactly four letters (cf. Section 3). We consider this outcome for the full class of E-pattern languages as particularly interesting as it contrasts with the results presented in [14] and [15]. The first proves the class of E-pattern languages not to be learnable for binary alphabets since even its subclass of terminal-free E-pattern languages (generated by patterns that consist of variables only) is not learnable for these alphabets. Contrary to this, the latter shows that the class of terminal-free E-pattern languages is inferrable if the corresponding terminal alphabet contains more than two letters. Consequently, with the result of the present paper in mind, for E-pattern languages there obviously is no general way to extend positive findings for the terminal-free subclass on the full class. The method we use is similar to the argumentation in [14], i.e. we give for both types of alphabets a respective example pattern with a certain property which can mislead any potential learning strategy. The foundations of this way of reasoning – that, as in [14], is solely made possible by an appropriate alphabet size and the nondeterminism of E-pattern languages – are explained in Section 2. Finally, in Section 4 one of our example patterns is shown to be applicable to the examinations on the equivalence problem by Ohlebusch and Ukkonen in [12], disproving the central conjecture given therein.

2 Preliminaries

In order to keep this paper largely self-contained we now introduce a number of definitions and basic properties. For standard mathematical notions and recursion-theoretic terms not defined explicitly, we refer to [18]; for unexplained aspects of formal language theory, [19] may be consulted.

$\mathbb{N}$ is the set of natural numbers, $\{0, 1, 2, \dots\}$. For an arbitrary set A of symbols, A^+ denotes the set of all non-empty words over A and A^* the set of all (empty and non-empty) words over A. Any set $L \subseteq A^*$ is a *language* over an alphabet A. We designate the *empty* word as e. For the word that results from the n-fold concatenation of a letter $\mathtt{a}$ or of a word w we write $\mathtt{a}^n$ or w^n, respectively. The size of a set A is denoted by $|A|$ and the length of a word w by $|w|$; $|w|_\mathtt{a}$ is the frequency of a letter $\mathtt{a}$ in a word w.

For any word w that contains at least one occurrence of a letter $\mathtt{a}$ we define the following subwords: $[w/\,\mathtt{a}]$ is the prefix of w up to (but not including) the leftmost occurrence of the letter $\mathtt{a}$ and $[\mathtt{a}\,\backslash w]$ is the suffix of w beginning with the first letter that is to the right of the leftmost occurrence of $\mathtt{a}$ in w. Thus, the specified subwords satisfy $w = [w/\,\mathtt{a}]\ \mathtt{a}\ [\mathtt{a}\,\backslash w]$; e.g., for $w = \mathtt{b\,c\,a\,a\,b}$, the subwords read $[w/\,\mathtt{a}] = \mathtt{b\,c}$ and $[\mathtt{a}\,\backslash w] = \mathtt{a\,b}$.

We proceed with the pattern specific terminology. Σ is a finite or infinite alphabet of *terminal* symbols and $X = \{x_1, x_2, x_3, \dots\}$ an infinite set of *variables*, $\Sigma \cap X = \emptyset$. Henceforth, we use lower case letters in typewriter font, e.g. $\mathtt{a}, \mathtt{b}, \mathtt{c}$, as terminal symbols exclusively; words of terminal symbols are named as u, v, or w. For every $j \geq 1$, the variable y_j is *unspecified*, i.e. there may exist indices k, k' such that $k \neq k'$, but $y_k = y_{k'}$. For unspecified terminal symbols we use upper case letters in typewriter font, such as $\mathtt{A}$.

A *pattern* is a non-empty word over $\Sigma \cup X$, a *terminal-free pattern* is a non-empty word over X; naming patterns we use lower case letters from the beginning of the Greek alphabet. $\mathrm{var}(\alpha)$ denotes the set of all variables of a pattern α. We write Pat_Σ for the set $(\Sigma \cup X)^+$ and we use Pat instead of Pat_Σ if Σ is understood. The pattern $\chi(\alpha)$ derives from any $\alpha \in \mathrm{Pat}$ removing all terminal symbols; e.g., $\chi(x_1 x_1 \, \mathtt{a} \, x_2 \, \mathtt{b}) = x_1 x_1 x_2$.

Following [5], we designate two patterns α, β as *similar* if and only if $\alpha = \alpha_0 \, u_1 \, \alpha_1 \, u_2 \, \dots \, \alpha_{m-1} \, u_m \, \alpha_m$ and $\beta = \beta_0 \, u_1 \, \beta_1 \, u_2 \, \dots \, \beta_{m-1} \, u_m \, \beta_m$ with $m \in \mathbb{N}$, $\alpha_i, \beta_i \in X^+$ for $1 \leq i < m$, $\alpha_0, \beta_0, \alpha_m, \beta_m \in X^*$ and $u_i \in \Sigma^+$ for $i \leq m$; in other words, we call patterns similar if and only if their terminal substrings coincide.

A *substitution* is a morphism $\sigma : (\Sigma \cup X)^* \longrightarrow \Sigma^*$ such that $\sigma(\mathtt{a}) = \mathtt{a}$ for every $\mathtt{a} \in \Sigma$. An *inverse substitution* is a morphism $\bar{\sigma} : \Sigma^* \longrightarrow X^*$. The *E-pattern language* $L_\Sigma(\alpha)$ of a pattern α is defined as the set of all $w \in \Sigma^*$ such that $\sigma(\alpha) = w$ for some substitution σ. For any word $w = \sigma(\alpha)$ we say that σ *generates* w, and for any language $L = L_\Sigma(\alpha)$ we say that α generates L. If there is no need to give emphasis to the concrete shape of Σ we denote the E-pattern language of a pattern α simply as $L(\alpha)$. We use ePAT_Σ (or ePAT for short) as an abbreviation for the full class of E-pattern languages over an alphabet Σ.

Following [11], we designate a pattern α as *succinct* if and only if $|\alpha| \leq |\beta|$ for all patterns β with $L(\beta) = L(\alpha)$. The pattern $\beta = x_1 x_2 x_1 x_2$, for instance, generates the same language as the pattern $\alpha = x_1 x_1$, and therefore β is not succinct; α is succinct because there does not exist any shorter pattern than α that exactly describes its language.

According to the studies of Mateescu and Salomaa on the nondeterminism of pattern languages (cf. [10]) we denote a word w as *ambiguous* (in respect of a pattern α) if and only if there exist two substitutions σ and σ' such that $\sigma(\alpha) = w = \sigma'(\alpha)$, but $\sigma(x_i) \neq \sigma'(x_i)$ for some $x_i \in \mathrm{var}(\alpha)$. The word $w = \mathtt{aaba}$, for instance, is ambiguous in respect of the pattern $\alpha = x_1 \mathtt{a} \, x_2$ since it can be generated by several substitutions, such as σ and σ' with $\sigma(x_1) = \mathtt{a}$, $\sigma(x_2) = \mathtt{ba}$ and $\sigma'(x_1) = e$, $\sigma'(x_2) = \mathtt{aba}$.

We now proceed with some decidability problems on E-pattern languages: Let $\mathrm{ePAT}^\star$ be any set of E-pattern languages. We say that the *inclusion problem* for $\mathrm{ePAT}^\star$ is *decidable* if and only if there exists a computable function which, given two arbitrary patterns α, β with $L(\alpha), L(\beta) \in \mathrm{ePAT}^\star$, decides whether or not $L(\alpha) \subseteq L(\beta)$. Correspondingly, the *equivalence problem* is decidable if and only if there exists another computable function which for every pair of patterns α, β with $L(\alpha), L(\beta) \in \mathrm{ePAT}^\star$ decides whether or not $L(\alpha) = L(\beta)$. Obviously, the decidability of the inclusion implies the decidability of the equivalence. The decidability of the equivalence problem for ePAT has not been resolved yet (cf. Section 4), whereas the inclusion problem is known to be undecidable (cf. [8]). Under certain circumstances, however, the inclusion problem is decidable; this is a consequence of the following fact:

Fact 1 (Ohlebusch, Ukkonen [12]). *Let Σ be an alphabet and α, β two arbitrary similar patterns such that Σ contains two distinct letters not occurring in α and β. Then $L_\Sigma(\beta) \subseteq L_\Sigma(\alpha)$ iff there exists a morphism $\phi : \mathrm{var}(\alpha)^* \longrightarrow \mathrm{var}(\beta)^*$ with $\phi(\alpha) = \beta$.*

In particular, Fact 1 implies the decidability of the inclusion problem for the class of terminal-free E-pattern languages if the alphabet contains at least two distinct letters (shown in [8]).

This paper exclusively deals with language theoretical properties of E-pattern languages. Both motivation and interpretation of our examination, however, are based on learning theory, and therefore we consider it useful to provide an adequate background. To this end, we now introduce our notions on Gold's learning model (cf. [6]) and begin with a specification of the objects to be learned. In this regard, we restrict ourselves to any *indexable class of non-empty languages*; a class $\mathcal{L}$ of languages is indexable if and only if there exists an *indexed family (of non-empty recursive languages)* $(L_i)_{i\in\mathbb{N}}$ such that $\mathcal{L} = \{L_i \mid i \in \mathbb{N}\}$ – this means that the *membership* is uniformly decidable for $(L_i)_{i\in\mathbb{N}}$, i.e. there is a total and computable function which, given any pair of an index $i \in \mathbb{N}$ and a word $w \in \Sigma^*$, decides whether or not $w \in L_i$. Concerning the learner's input, we exclusively consider inference from positive data given as *text*. A text for an arbitrary language L is any total function $t : \mathbb{N} \longrightarrow \Sigma^*$ satisfying $\{t(n) \mid n \in \mathbb{N}\} = L$. For any text t, any $n \in \mathbb{N}$ and a symbol $\diamond \notin \Sigma$, $t^n \in (\Sigma \cup \{\diamond\})^+$ is a coding of the first $n+1$ values of t, i.e. $t^n := t(0) \diamond t(1) \diamond t(2) \ldots \diamond t(n)$. Last, the learner and the learning goal need to be explained: Let the *learner* (or: the *learning strategy*) S be any total computable function that, for a given text t, successively reads t^0, t^1, t^2, etc. and returns a corresponding stream of natural numbers $S(t^0)$, $S(t^1)$, $S(t^2)$, and so on. For a language L_j and a text t for L_j, we say that S *identifies* L_j *from* t if and only if there exist natural numbers n_0 and j' such that, for every $n \geq n_0$, $S(t^n) = j'$ and, additionally, $L_{j'} = L_j$. An indexed family $(L_i)_{i\in\mathbb{N}}$ is *learnable (in the limit)* – or: *inferrable from positive data*, or: $(L_i)_{i\in\mathbb{N}} \in$ LIM-TEXT for short – if and only if there is a learning strategy S identifying each language in $(L_i)_{i\in\mathbb{N}}$ from any corresponding text. Finally, we call an indexable class $\mathcal{L}$ of languages learnable (in the limit) or inferrable from positive data if and only if there is a learnable indexed family $(L_i)_{i\in\mathbb{N}}$ with $\mathcal{L} = \{L_i \mid i \in \mathbb{N}\}$. In this case we write $\mathcal{L} \in$ LIM-TEXT for short.

In fact, the specific learning model given above – that largely is based on [2] – is just a special case of Gold's learning model, which frequently is considered for more general applications as well. For numerous different analyses the elements of our definition are modified or generalised, such as the objects to be learned (e.g., using arbitrary classes of languages instead of indexed families), the learning goal (e.g., asking for a semantic instead of a syntactic convergence), or the output of the learner (choosing a general *hypothesis space* instead of the indexed family).

Concerning the latter point we state that for the case when the LIM-TEXT model is applied to an indexed family, the choice of a general hypothesis spaces instead of the indexed family itself does not yield any additional learning power. For information on suchlike aspects, see [24].

Angluin has introduced some criteria on indexed families that reduce learnability to a particular language theoretical aspect (cf. [2]) and thereby facilitate our approach to learnability questions. For our purposes, the following is sufficient (combining Condition 2 and Corollary 1 of the referenced paper):

Fact 2 (Angluin [2]). *Let $(L_i)_{i \in \mathbb{N}}$ be an arbitrary indexed family of non-empty recursive languages. If $(L_i)_{i \in \mathbb{N}} \in$ LIM-TEXT then for every $j \in \mathbb{N}$ there exists a set T_j such that*

- $T_j \subseteq L_j$,
- *T_j is finite, and*
- *there does not exist a $j' \in \mathbb{N}$ with $T_j \subseteq L_{j'} \subset L_j$.*

If there exists a set T_j satisfying the conditions of Fact 2 then it is called a *telltale* (for L_j) (in respect of $(L_i)_{i \in \mathbb{N}}$).

The importance of telltales – that, at first glance, do not show any connection to the learning model – is caused by the need of avoiding *overgeneralisation* in the inference process, i.e. the case that the strategy outputs an index of a language which is a proper superset of the language to be learned and therefore, as the input consists of positive data only, is unable to detect its mistake. Thus, every language L_j in a learnable indexed family necessarily contains a finite set of words which, in the context of the indexed family, may be interpreted as a signal distinguishing the language from all languages that are subsets of L_j.

With regard to E-pattern languages, Fact 2 is applicable because ePAT is an indexable class of non-empty languages. This is evident as, first, a recursive enumeration of all patterns can be constructed with little effort and, second, the decidability of the membership problem for any pattern $\alpha \in$ Pat and word $w \in \Sigma^*$ is guaranteed since the search space for a successful substitution of α is bounded by the length of w.

Thus, we can conclude this section with a naming for a particular type of patterns that has been introduced in [14] and that directly aims at the content of Fact 2: A pattern β is a *passe-partout* (for a pattern α and a finite set W of words) if and only if $W \subseteq L(\beta)$ and $L(\beta) \subset L(\alpha)$. Consequently, if there exists such a passe-partout β then W is not a telltale for $L(\alpha)$.

3 The Main Result

When asking for the learnability of the class of E-pattern languages then, because of the different results on unary, binary and infinite terminal alphabets (cf. [11] and [14]), it evidently is necessary to specify the size of the alphabet. Keeping this in mind, there are some results on the learnability of subclasses that are worth to be taken into consideration, namely [20] and [15]. The first shows that the class of *regular* E-pattern languages is learnable; these are languages generated by patterns α with $|\alpha|_{x_j} = 1$ for all $x_j \in \text{var}(\alpha)$. Thus, roughly speaking, there is a way to algorithmically detect the position and the shape of the terminal symbols in the pattern from positive data. On the other hand, the latter publication shows that the class of terminal-free E-pattern languages is learnable if and only if the terminal alphabet does not consist of exactly two letters, or, in other words, that it is possible to extract the dependencies of variables for appropriate alphabets. However, our main result states that these theorems are only valid in their own context (i.e. the respective subclasses) and, consequently, that the combination of both approaches is impossible:

Theorem 1. *Let Σ be an alphabet, $|\Sigma| \in \{3, 4\}$. Then* $\text{ePAT}_\Sigma \notin \text{LIM-TEXT}$.

The proof of this theorem is given in the subsequent section.

Thus, with Theorem 1 and the results in [11] and [14], the learnability of the class of E-pattern languages is resolved for infinite alphabets and for finite alphabets with up to four letters. Concerning finite alphabets with five or more distinct letters we conjecture – as an indirect consequence of Section 3.1 – that the question of learnability for all of them can be answered in the same way:

Conjecture 1. Let Σ_1, Σ_2 be arbitrary finite alphabets with at least five letters each. Then $\text{ePAT}_{\Sigma_1} \in \text{LIM-TEXT}$ iff $\text{ePAT}_{\Sigma_2} \in \text{LIM-TEXT}$.

3.1 Proof of the Main Result

First, we give an elementary lemma on morphisms, that can be formulated in several equivalent ways; however, with regard to the needs of the subsequent reasoning on Lemma 2 and Lemma 3 (that provide the actual proof of Theorem 1), we restrict ourselves to a rather special statement on mappings between terminal-free patterns. Although the fact specified therein may be considered evident we additionally give an appropriate proof sketch in order to keep this paper self-contained.

Lemma 1. *Let α, β be terminal-free patterns and ϕ, ψ morphisms with $\phi(\alpha) = \beta$ and $\psi(\beta) = \alpha$. Then either $\psi(\phi(x_j)) = x_j$ for every $x_j \in \text{var}(\alpha)$ or there exists an $x_{j'} \in \text{var}(\alpha)$ such that $|\psi(\phi(x_{j'}))| \geq 2$ and $x_{j'} \in \text{var}(\psi(\phi(x_{j'})))$.*

We call any $x_{j'}$ satisfying these two conditions an *anchor variable* (in respect of ϕ and ψ).

Proof. Let $\alpha := y_1 y_2 y_3 \dots y_m$; then $\beta = \phi(y_1)\phi(y_2)\phi(y_3)\dots\phi(y_m)$. Let y_{k_0} be the leftmost variable such that $\psi(\phi(y_{k_0})) \neq y_{k_0}$. Now assume to the contrary there is no anchor variable in α. Then $\psi(\phi(y_{k_0}))$ necessarily equals e as otherwise $\psi(\beta) \neq \alpha$. Hence, $|\psi(\phi(y_1))\,\psi(\phi(y_2))\,\psi(\phi(y_3))\,\dots\,\psi(\phi(y_{k_0}))| = k_0 - 1$, and obviously, as there is no anchor variable in α, $|\psi(\phi(y_1))\psi(\phi(y_2))\psi(\phi(y_3))\dots\psi(\phi(y_k))| \leq k-1$ for every $k > k_0$. Consequently, $|\psi(\beta)| < |\alpha|$ and therefore $\psi(\beta) \neq \alpha$. This contradiction proves the lemma. □

We now proceed with the patterns that are crucial for our proof of Theorem 1. Contrary to the simply structured pattern used in [14] as an instrument for the negative result on binary alphabets, the examples given here unfortunately have to be rather sophisticated:

Definition 1. *The patterns* $\alpha_{\mathtt{abc}}$ *and* $\alpha_{\mathtt{abcd}}$ *are given by*

$$\alpha_{\mathtt{abc}} := x_1 \ \mathtt{a} \ x_2 \, x_3^2 \, x_4^2 \, x_5^2 \, x_6^2 \ \mathtt{a} \ x_7 \ \mathtt{a} \ x_2 \, x_8^2 \, x_4^2 \, x_5^2 \, x_6^2 \, ,$$
$$\alpha_{\mathtt{abcd}} := x_1 \ \mathtt{a} \ x_2 \, x_3^2 \, x_4^2 \, x_5^2 \, x_6^2 \, x_7^2 \, x_8 \ \mathtt{b} \ x_9 \ \mathtt{a} \ x_2 \, x_{10}^2 \, x_4^2 \, x_5^2 \, x_6^2 \, x_{11}^2 \, x_8 \ \mathtt{b} \ x_{12} \, .$$

$\alpha_{\mathtt{abc}}$ is used in Lemma 2 for the proof of Theorem 1 in case of alphabets with exactly three letters and $\alpha_{\mathtt{abcd}}$ in Lemma 3 for those with four. In these lemmata we show that $L(\alpha_{\mathtt{abc}})$ and $L(\alpha_{\mathtt{abcd}})$ for their particular alphabets do not have any telltale in respect of ePAT.

First, due to the intricacy of these patterns, we consider it helpful for the understanding of the proofs of the lemmata to briefly discuss the meaning of some of their variables and terminal symbols in our reasoning; we focus on $\alpha_{\mathtt{abc}}$ since $\alpha_{\mathtt{abcd}}$ is a natural extension thereof. Our argumentation on the lemmata utilises the insight that, with regard to E-pattern languages, the ambiguity of a word decides on the question of whether this word can be a useful part of a telltale. For instance, concerning the pattern $\alpha_0 := x_4^2 x_5^2 x_6^2$, that makes up the core of our example patterns, it is shown in [14] and [15] that any telltale of $L(\alpha_0)$ necessarily has to contain particular words which consist of three distinct letters in order to avoid a specific and unwanted kind of ambiguity. However, if for any substitution σ that is applied to $\alpha_1 := x_1 \, \mathtt{a} \, x_2 x_3^2 \alpha_0$ – which is a prefix of $\alpha_{\mathtt{abc}}$ – $\sigma(\alpha_0)$ contains all three letters of the alphabet and, thus, includes the letter a then $\sigma(\alpha_1)$ again is ambiguous and always may be generated by a second substitution σ' with $\sigma'(\alpha_0) = e$, $\sigma'(x_1) = \sigma(x_1 \, \mathtt{a} \, x_2 x_3^2)[\sigma(\alpha_0)/\,\mathtt{a}]$, $\sigma'(x_2) = [\mathtt{a} \backslash \sigma(\alpha_0)]$. With σ', in turn, we can give an inverse substitution leading to a tailor-made pattern that assuredly can be part of a passe-partout. Thus, for α_1 we can state the desired gap between, on the one hand, the need of substituting α_0 by three different letters and, on the other hand, the ambiguity of all words that conform to this requirement. However, due to the unique variable x_2 in α_1, the language generated by α_1 evidently equals that of $\alpha_2 := x_1 \, \mathtt{a} \, x_2$, turning the core substring α_0 to be redundant. Therefore, α_1 has to occur at least twice in the pattern (with an optional separating occurrence of the letter a). Since in the pattern $\alpha_1 \, \mathtt{a} \, \alpha_1$ still both occurrences of the substring α_0 are redundant, the second occurrence of α_1 is transformed into $\alpha_1' := x_7 \, \mathtt{a} \, x_2 x_8^2 \alpha_0$. Hence, $\alpha_{\mathtt{abc}} = \alpha_1 \, \mathtt{a} \, \alpha_1'$.

With regard to $\alpha_{\mathtt{abcd}}$, the underlying principle is similar. As stated above, three distinct letters are needed for an appropriate telltale substitution σ of α_0. However, if b, c, d are chosen as these letters, the desired ambiguity of $\sigma(\alpha_1)$ cannot be guaranteed. Hence, α_1 in $\alpha_{\mathtt{abcd}}$ is extended to $\hat{\alpha}_1 := \alpha_1 x_7^2 x_8 \, \mathtt{b} \, x_9$, such that every $\sigma(\hat{\alpha}_1)$ is ambiguous as soon as $\sigma(\alpha_0)$ contains the letters a or b. Furthermore, due to the reasons described above, a modification of $\hat{\alpha}_1$ serves as suffix of $\alpha_{\mathtt{abcd}}$, namely $\hat{\alpha}_1' := x_9 \, \mathtt{a} \, x_2 x_{10}^2 \alpha_0 x_{11}^2 x_8 \, \mathtt{b} \, x_{12}$. Contrary to the structure of $\alpha_{\mathtt{abc}}$, the prefix $\hat{\alpha}_1$ and the suffix $\hat{\alpha}_1'$ in this case are not separated by a terminal symbol, but they are overlapping.

Now we specify and formalise the approach discussed above:

Lemma 2. *Let $\Sigma := \{\mathtt{a}, \mathtt{b}, \mathtt{c}\}$. Then for $\alpha_{\mathtt{abc}}$ and for every finite $W \subset L_\Sigma(\alpha_{\mathtt{abc}})$ there exists a passe-partout $\beta \in$* Pat.

Proof. If W is empty then the claim of Lemma 2 holds trivially. Hence, let $W = \{w_1, w_2, w_3, \ldots, w_n\}$ be non-empty. Then, as $W \subset L_\Sigma(\alpha_{\mathtt{abc}})$, for every $w_i \in W$ there exists a substitution σ_i satisfying $\sigma_i(\alpha_{\mathtt{abc}}) = w_i$. Using these σ_i the following procedure constructs a passe-partout $\beta \in$ Pat:

Initially, we define

$$\beta_0 := \gamma_{1,0}\ \mathtt{a}\ \gamma_{2,0}\ \gamma_{3,0}^2\ \gamma_{4,0}^2\ \gamma_{5,0}^2\ \gamma_{6,0}^2\ \mathtt{a}\ \gamma_{7,0}\ \mathtt{a}\ \gamma_{2,0}\ \gamma_{8,0}^2\ \gamma_{4,0}^2\ \gamma_{5,0}^2\ \gamma_{6,0}^2$$

with $\gamma_{j,0} := e$ for every j, $1 \leq j \leq 8$.

For every $w_i \in W$ we define an inverse substitution $\bar{\sigma}_i : \Sigma^* \longrightarrow X^*$ by

$$\bar{\sigma}_i(\mathtt{A}) := \begin{cases} x_{3i-2} & , \quad \mathtt{A} = \mathtt{a}\,, \\ x_{3i-1} & , \quad \mathtt{A} = \mathtt{b}\,, \\ x_{3i} & , \quad \mathtt{A} = \mathtt{c}\,. \end{cases}$$

For every $i = 1, 2, 3, \ldots, n$ we now consider the following cases:

Case 1: There is no $\mathtt{A} \in \Sigma$ with $|\sigma_i(x_6)|_\mathtt{A} = 1$ and $|\sigma_i(\chi(\alpha_{\mathtt{abc}}))|_\mathtt{A} = 4$
Define $\gamma_{j,i} := \gamma_{j,i-1}\ \bar{\sigma}_i(\sigma_i(x_j))$ for every j, $1 \leq j \leq 8$.

Case 2: There is an $\mathtt{A} \in \Sigma$ with $|\sigma_i(x_6)|_\mathtt{A} = 1$ and $|\sigma_i(\chi(\alpha_{\mathtt{abc}}))|_\mathtt{A} = 4$

Case 2.1: $\mathtt{A} = \mathtt{a}$

Define
$$\begin{aligned} \gamma_{1,i} &:= \gamma_{1,i-1}\ \bar{\sigma}_i(\sigma_i(x_1\ \mathtt{a}\ x_2\ x_3^2\ x_4^2\ x_5^2))\ \bar{\sigma}_i([\sigma_i(x_6^2)/\ \mathtt{a}])\,, \\ \gamma_{2,i} &:= \gamma_{2,i-1}\ \bar{\sigma}_i([\mathtt{a} \backslash \sigma_i(x_6^2)])\,, \\ \gamma_{7,i} &:= \gamma_{7,i-1}\ \bar{\sigma}_i(\sigma_i(x_7\ \mathtt{a}\ x_2\ x_8^2\ x_4^2\ x_5^2))\ \bar{\sigma}_i([\sigma_i(x_6^2)/\ \mathtt{a}])\,, \\ \gamma_{j,i} &:= \gamma_{j,i-1},\ j \in \{3,4,5,6,8\}\,. \end{aligned}$$

Case 2.2: $\mathtt{A} = \mathtt{b}$

Case 2.2.1: $\sigma_i(x_4^2\ x_5^2) \in \{\mathtt{a}\}^* \cup \{\mathtt{c}\}^*$

Define
$$\begin{aligned} \gamma_{4,i} &:= \gamma_{4,i-1}\ \bar{\sigma}_i(\sigma_i(x_4\ x_5))\,, \\ \gamma_{5,i} &:= \gamma_{5,i-1}\ \bar{\sigma}_i(\sigma_i(x_6))\,, \\ \gamma_{6,i} &:= \gamma_{6,i-1}\,, \\ \gamma_{j,i} &:= \gamma_{j,i-1}\ \bar{\sigma}_i(\sigma_i(x_j)),\ j \in \{1,2,3,7,8\}\,. \end{aligned}$$

Case 2.2.2: $\sigma_i(x_4^2\ x_5^2) \in \{\mathtt{a}, \mathtt{c}\}^+ \setminus (\{\mathtt{a}\}^+ \cup \{\mathtt{c}\}^+)$

Define
$$\begin{aligned} \gamma_{1,i} &:= \gamma_{1,i-1}\ \bar{\sigma}_i(\sigma_i(x_1\ \mathtt{a}\ x_2\ x_3^2))\ \bar{\sigma}_i([\sigma_i(x_4^2\ x_5^2)/\ \mathtt{a}])\,, \\ \gamma_{2,i} &:= \gamma_{2,i-1}\ \bar{\sigma}_i([\mathtt{a} \backslash \sigma_i(x_4^2\ x_5^2\ x_6^2)])\,, \\ \gamma_{7,i} &:= \gamma_{7,i-1}\ \bar{\sigma}_i(\sigma_i(x_7\ \mathtt{a}\ x_2\ x_8^2))\ \bar{\sigma}_i([\sigma_i(x_4^2\ x_5^2)/\ \mathtt{a}])\,, \\ \gamma_{j,i} &:= \gamma_{j,i-1},\ j \in \{3,4,5,6,8\}\,. \end{aligned}$$

Case 2.3: $\mathtt{A} = \mathtt{c}$

Adapt case 2.2 replacing $\mathtt{c}$ by $\mathtt{b}$ in the predicates of cases 2.2.1 and 2.2.2.

Finally, define

$$\beta_i := \gamma_{1,i}\ \mathtt{a}\ \gamma_{2,i}\,\gamma_{3,i}^2\,\gamma_{4,i}^2\,\gamma_{5,i}^2\,\gamma_{6,i}^2\ \mathtt{a}\ \gamma_{7,i}\ \mathtt{a}\ \gamma_{2,i}\,\gamma_{8,i}^2\,\gamma_{4,i}^2\,\gamma_{5,i}^2\,\gamma_{6,i}^2\ .$$

When this has been accomplished for every i, $1 \le i \le n$, then define $\beta := \beta_n$.

Now, in order to conclude the proof, the following has to be shown: β is a passe-partout for $\alpha_{\mathtt{abc}}$ and W, i.e.

1. $W \subseteq L(\beta)$ and
2. $L(\beta) \subset L(\alpha_{\mathtt{abc}})$.

ad 1. For every i, $1 \le i \le n$, we define a substitution σ_i' by

$$\sigma_i'(x_j) := \begin{cases} \mathtt{a} & , \quad j = 3i-2\,, \\ \mathtt{b} & , \quad j = 3i-1\,, \\ \mathtt{c} & , \quad j = 3i\,, \\ e & , \quad \text{else}\,. \end{cases}$$

If w_i satisfies case 1 then obviously $\sigma_i'(\beta) = w_i$; if w_i satisfies case 2 then w_i necessarily is ambiguous and therefore in that case $\sigma_i'(\beta) = w_i$ as well. Thus, $W \subseteq L(\beta)$.

ad 2. Obviously, $\alpha_{\mathtt{abc}}$ and β are similar and there are two letters in Σ, namely $\mathtt{b}$ and $\mathtt{c}$, that do not occur in these patterns. Consequently, the inclusion criterion given in Fact 1 is applicable. According to this, $L(\beta) \subseteq L(\alpha_{\mathtt{abc}})$ since there exists a morphism $\phi : \mathrm{var}(\alpha_{\mathtt{abc}}) \longrightarrow \mathrm{var}(\beta)^*$ with $\phi(\alpha_{\mathtt{abc}}) = \beta$, given by $\phi(x_j) = \gamma_{j,n}$ for every $x_j \in \mathrm{var}(\alpha_{\mathtt{abc}})$.

We now prove that $L(\beta)$ is a proper subset of $L(\alpha_{\mathtt{abc}})$. More precisely, we show that there is no morphism $\psi : \mathrm{var}(\beta) \longrightarrow \mathrm{var}(\alpha_{\mathtt{abc}})^*$ with $\psi(\beta) = \alpha_{\mathtt{abc}}$. For that purpose, assume to the contrary there is such a morphism ψ. Then, as there is no variable in $\mathrm{var}(\alpha_{\mathtt{abc}})$ with more than four occurrences in $\alpha_{\mathtt{abc}}$, $\psi(x_k) = e$ for all $x_k \in \mathrm{var}(\beta)$ with $|\beta|_{x_k} \ge 5$. With regard to the variables in $\mathrm{var}(\gamma_{6,n})$, this means the following: If every letter in $\sigma_i(x_6)$ occurs more than four times in $\sigma_i(\chi(\alpha_{\mathtt{abc}}))$ then case 1 is satisfied and, consequently, every variable that is added to $\gamma_{6,i}$ occurs at least five times in β. If any letter $\mathtt{A}$ in $\sigma_i(x_6)$ occurs exactly four times in $\sigma_i(\chi(\alpha_{\mathtt{abc}}))$ – and, obviously, it must be at least four times as $|\,\alpha_{\mathtt{abc}}\,|_{x_6} = 4$ – then case 2 is applied, which, enabled by the ambiguity of w_i in that case, arranges the newly added components of $\gamma_{6,i}$ such that $\bar{\sigma}_i(\sigma_i(\mathtt{A}))$ is shifted to a different $\gamma_{j,i}$. Consequently, $|\beta|_{x_k} \ge 5$ for all $x_k \in \mathrm{var}(\gamma_{6,n})$ and, therefore, $\psi(\gamma_{6,n}) = e \ne x_6$. Hence, we analyse whether or not $\mathrm{var}(\alpha_{\mathtt{abc}})$ contains an anchor variable $x_{j'}$ in respect of ϕ and ψ (cf. Lemma 1). Evidently, $j' \notin \{1,7\}$; for $j' \in \{3,4,5,8\}$, $x_{j'}$ being an anchor variable implies that $\psi(\gamma_{j',n}^2) = x_k x_{k'} \delta x_k x_{k'} \delta$ with variables $x_k, x_{k'}$ and $\delta \in X^*$, but there is no substring in $\alpha_{\mathtt{abc}}$ that equals the given shape of $\psi(\gamma_{j',n}^2)$. Finally, x_2 cannot be an anchor variable since $\psi(\gamma_{2,n})$ had to equal both $x_2 x_3 \delta$ and $x_2 x_8 \delta$ for a $\delta \in X^*$. Consequently, there is no anchor variable in $\mathrm{var}(\alpha_{\mathtt{abc}})$. This contradicts $\psi(\gamma_{6,n}) = e \ne x_6$ and therefore the assumption is incorrect. Thus, $L(\beta) \not\supseteq L(\alpha_{\mathtt{abc}})$ and, finally, $L(\beta) \subset L(\alpha_{\mathtt{abc}})$. □

Lemma 3. *Let* $\Sigma := \{\mathtt{a}, \mathtt{b}, \mathtt{c}, \mathtt{d}\}$. *Then for* $\alpha_{\mathtt{abcd}}$ *and for every finite* $W \subset L_\Sigma(\alpha_{\mathtt{abcd}})$ *there exists a passe-partout* $\beta \in \mathrm{Pat}$.

Proof. We can argue similar to the proof of Lemma 2: For an empty W the claim of Lemma 2 holds obviously. For any non-empty $W = \{w_1, w_2, w_3, \dots, w_n\} \subset L_\Sigma(\alpha_{\mathtt{abcd}})$ there exist substitutions σ_i, $1 \leq i \leq n$, satisfying $\sigma_i(\alpha_{\mathtt{abcd}}) = w_i$. With these σ_i we give the following procedure that constructs a passe-partout $\beta \in \mathrm{Pat}$:

Initially, we define

$$\beta_0 := \gamma_{1,0}\ \mathtt{a}\ \gamma_{2,0}\ \gamma_{3,0}^2\ \gamma_{4,0}^2\ \gamma_{5,0}^2\ \gamma_{6,0}^2\ \gamma_{7,0}^2\ \gamma_{8,0}\ \mathtt{b}\ \gamma_{9,0}\ \mathtt{a}\ \gamma_{2,0}\ \gamma_{10,0}^2\ \gamma_{4,0}^2\ \gamma_{5,0}^2\ \gamma_{6,0}^2\ \gamma_{11,0}^2\ \gamma_{8,0}\ \mathtt{b}\ \gamma_{12,0}$$

with $\gamma_{j,0} := e$ for every j, $1 \leq j \leq 12$.

For every $w_i \in W$ we define an inverse substitution $\bar{\sigma}_i : \Sigma^* \longrightarrow X^*$ by

$$\bar{\sigma}_i(\mathtt{A}) := \begin{cases} x_{4i-3} & , \quad \mathtt{A} = \mathtt{a}\,, \\ x_{4i-2} & , \quad \mathtt{A} = \mathtt{b}\,, \\ x_{4i-1} & , \quad \mathtt{A} = \mathtt{c}\,, \\ x_{4i} & , \quad \mathtt{A} = \mathtt{d}\,. \end{cases}$$

For every $i = 1, 2, 3, \dots, n$ we now consider the following cases:

Case 1: There is no $\mathtt{A} \in \Sigma$ with $|\sigma_i(x_6)|_{\mathtt{A}} = 1$ and $|\sigma_i(\chi(\alpha_{\mathtt{abcd}}))|_{\mathtt{A}} = 4$
Define $\gamma_{j,i} := \gamma_{j,i-1}\ \bar{\sigma}_i(\sigma_i(x_j))$ for every j, $1 \leq j \leq 12$.

Case 2: There is an $\mathtt{A} \in \Sigma$ with $|\sigma_i(x_6)|_{\mathtt{A}} = 1$ and $|\sigma_i(\chi(\alpha_{\mathtt{abcd}}))|_{\mathtt{A}} = 4$

Case 2.1: $\mathtt{A} = \mathtt{a}$

$$\begin{aligned} \text{Define } \gamma_{1,i} &:= \gamma_{1,i-1}\ \bar{\sigma}_i(\sigma_i(x_1\ \mathtt{a}\ x_2\ x_3^2\ x_4^2\ x_5^2))\ \bar{\sigma}_i([\sigma_i(x_6^2)/\,\mathtt{a}])\,, \\ \gamma_{2,i} &:= \gamma_{2,i-1}\ \bar{\sigma}_i([\mathtt{a}\,\backslash\sigma_i(x_6^2)])\,, \\ \gamma_{9,i} &:= \gamma_{9,i-1}\ \bar{\sigma}_i(\sigma_i(x_9\ \mathtt{a}\ x_2\ x_{10}^2\ x_4^2\ x_5^2))\ \bar{\sigma}_i([\sigma_i(x_6^2)/\,\mathtt{a}])\,, \\ \gamma_{j,i} &:= \gamma_{j,i-1},\ j \in \{3,4,5,6,10\}\,, \\ \gamma_{j,i} &:= \gamma_{j,i-1}\ \bar{\sigma}_i(\sigma_i(x_j)),\ j \in \{7,8,11,12\}\,. \end{aligned}$$

Case 2.2: $\mathtt{A} = \mathtt{b}$

$$\begin{aligned} \text{Define } \gamma_{8,i} &:= \gamma_{8,i-1}\ \bar{\sigma}(\sigma_i(x_4^2\ x_5^2))\ \bar{\sigma}_i([\sigma_i(x_6^2)/\,\mathtt{b}])\,, \\ \gamma_{9,i} &:= \gamma_{9,i-1}\ \bar{\sigma}_i([\mathtt{b}\,\backslash\sigma_i(x_6^2\ x_7^2\ x_8\ \mathtt{b}\ x_9)])\,, \\ \gamma_{12,i} &:= \gamma_{12,i-1}\ \bar{\sigma}_i([\mathtt{b}\,\backslash\sigma_i(x_6^2\ x_{11}^2\ x_8\ \mathtt{b}\ x_{12})])\,, \\ \gamma_{j,i} &:= \gamma_{j,i-1},\ j \in \{4,5,6,7,11\}\,, \\ \gamma_{j,i} &:= \gamma_{j,i-1}\ \bar{\sigma}_i(\sigma_i(x_j)),\ j \in \{1,2,3,10\}\,. \end{aligned}$$

Case 2.3: $\mathtt{A} = \mathtt{c}$

Case 2.3.1: $\sigma_i(x_4^2\ x_5^2) \in \{\mathtt{a}\}^* \cup \{\mathtt{b}\}^* \cup \{\mathtt{d}\}^*$

$$\begin{aligned} \text{Define } \gamma_{4,i} &:= \gamma_{4,i-1}\ \bar{\sigma}_i(\sigma_i(x_4\ x_5))\,, \\ \gamma_{5,i} &:= \gamma_{5,i-1}\ \bar{\sigma}_i(\sigma_i(x_6))\,, \\ \gamma_{6,i} &:= \gamma_{6,i-1}\,, \\ \gamma_{j,i} &:= \gamma_{j,i-1}\ \bar{\sigma}_i(\sigma_i(x_j)),\ j \in \{1,2,3,7,8,9,10,11,12\}\,. \end{aligned}$$

Case 2.3.2: $\sigma_i(x_4^2\, x_5^2) \in \{\mathtt{a}, \mathtt{d}\}^+ \setminus (\{\mathtt{a}\}^+ \cup \{\mathtt{d}\}^+)$

Define $\gamma_{1,i} := \gamma_{1,i-1}\ \bar{\sigma}_i(\sigma_i(x_1\ \mathtt{a}\ x_2\, x_3^2))\ \bar{\sigma}_i([\sigma_i(x_4^2\, x_5^2)/\,\mathtt{a}])\,,$

$\gamma_{2,i} := \gamma_{2,i-1}\ \bar{\sigma}_i([\mathtt{a}\,\backslash \sigma_i(x_4^2\, x_5^2\, x_6^2)])\,,$

$\gamma_{9,i} := \gamma_{9,i-1}\ \bar{\sigma}_i(\sigma_i(x_9\ \mathtt{a}\ x_2\, x_{10}^2))\ \bar{\sigma}_i([\sigma_i(x_4^2\, x_5^2)/\,\mathtt{a}])\,,$

$\gamma_{j,i} := \gamma_{j,i-1},\ j \in \{3, 4, 5, 6, 10\}\,,$

$\gamma_{j,i} := \gamma_{j,i-1}\ \bar{\sigma}_i(\sigma_i(x_j)),\ j \in \{7, 8, 11, 12\}\,.$

Case 2.3.3: $\sigma_i(x_4^2\, x_5^2) \in \{\mathtt{a}, \mathtt{b}, \mathtt{d}\}^+ \setminus (\{\mathtt{a}\}^+ \cup \{\mathtt{b}\}^+ \cup \{\mathtt{d}\}^+ \cup \{\mathtt{a}, \mathtt{d}\}^+)$

Define $\gamma_{8,i} := \gamma_{8,i-1}\ \bar{\sigma}([\sigma_i(x_4^2\, x_5^2)/\,\mathtt{b}])\,,$

$\gamma_{9,i} := \gamma_{9,i-1}\ \bar{\sigma}_i([\mathtt{b}\,\backslash \sigma_i(x_4^2\, x_5^2\, x_6^2\, x_7^2\, x_8\ \mathtt{b}\ x_9)])\,,$

$\gamma_{12,i} := \gamma_{12,i-1}\ \bar{\sigma}_i([\mathtt{b}\,\backslash \sigma_i(x_4^2\, x_5^2\, x_6^2\, x_{11}^2\, x_8\ \mathtt{b}\ x_{12})])\,,$

$\gamma_{j,i} := \gamma_{j,i-1},\ j \in \{4, 5, 6, 7, 11\}\,,$

$\gamma_{j,i} := \gamma_{j,i-1}\ \bar{\sigma}_i(\sigma_i(x_j)),\ j \in \{1, 2, 3, 10\}\,.$

Case 2.4: $\mathtt{A} = \mathtt{d}$

Adapt case 2.3 replacing $\mathtt{d}$ by $\mathtt{c}$ in the predicates of cases 2.3.1, 2.3.2 and 2.3.3.

Finally, define

$$\beta_i := \gamma_{1,i}\ \mathtt{a}\ \gamma_{2,i}\, \gamma_{3,i}^2\, \gamma_{4,i}^2\, \gamma_{5,i}^2\, \gamma_{6,i}^2\, \gamma_{7,i}^2\, \gamma_{8,i}\ \mathtt{b}\ \gamma_{9,i}\ \mathtt{a}\ \gamma_{2,i}\, \gamma_{10,i}^2\, \gamma_{4,i}^2\, \gamma_{5,i}^2\, \gamma_{6,i}^2\, \gamma_{11,i}^2\, \gamma_{8,i}\ \mathtt{b}\ \gamma_{12,i}\,.$$

When this has been accomplished for every i, $1 \leq i \leq n$, then define $\beta := \beta_n$.

For the proof that β indeed is a passe-partout for α_{abcd} and W, see the proof of Lemma 2, mutatis mutandis. □

Concluding the proof of Theorem 1, we state that it directly follows from Lemma 2, Lemma 3, and Fact 2: Obviously, any indexed family $(L_i)_{i \in \mathbb{N}}$ with $\{L_i \mid i \in \mathbb{N}\} = \text{ePAT}$ necessarily contains all languages generated by potential passe-partouts for α_{abc} and α_{abcd}, respectively. Thus, $L_\Sigma(\alpha_{\mathsf{abc}})$ has no telltale in respect of ePAT_Σ if $|\Sigma| = 3$ and $L_\Sigma(\alpha_{\mathsf{abcd}})$ has no telltale in respect of ePAT_Σ if $|\Sigma| = 4$. Consequently, ePAT_Σ is not learnable for these two types of alphabets.

3.2 Some Remarks

Clearly, both procedures constructing the passe-partouts implement only one out of many possibilities. The definition of the $\gamma_{j,i}$ in case 2.3.1 in the proof of Lemma 3, for instance, could be separated in cases 2.3.1.1 and 2.3.1.2 depending on the question whether or not $\sigma_i(x_4^2 x_5^2) \in \{\mathtt{a}\}^+$. If so then case 2.3.1.1 could equal case 2.3.2, possibly leading to a different passe-partout. It can be seen easily that there are numerous other options like this. On the other hand, there are infinitely many different succinct patterns that can act as a substitute for α_{abc} and α_{abcd} in the respective lemmata. Some of these patterns, for instance, can be constructed replacing in α_{abc} and α_{abcd} the substring $\alpha_0 = x_4^2 x_5^2 x_6^2$ by any $\alpha_0' = x_p^2 x_{p+1}^2 \ldots x_{p+q}^2$, $p > \max\{j \mid x_j \in \text{var}(\alpha_{\mathsf{abcd}})\}$, $q \geq 4$. Hence, the phenomenon described in Lemma 2 and Lemma 3 is ubiquitous in ePAT. Therefore we give some brief considerations concerning the question on the shortest patterns generating a language without telltale in respect of ePAT. Obviously, even for the proof concept of Lemma 2 and Lemma 3, shorter patterns are suitable. In $\alpha_{\mathtt{abc}}$, e.g., the substring x_3^2 and the separating terminal symbol $\mathtt{a}$ in the middle of the pattern can be removed without loss of applicability; for $\alpha_{\mathtt{abcd}}$, e.g., the substrings x_3^2 and x_7^2 can be mentioned. Nevertheless, we consider both patterns in the given shape easier to grasp, and, moreover, we assume that the indicated steps for shortening $\alpha_{\mathtt{abc}}$ and $\alpha_{\mathtt{abcd}}$ lead to patterns with minimum length:

Conjecture 2. Let the alphabets Σ_1 and Σ_2 be given by $\Sigma_1 := \{\mathtt{a}, \mathtt{b}, \mathtt{c}\}$ and $\Sigma_2 := \{\mathtt{a}, \mathtt{b}, \mathtt{c}, \mathtt{d}\}$. Let the patterns $\alpha_{\mathtt{abc}}'$ and $\alpha_{\mathtt{abcd}}'$ be given by

$$\alpha_{\mathtt{abc}}' := x_1 \; \mathtt{a} \; x_2 \, x_4^2 \, x_5^2 \, x_6^2 \, x_7 \; \mathtt{a} \; x_2 \, x_8^2 \, x_4^2 \, x_5^2 \, x_6^2,$$

$$\alpha_{\mathtt{abcd}}' := x_1 \; \mathtt{a} \; x_2 \, x_4^2 \, x_5^2 \, x_6^2 \, x_8 \; \mathtt{b} \; x_9 \; \mathtt{a} \; x_2 \, x_{10}^2 \, x_4^2 \, x_5^2 \, x_6^2 \, x_{11}^2 \, x_8 \; \mathtt{b} \; x_{12}.$$

Then $L_{\Sigma_1}(\alpha_{\mathtt{abc}}')$ has no telltale in respect of ePAT_{Σ_1}, $L_{\Sigma_2}(\alpha_{\mathtt{abcd}}')$ has no telltale in respect of ePAT_{Σ_2} and there do not exist any shorter patterns in Pat with this respective property.

Finally, we emphasise that we consider it necessary to prove our result for both alphabet types separately. Obviously, for our way of reasoning, this is caused by the fact that the proof of Lemma 2 cannot be conducted with $\alpha_{\mathtt{abcd}}$ since this pattern – in combination with any passe-partout an adapted procedure could generate – does not satisfy the conditions of Fact 1 for alphabets with three letters. In effect, the problem is even more fundamental: Assume there are two alphabets Σ_1 and Σ_2 with $\Sigma_1 \subset \Sigma_2$. If for some $\alpha \in \text{Pat}_{\Sigma_1}$ there is no telltale $T_\alpha \subseteq L_{\Sigma_2}(\alpha)$ – as shown to be true for $\alpha_{\mathtt{abcd}}$ – then, at first glance, it seems natural to expect the same for $L_{\Sigma_1}(\alpha)$ since $L_{\Sigma_1}(\alpha) \subset L_{\Sigma_2}(\alpha)$. These considerations, however, immediately are disproven, for instance, by the fact that ePAT is learnable for unary, but not for binary alphabets (cf. [11] and [14]). This can be illustrated easily, e.g., by $\alpha_{\mathtt{abc}}$ and the pattern $\alpha = \mathtt{a}\,\mathtt{a}\,x_1\,\mathtt{a}$. With $\Sigma_1 = \{\mathtt{a}\}$ and $\Sigma_2 = \{\mathtt{a}, \mathtt{b}\}$ we may state $L_{\Sigma_1}(\alpha) = L_{\Sigma_1}(\alpha_{\mathtt{abc}})$, but $L_{\Sigma_2}(\alpha) \subset L_{\Sigma_2}(\alpha_{\mathtt{abc}})$. Thus, for Σ_1 both patterns generate the same language and, consequently, they have the same telltale, whereas any telltale for $L_{\Sigma_2}(\alpha_{\mathtt{abc}})$ has to contain a word that is not in $L_{\Sigma_2}(\alpha)$. The changing equivalence of E-pattern languages is a well-known fact for pairs of alphabets if the smaller one contains at most two distinct letters, but, concerning those pairs with three or more letters each, [12] conjectures that the situation stabilises. This is examined in the following section.

4 $\alpha_{\mathtt{abcd}}$ and the Equivalence Problem

The equivalence problem for E-pattern languages – one of the most prominent and well discussed open problems on this subject – has first been examined in [7] and later in [8], [5], and [12]. The latter authors conjecture that, for patterns $\alpha, \beta \in \text{Pat}$ and any alphabet Σ, $|\Sigma| \geq 3$, $L_\Sigma(\alpha) = L_\Sigma(\beta)$ if and only if there are morphisms $\phi : \text{var}(\alpha) \longrightarrow \text{var}(\beta)$ and $\psi : \text{var}(\beta) \longrightarrow \text{var}(\alpha)$ such that $\phi(\alpha) = \beta$

and $\psi(\beta) = \alpha$ (cf. [12], paraphrase of Conjecture 1). Furthermore, derived from Fact 1 and Theorem 5.3 of [7], the authors state that the equivalence problem is decidable if the following question (cf. [12], Open Question 2) has a positive answer: For arbitrary alphabets Σ_1, Σ_2 with $|\Sigma_1| \geq 3$ and $\Sigma_2 = \Sigma_1 \cup \{\mathtt{d}\}$, $\mathtt{d} \notin \Sigma_1$, and patterns $\alpha, \beta \in \mathrm{Pat}_{\Sigma_1}$, does the following statement hold: $L_{\Sigma_1}(\alpha) = L_{\Sigma_1}(\beta)$ iff $L_{\Sigma_2}(\alpha) = L_{\Sigma_2}(\beta)$? In other words: Is the equivalence of E-pattern languages *preserved under alphabet extension*?

We now show that for $|\Sigma_1| = 3$ this question has an answer in the negative, using $\alpha_{\mathtt{abcd}}$ – which for the learnability result in Section 3 is applied to $|\Sigma| = 4$ – and the following pattern: $\alpha_{\sim} := x_1 \; \mathtt{a} \; x_2 x_3^2 x_4^2 x_7^2 \; x_8 \; \mathtt{b} \; x_9 \; \mathtt{a} \; x_2 x_{10}^2 x_4^2 x_{11}^2 \; x_8 \; \mathtt{b} \; x_{12}$.

Theorem 2. *Let the alphabets Σ_1 and Σ_2 be given by $\Sigma_1 := \{\mathtt{a}, \mathtt{b}, \mathtt{c}\}$ and $\Sigma_2 \supseteq \{\mathtt{a}, \mathtt{b}, \mathtt{c}, \mathtt{d}\}$. Then $L_{\Sigma_1}(\alpha_{\mathtt{abcd}}) = L_{\Sigma_1}(\alpha_{\sim})$, but $L_{\Sigma_2}(\alpha_{\mathtt{abcd}}) \neq L_{\Sigma_2}(\alpha_{\sim})$.*

Proof. We first show that $L_{\Sigma_1}(\alpha_{\mathtt{abcd}}) = L_{\Sigma_1}(\alpha_{\sim})$. Let $\sigma : (\Sigma_1 \cup X)^* \longrightarrow \Sigma_1$ be any substitution that is applied to $\alpha_{\sim}$. Then, obviously, the substitution σ' with $\sigma'(x_j) = \sigma(x_j)$ for all $x_j \in \mathrm{var}(\alpha_{\sim})$ and $\sigma'(x_j) = e$ for all $x_j \notin \mathrm{var}(\alpha_{\sim})$ leads to $\sigma'(\alpha_{\mathtt{abcd}}) = \sigma(\alpha_{\sim})$ and, thus, $L_{\Sigma_1}(\alpha_{\sim}) \subseteq L_{\Sigma_1}(\alpha_{\mathtt{abcd}})$.

Now, let σ be any substitution that is applied to $\alpha_{\mathtt{abcd}}$. We give a second substitution σ' that leads to $\sigma'(\alpha_{\sim}) = \sigma(\alpha_{\mathtt{abcd}})$ and, thus, $L_{\Sigma_1}(\alpha_{\sim}) = L_{\Sigma_1}(\alpha_{\mathtt{abcd}})$:

Case 1: $\sigma(x_4^2 \, x_5^2 \, x_6^2) \in \{\mathtt{a}, \mathtt{b}, \mathtt{c}\}^+ \setminus \{\mathtt{b}, \mathtt{c}\}^+$

Define $\sigma'(x_1) := \sigma(x_1 \; \mathtt{a} \; x_2 \, x_3^2) \, [\sigma(x_4^2 \, x_5^2 \, x_6^2) / \, \mathtt{a}]$,

$\sigma'(x_2) := [\mathtt{a} \setminus \sigma(x_4^2 \, x_5^2 \, x_6^2)]$,

$\sigma'(x_9) := \sigma(x_9 \; \mathtt{a} \; x_2 \, x_{10}^2) \, [\sigma(x_4^2 \, x_5^2 \, x_6^2) / \, \mathtt{a}]$,

$\sigma'(x_j) := \sigma(x_j)$, $j \in \{7, 8, 11, 12\}$,

$\sigma'(x_j) := e$, $j \in \{3, 4, 10\}$.

Case 2: $\sigma(x_4^2 \, x_5^2 \, x_6^2) \in \{\mathtt{b}, \mathtt{c}\}^+ \setminus \{\mathtt{c}\}^+$

Define σ' symmetrically to case 1 using x_9 for x_1, x_8 for x_2, and x_{12} for x_9 (cf., e.g., case 2.2 in the proof of Lemma 3).

Case 3: $\sigma(x_4^2 \, x_5^2 \, x_6^2) \in \{\mathtt{c}\}^*$

Define $\sigma'(x_4) = \sigma(x_4 \, x_5 \, x_6)$ and $\sigma'(x_j) = \sigma(x_j)$ for $x_j \in \mathrm{var}(\alpha_{\sim})$, $j \neq 4$.

The proof for $L_{\Sigma_2}(\alpha_{\sim}) \neq L_{\Sigma_2}(\alpha_{\mathtt{abcd}})$ uses Fact 1 and Lemma 1 and is similar to the argumentation on $L(\beta) \subset L(\alpha_{\mathtt{abc}})$ in the proof of Lemma 2. □

Moreover, the reasoning on Theorem 2 reveals that Conjecture 1 in [12] – as cited above – is incorrect:

Corollary 1. *Let Σ be an alphabet, $|\Sigma| = 3$. Then $L_{\Sigma}(\alpha_{\mathtt{abcd}}) = L_{\Sigma}(\alpha_{\sim})$ and there exists a morphism $\phi : \mathrm{var}(\alpha_{\mathtt{abcd}}) \longrightarrow \mathrm{var}(\alpha_{\sim})$ with $\phi(\alpha_{\mathtt{abcd}}) = \alpha_{\sim}$, but there does not exist any morphism $\psi : \mathrm{var}(\alpha_{\sim}) \longrightarrow \mathrm{var}(\alpha_{\mathtt{abcd}})$ with $\psi(\alpha_{\sim}) = \alpha_{\mathtt{abcd}}$.*

Note that the argumentation on Theorem 2 and Corollary 1 can be conducted with a pattern that is shorter than $\alpha_{\mathtt{abcd}}$ (e.g., by removing x_6).

In [16], that solely examines the above questions for the transition between alphabets with four and alphabets with five letters, some methods of the present section are adopted and, thus, they are explained in more detail.

References

[1] D. Angluin. Finding patterns common to a set of strings. *J. Comput. Syst. Sci.*, 21:46–62, 1980.
[2] D. Angluin. Inductive inference of formal languages from positive data. *Inf. Control*, 45:117–135, 1980.
[3] D. Angluin and C. Smith. Inductive inference: Theory and methods. *Comput. Surv.*, 15:237–269, 1983.
[4] Ja.M. Barzdin and R.V. Freivald. On the prediction of general recursive functions. *Soviet Math. Dokl.*, 13:1224–1228, 1972.
[5] G. Dány and Z. Fülöp. A note on the equivalence problem of E-patterns. *Inf. Process. Lett.*, 57:125–128, 1996.
[6] E.M. Gold. Language identification in the limit. *Inf. Control*, 10:447–474, 1967.
[7] T. Jiang, E. Kinber, A. Salomaa, K. Salomaa, and S. Yu. Pattern languages with and without erasing. *Int. J. Comput. Math.*, 50:147–163, 1994.
[8] T. Jiang, A. Salomaa, K. Salomaa, and S. Yu. Decision problems for patterns. *J. Comput. Syst. Sci.*, 50:53–63, 1995.
[9] S. Lange and R. Wiehagen. Polynomial-time inference of arbitrary pattern languages. *New Generat. Comput.*, 8:361–370, 1991.
[10] A. Mateescu and A. Salomaa. Finite degrees of ambiguity in pattern languages. *RAIRO Inform. théor.*, 28(3–4):233–253, 1994.
[11] A.R. Mitchell. Learnability of a subclass of extended pattern languages. In *Proc. COLT 1998*, pages 64–71, 1998.
[12] E. Ohlebusch and E. Ukkonen. On the equivalence problem for E-pattern languages. *Theor. Comp. Sci.*, 186:231–248, 1997.
[13] D. Reidenbach. A non-learnable class of E-pattern languages. *Theor. Comp. Sci.*, to appear.
[14] D. Reidenbach. A negative result on inductive inference of extended pattern languages. In *Proc. ALT 2002*, volume 2533 of *LNAI*, pages 308–320, 2002.
[15] D. Reidenbach. A discontinuity in pattern inference. In *Proc. STACS 2004*, volume 2996 of *LNCS*, pages 129–140, 2004.
[16] D. Reidenbach. On the equivalence problem for E-pattern languages over four letters. In *Proc. MFCS 2004*, *LNCS*, 2004. Submitted.
[17] R. Reischuk and T. Zeugmann. Learning one-variable pattern languages in linear average time. In *Proc. COLT 1998*, pages 198–208, 1998.
[18] H. Rogers. *Theory of Recursive Functions and Effective Computability.* MIT Press, Cambridge, Mass., 1992. 3rd print.
[19] G. Rozenberg and A. Salomaa. *Handbook of Formal Languages*, volume 1. Springer, Berlin, 1997.
[20] T. Shinohara. Polynomial time inference of extended regular pattern languages. In *Proc. RIMS Symp.*, volume 147 of *LNCS*, pages 115–127, 1982.
[21] T. Shinohara and S. Arikawa. Pattern inference. In *Algorithmic Learning for Knowledge-Based Systems*, volume 961 of *LNAI*, pages 259–291. Springer, 1995.
[22] A. Thue. Über unendliche Zeichenreihen. *Kra. Vidensk. Selsk. Skrifter. I Mat. Nat. Kl.*, 7, 1906.
[23] R. Wiehagen and T. Zeugmann. Ignoring data may be the only way to learn efficiently. *J. Exp. Theor. Artif. Intell.*, 6:131–144, 1994.
[24] T. Zeugmann and S. Lange. A guided tour across the boundaries of learning recursive languages. In *Algorithmic Learning for Knowledge-Based Systems*, volume 961 of *LNAI*, pages 190–258. Springer, 1995.

Replacing Limit Learners with Equally Powerful One-Shot Query Learners

Steffen Lange[1] and Sandra Zilles[2]

[1] Fachhochschule Darmstadt,
FB Informatik, Haardtring 100, 64295 Darmstadt, Germany,
s.lange@fbi.fh-darmstadt.de
[2] Technische Universität Kaiserslautern,
FB Informatik, Postfach 3049, 67653 Kaiserslautern, Germany,
zilles@informatik.uni-kl.de

Abstract. Different formal learning models address different aspects of human learning. Below we compare *Gold-style learning*—interpreting learning as a *limiting process* in which the learner may change its mind arbitrarily often before converging to a correct hypothesis—to *learning via queries*—interpreting learning as a *one-shot process* in which the learner is required to identify the target concept with just one hypothesis. Although these two approaches seem rather unrelated at first glance, we provide characterizations of different models of Gold-style learning (learning in the limit, conservative inference, and behaviourally correct learning) in terms of query learning. Thus we describe the circumstances which are necessary to replace limit learners by equally powerful one-shot learners. Our results are valid in the general context of learning indexable classes of recursive languages.
In order to achieve the learning capability of Gold-style learners, the crucial parameters of the query learning model are the type of queries (membership, restricted superset, or restricted disjointness queries) and the underlying hypothesis space (uniformly recursive, uniformly r. e., or uniformly 2-r. e. families). The characterizations of Gold-style language learning are formulated in dependence of these parameters.

1 Introduction

Undeniably, there is no formal scheme spanning all aspects of human learning. Thus each learning model analysed within the scope of learning theory addresses only special facets of our understanding of learning.

For example, Gold's [8] model of *identification in the limit* is concerned with learning as a limiting process of creating, modifying, and improving hypotheses about a target concept. These hypotheses are based upon instances of the target concept offered as information. In the limit, the learner is supposed to stabilize on a correct guess, but during the learning process one will never know whether or not the current hypothesis is already correct. Here the ability to change its mind is a crucial feature of the learner.

J. Shawe-Taylor and Y. Singer (Eds.): COLT 2004, LNAI 3120, pp. 155–169, 2004.

In contrast to that, Angluin's [2,3] model of *learning with queries* focusses learning as a finite process of interaction between a learner and a teacher. The learner asks questions of a specified type about the target concept and the teacher—having the target concept in mind—answers these questions truthfully. After finitely many steps of interaction the learner is supposed to return its sole hypothesis—correctly describing the target concept. Here the crucial features of the learner are its ability to demand special information on the target concept and its restrictiveness in terms of mind changes. Since a query learner is required to identify the target concept with just a single hypothesis, we refer to this phenomenon as *one-shot learning*.

Our analysis concerns common features and coincidences between these two seemingly unrelated approaches, thereby focussing our attention on the identification of formal languages, ranging over indexable classes of recursive languages, as target concepts, see [1,10,14]. In case such coincidences exist, their revelation might allow for transferring theoretically approved insights from one model to the other. In this context, our main focus will be on characterizations of Gold-style language learning in terms of learning via queries. Characterizing different types of Gold-style language learning in such a way, we will point out interesting correspondences between the two models. In particular, our results demonstrate how learners identifying languages in the limit can be replaced by one-shot learners without loss of learning power. That means, under certain circumstances the capability of limit learners is equal to that of one-shot learners using queries.

The crucial question in this context is what abilities of the teacher are required to achieve the learning capability of Gold-style learners for query learners. In particular, it is of importance which types of queries the teacher is able to answer (and thus the learner is allowed to ask). This addresses two facets: first, the kind of information prompted by the queries (we consider membership, restricted superset, and restricted disjointness queries) and second, the hypothesis space used by the learner to formulate its queries and hypotheses (we consider uniformly recursive, uniformly r. e., and uniformly 2-r. e. families). Note that both aspects affect the demands on the teacher.

Our characterizations reveal the corresponding necessary requirements that have to be made on the teacher. Thereby we formulate coincidences of the learning capabilities assigned to Gold-style learners and query learners in a quite general context, considering three variants of Gold-style language learning. Moreover, we compare our results to several insights in Gold-style learning via oracles, see [13] for a formal background. As a byproduct of our analysis, we provide a special indexable class of recursive languages which can be learned in a behaviourally correct manner[1] in case a uniformly r. e. family is chosen as a hypothesis space, but which is not learnable in the limit, no matter which hypothesis space is chosen. Although such classes have already been offered in the literature, see [1], up to now all examples—to the authors' knowledge—are defined via diagonalisation

[1] Behaviourally correct learning is a variant of learning in the limit, see for example [7,4,13]. A definition is given later on.

in a rather involved manner. In contrast to that, the class we provide below is very simply and explicitly defined without any diagonal construction.

2 Preliminaries and Basic Results

2.1 Notations

Familiarity with standard mathematical, recursion theoretic, and language theoretic notions and notations is assumed, see [12,9]. From now on, a fixed finite alphabet Σ with $\{a, b\} \subseteq \Sigma$ is given. A *word* is any element from Σ^* and a *language* any subset of Σ^*. The *complement* $\overline{L}$ of a language L is the set $\Sigma^* \setminus L$. Any infinite sequence $t = (w_i)_{i \in \mathbb{N}}$ with $\{w_i \mid i \in \mathbb{N}\} = L$ is called a *text* for L.

A family $(A_i)_{i \in \mathbb{N}}$ of languages is *uniformly recursive* (*uniformly r. e.*) if there is a recursive (partial recursive) function f such that $A_i = \{w \in \Sigma^* \mid f(i, w) = 1\}$ for all $i \in \mathbb{N}$. A family $(A_i)_{i \in \mathbb{N}}$ is *uniformly 2-r. e.*, if there is a recursive function g such that $A_i = \{w \in \Sigma^* \mid g(i, w, n) = 1 \text{ for all but finitely many } n\}$ for all $i \in \mathbb{N}$. Note that for uniformly recursive families membership is uniformly decidable.

Let $\mathcal{C}$ be a class of recursive languages over Σ^*. $\mathcal{C}$ is said to be an *indexable class of recursive languages* (in the sequel we will write *indexable class* for short), if there is a uniformly recursive family $(L_i)_{i \in \mathbb{N}}$ of all and only the languages in $\mathcal{C}$. Such a family will subsequently be called an *indexing* of $\mathcal{C}$.

A family $(T_i)_{i \in \mathbb{N}}$ of *finite* languages is *recursively generable*, if there is a recursive function that, given $i \in \mathbb{N}$, enumerates all elements of T_i and stops.

In the sequel, let φ be a Gödel numbering of all partial recursive functions and Φ the associated Blum complexity measure, see [5].

2.2 Gold-Style Language Learning

Let $\mathcal{C}$ be an indexable class, $\mathcal{H} = (L_i)_{i \in \mathbb{N}}$ any uniformly recursive family (called *hypothesis space*), and $L \in \mathcal{C}$. An *inductive inference machine* (*IIM*) M is an algorithmic device that reads longer and longer initial segments σ of a text and outputs numbers $M(\sigma)$ as its hypotheses. An IIM M returning some i is construed to hypothesize the language L_i. Given a text t for L, M *identifies* L *from* t *with respect to* $\mathcal{H}$ *in the limit*, if the sequence of hypotheses output by M, when fed t, stabilizes on a number i (i. e., past some point M always outputs the hypothesis i) with $L_i = L$. M *identifies* $\mathcal{C}$ *in the limit from text* with respect to $\mathcal{H}$, if it identifies every $L' \in \mathcal{C}$ from every corresponding text. $LimTxt_{\text{rec}}$ denotes the collection of all indexable classes $\mathcal{C}'$ for which there are an IIM M' and a uniformly recursive family $\mathcal{H}'$ such that M' identifies $\mathcal{C}'$ in the limit from text with respect to $\mathcal{H}'$. A quite natural and often studied modification of $LimTxt_{\text{rec}}$ is defined by the model of *conservative inference*, see [1]. M is a *conservative* IIM for $\mathcal{C}$ with respect to $\mathcal{H}$, if M performs only justified mind changes, i. e., if M, on some text t for some $L \in \mathcal{C}$, outputs hypotheses i and later j, then M must have seen some element $w \notin L_i$ before returning j. The collection of all indexable classes identifiable from text by a conservative IIM is denoted by $ConsvTxt_{rec}$. Note that $ConsvTxt_{rec} \subset LimTxt_{rec}$ [14]. Since we consider learning from text only, we will assume in the sequel that all languages to be learned are *non-empty*. One main aspect of human learning is modelled in the approach of learning in the limit: the ability to change one's mind during learning. Thus learning is considered as a process in which the learner may change its hypothesis arbitrarily often until reaching its final correct guess. In particular, it is in general impossible to find out whether or not the final hypothesis has been reached, i. e., whether or not a success in learning has already eventuated.

Note that in the given context, where only uniformly recursive families are considered as hypothesis spaces for indexable classes, $LimTxt_{rec}$ coincides with the collection of all indexable classes identifiable from text in a behaviourally correct manner, see [7]: If $\mathcal{C}$ is an indexable class, $\mathcal{H} = (L_i)_{i\in\mathbb{N}}$ a uniformly recursive family, M an IIM, then M is a *behaviourally correct* learner for $\mathcal{C}$ from text with respect to $\mathcal{H}$, if for each $L \in \mathcal{C}$ and each text t for $\mathcal{C}$, all but finitely many outputs i of M when fed t fulfil $L_i = L$. Here M may alternate different correct hypotheses arbitrarily often instead of converging to a single hypothesis. Defining the notion $BcTxt_{rec}$ correspondingly as usual yields $BcTxt_{rec} = LimTxt_{rec}$ (a folklore result). In particular, each IIM *BcTxt*-identifying an indexable class $\mathcal{C}'$ in some uniformly recursive family $\mathcal{H}'$ can be modified to an IIM *LimTxt*-identifying $\mathcal{C}'$ in $\mathcal{H}'$.

This coincidence no longer holds, if more general types of hypothesis spaces are considered. Assume $\mathcal{C}$ is an indexable class and $\mathcal{H}^+ = (U_i)_{i\in\mathbb{N}}$ is any uniformly r. e. family of languages comprising $\mathcal{C}$. Then it is also conceivable to use $\mathcal{H}^+$ as a hypothesis space. $LimTxt_{r.e.}$ ($BcTxt_{r.e.}$) denotes the collection of all indexable classes learnable as in the definition of $LimTxt_{rec}$ ($BcTxt_{rec}$), if the demand for a uniformly recursive family $\mathcal{H}$ as a hypothesis space is loosened to demanding a uniformly r. e. family $\mathcal{H}^+$ as a hypothesis space. Interestingly, $LimTxt_{rec} = LimTxt_{r.e.}$ (a folklore result), i. e., in learning in the limit, the capabilities of IIMs do not increase, if the constraints concerning the hypothesis space are weakened by allowing for arbitrary uniformly r. e. families. In contrast to that, in the context of *BcTxt*-identification, weakening these constraints yields an add-on in learning power, i. e., $BcTxt_{rec} \subset BcTxt_{r.e.}$. In particular, $LimTxt_{rec} \subset BcTxt_{r.e.}$ and so *LimTxt*- and *BcTxt*-learning no longer coincide for identification with respect to arbitrary uniformly r. e. families, see also [4,1].

Hence, in what follows, our analysis of Gold-style language learning will focus on the inference types $LimTxt_{rec}$, $ConsvTxt_{rec}$, and $BcTxt_{r.e.}$.

The main results of our analysis will be characterizations of these inference types in the query learning model. For that purpose we will make use of well-known characterizations concerning so-called families of *telltales*, see [1].

Definition 1. *Let $(L_i)_{i\in\mathbb{N}}$ be a uniformly recursive family and $(T_i)_{i\in\mathbb{N}}$ a family of finite non-empty sets. $(T_i)_{i\in\mathbb{N}}$ is called a family of telltales for $(L_i)_{i\in\mathbb{N}}$ iff for all $i, j \in \mathbb{N}$:*

1. *$T_i \subseteq L_i$.*
2. *If $T_i \subseteq L_j \subseteq L_i$, then $L_j = L_i$.*

The concept of telltale families is the best known notion to illustrate the specific differences between indexable classes in $LimTxt_{\text{rec}}$, $ConsvTxt_{\text{rec}}$, and $BcTxt_{\text{r.e.}}$. Telltale families and their algorithmic structure have turned out to be characteristic for identifiability in our three models, see [1,10,14,4]:

Theorem 1. *Let $\mathcal{C}$ be an indexable class of languages.*

1. $\mathcal{C} \in LimTxt_{\text{rec}}$ *iff there is an indexing of $\mathcal{C}$ possessing a uniformly r. e. family of telltales.*
2. $\mathcal{C} \in ConsvTxt_{\text{rec}}$ *iff there is a uniformly recursive family comprising $\mathcal{C}$ and possessing a recursively generable family of telltales.*
3. $\mathcal{C} \in BcTxt_{\text{r.e.}}$ *iff there is an indexing of $\mathcal{C}$ possessing a family of telltales.*

The notion of telltales is closely related to the notion of *locking sequences*, see [6]. If $\mathcal{H} = (U_i)_{i \in \mathbb{N}}$ is a hypothesis space, M an IIM, and L a language, then any finite text segment σ of L is called a $LimTxt$-locking sequence for M and L (a $BcTxt$-locking sequence for M, L and $\mathcal{H}$), if $M(\sigma) = M(\sigma\sigma')$ ($U_{M(\sigma)} = U_{M(\sigma\sigma')}$) for all finite text segments σ' of L. If L is $LimTxt$-learned by M ($BcTxt$-learned by M) respecting $\mathcal{H}$, then there exists a $LimTxt$-locking sequence σ for M and L (a $BcTxt$-locking sequence for M, L, and $\mathcal{H}$). Moreover, $U_{M(\sigma)} = L$ must be fulfilled for each such locking sequence.

2.3 Language Learning Via Queries

In the query learning model, a learner has access to a teacher that truthfully answers queries of a specified kind. A *query learner* M is an algorithmic device that, depending on the reply on the previous queries, either computes a new query or returns a hypothesis and halts, see [2]. Its queries and hypotheses are coded as natural numbers; both will be interpreted with respect to an underlying *hypothesis space*. When learning an indexable class $\mathcal{C}$, any indexing $\mathcal{H} = (L_i)_{i \in \mathbb{N}}$ of $\mathcal{C}$ may form a hypothesis space. So, as in the original definition, see [2], when learning $\mathcal{C}$, M is only allowed to query languages belonging to $\mathcal{C}$.

More formally, let $\mathcal{C}$ be an indexable class, let $L \in \mathcal{C}$, let $\mathcal{H} = (L_i)_{i \in \mathbb{N}}$ be an indexing of $\mathcal{C}$, and let M be a query learner. *M learns L with respect to $\mathcal{H}$ using some type of queries* if it eventually halts and its only hypothesis, say i, correctly describes L, i. e., $L_i = L$. So M returns its unique and correct guess i after only finitely many queries. Moreover, *M learns $\mathcal{C}$ with respect to $\mathcal{H}$ using some type of queries*, if it learns every $L' \in \mathcal{C}$ with respect to $\mathcal{H}$ using queries of the specified type. Below we consider, for learning a target language L:

Membership queries. The input is a string w and the answer is 'yes' or 'no', depending on whether or not w belongs to L.

Restricted superset queries. The input is an index of a language $L' \in \mathcal{C}$. The answer is 'yes' or 'no', depending on whether or not L' is a superset of L.

Restricted disjointness queries. The input is an index of a language $L' \in \mathcal{C}$. The answer is 'yes' or 'no', depending on whether or not L' and L are disjoint.[2]

[2] The term "restricted" is used to distinguish these types of query learning from learning with superset (disjointness) queries, where, together with each negative answer the learner is provided a counterexample, i. e., a word in $L \setminus L_j$ (in $L \cap L_j$).

MemQ, *rSupQ*, and *rDisQ* denote the collections of all indexable classes $\mathcal{C}'$ for which there are a query learner M' and a hypothesis space $\mathcal{H}'$ such that M' learns $\mathcal{C}'$ with respect to $\mathcal{H}'$ using membership, restricted superset, and restricted disjointness queries, respectively. In the sequel we will omit the term "restricted" for convenience. In the literature, see [2,3], more types of queries such as (restricted) subset queries and equivalence queries have been analysed, but in what follows we concentrate on the three types explained above.

Note that, in contrast to the Gold-style models introduced above, learning via queries focusses the aspect of one-shot learning, i. e., it is concerned with learning scenarios in which learning may eventuate without mind changes.

Having a closer look at the different models of query learning, one easily finds negative learnability results. For instance, the class $\mathcal{C}_{\text{sup}}$ consisting of the language $L^* = \{a\}^* \cup \{b\}$ and all languages $\{a^k \mid k \leq i\}$, $i \in \mathbb{N}$, is not learnable with superset queries. Assume a query learner M learns $\mathcal{C}_{\text{sup}}$ with superset queries in an indexing $(L_i)_{i\in\mathbb{N}}$ of $\mathcal{C}$ and consider a scenario for M learning L^*. Obviously, a query j is answered 'yes', iff $L_j = L^*$. After finitely many queries, M hypothesizes L^*. Now let i be maximal, such that a query j with $L_j = \{a^k \mid k \leq i\}$ has been posed. The above scenario is also feasible for the language $\{a^k \mid k \leq i+1\}$. Given this language as a target, M will return a hypothesis representing L^* and thus fail. This yields a contradiction, so $\mathcal{C}_{\text{sup}} \notin rSupQ$.

Moreover, as can be verified easily, the class $\mathcal{C}_{\text{dis}}$ consisting only of the languages $\{a\}$ and $\{a, b\}$ is not learnable with disjointness queries.

Both examples point to a drawback of Angluin's query model, namely the demand that a query learner is restricted to pose queries concerning languages contained in the class of possible target languages. Note that the class $\mathcal{C}_{\text{sup}}$ would be learnable with superset queries, if it was additionally permitted to query the language $\{a\}^*$, i. e., to ask whether or not this language is a superset of the target language. Similarly, $\mathcal{C}_{\text{dis}}$ would be learnable with disjointness queries, if it was additionally permitted to query the language $\{b\}$. That means there are very simple classes of languages, for which any query learner must fail just because it is barred from asking the "appropriate" queries.

To overcome this drawback, it seems reasonable to allow the query learner to formulate its queries with respect to any uniformly recursive family comprising the target class $\mathcal{C}$. So let $\mathcal{C}$ be an indexable class. An *extra query learner* for $\mathcal{C}$ is permitted to query languages in any uniformly recursive family $(L'_i)_{i\in\mathbb{N}}$ comprising $\mathcal{C}$. We say that $\mathcal{C}$ is learnable with extra superset (disjointness) queries respecting $(L'_i)_{i\in\mathbb{N}}$ iff there is an extra query learner M learning $\mathcal{C}$ with respect to $(L'_i)_{i\in\mathbb{N}}$ using superset (disjointness) queries concerning $(L'_i)_{i\in\mathbb{N}}$. Then $rSupQ_{\text{rec}}$ ($rDisQ_{\text{rec}}$) denotes the collection of all indexable classes $\mathcal{C}$ learnable with extra superset (disjointness) queries respecting a uniformly recursive family.

Our classes $\mathcal{C}_{\text{sup}}$ and $\mathcal{C}_{\text{dis}}$ witness $rSupQ \subset rSupQ_{\text{rec}}$ and $rDisQ \subset rDisQ_{\text{rec}}$. Note that both classes would already be learnable, if in addition to the superset (disjointness) queries the learner was allowed to ask a membership query for the word b. So the capabilities of *rSupQ*-learners (*rDisQ*-learners) already increase with the additional permission to ask membership queries. Yet, as Theorem 2 shows, combining superset or disjointness queries with membership queries does not yield the same capability as extra queries do. For convenience, denote the family of classes which are learnable with a combination of superset (disjointness) queries and membership queries by *rSupMemQ* (*rDisMemQ*).

Theorem 2. *1.* $rSupQ \subset rSupMemQ \subset rSupQ_{\rm rec}$.
2. $rDisQ \subset rDisMemQ \subset rDisQ_{\rm rec}$.

Proof. ad 1. $rSupQ \subseteq rSupMemQ$ is evident; the class $\mathcal{C}_{\rm sup}$ yields the inequality.

In order to prove $rSupMemQ \subseteq rSupQ_{\rm rec}$, note that, for any word w and any language L, $w \in L$ iff $\Sigma^* \setminus \{w\} \not\supseteq L$. This helps to simulate membership queries with extra superset queries. Further details are omitted.

$rSupQ_{\rm rec} \setminus rSupMemQ \neq \emptyset$ is witnessed by the class $\mathcal{C}$ of all languages L_k and $L_{k,l}$ for $k, l \in \mathbb{N}$, where $L_k = \{a^k b^z \mid z \in \mathbb{N}\}$, $L_{k,l} = L_k$, if $\varphi_k(k)$ is undefined, and $L_{k,l} = \{a^k b^z \mid z \leq \Phi_k(k) \ \vee \ z > \Phi_k(k) + l\}$, if $\varphi_k(k)$ is defined, see [10].

To verify $\mathcal{C} \in rSupQ_{\rm rec}$ choose a uniformly recursive family comprising $\mathcal{C}$ and all languages $L_k^* = \{a^k b^z \mid z \leq \Phi_k(k)\}$, $k \in \mathbb{N}$. Note that $L_k^* \in \mathcal{C}$ iff $\varphi_k(k)$ is undefined. An $rSupQ_{\rm rec}$-learner M for $\mathcal{C}$ may act on the following instructions.

- For $k = 0, 1, 2, \ldots$ ask a superset query concerning L_k, until the answer 'yes' is received for the first time, i. e., until some k with $L_k \supseteq L$ is found.
- Pose a superset query concerning the language L_k^*. (* Note that L_k^* is a superset of the target language iff L_k^* is infinite iff $\varphi_k(k)$ is undefined. *)
  If the answer is 'yes', then output a hypothesis representing L_k and stop.
  If the answer is 'no' (* in this case $\varphi_k(k)$ is defined *), then compute $\Phi_k(k)$.
  Pose a superset query concerning $L_{k,1}$. (* Note that, for any target language $L \subseteq L_k$, this query will be answered with 'yes' iff $a^k b^{\Phi_k(k)+1} \notin L$. *)
    If the answer is 'no', then output a hypothesis representing L_k and stop.
    If the answer is 'yes', then, for any $l = 2, 3, 4, \ldots$, pose a superset query concerning $L_{k,l}$. As soon as such a query is answered with 'no', for some l, output a hypothesis representing $L_{k,l-1}$ and stop.

The details verifying that M learns $\mathcal{C}$ with extra superset queries are omitted.

In contrast to that one can show that $\mathcal{C} \notin rSupMemQ$. Otherwise the halting problem with respect to φ would be decidable. Details are omitted.

Hence $rSupMemQ \subset rSupQ_{\rm rec}$.

ad 2. $rDisQ \subseteq rDisMemQ$ is obvious; the class $\mathcal{C}_{\rm dis}$ yields the inequality.

In order to prove $rDisMemQ \subseteq rDisQ_{\rm rec}$, note that, for any word w and any language L, $w \in L$ iff $\{w\}$ and L are not disjoint. This helps to simulate membership queries with extra disjointness queries. Further details are omitted.

To prove the existence of a class in $rDisQ_{\rm rec} \setminus rDisMemQ$, define an indexable class $\mathcal{C}$ consisting of $L_0 = \{b\}$ and all languages $L_{i+1} = \{a^{i+1}, b\}$, $i \in \mathbb{N}$.

To show that $\mathcal{C} \in rDisQ_{\rm rec}$ choose a uniformly recursive family comprising $\mathcal{C}$ as well as $\{a\}^*$ and all languages $\{a^{i+1}\}$, $i \in \mathbb{N}$. A learner M identifying $\mathcal{C}$ with extra disjointness queries may work according to the following instructions.

Pose a disjointness query concerning $\{a\}^*$. (* Note that the only possible target language disjoint with $\{a\}^*$ is L_0. *)
If the answer is 'yes', then return a hypothesis representing L_0 and stop.

If the answer is 'no', then, for $i = 0, 1, 2, \ldots$ ask a disjointness query concerning $\{a^{i+1}\}$, until the answer 'no' is received for the first time. (* Note that this must eventually happen. *) As soon as such a query is answered with 'no', for some i, output a hypothesis representing L_{i+1} and stop.

The details verifying that M learns $\mathcal{C}$ with extra disjointness queries are omitted.

In contrast one can show that $\mathcal{C} \notin rDisMemQ$. For that purpose, to deduce a contradiction, assume that there is a query learner identifying $\mathcal{C}$ with disjointness and membership queries respecting an indexing $(L'_i)_{i\in\mathbb{N}}$ of $\mathcal{C}$. Consider a learning scenario of M for the target language L_0. Obviously, each disjointness query is answered with 'no'; a membership query for a word w is answered with 'no' iff $w \neq b$. After finitely many queries, M must return a hypothesis representing L_0. Now let i be maximal, such that a membership query concerning a word a^i has been posed. The scenario described above is also feasible for the language $\{a^{i+1}, b\}$. If this language constitutes the target, then M will return a hypothesis representing L^* and thus fail. This yields the desired contradiction.

Hence $rDisMemQ \subset rDisQ_{\mathrm{rec}}$. □

3 Characterizations of Gold-Style Inference Types

3.1 Characterizations in the Query Model

One main difference between Gold-style and query learning lies in the question whether or not a current hypothesis of a learner is already correct. A Gold-style learner is allowed to change its mind arbitrarily often (thus in general this question can not be answered), whereas a query learner has to find a correct representation of the target object already in the first guess, i.e., within "one shot" (and thus the question can always be answered in the affirmative). Another difference is certainly the kind of information provided during the learning process. So, at first glance, these models seem to focus on very different aspects of human learning and do not seem to have much in common.

Thus the question arises, whether there are any similarities in these models at all and whether there are aspects of learning both models capture. This requires a comparison of both models concerning the capabilities of the corresponding learners. In particular, one central question in this context is whether Gold-style (limit) learners can be replaced by equally powerful (one-shot) query learners. The rather trivial examples of classes not learnable with superset or disjointness queries already show that quite general hypothesis spaces—such as in learning with extra queries—are an important demand, if such a replacement shall be successful. In other words, we demand a more potent teacher, able to answer more general questions than in Angluin's original model. Astonishingly, this demand is already sufficient to coincide with the capabilities of conservative limit learners: in [11] it is shown that the collection of indexable classes learnable with extra superset queries coincides with $ConsvTxt_{\mathrm{rec}}$. And, moreover, this also holds for the collection of indexable classes learnable with extra disjointness queries.

Theorem 3. $rSupQ_{\mathrm{rec}} = rDisQ_{\mathrm{rec}} = ConsvTxt_{\mathrm{rec}}$.

Proof. $rSupQ_{\text{rec}} = ConsvTxt_{\text{rec}}$ holds by [11]. Thus it remains to prove that $rSupQ_{\text{rec}} = rDisQ_{\text{rec}}$. For that purpose let $\mathcal{C}$ be any indexable class.

First assume $\mathcal{C} \in rDisQ_{\text{rec}}$. Then there is a uniformly recursive family $(L_i)_{i\in\mathbb{N}}$ and a query learner M, such that M learns $\mathcal{C}$ with extra disjointness queries with respect to $(L_i)_{i\in\mathbb{N}}$. Now define $L'_{2i} = L_i$ and $L'_{2i+1} = \overline{L_i}$ for all $i \in \mathbb{N}$.

Suppose L is a target language. A query learner M' identifying L with extra superset queries respecting $(L'_i)_{i\in\mathbb{N}}$ is defined via the following instructions:

- Simulate M when learning L.
- If M poses a disjointness query concerning L_i, then pose a superset query concerning L'_{2i+1} to your teacher. If the answer is 'yes', then transmit the answer 'yes' to M. If the answer is 'no', then transmit the answer 'no' to M. (* Note that $L_i \cap L = \emptyset$ iff $L \subseteq \overline{L_i}$ iff $L'_{2i+1} \supseteq L$. *)
- If M hypothesizes L_i, then output a representation for L'_{2i}.

It is not hard to verify that M' learns $\mathcal{C}$ with extra superset queries with respect to $(L'_i)_{i\in\mathbb{N}}$. Hence $\mathcal{C} \in rSupQ_{\text{rec}}$. This implies $rDisQ_{\text{rec}} \subseteq rSupQ_{\text{rec}}$.

The opposite inclusion $rSupQ_{\text{rec}} \subseteq rDisQ_{\text{rec}}$ is verified analogously. □

As initially in Gold-style learning, we have only considered uniformly recursive families as hypothesis spaces for query learners. Similarly to the notion of $BcTxt_{\text{r.e.}}$, it is conceivable to permit more general hypothesis spaces also in the query model, i. e., to demand an even more potent teacher. Thus, by $rSupQ_{\text{r.e.}}$ ($rDisQ_{\text{r.e.}}$) we denote the collection of all indexable classes which are learnable with superset (disjointness) queries respecting a uniformly r. e. family. Interestingly, this relaxation helps to characterize learning in the limit in terms of query learning.

Theorem 4. $rDisQ_{\text{r.e.}} = LimTxt_{\text{rec}}$.

Proof. First we show $rDisQ_{\text{r.e.}} \subseteq LimTxt_{\text{rec}}$. For that purpose, let $\mathcal{C} \in rDisQ_{\text{r.e.}}$ be an indexable class. Fix a uniformly r. e. family $(U_i)_{i\in\mathbb{N}}$ and a query learner M identifying $\mathcal{C}$ with disjointness queries with respect to $(U_i)_{i\in\mathbb{N}}$.

The following IIM M' $LimTxt$-identifies $\mathcal{C}$ with respect to $(U_i)_{i\in\mathbb{N}}$. Given a text segment σ of length n, M' interacts with M simulating a learning process for n steps. In step k, $k \le n$, depending on how M' has replied to the previous queries posed by M, the learner M computes either (i) a new query i or (ii) a hypothesis i. In case (ii), M' returns the hypothesis i and stops simulating M. In case (i), M' checks whether there is a word in σ, which is found in U_i within n steps. If such a word exists, M' transmits the answer 'no' to M; else M' transmits the answer 'yes' to M. If $k < n$, M executes step $k+1$, else M' returns any auxiliary hypothesis and stops simulating M. Given segments σ of a text for some target language, if their length n is large enough, M' answers all queries of M correctly and M returns its sole hypothesis within n steps. So, the hypotheses returned by M' stabilize on this correct guess.

Hence $\mathcal{C} \in LimTxt_{\text{r.e.}} (= LimTxt_{\text{rec}})$ and therefore $rDisQ_{\text{r.e.}} \subseteq LimTxt_{\text{rec}}$.

Second we show that $LimTxt_{\text{rec}} \subseteq rDisQ_{\text{r.e.}}$. So let $\mathcal{C} \in LimTxt_{\text{rec}}$ be an indexable class. Fix an indexing $\mathcal{H} = (L_i)_{i\in\mathbb{N}}$ of $\mathcal{C}$ and an IIM M, such that M $LimTxt$-identifies $\mathcal{C}$ with respect to $\mathcal{H}$.

Let $(U_i)_{i\in\mathbb{N}}$ be any Gödel numbering of all r.e. languages and $(w_x)_{x\in\mathbb{N}}$ an effective enumeration of Σ^*. Suppose $L \in \mathcal{C}$ is the target language. An *rDisQ*-learner M' for L with respect to $(U_i)_{i\in\mathbb{N}}$ is defined to act on the following instructions, starting in step 0. Note that Gödel numbers (representations in $(U_i)_{i\in\mathbb{N}}$) can be computed for all queries to be asked. Step n reads as follows:

- Ask disjointness queries for $\{w_0\}, \dots, \{w_n\}$. Let $L_{[n]}$ be the set of words w_x, $x \le n$, for which the corresponding query is answered with 'no'. (* Note that $L_{[n]} = L \cap \{w_x \mid x \le n\}$. *)
- Let $(\sigma_x^n)_{x\in\mathbb{N}}$ be an effective enumeration of all finite text segments for $L_{[n]}$. For all $x, y \le n$ pose a disjointness query for $\overline{L_{M(\sigma_x^y)}}$ and thus build $\mathrm{Cand}_n = \{\sigma_x^y \mid x, y \le n \text{ and } \overline{L_{M(\sigma_x^y)}} \cap L = \emptyset\}$ from the queries answered with 'yes'. (* Note that $\mathrm{Cand}_n = \{\sigma_x^y \mid x, y \le n \text{ and } L \subseteq L_{M(\sigma_x^y)}\}$. *)
- For all $\sigma \in \mathrm{Cand}_n$, pose a disjointness query for the language

$$U'_\sigma = \begin{cases} \Sigma^*, & \text{if } M(\sigma\sigma') \neq M(\sigma) \text{ for some text segment } \sigma' \text{ of } L_{M(\sigma)}, \\ \emptyset, & \text{otherwise}. \end{cases}$$

  (* Note that U'_σ is uniformly r.e. in σ and $U'_\sigma \cap L = \emptyset$ iff σ is a *LimTxt*-locking sequence for M and $L_{M(\sigma)}$. *)
  If all these disjointness queries are answered with 'no', then go to step $n+1$. Otherwise, if $\sigma \in \mathrm{Cand}_n$ is minimal fulfilling $U'_\sigma \cap L = \emptyset$, then return a hypothesis representing $L_{M(\sigma)}$ and stop.

M' identifies L with disjointness queries respecting $(U_i)_{i\in\mathbb{N}}$, because *(i)* M' eventually returns a hypothesis and *(ii)* this hypothesis is correct for L. To prove *(i)*, note that M is a *LimTxt*-learner for L respecting $(L_i)_{i\in\mathbb{N}}$. So there are i, x, y such that $M(\sigma_x^y) = i$, $L_i = L$, and σ_x^y is a *LimTxt*-locking sequence for M and L. Then $U'_{\sigma_x^y} = \emptyset$ and the corresponding disjointness query is answered with 'yes'. Thus M' returns a hypothesis. To prove *(ii)*, assume M' returns a hypothesis representing $L_{M(\sigma)}$ for some text segment σ of L. Then, by definition of M', $L \subseteq L_{M(\sigma)}$ and σ is a *LimTxt*-locking sequence for M and $L_{M(\sigma)}$. In particular, σ is a *LimTxt*-locking sequence for M and L. Since M learns L in the limit from text, this implies $L = L_{M(\sigma)}$. Hence the hypothesis M' returns is correct for L.

Therefore $\mathcal{C} \in rDisQ_{\text{r.e.}}$ and $LimTxt_{\text{rec}} \subseteq rDisQ_{\text{r.e.}}$. □

Reducing the constraints concerning the hypothesis spaces even more, let $rSupQ_{\text{2-r.e.}}$ ($rDisQ_{\text{2-r.e.}}$) denote the collection of all indexable classes which are learnable using superset (disjointness) queries with respect to a uniformly 2-r.e. family.[3] This finally allows for a characterization of the classes in $BcTxt_{\text{r.e.}}$.

Theorem 5. $rSupQ_{\text{2-r.e.}} = rDisQ_{\text{2-r.e.}} = BcTxt_{\text{r.e.}}$.

Proof. First we show $rSupQ_{\text{2-r.e.}} \subseteq BcTxt_{\text{r.e.}}$ and $rDisQ_{\text{2-r.e.}} \subseteq BcTxt_{\text{r.e.}}$. For that purpose, let $\mathcal{C} \in rSupQ_{\text{2-r.e.}}$ ($\mathcal{C} \in rDisQ_{\text{2-r.e.}}$) be an indexable class, $(L_i)_{i\in\mathbb{N}}$ an indexing of $\mathcal{C}$. Fix a uniformly 2-r.e. family $(V_i)_{i\in\mathbb{N}}$ and a query learner M identifying $\mathcal{C}$ with superset (disjointness) queries respecting $(V_i)_{i\in\mathbb{N}}$.

[3] With analogous definitions for Gold-style learning one easily obtains $LimTxt_{\text{2-r.e.}} = LimTxt_{\text{r.e.}} = LimTxt_{\text{rec}}$ and $BcTxt_{\text{2-r.e.}} = BcTxt_{\text{r.e.}}$.

To obtain a contradiction, assume that $\mathcal{C} \notin BcTxt_{\text{r.e.}}$. By Theorem 1, $(L_i)_{i\in\mathbb{N}}$ does not possess a telltale family. In other words, there is some $i \in \mathbb{N}$, such that for any finite set $W \subseteq L_i$ there exists some $j \in \mathbb{N}$ satisfying $W \subseteq L_j \subset L_i$. $(*)$

Consider M when learning L_i. In the corresponding learning scenario S

- M poses queries representing $V_{i_1^-}, \ldots, V_{i_k^-}, V_{i_1^+}, \ldots, V_{i_m^+}$ (in some order);
- the answers are 'no' for $V_{i_1^-}, \ldots, V_{i_k^-}$ and 'yes' for $V_{i_1^+}, \ldots, V_{i_m^+}$;
- afterwards M returns a hypothesis representing L_i.

That means, for all $z \in \{1, \ldots, k\}$, we have $V_{i_z^-} \not\supseteq L_i$ ($V_{i_z^-} \cap L_i \neq \emptyset$). In particular, for all $z \in \{1, \ldots, k\}$, there is a word $w_z \in L_i \backslash V_{i_z^-}$ ($w_z \in V_{i_z^-} \cap L_i$). Let $W = \{w_1, \ldots, w_k\} (\subseteq L_i)$. By $(*)$ there is some $j \in \mathbb{N}$ satisfying $W \subseteq L_j \subset L_i$.

Now note that the above scenario S is also feasible for L_j: $w_z \in L_j$ implies $V_{i_z^-} \not\supseteq L_j$ ($V_{i_z^-} \cap L_j \neq \emptyset$) for all $z \in \{1, \ldots, k\}$. $V_{i_z^+} \supseteq L_i$ ($V_{i_z^+} \cap L_i = \emptyset$) implies $V_{i_z^+} \supseteq L_j$ ($V_{i_z^+} \cap L_j = \emptyset$) for all $z \in \{1, \ldots, m\}$. Thus all queries in S are answered truthfully for L_j. Since M hypothesizes L_i in the scenario S, and $L_i \neq L_j$, M fails to identify L_j. This is the desired contradiction.

Hence $\mathcal{C} \in BcTxt_{\text{r.e.}}$, so $rSupQ_{\text{2-r.e.}} \subseteq BcTxt_{\text{r.e.}}$, $rDisQ_{\text{2-r.e.}} \subseteq BcTxt_{\text{r.e.}}$.

Second we show that $BcTxt_{\text{r.e.}} \subseteq rSupQ_{\text{2-r.e.}}$ and $BcTxt_{\text{r.e.}} \subseteq rDisQ_{\text{2-r.e.}}$. So let $\mathcal{C} \in BcTxt_{\text{r.e.}}$ be an indexable class. Fix a uniformly r. e. family $(U_i)_{i\in\mathbb{N}}$ and an IIM M, such that M $BcTxt_{\text{r.e.}}$-identifies $\mathcal{C}$ with respect to $(U_i)_{i\in\mathbb{N}}$.

Let $(V_i)_{i\in\mathbb{N}}$ be a uniformly 2-r. e. family such that indices can be computed for all queries to be asked below. Let $(w_x)_{x\in\mathbb{N}}$ an effective enumeration of Σ^*.

Assume $L \in \mathcal{C}$ is the target language. A query learner M' identifying L with superset (disjointness) queries respecting $(V_i)_{i\in\mathbb{N}}$ is defined according to the following instructions, starting in step 0. Step n reads as follows:

- Ask superset queries for $\Sigma^* \backslash \{w_i\}$ (disjointness queries for $\{w_i\}$) for all $i \leq n$. Let $L_{[n]}$ be the set of words w_x, $x \leq n$, for which the corresponding query is answered with 'no'. (* Note that $L_{[n]} = L \cap \{w_x \mid x \leq n\}$. *)
- Let $(\sigma_x^n)_{x\in\mathbb{N}}$ be an effective enumeration of all finite text segments for $L_{[n]}$. For all $x, y \leq n$ pose a superset query for $U_{M(\sigma_x^y)}$ (a disjointness query for $\overline{U_{M(\sigma_x^y)}}$) and thus build $\text{Cand}_n = \{\sigma_x^y \mid x, y \leq n \text{ and } U_{M(\sigma_x^y)} \supseteq L\} = \{\sigma_x^y \mid x, y \leq n \text{ and } \overline{U_{M(\sigma_x^y)}} \cap L = \emptyset\}$ from the queries answered with 'yes'.
- For all $\sigma \in \text{Cand}_n$, pose a superset (disjointness) query for the language

  $$V'_\sigma = \begin{cases} \Sigma^*, & \text{if } U_{M(\sigma)} \neq U_{M(\sigma\sigma')} \text{ for some text segment } \sigma' \text{ of } U_{M(\sigma)}, \\ \emptyset, & \text{otherwise}. \end{cases}$$

  (* Note that V'_σ is uniformly 2-r. e. in σ and $V'_\sigma \not\supseteq L$ iff $V'_\sigma \cap L = \emptyset$ iff σ is a *BcTxt*-locking sequence for M and $U_{M(\sigma)}$. *)

  If all these superset queries are answered with 'yes' (all these disjointness queries are answered with 'no'), then go to step $n+1$. Otherwise, if $\sigma \in \text{Cand}_n$ is minimal fulfilling $V'_\sigma \not\supseteq L$ and thus $V'_\sigma \cap L = \emptyset$, then return a hypothesis representing $U_{M(\sigma)}$ and stop.

M' learns L with superset (disjointness) queries in $(V_i)_{i\in\mathbb{N}}$, because *(i)* M' eventually returns a hypothesis and *(ii)* this hypothesis is correct for L. To prove *(i)*, note that M is a *BcTxt*-learner for L in $(U_i)_{i\in\mathbb{N}}$. So there are x, y such that

$U_{M(\sigma_x^y)} = L$ and σ_x^y is a *BcTxt*-locking sequence for M, L, and $(U_i)_{i\in\mathbb{N}}$. Then $V'_{\sigma_x^y} = \emptyset$ and the corresponding superset query is answered with 'no' (the disjointness query with 'yes'). Thus M' returns a hypothesis. To prove *(ii)*, suppose M' returns a hypothesis representing $U_{M(\sigma)}$ for a text segment σ of L. Then, by definition of M', σ is a *BcTxt*-locking sequence for M, $U_{M(\sigma)}$, and $(U_i)_{i\in\mathbb{N}}$. In particular, σ is a *BcTxt*-locking sequence for M, L, and $(U_i)_{i\in\mathbb{N}}$. As M *BcTxt*-learns L, this implies $L = U_{M(\sigma)}$ and the hypothesis of M' is correct for L.

Therefore $\mathcal{C} \in rSupQ_{\text{2-r.e.}} \cap rDisQ_{\text{2-r.e.}}$, and thus $BcTxt_{\text{r.e.}} \subseteq rSupQ_{\text{2-r.e.}}$ and $BcTxt_{\text{r.e.}} \subseteq rDisQ_{\text{2-r.e.}}$. □

3.2 Characterizations in the Model of Learning with Oracles – A Comparison

In our characterizations we have seen that the capability of query learners strongly depends on the hypothesis space and thus on the demands concerning the abilities of the teacher. Of course a teacher might have to be more potent to answer questions with respect to some uniformly r. e. family than to work in some uniformly recursive family. For instance, teachers of the first kind might have to be able to solve the halting problem with respect to some Gödel numbering. In other words, the learner might use such a teacher as an *oracle* for the halting problem. The problem we consider in the following is to specify nonrecursive sets $A \subseteq \mathbb{N}$ such that A-recursive[4] query learners using uniformly recursive families as hypothesis spaces are as powerful as recursive learners using uniformly r. e. or uniformly 2-r. e. families. For instance, we know that $rDisQ_{\text{rec}} \subset rDisQ_{\text{r.e.}} = LimTxt_{\text{rec}}$. So we would like to specify a set A, such that $LimTxt_{\text{rec}}$ equals the collection of all indexable classes which can be identified with A-recursive $rDisQ_{\text{rec}}$-learners. The latter collection will be denoted by $rDisQ_{\text{rec}}[A]$. Subsequently, similar notions are used correspondingly.

In the Gold-style model, the use of oracles has been analysed for example in [13]. Most of the claims below use K-recursive or Tot-recursive learners, where $K = \{i \mid \varphi_i(i) \text{ is defined}\}$ and $Tot = \{i \mid \varphi_i \text{ is a total function}\}$. Concerning coincidences in Gold-style learning, the use of oracles is illustrated by Lemma 1.

Lemma 1. *1.* [13] $ConsvTxt_{\text{rec}}[K] = LimTxt_{\text{rec}}$.
2. $ConsvTxt_{\text{rec}}[Tot] = LimTxt_{\text{rec}}[K] = BcTxt_{\text{r.e.}}$.
3. $BcTxt_{\text{r.e.}}[A] = BcTxt_{\text{r.e.}}$ *for all* $A \subseteq \mathbb{N}$.

Proof. ad 3. Let $A \subseteq \mathbb{N}$. By definition $BcTxt_{\text{r.e.}} \subseteq BcTxt_{\text{r.e.}}[A]$. Thus it remains to prove the opposite inclusion, namely $BcTxt_{\text{r.e.}}[A] \subseteq BcTxt_{\text{r.e.}}$. For that purpose let $\mathcal{C} \in BcTxt_{\text{r.e.}}[A]$ be an indexable class. Fix an A-recursive IIM M such that $\mathcal{C}$ is $BcTxt_{\text{r.e.}}$-learned by M. Moreover, let $(L_i)_{i\in\mathbb{N}}$ be an indexing of $\mathcal{C}$.

Striving for a contradiction, assume $\mathcal{C} \notin BcTxt_{\text{r.e.}}$. By Theorem 1, $(L_i)_{i\in\mathbb{N}}$ does not possess a telltale family. In other words, there is some $i \in \mathbb{N}$, such that for any finite set $W \subseteq L_i$ there exists some $j \in \mathbb{N}$ satisfying $W \subseteq L_j \subset L_i$.

[4] A-recursive means recursive with the help of an oracle for the set A.

Since M is a $BcTxt$-learner for L_i in some hypothesis space $\mathcal{H}$, there must be a $BcTxt$-locking sequence σ for M, L_i, and $\mathcal{H}$. If W denotes the set of words occurring in σ, there is some language $L_j \in \mathcal{C}$ with $W \subseteq L_j \subset L_i$. Thus σ is a $BcTxt$-locking sequence for M, L_j, and $\mathcal{H}$. In particular, M fails to $BcTxt_{\text{r.e.}}$-identify L_j. This yields the contradiction. Hence $BcTxt_{\text{r.e.}}[A] = BcTxt_{\text{r.e.}}$.

ad 2. The proofs of $ConsvTxt_{\text{rec}}[Tot] \subseteq BcTxt_{\text{r.e.}}$, $LimTxt_{\text{rec}}[K] \subseteq BcTxt_{\text{r.e.}}$ are obtained by similar means as the proof of 3. It suffices to use Theorem 1 for $ConsvTxt_{\text{rec}}$ and $LimTxt_{\text{rec}}$ instead of the accordant statement for $BcTxt_{\text{r.e.}}$. Note that $LimTxt_{\text{rec}}[K] = BcTxt_{\text{r.e.}}$ is already verified in [4].

Next we prove $BcTxt_{\text{r.e.}} \subseteq ConsvTxt_{\text{rec}}[Tot]$ and $BcTxt_{\text{r.e.}} \subseteq LimTxt_{\text{rec}}[K]$. For that purpose, let $\mathcal{C}$ be an indexable class in $BcTxt_{\text{r.e.}}$. By Theorem 1 there is an indexing $(L_i)_{i\in\mathbb{N}}$ of $\mathcal{C}$ which possesses a family of telltales. Next we show:

(i) $(L_i)_{i\in\mathbb{N}}$ possesses a Tot-recursively generable (uniformly K-r. e.) family of telltales.

(ii) A $ConsvTxt_{\text{rec}}$-learner ($LimTxt_{\text{rec}}$-learner) for $\mathcal{C}$ can be computed from any recursively generable (uniformly r. e.) family of telltales for $(L_i)_{i\in\mathbb{N}}$.

To prove *(i)*, Let $(w_x)_{x\in\mathbb{N}}$ be an effective enumeration of all words in Σ^*. Given $i \in \mathbb{N}$, let a function f_i enumerate a set T_i as follows.

- $f_i(0) = w_z$ for $z = \min\{x \mid w_x \in L_i\}$.
- If $f_i(0), \ldots, f_i(n)$ are computed, then test whether or not there is some $j \in \mathbb{N}$ (some $j \leq n$), such that $\{f_i(0), \ldots, f_i(n)\} \subseteq L_j \subset L_i$. (* Note that this test is Tot-recursive (K-recursive). *)
- If such a number j exists, then $f_i(n+1) = w_z$ for $z = \min\{x \mid w_x \in L_i \setminus \{f_i(0), \ldots, f_i(n)\}\}$. If no such number j exists, then $f_i(n+1) = f_i(n)$.

With $T_i = \{f_i(x) \mid x \in \mathbb{N}\}$, it is not hard to verify that $(T_i)_{i\in\mathbb{N}}$ is a Tot-recursively generable (uniformly K-r. e.) family of telltales for $(L_i)_{i\in\mathbb{N}}$. Here note that, in the case of using a Tot-oracle, $T_i = \{f_i(x) \mid f_i(y+1) \neq f_i(y) \text{ for all } y < x\}$.

Finally, *(ii)* holds since Theorem 1.1/1.2 has a constructive proof, see [1,10].

Claims *(i)* and *(ii)* imply $\mathcal{C} \in ConsvTxt_{\text{rec}}[Tot]$ and $\mathcal{C} \in LimTxt_{\text{rec}}[K]$. So $BcTxt_{\text{r.e.}} \subseteq ConsvTxt_{\text{rec}}[Tot]$ and $BcTxt_{\text{r.e.}} \subseteq LimTxt_{\text{rec}}[K]$. □

Since this proof is constructive as are the proofs of our characterizations above, we can deduce results like for example $rDisQ_{\text{rec}}[K] = LimTxt_{\text{rec}}$: Given $\mathcal{C} \in LimTxt_{\text{rec}}$, a K-recursive conservative IIM for $\mathcal{C}$ can be constructed from a $LimTxt_{\text{rec}}$-learner for $\mathcal{C}$. Moreover, a $rDisQ_{\text{rec}}$-learner for $\mathcal{C}$ can be constructed from a conservative IIM for $\mathcal{C}$. Thus, a K-recursive $rDisQ_{\text{rec}}$-learner for $\mathcal{C}$ can be constructed from a $LimTxt_{\text{rec}}$-learner. Similar results are obtained by combining Lemma 1 with our characterizations above. This proves the following theorem.

Theorem 6. *1.* $rSupQ_{\text{rec}}[K] = rDisQ_{\text{rec}}[K] = LimTxt_{\text{rec}}$.
2. $rSupQ_{\text{rec}}[Tot] = rDisQ_{\text{rec}}[Tot] = BcTxt_{\text{r.e.}}$.
3. $rSupQ_{\text{2-r.e.}}[A] = rDisQ_{\text{2-r.e.}}[A] = BcTxt_{\text{r.e.}}$ *for all* $A \subseteq \mathbb{N}$.

4 Discussion

Our characterizations have revealed a correspondence between Gold-style learning and learning via queries—between limiting and one-shot learning processes.

Crucial in this context is that the learner may ask the "appropriate" queries. Thus the choice of hypothesis spaces and, correspondingly, the ability of the teacher is decisive. If the teacher is potent enough to answer disjointness queries in some uniformly r. e. family of languages, then, by Theorem 4, learning with disjointness queries coincides with learning in the limit. Interestingly, given uniformly recursive or uniformly 2-r. e. families as hypothesis spaces, disjointness and superset queries coincide respecting the learning capabilities. As it turns out, this coincidence is not valid, if the hypothesis space may be any uniformly r. e. family. That means, $rDisQ_{\text{r.e.}}$ (and $LimTxt_{\text{rec}}$) is not equal to the collection of all indexable classes learnable with superset queries in uniformly r. e. families.

Theorem 7. $LimTxt_{\text{rec}} \subset rSupQ_{\text{r.e.}}$.

Proof. To verify $LimTxt_{\text{rec}} \subseteq rSupQ_{\text{r.e.}}$, the proof of $LimTxt_{\text{rec}} \subseteq rDisQ_{\text{r.e.}}$ can be adapted. It remains to quote a class in $rSupQ_{\text{r.e.}} \setminus LimTxt_{\text{rec}}$.

Let, for all $k, n \in \mathbb{N}$, $\mathcal{C}_{\text{lim}}$ contain the languages $L_k = \{a^k b^z \mid z \geq 0\}$ and

$$L_{k,n} = \begin{cases} \{a^k b^z \mid z \leq m\}, & \text{if } m \leq n \text{ is minimal such} \\ & \text{that } \varphi_k(m) \text{ is undefined}, \\ \{a^k b^z \mid z \leq n\} \cup \{b^{n+1} a^{y+1}\}, & \text{if } \varphi_k(x) \text{ is defined for all } x \leq n \\ & \text{and } y = \max\{\Phi_k(x) \mid x \leq n\}. \end{cases}$$

$\mathcal{C}_{\text{lim}}$ is an indexable class; the proof is omitted due to the space constraints.

To show $\mathcal{C}_{\text{lim}} \in rSupQ_{\text{r.e.}}$, let $(U_i)_{i \in \mathbb{N}}$ be a Gödel numbering of all r. e. languages. Assume $L \in \mathcal{C}$ is the target language. A learner M identifying L with superset queries respecting $(U_i)_{i \in \mathbb{N}}$ is defined to act on the following instructions:

- For $k = 0, 1, 2, \ldots$ ask a superset query concerning $L_k \cup \{b^r a^s \mid r, s \in \mathbb{N}\}$, until the answer 'yes' is received for the first time.
- Pose a superset query concerning the language L_k.
  If the answer is 'no', then, for $r, s = 0, 1, 2, \ldots$ ask a superset query concerning $L_k \cup \{b^{r+1} a^{s+1}\}$, until the answer 'yes' is received for the first time. Output a hypothesis representing $L_{k,r}$ and stop.
  If the answer is 'yes', then pose a superset query for the language

$$U'_k = \begin{cases} \{a^k b^z \mid z \leq n\}, & \text{if } n \text{ is minimal, such that } \varphi_k(n) \text{ is undefined}, \\ \{a^k b^z \mid z \geq 0\}, & \text{if } \varphi_k \text{ is a total function}. \end{cases}$$

  (* Note that U'_k is uniformly r. e. in k. U'_k is a superset of L iff $U'_k = L$. *)
  If the answer is 'yes', then return a hypothesis representing U'_k and stop.
  If the answer is 'no', then return a hypothesis representing L_k and stop.

The details proving that M $rSupQ$-identifies $\mathcal{C}_{\text{lim}}$ respecting $(U_i)_{i \in \mathbb{N}}$ are omitted.

Finally, $\mathcal{C}_{\text{lim}} \notin LimTxt_{\text{rec}}$ holds, since otherwise Tot would be K-recursive. To verify this, assume M is an IIM learning $\mathcal{C}_{\text{lim}}$ in the limit from text. Let $k \geq 0$. To decide whether or not φ_k is a total function, proceed as follows:

Let σ be a $LimTxt$-locking sequence for M and L_k. (* Note that σ exists by assumption and thus can be found by a K-recursive procedure. *) If there is some $x \leq \max\{z \mid a^k b^z \text{ occurs in } \sigma\}$, such that $\varphi_k(x)$ is undefined (* also a K-recursive test *), then return '0'. Otherwise return '1'.

It remains to show that φ_k is total, if this procedure returns '1'. So let the procedure return '1'. Assume φ_k is not total and n is minimal, such that $\varphi_k(n)$ is undefined. By definition, the language $L = \{a^k b^z \mid z \leq n\}$ belongs to $\mathcal{C}_{\mathrm{lim}}$. Then the sequence σ found in the procedure is also a text segment for L and by choice—since $L \subset L_k$—a *LimTxt*-locking sequence for M and L. As $M(\sigma)$ is correct for L_k, M fails to identify L. This is a contradiction; hence φ_k is total.

Thus the set *Tot* is K-recursive—a contradiction. So $\mathcal{C}_{\mathrm{lim}} \notin \mathit{LimTxt}_{\mathrm{rec}}$. □

Since $\mathit{rSupQ}_{\mathrm{r.e.}} \subseteq \mathit{rSupQ}_{2\text{-r.e.}}$, one easily obtains $\mathit{rSupQ}_{\mathrm{r.e.}} \subseteq \mathit{BcTxt}_{\mathrm{r.e.}}$. Whether or not these two collections are equal, remains an open question. Still it is possible to prove that any indexable class containing just infinite languages is in $\mathit{rSupQ}_{\mathrm{r.e.}}$ iff it is in $\mathit{BcTxt}_{\mathrm{r.e.}}$. We omit the proof. In contrast to that there are classes of only infinite languages in $\mathit{BcTxt}_{\mathrm{r.e.}} \setminus \mathit{LimTxt}_{\mathrm{rec}}$.

Moreover, note that the indexable class $\mathcal{C}_{\mathrm{lim}}$ defined in the proof of Theorem 7 belongs to $\mathit{BcTxt}_{\mathrm{r.e.}} \setminus \mathit{LimTxt}_{\mathrm{rec}}$. Up to now, the literature has not offered many such classes. The first example can be found in [1], but its definition is quite involved and uses a diagonalisation. In contrast to that, $\mathcal{C}_{\mathrm{lim}}$ is defined compactly and explicitly without a diagonal construction and is—to the authors' knowledge—the first such class known in $\mathit{BcTxt}_{\mathrm{r.e.}} \setminus \mathit{LimTxt}_{\mathrm{rec}}$.

References

1. D. Angluin. Inductive inference of formal languages from positive data. *Inform. Control*, 45:117–135, 1980.
2. D. Angluin. Queries and concept learning. *Machine Learning*, 2:319–342, 1988.
3. D. Angluin. Queries revisited. *Theoret. Comput. Sci.*, 313:175–194, 2004.
4. G. Baliga, J. Case, S. Jain. The synthesis of language learners. *Inform. Comput.*, 152:16–43, 1999.
5. M. Blum. A machine-independent theory of the complexity of recursive functions. *J. ACM*, 14:322–336, 1967.
6. L. Blum, M. Blum. Toward a mathematical theory of inductive inference. *Inform. Control*, 28:125–155, 1975.
7. J. Case, C. Lynes. Machine inductive inference and language identification. In: *Proc. ICALP 1982*, LNCS 140, 107–115, Springer, 1982.
8. E.M. Gold. Language identification in the limit. *Inform. Control*, 10:447–474, 1967.
9. J.E. Hopcroft, J.D. Ullman. *Introduction to Automata Theory, Languages, and Computation.* Addison-Wesley Publishing Company, 1979.
10. S. Lange, T. Zeugmann. Language learning in dependence on the space of hypotheses. In: *Proc. COLT 1993*, 127–136, ACM Press, 1993.
11. S. Lange, S. Zilles. On the learnability of erasing pattern languages in the query model. In: *Proc. ALT 2003*, LNAI 2842, 129–143, Springer, 2003.
12. H. Rogers, Jr. *Theory of Recursive Functions and Effective Computability*, MIT Press, 1987.
13. F. Stephan. *Degrees of Computing and Learning.* Habilitationsschrift, Ruprecht-Karls-Universität, Heidelberg, 1999.
14. T. Zeugmann, S. Lange. A guided tour across the boundaries of learning recursive languages. In: *Algorithmic Learning for Knowledge-Based Systems*, LNAI 961, 190–258, Springer, 1995.

Concentration Bounds for Unigrams Language Model

Evgeny Drukh and Yishay Mansour

School of Computer Science, Tel Aviv University, Tel Aviv, Israel
{drukh,mansour}@post.tau.ac.il

Abstract. We show several PAC-style concentration bounds for learning unigrams language model. One interesting quantity is the probability of all words appearing exactly k times in a sample of size m. A standard estimator for this quantity is the Good-Turing estimator. The existing analysis on its error shows a PAC bound of approximately $O\left(\frac{k}{\sqrt{m}}\right)$. We improve its dependency on k to $O\left(\frac{\sqrt[4]{k}}{\sqrt{m}} + \frac{k}{m}\right)$. We also analyze the empirical frequencies estimator, showing that its PAC error bound is approximately $O\left(\frac{1}{k} + \frac{\sqrt{k}}{m}\right)$. We derive a combined estimator, which has an error of approximately $O\left(m^{-\frac{2}{5}}\right)$, for any k.
A standard measure for the quality of a learning algorithm is its expected per-word log-loss. We show that the leave-one-out method can be used for estimating the log-loss of the unigrams model with a PAC error of approximately $O\left(\frac{1}{\sqrt{m}}\right)$, for any distribution.
We also bound the log-loss a priori, as a function of various parameters of the distribution.

1 Introduction and Overview

Natural language processing (NLP) has developed rapidly over the last decades. It has a wide range of applications, including speech recognition, optical character recognition, text categorization and many more. The theoretical analysis has also advanced significantly, though many fundamental questions remain unanswered. One clear challenge, both practical and theoretical, concerns deriving stochastic models for natural languages.

Consider a simple language model, where the distribution of each word in the text is assumed to be independent. Even for such a simplistic model, fundamental questions relating sample size to the learning accuracy are already challenging. This is mainly due to the fact that the sample size is almost always insufficient, regardless of how large it is.

To demonstrate this phenomena, consider the following example. We would like to estimate the distribution of first names in the university. For that, we are given the names list of a graduate seminar: Alice, Bob, Charlie, Dan, Eve, Frank, two Georges, and two Henries. How can we use this sample to estimate the

J. Shawe-Taylor and Y. Singer (Eds.): COLT 2004, LNAI 3120, pp. 170–185, 2004.

distribution of students' first names? An empirical frequency estimator would assign Alice the probability of 0.1, since there is one Alice in the list of 10 names, while George, appearing twice, would get estimation of 0.2. Unfortunately, unseen names, such as Michael, will get an estimation of 0. Clearly, in this simple example the empirical frequencies are unlikely to estimate well the desired distribution.

In general, the empirical frequencies estimate well the probabilities of popular names, but are rather inaccurate for rare names. Is there a sample size, which assures us that all the names (or most of them) will appear enough times to allow accurate probabilities estimation? The distribution of first names can be conjectured to follow the Zipf's law. In such distributions, there will be a significant fraction of rare items, as well as a considerable number of non-appearing items, in any sample of reasonable size. The same holds for the language unigrams model, which tries to estimate the distribution of single words. As it has been observed empirically on many occasions ([2], [5]), there are always many rare words and a considerable number of unseen words, regardless of the sample size. Given this observation, a fundamental issue is to estimate the distribution the best way possible.

1.1 Good-Turing Estimators

An important quantity, given a sample, is the probability mass of unseen words (also called "the missing mass"). Several methods exist for smoothing the probability and assigning probability mass to unseen items. The almost standard method for estimating the missing probability mass is the Good-Turing estimator. It estimates the missing mass as the total number of unique items, divided by the sample size. In the names example above, the Good-Turing missing mass estimator is equal 0.6, meaning that the list of the class names does not reflect the true distribution, to put it mildly. The Good-Turing estimator can be extended for higher orders, that is, estimating the probability of all names appearing exactly k times. Such estimators can also be used for estimating the probability of individual words.

The Good-Turing estimators date to World War II, and were published at 1953 ([10], [11]). They have been extensively used in language modeling applications since then ([2], [3], [4], [15]). However, their theoretical convergence rate in various models has been studied only in the recent years ([17], [18], [19], [20], [22]). For estimation of the probability of all words appearing exactly k times in a sample of size m, [19] shows a PAC bound on Good-Turing estimation error of approximately $O\left(\frac{k}{\sqrt{m}}\right)$.

One of our main results improves the dependency on k of this bound to approximately $O\left(\frac{\sqrt[4]{k}}{\sqrt{m}} + \frac{k}{m}\right)$. We also show that the empirical frequencies estimator has an error of approximately $O\left(\frac{1}{k} + \frac{\sqrt{k}}{m}\right)$, for large values of k. Based on the two estimators, we derive a combined estimator with an error of approximately $O\left(m^{-\frac{2}{5}}\right)$, for any k. We also derive a weak lower bound of $\Omega\left(\frac{\sqrt[4]{k}}{\sqrt{m}}\right)$ for an error of any estimator based on an independent sample.

Our results give theoretical justification for using the Good-Turing estimator for small values of k, and the empirical frequencies estimator for large values of k. Though in most applications the Good-Turing estimator is used for very small values of k (e.g. $k \leq 5$, as in [15] or [2]), we show that it is fairly accurate in a much wider range.

1.2 Logarithmic Loss

The Good-Turing estimators are used to approximate the probability mass of all the words with a certain frequency. For many applications, estimating this probability mass is not the main optimization criteria. Instead, a certain distance measure between the true and the estimated distributions needs to be minimized.

The most popular distance measure widely used in NLP applications is the *Kullback-Leibler (KL) divergence*. For $P = \{p_x\}$ and $Q = \{q_x\}$, two distributions over some set X, this measure is defined as $\sum_x p_x \ln \frac{p_x}{q_x}$. An equivalent measure, up to the entropy of P, is the *logarithmic loss* (*log-loss*), which equals $\sum_x p_x \ln \frac{1}{q_x}$.

Many NLP applications use the value of *log-loss* to evaluate the quality of the estimated distribution. However, the *log-loss* cannot be directly calculated, since it depends on the underlying distribution, which is unknown. Therefore, estimating *log-loss* using the sample is important, although the sample cannot be independently used for both estimating the distribution and testing it. The *hold-out* estimation splits the sample into two parts: training and testing. The training part is used for learning the distribution, whereas the testing sample is used for evaluating the average per-word log-loss. The main disadvantage of this method is the fact that it uses only part of the available information for learning, whereas in practice one would like to use all the sample.

A widely used general estimation method is called *leave-one-out*. Basically, it means averaging all the possible estimations, where a single item is chosen for testing, and the rest is used for training. This procedure has an advantage of using the entire sample, in addition it is rather simple and usually can be easily implemented. The existing theoretical analysis of the *leave-one-out* method ([14], [16]) shows general PAC-style concentration bounds for the generalization error. However, these techniques are not applicable in our setting.

We show that the *leave-one-out* estimation error for the *log-loss* is approximately $O\left(\frac{1}{\sqrt{m}}\right)$, for any underlying distribution. In addition, we show a PAC bound for the *log-loss*, as a function of various parameters of the distribution.

1.3 Model and Semantics

We denote the set of all words as V, and $N = |V|$. Let P be a distribution over V, where p_w is the probability of a word $w \in V$. Given a sample S of size m, drawn i.i.d. using P, we denote the number of appearances of a word w in

S as c_w^S, or simply c_w, when a sample S is clear from the context[1]. We define $S_k = \{w \in V : c_w^S = k\}$, and $n_k = |S_k|$.

For a claim Φ regarding a sample S, we write $\forall^\delta S\ \Phi[S]$ for $P(\Phi[S]) \geq 1 - \delta$. For some PAC bound function $f(\cdot)$, we write $\tilde{O}(f(\cdot))$ for $O\left(f(\cdot)\left(\ln \frac{m}{\delta}\right)^c\right)$, where $c > 0$ is some constant, and δ is the PAC error probability.

Due to lack of space, some of the proofs are omitted. Detailed proofs can be found at [7].

2 Concentration Inequalities

In this section we state several standard Chernoff-style concentration inequalities. We also show some of their corollaries regarding the maximum-likelihood approximation of p_w by $\hat{p}_w = \frac{c_w}{m}$.

Lemma 1. *(Hoeffding's inequality: [13], [18]) Let $Y = Y_1, \ldots, Y_n$ be a set of n independent random variables, such that $Y_i \in [b_i, b_i + d_i]$. Then, for any $\epsilon > 0$,*

$$P\left(\left|\sum_i Y_i - E\left[\sum_i Y_i\right]\right| > \epsilon\right) \leq 2\ \exp\left(-\frac{2\epsilon^2}{\sum_i d_i^2}\right)$$

This inequality has an extension for various functions of $\{Y_1, \ldots, Y_n\}$, which are not necessarily the sum.

Lemma 2. *(Variant of McDiarmid's inequality: [21], [6]) Let $Y = Y_1, \ldots, Y_n$ be a set of n independent random variables, and $f(Y)$ such that any change of Y_i value changes $f(Y)$ by at most d_i. Let $d = \max_i d_i$. Then,*

$$\forall^\delta Y: \qquad |f(Y) - E[f(Y)]| \leq d\sqrt{\frac{n \ln \frac{2}{\delta}}{2}}$$

Lemma 3. *(Angluin-Valiant bound: [1], [18]) Let $Y = Y_1, \ldots, Y_n$ be a set of n independent random variables, where $Y_i \in [0, B]$. Let $\mu = E\left[\sum_i Y_i\right]$. Then, for any $\epsilon > 0$,*

$$P\left(\left|\sum_i Y_i - \mu\right| > \epsilon\right) \leq 2\exp\left(-\frac{\epsilon^2}{(2\mu + \epsilon)B}\right)$$

The next lemma shows an explicit upper bound on the binomial distribution probability[2].

[1] Unless mentioned otherwise, all further sample-dependent definitions depend on the sample S.

[2] Its proof is based on Stirling approximation directly, though local limit theorems could be used. This form of bound is needed for the proof of Theorem 4.

Lemma 4. *Let $X \sim Bin(n,p)$ be a binomial random variable, i.e. a sum of n i.i.d. Bernoulli random variables with $p \in (0,1)$. Let $\mu = E[X] = np$. For $x \in (0,n]$, there exist some $T_x = \exp\left(\frac{1}{12x} + O\left(\frac{1}{x^2}\right)\right)$, such that $\forall k \in \{0,\ldots,n\}$, we have $P(X=k) \leq \frac{1}{\sqrt{2\pi\mu(1-p)}}\frac{T_n}{T_\mu T_{n-\mu}}$. For integral values of μ, the equality is achieved at $k=\mu$. (Note that for $x \geq 1$, we have $T_x = \Theta(1)$.)*

The next lemma (by Hoeffding, [12]) deals with the number of successes in independent trials.

Lemma 5. *([12], Theorem 5) Let $Y_1,\ldots,Y_n \in \{0,1\}$ be a sequence of independent trials, with $p_i = E[Y_i]$. Let $X = \sum_i Y_i$ be the number of successes, and $p = \frac{1}{n}\sum_i p_i$ be the average trial success probability. For any integers b and c such that $0 \leq b \leq np \leq c \leq n$, we have:*

$$\sum_{k=b}^{c}\binom{n}{k}p^k(1-p)^{n-k} \leq P(b \leq X \leq c) \leq 1$$

Using the above lemma, the next lemma shows a general concentration bound for a sum of arbitrary real-valued functions of a multinomial distribution components. We show that with a small penalty, any Chernoff-style bound pretending the components being independent is valid[3]. We recall that c_w^S, or equivalently c_w, is the number of appearances of the word w in a sample S of size m.

Lemma 6. *Let $\{c'_w \sim Bin(m,p_w) : w \in V\}$ be independent binomial random variables. Let $\{f_w(x) : w \in V\}$ be a set of real valued functions. Let $F = \sum_w f_w(c_w)$ and $F' = \sum_w f_w(c'_w)$. For any $\epsilon > 0$,*

$$P\left(|F - E[F]| > \epsilon\right) \leq 3\sqrt{m}\, P\left(|F' - E[F']| > \epsilon\right)$$

The following lemmas provide concentration bounds for maximum-likelihood estimation of p_w by $\frac{c_w}{m}$.

Lemma 7. *Let $\delta > 0$, and $\lambda \geq 3$. We have $\forall^\delta S$:*

$$\forall w \in V,\ \text{s.t.}\ mp_w \geq 3\ln\tfrac{2m}{\delta},\quad |mp_w - c_w| \leq \sqrt{3mp_w \ln\frac{2m}{\delta}}$$

$$\forall w \in V,\ \text{s.t.}\ mp_w > \lambda\ln\tfrac{2m}{\delta},\quad c_w > \left(1 - \sqrt{\frac{3}{\lambda}}\right)mp_w$$

Lemma 8. *Let $\delta \in (0,1)$, and $m > 1$. Then, $\forall^\delta S$: $\forall w \in V$ such that $mp_w \leq 3\ln\frac{m}{\delta}$, we have $c_w \leq 6\ln\frac{m}{\delta}$.*

[3] The *negative association* analysis ([8]) shows that a sum of negatively associated variables must obey Chernoff-style bounds pretending that the variables are independent. The components of a multinomial distribution are negatively associated. Therefore, any Chernoff-style bound is valid for their sum, as well as for the sum of monotone functions of the components. In some sense, our result extends this notion, since it does not require the functions to be monotone.

3 Hitting Mass Estimation

In this section our goal is to estimate the probability of the set of words appearing exactly k times in the sample, which we call "the hitting mass". We analyze the Good-Turing estimator, the empirical frequencies estimator, and the combined estimator.

Definition 1. *We define the hitting mass and its estimators as:* [4]

$$M_k = \sum_{w \in S_k} p_w \qquad \hat{M}_k = \left(\frac{k}{m}\right) n_k \qquad G_k = \left(\frac{k+1}{m-k}\right) n_{k+1}$$

The outline of this section is as follows. Definition 3 slightly redefines the hitting mass and its estimators. Lemma 9 shows that this redefinition has a negligible influence. Then, we analyze the estimation errors using the concentration inequalities from Section 2.

The expectation of the Good-Turing estimator error is bounded as in [19]. Lemma 14 bounds the deviation of the error, using the negative association analysis. A tighter bound, based on Lemma 6, is achieved at Theorem 1. Theorem 2 analyzes the error of the empirical frequencies estimator. Theorem 3 refers to the combined estimator. Finally, Theorem 4 shows a weak lower bound for the hitting mass estimation.

Definition 2. *For any $w \in V$ and $i \in \{0, \cdots, m\}$, we define $X_{w,i}$ as a random variable equal 1 if $c_w = i$, and 0 otherwise.*

Definition 3. *Let $\alpha > 0$ and $k > 3\alpha^2$. We define $I_{k,\alpha} = \left[\frac{k-\alpha\sqrt{k}}{m}, \frac{k+1+\alpha\sqrt{k+1}}{m}\right]$, and $V_{k,\alpha} = \{w \in V : p_w \in I_{k,\alpha}\}$. We define:*

$$M_{k,\alpha} = \sum_{w \in S_k \cap V_{k,\alpha}} p_w = \sum_{w \in V_{k,\alpha}} p_w X_{w,k}$$

$$G_{k,\alpha} = \frac{k+1}{m-k} |S_{k+1} \cap V_{k,\alpha}| = \frac{k+1}{m-k} \sum_{w \in V_{k,\alpha}} X_{w,k+1}$$

$$\hat{M}_{k,\alpha} = \frac{k}{m} |S_k \cap V_{k,\alpha}| = \frac{k}{m} \sum_{w \in V_{k,\alpha}} X_{w,k}$$

By Lemma 7 and Lemma 8, for large values of k the redefinition coincides with the original definition with high probability:

Lemma 9. *For $\delta > 0$, let $\alpha = \sqrt{6 \ln \frac{4m}{\delta}}$. For $k > 18 \ln \frac{4m}{\delta}$, we have $\forall^\delta S$: $M_k = M_{k,\alpha}$, $G_k = G_{k,\alpha}$, and $\hat{M}_k = \hat{M}_{k,\alpha}$.*

---

[4] The Good-Turing estimator is usually defined as $(\frac{k+1}{m}) n_{k+1}$. The two definitions are almost identical for small values of k. Following [19], we use our definition, which makes the calculations slightly simpler.

Since the minimal probability of a word in $V_{k,\alpha}$ is $\Omega\left(\frac{k}{m}\right)$, we derive:

Lemma 10. *Let $\alpha > 0$ and $k > 3\alpha^2$. Then, $|V_{k,\alpha}| = O\left(\frac{m}{k}\right)$.*

Using Lemma 4, we derive:

Lemma 11. *Let $\alpha > 0$ and $3\alpha^2 < k \leq \frac{m}{2}$. Let $w \in V_{k,\alpha}$. Then, $E[X_{w,k}] = P(c_w = k) = O\left(\frac{1}{\sqrt{k}}\right)$.*

3.1 Good-Turing Estimator

The following lemma, based on the definition of the binomial distribution, was shown in Theorem 1 of [19].

Lemma 12. *For any $k < m$, and $w \in V$, we have:*

$$p_w P(c_w = k) = \frac{k+1}{m-k} P(c_w = k+1)(1 - p_w)$$

The following lemma bounds the expectations of the redefined hitting mass, its Good-Turing estimator, and their difference.

Lemma 13. *Let $\alpha > 0$ and $3\alpha^2 < k < \frac{m}{2}$. We have $E[M_{k,\alpha}] = O\left(\frac{1}{\sqrt{k}}\right)$, $E[G_{k,\alpha}] = O\left(\frac{1}{\sqrt{k}}\right)$, and $|E[G_{k,\alpha}] - E[M_{k,\alpha}]| = O\left(\frac{\sqrt{k}}{m}\right)$.*

Using the *negative association* notion, we can show a preliminary bound for Good-Turing estimation error:

Lemma 14. *For $\delta > 0$ and $18 \ln \frac{8m}{\delta} < k < \frac{m}{2}$, we have $\forall^\delta S$:*

$$|G_k - M_k| = O\left(\sqrt{\frac{k \ln \frac{1}{\delta}}{m}}\right)$$

Lemma 15. *Let $\delta > 0$, $k > 0$. Let $U \subseteq V$. Let $\{b_w : w \in U\}$ be a set of weights, such that $b_w \in [0, B]$. Let $X_k = \sum_{w \in U} b_w X_{w,k}$, and $\mu = E[X_k]$. We have:*

$$\forall^\delta S,\ |X_k - \mu| \leq \max\left\{\sqrt{4B\mu \ln\left(\frac{6\sqrt{m}}{\delta}\right)}, 2B \ln\left(\frac{6\sqrt{m}}{\delta}\right)\right\}$$

Proof. By Lemma 6, combined with Lemma 3, we have:

$$\begin{aligned} P(|X_k - \mu| > \epsilon) &\leq 6\sqrt{m}\ \exp\left(-\frac{\epsilon^2}{B(2\mu + \epsilon)}\right) \\ &\leq \max\left\{6\sqrt{m}\ \exp\left(-\frac{\epsilon^2}{4B\mu}\right), 6\sqrt{m}\ \exp\left(-\frac{\epsilon}{2B}\right)\right\}, \end{aligned} \quad (1)$$

where (1) follows by considering $\epsilon \leq 2\mu$ and $\epsilon > 2\mu$ separately. The lemma follows substituting $\epsilon = \max\left\{\sqrt{4B\mu \ln\left(\frac{6\sqrt{m}}{\delta}\right)}, 2B \ln\left(\frac{6\sqrt{m}}{\delta}\right)\right\}$. □

We now derive the concentration bound on the error of the Good-Turing estimator.

Theorem 1. *For $\delta > 0$ and $18 \ln \frac{8m}{\delta} < k < \frac{m}{2}$, we have $\forall^{\delta} S$:*

$$|G_k - M_k| = O\left(\sqrt{\frac{\sqrt{k}\ln\frac{m}{\delta}}{m}} + \frac{k \ln \frac{m}{\delta}}{m}\right)$$

Proof. Let $\alpha = \sqrt{6 \ln \frac{8m}{\delta}}$. Using Lemma 9, we have $\forall^{\frac{\delta}{2}} S$: $G_k = G_{k,\alpha}$, and $M_k = M_{k,\alpha}$. Recall that $M_{k,\alpha} = \sum_{w \in V_{k,\alpha}} p_w X_{w,k}$ and $G_{k,\alpha} = \sum_{w \in V_{k,\alpha}} \frac{k+1}{m-k} X_{w,k+1}$. Both $M_{k,\alpha}$ and $G_{k,\alpha}$ are linear combinations of $X_{w,k}$ and $X_{w,k+1}$, respectively, where the coefficients' magnitude is $O\left(\frac{k}{m}\right)$, and the expectation, by Lemma 13, is $O\left(\frac{1}{\sqrt{k}}\right)$. By Lemma 15, we have:

$$\forall^{\frac{\delta}{4}} S,\ |M_{k,\alpha} - E[M_{k,\alpha}]| = O\left(\sqrt{\frac{\sqrt{k}\ln\frac{m}{\delta}}{m}} + \frac{k \ln \frac{m}{\delta}}{m}\right) \tag{2}$$

$$\forall^{\frac{\delta}{4}} S,\ |G_{k,\alpha} - E[G_{k,\alpha}]| = O\left(\sqrt{\frac{\sqrt{k}\ln\frac{m}{\delta}}{m}} + \frac{k \ln \frac{m}{\delta}}{m}\right) \tag{3}$$

Combining (2), (3), and Lemma 13, we have $\forall^{\delta} S$:

$$\begin{aligned} |G_k - M_k| &= |G_{k,\alpha} - M_{k,\alpha}| \\ &\leq |G_{k,\alpha} - E[G_{k,\alpha}]| + |M_{k,\alpha} - E[M_{k,\alpha}]| + |E[G_{k,\alpha}] - E[M_{k,\alpha}]| \\ &= O\left(\sqrt{\frac{\sqrt{k}\ln\frac{m}{\delta}}{m}} + \frac{k \ln \frac{m}{\delta}}{m} + \frac{\sqrt{k}}{m}\right) = O\left(\sqrt{\frac{\sqrt{k}\ln\frac{m}{\delta}}{m}} + \frac{k \ln \frac{m}{\delta}}{m}\right), \end{aligned}$$

which completes the proof. □

3.2 Empirical Frequencies Estimator

In this section we bound the error of the empirical frequencies estimator $\hat{M}_k$.

Theorem 2. *For $\delta > 0$ and $18 \ln \frac{8m}{\delta} < k < \frac{m}{2}$, we have:*

$$\forall^{\delta} S,\ |M_k - \hat{M}_k| = O\left(\frac{\sqrt{k}\left(\ln\frac{m}{\delta}\right)^{\frac{3}{2}}}{m} + \frac{\sqrt{\ln\frac{m}{\delta}}}{k}\right)$$

Proof. Let $\alpha = \sqrt{6 \ln \frac{8m}{\delta}}$. By Lemma 9, we have $\forall^{\frac{\delta}{2}} S$: $\hat{M}_k = \hat{M}_{k,\alpha}$, and $M_k = M_{k,\alpha}$. Let $V_{k,\alpha}^{-} = \{w \in V_{k,\alpha} : p_w < \frac{k}{m}\}$, and $V_{k,\alpha}^{+} = \{w \in V_{k,\alpha} : p_w > \frac{k}{m}\}$. Let

$$X_- = \sum_{w \in V_{k,\alpha}^-} \left(\frac{k}{m} - p_w \right) X_{w,k}, \qquad X_+ = \sum_{w \in V_{k,\alpha}^+} \left(p_w - \frac{k}{m} \right) X_{w,k},$$

and let $X_?$ specify either X_- or X_+. By the definition, for $w \in V_{k,\alpha}$ we have $\left|\frac{k}{m} - p_w\right| = O\left(\frac{\alpha\sqrt{k}}{m}\right)$. By Lemma 10, $|V_{k,\alpha}| = O\left(\frac{m}{k}\right)$. By Lemma 11, for $w \in V_{k,\alpha}$ we have $E[X_{w,k}] = O\left(\frac{1}{\sqrt{k}}\right)$. Therefore,

$$|E[X_?]| \leq \sum_{w \in V_{k,\alpha}} \left| \frac{k}{m} - p_w \right| E[X_{w,k}] = O\left(\frac{m}{k} \frac{\alpha\sqrt{k}}{m} \frac{1}{\sqrt{k}} \right) = O\left(\frac{\alpha}{k}\right) \tag{4}$$

Both X_- and X_+ are linear combinations of $X_{w,k}$, where the coefficients are $O\left(\frac{\alpha\sqrt{k}}{m}\right)$ and the expectation is $O\left(\frac{\alpha}{k}\right)$. Therefore, by Lemma 15, we have:

$$\forall^{\frac{\delta}{4}} S: \qquad |X_? - E[X_?]| = O\left(\sqrt{\frac{\alpha^4}{m\sqrt{k}}} + \frac{\alpha^3\sqrt{k}}{m} \right) \tag{5}$$

By the definition of X_- and X_+, $M_{k,\alpha} - \hat{M}_{k,\alpha} = X_+ - X_-$. Combining (4) and (5), we have $\forall^{\delta} S$:

$$\begin{aligned} |M_k - \hat{M}_k| &= |M_{k,\alpha} - \hat{M}_{k,\alpha}| = |X_+ - X_-| \\ &\leq |X_+ - E[X_+]| + E[X_+] + |X_- - E[X_-]| + E[X_-] \\ &= O\left(\sqrt{\frac{\alpha^4}{m\sqrt{k}}} + \frac{\alpha^3\sqrt{k}}{m} + \frac{\alpha}{k} \right) = O\left(\frac{\sqrt{k}\left(\ln\frac{m}{\delta}\right)^{\frac{3}{2}}}{m} + \frac{\sqrt{\ln\frac{m}{\delta}}}{k} \right), \end{aligned}$$

since $\sqrt{ab} = O(a+b)$, and we use $a = \frac{\alpha^3\sqrt{k}}{m}$ and $b = \frac{\alpha}{k}$. □

3.3 Combined Estimator

In this section we combine the Good-Turing estimator with the empirical frequencies to derive a combined estimator, which is accurate for all values of k.

Definition 4. *We define $\tilde{M}_k$, a combined estimator for M_k, by:*

$$\tilde{M}_k = \begin{cases} G_k & k \leq m^{\frac{2}{5}} \\ \hat{M}_k & k > m^{\frac{2}{5}} \end{cases}$$

Lemma 16. *(Theorem 3 at [19]) Let $k \in \{0, \ldots, m\}$. For any $\delta > 0$, we have:*

$$\forall^\delta S: \qquad |G_k - M_k| = O\left(\sqrt{\frac{\ln\frac{1}{\delta}}{m}}\left(k + \ln\frac{m}{\delta}\right)\right)$$

The following theorem shows that $\tilde{M}_k$ has an error bounded by $\tilde{O}\left(m^{-\frac{2}{5}}\right)$, for any k. For small k, we use Lemma 16. Theorem 1 is used for $18\ln\frac{8m}{\delta} < k \leq m^{\frac{2}{5}}$. Theorem 2 is used for $m^{\frac{2}{5}} < k < \frac{m}{2}$. The complete proof also handles $k \geq \frac{m}{2}$.

Theorem 3. *Let $\delta > 0$. For any $k \in \{0, \ldots, m\}$, we have:*

$$\forall^\delta S, |\tilde{M}_k - M_k| = \tilde{O}\left(m^{-\frac{2}{5}}\right)$$

The following theorem shows a weak lower bound for approximating M_k. It applies to estimating M_k based on a different independent sample. This is a very "weak" notation, since G_k, as well as $\hat{M}_k$, are based on the same sample as M_k.

Theorem 4. *Suppose that the vocabulary consists of $\frac{m}{k}$ words distributed uniformly (i.e. $p_w = \frac{k}{m}$), where $1 \ll k \ll m$. The variance of M_k is $\Theta\left(\frac{\sqrt{k}}{m}\right)$.*

4 Leave-One-Out Estimation of Log-Loss

Many NLP applications use log-loss as the learning performance criteria. Since the log-loss depends on the underlying probability P, its value cannot be explicitly calculated, and must be approximated. The main result of this section, Theorem 5, is an upper bound on the leave-one-out estimation of the log-loss, assuming a general family of learning algorithms.

Given a sample $S = \{s_1, \ldots, s_m\}$, the goal of a learning algorithm is to approximate the true probability P by some probability Q. We denote the probability assigned by the learning algorithm to a word w by q_w.

Definition 5. *We assume that any two words with equal sample frequency are assigned equal probabilities in Q, and therefore denote q_w by $q(c_w)$. Let the log-loss of a distribution Q be:*

$$L = \sum_{w \in V} p_w \ln\frac{1}{q_w} = \sum_{k \geq 0} M_k \ln\frac{1}{q(k)}$$

Let the leave-one-out estimation, q'_w, be the probability assigned to w, when one of its instances is removed. We assume that any two words with equal sample *frequency are assigned equal leave-one-out probability estimation, and therefore denote q'_w by $q'(c_w)$. We define the leave-one-out estimation of the log-loss as:*

$$L_{leave-one} = \sum_{w \in V} \frac{c_w}{m} \ln \frac{1}{q'_w} = \sum_{k>0} \frac{kn_k}{m} \ln \frac{1}{q'(k)}$$

Let $L_w = L(c_w) = \ln \frac{1}{q(c_w)}$, and $L'_w = L'(c_w) = \ln \frac{1}{q'(c_w)}$. Let $L_{max} =$ $\max_k \max \{L(k), L'(k+1)\}$.

In this section we discuss a family of learning algorithms, that receive the sample as an input. Assuming an accuracy parameter δ, we require the following properties to hold:

1. Starting from a certain number of appearances, the estimation is close to the sample frequency. Specifically, for some $\alpha, \beta \in [0,1]$,

$$\forall k \geq \ln\left(\frac{4m}{\delta}\right), \quad q(k) = \frac{k-\alpha}{m-\beta} \tag{6}$$

2. The algorithm is stable when a word is extracted from the sample:

$$\forall m, \qquad 2 \leq k \leq 10 \ln \tfrac{4m}{\delta}, \qquad |L'(k+1) - L(k)| = O\left(\frac{1}{m}\right) \tag{7}$$

$$\forall m, \forall S \text{ s.t. } n_1^S > 0,\ k \in \{0,1\}, \quad |L'(k+1) - L(k)| = O\left(\frac{1}{n_1^S}\right) \tag{8}$$

An example of such an algorithm is the following leave-one-out algorithm (we assume that the vocabulary is large enough so that $n_0 + n_1 > 0$):

$$q_w = \begin{cases} \frac{N-n_0-1}{(n_0+n_1)(m-1)} & c_w \leq 1 \\ \frac{c_w-1}{m-1} & c_w \geq 2 \end{cases}$$

The next lemma shows that the expectation of the leave-one-out method is a good approximation for the per-word expectation of the logarithmic loss.

Lemma 17. *Let $0 \leq \alpha \leq 1$, and $y \geq 1$. Let $B_n \sim Bin(n,p)$ be a binomial random variable. Let $f_y(x) = \ln(\max(x,y))$. Then,*

$$0 \leq E\left[pf_y(B_n - \alpha) - \frac{B_n}{n} f_y(B_n - \alpha - 1)\right] \leq \frac{3p}{n}$$

Sketch of Proof. For a real valued function F (here $F(x) = f_y(x - \alpha)$), we have:

$$E\left[\frac{B_n}{n}F(B_n - 1)\right] = \sum_{x=0}^{n}\binom{n}{x}p^x(1-p)^{n-x}\frac{x}{n}F(x-1)$$
$$= p\sum_{x=1}^{n}\binom{n-1}{x-1}p^{x-1}(1-p)^{(n-1)-(x-1)}F(x-1)$$
$$= pE[F(B_{n-1})] ,$$

where we used $\binom{n}{x}\frac{x}{n} = \binom{n-1}{x-1}$. The rest of the proof follows by algebraic manipulations, and the definition of the binomial distribution (see [7] for details). □

Lemma 18. *Let $\delta > 0$. We have $\forall^\delta S$: $n_2 = O\left(\left(\sqrt{m \ln \frac{1}{\delta}} + n_1\right) \ln \frac{m}{\delta}\right)$.*

Theorem 5. *For $\delta > 0$, we have:*

$$\forall^\delta S, |L - L_{leave-one}| = O\left(L_{max}\sqrt{\frac{(\ln \frac{m}{\delta})^4 \ln \frac{\ln \frac{m}{\delta}}{\delta}}{m}}\right)$$

Proof. Let $y_w = \left(1 - \sqrt{\frac{3}{5}}\right) p_w m - 2$. By Lemma 7, with $\lambda = 5$, we have $\forall^{\frac{\delta}{2}} S$:

$$\forall w \in V : p_w > \frac{3 \ln \frac{4m}{\delta}}{m}, \qquad \left|p_w - \tfrac{c_w}{m}\right| \le \sqrt{\frac{3p_w \ln \frac{4m}{\delta}}{m}} \tag{9}$$

$$\forall w \in V : p_w > \frac{5 \ln \frac{4m}{\delta}}{m}, \; c_w > y_w + 2 \ge (5 - \sqrt{15}) \ln \tfrac{4m}{\delta} > \ln \tfrac{4m}{\delta} \tag{10}$$

Let $V_H = \left\{w \in V : p_w > \frac{5 \ln \frac{4m}{\delta}}{m}\right\}$ and $V_L = V \setminus V_H$. We have:

$$|L - L_{leave-one}| \le \left|\sum_{w \in V_H}\left(p_w L_w - \frac{c_w}{m}L'_w\right)\right| + \left|\sum_{w \in V_L}\left(p_w L_w - \frac{c_w}{m}L'_w\right)\right| \tag{11}$$

We start by bounding the first term of (11). By (10), we have $\forall w \in V_H, c_w > y_w + 2 > \ln \frac{4m}{\delta}$. Assumption (6) implies that $q_w = \frac{c_w - \alpha}{m - \beta}$, therefore $L_w = \ln \frac{m-\beta}{c_w - \alpha} = \ln \frac{m-\beta}{\max(c_w - \alpha, y_w)}$, and $L'_w = \ln \frac{m-1-\beta}{c_w - 1 - \alpha} = \ln \frac{m-1-\beta}{\max(c_w - 1 - \alpha, y_w)}$. Let

$$Err_w^H = \frac{c_w}{m} \ln \frac{m - \beta}{\max(c_w - 1 - \alpha, y_w)} - p_w \ln \frac{m - \beta}{\max(c_w - \alpha, y_w)}$$

We have:

$$\left|\sum_{w\in V_H}\left(\frac{c_w}{m}L'_w - p_w L_w\right)\right| = \left|\sum_{w\in V_H} Err^H_w + \ln\frac{m-1-\beta}{m-\beta}\sum_{w\in V_H}\frac{c_w}{m}\right|$$
$$\leq \left|\sum_{w\in V_H} Err^H_w\right| + O\left(\frac{1}{m}\right) \qquad (12)$$

We bound $\left|\sum_{w\in V_H} Err^H_w\right|$ using McDiarmid's inequality. As in Lemma 17, let $f_w(x) = \ln(\max(x, y_w))$. We have:

$$E\left[Err^H_w\right] = \ln(m-\beta)E\left[\frac{c_w}{m} - p_w\right] + E\left[p_w f_w(c_w - \alpha) - \frac{c_w}{m} f_w(c_w - 1 - \alpha)\right]$$

The first expectation equals 0, the second can be bounded using Lemma 17:

$$\left|\sum_{w\in V_H} E\left[Err^H_w\right]\right| \leq \sum_{w\in V_H}\frac{3p_w}{m} = O\left(\frac{1}{m}\right) \qquad (13)$$

In order to use McDiarmid's inequality, we bound the change of $\sum_{w\in V_H} Err^H_w$ as a function of a single change in the sample. Suppose that a word u is replaced by a word v. This results in decrease for c_u, and increase for c_v. Recalling that $y_w = \Omega(mp_w)$, the change of Err^H_u, as well as the change of Err^H_v, is bounded by $O\left(\frac{\ln m}{m}\right)$ (see [7] for details).

By (12), (13), and Lemma 2, we have $\forall^{\frac{\delta}{16}} S$:

$$\left|\sum_{w\in V_H}\left(\frac{c_w}{m}L'_w - p_w L_w\right)\right| = O\left(\sqrt{\frac{(\ln m)^2 \ln\frac{1}{\delta}}{m}}\right) \qquad (14)$$

Next, we bound the second term of (11). By Lemma 8, we have $\forall^{\frac{\delta}{4}} S$:

$$\forall w \in V \; s.t. \; p_w \leq \frac{3\ln\frac{4m}{\delta}}{m}, \; c_w \leq 6\ln\frac{4m}{\delta} \qquad (15)$$

Let $b = 5\ln\frac{4m}{\delta}$. By (9) and (15), for any w such that $p_w \leq \frac{b}{m}$, we have:

$$\frac{c_w}{m} \leq \max\left\{p_w + \sqrt{\frac{3p_w\ln\frac{4m}{\delta}}{m}}, \frac{6\ln\frac{4m}{\delta}}{m}\right\} \leq \frac{(5+\sqrt{3*5})\ln\frac{4m}{\delta}}{m} < \frac{2b}{m}$$

Therefore $\forall w \in V_L$, we have $c_w < 2b$. Let $n_k^L = |V_L \cap S_k|$, $G_{k-1}^L = \frac{k}{m-k+1} n_k^L$, and $M_k^L = \sum_{w \in V_L \cap S_k} p_w$. Using algebraic manipulations (see [7] for details), we have:

$$\left| \sum_{w \in V_L} \left(\frac{c_w}{m} L'_w - p_w L_w \right) \right| = \left| \sum_{k=1}^{2b} \frac{k n_k^L}{m} L'(k) - \sum_{k=0}^{2b-1} M_k^L L(k) \right|$$
$$\leq \sum_{k=0}^{2b-1} G_k^L |L'(k+1) - L(k)| + \sum_{k=0}^{2b-1} |G_k^L - M_k^L| L(k) + O\left(\frac{b L_{max}}{m} \right) \quad (16)$$

The first sum of (16) is bounded using (7), (8), and Lemma 18 (with accuracy $\frac{\delta}{16}$). The second sum of (16) is bounded using Lemma 16 separately for every $k < 2b$ with accuracy $\frac{\delta}{16b}$. Since the proof of Lemma 16 also holds for G_k^L and M_k^L (instead of G_k and M_k), we have $\forall^{\frac{\delta}{8}} S$, for every $k < 2b$, $|G_k^L - M_k^L| = O\left(b\sqrt{\frac{\ln \frac{b}{\delta}}{m}} \right)$. Therefore (the details can be found at [7]),

$$\left| \sum_{w \in V_L} \left(\frac{c_w}{m} L'_w - p_w L_w \right) \right| = O\left(L_{max} \sqrt{\frac{b^4 \ln \frac{b}{\delta}}{m}} \right) \quad (17)$$

The proof follows by combining (11), (14), and (17). □

5 Log-Loss A Priori

Section 4 bounds the error of the leave-one-out estimation of the log-loss. In this section we analyze the log-loss itself. We denote the learning error (equivalent to the log-loss) as the KL-divergence between the true and the estimated distribution. We refer to a general family of learning algorithms, and show an upper bound for the learning error.

Let $\alpha \in (0,1)$ and $\tau \geq 1$. We define an (absolute discounting) algorithm $A_{\alpha,\tau}$, which "removes" $\frac{\alpha}{m}$ probability mass from words appearing at most τ times, and uniformly spreads it among the unseen words. We denote by $n_{1\ldots\tau} = \sum_{i=1}^{\tau} n_i$ the number of words with count between 1 and τ. The learned probability Q is defined by :

$$q_w = \begin{cases} \frac{\alpha n_{1\ldots\tau}}{m n_0} & c_w = 0 \\ \frac{c_w - \alpha}{m} & 1 \leq c_w \leq \tau \\ \frac{c_w}{m} & \tau < c_w \end{cases}$$

Theorem 6. *For any $\delta > 0$ and $\lambda > 3$, such that $\tau < (\lambda - \sqrt{3\lambda}) \ln \frac{8m}{\delta}$, let $x = \frac{\lambda \ln \frac{8m}{\delta}}{m}$ and $N_x = |\{w \in V : p_w > x\}|$. Then, the learning error of $A_{\alpha,\tau}$ is bounded $\forall^\delta S$ by:*

$$0 \leq \sum_{w \in V} p_w \ln \left(\frac{p_w}{q_w} \right) = \tilde{O} \left(M_0 \ln N + x\sqrt{m} + \frac{N_x}{m} \right)$$

Since N_x counts only words with $p_w > x$, it is bounded by $\frac{1}{x}$. Therefore, $x = m^{-\frac{3}{4}}$ gives a bound of $\tilde{O}\left(M_0 \ln N + m^{-\frac{1}{4}}\right)$. Lower loss can be achieved for specific distributions, such as those with small M_0 and small N_x (for some reasonable x).

Acknowledgements. We are grateful to David McAllester for his important contributions in the early stages of this research.

References

1. D. Angluin and L. G. Valiant. Fast Probabilistic Algorithms for Hamiltonian Circuits and matchings, In *Journal of Computer and System Sciences*, 18:155-193, 1979.
2. S. F. Chen, Building Probabilistic Models for Natural Language, *Ph.D. Thesis*, Harvard University, 1996.
3. S. F. Chen and J. Goodman, An Empirical Study of Smoothing Techniques for Language Modeling, *Technical Report* TR-10-98, Harvard University, 1998.
4. K. W. Church and W. A. Gale, A Comparison of the Enhanced Good-Turing and Deleted Estimation Methods for Estimating Probabilities of English Bigrams, In *Computer Speech and Language*, 5:19-54, 1991.
5. J. R. Curran and M. Osborne, A Very Very Large Corpus Doesn't Always Yield Reliable Estimates, In *Proceedings of the Sixth Conference on Natural Language Learning*, pages 126-131, 2002.
6. L. Devroye, L. Györfi, and G. Lugosi, A Probabilistic Theory of Pattern Recognition, *Springer-Verlag, New York*, 1996.
7. E. Drukh, Concentration Bounds for Unigrams Language Model, *M.Sc. Thesis*, Tel Aviv University, 2004.
8. D. P. Dubhashi and D. Ranjan, Balls and Bins: A Study in Negative Dependence, In *Random Structures and Algorithms*, 13(2):99-124, 1998.
9. W. Gale, Good-Turing Smoothing Without Tears, In *Journal of Quantitative Linguistics*, 2:217–37, 1995.
10. I. J. Good, The Population Frequencies of Species and the Estimation of Population Parameters, In *Biometrika*, 40(16):237-264, 1953.
11. I. J. Good, Turing's Anticipation of Empirical Bayes in Connection with the Cryptanalysis of the Naval Enigma, In *Journal of Statistical Computation and Simulation*, 66(2):101-112, 2000.
12. W. Hoeffding, On the Distribution of the Number of Successes in Independent Trials, In *Annals of Mathematical Statistics*, 27:713-721, 1956.

13. W. Hoeffding, Probability Inequalities for Sums of Bounded Random Variables, In *Journal of the American Statistical Association*, 58:13-30, 1963.
14. S. B. Holden, PAC-like Upper Bounds for the Sample Complexity of Leave-One-Out Cross-Validation, In *Proceesings of the Ninth Annual ACM Workshop on Computational Learning Theory*, pages 41-50, 1996.
15. S. M. Katz, Estimation of Probabilities from Sparse Data for the Language Model Component of a Speech Recognizer, In *IEEE Transactions on Acoustics, Speech and Signal Processing*, 35(3):400-401, 1987.
16. M. Kearns and D. Ron, Algorithmic Stability and Sanity-Check Bounds for Leave-One-Out Cross-Validation, In *Neural Computation*, 11(6):1427-1453, 1999.
17. S. Kutin, Algorithmic Stability and Ensemble-Based Learning, *Ph.D. Thesis*, University of Chicago, 2002.
18. D. McAllester and L. Ortiz, Concentration Inequalities for the Missing Mass and for Histogram Rule Error, In *Journal of Machine Learning Research, Special Issue on Learning Theory*, 4(Oct):895-911, 2003.
19. D. McAllester and R. E. Schapire, On the Convergence Rate of Good-Turing Estimators, In *Proceedings of the Thirteenth Annual Conference on Computational Learning Theory*, pages 1-6, 2000.
20. D. McAllester and R. E. Schapire, Learning Theory and Language Modeling, In *Seventeenth International Joint Conference on Artificial Intelligence*, 2001.
21. C. McDiarmid, On the Method of Bounded Differences, In *Surveys in Combinatorics 1989*, Cambridge University Press, Cambridge, 148-188, 1989.
22. A. Orlitsky, N. P. Santhanam, and J. Zhang, Always Good Turing: Asymptotically Optimal Probability Estimation, In *Science*, 302(Oct):427-431, 2003 (in Reports).

Inferring Mixtures of Markov Chains

Tuğkan Batu*[1], Sudipto Guha[2], and Sampath Kannan**[2]

[1] Department of Computer Sciences, University of Texas, Austin, TX.
batu@cs.utexas.edu

[2] Department of Computer and Information Science, University of Pennsylvania, Philadelphia, PA.
{sudipto,kannan}@cis.upenn.edu

Abstract. We define the problem of inferring a "mixture of Markov chains" based on observing a stream of interleaved outputs from these chains. We show a sharp characterization of the inference process. The problems we consider also has applications such as gene finding, intrusion detection, etc., and more generally in analyzing interleaved sequences.

1 Introduction

In this paper we study the question of inferring Markov chains from a stream of interleaved behavior. We assume that the constituent Markov chains output their current state. The sequences of states thus obtained are interleaved by some switching mechanism (such as a natural mixture model). Observe that if we only observe a (probabilistic) function of the current state, the above problem already captures hidden Markov models and probabilistic automata, and is computationally intractable as shown by Abe and Warmuth [1]. Our results can therefore be interpreted as providing an analytical inference mechanism for one class of hidden Markov models. The closely related problem of learning switching distributions is studied by Freund and Ron [10].

Thiesson et al. study learning mixtures of Bayesian networks and DAG models [16,17]. In related works, learning mixtures of Gaussian distributions are studied in [6,3]. The hidden Markov model, pioneered in speech recognition (see [14,4]) has been the obvious choice for modeling sequential patterns. Related Hierarchical Markov models [11] were proposed for graphical modeling. Mixture models have been studied considerably in the context of learning and even earlier in the context of pattern recognition [8]. To the best of our knowledge, mixture models of Markov chains have not been explored.

Our motivation for studying the problem is in understanding interleaved processes that can be modeled by discrete-time Markov chains. The interleaving process controls a token which it hands off to one of the component processes

* This work was supported by ARO DAAD 19-01-1047 and NSF CCR01-05337.
** This work was supported by NSF CCR98-20885 and NSF CCR01-05337.

J. Shawe-Taylor and Y. Singer (Eds.): COLT 2004, LNAI 3120, pp. 186–199, 2004.

at each time step. A component process that receives the token makes a transition, outputs its state, and returns the token. We consider several variants of the interleaving process. In the simplest, tokens are handed off to the component processes with fixed probabilities independent of history. A more general model is where these hand-off probabilities are dependent on the chain of the state that was generated last. The following are potential applications of our framework.

- The problem of *intrusion detection* is the problem of observing a stream of packets and deciding if some improper use is being made of system resources.[1] We can attempt to model the background (good) traffic and the intrusive traffic being different Markov processes. We then model the overall traffic as a random mixture of these two types of traffic. The problem of *fraud detection* arises in this context as well; see [7,18,12,9] for models on intrusion and fraud detection.
- Given a genome sequence (a sequence from a chromosome) the problem is to locate the regions of this sequence (called *exons*) that collectively represent a gene. Again, precise defining characteristics are not known for exons and the regions in between them called *introns*. However, a number of papers have attempted to identify statistical differences between these two types of segments. Because the presence of a nucleotide at one position affects the distribution of nucleotides at neighboring positions one needs to model these distributions (at least) as first-order Markov chains rather than treating each position independently. In fact, fifth-order Markov chains and Generalized Hidden Markov Models (GHMMs) are used by gene finding programs such as GENSCAN [5].
- The problem of validation and mining of log-files of transactions arises in e-commerce applications [2,15]. The user interacts with a server and the only information is available at the server end is a transcript of the interleaved interactions of multiple users . Typically searches/queries/requests are made in "sessions" by the same user; but there is no obvious way to determine if two requests correspond to the same user or different ones. Complete information is not always available (due to proxies or explicit privacy concerns) and at times unreliable. See [13] for a survey of issues in this area.

The common theme of the above problems is the analysis of a sequence that arises from a process which is not completely known. Furthermore the problem is quite simple if *exactly one* process is involved. The complexity of these problems arise from the interleaving of the two or more processes due to probabilistic linearization of parallel processes rather than due to adversarial intervention.

---

[1] We do not have a precise definition of what constitutes such intrusion but we expect that experts "will know it when they see it."

1.1 Our Model

Let $M^{(1)}, M^{(2)}, \ldots, M^{(k)}$ be Markov chains where Markov chain $M^{(l)}$ has state space V_l for $l = 1, 2, \ldots, k$. The inference algorithm has no *a priori* knowledge of which states belong to which Markov chains. In fact, identifying the set of states in each chain is the main challenge in the inference problem.

One might be tempted to "simplify" the picture by saying that the process generating the data is a *single* Markov chain on the cross-product state space. Note, however, that at each step we only observe one component of the state of this cross-product chain and hence with this view, we are faced with the problem of inferring a hidden Markov model. Our results can therefore be interpreted as providing an analytical inference mechanism for one class of hidden Markov models where the hiding function projects a state in a product space to an appropriate component. We consider two mixture models.

- In the simpler mixture model, we assume that there are probability values $\alpha_1, \ldots, \alpha_k$ summing to 1 such that at each time step, Markov chain $M^{(i)}$ is chosen with probability α_i. The choices at different time steps are assumed to be independent. *Note that the number k of Markov chains (and, necessarily, the mixing probabilities) are not known in advance.*

- A more sophisticated mixture model, for example, in the case of modeling exons and introns, would be to assume that at any step the current chain determines according to some probability distribution which Markov chain (including itself) will be chosen in the next step. We call this more sophisticated model the *chain-dependent mixture model.*

We assume that all Markov chains considered are *ergodic* which means that there is a k_0 such that every entry in M^k is non-zero for $k \geq k_0$. Informally, this means that there is a non-zero probability of eventually getting from any state i to any state j and that the chain is *aperiodic.* We also assume that the *cover time*[2] of each of the Markov chains is bounded by τ, a polynomial in the maximum number of states in any chain — these restrictions are necessary to estimate the edge transition probabilities of any Markov chain in polynomial time. Furthermore, since we cannot infer arbitrary real probabilities exactly based on polynomially many observations, we will assume that all probabilities involved in the problem are of the form p/q where all denominators are bounded by some bound Q. As long as we are allowed to observe a stream whose length is some suitable polynomial in Q, we will infer the Markov chains exactly with high probability.

[2] The cover time is the maximum over all vertices u of the expected number of steps required by a random walk that starts at u and ends on visiting every vertex in the graph. For a Markov chain M, if we are at vertex v we choose the next vertex to be v' with probability $M_{vv'}$.

1.2 Our Results

We first consider the version of the inference problem where the Markov chains have pairwise-disjoint state sets in the chain-dependent mixture model. In this model, the interleaving process is itself a Markov Chain whose cover time we denote by τ_1. We show the following result in Section 3.

Theorem 1. *For Markov chains over disjoint state sets and the chain-dependent mixture model, we can infer a model of the source that is observationally equivalent, to the original source, i.e., that the inferred model generates the exact same distribution as the target model. We make the assumption that* α_{ii}*, i.e., the probability of observing the next label from the same Markov process is non-zero. We require a stream of length* $O(\tau^2\tau_1^2Q^2)$*, where* Q *is the upper bound on the denominator of any probability represented as a fraction, and* τ_1, τ *are upper bounds on the cover times of the interleaving and constituent processes, respectively.*

We can easily show that our upper bound in Theorem 1 is a polynomial function of the minimum length required to estimate each of the probabilities. Next, we prove that it is necessary to restrict to disjoint-state-set Markov chains to achieve polynomial-time inference schemes.

Theorem 2. *Inferring chain dependent mixture of Markov chains is computationally intractable. In particular, we show that the inference of two state probablistic automata (with variable alphabet size) can be represented in this model.*

The question about the inference of simple probabilistic mixture of Markov chains with overlapping state spaces arises naturally as a consequence of the above two theorems. Although we do not get as general a result as Theorem 1, we show the following in Section 4, providing evidence towards a positive result.

Theorem 3. *For two Markov chains on non-disjoint state sets, we can infer the chains in the simple mixture model with a stream of length* $O(\text{poly}(n))$ *where* n *is the total number of states in both chains, provided that there is a state* i_s *that occurs in only one chain, say* $M^{(1)}$*, and satisfies the technical condition:*

$$\textit{either } M^{(1)}_{i_s j} > S_1(j) \textit{ or } M^{(1)}_{i_s j} = 0 \quad \textit{for all states } j$$

where S_1 *is the stationary distribution of* $M^{(1)}$*.*

To make sense of the technical condition above consider the special case where the Markov chain is a random walk in a graph. The condition above is satisfied if there is a state that occurs in only one graph that has a small degree. This condition sounds plausible in many applications.

2 Preliminaries and Notation

We identify the combined state space of the given Markov chains with the set $[n] \stackrel{\text{def}}{=} \{1, \ldots, n\}$. Suppose $M^{(1)}, \ldots, M^{(k)}$ are finite-state ergodic Markov chains in discrete time with state space $V_l \subseteq [n]$ corresponding to $M^{(l)}$. We consider two possible cases—one where the state spaces of the individual Markov chains are disjoint and the other where they are allowed to overlap. Suppose each Markov chain outputs its current state after it makes a transition. The first and the simpler mixture model that we consider generates streams with the alphabet $[n]$ in the following manner. Let $\alpha_1, \ldots, \alpha_k$ be such that $\sum_l \alpha_l = 1$. Assume that initial states are chosen for each of the Markov chains arbitrarily. The stream is generated by interleaving the outputs of Markov chains $M^{(1)}, \ldots, M^{(k)}$. For each stream element, an index l is chosen according to the distribution defined by α_l's. Then, $M^{(l)}$ is allowed to make a transition from its previous state and its output is appended to the stream. Define $S_l(i)$ to be the probability of i in the stationary distribution of $M^{(l)}$.

A more general mixture model we explore is where the probability distribution for choosing the Markov chain that will make a transition next is dependent on the chain of the last output state. For $i, j \in [n]$, we use α_{ij} to denote the probability that the control is handed off to Markov chain that j belongs to when the last output was i. Note that for states i_1, i_2 in the same chain, $\alpha_{i_1 j} = \alpha_{i_2 j}$ and $\alpha_{j i_1} = \alpha_{j i_2}$ for all states $j \in [n]$. Since we use this mixture model only for Markov chains with disjoint state spaces, α_{ij}'s are well defined.

We will sometimes denote the interleaving process by $\mathcal{I}$. Then we can denote the entire interleaved Markov process by a tuple, $\langle M^{(1)}, M^{(2)}, \ldots, M^{(k)}; \mathcal{I} \rangle$.

Let $\hat{T}_i$ denote the (relative) frequency of occurrence of the state i. Given a pattern $\langle ij \rangle$ let $\hat{T}_{ij}$ be the frequency of j occurring immediately after i. Likewise define $\hat{T}_{ijs}$ to be the frequency of the pattern $\langle ijs \rangle$.

We define the problem of inferring mixtures of Markov chains as given a stream generated as described above, constructing the transition matrices for the underlying Markov chains as well as the mixing parameters. The problem reduces to identifying the partitioning of the state space—since given a partitioning we can project the data on each of the partitions and identify the transition probabilities.

It is also clear that if two Markov chain mixtures produce each finite length stream with equal probability, then they are indistinguishable by our techniques. Consequently we need a notion of *observational equivalence.*

Definition 1. *Two interleaved processes $\mathcal{P} = \langle M^{(1)}, \ldots, M^{(k)}; \mathcal{I} \rangle$ and $\mathcal{P}' = \langle M'^{(1)}, \ldots, M'^{(k')}; \mathcal{I}' \rangle$ are* observationally indistinguishable *if there is an assignment of initial state probabilities to each chain of $\mathcal{P}'$ for every assignment of initial states to the chains in $\mathcal{P}$ such that for any finite sequence in $[n]^*$ the probability of the sequence being produced by $\mathcal{P}$ is equal to the probability of the sequence being produced by $\mathcal{P}'$.*

Note that we have no hope of disambiguating between observationally equivalent processes. We provide an example of such pairs of processes:

Example. Let process $\mathcal{P} = \langle M^{(1)}, M^{(2)}; \mathcal{I} \rangle$ where $M^{(1)}$ is the trivial single-state Markov chain on state 1 and $M^{(2)}$ is the trivial single-state Markov chain on state 2. Let $\mathcal{I}$ be the process which chooses each chain with probability $\frac{1}{2}$ at each step.

Let process $\mathcal{P}' = \langle M'; \mathcal{I}' \rangle$ where $\mathcal{I}'$ trivially always chooses M' and M' is a 2-state process which has probability $\frac{1}{2}$ for all transitions. $\mathcal{P}$ and $\mathcal{P}'$ are observationally indistinguishable.

Definition 2. *A Markov chain $M^{(1)}$ is defined to be reducible to* one-step mixing *if for all $i, j \in V_1$ we have $M^{(1)}_{ij} = S_1(j)$, i.e., the next state distribution is also the stationary distribution.*

Proposition 1. *If $M^{(1)}$ is reducible to one-step mixing, where $|V_1| = z$, the interleaved process $\mathcal{P} = \langle M^{(1)}, \ldots, M^{(k)}; \mathcal{I} \rangle$ is observationally indistinguishable from $\mathcal{P}' = \langle M^{(1)}_1, M^{(1)}_2, \ldots M^{(1)}_z, M^{(2)}, \ldots, M^{(k)}; \mathcal{I}' \rangle$ for some interleaving process $\mathcal{I}'$, where $M^{(1)}_r$ indicates the Markov chain defined on the single state $r \in V_1$.*

The interleaving process $\mathcal{I}'$ is defined as follows: If in $\mathcal{I}$ the probability of transition from some chain into $M^{(1)}$ in $\mathcal{P}$ is α, in $\mathcal{I}'$ the probability of transition from the same chain to $M^{(1)}_j$ is $\alpha S_1(j)$. Transition probabilities from $M^{(1)}_j$ are the same in $\mathcal{I}'$ as the transition probabilities from $M^{(1)}$ in $\mathcal{I}$.
Remark: Note that a one-step-mixing Markov chain is a zeroth-order Markov chain and a random walk on it is akin to drawing independent samples from a distribution. Nevertheless, we use this terminology to highlight the fact that such chains are a special pathological case for our algorithms.

3 Markov Chains on Disjoint State Spaces

In this section, we consider the problem of inferring mixtures of Markov chains when state spaces are pairwise disjoint. To begin with, we will assume the simpler mixture model. In Section 3.2, we show how our techniques extend to the chain-dependent mixture model.

3.1 The Simple Mixture Model

Our algorithm will have two stages. In the first stage, our algorithm will discover the partition of the whole state space $[n]$ into sets $\hat{V}_1, \ldots, \hat{V}_m$ which are the state spaces of the component Markov chains. Then, it is easy to infer the transition probabilities between states by looking at the substream corresponding to states in each $\hat{V}_l$. Once we infer the partition of the states, the mixing parameter α_l's can be estimated accurately from the fraction of states in $\hat{V}_l$ within the stream.

The main idea behind our algorithm is that certain patterns of states occur with different probabilities depending on whether the states in the pattern come from the same chain or from different chains. We make this idea precise and describe the algorithm in what follows.

Recall that S_l is the stationary distribution vector for the Markov chain $M^{(l)}$ extended to $[n]$. It is well know that the probability that Markov chain $M^{(l)}$ visits a state i tends to $S_l(i)$ as time goes to infinity. It follows that in our mixture model, the probability that we see a state i in our stream tends to

$$S(i) \stackrel{\text{def}}{=} \alpha_l S_l(i)$$

where l is such that $i \in V_l$. Note that l is unique since the state spaces are disjoint. Hence, one can get an estimate $\hat{T}_i$ for $S(i)$ by observing the frequencies[3] of each state i in the stream. The accuracy of this estimate is characterized by the following lemma.

Lemma 1. *For all i, the estimate $\hat{S}(i)$ is within $e^{-O(t)}$ of $\hat{T}_i$ when the length of the stream is at least $\tau t/(\min_i(\alpha_i))$ where τ is maximum cover time of any chain.*

We make the following key observations.

Proposition 2. *For $i, j \in V_l$, we expect to see the pattern $\langle ij \rangle$ in the stream with the frequency $\alpha_l S(i) M_{ij}^{(l)}$.*

In particular, if states i and j belong to the same Markov chain but the transition probability from i to j is 0, the pattern $\langle ij \rangle$ will not occur in the stream.

Proposition 3. *For states i and j from separate Markov chains, we expect the frequency of the pattern $\langle ij \rangle$, $\hat{T}_{ij}$ to be equal to $\hat{T}_i \hat{T}_j$.*

There is an important caveat to the last proposition. In order to accurately measure the frequencies of patterns $\langle ij \rangle$ where i and j occur in different Markov chain, it is necessary to look at positions in the stream that are sufficiently spaced to allow mixing of the component Markov chains. Consequently, we fix *a priori*, positions in the stream which are $\Omega(\tau Q)$ apart where τ is the maximum cover time and Q is the upper bound on the denominator of any probability represented as a fraction. We then sample these positions to determine the estimate on the frequency of various patterns.
Since the values of $\hat{S}$ and $\hat{T}$ are only estimates, we will use the notation "$\approx$" when we are comparing equalities relating such values. By the argument given in Lemma 1, these estimation errors will not lead us to wrong deductions, provided

[3] Here and elsewhere in the paper "frequency" refers to an estimated probability, i.e., it is a ratio of the observed number of successes to the total number of trials where the definition of "success" is evident from the context

that the estimates are based on a long enough stream. Using the estimates $\hat{S}(\cdot)$ and the frequency $\hat{T}_{ij}$ one can make the following deduction:

- If $\hat{T}_{ij} \not\approx \hat{T}_i\hat{T}_j$, then i, j belong to the same chain.

In the case that $i, j \in V_l$ and $\alpha_l M_{i,j}^{(l)} = S(j)$, or equivalently $M_{i,j}^{(l)} = S_l(j)$. the criterion above does not suffice to provide us with clear evidence that i and j belong to the same Markov Chain and not to different Markov Chains. The next proposition may be used to disambiguate such cases.

Proposition 4. *Suppose $i, j \in V_l$ such that $M_{ij}^{(l)} \neq S_l(j)$. Suppose for a state p we cannot determine if $p \in V_l$ using the test above,[4] then $p \in V_l$ if and only if pattern $\langle ipj \rangle$ has the frequency $S(i)S(p)S(j)$, which translates to the test $\hat{T}_{ipj} \approx \hat{T}_i\hat{T}_p\hat{T}_j$.*

Proof. If $p \in V_l$, then $\alpha_l M_{ip}^{(l)} = S(p)$ by the assumption $\hat{T}_{ip} \approx \hat{S}(i)\hat{S}(p)$. Similarly, $\alpha_l M_{pj}^{(l)} = S(j)$. Therefore, the frequency of the pattern $\langle ipj \rangle$ in the stream is expected to be $\alpha_l^2 S(i) M_{ip}^{(l)} M_{pj}^{(l)} = S(i)S(p)S(j)$. In the case $p \notin V_l$, the same frequency is expected to be $\alpha_l S(i)S(p)M_{ij}^{(l)}$. These two expectation are separated since $\alpha_l M_{ij}^{(l)} \neq S(j)$ by the assumption.

Next, we give the subroutine `Grow_Components` that constructs a partition of $[n]$ using the propositions above and the frequencies $\hat{T}$. The algorithms uses the notation $C(i)$ to denote the component to which i belongs to.

```
Grow_Components(T̂)
Initialize: ∀i ∈ [n], C(i) ← {i}
Phase 1:
   For all i, j ∈ [n]
     If T̂_ij ≉ T̂_i T̂_j then
       Union(C(i), C(j))
Phase 2:
   For all i, j, p ∈ [n] such that T̂_ij ≉ T̂_i T̂_j and T̂_ipj ≈ T̂_i T̂_p T̂_j
       Union(C(i), C(p))
Return: the partition defined by C(·)'s
```

Lemma 2 (Soundness). *At the end of* `Grow_Components`, *if $C(i) = C(j)$ for some i, j, then there exists l such that $i, j \in V_l$.*

Proof. At the start of the subroutine, every state is initialized to be a component by itself. In Phase 1, two components are merged when there is definite evidence that the components belong to the same Markov chain by Proposition 2 or Proposition 3. In Phase 2, $\hat{T}_{ij} \not\approx \hat{T}_i\hat{T}_j$ implies that i and j are in the same component and hence Proposition 4 applies and shows the correctness of the union operation performed.

[4] i.e., $\hat{T}_{ip} \approx \hat{S}(i)\hat{S}(p) \approx \hat{T}_{pi}$ and $\hat{T}_{jp} \approx \hat{S}(j)\hat{S}(p) \approx \hat{T}_{pj}$.

Lemma 3 (Completeness). *At the end of* `Grow_Components`, *$C(i) = C(j)$ for all i, j such that $i, j \in V_l$ for some l and $M^{(l)}_{i'j'} \neq S_l(j')$ for some $i', j' \in V_l$.*

Proof. First notice that our algorithm will identify i' and j' as being in the same component in phase 1. Now if either $M^{(l)}_{i'i} \neq S_l(i)$ or $M^{(l)}_{ij'} \neq S_l(j')$ we would have identified i as belonging to the same component as i' and j' in phase 1. Otherwise, phase 2 allows us to make this determination. The same argument holds for j as well. Thus, i and j will be known to belong to the component as i' and hence to each other's component.

```
Infer_Disjoint_MC_Mixtures(X)
  Compute T̂_i, T̂_ij and T̂_ipj
  Let V̂_1, ..., V̂_m be the partition Grow_Components(T̂) returns
  For each 1 ≤ l ≤ m
    Considering the substream of X formed by all i ∈ V̂_l, calculate
      estimates for the transition probabilities involving i, j ∈ V̂_l.
```

At this point, we can claim that our algorithm identifies the irreducible Markov chains $M^{(l)}$ in the mixture (and their parameters). For other chains which have not been merged, from the contrapositive of the statement of Lemma 3 it must be the case that for all $i', j' \in V_l$ we have $M^{(l)}_{i'j'} = S_l(j')$, and the chains reduce to one-step mixing processes.

Theorem 4. *The model output by the algorithm is observationally equivalent to the true model with very high probability.*

3.2 Chain-Dependent Mixture Model

We now consider the model where the mixing process chooses the next chain with probabilities that are dependent on the chain that last made a transition. As in our algorithm for the simple mixture model, we will start with each state in a set by itself, and keep growing components by merging state sets as long as we can.

Definition 3. *A triple (i, j, s) satisfying $\hat{T}_{ij}\hat{T}_{js} \not\approx \hat{T}_{ijs}\hat{T}_j$ is termed as a* revealing triple, *otherwise a triple is called* non-revealing.

The following lemma ensues from case analysis.

Lemma 4. *If (i, j, s) is a revealing triple then i and s belong to the same chain and j belongs to a different chain.*

The algorithm, in the first part, will keep combining the components of the first two states in revealing triples, till no further merging is possible. Since the above test is sound, we will have a partition at the end which is possibly finer than the actual partition. That is, the state set of each of the original chains is the union of some of the parts in our partition. We can show the following:

Lemma 5. *If $i, s \in M^{(l)}$, $j \in M^{(k)}, k \neq l$, $M_{is}^{(l)} \neq S_l(s)$ and $\alpha_{ij} \cdot \alpha_{js} \neq 0$ then (i, j, s) is a revealing triple.*

Proof. Given i, j, s as in the statement consider the left hand side of the inequality in Lemma 4. $\hat{T}_{ij}\hat{T}_{js} \approx \hat{T}_i \alpha_{ij} S_k(j) \hat{T}_j \alpha_{js} S_l(s)$ and the right hand side, $\hat{T}_{ijs}\hat{T}_j \approx \hat{T}_i \alpha_{ij} S_k(j) \alpha_{js} M_{is}^{(l)} \hat{T}_j$. Evidently, these two expressions are not equal whenever $M_{is}^{(l)} \neq S_l(s)$.

The contrapositive of the above Lemma shows that if the triple (i, j, s) is a non-revealing triple where i and s belong to the same chain and $\hat{T}_{ij}\hat{T}_{js} \not\approx 0$ then it must be the case that j belongs to the same chain as i and s. This suggests the following merging algorithm:

```
Grow_Components_2(T̂)
Initialize: ∀i ∈ [n], C(i) ← {i}
Phase 1:
   For all i, j, s ∈ [n]
     If T̂_ij T̂_js ≉ T̂_ijs T̂_j then
       Union(C(i), C(s))
Phase 2:
   For all i, j, s ∈ [n] such that i, s ∈ C(i) ≠ C(j)
     If T̂_ij T̂_js ≈ T̂_ijs T̂_j ≉ 0 then
     Union(C(i), C(j))
Return: the partition defined by C(·)'s
```

Thus if the condition $\alpha_{ij}\alpha_{ji} \neq 0$ is satisfied and the Markov chain of i is not united in a single component, it must be the case that the Markov chain in question is observationally reducible to one step mixing. Thus the only remaining case to consider are (irreducible) Markov chains (containing i) such that for any other chain (containing j) it must be that $\alpha_{ij}\alpha_{ji} = 0$.
To handle Markov chains $M^{(l)}$ such that for all $l' \neq l$ and $j \in M^{(l')}$, we have $\alpha_{ij}\alpha_{ji} = 0$ the algorithm, in the second part, will perform the following steps:

1. Let $F_i(j) = \hat{T}_{ij}/\hat{T}_i$, i.e., the relative frequency that the next label after an i is j.
2. For all pairs i, j such that $\hat{T}_{ij} \neq 0$, and i and j are still singleton components, start with $D_{ij} = \{i, j\}$.
   a) If for some state p, $F_i(p) \not\approx F_j(p)$, then include p in D_{ij}.
   b) If for some state q, $\frac{F_q(i)}{F_q(j)} \not\approx \frac{T_i}{T_j}$, then include q in D_{ij}.
3. Keep applying the above rules above using all pairs in a component so far until D_{ij} does not change any more.
4. For each starting pair i, j, a set D_{ij} of states will be obtained at the end of this phase. Let $\mathcal{D}$ be the collection of those D_{ij}'s that are minimal.
5. Merge the components corresponding to the elements belonging to $D_{ij} \in \mathcal{D}$.

Lemma 6. *For states i and j from separate Markov chains, $D_{ij} \notin \mathcal{D}$.*

Proof. For any state s in the same chain $M^{(l)}$ as i, $F_{js} = 0$, because $\alpha_{js} = 0$. Therefore, the second closure rule will eventually include all the states from $M^{(l)}$ to D_{ij}. On the other hand for states i, v such that $v \in M^{(l)}$, D_{iv} will contain states only from $M^{(l)}$. Hence, as $D_{iv} \subset D_{ij}$, D_{ij} will not be minimal.

Now we know that each set in $\mathcal{D}$ is a subset of the state space of a Markov chain. Thus, we get

Theorem 5. *Let $\langle M^{(1)}, M^{(2)}, \ldots, M^{(k)}; \mathcal{I}\rangle$ be an interleaved process with chain-dependent mixing and no one-step-mixing Markov chains. If for all $l \in [k]$, $\alpha_{ii} \neq 0$ for $i \in M^{(l)}$, then we can infer a model observationally equivalent to the true model.*

3.3 A Negative Result

Suppose H is a two state probabilistic automaton where the transition probabilities are H_{ija} where $i, j \in \{1, 2\}$. Let $\{a\} = L$ be the collection of all possible labels output.

Consider the following mixture process: We will create two Markov chains $M_1^{(a)}, M_2^{(a)}$ for each label $a \in L$. Each of the Markov chains $M_1^{(a)}, M_2^{(a)}$ is a markov chain with a single state corresponding to the label a. The transition probability from chain $M_i^{(a)}$ to $M_j^{(b)}$ is H_{ijb}.

Clearly the "states" of the Markov chains $M_1^{(a)}, M_2^{(a)}$ overlap – and it is easy to see that the probability of observing a sequence of labels as the output of H is the same as observing the sequence in the interleaved mixture of the Markov chains. Since the estimation of H is intractable [1], even for two states (but variable size alphabet), we can conclude:

Theorem 6. *Identifying interleaving Markov chains with overlapping state spaces under the chain dependent mixture model is computationally intractable.*

4 Non-disjoint State Spaces

In the previous section we showed that in the chain dependent mixture model we have a reasonably sharp characterization. A natural question that arises from the negative result is: *can we characterize under what conditions can we infer the mixture of non-disjoint Markov chains, even for two chains ?* A first step towards the goal would be to understand the simple mixture model.

Consider the most extreme case of overlap where we have a mixture of two identical Markov chains. The frequency of states in the sequence gives an estimate of the stationary distribution S of each chain which is also the overall stationary distribution. Note that $M_{ij}^{(l)} = M_{ij}$ for all i, j.

Consider the pattern $\langle ij\rangle$. This pattern can arise because there was a transition from i to j in some chain $M^{(l)}$ or it can arise because we first observed i and control shifted to the other chain and we observed j. Let α_l be the probability that the mixing process chooses $M^{(l)}$. Then,

$$\hat{T}_{ij} \approx \sum_{c=1}^{k} \alpha_c S(i)((\alpha_c M_{ij}) + (1-\alpha_c)S(j)).$$

Letting $w = \sum_c \alpha_c^2$ we can simplify the above equation to get: $\hat{T}_{ij} = S(i)[wM_{ij} + (1-w)S(j)] = S(i)[w(M_{ij} - S(j)) + S(j)]$. Rearranging terms we have $M_{ij} = \frac{\frac{\hat{T}_{ij}}{S_i} - S_j}{w} + S_j$. Any value of w that results in $0 \leq M_{ij} \leq 1$ for all i, j leads to an observationally equivalent process to the one actually generating the stream. The set of possible w's is not empty since, in particular, $w = 1$ leads to $M_{ij} = \frac{\hat{T}_{ij}}{S_i}$ corresponding to having just one Markov chain with these transition probabitlities.

What we see above is that the symmetries in the problem introduced by assuming that all Markov chains are identical facilitate the inference of an observationally equivalent process. The general situation is more complicated even for two Markov chains.

We consider the mixtures of two Markov chains with non-disjoint state spaces. We give an algorithm for this case under a technical condition that requires a special state. Namely, we require that there is a state i_s that is exclusively in one of the Markov chains, say $M^{(1)}$, and

$$\text{either } M^{(1)}_{i_s j} > S_1(j) \text{ or } M^{(1)}_{ij} = 0 \text{ for all } j \in V_1.$$

Let α_1, α_2 be the mixture probabilities. Then, considering the four possible ways of $\langle ij \rangle$ occurring in the stream, we get

$$\hat{T}_{ij} = \alpha_1^2 S_1(i) M^{(1)}_{ij} + \alpha_1\alpha_2 \left(S_1(i)S_2(j) + S_2(i)S_1(j)\right) + \alpha_2^2 S_2(i) M^{(2)}_{ij}.$$

Let $A_{ij} \stackrel{\text{def}}{=} \hat{T}_{ij} - (SS^T)_{ij}$ where $S = \alpha_1 S_1 + \alpha_2 S_2$ as before. Then, we can write

$$A_{ij} = \alpha_1^2 S_1(i) \left(M^{(1)}_{ij} - S_1(j)\right) + \alpha_2^2 S_2(i) \left(M^{(2)}_{ij} - S_2(j)\right).$$

Consider the state i_s required by the technical condition. For any state j such that $M^{(1)}_{i_s j} > 0$, we have $A_{i_s j} = \alpha_1^2 S_1(i_s) \left(M^{(1)}_{i_s j} - S_1(j)\right) > 0$. For any other state j with $S_1(j) > 0$, $A_{i_s j} = -\alpha_1^2 S_1(i_s) S_1(j) < 0$. Finally, $A_{i_s j} = 0$ for all the remaining states.

Since $S(i_s) = \alpha_1 S_1(i_s)$, for each $j \in [n]$, we can infer $\alpha_1 S_1(j)$ from the observations above. Hence, we can infer $\alpha_2 S_2(j)$ for each j by $S(j) = \alpha_1 S_1(j) + \alpha_2 S_2(j)$. Since we know the vectors S_1, S_2, we can now calculate $M_{ij} \stackrel{\text{def}}{=} \alpha_1 M^{(1)}_{ij} + \alpha_2 M^{(2)}_{ij}$ for all i, j pairs.

If state i or j exclusively belongs to one of the Markov chains, M_{ij} gives the product of the appropriate mixing parameter and the transition probability. In the case when both states i and j are common between the Markov chains, we will use the frequency $\hat{T}_{ii_sj}$ of pattern $\langle ii_sj \rangle$ to infer $M_{ij}^{(1)}$ and $M_{ij}^{(2)}$.

The frequency of the pattern $\langle ii_sj \rangle$ is expected to be

$$\hat{T}_{ii_sj} \approx \alpha_1^2 S_1(i) M_{ii_s}^{(1)} (\alpha_2 S_2(j) + \alpha_1 M_{i_sj}^{(1)}) + \alpha_1 \alpha_2 S_2(i) S_1(i_s) (\alpha_1 M_{i_sj}^{(1)} + \alpha_2 M_{ij}^{(2)}).$$

Note that all but the last term is already inferred by the algorithm. Therefore, $\alpha_2 M_{ij}^{(2)}$, hence $\alpha_1 M_{ij}^{(1)}$, can be calculated.

Finally, using the next state distribution for the state i_s, we can calculate α_1 and α_2. This completes the description of our algorithm.

5 Conclusions and Open Problems

In this paper we have taken the first steps towards understanding the behavior of a mixture of Markov chains. We believe that there are many more problems to be explored in this area which are both mathematically challenging and practically interesting.

A natural open question is the condition $\alpha_{ii} \neq 0$, i.e., there is a non-zero probability of observing the next label from the same Markov chain. We note that Freund and Ron had made a similar assumption that α_{ii} is large, which allowed then to obtain "pure" runs from each of the chains. It is conceivable that the inference problem of disjoint state Markov chains becomes intractable after we allow $\alpha_{ii} = 0$.

Another interesting question is the optimizing the length of the observation required for inference – or if sufficient lengths are not available then compute the best partial inference possible. This is interesting even for small ~ 50 states and a possible solution may be trade off computation or storage against observation length.

References

1. Naoki Abe and Manfred Warmuth. On the computational complexity of approximating distributions by probabilistic automata. *Machine Learning*, 1992. (to appear in the special issue for COLT 1990).
2. Serge Abiteboul, Victor Vianu, Brad Fordham, and Yelena Yesha. Relational transducers for electronic commerce. pages 179–187, 1998.
3. Sanjeev Arora and Ravi Kannan. Learning mixtures of arbitrary gaussians. In *ACM Symposium on Theory of Computing*, pages 247–257, 2001.
4. Y. Bengio and P. Frasconi. Input-output HMM's for sequence processing. *IEEE Transactions on Neural Networks*, 7(5):1231–1249, September 1996.
5. C.B. Burge and S. Karlin. Finding the genes in genomic dna. *J. Mol. Bio.*, 268:78–94, 1997.
6. Sanjoy Dasgupta. Learning mixtures of gaussians. Technical Report CSD-99-1047, University of California, Berkeley, May 19, 1999.
7. Dorothy E. Denning. An intrusion-detection model. *Transactions of software engineering*, 13(2):222–232, 1987.

8. R. O. Duda and P. E. Hart. *Pattern Classification and Scene Analysis*. John Wiley and Sons, New York, 1974.
9. Tom Fawcett and Foster J. Provost. Adaptive fraud detection. *Data Mining and Knowledge Discovery*, 1(3):291–316, 1997.
10. Yoav Freund and Dana Ron. Learning to model sequences generated by switching distributions. In *Proceedings of the 8th Annual Conference on Computational Learning Theory (COLT'95)*, pages 41–50, New York, NY, USA, July 1995. ACM Press.
11. Charles Kervrann and Fabrice Heitz. A hierarchical Markov modeling approach for the segmentation and tracking of deformable shapes. *Graphical models and image processing: GMIP*, 60(3):173–195, 1998.
12. Wenke Lee, Salvatore J. Stolfo, and Kui W. Mok. A data mining framework for building intrusion detection models. In *IEEE Symposium on Security and Privacy*, pages 120–132, 1999.
13. Alon Y. Levy and Daniel S. Weld. Intelligent internet systems. *Artificial Intelligence*, 118(1-2):1–14, 2000.
14. Lawrence R. Rabiner. A tutorial on hidden markov models and selected applications in speech recognition. *Proceedings of the IEEE*, 77(2), 1989.
15. Marc Spielmann. Verification of relational transducers for electronic commerce. In *Symposium on Principles of Database Systems*, pages 92–103, 2000.
16. B. Thiesson, C. Meek, D. Chickering, and D. Heckerman. Learning mixtures of Bayesian networks. Technical Report MSR-TR-97-30, Microsoft Research, Redmond, WA, 1997.
17. Bo Thiesson, Christopher Meek, David Maxwell Chickering, and David Heckerman. Learning mixtures of DAG models. In Gregory F. Cooper and Serafín Moral, editors, *Proceedings of the 14th Conference on Uncertainty in Artificial Intelligence (UAI-98)*, pages 504–513, San Francisco, July 24–26 1998. Morgan Kaufmann.
18. Christina Warrender, Stephanie Forrest, and Barak A. Pearlmutter. Detecting intrusions using system calls: Alternative data models. In *IEEE Symposium on Security and Privacy*, pages 133–145, 1999.

PExact = Exact Learning

Dmitry Gavinsky and Avi Owshanko

[1] Department of Computer Science
University of Calgary
Calgary, Alberta, Canada, T2N 1N4
gavinsky@cpsc.ucalgary.ca

[2] Departments of Computer Science
Technion
Haifa, Israel, 32000
avshash@cs.technion.ac.il

Abstract. The Probably Exact model (PExact) is a relaxation of the Exact model, introduced in by Bshouty. In this paper, we show that the PExact model is equivalent to the Exact model.
We also show that in the Exact model, the adversary (oracle) gains no additional power from knowing the learners' coin tosses a-priory.

1 Introduction

In this paper we examine the *Probably Exact* (PExact) model introduced by Bshouty in [5] (called PEC there). This model lies between Valiant's PAC model [12] and Angulin's Exact model [1].

We show that the PExact model is equivalent to the Exact model, thus extending the results by Bshouty et. al. [8] who showed the PExact model is stronger than the PAC model (under the assumption that one way functions exist), as well as that the deterministic Exact model (where the learning algorithm is deterministic) is equivalent to the deterministic PExact model.

The PExact model is a variant of the Exact model, in which each counterexample to an equivalence query is drawn according to a distribution, rather than maliciously chosen. The main advantage of the PExact model is that the teacher is not an adversary. For achieving lower bounds in the Exact model, (like those given by Bshouty in [5]), we must consider a malicious adversary with unbounded computational power that actively adapts its behavior. On the other hand, in the PExact model the only role of the adversary is to choose a target and a distribution. After that the learning algorithm starts learning without any additional adversarial influence.

For removing randomness from the PExact model, we introduce a new variation of the model introduced by Ben-David et. al. in [3]. We call this the *Ordered Exact* (OExact) model. This model is similar to the PExact model, where instead of a distribution function we have an ordered set. Each time the OExact oracle gets an equivalence query, it returns the lowest indexed counterexample, instead of randomly or maliciously choosing one.

J. Shawe-Taylor and Y. Singer (Eds.): COLT 2004, LNAI 3120, pp. 200–209, 2004.

Another model we consider in this work is the random-PExact model, introduced by Bshouty and Gavinsky [7]. The random-PExact model is a relaxation of the PExact model that allows the learner to use random hypotheses. We will show that for every algorithm A that uses some restricted random hypothesis for efficiently learning the concept class C in the random-PExact model, there exists an algorithm ALG that efficiently learns C in the Exact model.

In additional we show that the adversary does not gain any additional power by knowing all coin tosses in advance. In other words, we show that offline-Exact learning = Exact learning.

In [8] Bshouty et al. showed that Exact-learnable $\Rightarrow$ PExact-learnable $\Rightarrow$ PAC-learnable. Based on Blum construction [4] they also showed that under the standard cryptographic assumptions (that one-way functions exist), PExact-learnable $\neq$ PAC-learnable. In [7], Bshouty and Gavinsky showed that under polybit distributions, PExact-learnable = PAC-learnable. In this work we will exploit the exponential probabilities to show that PExact-learnable $\Rightarrow$ Exact-learnable.

Another model residing between the PAC model and the PExact model is the PAExact model introduced by Bshouty et al. in [8]. The PAExact model is similar to the PExact model, but allows the learner some exponentially small final error (as opposed to the exact target identification required in PExact). Bshouty and Gavinsky [7] showed that PAExact-learnable = PAC-learnable using boosting algorithms based on [11] and [10]. In [6], Bshouty improves the error factor and gives a more simple algorithm for boosting process.

The following chart indicates relations between the models.

$$\begin{array}{ccc} Exact & & PAExact \\ \| & \not\Leftarrow\!\!\!\Rightarrow & \| \\ PExact & & PAC \end{array}$$

We note that this work represents results independently obtained by the authors. This joint publication has evolved from a manuscript by Avi Owshanko; the other author's original manuscript [9] may be found at his web page.

2 Preliminaries

In the following we formally define the models we use. We will focus on exact learning of concept classes. In this setting, there exists some learning algorithm A with the goal of exactly identifying some target concept t out of the concept class C over a domain X. In this paper we consider only finite and countable infinite domains X. The learner A has full knowledge of the domain X and of the concept class C, but does not have any a-priory knowledge about the target class t. As each concept $t \in C$ is a subset of the domain X, we will refer to it as a function $t : X \to \{0, 1\}$.

For learning the target concept, the learner can ask some teacher (also referred to as an oracle) several kinds of queries about the target. The teacher can be regarded as an adversary with unlimited computational power and full knowledge of all that the learner knows. The adversary must always answer queries honestly, though it may choose the worst (correct) answer. If the adversary knows in advance all the learner's coin tosses, we call the adversary an *offline adversary* and call the model an *offline-model.*

In this paper we will focus on efficient learning under several models. Whenever we write *efficient learning* of some target t with success probability δ, we mean that the learning algorithm receives the answer "Equivalent" after time polynomial in $size_C(t)$, $\log(1/\delta)$ and b (the size of the longest answer that the teacher returns).

We now give the formal definitions of Exact learning [12], PExact learning [5] and a new model we denote OExact (which is a variation over the model considered in [3]).

We say that a concept class C is *learnable* in some model if there exists some algorithm A such that for every target $t \in C$, and each confidence level δ, A efficiently learns t with the help of the teacher, with success probability greater than $1 - \delta$. We say that a learner is *random* if it uses coin tosses and *deterministic* otherwise.

In the ***Exact*** model, the learner A supplies the adversary with some hypothesis h (such that h can be computed efficiently for every point x in X) and the adversary either says "Equivalent", or returns a counterexample, $x \in X$ such that $t(x) \neq h(x)$.

In the ***PExact*** (probably exact) model, the PExact teacher holds some probability distribution D over X, as well as the target $t \in C$. Both the target and the distribution functions are determined before the learning process starts and stay fixed for the duration of the learning process. The learner can supply the teacher with some hypothesis h and the teacher either returns "Equivalent" (when $Pr_D[h(x) \neq t(x)] = 0$), or returns some counterexample x. The counterexample is randomly chosen, under the distribution D induced over all erroneous points $x \in X$ (that is $h(x) \neq t(x)$).

In the ***OExact*** (ordered exact) model, the OExact oracle holds some finite well ordered set $S \subseteq X$. For each query of the algorithm A , the OExact oracle returns $x \in S$ where x is the smallest member of S such that $h(x) \neq t(x)$. For every member $x \in S$, we let $Ord(S, x)$ denotes the number of elements in S that are smaller than x (for example, for x_0 the smallest member of S, $Ord(S, x_0) = 0$).

For the PExact model, There exists some relaxed variation of the PExact model, denoted ***random-PExact***, introduced by Bshouty and Gavinsky [7]. In this setting, the algorithm A may use a random hypothesis. A random hypothesis $h_r : X \times R \to \{0, 1\}$ is a function such that for every input $x_0 \in X$ it randomly uniformly chooses $r_0 \in R$ and returns $h_{r_0}(x_0)$. As before, the teacher may either answer "Equivalent" (when $\forall x \in X : Pr_D[h_r(x) \neq t(x)] = 0$) or returns some counterexample x. For choosing the counterexample, the teacher keeps randomly choosing points x in X according to the distribution D until the first point such that $h_r(x) \neq t(x)$. For the Exact (OExact) model, the adversary returns some (the smallest) point $x \in X$ ($x \in S$) such that $Pr[h_r(x) \neq t(x)] > 0$.

We will also use the following inequality:

Theorem 1 (Chernoff inequality). *Let $Y_1, Y_2, \ldots, Y_n$ be n independent random variables such that for $1 \leq i \leq n$, $\mathbf{Pr}[Y_i = 1] = p_i$, where $0 < p_i < 1$. Then, for $Y = \Sigma_{i=1}^n Y_i$, $\mu = \mathbf{E}\,[Y] = \Sigma_{i=1}^n p_i$, and $0 < \lambda \leq 1$,*

$$Pr[Y < (1-\lambda)\mu] < e^{-\mu\lambda^2/2}$$

3 The Learning Algorithm

In this section we introduce a scheme relying on majority vote to turn every algorithm A that efficiently learns a concept class C in the PExact model into an algorithm ALG that can learn C in the Exact model.

We will rely on the fact that you can fool most of the people some of the time, or some of the people most of the time, but you can never fool most of the people most of the time. Consider some algorithm A where for every target $t \in C$, there exists some bound T, such that A makes no more than T mistakes with some probability p. When we run two copies of A , the probability that both make mistakes on the same T points (in the same order) is p^2. When running k copies of A , the probability that all make mistakes on the same points is p^k. But this fact is not enough for building a new algorithm, because it is not enough for us to know that there is a possible error, but we need to label every point correctly. Hence we need to have that the number of points such that more than half the running copies of A mislabel is bounded by some factor of T. We will prove that if A is an efficient PExact algorithm, then there exists some such (efficient) bound T for every target $t \in C$, and that the number of errors is no more than $4T$.

Because the learner does not know the target t in advance, it must find this bound T dynamically, using a standard doubling technique — each iteration doubling the allowable mistakes number (and the number of copies of A) until successfully learning t. The full algorithm can be viewed in figure 1

We start by showing that A is an efficient learning algorithm in the OExact model. That way, we can remove the element of randomness that is inherent to the PExact model.

Lemma 2. *If A learns every target t in C using less than $T(t)$ steps, with the aid of a PExact teacher with confidence greater than* 0.95*, then there exists an algorithm A', (a copy of A), that learns every target t in C using less than $T(t)$ steps, with the aid of an OExact teacher with confidence greater than* 0.9.

Proof: In this proof we build for every well ordered set S and every target $t \in C$ a step probability function D_S that will force the PExact oracle to behave the same as the OExact oracle (with high probability).

We will run both algorithms A and A' in parallel, where both use the same random strings (when they are random algorithms). Let k be the size of S and

ALG

1. Init $k \leftarrow 4$
2. *Do*
3. – Init $\mathcal{P} \leftarrow \emptyset$, $count \leftarrow 0$
4. – Let $\mathcal{A} \leftarrow \{\mathcal{A}_\infty, \mathcal{A}_\in, \ldots, \mathcal{A}_\|\}$ [where each A_i is a copy of A]
5. – Init each copy A_i in $\mathcal{A}$.
6. – *While* $(count < k)$
7. -- Run each copy $A_i \in \mathcal{A}$ until it asks an equivalence query,
   -- terminates, or executed more than $k/4$ steps.
8. -- Remove from $\mathcal{A}$ all copies A_i that either terminated unsuccessfully
   -- or executed more than $k/4$ steps.
9. -- *If* there exists some copy $A_i \in \mathcal{A}$ asking an equivalence query with
   -- an hypothesis h_i that is not consistent with $\mathcal{P}$
10. -- Let $(y, label(y), c)$ be a counterexample with the lowest index c.
11. -- Give $(y, label(y))$ as a counterexample to A_i
12. -- Jump back to step 7
13. -- End *If*
14. -- Let $h = majority\{h_1, h_2, \ldots, h_k\}$
   -- [where h_i is A_i's hypothesis at this point].
15. -- Let $x \leftarrow EQ(h)$. *If* $x =$ "Equivalent", return h as the answer
   -- *else*, Add $(x, label(x), count)$ to $\mathcal{P}$
16. -- Let $count \leftarrow count + 1$
17. – End *While*
18. – Let $k \leftarrow 2k$
19. *While* the hypothesis h is not equivalent to the target.

Fig. 1. The learning algorithm

let l denotes $T(t)$. We define the probability distribution D_S as follows (recall that $Ord(S, x)$ denotes the number of elements in S that are smaller than x).

$$D_S(x) = \begin{cases} 0 & x \notin S \\ \frac{(40l+2)^{-Ord(S,x)}}{\Sigma_{i=1}^{k}(40l+2)^{-i}} & x \in S \end{cases}$$

Consider the case that both A and A' ask their teachers some equivalence query using the same hypothesis h. Let x be the counterexample that the OExact teacher returns to A'. By definition of the OExact model, x is the smallest counterexample in S. The probability that the PExact teacher returns to A a counterexample y such that $y \neq x$ (and $Ord(S, y) > Ord(S, x)$) is less than

$$\sum_{j=Ord(S,x)+1}^{k} \frac{(40l+2)^{-j}}{\Sigma_{i=1}^{k}(40l+2)^{-i}} < \frac{2}{40l+2} \cdot \frac{(40l+2)^{-Ord(S,x)}}{\Sigma_{i=1}^{k}(40l+2)^{-i}} = \frac{D_S(x)}{20l+1}$$

Hence, the PExact oracle returns the lowest indexed counterexample x with probability greater than $1 - \frac{1}{20l}$.

We can conclude that the PExact and the OExact teachers return the same answer with probability greater than $1 - \frac{1}{20l}$, and the probability for l such consequent answers is greater than

$$\left(1 - \frac{1}{20l}\right)^l \approx e^{-1/20} > 0.95.$$

Because both A and A' hold the same random string, they will both behave the same (ask the same queries) until the first time that the teachers give different answers. On the other hand, A learns t using less than $T(t)$ steps with confidence of 0.95. So we can conclude that with confidence greater than $0.95 \cdot 0.95 > 0.9$, A' learns t in the OExact model using less than $T(t)$ steps. ∎

Our next step is to show that if A is an efficient OExact learning algorithm, then ALG learns C in the Exact model.

Lemma 3. *Let X be a finite domain. If A learns every class t in C using less than $T(t)$ steps, with the aid of an OExact teacher with confidence level greater than 0.9, then ALG learns every t in C with the aid of an offline-exact teacher, with probability greater than $1 - \delta$ using less than*

$$O((\log(1/\delta) + T(t)\log(|X|) + \log(|C|))^2)$$

steps.

Proof: Let l denotes $T(t)$ and let $m \geq m_0 = 20(\ln(1/\delta) + 4l\ln(|X|) + \ln(|C|))$. Consider running $3m$ copies of the learning algorithm A , over some given ordered set S of size $4l$. We shall calculate the probability that m of these copies need more than l steps to exact learn t.

Using Chernoff inequality (1), we have $n = 3m$, $\mu = 0.9 \cdot 3m = 2.7m$, and $\lambda > 0.2$:

$$Pr[Y < 2m] < e^{-2.7m\cdot(0.2)^2/2} < e^{-0.05m} \leq \frac{\delta}{|X|^{4l} \cdot |C|}. \quad (1)$$

Next we define the following property:
Property I: *The probability that there exists some target $t \in C$ and some ordered set S of size $4l$ such that more than m copies of A will need more than l steps to learn t is less than δ.*

The reasoning behind this claim is as follows. Assume that all $3m$ copies of A have a sequence of random bits. We let the adversary know these random bits and look for some target $t \in C$ and some ordered set S that will cause more than m copies to fail. The number of possible target concepts $t \in C$ is $|C|$ and the number of possible ordered sets is less than $|X|^{4l}$. On the other hand, the probability for some set to cause more than m copies to fail for some target t is less than $\frac{\delta}{|X|^{4l}\cdot|C|}$ by (1). Hence the probability for the existence of such a bad target t and ordered set S is less than

$$\frac{\delta}{|X|^{4l} \cdot |C|} \cdot |X|^{4l} \cdot |C| = \delta.$$

and property I holds.

We now consider *ALG* 's main loop (steps 6-17 in figure 1) when $6m_0 \geq k \geq 3m_0$ (*ALG* reaches this loop after after $O(k^2)$ steps, unless it already received the answer "Equivalent"). Assume that *ALG* receives $4l$ counterexamples in this loop (recall that $4l < k$). Note that this set of counterexamples defines an ordered set S of size $4l$ (we order the counterexamples chronologically). Because each such counterexample is given to at least half the currently running copies of A , at least m copies of A received at least l counterexamples (or executed more than $k/4 > l$ steps). But property I states that there exists such a set of counterexamples with probability smaller than δ.

So we conclude that with probability greater than $1 - \delta$, *ALG* learns t in the Exact model when $6m_0 \geq k$, where the number of steps is bounded by

$$O(m_0^2) = O((\log(1/\delta) + T(t)\log(|X|) + \log(|C|))^2).$$

■

Our next step is to remove the size of the domain X and the concept class C from the complexity analysis.

Lemma 4. *If A learns every class t in C using less than $T(t)$ steps, with the aid of an OExact teacher with confidence level greater than* 0.9, *then ALG learns every t in C with the aid of an offline-exact teacher, with probability greater than* $1 - \delta$ *using less than*

$$O((\log(1/\delta) + T(t)(size(t) + b))^2)$$

steps, where b is the size of the longest counterexample that the teacher returns.

Proof: For some set Q, we let Q^b denotes all members of Q that are represented by no more than b bits. By definition, $|Q^b| < 2^{b+1}$. By lemma 3, there exists some constant c, such that for every finite domain X, *ALG* learns every t in C with the aid of an offline-exact teacher with probability greater than $1 - \delta$ using less than $c \cdot (\log(1/\delta) + T(t)\log(|X|) + \log(|C|))^2$ steps.

Let us consider the case that the longest counterexample b, or the size of the target t ($size_C(t)$) is at least 2^i and less than 2^{i+1}. We let d denotes 2^i. So we have that $d < size(t) + b$. Applying lemma 3, we get that *ALG* learns t with probability greater than $1 - \delta/d$, using less than

$$\begin{aligned} & c \cdot (\log(1/\delta) + T(t)\log(|X|) + \log(|C|))^2 \\ < & \; c \cdot (\log(1/\delta) + T(t)\log(d) + log(d))^2 \\ = & \; c \cdot (\log(1/\delta) + (T(t) + 1)(size(t) + b))^2 \end{aligned}$$

steps. Hence, the probability to find some $d = 2^i$ such that *ALG* will be forced to use more than $c \cdot (poly(size(t)) \cdot \log^2(d/\delta) \cdot 16d^4)$ steps is less than:

$$1 - \prod_{i=1}^{\infty}(1 - \frac{\delta}{2^i}) \leq \sum_{i=1}^{\infty}(\frac{\delta}{2^i}) \leq \delta$$

and the lemma holds. ■

At this point we can conclude that:

Theorem 5. *PExact = offline-Exact learning.*

Proof: This theorem immediately follows from lemmas 2 and 4. In lemma 2 we showed that every algorithm A that efficiently learns the class C in the PExact model with probability greater than 0.95 also efficiently learns C in the OExact model with probability greater than 0.9. In lemma 4 we showed that if A efficiently learns C in the OExact model with probability greater than 0.9, the algorithm ALG efficiently learns C in the offline-Exact model with any needed confidence level $1-\delta$. On the other hand, Bshouty et. al. [8] already showed that $Exact \Rightarrow PExact$. Hence the theorem holds. ∎

An additional interesting result following immediately from theorem 5 is:

Corollary 6. *Exact = offline-Exact learning.*

4 Handling the Random Model

We now show that if A is an efficient algorithm for learning C in the random-PExact model and if A follows some constraints, then ALG learns C in the Exact model. Namely, we will show that if we can efficiently determine for every hypothesis h_r that A produces and for every $x \in X$ whether $0 < E[h_r(x)] < 1$ or not, then if A learns C in the random-PExact model, ALG learns C in the Exact model. As in the previous section, we start by showing that random-PExact = OExact.

Lemma 7. *If A efficiently learns C in the random-PExact model with probability greater than 0.95, then A efficiently learns C in the OExact model with probability greater than 0.9.*

Proof: This proof is similar to that of Lemma 2. For every target $t \in C$ and every order $S \in X$ we build a step distribution function that will force the random-PExact oracle to behave in the same way as the OExact oracle.

Let k be the size of S and assume that that A needs $l = poly(size(t))$ Consider running A for l steps in the OExact model until A executes l steps (or terminates successfully). Let h_r^i denotes A's hypothesis after the i's step. Because the number of steps is bounded by l, there exists some $0 < \lambda < 1$ such that for all members $x \in S$ and all steps $0 \le i \le l$,

$$(E[h_r^i(x)] = 0) \vee (E[h_r^i(x)] = 1) \vee (\lambda < E[h_r^i(x)] < 1 - \lambda).$$

Using this value λ, We define the probability distribution D_S as follows

$$D_S(x) = \begin{cases} 0 & x \notin S \\ \left(\frac{\lambda}{40l+2}\right)^{Ord(S,x)} \cdot \frac{1}{\Sigma_{i=1}^{k}\left(\frac{\lambda}{40l+2}\right)^i} & x \in S \end{cases}$$

For every x member of S , We let $Y(x) \subset S$ denotes all members of S larger than x in the order S. By definition of D_S, we have

$$D_S(x) > \frac{\lambda}{20l+1} \cdot \Sigma_{y \in Y(x)} D_S(y).$$

From this point on, the proof is similar to that of Lemma 2. The probability to receive the smallest possible x as the counterexample in the random-PExact model under the probability distribution D_S is (at least) $\frac{1}{20l+1}$, and the probability that the random-PExact oracle behaves the same as the OExact oracle for all l steps is greater than 0.95. So we conclude that A learns C in the OExact model with probability greater than 0.9. ∎

After we showed that random-PExact = OExact, we can apply the same proofs as in the previous section to receive the following result:

Theorem 8. *If A efficiently learns C in the random-PExact model, and if for every hypothesis h_r that A holds and every $x \in X$ we can (efficiently) determine whether $0 < E[h_r(x)] < 1$ or not, then ALG efficiently learns C in the Exact model.*

Proof: The proof is similar to that of the theorem 5. We can still emulate the way that the OExact oracle behaves, because for every hypothesis h_r and every $x \in X$ we can efficiently determine whether $0 < E[h_r(x)] < 1$ or not. When h_r can assign x both values, we can give x as a counterexample. Otherwise, we can choose any random string r (for example all bits are zero) and calculate the value of $h_r(x)$. Also note that if x is a counterexample for ALG , then at least half of the running copies of A can receive x as a counterexample. So we can use both lemmas 2 and 4. The rest of the proof is similar. ∎

5 Conclusions and Open Problems

In this paper we showed that PExact = Exact learning, thus allowing the use of a model without an adaptive adversary, in order to prove computational lower bounds. We also showed that a limited version of random-PExact is equivalent to that of the Exact model. An interesting question left open is whether the random-PExact is strictly stronger than the Exact model or not (assuming that $P \neq NP$).

The second result we gave is that even when the adversary knows all the learner's coin tosses in advance (the offline-Exact model), it does not gain any additional computational power. This results also holds when the learner has the help of a membership oracle, but it is not known whether this still holds when the membership oracle is limited, such as in [2].

References

[1] D. Angluin. Queries and concept learning. *Machine Learning*, 75(4):319-342, 1988.
[2] D. Angluin and D. Slonim. (1994). Randomly Fallible Teachers: Learning Monotone DNF with an Incomplete Membership Oracle. *Machine Learning*, 14:7-26.
[3] Shai Ben-David, Eyal Kushilevitz, Yishay Mansour. Online Learning versus Offline Learning. *Machine Learning* 29(1): 45-63, 1997.
[4] A. Blum. Separating distribution-free and mistake-bound learning models over the boolean domain. *SIAM Journal on Computing 23(5)*, pp. 990-1000, 1994.

[5] N. H. Bshouty. Exact learning of formulas in parallel. *Machine Learning* 26, pp. 25-41, 1997.
[6] N. H. Bshouty. A Booster for the PAExact Model.
[7] N. H. Bshouty, D. Gavinsky. PAC = PAExact and other Equivalent Models in Learning. *Proceedings of the 43th Annual Symposium on Foundations of Computer Science*, pp. 167-176, 2002.
[8] N. H. Bshouty, J. Jackson, C. Tamon. Exploring learnability between exact and PAC. *Proceedings of the 15th Annual Conference on Computational Learning Theory*, 2002.
[9] D. Gavinsky. Exact = PExact. 2004.
http://pages.cpsc.ucalgary.ca/~gavinsky/papers/papers.html
[10] Y. Mansour and D. McAllester, Boosting using Branching Programs, Proceedings of the 13th Annual Conference on Computational Learning Theory, pp. 220-224, 2000.
[11] R. E. Schapire, The strength of weak learnability, *Machine Learning, 5(2)* pp. 197-227, 1990.
[12] L. G. Valiant. (1984) A theory of the learnable. *communications of the ACM, 27:1134-1142.*

Learning a Hidden Graph Using $O(\log n)$ Queries Per Edge

Dana Angluin and Jiang Chen

Department of Computer Science, Yale University
{angluin,criver}@cs.yale.edu

Abstract. We consider the problem of learning a general graph using edge-detecting queries. In this model, the learner may query whether a set of vertices induces an edge of the hidden graph. This model has been studied for particular classes of graphs by Kucherov and Grebinski [1] and Alon *et al.*[2], motivated by problems arising in genome sequencing. We give an adaptive deterministic algorithm that learns a general graph with n vertices and m edges using $O(m \log n)$ queries, which is tight up to a constant factor for classes of non-dense graphs. Allowing randomness, we give a 5-round Las Vegas algorithm using $O(m \log n + \sqrt{m} \log^2 n)$ queries in expectation. We give a lower bound of $\Omega((2m/r)^{r/2})$ for learning the class of non-uniform hypergraphs of dimension r with m edges. For the class of r-uniform hypergraphs with bounded degree d, where $d \leq n^{1/(r-1)}/(2r^{1+2/(r-1)})$, we give a non-adaptive Monte Carlo algorithm using $O(dn \log n)$ queries, which succeeds with probability at least $1-n^{-c}$, where c is any constant.

1 Introduction

The problem of learning a hidden graph is the following. Imagine that there is a graph $G = (V, E)$ whose vertices are known to us and whose edges are not. We wish to determine all the edges of G by making *edge-detecting queries* of the following form

$$Q_G(S): \textit{does } S \textit{ include at least one edge of } G?$$

where $S \subseteq V$. The query $Q_G(S)$ is answered 1 or 0, indicating whether S contains both ends of at least one edge of G or not. We abbreviate $Q_G(S)$ to $Q(S)$ whenever the choice of G is clear from the context. The edges and non-edges of G are completely determined by the answers to $Q(\{u, v\})$ for all unordered pairs of vertices u and v; however, we seek algorithms that use significantly fewer queries when G is not dense.

This type of query may be motivated by the following scenario. We are given a set of chemicals, some pairs of which react and others don't. When multiple chemicals are combined in one test tube, a reaction is detectable if and only if at least one pair of the chemicals in the tube react. The task is to identify which pairs react using as few experiments as possible. The time needed to compute which experiments to do is a secondary consideration, though it is polynomial for the algorithms we present.

An important aspect of an algorithm in this model is its adaptiveness. An algorithm is *non-adaptive* if the whole set of queries it makes is chosen before the answers to any

J. Shawe-Taylor and Y. Singer (Eds.): COLT 2004, LNAI 3120, pp. 210–223, 2004.

queries are known. An algorithm is *adaptive* if the choice of later queries may depend on the answers to earlier queries. Although adaptiveness is powerful, non-adaptiveness is desirable in practice to permit the queries (or experiments) to be parallelized. A *multiple-round algorithm* consists of a sequence of rounds in which the set of queries made in a given round may depend only on the answers to queries asked in preceding rounds. Since the queries in each round may be parallelized, it is desirable to keep the number of rounds small. A non-adaptive algorithm is a 1-round algorithm.

Another important aspect of an algorithm is what assumptions may be made about the graph G; this is modeled by assuming that G is drawn from a known class of graphs. Previous work has mainly concentrated on identifying a graph G drawn from the class of graphs isomorphic to a fixed known graph. The cases of Hamiltonian cycles and matchings have specific applications to genome sequencing, which are explained in the papers cited below. Grebinski and Kucherov [1] give a deterministic adaptive algorithm for learning Hamiltonian cycles using $O(n \log n)$ queries. Beigel *et al.*[3] describe a 8-round deterministic algorithm for learning matchings using $O(n \log n)$ queries, which has direct application in genome sequencing projects. Alon *et al.*[2] give a 1-round Monte Carlo algorithm for learning matchings using $O(n \log n)$ queries, which succeeds with probability at least $1 - n^{-c}$. On the other hand, they show a lower bound of $\Omega(\binom{n}{2})$ for learning matchings with a deterministic 1-round algorithm. They also give a nearly matching upper bound in this setting. Alon and Asodi [4] give bounds for learning stars and cliques with a deterministic 1-round algorithm. Considerable effort has been devoted to optimizing the implied constants in these results.

In this paper, we are interested in the power of edge-detecting queries from a more theoretical point of view. In particular, we consider the problem of learning more general classes of graphs. Because of this focus, in this paper, we are more interested in asymptotic results than optimizing constants.

Let n denote the number of vertices and m the number of edges of G. Clearly n is known to the algorithm (since V is known), but m may not be. In Section 3, we give a deterministic adaptive algorithm to learn any graph using $O(m \log n)$ queries. The algorithm works without assuming m is known. For Hamiltonian cycles, matchings, and stars, our algorithm uses $O(n \log n)$ queries. In Section 4, we give a 1-round Monte Carlo algorithm for all graphs of degree at most d using $O(dn \log n)$ queries that succeeds with probability at least $1-n^{-c}$ assuming d is known. Note Hamiltonian cycles and matchings are both degree bounded by constants. This algorithm takes $O(n \log n)$ queries in both cases. In Section 5, we consider constant-round algorithms for general non-dense graphs. W first briefly describe a 4-round Las Vegas algorithm using $O(m \log n + \sqrt{m} \log^2 n)$ queries in expectation, assuming m is known. If m is not known, we give a 5-round Las Vegas algorithm that uses as many queries. Note $O(\sqrt{m} \log^2 n)$ is negligible when $m = \Omega(\log^2 n)$. Therefore, the 5-round algorithm achieves $O(\log n)$ queries per edge unless the graph is very sparse, i.e. $m = o(\log^2 n)$.

In Section 6 we consider the problem of learning hypergraphs. The information-theoretic the lower bound implies that $\Omega(rm \log n)$ queries are necessary for learning the class of hypergraphs of dimension r with m edges. We show further that no algorithm can learn this class of hypergraphs using $o((2m/r)^{r/2})$ queries. However, non-uniformity of hypergraphs does play an important role in our construction of lower bound. Thus we leave the problem of the existence of an algorithm for r-uniform hypergraphs with m edges using $O(rm \log n)$ queries open. On the other hand, we show that hypergraphs of bounded degree d, where $d \leq n^{1/(r-1)}/(2r^{1+2/(r-1)})$, are learnable with $O(dn \log n)$ queries using a Monte Carlo algorithm, which succeeds with probability at least $1-n^{-c}$.

The graph learning problem may also be viewed as the problem of learning a monotone disjunctive normal form (DNF) boolean formula with terms of size 2 using membership queries only. Each vertex of G is represented by a variable and each edge by a term containing the two variables associated with the endpoints of the edge. A membership query assigns 1 or 0 to each variable, and is answered 1 if the assignment satisfies at least one term, and 0 otherwise, that is, if the set of vertices corresponding to the variables assigned 1 contains both endpoints of at least one edge of G. Similarly, a hyperedge with r vertices corresponds to a term with r variables. Thus, our results apply also to learning the corresponding classes of monotone DNF formulas using membership queries. The graph-theoretic formulation provides useful intuitions.

2 Preliminaries

A hypergraph is a pair $H = (V, E)$ such that E is a subset of the power set of V, where V is the set of vertices and E is the set of edges. A set S is an *independent set* of G if it contains no edge of H. The *degree* of a vertex is the number of edges of H that contain it. If S is a set of vertices, then the *neighbors* of S are all those vertices v not in S such that $\{u, v\}$ is contained in an edge of H for some $u \in S$. We denote the set of neighbors of S by $\Gamma(S)$. The dimension of a hypergraph H is the cardinality of the largest set in E. H is said to be r-uniform if E contains only sets of size r. In a r-uniform hypergraph, a set of vertices of size r is called a *non-edge* if it is not an edge of H.

A undirected simple graph G with no self loops is a just 2-uniform hypergraph. Thus the edges of $G = (V, E)$ may be considered to be a subset of the set of all unordered pairs of vertices of G. A c-coloring of a graph G is a function from V to $\{1, 2, \ldots, c\}$ such that no edge of G has both endpoints mapped to the same color. The set of vertices assigned the same color by a coloring is a *color class* of the coloring.

We *divide a set S in half* by partitioning it arbitrarily into two sets S_1 and S_2 such that $|S_1| = \lfloor |S|/2 \rfloor$ and $|S_2| = \lceil |S|/2 \rceil$.

Here are two inequalities that we use.

Proposition 1. *If* $0 \leq x \leq 1$, *then*

$$1 - x \leq e^{-x}.$$

Proposition 2. *If* $0 < x \leq 1$,

$$(1-x)^{\frac{1}{x}} \geq \frac{2(1-x)}{e(2-x)} \geq \frac{(1-x)}{e}.$$

3 An Adaptive Algorithm

The main result of this section is the following.

Theorem 1. *There is a deterministic adaptive algorithm that identifies any graph G drawn from the class of all graphs with n vertices using $O(m \log n)$ edge-detecting queries, where m is the number of edges of G.*

By a counting argument, this upper bound is tight up to a constant factor for certain classes of non-dense graphs.

Theorem 2. *$\Omega(\epsilon m \log n)$ edge-detecting queries are required to identify a graph G drawn from the class of all graphs with n vertices and $m = n^{2-\epsilon}$ edges.*

We begin by presenting a simple adaptive algorithm for the case of finding the edges between two known independent sets of vertices in G using $O(\log n)$ queries per edge. This algorithm works without priori knowledge about s.

Lemma 1. *Assume that S_1 and S_2 are two known, nonempty independent sets of vertices in G. Also assume that $|S_1| \leq |S_2|$ and there are s edges between S_1 and S_2, where $s > 0$. Then these edges can be identified by a deterministic adaptive algorithm using no more than $4s(\log |S_2| + 1)$ edge-detecting queries.*

Proof. We describe a recursive algorithm whose inputs are the two sets S_1 and S_2. If both S_1 and S_2 are singleton sets, then there is one edge connecting the unique vertex in S_1 to the unique vertex in S_2.

If exactly one of S_1 and S_2 is a singleton, suppose w.l.o.g it is S_1. Divide S_2 into halves S_{21} and S_{22} and query the two sets $S_1 \cup S_{21}$ and $S_1 \cup S_{22}$. For $j = 1, 2$, solve the problem recursively for S_1 and S_{2j} if the query on $S_1 \cup S_{2j}$ is answered 1.

Otherwise, both S_1 and S_2 contain more than one vertex. Divide each S_i into halves S_{i1} and S_{i2} and query the four sets $S_{1j} \cup S_{2k}$ for $j = 1, 2$ and $k = 1, 2$. For each query that is answered 1, solve the problem recursively for S_{1j} and S_{2k}.

If we consider the computation tree for this algorithm, the maximum depth does not exceed $\log |S_2| + 1$ and there are at most s leaves in the tree (corresponding to the s edges of G that are found.) At each internal node of the computation tree, the algorithm asks at most 4 queries. Therefore, the algorithm asks at most $4s(\log |S_2| + 1)$ queries. □

If S_1 and S_2 are not independent sets in G, the problem is more complex because we must eliminate interference from the edges of G induced by S_1 or S_2. If we happen to know the edges of G induced by S_1 and S_2, and we color the two induced graphs, then each color class is an independent set in G. Then the edges between a color class in S_1 and a color class in S_2 can be identified using the algorithm in *Lemma 1*. Because every edge between S_1 and S_2 belongs to one such pair, it suffices to consider all such pairs. The next lemma formalizes this idea.

Lemma 2. *For $i = 1, 2$ assume that S_i is a set of vertices that includes s_i edges of G, where s_1 and s_2 are not both 0, and assume that these edges are known. Also assume that $|S_1| \leq |S_2|$ and there are $s > 0$ edges between S_1 and S_2. Then these edges can be identified adaptively using no more than $4(s \log |S_2| + s + s_1 + s_2)$ edge-detecting queries.*

We observe the following fact about vertex coloring.

Fact 1. *A graph with m edges can be $\lfloor \sqrt{2m}+1 \rfloor$-colored. Furthermore, the coloring can be constructed in polynomial time.*

To see this, we successively collapse pairs of vertices not joined by an edge until we obtain the complete graph on t vertices, which can be t-colored and has $t(t-1)/2 \leq m$ edges. This yields a t-coloring of the original graph because no edge joins vertices that are collapsed into the same final vertex.

Proof. (of *Lemma 2*) Using the preceding *Fact 1*, for $i = 1, 2$, we may color the subgraph of G induced by S_i using at most $\lfloor \sqrt{2s_i}+1 \rfloor$ colors. Each color class is an independent set in G. The edges between S_1 and S_2 can be divided into the sets of edges between pairs of color classes from S_1 and S_2. For each pair of color classes, one from S_1 and one from S_2, we query the union of the two classes to determine whether there is any edge of G between the two classes. If so, then using the algorithm in *Lemma 2*, we can identify the edges between the two classes with no more than $4(\log|S_2|+1)$ queries per edge. To query the union of each pair of color classes requires at most $(\lfloor \sqrt{2s_1}+1 \rfloor)(\lfloor \sqrt{2s_2}+1 \rfloor)$ queries, which does not exceed $(1+\sqrt{2})(s_1+s_2)+1$. Thus, in total, we use no more than $4(s\log|S_2|+s+s_1+s_2)$ edge-detecting queries. □

Now we are able to present our adaptive algorithm to learn a general graph $G = (V, E)$ with $O(\log n)$ queries per edge. One query with the set V suffices to determine whether E is empty, so we assume that $|E| > 0$.

Algorithm 1 *(Adaptive algorithm)*

1: If $|V| = 2$, mark the pair of vertices in V as an edge and return.
2: Divide V into halves S_1 and S_2. Ask $Q(S_1)$ and $Q(S_2)$.
3: Recursively solve the problem for S_i if $Q(S_i) = 1$, for $i = 1, 2$.
4: Use the algorithm in *Lemma 2* to identify the edges between S_1 and S_2.

Proof. (of *Theorem 1*) We give an inductive proof that the algorithm uses no more than $12m\log n$ edge-detecting queries to learn a graph G with n vertices and $m > 0$ edges. This clearly holds when $n = 2$. Assume that for some $n \geq 3$, every graph with $n' < n$ vertices and $m' > 0$ edges is learnable with at most $12m'\log n'$ edge-detecting queries. Assume S_i includes s_i edges of G, for $i = 1, 2$. Since $|S_2| \geq |S_1|$, the number of queries required to learn G is at most

$$(12(s_1+s_2)+4(m-s_1-s_2))\log|S_2|+4m+2$$

using the inductive hypothesis and *Lemma 2*.

We know that $\log|S_2| \leq \log((n+1)/2) \leq \log n - 1/2$, when $n \geq 3$. Then for $n \geq 3$, the above expression is at most $12m\log n$ because $m \geq 1$. This concludes the induction. □

This shows that any graph is adaptively learnable using $O(\log n)$ queries per edge. This algorithm can be parallelized into $O(\log^2 n)$ nonadaptive rounds; in subsequent sections we develop randomized algorithms that achieve a constant number of rounds.

4 Bounded Degree Graphs

In this section, we present a randomized non-adaptive algorithm to learn any graph with bounded degree d, where we assume that $d = o(n)$ and d is known to the algorithm. The algorithm uses $O(dn \log n)$ queries and succeeds with probability at least $1 - n^{-c}$. Our algorithm is a generalization of that of Alon *et al.*[2] to learn a hidden matching using $O(n \log n)$ queries. In contrast to their results, we use sampling with replacement and do not attempt to optimize the constants, as our effort is to map out what is possible in the general case.

The key observation is that every pair of vertices in S is discovered to be a non-edge of G if $Q(S) = 0$. The algorithm asks a set of $O(dn \log n)$ queries with random sets of vertices with the goal of discovering all of the non-edges of G.

For a probability p, a *p-random* set P is obtained by including each vertex independently with probability p. Each query is an independently chosen p-random set. After all the queries are answered, those pairs of vertices that have not been discovered to be non-edges are output as edges in G. The algorithm may fail by not discovering some non-edge of G, and we bound the probability of failure by n^{-c} for an appropriate choice of p and number of queries.

For a given non-edge $\{u, v\}$ in G, the probability that both u and v are included in a p-random set P is p^2. Given that u and v are included in P, the probability that P has no edge of G is bounded below using the following lemma. Let $N_G(p)$ denote the probability that a p-random set includes no edge of G.

Lemma 3. *Suppose I is an independent set in G, and $\Gamma(I)$ is the set of neighbors of vertices in I. Suppose P is a p-random set. $Pr\{Q(P) = 0 | I \subseteq P\}$ is at least*

$$(1 - p)^{|\Gamma(I)|} \cdot N_G(p).$$

Proof. Let G' be the induced subgraph of G on $V - I - \Gamma(I)$. It is easy to verify that $N_{G'}(p) \geq N_G(p)$. Independence in the selection of the vertices in P implies that $Pr\{Q(P) = 0 | I \subseteq P\}$ is the product of the probability that P contains no vertices in $\Gamma(I)$, which is $(1 - p)^{|\Gamma(I)|}$, and the probability that given the previous event P has no edge of G, which is $N_{G'}(p)$. □

By the union bound, we know that $N_G(p) \geq 1 - mp^2$. Also, $\Gamma(\{u, v\}) \leq 2d$ because the degree of each vertex of G is bounded by d. Therefore,

$$\begin{aligned} Pr\{Q(P) = 0 | u, v \in P\} &\geq (1 - p)^{2d}(1 - mp^2) \\ &\geq 1 - 2dp - mp^2 \end{aligned}$$

Since d is asssumed to be known to the algorithm, we choose $p = 1/\sqrt{dn}$. Then the above expression is at least $1 - 2\sqrt{d/n} - m/dn \geq 1/2 - o(1)$. (Recall that we assume $d = o(n)$). Therefore, the probability $\{u, v\}$ is shown to be a non-edge of G by one random query is at least

$$p^2 \cdot (\frac{1}{2} - o(1)) = \frac{1}{2dn} \cdot (1 - o(1))$$

The probability that a non-edge $\{u, v\}$ is not discovered to be a non-edge using $6(1 + o(1)) \cdot dn \ln n$ queries is at most n^{-3} (using *Proposition 1*). Thus, the probability that some non-edge of G is not discovered after this many queries is bounded by n^{-1}. Note that we can decrease this probability to n^{-c} by asking c times more queries.

Therefore, we have proved the following.

Theorem 3. *There is a Monte Carlo non-adaptive algorithm that identifies any graph G drawn from the class of graphs with bounded degree d with probability at least $1 - n^{-c}$ using $O(dn \log n)$ edge-detecting queries, where n is the number of vertices and c is any constant.*

For d-regular graphs, this algorithm uses $O(m \log n)$ queries. In particular, for matchings and Hamiltonian cycles, the algorithm uses $O(n \log n)$ queries.

5 Constant-Round Algorithms

The algorithm in the previous section is not query-efficient when G is far from regular, e.g. we get a bound of $O(n^2 \log n)$ to learn a star with only $n - 1$ total edges, because the maximum degree is large. To obtain a query-efficient algorithm for a more general class of graphs, we consider constant-round algorithms, in which the set of queries in a given round may depend on the answers to queries in preceding rounds. For each round of the algorithm, a *pseudo-edge* is any pair of vertices that has not been discovered to be a non-edge of G in any preceding round; this includes all the edges of G and all the (as yet) undiscovered non-edges of G.

In a multiple-round algorithm, there is the option of a a final *cleanup* round, in which we ask a query for each remaining pseudo-edge, yielding a Las Vegas algorithm instead of a Monte Carlo algorithm. For example, if we add a cleanup round to the algorithm in the previous section, we get a 2-round Las Vegas algorithm that always answers correctly and uses $O(dn \log n)$ queries in expectation.

The algorithm in the previous section assumes d is known. In this section, we first sketch the intuitions of a 4-round Las Vegas algorithm that learns a general graph using an expected $O(m \log n + \sqrt{m} \log^2 n)$ queries, assuming m is known. We then develop a 5-round Las Vegas algorithm that learns a general graph using as many queries without assuming m is known.

Each vertex of G is classified as a *low-degree vertex*, if its degree does not exceed $\sqrt{m}$, or a *high-degree vertex* otherwise. A non-edge of G is a *low-degree non-edge* if both vertices in the pair are low-degree vertices.

For the first round we choose the sample probability $p = 1/\sqrt{2m}$. (Recall that we are assuming m is known in this sketch.) Using *Lemma 3*, the probability that a particular low-degree non-edge of G is shown to be a non-edge by a query with a p-random set is at least

$$p^2 \cdot (1 - p)^{\sqrt{m}} (1 - m \cdot p^2)$$

which is $\Omega(1/m)$. Thus, $O(m \log n)$ queries with p-random sets suffice to identify all the low-degree non-edges of G in the first round with probability at least $1 - n^{-2}$.

Because the number of high-degree vertices is at most $2\sqrt{m}$, we can afford to query all pairs of them in the cleanup round. We therefore concentrate on non-edges containing one high-degree and one low-degree vertex. To discover these non-edges, we need a smaller sampling probability ($p = o(1/\sqrt{m})$), but choosing a sample probability that is too small runs the risk of requiring too many queries.

The right choice of a sampling probability p differs with the degree of each individual high-degree vertex, so in the second round we estimate such p's. In the third round, we use the estimated p's to identify non-edges containing a high-degree and a low-degree vertex. In the cleanup round we ask queries on every remaining pseudo-edge. In fact, since the actual degrees of the vertices are not known, the sets of high-degree and low-degree vertices must be approximated.

The above sketches the intuitions for a 4-round algorithm when m is known. If m is unknown, one plausible idea would be to try to estimate m sufficiently accurately by random sampling in the first round, and then proceed with the algorithm sketched above. This idea does not seem to work, but analyzing it motivates the development of our final 5-round algorithm.

First we have the following "obvious" lemma: as we increase the sampling probability p, we are more likely to include an edge of G in a p-random set. It can be proved by expressing $N_G(p)$ as a sum over all independent sets in G, grouped by their sizes, and differentiating with respect to p.

Lemma 4. *Assuming $m > 0$, $N_G(p)$ is strictly decreasing as p increases.*

It follows that since $N_G(0) = 1$ and $N_G(1) = 0$, there exists a unique $p_*(G)$ such that $N(p_*(G)) = 1/2$. In other words, $p_*(G)$ is the sampling probability p that makes an edge-detecting query with a p-random set equally likely to return 0 or 1, maximizing the information content of such queries.

It is plausible to think that $p_*(G)$ will reveal much about m. However, $p_*(G)$ also depends strongly on the topology of G. Consider the following two graphs: G_M, a matching with m edges, and G_S, a star with m edges. We have

$$N_{G_M}(p) = (1 - p^2)^m$$
$$N_{G_S}(p) = 1 - p + p(1 - p)^m$$

Therefore, we have $p_*(G_M) = O(1/\sqrt{m})$ but $p_*(G_S) > 1/2$. We believe that such a gap in $p_*(G)$'s of two different topologies lies behind the difficulty of estimating m in one round.

Although our effort to estimate m has been thwarted, $p_*(G)$ turns out to be the sampling probability that will help us identify most of the non-edges in the graph. We will use $N(p)$ instead of $N_G(p)$ and p_* instead of $p_*(G)$ when the choice of G is clear from the context.

First, we have rough upper and lower bounds for p_*.

$$\frac{1}{\sqrt{2m}} \leq p_* \leq \frac{\sqrt{2}}{2},$$

observing that $1 - mp^2 \leq N(p) \leq 1 - p^2$. The fact that p_* helps us identify most of the non-edges is made clear in the following two lemmas.

Lemma 5. *Let $\{u, v\}$ be a non-edge of G in which the degrees of u and v do not exceed $2/p_*$. Then a query on a p_*-random set identifies $\{u, v\}$ as a non-edge with probability at least $\Omega(1/m)$.*

Proof. According to *Lemma 3*, the probability that the non-edge $\{u, v\}$ is identified by a query on a p_*-random set is at least

$$p_*^2(1-p_*)^{4/p_*} \cdot N(p_*)$$

We know that $p_* \leq \sqrt{2}/2$. According to *Proposition 2*, $(1-p_*)^{4/p_*} = \Omega(1)$. Combining this with the facts that $p_* \geq 1/\sqrt{2m}$ and $N(p_*) = 1/2$, we have that the probability is $\Omega(1/m)$. □

Examining the proof of *Lemma 5* we can see that rather than requiring the sampling probability p be exactly p_*, it is sufficient to require upper and lower bounds as follows: $p = \Omega(1/\sqrt{m})$ and $p \leq p_*$.

Corollary 1. *We can identify with probability at least $\Omega(1/m)$ any non-edge with the degrees of both ends no more than $2/p_*$ by a query on a p-random set, where $p = \Omega(1/\sqrt{m})$ and $p \leq p_*$.*

Lemma 6. *There are at most $1/p_*$ vertices that have degree more than $2/p_*$.*

Proof. Suppose that there are h vertices that have degree more than $2/p_*$. Let P be a p_*-random set. Given that one of the h vertices is included in P, the probability that P has no edge in G is at most $(1-p_*)^{2/p_*} \leq 1/e^2$. The probability that P contains none of the h vertices is at most $(1-p_*)^h$. Therefore, the probability P has no edge of G is at most

$$\begin{aligned}
&(1-(1-p_*)^h) \cdot \frac{1}{e^2} + (1-p_*)^h \cdot 1 \\
\leq &\frac{1}{e^2}(1+(e^2-1) \cdot e^{-p_* h})
\end{aligned}$$

which should be no less than $1/2$. Thus we have $e^{-p_* h} \geq 1/e$. Therefore $h \leq 1/p_*$. □

Recalling that $p_* \geq 1/\sqrt{2m}$, we have the following.

Corollary 2. *There are at most $O(\sqrt{m})$ vertices that have degrees more than $2/p_*$.*

The 5-round algorithm is shown in *Algorithm 2*. Its correctness is guaranteed by the cleanup round, so our task is to bound the expected number of queries. For this analysis, we call a vertex a *low-degree vertex* if its degree is at most $2/p_*$ and call it a *high-degree* vertex otherwise. The non-edges consisting of two low-degree vertices are called *low-degree non-edges*. In the following, we will show that each round will succeed with probability at least $1 - n^{-2}$ given that the previous rounds succeed.

First we show that with high probability p' exists and satisfies our requirement for the second round.

Algorithm 2 the 5-round algorithm

1. (**Estimate** p_*) Let $p_i = 2^i/n$ for $i = 0, \ldots, \lfloor \log n \rfloor$. For each i, choose and query a p_i-random set $\Theta(\log n)$ times. Let the average outcome of edge-detecting queries on p_i-random sets be $1 - \hat{N}_i$. Let $p' = (1/2) \min \{p_i | \hat{N}_i \leq 5/8\}$. Go to the 5th round if p' doesn't exist.
2. (**Low-degree edges**) Choose and query a p'-random set $\Theta((1/p'2) \log n)$ times.
3. (**Degree estimation of high-degree vertices**) Let E' be the set of pseudo-edges after the second round. Let $G' = (V, E')$.
   a) Divide V into two sets H and L according to their degrees in G'. L contains the vertices that have degrees at most $3/p'$ and H contains the rest of the vertices.
   b) For each vertex u in H and each p_i, query $\Theta(\log n)$ times the union of $\{u\}$ and a p_i-random set.
   c) Let $1 - \hat{N_i^u}$ be the average outcome of random queries with probability p_i on vertex u. Let $p_u = \max \{p_i | \hat{N_i^u} \geq 1/5 + 1/(2e)\}$ if p_u exists.
4. (**Edges between high-degree and low-degree vertices**) For each vertex $u \in H$ such that p_u exists, query the union of $\{u\}$ and a p_u-random set $\Theta((1/p_u) \log n)$ times.
5. (**Cleanup**) Query every remaining pseudo-edge.

Lemma 7. *$p' \leq p_*$ and $p' = \Omega(1/\sqrt{m})$ with probability at least $1 - n^{-2}$.*

Proof. Let $p_j = \min\{p_i | p_i \geq p_*\}$. Obviously p_j exists and we have $p_j \leq 2p_*$. First we observe that with high probability

$$p' \leq \frac{1}{2} p_j \leq p_*$$

The probability that the above inequality is violated is $Pr[p' > (1/2)p_j] \leq Pr[\hat{N}_j > 5/8]$. We know that $N(p_j) \leq N(p_*) \leq 1/2$. According to Hoeffding's inequality [5], we can make the probability at most $1/(2n^2)$ by asking $\Theta(\log n)$ queries.

Also by Hoeffding's inequality, we have $Pr[N(2p') > 3/4] \leq 1/(2n^2)$. Therefore, we have $1 - m(2p')^2 \leq N(2p') \leq 3/4$, and hence $p' \geq 1/(4\sqrt{m})$. Thus with probability at least $1 - n^{-2}$, we have $1/4\sqrt{m} \leq p' \leq p_*$. □

Using *Corollary 1*, we can conclude that if the above inequalities are true, by asking $\Theta(m \log n)$ queries, we can guarantee with probability at least $1 - n^{-4}$ that a given low-degree non-edge is identified in the second round. So we can guarantee with probability at least $1 - n^{-2}$ that every low-degree non-edge is identified in the second round.

Suppose that we identify all of the low-degree non-edges in the second round. All the low-degree vertices must fall into L, since their degrees in G' are at most $3/p_*$ (which is at most $|H| \leq 1/p_*$ more than their true degrees).

However, L may also contain some high-degree vertices. At most $1/p_*$ high-degree vertices fall into L, and their degrees are bounded by $3/p'$. Note that both $1/p'$ and $1/p_*$ are $O(\sqrt{m})$. The total number of pseudo-edges incident with high-degree vertices in L is therefore bounded by $O(m)$. Also, the number of pseudo-edges between pairs of vertices in H is bounded by $O(m)$. As stated before, they can be identified in the cleanup round with $O(m)$ queries. We will therefore analyze only the behavior of non-edges between vertices in H and low-degree vertices in L in the third and fourth round.

We will now show p_u is what we want for each vertex $u \in H$. Let d_u denote the degree of vertex u.

Lemma 8. *For each* $u \in H$, $1/(10d_u) \leq p_u \leq 1/d_u$ *with probability at least* $1 - n^{-3}$, *given that the algorithm succeeds in the first and second rounds.*

Proof. Denote by $N^u(p)$ the probability that the union of $\{u\}$ and a p-random set has no edge. According to Hoeffding's inequality, by asking $\Theta(\log n)$ queries we can make $N^u(p_u) \geq 1/e$ true with probability at least $1 - (1/3)n^{-3}$. Note that $N^u(p_u) \leq (1 - p_u)^{d_u} \leq e^{-p_u d_u}$. Thus we can conclude that $p_u \leq 1/d_u$ is true with probability at least $1 - (1/3)n^{-3}$.

Assume $p_j^u = max\{p_i | N^u(p_i) \geq 2/5\}$. First we observe that with high probability that $p_u \geq p_j^u$. The probability this inequality is violated is

$$Pr[p_u \geq p_j^u] \geq Pr[N^u(p_j) < 1/5 + 1/2e]$$

By Hoeffding's inequality, the probability can be made no more than $(1/3)n^{-3}$ by asking $\Theta(\log n)$ queries.

According to our choice of p_j^u, we have $N^u(p_{j+1}^u) < 2/5$. By *Lemma 3* we know that

$$N^u(p_{j+1}^u) \geq (1 - 2p_j^u)^{d_u} \cdot N(2p_j^u)$$

As we just showed, $p_u \geq p_j^u$ is true with probability at least $1 - (1/3)n^{-3}$. Therefore, with probability at least $1 - (1/3)n^{-3}$

$$\begin{aligned} \frac{2}{5} > N^u(p_{j+1}^u) &\geq (1 - 2p_u)^{d_u} \cdot N(2p_u) \\ &\geq (1 - 2p_u d_u) \cdot N(2p_u) \end{aligned}$$

Since we already showed that $p_u \leq 1/d_u$ is true with probability at least $1-(1/3)n^{-3}$ and we know that $\forall u \in H, d_u \geq 2/p_*$, we have

$$N(2p_u) \geq N(\frac{2}{d_u}) \geq N(p_*) \geq \frac{1}{2}$$

is true with probability at least $1-(1/3)n^{-3}$. Thus we can conclude that $p_u \geq 1/(10d_u)$ with probability at least $1 - (2/3)n^{-3}$. □

In the third round, we can guarantee that $1/(10d_u) \leq p_u \leq 1/d_u$ is true for every $u \in H$ with probability at least $1 - n^{-2}$.

Let's assume the above inequality is true for every $u \in H$. Suppose v is a low-degree vertex and $\{u, v\}$ is a non-edge. Let P be a p_u-random set.

$$Pr\{Q(P \cup \{u, v\}) = 0\} \geq (1 - p_u)^{d_u + 2/p_*} \cdot N(p_u)$$

Since $p_u \leq 1/d_u \leq p_*/2$, we have both $(1 - p_u)^{d_u + 2/p_*} = \Omega(1)$ and $N(p_u) = \Omega(1)$. The probability that we choose v in one random query is p_u, which is $\Omega(1/d_u)$. Therefore, the probability $\{u, v\}$ is identified in one random query concerning u is $\Omega(1/d_u)$. By querying the union of $\{u\}$ and a p_u-random set $\Theta(d_u \log n)$ times, we can guarantee that $\{u, v\}$ is identified as a non-edge with probability at least $1 - n^{-4}$. Therefore, given that rounds one, two and three succeed, round four identifies every non-edge $\{u, v\}$ with $u \in H$ and v a low degree vertex, with probability at least $1 - n^{-2}$.

Given that the algorithm succeeds in rounds one through four, the only pseudo-edges that remain are either edges of G or non-edges between pairs of vertices in H or non-edges incident with the high degree vertices in L. As shown above, the total number of such non-edges is $O(m)$.

Finally, we bound the expected number of queries used by the algorithm. It is clear that in the event that each round succeeds, the first round uses $O(\log^2 n)$ queries; the second round uses $O(m \log n)$ queries; the third round uses $O(\sqrt{m} \log^2 n)$ queries; the fourth round uses $O(\sum_{u \in H} d_u \log n) = O(m \log n)$ queries; the fifth round uses $O(m)$ queries. The probability that each round fails is bounded by n^{-2}. The maximum number of queries used in case of failures is $O(n^2 \log n)$. Therefore in expectation the algorithm uses $O(m \log n + \sqrt{m} \log^2 n)$ queries. Note that this bound is $O(m \log n)$ if m is $\Omega(\log^2 n)$.

Therefore, we have the following theorem.

Theorem 4. *There is a Las Vegas 5-round algorithm that identifies any graph G drawn from the class of all graphs with n vertices and m edges using $O(m \log n + \sqrt{m} \log^2 n)$ edge-detecting queries in expectation.*

6 Hypergraph Learning

In this section, we consider the problem of learning hypergraphs with edge-detecting queries. An edge-detecting query $Q_H(S)$ where H is a hypergraph is answered 1 or 0 indicating whether S contains all vertices of at least one hyperedge of H or not. The information-theoretic lower bound implies that any algorithm takes at least $\Omega(rm \log n)$ queries to learn hypergraphs of dimension r with m edges. We show that no algorithm can learn hypergraphs of dimension r with m edges using $o((2m/r)^{r/2})$ queries if we allow the hypergraph to be non-uniform, even if we allow randomness. When m is large, say $\omega(r \log^2 n)$, this implies that there is no algorithm using only $O(r \log n)$ queries per edge when $r \geq 3$.

For uniform hypergraphs, we show that the algorithm in Section 4 for graphs can be generalized to sparse hypergraphs. However, the sparsity requirement for hypergraphs is more severe. Recall that we assume $d = o(n)$ in Section 4. For hypergraphs, we require $d \leq n^{1/(r-1)}/(2r^{1+2/(r-1)})$.

Theorem 5. *$\Omega((2m/r)^{r/2})$ edge-detecting queries are required to identify a hypergraph H drawn from the class of all hypergraphs of dimension r with n vertices and m edges.*

Proof. We generalize the lower bound argument from [6] for learning monotone DNF formulas using membership queries. Let r and k be integers greater than 1. Let $V_1, \ldots, V_r$

be pairwise disjoint sets containing k vertices each. For $1 \leq i \leq r$ let $E_i = \{(u,v)|u,v \in V_i, u \neq v\}$. Thus, E_i is a clique of 2-edges on the vertices V_i. Consider a hypergraph H with vertices V including each V_i and edges

$$E = \bigcup_{i=1}^{r} E_i \cup \{v_1, v_2, \ldots, v_r\}.$$

where $v_i \in V_i$ for $1 \leq i \leq r$. There are k^r such hypergraphs, one for each choice of an r-edge.

Even knowing the form of the hypergraph and the identity of the sets of vertices V_i, the learning algorithm must ask at least $k^r - 1$ queries if the adversary is adaptive. Every query that contains more than one vertex from some V_i is answered 1; therefore, only queries that contain exactly one vertex from each V_i yield any information about the r-edge characterizing H. An adversary may maintain a set $R \subseteq V_1 \times \ldots \times V_r$ consisting of the r-edges not queried so far. Each query with an r-edge may be answered 0 until $|R| = 1$, which means that the learning algorithm must make at least $k^r - 1$ queries to learn H. In terms of m, this is $\Omega((2m/r)^{r/2})$.

Even if the adversary is constrained to make a random choice of an r-edge T at the start of the algorithm and answer consistently with it, we show that $\Omega((2m/r)^{r/2})$ queries are necessary. Suppose $S_1, S_2, \ldots, S_q$ is the sequence of r-edges a randomized algorithm makes queries on. It is easy to see that $Pr\{S_1 = T\} = 1/k^r$. And also we have $Pr\{S_{i+1} = T|S_j \neq T, j \leq i\} \leq 1/(k^r - i)$ since each r-edge is equally likely to be T. Therefore, the probability that none of S_i's equals T is at least $(k^r - q)/k^r$. When $q \leq k^r/2$, this is at least 1/2. □

We now present a randomized non-adaptive algorithm for r-uniform hypergraphs with bounded degree d, generalizing the algorithm for degree bounded graphs in Section 4. The algorithm uses $O(dn \log n)$ queries and succeeds with probability n^{-1} assuming d is known and $d \leq n^{1/(r-1)}/(2r^{1+2/(r-1)})$. The algorithm asks queries on independently chosen p-random sets. Let P be a p-random set. Let w be a non-edge of H. Thus $Pr\{w \subseteq P\} = p^r$. Consider the set E' of hyperedges that have nonempty intersection with w. By uniformity, each such hyperedge contains a vertex that is not in w. Let L be a set that contains one such vertex from each hyperedge in E'. Thus $|L| \leq |E'| \leq dr$. The probability that P includes no edge in E' given that $w \subseteq P$ is at least $(1-p)^{|L|} \leq (1-p)^{dr}$. Let H' be the induced hypergraph on $V - L - w$. Since H' has at most m edges, the probability P contains no edge in H' is at least $1 - mp^r$. Therefore, we have

$$\begin{aligned} Pr\{Q_H(P) = 0|w \subseteq P\} \geq & p^r(1-p)^{dr}(1-mp^r) \\ \geq & p^r(1-drp)(1-mp^r) \end{aligned}$$

Choose $p = 1/(2dn/r)^{1/r}$. Since $mr \leq dn$, $1 - mp^r \geq 1/2$. When $d \leq n^{1/(r-1)}/(2r^{1+2/(r-1)})$, $1 - drp \geq 1/2$. Therefore, the above probability is at least $r/(8dn)$. The probability that w is not discovered to be a non-edge after $8dn(r+1)/r \ln n$ queries is at most $n^{-(r+1)}$. The probability that some non-edge in H is not discovered after this many queries is bounded by n^{-1}. We can decrease this probability to n^{-c} by asking c times more queries.

Theorem 6. *There is a Monte Carlo non-adaptive algorithm that identifies any graph G drawn from the class of all graphs bounded degree d, where $d \leq n^{1/(r-1)}/(2r^{1+2/(r-1)})$, with probability at least $1 - n^{-c}$ using $O(dn \log n)$ queries, where n is the number of vertices and c is some constant.*

7 Open Problems

We leave the following problems open. Reduce the number of queries needed for Algorithm 2 from $O(m \log n + \sqrt{m} \log^2 n)$ to $O(m \log n)$. Reduce the number of rounds of Algorithm 2 without substantially increasing the number of queries. Find an algorithm that learns the class of r-uniform hypergraphs with m edges using $O(rm \log n)$ queries or show it is impossible.

References

1. Grebinski, V., Kucherov, G.: Optimal query bounds for reconstructing a Hamiltonian Cycle in complete graphs. In: Fifth Israel Symposium on the Theory of Computing Systems. (1997) 166–173
2. Alon, N., Beigel, R., Kasif, S., Rudich, S., Sudakov, B.: Learning a hidden matching. In: The 43rd Annual IEEE Symposium on Foundations of Computer Science. (2002) 197–206
3. Beigel, R., Alon, N., Kasif, S., Apaydin, M.S., Fortnow, L.: An optimal procedure for gap closing in whole genome shotgun sequencing. In: RECOMB. (2001) 22–30
4. Alon, N., Asodi, V.: Learning a hidden subgraph. http://www.math.tau.ac.il/~nogaa/PDFS/hidden4.pdf (2003)
5. Hoeffding, W.: Probability inequalities for sums of bounded random variables. Journal of the American Statistical Association **58** (1963) 13–30
6. Aigner, M.: Combinatorial Search. Wiley Teubner (1988)

Toward Attribute Efficient Learning of Decision Lists and Parities

Adam R. Klivans*[1] and Rocco A. Servedio[2]

[1] Divsion of Engineering and Applied Sciences
Harvard University
Cambridge, MA 02138
klivans@eecs.harvard.edu

[2] Department of Computer Science
Columbia University
New York, NY 10027, USA
rocco@cs.columbia.edu

Abstract. We consider two well-studied problems regarding attribute efficient learning: learning decision lists and learning parity functions. First, we give an algorithm for learning decision lists of length k over n variables using $2^{\tilde{O}(k^{1/3})} \log n$ examples and time $n^{\tilde{O}(k^{1/3})}$. This is the first algorithm for learning decision lists that has both subexponential sample complexity and subexponential running time in the relevant parameters. Our approach is based on a new construction of low degree, low weight polynomial threshold functions for decision lists. For a wide range of parameters our construction matches a lower bound due to Beigel for decision lists and gives an essentially optimal tradeoff between polynomial threshold function degree and weight.

Second, we give an algorithm for learning an unknown parity function on k out of n variables using $O(n^{1-1/k})$ examples in poly(n) time. For $k = o(\log n)$ this yields the first polynomial time algorithm for learning parity on a superconstant number of variables with sublinear sample complexity. We also give a simple algorithm for learning an unknown size-k parity using $O(k \log n)$ examples in $n^{k/2}$ time, which improves on the naive n^k time bound of exhaustive search.

1 Introduction

An important goal in machine learning theory is to design *attribute efficient* algorithms for learning various classes of Boolean functions. A class C of Boolean functions over n variables $x_1, \ldots, x_n$ is said to be *attribute-efficiently learnable* if there is a poly(n) time algorithm which can learn any function $f \in C$ using a number of examples which is polynomial in the "size" (description length) of the function f to be learned, rather than in n, the number of features in the domain over which learning takes place. (Note that the running time of

* Supported by a National Science Foundation Mathematical Sciences Postdoctoral Research Fellowship.

J. Shawe-Taylor and Y. Singer (Eds.): COLT 2004, LNAI 3120, pp. 224–238, 2004.

the learning algorithm must in general be at least n since each example is an n-bit vector.) Thus an attribute efficient learning algorithm for e.g. the class of Boolean conjunctions must be able to learn any Boolean conjunction of k literals over $x_1, \ldots, x_n$ using poly$(k, \log n)$ examples, since $k \log n$ bits are required to specify such a conjunction.

A longstanding open problem in machine learning, posed first by Blum in 1990 [4,5,7,8] and again by Valiant in 1998 [33], is whether or not there exist attribute efficient algorithms for learning *decision lists*, which are essentially nested "if-then-else" statements (we give a precise definition in Section 2). One motivation for considering the problem comes from the *infinite attribute model* introduced in [4]. Blum *et al.* [7] showed that for many concept classes (including decision lists) attribute efficient learnability in the standard n-attribute model is equivalent to learnability in the infinite attribute model. Since simple classes such as disjunctions and conjunctions are attribute efficiently learnable (and hence learnable in the infinite attribute model), this motivated Blum [4] to ask whether the richer class of decision lists is thus learnable as well. Several researchers [5,8, 10,26,29] have since considered this problem; we summarize this previous work in Section 1.2. More recently, Valiant [33] relates the problem of learning decision lists attribute efficiently to questions about human learning abilities.

Another outstanding challenge in machine learning is to determine whether there exist attribute efficient algorithms for learning *parity functions*. The parity function on a set of 0/1-valued variables $x_{i_1}, \ldots, x_{i_k}$ takes value $+1$ or -1 depending on whether $x_{i_1} + \cdots + x_{i_k}$ is even or odd. As with decision lists, a simple PAC learning algorithm is known for the class of parity functions but no attribute efficient algorithm is known.

1.1 Our Results

We give the first learning algorithm for decision lists that is subexponential in both sample complexity (in the relevant parameters k and $\log n$) and running time (in the relevant parameter k). Our results demonstrate for the first time that it is possible to simultaneously avoid the "worst case" in both sample complexity and running time, and thus suggest that it may perhaps be possible to learn decision lists attribute efficiently. Our main learning result for decision lists is:

Theorem 1. *There is an algorithm which learns length-k decision lists over $\{0,1\}^n$ with mistake bound $2^{\tilde{O}(k^{1/3})} \log n$ and time $n^{\tilde{O}(k^{1/3})}$.*

This bound improves on the sample complexity of Littlestone's well-known Winnow algorithm [21] for all k and improves on its runtime as well for $k = \Omega(\log^{3/2} n)$; see Section 1.2.

We prove Theorem 1 in two parts; first we generalize the Winnow algorithm for learning linear threshold functions to learn *polynomial threshold functions* (PTFs). In recent work on learning DNF formulas [18], intersections of halfspaces [17], and Boolean formulas of superconstant depth [27], PTFs of degree d have been learned in time $n^{O(d)}$ by using polynomial time linear programming algorithms such as the Ellipsoid algorithm (see e.g. [18]). In contrast, since we want to achieve low sample complexity as well as an $n^{O(d)}$ runtime, we use a generalization of the Winnow algorithm to learn PTFs. This generalization has sample complexity and running time bounds which depend on the degree and the total magnitude of the integer coefficients (i.e. the weight) of the PTF:

Theorem 2. *Let C be a class of Boolean functions over $\{0,1\}^n$ with the property that each $f \in C$ has a PTF of degree at most d and weight at most W. Then there is an online learning algorithm for C which runs in n^d time per example and has mistake bound $O(W^2 \cdot d \cdot \log n)$.*

This reduces the decision list learning problem to a problem of representing decision lists with PTFs of low weight and low degree. To this end we prove:

Theorem 3. *Let L be a decision list of length k. Then L is computed by a polynomial threshold function of degree $\tilde{O}(k^{1/3})$ and weight $2^{\tilde{O}(k^{1/3})}$.*

Theorem 1 follows directly from Theorems 2 and 3. We emphasize that Theorem 3 does *not* follow from previous results [18] on representing DNF formulas as PTFs; the PTF construction from [18] in fact has exponentially larger weight ($2^{2^{\tilde{O}(k^{1/3})}}$ rather than $2^{\tilde{O}(k^{1/3})}$) than the construction in this paper.

Our PTF construction is essentially optimal in the tradeoff between degree and weight which it achieves. In 1994 Beigel [3] gave a lower bound showing that any degree d PTF for a certain decision list must have weight $2^{\Omega(n/d^2)}$. [1] For $d = n^{1/3}$, Beigel's lower bound implies that our construction in Theorem 3 is essentially the best possible.

For parity functions, we give an $O(n^4)$ time algorithm which can PAC learn an unknown parity on k variables out of n using $\tilde{O}(n^{1-1/k})$ examples. To our knowledge this is the first algorithm for learning parity on a superconstant number of variables with sublinear sample complexity. Our algorithm works by finding a "low weight" solution to a system of m linear equations (corresponding to a set of m examples). We prove that with high probability we can find a solution of weight $O(n^{1-1/k})$ irrespective of m. Thus by taking m to be only slightly larger than $n^{1-1/k}$, standard arguments show that our solution is a good hypothesis.

We also describe a simple algorithm, due to Dan Spielman, for learning an unknown parity on k variables using $O(k \log n)$ examples and $\tilde{O}(n^{k/2})$ time. This gives a square root runtime improvement over a naive $O(n^k)$ exhaustive search.

1.2 Previous Results

In previous work several algorithms with different performance bounds (runtime and sample complexity) have been given for learning length-k decision lists.

[1] Krause [20] claims a lower bound of degree d and weight $2^{\Omega(n/d)}$ for a particular decision list; this claim, however, is in error.

- Rivest [28] gave the first algorithm for learning decision lists in Valiant's PAC model of learning from random examples. Littlestone [5] later gave an analogue of Rivest's algorithm in the online learning model. The algorithm can learn any decision list of length k in $O(kn^2)$ time using $O(kn)$ examples.
- A brute-force approach is to maintain the set of all length-k decision lists which are consistent with the examples seen so far, and to predict at each stage using majority vote over the surviving hypotheses. This "halving algorithm" (proposed in various forms in [1,2,24]) can learn decision lists of length k using only $O(k \log n)$ examples, but the running time is $n^{O(k)}$.
- Several researchers [5,33] have observed that Winnow can learn length-k decision lists from $2^{O(k)} \log n$ examples in time $2^{O(k)} n \log n$. This follows from the fact that any decision list of length k can be expressed as a linear threshold function with integer coefficients of magnitude $2^{\Theta(k)}$.
- Finally, several researchers have considered the special case of learning a length-k decision list in which the output bits of the list have at most D alternations. Valiant [33] and Nevo and El-Yaniv [26] have given refined analyses of Winnow's performance for this case (see also Dhagat and Hellerstein [10]). However, for the general case where D can be as large as k, these results do not improve on the standard Winnow analysis described above.

Note that all of these earlier algorithms have an exponential dependence on the relevant parameter(s) (k and $\log n$ for sample complexity, k for running time) for either the running time or the sample complexity.

Little previous work has been published on learning parity functions attribute efficiently in the PAC model. The standard PAC learning algorithm for parity (based on solving a system of linear equations) is due to Helmbold *et al.* [15]; however this algorithm is not attribute efficient since it uses $\Omega(n)$ examples regardless of k. Several authors have considered learning parity attribute efficiently in a model where the learner is allowed to make membership queries. Attribute efficient learning is easier in this framework since membership queries can help identify relevant variables. Blum et al. [7] give a randomized polynomial time membership-query algorithm for learning parity on k variables using only $O(k \log n)$ examples, and these results were later refined by Uehara *et al.* [32].

In Section 2 we give necessary background. In Section 3 we show how to reduce the decision list learning problem to a problem of finding suitable PTF representations of decision lists (Theorem 2). In Section 4 we give our PTF construction for decision lists (Theorem 3). In Section 5 we discuss the connection between Theorem 3 and Beigel's ODDMAXBIT lower bound. In Section 6 we give our results on learning parity functions, and we conclude in Section 7.

2 Preliminaries

Attribute efficient learning has been chiefly studied in the *on-line mistake-bound* model of concept learning which was introduced in [21,23]. In this model learning proceeds in a series of trials, where in each trial the learner is given an unlabelled boolean example $x \in \{0,1\}^n$ and must predict the value $f(x)$ of the unknown target function f. After each prediction the learner is given the true value of $f(x)$ and can update its hypothesis before the next trial begins. The *mistake bound* of a learning algorithm on a target concept c is the worst-case number of mistakes that the algorithm makes over all (possibly infinite) sequences of examples, and the mistake bound of a learning algorithm on a concept class (class of Boolean functions) C is the worst-case mistake bound across all functions $f \in C$. The running time of a learning algorithm A for a concept class C is defined as the product of the mistake bound of A on C times the maximum running time required by A to evaluate its hypothesis and update its hypothesis in any trial.

Our main interests are the classes of *decision lists* and *parity functions.* A decision list L of length k over the Boolean variables $x_1, \dots, x_n$ is represented by a list of k pairs and a bit $(\ell_1, b_1), (\ell_2, b_2), \dots, (\ell_k, b_k), b_{k+1}$ where each ℓ_i is a literal and each b_i is either -1 or 1. Given any $x \in \{0,1\}^n$, the value of $L(x)$ is b_i if i is the smallest index such that ℓ_i is made true by x; if no ℓ_i is true then $L(x) = b_{k+1}$. A parity function of length k is defined by a set of variables $S \subset \{x_1, \dots, x_n\}$ such that $|S| = k$. The parity function $\chi_S(x)$ takes value 1 (-1) on inputs which set an even (odd) number of variables in S to 1.

Given a concept class C over $\{0,1\}^n$ and a Boolean function $f \in C$, let size(f) denote the description length of f under some reasonable encoding scheme. We say that a learning algorithm A for C in the mistake-bound model is *attribute-efficient* if the mistake bound of A on any concept $f \in C$ is polynomial in size(f). In particular, the description length of a length k decision list (parity) is $O(k \log n)$, and thus we would ideally like to have poly(n)-time algorithms which learn decision lists (parities) of length k with a mistake bound of poly$(k, \log n)$.

(We note here that attribute efficiency has also been studied in other learning models, namely Valiant's Probably Approximately Correct (PAC) model of learning from random examples. Standard conversion techniques are known [1, 14,22] which can be used to transform any mistake bound algorithm into a PAC learning algorithm. These transformations essentially preserve the running time of the mistake bound algorithm, and the sample size required by the PAC algorithm is essentially the mistake bound. Thus, positive results for mistake bound learning, such as those we give for decision lists in this paper, directly yield corresponding positive results for the PAC model.)

Finally, our results for decision lists are achieved by a careful analysis of *polynomial threshold functions.* Let f be a Boolean function $f : \{0,1\}^n \to \{-1,1\}$ and let p be a polynomial in n variables with integer coefficients. Let d denote the degree of p and let W denote the sum of the absolute values of p's integer coefficients. If the sign of $p(x)$ equals $f(x)$ for every $x \in \{0,1\}^n$, then we say that p is a *polynomial threshold function (PTF) of degree d and weight W* for f.

3 Expanded-Winnow: Learning Polynomial Threshold Functions

Littlestone [21] introduced the online Winnow algorithm and showed that it can attribute efficiently learn Boolean conjunctions, disjunctions, and low weight linear threshold functions. Throughout its execution Winnow maintains a linear threshold function as its hypothesis; at the heart of the algorithm is an update rule which makes a multiplicative update to each coefficient of the hypothesis each time a mistake is made. Since its introduction Winnow has been intensively studied from both applied and theoretical standpoints (see e.g. [6,12,16,30]).

The following theorem (which, as noted in [33], is implicit in Littlestone's analysis in [21]) gives a mistake bound for Winnow for linear threshold functions:

Theorem 4. *Let $f(x)$ be the linear threshold function $sign(\sum_{i=1}^{n} w_i x_i - \theta)$ over inputs $x \in \{0,1\}^n$ where θ and $w_1, \ldots, w_n$ are integers. Let $W = \sum_{i=1}^{n} |w_i|$. Then Winnow learns $f(x)$ with mistake bound $O(W^2 \log n)$, and uses n time steps per example.*

We will use a generalization of the Winnow algorithm, which we call Expanded-Winnow, to learn *polynomial* threshold functions of degree at most d. Our generalization introduces $\sum_{i=1}^{d} \binom{n}{d}$ new variables (one for each monomial of degree up to d) and runs Winnow to learn a linear threshold function over these new variables. More precisely, in each trial we convert the n-bit received example $x = (x_1, \ldots, x_n)$ into a $\sum_{i=1}^{d} \binom{n}{d}$ bit expanded example (where the bits in the expanded example correspond to monomials over $x_1, \ldots, x_n$), and we give the expanded example to Winnow. Thus the hypothesis which Winnow maintains – a linear threshold function over the space of expanded features – is a polynomial threshold function of degree d over the original n variables $x_1, \ldots, x_n$. Theorem 2, which follows directly from Theorem 4, summarizes the performance of Expanded-Winnow:

Theorem 2 *Let C be a class of Boolean functions over $\{0,1\}^n$ with the property that each $f \in C$ has a polynomial threshold function of degree at most d and weight at most W. Then Expanded-Winnow algorithm runs in n^d time per example and has mistake bound $O(W^2 \cdot d \cdot \log n)$ for C.*

Theorem 2 shows that the degree of a polynomial threshold function strongly affects Expanded-Winnow's running time, and the weight of a polynomial threshold function strongly affects its sample complexity.

4 Constructing PTFs for Decision Lists

In previous constructions of polynomial threshold functions for computational learning theory applications [18,17,27] the sole goal has been to minimize the degree of the polynomials regardless of the size of the coefficients. As one example, the construction of [18] of $\tilde{O}(n^{1/3})$ degree PTFs for DNF formulae yields polynomials whose coefficients can be *doubly exponential* in the degree. In contrast, we must now construct PTFs that have low degree and low weight.

We give two constructions of PTFs for decision lists, each of which has relatively low degree and relatively low weight. We then combine these to achieve an optimal construction with improved bounds on both degree and weight.

4.1 Outer Construction

Let L be a decision list of length k over variables $x_1, \dots, x_k$. We first give a simple construction of a degree h, weight $\frac{2k}{h} 2^{(k/h+h)}$ PTF for L which is based on breaking the list L into sublists. We call this construction the "outer construction" since we will ultimately combine this construction with a different construction for the "inner" sublists.

We begin by showing that L can be expressed as a threshold of *modified decision lists* which we now define. The set $\mathcal{B}_h$ of modified decision lists is defined as follows: each function in $\mathcal{B}_h$ is a decision list $(\ell_1, b_1), (\ell_2, b_2), \dots, (\ell_h, b_h), 0$ where each ℓ_i is some literal over $x_1, \dots, x_n$ and each $b_i \in \{-1, 1\}$. Thus the only difference between a modified decision list $f \in \mathcal{B}_h$ and a normal decision list of length h is that the final output value is 0 rather than $b_{h+1} \in \{-1, +1\}$.

Without loss of generality we may suppose that the list L is $(x_1, b_1), \dots, (x_k, b_k), b_{k+1}$. We break L sequentially into k/h blocks each of length h. Let $f_i \in \mathcal{B}_h$ be the modified decision list which corresponds to the i-th block of L, i.e. f_i is the list $(x_{(i-1)h+1}, b_{(i-1)h+1}), \dots, (x_{(i+1)h}, b_{(i+1)h}), 0$. Intuitively f_i computes the ith block of L and equals 0 only if we "fall of the edge" of the ith block. We then have the following straightforward claim:

Claim. The decision list L is eqivalent to

$$\operatorname{sign}\left(\sum_{i=1}^{k/h} 2^{k/h-i+1} f_i(x) \; + \; b_{k+1} \right). \tag{1}$$

Proof. Given an input $x \neq 0^k$ let $r = (i-1)h + c$ be the first index such that x_r is satisfied. It is easy to see that $f_j(x) = 0$ for $j < i$ and hence the value in (1) is $2^{k/h-i+1} b_r + \sum_{j=i+1}^{k/h} 2^{k/h-j+1} f_j(x) \; + \; b_{k+1}$, the sign of which is easily seen to be b_r. Finally if $x = 0^k$ then the argument to (1) is b_{k+1}. □

Note: It is easily seen that we can replace the 2 in formula (1) by a 3; this will prove useful later.

As an aside, note that Claim 4.1 can already be used to obtain a tradeoff between running time and sample complexity for learning decision lists. The class $\mathcal{B}_h$ contains at most $(4n)^h$ functions. Thus as in Section 3 it is possible to run the Winnow algorithm using the functions in $\mathcal{B}_h$ as the base features for Winnow. (So for each example x which it receives, the algorithm would first compute the value of $f(x)$ for each $f \in \mathcal{B}_h$, and would then use this vector of $(f(x))_{f \in \mathcal{B}_h}$ values as the example point for Winnow.) A direct analogue of Theorem 2 now implies that Expanded-Winnow (run over this expanded feature space of functions from $\mathcal{B}_h$) can be used to learn L_k in time $n^{O(h)} 2^{O(k/h)}$ with mistake bound $2^{O(k/h)} h \log n$.

However, it will be more useful for us to obtain a PTF for L. We can do this from Claim 4.1 as follows:

Theorem 5. *Let L be a decision list of length k. For any $h < k$ we have that L is computed by a polynomial threshold function of degree h and weight $4 \cdot 2^{k/h+h}$.*

Proof. Consider the first modified decision list $f_1 = (\ell_1, b_1), (\ell_2, b_2), \ldots, (\ell_h, b_h), 0$ in the expression (1). For ℓ a literal let $\tilde{\ell}$ denote x if ℓ is an unnegated variable x and let $\tilde{\ell}$ denote $1 - x$ if if ℓ is a negated variable $\overline{x}$. We have that for all $x \in \{0,1\}^h$, $f_1(x)$ is computed exactly by the polynomial

$$f_1(x) = \tilde{\ell}_1 b_1 + (1-\tilde{\ell}_1)\tilde{\ell}_2 b_2 + (1-\tilde{\ell}_1)(1-\tilde{\ell}_2)\tilde{\ell}_3 b_3 + \cdots + (1-\tilde{\ell}_1)\cdots(1-\tilde{\ell}_{h-1})\tilde{\ell}_h b_h.$$

This polynomial has degree h and has weight at most 2^{h+1}. Summing these polynomial representations for $f_1, \ldots, f_{k/h}$ as in (1) we see that the resulting PTF given by (1) has degree h and weight at most $2^{k/h+1} \cdot 2^{h+1} = 4 \cdot 2^{k/h+h}$. □

Specializing to the case $h = \sqrt{k}$ we obtain:

Corollary 1. *Let L be a decision list of length k. Then L is computed by a polynomial threshold function of degree $k^{1/2}$ and weight $4 \cdot 2^{2k^{1/2}}$.*

We close this section by observing that an intermediate result of [18] can be used to give an alternate proof of Corollary 1 with slightly weaker parameters; however our later proofs require the construction given in this section.

4.2 Inner Approximator

In this section we construct low degree, low weight polynomials which approximate (in the L_∞ norm) the modified decision lists from the previous subsection. Moreover, the polynomials we construct are exactly correct on inputs which "fall off the end":

Theorem 6. *Let $f \in \mathcal{B}_h$ be a modified decision list of length h (without loss of generality we may assume that f is $(x_1, b_1), \ldots, (x_h, b_h), 0$). Then there is a degree $2\sqrt{h}\log h$ polynomial p such that*

- *for every input $x \in \{0,1\}^h$ we have $|p(x) - f(x)| \leq 1/h$.*
- *$p(0^h) = f(0^h) = 0$.*

Proof. As in the proof of Theorem 5 we have that

$$f(x) = b_1 x_1 + b_2(1-x_1)x_2 + \cdots + b_h(1-x_1)\cdots(1-x_{h-1})x_h.$$

We will construct a lower (roughly $\sqrt{h}$) degree polynomial which closely approximates f. Let T_i denote $(1-x_1)\ldots(1-x_{i-1})x_i$, so we can rewrite f as

$$f(x) = b_1 T_1 + b_2 T_2 + \cdots + b_h T_h.$$

We approximate each T_i separately as follows: set $A_i(x) = h - i + x_i + \sum_{j=1}^{i-1}(1-x_j)$. Note that for $x \in \{0,1\}^h$, we have $T_i(x) = 1$ iff $A_i(x) = h$ and $T_i(x) = 0$ iff $0 \leq A_i(x) \leq h-1$. Now define the polynomial

$$Q_i(x) = q\left(A_i(x)/h\right) \qquad \text{where} \qquad q(y) = C_d\left(y\left(1 + 1/h\right)\right).$$

As in [18], here $C_d(x)$ is the dth Chebyshev polynomial of the first kind (a univariate polynomial of degree d) with d set to $\lceil\sqrt{h}\rceil$. We will need the following facts about Chebyshev polynomials [9]:

- $|C_d(x)| \leq 1$ for $|x| \leq 1$ with $C_d(1) = 1$;
- $C'_d(x) \geq d^2$ for $x > 1$ with $C'_d(1) = d^2$.
- The coefficients of C_d are integers each of whose magnitude is at most 2^d.

These first two facts imply that $q(1) \geq 2$ but $|q(y)| \leq 1$ for $y \in [0, 1 - \frac{1}{h}]$. We thus have that $Q_i(x) = q(1) \geq 2$ if $T_i(x) = 1$ and $|Q_i(x)| \leq 1$ if $T_i(x) = 0$. Now define $P_i(x) = \left(\frac{Q_i(x)}{q(1)}\right)^{2 \log h}$. This polynomial is easily seen to be a good approximator for T_i: if $x \in \{0,1\}^h$ is such that $T_i(x) = 1$ then $P_i(x) = 1$, and if $x \in \{0,1\}^h$ is such that $T_i(x) = 0$ then $|P_i(x)| < \left(\frac{1}{2}\right)^{2 \log h} < \frac{1}{h^2}$.

Now define $R(x) = \sum_{i=1}^{\ell} b_i P_i(x)$ and $p(x) = R(x) - R(0^h)$. It is clear that $p(0^h) = 0$. We will show that for every input $0^h \neq x \in \{0,1\}^h$ we have $|p(x) - f(x)| \leq 1/h$. Fix some such x; let i be the first index such that $x_i = 1$. As shown above we have $P_i(x) = 1$. Moreover, by inspection of $T_j(x)$ we have that $T_j(x) = 0$ for all $j \neq i$, and hence $|P_j(x)| < \frac{1}{h^2}$. Consequently the value of $R(x)$ must lie in $[b_i - \frac{h-1}{h^2}, b_i + \frac{h-1}{h^2}]$. Since $f(x) = b_i$ we have that $p(x)$ is an L_∞ approximator for $f(x)$ as desired.

Finally, it is straightforward to verify that $p(x)$ has the claimed degree. □

Strictly speaking we cannot discuss the weight of the polynomial p since its coefficients are rational numbers but not integers. However, by multiplying p by a suitable integer (clearing denominators) we obtain an integer polynomial with essentially the same properties. Using the third fact about Chebyshev polynomials from our proof above, we have that $q(1)$ is a rational number N_1/N_2 where N_1, N_2 are each integers of magnitude $h^{O(\sqrt{h})}$. Each $Q_i(x)$ for $i = 1, \ldots, h$ can be written as an integer polynomial (of weight $h^{O(\sqrt{h})}$) divided by $h^{\sqrt{h}}$. Thus each $P_i(x)$ can be written as $\tilde{P}_i(x)/(h^{\sqrt{h}} N_1)^{2 \log h}$ where $\tilde{P}_i(x)$ is an integer polynomial of weight $h^{O(\sqrt{h} \log h)}$. It follows that $p(x)$ equals $\tilde{p}(x)/C$, where C is an integer which is at most $2^{O(h^{1/2} \log^2 h)}$ and $\tilde{p}$ is a polynomial with integer coefficients and weight $2^{O(h^{1/2} \log^2 h)}$. We thus have

Corollary 2. *Let $f \in \mathcal{B}_h$ be a modified decision list of length h. Then there is an integer polynomial $p(x)$ of degree $2\sqrt{h} \log h$ and weight $2^{O(h^{1/2} \log^2 h)}$ and an integer $C = 2^{O(h^{1/2} \log^2 h)}$ such that*

- *for every input $x \in \{0,1\}^h$ we have $|p(x) - Cf(x)| \leq C/h$.*
- *$p(0^h) = f(0^h) = 0$.*

The fact that $p(0^h)$ is exactly 0 will be important in the next subsection when we combine the inner approximator with the outer construction.

4.3 Composing the Constructions

In this section we combine the two constructions from the previous subsections to obtain our main polynomial threshold construction:

Theorem 7. *Let L be a decision list of length k. Then for any $h < k$, L is computed by a polynomial threshold function of degree $O(h^{1/2} \log h)$ and weight $2^{O(k/h + h^{1/2} \log^2 h)}$.*

Proof. We suppose without loss of generality that L is the decision list $(x_1, b_1), \ldots, (x_k, b_k), b_{k+1}$. We begin with the outer construction: from the note following Claim 4.1 we have that

$$L(x) = \operatorname{sign}\left(C \left[\sum_{i=1}^{k/h} 3^{k/h-i+1} f_i(x) \ + \ b_{k+1} \right] \right)$$

where C is the value from Corollary 2 and each f_i is a modified decision list of length h computing the restriction of L to its ith block as defined in Subsection 4.1. Now we use the inner approximator to replace each Cf_i above by p_i, the approximating polynomial from Corollary 2, i.e. consider $\operatorname{sign}(H(x))$ where

$$H(x) = \sum_{i=1}^{k/h} (3^{k/h-i+1} p_i(x)) \ + \ Cb_{k+1}.$$

We will show that $\operatorname{sign}(H(x))$ is a PTF which computes L correctly and has the desired degree and weight.

Fix any $x \in \{0,1\}^k$. If $x = 0^k$ then by Corollary 2 each $p_i(x)$ is 0 so $H(x) = Cb_{k+1}$ has the right sign. Now suppose that $r = (i-1)h + c$ is the first index such that $x_r = 1$. By Corollary 2, we have that

- $3^{k/h-j+1} p_j(x) = 0$ for $j < i$;
- $3^{k/h-i+1} p_i(x)$ differs from $3^{k/h-i+1} C b_r$ by at most $C 3^{k/h-i+1} \cdot \frac{1}{h}$;
- The magnitude of each value $3^{k/h-j+1} p_j(x)$ is at most $C 3^{k/h-j+1} (1 + \frac{1}{h})$ for $j > i$.

Combining these bounds, the value of $H(x)$ differs from $3^{k/h-i+1} C b_r$ by at most

$$C \left(\frac{3^{k/h-i+1}}{h} + \left(1 + \frac{1}{h}\right) \left[3^{k/h-i} + 3^{k/h-i-1} + \cdots + 3 \right] + 1 \right)$$

which is easily seen to be less than $C 3^{k/h-i+1}$ in magnitude. Thus the sign of $H(x)$ equals b_r, and consequently $\operatorname{sign}(H(x))$ is a valid polynomial threshold representation for $L(x)$. Finally, our degree and weight bounds from Corollary 2 imply that the degree of $H(x)$ is $O(h^{1/2} \log h)$ and the weight of $H(x)$ is $2^{O(k/h) + O(h^{1/2} \log^2 h)}$, and the theorem is proved. □

Taking $h = k^{2/3} / \log^{4/3} k$ in the above theorem we obtain our main result on representing decision lists as polynomial threshold functions:

Theorem 3 *Let L be a decision list of length k. Then L is computed by a polynomial threshold function of degree $k^{1/3} \log^{1/3} k$ and weight $2^{O(k^{1/3} \log^{4/3} k)}$.*

Theorem 3 immediately implies that Expanded-Winnow can learn decision lists of length k using $2^{\tilde{O}(k^{1/3})} \log n$ examples and time $n^{\tilde{O}(k^{1/3})}$.

4.4 Application to Learning Decision Trees

In 1989 Ehrenfeucht and Haussler [11] gave an a time $n^{O(\log s)}$ algorithm for learning decision trees of size s over n variables. Their algorithm uses $n^{O(\log s)}$ examples, and they asked if the sample complexity could be reduced to poly(n, s). We can apply our techniques here to give an algorithm using $2^{\tilde{O}(s^{1/3})} \log n$ examples, if we are willing to spend $n^{\tilde{O}(s^{1/3})}$ time:

Theorem 8. *Let D be a decision tree of size s over n variables. Then D can be learned with mistake bound $2^{\tilde{O}(s^{1/3})} \log n$ in time $n^{\tilde{O}(s^{1/3})}$.*

The proof is omitted because of space limitations in these proceedings.

5 Lower Bounds for Decision Lists

Here we observe that our construction from Theorem 7 is essentially optimal in terms of the tradeoff it achieves between polynomial threshold function degree and weight.

In [3], Beigel constructs an oracle separating PP from P^{NP}. At the heart of his construction is a proof that any low degree PTF for a particular decision list, called the $\mathrm{ODDMAXBIT}_n$ function, must have large weights:

Definition 1. *The $\mathrm{ODDMAXBIT}_n$ function on input $x = x_1, \ldots, x_n \in \{0, 1\}^n$ equals $(-1)^i$ where i is the index of the first nonzero bit in x.*

It is clear that the $\mathrm{ODDMAXBIT}_n$ function is equivalent to a decision list $(x_1, -1), (x_2, 1), (x_3, -1), \ldots, (x_n, (-1)^n), (-1)^{n+1}$ of length n. The main technical theorem which Beigel proves in [3] states that any polynomial threshold function of degree d computing $\mathrm{ODDMAXBIT}_n$ must have weight $2^{\Omega(n/d^2)}$:

Theorem 9. *Let p be a degree d PTF with integer coefficients which computes $\mathrm{ODDMAXBIT}_n$. Then $w = 2^{\Omega(n/d^2)}$ where w is the weight of p.*

(As stated in [3] the bound is actually $w \geq \frac{1}{s} 2^{\Omega(n/d^2)}$ where s is the number of nonzero coefficients in p. Since $s \leq w$ this implies the result as stated above.)

A lower bound of $2^{\Omega(n)}$ on the weight of any linear threshold function ($d = 1$) for $\mathrm{ODDMAXBIT}_n$ has long been known [25]; Beigel's proof generalizes this lower bound to all $d = O(n^{1/2})$. A matching upper bound of $2^{O(n)}$ on weight for $d = 1$ has also long been known [25]. Our Theorem 7 gives an upper bound which matches Beigel's lower bound (up to logarithmic factors) for all $d = O(n^{1/3})$:

Observation 10 *For any $d = O(n^{1/3})$ there is a polynomial threshold function of degree d and weight $2^{\tilde{O}(n/d^2)}$ which computes $\mathrm{ODDMAXBIT}_n$.*

Proof. Set $d = h^{1/2} \log h$ in Theorem 7. The weight bound given by Theorem 7 is $2^{O(\frac{n \log^2 d}{d^2} + d \log d)}$ which is $\tilde{O}(n/d^2)$ for $d = O(n^{1/3})$. □

Note that since the $\mathrm{ODDMAXBIT}_n$ function has a polynomial size DNF, Beigel's lower bound gives a polynomial size DNF f such that any degree $\tilde{O}(n^{1/3})$ polynomial threshold function for f must have weight $2^{\tilde{\Omega}(n^{1/3})}$. This suggests that the Expanded-Winnow algorithm cannot learn polynomial size DNF in $2^{\tilde{O}(n^{1/3})}$ time from $2^{n^{1/3-\epsilon}}$ examples for any $\epsilon > 0$, and thus suggests that improving the sample complexity of the DNF learning algorithm from [18] while maintaining its $2^{\tilde{O}(n^{1/3})}$ running time may be difficult.

6 Learning Parity Functions

6.1 A Polynomial Time Algorithm

Recall that the standard algorithm for learning parity functions works by viewing a set of m labelled examples as a set of m linear equations over GF(2). Gaussian elimination is used to solve the system and thus find a consistent parity. Even though there exists a solution of weight at most k (since the target parity is of size k), Gaussian elimination applied to a system of m equations in n variables over $GF(2)$ may yield a solution of weight as large as $\min(m, n)$. Thus this standard algorithm and analysis give an $O(n)$ sample complexity bound for learning a parity of length at most k.

We now describe a simple poly(n)-time algorithm for PAC learning an unknown size-k parity using $\tilde{O}(n^{1-1/k})$ examples. As far as we know this is the first improvement on the standard algorithm and analysis described above.

Theorem 11. *The class of all parity functions on at most k variables is PAC learnable in $O(n^4)$ time using $O(n^{1-1/k} \log n)$ examples. The hypothesis output by the learning algorithm is a parity function on $O(n^{1-1/k})$ variables.*

Proof. If $k = \Omega(\log n)$ then the standard algorithm suffices to prove the claimed bound. We thus assume that $k = o(\log n)$.

Let H be the set of all parity functions of size at most $n^{1-1/k}$. Note that $|H| \leq n^{n^{1-1/k}}$ so $\log |H| \leq n^{1-1/k} \log n$. Consider the following algorithm:

1. Choose $m = 1/\epsilon(\log |H| + \log(1/\delta))$ examples. Express each example as a linear equation over n variables mod 2 as described above.
2. Randomly choose a set of $n - n^{1-1/k}$ variables and assign them the value 0.
3. Use Gaussian elimination to attempt to solve the resulting system of equations on the remaining $n^{1-1/k}$ variables. If the system has a solution, output the corresponding parity (of size at most $n^{1-1/k}$) as the hypothesis. If the system has no solution, output "FAIL."

If the simplified system of equations has a solution, then by a standard Occam's Razor argument this solution is a good hypothesis. We will show that the simplified system has a solution with probability $\Omega(1/n)$. The theorem follows by repeating steps 2 and 3 of the above algorithm until a solution is found (an expected $O(n)$ repetitions will suffice).

Let V be the set of k relevant variables on which the unknown parity function depends. It is easy to see that as long as no variable in V is assigned a 0, the resulting simplified system of equations will have a solution. Let $\ell = n^{1-1/k}$. The probability that in Step 2 the $n-\ell$ variables chosen do not include any variables in V is exactly $\binom{n-k}{n-\ell}/\binom{n}{\ell}$ which equals $\binom{n-k}{\ell-k}/\binom{n}{\ell}$. Expanding binomial coefficients we have

$$\frac{\binom{n-k}{\ell-k}}{\binom{n}{\ell}} = \prod_{i=1}^{k} \frac{\ell-k+i}{n-k+i} > \left(\frac{\ell-k}{n-k}\right)^k = \left(\frac{\ell}{n}\right)^k \left(\frac{1-\frac{k}{\ell}}{1-\frac{k}{n}}\right)^k$$
$$= \frac{1}{n} \cdot \left[\left(1-\frac{k}{\ell}\right)\left(1+\frac{2k}{n}\right)\right]^k > \frac{1}{n}\left(1-\frac{k}{\ell}\right)^k > \frac{1}{n}\left(1-\frac{k^2}{\ell}\right) > \frac{1}{2n}$$

which proves the theorem. □

6.2 An $\tilde{O}(n^{k/2})$ Time Attribute Efficient Algorithm

Dan Spielman [31] has observed that it is possible to improve on the n^k time bound of a naive search algorithm for learning parity using $k \log n$ examples:

Theorem 12 (Spielman). *The class of all size-k parity functions is PAC learnable in $\tilde{O}(n^{k/2})$ time from $O(k \log n)$ examples, using size-k parities as the hypothesis class.*

Proof. By Occam's Razor we need only show that given a set of $m = O(k \log n)$ labelled examples, a consistent size-k parity can be found in $\tilde{O}(n^{k/2})$ time.

Given a labelled example $(x_1, \dots, x_n; y)$ we will view y as an $(n+1)$st attribute x_{n+1}. Thus our task is to find a set of $(k+1)$ attributes $x_{i_1}, \dots, x_{i_{k+1}}$, one of which must be x_{n+1}, which sum to 0 in every example in the sample.

Let $(x^1; y_1), \dots (x^m; y_m)$ be the labelled examples in our sample. Given a subset S of variables, let v_S denote the length-m binary vector $(\chi_S(x^1), \dots, \chi_S(x^m))$ obtained by computing the parity function χ_S on each example in our sample.

We construct two lists, each containing $\binom{n}{k/2}$ vectors of length m. The first list contains all the vectors v_S where S ranges over all $k/2$-element subsets of $\{x_1, \dots, x_n\}$. The second list contains all the vectors $v_{S \cup \{x_{n+1}\}}$ where S again ranges over all $k/2$-element subsets of $\{x_1, \dots, x_n\}$.

After sorting these two lists of vectors, which takes $\tilde{O}(n^{k/2})$ time, we scan through them in parallel in time linear in the length of the lists and find a pair of vectors v_{S_1} from the first list and $v_{S_2 \cup \{x_{n+1}\}}$ from the second list which are the same. (Note that any decomposition of the target parity into two subsets S_1 and S_2 of $k/2$ variables each will give such a pair). The set $S_1 \cup S_2$ is then a consistent parity of size k. □

7 Future Work

An obvious goal for future work is to improve our algorithmic results for learning decision lists. As a first step, one might attempt to extend the tradeoffs we achieve: is it possible to learn decision lists of length k in $n^{k^{1/2}}$ time from poly$(k, \log n)$ examples?

Another goal is to extend our results for decision lists to broader concept classes. In particular, it would be interesting to obtain analogues of our algorithmic results for learning general linear threshold functions (independent of their weight). We note here that Goldmann *et al.* [13] have given a linear threshold function over $\{-1,1\}^n$ for which any polynomial threshold function must have weight $2^{\Omega(n^{1/2})}$ regardless of its degree. Moreover Krause and Pudlak [19] have shown that any Boolean function which has a polynomial threshold function over $\{0,1\}^n$ of weight w has a polynomial threshold function over $\{-1,1\}^n$ of weight n^2w^4. These results imply that *representational* results akin to Theorem 3 for general linear threshold functions must be quantitatively weaker than Theorem 3; in particular, there is a linear threshold function over $\{0,1\}^n$ with k nonzero coefficients for which any polynomial threshold function, regardless of degree, must have weight $2^{\Omega(k^{1/2})}$.

For parity functions many questions remain as well: can we learn parity functions on $k = \Theta(\log n)$ variables in polynomial time using a sublinear number of examples? Can we learn size-k parities in polynomial time using fewer than $n^{1-1/k}$ examples? Can we learn size-k parities from $O(k \log n)$ examples in time $\tilde{O}(n^{k/3})$? Progress on any of these fronts would be quite interesting.

Acknowledgements. We thank Les Valiant for his observation that Claim 4.1 can be reinterpreted in terms of polynomial threshold functions, and we thank Jean Kwon for suggesting the Chebychev polynomial. We thank Dan Spielman for allowing us to include his proof of Theorem 12.

References

[1] D. Angluin. Queries and concept learning. *Machine Learning*, 2:319–342, 1988.
[2] J. Barzdin and R. Freivald. On the prediction of general recursive functions. *Soviet Mathematics Doklady*, 13:1224–1228, 1972.
[3] R. Beigel. When do extra majority gates help? polylog(n) majority gates are equivalent to one. *Computational Complexity*, 4:314–324, 1994.
[4] A. Blum. Learning boolean functions in an infinite attribute space. In *Proceedings of the Twenty-Second Annual Symposium on Theory of Computing*, pages 64–72, 1990.
[5] A. Blum. On-line algorithms in machine learning. available at `http://www.cs.cmu.edu/~avrim/Papers/pubs.html`, 1996.
[6] A. Blum. Empirical support for winnow and weighted-majority algorithms: results on a calendar scheduling domain. *Machine Learning*, 26:5–23, 1997.
[7] A. Blum, L. Hellerstein, and N. Littlestone. Learning in the presence of finitely or infinitely many irrelevant attributes. *Journal of Computer and System Sciences*, 50:32–40, 1995.
[8] A. Blum and P. Langley. Selection of relevant features and examples in machine learning. *Artificial Intelligence*, 97(1-2):245–271, 1997.
[9] E. Cheney. *Introduction to approximation theory.* McGraw-Hill, New York, New York, 1966.

[10] A. Dhagat and L. Hellerstein. Pac learning with irrelevant attributes. In *Proceedings of the Thirty-Fifth Annual Symposium on Foundations of Computer Science*, pages 64–74, 1994.
[11] A. Ehrenfeucht and D. Haussler. Learning decision trees from random examples. *Information and Computation*, 82(3):231–246, 1989.
[12] A.R. Golding and D. Roth. A winnow-based approach to spelling correction. *Machine Learning*, 34:107–130, 1999.
[13] M. Goldmann, J. Hastad, and A. Razborov. Majority gates vs. general weighted threshold gates. *Computational Complexity*, 2:277–300, 1992.
[14] D. Haussler. Space efficient learning algorithms. Technical Report UCSC-CRL-88-2, University of California at Santa Cruz, 1988.
[15] D. Helmbold, R. Sloan, and M. Warmuth. Learning integer lattices. *SIAM Journal on Computing*, 21(2):240–266., 1992.
[16] J. Kivinen, M. Warmuth, and P. Auer. The perceptron algorithm vs. winnow: linear vs. logarithmic mistake bounds when few input variables are relevant. *Artificial Intelligence*, 97(1-2):325–343, 1997.
[17] A. Klivans, R. O'Donnell, and R. Servedio. Learning intersections and thresholds of halfspaces. In *Proceedings of the 43rd Annual Symposium on Foundations of Computer Science*, 2002.
[18] A. Klivans and R. Servedio. Learning dnf in time $2^{\tilde{o}(n^{1/3})}$. In *Proceedings of the Thirty-Third Annual Symposium on Theory of Computing*, pages 258–265, 2001.
[19] M. Krause and P. Pudlak. Computing boolean functions by polynomials and threshold circuits. *Computational Complexity*, 7(4):346–370, 1998.
[20] Matthias Krause. On the computational power of boolean decision lists. *Lecture Notes in Computer Science (STACS 2002)*, 2285, 2002.
[21] N. Littlestone. Learning quickly when irrelevant attributes abound: a new linear-threshold algorithm. *Machine Learning*, 2:285–318, 1988.
[22] N. Littlestone. From online to batch learning. In *Proceedings of the Second Annual Workshop on Computational Learning Theory*, pages 269–284, 1989.
[23] N. Littlestone. *Mistake bounds and logarithmic linear-threshold learning algorithms.* PhD thesis, University of California at Santa Cruz, 1989.
[24] T. Mitchell. Generalization as search. *Artificial Intelligence*, 18:203–226, 1982.
[25] J. Myhill and W. Kautz. On the size of weights required for linear-input switching functions. *IRE Trans. on Electronic Computers*, EC10(2):288–290, 1961.
[26] Z. Nevo and R. El-Yaniv. On online learning of decision lists. *Journal of Machine Learning Research*, 3:271–301, 2002.
[27] R. O'Donnell and R. Servedio. New degree bounds for polynomial threshold functions. Proceedings of the 35th ACM Symposium on Theory of Computing, 2003.
[28] R. Rivest. Learning decision lists. *Machine Learning*, 2(3):229–246, 1987.
[29] R. Servedio. Computational sample complexity and attribute-efficient learning. *Journal of Computer and System Sciences*, 60(1):161–178, 2000.
[30] R. Servedio. Perceptron, Winnow and PAC learning. *SIAM Journal on Computing*, 31(5):1358–1369, 2002.
[31] D. Spielman. Personal communication, 2003.
[32] R. Uehara, K. Tsuchida, and I. Wegener. Optimal attribute-efficient learning of disjunction, parity, and threshold functions. In *Proceedings of the Third European Conference on Computational Learning Theory*, pages 171–184, 1997.
[33] L. Valiant. Projection learning. *Machine Learning*, 37(2):115–130, 1999.

Learning Over Compact Metric Spaces

H. Quang Minh[1] and Thomas Hofmann[2]

[1] Department of Mathematics
Brown University, Providence RI 02912-1917 USA
minh@math.brown.edu
[2] Department of Computer Science
Brown University, Providence RI 02912-1910, USA
th@cs.brown.edu

Abstract. We consider the problem of learning on a compact metric space X in a functional analytic framework. For a dense subalgebra of $Lip(X)$, the space of all Lipschitz functions on X, the Representer Theorem is derived. We obtain exact solutions in the case of least square minimization and regularization and suggest an approximate solution for the Lipschitz classifier.

1 Introduction

One important direction of current machine learning research is the generalization of the Support Vector Machine paradigm to handle the case where the input space is an arbitrary metric space. One such generalization method was suggested recently in [2], [5]: we embed the input space X into a Banach space E and the hypothesis space of decisions functions on X into the dual space E^* of linear functionals on E. In [5], the hypothesis space is $Lip(X)$, the space of all bounded Lipschitz functions on X. The input space X itself is embedded into the space $AE(X_0)$ of molecules on X_0, which up to isometry, is the largest Banach space that X embeds into isometrically [6].

The Representer Theorem, which is essential in the formulation of the solutions of Support Vector Machines, was, however, not achieved in [2]. In order to obtain this theorem, it is necessary to restrict ourselves to subspaces of $Lip(X)$ consisting of functions of a given explicit form. In this paper, we introduce a general method for deriving the Representer Theorem and apply it to a dense subalgebra of $Lip(X)$. We then use the theorem to solve a problem of least square minimization and regularization on the subalgebra under consideration. Our approach can be considered as a generalization of the Lagrange polynomial interpolation formulation. It is substantially different from that in [5], which gives solutions that are minimal Lipschitz extensions (section 6.1).

Throughout the paper, (X, d) will denote a compact metric space and $S = \{(x_i, y_i)\}_{i=1}^n \subset (X \times \mathbb{R})^n$ a sample of length n.

J. Shawe-Taylor and Y. Singer (Eds.): COLT 2004, LNAI 3120, pp. 239–254, 2004.

1.1 The Representer Theorem

The Representer Theorem is not magic, neither is it an exclusive property of Support Vector Machines and Reproducing Kernel Hilbert Spaces. It is a direct consequence of the fact that our training data is finite. A general method to derive the Representer Theorem is as follows. Let $\mathcal{F}$ be a normed space of real-valued functions on X. Consider the evaluation operator

$$A_S : \mathcal{F} \to \mathbb{R}^n \tag{1}$$

defined by

$$A_S(f) = (f(x_1), \dots, f(x_n)) \tag{2}$$

Consider the problem of minimizing the following functional over $\mathcal{F}$:

$$I_S(f) = \sum_{i=1}^{n} V(f(x_i), y_i) \tag{3}$$

with V being a convex, lower semicontinuous loss function. Let $ker(A_S)$ denote the kernel of the map A_S, defined by

$$ker(A_S) = \{f \in \mathcal{F} : A_S(f) = (f(x_1), \dots, f(x_n)) = (0, \dots, 0)\} \tag{4}$$

Clearly, the problem of minimizing I_S over $\mathcal{F}$ is equivalent to minimizing I_S over the quotient space $\mathcal{F}/ker(A_S)$, which being isomorphic to the image $Im(A_S) \subset \mathbb{R}^n$, is finite dimensional. Let $\mathcal{F}_n$ be the complementary subspace of $ker(A_S)$

$$\mathcal{F} = \mathcal{F}_n \oplus ker(A_S) \tag{5}$$

that is a linear subspace of $\mathcal{F}$ such that $\mathcal{F}_n \cap ker(A_S) = \{0\}$ and every $f \in \mathcal{F}$ admits a unique decomposition

$$f = f_n + r \tag{6}$$

where $f_n \in \mathcal{F}_n$ and $r \in ker(A_S)$. Clearly we have $f - f_n \in ker(A_S)$. Consider the equivalent relation on the quotient space $\mathcal{F}/ker(A_S)$ defined by

$$f \sim f_0 \Longleftrightarrow f \in [f_0] \Longleftrightarrow A_S f = A_S f_0 \Longleftrightarrow f - f_0 \in ker(A_S) \tag{7}$$

Thus $f \sim f_0$ iff they have the same projection onto $\mathcal{F}_n$. Hence $\mathcal{F}/ker(A_S) \cong \mathcal{F}_n$ via the identification.

$$[f] \to f_n \tag{8}$$

We are led to the following fundamental result:

Theorem 1. *There is* ***always*** *a minimizer of I_S, if one exists, lying in a finite dimensional subspace $\mathcal{F}_n$ of $\mathcal{F}$, with dimension at most n. The space $\mathcal{F}_n$ is the complementary subspace of $ker(A_S)$.*

Proof. From the preceding discussion, it clearly follows that the problem of minimizing I_S over $\mathcal{F}$ is equivalent to minimizing I_S over the subspace $\mathcal{F}_n$. This subspace has dimension at most n

$$dim(\mathcal{F}_n) = dim(\mathcal{F}/ker(A_S)) \leq n$$

Thus if I_S has minimizers in $\mathcal{F}$, then it must have one minimizer lying in $\mathcal{F}_n$. □

Corollary 1. *Suppose the problem of minimizing I_S over $\mathcal{F}_n$ has a set of solutions F^*, then the set of all minimizers of I_S over $\mathcal{F}$ has the form*

$$F^* + ker(A_S) = \{f^* + r \mid f^* \in F^*, r \in ker(A_S)\} \tag{9}$$

Proof. This is obvious. □

Consider now the problem of minimizing the regularized functional

$$I_{S,\gamma}(f) = \sum_{i=1}^{n} V(f(x_i), y_i) + \gamma \Omega(f) \tag{10}$$

where Ω is a strictly convex, coercive functional on $\mathcal{F}$. We have another key result:

Theorem 2. *The functional $I_{S,\gamma}$ has a unique minimizer in $\mathcal{F}$. Assume further that the regularizer Ω satisfies:*

$$\Omega(f) = \Omega(f_n + r) \geq \Omega(f_n) \tag{11}$$

for all $f \in \mathcal{F}$, where $f_n \in \mathcal{F}_n$ and $r \in ker(A_S)$. Then this minimizer lies in the finite dimensional subspace $\mathcal{F}_n$.

Proof. The existence and uniqueness of the minimizer f^* is guaranteed by the coercivity and strict convexity of the regularizer Ω, respectively. If furthermore, $\Omega(f_n + r) \geq \Omega(f_n)$ then for all $f \in \mathcal{F}$:

$$I_{S,\gamma}(f) \geq I_{S,\gamma}(f_n)$$

Thus a function f^* minimizing $I_{S,\gamma}$ must lie in the finite dimensional subspace $\mathcal{F}_n$ of $\mathcal{F}$. □

Without the assumption of strict convexity and coercivity of the functional Ω, we can no longer state the uniqueness or existence of the minimizer, but we still have the following result

Theorem 3. *Suppose the functional Ω satisfies*

$$\Omega(f) = \Omega(f_n + r) \geq \Omega(f_n) \tag{12}$$

for all $f \in \mathcal{F}$, where $f_n \in \mathcal{F}_n$ and $r \in ker(A_S)$, with equality iff $r = 0$. If the problem of minimizing $I_{S,\gamma}$ over $\mathcal{F}$ has a solution f^*, it must lie in the finite dimensional subspace $\mathcal{F}_n$.

Proof. This is similar to the above theorem. □

Having the above key results, the Representer Theorem can then be obtained if we can exhibit a basis for the above finite dimensional subspace $\mathcal{F}_n$ via the data points x_i $(1 \leq i \leq n)$.

Example 1 (RKHS). Let $\mathcal{F} = \mathcal{H}_K$ be the reproducing kernel Hilbert space induced by a Mercer kernel K, then from the reproducing property $f(x) = \langle f, K(x,.)\rangle$, it follows that

$$ker(A_S) = span\{K(x_i,.)_{i=1}^n\}^\perp$$

From the unique orthogonal decomposition

$$\mathcal{H}_K = span\{K(x_i,.)_{i=1}^n\} \oplus span\{K(x_i,.)_{i=1}^n\}^\perp$$

it follows that $\mathcal{F}_n = span\{K(x_i,.)_{i=1}^n\}$. □

In section 2, we apply the above framework to derive the Representer Theorem for the special case $\mathcal{F}$ is the vector space of all algebraic polynomials on a compact subset of the real line $\mathbb{R}$. We then generalize this result to the case of a general compact metric space in sections 3 and 4.

2 Learning Over Compact Subsets of $\mathbb{R}$

Let $X \subset \mathbb{R}$ be compact. Let $P(X)$ be the vector space of all algebraic polynomials on X, then $P(X)$ is dense in $C(X)$ according to Weierstrass Approximation Theorem:

Theorem 4 (Weierstrass Approximation Theorem). *Each continuous function $f \in C(X)$ is uniformly approximable by algebraic polynomials: for each $\epsilon > 0$, there is a polynomial $p \in P(X)$ such that*

$$|f(x) - p(x)| < \epsilon \tag{13}$$

for all $x \in X$.

Consider the problem of minimizing the functional I_S over $P(X)$.

Lemma 1.

$$ker(A_S) = \{f \in P(X) : f(x) = (x - x_1)\dots(x - x_n)r_n(x)\} \tag{14}$$

for some $r_n \in P(X)$. Let $P_n(X) = span\{1, (x - x_1), (x - x_1)(x - x_2), \dots, (x - x_1)\dots(x - x_{n-1})\}$, then $P(X)$ admits the following unique decomposition

$$P(X) = P_n(X) \oplus ker(A_S) \tag{15}$$

Proof. First we note that $f \in ker(A_S) \iff (f(x_1), \dots, f(x_n)) = (0, \dots, 0)$ iff x_i $(1 \leq i \leq n)$ is a zero of f iff f contains the linear factor $(x - x_i)$ $(1 \leq i \leq n)$, hence the form of $ker(A_S)$.

To prove the unique decomposition, we apply the Taylor expansion to f, with centers $x_1, \dots, x_n$ successively:

$$f(x) = c_0 + (x - x_1)r_1(x) = c_0 + (x - x_1)[c_1 + (x - x_2)r_2(x)]$$
$$= c_0 + c_1(x - x_1) + (x - x_1)(x - x_2)r_2(x) = \cdots =$$
$$= c_0 + c_1(x - x_1) + c_2(x - x_1)(x - x_2) + \ldots + c_{n-1}(x - x_1)\ldots(x - x_{n-1})$$
$$+(x - x_1)\ldots(x - x_n)r_n(x)$$

with $c_i \in \mathbb{R}$ $(0 \leq i \leq n-1)$. □

The basis $\{\prod_{j=1}^{i}(x - x_j)\}_{i=0}^{n-1}$ for $P_n(X)$ is not symmetric in the x_i's. Let us construct a symmetric basis for this subspace.

Lemma 2.

$$P_n(X) = span\{\prod_{j \neq i}(x - x_j)\}_{i=1}^{n} \tag{16}$$

Proof. Let $f = \sum_{i=0}^{n-1} c_i \prod_{j=1}^{i}(x - x_j)$. Define the function

$$g^*(x) = \sum_{i=1}^{n} d_i \prod_{j \neq i}(x - x_j) \tag{17}$$

with

$$d_i = \frac{\sum_{j=0}^{i-1} c_j \prod_{k=1}^{j}(x_i - x_k)}{\prod_{j \neq i}(x_i - x_j)} \tag{18}$$

It is straightforward to verify that $f^*(x_i) = g^*(x_i)$ $(1 \leq i \leq n)$. Since f^* and g^* have degree $n-1$, it follows that $f^* = g^*$. □

We arrive at the following Representer Theorem for the space $P(X)$:

Theorem 5 (Representer Theorem). *The problem of minimizing the functional I_S over space $P(X)$ is equivalent to minimizing I_S over the finite-dimensional subspace $P_n(X) = span\{\prod_{j \neq i}(x - x_j)\}_{i=1}^{n}$. Suppose the latter problem has a set of solutions F^*, then the set of all minimizers of $I_S(f)$ over $P(X)$ has the form:*

$$F^* + ker(A_S) = \{f^* + (x - x_1)\ldots(x - x_n)r_n \,|f^* \in F^*, r_n \in P(X)\} \tag{19}$$

Each $f^* \in F^*$ admits a unique representation:

$$f^* = \sum_{i=1}^{n} c_i \prod_{j \neq i}(x - x_j) \tag{20}$$

for $c_i \in \mathbb{R}$ $(1 \leq i \leq n)$.

Proof. This is a special case of theorem 1, with $\mathcal{F}_n = P_n(X)$. □

3 The Stone-Weierstrass Theorem

Let us now consider the general case where X is a compact metric space. We then have Stone's generalization of Weierstrass Approximation Theorem. For a very accessible treatment of this topic, we refer to [1].

Definition 1 (Algebra). *A real algebra is a vector space $\mathcal{A}$ over $\mathbb{R}$ together with a binary operation representing multiplication: $x, y \in \mathcal{A} \to xy \in \mathcal{A}$ satisfying:*

(i) Bilinearity: for all $a, b \in \mathbb{R}$ and all $x, y, z \in \mathcal{A}$:

$$(a.x + b.y)z = a.xz + b.yz$$

$$x(a.y + b.z) = a.xy + b.xz$$

(ii) Associativity: $x(yz) = (xy)z$

The multiplicative identity, if it exists, is called the unit of the algebra. An algebra with unit is called a unital algebra. A complex algebra over $\mathbb{C}$ is defined similarly.

Definition 2 (Normed algebra-Banach algebra). *A normed algebra is a pair $(\mathcal{A}, || \ ||)$ consisting of an algebra $\mathcal{A}$ together with a norm $|| \ || : \mathcal{A} \to [0, \infty)$ satisfying*

$$||xy|| \leq ||x|| \, ||y|| \tag{21}$$

A Banach algebra is a normed algebra that is a Banach space relative to its given norm.

Example 2. $C(X)$: Let X be a compact Hausdorff space. We have the unital algebra $C(X)$ of all real-valued functions on X, with multiplication and addition being defined pointwise:

$$fg(x) = f(x)g(x) \text{ and } (f + g)(x) = f(x) + g(x)$$

Relative to the supremum norm $|| \ ||_\infty$, $C(X)$ is a commutative Banach algebra with unit.

Definition 3 (Separation). *Let X be a metric space. Let $\mathcal{A}$ be a set of real-valued functions on X. $\mathcal{A}$ is said to separate the points of X if for each pair x, y of distinct points of X there exists a function $f \in \mathcal{A}$ such that $f(x) \neq f(y)$.*

Theorem 6 (Stone-Weierstrass Theorem). *Let X be a compact metric space and $\mathcal{A}$ a subalgebra of $C(X)$ that contains the constant functions and separates the points of X. Then $\mathcal{A}$ is dense in the Banach space $C(X)$.*

4 Learning Over Compact Metric Spaces

Let (X, d) be a compact metric space containing at least two points.

Proposition 1. *Let $\mathcal{A}$ be the subalgebra of $C(X)$ generated by the family*

$$\{1, \phi_x : t \to d(x,t)\}_{x \in X} \tag{22}$$

where 1 denote the constant function with value 1, then $\mathcal{A}$ is dense in $C(X)$.

Proof. By the Stone-Weierstrass Theorem, we need to verify that $\mathcal{A}$ separates the points of X. Let t_1, t_2 be two distinct points in X, so that $d(t_1, t_2) \neq 0$. Suppose that $d(x, t_1) = d(x, t_2)$ for all $x \in X$. Let $x = t_1$, we then obtain:

$$d(t_1, t_2) = d(t_1, t_1) = 0$$

a contradiction. Thus there must exist $x \in X$ such that $d(x, t_1) \neq d(x, t_2)$, showing that $\mathcal{A}$ separates the points in X. □

Consider the algebra $\mathcal{A}$ defined in the above proposition and the problem of minimizing I_S over $\mathcal{A}$.

Lemma 3. *Each $f \in \mathcal{A}$ can be expressed in the form:*

$$f = g + d(x_1, .) \dots d(x_n, .) f_{n+1} \tag{23}$$

where

$$g = f_1 + d(x_1, .)f_2 + d(x_1, .)d(x_2, .)f_3 + \dots + d(x_1, .)d(x_2, .) \dots d(x_{n-1}, .)f_n \tag{24}$$

and $f_{n+1} \in \mathcal{A}$, $f_i \in \mathcal{A}/\langle d(x_i, .)\rangle$ with $\langle d(x_i, .)\rangle$ being the ideal generated by $d(x_i, .)$, $1 \leq i \leq n$.

Proof. This is similar to a Taylor expansion: clearly there is $f_i \in \mathcal{A}/\langle d(x_i, .)\rangle$ such that

$$f = f_1 + d(x_1, .)r_1 = f_1 + d(x_1, .)[f_2 + d(x_2, .)r_2]$$
$$= f_1 + d(x_1, .)f_2 + d(x_1, .)d(x_2, .)r_2$$

Continuing in this way we obtain the lemma. □

Since $f(x_i) = g(x_i)$ $(1 \leq i \leq n)$, minimizing I_S over $\mathcal{A}$ is equivalent to minimizing I_S over all f of the form:

$$f = f_1 + d(x_1, .)f_2 + d(x_1, .)d(x_2, .)f_3 + \dots + d(x_1, .)d(x_2, .) \dots d(x_{n-1}, .)f_n \tag{25}$$

with $f_i \in \mathcal{A}/\langle d(x_i, .)\rangle$. From the above equation, we obtain for $1 \leq i \leq n$:

$$f(x_i) = \sum_{j=1}^{i} f_j(x_i) \prod_{k=1}^{j-1} d(x_k, x_i) \tag{26}$$

It is straightforward to verify that

$$f = \sum_{k=1}^{n} \sum_{i=k}^{n} f_k(x_i) \frac{\prod_{j \neq i} d(x_j, .)}{\prod_{j=k, j \neq i}^{n} d(x_j, x_i)} \tag{27}$$

From the above general expression for f, it follows that there are constants $c_i \in \mathbb{R}$ $(1 \leq i \leq n)$ such that

$$f = \sum_{i=1}^{n} c_i \prod_{j \neq i} d(x_j, .) \tag{28}$$

Let $P_n(X)$ denote the n-dimensional subspace of $\mathcal{A}$ defined by

$$P_n(X) = span\{\prod_{j \neq i} d(x_j, .)\}_{i=1}^{n} \tag{29}$$

We have proved the following theorem:

Theorem 7 (Representer Theorem). *The problem of minimizing the functional I_S over $\mathcal{A}$ is equivalent to minimizing I_S over the n-dimensional subspace $P_n(X) = span\{\prod_{j \neq i} d(x_j, .)\}_{i=1}^{n}$. Suppose the latter problem has a set of solutions F^*, then the set of minimizer of I_S over $\mathcal{A}$ has the form*

$$\{f^* + d(x_1, .) \ldots d(x_n, .) f_{n+1} : f^* \in F^*, f_{n+1} \in \mathcal{A}\} \tag{30}$$

Each $f^* \in F^*$ admits a unique representation

$$f^* = \sum_{i=1}^{n} c_i \prod_{j \neq i} d(x_j, .) \tag{31}$$

for $c_i \in \mathbb{R}$ $(1 \leq i \leq n)$. Let Ω be as in theorem 2, then the problem of minimizing the functional $I_{S,\gamma}$ over $\mathcal{A}$ has a unique solution lying in $P_n(X)$.

Proof. This is a special case of theorems 1 and 2, with $\mathcal{F}_n = P_n(X)$. □

We now show that the algebra $\mathcal{A}$ consists of Lipschitz functions and that it is dense in the space $Lip(X)$ of all Lipschitz functions on X, in the supremum norm:

Lemma 4. *For each $x \in X$, the function $\phi_x : t \to d(x, t)$ is Lipschitz with Lipschitz constant $L(\phi_x) = 1$.*

Proof. Let $t_1, t_2 \in X$. From the triangle inequality, we have:

$d(x, t_1) \leq d(x, t_2) + d(t_2, t_1) \Rightarrow d(x, t_1) - d(x, t_2) \leq d(t_1, t_2)$

Similarly, we have $d(x, t_2) - d(x, t_1) \leq d(t_1, t_2)$. It follows that

$|\phi_x(t_1) - \phi_x(t_2)| = |d(x, t_1) - d(x, t_2)| \leq d(t_1, t_2)$

with equality iff $t_1 = x$ or $t_2 = x$. Thus ϕ_x is a Lipschitz function with Lipschitz constant $L(\phi_x) = 1$. □

Proposition 2. *Let X be a compact metric space and $\mathcal{A}$ defined as above. Then $\mathcal{A}$ consists of Lipschitz functions and $\mathcal{A}$ is dense in $Lip(X)$ in the supremum norm.*

Proof. Since Lipschitz functions are closed under addition, scalar multiplication, and for X bounded, pointwise multiplication (see appendix), it follows from the above lemma that $\mathcal{A}$ consists of Lipschitz functions, that is $\mathcal{A}$ is a subalgebra of $Lip(X)$. Since for compact X, both $\mathcal{A}$ and $Lip(X)$ are dense in $C(X)$ in the supremum norm, it follows that $\mathcal{A}$ is dense in $Lip(X)$ in the supremum norm. □

5 Least Square Minimization and Regularization

5.1 Least Square Minimization

Let $S = \{(x_i, y_i)\}_{i=1}^n \in (X \times \mathbb{R})^n$ be a training sample of length n. Consider the problem of minimizing the empirical square error over $\mathcal{A}$:

$$I_S(f) = \frac{1}{n}\sum_{i=1}^{n}(f(x_i) - y_i)^2 \tag{32}$$

or equivalently

$$I_S(f) = \sum_{i=1}^{n}(f(x_i) - y_i)^2 \tag{33}$$

By the Representer Theorem, this is equivalent to minimizing the functional $I_S(f)$ over the finite dimensional subspace $P_n(X)$. Let $f = \sum_{i=1}^n c_i \prod_{j\neq i} d(x_j, .) \in Lip(X)$. Let

$$M_i = \prod_{j\neq i} d(x_j, x_i)$$

then clearly

$$f(x_i) = c_i M_i$$

Theorem 8. *The problem of minimizing the functional $I_S(f)$ over the finite dimensional subspace $P_n(X)$ has a unique solution*

$$f^* = \sum_{i=1}^{n} \frac{y_i}{M_i}\prod_{j\neq i} d(x_j, .) = \sum_{i=1}^{n} y_i \frac{\prod_{j\neq i} d(x_j, .)}{\prod_{j\neq i} d(x_j, x_i)} \tag{34}$$

Proof. Each $f \in P_n(X)$ has the form: $f = \sum_{i=1}^n c_i \prod_{j\neq i} d(x_j, .)$. Thus

$$f(x_i) = c_i \prod_{j\neq i} d(x_j, x_i) = c_i M_i$$

Clearly the smallest value that $I_S(f)$ assumes is zero, which occurs iff

$$f(x_i) = y_i \Longleftrightarrow c_i M_i = y_i \Longleftrightarrow c_i = \frac{y_i}{M_i}$$

This gives us the desired minimizer f^*. □

Remark 1. Let $\phi_i(x) = \frac{\prod_{j\neq i} d(x_j,.)}{\prod_{j\neq i} d(x_j,x_i)}$, then we have

$$\phi_i(x_j) = \delta_{ij} \text{ and } f^*(x) = \sum_{i=1}^n y_i \phi_i(x)$$

In the case $X \subset \mathbb{R}$, these functions are precisely the Lagrange interpolation polynomials and we recover the Lagrange interpolation formula.

5.2 Least Square Regularization

The minimization process above always gives an exact interpolation, which may lead to the undesirable phenomenon of overfitting. Hence we consider the following regularization problem. Each function $f \in \mathcal{A}$ has the form $f = \sum_{J\subset I} c_J \prod_{j\in J} d(x_j,.)$ where I is a finite index set. Consider the functional $\Omega : \mathcal{A} \to \mathbb{R}$ defined by

$$\Omega(f) = \sum_{J\subset I} |c_J|^2 \tag{35}$$

Lemma 5. *Let $f \in \mathcal{A}$ with the decomposition: $f = g + d(x_1,.)\dots d(x_n,.)f_{n+1}$ where $g \in P_n(X)$ and $f_{n+1} \in \mathcal{A}$. Then $\Omega(f) = \Omega(g) + \Omega(f_{n+1})$.*

Proof. This is obvious. □

Lemma 6. *The functional Ω is strictly convex.*

Proof. This follows from the strict convexity of the square function. □

Lemma 7. *Let $f = \sum_{J\subset I} c_J \prod_{j\in J} d(x_j,.) \in \mathcal{A}$. Then*

$$||f||_\infty \leq \sum_{J\subset I} |c_J| diam(X)^{|J|} \leq (\sum_{J\subset I} diam(X)^{2|J|})^{1/2} (\sum_{J\subset I} |c_J|^2)^{1/2} \tag{36}$$

The functional Ω is coercive in the supremum norm:

$$\lim_{||f||_\infty \to\infty} \Omega(f) = \infty \tag{37}$$

Proof. We have

$$||\prod_{j\in J} d(x_j,.)||_\infty \leq diam(X)^{|J|}$$

It follows that

$$||f||_\infty \leq \sum_{J \subset I} |c_J| diam(X)^{|J|} \leq (\sum_{J \subset I} diam(X)^{2|J|})^{1/2} (\sum_{J \subset I} |c_J|^2)^{1/2}$$

Thus $||f||_\infty \to \infty$ implies that $\sum_{J \subset I} |c_J|^2 \to \infty$ as well, showing that Ω is coercive in the supremum norm. □

Lemma 8. *Let* $f = d(x_1, .) \ldots d(x_k, .)$. *Then*

$$L(f) \leq k diam(X)^{k-1} \tag{38}$$

Let $f = \sum_{J \subset I} c_J \prod_{j \in J} d(x_j, .)$. *Then there is a constant* $C > 0$ *such that*

$$L(f) \leq C \sum_{J \subset I} |c_J| \leq C (\sum_{J \subset I} 1)^{1/2} (\sum_{J \subset I} |c_J|^2)^{1/2} \tag{39}$$

In particular, for $f = \sum_{i=1}^n c_i \prod_{j \neq i} d(x_j, .)$, *we have*

$$L(f) \leq C \sum_{i=1}^n |c_i| \leq C \sqrt{n} (\sum_{i=1}^n |c_i|^2)^{1/2} \tag{40}$$

Proof. The first inequality follows from a standard induction argument. This and the Cauchy-Schwarz inequality imply the other inequalities. □

Consider the problem of minimizing the regularized functional:

$$I_{S,\gamma}(f) = \sum_{i=1}^n (f(x_i) - y_i)^2 + \gamma \Omega(f) \tag{41}$$

with regularization parameter $\gamma > 0$. By lemmas 7 and 8, this regularization process aims to minimize $\sum_{i=1}^n (f(x_i) - y_i)^2$ and penalize $||f||_\infty$ and $L(f)$ simultaneously.

Theorem 9. *The problem of minimizing the regularized functional* $I_{S,\gamma}(f)$ *over the algebra* $\mathcal{A}$ *has a unique solution* f^* *which lies in the finite dimensional subspace* $P_n(X)$:

$$f^* = \sum_{i=1}^n \frac{y_i M_i}{\gamma + M_i^2} \prod_{j \neq i} d(x_j, .) \tag{42}$$

Proof. The functional Ω is strictly convex and coercive in the supremum norm on $\mathcal{A}$ and satisfies $\Omega(f) = \Omega(g) + \Omega(f_{n+1}) \geq \Omega(g)$. Thus by the Representer Theorem, there is a unique solution minimizing $I_{S,\gamma}(f)$, which lies in the finite dimensional subspace $P_n(X)$. We have for $f \in P_n(X)$:

$$I_{S,\gamma}(f) = \sum_{i=1}^n [(c_i M_i - y_i)^2 + \gamma c_i^2] = \sum_{i=1}^n [c_i^2 (\gamma + M_i^2) - 2 c_i M_i y_i + y_i^2]$$

Differentiating and setting $\frac{\partial I}{c_i} = 2c_i(\gamma + M_i^2) - 2M_i y_i = 0$, we obtain

$$c_i = \frac{y_i M_i}{\gamma + M_i^2}$$

as claimed. □

6 The Lipschitz Classifier

Let $(x_i, y_i)_{i=1}^n \subset (X \times \{\pm 1\})^n$ be a set of training data, with the assumption that both classes ± 1 are present. Let $X_0 = X \cup \{e\}$ where e is a distinguished base point with the metric $d^{X_0}|_{X \times X} = d$ and $d^{X_0}(x, e) = diam(X)$ for $x \in X$. It is straightforward to show that

Proposition 3 ([5]). *Lip(X) is isometrically isomorphic to $Lip_0(X_0)$ via the map $\psi : Lip(X) \to Lip_0(X_0)$ defined by $(\psi f)(x) = f(x)$ for $x \in X$ and $(\psi f)(e) = 0$. One has $||f||_L = L(\psi f)$.*

Proposition 4 ([6]). *X embeds isometrically into the Banach space $AE(X_0)$, via the map $\Phi(x) = m_x = m_{xe} = \chi_x - \chi_e$. $Lip_0(X_0)$ embeds isometrically into the dual space $AE(X_0)^*$, via the map $T : Lip_0(X_0) \to AE(X_0)^*$ defined by $\langle Tf, m\rangle = \sum_{x \in X} f(x)m(x)$ for all $f \in Lip_0(X_0)$, all $m \in AE(X_0)$. Clearly $f(x) = \langle Tf, m_x\rangle$ for all $x \in X$.*

The problem of finding a decision function $f \in Lip(X)$ separating the points x_i's in X is then equivalent to that of finding the corresponding linear functional $Tf \in AE(X_0)^*$ separating the corresponding molecules m_{x_i}, that is a hyperplane Hf defined by $Hf = \{m \in AE(X_0) : \langle Tf, m\rangle = 0\}$. It is straightforward to show the following

Proposition 5 (Margin of the Lipschitz Classifier [5]). *Assume that the hyperplane is normalized such that $\min_{1 \le i \le n} |f(x_i)| = 1$ and suppose that $y_i f(x_i) \ge 1$ $(1 \le i \le n)$. Then*

$$\rho = \inf_{1 \le i \le n, m_h \in Hf} ||m_{x_i} - m_h||_{AE} \ge \frac{1}{L(f)} \tag{43}$$

Thus the following algorithm then corresponds to a large margin algorithm in the space $AE(X_0)$:

Algorithm 1 ([5])

$$Minimize_{f \in Lip(X)} L(f) \quad \textit{subject to } y_i f(x_i) \ge 1 \ (1 \le i \le n) \tag{44}$$

The solutions of this algorithm are precisely the minimal Lipschitz extensions of the function $f : \{x_i\}_{i=1}^n \to \{\pm 1\}$ with $f(x_i) = y_i$, as we show below.

6.1 Minimal Lipschitz Extensions

The following was shown simultaneously in 1934 by McShane [4] and Whitney [7].

Proposition 6 (Minimal Lipschitz Extension-MLE). *Let (X, d) denote an arbitrary metric space and let E be any nonempty subset of X. Let $f : E \to \mathbb{R}$ be a Lipschitz function. Then there exists a **minimal Lipschitz extension** of f to X, that is a Lipschitz function $h : X \to \mathbb{R}$ such that $h|_E = f$ and $L(h) = L(f)$.*

Proof. Two such minimal Lipschitz extensions were constructed explicitly in [4] and [7]:

$$\overline{f}(x) = \inf_{y \in E}\{f(y) + L(f)d(x,y)\} \tag{45}$$

$$\underline{f}(x) = \sup_{y \in E}\{f(y) - L(f)d(x,y)\} \tag{46}$$

Furthermore, if u is any minimal Lipschitz extension of f to X, then for all $x \in X$:

$$\underline{f}(x) \leq u(x) \leq \overline{f}(x) \tag{47}$$

We refer to the above references for detail. □

Let us return to the classification problem. Let $E = \{x_i\}_{i=1}^n$ and $f : E \to \{\pm 1\}$ be defined by $f(x_i) = y_i$. Let X^+ and X^- denote the sets of training points with positive and negative labels, respectively. Let $d(X^+, X^-) = \inf_{x \in X^+, x' \in X^-} d(x, x')$. It is straightforward to see that f is Lipschitz with Lipschitz constant $L^* = \frac{2}{d(X^+,X^-)}$. The above proposition gives two of f's minimal Lipschitz extensions:

$$\overline{f}(x) = \min_i\{y_i + L^* d(x, x_i)\} \text{ and } \underline{f}(x) = \max_i\{y_i - L^* d(x, x_i)\}$$

These are precisely the solutions of the above algorithm in [5].

Remark 2. The notion of minimal Lipschitz extension is not completely satisfactory. Firstly, it is not unique. Secondly, and more importantly, it involves only the global Lipschitz constant and ignores what may happen locally. For a discussion of this phenomenon, we refer to [3].

6.2 A Variant of the Lipschitz Classifier

The problem of computing the Lipschitz constants for a class of functions is nontrivial in general. It is easier to obtain an upper bound for $L(f)$ and minimize it instead. Let us consider this approach with the algebra $\mathcal{A}$, which is dense in $Lip(X)$ in the supremum norm as shown above.

From the above upper bound on $L(f)$, instead of minimizing $L(f)$, we can minimize $\sum_{J \subset I} |c_J|$. We obtain the following algorithm:

Algorithm 2

$$Minimize_{I \subset \mathbb{N}} \sum_{J \subset I} |c_J| \; subject\ to\ y_i f(x_i) \geq 1 \; (1 \leq i \leq n) \tag{48}$$

The functional $\Omega : \mathcal{A} \to \mathbb{R}$ defined by

$$\Omega(f) = \sum_{J \subset I} |c_J| \tag{49}$$

clearly satisfies $\Omega(g + d(x_1, .) \dots d(x_n, .)f_{n+1}) \geq \Omega(g)$ for all $g \in P_n(X)$ and $f_{n+1} \in \mathcal{A}$, with equality iff $f_{n+1} = 0$. Thus by theorem 3, we have the equivalent problem:

Algorithm 3

$$\textit{Minimize} \sum_{i=1}^{n} |c_i| \ \textit{subject to} \ y_i c_i M_i \geq 1 \ (1 \leq i \leq n) \tag{50}$$

According to lemma 7, the functional Ω is coercive in the $|| \ ||_\infty$ norm, thus the problem has a solution. Let us show that it is unique and find its explicit form.

Theorem 10. *The above minimization problem has a unique solution*

$$f^* = \sum_{i=1}^{n} \frac{y_i}{M_i} \prod_{j \neq i} d(x_j, .) = \sum_{i=1}^{n} y_i \frac{\prod_{j \neq i} d(x_j, .)}{\prod_{j \neq i} d(x_j, x_i)} \tag{51}$$

Proof. $\sum_{i=1}^{n} |c_i|$ is obviously minimum when $y_i c_i M_i = 1$, implying that

$$c_i = \frac{y_i}{M_i}$$

as we claimed. □

Remark 3. Clear we have $f(x_i) = y_i$. From lemma 8, we have $L(f) \leq C \sum_{i=1}^{n} |c_i|$. Thus it follows that

$$\rho \geq \frac{1}{L(f)} \geq \frac{1}{C} \frac{1}{\sum_{i=1}^{n} |c_i|}$$

Thus the above algorithm can also be viewed as a large margin algorithm as well.

7 Conclusion

We presented a general method for deriving the Representer Theorem in learning algorithms. The method is applied to a dense subalgebra of the space of Lipschitz functions on a general compact metric space X. We then used the Representer Theorem to obtain solutions to several special minimization and regularization problems. This approach may be used to obtain solutions when minimizing other functionals over other function spaces as well. We plan to continue with a more systematic regularization method and comprehensive analysis of our approach in future research.

A Lipschitz Functions and Lipschitz Spaces

We review some basic properties of Lipschitz functions and the corresponding function spaces. For detail treatment we refer to [6]. Let X be a metric space. A function $f : X \to \mathbb{R}$ (or $\mathbb{C}$) is called Lipschitz if there is a constant L such that for all $x, y \in X$:

$$|f(x) - f(y)| \leq Ld(x, y) \tag{52}$$

The smallest such L is called the Lipschitz constant of f, denoted by $L(f)$. We have

$$L(f) = \sup_{x \neq y} \frac{|f(x) - f(y)|}{d(x, y)} \tag{53}$$

Proposition 7 ([6]). *Let X be a metric space and f, g, f_n ($n \in \mathbb{N}$) be Lipschitz functions from X into $\mathbb{R}$ (or $\mathbb{C}$). Then:*

(a) $L(af) = |a|L(f)$ for all $a \in \mathbb{R}$

(b) $L(f + g) \leq L(f) + L(g)$

Proposition 8 ([6]). *Let X be a metric space and $f, g : X \to \mathbb{R}$ ($\mathbb{C}$) be bounded Lipschitz functions. Then*

(a) $L(fg) \leq ||f||_\infty L(g) + ||g||_\infty L(f)$

(b) If $diam(X) < \infty$, then the product of any two scalar-valued Lipschitz functions is again Lipschitz.

Definition 4 ([6]). *Let X be a metric space. $Lip(X)$ is the space of all bounded Lipschitz functions on X equipped with the Lipschitz norm:*

$$||f||_L = \max\{||f||_\infty, L(f)\}$$

If $\mathcal{X}$ is a bounded metric space, that is $diam(X) < \infty$, we follow [5] and define:

$$||f||_L = \max\{\tfrac{||f||_\infty}{diam(X)}, L(f)\}$$

Theorem 11 ([6]). *$Lip(X)$ is a Banach space. If X is compact, then $Lip(X)$ is dense in $C(X)$ in the supremum norm.*

Definition 5. *Let X_0 be a pointed metric space, with a distinguished base point e. Then we define*

$$Lip_0(X_0) = \{f \in Lip(X_0) : f(e) = 0\} \tag{54}$$

On this space, $L(f)$ is a norm.

Definition 6 (Arens-Eells Space). *Let X be a metric space. A* **molecule** *of X is a function $m : X \to \mathbb{R}$ (or $\mathbb{C}$) that is supported on a finite set of X and that satisfies:*

$$\sum_{x \in \mathcal{X}} m(x) = 0$$

For $x, y \in X$, define the molecule $m_{xy} = \chi_x - \chi_y$, where χ_x and χ_y denote the characteristic functions of the singleton sets $\{x\}$ and $\{y\}$. On the set of molecules, consider the norm:

$$||m||_{AE} = \inf\{\sum_{i=1}^{n} |a_i| d(x_i, y_i) : m = \sum_{i=1}^{n} a_i m_{x_i y_i}\}$$

The Arens-Eells space $AE(X)$ is defined to be the completion of the space of molecules under the above norm.

References

1. D. Bridges, *Foundations of Real and Abstract Analysis*, Graduate Texts in Mathematics 174, Springer, New York, 1998.
2. M. Hein and O. Bousquet, Maximal Margin Classification for Metric Spaces, *Proceedings of the 16th Conference on Learning Theory (COLT 2003)*, Washington DC, August 2003.
3. P. Juutinen, Absolutely Minimizing Lipschitz Extensions on a Metric Space, *Annales Academiæ Scientiarum Fennicæ Mathematica*, vol. 27, pages 57-67, 2002.
4. E.J. McShane, Extension of Range of Functions, *Bulletin of the American Mathematical Society*, vol. 40, pages 837-842, 1934.
5. U. von Luxburg and O. Bousquet, Distance-Based Classification with Lipschitz Functions, *Proceedings of the 16th Conference on Learning Theory (COLT 2003)*, Washington DC, August 2003.
6. N. Weaver, *Lipschitz Algebras*, World Scientific, Singapore, 1999.
7. H. Whitney, Analytic Extensions of Differentiable Functions Defined in Closed Sets, *Transactions of the American Mathematical Society*, vol. 36, no. 1, pages 63-89, 1934.

A Function Representation for Learning in Banach Spaces*

Charles A. Micchelli[1] and Massimiliano Pontil[2]

[1] Department of Mathematics and Statistics
State University of New York, The University at Albany
1400 Washington Avenue, Albany, NY, 12222, USA
cam@math.albany.edu
[2] Department of Computer Sciences
University College London
Gower Street, London WC1E 6BT, England, UK
m.pontil@cs.ucl.ac.uk

Abstract. Kernel–based methods are powerful for high dimensional function representation. The theory of such methods rests upon their attractive mathematical properties whose setting is in Hilbert spaces of functions. It is natural to consider what the corresponding circumstances would be in Banach spaces. Led by this question we provide theoretical justifications to enhance kernel–based methods with function composition. We explore regularization in Banach spaces and show how this function representation naturally arises in that problem. Furthermore, we provide circumstances in which these representations are dense relative to the uniform norm and discuss how the parameters in such representations may be used to fit data.

1 Introduction

Kernel–based methods have in recent years been a focus of attention in Machine Learning. They consist in choosing a kernel $K : D \times D \to \mathbb{R}$ which provides functions of the form

$$\sum_{j \in \mathbb{Z}_m} c_j K(x_j, \cdot) \tag{1.1}$$

whose parameters $D_m = \{x_j : j \in \mathbb{Z}_m\} \subseteq D$ and $c = \{c_j : j \in \mathbb{Z}_m\} \subset \mathbb{R}$ are used to learn an unknown function f. Here, we use the notation $\mathbb{Z}_m = \{0, \ldots, m-1\}$. Typically K is chosen to be a reproducing kernel of some Hilbert space. Although this is *not* required, it does provide (1.1) with a Hilbert space justification. The *simplicity* of the functional form (1.1) and its ability to address *efficiently high dimensional* learning tasks make it very attractive. Since it arises from Hilbert space considerations it is natural to inquire what may transpire in other Banach spaces. The goal of this paper is to study this question, especially learning algorithms based on regularization in a Banach space. A consequence

* This work was supported by NSF Grant No. ITR-0312113.

J. Shawe-Taylor and Y. Singer (Eds.): COLT 2004, LNAI 3120, pp. 255–269, 2004.

of our remarks here is that *function composition* should be introduced in the representation (1.1). That is, we suggest the use of the *nonlinear* functional form

$$\phi\left(\sum_{j\in\mathbb{Z}_m} c_j g_j\right) \tag{1.2}$$

where $\phi : \mathbb{R} \to \mathbb{R}$ and for $j \in Z_m$, $g_j : D \to \mathbb{R}$ are prescribed functions, for example (but not necessarily so) $g_j = K(x_j, \cdot)$. In section 2 we provide an *abstract* framework where in a particular case the functional form (1.2) naturally arises. What we say here is a compromise between the generality in which we work and our desire to provide useful functional forms for Machine Learning.

We consider the problem of learning a function f in a Banach space from a set of continuous linear functionals $L_j(f) = y_j$, $j \in \mathbb{Z}_m$. Typically in Machine Learning there is available function values for learning, that is, the L_j are point evaluation functionals. However, there are many practical problems where such information is not readily available, for example tomography or EXAFS spectroscopy, [15]. Alternatively, it may be of practical advantage to use "local" averages of f as observed information. This idea is investigated in [23, c. 8] in the context of support vector machines. Perhaps, even more compelling is the question of what may be the "best" m observations that should be made to learn a function. For example, is it better to know function values or Fourier coefficients of a periodic function? These and related questions are addressed in [18] and lead us here to deal with linear functionals other than function values for Machine Learning.

We are especially interested in the case when the samples y_j, $j \in \mathbb{Z}_m$ are known to be noisy so that it is appropriate to estimate f as the minimizer in some Banach space of a regularization functional of the form

$$E(f) := \sum_{j\in\mathbb{Z}_m} Q(y_j, L_j(f)) + H(\|f\|) \tag{1.3}$$

where $H : \mathbb{R}_+ \to \mathbb{R}_+$ is a strictly increasing function, and $Q : \mathbb{R} \times \mathbb{R} \to \mathbb{R}_+$ is some prescribed *loss function*. If the Banach space is a reproducing kernel Hilbert space, the linear functionals $L_j, j \in \mathbb{Z}_m$ are chosen to be point evaluations. In this case a minimizer of (1.3) has the form in equation (1.1), a fact which is known as the representer theorem, see e.g. [22,25], which we generalize here to any Banach space.

We note that the problem of minimizing a regularization functional of the form (1.3) in a *finite dimensional* Banach has been considered in the case of support vector machines in [1] and in more general cases in [26]. Finite dimensional Banach spaces have been also considered in the context of on–line learning, see e.g. [9]. Learning in infinite dimensional Banach spaces has also been considered. For example, [7] considers learning a univariate function in L_p spaces, [2] addresses learning in non–Hilbert spaces using point evaluation with kernels, and [24,6] propose large margin algorithms in a metric input space by embedding this space into certain Banach spaces of functions.

Since the functions (1.2) do not form a linear space as we vary $c \in \mathbb{R}^m$, we may also enhance them by *linear superposition* to obtain functions of the form

$$\sum_{j \in \mathbb{Z}_n} a_j \phi \left(\sum_{k \in \mathbb{Z}_m} c_{jk} g_k \right) \tag{1.4}$$

where $\{a_j : j \in \mathbb{Z}_n\} \subset \mathbb{R}$ and $\{c_{jk} : j \in \mathbb{Z}_n, k \in \mathbb{Z}_m\} \subset \mathbb{R}$ are real–valued parameters. This functional form has flexibility and simplicity. In particular, when the functions $\{g_j : j \in \mathbb{Z}_{m+1}\}$ are chosen to be a basis for *linear functions* on $\mathbb{R}^m$, (1.4) corresponds to feed–forward neural networks with one hidden layer, see for example [12].

In section 3 we address the problem of when functions of the form in equation (1.4) are dense in the space of continuous functions in the uniform norm. Finally, in section 4 we present some preliminary thoughts about the problem of choosing the parameters in (1.4) from prescribed linear constraints.

2 Regularization and Minimal Norm Interpolation

Let $\mathcal{X}$ be a Banach space and $\mathcal{X}^*$ its dual, that is, the space of bounded linear functionals $L : \mathcal{X} \to \mathbb{R}$ with the norm $\|L\| := \sup\{L(x) : \|x\| \leq 1\}$. Given a set of examples $\{(L_j, y_j) : j \in \mathbb{Z}_m\} \subset \mathcal{X} \times \mathbb{R}$ and a prescribed function $V : \mathbb{R}^m \times \mathbb{R}_+ \to \mathbb{R}$ which is *strictly increasing* in its last argument (for every choice of its first argument) we consider the problem of minimizing the functional $E : \mathcal{X} \to \mathbb{R}$ defined for $x \in \mathcal{X}$ as

$$E(x) := V\left((L_j(x) : j \in \mathbb{Z}_m), \|x\|\right) \tag{2.5}$$

over all elements x in $\mathcal{X}$ (here V contains the information about the y_j). A special case of this problem is covered by a functional of the form (1.3). Suppose that x_0 is the solution to the above problem, x is any element of $\mathcal{X}$ such that $L_j(x) = y_j, j \in \mathbb{Z}_m$ where we set $y_j := L_j(x_0), j \in \mathbb{Z}_m$. By the definition of x_0 we have that

$$V(y, \|x_0\|) \leq V(y, \|x\|)$$

and so

$$\|x_0\| = \min\{\|x\| : L_j(x) = y_j, j \in \mathbb{Z}_m,\ x \in \mathcal{X}\}. \tag{2.6}$$

This observation is the motivation for our study of problem (2.6) which is usually called minimal norm interpolation. Note that this conclusion even holds when $\|x\|$ is replaced by *any* functional of x.

We make no claim for originality in our ensuing remarks about this problem which have been chosen to show the usefulness of the representation (1.2). Indeed, we are roaming over well–trodden ground.

Thus, given data $\{y_j : j \in \mathbb{Z}_m\} \subset \mathbb{R}\backslash\{0\}$, we consider the minimum norm interpolation (MNI) problem

$$\mu := \inf\left\{\|x\| : L_j(x) = y_j,\ j \in \mathbb{Z}_m,\ x \in \mathcal{X}\right\}. \tag{2.7}$$

We always require in (2.7) that corresponding to the prescribed data $y := (y_j : j \in \mathbb{Z}_m)$ there is at least one $x \in \mathcal{X}$ for which the linear constraints in (2.7) are satisfied. In addition, we may assume that the linear functionals $\{L_j : j \in \mathbb{Z}_m\}$ are *linearly independent.* This means that whenever $a := (a_j : j \in \mathbb{Z}_m)$ is such that $\sum_{j \in \mathbb{Z}_m} a_j L_j = 0$ then $a = 0$. Otherwise, we can "thin" the set of linear functionals to a linearly independent set.

We say that the linear functional $L \in \mathcal{X}^* \backslash \{0\}$ *peaks* at $x \in \mathcal{X} \backslash \{0\}$, if $L(x) = \|L\| \|x\|$. Let us also say that x peaks at L, if L peaks at x. A consequence of the Hahn–Banach Theorem, see for example [21, p. 223], is that for *every* $x \in \mathcal{X}$ there always exists an $L \in \mathcal{X}^*$ which peaks at x and so, $\|x\| = \max\{L(x) : \|L\| \leq 1, L \in \mathcal{X}^*\}$, see [21, p. 226, Prop. 6]. On the other hand, the supremum in the definition of $\|L\|$ is not always achieved, unless L peaks at some $x \in \mathcal{X} \backslash \{0\}$. We also recall that $\mathcal{X}$ is *weakly compact* if, for every *norm bounded* sequence $\{x_n : n \in \mathbb{Z}_+\} \subset \mathcal{X}$ there exists a *weakly* convergent subsequence $\{x'_n : n \in \mathbb{N}\}$, that is, there is an $x \in \mathcal{X}$ such that for every $L \in \mathcal{X}^*$ $\lim_{n \to \infty} L(x'_n) = L(x)$. When $\mathcal{X}$ is weakly compact then for *every* $L \in \mathcal{X}^*$ there is always an $x \in \mathcal{X}$ which peaks at L. Recall that a Banach space $\mathcal{X}$ is reflexive, that is, $(\mathcal{X}^*)^* = \mathcal{X}$ if and only if $\mathcal{X}$ is weakly compact, see [16, p. 127, Thm. 3.6] and it is known that any weakly compact normed linear spaces always admit a minimal norm interpolant.

If $\mathcal{M}$ is a closed subspace of $\mathcal{X}$, we define the distance of x to $\mathcal{M}$ as

$$d(x, \mathcal{M}) := \min\{\|x - t\| : t \in \mathcal{M}\}.$$

In particular, if we choose $\mathcal{M}_0 := \{x : x \in \mathcal{X}, L_j(x) = 0, j \in \mathbb{Z}_m\}$ and *any* $w \in \mathcal{X}$ such that $L_j(w) = y_j, j \in \mathbb{Z}_m$ then we have that

$$d(w, \mathcal{M}_0) = \mu. \tag{2.8}$$

Theorem 1. *x_0 is a solution of (2.7) if and only if $L_j(x_0) = y_j, j \in \mathbb{Z}_m$ and there exists $(c_j : j \in \mathbb{Z}_m) \in \mathbb{R}^m$ such that the linear functional $\sum_{j \in \mathbb{Z}_m} c_j L_j$ peaks at x_0.*

Proof. We choose in (2.8) $w = x_0$ so that $L_j(x_0) = y_j, j \in \mathbb{Z}_m$ and $\|x_0\| = d(x_0, \mathcal{M}_0)$. Using the basic duality principle for the distance (2.8), see for example [8], we conclude that

$$\|x_0\| = \max\{L(x_0) : L(x) = 0,\ x \in \mathcal{M}_0, \|L\| \leq 1\}. \tag{2.9}$$

However, L vanishes on $\mathcal{M}_0$ if and only if there exists $(c_j : j \in \mathbb{Z}_m) \in \mathbb{R}^m$ such that $L = \sum_{j \in \mathbb{Z}_m} c_j L_j$ and by (2.9) there is such an L which peaks at x_0.

On the other hand, if for some $(c_j : j \in \mathbb{Z}_m) \in \mathbb{R}^m$ the linear functional $\sum_{j \in \mathbb{Z}_m} c_j L_j$ peaks at x_0 with $L_j(x_0) = y_j, j \in \mathbb{Z}_m$ we have, for every $t \in \mathcal{M}_0$, that

$$\left\| \sum_{j \in \mathbb{Z}_m} c_j L_j \right\| \|x_0\| = \sum_{j \in \mathbb{Z}_m} c_j L_j(x_0) = \sum_{j \in \mathbb{Z}_m} c_j L_j(x_0 + t) \leq \|x_0 + t\| \left\| \sum_{j \in \mathbb{Z}_m} c_j L_j \right\|$$

and so, x_0 is a minimal norm interpolant. $\square$

This theorem tells us if x_0 solves the MNI problem then there exists $\{c_j, j \in N_m\} \subset \mathbb{R}$ such that $\|x_0\| = \sum_{j\in\mathbb{Z}_m} c_j L_j(x_0) = \sum_{j\in\mathbb{Z}_m} c_j y_j$. How do we find the the parameters $\{c_j : j \in \mathbb{Z}_m\}$? This is described next.

Theorem 2. *If $\mathcal{X}$ be a Banach space then*

$$\min\left\{\left\|\sum_{j\in\mathbb{Z}_m} c_j L_j\right\| : \sum_{j\in\mathbb{Z}_m} c_j y_j = 1\right\} = 1/\mu. \tag{2.10}$$

In addition, if $\mathcal{X}$ is weakly compact and $\hat{c}$ is the solution to (2.10) then there exists $\hat{x} \in \mathcal{X}$ such that $\|\hat{x}\| = 1$, $L_j(\hat{x}) = y_j/\mu, j \in \mathbb{Z}_m$ and $\sum_{j\in\mathbb{Z}_m} \hat{c}_j L_j(\hat{x}) = \|\sum_{j\in\mathbb{Z}_m} \hat{c}_j L_j\|$.

Proof. Since the function $H : \mathbb{R}^m \to \mathbb{R}_+$ defined for each $c = (c_j : j \in \mathbb{Z}_m)$ by $H(c) := \|\sum_{j\in\mathbb{Z}_m} c_j L_j\|$ is continuous, homogeneous and nonzero for $c \neq 0$, it tends to infinity as $c \to \infty$, so the minimum in (2.10) exists. The proof of (2.10) is transparent from our remarks in Theorem 1. Indeed, for every $w \in \mathcal{X}$ such that $L_j(w) = y_j$, $j \in \mathbb{Z}_m$ we have that $\mu = d(w, \mathcal{M}_0)$ and

$$\mu = \max\{L(w) : L(x) = 0, x \in \mathcal{M}_0, \|L\| \leq 1\}.$$

Moreover, since L vanishes on $\mathcal{M}_0$ if and only if $L = \sum_{j\in\mathbb{Z}_m} c_j L_j$ for some $c = (c_j : j \in \mathbb{Z}_m)$, the right hand side of this equation becomes

$$\max\left\{\sum_{j\in\mathbb{Z}_m} c_j y_j : \left\|\sum_{j\in\mathbb{Z}_m} c_j L_j\right\| \leq 1\right\} = \left(\min\left\{\left\|\sum_{j\in\mathbb{Z}_m} c_j L_j\right\| : \sum_{j\in\mathbb{Z}_m} c_j y_j = 1\right\}\right)^{-1}$$

from which equation (2.10) follows.

For vectors $c = (c_j : j \in \mathbb{Z}_m)$, $d = (d_j : j \in \mathbb{Z}_m)$ in $\mathbb{R}^m$, we let $c \cdot d = \sum_{j\in\mathbb{Z}_m} c_j d_j$, the standard inner product on $\mathbb{R}^m$. Let $\hat{c} := (\hat{c}_j : j \in \mathbb{Z}_m)$ be a solution to the minimization problem (2.10) and consider the linear functional

$$\hat{L} := \sum_{j\in\mathbb{Z}_m} \hat{c}_j L_j.$$

This solution is characterized by the fact that the right directional derivative of the function H at $\hat{c}$ along *any* vector $a = (a_j : j \in \mathbb{Z}_m)$ perpendicular to y is nonnegative. That is, we have that

$$H'(\hat{c}; a) := \lim_{\lambda\to 0^+} \frac{H(\hat{c} + \lambda a) - H(\hat{c})}{\lambda} \geq 0 \tag{2.11}$$

when $a \cdot y = 0$. This derivative can be computed to be

$$H'(\hat{c}; a) = \max\left\{\sum_{j=1}^{m} a_j L_j(x) : \|x\| \leq 1\right\} \tag{2.12}$$

see [13]. We introduce the convex and the compact set $\mathcal{C} := \{(L_j(x) : j \in \mathbb{Z}_m) : \|x\| \leq 1\} \subset \mathbb{R}^m$. If a is perpendicular to y then, by the inequality (2.11) and the formula (2.12), we have that

$$\max\{a \cdot v : v \in \mathcal{C}\} \geq 0. \tag{2.13}$$

We shall now prove that the line $\mathcal{L} := \{\lambda y : \lambda \in \mathbb{R}\}$ intersects $\mathcal{C}$. Suppose to the contrary that it does not. So, there exists an hyperplane $\{z : u \cdot z + \tau = 0\}$ where $u \in \mathbb{R}^m$ and $\tau \in \mathbb{R}$, which separates these sets, that is

$$(i)\ \ u \cdot z + \tau > 0,\ z \in \mathcal{L}, \qquad (ii)\ \ u \cdot z + \tau \leq 0,\ z \in \mathcal{C}$$

see [21]. From condition (i) we conclude that u is perpendicular to y and $\tau > 0$ while (ii) implies that $\max\{u \cdot v : v \in \mathcal{C}\} < 0$. This is in contradiction to (2.13). Hence, there is an $\hat{x}$ such that $L_j(\hat{x}) = y_j/\mu, j \in \mathbb{Z}_m$, $\hat{L}(\hat{x}) = \|\hat{L}\|$ and $\|\hat{x}\| = 1$. Therefore, it must be that $x_0 := \mu\hat{x}$ is a MNS. □

This theorem leads us to a method to identify the MNS in a reflexive smooth Banach space $\mathcal{X}$. Recall that a reflexive Banach space $\mathcal{X}$ is *smooth* provided that for every $L \in \mathcal{X}^* \backslash \{0\}$ there is *unique* $x_L \in \mathcal{X}$ which peaks at L.

Corollary 1. *If $\mathcal{X}$ is a smooth reflexive Banach space, $\hat{L} := \sum_{j \in \mathbb{Z}_m} \hat{c}_j L_j$ is the solution to (2.10) and $\hat{L}$ peaks at x_L with $\|x_L\| = 1$ then $x_0 := \mu x_L$ is the unique solution to (2.7) and $\mu = 1/\|\hat{L}\|$.*

We wish to note some important examples of the above results. The first to consider is naturally a Hilbert space $\mathcal{X}$. In this case $\mathcal{X}$ is reflexive and $\mathcal{X}^*$ can be identified with $\mathcal{X}$, that is, for each $L_j \in \mathcal{X}^*$, there is a *unique* $x^j \in \mathcal{X}$ such that $L_j(x) = (x^j, x), x \in \mathcal{X}$. Thus, $\hat{x} = \sum_{j \in \mathbb{Z}_m} c_j x^j$ solves the dual problem when $(x^j, x) = \lambda y_j, j \in \mathbb{Z}_m$, $\lambda = \|\hat{x}\|^2$ and $x_0 = \hat{x}/\|\hat{x}\|$ is the minimal norm solution.

The Hilbert space case does not show the value of function composition appearing in (1.2). A better place to reveal this is in the context of Orlicz spaces. The theory of such spaces is discussed in several books, see e.g [17,20], and minimal norm interpolation is studied in [3]. We review these ideas in the context of Corollary 1. Let $\omega : [0, \infty) \to [0, \infty)$ be a convex and continuously differentiable function on $[0, \infty)$ such that $\lim_{s \to \infty} \omega'(s) = \infty$ and $\omega(0) = \omega'_+(0) = 0$ where ω'_+ is the right derivative of ω. Such a function is sometimes known as a Young function. We will also assume that the function $s \mapsto s\omega'(s/\omega(s))$, $s \in [0, \infty)$ is bounded on $[k, \infty)$ for some $k \in [0, \infty)$. Let $(D, \mathcal{B}, \mu)$ be a finite measure space, see [21, p. 286], $L^0(\mu)$ the space of measurable functions $f : D \to \mathbb{R}$, and denote by $\mathcal{L}_\omega$ the convex hull of the set

$$\left\{ f \in L^0(\mu) : \int_D \omega(|f(t)|) d\mu(t) < \infty \right\}.$$

The space $\mathcal{L}_\omega$ can be made into a normed space by introducing, for every $f \in \mathcal{L}_\omega$ the norm

$$\|f\|_\omega := \inf \left\{ \lambda \geq 0 : \int_D \omega\left(\frac{|f(t)|}{\lambda}\right) d\mu(t) \leq 1 \right\}.$$

The dual of $\mathcal{L}_\omega$ is the space $\mathcal{L}_{\omega^*}$ where ω^* is the complementary function of ω which is given by the formula

$$\omega^*(s) = \int_0^s (\omega')^{-1}(\xi)d\xi, \ s \in [0, \infty).$$

For every $f \in \mathcal{L}_\omega$ and $g \in \mathcal{L}_{\omega^*}$ there also holds the Orlicz inequality

$$|(f, g)| \leq \|f\|_\omega \|g\|_{\omega^*}$$

where we have defined $(f, g) := \int_D f(t)g(t)d\mu(t)$. The Orlicz inequality becomes an equality if and only if

$$f = \lambda(\omega^*)'(|g|)\text{sign}(g), \tag{2.14}$$

for some $\lambda \in \mathbb{R}$. This means that the linear functional represented by $g \in \mathcal{L}_{\omega^*}$ peaks at f if and only if f satisfies equation (2.14). Moreover, under the above conditions on ω, $\mathcal{L}_\omega$ is reflexive and smooth. Thus the hypothesis of Corollary 1 is satisfied and we conclude that the unique solution to (2.7) is given by $f = \lambda\phi_\omega(\sum_{j\in\mathbb{Z}_m} c_j g_j)$ where ϕ_ω is defined for $t \in \mathbb{R}$ as

$$\phi_\omega(t) = (\omega^*)'(|t|)\text{sign}(t) \tag{2.15}$$

and the coefficients λ, $c_j, j \in \mathbb{Z}_m$ solve the system of *nonlinear* equations $(f, g_j) = y_j, \ j \in \mathbb{Z}_m$.

As a special case consider the choice $\omega(s) = s^p/p, p > 1, \ s \in [0, \infty)$. In this case $\mathcal{L}_\omega = \mathcal{L}^p$, the space of functions whose p power is integrable, and the dual space is $\mathcal{L}^q$ where $1/p + 1/q = 1$, [21]. Since $\omega^*(s) = s^q/q, \ s \in [0, \infty)$, the solution to equations (2.5) and (2.7) has the form $f = \lambda\phi_q(\sum_{j\in\mathbb{Z}_m} \hat{c}_j g_j)$ where for all $t \in \mathbb{R}$ ϕ_q is defined by the equation

$$\phi_q(t) := |t|^{q-1}\text{sign}(t). \tag{2.16}$$

3 Learning All Continuous Functions: Density

An important feature of any learning algorithm is its ability to enhance accuracy by increasing the *number of parameters* in the model. Below we present a sufficient condition on the functions ϕ and $\{g_j : j \in \mathbb{Z}_m\}$ so that the functions in (1.4) can approximate any continuous real–valued function within any given tolerance on a compact set $D \subseteq \mathbb{R}^d$. For related material see [19]. Let us formulate our observation.

We use $\mathcal{C}(D)$ for the space of all continuous functions on the set D and for any $f \in \mathcal{C}(D)$ we set $\|f\|_D := \max\{|f(x)| : x \in D)\}$. For any subset $\mathcal{T}$ of $\mathcal{C}(D)$ we use *span*$(\mathcal{T})$ to denote the smallest *closed* linear subspace of $\mathcal{C}(D)$ containing $\mathcal{T}$. We enumerate vectors in $\mathbb{R}^m$ by superscripts and use $g := (g_j : j \in \mathbb{Z}_m)$ for the vector–valued map $g : D \to \mathbb{R}^m$ whose coordinates are built from the functions in $\mathcal{G} := \{g_j : j \in \mathbb{Z}_m\}$. This allows us to write the functions in (1.4) as

$$\sum_{j\in\mathbb{Z}_n} a_j \phi(c^j \cdot g). \tag{3.17}$$

For any two subsets $\mathcal{A}$ and $\mathcal{B}$ of $\mathcal{C}(D)$ we use $\mathcal{A} \cdot \mathcal{B}$ for the set defined by $\mathcal{A} \cdot \mathcal{B} := \{fg : f \in \mathcal{A}, g \in \mathcal{B}\}$ and, for every $k \in \mathbb{N}$, $\mathcal{A}^k$ denotes the set $\{f^k : f \in \mathcal{A}\}$. Given any $\phi \in \mathcal{C}(D)$ we let $\mathcal{M}(\phi)$ be the smallest closed linear subspace containing all the functions (3.17). Note that m is fixed while $\mathcal{M}(\phi)$ contains all the functions (3.17) for *any* n. We use $\mathcal{A}_\mathcal{G}$ for the smallest subalgebra in $\mathcal{C}(D)$ which contains $\mathcal{G}$, that is, the direct sum $\oplus_{k \in \mathbb{N}} \mathcal{G}^k$. We seek conditions on ϕ and g so that $\mathcal{M}(\phi) = \mathcal{C}(D)$ and we prepare for our observation with two lemmas.

Lemma 1. *If $\phi \in \mathcal{C}(D) \backslash \{0\}$ and $1 \in span(\mathcal{G})$ then $1 \in \mathcal{M}(\phi)$.*

Proof. By hypothesis, there is a $t \in \mathbb{R}$ such that $\phi(t) \neq 0$ and a $c \in \mathbb{R}^m$ such that $c \cdot g = t$. Hence we have that $1 = \frac{1}{\phi(t)} \phi(c \cdot g) \in \mathcal{M}(\phi)$. □

Lemma 2. *If $\phi' \in \mathcal{C}(D)$ then $\mathcal{M}(\phi') \cdot \mathcal{G} \subseteq \mathcal{M}(\phi)$.*

Proof. We choose any function f of the form

$$f = \sum_{j \in \mathbb{Z}_n} a_j \phi'(c^j \cdot g)$$

where $a = (a_j : j \in \mathbb{Z}_n) \in \mathbb{R}^n$ and $\{c^j : j \in \mathbb{Z}_n\} \subset \mathbb{R}^m$. For any $d \in \mathbb{R}^m$ we define the function $q = d \cdot g$. Let us show that $f \cdot q \in \mathcal{M}(\phi)$. To this end, we define for $t \in \mathbb{R}$ the function

$$h_t := \sum_{j \in \mathbb{Z}_n} a_j \phi((c^j + td) \cdot g)$$

and observe that $\lim_{t \to 0} t^{-1}(h_t - h_0) = f \cdot q$. Since $\{h_t - h_0 : t \in \mathbb{R}\} \subseteq \mathcal{M}(\phi)$, the result follows. □

We say that $\mathcal{G}$ separates points on $\mathcal{D}$ when the map $g : D \to \mathbb{R}^m$ is injective. Recall that an algebra $\mathcal{A} \subseteq C(D)$ *separates points* provided for each pair of distinct points x and $y \in D$ there is an $f \in \mathcal{A}$ such that $f(x) \neq f(y)$.

Theorem 3. *If $\phi \in \mathcal{C}^\infty(\mathbb{R})$, ϕ is not a polynomial, $1 \in span(\mathcal{G})$ and $\mathcal{G}$ separates points then $\mathcal{M}(\phi) = \mathcal{C}(D)$.*

Proof. Our hypothesis implies that $\mathcal{A}_\mathcal{G}$ separates points and contains constants. Hence, the Stone–Weierstrass Theorem, see for example [21], implies that the algebra $\mathcal{A}_\mathcal{G}$ is dense in $\mathcal{C}(D)$. Thus, the result will follow as soon as we show that $\mathcal{A}_\mathcal{G} \subseteq \mathcal{M}(\phi)$. Since $\phi \in \mathcal{C}^\infty(\mathbb{R})$ Lemma 2 implies for any positive integer k that

$$\mathcal{M}(\phi^{(k)}) \cdot \mathcal{G}^k \subseteq \mathcal{M}(\phi).$$

Using Lemma 1 and the fact that ϕ is not a polynomial the above inclusion implies that $\mathcal{G}^k \subseteq \mathcal{M}(\phi)$. Consequently, we conclude that

$$\mathcal{A}_\mathcal{G} = \bigoplus_{k \in \mathbb{N}} \mathcal{G}^k \subseteq \mathcal{M}(\phi).$$

□

We remark that the idea for the proof of Lemma 2 is borrowed from [4] where only the case that $span(\mathcal{G})$ is linear functions on $\mathbb{R}^{m-1}$ and D is a subset of $\mathbb{R}^m$ is treated. We also recommend [12] for a Fourier analysis approach to density and [10] which may allow for the removable of our hypothesis that $\phi \in \mathcal{C}^\infty(D)$.

In Theorem 3 above m is fixed and we enhance approximation of an arbitrary function by functions of the special type (1.4) by adjusting n. Next, we provide another density result where m is allowed to vary, but in this case, g is chosen in a specific fashion from the reproducing kernel of a Hilbert space $\mathcal{H}$ of real–valued functions on D contained in $\mathcal{C}(D)$. Indeed, let K be the reproducing kernel for $\mathcal{H}$ which is jointly continuous on $D \times D$. There are useful cases when $\mathcal{H}$ is endowed with a *semi–norm*, that is, there are nontrivial functions in $\mathcal{H}$ with norm zero, see e.g [25]. To ensure that these cases are covered by our results below we specify a finite number of functions $\{k_j : j \in \mathbb{Z}_r\}$ and consider functions of the form

$$\sum_{j \in \mathbb{Z}_m} c_j K(\cdot, x_j) + \sum_{j \in \mathbb{Z}_r} c_{j+m} k_j. \tag{3.18}$$

We use $\mathcal{K}$ for the smallest closed linear subspace of $\mathcal{C}(D)$ which contains all the functions in (3.18) for any m and $c = (c_j : j \in \mathbb{Z}_{m+r}) \in \mathbb{R}^{m+r}$. Here the samples $D_m := \{x_j : j \in \mathbb{Z}_m\}$ are chosen in D and, in the spirit of our previous discussion we compose the function in (3.18) with a function ϕ to obtain functions of the form

$$\phi(\sum_{j \in \mathbb{Z}_m} c_j K(\cdot, x_j) + \sum_{j \in \mathbb{Z}_r} c_{j+m} k_j).$$

We write this function as $\phi(c \cdot w)$ where $c \in \mathbb{R}^{m+r}$ and the coordinates of the vector map $w : D \to \mathbb{R}^{m+r}$ are defined as $w_j = K(\cdot, x_j), j \in \mathbb{Z}_m$ and $w_{j+m} = k_j, j \in \mathbb{Z}_r$. We let $\mathcal{K}(\phi)$ be the smallest closed linear subspace containing all these functions. Our next result provides a sufficient condition on ϕ and w such that $\mathcal{K}(\phi)$ is dense in $\mathcal{C}(D)$. To this end we write K in the "Mercer form"

$$K(x, y) = \sum_{\ell \in \mathbb{Z}_+} \lambda_\ell \phi_\ell(x) \phi_\ell(y), \;\; x, y \in D \tag{3.19}$$

where we may as well assume that $\lambda_\ell \neq 0$ for all $\ell \in \mathbb{Z}_+$. Here, we demand that $\{\phi_\ell : \ell \in \mathbb{Z}_+\} \subseteq \mathcal{C}(D)$ and we require the series above converges *uniformly* on $D \times D$. We also require that the set $J = \{\ell : \lambda_\ell < 0\}$ has the property that

$$\{\phi_\ell : \ell \in J\} \subseteq span\{k_j : j \in \mathbb{Z}_r\} \tag{3.20}$$

and that $\mathcal{U} := span\{\phi_\ell : \ell \in \mathbb{Z}_+\} = \mathcal{C}(D)$. When these conditions holds we call *K acceptable*.

Theorem 4. *If K is acceptable, $1 \in \mathcal{K}(\phi')$ and $\phi' \in \mathcal{C}(D) \backslash \{0\}$ then $\mathcal{K}(\phi) = \mathcal{C}(D)$.*

Proof. We establish this fact by showing that there is no *nontrivial* linear functional L which has the property that

$$L(g) = 0 \tag{3.21}$$

for every $g \in \mathcal{K}(\phi)$, see for example [21]. Let c and w be as above. We choose $b \in \mathbb{R}$, $y \in D$ and $g = \phi(c \cdot w + bK(\cdot, y))$. Now, differentiate both sides of equation (3.21) with respect to b and evaluate the resulting equation at $b = 0$ to obtain the equation

$$L(\phi'(c \cdot w)K(\cdot, y)) = 0, \ y \in D. \tag{3.22}$$

On the other hand, differentiating (3.21) with respect to c_{j+m}, $j \in \mathbb{Z}_r$ gives the equation

$$L(\phi'(c \cdot w)k_\ell) = 0, \ \ell \in \mathbb{Z}_r. \tag{3.23}$$

We shall use these equations in a moment. First, we observe that by hypothesis there exists a $t \in \mathbb{R}$ such that $\phi'(t) \neq 0$ and for every $\epsilon > 0$ there exists $f \in \mathcal{K}(\phi')$ given, for some $m \in \mathbb{N}$, $\{a_j : j \in \mathbb{Z}_n\} \subset \mathbb{R}$, $\{d_j : j \in \mathbb{Z}_n\} \subset \mathbb{R}^m$, by the formula

$$f = \sum_{j \in \mathbb{Z}_n} a_j \phi'(d^j \cdot w) \tag{3.24}$$

such that $|\phi'(t) - f| \leq \epsilon$ on D. We now evaluate the equations (3.22) and (3.23) at $c = d^j, j \in \mathbb{Z}_n$ and combine the resulting equations to obtain

$$L(fK(\cdot, y)) = 0, \ y \in D, \qquad L(fk_\ell) = 0, \ \ell \in \mathbb{Z}_r.$$

We let M be a constant chosen big enough so that for all x and $y \in D$, $|K(x, y)| \leq M$, and $|k_\ell(x)| \leq M, \ell \in \mathbb{Z}_r$. We rewrite (3.22) in the form

$$0 = L((f - \phi'(t))K(\cdot, y)) + \phi'(t)L(K(\cdot, y))$$

from which we obtain the inequalities

$$|\phi'(t)L(K(\cdot, y))| \leq \epsilon \|L\| M, \ y \in D, \qquad |\phi'(t)L(k_\ell)| \leq \epsilon \|L\| M, \ \ell \in \mathbb{Z}_r.$$

Since ϵ is arbitrary we conclude for all $y \in D$ that $L((K(\cdot, y)) = 0, \ y \in D$ and $L(k_\ell) = 0, \ \ell \in \mathbb{Z}_r$. Thus, using the Mercer representation for K we conclude, for all $y \in D$, that

$$\sum_{j \notin J} \lambda_j \phi_j(y) L(\phi_j) = 0. \tag{3.25}$$

Next, we apply L to both sides of (3.25) and obtain that $\sum_{j \notin J} \lambda_j |L(\phi_j)|^2 = 0$ which implies that $L(\phi_j) = 0, \ j \in \mathbb{Z}_+$. However, since $span\{\phi_j : j \in \mathbb{Z}_+\} = \mathcal{C}(D)$, it follows that $L = 0$, which proves the result. □

We remark that the proof of this theorem yields for any $f \in \mathcal{C}(D)$ the fact that

$$d(f, \mathcal{K}(\phi)) \leq d(f, \mathcal{K}) = d(f, \mathcal{U}).$$

Note that if $\phi(t) = t$ the hypothesis that $1 \in \mathcal{K}(\phi')$ is automatically satisfied. We provide another sufficient condition for this requirement to hold.

Lemma 3. *If* $1 \in \mathcal{K}$ *and* $\phi \in \mathcal{C}(\mathbb{R}) \backslash \{0\}$ *then* $1 \in \mathcal{K}(\phi)$.

Proof. We choose some $t \in \mathbb{R}$ such that $\phi(t) \neq 0$ and some $\epsilon > 0$. There is a $\delta > 0$ such that whenever $|t - s| \leq \epsilon$, $s \in \mathbb{R}$ it follows that $|\phi(t) - \phi(s)| \leq \epsilon$. Since $1 \in \mathcal{K}$, there is a $d \in \mathbb{R}^{m+r}$ and $D_m \subset \mathcal{D}$ so that $|t - d \cdot w| \leq \delta$ uniformly on D. Hence it follows that $|\phi(t) - \phi(d \cdot w)| \leq \epsilon$ uniformly on D which proves the result. □

As an example of the theorem above we choose $D = [-\pi, \pi]^d$, $d \in \mathbb{N}$, $\phi(t) = t$, $t \in \mathbb{R}$, K a $2\pi-$periodic translation kernel, that is, $K(x, y) = h(x - y)$, $x, y \in D$, where $h : [-\pi, \pi]^d \to \mathbb{R}$ is even, continuous, and $2\pi-$periodic, and $r = 0$. To ensure that K is a reproducing kernel we assume h has a uniformly convergent Fourier series,

$$h(x) = \sum_{n \in \mathbb{Z}^d_+} a_n \cos(n \cdot x), \quad x \in \mathbb{R}^d \tag{3.26}$$

where $a_n \geq 0$, $n \in \mathbb{Z}^d_+$. In this case we have the Mercer representation for K

$$K(x, y) = \sum_{n \in \mathbb{Z}^d_+} a_n \sin(n \cdot x) \sin(n \cdot y) + \sum_{n \in \mathbb{Z}^d_+} a_n \cos(n \cdot x) \cos(n \cdot y), \quad x, y \in \mathbb{R}^d$$

In addition, if $a_n > 0$ for all $n \in \mathbb{Z}^d_+$, the functions appearing in this representation are dense in the $2\pi-$periodic functions in $\mathcal{C}(D)$, we conclude that $\mathcal{K}$ is dense in $\mathcal{C}(D)$ as well.

We remark that the method of proof of Theorem 4 can be extended to other function spaces, for instance $\mathcal{L}^p$ spaces. This would require that (3.19) holds relative to the convergence in that space and that the set of functions $\{\phi_n : n \in \mathbb{Z}_+\}$ are dense in it.

4 Learning Any Set of Finite Data: Interpolation

In this section we discuss the possibility of adjusting the parameters in our model (1.4) to satisfy some prescribed linear constraints. This is a complex issue as it leads to the problem of solving *nonlinear* equations. Our observations, although incomplete, provide some instances in which this may be accomplished as well as an algorithm which may be useful to accomplish this goal. Let us first describe our setup. We start with the function

$$f := \sum_{j \in \mathbb{Z}_n} a_j \phi(c^j \cdot g)$$

where $\{a_j : j \in \mathbb{Z}_n\} \subset \mathbb{R}$ and $\{c^j : j \in \mathbb{Z}_n\} \subset \mathbb{R}^m$ are to be specified by some linear constraint. The totality of scalar parameters in this representation is $n(m+1)$. To use these parameters we suppose there is available data vectors $\{y^j : j \in \mathbb{Z}_n\} \subset \mathbb{R}^m$ and linear operators $L^s : \mathcal{C}(D) \to \mathbb{R}^m, s \in \mathbb{Z}_n$ that lead to the nonlinear equations

$$\sum_{j \in \mathbb{Z}_n} a_j L^s(\phi(c^j \cdot g)) = y^s, \ s \in \mathbb{Z}_n. \tag{4.27}$$

There are mn scalar equations here and the remaining degrees of freedom will be used to specify the Euclidean norm of the vectors $c^j, j \in \mathbb{Z}_n$. We shall explain this in a moment. It is convenient to introduce for each $s \in \mathbb{Z}_m$ the operator $B_s : \mathbb{R}^m \to \mathbb{R}^m$ defined for any $c \in \mathbb{R}^m$ by the equation

$$B_s(c) = L^s(\phi(c \cdot g)), \ s \in \mathbb{Z}_n. \tag{4.28}$$

Therefore, the equations (4.27) take the form

$$\sum_{j \in \mathbb{Z}_n} a_j B_s(c^j) = y^s, \ s \in \mathbb{Z}_n. \tag{4.29}$$

Our first result covers the case $n = 1$.

Theorem 5. *If $\phi \in \mathcal{C}(\mathbb{R})$ is an odd function and B_0 only vanishes on $\mathbb{R}^m$ at 0 then for any $y^0 \in \mathbb{R}^m$ and $r > 0$ there is a $c^0 \in \mathbb{R}^m$ with $c^0 \cdot c^0 = r_0^2$ and $a_0 \in \mathbb{R}$ such that $a_0 B_0(c^0) = y^0$.*

Proof. We choose linearly independent vectors $\{w^j : j \in \mathbb{Z}_{m-1}\} \subset \mathbb{R}^m$ perpendicular to y^0 and construct the map $H : \mathbb{R}^m \to \mathbb{R}^{m-1}$ by setting for $c \in \mathbb{R}^m$

$$H(c) := (w^j \cdot B_0(c) : j \in \mathbb{Z}_{m-1}).$$

We restrict H to the sphere $c \cdot c = r_0$. Since H is an odd continuous map by the Borsuk antipodal mapping theorem, see for example [11], there is a $c^0 \in \mathbb{R}^m$ with $c^0 \cdot c^0 = r_0^2$ such that $H(c^0) = 0$. Hence, $B_0(c^0) = uy^0$ for some scalar $u \in \mathbb{R}$. Since B_0 vanishes only at the origin we have that $u \neq 0$ and, so, setting $a_0 = u^{-1}$ proves the result. □

We remark that the above theorem extends our observation in (2.16). Indeed, if we choose $\phi := \phi_q$ and use the linear operator $L^0 : \mathcal{L}^p \to \mathbb{R}^m$ defined for each $f \in \mathcal{L}^p$ as $L^0(f) := ((f, g_j) : j \in \mathbb{Z}_m)$, then the above result reduces to (2.16). However, note that Theorem 5 even in this special case is *not* proven by the analysis of a variational problem.

We use Theorem 5 to propose an iterative method to solve the system of equations (4.29). We begin with an initial guess $a^0 = (a_j^0 : j \in \mathbb{Z}_n)$ and vectors $\{c^{j,0} : j \in \mathbb{Z}_n\}$ with $c^{j,0} \cdot c^{j,0} = r_j, j \in \mathbb{Z}_n$. We now update these parameters by explaining how to construct $a^1 = (a_j^1 : j \in \mathbb{Z}_n)$ and vectors $\{c^{j,1} : j \in \mathbb{Z}_n\}$. First, we define a_0^1 and $c^{0,1}$ by solving the equation

$$a_0^1 B_0(c^{0,1}) + \sum_{j \in \mathbb{Z}_{n-1}} a_{j+1}^0 B_0(c^{j+1,0}) = y^0.$$

whose solution is assured by Theorem 5. Now, suppose we have found $a_0^1, \ldots, a_{r-1}^1, c^{0,1}, \ldots, c^{r-1,1}$ for some integer $1 \leq r < n-1$. We then solve the equation

$$\sum_{j \in \mathbb{Z}_{r+1}} a_j^1 B_r(c^{j,1}) + \sum_{j \in \mathbb{Z}_{n-r-1}} a_{j+r+1}^0 B_r(c^{j+r+1,0}) = y^r$$

for a_r^1 and $c^{r,1}$ until we reach $r = n-1$. In this manner, we construct a sequence of vectors $a^k \in \mathbb{R}^n$ and $c^{j,k} \in \mathbb{R}^m, k \in \mathbb{Z}_+, j \in \mathbb{Z}_n$ such that for all $k \in \mathbb{Z}_+$ and $r \in \mathbb{Z}_n$,

$$\sum_{j \in \mathbb{Z}_{r+1}} a_j^{k+1} B_r(c^{j,k+1}) + \sum_{j \in \mathbb{Z}_{n-r-1}} a_{j+r+1}^{k+1} B_r(c^{j+r+1,k}) = y^r. \tag{4.30}$$

We do not know whether or not this iterative method converges in the generality presented. However, below we provide a sufficient condition for which the sequences generated above remain bounded.

Corollary 2. *If there is an $s \in \mathbb{Z}_n$ such that whenever $\{c^j : j \in \mathbb{Z}_n\} \subset \mathbb{R}^m$, $b = (b_j : j \in \mathbb{Z}_n) \in \mathbb{R}^n$ with $c^j \cdot c^j > 0, j \in \mathbb{Z}_n$ and*

$$\sum_{j \in \mathbb{Z}_n} b_j B_s(c^j) = 0 \tag{4.31}$$

it follows that $b = 0$, then the sequence $\{a_j^k : j \in \mathbb{Z}_n\}$ defined in (4.28) is bounded.

Proof. Without loss of generality we assume, by reordering the equations, that $s = n-1$. The last equation in (4.30), corresponding to $r = n-1$, allows us to observe that the coefficients $\{a_j^{k+1} : j \in \mathbb{Z}_n\}$ remain bounded during the updating procedure. To confirm this, we set $\gamma_k = \sum_{j \in \mathbb{Z}_n} |a_j^{k+1}|$ and divide both sides of (4.30) by γ_k. If the sequence $\{a_j^{k+1} : k \in \mathbb{N}\}$ is not bounded we obtain, in the limit as $k \to \infty$ through a subsequence, that

$$\sum_{j \in \mathbb{Z}_n} \tilde{a}_j B_s(\tilde{c}^j) = 0 \tag{4.32}$$

where the constants $\tilde{a}_j$, $j \in \mathbb{Z}_n$ satisfy $\sum_{j \in \mathbb{Z}_n} |\tilde{a}_j| = 1$, which in contradiction with our hypothesis. □

5 Discussion

We have proposed a framework for learning in a Banach space and establish a representation theorem for the solution of regularization–based learning algorithms. This naturally extends the representation theorem in Hilbert spaces which is central in developing kernel–based methods. The framework builds on a link between regularization and minimal norm interpolation, a key concept in function estimation and interpolation. For concrete Banach spaces such as Orlicz spaces, our result leads to the functional representation (1.2). We have studied the density property of this functional representation and its extension.

There are important directions that should be explored in the context presented in this paper. First, it would be valuable to extend on–line and batch learning algorithms which have already been studies for finite dimensional Banach spaces (see e.g. [1,9,26]) within the general framework discussed here.

For example, in [14] we consider the hinge loss function used in support vector machines and an appropriate H to identify the dual of the minimization problem (1.3) and report of our numerical experience with it.

Second, it would be interesting to study error bounds for learning in Banach spaces. This study will involve both the sample as well the approximation error, and should uncover advantage or disadvantages of learning in Banach spaces in comparison to Hilbert spaces which are not yet understood.

Finally, we believe that the framework presented here remains valid when problems (2.5) and (2.7) are studied subject to additional *convex constraints.* These may be available in form of prior knowledge on the function we seek to learn. Indeed constrained minimal norm interpolation has been studied in Hilbert spaces, see [15] and [5] for a review. It would be interesting to extend these idea to regularization in Banach spaces. As an example, consider the problem of learning a *nonnegative* function f in the Hilbert space $\mathcal{H} := \mathcal{L}^2(D)$ from the data $\{y_j = \int_D f(t)g_j(t)dt : j \in \mathbb{Z}_m\}$. Then, any minimizer of the regularization functional of the form (1.3) in $\mathcal{H}$ (where $L_j(f) := \int_D f(t)g_j(t)dt$) subject to the additional nonnegativity constraint, has the form in equation (1.2) where $\phi(t) = \max(t, 0)$, $t \in \mathbb{R}$, see Theorem 2.3 in [15] for a proof.

Acknowledgements. We are grateful to Benny Hon and Ding-Xuan Zhou of the Mathematics Department at City University of Hong Kong for providing both of us with the opportunity to complete this work in a scientifically stimulating and friendly environment.

References

1. K. Bennett and Bredensteiner. Duality and geometry in support vector machine classifiers. Proc. of the 17–th Int. Conf. on Machine Learning, P. Langley Ed., Morgan Kaufmann, pp. 57–63, 2000.
2. S. Canu, X. Mary, and A. Rakotomamonjy. Functional learning through kernel. In *Advances in Learning Theory: Methods, Models and Applications*, J. Suykens et al. Eds., NATO Science Series III: Computer and Systems Sciences, Vol. 190, pp 89–110, IOS Press, Amsterdam 2003.
3. J.M. Carnicer and J. Bastero. On best interpolation in Orlicz spaces. *Approx. Theory and its Appl.*, 10(4), pp. 72–83, 1994.
4. W. Dahmen and C.A. Micchelli. Some remarks on ridge functions. *Approx. Theory and its Appl.*, 3, pp. 139–143, 1987.
5. F. Deutsch. *Best Approximation in inner Product Spaces* CMS Books in Mathematics, Springer, 2001.
6. M. Hein and O. Bousquet. Maximal Margin Classification for Metric Spaces. In Proc. of the 16–th Annual Conference on Computational Learning Theory (COLT), 2003.
7. D. Kimber and P. M. Long. On-line learning of smooth functions of a single variable. *Theoretical Computer Science*, 148(1), pp. 141–156, 1995.
8. G.G. Lorenz. *Approximation of Functions.* Chelsea, 2nd ed., 1986.
9. C. Gentile. A new approach to maximal margin classification algorithms. *Journal of Machine Learning Research*, 2, pp. 213–242, 2001.

10. M. Leshno, V. Ya. Lin, A. Pinkus, and S. Schocken. Multilayer Feedforward Networks with a Non–Polynomial Activation Function can Approximate any Function. *Neural Networks*, 6, pp. 861–867, 1993.
11. J. Matousek. *Using the Borsuk-Ulam Theorem: Lectures on Topological Methods in Combinatorics and Geometry.* Springer-Verlag, Berlin, 2003.
12. H.N. Mhaskar and C.A. Micchelli. Approximation by superposition of sigmoidal functions. *Advances in Applied Mathematics*, 13, pp. 350–373, 1992.
13. C.A. Micchelli and M. Pontil. A function representation for learning in Banach spaces. Research Note RN/04/05, Dept of Computer Science, UCL, February 2004.
14. C.A. Micchelli and M. Pontil. Regularization algorithms for learning theory. Working paper, Dept of Computer Science, UCL, 2004.
15. C. A. Micchelli and F. I. Utreras. Smoothing and interpolation in a convex subset of a hilbert space. *SIAM J. of Scientific and Statistical Computing*, 9, pp. 728–746, 1988.
16. T.J. Morrison. *Functional Analysis: An Introduction to Banach Space Theory.* John Wiley Inc., New York, 2001.
17. W. Orlicz. *Linear Functional Analysis.* World Scientific, 1990.
18. A. Pinkus. *n–Widths in Approximation Theory.* Ergebnisse, Springer–Verlag, 1985.
19. A. Pinkus. Approximation theory of the MLP model in neural networks. *Acta Numerica* 8, pp. 143–196, 1999.
20. M.M. Rao and Z.D. R. Ren. *Theory of Orlicz Spaces.* Marcel Dekker, Inc. 1992.
21. H.L. Royden. *Real Analysis.* Macmillan Publishing Company, New York, 3rd edition, 1988.
22. B. Schölkopf and A.J. Smola. *Learning with Kernels.* The MIT Press, Cambridge, MA, USA, 2002.
23. V. Vapnik. *The Nature of Statistical Learning Theory.* 2–nd edition, Springer, New York, 1999.
24. U. von Luxburg and O. Bousquet. Distance–based classification with Lipschitz functions. In Proc. of the 16–th Annual Conference on Computational Learning Theory (COLT), 2003.
25. G. Wahba. *Splines Models for Observational Data.* Series in Applied Mathematics, Vol. 59, SIAM, Philadelphia, 1990.
26. T. Zhang. On the dual formulation of regularized linear systems with convex risks. *Machine Learning*, 46, pp. 91–129, 2002.

Local Complexities for Empirical Risk Minimization

Peter L. Bartlett[1], Shahar Mendelson[2], and Petra Philips[2]

[1] Division of Computer Science and Department of Statistics
University of California, Berkeley
367 Evans Hall #3860, Berkeley, CA 94720-3860
bartlett@stat.berkeley.edu

[2] RSISE, The Australian National University
Canberra, 0200 Australia
shahar.mendelson@anu.edu.au, petra.philips@anu.edu.au

Abstract. We present sharp bounds on the risk of the empirical minimization algorithm under mild assumptions on the class. We introduce the notion of isomorphic coordinate projections and show that this leads to a sharper error bound than the best previously known. The quantity which governs this bound on the empirical minimizer is the largest fixed point of the function $\xi_n(r) = \mathbb{E}\sup\{|\mathbb{E}f - \mathbb{E}_n f| : f \in F, \mathbb{E}f = r\}$. We prove that this is the best estimate one can obtain using "structural results", and that it is possible to estimate the error rate from data. We then prove that the bound on the empirical minimization algorithm can be improved further by a direct analysis, and that the correct error rate is the maximizer of $\xi'_n(r) - r$, where $\xi'_n(r) = \mathbb{E}\sup\{\mathbb{E}f - \mathbb{E}_n f : f \in F, \mathbb{E}f = r\}$.

Keywords: Statistical learning theory, empirical risk minimization, generalization bounds, concentration inequalities, isomorphic coordinate projections, data-dependent complexity.

1 Introduction

Error bounds for learning algorithms measure the probability that a function produced by the algorithm has a small error. Sharp bounds give an insight into the parameters that are important for learning and allow one to assess accurately the performance of learning algorithms. The bounds are usually derived by studying the relationship between the expected and the empirical error. It is now a standard result that, for every function, the deviation of the expected from the empirical error is bounded by a complexity term which measures the size of the function class from which the function was chosen. Complexity terms which measure the size of the entire class are called *global complexity measures*, and two such examples are the VC-dimension and the Rademacher averages of the function class (note that there is a key difference between the two; the VC-dimension is independent of the underlying measure, and thus captures the

J. Shawe-Taylor and Y. Singer (Eds.): COLT 2004, LNAI 3120, pp. 270–284, 2004.

worst case scenario, while the Rademacher averages are measure dependent and lead to sharper bounds).

Moreover, estimates which are based on comparing the empirical and the actual structures (for example empirical vs. actual means) uniformly over the class are loose, because this condition is stronger than necessary. Indeed, in the case of the empirical risk minimization algorithm, it is more likely that the algorithm produces functions with a small expectation, and thus one only has to consider a small subclass. Taking that into account, error bounds should depend only on the complexity of the functions with small error or variance. Such bounds in terms of *local complexity measures* were established in [10,15,13,2,9].

In this article we will show that by imposing very mild structural assumptions on the class, these local complexity bounds can be improved further. We will state the best possible estimates which can be obtained by a comparison of empirical and actual structures. Then, we will pursue the idea of leaving the "structural approach" and analyzing the empirical minimization algorithm directly. The reason for this is that structural results comparing the empirical and actual structures on the class have a limitation. It turns out that if one is too close to the true minimizer the class is too rich at that scale and the structures are not close at a small enough scale to yield a useful bound. On the other hand, with the empirical minimizer one can go beyond the structural limit.

We consider the following setting and notation: let $\mathcal{X} \times \mathcal{Y}$ be a measurable space, and let P be an unknown probability distribution on $\mathcal{X} \times \mathcal{Y}$. Let $((X_1, Y_1), ..., (X_n, Y_n)) \in (\mathcal{X} \times \mathcal{Y})^n$ be a finite training sample, where each pair (X_i, Y_i) is generated independently according to P. The goal of a learning algorithm is to estimate a function $h : \mathcal{X} \longrightarrow \mathcal{Y}$ (based on the sample), which predicts the value of Y given X. The possible choices of functions are all in a function class H, called the hypothesis class. A quantitative measure of how accurate a function $h \in H$ approximates Y is given by a loss function $l : \mathcal{Y}^2 \longrightarrow \mathbb{R}$. Typical examples of loss functions are the 0-1 loss for classification defined by $l(r, s) = 0$ if $r = s$ and $l(r, s) = 1$ if $r \neq s$ or the square-loss for regression tasks $l(r, s) = (r - s)^2$. In what follows we will assume a bounded loss function and therefore, without loss of generality, $l : \mathcal{Y}^2 \longrightarrow [-b, b]$. For every $h \in H$ we define the associated loss function $l_h : (\mathcal{X} \times \mathcal{Y}) \longrightarrow [-b, b]$, $l_h(x, y) = l(h(x), y)$ and denote by $F = \{l_h : (\mathcal{X} \times \mathcal{Y}) \longrightarrow [-b, b] \, : \, h \in H\}$ the loss class associated with the learning problem. The best estimate $h^* \in H$ is the one for which the expected loss (also called risk) is as small as possible, that is, $\mathbb{E} l_{h*} = \inf_{h \in H} \mathbb{E} l_h$, and we will assume that such an h^* exists and is unique. We call $F' = \{l_h - l_{h^*} : h \in H\}$ the excess loss class. Note that all functions in F' have a non-negative expectation, though they can take negative values, and that $0 \in F'$.

Empirical risk minimization algorithms are based on the philosophy that it is possible to approximate the expectation of the loss functions using their empirical mean, and choose instead of h^* the function $\hat{h} \in H$ for which $\frac{1}{n} \sum_{i=1}^{n} l_{\hat{h}}(x_i, y_i) \approx \inf_{h \in H} \frac{1}{n} \sum_{i=1}^{n} l_h(x_i, y_i)$. Such a function is called the empirical minimizer.

In studying the loss class F we will simplify notation and assume that F consists of bounded, real-valued functions defined on a measurable set $\mathcal{X}$, that is, instead of $\mathcal{X} \times \mathcal{Y}$ we only write $\mathcal{X}$. Let $X_1, \ldots, X_n$ be independent random variables distributed according to P. For every $f \in F$, we denote by

$$P_n f = \mathbb{E}_n f = \frac{1}{n} \sum_{i=1}^{n} f(X_i), \qquad Pf = \mathbb{E} f, \qquad R_n f = \frac{1}{n} \sum_{i=1}^{n} \sigma_i f(X_i),$$

where $\mathbb{E} f$ is the expectation of the random variable $f(X)$ with respect to P and $\sigma_1, \ldots, \sigma_n$ are independent Rademacher random variables, that is, symmetric, $\{-1, 1\}$-valued random variables. We further denote

$$\|P - P_n\|_F = \sup_{f \in F} |\mathbb{E} f - \mathbb{E}_n f|, \qquad R_n F = \sup_{f \in F} R_n f.$$

The Rademacher averages of the class F are defined as $\mathbb{E} R_n F$, where the expectation is taken with respect to all random variables X_i and σ_i. An empirical version of the Rademacher averages is obtained by conditioning on the sample,

$$\mathbb{E}_\sigma R_n F = \mathbb{E} \left(\sup_{f \in F} \frac{1}{n} \sum_{i=1}^{n} \sigma_i f(X_i) \,\middle|\, X_1, \ldots, X_n \right).$$

Let

$$F_r = \{f \in F : \mathbb{E} f = r\}, \qquad F^n_{r_1, r_2} = \{f \in F : r_1 \leq \mathbb{E}_n f \leq r_2\}.$$

For a given sample, denote by $\hat{f}$ the corresponding empirical risk minimizer, that is, a function that satisfies: $\mathbb{E}_n \hat{f} = \min_{f \in F} \mathbb{E}_n f$. If the minimum does not exist, we denote by $\hat{f} \in F$ any ρ-approximate empirical minimizer, which is a function satisfying

$$\mathbb{E}_n \hat{f} \leq \inf_{f \in F} \mathbb{E}_n f + \rho,$$

where $\rho \geq 0$. Denote the conditional expectation $\mathbb{E}(\hat{f}(X) | X_1, \ldots, X_n)$ by $\mathbb{E} \hat{f}$.

In the following we will show that if the class F is star-shaped and the variance of every function can be bounded by a reasonable function of its expectation, then the quantity which governs both the structural behaviour of the class and the error rate of the empirical minimizer is the function

$$\xi_n(r) = \mathbb{E} \sup_{f \in F_r} |\mathbb{E} f - \mathbb{E}_n f| = \mathbb{E} \|P - P_n\|_{F_r},$$

or minor modifications of $\xi_n(r)$. Observe that this function measures the expectation of the empirical process $\|P - P_n\|$ indexed by the subset F_r. In the classical result, involving a global complexity measure, the resulting bounds are given in terms of $\mathbb{E} \|P - P_n\|$ indexed by the whole set F, and in [10,15,13,2,9] in terms of the fixed point of $\mathbb{E} \|P - P_n\|$ indexed by the subsets $\{f \in F : \mathbb{E} f \leq r\}$ or $\{f \in F : \mathbb{E} f^2 \leq r\}$, which are all larger sets than F_r. For an empirical minimizer, these structural comparisons lead to the estimate that $\mathbb{E} \hat{f}$ is essentially bounded by $r^* = \inf \left\{ r : \xi_n(r) \leq \frac{r}{4} \right\}$. This result can be improved further: we show that the loss of the empirical minimizer is concentrated around the value $s^* = \mathrm{argmax}\{\xi'_n(r) - r\}$, where $\xi'_n(r) = \mathbb{E} \sup \{\mathbb{E} f - \mathbb{E}_n f : f \in F_r\}$.

2 Preliminaries

In order to obtain the desired results we will require some minor structural assumptions on the class, namely, that F is star-shaped around 0 and satisfies a Bernstein condition.

Definition 1. *We say that F is a (β, B)-Bernstein class with respect to the probability measure P (where $0 < \beta \leq 1$ and $B \geq 1$), if every $f \in F$ satisfies*

$$\mathbb{E}f^2 \leq B(\mathbb{E}f)^\beta.$$

We say that F has Bernstein type β with respect to P if there is some constant B for which F is a (β, B)-Bernstein class.

There are many examples of loss classes for which this assumption can be verified. For example, for nonnegative bounded loss functions, the associated loss function classes satisfy this property with $\beta = 1$. For convex classes of functions bounded by 1, the associated excess squared-loss class satisfies this property as well with $\beta = 1$, a result that was first shown in [12] and improved and extended in [16,3] e.g. to other power types of excess losses.

Definition 2. *F is called star-shaped around 0 if for every $f \in F$ and $0 \leq \alpha \leq 1$, $\alpha f \in F$.*

We can always make a function star-shaped by replacing F with $\mathrm{star}(F, 0) = \{\alpha f : f \in F, 0 \leq \alpha \leq 1\}$. Although $F \subset \mathrm{star}(F, 0)$, one can show that the complexity measure $\xi_n(r)$ does not increase too much. For star-shaped classes, the function $\xi_n(r)/r$ is non-increasing, a property which will allow us to estimate the largest fixed point of $\xi_n(r)$:

Lemma 1. *If F is star-shaped around 0, then for any $0 < r_1 < r_2$,*

$$\frac{\xi_n(r_1)}{r_1} \geq \frac{\xi_n(r_2)}{r_2}.$$

In particular, if for some α, $\xi_n(r) \geq \alpha r$ then for all $0 < r' \leq r$, $\xi_n(r') \geq \alpha r'$.

Proof: Fix $\tau = (X_1, ..., X_n)$ and without loss of generality, suppose that $\sup_{f \in F_{r_2}} |\mathbb{E}f - \mathbb{E}_n f|$ is attained at f. Then $f' = \frac{r_1}{r_2} f \in F_{r_1}$ satisfies

$$|\mathbb{E}f' - \mathbb{E}_n f'| = \frac{r_1}{r_2} \sup_{f \in F_{r_2}} |\mathbb{E}f - \mathbb{E}_n f|.$$

■

The tools used in the proofs of this article are mostly concentration inequalities. We first state the main concentration inequality used in this article, which is a version of Talagrand's inequality [21,20,11].

Theorem 1. *Let F be a class of functions defined on $\mathcal{X}$ and set P to be a probability measure such that for every $f \in F$, $\|f\|_\infty \leq b$ and $\mathbb{E}f = 0$. Let $X_1, ..., X_n$ be independent random variables distributed according to P and set $\sigma^2 = n \sup_{f\in F} \mathrm{var}[f]$. Define*

$$Z = \sup_{f\in F} \sum_{i=1}^{n} f(X_i),$$

$$\bar{Z} = \sup_{f\in F} \left| \sum_{i=1}^{n} f(X_i) \right| .$$

Then there is an absolute constant K such that, for every $x > 0$ and every $\rho > 0$, the following holds:

$$Pr\left(\left\{Z \geq (1+\rho)\mathbb{E}Z + \sigma\sqrt{Kx} + K(1+\rho^{-1})bx\right\}\right) \leq e^{-x},$$
$$Pr\left(\left\{Z \leq (1-\rho)\mathbb{E}Z - \sigma\sqrt{Kx} - K(1+\rho^{-1})bx\right\}\right) \leq e^{-x},$$

and the same inequalities hold for $\bar{Z}$.

The inequality for $\bar{Z}$ is due to Massart [14]. The one sided versions were shown by Rio [19] and Klein [7]. For $b = 1$, the best estimates on the constants in all cases are due to Bousquet [6].

Setting $\bar{Z} = \|P - P_n\|_F$ we obtain the following corollary:

Corollary 1. *For any class of functions F, and every $x > 0$, if*

$$\lambda \geq C \max\left\{\mathbb{E}\|P - P_n\|_F, \sigma_F\sqrt{\frac{x}{n}}, \frac{bx}{n}\right\}, \tag{1}$$

where $\sigma_F^2 = \sup_{f\in F} \mathrm{var}[f]$ and $b = \sup_{f\in F} \|f\|_\infty$, then with probability at least $1 - e^{-x}$, every f in F satisfies

$$|\mathbb{E}f - \mathbb{E}_n f| \leq \lambda.$$

This global estimate is essentially the result obtained in [8,1,18]. It is a worst-case result in the sense that it holds uniformly over the entire class, but $\mathbb{E}\|P - P_n\|_F$ is a better measure of complexity than the VC-dimension since it is measure dependent and it is well known that for binary valued classes, $\mathbb{E}\|P - P_n\|_F \leq c\sqrt{VC(F)/n}$. One way of understanding this result is as a method to compare the empirical and actual structure on the class additively up to λ. Condition (1) arises from the two extra terms in Talagrand's concentration inequality. The result is sharp since it can be shown that for large enough n, $\mathbb{E}\|P - P_n\|_F \geq \sigma_F\sqrt{x/n}$, and that with high probability $\|P - P_n\|_F \geq c\mathbb{E}\|P - P_n\|_F$ for a suitable absolute constant c, see e.g. [4]. Therefore, asymptotically, the difference of empirical and actual structures in this sense is controlled by the global quantity $\mathbb{E}\|P - P_n\|_F$, and the error rate obtained using this approach cannot decay faster than $O(1/\sqrt{n})$. In particular, for any ρ-approximate empirical minimizer, if r satisfies the global condition of the theorem, then with probability at least $1 - e^{-x}$, $\mathbb{E}\hat{f} \leq \mathbb{E}_n \hat{f} + \rho + r$.

The following symmetrization theorem states that the expectation of $\|P - P_n\|_F$ is upper bounded by the Rademacher averages of F, see for example [17].

Theorem 2. *Let F be a class of functions defined on $\mathcal{X}$, set P to be a probability measure on $\mathcal{X}$ and $X_1, ..., X_n$ independent random variables distributed according to P. Then,*

$$\mathbb{E} \|P - P_n\|_F \leq 2\mathbb{E} R_n F .$$

The next lemma, following directly from a theorem in [5], shows that the Rademacher averages of a class can be upper bounded by the empirical Rademacher averages of this class. The following formulation can be found in [2].

Theorem 3. *Let F be a class of bounded functions defined on $\mathcal{X}$ taking values in $[a, b]$, P a probability measure on $\mathcal{X}$, and $X_1, ..., X_n$ be independent random variables distributed according to P. Then, for any $0 \leq \alpha \leq 1$ and $x > 0$, with probability at least $1 - e^{-x}$,*

$$\mathbb{E} R_n F \leq \frac{1}{1-\alpha} \mathbb{E}_\sigma R_n F + \frac{(b-a)x}{4n\alpha(1-\alpha)} .$$

3 Isomorphic Coordinate Projections

We now introduce a multiplicative (rather than additive, as in Corollary 1) notion of similarity of the expected and empirical means which characterizes the fact that, for the given sample, for all functions in the class, $|\mathbb{E}f - \mathbb{E}_n f|$ is at most a constant times its expectation.

Definition 3. *For $\tau = (X_1, \ldots, X_n)$, we say that the coordinate projection $\Pi_\tau : f \mapsto (f(X_1), \ldots, f(X_n))$ is an ϵ-isomorphism if for every $f \in F$,*

$$(1 - \epsilon)\mathbb{E}f \leq \mathbb{E}_n f \leq (1 + \epsilon)\mathbb{E}f.$$

We observe that for star-shaped classes, if, for a given sample τ, a coordinate projection Π_τ is an ϵ-isomorphism on the subset F_r, then the same holds for the larger set $\{f \in F : \mathbb{E}f \geq r\}$.

Lemma 2. *Let F be star-shaped around 0 and let $\tau \in \mathcal{X}^n$. For any $r > 0$ and $0 < \epsilon < 1$, the projection Π_τ is an ϵ-isomorphism of F_r if and only if it is an ϵ-isomorphism of $\{f \in F : \mathbb{E}f \geq r\}$.*

Proof: Let $f \in F$ such that $\mathbb{E}f = t > r$, and since F is star-shaped around 0, $g = rf/t \in F_r$; hence, $(1-\epsilon)\mathbb{E}f \le \mathbb{E}_n f \le (1+\epsilon)\mathbb{E}f$ if and only if the same holds for g. ∎

Thus, for star-shaped classes, it suffices to analyze this notion of similarity on the subsets F_r. The next result, which establishes this fact, follows from Theorem 1. It states that for every subset F_r, if $\xi_n(r)$ is slightly smaller than r then most projections are ϵ-isomorphisms on F_r (and by Lemma 2 also on $\{f \in F : \mathbb{E}f \ge r\}$). On the other hand, if $\xi_n(r)$ is slightly larger than r, most projections are not ϵ-isomorphisms. Hence, at the value of r for which $\xi_n(r) \sim r$, there occurs a phase transition: above that point the class is small enough and a structural result can be obtained. Below the point, the class F_r, which consists of scaled down versions of all functions $\{f \in F : \mathbb{E}f > r\}$ and "new atoms" with $\mathbb{E}f = r$, is too saturated and statistical control becomes impossible.

Theorem 4. *There is an absolute constant c for which the following holds. Let F be a class of functions, such that for every $f \in F$, $\|f\|_\infty \le b$. Assume that F is a (β, B)-Bernstein class. Suppose $r \ge 0$, $0 < \epsilon < 1$, and $0 < \alpha < 1$ satisfy*

$$r \ge c \max\left\{\frac{bx}{n\alpha^2\epsilon}, \left(\frac{Bx}{n\alpha^2\epsilon^2}\right)^{1/(2-\beta)}\right\}.$$

1. *If $\mathbb{E}\|P - P_n\|_{F_r} \ge (1+\alpha)r\epsilon$, then*

$$\Pr\{\Pi_\tau \textit{ is not an } \epsilon\textit{-isomorphism of } F_r\} \ge 1 - e^{-x}.$$

2. *If $\mathbb{E}\|P - P_n\|_{F_r} \le (1-\alpha)r\epsilon$, then*

$$\Pr\{\Pi_\tau \textit{ is an } \epsilon\textit{-isomorphism of } F_r\} \ge 1 - e^{-x}.$$

Proof: The proof follows in a straightforward way from Theorem 1. Define $Z = n\|P - P_n\|_{F_r}$, set $\sigma^2 = n \sup_{f \in F_r} \operatorname{var}[f]$ and note that Π_τ is an ϵ-isomorphism of F_r if and only if $Z \le \epsilon r n$.

To prove the first part of our claim, recall that by Theorem 1, for every $\rho, x > 0$, with probability larger than $1 - e^{-x}$,

$$Z > (1-\rho)\mathbb{E}Z - \sigma\sqrt{Kx} - K\left(1 + \frac{1}{\rho}\right)bx.$$

To ensure that $Z > \epsilon r n$, select $\rho = \alpha/(2(1+\alpha))$, and observe that by the assumption that F is a Bernstein class, it suffices to show that

$$\frac{1}{2}\alpha n r\epsilon \ge (Bnr^\beta Kx)^{1/2} + K\left(1 + \frac{2(1+\alpha)}{\alpha}\right)xb,$$

which holds by the condition on r.

The second part of the claim also follows from Theorem 1: for every $\rho, x > 0$, with probability larger than $1 - e^{-x}$,

$$Z < (1+\rho)\mathbb{E}Z + \sigma\sqrt{Kx} + K\left(1 + \frac{1}{\rho}\right)bx.$$

Choosing $\rho = \alpha/(2(1-\alpha))$, we see that $Z < nr\epsilon$ if

$$\frac{1}{2}\alpha nr\epsilon \geq (Bnr^{\beta}Kx)^{1/2} + K\left(1 + \frac{2(1-\alpha)}{\alpha}\right)xb,$$

so the condition on r again suffices. ∎

Corollary 2. *Let F be a class of functions bounded by b, which is star-shaped around 0 and is a (β, B)-Bernstein class. Then there exists an absolute constant c for which the following holds.If $0 < \epsilon, \alpha < 1$, and $r, x > 0$, satisfy*

$$r \geq \max\left\{\frac{\xi_n(r)}{(1-\alpha)\epsilon}, c\frac{bx}{n\alpha^2\epsilon}, c\left(\frac{Bx}{n\alpha^2\epsilon^2}\right)^{1/(2-\beta)}\right\}, \tag{2}$$

then with probability at least $1 - e^{-x}$, every $f \in F$ satisfies

$$\mathbb{E}f \leq \max\left\{\frac{\mathbb{E}_n f}{1-\epsilon}, r\right\}.$$

Proof: The proof follows directly from Theorem 4. ∎

Clearly, Corollary 2 is an improvement on the result in Corollary 1 for most interesting loss classes, for which $0 < \beta \leq 1$. The condition (2) allows one to control the expectation of the empirical minimizer asymptotically up to the scale $O(1/n^{1/2-\beta})$, and for classes with $\beta = 1$ even at the best possible scale $O(1/n)$, as opposed to $O(1/\sqrt{n})$ in Corollary 1. The quantity $\xi_n(r) = \mathbb{E}\left\|P - P_n\right\|_{F_r}$ is also an improvement on $\lambda \sim \mathbb{E}\left\|P - P_n\right\|_F$ from Corollary 1, since the supremum is taken only on the subset F_r which can be much smaller than F.

Corollary 2 also improves the localized results from [2]. In [2] the indexing set is the set of functions with a small variance, $\{f \in F : Pf^2 \leq r\}$, or a sub-root function upper bounding the empirical process indexed by $\{f \in F : Pf \leq r\}$. The advantage of Corollary 2 is that the indexing set F_r is smaller, and that the upper bound in terms of the fixed point can be proved without assuming the sub-root property. The property of $\xi_n(r)$ in Lemma 1, a "sub-linear" property, is sufficient to lead to the following estimate on the empirical minimizer:

Theorem 5. *Let F be a (β, B)-Bernstein class of functions bounded by b which is star-shaped around 0. Then there is an absolute constant c such that if*

$$r' = \max\left\{\inf\left\{r : \xi_n(r) \leq r/4\right\}, \frac{cbx}{n}, c\left(\frac{Bx}{n}\right)^{1/(2-\beta)}\right\},$$

then with probability at least $1-e^{-x}$, a ρ-approximate empirical minimizer $\hat{f} \in F$ satisfies

$$\mathbb{E}\hat{f} \leq \max\{2\rho, r'\}.$$

Proof: The proof follows from Corollary 2 by taking $\epsilon = \alpha = 1/2$ and $r = r'$. In particular, Lemma 1 shows that if $r' \geq \inf\left\{r : \xi_n(r) \leq \frac{r}{4}\right\}$, then $\xi_n(r') \leq r'/4$. Thus, with large probability, if $f \in F$ satisfies $\mathbb{E}f \geq r'$, then $\mathbb{E}f \leq 2\mathbb{E}_n f$. Since $\hat{f}$ is a ρ-approximate empirical minimizer and F is star-shaped at 0, it follows that $\mathbb{E}_n \hat{f} \leq \rho$, so either $\mathbb{E}f \leq r'$ or $\mathbb{E}f \leq 2\rho$, as claimed. ■

Thus, with high probability, $r^* = \inf\left\{r : \xi_n(r) \leq \frac{r}{4}\right\}$ is an upper bound for $\mathbb{E}\hat{f}$, as long as $r^* \geq c/n$.

This result holds in particular for any empirical minimizer of the excess loss class if the true minimizer f^* exists. In this case, $0 \in F$, and any empirical minimizer over F is also an empirical minimizer over star$(F, 0)$.

Data-Dependent Estimation of $\xi_n(r)$ and r^*

The next question we wish to address is how to estimate the function $\xi_n(r)$ and the fixed point

$$r^* = \inf\left\{r : \xi_n(r) \leq \frac{r}{4}\right\}$$

empirically, in cases where the global complexity of the function class, for example the covering numbers or the combinatorial dimension, is not known.

To estimate r^* we will find an empirically computable function $\hat{\xi}_n(r)$ which is, with high probability, an upper bound for the function $\xi_n(r)$. Therefore, it will hold that its fixed point $\hat{r}^* = \inf\{r : \hat{\xi}_n(r) \leq \frac{r}{4}\}$ is with high probability an upper bound for r^*. Since $\hat{\xi}_n(r)/r$ will be a non-increasing function, we will be able to determine $\hat{r}^*$ using a binary search algorithm.

Assume that F is a star-shaped (β, B)-Bernstein class and $\sup_{f \in F} \|f\|_\infty \leq b$. Let $\tau = (X_1, ..., X_n)$ be a sample, where each X_i is drawn independently according to P.

From Theorem 4, for $\alpha = 1/2, \epsilon = 1/2$, if $r \geq c \max\left\{\frac{bx}{n}, \left(\frac{Bx}{n}\right)^{1/(2-\beta)}\right\}$ and $\xi_n(r) \leq \frac{r}{4}$, then with probability larger than $1 - e^{-x}$, every $f \in F_r$ satisfies that

$$\forall f \in F_r : \mathbb{E}_n f \in \left[\frac{r}{2}, \frac{3r}{2}\right].$$

Since F is star-shaped, and by Lemma 1, it holds that $\xi_n(r) \leq \frac{r}{4}$ if and only if $r \geq r^*$. Therefore, if $r \geq \max\left\{r^*, \frac{cbx}{n}, c\left(\frac{Bx}{n}\right)^{1/(2-\beta)}\right\}$, then with probability larger than $1 - e^{-x}$, $F_r \subset F^n_{\frac{r}{2}, \frac{3r}{2}}$, which implies that

$$\mathbb{E}_\sigma R_n(F_r) \leq \mathbb{E}_\sigma R_n\left(F^n_{\frac{r}{2}, \frac{3r}{2}}\right),$$

where $F^n_{r_1, r_2} = \{f \in F : r_1 \leq \mathbb{E}_n f \leq r_2\}$.

By symmetrization (Theorem 2) and concentration of Rademacher averages around their mean (Theorem 3), it follows that with probability at least $1 - 2e^{-x}$,

$$\xi_n(r) \leq 2\mathbb{E}R_n(F_r) \leq 4\mathbb{E}_\sigma R_n(F_r) + \frac{bx}{n} \leq 4\mathbb{E}_\sigma R_n\left(F^n_{\frac{r}{2}, \frac{3r}{2}}\right) + \frac{r}{c},$$

where we used the fact that $r \geq \frac{cbx}{n}$ (and clearly we can assume that $c > 8$).

Set

$$r' = \max\left\{r^*, \frac{cbx}{n}, c\left(\frac{Bx}{n}\right)^{1/(2-\beta)}\right\}, \text{and}$$

$$R = \left\{\frac{1}{n}, \frac{2}{n}, \ldots, \frac{\lceil bn \rceil}{n}\right\} \cap \left[\frac{\lfloor r'n \rfloor}{n}, \frac{\lceil bn \rceil}{n}\right].$$

Applying the union bound, and since $|R| \leq bn+1$, with probability at least $1-2(bn+1)e^{-x}$, $\xi_n(r) \leq 4\mathbb{E}_\sigma R_n\left(F^n_{\frac{r}{2},\frac{3r}{2}}\right) + \frac{r}{c}$ for every $r \in R$. By Lemma 1, if $r \in [k/n, (k+1)/n]$, then $\xi_n(r) \leq \xi_n\left(\frac{k}{n}\right)\frac{nr}{k}$, and thus, with probability at least $1-2(bn+1)e^{-x}$, every $r \in [r', b]$ satisfies

$$\xi_n(r) \leq \xi_n\left(\frac{k}{n}\right)\frac{nr}{k} \leq \left(4\mathbb{E}_\sigma R_n\left(F^n_{\frac{k}{2n},\frac{3k}{2n}}\right) + \frac{k}{cn}\right)\frac{nr}{k} \leq 8\mathbb{E}_\sigma R_n\left(F^n_{c_1 r, c_2 r}\right) + \frac{r}{c},$$

where c_1, c_2 are positive constants. We define therefore

$$\hat{\xi}_n(r) = 8\mathbb{E}_\sigma R_n\left(F^n_{c_1 r, c_2 r}\right) + \frac{r}{c}.$$

Then it follows that with probability at least $1-2(bn+1)e^{-x}$

$$\forall r \in [r', b] : \xi_n(r) \leq \hat{\xi}_n(r).$$

Let $\hat{r}^* = \inf\{r : \hat{\xi}_n(r) \leq \frac{r}{4}\}$, then we know that with probability at least $1-2(bn+1)e^{-x}$, $\hat{r}^* \geq r^*$. Since $\hat{\xi}_n(r)/r$ is non-increasing, it follows that $r \geq \hat{r}^*$ if and only if $\hat{\xi}_n(r) \leq \frac{r}{4}$.

With this, given a sample of size n, we are ready to state the following algorithm to estimate the upper bound on $\hat{r}^*$ based on the data:

Algorithm RSTAR(F, $X_1, \ldots, X_n$)

Set $r_L = 0$, $r_R = b$.
If $\hat{\xi}_n(r_R) \leq r_R/4$ then
  for $l = 0$ to $\lceil \log_2 bn \rceil$
    set $r = \frac{r_R - r_L}{2}$;
    if $\hat{\xi}_n(r) > r/4$ then set $r_L = r$,
      else set $r_R = r$.
Output $\bar{r} = r_R$.

By the construction, $\bar{r} - \frac{1}{n} \leq \hat{r}^* \leq \bar{r}$. For every n and every sample, with probability larger than $1-2(bn+1)e^{-x}$, $r^* \leq \bar{r}$.

Theorem 6. *Let F be a (β, B)-Bernstein class of functions bounded by b which is star-shaped around 0. With probability at least $1-(2bn+3)e^{-x}$, a ρ-approximate empirical minimizer $\hat{f} \in F$ satisfies*

$$\mathbb{E}\hat{f} \leq \max\{2\rho, r''\},$$

where

$$r'' = \max\left\{\bar{r}, \frac{cbx}{n}, c\left(\frac{Bx}{n}\right)^{1/(2-\beta)}\right\},$$

and $\bar{r} = RSTAR(F, \tau)$.

RSTAR(F, τ) is essentially the fixed point of the $\mathbb{E}_\sigma R_n\left(F^n_{c_1 r, c_2 r}\right)$. This function measures the complexity of the function class $F^n_{c_1 r, c_2 r}$ which is the subset of functions having the empirical mean in an interval whose length is proportional to r. The main difference from the data-dependent estimates in [2] is that instead of taking the whole empirical ball, here we only measure the complexity of an empirical "belt" around r, since $c_1 r > 0$.

We can tighten this bound further by narrowing the size of the belt by replacing the empirical set $F^n_{r/2,3r/2}$ with $F^n_{r-r/\log n, r+r/\log n}$. The price we pay is an extra $\log n$ factor.

With the same reasoning as before, by Theorem 4 for $\alpha = 1/2, \epsilon = 1/\log n$, and since F is star-shaped, then, if $r \geq \max\left\{r^*, \frac{cbx \log n}{n}, c\left(\frac{Bx \log^2 n}{n}\right)^{1/(2-\beta)}\right\}$, with probability larger than $1 - e^{-x}$, $F_r \subset F^n_{r-r/\log n, r+r/\log n}$. We define

$$\hat{\xi}_n(r) = \left(4\mathbb{E}_\sigma R_n\left(F^n_{k/n - k/(n\log n), k/n + k/(n \log n)}\right) + \frac{k}{cn \log n}\right)\frac{n}{k} r,$$

if $r \in [k/n, (k+1)/n]$. Again, with probability at least $1 - 2(bn+1)e^{-x}$, it holds that for all $r \in [r', b] : \xi(r) \leq \hat{\xi}_n(r)$, where

$$r' = \max\left\{r^*, \frac{cbx \log n}{n}, c\left(\frac{Bx \log^2 n}{n}\right)^{1/(2-\beta)}\right\}.$$

Since $\hat{\xi}_n(r)/r$ is non-increasing, we can compute

$$\hat{r}^* = \inf\left\{r : \hat{\xi}_n(r) \leq \frac{r}{2 \log n}\right\}$$

with a slight modification of RSTAR (we replace the test in the if-clause, $\hat{\xi}_n(r) > r/4$, with $\hat{\xi}_n(r) > r/2 \log n$). For every n and every sample of size n, with probability larger than $1 - 2(bn+1)e^{-x}$, $r^* \leq \bar{r}$.

4 Direct Concentration Result for Empirical Minimizers

In this section we will now show that a direct analysis of the empirical minimizer leads to sharper estimates than those obtained in the previous section. We will show that $\mathbb{E}\hat{f}$ is concentrated around the value $s^* = \text{argmax}\{\xi'_n(r) - r\}$, where

$$\xi'_n(r) = \mathbb{E} \sup\left\{\mathbb{E}f - \mathbb{E}_n f : f \in F, \mathbb{E}f = r\right\}.$$

To understand why it makes sense to expect that with high probability $\mathbb{E}\hat{f} \sim s^*$, fix one value of r such that $\xi_n'(s^*) - s^* > \xi_n'(r) - r$. Consider a perfect situation in which one could say that with high probability,

$$\xi_n'(r) \sim \sup\{\mathbb{E}f - \mathbb{E}_n f : f \in F, \mathbb{E}f = r\} = r - \inf\{\mathbb{E}_n f : f \in F, \mathbb{E}f = r\}.$$

(Of course, this is not the case, as Talagrand's inequality contains additional terms which blow-up as the multiplicative constant represented by $\sim$ tends to one; this fact is the crux of the proof.) In that case, it would follow that

$$-\inf\{\mathbb{E}_n f : f \in F, \mathbb{E}f = s^*\} > -\inf\{\mathbb{E}_n f : f \in F, \mathbb{E}f = r\}$$

and the empirical minimizer will not be in F_r. In a similar manner, one has to rule out all other values of r, and to that end we will have to consider a belt around s^* rather than s^* itself.

For $\epsilon > 0$, define

$$r_{\epsilon,+} = \sup\left\{0 \le r \le b : \xi_n'(r) - r \ge \sup_s\left(\xi_n'(s) - s\right) - \epsilon\right\},$$

$$r_{\epsilon,-} = \inf\left\{0 \le r \le b : \xi_n'(r) - r \ge \sup_s\left(\xi_n'(s) - s\right) - \epsilon\right\}.$$

The following theorem is the main result:

Theorem 7. *For any $c_1 > 0$, there is a constant c (depending only on c_1) such that the following holds. Let F be a (β, B)-Bernstein class that is star-shaped at 0. Define $r_{\epsilon,+}$, and $r_{\epsilon,-}$ as above, and set*

$$r' = \max\left\{\inf\{r : \xi_n'(r) \le r/4\}, \frac{cb(x+\log n)}{n}, c\left(\frac{B(x+\log n)}{n}\right)^{1/(2-\beta)}\right\}.$$

For $0 < \rho < r'/2$, let $\hat{f}$ denote a ρ-approximate empirical risk minimizer. If

$$\epsilon \ge c\left(\max\left\{\sup_s\left(\xi_n'(s) - s\right), r'^{\beta}\right\}\frac{(B+b)(x+\log n)}{n}\right)^{1/2} + \rho,$$

then

1. *With probability at least $1 - e^{-x}$,*

$$\mathbb{E}\hat{f} \le \max\left\{\frac{1}{n}, r_{\epsilon,+}\right\}.$$

2. *If*

$$\xi_n'(0, c_1/n) < \sup_s\left(\xi_n'(s) - s\right) - \epsilon,$$

then with probability at least $1 - e^{-x}$,

$$\mathbb{E}\hat{f} \ge r_{\epsilon,-}.$$

Note that this result is considerably sharper than the bound resulting from Theorem 5, as long as the function $\xi_n'(r) - r$ is not flat. (This corresponds to no "significant atoms" appearing at a scale below some r_0, and thus, for $r < r_0$, F_r is just a scaled down version of F_{r_0}; if $\xi_n'(r) - r$ is flat, the two bounds will be of the same order of magnitude.)

Indeed, by Lemma 1, since $\xi_n'(r)/r$ is non-increasing,

$$\inf\{r : \xi_n'(r) \le r\} \le \inf\left\{r : \xi_n'(r) \le \frac{r}{4}\right\}.$$

Clearly, $\xi_n'(r) \ge 0$, since $\xi_n'(r) \ge \mathbb{E}(\mathbb{E}f - \mathbb{E}_n f) = 0$ for any fixed function, and thus $0 \le s^* \le \inf\{r : \xi_n'(r) \le r\} \le r*$. The same argument shows that if $\xi_n'(r) - r$ is not "flat" then $s^* \ll r$. Now, for $\beta = 1$, $\epsilon \sim \sqrt{\frac{s^*}{n}} \ll s^*$ and $r_{\epsilon,+}, r_{\epsilon,-}$ will be of the order of s^*.

5 Discussion

Now, we will give an example which shows that, for any given sample size n, we can construct a function class and a probability measure such that the bound on the empirical minimizer differs significantly when using r^* from Section 3 versus s^* from Section 4.

We first prove the existence of two types of function classes, which are both bounded and Bernstein.

Lemma 3. *For every positive integer n and all $m \ge 2(n^2 + n)$, the following holds. If P is the uniform probability measure on $\{1, ..., m\}$, then for every $\frac{1}{n} \le \lambda \le 1/2$ there exists a function class G_λ such that*

1. *For every $g \in G_\lambda$, $-1 \le g(x) \le 1$, $\mathbb{E}g = \lambda$ and $\mathbb{E}g^2 \le 2\mathbb{E}g$.*
2. *For every set $\tau \subset \{1, ..., m\}$ with $|\tau| \le n$, there is some $g \in G_\lambda$ such that for every $i \in \tau$, $g(i) = -1$.*

Also, there exists a function class H_λ such that

1. *For every $h \in H_\lambda$, $0 \le h(x) \le 1$, $\mathbb{E}h = \lambda$.*
2. *For every set $\tau \subset \{1, ..., m\}$ with $|\tau| \le n$, there is some $h \in H_\lambda$ such that for every $i \in \tau$, $h(i) = 0$.*

Proof: The proof is constructive. Let $J \subset \{1, ..., m\}$, $|J| = n$; for every $I \subset J$ define $g = g_{I,J}$ in the following manner. For $i \in I$, set $g(i) = 1$, if $i \in J \backslash I$, set $g(i) = -1$, and for $i \notin J$ put $g(i) = t$, where

$$t = \frac{\lambda m + |J \backslash I| - |I|}{m - n}.$$

Observe that if $m \ge n^2 + 2n$, then $0 < t \le 2\lambda \le 1$ for every I, J. By the definition of t, $\mathbb{E}g_{I,J} = \lambda$, and

$$\begin{aligned}\mathbb{E}g^2 &= \frac{1}{m}\left(|I| - |J \backslash I| + t^2(m-n) + 2|J \backslash I|\right) \le \mathbb{E}g + \frac{2|J \backslash I|}{m} \\ &\le \mathbb{E}g + 2\frac{n}{m} < \mathbb{E}g + \frac{1}{n} \le 2\mathbb{E}g,\end{aligned}$$

where the last inequality holds because $\mathbb{E}g = \lambda \ge 1/n$, and $m \ge 2n^2$.

The second property of G_λ is clear by the construction, and the claims regarding H_λ can be verified using a similar argument. ∎

Given a sample size n, we can choose a large enough m and the uniform probability measure P on $\{1,\ldots,m\}$, and define the function class $F = \text{star}(\tilde{F}, 0)$, where $\tilde{F} = H_{1/4} \cup G_{1/n}$ from Lemma 3. F is star-shaped and (1,2) Bernstein.

Theorem 8. *If $0 < \delta < 1$ and $n > N_0(\delta)$, then for any corresponding $F = star(\tilde{F}, 0)$ as above, the following holds:*

1. *For every $X_1, ..., X_n$ there is a function $f \in F$ with $\mathbb{E}f = 1/4$ and $\mathbb{E}_n f = 0$.*
2. *For the class F, the function ξ'_n satisfies*

$$\xi'_n(r) = \begin{cases} (n+1)r & \text{if } 0 < r \leq 1/n, \\ r & \text{if } 1/n < r \leq 1/4, \\ 0 & \text{if } r > 1/4. \end{cases}$$

   Thus, $\inf\{r > 0 : \xi'_n(r) \leq r/4\} = 1/4$.
3. *If $\hat{f}$ is a ρ-approximate empirical minimizer, where $0 < \rho < 1/8$, then with probability larger than $1 - \delta$,*

$$\frac{1}{n}\left(1 - c\sqrt{\frac{\log n}{n}} - \rho\right) \leq \mathbb{E}\hat{f} \leq \frac{1}{n}.$$

The proof can be found in [4].

References

1. P.L. Bartlett, S. Boucheron, G. Lugosi: Model selection and error estimation. Machine Learning 48, 85-113, 2002.
2. P.L. Bartlett, O. Bousquet, S. Mendelson: Local Rademacher Complexities. Submitted, 2002 (available at http://www.stat.berkeley.edu/~bartlett/publications/recent-pubs.html).
3. P.L. Bartlett, M.I. Jordan, J.D. McAuliffe: Convexity, classification, and risk bounds. Tech. Rep. 638, Dept. of Stat., U.C. Berkeley, 2003.
4. P.L. Bartlett, S. Mendelson: Empirical minimization. Submitted, 2003 (available at http://axiom.anu.edu.au/~shahar).
5. S. Boucheron, G. Lugosi, P. Massart: Concentration inequalities using the entropy method. Ann. of Prob. 31, 1583-1614, 2003.
6. O. Bousquet: Concentration Inequalities and Empirical Processes Theory Applied to the Analysis of Learning Algorithms. PhD. Thesis, 2002.
7. T. Klein: Une inégalité de concentration gauche pour les processus empiriques. C. R. Math. Acad. Sci. Paris 334(6), 501-504, 2002.
8. V. Koltchinskii, Rademacher penalties and structural risk minimization. IEEE Trans. on Info. Th. 47(5), 1902-1914, 2001.
9. V. Koltchinskii: Local Rademacher Complexities and Oracle Inequalities in Risk Minimization. Tech. Rep., Univ. of New Mexico, August 2003.

10. V. Koltchinskii and D. Panchenko, Rademacher processes and bounding the risk of function learning. In E. Gine and D. Mason and J. Wellner (Eds.), *High Dimensional Probability II*, 443-459, 2000.
11. M. Ledoux: *The concentration of measure phenomenon.* Mathematical Surveys and Monographs, Vol 89, AMS, 2001.
12. W.S. Lee, P.L. Bartlett, R.C. Williamson: The Importance of Convexity in Learning with Squared Loss. IEEE Trans. on Info Th., 44(5), 1974-1980, 1998.
13. G. Lugosi and M. Wegkamp, Complexity regularization via localized random penalties. Ann. of Stat., to appear, 2003.
14. P. Massart: About the constants in Talagrand's concentration inequality for empirical processes. Ann. of Prob., 28(2), 863-884, 2000.
15. P. Massart. Some applications of concentration inequalities to statistics. Ann. de la Faculté des Sciences de Toulouse, IX: 245-303, 2000.
16. S. Mendelson, Improving the sample complexity using global data. IEEE Trans. on Info. Th. 48(7), 1977-1991, 2002.
17. S. Mendelson: A few notes on Statistical Learning Theory. In *Proc. of the Machine Learning Summer School, Canberra 2002, S. Mendelson and A. J. Smola (Eds.)*, LNCS 2600, Springer, 2003.
18. S. Mendelson, Rademacher averages and phase transitions in Glivenko-Cantelli classes. IEEE Transactions on Information Theory 48(1), 251-263, 2002.
19. E. Rio: Inégalités de concentration pour les processus empiriques de classes de parties. Probab. Theory Related Fields 119(2), 163-175, 2001.
20. M. Talagrand: New concentration inequalities in product spaces. Invent. Math., 126, 505-563, 1996.
21. M. Talagrand: Sharper bounds for Gaussian and empirical processes. Ann. of Prob., 22(1), 28-76, 1994.

Model Selection by Bootstrap Penalization for Classification

Magalie Fromont

Université Paris XI
Laboratoire de mathématiques, Bât. 425
91405 Orsay Cedex, France
magalie.fromont@math.u-psud.fr

Abstract. We consider the binary classification problem. Given an i.i.d. sample drawn from the distribution of an $\mathcal{X} \times \{0,1\}$-valued random pair, we propose to estimate the so-called *Bayes classifier* by minimizing the sum of the empirical classification error and a penalty term based on Efron's or i.i.d. weighted bootstrap samples of the data. We obtain exponential inequalities for such bootstrap type penalties, which allow us to derive non-asymptotic properties for the corresponding estimators. In particular, we prove that these estimators achieve the global minimax risk over sets of functions built from Vapnik-Chervonenkis classes. The obtained results generalize Koltchinskii [12] and Bartlett, Boucheron, Lugosi's [2] ones for Rademacher penalties that can thus be seen as special examples of bootstrap type penalties.

1 Introduction

Let (X, Y) be a random pair with values in a measurable space $\Xi = \mathcal{X} \times \{0,1\}$. Given n independent copies $(X_1, Y_1), \ldots, (X_n, Y_n)$ of (X, Y), we aim at constructing a *classification rule* that is a function which would give the value of Y from the observation of X. More precisely, in statistical terms, we are interested in the estimation of the function s minimizing the classification error $\mathbb{P}[t(X) \neq Y]$ over all the measurable functions $t : \mathcal{X} \to \{0,1\}$. The function s is called the *Bayes classifier* and it is also defined by $s(x) = \mathbb{I}_{\mathbb{P}[Y=1|X=x]>1/2}$.

Given a class S of measurable functions from $\mathcal{X}$ to $\{0,1\}$, an estimator $\hat{s}$ of s is determined by minimization of the empirical classification error $\gamma_n(t) = n^{-1}\sum_{i=1}^{n} \mathbb{I}_{t(X_i)\neq Y_i}$ over all the functions t in S. This method has been introduced in learning problems by Vapnik and Chervonenkis [25]. However, it poses the problem of the choice of the class S. To provide an estimator with classification error close to the optimal one, S has to be large enough so that the error of the best function in S is close to the optimal error, while it has to be small enough so that finding the best candidate in S from the data $(X_1, Y_1), \ldots, (X_n, Y_n)$ is still possible. In other words, one has to choose a class S which achieves the best trade-off between the approximation error and the estimation error.

J. Shawe-Taylor and Y. Singer (Eds.): COLT 2004, LNAI 3120, pp. 285–299, 2004.

One approach proposed to solve this question is the method of *Structural Risk Minimization* (SRM) initiated by Vapnik [27] and also known as *Complexity regularization* (see [1] for instance). It consists in selecting among a given collection of functions sets the set S minimizing the sum of the empirical classification error of the estimator $\hat{s}$ and a penalty term taking the complexity of S into account. The quantities generally used to measure the complexity of some class S of functions from $\mathcal{X}$ to $\{0,1\}$ are the *Shatter coefficients* of the associated class of sets $\mathcal{C} = \{\{x \in \mathcal{X},\ t(x) = 1\},\ t \in S\}$ given by:

$$\text{for } k \geq 1,\ \mathbb{S}(\mathcal{C}, k) = \max_{x_1,\ldots,x_k \in \mathcal{X}} |\ \{\{x_1, \ldots, x_k\} \cap C,\ C \in \mathcal{C}\}\ |,$$

and the *Vapnik-Chervonenkis dimension* of $\mathcal{C}$ defined as:

$$V(\mathcal{C}) = \infty \text{ if for all } k \geq 1,\ \mathbb{S}(\mathcal{C}, k) = 2^k,$$
$$V(\mathcal{C}) = \sup\left\{k \geq 1,\ \mathbb{S}(\mathcal{C}, k) = 2^k\right\} \text{ else.}$$

Considering a collection $\{S_m,\ m \in \mathbb{N}^*\}$ of classes of functions from $\mathcal{X}$ to $\{0,1\}$ and setting $\mathcal{C}_m = \{\{x \in \mathcal{X},\ t(x) = 1\},\ t \in S_m\}$ for all m in $\mathbb{N}^*$, Lugosi and Zeger [17] study the standard penalties of the form

$$\text{pen}(m) = \kappa\sqrt{(\log \mathbb{S}(\mathcal{C}_m, n^2) + m)/n},$$

which are approximately $\kappa'\sqrt{(V(\mathcal{C}_m)\log n + m)/n}$. By using an inequality due to Devroye, they prove that if the classes $\mathcal{C}_m$ are Vapnik-Chervonenkis classes (that is if they have a finite VC-dimension) such that the sequence $(V(\mathcal{C}_m))_{m\in\mathbb{N}^*}$ is strictly increasing, and if the Bayes classifier s belongs to the union of the S_m's, there exists an integer k such that the expected classification error of the rule obtained by SRM with such penalties differs from the optimal error $\mathbb{P}\left[s(X) \neq Y\right]$ by a term not larger than a constant times $\sqrt{V(\mathcal{C}_k)\log n/n}$. This upper bound is optimal in a global minimax sense up to a logarithmic factor. Given a class S of functions from $\mathcal{X}$ to $\{0,1\}$ where $\mathcal{C} = \{\{x \in \mathcal{X},\ t(x) = 1\},\ t \in S\}$ is a VC-class with VC-dimension $V(\mathcal{C})$, Vapnik and Chervonenkis [26] actually prove that there exist some constants κ_1 and κ_2 such that for any classification rule $\hat{s}$ with classification error $L_{\hat{s}}$,

$$\sup_{P,s\in S}\mathbb{E}\left[L_{\hat{s}} - \mathbb{P}\left[s(X) \neq Y\right]\right] \geq \kappa_1\sqrt{V(\mathcal{C})/n},\ \forall n \geq \kappa_2 V(\mathcal{C}).$$

We explain in the next section how the choice of the penalty terms is connected with the calibration of an upper bound for the quantity $\sup_{t\in S}|\gamma_n(t) - \mathbb{P}\left[t(X) \neq Y\right]|$. Unfortunately, in addition to the fact that their computation is generally complicated, the penalties based on the Shatter coefficients or the VC-dimensions have the disadvantage to be deterministic and to overestimate this quantity for specific data distributions. This remark has led many authors to introduce *data-driven* penalties (see for example [6], [15], [5]). Inspired by the method of Rademacher symmetrization commonly used in the empirical processes theory, Koltchinskii [12] and Bartlett, Boucheron, Lugosi [2] independently propose the so-called *Rademacher penalties*. They prove oracle type inequalities showing that such random penalties provide optimal classification rules in a global minimax sense over sets of functions built from Vapnik-Chervonenkis classes. Lozano [14] gives the experimental evidence that, for the intervals model selection problem, Rademacher penalization outperforms SRM and cross validation over a wide range of sample sizes. Bartlett, Boucheron and Lugosi [2] also study Rademacher penalization from a practical point of view by comparing it with other kinds of data-driven methods.

Whereas the methods of Rademacher penalization are now commonly used in the statistical learning theory, they are not so popular yet in the applied statistics community. In fact, statisticians often prefer to stick with resampling tools such as bootstrap or jacknife in practice. We here aim at making the connection between the two approaches. We investigate a new family of penalties based on classical bootstrap processes such as Efron's or i.i.d. weighted bootstrap ones while attending to placing Rademacher penalties among this family.

The paper is organized as follows. In Section 2, we present the model selection by penalization approach and explain how to choose a penalty function. We introduce and study in Section 3 some penalties based on Efron's bootstrap samples of the observations. We establish oracle type inequalities and, from a maximal inequality stated in Section 5, some (global) minimax properties for the corresponding classification rules. Section 4 is devoted to various symmetrized bootstrap penalizations: similar results are obtained, generalizing Koltchinskii and Bartlett, Boucheron, Lugosi's ones. We finally give in Section 6 a discussion about these results.

2 Model Selection

We describe here the model selection by penalization approach to construct classification rules or estimators of the Bayes classifier s. In the following, we denote by $\mathcal{S}$ the set of all the measurable functions $t : \mathcal{X} \to \{0,1\}$ and by P the distribution of (X,Y). Given a countable collection $\{S_m, m \in \mathcal{M}\}$ of classes of functions in $\mathcal{S}$ (the *models*) and $\rho_n \geq 0$, for any m in $\mathcal{M}$, we can construct some approximate minimum contrast estimator $\hat{s}_m$ in S_m satisfying:

$$\gamma_n(\hat{s}_m) \leq \inf_{t \in S_m} \gamma_n(t) + \rho_n/2.$$

We thus obtain a collection $\{\hat{s}_m, m \in \mathcal{M}\}$ of possible classification rules and at this stage, the issue is to choose among this collection the "best" rule in terms of risk minimization. Let l be the loss function defined by:

$$l(u,v) = \mathbb{E}\left[\mathbb{I}_{v(X) \neq Y} - \mathbb{I}_{u(X) \neq Y}\right], \text{ for all } u, v \text{ in } \mathcal{S}.$$

Notice that, by definition of s, $l(s,t)$ is nonnegative for every t in $\mathcal{S}$. The risk of any estimator $\hat{s}_m$ of s is given by $\mathbb{E}\left[l(s,\hat{s}_m)\right]$. Ideally, we would like to select some element $\bar{m}$ (the *oracle*) in $\mathcal{M}$ minimizing

$$\mathbb{E}\left[l(s,\hat{s}_m)\right] = l(s,s_m) + \mathbb{E}\left[l(s_m,\hat{s}_m)\right],$$

where for every m in $\mathcal{M}$, s_m denotes some function in S_m such that $l(s,s_m) = \inf_{t \in S_m} l(s,t)$. However, such an oracle $\bar{m}$ necessarily depends on the unknown distribution of (X, Y). This leads us to use the method of model selection by penalization which originates in Mallows' C_p and Akaike's heuristics.

The purpose of this method is actually to provide a criterion which allows to select, only from the data, an element $\hat{m}$ in $\mathcal{M}$ mimicking the oracle. Considering some *penalty function* pen : $\mathcal{M} \to \mathbb{R}_+$, we choose $\hat{m}$ such that:

$$\gamma_n(\hat{s}_{\hat{m}}) + \text{pen}(\hat{m}) \leq \inf_{m \in \mathcal{M}} \{\gamma_n(\hat{s}_m) + \text{pen}(m)\} + \rho_n/2,$$

and we finally take as "best" rule the so-called *approximate minimum penalized contrast estimator*

$$\tilde{s} = \hat{s}_{\hat{m}}. \tag{1}$$

We then have to determine some penalty function such that the risk of the approximate minimum penalized contrast estimator $\tilde{s}$ is of the same order as

$$\inf_{m \in \mathcal{M}} \mathbb{E}\left[l(s, \hat{s}_m)\right] = \inf_{m \in \mathcal{M}} \{l(s, s_m) + \mathbb{E}\left[l(s_m, \hat{s}_m)\right]\}$$

or, failing that, at most of the same order as $\inf_{m \in \mathcal{M}}\{l(s, s_m) + \sqrt{V_m/n}\}$ when for each m in $\mathcal{M}$, $S_m = \{\mathbb{I}_C, C \in \mathcal{C}_m\}$, $\mathcal{C}_m$ being a VC-class with VC-dimension V_m. Indeed, as cited in the introduction, Vapnik and Chervonenkis [26] proved that the global minimax risk over such a class S_m defined by $\inf_{\hat{s}} \sup_{P, s \in S_m} \mathbb{E}\left[l(s, \hat{s})\right]$ is of order $\sqrt{V_m/n}$ as soon as $n \geq \kappa V_m$, for some absolute constant κ.

The various strategies to determine adequate penalty functions rely on the same basic inequality that we present below. Let us fix m in $\mathcal{M}$ and introduce the centered empirical contrast defined for all t in $\mathcal{S}$ by $\overline{\gamma_n}(t) = \gamma_n(t) - \mathbb{E}\left[\mathbb{I}_{t(X) \neq Y}\right]$. Since

$$l(s_m, \hat{s}_{\hat{m}}) = \overline{\gamma_n}(s_m) - \gamma_n(s_m) - \overline{\gamma_n}(\hat{s}_{\hat{m}}) + \gamma_n(\hat{s}_{\hat{m}}),$$

by definition of $\hat{m}$ and $\hat{s}_m$, it is easy to see that

$$l(s, \tilde{s}) \leq l(s, s_m) + \overline{\gamma_n}(s_m) + \text{pen}(m) - \overline{\gamma_n}(\hat{s}_{\hat{m}}) - \text{pen}(\hat{m}) + \rho_n \tag{2}$$

holds whatever the penalty function. Looking at the problem from a global minimax point of view, since $\mathbb{E}\left[\overline{\gamma_n}(s_m)\right] = 0$, it is then a matter of choosing a penalty such that $\text{pen}(\hat{m})$ compensates for $-\overline{\gamma_n}(\hat{s}_{\hat{m}})$ and such that $\mathbb{E}\left[\text{pen}(m)\right]$ is of order at most $\sqrt{V_m/n}$ in the VC-case. Hence, we need to control $-\overline{\gamma_n}(t)$ uniformly for t in S_m and m in $\mathcal{M}$ or $\sup_{t \in S_m}(-\overline{\gamma_n}(t))$ uniformly for m in $\mathcal{M}$, and the concentration inequalities appear as the appropriate tools.

Since we deal with a bounded contrast, we can use the so-called McDiarmid's [22] inequality that we recall here.

Theorem 1 (McDiarmid). *Let $X_1, \ldots, X_n$ be independent random variables taking values in a set A, and assume that $\phi : A^n \to \mathbb{R}$ satisfies:*

$$\sup_{x_1, \ldots, x_n, x_i' \in A} |\phi(x_1, \ldots, x_n) - \phi(x_1, \ldots, x_{i-1}, x_i', x_{i+1}, \ldots, x_n)| \leq c_i,$$

for all $i \in \{1, \ldots, n\}$. Then for all $x > 0$, the two following inequalities hold:

$$\mathbb{P}\left[\phi(X_1, \ldots, X_n) \geq \mathbb{E}\left[\phi(X_1, \ldots, X_n)\right] + x\right] \leq \exp\left(-2x^2/\textstyle\sum_{i=1}^n c_i^2\right),$$

$$\mathbb{P}\left[\phi(X_1, \ldots, X_n) \leq \mathbb{E}\left[\phi(X_1, \ldots, X_n)\right] - x\right] \leq \exp\left(-2x^2/\textstyle\sum_{i=1}^n c_i^2\right).$$

We can thus see that for all m in $\mathcal{M}$, $\sup_{t\in S_m}(-\overline{\gamma_n}(t))$ concentrates around its expectation. A well-chosen estimator of an upper bound for $\mathbb{E}[\sup_{t\in S_m}(-\overline{\gamma_n}(t))]$, with expectation of order $\sqrt{V_m/n}$ in the VC-case, may therefore be a good penalty.

In this paper, we focus on penalties based on weighted empirical processes. The ideas developed here have been initiated by Koltchinskii [12] and Bartlett, Boucheron, Lugosi's [2] works.

Let ξ_1^n denote the sample $(X_1,Y_1),\ldots,(X_n,Y_n)$. Starting from the symmetrization tools used in the empirical processes theory, Koltchinskii [12] and Bartlett, Boucheron and Lugosi [2] propose a penalty based on the random variable $\hat{R}_m = 2\mathbb{E}\left[\sup_{t\in S_m} n^{-1}\sum_{i=1}^n \varepsilon_i \mathbb{I}_{t(X_i)\neq Y_i}\middle|\xi_1^n\right]$, where $\varepsilon_1,\ldots,\varepsilon_n$ is a sequence of independent identically distributed Rademacher variables such that $\mathbb{P}[\varepsilon_i=1]=\mathbb{P}[\varepsilon_i=-1]=1/2$ and the ε_i's are independent of ξ_1^n. More precisely, they take $\mathcal{M}=\mathbb{N}^*$ and they consider the minimum penalized contrast estimator $\tilde{s}$ given by (1) with $\mathrm{pen}(m)=\hat{R}_m + c_1\sqrt{\log m/n}$, for some absolute, positive constant c_1. Setting $L_t=\mathbb{P}[t(X)\neq Y]$, they prove that there exists some constant $c_2>0$ such that

$$\mathbb{E}[L_{\tilde{s}}] \leq \inf_{m\in\mathcal{M}}\left\{\inf_{t\in S_m} L_t + \mathbb{E}[\mathrm{pen}(m)]\right\} + \frac{c_2}{\sqrt{n}} + \rho_n,$$

which can be translated in terms of risk bounds as follows:

$$\mathbb{E}[l(s,\tilde{s})] \leq \inf_{m\in\mathcal{M}}\{l(s,s_m)+\mathbb{E}[\mathrm{pen}(m)]\} + \frac{c_2}{\sqrt{n}} + \rho_n.$$

Moreover, it is well known (see [19] for instance) that if the collection $\{S_m, m\in\mathcal{M}\}$ of models is taken such that each $\mathcal{C}_m=\{\{x\in\mathcal{X}, t(x)=1\}, t\in S_m\}$ is a VC-class of subsets of $\mathcal{X}$ with VC-dimension V_m, then $\mathbb{E}[\hat{R}_m]$ is of order $\sqrt{V_m/n}$.

Our purpose is to extend this study by investigating penalty functions based on random variables of the form $\mathbb{E}\left[\sup_{t\in S_m} n^{-1}\sum_{i=1}^n Z_i\mathbb{I}_{t(X_i)\neq Y_i}\middle|\xi_1^n\right]$, with various random weights $Z_1,\ldots,Z_n$.

To avoid dealing with measurability issues, we assume that all the classes of functions considered in the paper are at most countable.

3 Efron's Bootstrap Penalization

Setting $\xi_i=(X_i,Y_i)$ for all i in $\{1,\ldots,n\}$, let P_n be the empirical process associated with the sample $\xi_1^n=(\xi_1,\ldots,\xi_n)$ and defined by $P_n(f)=n^{-1}\sum_{i=1}^n f(\xi_i)$. Let $P(f)=\mathbb{E}[f(X,Y)]$. For every m in $\mathcal{M}$, denote by $\mathcal{F}_m$ the class of functions $\{f:\Xi\to\{0,1\}, f(x,y)=\mathbb{I}_{t(x)\neq y}, t\in S_m\}$. As explained above with (2), we determine an adequate penalty function by controlling $\sup_{t\in S_m}(-\overline{\gamma_n}(t)) = \sup_{f\in\mathcal{F}_m}(P-P_n)(f)$ uniformly for m in $\mathcal{M}$. Since McDiarmid's inequality allows to prove that each supremum concentrates around its expectation, we only need to estimate $\mathbb{E}[\sup_{f\in\mathcal{F}_m}(P-P_n)(f)]$. Introduce now the Efron's bootstrap sample $\xi_{n,1}^*=(X_{n,1}^*,Y_{n,1}^*),\ldots,\xi_{n,n}^*=(X_{n,n}^*,Y_{n,n}^*)$ given by

$$\xi_{n,i}^* = \sum_{j=1}^n \xi_j \mathbb{I}_{U_i\in](j-1)/n, j/n]},$$

where $(U_1, \ldots, U_n)$ is a sample of n i.i.d. random variables uniformly distributed on $]0,1[$ independent of ξ_1^n. Denote by P_n^b the corresponding empirical process.

According to the asymptotic results due to Giné and Zinn [10], we can expect that $\mathbb{E}[\sup_{f\in\mathcal{F}_m}(P-P_n)(f)]$ is well approximated by $\mathbb{E}[\sup_{f\in\mathcal{F}_m}(P_n-P_n^b)(f)|\xi_1^n]$. In fact, starting from the observation that $\mathbb{E}[\sup_{f\in\mathcal{F}_m}(P_n-P_n^b)(f)|\xi_1^n]$ can be written as $\mathbb{E}\left[\sup_{f\in\mathcal{F}_m} n^{-1}\sum_{i=1}^n (1-M_{n,i})f(\xi_i)\middle|\xi_1^n\right]$, where $(M_{n,1},\ldots,M_{n,n})$ is a multinomial vector with parameters $(n,n^{-1},\ldots,n^{-1})$, using McDiarmid's inequality again, we can obtain an exponential bound for

$$\mathbb{E}\left[\sup_{f\in\mathcal{F}_m}(P-P_n)(f)\right] - 2e\mathbb{E}\left[\sup_{f\in\mathcal{F}_m}(P_n-P_n^b)(f)\middle|\xi_1^n\right],$$

and a fortiori for $\left(\sup_{f\in\mathcal{F}_m}(P-P_n)(f) - 2e\mathbb{E}\left[\sup_{f\in\mathcal{F}_m}(P_n-P_n^b)(f)\middle|\xi_1^n\right]\right)$.

Proposition 1. *Let $\mathcal{F}$ be some countable set of measurable functions from Ξ to $[0,1]$. For any $x>0$, the following inequality holds:*

$$\mathbb{P}\left[\sup_{f\in\mathcal{F}}(P-P_n)(f) - 2e\mathbb{E}\left[\sup_{f\in\mathcal{F}}(P_n-P_n^b)(f)\middle|\xi_1^n\right] \geq 5\sqrt{\frac{x}{2n}}\right] \leq e^{-x}.$$

Proof. Let $M_n = (M_{n,1},\ldots,M_{n,n})$ with $M_{n,i} = \sum_{j=1}^n \mathbb{I}_{U_j\in](i-1)/n,i/n]}$ for all $i\in\{1,\ldots,n\}$. M_n is a multinomial vector with parameters $(n,n^{-1},\ldots,n^{-1})$ independent of ξ_1^n and the bootstrap empirical process P_n^b can be written as: $P_n^b(f) = n^{-1}\sum_{i=1}^n M_{n,i}f(\xi_i)$. By Jensen's inequality, we get:

$$\begin{aligned}
\mathbb{E}\left[\sup_{f\in\mathcal{F}}(P-P_n)(f)\right] &\leq \frac{1}{\mathbb{P}\left[M_{n,1}=2\right]}\mathbb{E}\left[\sup_{f\in\mathcal{F}}\frac{1}{n}\sum_{i=1}^n \mathbb{E}\left[(P(f)-f(\xi_i))\mathbb{I}_{M_{n,i}=2}\middle|\xi_1^n\right]\right] \\
&\leq 2e\mathbb{E}\left[\sup_{f\in\mathcal{F}}\frac{1}{n}\sum_{i=1}^n(P(f)-f(\xi_i))\mathbb{I}_{M_{n,i}=2}\right] \\
&\leq 2e\mathbb{E}\left[\sup_{f\in\mathcal{F}}\frac{1}{n}\sum_{i=1}^n(P(f)-f(\xi_i))(M_{n,i}-1)\mathbb{I}_{M_{n,i}=2}\right] \\
&\leq 2e\mathbb{E}\left[\mathbb{E}\left[\sup_{f\in\mathcal{F}}\frac{1}{n}\sum_{i=1}^n(P(f)-f(\xi_i))(M_{n,i}-1)\mathbb{I}_{M_{n,i}=2}\middle|M_n\right]\right].
\end{aligned}$$

It is well known that if U and V are random variables such that for all g in a class of functions $\mathcal{G}$, $g(U)$ and $g(V)$ are independent and $\mathbb{E}\left[g(V)\right]=0$, then

$$\mathbb{E}\left[\sup_{g\in\mathcal{G}}g(U)\right] \leq \mathbb{E}\left[\sup_{g\in\mathcal{G}}(g(U)+g(V))\right]. \tag{3}$$

Since M_n is independent of ξ_1^n, for all f in $\mathcal{F}$, conditionnally given M_n, $\sum_{i=1}^n(P(f)-f(\xi_i))(M_{n,i}-1)\mathbb{I}_{M_{n,i}=2}$ and $\sum_{i=1}^n(P(f)-f(\xi_i))(M_{n,i}-1)\mathbb{I}_{M_{n,i}\neq 2}$ are centered and independent. So, applying (3) conditionnally given M_n, one gets:

$$\mathbb{E}\left[\sup_{f\in\mathcal{F}}(P-P_n)(f)\right] \leq 2e\mathbb{E}\left[\sup_{f\in\mathcal{F}}n^{-1}\sum_{i=1}^n(P(f)-f(\xi_i))(M_{n,i}-1)\right],$$

that is

$$\mathbb{E}\left[\sup_{f\in\mathcal{F}}(P-P_n)(f)\right] \le 2e\mathbb{E}\left[\sup_{f\in\mathcal{F}}(P_n-P_n^b)(f)\right]. \tag{4}$$

One can see by straightforward computations that the variable $\phi(\xi_1,\dots,\xi_n) = \sup_{f\in\mathcal{F}}(P-P_n)(f) - 2e\mathbb{E}\left[\sup_{f\in\mathcal{F}}(P_n-P_n^b)(f)\middle|\xi_1^n\right]$ satisfies the assumptions of McDiarmid's inequality with $c_i = 5/n$ for all $i \in \{1,\dots,n\}$. We thus have:

$$\mathbb{P}\Big[\sup_{f\in\mathcal{F}}(P-P_n)(f) - 2e\mathbb{E}\left[\sup_{f\in\mathcal{F}}(P_n-P_n^b)(f)\middle|\xi_1^n\right] \\ \ge \mathbb{E}\left[\sup_{f\in\mathcal{F}}(P-P_n)(f) - 2e\,\sup_{f\in\mathcal{F}}(P_n-P_n^b)(f)\right] + 5\sqrt{x/2n}\Big] \le e^{-x},$$

and Proposition 1 follows from (4).

From this bound, we can derive non-asymptotic properties for the minimum penalized contrast estimator obtained via an Efron's bootstrap based penalty.

Theorem 2. *Let $\xi_1^n = (X_1,Y_1),\dots,(X_n,Y_n)$ be a sample of n independent copies of a couple of variables (X,Y) with values in $\mathcal{X}\times\{0,1\}$ and with joint distribution P. Let $\xi_n^* = (X_{n,1}^*,Y_{n,1}^*),\dots,(X_{n,n}^*,Y_{n,n}^*)$ be the Efron's bootstrap sample defined for i in $\{1,\dots,n\}$ by:*

$$(X_{n,i}^*,Y_{n,i}^*) = \sum_{j=1}^n (X_j,Y_j)\mathbb{I}_{U_i\in](j-1)/n,j/n]},$$

where $(U_1,\dots,U_n)$ is a sample of n i.i.d. random variables uniformly distributed on $[0,1]$ independent of ξ_1^n. Let

$$\gamma_n(t) = n^{-1}\sum_{i=1}^n \mathbb{I}_{t(X_i)\ne Y_i} \text{ and } \gamma_n^b(t) = n^{-1}\sum_{i=1}^n \mathbb{I}_{t(X_{n,i}^*)\ne Y_{n,i}^*}.$$

Consider a countable collection $\{S_m, m\in\mathcal{M}\}$ of classes of functions in $\mathcal{S}$ and a family $(x_m)_{m\in\mathcal{M}}$ of nonnegative weights such that for some absolute constant Σ, $\sum_{m\in\mathcal{M}} e^{-x_m} \le \Sigma$. Introduce the loss function $l(s,t) = \mathbb{E}\left[\mathbb{I}_{t(X)\ne Y} - \mathbb{I}_{s(X)\ne Y}\right]$ and assume that for each m in $\mathcal{M}$, there exists a minimizer s_m of $l(s,.)$ over S_m. Choose the penalty function such that

$$pen(m) = 2e\mathbb{E}\left[\sup_{t\in S_m}\left(\gamma_n(t)-\gamma_n^b(t)\right)\middle|\xi_1^n\right] + 5\sqrt{\frac{x_m}{2n}}.$$

The approximate minimum penalized contrast estimator $\tilde{s}$ given by (1) satisfies:

$$\mathbb{E}\left[l(s,\tilde{s})\right] \le \inf_{m\in\mathcal{M}}\left\{l(s,s_m) + \mathbb{E}\left[pen(m)\right]\right\} + \frac{5\Sigma}{2}\sqrt{\frac{\pi}{2n}} + \rho_n.$$

Moreover, if for all m in $\mathcal{M}$, $S_m = \{\mathbb{I}_C,\ C\in\mathcal{C}_m\}$, where $\mathcal{C}_m$ is a VC-class with VC-dimension $V_m \ge 1$, assuming that $n \ge 4$, there exists some positive, absolute constant κ such that

$$\mathbb{E}\left[l(s,\tilde{s})\right] \le \inf_{m\in\mathcal{M}}\left\{l(s,s_m) + \kappa\left(\sqrt{\frac{V_m}{n}} + \frac{V_m}{n}\log^2 n + \sqrt{\frac{x_m}{n}}\right)\right\} + \rho_n.$$

Comments:
(i) The risk bounds obtained here are similar to the ones proved by Koltchinskii and Bartlett, Boucheron, Lugosi in the Rademacher penalization context. In particular, we have the following minimax result.

Consider a collection $\{S_m,\ m \in \mathcal{M}\}$ of at most n classes of functions from $\mathcal{X}$ to $\{0,1\}$ such that for each m in $\mathcal{M}$, $S_m = \{\mathbb{I}_C,\ C \in \mathcal{C}_m\}$, $\mathcal{C}_m$ being a VC-class with VC-dimension $V_m \geq 1$. If the Bayes classifier s associated with (X,Y) is in some S_{m_0}, the approximate minimum penalized contrast estimator $\tilde{s}$ obtained from the above Efron's bootstrap penalization satisfies:

$$\mathbb{E}\left[l(s,\tilde{s})\right] \leq \kappa' \left(\sqrt{\frac{V_{m_0}}{n}} + \sqrt{\frac{\log n}{n}} + \frac{V_{m_0}}{n} \log^2 n \right) + \rho_n.$$

This implies that when $\log n \leq V_{m_0} \leq n/\log^4 n$ holds and when ρ_n is at most $n^{-1/2}$, $\tilde{s}$ achieves, up to a constant, the global minimax risk over S_{m_0}.
(ii) The constant $2e$ in the expression of the penalty term is due to technical reasons, but all the experiments that we have carried out show that it is too pessimistic. These experiments indeed lead us to think that the real constant is about 1 and to take in practice a penalty equal to $\mathbb{E}[\sup_{t\in S_m} (\gamma_n(t) - \gamma_n^b(t))\,|\xi_1^n]$.

Proof. Let us prove the first part of Theorem 2. Recall that for any m in $\mathcal{M}$, $\tilde{s}$ satisfies the inequality (2):

$$l(s,\tilde{s}) \leq l(s,s_m) + \overline{\gamma_n}(s_m) + \mathrm{pen}(m) - \overline{\gamma_n}(\hat{s}_{\hat{m}}) - \mathrm{pen}(\hat{m}) + \rho_n,$$

with $\overline{\gamma_n}(t) = \gamma_n(t) - \mathbb{E}\left[\mathbb{I}_{t(X)\neq Y}\right]$. Let $\hat{B}_m = 2e\mathbb{E}\left[\sup_{t\in S_m}(\gamma_n(t) - \gamma_n^b(t))\middle|\xi_1^n\right]$. Introduce a family $(x_m)_{m\in\mathcal{M}}$ of nonnegative weights such that for some absolute constant Σ, $\sum_{m\in\mathcal{M}} e^{-x_m} \leq \Sigma$. Applying Proposition 1 with $\mathcal{F} = \{(x,y) \to \mathbb{I}_{t(x)\neq y},\ t \in S_{m'}\}$ and $x = x_{m'} + \zeta$ for every m' in $\mathcal{M}$, we obtain that for all $\zeta > 0$, except on a set of probability not larger than $\Sigma e^{-\zeta}$,

$$\sup_{t\in S_{m'}} (-\overline{\gamma_n}(t)) \leq \hat{B}_{m'} + 5\sqrt{\frac{x_{m'}+\zeta}{2n}} \quad \forall m' \in \mathcal{M}.$$

This implies that, except on a set of probability not larger than $\Sigma e^{-\zeta}$,

$$l(s,\tilde{s}) \leq l(s,s_m) + \overline{\gamma_n}(s_m) + \mathrm{pen}(m) + \hat{B}_{\hat{m}} + 5\sqrt{\frac{x_{\hat{m}}}{2n}} - \mathrm{pen}(\hat{m}) + \rho_n + 5\sqrt{\frac{\zeta}{2n}}$$

holds. Therefore, if $\mathrm{pen}(m) \geq \hat{B}_m + 5\sqrt{x_m/2n}$,

$$\mathbb{P}\left[l(s,\tilde{s}) \geq l(s,s_m) + \overline{\gamma_n}(s_m) + \mathrm{pen}(m) + \rho_n + 5\sqrt{\frac{\zeta}{2n}}\right] \leq \Sigma e^{-\zeta},$$

which leads by integration with respect to ζ to:

$$\mathbb{E}\left[\left(l(s,\tilde{s}) - l(s,s_m) - \overline{\gamma_n}(s_m) - \mathrm{pen}(m) - \rho_n\right)^+\right] \leq \frac{5\Sigma}{2}\sqrt{\frac{\pi}{2n}}.$$

Since $\mathbb{E}\left[\overline{\gamma_n}(s_m)\right] = 0$, we obtain that

$$\mathbb{E}\left[l(s, \tilde{s})\right] \leq l(s, s_m) + \mathbb{E}\left[\text{pen}(m)\right] + \frac{5\Sigma}{2}\sqrt{\frac{\pi}{2n}} + \rho_n,$$

which gives, since m can be taken arbitrarily in $\mathcal{M}$, the expected risk bound.

Let us now look for an upper bound for $\mathbb{E}[\hat{B}_m]$ when for all m in $\mathcal{M}$, $S_m = \{\mathbb{I}_C,\ C \in \mathcal{C}_m\}$, $\mathcal{C}_m$ being a VC-class with VC-dimension $V_m \geq 1$. In view of Theorem 4, the main difficulty lies in the fact that the variables $(1-M_{n,i})$ are not independent. To remove the dependence, we use the classical tool of Poissonization. Let N be a Poisson random variable with parameter n independent of ξ_1^n and $(U_1, \ldots, U_n)$, and for all $i \in \{1, \ldots, n\}$, $N_i = \sum_{j=1}^{N} \mathbb{I}_{U_j \in](i-1)/n, i/n]}$. The N_i's are independent identically distributed Poisson random variables with parameter 1 and we see that

$$\mathbb{E}\left[\hat{B}_m\right] \leq \frac{2e}{n}\mathbb{E}\left[\sup_{t \in S_m} \sum_{i=1}^{n} (1-N_i)\mathbb{I}_{t(X_i) \neq Y_i}\right] + \frac{2e}{n}\mathbb{E}\left[\sum_{i=1}^{n} |N_i - M_{n,i}|\right].$$

Since $\sum_{i=1}^{n} |N_i - M_{n,i}| = |N - n|$, we get:

$$\mathbb{E}\left[\hat{B}_m\right] \leq \frac{2e}{n}\mathbb{E}\left[\sup_{t \in S_m} \sum_{i=1}^{n} (1-N_i)\mathbb{I}_{t(X_i) \neq Y_i}\right] + \frac{2e}{\sqrt{n}}. \tag{5}$$

Furthermore, the $(1-N_i)$'s are i.i.d. centered real random variables satisfying the moments condition (7) with $v = 1$ and $c = 1$ and Theorem 4 allows to conclude.

4 Symmetrized Bootstrap Penalization

Noting that the bootstrap empirical process satisfies $P_n^b(f) = n^{-1}\sum_{i=1}^{n} M_{n,i} f(\xi_i)$, where $(M_{n,1}, \ldots, M_{n,n})$ is a multinomial vector with parameters $(n, n^{-1}, \ldots, n^{-1})$, Efron [8] suggests considering other ways to bootstrap. Let $W_n = (W_{n,1}, \ldots, W_{n,n})$ denote a vector of n exchangeable and nonnegative random variables independent of the ξ_i's and satisfying $\sum_{i=1}^{n} W_{n,i} = n$. Then $P_n^w(f) = n^{-1}\sum_{i=1}^{n} W_{n,i} f(\xi_i)$ defines a weighted bootstrap empirical process. Præstgaard and Wellner [23] obtain, for such processes, some results that extend the ones due to Giné and Zinn [10]. The best known and most often used example is the i.i.d. weighted bootstrap which is defined by $W_{n,i} = V_i/\overline{V_n}$, where $V_1, \ldots, V_n$ are i.i.d. positive random variables and $\overline{V_n} = n^{-1}\sum_{j=1}^{n} V_j$. This is the case in which we are interested in this section. With the same notations as in the previous section, from Præstgaard and Wellner's results, we could expect that $\mathbb{E}\left[\sup_{f \in \mathcal{F}_m} (P - P_n)(f)\right]$ is sufficiently well approximated by $\sqrt{\mathbb{E}[V_1^2]/\text{Var}[V_1]}\,\mathbb{E}\left[\sup_{f \in \mathcal{F}_m} (P_n - P_n^w)\middle|\xi_1^n\right]$, but we could not prove it in a general way. However, considering here the symmetrized bootstrap process $(P_n^w - P_n^{w'})$, where $P_n^{w'}$ is the i.i.d. weighted bootstrap process associated with an independent copy $(V_1', \ldots, V_n')$ of $(V_1, \ldots, V_n)$, allows us to use some symmetrization tools that generalize those cited in [12] and [2] and lead to the following result.

Proposition 2. *Consider some countable set $\mathcal{F}$ of measurable functions from Ξ to $[0,1]$. Let $Z_1,\dots,Z_n$ be a sequence of i.i.d. symmetric variables independent of ξ_1^n and such that $\mathbb{E}[|Z_1|]<+\infty$. For any $x>0$,*

$$\mathbb{P}\left[\sup_{f\in\mathcal{F}}(P-P_n)(f)-\frac{2}{n\mathbb{E}[|Z_1|]}\mathbb{E}\Big[\sup_{f\in\mathcal{F}}\sum_{i=1}^n Z_i f(\xi_i)\Big|\xi_1^n\Big]\geq 3\sqrt{\frac{x}{2n}}\right]\leq e^{-x}.$$

We can then get an exponential bound for

$$\sup_{f\in\mathcal{F}_m}(P-P_n)(f)-\frac{2\mathbb{E}[V_1]}{\mathbb{E}[|V_1-V_1'|]}\mathbb{E}\Big[\sup_{f\in\mathcal{F}_m}(P_n^w-P_n^{w'})(f)\Big|\xi_1^n\Big],$$

provided that the V_i's satisfy some moments conditions precised below. The same arguments lead furthermore to other kinds of penalties involving symmetric variables or symmetrized Efron's bootstrap processes.

Theorem 3 provides an upper bound for the risk of the approximate minimum penalized contrast estimators obtained via such penalties.

Theorem 3. *Assume that $n\geq 4$ and let $\xi_1^n=(X_1,Y_1),\dots,(X_n,Y_n)$ be a sample of n independent copies of a couple of variables (X,Y) with values in $\mathcal{X}\times\{0,1\}$ and with joint distribution P. Let $(W_{n,1},\dots,W_{n,n})$, $(W'_{n,1},\dots,W'_{n,n})$ and η defined by one of the three following propositions:*
1. For all $i\in\{1,\dots,n\}$, $W_{n,i}=V_i$, $W'_{n,i}=V'_i$ and $\eta=1/\mathbb{E}[|V_1-V'_1|]$, where $V_1^n=(V_1,\dots,V_n)$ is a sample of n i.i.d. nonnegative random variables independent of ξ_1^n and satisfying

$$\forall k\geq 2,\ \mathbb{E}\left[|V_1|^k\right]\leq\frac{k!}{2}vc^{k-2},\tag{6}$$

for $v>0$ and $c>0$, $(V'_1,\dots,V'_n)$ is a copy of V_1^n independent of V_1^n and ξ_1^n.
2. $\eta=1$ and for all $i\in\{1,\dots,n\}$, $W_{n,i}=M_{n,i}$, $W'_{n,i}=M'_{n,i}$, where $M_n=(M_{n,1},\dots,M_{n,n})$ is a multinomial vector with parameters $(n,n^{-1},\dots,n^{-1})$ independent of ξ_1^n and $(M'_{n,1},\dots,M'_{n,n})$ is a copy of M_n independent of M_n and ξ_1^n.
3. For all $i\in\{1,\dots,n\}$, $W_{n,i}=V_i/\overline{V_n}$, $W'_{n,i}=V'_i/\overline{V'_n}$ and $\eta=\mathbb{E}[V_1]/\mathbb{E}[|V_1-V'_1|]$, where $V_1^n=(V_1,\dots,V_n)$ is a sample of n i.i.d. positive random variables independent of ξ_1^n satisfying (6), $(V'_1,\dots,V'_n)$ is a copy of V_1^n independent of V_1^n and ξ_1^n.
Consider a countable collection $\{S_m,m\in\mathcal{M}\}$ of classes of functions in $\mathcal{S}$ and a family $(x_m)_{m\in\mathcal{M}}$ of nonnegative weights such that $\sum_{m\in\mathcal{M}}e^{-x_m}\leq\Sigma$, for some absolute constant Σ. Introduce the loss function $l(s,t)=\mathbb{E}\left[\mathbb{I}_{t(X)\neq Y}-\mathbb{I}_{s(X)\neq Y}\right]$ and assume that for each m in $\mathcal{M}$, there exists a minimizer s_m of $l(s,.)$ over S_m. Choose a penalty function such that

$$pen(m)=\frac{2\eta}{n}\mathbb{E}\left[\sup_{t\in S_m}\sum_{i=1}^n(W_{n,i}-W'_{n,i})\mathbb{I}_{t(X_i)\neq Y_i}\Big|\xi_1^n\right]+3\sqrt{\frac{x_m}{2n}}.$$

The approximate minimum penalized contrast estimator $\tilde{s}$ given by (1) satisfies:

$$\mathbb{E}[l(s,\tilde{s})]\leq\inf_{m\in\mathcal{M}}\{l(s,s_m)+\mathbb{E}[pen(m)]\}+\frac{3\Sigma}{2}\sqrt{\frac{\pi}{2n}}+\frac{\nu}{\sqrt{n}}+\rho_n,$$

where ν is some constant which may depend on $v, c, \mathbb{E}[V_1]$ and $\mathbb{E}[|V_1 - V_1'|]$. Moreover, if for all m, $S_m = \{\mathbb{I}_C, C \in \mathcal{C}_m\}$, where $\mathcal{C}_m$ is a VC-class with VC-dimension $V_m \geq 1$, there exists some positive constant $\nu'(v, c, \mathbb{E}[V_1], \mathbb{E}[|V_1 - V_1'|])$ such that

$$\mathbb{E}[l(s,\tilde{s})] \leq \inf_{m\in\mathcal{M}} \left\{ l(s,s_m) + \nu' \left(\sqrt{\frac{V_m}{n}} + \frac{V_m}{n}\log^2 n + \sqrt{\frac{x_m}{n}} \right) \right\} + \rho_n,$$

and if $(W_{n,1},\ldots,W_{n,n})$, $(W'_{n,1},\ldots,W'_{n,n})$ are defined as in the cases 1 or 3 with $(V_1 - V_1')$ satisfying $\mathbb{E}\left[e^{\lambda(V_1 - V_1')}\right] \leq e^{\lambda^2/2}$ for any $\lambda > 0$,

$$\mathbb{E}[l(s,\tilde{s})] \leq \inf_{m\in\mathcal{M}} \left\{ l(s,s_m) + \nu' \left(\sqrt{\frac{V_m}{n}} + \sqrt{\frac{x_m}{n}} \right) \right\} + \rho_n.$$

Comments:
(i) The structure of the risk upper bound derived here is essentially the same as the bound achieved by the approximate minimum penalized contrast estimator considered in Theorem 2, so one can see in the same way that it is optimal in a global minimax sense over sets of functions based on VC-classes.
(ii) As in Theorem 2, we shall also remark that the factor 2 in the penalty term, which comes from symmetrization inequalities, is pessimistic. A practical study actually shows that the real factor is closer to 1.
(iii) The subgaussian inequality $\mathbb{E}\left[e^{\lambda Z}\right] \leq e^{\lambda^2/2}$ for all $\lambda > 0$ is essentially satisfied by the Gaussian and Rademacher variables. We can then deduce from Theorem 3 Koltchinskii [12] and Bartlett, Boucheron, Lugosi's [2] result about Rademacher penalization.

Proof. The key point of the proof is the computation of an exponential inequality for

$$\sup_{t\in S_m}(-\overline{\gamma_n}(t)) - 2\eta\,\mathbb{E}\left[\sup_{t\in S_m} n^{-1}\textstyle\sum_{i=1}^n (W_{n,i} - W'_{n,i})\mathbb{I}_{t(X_i)\neq Y_i} \middle| \xi_1^n\right],$$

in the three considered cases.

For the first case, a direct application of Proposition 2 provides such an inequality. For the second case, as in (5) we can use Poissonization to remove the dependence between the $(M_{n,i} - M'_{n,i})$'s and to apply Proposition 2. The fact that $\mathbb{E}[|N_1 - N_1'|] \geq 1$ for every independent Poisson variables N_1 and N_1' with parameter 1 finally leads to an appropriate inequality. For the third case, we still have to remove the dependence between the $(W_{n,i} - W'_{n,i})$'s. To do this, we notice that if $\hat{W}_m = 2\eta\mathbb{E}\left[\sup_{t\in S_m} n^{-1}\sum_{i=1}^n (W_{n,i} - W'_{n,i})\mathbb{I}_{t(X_i)\neq Y_i} \middle| \xi_1^n\right]$:

$$\left| \frac{2}{n\mathbb{E}[|V_1 - V_1'|]}\mathbb{E}\left[\sup_{t\in S_m}\sum_{i=1}^n (V_i - V_i')\,\mathbb{I}_{t(X_i)\neq Y_i} \middle| \xi_1^n \right] - \hat{W}_m \right| \leq \frac{4\mathbb{E}\left[\frac{V_1}{\overline{V_n}}\left|\overline{V_n} - \mathbb{E}[V_1]\right|\right]}{\mathbb{E}[|V_1 - V_1'|]}.$$

Moreover, successive applications of the special version of Bernstein's inequality proposed by Birgé and Massart [4] lead to an exponential bound which gives by integration (see [9] for further details):

$$\mathbb{E}\left[(V_1/\overline{V_n})\left|\overline{V_n} - \mathbb{E}[V_1]\right|\right] \leq C(v, c, \mathbb{E}[V_1])/\sqrt{n}.$$

We can then use Proposition 2. In all cases, we obtain for all $x > 0$, for all $m \in \mathcal{M}$,

$$\mathbb{P}\left[\sup_{t\in S_m}(-\overline{\gamma_n}(t)) - \frac{2\eta}{n}\mathbb{E}\left[\sup_{t\in S_m}\sum_{i=1}^{n}(W_{n,i}-W'_{n,i})\mathbb{I}_{t(X_i)\neq Y_i}\left|\xi_1^n\right.\right] \geq 3\sqrt{\frac{x}{2n}} + \frac{\nu}{\sqrt{n}}\right] \leq e^{-x},$$

where ν is a constant which may depend on v, c, $\mathbb{E}[V_1]$ and $\mathbb{E}[|V_1 - V_1'|]$. We conclude in the same way as in the proof of Theorem 2. The risk bound in the VC-case follows from Theorem 4.

5 A Maximal Inequality

Our purpose in this section is to provide a maximal inequality for weighted empirical processes. To do this, we first need the chaining result stated below. We set for all $a = (a_1, \dots, a_n)$ in $\mathbb{R}^n$, $\|a\|_2^2 = \sum_{i=1}^n a_i^2$. For $\varepsilon > 0$ and $\mathcal{A} \subset \mathbb{R}^n$, let $H_2(\varepsilon, \mathcal{A})$ denote the logarithm of the maximal number N of elements $\{a^{(1)}, \dots, a^{(N)}\}$ in $\mathcal{A}$ such that for every $l, l' \in \{1, \dots, N\}, l \neq l'$, $\|a^{(l)} - a^{(l')}\|_2^2 > \varepsilon^2$.

Lemma 1. *Let $\mathcal{A}$ be some subset of $[0,1]^n$ and $Z_1, \dots, Z_n$ i.i.d. centered real random variables. Let $\delta > 0$ such that $sup_{a\in\mathcal{A}}\|a\|_2 \leq \delta$ and assume that there exist some positive constants v and c such that the Z_i's satisfy the condition:*

$$\forall k \geq 2,\ \mathbb{E}\left[|Z_1|^k\right] \leq \frac{k!}{2} v c^{k-2}. \tag{7}$$

Then, one has

$$\mathbb{E}\left[\sup_{a\in\mathcal{A}}\sum_{i=1}^{n} a_i Z_i\right] \leq 3\sum_{j=0}^{+\infty}\left(\delta\sqrt{v}2^{-j}\sqrt{H_2\left(2^{-(j+1)}\delta, \mathcal{A}\right)} + c(2^{-j}\delta \wedge 1) H_2\left(2^{-(j+1)}\delta, \mathcal{A}\right)\right),$$

and if for all $\lambda \geq 0$, $\mathbb{E}\left[e^{\lambda Z_1}\right] \leq e^{\lambda^2/2}$,

$$\mathbb{E}\left[sup_{a\in\mathcal{A}}\textstyle\sum_{i=1}^n a_i Z_i\right] \leq 3\textstyle\sum_{j=0}^{+\infty} 2^{-j}\delta\sqrt{H_2\left(2^{-(j+1)}\delta, \mathcal{A}\right)}.$$

The proof of this lemma is inspired by Lemma 15 in [20]. It is based on Birgé and Massart's [4] version of Bernstein's inequality and Lemma 2 in [20] which follows from an argument due to Pisier. We can then prove the following theorem.

Theorem 4. *Let $\xi_1^n = (X_1, Y_1), \dots, (X_n, Y_n)$ be a sample of n independent copies of a couple of variables (X, Y) with values in $\mathcal{X} \times \{0, 1\}$. Introduce n i.i.d. real random variables $Z_1, \dots, Z_n$ centered, independent of ξ_1^n and satisfying the moments condition (7) for some positive constants v and c. Let $S_m = \{\mathbb{I}_C, C \in \mathcal{C}_m\}$ where $\mathcal{C}_m$ is a VC-class with VC-dimension V_m and assume that $n \geq 4$. There exist some absolute constants κ_1 and κ_2 such that:*

$$\mathbb{E}\left[\frac{1}{n}\sup_{t\in S_m}\sum_{i=1}^{n} Z_i \mathbb{I}_{t(X_i)\neq Y_i}\right] \leq \kappa_1\sqrt{v}\sqrt{\frac{V_m}{n}} + \kappa_2 c\frac{V_m}{n}\log^2 n, \tag{8}$$

and if for all $\lambda \geq 0$, $\mathbb{E}\left[e^{\lambda Z_1}\right] \leq e^{\lambda^2/2}$, *then*

$$\mathbb{E}\left[n^{-1} sup_{t \in S_m} \sum_{i=1}^{n} Z_i \mathbb{I}_{t(X_i) \neq Y_i}\right] \leq \kappa_1 \sqrt{V_m/n}.$$

Proof. Considering $\mathcal{B}_m = \{\{(x,y) \in \mathcal{X} \times \{0,1\},\ \mathbb{I}_C(x) \neq y\},\ C \in \mathcal{C}_m\}$ and the set $\mathcal{A}_m = \{(\mathbb{I}_B(X_1,Y_1),\ldots,\mathbb{I}_B(X_n,Y_n)),\ B \in \mathcal{B}_m\}$, one has

$$\mathbb{E}\left[\sup_{t \in S_m} \sum_{i=1}^{n} Z_i \mathbb{I}_{t(X_i) \neq Y_i}\right] = \mathbb{E}\left[\sup_{a \in \mathcal{A}_m} \sum_{i=1}^{n} a_i Z_i\right].$$

Moreover, $\sup_{a \in \mathcal{A}_m} \|a\|_2 \leq \sqrt{n}$, and by definition of $\mathcal{A}_m$, for $\varepsilon > 0$, $H_2\left(\sqrt{n}\varepsilon, \mathcal{A}_m\right) = H(\varepsilon, \mathcal{B}_m, P_n)$, where $H(\varepsilon, \mathcal{B}_m, P_n)$ is the $\varepsilon-$metric entropy of $\mathcal{B}_m$ with respect to the empirical measure $n^{-1}\sum_{i=1}^{n} \delta_{(X_i,Y_i)}$. For any probability measure Q, the $\varepsilon-$metric entropy $H(\varepsilon, \mathcal{B}_m, Q)$ of $\mathcal{B}_m$ with respect to Q is the logarithm of the maximal number N of elements $\{b^{(1)},\ldots,b^{(N)}\}$ in $\{\mathbb{I}_B,\ B \in \mathcal{B}_m\}$ such that for all $l, l' \in \{1,\ldots,N\}$, $l \neq l'$, $\mathbb{E}_Q(b^{(l)} - b^{(l')})^2 > \varepsilon^2$. Let us denote by $H(\varepsilon, \mathcal{B}_m)$ the universal $\varepsilon-$metric entropy of $\mathcal{B}_m$ that is $H(\varepsilon, \mathcal{B}_m) = \sup_Q H(\varepsilon, \mathcal{B}_m, Q)$, where the supremum is taken over all the probabilty measures on $\mathcal{X} \times \{0,1\}$. For all j in $\mathbb{N}$,

$$H_2\left(\sqrt{n}2^{-(j+1)}, \mathcal{A}_m\right) \leq H(2^{-(j+1)}, \mathcal{B}_m).$$

Furthermore, since $\mathcal{B}_m$ is a VC-class with VC-dimension not larger than V_m, Haussler's [11] bound gives:

$$H(2^{-(j+1)}, \mathcal{B}_m) \leq \kappa V_m\left(1 + (j+1)\log 2\right)\ \forall j \in \mathbb{N},$$

for some positive constant κ. Hence, from Lemma 1 we get:

$$\mathbb{E}\left[\sup_{t \in S_m} \sum_{i=1}^{n} Z_i \mathbb{I}_{t(X_i) \neq Y_i}\right] \leq 3 \sum_{j=0}^{+\infty} \Big(\sqrt{v\kappa}2^{-j}\sqrt{nV_m\left(1 + (j+1)\log 2\right)}$$
$$+c\kappa(2^{-j}\sqrt{n} \wedge 1)V_m\left(1 + (j+1)\log 2\right)\Big),$$

which leads by some direct computations to the upper bound (8). The upper bound in the subgaussian case is obtained in the same way.

6 Conclusion

In this conclusion, we wish to point out that the theoretical results presented here do not allow to come out in favour of one of the investigated penalization schemes. In particular, as we consider the problem from the global minimax point of view, we can not decide between Rademacher and bootstrap type penalties.

Nevertheless, it is now admitted that the global minimax risk is not an ideal bench mark to evaluate the relevance of classification rules, since it may overestimate the risk in some situations. Vapnik and Chervonenkis' [26] results in the so called *zero-error case* first raised this question. Devroye and Lugosi [7] then confirmed these reserves. They proved that for $S = \{\mathbb{I}_C, C \in \mathcal{C}\}$ where $\mathcal{C}$

is a VC-class with VC-dimension $V(\mathcal{C})$, setting $L_t = \mathbb{P}[t(X) \neq Y]$ and fixing L^* in $]0, 1/2[$, there exist some constants κ_1 and κ_2 such that for any classification rule $\hat{s}$, if $\kappa_1 L^*(1-2L^*)^2 \geq V(\mathcal{C})/n$,

$$\sup_{P, \inf_{t\in S} L_t = L^*} \mathbb{E}[L_{\hat{s}} - L^*] \geq \kappa_2 \sqrt{L^* V(\mathcal{C})/n}.$$

The localized versions of Rademacher penalization recently proposed by Koltchinskii and Panchenko [13], Bartlett, Bousquet and Mendelson [3] and Lugosi and Wegkamp [16] allow to construct classification rules satisfying oracle type inequalities with the appropriate dependence on L^*. In the same spirit, we could introduce some localized bootstrap penalties. This would entail improving the inequality given in Proposition 1 under propitious conditions, for example when the classification error is small. Boucheron, Lugosi and Massart's [5] concentration inequality seems to be the adequate tool, though it can not be directly applied because of the dependence between the weights involved in the bootstrap processes. Some refined Poissonization techniques may allow us to overcome this difficulty.

However, by further analyzing the problem, Mammen and Tsybakov [18], Tsybakov [24] and Massart and Nedelec's [21] works highlight the fact that one can describe the minimax risk more precisely for some pairs (X, Y) satisfying a prescribed margin condition. Massart and Nedelec [21] prove that if for every $h \in [0, 1]$, $\mathcal{P}(h, S)$ denotes the set of the distributions P such that $s \in S$ and (X, Y) satisfies the margin condition $|2\mathbb{E}[Y|X=x] - 1| \geq h$ for all x in $\mathcal{X}$, if $2 \leq V(\mathcal{C}) \leq n$,

$$\inf_{\hat{s}} \sup_{P\in\mathcal{P}(h,S)} \mathbb{E}\left[l(s, \hat{s})\right] \geq \kappa_3 \left(V(\mathcal{C})/(nh) \wedge \sqrt{V(\mathcal{C})/n} \right).$$

In view of these works, a desirable goal would be to develop some estimation procedures which lead to classification rules adapting better to the margin. Localized versions of Rademacher or bootstrap penalization may provide such procedures. But these methods essentially have a theoretical interest.

We are hopeful that the connection made here between Rademacher penalization and the bootstrap approach, which takes advantage of its intuitive qualities, provides new lines of research towards more operational methods of construction of "margin adaptive" classification rules.

Acknowledgements. The author wishes to thank Stéphane Boucheron and Pascal Massart for many interesting and helpful discussions.

References

1. Barron A.R. Logically smooth density estimation. Technical Report 56, Dept. of Statistics, Stanford Univ. (1985)
2. Bartlett P., Boucheron S. and Lugosi G. Model selection and error estimation. *Mach. Learn.* **48** (2002) 85–113
3. Bartlett P., Bousquet O. and Mendelson S. Localized Rademacher complexities. *Proc. of the 15th annual conf. on Computational Learning Theory* (2002) 44–58

4. Birgé L., Massart P. Minimum contrast estimators on sieves: exponential bounds and rates of convergence. *Bernoulli* **4** (1998) 329–375
5. Boucheron S., Lugosi G., Massart P. A sharp concentration inequality with applications. *Random Struct. Algorithms* **16** (2000) 277–292
6. Buescher K.L, Kumar P.R. Learning by canonical smooth estimation. I: Simultaneous estimation, II: Learning and choice of model complexity. *IEEE Trans. Autom. Control* **41** (1996) 545–556, 557–569
7. Devroye L., Lugosi G. Lower bounds in pattern recognition and learning. *Pattern Recognition* **28** (1995) 1011–1018
8. Efron B. *The jackknife, the bootstrap and other resampling plans.* CBMS-NSF Reg. Conf. Ser. Appl. Math. **38** (1982)
9. Fromont M. *Quelques problèmes de sélection de modèles : construction de tests adaptatifs, ajustement de pénalités par des méthodes de bootstrap (Some model selection problems: construction of adaptive tests, bootstrap penalization).* Ph. D. thesis, Université Paris XI (2003)
10. Giné E., Zinn J. Bootstrapping general empirical measures. *Ann. Probab.* **18** (1990) 851–869
11. Haussler D. Sphere packing numbers for subsets of the Boolean n-cube with bounded Vapnik-Chervonenkis dimension. *J. Comb. Theory* **A 69** (1995) 217–232
12. Koltchinskii V. Rademacher penalties and structural risk minimization. *IEEE Trans. Inf. Theory* **47** (2001) 1902–1914
13. Koltchinskii V., Panchenko D. Rademacher processes and bounding the risk of function learning. *High dimensional probability II. 2nd international conference,* Univ. of Washington, DC, USA (1999)
14. Lozano F. Model selection using Rademacher penalization. *Proceedings of the 2nd ICSC Symp. on Neural Computation.* Berlin, Germany (2000)
15. Lugosi G., Nobel A.B. Adaptive model selection using empirical complexities. *Ann. Statist.* **27** (1999) 1830–1864
16. Lugosi G., Wegkamp M. Complexity regularization via localized random penalties. Preprint (2003)
17. Lugosi G., Zeger K. Concept learning using complexity regularization. *IEEE Trans. Inf. Theory* **42** (1996) 48–54
18. Mammen E., Tsybakov A. Smooth discrimination analysis. *Ann. Statist.* **27** (1999) 1808–1829
19. Massart P. Some applications of concentration inequalities to statistics. *Ann. Fac. Sci. Toulouse* **9** (2000) 245–303
20. Massart P. *Concentration inequalities and model selection.* Lectures given at the St-Flour summer school of Probability Theory. To appear in Lect. Notes Math. (2003)
21. Massart P., Nedelec E. Risk bounds for statistical learning. Preprint (2003)
22. McDiarmid C. On the method of bounded differences. *Surveys in combinatorics (Lond. Math. Soc. Lect. Notes)* **141** (1989) 148–188
23. Præstgaard J., Wellner J.A. Exchangeably weighted bootstraps of the general empirical process. *Ann. Probab.* **21** (1993) 2053–2086
24. Tsybakov A. Optimal aggregation of classifiers in statistical learning. Preprint (2001)
25. Vapnik V.N., Chervonenkis A.Ya. On the uniform convergence of relative frequencies of events to their probabilities. *Theor. Probab. Appl.* **16** (1971) 264–280
26. Vapnik V. N., Chervonenkis A. Ya. *Teoriya raspoznavaniya obrazov. Statisticheskie problemy obucheniya.* Nauka, Moscow (1974)
27. Vapnik V.N. *Estimation of dependences based on empirical data.* New York, Springer-Verlag (1982)

Convergence of Discrete MDL for Sequential Prediction

Jan Poland and Marcus Hutter

IDSIA, Galleria 2, CH-6928 Manno (Lugano), Switzerland*
{jan,marcus}@idsia.ch

Abstract. We study the properties of the Minimum Description Length principle for sequence prediction, considering a two-part MDL estimator which is chosen from a countable class of models. This applies in particular to the important case of *universal sequence prediction*, where the model class corresponds to all algorithms for some fixed universal Turing machine (this correspondence is by enumerable semimeasures, hence the resulting models are stochastic). We prove convergence theorems similar to Solomonoff's theorem of universal induction, which also holds for general Bayes mixtures. The bound characterizing the convergence speed for MDL predictions is exponentially larger as compared to Bayes mixtures. We observe that there are at least *three* different ways of using MDL for prediction. One of these has worse prediction properties, for which predictions only converge if the MDL estimator stabilizes. We establish sufficient conditions for this to occur. Finally, some immediate consequences for complexity relations and randomness criteria are proven.

1 Introduction

The Minimum Description Length (MDL) principle is one of the most important concepts in Machine Learning, and serves as a scientific guide, in general. In particular, the process of building a model for any kind of given data is governed by the MDL principle in the majority of cases. The following illustrating example is probably familiar to many readers: A Bayesian net (or neural network) is constructed from (trained with) some data. We may just determine (train) the net in order to fit the data as closely as possible, then we are describing the data very precisely, but disregard the description of the net itself. The resulting net is a maximum likelihood estimator. Alternatively, we may *simultaneously* minimize the "residual" description length of the data given the net *and* the description length of the net. This corresponds to minimizing a *regularized* error term, and the result is a maximum a posteriori or MDL estimator. The latter way of modelling is not only superior to the former in most applications, it is also conceptually appealing since it implements the simplicity principle, Occam's razor.

The MDL method has been studied on all possible levels from very concrete and highly tuned practical applications up to general theoretical assertions (see

* This work was supported by SNF grant 2100-67712.02.

J. Shawe-Taylor and Y. Singer (Eds.): COLT 2004, LNAI 3120, pp. 300–314, 2004.

e.g. [1,2,3]). The aim of this work is to contribute to the theory of MDL. We regard Bayesian or neural nets or other models as just some particular class of models. We identify (probabilistic) models with *(semi)measures*, *data* with the initial part of a *sequence* $x_1, x_2, \ldots, x_{t-1}$, and the task of learning with the problem of *predicting* the next symbol x_t (or more symbols). The sequence $x_1, x_2, \ldots$ itself is generated by some *true* but unknown *distribution* μ.

An two-part MDL estimator for some string $x = x_1, \ldots, x_{t-1}$ is then some short description of the semimeasure, while simultaneously the probability of the data under the related semimeasure is large. Surprisingly little work has been done on this general setting of sequence *prediction* with MDL. In contrast, most work addresses MDL for *coding and modeling*, or others, see e.g. [4,5,6, 7]. Moreover, there are some results for the prediction of independently identically distributed (i.i.d.) sequences, see e.g. [6]. There, discrete model classes are considered, while most of the material available focusses on continuous model classes. In our work we will study countable classes of *arbitrary* semimeasures.

There is a strong motivation for considering both countable classes and semimeasures: In order to derive performance guarantees one has to assume that the model class contains the true model. So the larger we choose this class, the less restrictive is this assumption. From a computational point of view the largest relevant class is the class of *all* lower-semicomputable semimeasures. We call this setup *universal sequence prediction*. This class is at the foundations of and has been intensely studied in Algorithmic Information Theory [8,9,10]. Since algorithms do not necessarily halt on each string, one is forced to consider the more general class of semimeasures, rather than measures. Solomonoff [11,12] defined a universal induction system, essentially based on a Bayes mixture over this class (see [13,14] for recent developments). There seems to be no work on MDL for this class, which this paper intends to change. What has been studied intensely in [15] is the so called one-part MDL over the class of deterministic computable models (see also Section 7).

The paper is structured as follows. Section 2 establishes basic definitions. In Section 3, we introduce the MDL estimator and show how it can be used for sequence prediction in at least three ways. Sections 4 and 5 are devoted to convergence theorems. In Section 6, we study the stabilization properties of the MDL estimator. The setting of universal sequence prediction is treated in Section 7. Finally, Section 8 contains the conclusions.

2 Prerequisites and Notation

We build on the notation of [9] and [15]. Let the alphabet $\mathcal{X}$ be a finite set of symbols. We consider the spaces $\mathcal{X}^*$ and $\mathcal{X}^\infty$ of finite strings and infinite sequences over $\mathcal{X}$. The initial part of a sequence up to a time $t \in \mathbb{N}$ or $t-1 \in \mathbb{N}$ is denoted by $x_{1:t}$ or $x_{<t}$, respectively. The empty string is denoted by ϵ.

A *semimeasure* is a function $\nu : \mathcal{X}^* \to [0,1]$ such that

$$\nu(\epsilon) \leq 1 \text{ and } \nu(x) \geq \sum_{a \in \mathcal{X}} \nu(xa) \text{ for all } x \in \mathcal{X}^* \quad (1)$$

holds. If equality holds in both inequalities of (1), then we have a *measure*. Let $\mathcal{C}$ be a countable class of (semi)measures, i.e. $\mathcal{C} = \{\nu_i : i \in I\}$ with finite or infinite index set $I \subseteq \mathbb{N}$. A (semi)measure $\tilde{\nu}$ *dominates* the class $\mathcal{C}$ iff for all $\nu_i \in \mathcal{C}$ there is a constant $c(\nu_i) > 0$ such that $\nu(x) \geq c(\nu_i) \cdot \nu_i(x)$ holds for all $x \in \mathcal{X}^*$. The dominant semimeasure $\tilde{\nu}$ need not be contained in $\mathcal{C}$, but if it is, we call it a *universal* element of $\mathcal{C}$.

Let $\mathcal{C}$ be a countable class of (semi)measures, where each $\nu \in \mathcal{C}$ is associated with a weight $w_\nu > 0$ and $\sum_\nu w_\nu \leq 1$. We may interpret the weights as a *prior* on $\mathcal{C}$. Then it is obvious that the Bayes mixture

$$\xi(x) = \xi_{[\mathcal{C}]}(x) = \sum_{\nu \in \mathcal{C}} w_\nu \nu(x), \; x \in \mathcal{X}^*, \tag{2}$$

dominates $\mathcal{C}$. Assume that there is some measure $\mu \in \mathcal{C}$, the *true distribution*, generating sequences $x_{<\infty} \in \mathcal{X}^\infty$. Normally μ is unknown. (Note that we require μ to be a measure, while $\mathcal{C}$ may contain also semimeasures in general. This is motivated by the setting of universal sequence prediction as already indicated.) If some initial part $x_{<t}$ of a sequence is given, the probability of observing $x_t \in \mathcal{X}$ as a next symbol is given by

$$\mu(x_t|x_{<t}) = \frac{\mu(x_{<t}x_t)}{\mu(x_{<t})} \text{ if } \mu(x_{<t}) > 0 \;\text{ and }\; \mu(x_t|x_{<t}) = 0 \text{ if } \mu(x_{<t}) = 0. \tag{3}$$

The case $\mu(x_{<t}) = 0$ is stated only for well-definedness, it has probability zero. Note that $\mu(x_t|x_{<t})$ can depend on $x_{<t}$. We may generally define the quantity (3) for *any* function $\varphi : \mathcal{X}^* \to [0, 1]$, we call $\varphi(x_t|x_{<t}) = \frac{\varphi(x_{1:t})}{\varphi(x_{<t})}$ the *φ-prediction*. Clearly, this is not necessarily a probability on $\mathcal{X}$ for general φ. For a semimeasure ν in particular, the ν-prediction $\nu(\cdot|x_{<t})$ is a semimeasure on $\mathcal{X}$.

We define the *expectation* with respect to the true probability μ: Let $n \geq 0$ and $f : \mathcal{X}^n \to \mathbb{R}$ be a function, then

$$\mathbf{E}\, f = \mathbf{E}\, f(x_{1:n}) = \sum_{x_{1:n} \in \mathcal{X}^n} \mu(x_{1:n}) f(x_{1:n}). \tag{4}$$

Generally, we may also define the expectation as an integral over infinite sequences. But since we won't need it, we can keep things simple. We can now state a central result about prediction with Bayes mixtures in a form independent of Algorithmic Information Theory.

Theorem 1. *For any class of (semi)measures $\mathcal{C}$ containing the true distribution μ and any $n \geq 1$, we have*

$$\sum_{t=1}^{n} \mathbf{E} \sum_{a \in \mathcal{X}} \Big(\mu(a|x_{<t}) - \xi(a|x_{<t})\Big)^2 \;\leq\; \ln w_\mu^{-1}. \tag{5}$$

This was found by Solomonoff ([12]) for universal sequence prediction. A proof is also given in [9] (only for binary alphabet) or [16] (arbitrary alphabet).

It is surprisingly simple once Lemma 7 is known. A few lines analogous to (8) and (9) exploiting the dominance of ξ are sufficient.

The bound (5) asserts convergence of the ξ-predictions to the μ-predictions *in mean sum (i.m.s.)*, since we define

$$\varphi \stackrel{i.m.s.}{\longrightarrow} \mu \quad \Longleftrightarrow \quad \exists\, C>0: \sum_{t=1}^{\infty} \mathbf{E} \sum_{a\in\mathcal{X}} \Big(\mu(a|x_{<t}) - \varphi(a|x_{<t})\Big)^2 \leq C. \qquad (6)$$

Convergence i.m.s. implies convergence with μ-probability one (w.μ-p.1), since otherwise the sum would be infinite. Moreover, convergence i.m.s. provides a rate or speed of convergence in the sense that the expected number of times t in which $\varphi(a|x_{<t})$ deviates more than ε from $\mu(a|x_{<t})$ is finite and bounded by C/ε^2 and the probability that the number of ε-deviations exceeds $\frac{C}{\varepsilon^2\delta}$ is smaller than δ. If the quadratic differences were monotonically decreasing (which is usually not the case), we could even conclude convergence faster than $\frac{1}{t}$.

Probabilities vs. Description Lengths. By the Kraft inequality, each (semi)measure can be associated with a code length or *complexity* by means of the negative logarithm, where all (binary) codewords form a prefix-free set. The converse holds as well. E.g. for the weights w_ν with $\sum w_\nu \leq 1$, codes of lengths $\lceil -\log_2 w_\nu \rceil$ can be found. It is often only a matter of notational convenience if description lengths or probabilities are used, but description lengths are generally preferred in Algorithmic Information Theory. Keeping the equivalence in mind, we will develop the general theory in terms of probabilities, but formulate parts of the results in universal sequence prediction rather in terms of complexities.

3 MDL Estimator and Predictions

Assume that $\mathcal{C}$ is a countable class of semimeasures together with weights $(w_\nu)_{\nu\in\mathcal{C}}$, and $x \in \mathcal{X}^*$ is some string. Then the *maximizing element* ν^x, often called MAP estimator, is defined as

$$\nu^x = \nu^x_{[\mathcal{C}]} = \arg\max_{\nu\in\mathcal{C}} \{w_\nu \nu(x)\}.$$

In fact the maximum is attained since for each $\varepsilon \in (0,1)$ only a finite number of elements fulfil $w_\nu \nu(x) > \varepsilon$. Observe immediately the correspondence in terms of *description lengths* rather than *probabilities*: $\nu^x = \arg\min_{\nu\in\mathcal{C}} \big\{ -\log_2 w(\nu) - \log_2 \nu(x)\big\}$. Then the *minimum description length principle* is obvious: ν^x minimizes the joint description length of the model plus the data given the model[1]

[1] Precisely, we define a MAP (maximum a posteriori) estimator. For two reasons, information theorists and statisticians would not consider our definition as MDL in the strong sense. First, MDL is often associated with a specific prior. Second, when coding some data x, one can exploit the fact that once the model ν^x is specified, only data which leads to the maximizing element ν^x needs to be considered. This allows for a description shorter than $\log_2 \nu^x(x)$. Since however most authors refer to MDL, we will keep using this general term instead of MAP, too.

(see the last paragraph of the previous section). As explained before, we stick to the product notation.

For notational simplicity we set $\nu^*(x) = \nu^x(x)$. The *two-part MDL estimator* is defined by

$$\varrho(x) = \varrho_{[\mathcal{C}]}(x) = w_{\nu^x}\nu^x(x) = \max_{\nu\in\mathcal{C}}\{w_\nu \nu(x)\}.$$

So ϱ chooses the maximizing element with respect to its argument. We may also use the version $\varrho^y(x) := w_{\nu^y}\nu^y(x)$ for which the choice depends on the superscript instead of the argument. For each $x, y \in \mathcal{X}^*$, $\xi(x) \geq \varrho(x) \geq \varrho^y(x)$ is immediate.

We can define MDL predictors according to (3). There are *at least three* possible ways to use MDL for prediction.

Definition 2. *The* dynamic *MDL predictor is defined as*

$$\varrho(a|x) = \frac{\varrho(xa)}{\varrho(x)} = \frac{\varrho^{xa}(xa)}{\varrho^x(x)}.$$

That is, we look for a short description of xa and relate it to a short description of $x = x_{<t}$. We call this dynamic since for each possible a we have to find a new MDL estimator. This is the closest correspondence to the ξ-predictor.

Definition 3. *The* static *MDL predictor is given by*

$$\varrho^{\text{static}}(a|x) = \varrho^x(a|x) = \frac{\varrho^x(xa)}{\varrho(x)} = \frac{\varrho^x(xa)}{\varrho^x(x)} = \frac{\nu^x(xa)}{\nu^x(x)}.$$

Here obviously only one MDL estimator ϱ^x has to be identified, which may be more efficient in practice.

Definition 4. *The* hybrid *MDL predictor is given by $\varrho^{\text{hyb}}(a|x) = \frac{\nu^*(xa)}{\nu^*(x)}$. This can be paraphrased as "do dynamic MDL and drop the weights". It is somewhat in-between static and dynamic MDL.*

The range of the static MDL predictor is obviously contained in $[0,1]$. For the dynamic MDL predictor, this holds by $\varrho^x(x) \geq \varrho^{xa}(x) \geq \varrho^{xa}(xa)$, while for the hybrid MDL predictor it is generally false.

Static MDL is omnipresent in machine learning and applications. In fact, many common prediction algorithms can be abstractly understood as static MDL, or rather as approximations. Namely, if a prediction task is accomplished by building a *model* such as a neural network with a suitable regularization to prevent "overfitting", this is just searching an MDL estimator within a certain class of distributions. After that, only this model is used for prediction. Dynamic and hybrid MDL are applied more rarely due to their larger computational effort. For example, the similarity metric proposed in [17] can be interpreted as (a deterministic variant of) dynamic MDL. For hybrid MDL, we will see that the prediction properties are worse than for dynamic and static MDL.

We will need to convert our MDL predictors to *measures* on $\mathcal{X}$ by means of *normalization*. If $\varphi : \mathcal{X}^* \to [0,1]$ is any function, then

$$\varphi_{norm}(a|x_{<t}) = \frac{\varphi(a|x_{<t})}{\sum_{a'\in\mathcal{X}} \varphi(a'|x_{<t})} = \frac{\varphi(x_{<t}a)}{\sum_{a'\in\mathcal{X}} \varphi(x_{<t}a')}$$

(assume that the denominator is different from zero, which is always true with probability 1 if φ is an MDL predictor). This procedure is known as *Solomonoff normalization* ([12,9]) and results in $\nu_{norm}(x_{1:n}) = \nu(x_{1:n})/\big[\nu(\epsilon)N_\nu(x_{<n})\big]$, where

$$N_\nu(x) = \prod_{t=1}^{\ell(x)+1} \frac{\sum_{a\in\mathcal{X}} \nu(x_{<t}a)}{\nu(x_{<t})} \tag{7}$$

is the normalizer. Before proceeding with the theory, an example is in order.

Example 5. Let $n \in \mathbb{N}$, $\mathcal{X} = \{1,\ldots,n\}$, and

$$\mathcal{C} = \Big\{\nu_\vartheta(x_{1:t}) = \vartheta_{x_1}\cdot\ldots\cdot\vartheta_{x_t} : \vartheta \in \Theta\Big\} \quad \text{with} \quad \Theta = \Big\{\vartheta \in ([0,1]\cap\mathbb{Q})^n : \sum_{i=1}^n \vartheta_i = 1\Big\}$$

be the set of all rational probability vectors with any prior $(w_\vartheta)_{\vartheta\in\Theta}$. Each $\vartheta \in \Theta$ generates sequences $x_{<\infty}$ of *independently identically distributed (i.i.d)* random variables such that $P(x_t = i) = \vartheta_i$ for all $t \geq 1$ and $1 \leq i \leq n$. If $x_{1:t}$ is the initial part of a sequence and $\alpha \in \Theta$ is defined by $\alpha_i = |\{s \leq t : x_s = i\}|$, then it is easy to see that

$$\nu^{x_{1:t}} = \arg\max_{\vartheta\in\Theta} \big\{w(\vartheta) \cdot \exp\big[-t\cdot D(\alpha\|\vartheta)\big]\big\},$$

where $D(\alpha\|\vartheta) = \sum_{i=1}^n \alpha_i \ln\frac{\alpha_i}{\vartheta_i}$ is the *Kullback-Leibler divergence*. If $|\mathcal{X}| = 2$, then Θ is also called a *Bernoulli class*, and one usually takes the binary alphabet $\mathcal{X} = \mathbb{B} = \{0,1\}$ in this case.

4 Dynamic MDL

We can start to develop results. It is surprisingly easy to give a convergence proof w.p.1 of the non-normalized dynamic MDL predictions based on martingales. However we omit it, since it does not include a convergence speed assertion as i.m.s. results do, nor does it yield an off-sequence statement about $\varrho(a|x_{<t})$ for $a \neq x_t$ which is necessary for prediction.

Lemma 6. *For an arbitrary class of (semi)measures $\mathcal{C}$, we have*

$$(i) \quad \varrho(x) - \sum_{a\in\mathcal{X}} \varrho(xa) \;\leq\; \xi(x) - \sum_{a\in\mathcal{X}} \xi(xa) \text{ and}$$
$$(ii) \quad \varrho^x(x) - \sum_{a\in\mathcal{X}} \varrho^x(xa) \;\leq\; \xi(x) - \sum_{a\in\mathcal{X}} \xi(xa)$$

for all $x \in \mathcal{X}^*$. In particular, $\xi - \varrho$ is a semimeasure.

Proof. For all $x \in \mathcal{X}^*$, with $f := \xi - \varrho$ we have

$$\sum_{a\in\mathcal{X}} f(xa) = \sum_{a\in\mathcal{X}} \Big(\xi(xa) - \varrho(xa)\Big) \leq \sum_{a\in\mathcal{X}} \Big(\xi(xa) - \varrho^x(xa)\Big)$$
$$= \sum_{\nu\in\mathcal{M}\setminus\{\nu^x\}} \sum_{a\in\mathcal{X}} w_\nu \nu(xa) \leq \sum_{\nu\in\mathcal{M}\setminus\{\nu^x\}} w_\nu \nu(x) = \xi(x) - \varrho(x) = f(x).$$

The first inequality follows from $\varrho^x(xa) \leq \varrho(xa)$, and the second one holds since all ν are semimeasures. Finally, $f(x) = \xi(x) - \varrho(x) = \sum_{\nu\in\mathcal{M}\setminus\{\nu^x\}} w_\nu \nu(x) \geq 0$ and $f(\epsilon) = \xi(\epsilon) - \varrho(\epsilon) \leq 1$. Hence f is a semimeasure. □

Lemma 7. *Let μ and $\tilde{\mu}$ be measures on $\mathcal{X}$, then*

$$\sum_{a\in\mathcal{X}} \big(\mu(a) - \tilde{\mu}(a)\big)^2 \leq \sum_{a\in\mathcal{X}} \mu(a) \ln \frac{\mu(a)}{\tilde{\mu}(a)}.$$

See e.g. [16, Sec.3.2] for a proof.

Theorem 8. *For any class of (semi)measures $\mathcal{C}$ containing the true distribution μ and for all $n \in \mathbb{N}$, we have*

$$\sum_{t=1}^{n} \mathbf{E} \sum_{a\in\mathcal{X}} \big(\mu(a|x_{<t}) - \varrho_{norm}(a|x_{<t})\big)^2 \leq w_\mu^{-1} + \ln w_\mu^{-1}.$$

That is, $\varrho_{norm}(a|x_{<t}) \stackrel{i.m.s.}{\longrightarrow} \mu(a|x_{<t})$ (see (6)), which implies $\varrho_{norm}(a|x_{<t}) \to \mu(a|x_{<t})$ with μ-probability one.

Proof. From Lemma 7, we know

$$\sum_{t=1}^{n} \mathbf{E} \sum_{a\in\mathcal{X}} \big(\mu(a|x_{<t}) - \varrho_{norm}(a|x_{<t})\big)^2 \leq \sum_{t=1}^{n} \mathbf{E} \sum_{a\in\mathcal{X}} \mu(a|x_{<t}) \ln \frac{\mu(a|x_{<t})}{\varrho_{norm}(a|x_{<t})}$$
$$= \sum_{t=1}^{n} \mathbf{E} \ln \frac{\mu(x_t|x_{<t})}{\varrho_{norm}(x_t|x_{<t})} = \sum_{t=1}^{n} \mathbf{E} \left[\ln \frac{\mu(x_t|x_{<t})}{\varrho(x_t|x_{<t})} + \ln \frac{\sum_{a\in\mathcal{X}} \varrho(x_{<t}a)}{\varrho(x_{<t})}\right]. \quad (8)$$

Then we can estimate

$$\sum_{t=1}^{n} \mathbf{E} \ln \frac{\mu(x_t|x_{<t})}{\varrho(x_t|x_{<t})} = \mathbf{E} \ln \prod_{t=1}^{n} \frac{\mu(x_t|x_{<t})}{\varrho(x_t|x_{<t})} = \mathbf{E} \ln \frac{\mu(x_{1:n})}{\varrho(x_{1:n})} \leq \ln w_\mu^{-1}, \quad (9)$$

since always $\frac{\mu}{\varrho} \leq w_\mu^{-1}$. Moreover, by setting $x = x_{<t}$, using $\ln u \leq u - 1$, adding an always positive max-term, and finally using $\frac{\mu}{\varrho} \leq w_\mu^{-1}$ again, we obtain

$$\mathbf{E} \ln \frac{\sum_a \varrho(x_{<t}a)}{\varrho(x_{<t})} \leq \mathbf{E}\left[\frac{\sum_a \varrho(xa)}{\varrho(x)} - 1\right] = \sum_{\ell(x)=t-1} \frac{\mu(x)\Big[\big(\sum_a \varrho(xa)\big) - \varrho(x)\Big]}{\varrho(x)}$$

$$\leq \sum_{\ell(x)=t-1} \frac{\mu(x)\Big[\,(\sum_{a\in\mathcal{X}} \varrho(xa)) - \varrho(x) + \max\big\{0, \varrho(x) - \sum_{a\in\mathcal{X}} \varrho(xa)\big\}\Big]}{\varrho(x)}$$

$$\leq w_\mu^{-1} \sum_{\ell(x)=t-1} \left[\Big(\sum_{a\in\mathcal{X}} \varrho(xa)\Big) - \varrho(x) + \max\Big\{0, \varrho(x) - \sum_{a\in\mathcal{X}} \varrho(xa)\Big\}\right]. \quad (10)$$

We proceed by observing

$$\sum_{t=1}^{n} \sum_{\ell(x)=t-1} \Big[\Big(\sum_{a\in\mathcal{X}} \varrho(xa)\Big) - \varrho(x)\Big] = \sum_{t=1}^{n} \Big[\sum_{\ell(x)=t} \varrho(x) - \sum_{\ell(x)=t-1} \varrho(x)\Big] = \Big[\sum_{\ell(x)=n} \varrho(x)\Big] - \varrho(\epsilon) \quad (11)$$

which is true since for successive t the positive and negative terms cancel. From Lemma 6 we know $\varrho(x) - \sum_{a\in\mathcal{X}} \varrho(xa) \leq \xi(x) - \sum_{a\in\mathcal{X}} \xi(xa)$ and therefore

$$\sum_{t=1}^{n} \sum_{\ell(x)=t-1} \max\Big\{0, \varrho(x) - \sum_{a\in\mathcal{X}} \varrho(xa)\Big\} \leq \sum_{t=1}^{n} \sum_{\ell(x)=t-1} \max\Big\{0, \xi(x) - \sum_{a\in\mathcal{X}} \xi(xa)\Big\}$$

$$= \sum_{t=1}^{n} \sum_{\ell(x)=t-1} \Big[\xi(x) - \sum_{a\in\mathcal{X}} \xi(xa)\Big] = \xi(\epsilon) - \sum_{\ell(x)=n} \xi(x). \quad (12)$$

Here we have again used the fact that positive and negative terms cancel for successive t, and moreover the fact that ξ is a semimeasure. Combining (10), (11) and (12), and observing $\varrho \leq \xi \leq 1$, we obtain

$$\sum_{t=1}^{n} \mathbf{E} \ln \frac{\sum_a \varrho(x_{<t}a)}{\varrho(x_{<t})} \leq w_\mu^{-1} \left[\xi(\epsilon) - \varrho(\epsilon) + \sum_{\ell(x)=n} \Big(\varrho(x) - \xi(x)\Big)\right] \leq w_\mu^{-1}\xi(\epsilon) \leq w_\mu^{-1}. \quad (13)$$

Therefore, (8), (9) and (13) finally prove the assertion. □

This is the first convergence result in mean sum, see (6). It implies both on-sequence and off-sequence convergence. Moreover, it asserts the convergence is "fast" in the sense that the sum of the total expected deviations is bounded by $w_\mu^{-1} + \ln w_\mu^{-1}$. Of course, w_μ^{-1} can be very large, namely 2 to the power of complexity of μ. The following example will show that this bound is sharp (save for a constant factor). Observe that in the corresponding result for mixtures, Theorem 1, the bound is much smaller, namely $\ln w_\mu^{-1}$ = complexity of μ.

Example 9. Let $\mathcal{X} = \{0,1\}$, $N \geq 1$ and $\mathcal{C} = \{\nu_1, \ldots, \nu_{N-1}, \mu\}$. Each ν_i is a deterministic measure concentrated on the sequence $1^{i-1}0^\infty$, while the true distribution μ is deterministic and concentrated on $x_{<\infty} = 1^\infty$. Let $w_{\nu_i} = w_\mu = \frac{1}{N}$ for all i. Then μ generates $x_{<\infty}$, and for each $t \leq N-1$ we have $\varrho_{norm}(0|x_{<t}) = \varrho_{norm}(1|x_{<t}) = \frac{1}{2}$. Hence, $\sum_t \mathbf{E} \sum_a \big(\mu(a|x_{<t}) - \varrho_{norm}(a|x_{<t})\big)^2 = \frac{1}{2}(N-1) \approx \frac{1}{2} w_\mu^{-1}$ for large N. Here, μ is Bernoulli, while the ν_i are not. It might be surprising at a first glance that there are even classes $\mathcal{C}$ containing *only* Bernoulli distributions, where the exponential bound is sharp [18].

Theorem 10. *For any class of (semi)measures $\mathcal{C}$ containing the true distribution μ, we have*

$$(i)\ \sum_{t=1}^{\infty}\mathbf{E}\left|\ln\sum_{a\in\mathcal{X}}\varrho(a|x_{<t})\right| \ \leq\ 2w_\mu^{-1} \quad\text{and}$$

$$(ii)\ \sum_{t=1}^{\infty}\mathbf{E}\sum_{a\in\mathcal{X}}\left|\varrho_{norm}(a|x_{<t})-\varrho(a|x_{<t})\right| \ =\ \sum_{t=1}^{\infty}\mathbf{E}\left|1-\sum_{a\in\mathcal{X}}\varrho(a|x_{<t})\right| \ \leq\ 2w_\mu^{-1}.$$

Consequently, $\varrho(a|x_{<t}) \stackrel{i.m.s.}{\longrightarrow} \mu(a|x_{<t})$*, and for almost all* $x_{<\infty}\in\mathcal{X}^\infty$*, the normalizer* N_ϱ *defined in (7) converges to a number which is finite and greater than zero, i.e.* $0<N_\varrho(x_{<\infty})<\infty$.

Proof. (i) Define $u^+=\max\{0,u\}$ for $u\in\mathbb{R}$, then for $x:=x_{<t}\in\mathcal{X}^{t-1}$ we have

$$\begin{aligned}
\mathbf{E}\left|\ln\sum_{a\in\mathcal{X}}\varrho(a|x)\right| &= \mathbf{E}\left|\ln\frac{\sum_a\varrho(xa)}{\varrho(x)}\right| = \mathbf{E}\left[\left(\ln\frac{\sum_a\varrho(xa)}{\varrho(x)}\right)^+ + \left(\ln\frac{\varrho(x)}{\sum_a\varrho(xa)}\right)^+\right]\\
&\leq\ \mathbf{E}\frac{\left(\sum_a\varrho(xa)-\varrho(x)\right)^+}{\varrho(x)} + \mathbf{E}\frac{\left(\varrho(x)-\sum_a\varrho(xa)\right)^+}{\sum_a\varrho(xa)}\\
&=\ \sum_{\ell(x)=t-1}\frac{\mu(x)\left(\sum_a\varrho(xa)-\varrho(x)\right)^+}{\varrho(x)} + \sum_{\ell(x)=t-1}\frac{\mu(x)\left(\varrho(x)-\sum_a\varrho(xa)\right)^+}{\sum_a\varrho(xa)}\\
&\leq\ w_\mu^{-1}\sum_{\ell(x)=t-1}\left(\textstyle\sum_a\varrho(xa)-\varrho(x)\right)^+ + w_\mu^{-1}\sum_{\ell(x)=t-1}\left(\varrho(x)-\textstyle\sum_a\varrho(xa)\right)^+\\
&=\ w_\mu^{-1}\sum_{\ell(x)=t-1}\left[\textstyle\sum_a\varrho(xa)-\varrho(x)+2\left(\varrho(x)-\sum_a\varrho(xa)\right)^+\right].
\end{aligned}$$

Here, $|u|=u^++(-u)^+=-u+2u^+$, $\ln u\leq u-1$, and $\varrho\geq w_\mu\mu$ have been used, the latter implies also $\sum_a\varrho(xa)\geq w_\mu\sum_a\mu(xa)=w_\mu\mu(x)$. The last expression in this (in)equality chain, when summed over $t=1...\infty$ is bounded by $2w_\mu^{-1}$ by essentially the same arguments (10) - (13) as in the proof of Theorem 8.

(ii) Let again $x:=x_{<t}$ and use $\varrho_{norm}(a|x)=\varrho(a|x)/\sum_b\varrho(b|x)$ to obtain

$$\begin{aligned}
\sum_a\left|\varrho_{norm}(a|x)-\varrho(a|x)\right| &= \sum_a\frac{\varrho(a|x)}{\sum_b\varrho(b|x)}\left|1-\sum_b\varrho(b|x)\right| = \left|1-\sum_b\varrho(b|x)\right|\\
&= \frac{\left(\sum_a\varrho(xa)-\varrho(x)\right)^+}{\varrho(x)} + \frac{\left(\varrho(x)-\sum_a\varrho(xa)\right)^+}{\varrho(x)}.
\end{aligned}$$

Then take the expectation $\mathbf{E}$ and the sum $\sum_{t=1}^\infty$ and proceed as in (i). Finally, $\varrho(a|x_{<t})\stackrel{i.m.s.}{\longrightarrow}\mu(a|x_{<t})$ follows by combining (ii) with Theorem 8, and by (i), $\sum_1^n\left|\ln\frac{\sum_a\varrho(x_{<t}a)}{\varrho(x_{<t})}\right|$ is bounded in n with μ-probability 1, thus the same is true for $\ln N_\varrho(x_{<\infty})=\sum_1^\infty\ln\frac{\sum_{a\in\mathcal{X}}\varrho(x_{<t}a)}{\varrho(x_{<t})}$. □

5 Static MDL

So far, we have considered dynamic MDL from Definition 2. We turn now to the static variant (Definition 3), which is usually more efficient and thus preferred in practice.

Theorem 11. *For any class of (semi)measures $\mathcal{C}$ containing the true distribution μ, we have*

$$\sum_{t=1}^{\infty}\mathbf{E}\sum_{a\in\mathcal{X}}\left|\varrho_{norm}^{x_{<t}}(a|x_{<t})-\varrho^{x_{<t}}(a|x_{<t})\right| = \sum_{t=1}^{\infty}\mathbf{E}\left|1-\sum_{a\in\mathcal{X}}\varrho^{x_{<t}}(a|x_{<t})\right| \leq w_\mu^{-1}.$$

Proof. We proceed in a similar way as in the proof of Theorem 8, (10) - (12). From Lemma 6, we know $\varrho(x)-\sum_a\varrho^x(xa) \leq \xi(x)-\sum_a\xi(xa)$. Then

$$\sum_{t=1}^{n}\mathbf{E}\left|1-\sum_{a\in\mathcal{X}}\varrho^{x_{<t}}(a|x_{<t})\right| = \sum_{t=1}^{n}\mathbf{E}\frac{\varrho(x_{<t})-\sum_{a\in\mathcal{X}}\varrho^{x_{<t}}(x_{<t}a)}{\varrho(x_{<t})}$$

$$=\sum_{t=1}^{n}\sum_{\ell(x)=t-1}\mu(x)\frac{\varrho(x)-\sum_{a\in\mathcal{X}}\varrho^x(xa)}{\varrho(x)} \leq w_\mu^{-1}\sum_{t=1}^{n}\sum_{\ell(x)=t-1}\left[\varrho(x)-\sum_{a\in\mathcal{X}}\varrho^x(xa)\right]$$

$$\leq w_\mu^{-1}\sum_{t=1}^{n}\sum_{\ell(x)=t-1}\left[\xi(x)-\sum_{a\in\mathcal{X}}\xi(xa)\right] \leq w_\mu^{-1}\left[\xi(\epsilon)-\sum_{\ell(x)=n}\xi(x)\right] \leq w_\mu^{-1}.$$

for all $n\in\mathbb{N}$. This implies the assertion. Again we have used $\frac{\mu}{\varrho}\leq w_\mu^{-1}$ and the fact that positive and negative terms cancel for successive t. □

Corollary 12. *Let $\mathcal{C}$ contain the true distribution μ, then*

$$\begin{aligned}
\textstyle\sum_t\mathbf{E}\sum_a\left(\mu(a|x_{<t})-\varrho_{norm}(a|x_{<t})\right)^2 &\leq 2w_\mu^{-1},\\
\textstyle\sum_t\mathbf{E}\sum_a\left(\mu(a|x_{<t})-\varrho(a|x_{<t})\right)^2 &\leq 8w_\mu^{-1},\\
\textstyle\sum_t\mathbf{E}\sum_a\left(\mu(a|x_{<t})-\varrho^{x_{<t}}(a|x_{<t})\right)^2 &\leq 21w_\mu^{-1},\\
\textstyle\sum_t\mathbf{E}\sum_a\left(\mu(a|x_{<t})-\varrho_{norm}^{x_{<t}}(a|x_{<t})\right)^2 &\leq 32w_\mu^{-1}.
\end{aligned}$$

Proof. This follows by combining the assertions of Theorems 8 - 11 with the triangle inequality. For static MDL, use in addition $\sum_a\left|\varrho(a|x)-\varrho^x(a|x)\right| = \left|\sum_a\varrho(a|x)-\sum_a\varrho^x(a|x)\right| \leq \left|\sum_a\varrho(a|x)-1\right|+\left|1-\sum_a\varrho^x(a|x)\right|$ which follows from $\varrho(xa)\geq\varrho^x(xa)$. □

This corollary recapitulates our results and states convergence i.m.s (and therefore also with μ-probability 1) for all combinations of un-normalized/normalized and dynamic/static MDL predictions.[2]

[2] We briefly discuss the choice of the total expected square error for measuring speed of convergence. The expected Kullback-Leibler distance may seem more natural in

6 Hybrid MDL and Stabilization

We now turn to the hybrid MDL variant (see Definition 4). So far we have not cared about what happens if two or more (semi)measures obtain the same value $w_\nu \nu(x)$ for some string x. In fact, for the previous results, the *tie-breaking strategy* can be completely arbitrary. This need not be so for all thinkable prediction methods other than static and dynamic MDL, as the following example shows.

Example 13. Let $\mathcal{X} = \mathbb{B}$ and $\mathcal{C}$ contain only two measures, the uniform measure λ which is defined by $\lambda(x) = 2^{-\ell(x)}$, and another measure ν having $\nu(1x) = 2^{-\ell(x)}$ and $\nu(0x) = 0$. The respective weights are $w_\lambda = \frac{2}{3}$ and $w_\nu = \frac{1}{3}$. Then, for each x starting with 1, we have $w_\nu \nu(x) = w_\lambda \lambda(x) = \frac{1}{3} 2^{-\ell(x)+1}$. Therefore, for all $x_{<\infty}$ starting with 1 (a set which has uniform measure $\frac{1}{2}$), we have a tie. If the maximizing element ν^* is chosen to be λ for even t and ν for odd t, then both static and dynamic MDL constantly predict probabilities of $\frac{1}{2}$ for all $a \in \mathbb{B}$. However, the hybrid MDL predictor values $\frac{\nu^*(x_{<t}a)}{\nu^*(x_{<t})}$ oscillate between $\frac{1}{4}$ and 1.

If the ambiguity in the tie-breaking process is removed, e.g. if always the measure with the larger weight w_ν is been chosen, then the hybrid MDL predictor *does* converge for this example. If there are more (semi)measures in the class and there remains still a tie of shortest programs, an arbitrary program can be selected, since then the respective measures are equal, too. In the following, we assume that this tie-breaking rule is applied.

Do the hybrid MDL predictions always converge then? This is equivalent to asking if the process of selecting a maximizing element eventually *stabilizes*. If there is no stabilization, then hybrid MDL will necessarily fail as soon as the weights are not equal. A possible counterexample could consist of two measures the fraction of which oscillates perpetually around a certain value. This can indeed happen.

Example 14. Let $\mathcal{X}$ be binary, $\mu(x) = \prod_{i=1}^{\ell(x)} \mu_i(x_i)$ and $\nu(x) = \prod_{i=1}^{\ell(x)} \nu_i(x_i)$ with

$$\mu_i(1) = 1 - 2^{-2\lceil \frac{i}{2} \rceil} \text{ and } \nu_i(1) = 1 - 2^{-2\lceil \frac{i+1}{2} \rceil + 1}.$$

Then one can easily see that $\mu(111\ldots) = \prod_1^\infty \mu_i(1) > 0$, $\nu(111\ldots) = \prod_1^\infty \nu_i(1) > 0$, and $\frac{\nu(111\ldots)}{\mu(111\ldots)}$ is convergent but oscillates around its limit. Therefore, we can set w_μ and w_ν appropriately to prevent the maximizing element from stabilizing on $x_{<\infty} = 111\ldots$ (Moreover, each sequence having positive measure under μ and ν contains eventually only ones, and the quotient oscillates.)

the light of our proofs. However, this quantity behaves well only under dynamic MDL, not static MDL. To see this, let $\mathcal{C}$ be the class of all computable Bernoulli distributions and μ the measure having $\mu(0) = \mu(1) = \frac{1}{2}$. Then the sequence $x = 0^n$ has nonzero probability. For sufficiently large n, $\nu^x = \nu_0$ holds (typically already for small n), where ν_0 is the distribution generating only 0. Then $D(\mu \| \nu^x) = \infty$, and the expectation is ∞, too. The quadratic distance behaves locally like the Kullback-Leibler distance (Lemma 7), but otherwise is bounded and thus more convenient.

The reason for the oscillation in this example is the fact that measures μ and ν are asymptotically very similar. One can also achieve a similar effect by constructing a measure which is *dependent* on the past. This shows in particular that we need both parts of the following definition which states properties sufficient for a positive result.

Definition 15. *(i) A (semi)measure ν on $\mathcal{X}^\infty$ is called* factorizable *if there are (semi)measures ν_i on $\mathcal{X}$ such that $\nu(x) = \prod_{i=1}^{\ell(x)} \nu_i(x_i)$ for all $x \in \mathcal{X}^*$. That is, the symbols of sequences $x_{<\infty}$ generated by ν are independent.*
(ii) A factorizable (semi)measure $\mu = \prod \mu_i$ is called uniformly stochastic, *if there is some $\delta > 0$ such that at each time i the probability of all symbols $a \in \mathcal{X}$ is either 0 or at least δ. That is, $\mu_i(a) > 0 \Rightarrow \mu_i(a) \geq \delta$ for all $a \in \mathcal{X}$ and $i \geq 1$.*

In particular, all deterministic measures are uniformly stochastic. Another simple example of a uniformly stochastic measure is a probability distribution which generates alternately random bits by fair coin flips and the digits of the binary representation of π.

Theorem 16. *Let $\mathcal{C}$ be a countable class of factorizable (semi)measures and μ be uniformly stochastic. Then the maximizing element stabilizes almost surely.*

We omit the proof. So in particular, under the conditions of Theorem 16, the hybrid MDL predictions converge almost surely. No statement about the convergence speed can be made.

7 Complexities and Randomness

In this section, we concentrate on universal sequence prediction. It was mentioned already in the introduction that this is one interesting application of the theory developed so far. So $\mathcal{C} = \mathcal{M}$ is the countable set of all enumerable (i.e. lower semicomputable) semimeasures on $\mathcal{X}^*$. (Algorithms are identified with semimeasures rather than measures since they need not terminate.) $\mathcal{M}$ contains stochastic models in general, and in particular all models for computable deterministic sequences. One can show that this class $\mathcal{M}$ is determined by *all* algorithms on some fixed universal monotone Turing machine U [9, Th. 4.5.2]. By this correspondence, each semimeasure $\nu \in \mathcal{M}$ is assigned a *canonical weight* $w_\nu = 2^{-K(\nu)}$ (where $K(\nu)$ is the Kolmogorov complexity of ν, see [9, Eq. 4.11]), and $\sum w_\nu \leq 1$ holds. We will assume programs to be *binary*, i.e. $p \in \mathbb{B}^*$, in contrast to outputs, which are strings $x \in \mathcal{X}^*$.

The MDL definitions in Section 3 directly transfer to this setup. All our results (Theorems 8 - 11) therefore apply to $\varrho = \varrho_{[\mathcal{M}]}$ if the true distribution μ is a measure, which is not very restrictive. Then μ is necessarily computable. Also, Theorem 1 implies Solomonoff's important *universal induction* theorem: ξ converges to the true distribution i.m.s., if the latter is computable. Note that the Bayes mixture ξ is within a multiplicative constant of the *Solomonoff-Levin prior* $M(x)$, which is the algorithmic probability that U produces an output starting with x if its input is random.

In addition to $\mathcal{M}$, we also consider the set of all recursive measures $\tilde{\mathcal{M}}$ together with the same canonical weights, and the mixture $\tilde{\xi}(x) = \sum_{\nu \in \tilde{\mathcal{M}}} w_\nu \nu(x)$. Likewise, define $\tilde{\varrho} = \varrho_{[\tilde{\mathcal{M}}]}$. Then we obviously have $\tilde{\varrho}(x) \leq \tilde{\xi}(x) \leq \xi(x)$ and $\varrho(x) \leq \xi(x)$ for all $x \in \mathcal{X}^*$. It is even immediate that $\xi(x) \stackrel{\times}{\leq} \varrho(x)$ since $\xi \in \mathcal{M}$. Here, by $f \stackrel{\times}{\leq} g$ we mean $f \leq g \cdot O(1)$, "$\stackrel{\times}{\geq}$" and "$\stackrel{\times}{=}$" are defined analogously.

Moreover, for any string $x \in \mathcal{X}^*$, there is also a *universal one-part MDL estimator* $m(x) = 2^{-Km(x)}$ derived from the monotone complexity $Km(x) = \min\{\ell(p) : U(p) = x*\}$. (I.e. the monotone complexity is the length of the shortest program such that U's output starts with x.) The minimal program p defines a measure ν with $\nu(x) = 1$ and $w_\nu \geq 2^{-\ell(p)} \cdot O(1)$ (recall that programs are binary). Therefore, $m(x) \stackrel{\times}{\leq} \tilde{\varrho}(x)$ for all $x \in \mathcal{X}^*$. Together with the following proposition, we thus obtain

$$m(x) \stackrel{\times}{=} \tilde{\varrho}(x) \stackrel{\times}{\leq} \tilde{\xi}(x) \stackrel{\times}{\leq} \varrho(x) \stackrel{\times}{=} \xi(x) \text{ for all } x \in \mathcal{X}^*. \tag{14}$$

Proposition 17. *We have $\tilde{\varrho}(x) \stackrel{\times}{\leq} m(x)$ for all $x \in \mathcal{X}^*$.*

Proof. (Sketch only.) It is not hard to show that given a string $x \in \mathcal{X}^*$ and a recursive measure ν (which in particular may be the MDL descriptor $\nu^*(x)$) it is possible to specify a program p of length at most $-\log_2 w_\nu - \log_2 \nu(x) + c$ that outputs a string starting with x, where constant c is independent of x and ν. This is done via arithmetic encoding. Alternatively, it is also possible to prove the proposition indirectly using [9, Th.4.5.4]. This implies that $m(x) \stackrel{\times}{\geq} w_\nu \nu(x)$ for all $x \in \mathcal{X}^*$ and all recursive measures ν. Then, also $m(x) \stackrel{\times}{\geq} \max\{w_\nu \nu(x)\}$ holds. □

On the other hand, we know from [19] that $m \stackrel{\times}{\neq} \xi$. Therefore, at least one of the two inequalities in (14) must be proper.

Problem 18. Which of the inequalities $\tilde{\varrho} \stackrel{\times}{\leq} \tilde{\xi}$ and $\tilde{\xi} \stackrel{\times}{\leq} \varrho$ is proper (or are both)?

Equation (14) also has an easy consequence in terms of randomness criteria.

Proposition 19. *A sequence $x_{<\infty} \in \mathcal{X}^\infty$ is Martin-Löf random with respect to some computable measure μ iff for any $f \in \{m, \tilde{\varrho}, \tilde{\xi}, r, M\}$ there is a constant $C > 0$ such that $f(x_{1:n}) \leq C\mu(x_{1:n})$ for all $n \in \mathbb{N}$ holds.*

Proof. It is a standard result that if $x_{<\infty}$ is random then $M(x_{1:n}) \leq C\mu(x_{1:n})$ for some C [20, Th.3]. Then by (14), $f(x_{1:n}) \stackrel{\times}{\leq} \mu(x_{1:n})$ for all f. Conversely, if $f(x_{1:n}) \stackrel{\times}{\leq} \mu(x_{1:n})$ for some f, then there is C such that $m(x_{1:n}) \leq C\mu(x_{1:n})$. This implies μ-randomness of $x_{<\infty}$ ([20, Th.2] or [9, p295]). □

Interestingly, these randomness criteria partly depend on the weights. The criteria for $\tilde{\xi}$ and $\tilde{\varrho}$ are not equivalent any more if weights other than the canonical weights are used, as the following example will show. In contrast, for ξ and ϱ there is no weight dependency as long as the weights are strictly greater than zero, since $\xi \in \mathcal{M}$.

Example 20. There are other randomness criteria than Martin-Löf randomness, e.g. rec-randomness. A rec-random sequence $x_{<\infty}$ (with respect to the uniform distribution) satisfies $\nu(x_{1:n}) \leq c(\nu)2^{-n}$ for each computable measure ν and for all n. It is obvious that Martin-Löf random sequences are also rec-random. The converse does not hold, there are sequences $x_{<\infty}$ that are rec-random but not Martin-Löf random, as shown e.g. in [21,22].

Let $x_{<\infty}$ be such a sequence, i.e. $\nu(x_{1:n}) \leq c(\nu)2^{-n}$ for all computable measures ν and for all n, but where $x_{<\infty}$ is not Martin-Löf random. Let $\nu_1, \nu_2, \ldots$ be a (non-effective) enumeration of all computable measures. Define $w'_i = 2^{-i}c(\nu_i)^{-1}$. Then

$$\tilde{M}'(x_{1:n}) = \sum_{i=1}^{\infty} w'_i \nu_i(x_{1:n}) \leq \sum_{i=1}^{\infty} 2^{-i} c(\nu_i)^{-1} c(\nu_i) 2^{-n} = 2^{-n} \text{ for all } n,$$

i.e. $x_{<\infty}$ is $\tilde{M}'$-random. Thus, $x_{<\infty}$ is also $\tilde{r}'$-random with $\tilde{r}' = \max_i\{w'_i \nu_i\}$.

8 Conclusions

We have proven convergence theorems for MDL prediction for arbitrary countable classes of semimeasures, the only requirement being that the true distribution μ is a measure. Our results hold for both static and dynamic MDL and provide a statement about convergence speed in mean sum. This also yields both on-sequence and off-sequence assertions. Our results are to our knowledge the strongest available for the discrete case.

Compared to the bound for Bayes mixture prediction prediction in Theorem 1, the error bounds for MDL are exponentially worse, namely w_μ^{-1} instead of $\ln w_\mu^{-1}$. Our bounds are sharp in general, as Example 9 shows. There are even classes of Bernoulli distributions where the exponential bound is sharp [18].

In the case of continuously parameterized model classes, finite error bounds do not hold [6,4], but the error grows slowly as $\ln n$. Under additional assumptions (i.i.d. for instance) and with a reasonable prior, one can prove similar behavior of MDL and Bayes mixture predictions [5]. In this sense, MDL converges as fast as a Bayes mixture there. This fast convergence even holds for the "slow" Bernoulli example in [18]. However in Example 9, the error grows as n, which shows that the Bayes mixture can be superior to MDL in general.

References

1. Wallace, C.S., Boulton, D.M.: An information measure for classification. Computer Jrnl. **11** (1968) 185–194
2. Rissanen, J.J.: Modeling by shortest data description. Automatica **14** (1978) 465–471
3. Grünwald, P.D.: The Minimum Discription Length Principle and Reasoning under Uncertainty. PhD thesis, Universiteit van Amsterdam (1998)
4. Barron, A.R., Rissanen, J.J., Yu, B.: The minimum description length principle in coding and modeling. IEEE Transactions on Information Theory **44** (1998) 2743–2760
5. Rissanen, J.J.: Fisher Information and Stochastic Complexity. IEEE Trans on Information Theory **42** (1996) 40–47
6. Barron, A.R., Cover, T.M.: Minimum complexity density estimation. IEEE Transactions on Information Theory **37** (1991) 1034–1054
7. Rissanen, J.J.: Hypothesis selection and testing by the MDL principle. The Computer Journal **42** (1999) 260–269
8. Zvonkin, A.K., Levin, L.A.: The complexity of finite objects and the development of the concepts of information and randomness by means of the theory of algorithms. Russian Mathematical Surveys **25** (1970) 83–124
9. Li, M., Vitányi, P.M.B.: An introduction to Kolmogorov complexity and its applications. 2nd edn. Springer (1997)
10. Calude, C.S.: Information and Randomness. 2nd edn. Springer, Berlin (2002)
11. Solomonoff, R.J.: A formal theory of inductive inference: Part 1 and 2. Inform. Control **7** (1964) 1–22, 224–254
12. Solomonoff, R.J.: Complexity-based induction systems: comparisons and convergence theorems. IEEE Trans. Inform. Theory **IT-24** (1978) 422–432
13. Hutter, M.: New error bounds for Solomonoff prediction. Journal of Computer and System Sciences **62** (2001) 653–667
14. Hutter, M.: Optimality of universal Bayesian prediction for general loss and alphabet. Journal of Machine Learning Research **4** (2003) 971–1000
15. Hutter, M.: Sequence prediction based on monotone complexity. In: Proceedings of the 16th Annual Conference on Learning Theory (COLT-2003). Lecture Notes in Artificial Intelligence, Berlin, Springer (2003) 506–521
16. Hutter, M.: Convergence and error bounds of universal prediction for general alphabet. Proceedings of the 12th Eurpean Conference on Machine Learning (ECML-2001) (2001) 239–250
17. Li, M., Chen, X., Li, X., Ma, B., Vitányi, P.M.B.: The similarity metric. In: Proc. 14th ACM-SIAM Symposium on Discrete Algorithms (SODA). (2003)
18. Poland, J., Hutter, M.: On the convergence speed of MDL predictions for Bernoulli sequences. preprint (2004)
19. Gács, P.: On the relation between descriptional complexity and algorithmic probability. Theoretical Computer Science **22** (1983) 71–93
20. Levin, L.A.: On the notion of a random sequence. Soviet Math. Dokl. **14** (1973) 1413–1416
21. Schnorr, C.P.: Zufälligkeit und Wahrscheinlichkeit. Volume 218 of Lecture Notes in Mathematics. Springer, Chichester, England (1971)
22. Wang, Y.: Randomness and Complexity. PhD thesis, Ruprecht-Karls-Universität Heidelberg (1996)

On the Convergence of MDL Density Estimation

Tong Zhang

IBM T.J. Watson Research Center
Yorktown Heights, NY, 10598, USA
tzhang@watson.ibm.com

Abstract. We present a general information exponential inequality that measures the statistical complexity of some deterministic and randomized density estimators. Using this inequality, we are able to improve classical results concerning the convergence of two-part code MDL in [1]. Moreover, we are able to derive clean finite-sample convergence bounds that are not obtainable using previous approaches.

1 Introduction

The purpose of this paper is to study a class of complexity minimization based density estimation methods using a generalization of ϵ-entropy which we call KL-complexity. Specifically, we derive a simple yet general information theoretical inequality that can be used to measure the convergence behavior of some randomized estimation methods. Consequences of this very basic inequality will then be explored. In particular, we apply this analysis to the two-part code MDL density estimator studied in [1], and refine their results.

We shall first introduce basic notations used in the paper. Consider a sample space $\mathcal{X}$ and a measure μ on $\mathcal{X}$ (with respect to some σ-field). In statistical inferencing, the nature picks a probability measure Q on $\mathcal{X}$ which is unknown. We assume that Q has a density q with respect to μ. In density estimation, the statistician considers a set of probability densities $p(\cdot|\theta)$ (with respect to μ on $\mathcal{X}$) indexed by $\theta \in \Gamma$.[1] Throughout this paper, we always denote the true underlying density by q, which may not belong to the model class Γ. Given Γ, the goal of the statistician is to select a density $p(\cdot|\theta) \in \Gamma$ based on the observed data $X = \{X_1, \ldots, X_n\} \in \mathcal{X}^n$, such that $p(\cdot|\theta)$ is as close to q as possible when measured by a certain distance function (to be specify later).

In the framework considered in this paper, we assume that there is a prior distribution $d\pi(\theta)$ on the parameter space Γ that is independent of the observed data. For notational simplicity, we shall call any observation X dependent probability density $\hat{w}_X(\theta)$ on Γ (measurable on $\mathcal{X}^n \times \Gamma$) with respect to $d\pi(\theta)$ a *posterior randomization measure*. In particular, a posterior randomization measure in our sense is not limited to the *Bayesian posterior distribution*, which has a specific meaning. We are interested in the density estimation performance of

[1] Without causing any confusion, we may also occasionally denote the model family $\{p(\cdot|\theta) : \theta \in \Gamma\}$ by the same symbol Γ.

J. Shawe-Taylor and Y. Singer (Eds.): COLT 2004, LNAI 3120, pp. 315–330, 2004.

randomized estimators that draw θ according to posterior randomization measure $\hat{w}_X(\theta)$ obtained from a class of density estimation schemes. We should note that in this framework, our density estimator is completely characterized by the associated posterior randomization density $\hat{w}_X(\theta)$.

2 Information Complexity Minimization Method

We introduce an information theoretical complexity measure of randomized estimators represented as posterior randomization densities.

Definition 1. *Consider a probability density $w(\cdot)$ on Γ with respect to π. The KL-divergence $D_{KL}(wd\pi||d\pi)$ is defined as:*

$$D_{KL}(wd\pi||d\pi) = \int_\Gamma w(\theta) \ln w(\theta) d\pi(\theta).$$

The definition becomes the differential entropy for measures on a real-line, when we choose the uniform prior. If we place the prior uniformly on an ϵ-net of the parameter space, then the KL-compleixty becomes ϵ-entropy. KL-divergence is a rather standard information theoretical concept. We will later show that it can be used to measure the complexity of a randomized estimator. We call such a measure the *KL-complexity* or *KL-entropy* of a randomized estimator.

For a real-valued function $f(\theta)$ on Γ, we denote by $\mathbf{E}_\pi f(\theta)$ the expectation of $f(\cdot)$ with respect to π. Similarly, for a real-valued function $\ell(x)$ on $\mathcal{X}$, we denote by $\mathbf{E}_q\, \ell(x)$ the expectation of $\ell(\cdot)$ with respect the true underlying distribution q. We also use $\mathbf{E}_X$ to denote the expectation with respect to the observation X (n independent samples from q).

The MDL method (7) which we will study in Section 5 can be regarded as a special case of a general class of estimation methods which we refer to as *Information Complexity Minimization*. The method produces a posterior randomization density. Let S be a pre-defined set of densities on Γ with respect to the prior π. We consider a general information complexity minimization estimator:

$$\hat{w}_X^S = \arg\min_{w \in S} \left[-\mathbf{E}_\pi\, w(\theta) \sum_{i=1}^n \ln p(X_i|\theta) + \lambda D_{KL}(wd\pi||d\pi) \right]. \tag{1}$$

If we let S be the set of all possible posterior randomization measures, then the estimator leads to the Bayesian posterior distribution with $\lambda = 1$ (see [11]). Therefore bounds obtained for (1) can also be applied to Bayesian posterior distributions. Instead of focusing on the more special MDL method presented later in (7), we shall develop our analysis for the general formulation in (1).

3 The Basic Information Theoretical Inequality

The key ingredient of our analysis using KL-complexity is a well-known convex duality, which has already been used in some recent machine learning papers to study sample complexity bounds [5,7].

Proposition 1. *Assume that $f(\theta)$ is a measurable real-valued function on Γ, and $w(\theta)$ is a density with respect to π, we have $\mathbf{E}_\pi\, w(\theta) f(\theta) \le D_{KL}(w d\pi || d\pi) + \ln \mathbf{E}_\pi \exp(f(\theta))$.*

The basis of the paper is the following lemma, where we assume that $\hat{w}_X(\theta)$ is a posterior randomization measure (density with respect to π that depends on X and measurable on $\mathcal{X}^n \times \Gamma$).

Lemma 1 (Information Exponential Inequality). *Consider any posterior randomization density $\hat{w}_X(\theta)$. Let α and β be two real numbers. The following inequality holds for all measurable real-valued functions $L_X(\theta)$ on $\mathcal{X}^n \times \Gamma$:*

$$\mathbf{E}_X \exp\left[\mathbf{E}_\pi \hat{w}_X(\theta)(L_X(\theta) - \alpha \ln \mathbf{E}_X e^{\beta L_X(\theta)}) - D_{KL}(\hat{w}_X d\pi || d\pi)\right] \le \mathbf{E}_\pi \frac{\mathbf{E}_X e^{L_X(\theta)}}{\mathbf{E}_X^\alpha e^{\beta L_X(\theta)}}.$$

where $\mathbf{E}_X$ is the expectation with respect to the observation X.

Proof. From Proposition 1, we obtain

$$\begin{aligned}\hat{L}(X) =& \mathbf{E}_\pi \hat{w}_X(\theta)(L_X(\theta) - \alpha \ln \mathbf{E}_X e^{\beta L_X(\theta)}) - D_{KL}(\hat{w}_X d\pi || d\pi) \\ \le& \ln \mathbf{E}_\pi \exp(L_X(\theta) - \alpha \ln \mathbf{E}_X e^{\beta L_X(\theta)}).\end{aligned}$$

Now applying Fubini's theorem to interchange the order of integration, we have:

$$\mathbf{E}_X e^{\hat{L}(X)} \le \mathbf{E}_X \mathbf{E}_\pi e^{L_X(\theta) - \alpha \ln \mathbf{E}_X \exp(\beta L_X(\theta))} = \mathbf{E}_\pi \frac{\mathbf{E}_X e^{L_X(\theta)}}{\mathbf{E}_X^\alpha e^{\beta L_X(\theta)}}.$$

□

Remark 1. The main technical ingredients of the proof are motivated from techniques in the recent machine learning literature. The general idea for analyzing randomized estimators using Fubini's theorem and decoupling was already in [10]. The specific decoupling mechanism using Proposition 1 appeared in [5,7] for related problems. A simplified form of Lemma 1 was used in [11] to analyze Bayesian posterior distributions.

The following bound is a straight-forward consequence of Lemma 1. Note that for density estimation, the loss $\ell_\theta(x)$ has a form of $\ell(p(x|\theta))$, where $\ell(\cdot)$ is a scaled log-loss.

Theorem 1 (Information Posterior Bounds). *Using the notation of Lemma 1. Let $X = \{X_1, \dots, X_n\}$ be n-samples that are independently drawn from q. Consider a measurable function $\ell_\theta(x) : \Gamma \times \mathcal{X} \to R$. Consider real numbers α and β, and define*

$$c_n(\alpha, \beta) = \frac{1}{n} \ln \mathbf{E}_\pi \left(\frac{\mathbf{E}_q e^{-\ell_\theta(x)}}{\mathbf{E}_q^\alpha e^{-\beta \ell_\theta(x)}} \right)^n.$$

Then $\forall t$, the following event holds with probability at least $1 - \exp(-t)$:

$$-\alpha \mathbf{E}_\pi \hat{w}_X(\theta) \ln \mathbf{E}_q\, e^{-\beta \ell_\theta(x)} \le \frac{\mathbf{E}_\pi\, \hat{w}_X(\theta) \sum_{i=1}^n \ell_\theta(X_i) + D_{KL}(\hat{w}_X d\pi || d\pi) + t}{n} + c_n(\alpha, \beta).$$

Moreover, we have the following expected risk bound:

$$-\alpha \mathbf{E}_X \mathbf{E}_\pi \hat{w}_X(\theta) \ln \mathbf{E}_q e^{-\beta \ell_\theta(x)} \leq \mathbf{E}_X \frac{\mathbf{E}_\pi \hat{w}_X(\theta) \sum_{i=1}^n \ell_\theta(X_i) + D_{KL}(\hat{w}_X d\pi || d\pi)}{n} + c_n(\alpha, \beta).$$

Proof. We use the notation of Lemma 1, with $L_X(\theta) = -\sum_{i=1}^n \ell_\theta(X_i)$. If we define $\hat{L}(X) = \mathbf{E}_\pi \hat{w}_X(\theta)(L_X(\theta) - \alpha \ln \mathbf{E}_X e^{\beta L_X(\theta)}) - D_{KL}(\hat{w}_X d\pi || d\pi)$, then by Lemma 1, we have $\mathbf{E}_X e^{\hat{L}(X)} \leq e^{nc_n(\alpha,\beta)}$. This implies $\forall \epsilon$: $e^\epsilon P(\hat{L}(X) > \epsilon) \leq e^{nc_n(\alpha,\beta)}$. Let $t = -\ln(1 - P(\hat{L}(X) \leq \epsilon))$, we obtain $\epsilon \leq nc_n(\alpha, \beta) + t$. Therefore with probability at least $1 - e^{-t}$, $\hat{L}(X) \leq \epsilon \leq nc_n(\alpha, \beta) + t$. Rearranging, we obtain the first inequality of the theorem.

To prove the second inequality, we still start with $\mathbf{E}_X e^{\hat{L}(X)} \leq e^{nc_n(\alpha,\beta)}$ from Lemma 1. From Jensen's inequality with the convex function e^x, we obtain $e^{\mathbf{E}_X \hat{L}(X)} \leq \mathbf{E}_X e^{\hat{L}(X)} \leq e^{nc_n(\alpha,\beta)}$. That is, $\mathbf{E}_X \hat{L}(X) \leq nc(\alpha, \beta)$. Rearranging, we obtain the desired bound. □

Remark 2. The special case of Theorem 1 with $\alpha = \beta = 1$ is very useful since in this case, the term $c_n(\alpha, \beta)$ vanishes. In fact, in order to obtain the correct rate of convergence for non-parametric problems, it is sufficient to choose $\alpha = \beta = 1$. The more complicated case with general α and β is only needed for parametric problems, where we would like to obtain a convergence rate of the order $O(1/n)$. In such cases, the choice of $\alpha = \beta = 1$ would lead to a rate of $O(\ln n/n)$, which is suboptimal.

4 Bounds for Information Complexity Minimization

Consider the Information Complexity Minimization (1). Given the true density q, if we define

$$\hat{R}_\lambda(w) = \frac{1}{n} \mathbf{E}_\pi w(\theta) \sum_{i=1}^n \ln \frac{q(X_i)}{p(X_i|\theta)} + \frac{\lambda}{n} D_{KL}(w d\pi || d\pi), \tag{2}$$

then it is clear that

$$\hat{w}_X^S = \arg\min_{w \in S} \hat{R}_\lambda(w).$$

The above estimation procedure finds a randomized estimator by minimizing the regularized empirical risk $\hat{R}_\lambda(w)$ among all possible densities with respect to the prior π in a pre-defined set S.

The purpose of this section is to study the performance of the estimator defined in (2) using Theorem 1. For simplicity, we shall only study the expected performance using the second inequality, although similar results can be obtained using the first inequality (which leads to exponential probability bounds).

One may define the true risk of w by replacing the empirical expectation in (1) with the true expectation with respect to q:

$$R_\lambda(w) = \mathbf{E}_\pi\, w(\theta) D_{KL}(q||p(\cdot|\theta)) + \frac{\lambda}{n} D_{KL}(w d\pi||d\pi), \tag{3}$$

where $D_{KL}(q||p) = \mathbf{E}_q \ln(q(x)/p(x))$ is the KL-divergence between q and p. The information complexity minimizer in (1) can be regarded as an approximate solution to (3) using empirical expectation.

Using empirical process techniques, one can typically expect to bound $R_\lambda(w)$ in terms of $\hat{R}_\lambda(w)$. Unfortunately, it does not work in our case since $D_{KL}(q||p)$ is not well-defined for all p. This implies that as long as w has non-zero concentration around a density p with $D_{KL}(q||p) = +\infty$, then $R_\lambda(w) = +\infty$. Therefore we may have $R_\lambda(\hat{w}_X^S) = +\infty$ with non-zero probability even when the sample size approaches infinity.

A remedy is to use a distance function that is always well-defined. In statistics, one often considers the ρ-divergence for $\rho \in (0,1)$, which is defined as:

$$D_\rho(q||p) = \frac{1}{\rho(1-\rho)} \mathbf{E}_q \left[1 - \left(\frac{p(x)}{q(x)} \right)^\rho \right]. \tag{4}$$

This divergence is always well-defined and $D_{KL}(q||p) = \lim_{\rho\to 0} D_\rho(q||p)$. In the statistical literature, convergence results were often specified under the Hellinger distance ($\rho = 0.5$). In this paper, we specify convergence results with general ρ. We shall mention that bounds derived in this paper will become trivial when $\rho \to 0$. This is consistent with the above discussion since R_λ (corresponding to $\rho = 0$) may not converge at all. However, under additional assumptions, such as the boundedness of q/p, $D_{KL}(q||p)$ exists and can be bounded using the ρ-divergence $D_\rho(q||p)$.

The following bounds imply that up to a constant, the ρ-divergence with any $\rho \in (0,1)$ is equivalent to the Hellinger distance. Therefore a convergence bound in any ρ-divergence implies a convergence bound of the same rate in the Hellinger distance. Since this result is not crucial in our analysis, we skip the proof due to the space limitation.

Proposition 2. *We have the following inequalities* $\forall \rho \in [0,1]$*:*

$$\max(\rho, 1-\rho) D_\rho(q||p) \geq \frac{1}{2} D_{1/2}(q||p) \geq \min(\rho, 1-\rho) D_\rho(q||p).$$

4.1 A General Convergence Bound

The following general theorem is an immediate consequence of Theorem 1. Most of our later discussions can be considered as interpretations of this theorem under various different conditions.

Theorem 2. *Consider the estimator $\hat{w}_X^S$ defined in (1). Let $\alpha > 0$. Then $\forall \rho \in (0,1)$ and $\gamma \geq \rho$ such that $\lambda' = \frac{\lambda\gamma - 1}{\gamma - \rho} \geq 0$, we have:*

$$\begin{aligned}\mathbf{E}_X \mathbf{E}_\pi \hat{w}_X^S(\theta) D_\rho(q\|p(\cdot|\theta)) \leq & \frac{-1}{\rho(1-\rho)} \mathbf{E}_X \mathbf{E}_\pi \hat{w}_X^S(\theta) \ln \mathbf{E}_q \left(\frac{p(x|\theta)}{q(x)}\right)^\rho \\ \leq & \frac{\gamma \inf_{w \in S} R_\lambda(w)}{\alpha\rho(1-\rho)} - \frac{\gamma - \rho}{\alpha\rho(1-\rho)} \mathbf{E}_X \hat{R}_{\lambda'}(\hat{w}_X^S) + \frac{c_{\rho,n}(\alpha)}{\alpha\rho(1-\rho)},\end{aligned}$$

where

$$c_{\rho,n}(\alpha) = \frac{1}{n} \ln \mathbf{E}_\pi \mathbf{E}_q^{(1-\alpha)n} \left(\frac{p(x|\theta)}{q(x)}\right)^\rho.$$

Proof Sketch. Consider an arbitrary data-independent density $w(\theta) \in S$ with respect to π, using (4), we can obtain from Theorem 1 the following chain of equations:

$$\begin{aligned}& \alpha\rho(1-\rho)\mathbf{E}_X \mathbf{E}_\pi \hat{w}_X^S(\theta) D_\rho(q\|p(\cdot|\theta)) \\ \leq & \alpha \mathbf{E}_X \mathbf{E}_\pi \hat{w}_X^S(\theta) \ln \frac{1}{1 - \rho(1-\rho) D_\rho(q\|p(\cdot|\theta))} \\ \leq & \mathbf{E}_X \left[\rho \mathbf{E}_\pi \hat{w}_X^S \sum_{i=1}^n \frac{1}{n} \ln \frac{q(X_i)}{p(X_i|\theta)} + \frac{D_{KL}(\hat{w}_X^S d\pi \| d\pi)}{n}\right] + c_{\rho,n}(\alpha) \\ \leq & \mathbf{E}_X \left[\gamma \hat{R}_\lambda(w) + (\rho - \gamma)\hat{R}_{\lambda'}(\hat{w}_X^S)\right] + c_{\rho,n}(\alpha),\end{aligned}$$

where $R_\lambda(w)$ is defined in (3). □

Remark 3. If $\gamma = \rho$ in Theorem 2, then we also require $\lambda\gamma = 1$, and let $\lambda' = 0$.

Consequences of this theorem will later be applied to MDL methods. Although the bound in Theorem 2 looks complicated, the most important part on the right hand side is the first term. The second term is only needed to handle the situation $\lambda \leq 1$. The requirement that $\gamma \geq \rho$ is to ensure that the second term is non-positive. Therefore in order to apply the theorem, we only need to estimate a lower bound of $\hat{R}_{\lambda'}(\hat{w}_X^S)$, which (as we shall see later) is much easier than obtaining an upper bound. The third term is mainly included to get the correct convergence rate of $O(1/n)$ for parametric problems, and can be ignored for non-parametric problems. The effect of this term is quite similar to using localized ϵ-entropy in the empirical process approach for analyzing the maximum-likelihood method (for example, see [8]). As a comparison, the KL-entropy in the first term corresponds to the global ϵ-entropy.

Note that one can easily obtain a simplified bound from Theorem 2 by choosing specific parameters so that both the second term and the third term vanish:

Corollary 1. *Consider the estimator $\hat{w}_X^S$ defined in (1). Assume that $\lambda > 1$ and let $\rho = 1/\lambda$, we have*

$$\mathbf{E}_X \mathbf{E}_\pi \hat{w}_X^S(\theta) D_\rho(q||p(\cdot|\theta)) \leq \frac{1}{1-\rho} \inf_{w \in S} R_\lambda(w).$$

Proof. We simply let $\alpha = 1$ and $\gamma = \rho$ in Theorem 2. □.

An important observation is that for $\lambda > 1$, the convergence rate is solely determined by the quantity $\inf_{w \in S} R_\lambda(w)$, which we shall refer to as the *model resolvability* associated with S.

4.2 Some Lower Bounds on $\mathbf{E}_X \hat{R}_{\lambda'}(\hat{w}_X^S)$

Lemma 2. *$\forall \lambda' \geq 1$: $\mathbf{E}_X \hat{R}_{\lambda'}(\hat{w}_X^S) \geq -\frac{\lambda'}{n} \geq 0$.*

Proof. See Appendix A. □

By combining the above estimate with Theorem 2, we obtain the following refinement of Corollary 1.

Corollary 2. *Consider the estimator $\hat{w}_X^S$ defined in (1). Assume that $\lambda > 1$, then $\forall \rho \in (0, 1/\lambda]$:*

$$\mathbf{E}_X \mathbf{E}_\pi \hat{w}_X^S(\theta) D_\rho(q||p(\cdot|\theta)) \leq \frac{1}{\rho(\lambda - 1)} \inf_{w \in S} R_\lambda(w).$$

Proof. We simply let $\alpha = 1$ and $\gamma = (1-\rho)/(\lambda - 1)$ in Theorem 2. Note that in this case, $\lambda' = 1$, and hence by Lemma 2, $\mathbf{E}_X \hat{R}_{\lambda'}(\hat{w}_X^S) \geq 0$. □

Note that Lemma 2 is only applicable for $\lambda' \geq 1$. If $\lambda' \leq 1$, then we need a discretization device, which generalizes the upper ϵ-covering number concept used in [2] for showing the consistency (or inconsistency) of Bayesian posterior distributions:

Definition 2. *The ϵ-upper bracketing number of Γ, denoted by $N(\Gamma, \epsilon)$, is the minimum number of non-negative functions $\{f_j\}$ on $\mathcal{X}$ with respect to μ such that $\mathbf{E}_q(f_j/q) = 1 + \epsilon$, and $\forall \theta \in \Gamma$, $\exists j$ such that $p(x|\theta) \leq f_j(x)$ a.e. $[\mu]$.*

The discretization device which we shall use in this paper is based on the following definition:

Definition 3. *An ϵ-upper discretization of Γ consists of a countable decomposition of Γ as measurable subsets $\{\Gamma_j\}$ such that $\cup_j \Gamma_j = \Gamma$ and $\mathbf{E}_q \sup_{\theta \in \Gamma_j}(p(x|\theta)/q(x)) \leq 1 + \epsilon$.*

Lemma 3. *Consider an ϵ-upper discretization $\{\Gamma_j\}$ of Γ. The following inequality is valid $\forall \lambda' \in [0, 1]$:*

$$\mathbf{E}_X \hat{R}_{\lambda'}(\hat{w}_X^S) \geq -\left[\frac{\ln \sum_j \pi(\Gamma_j)^{\lambda'}}{n} + \ln(1 + \epsilon)\right].$$

Proof. See Appendix B. □

Combine the above estimate with Theorem 2, we obtain the following simplified bound for $\lambda = 1$. Similar results can be obtained for $\lambda < 1$ but the case of $\lambda = 1$ is most interesting.

Corollary 3. *Consider the estimator defined in (1). Let $\lambda = 1$. Consider an ϵ-upper discretization $\{\Gamma_i\}$ of Γ. $\forall \rho \in (0,1)$ and $\forall \gamma \geq 1$, we have:*

$$\mathbf{E}_X \mathbf{E}_\pi \hat{w}_X^S(\theta) D_\rho(q||p(\cdot|\theta)) \leq \frac{\gamma \inf_{w \in S} R_\lambda(w)}{\rho(1-\rho)} + \frac{\gamma - \rho}{\rho(1-\rho)} \left[\frac{\ln \sum_j \pi(\Gamma_j)^{\frac{\gamma-1}{\gamma-\rho}}}{n} + \ln(1+\epsilon) \right].$$

Proof. We let $\alpha = 1$ in Theorem 2, and apply Lemma 3. □

Note that the above results immediately imply the following bound using ϵ-upper entropy by letting $\gamma \to 1$ with a finite ϵ-upper bracketing cover of size $N(\Gamma, \epsilon)$ as the discretization:

$$\mathbf{E}_X \mathbf{E}_\pi \hat{w}_X^S(\theta) D_\rho(q||p(\cdot|\theta)) \leq \frac{\inf_{w \in S} R_\lambda(w)}{\rho(1-\rho)} + \frac{1}{\rho} \inf_{\epsilon > 0} \left[\frac{\ln N(\Gamma, \epsilon)}{n} + \ln(1+\epsilon) \right]. \tag{5}$$

It is clear that Corollary 3 is significantly more general than the covering number result (5). We are able to deal with an infinite cover as long as the decay of the prior π is fast enough on the discretization so that $\sum_j \pi(\Gamma_j)^{(\gamma-1)/(\gamma-\rho)} < +\infty$.

4.3 Weak Convergence Bound

The case of $\lambda = 1$ is related to a number of important estimation methods in statistical applications such as the standard MDL and Bayesian methods. However, for an arbitrary prior π without any additional assumption such as the fast decay condition in Corollary 3, it is not possible to establish any convergence rate result in terms of Hellinger distance using the model resolvability quantity alone, as in the case of $\lambda > 1$ (Corollary 2). See Section 5.4 for an example demonstrating this claim. However, one can still obtain a weaker convergence result in this case. The following theorem essentially implies that the posterior randomization average $\mathbf{E}_\pi \hat{w}_X^S(\theta) p(\cdot|\theta)$ converges weakly to q as long as the model resolvability $\inf_{w \in S} R_\lambda(w) \to 0$ when $n \to \infty$.

Theorem 3. *Consider the estimator $\hat{w}_X^S$ defined in (1) with $\lambda = 1$. Then $\forall f : \mathcal{X} \to [-1, 1]$, we have:*

$$\mathbf{E}_X \left| \mathbf{E}_\pi \hat{w}_X^S(\theta) \mathbf{E}_{p(\cdot|\theta)} f(x) - \frac{1}{n} \sum_{i=1}^n f(X_i) \right| \leq 2A_n + \sqrt{2A_n},$$

where $A_n = \inf_{w \in S} \mathbf{E}_X R_\lambda(w) + \frac{\ln 2}{n}$.

Proof Sketch. Let $g_\epsilon(x) = 1 - \epsilon f(x)$, and $h_\epsilon(x) = \frac{q(x)}{p(x|\theta)g_\epsilon(x)}$, where $\epsilon \in (-1,1)$ is a parameter to be determined later. Note that $g_\epsilon(x) > 0$. Let $\alpha = \beta = 1$ and $L_X(\theta) = -\sum_{i=1}^n \ln h_\epsilon(X_i)$ in Lemma 1, we have

$$\mathbf{E}_X \exp\left[\mathbf{E}_\pi \hat{w}_X^S(\theta)\left(-\sum_{i=1}^n \ln h_\epsilon(X_i) - \ln \mathbf{E}_X \prod_{i=1}^n \frac{1}{h_\epsilon(X_i)}\right) - D_{KL}(\hat{w}_X^S d\pi || d\pi)\right] \le 1.$$

If we let

$$\Delta_\epsilon(X) = \mathbf{E}_\pi \hat{w}_X^S(\theta)\left(\sum_{i=1}^n \ln g_\epsilon(X_i) - n \ln \mathbf{E}_{p(\cdot|\theta)} g_\epsilon(x)\right),$$

then $\mathbf{E}_X e^{\Delta_\epsilon(X) - n\hat{R}_\lambda(\hat{w}_X^S)} \le 1$. This implies that $\mathbf{E}_X[e^{\Delta_\epsilon(X)} + e^{\Delta_{-\epsilon}(X)}]e^{-n\hat{R}_\lambda(\hat{w}_X^S)} \le 2$. Applying Jensen's inequality, we obtain

$$\mathbf{E}_X \ln[e^{\Delta_\epsilon(X)} + e^{\Delta_{-\epsilon}(X)}] \le n\mathbf{E}_X \hat{R}_\lambda(\hat{w}_X^S) + \ln 2 \le n \inf_{w \in S} R_\lambda(w) + \ln 2. \quad (6)$$

Consider $x \le y < 1$. We have the following inequalities (which follow from Taylor expansion) $x \le -\ln(1-x) \le x + \frac{x^2}{2(1-y)^2}$. This implies $\ln g_\epsilon(x) \ge -\epsilon f(x) - \frac{\epsilon^2}{2(1-|\epsilon|)^2}$ and $-\ln \mathbf{E}_{p(\cdot|\theta)} g_\epsilon(x) \ge \epsilon \mathbf{E}_{p(\cdot|\theta)} f(x)$. Therefore

$$\Delta_\epsilon(X) \ge \epsilon \mathbf{E}_\pi \hat{w}_X^S(\theta)\left(-\sum_{i=1}^n f(X_i) + n\mathbf{E}_{p(\cdot|\theta)} f(x)\right) - \frac{n\epsilon^2}{2(1-|\epsilon|)^2}.$$

A similar bound can be obtained for $\Delta_{-\epsilon}(X)$. Now substitute them into (6) and observe that $|x| \le \ln(e^x + e^{-x})$, we obtain

$$\mathbf{E}_X \left|\epsilon \mathbf{E}_\pi \hat{w}_X^S(\theta)\left(-\sum_{i=1}^n f(X_i) + n\mathbf{E}_{p(\cdot|\theta)} f(x)\right)\right| - \frac{n\epsilon^2}{2(1-|\epsilon|)^2} \le n \inf_{w \in S} \mathbf{E}_X R_\lambda(w) + \ln 2.$$

Let $|\epsilon| = \sqrt{2A_n}/(\sqrt{2A_n} + 1)$, we obtain the desired bound. □

5 MDL on Discrete Net

The minimum description length (MDL) method has been widely used in practice [6]. The version we consider here is the same as that of [1]. In fact, results in this section improve those of [1]. The MDL method considered in [1] can be regarded as a special case of information complexity minimization. The model space Γ is countable: $\theta \in \Gamma = \{1, 2, \ldots\}$. We denote the corresponding models $p(x|\theta = j)$ by $p_j(x)$. The prior π has a form $\pi = \{\pi_1, \pi_2, \ldots\}$ such that $\sum_j \pi_j = 1$, where we assume that $\pi_j > 0$ for each j. A randomized algorithm can be represented as a non-negative weight vector $w = [w_j]$ such that $\sum_j \pi_j w_j = 1$.

MDL gives a deterministic estimator, which corresponds to the set of weights concentrated on any one specific point k. That is, we can select S in (1) such that each weight w in S corresponds to an index $k \in \Gamma$ such that $w_k = 1/\pi_k$ and $w_j = 0$ when $j \neq k$. It is easy to check that $D_{KL}(wd\pi||d\pi) = \ln(1/\pi_k)$. The corresponding algorithm can thus be described as finding a probability density $p_{\hat{k}}$ with $\hat{k}$ obtained by

$$\hat{k} = \arg\min_k \left[\sum_{i=1}^{n} \ln \frac{1}{p_k(X_i)} + \lambda \ln \frac{1}{\pi_k} \right], \tag{7}$$

where $\lambda \geq 1$ is a regularization parameter. The first term corresponds to the description of the data, and the second term corresponds to the description of the model. The choice $\lambda = 1$ can be interpreted as minimizing the total description length, which corresponds to the standard MDL. The choice $\lambda > 1$ corresponds to heavier penalty on the model description, which makes the estimation method more stable. This modified MDL method was considered in [1] for which the authors obtained results on the asymptotic rate of convergence. However, no simple finite sample bounds were obtained. For the case of $\lambda = 1$, only weak consistency was shown. In the following, we shall improve these results using the analysis presented in Section 4.

5.1 Modified MDL under Global Entropy Condition

Consider the case $\lambda > 1$ in (7). We can obtain the following theorem from Corollary 2.

Theorem 4. *Consider the estimator $\hat{k}$ defined in (7). Assume that $\lambda > 1$, then $\forall \rho \in (0, 1/\lambda]$:*

$$\mathbf{E}_X D_\rho(q||p_{\hat{k}}) \leq \frac{1}{\rho(\lambda - 1)} \inf_k \left[D_{KL}(q||p_k) + \frac{\lambda}{n} \ln \frac{1}{\pi_k} \right].$$

Note that in [1], the term $r_{\lambda,n}(q) = \inf_k \left[D_{KL}(q||p_k) + \frac{\lambda}{n} \ln \frac{1}{\pi_k} \right]$ is referred to as *index of resolvability.* They showed (Theorem 4) that $D_{1/2}(q||p_{\hat{k}}) = O_p(r_{\lambda,n}(q))$ when $\lambda > 1$. Theorem 4 is a slight generalization of a result developed by Andrew Barron and Jonathan Li, which gave the same inequality but only for the case of $\lambda = 2$ and $\rho = 1/2$. The result, with a proof quite similar to what we presented here, can be found in [4] (Theorem 5.5, page 78).

Examples of index of resolvabilities for various function classes can be found in [1], which we shall not repeat in this paper. In particular, it is known that for non-parametric problems, with appropriate discretization, the rate matches the minimax rate such as those in [9].

5.2 Local Entropy Analysis

Although the bound based on the index of resolvability in Theorem 4 is quite useful for non-parametric problems (see [1] for examples), it does not handle the parametric case satisfactorily. To see this, we consider a one-dimensional parameter family indexed by $\theta \in [0,1]$, and we discretize the family using a uniform discrete net of size $N+1$: $\theta_j = j/N$ $(j=0,\ldots,N)$. If q is taken from the parametric family so that we can assume that $\inf_k D_{KL}(q||p_k) = O(N^{-2})$, then Theorem 4 with $\lambda = 2$, $\rho = 1/2$ and uniform prior on the net, becomes $\mathbf{E}_X D_{1/2}(q||p_{\hat{k}}) \leq O(N^{-2}) + \frac{4}{n}\ln\frac{1}{N}$. Now by choosing $N = O(n^{-1/2})$, we obtain a suboptimal convergence rate $\mathbf{E}_X D_{1/2}(q||p_{\hat{k}}) \leq O(\ln n/n)$. Note that convergence rates established in [1] for parametric examples are also of the order $O(\ln n/n)$.

The main reason for this sub-optimality is that the complexity measure $O(\ln N)$ or $O(-\ln \pi_k)$ corresponds to the globally defined entropy. However, readers who are familiar with the empirical process theory know that the rate of convergence of the maximum likelihood estimate is determined by local entropy which appeared in [3]. For non-parametric problems, it was pointed out in [9] that the worst case local entropy is the same order of the global entropy. Therefore a theoretical analysis which relies on global entropy (such as Theorem 4) leads to the correct worst case rate at least in the minimax sense. For parametric problems, at the $O(1/n)$ approximation level, local entropy is constant but the global entropy is $\ln n$. This leads to a $\ln(n)$ difference in the resulting bound.

Although it may not be immediately obvious how to define a localized counterpart of the index of resolvability, we can make a correction term which has the same effect. As pointed out earlier, this is essentially the role of the $c_{\rho,n}(\alpha)$ term in Theorem 2. We include a simplified version below, which can be obtained by choosing $\alpha = 1/2$, and $\gamma = \rho = 1/\lambda$.

Theorem 5. *Consider the estimator $\hat{k}$ defined in (7). Assume that $\lambda > 1$, and let $\rho = 1/\lambda$:*

$$\mathbf{E}_X D_\rho(q||p_{\hat{k}}) \leq \frac{2}{1-\rho}\inf_k \left[D_{KL}(q||p_k) + \frac{\lambda}{n}\ln\frac{\sum_j \pi_j \mathbf{E}_q^{n/2}\left(\frac{p_j(x)}{q(x)}\right)^\rho}{\pi_k}\right].$$

The bound relies on a localized version of the index of resolvability, with the global entropy $-\ln \pi_k$ replaced by a localized entropy $\ln \sum_j \pi_j \mathbf{E}_q^{n/2}\left(\frac{p_j(x)}{q(x)}\right)^\rho - \ln \pi_k$. Since

$$\ln \sum_j \pi_j \mathbf{E}_q^{n/2}\left(\frac{p_j(x)}{q(x)}\right)^\rho \leq \ln \sum_j \pi_j = 0,$$

the localized entropy is always smaller than the global entropy. Intuitively, we can see that if $p_j(x)$ is far away from $q(x)$, then $\mathbf{E}_q^{n/2}\left(\frac{p_j(x)}{q(x)}\right)^\rho$ is very small as $n \to \infty$. It follows that the summation in $\sum_j \pi_j \mathbf{E}_q^{n/2}\left(\frac{p_j(x)}{q(x)}\right)^\rho$ is mainly contributed by terms such that $D_\rho(q||p_j)$ is small. This is equivalent to a reweighting of prior π_k in such a way that we only count points that are localized within a small D_ρ ball of q.

This localization leads to the correct rate of convergence for parametric problems. The effect is similar to using localized entropy in the empirical process analysis. We consider the maximum likelihood estimate with a general one dimensional problem discussed at the beginning of the section with a uniform discretization consisted of $N+1$ points. For one-dimensional parametric problems, it is natural to assume that the number of k such that $\rho(1-\rho)D_\rho(q||p_k) \leq 1-\exp(-m^2/N^2)$ is $O(m)$ for $m \geq 1$. This implies that $\forall N = O(n^{1/2})$,

$$\ln \sum_j \mathbf{E}_q^{n/2} \left(\frac{p_j(x)}{q(x)}\right)^\rho \leq \ln \sum_m O(m)(e^{-m^2/N^2})^{n/2} = O(1).$$

Since $\pi_j = 1/N$, the localized entropy

$$\ln \frac{\sum_j \pi_j \mathbf{E}_q^{n/2} \left(\frac{p_j(x)}{q(x)}\right)^\rho}{\pi_k} = O(1)$$

is a constant when $N = O(n^{1/2})$. Therefore with a discretization size $N = O(n^{1/2})$, Theorem 5 implies a convergence rate of the correct order $O(1/n)$.

5.3 The Standard MDL ($\lambda = 1$)

The standard MDL with $\lambda = 1$ in (7) is more complicated to analyze. It is not possible to give a bound similar to Theorem 4 that only depends on the index of resolvability. As a matter of fact, no bound was established in [1]. As we will show later, the method can converge very slowly even if the index of resolvability is well-behaved.

However, it is possible to obtain bounds in this case under additional assumptions on the rate of decay of the prior π. The following theorem is a straightforward interpretation of Corollary 3, where we consider the family itself as an 0-upper discretization: $\Gamma_i = \{p_i\}$:

Theorem 6. *Consider the estimator defined in (7) with $\lambda = 1$. $\forall \rho \in (0,1)$ and $\forall \gamma \geq 1$, we have:*

$$\mathbf{E}_X D_\rho(q||p_{\hat{k}}) \leq \frac{\gamma \inf_k \left[D_{KL}(q||p_k) + \frac{1}{n}\ln\frac{1}{\pi_k}\right]}{\rho(1-\rho)} + \frac{\gamma - \rho}{\rho(1-\rho)n} \ln \sum_j \pi_j^{(\gamma-1)/(\gamma-\rho)}.$$

The above theorem only depends on the index of resolvability and decay of the prior π. If π has a fast decay in the sense of $\sum_j \pi_j^{(\gamma-1)/(\gamma-\rho)} < +\infty$ and does not change with respect to n, then the second term on the right hand side of Theorem 6 is $O(1/n)$. In this case the convergence rate is determined by the index of resolvability. The prior decay condition specified here is rather mild. This implies that the standard MDL is usually Hellinger consistent when used with care.

5.4 Slow Convergence of the Standard MDL

The purpose of this section is to illustrate that the index of resolvability cannot by itself determine the rate of convergence for the standard MDL. We consider a simple example related to the Bayesian inconsistency counter-example given in [2], with an additional randomization argument. Note that due to the randomization, we shall allow two densities in our model class to be identical. It is clear from the construction that this requirement is for convenience only, rather than anything essential.

Given a sample size n, and consider an integer m such that $m \gg n$. Let the space $\mathcal{X}$ consist of $2m$ points $\{1, \dots, 2m\}$. Assume that the truth q is the uniform distribution: $q(u) = 1/2m$ for $u = 1, \dots 2m$.

Consider a density class Γ' consisted of all densities p such that either $p(u) = 0$ or $p(u) = 1/m$. That is, a density p in Γ' takes value $1/m$ at m of the $2m$ points, and 0 elsewhere. Now let our model class Γ be consisted of the true density q with prior $1/4$, and 2^n densities p_j $(j = 1, \dots, 2^n)$ that are randomly (and uniformly) drawn from Γ', each with the same prior $3/2^{n+2}$.

We shall show that for a sufficiently large integer m, with large probability we will estimate one of the 2^n densities from Γ' with probability of at least $1 - e^{-1/2}$. Since the index of resolvability is $\ln 4/n$, which is small when n is large, the example implies that the convergence of the standard MDL method cannot be characterized by the index of resolvability alone.

Let $X = \{X_1, \dots, X_n\}$ be a set of n-samples from q and $\hat{p}$ be the estimator from (7) with $\lambda = 1$ and Γ randomly generated above. We would like to estimate $P(\hat{p} = q)$. By construction, $\hat{p} = q$ only when $\prod_{i=1}^{n} p_j(X_i) = 0$ for all $p_j \in \Gamma' \cap \Gamma$. Now pick m large enough such that $(m-n)^n/m^n \geq 0.5$, we have

$$\begin{aligned} P(\hat{p} = q) =& P\left(\forall p_j \in \Gamma' \cap \Gamma : \prod_{i=1}^{n} p_j(X_i) = 0\right) \\ =& \mathbf{E}_X\, P\left(\prod_{i=1}^{n} p_1(X_i) = 0 | X\right)^{2^n} \leq \mathbf{E}_X \left(1 - \left(\frac{m-n}{2m}\right)^n\right)^{2^n} \leq e^{-0.5}, \end{aligned}$$

where $|X|$ denotes the number of distinct elements in X. Therefore with a constant probability, we have $\hat{p} \neq q$ no matter how large n is.

This example shows that it is not possible to obtain any rate of convergence result using index of resolvability alone. In order to estimate convergence, it is thus necessary to make additional assumptions, such as the prior decay condition of Theorem 6. We shall also mention that from this example together with a construction scheme similar to that of the Bayesian inconsistency counter example in [2], it is not difficult to show that the standard MDL is not Hellinger consistent even when the index of resolvability approaches zero as $n \to \infty$. For simplicity, we skip the detailed construction in this paper.

5.5 Weak Convergence of the Standard MDL

Although Hellinger consistency cannot be obtained for standard MDL based on index of resolvability alone, it was shown in [1] that as $n \to \infty$, if the index of resolvability approaches zero, then $p_{\hat{k}}$ converges weakly to q. Therefore MDL is effectively weakly consistent as long as q belongs to the information closure of Γ. This result is a direct consequence of Theorem 3, which we shall restate here:

Theorem 7. *Consider the estimator defined in (7) with $\lambda = 1$. Then $\forall f : \mathcal{X} \to [-1, 1]$, we have:*

$$\mathbf{E}_X \left| \mathbf{E}_{p_{\hat{k}}} f(x) - \frac{1}{n} \sum_{i=1}^{n} f(X_i) \right| \leq 2A_n + \sqrt{2A_n},$$

where $A_n = \inf_k \left[D_{KL}(q||p_k) + \frac{1}{n} \ln \frac{1}{\pi_k} \right] + \frac{\ln 2}{n}$.

Note that this theorem essentially implies that the standard MDL estimator is weakly consistent as long as the index of resolvability approaches zero when $n \to 0$. Moreover, it establishes a rate of convergence result which only depends on the index of resolvability. This theorem improves the consistency result in [1], where no rate of convergence results were established, and f was assumed to be an indicator function.

6 Discussions

This paper studies certain randomized (and deterministic) density estimation methods which we call information complexity minimization. We introduced a general KL-complexity based convergence analysis, and demonstrated that the new approach can lead to simplified and improved convergence results for two-part code MDL, which improves the classifical results in [1].

An important observation from our study is that generalized information complexity minimization methods with regularization parameter $\lambda > 1$ are more robust than the corresponding standard methods with $\lambda = 1$. That is, their convergence behavior is completely determined by the local prior density around the true distribution measured by the model resolvability $\inf_{w \in S} R_\lambda(w)$. For MDL, this quantity (index of resolvability) is well-behaved if we put a not too small prior mass at a density that is close to the truth q. We have also demonstrated through an example that the standard MDL does not have this desirable property in that even we can guess the true density by putting a relatively large prior mass at the true density q, we may not estimate q very well as long as there exits a bad (random) prior structure even at places very far from the truth q.

References

1. Andrew Barron and Thomas Cover. Minimum complexity density estimation. *IEEE Transactions on Information Theory*, 37:1034–1054, 1991.
2. Andrew Barron, Mark J. Schervish, and Larry Wasserman. The consistency of posterior distributions in nonparametric problems. *Ann. Statist.*, 27(2):536–561, 1999.
3. Lucien Le Cam. Convergence of estimates under dimensionality restrictions. *The Annals of Statistics*, 1:38–53, 1973.
4. J.Q. Li. *Estimation of Mixture Models.* PhD thesis, The Department of Statistics. Yale University, 1999.
5. Ron Meir and Tong Zhang. Generalization error bounds for Bayesian mixture algorithms. *Journal of Machine Learning Research*, 4:839–860, 2003.
6. J. Rissanen. *Stochastic complexity and statistical inquiry.* World Scientific, 1989.
7. M. Seeger. PAC-Bayesian generalization error bounds for Gaussian process classification. *JMLR*, 3:233–269, 2002.
8. S.A. van de Geer. *Empirical Processes in M-estimation.* Cambridge University Press, 2000.
9. Yuhong Yang and Andrew Barron. Information-theoretic determination of minimax rates of convergence. *The Annals of Statistics*, 27:1564–1599, 1999.
10. Tong Zhang. Theoretical analysis of a class of randomized regularization methods. In *COLT 99*, pages 156–163, 1999.
11. Tong Zhang. Learning bounds for a generalized family of Bayesian posterior distributions. In *NIPS 03*, 2004. to appear.

A Proof of Lemma 2

Applying the convex duality in Proposition 1 with $f(x) = -\frac{1}{\lambda'}\sum_{i=1}^n \ln \frac{q(X_i)}{p(X_i|\theta)}$, we obtain

$$\hat{R}_{\lambda'}(\hat{w}_X^S) \geq -\frac{\lambda'}{n} \ln \mathbf{E}_\pi \exp\left(-\frac{1}{\lambda'}\sum_{i=1}^n \ln \frac{q(X_i)}{p(X_i|\theta)}\right).$$

Taking expectation and using Jensen's inequality with the convex function $\psi(x) = -\ln(x)$, we obtain

$$\mathbf{E}_X \hat{R}_{\lambda'}(\hat{w}_X^S) \geq -\frac{\lambda'}{n} \ln \mathbf{E}_X \mathbf{E}_\pi \exp\left(-\frac{1}{\lambda'}\sum_{i=1}^n \ln \frac{q(X_i)}{p(X_i|\theta)}\right) \geq 0.$$

B Proof of Lemma 3

The proof is similar to that of Lemma 2, but with a slightly different estimate. We again start with the inequality

$$\hat{R}_{\lambda'}(\hat{w}_X^S) \geq -\frac{\lambda'}{n} \ln \mathbf{E}_\pi \exp\left(-\frac{1}{\lambda'}\sum_{i=1}^n \ln \frac{q(X_i)}{p(X_i|\theta)}\right).$$

Taking expectation and using Jensen's inequality with the convex function $\psi(x) = -\ln(x)$, we obtain

$$\begin{aligned}
-\mathbf{E}_X \hat{R}_{\lambda'}(\hat{w}_X^S) \leq & \frac{1}{n} \ln \mathbf{E}_X \mathbf{E}_\pi^{\lambda'} \exp\left(-\frac{1}{\lambda'}\sum_{i=1}^n \ln\frac{q(X_i)}{p(X_i|\theta)}\right) \\
\leq & \frac{1}{n} \ln \mathbf{E}_X \left[\sum_j \pi(\Gamma_j) \exp\left(-\frac{1}{\lambda'}\sum_{i=1}^n \ln\frac{q(X_i)}{\sup_{\theta\in\Gamma_j} p(X_i|\theta)}\right)\right]^{\lambda'} \\
\leq & \frac{1}{n} \ln \mathbf{E}_X \left[\sum_j \pi(\Gamma_j)^{\lambda'} \exp\left(-\sum_{i=1}^n \ln\frac{q(X_i)}{\sup_{\theta\in\Gamma_j} p(X_i|\theta)}\right)\right] \\
= & \frac{1}{n} \ln \left[\sum_j \pi(\Gamma_j)^{\lambda'} \mathbf{E}_X \prod_{i=1}^n \frac{\sup_{\theta\in\Gamma_j} p(X_i|\theta)}{q(X_i)}\right] \\
\leq & \frac{1}{n} \ln \left[\sum_j \pi(\Gamma_j)^{\lambda'} (1+\epsilon)^n\right].
\end{aligned}$$

The third inequality follows from the fact that $\forall\lambda' \in [0,1]$ and positive numbers $\{a_j\}$: $(\sum_j a_j)^{\lambda'} \leq \sum_j a_j^{\lambda'}$.

Suboptimal Behavior of Bayes and MDL in Classification Under Misspecification

Peter Grünwald[1] and John Langford[2]

[1] CWI Amsterdam
pdg@cwi.nl
www.grunwald.nl
[2] TTI-Chicago
jcl@cs.cmu.edu
hunch.net/~\/jl/.

Abstract. We show that forms of Bayesian and MDL inference that are often applied to classification problems can be *inconsistent*. This means there exists a learning problem such that for all amounts of data the generalization errors of the MDL classifier and the Bayes classifier relative to the Bayesian posterior both remain bounded away from the smallest achievable generalization error.

1 Introduction

Overfitting is a central concern of machine learning and statistics. Two frequently used learning methods that in many cases 'automatically' protect against overfitting are Bayesian inference [5] and the Minimum Description Length (MDL) Principle [21,2,11]. We show that, when applied to classification problems, some of the standard variations of these two methods can be *inconsistent* in the sense that they *asymptotically overfit*: there exist scenarios where, no matter how much data is available, the generalization error of a classifier based on MDL or the full Bayesian posterior does not converge to the minimum achievable generalization error within the set of classifiers under consideration.

Some Caveats and Warnings. These result must be interpreted carefully. There exist many different versions of MDL and Bayesian inference, only some of which are covered. For the case of MDL, we show our result for a two-part form of MDL that has often been used for classification. For the case of Bayes, our result may appear to contradict some well-known Bayesian consistency results [6]. Indeed, our result only applies to a 'pragmatic' use of Bayes, where the set of hypotheses under consideration are *classifiers*: functions mapping each input X to a discrete class label Y. To apply Bayes rule, these classifiers must be converted into conditional probability distributions. We do this conversion in a standard manner, crossing a prior on classifiers with a prior on error rates for these classifiers. This may lead to (sometimes subtly) 'misspecified' probability models not containing the 'true' distribution D. Thus, our result may be restated

J. Shawe-Taylor and Y. Singer (Eds.): COLT 2004, LNAI 3120, pp. 331–347, 2004.

as 'Bayesian methods for classification can be inconsistent under misspecification for common classification probability models'. The result is still interesting, since (1) even under misspecification, Bayesian inference is known to be consistent under fairly broad conditions – we provide an explicit context in which it is not; (2) in practice, Bayesian inference is used frequently for classification under misspecification – see Section 6.

1.1 A Preview

Classification Problems. A classification problem is defined on an input (or feature) domain $\mathcal{X}$ and output domain (or class label) $\mathcal{Y} = \{0, 1\}$. The problem is defined by a probability distribution D over $\mathcal{X} \times \mathcal{Y}$. A classifier is a function $c : \mathcal{X} \to \mathcal{Y}$ The error rate of any classifier is quantified as:

$$e_D(c) = E_{(x,y)\sim D} I(c(x) \neq y)$$

where $(x, y) \sim D$ denotes a draw from the distribution D and $I(\cdot)$ is the indicator function which is 1 when its argument is true and 0 otherwise.

The goal is to find a classifier which, as often as possible according to D, correctly predicts the class label given the input feature. Typically, the classification problem is solved by searching for some classifier c in a limited subset $\mathcal{C}$ of all classifiers using a sample $S = (x_1, y_1), \ldots, (x_m, y_m) \sim D^m$ generated by m independent draws from the distribution D. Naturally, this search is guided by the *empirical error rate*. This is the error rate on the subset S defined by:

$$\hat{e}_S(c) := E_{(x,y)\sim S} I(c(x) \neq y) = \frac{1}{|S|} \sum_{(x,y)\in S} I(c(x) \neq y).$$

where $(x, y) \sim S$ denotes a sample drawn from the uniform distribution on S. Note that $\hat{e}_S(c)$ is a random variable dependent on a draw from D^m. In contrast, $e_D(c)$ is a number (an expectation) relative to D.

The Basic Result. Our basic result is that certain classifier learning algorithms may not behave well as a function of the information they use, even when given infinitely many samples to learn from. The learning algorithms we analyze are "Bayesian classification" (Bayes), "Maximum a Posteriori classification" (MAP), and "Minimum Description Length classification" (MDL). These algorithms are precisely defined later. Functionally they take as arguments a training sample S and a "prior" P which is a probability distribution over a set of classifiers $\mathcal{C}$. In Section 3 we state our basic result, Theorem 2. The theorem has the following corollary, indicating suboptimal behavior of Bayes and MDL:

Corollary 1. (Classification Inconsistency) *There exists an input domain $\mathcal{X}$, a prior P always nonzero on a countable set of classifiers $\mathcal{C}$, a learning problem D, and a constant $K > 0$ such that the Bayesian classifier $c_{\text{BAYES}(P,S)}$, the*

MAP classifier $c_{\text{MAP}(P,S)}$, *and the MDL classifier* $c_{\text{MDL}(P,S)}$ *are asymptotically* K*-suboptimal. That is, for each* $\mathbf{e} \in \{e_D(c_{\text{BAYES}(P,S)}), e_D(c_{\text{MAP}(P,S)}), e_D(c_{\text{MDL}(P,S)})\}$, *we have*

$$\lim_{m\to\infty} \Pr_{S\sim D^m}\left(\mathbf{e} > K + \inf_{c\in\mathcal{C}} e_D(c)\right) = 1.$$

How dramatic is this result? We may ask (1) are the priors P for which the result holds natural; (2) how large can the constant K become and how small can $\inf_{c\in\mathcal{C}} e_D(c)$ be? (3) perhaps demanding an algorithm which depends on the prior P and the sample S to be consistent (asymptotically optimal) is too strong? The short answer to (1) and (2) is: the priors P have to satisfy several requirements, but they correspond to priors often used in practice. K can be quite large and $\inf_c e_D(c)$ can be quite small - see Section 5.1 and Figure 1.

The answer to (3) is that there do exist simple algorithms which are consistent. An example is the algorithm which minimizes the Occam's Razor bound (ORB) [7], Section 4.2.

Theorem 1. (ORB consistency) *For all priors P nonzero on a set of classifiers $\mathcal{C}$, for all learning problems D, and all constants $K > 0$ the ORB classifier* $c_{\text{ORB}(P,S)}$ *is asymptotically K-optimal:*

$$\lim_{m\to\infty} \Pr_{S\sim D^m}\left(e_D(c_{\text{ORB}(P,S)}) > K + \inf_{c\in\mathcal{C}} e_D(c)\right) = 0.$$

The remainder of this paper first defines precisely what we mean by the above classifiers. It then states the main inconsistency theorem which implies the above corollary, as well as a theorem that provides an upper-bound on how badly Bayes can behave. In Section 4 we prove our theorems. Variations of the result are discussed in Section 5.1. A discussion of the result from a Bayesian point of view is given in Section 6.

2 Some Classification Algorithms

The basic inconsistency result is about particular classifier learning algorithms which we define next.

The Bayesian Classification Algorithm. The Bayesian approach to inference starts with a prior probability distribution P over a set of distributions $\mathcal{P}$ which typically represents a measure of "belief" that some $p \in \mathcal{P}$ is the process generating data. Bayes' rule states that, given sample data S, the posterior probability $P(\cdot \mid S)$ that some p is the process generating the data is:

$$P(p \mid S) = \frac{p(S)P(p)}{P(S)}.$$

where $P(S) := E_{p\sim P}\, p(S)$. In classification problems with sample size $m = |S|$, each $p \in \mathcal{P}$ is a distribution on $(\mathcal{X} \times \mathcal{Y})^m$ and the outcome $S = (x_1, y_1), \dots, (x_m, y_m)$ is the sequence of labeled examples.

If we intend to perform classification based on a set of classifiers $\mathcal{C}$ rather than distributions $\mathcal{P}$, it is natural to introduce a "prior" $P(c)$ that a particular classifier $c : \mathcal{X} \to \{0,1\}$ is the best classifier for solving some learning problem. This, of course, is *not* a Bayesian prior in the conventional sense because classifiers do not induce a measure over the training data. It is the standard method of converting a "prior" over classifiers into a Bayesian prior over distributions on the observations which our inconsistency result applies to.

One common conversion [14,22,12] transforms the set of classifiers $\mathcal{C}$ into a simple logistic regression model – the precise relationship to logistic regression is discussed in Section 5.2. In our case $c(x) \in \{0,1\}$ is binary valued, and then (but only then) the conversion amounts to assuming that the error rate θ of the optimal classifier is independent of the feature value x. This is known as "homoskedasticity" in statistics and "label noise" in learning theory. More precisely, it is assumed that, for the optimal classifier $c \in C$, there exists some θ such that $\forall x \; P(c(x) \neq y) = \theta$. Given this assumption, we can construct a conditional probability distribution $p_{c,\theta}$ over the labels given the unlabeled data:

$$p_{c,\theta}(y^m \mid x^m) = \theta^{m\hat{e}_S(c)}(1-\theta)^{m-m\hat{e}_S(c)}. \tag{1}$$

For each fixed $\theta < 0.5$, the log likelihood $\log p_{c,\theta}(y^m \mid x^m)$ is linearly decreasing in the empirical error that c makes on S. By differentiating with respect to θ, we see that for fixed c, the likelihood (1) is maximized by setting $\theta := \hat{e}_S(c)$, giving

$$\log \frac{1}{p_{c,\hat{e}_S(c)}(y^m \mid x^m)} = mH(\hat{e}_S(c)). \tag{2}$$

where H is the binary entropy $H(\mu) = -\mu \log \mu - (1-\mu)\log(1-\mu)$, which is strictly increasing for $\hat{e}_S(c) \in [0, 0.5)$. We further assume that *some* distribution p_x on $\mathcal{X}^m$ generates the x-values[1]. We can apply Bayes rule to get a posterior on $p_{c,\theta}$, denoted as $P(c,\theta \mid S)$, without knowing p_x, since the $p_x(x^m)$-factors cancel:

$$P(c,\theta \mid S) = \frac{p_{c,\theta}(y^m|x^m)p_x(x^m)P(c,\theta)}{P(y^m \mid x^m)p_x(x^m)} = \frac{p_{c,\theta}(y^m|x^m)P(c,\theta)}{E_{c,\theta\sim P}\,p_{c,\theta}(y^m \mid x^m)}. \tag{3}$$

To make (3) applicable, we need to incorporate a prior measure on the joint space $\mathcal{C} \times [0,1]$ of classifiers and θ-parameters. In the next section we discuss the priors under which our theorems hold.

Bayes rule (3) is formed into a classifier learning algorithm by choosing the most likely label given the input x and the posterior $P(\cdot|S)$:

$$c_{\text{BAYES}(P,S)}(x) := \begin{cases} 1 & \text{if } E_{c,\theta\sim P(\cdot|S)}\,p_{c,\theta}(Y=1|X=x) \geq \frac{1}{2}, \\ 0 & \text{otherwise.} \end{cases} \tag{4}$$

[1] And, in particular that this distribution is independent of c and θ.

The MAP classification Algorithm. The integrations of the full Bayesian classifier can be too computationally intensive, so we sometimes predict using the Bayesian Maximum A Posteriori (MAP) classifier. This classifier is given by:

$$c_{\mathrm{MAP}(P,S)} = \arg\max_{c\in\mathcal{C}} \max_{\theta\in[0,1]} P(c,\theta \mid S) = \arg\max_{c\in\mathcal{C}} \max_{\theta\in[0,1]} p_{c,\theta}(y^m \mid x^m) P(c,\theta)$$

with ties broken arbitrarily. Integration over $\theta \in [0,1]$ being much less problematic than summation over $c \in \mathcal{C}$, one sometimes uses a learning algorithm which integrates over θ (like full Bayes) but maximizes over c (like MAP):

$$c_{\mathrm{SMAP}(P,S)} = \arg\max_{c\in\mathcal{C}} P(c \mid S) = \arg\max_{c\in\mathcal{C}} E_{\theta\sim P(\theta)} p_{c,\theta}(y^m \mid x^m) P(c \mid \theta).$$

The MDL Classification Algorithm. The MDL approach to classification is transplanted from the MDL approach to density estimation. There is no such thing as a 'definition' of MDL for classification because the transplant has been performed in various ways by various authors. Nonetheless, most implementations are essentially equivalent to the following algorithm [20,21,15,12]:

$$c_{\mathrm{MDL}(P,S)} = \arg\min_{c\in\mathcal{C}} \log\frac{1}{P(c)} + \log\binom{m}{m\hat{e}_S(c)}. \tag{5}$$

The quantity minimized has a coding interpretation: it is the number of bits required to describe the classifier plus the number of bits required to describe the labels on S given the classifier and the unlabeled data. We call $-\log P(c) + \log\binom{m}{m\hat{e}_S(c)}$ the *two-part MDL codelength* for encoding data S with classifier c.

3 Main Theorems

In this section we prove the basic inconsistency theorem. We prove inconsistency for some countable set of classifiers $\mathcal{C} = \{c_0, c_1, \ldots\}$ which we define later. The inconsistency is attained for priors with 'heavy tails', satisfying

$$\log\frac{1}{P(c_k)} \le \log k + o(\log k). \tag{6}$$

This condition is satisfied, by, for example, Rissanen's *universal prior for the integers*, [21]. The sensitivity of our result to the choice of prior is analyzed further in Section 5.1. The prior on θ can be any distribution on $[0,1]$ with a continuously differentiable density P bounded away from 0, i.e. for some $\gamma > 0$,

$$\text{for all } \theta \in [0,1], P(\theta) > \gamma. \tag{7}$$

For example, we may take the uniform distribution with $P(\theta) \equiv 1$. We assume that the priors $P(\theta)$ on $[0,1]$ and the prior $P(c)$ on $\mathcal{C}$ are independent, so that $P(c,\theta) = P(c)P(\theta)$. In the theorem, $H(\mu) = -\mu\log\mu - (1-\mu)\log(1-\mu)$ stands for the binary entropy of a coin with bias μ.

Theorem 2. (Classification Inconsistency) *There exists an input space $\mathcal{X}$ and a countable set of classifiers $\mathcal{C}$ such that the following holds: let P be any prior satisfying (6) and (7). For all $\mu \in (0, 0.5)$ and all $\mu' \in [\mu, H(\mu)/2)$, there exists a D with $\min_{c \in \mathcal{C}} e_D(c) = \mu$ such that, for all large m, all $\delta > 0$,*

$$\Pr_{S \sim D^m}\left(e_D(c_{\mathrm{MAP}(P,S)}) = \mu'\right) \geq 1 - a_m$$
$$\Pr_{S \sim D^m}\left(e_D(c_{\mathrm{SMAP}(P,S)}) = \mu'\right) \geq 1 - a_m$$
$$\Pr_{S \sim D^m}\left(e_D(c_{\mathrm{MDL}(P,S)}) = \mu'\right) \geq 1 - a_m,$$
$$\Pr_{S \sim D^m}\left(e_D(c_{\mathrm{BAYES}(P,S)}) \geq \mu' - \delta\right) \geq 1 - a_m, \qquad \text{where } a_m = 3\exp(-2\sqrt{m}).$$

The theorem states that Bayes is inconsistent for *all large* m on a fixed distribution D. This is a significantly more difficult statement than "for all (large) m, there exists a learning problem where Bayes is inconsistent"[2]. Differentiation of $0.5H(\mu) - \mu$ shows that the maximum discrepancy between $e_D(c_{\mathrm{MAP}(P,S)})$ and μ is achieved for $\mu = 1/5$. With this choice of μ, $0.5H(\mu) - \mu = 0.1609\ldots$ so that, by choosing μ' arbitrarily close to $H(\mu)$, the discrepancy $\mu' - \mu$ comes arbitrarily close to $0.1609\ldots$. These findings are summarized in Figure 1.

How large can the discrepancy between $\mu = \inf_c e_D(c)$ and $\mu' = e_D(c_{\mathrm{BAYES}(P,S)})$ be in the large m limit, for general learning problems? Our next theorem, again summarized in Figure 1, gives an upperbound, namely, $\mu' < H(\mu)$:

Theorem 3. (Maximal Inconsistency of Bayes) *Let S^i be the sequence consisting of the first i examples $(x_1, y_1), \ldots, (x_i, y_i)$. For all priors P nonzero on a set of classifiers $\mathcal{C}$, for all learning problems D with $\inf_{c \in \mathcal{C}} e_D(c) = \mu$, for all $\delta > 0$, for all large m, with D^m-probability $\geq 1 - \exp(-2\sqrt{m})$,*

$$\frac{1}{m}\sum_{i=1}^{m}\left|y_i - c_{\mathrm{BAYES}(P,S^{i-1})}(x_i)\right| \leq H(\mu) + \delta.$$

The theorem says that for large m, the total number of mistakes when successively classifying y_i given x_i made by the Bayesian algorithm based on S^{i-1}, divided by m, is not larger than $H(\mu)$. By the law of large numbers, it follows that for large m, $e_D(c_{\mathrm{BAYES}(P,S^{i-1})}(x_i))$, *averaged* over all i, is no larger than $H(\mu)$. Thus, it is not ruled out that sporadically, for some i, $e_D(c_{\mathrm{BAYES}(P,S^{i-1})}(x_i)) > H(\mu)$; but this must be 'compensated' for by most other i. We did not find a proof that $e_D(c_{\mathrm{BAYES}(P,S^{i-1})}(x_i)) < H(\mu)$ for *all* large i.

4 Proofs

In this section we present the proofs of our three theorems. Theorem 2 and 3 both make use of the following lemma:

[2] In fact, a meta-argument can be made that *any* nontrivial learning algorithm is 'inconsistent' in this sense for finite m.

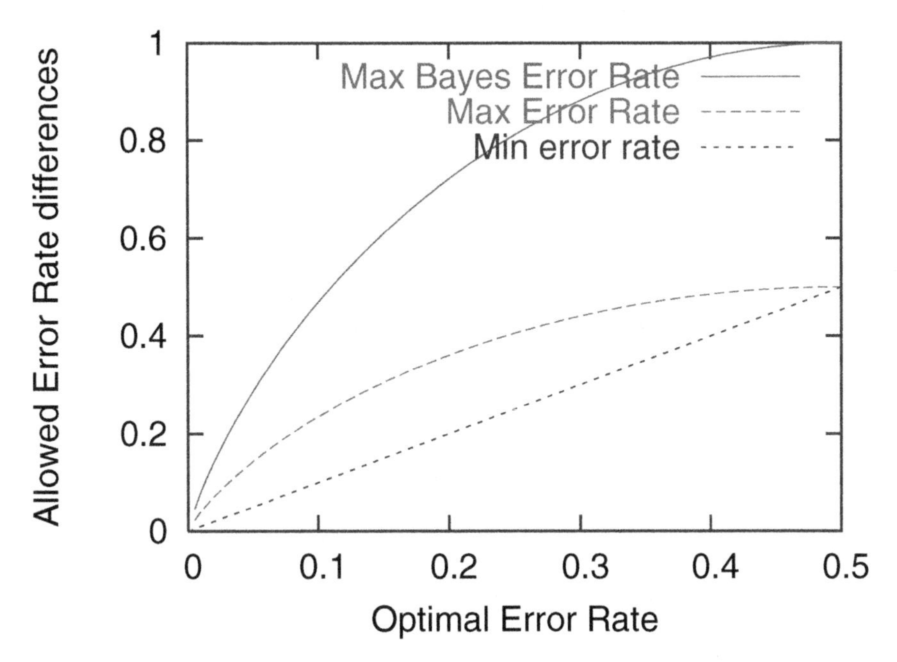

Fig. 1. A graph depicting the set of asymptotically allowed error rates for different classification algorithms. The x-axis depicts the optimal classifier's error rate μ (also shown as the straight line). The lower curve is just $0.5H(\mu)$ and the upper curve is $H(\mu)$. Theorem 2 says that any (μ, μ') between the straight line and the lower curve can be achieved for some learning problem D and prior P. Theorem 3 shows that the Bayesian learner can never have asymptotic error rate μ' above the upper curve.

Lemma 1. *There exists $\gamma > 0$ such that for all classifiers c, $\alpha > 0$, $m > 0$, all $S \sim D^m$ satisfying $\alpha + 1/\sqrt{m} < \hat{e}_S(c) \leq 0.5$, all priors satisfying (7):*

$$\log \frac{1}{P(y^m \mid x^m, c, \hat{e}_S(c))} \leq \log \frac{1}{P(y^m \mid x^m, c)} \leq$$
$$\log \frac{1}{P(y^m \mid x^m, c, \hat{e}_S(c))} + \frac{1}{2} \log m + \frac{1}{2} \frac{1}{\alpha(1-\alpha)} - \log \gamma. \quad (8)$$

Proof. **(sketch)** For the first inequality, note

$$\log \frac{1}{P(y^m \mid x^m, c)} = \log \frac{1}{\int P(y^m \mid x^m, c, \theta) P(\theta) d\theta} \geq \log \frac{1}{P(y^m \mid x^m, c, \hat{e}_S(c))},$$

since the likelihood $P(y^m \mid x^m, c, \theta)$ is maximized at $\theta = \hat{e}_S(c)$. For the second inequality, note that

$$\int_0^1 P(y^m \mid x^m, c, \theta) P(\theta) d\theta \geq \int_{\hat{e}_S(c) - 1/\sqrt{m}}^{\hat{e}_S(c) + 1/\sqrt{m}} \exp\bigl(\log P(y^m \mid x^m, c, \theta) + \log P(\theta)\bigr) d\theta.$$

We obtain (8) by expanding $\log P(y^m \mid x^m, c, \theta)$ around the maximum $\theta = \hat{e}_S(c)$ using a second-order Taylor approximation. See, [2] for further details.

4.1 Inconsistent Learning Algorithms: Proof of Theorem 2

Below we first define the particular learning problem that causes inconsistency. We then analyze the performance of the algorithms on this learning problem.

The Learning Problem. For given μ and $\mu' \geq \mu$, we construct a learning problem and a set of classifiers $\mathcal{C} = \{c_0, c_1, \ldots\}$ such that c_0 is the 'good' classifier with $e_D(c_0) = \mu$ and $c_1, c_2, \ldots$ are all 'bad' classifiers with $e_D(c_j) = \mu' \geq \mu$. $\mathcal{X}$ consists of one binary feature per classifier[3], and the classifiers simply output the value of their special feature. The underlying distribution D is constructed in terms of μ and μ' and a proof parameter $\mu_{\text{hard}} \geq \frac{1}{2}$ (the error rate for "hard" examples). To construct an example (x, y), we first flip a fair coin to determine y, so $y = 1$ with probability 1/2. We then flip a coin with bias $p_{\text{hard}} := \frac{\mu'}{\mu_{\text{hard}}}$ which determines if this is a "hard" example or an "easy" example. Based upon these two coin flips, each x_j is independently generated based on the following 3 cases.

1. For a "hard" example, and for each classifier c_j with $j \geq 1$, set $x_j = |1 - y|$ with probability μ_{hard} and $x_j = y$ otherwise.
2. For an "easy" example, and every $j \geq 1$ set $x_j = y$.
3. For the "good" classifier c_0 (with true error rate μ), set $x_0 = |1 - y|$ with probability μ and $x_0 = y$ otherwise.

The error rates of each classifier are $e_D(c_0) = \mu$ and $e_D(c_j) = \mu'$ for all $j \geq 1$.

Bayes and MDL are inconsistent. We now prove Theorem 2. In Stage 1 we show that there exists a k_m such that for every value of m, with probability converging to 1, there exists some 'bad' classifier c_j with $0 < j \leq k_m$ that has 0 empirical error. In Stage 2 we show that the prior of this classifier is large enough so that its posterior is exponentially larger than that of the good classifier c_0, showing the convergence $e_D(c_{\text{MAP}(P,S)}) \to \mu'$. In Stage 3 we sketch the convergences $e_D(c_{\text{SMAP}(P,S)}) \to \mu'$, $e_D(c_{\text{MDL}(P,S)}) \to \mu'$, $e_D(c_{\text{BAYES}(P,S)}) \to \mu'$.

Stage 1. Let m_{hard} denote the number of hard examples generated within a sample S of size m. Let k be a positive integer and $\mathcal{C}_k = \{c_j \in \mathcal{C} : 1 \leq j \leq k\}$.

[3] This input space has a countably infinite size. The Bayesian posterior is still computable for any finite m if we order the features according to the prior of the associated classifier. We need only consider features which have an associated prior greater than $\frac{1}{2^m}$ since the minus log-likelihood of the data is always less than m bits. Alternatively, we could use stochastic classifiers and a very small input space.

For all $\epsilon > 0$ and $m \geq 0$, we have:

$$\begin{aligned}
&\Pr_{S\sim D^m}(\forall c \in \mathcal{C}_k :\ \hat{e}_S(c) > 0) \\
&\overset{(a)}{=} \Pr_{S\sim D^m}\left(\forall c \in \mathcal{C}_k :\ \hat{e}_S(c) > 0 \mid \frac{m_{\text{hard}}}{m} > p_{\text{hard}} + \epsilon\right) \Pr_{S\sim D^m}\left(\frac{m_{\text{hard}}}{m} > p_{\text{hard}} + \epsilon\right) \\
&+ \Pr_{S\sim D^m}\left(\forall c \in \mathcal{C}_k :\ \hat{e}_S(c) > 0 \mid \frac{m_{\text{hard}}}{m} \leq p_{\text{hard}} + \epsilon\right) \Pr_{S\sim D^m}\left(\frac{m_{\text{hard}}}{m} \leq p_{\text{hard}} + \epsilon\right) \\
&\overset{(b)}{\leq} e^{-2m\epsilon^2} + \Pr_{S\sim D^m}\left(\forall c \in \mathcal{C}_k :\ \hat{e}_S(c) > 0 \mid \frac{m_{\text{hard}}}{m} \leq p_{\text{hard}} + \epsilon\right) \\
&\overset{(c)}{\leq} e^{-2m\epsilon^2} + (1 - (1 - \mu_{\text{hard}})^{m(p_{\text{hard}}+\epsilon)})^k \overset{(d)}{\leq} e^{-2m\epsilon^2} + e^{-k(1-\mu_{\text{hard}})^{m(p_{\text{hard}}+\epsilon)}}. \quad (9)
\end{aligned}$$

Here (a) follows because $P(a) = \sum_b P(a|b)P(b)$. (b) follows by $\forall a, P :\ P(a) \leq 1$ and the Chernoff bound. (c) holds since $(1-(1-\mu_{\text{hard}})^{m(p_{\text{hard}}+\epsilon)})^k$ is monotonic in ϵ, and (d) by $\forall x \in [0,1], k > 0 :\ \ (1-x)^k \leq e^{-kx}$. We now set $\epsilon_m := m^{-0.25}$ and $k(m) = \frac{2m\epsilon_m^2}{(1-\mu_{\text{hard}})^{m(p_{\text{hard}}+\epsilon_m)}}$. Then (9) becomes

$$\Pr_{S\sim D^m}(\forall c \in \mathcal{C}_{k(m)} :\ \hat{e}_S(c) > 0) \leq 2e^{-2\sqrt{m}} \quad (10)$$

On the other hand, by the Chernoff bound we have $\Pr_{S\sim D^m}(\hat{e}_S(c_0) < e_D(c_0) - \epsilon_m) \leq e^{-2\sqrt{m}}$ for the optimal classifier c_0. Combining this with (10) using the union bound, we get that, with D^m-probability larger than $1 - 3e^{-2\sqrt{m}}$, the following event holds:

$$\exists c \in \mathcal{C}_{k(m)} :\ \hat{e}_S(c) = 0 \text{ and } \hat{e}_S(c_0) \geq e_D(c_0) - \epsilon_m. \quad (11)$$

Stage 2. In the following derivation, we assume that the large probability event (11) holds. We show that this implies that for large m, the posterior on some $c^* \in \mathcal{C}_{k(m)}$ with $\hat{e}_S(c^*) = 0$ is greater than the posterior on c_0, which implies that the MAP algorithm is inconsistent. Taking the log of the posterior ratios, we get:

$$\log \frac{\max_\theta P(c_0, \theta \mid x^m, y^m)}{\max_\theta P(c^*, \theta \mid x^m, y^m)} = \log \frac{\max_\theta P(c_0)P(\theta)P(y^m \mid x^m, c_0, \theta)}{\max_\theta P(c^*)P(\theta)P(y^m \mid x^m, c^*, \theta)} =$$
$$\log \max_\theta P(c_0)P(\theta)P(y^m \mid x^m, c_0, \theta) - \log \max_\theta P(c^*)P(\theta)P(y^m \mid x^m, c^*, \theta). \quad (12)$$

Using (2) we see that the leftmost term is no larger than

$$\begin{aligned}
\log \left(\max_\theta P(c_0)P(\theta)\right) \cdot \left(\max_{\theta'} P(y^m \mid x^m, c_0, \theta')\right) &= -mH(\hat{e}_S(c_0)) + O(1) \leq \\
-mH(e_D(c_0)) - Km\epsilon_m + O(1) &= -mH(\mu) - m^{0.75}K + O(1) \quad (13)
\end{aligned}$$

where K is some constant. The last line follows because $H(\mu)$ is continuously differentiable in a small enough neighborhood around μ.

For the rightmost term in (12), by the condition on prior $p(\theta)$, (7),

$$-\log \max_\theta P(c^*)P(\theta)P(y^m \mid x^m, c^*, \theta) \leq -\log P(c^*) + \log \gamma. \quad (14)$$

Using condition (6) on prior $P(c^*)$ and using $c^* \in \mathcal{C}_{k(m)}$, we find:

$$\log \frac{1}{P(c^*)} \leq \log k(m) + o(\log k(m)), \tag{15}$$

where $\log k(m) = \log 2\sqrt{m} - (mp_{\text{hard}} + m^{0.25}) \log(1 - \mu_{\text{hard}})$. Choosing $\mu_{\text{hard}} = 1/2$, this becomes $\log k(m) = \frac{1}{2} \log m + 2m\mu' + m^{0.25} + O(1)$. Combining this with (15), we find that

$$\log \frac{1}{P(c^*)} \leq 2m\mu' + o(m) \tag{16}$$

which implies that (14), is no larger than $2m\mu' + o(m)$. Since $\mu' < H(\mu)/2$, the difference between the leftmost term (13) and the rightmost term (14) in (12) is less than 0 for large m, implying that then $e_D(c_{\text{MAP}(P,S)}) = \mu'$. We derived all this from (11) which holds with probability $\geq 1 - 3\exp(-2\sqrt{m})$. Thus, for all large m, $\Pr_{S \sim D^m}\left(c_{\text{MAP}(P,S)} = \mu'\right) \geq 1 - 3\exp(-2\sqrt{m})$, and the result follows.

Stage 3. **(sketch)** The proof that the integrated MAP classifier $c_{\text{SMAP}(P,S)}$ is inconsistent is similar to the proof for $c_{\text{MAP}(P,S)}$ that we just gave, except that (12) now becomes

$$\log P(c_0)P(y^m \mid x^m, c_0) - \log P(c^*)P(y^m \mid x^m, c^*). \tag{17}$$

By Lemma 1 we see that, if (11) holds, the difference between (12) and (17) is of order $O(\log m)$. The proof then proceeds exactly as for the MAP case.

To prove inconsistency of $c_{\text{MDL}(P,S)}$, note that the MDL code length of y^m given x^m according to c_0 is given by $\log \binom{m}{m\hat{e}_S(c_0)}$. If (11) holds, then a simple Stirling's approximation as in [12] or [15] shows that $\log \binom{m}{m\hat{e}_S(c_0)} = mH(\hat{e}_S(c_0)) - O(\log m)$. Thus, the difference between two-part codelengths achieved by c_0 and c^* is given by

$$-mH(\hat{e}_S(c_0)) + O(\log m) - \log P(c^*). \tag{18}$$

The proof then proceeds as for the MAP case, with (12) replaced by (18) and a few immediate adjustments.

To prove inconsistency of $c_{\text{BAYES}(P,S)}$, we take μ_{hard} not equal to $1/2$ but to $1/2 + \delta$ for some small $\delta > 0$. By taking δ small enough, the proof for $c_{\text{MAP}(P,S)}$ above goes through unchanged so that, with probability $\geq 1 - 3\exp(-2\sqrt{m})$, the Bayesian posterior puts all its weight, except for an exponentially small part, on a mixture of distributions $p_{c_j,\theta}$ whose Bayes classifier has error rate μ' and error rate on hard examples $> 1/2$. It can be shown that this implies that for large m, the classification error $c_{\text{BAYES}(P,S)}$ converges to μ'; we omit details.

4.2 A Consistent Algorithm: Proof of Theorem 1

In order to prove the theorem, we first state the Occam's Razor Bound classification algorithm, based on minimizing the bound given by the following theorem.

Theorem 4. *(Occam's Razor Bound) [7] For all priors P on a countable set of classifiers $\mathcal{C}$, for all distributions D, with probability $1-\delta$:*

$$\forall c: \quad e_D(c) \leq \hat{e}_S(c) + \sqrt{\frac{\ln \frac{1}{P(c)} + \ln \frac{1}{\delta}}{2m}}.$$

We state the algorithm here in a suboptimal form, which good enough for our purposes (see [18] for more sophisticated versions):

$$c_{\mathrm{ORB}(P,S)} := \arg\min_{c \in \mathcal{C}} \hat{e}_S(c) + \sqrt{\frac{\ln \frac{1}{P(c)} + \ln m}{2m}}.$$

Proof of Theorem 1. Set $\delta_m := 1/m$. It is easy to see that

$$\min_{c \in \mathcal{C}} e_D(c) + \sqrt{\frac{\ln \frac{1}{P(c)} + \ln m}{2m}}$$

is achieved for at least one $c \in \mathcal{C} = \{c_0, c_1, \ldots\}$. Among all $c_j \in \mathcal{C}$ achieving the minimum, let $\tilde{c}_m$ be the one with smallest index j. By the Chernoff bound, we have with probability at least $1 - \delta_m = 1 - 1/m$,

$$e_D(\tilde{c}_m) \geq \hat{e}_S(\tilde{c}_m) - \sqrt{\frac{\ln(1/\delta_m)}{2m}} = \hat{e}_S(\tilde{c}_m) - \sqrt{\frac{\ln m}{2m}}, \tag{19}$$

whereas by Theorem 4, with probability at least $1 - \delta_m = 1 - 1/m$,

$$e_D(c_{\mathrm{ORB}(P,S)}) \leq \min_{c \in \mathcal{C}} \hat{e}_S(c) + \sqrt{\frac{-\ln P(c) + \ln m}{2m}} \leq \hat{e}_S(\tilde{c}_m) + \sqrt{\frac{-\ln P(\tilde{c}_m) + \ln m}{2m}}.$$

Combining this with (19) using the union bound, we find that

$$e_D(c_{\mathrm{ORB}(P,S)}) \leq e_D(\tilde{c}_m) + \sqrt{\frac{-\ln P(\tilde{c}_m) + \ln m}{2m}} + \sqrt{\frac{\ln m}{2m}},$$

with probability at least $1 - 2/m$. The theorem follows upon noting that the right-hand side of this expression converges to $\inf_{c \in \mathcal{C}} e_D(c)$ with increasing m.

4.3 Proof of Theorem 3

Without loss of generality assume that c_0 achieves $\min_{c \in \mathcal{C}} e_D(c)$. Consider both the 0/1-loss and the log loss of sequentially predicting with the Bayes predictive distribution $P(Y_i = \cdot \mid X_i = \cdot, S^{i-1})$ given by $P(y_i \mid x_i, S^{i-1}) = E_{c,\theta \sim P(\cdot \mid S^{i-1})} p_{c,\theta}(y_i \mid x_i)$. Every time $i \in \{1, \ldots, m\}$ that the Bayes classifier based on S^{i-1} classifies y_i incorrectly, $P(y_i \mid x_i, S^{i-1})$ must be $\leq 1/2$ so that $-\log P(y_i \mid x_i, S^{i-1}) \geq 1$. Therefore,

$$\sum_{i=1}^{m} -\log P(y_i \mid x_i, S^{i-1}) \geq \sum_{i=1}^{m} |y_i - c_{\mathrm{BAYES}(P,S^{i-1})}(x_i)|. \tag{20}$$

On the other hand we have

$$\sum_{i=1}^{m} - \log P(y_i \mid x_i, S^{i-1}) = - \log \prod_{i=1}^{m} P(y_i \mid x_i, x^{i-1}, y^{i-1}) =$$
$$- \log \prod_{i=1}^{m} P(y_i \mid x^m, y^{i-1}) = - \log \prod_{i=1}^{m} \frac{P(y^i | x^m)}{P(y^{i-1} | x^m)} = - \log P(y^m \mid x^m) =$$
$$- \log \sum_{j=0,1,2\ldots} P(y^m \mid x^m, c_j) P(c_j) \leq - \log P(y^m \mid x^m, c_0) - \log P(c_0), \quad (21)$$

where the inequality follows because a sum is larger than each of its terms. By the Chernoff bound, for all small enough $\epsilon > 0$, with probability larger than $1 - 2\exp(-2m\epsilon^2)$, we have $|\hat{e}_S(c_0) - e_D(c_0)| < \epsilon$. We now set $\epsilon_m = m^{-0.25}$. Then, using Lemma 1, with probability larger than $1 - 2\exp(-2\sqrt{m})$, for all large m (21) is less than or equal to

$$- \log P(y^m \mid x^m, c_0, \hat{e}(c_0)) + \frac{1}{2} \log m + C_m \overset{(a)}{=} mH(\hat{e}_S(c_0)) + \frac{1}{2} \log m + C_m \leq$$
$$mH(e_D(c_0)) + Km^{0.75} + \frac{1}{2} \log m + C_m, \quad (22)$$

where $C_m = (e_D(c_0) - \epsilon_m - m^{-0.5})^{-1}(1 - e_D(c_0) + \epsilon_m + m^{-0.5})^{-1}$ and K is a constant not depending on $S = S^m$. Here (a) follows from Equation 2 and (b) follows because $H(\mu)$ is continuously differentiable in a neighborhood of μ.

Combining (22) with (20) and using $C_m = O(1)$ we find that with probability $\geq 1 - \exp(-2\sqrt{m})$, $\sum_{i=1}^{m} |y_i - c_{\text{BAYES}(P,S^{i-1})}(x_i)| \leq mH(e_D(c_0)) + o(m)$, QED.

5 Technical Discussion

5.1 Variations of Theorem 2 and Dependency on the Prior

Prior on classifiers. The requirement (6) that $-\log P(c_k) \geq \log k + o(\log k)$ is needed to obtain (16), which is the key inequality in the proof of Theorem 2. If $P(c_k)$ decreases at polynomial rate, but at a degree d larger than one, i.e. if

$$- \log P(c_k) = d \log k + o(\log k), \quad (23)$$

then a variation of Theorem 2 still applies but the maximum possible discrepancies between μ and μ' become much smaller: essentially, if we require $\mu \leq \mu' < \frac{1}{2d} H(\mu)$ rather than $\mu \leq \mu' < \frac{1}{2} H(\mu)$ as in Theorem 2, then the argument works for all priors satisfying (23). Since the derivative $dH(\mu)/d\mu \to \infty$ as $\mu \downarrow 0$, by setting μ close enough to 0 it is possible to obtain inconsistency for any fixed polynomial degree of decrease d. However, the higher d, the smaller $\mu = \inf_{c \in \mathcal{C}} e_D(c)$ must be to get any inconsistency with our argument.

Prior on error rates. Condition (7) on the prior on the error rates is satisfied for most reasonable priors. Some approaches to applying MDL to classification problems amount to assuming priors of the form $p(\theta^*) = 1$ for a single $\theta^* \in [0, 1]$. In that case, we can still prove a version of Theorem 2, but the maximum discrepancy between μ and μ' may now be either larger or smaller than $H(\mu)/2 - \mu$, depending on the choice of θ^*.

5.2 Properties of the Transformation from Classifiers to Distributions

Optimality and Reliability. Assume that the conditional distribution of y given x according to the 'true' underlying distribution D is defined for all $x \in \mathcal{X}$, and let $p_D(y|x)$ denote its mass function. Define $\Delta(p_{c,\theta})$ as the Kullback-Leibler (KL) divergence [9] between $p_{c,\theta}$ and the 'true' conditional distribution p_D:

$$\Delta(p_{c,\theta}) := \mathrm{KL}(p_D \| p_{c,\theta}) = E_{(x,y)\sim D}[-\log p_{c,\theta}(y|x) + \log p_D(y|x)].$$

Proposition 1. *Let $\mathcal{C}$ be any set of classifiers, and let $c^* \in \mathcal{C}$ achieve $\min_{c \in \mathcal{C}} e_D(c) = e_D(c^*)$.*

1. *If $e_D(c^*) < 1/2$, then*

$$\min_{c,\theta} \Delta(p_{c,\theta}) \text{ is uniquely achieved for } (c,\theta) = (c^*, e_D(c^*)).$$

2. *$\min_{c,\theta} \Delta(p_{c,\theta}) = 0$ iff $p_{c^*,e_D(c^*)}$ is 'true', i.e. if $\forall x, y : p_{c^*,e_D(c^*)}(y|x) = p_D(y|x)$.*

Property 1 follows since for each fixed c, $\min_{\theta \in [0,1]} \Delta(p_{c,\theta})$ is uniquely achieved for $\theta = e_D(c)$ (this follows by differentiation) and satisfies $\min_\theta \Delta(p_{c,\theta}) = \Delta(p_{c,e_D(c)}) = H(e_D(c)) - K_D$, where $K_D = E[\log p_D(y|x)]$ does not depend on c or θ, and $H(\mu)$ is monotonically increasing for $\mu < 1/2$. Property 2 follows from the information inequality [9].

Proposition 1 implies that our transformation is a good candidate for turning classifiers into probability distributions.

Namely, let $\mathcal{P} = \{p_\alpha : \alpha \in A\}$ be a set of i.i.d. distributions indexed by parameter set A and let $P(\alpha)$ be a prior on A. By the law of large numbers, for each $\alpha \in A$, $m^{-1} \log p_\alpha(y^m \mid x^m) P(\alpha) \to \mathrm{KL}(p_D \| p_\alpha)$. By Bayes rule, this implies that if the class $\mathcal{P}$ is 'small' enough so that the law of large numbers holds *uniformly* for all $p_\alpha \in \mathcal{P}$, then for all $\epsilon > 0$, the Bayesian posterior will concentrate, with probability 1, on the set of distributions in $\mathcal{P}$ within ϵ of the $p^* \in \mathcal{P}$ minimizing KL-divergence to D. In our case, if $\mathcal{C}$ is 'simple' enough so that the corresponding $\mathcal{P} = \{p_{c,\theta} : c \in \mathcal{C}, \theta \in [0,1]\}$ admits uniform convergence [12], then the Bayesian posterior asymptotically concentrates on the $p_{c^*,\theta^*} \in \mathcal{P} = \{p_{c,\theta}\}$ closest to D in KL-divergence. By Proposition 1, this p_{c^*,θ^*} corresponds to the $c^* \in \mathcal{C}$ with smallest generalization error rate $e_D(c^*)$ (p_{c^*,θ^*} is *optimal* for 0/1-loss), and for the $\theta^* \in [0,1]$ with $\theta^* = e_D(c^*)$ (p_{c^*,θ^*} gives a *reliable* impression of its prediction quality). This convergence to an optimal and reliable p_{c^*,θ^*} will happen if, for example, $\mathcal{C}$ has finite VC-dimension [12]. We can only get trouble as in Theorem 2 if we allow $\mathcal{C}$ to be of infinite VC-dimension.

Logistic regression interpretation. let $\mathcal{C}$ be a set of functions $\mathcal{X} \to \mathcal{Y}$, where $\mathcal{Y} \subseteq \mathbb{R}$ ($\mathcal{Y}$ does not need to be binary-valued). The corresponding logistic regression model is the set of conditional distributions $\{p_{c,\beta} : c \in \mathcal{C}; \beta \in \mathbb{R}\}$ of the form

$$p_{c,\beta}(1 \mid x) := \frac{e^{-\beta c(x)}}{1 + e^{-\beta c(x)}} \ ; \ p_{c,\beta}(0 \mid x) := \frac{1}{1 + e^{-\beta c(x)}}. \tag{24}$$

This is the standard construction used to convert classifiers with real-valued output such as support vector machines and neural networks into conditional distributions [14,22], so that Bayesian inference can be applied. By setting $\mathcal{C}$ to be a set of $\{0,1\}$-valued classifiers, and substituting $\beta = \ln(1-\theta) - \ln\theta$, we see that our construction is a special case of the logistic regression transformation (24). It may seem that (24) does not treat $y = 1$ and $y = 0$ on equal footing, but this is not so: we can alternatively define a symmetric version of (24) by defining, for each $c \in \mathcal{C}$, a corresponding $c' : \mathcal{X} \rightarrow \{-1, 1\}$, $c'(x) := 2c(x) - 1$. Then we can set

$$p_{c,\beta}(1 \mid x) := \frac{e^{-\beta c(x)}}{e^{\beta c(x)} + e^{-\beta c(x)}} \ ; \ p_{c,\beta}(-1 \mid x) := \frac{e^{\beta c(x)}}{e^{\beta c(x)} + e^{-\beta c(x)}}. \tag{25}$$

By setting $\beta' = 2\beta$ we see that $p_{c,\beta}$ as in (24) is identical to $p_{c,\beta'}$ as in (25), so that the two models really coincide.

6 Interpretation from a Bayesian Perspective

Bayesian Consistency. It is well-known that Bayesian inference is strongly consistent under very broad conditions. For example, when applied to our setting, the celebrated Blackwell-Dubins consistency theorem [6] says the following. Let $\mathcal{C}$ be countable and suppose D is such that, for some $c^* \in \mathcal{C}$ and $\theta^* \in [0,1]$, p_{c^*,θ^*} is equal to p_D, the true distribution/ mass function of y given x. Then with D-probability 1, the Bayesian posterior concentrates on c^*: $\lim_{m\rightarrow\infty} P(c^* \mid S^m) = 1$.

Consider now the learning problem underlying Theorem 2 as described in Section 4.1. Since c_0 achieves $\min_{c\in\mathcal{C}} e_D(c)$, it follows by part 1 of Proposition 1 that $\min_{c,\theta} \Delta(p_{c,\theta}) = \Delta(p_{c_0,e_D(c_0)})$. *If* $\Delta(p_{c_0,e_D(c_0)})$ were 0, then by part 2 of Proposition 1, Blackwell-Dubins would apply, and we would have $P(c_0 \mid S^m) \rightarrow 1$. Theorem 2 states that this does *not* happen. It follows that the premisse $\Delta(p_{c_0,e_D(c_0)}) = 0$ must be false. But since $\Delta(p_{c,\theta})$ is minimized for $(c_0, e_D(c_0))$, the Proposition implies that for *no* $c \in \mathcal{C}$ and *no* $\theta \in [0,1]$, $p_{c,\theta}$ is equal to $p_D(\cdot|\cdot)$ - in statistical terms, the model $\mathcal{P} = \{p_{c,\theta} : c \in \mathcal{C}, \theta \in [0,1]\}$ is *misspecified.*

Why is the result interesting for a Bayesian? Here we answer several objections that a Bayesian might have to our work.

Bayesian inference has never been designed to work under misspecification. So why is the result relevant?
We would maintain that in *practice*, Bayesian inference is applied *all the time* under misspecification in classification problems [12]. It is very hard to avoid

misspecification with Bayesian classification, since the modeler often has no idea about the noise-generating process. Even though it may be known that noise is not homoskedastic, it may be practically impossible to incorporate all ways in which the noise may depend on x into the prior.

It is already well-known that Bayesian inference can be inconsistent even if $\mathcal{P}$ is well-specified, *i.e. if it contains D [10]. So why is our result interesting?*
The (in)famous inconsistency results by Diaconis and Freedman [10] are based on nonparametric inference with uncountable sets $\mathcal{P}$. Their theorems require that the true p has small prior density, and in fact prior *mass* 0 (see also [1]). In contrast, Theorem 2 still holds if we assign $p_{c_0,e_D(c_0)}$ arbitrarily large prior mass < 1, which, by the Blackwell-Dubins theorem, guarantees consistency if $\mathcal{P}$ is well-specified. We show that consistency may *still* fail dramatically if $\mathcal{P}$ is misspecified. This is interesting because even under misspecification, Bayes is consistent under fairly broad conditions [8,16], in the sense that the posterior concentrates on a neighborhood of the distribution that minimizes KL-divergence to the true D. Thus, we feel our result is relevant at least from the *inconsistency under misspecification* interpretation.

So how can our result co-exist with theorems establishing Bayesian consistency under misspecification?
Such results are typically proved under either one of the following two assumptions:

1. The set of distributions $\mathcal{P}$ is 'simple', for example, finite-dimensional parametric. In such cases, ML estimation is usually also consistent - thus, for large m the role of the prior becomes negligible. In case $\mathcal{P}$ corresponds to a classification model $\mathcal{C}$, this would obtain, for example, if $\mathcal{C}$ were finite or had finite VC-dimension.
2. $\mathcal{P}$ may be arbitrarily large or complex, but it is *convex*: any finite mixture of elements of $\mathcal{P}$ is an element of $\mathcal{P}$. An example is the family of Gaussian mixtures with an arbitrary but finite number of components [17].

Our setup violates both conditions: $\mathcal{C}$ has infinite VC-dimension, and the corresponding $\mathcal{P}$ is not closed under taking mixtures. This suggests that we could make Bayes consistent again if, instead of $\mathcal{P}$, we would base inferences on its convex closure $\overline{\mathcal{P}}$. Computational difficulties aside,this approach will not work, since we now use the crucial part (1) of Proposition 1 will not hold any more: the conditional distribution in $\overline{\mathcal{P}}$ closest in KL-divergence to the true $p_D(y|x)$, when used for classification, may end up having larger generalization error (expected 0/1-loss) than the optimal classifier c^* in the set $\mathcal{C}$ on which $\mathcal{P}$ was based. We will give an explicit example of this in the journal version of this paper. Thus, with a prior on $\overline{\mathcal{P}}$, the Bayesian posterior will converge, but potentially it converges to a distribution that is suboptimal in the performance measure we are interested in.

How 'standard' is the conversion from classifiers to probability distributions on which our results are based?
One may argue that our notion of 'converting' classifiers into probability distributions is not always what Bayesians do in practice. For classifiers which produce *real-valued* output, such as neural networks and support vector machines, our transformation coincides with the logistic regression transformation, which is a standard Bayesian tool; see for example [14,22]. But our theorems are based on classifiers with 0/1-output. With the exception of decision trees, such classifiers have not been addresses frequently in the Bayesian literature. Decision trees have usually been converted to conditional distributions differently, by assuming a different noise rate *in each leaf* of the decision tree [13]. This makes the set of all decision trees on a given input space $\mathcal{X}$ coincide with the set of all conditional distributions on $\mathcal{X}$, and thus avoids the misspecification problem, at the cost of using a much larger model space.

Thus, this a weak point in our analysis: we use a transformation that has mostly been applied to real-valued classifiers, whereas our classifiers are 0/1-valued. Whether our inconsistency results can be extended in a natural way to classifiers with real-valued output remains to be seen. The fact that the Bayesian model corresponding to such neural networks will still typically be misspecified suggests (but does not prove) that similar scenarios may be constructed.

Acknowledgments. The ideas in this paper were developed in part during the workshop *Complexity and Inference*, held at the DIMACS center, Rutgers University, June 2003. We would like to thank Mark Hansen, Paul Vitányi and Bin Yu for organizing this workshop, and Dean Foster and Abraham Wyner for stimulating conversations during the workshop.

References

1. Andrew R. Barron. Information-theoretic characterization of Bayes performance and the choice of priors in parametric and nonparametric problems. In *Bayesian Statistics*, volume 6, pages 27–52. Oxford University Press, 1998.
2. Andrew R. Barron, Jorma Rissanen, and Bin Yu. The MDL Principle in coding and modeling. *IEEE Trans. Inform. Theory*, 44(6):2743–2760, 1998.
3. A.R. Barron. Complexity regularization with application to artificial neural networks. In *Nonparametric Functional Estimation and Related Topics*, pages 561–576. Kluwer Academic Publishers, 1990.
4. A.R. Barron and T.M. Cover. Minimum complexity density estimation. *IEEE Trans. Inform. Theory*, 37(4):1034–1054, 1991.
5. J.M. Bernardo and A.F.M Smith. *Bayesian theory.* John Wiley, 1994.
6. D. Blackwell and L. Dubins. Merging of opinions with increasing information. *The Annals of Mathematical Statistics*, 33:882–886, 1962.
7. A. Blumer, A. Ehrenfeucht, D. Haussler, and M. Warmuth. Occam's razor. *Information Processing Letters*, 24:377–380, April 1987.
8. O. Bunke and X. Milhaud. Asymptotic behaviour of Bayes estimates under possibly incorrect models. *The Annals of Statistics*, 26:617–644, 1998.

9. T.M. Cover and J.A. Thomas. *Elements of Information Theory*. Wiley, 1991.
10. P. Diaconis and D. Freedman. On the consistency of Bayes estimates. *The Annals of Statitics*, 14(1):1–26, 1986.
11. P. D. Grünwald. MDL tutorial. In P. D. Grünwald, I. J. Myung, and M. A. Pitt, editors, *Minimum Description Length: recent developments in theory and practice*, chapter 1. MIT Press, 2004. to appear.
12. P.D. Grünwald. *The Minimum Description Length Principle and Reasoning under Uncertainty*. PhD thesis, University of Amsterdam, The Netherlands, 1998.
13. D. Heckerman, D.M. Chickering, C. Meek, R. Rounthwaite, and C. Kadie. Dependency networks for inference, collaborative filtering, and data visualization. *Journal of Machine Learning Research*, 1:49–75, 2000.
14. M.I. Jordan. Why the logistic funtion? a tutorial discussion on probabilities and neural networks. Computational Cognitive Science Tech. Rep. 9503, MIT, 1995.
15. M. Kearns, Y. Mansour, A.Y. Ng, and D. Ron. An experimental and theoretical comparison of model selection methods. *Machine Learning*, 27:7–50, 1997.
16. Bas Kleijn and Aad van der Vaart. Misspecification in infinite-dimensional Bayesian statistics. submitted, 2004.
17. J.K. Li. *Estimation of Mixture Models*. PhD thesis, Yale University, Department of Statistics, 1997.
18. D. McAllester. PAC-Bayesian model averaging. In *Proceedings COLT '99*, 1999.
19. R. Meir and N. Merhav. On the stochastic complexity of learning realizable and unrealizable rules. *Machine Learning*, 19:241–261, 1995.
20. J. Quinlan and R. Rivest. Inferring decision trees using the minimum description length principle. *Information and Computation*, 80:227–248, 1989.
21. J. Rissanen. *Stochastic Complexity in Statistical Inquiry*. World Scientific, 1989.
22. M.E. Tipping. Sparse Bayesian learning and the relevance vector machine. *Journal of Machine Learning Research*, 1:211–244, 2001.
23. M. Viswanathan., C.S. Wallace, D.L. Dowe, and K.B. Korb. Finding cutpoints in noisy binary sequences - a revised empirical evaluation. In *Proc. 12th Australian Joint Conf. on Artif. Intelligence*, volume 1747 of *Lecture Notes in Artificial Intelligence (LNAI)*, pages 405–416, Sidney, Australia, 1999.
24. K. Yamanishi. A decision-theoretic extension of stochastic complexity and its applications to learning. *IEEE Trans. Inform. Theory*, 44(4):1424–1439, 1998.

Learning Intersections of Halfspaces with a Margin

A.R. Klivans and R.A. Servedio

[1] Divsion of Engineering and Applied Sciences, Harvard University
Cambridge, MA 02138
klivans@eecs.harvard.edu
[2] Department of Computer Science, Columbia University
New York, NY 10027, USA
rocco@cs.columbia.edu

Abstract. We give a new algorithm for learning intersections of halfspaces with a margin, i.e. under the assumption that no example lies too close to any separating hyperplane. Our algorithm combines random projection techniques for dimensionality reduction, polynomial threshold function constructions, and kernel methods. The algorithm is fast and simple. It learns a broader class of functions and achieves an exponential runtime improvement compared with previous work on learning intersections of halfspaces with a margin.

1 Introduction

The Perceptron algorithm and Perceptron Convergence Theorem are among the oldest and most famous results in machine learning. The Perceptron Convergence Theorem (see e.g. [10]) states that at most $4/\rho^2$ iterations of the Perceptron update rule are required in order to correctly classify any set S of examples which are consistent with some halfspace which has margin ρ on S. (Roughly speaking, this margin condition means that no example lies within distance ρ of the separating hyperplane; we give precise definitions later.)

Since halfspace learning is so widely used in machine learning algorithms and applications, it is of great interest to develop efficient algorithms for learning intersections of halfspaces and other more complex functions of halfspaces. While this problem has been intensively studied, progress to date has been quite limited; we give a brief overview of relevant previous work on learning intersections of halfspaces at the end of this section.

Our results: toward Perceptron-like performance for learning intersections of halfspaces. In this paper we take a perspective similar to that of the original Perceptron Convergence Theorem by highlighting the role of the margin; our goal is to obtain results analogous to the Perceptron Convergence Theorem for learning intersections of halfspaces with margin ρ. (Roughly speaking, an intersection of t halfspaces has margin ρ relative to a data set if each of the defining halfspaces has margin ρ on the data set; we give precise definitions

J. Shawe-Taylor and Y. Singer (Eds.): COLT 2004, LNAI 3120, pp. 348–362, 2004.

Table 1. Bounds on running time for learning intersections and arbitrary functions of t halfspaces with margin ρ. Each h_i is a halfspace over $\mathbf{R}^n$; in the second line f denotes an arbitrary Boolean function (not known a priori to the learner) on t bits. In each case the target function is assumed to have margin ρ.

	Arriaga & Vempala [3]	This Paper
$h_1 \wedge \cdots \wedge h_t$	$n \cdot \mathrm{poly}\left(\frac{\log t}{\rho}\right) + \left(\frac{\log t}{\rho}\right)^{\frac{t \log \frac{t}{\rho}}{\rho^2}}$	$n\left(\frac{t}{\rho}\right)^{t \log t \log \frac{1}{\rho}}$ or $n\left(\frac{\log t}{\rho}\right)^{\sqrt{\frac{1}{\rho}} \log t}$
$f(h_1, \ldots, h_t)$	———	$n\left(\frac{t}{\rho}\right)^{t^2 \log \frac{1}{\rho}}$

later.) The margin is a natural parameter to consider; previous work by Arriaga and Vempala [3] on learning intersections of halfspaces has explicitly studied the dependence on this parameter. Since the Perceptron algorithm learns a single halfspace in time $O(1/\rho^2)$, the ultimate goal in this framework would be an algorithm which can learn (say) an intersection of two halfspaces in time polynomial in $1/\rho$ as well.

Table 1 summarizes our main results. For any constant $t = O(1)$ number of halfspaces (in our opinion this is the most interesting case) our learning algorithm runs in $(1/\rho)^{O(\log 1/\rho)}$ time, i.e. quasipolynomial in $1/\rho$. This is an exponential improvement over Arriaga and Vempala's previous result [3] which was an algorithm that runs in $(1/\rho)^{\omega(1/\rho^2)}$ time. (Put another way, our algorithm can learn the intersection of $O(1)$ halfspaces with margin at least $1/2^{\sqrt{\log n}}$ in poly(n) time, whereas Arriaga and Vempala require the margin to be at least $\omega(1/\sqrt{\log n})$ to achieve poly(n) runtime.) In fact, we can learn any Boolean function of $t = O(1)$ halfspaces, not just an intersection of halfspaces, in $(1/\rho)^{O(\log 1/\rho)}$ time.

One can instead consider the number of halfspaces t as the relevant asymptotic parameter and view ρ as fixed at $\Theta(1)$. For this case we give an algorithm which has a $t^{O(\log \log t)}$ dependence on t; this algorithm can learn an intersection of $t = n^{1/\log \log n}$ many halfspaces in poly(n) time. In contrast, the previous algorithm of [3] has a $t^{\omega(t)}$ dependence on t and thus runs in poly(n) time only for $t = o(\frac{\log n}{\log \log n})$ many halfspaces.

As described below all our results are achieved using simple iterative algorithms (in fact using simple variants of the Perceptron algorithm!).

Our Approach. Our algorithm for learning an intersection of t halfspaces in $\mathbf{R}^n$ with margin ρ is given in Figure 1. The algorithm has three conceptual stages: (i) random projection, (ii) polynomial threshold function construction, and (iii) kernel methods used to learn polynomial threshold functions. We now give a brief overview of each of these stages.

Random Projection: Random projection for dimensionality reduction has emerged as a useful tool in many areas of CS theory. The key fact on which most of these applications are based is the Johnson-Lindenstrauss lemma [13] which shows that a random projection of a set of m points in $\mathbf{R}^n$ into $\mathbf{R}^k$ (with

Algorithm A($EX(c,\mathcal{D})$):

1. Let M be a $n \times k$ random projection matrix.
2. Draw m many examples from $EX(c,\mathcal{D})$ and project them to $\mathbf{R}^k$ using M.
3. Run the kernel Perceptron algorithm using the polynomial kernel $K_d(x,y) = (x \cdot y + 1)^d$ over the projected examples until a consistent hypothesis is obtained. Let h' be the kernel Perceptron hypothesis (a mapping from $\mathbf{R}^k$ to $\{-1,1\}$).
4. Output $h : \mathbf{R}^n \rightarrow \{-1,1\}$, $h(x) = \mathrm{sign}(h'(M^T x))$ as the final hypothesis.

Fig. 1. The algorithm is given access to a source $EX(c,\mathcal{D})$ of random labelled examples, where the target concept c is an intersection of t halfspaces over $\mathbf{R}^n$ which has margin ρ with respect to distribution $\mathcal{D}$. The values of m, k and d are given in Section 6.

$k \approx O(\frac{\log m}{\epsilon^2}))$ with high probability will not change pairwise distances by more than a $(1 \pm \epsilon)$ factor. Arriaga and Vempala [3] were the first to give learning algorithms based on random projections. Their key insight was that since the geometry of a sample does not change much under random projection, one can run learning algorithms in the low dimensional space $\mathbf{R}^k$ rather than $\mathbf{R}^n$ and thus get a computational savings.

As described in Section 3, the first step of our algorithm is to perform a random projection of the sample from $\mathbf{R}^n$ into a lower dimensional space $\mathbf{R}^k$ where k has no dependence on n. After this projection, with high probability we have data points in $\mathbf{R}^k$ which are labelled according to some intersection of halfspaces with margin $\rho/2$.

Polynomial Threshold Functions: Constructions of polynomial threshold functions (PTFs) have recently proved quite useful in computational learning theory; for example the DNF learning algorithm of [16] has at its heart the fact that any DNF formula can be expressed as a low degree thresholded polynomial $\mathrm{sign}(p(x))$. The second conceptual step of our algorithm is to construct a polynomial threshold function for an intersection of halfspaces over $\mathbf{R}^k$. We show in Section 4 that any intersection of halfspaces with margin $\rho/2$ over $\mathbf{R}^k$ can be expressed as a low-degree polynomial threshold function p over $\mathbf{R}^k$. Moreover, unlike previous analyses (which only gave degree bounds) we show that this PTF p has nonnegligible *PTF margin* (we define PTF margin in Section 2.2). We can thus view our projected data in $\mathbf{R}^k$ as being labelled according to some degree-d PTF over $\mathbf{R}^k$ which has nonnegligible PTF margin. (We emphasize that this is only a conceptual rather than an algorithmic step – the learning algorithm itself does not have to do anything at this stage!)

Kernel Methods: The third step is to learn the low-degree polynomial threshold function over $\mathbf{R}^k$. As shown in Section 5 we do this using the Perceptron algorithm with the standard polynomial kernel $K_d(x,y) = (1 + x \cdot y)^d$. The kernel Perceptron algorithm learns an implicit representation of a halfspace over an expanded feature space; here the expanded space has a feature for each monomial of degree up to d, and thus each example in $\mathbf{R}^k$ corresponds to a point in $\mathbf{R}^{\binom{k+d}{d}}$. We show that since there is a polynomial threshold function which correctly classifies the data in $\mathbf{R}^k$ with some PTF margin, there must be a halfspace over $\mathbf{R}^{\binom{k+d}{d}}$ which correctly classifies the expanded data with a margin, and thus we can use kernel Perceptron to learn.

Comparison with Previous Work. Many researchers have considered the problem of learning intersections of halfspaces. Efficient algorithms are known for learning intersections of halfspaces under the uniform distribution on the unit ball [7,21] and on the Boolean cube [15], but less is known about learning under more general probability distributions. Baum [4] gave an algorithm which learns an intersection of two origin-centered halfspaces under any symmetric distribution $\mathcal{D}$ (which satisfies $\mathcal{D}(x) = \mathcal{D}(-x)$ for all $x \in \mathbf{R}^n$), and Klivans *et al.* [15] gave a PTF-based algorithm which learns an intersection of $O(1)$ many poly(n)-weight halfspaces over $\{0,1\}^n$ in $n^{O(\log n)}$ time under any distribution.

The most closely related previous work is that of Arriaga and Vempala [3] who gave an algorithm for learning an intersection of halfspaces with margin ρ; see Table 1 for a comparison with their results. Their algorithm uses random projection to reduce dimensionality and then uses a brute-force search over all (combinatorially distinct) halfspaces over the sample data. In contrast, our algorithm combines polynomial threshold functions and kernel methods with random projections, and is able to achieve an exponential runtime savings over [3].

2 Preliminaries

2.1 Concepts and Margins

A *concept* is simply a Boolean function $c : \mathbf{R}^n \to \{-1, +1\}$. A *halfspace* over $\mathbf{R}^n$ is a Boolean function $h : \mathbf{R}^n \to \{-1, 1\}$ defined by a vector $w \in \mathbf{R}^n$ and a value $\theta \in \mathbf{R}$; given an input $x \in \mathbf{R}^n$, the value of $h(x)$ is $\text{sign}(w \cdot x - \theta)$, i.e. $h(x) = +1$ if $w \cdot x \geq \theta$ and $h(x) = -1$ if $w \cdot x < \theta$. An *intersection of t halfspaces $h_1, \ldots, h_t$* is the Boolean AND of these halfspaces, i.e. the value is 1 if $h_i(x) = 1$ for all $i = 1, \ldots, t$ and is -1 otherwise.

For two vectors $x, y \in \mathbf{R}^n$ we write $\|x - y\|$ to denote the Euclidean distance between x and y and we write S^{n-1} for the unit ball in $\mathbf{R}^n$. We have:

Definition 1. *Given $X \subset \mathbf{R}^n$ and a concept c over $\mathbf{R}^n$, write $\|X\|$ to denote* $\max_{z \in X} \|z\|$. *We say that c has* (geometric) margin ρ with respect to X *if*

$$\rho = \min\{\|z - y\| : z \in X, y \in \mathbf{R}^n, c(z) \neq c(y)\}/\|X\|.$$

Our definition of the geometric margin is similar to the notion of robustness defined in Arriaga and Vempala [3]; the difference is that we normalize by dividing by the radius of the data set $\|X\|$. In the case where $\|X\| = 1$ these notions coincide and the condition is simply that for every $z \in X$, every point within a ball of radius ρ around z has the same label as z under c.

For $\mathcal{D}$ a probability distribution over $\mathbf{R}^n$ we write $\text{Supp}(\mathcal{D})$ to denote the set $\{x \in \mathbf{R}^n : \mathcal{D}(x) > 0\}$. We say that c has *margin ρ with respect to distribution $\mathcal{D}$* if c has margin ρ on $\text{Supp}(\mathcal{D})$. Thus, for $\mathcal{D}$ a distribution where $\text{Supp}(\mathcal{D}) \subset S^{n-1}$, an intersection of t halfspaces has margin ρ with respect to $\mathcal{D}$ if every point in Supp($\mathcal{D}$) lies at least distance ρ away from each of the t separating hyperplanes.

Throughout this paper we assume that: (i) All halfspaces in our intersection of halfspaces learning problem are origin-centered, i.e. of the form $\text{sign}(w \cdot x - \theta)$ with $\theta = 0$ – this can be achieved by adding an $(n+1)$st coordinate to each example. (ii) All examples lie on the unit ball S^{n-1} – this can be achieved by adding a new coordinate so that all examples have the same norm and rescaling.

2.2 Polynomial Threshold Functions and PTF Margins

Let $f : \mathbf{R}^n \rightarrow \{-1, 1\}$ be a Boolean function and X be a subset of $\mathbf{R}^n$. A real polynomial p in n variables is said to be a *polynomial threshold function (PTF) for f over X* if $\text{sign}(p(x)) = f(x)$ for all $x \in X$. The *degree* of a polynomial threshold function p is simply the degree of the polynomial p. Polynomial threshold functions are well studied in the case where $X = \{0,1\}^n$ or $\{-1,1\}^n$ (see e.g. [5,16,18,20]) but we will consider other more general subsets X.

For $S \subseteq \{x_1, \ldots, x_n\}$ a multiset of variables, we write x_S to denote the monomial $\prod_{i \in S} x_i$. For $p(x) = \sum_S c_S x_S$ a polynomial, we write $\|p\|$ to denote $\sqrt{\sum_S c_S^2}$, i.e. the L_2 norm of the vector of coefficients of p. Given a PTF p over X, we define the *PTF margin of p over X* to be $\min\{|p(z)| : z \in X\}/\|p\|$. Note that if $p(x) = w \cdot x$ is a degree-1 polynomial which has $\|p\| = \sqrt{w_1^2 + \cdots + w_n^2} = 1$, then the PTF margin of p over X is equal to the geometric margin of $\text{sign}(p(x))$ over X (up to scaling by $\|X\|$). However in general for polynomials of degree greater than 1 these two notions are not equivalent.

2.3 The Perceptron Algorithm and Kernel Perceptron

Perceptron is a simple iterative algorithm which finds a linear separator for a labelled data set $X \subset \mathbf{R}^n$ if such a separator exists. The algorithm maintains a weight vector $w \in \mathbf{R}^n$ and a bias $\theta \in \mathbf{R}$ and updates these parameters additively after each example; see e.g. Chapter 2 of [10] for details. The Perceptron Convergence Theorem bounds the number of updates in terms of the maximum margin of any halfspace (the following is adapted from Theorem 2.3 of [10]):

Theorem 1. *Let $X \subset \mathbf{R}^n$ be a set of labelled examples such that there is some halfspace h (which need not be origin-centered) which has margin ρ over X. Then the Perceptron algorithm makes at most $\frac{4}{\rho^2}$ mistakes on X.*

Let $\phi : \mathbf{R}^n \rightarrow \mathbf{R}^N$ be a function which we call a *feature expansion*. We refer to $\mathbf{R}^n$ as the original feature space and $\mathbf{R}^N$ as the expanded feature space. The *kernel* corresponding to ϕ is the function $K(x, y) = \phi(x) \cdot \phi(y)$. The use of kernels in machine learning has received much research attention in recent years (see e.g. [10,12] and references therein).

Given a data set $X \subset \mathbf{R}^n$, it is well known (see e.g. [11]) that the Perceptron algorithm can be simulated over $\phi(X)$ in the expanded feature space $\mathbf{R}^N$ using the kernel function $K(x, y)$ to yield an implicit representation of a halfspace in

$\mathbf{R}^N$. If evaluating $K(x, y)$ takes time T and the Perceptron algorithm is simulated until M mistakes are made on a data set X with $|X| = m$, the time required is $O(mTM^2)$ (see e.g. [12,14]).

3 Random Projections

We say that an $n \times k$ matrix M is a *random projection matrix* if each entry of M is chosen independently and uniformly from $\{-1, 1\}$. We will use the following lemma from Arriaga and Vempala [3] (see Achlioptas [1] for similar results):

Lemma 1. *[3] Fix $\rho < 1$, $0 < c < \frac{1}{2}$ and $w \in \mathbf{R}^n$ with $\|w\| = 1$. Let M be an $n \times k$ random projection matrix. For any $x \in \mathbf{R}^n$ we have*

$$\Pr[w \cdot x - 2c \leq (M^T w) \cdot (M^T x) \leq w \cdot x + 2c] \geq 1 - 6e^{-(c^2 - c^3)k/4} \geq 1 - 6e^{-c^2 k/8}.$$

With this lemma in hand we can establish the main theorem on random projection which we will use:

Theorem 2. *Let X be a set of m points on S^{n-1} and let $h = sign(w \cdot x)$ be a halfspace which has margin ρ on X. Let $k \geq \frac{2048}{\rho^2} \log(\frac{18m}{\delta})$ and let M be a $n \times k$ random projection matrix. Let $M(X) \subset \mathbf{R}^k$ denote the projection of X under M and let $h' : \mathbf{R}^k \to \{-1, +1\}$ denote the function $h'(y) = sign((M^T w) \cdot y)$. Then with probability $1 - \delta$, the halfspace h' correctly classifies $M(X)$ with margin at least $\frac{\rho}{2}$ and we have $\frac{1}{2} \leq \|M(X)\| \leq 2$.*

Proof. We may assume that $\|w\| = 1$. After applying M to the points in X, we need to verify that Definition 1 is satisfied for h' with respect to the points in $M(X)$. Setting $c = \frac{\rho}{16}$ and setting k as above, taking $x = w$ in Lemma 1 we have that with probability at least $1 - \frac{\delta}{3m}$, $\|M^T w\|^2 \leq \|w\|^2 + \frac{\rho}{8} = 1 + \frac{\rho}{8}$, so $\|M^T w\| \leq 1 + \frac{\rho}{16}$.

Now for each point $z \in X$, applying Lemma 1 with $x = z$, with probability at least $1 - \frac{\delta}{3m}$ we have $(w \cdot z) - \frac{\rho}{8} \leq (M^T w) \cdot (M^T z) \leq (w \cdot z) + \frac{\rho}{8}$. Since $|(w \cdot z)| \geq \rho$, this gives $|(M^T w) \cdot (M^T z)| \geq \frac{7\rho}{8}$. Hence with probability at least $1 - \frac{\delta}{2}$ we have $\min\{\|z' - y\| : z' \in M(X), y \in \mathbf{R}^k, h'(z') \neq h'(y)\} \geq \min_{z \in X} |(M^T w) \cdot (M^T z)| / \|M^T w\| \geq \frac{7\rho/8}{1+\rho/16} \geq \frac{3\rho}{4}$. Lemma 1 similarly implies that $1 - \frac{\rho}{8} \leq \|M(X)\| \leq 1 + \frac{\rho}{16}$ with probability at least $1 - \frac{\delta}{2}$. Thus with probability $1 - \delta$, h' has margin at least $\frac{\rho}{2}$ on $M(X)$ and $\frac{1}{2} \leq \|M(x)\| \leq 2$. □

A union bound yields the following corollary:

Corollary 1. *Let X be a set of m points on S^{n-1} and let $H = \bigwedge_{i=1}^t h_i = sign(w^1 \cdot x) \wedge \ldots \wedge sign(w^t \cdot x)$ be an intersection of t halfspaces which has margin ρ on X. Let $k \geq \frac{2048}{\rho^2} \cdot \log(\frac{18mt}{\delta})$ and let M be a $n \times k$ random projection matrix. Let $M(X) \subset \mathbf{R}^k$ denote the projection of X under M and let $H' = \bigwedge_{i=1}^t sign((M^T w^i) \cdot y)$. Then with probability $1 - \delta$, the intersection of halfspaces H' correctly classifies $M(X)$ with margin at least $\frac{\rho}{2}$ and $\frac{1}{2} \leq \|M(X)\| \leq 2$.*

Thus with high probability the projected set of examples in $\mathbf{R}^k$ is classified by an intersection of halfspaces with margin $\frac{\ell}{2}$. It is easy to see that the corollary in fact holds for any Boolean function (not just intersections) of t halfspaces.

4 Polynomial Threshold Functions for Intersections of Halfspaces with a Margin

In this section we give several constructions of polynomial threshold functions for intersections of halfspaces with a margin. In each case we give a PTF and also a lower bound on the PTF margin of the polynomial threshold function which we construct. These PTF margin lower bounds will be useful when we analyze the performance of kernel methods for learning polynomial threshold functions.

In order to lower bound the PTF margin of a polynomial p we must upper bound $\|p\|$. Fact 3 helps obtain such upper bounds:[1]

Fact 3 *1. For $i = 1, \ldots, \ell$ let $q_i(x) = \sum_S c_{i,S} x_S$ be a degree-d polynomial over $x_1, \ldots, x_k$ with $\|q_i\|^2 \leq M$. Then $\|q_1(x) \ldots q_\ell(x)\|^2 \leq \binom{k+d}{d}^\ell M^\ell$.*
2. For $q_1, \ldots, q_\ell$ with $\|q_i\|^2 \leq M_i$, we have $\|q_1 + \cdots + q_\ell\|^2 \leq \ell(M_1 + \cdots + M_\ell)$.

4.1 Constructions Based on Rational Functions

Recall that a *rational function* is a quotient of two real polynomials, i.e. $Q(x) = a(x)/b(x)$. The *degree* of Q is defined as $\deg(a) + \deg(b)$. Building on results of Newman [17] on rational functions which approximate the function $|x|$, in [6] Beigel *et al.* gave a construction of a low-degree rational function which closely approximates the function $\operatorname{sgn}(x)$. We will use the following (Lemma 9 of [6]):

Lemma 2. *[6] For all integers $r, \ell \geq 1$ there is a univariate rational function $P_\ell^r(x) = \frac{a(x)}{b(x)}$ of degree $O(\ell \log r)$ with the following properties: (i) $P_\ell^r(x) \in [1, 1 + \frac{1}{r}]$ for all $x \in [1, 2^\ell]$; (ii) $P_\ell^r(x) \in [-1 - \frac{1}{r}, -1]$ for all $x \in [-2^\ell, -1]$; and (iii) Each coefficient of $a(x), b(x)$ has magnitude at most $2^{O(\ell^2 \log r)}$.*

The following theorem generalizes Theorem 24 in [15], which addresses the special case of intersections of low-weight halfspaces over the space $X = \{0, 1\}^n$:

Theorem 4. *Let X be a subset of $\mathbf{R}^k$ with $\frac{1}{2} \leq \|X\| \leq 2$ and $c : \mathbf{R}^k \to \{-1, 1\}$ be an intersection of t origin-centered halfspaces $h_1, \ldots, h_t$. If c has margin ρ on X then there is a polynomial threshold function of degree $d = O(t \log t \log \frac{1}{\rho})$ for c on X. If $d \leq k$ then this PTF has PTF margin $(\rho/k)^{O(t \log t \log 1/\rho)}$ on X.*

Proof. We must exhibit a polynomial $p(x)$ of the claimed degree such that for any $z \in X$ we have $\operatorname{sign}(p(z)) = c(z)$ and $\frac{|p(z)|}{\|p\|} \geq (k/\rho)^{O(t \log t \log 1/\rho)}$.

[1] Because of space restrictions all appendices are omitted in this version; see http://www.cs.columbia.edu/~rocco/p6_long.pdf for the full version.

Let $w^1 \cdot x = 0, \ldots, w^t \cdot x = 0$ be the t hyperplanes which define halfspaces $h_1, \ldots, h_t$; we may assume without loss of generality that each $\|w^i\| = 1$. Now consider the sum of rational functions

$$Q(x) = P^{2t}_{\log 4/\rho}(2(w^1 \cdot x)/\rho) + \cdots + P^{2t}_{\log 4/\rho}(2(w^t \cdot x)/\rho) - t + 1/2.$$

Fix any $z \in X$. Since c has margin ρ on X and $\frac{1}{2} \leq \|X\| \leq 2$, for each $i = 1, \ldots, t$ we have $\frac{\rho}{2} \leq \rho\|X\| \leq |w^i \cdot z| \leq \|w^i\| \cdot \|X\| \leq 2$ and hence $|2(w^i \cdot z)/\rho| \in [1, \frac{4}{\rho}]$. Consequently $P^{2t}_{\log 4/\rho}(\frac{2(w^i \cdot z)}{\rho})$ lies in $[1, 1+\frac{1}{2t}]$ if $h_i(z) = 1$ and lies in $[-1-\frac{1}{2t}, -1]$ if $h_i(z) = -1$. Thus if $h_i(z) = 1$ for all i we have $Q(z) \geq t - t + \frac{1}{2} = \frac{1}{2}$, and if $h_i(z) = -1$ for some i we have $Q(z) < -1 + (t-1) + \frac{(t-1)}{2t} - t + \frac{1}{2} < -\frac{1}{2}$. So $\text{sign}(Q(z)) = c(z)$ for all $z \in X$.

Since $Q(x)$ is a sum of t rational functions of degree $O(\log t \log \frac{1}{\rho})$, we can clear denominators and re-express $Q(x)$ as a single rational function $A(x)/B(x)$ of degree $O(t \log t \log \frac{1}{\rho})$. It follows that the function $p(x) = A(x)B(x)$, which is a polynomial of degree $O(t \log t \log \frac{1}{\rho})$, has $\text{sign}(p(z)) = \text{sign}(Q(z))$ as desired.

Now we must bound $\|p\|$. We have $\|\frac{2w^i \cdot x}{\rho}\|^2 = \frac{4}{\rho^2}$ so by part (1) of Fact 3 we have that $\|(\frac{2w^i \cdot x}{\rho})^j\|^2 \leq (\frac{4k}{\rho^2})^j$ for all j. By Lemma 2 we have that $P^{2t}_{\log 4/\rho}(x) = \frac{a(x)}{b(x)}$ where $a(x), b(x)$ are polynomials of degree $O(\log t \log \frac{1}{\rho})$ with coefficients of magnitude at most $2^{O((\log \frac{1}{\rho})^2 \log t)} = (\frac{1}{\rho})^{O(\log t \log 1/\rho)}$. It follows from part (2) of Fact 3 that $\|a(\frac{2w^i \cdot x}{\rho})\|^2 \leq (\frac{k}{\rho})^{O(\log t \log 1/\rho)} . (\frac{1}{\rho})^{O(\log t \log 1/\rho)}$ which equals $(\frac{k}{\rho})^{O(\log t \log 1/\rho)}$, and the same holds for $\|b(\frac{2w^i \cdot x}{\rho})\|^2$. Expressing $Q(x)$ as a rational function $A(x)/B(x)$, we have that $B(x) = \prod_{i=1}^t b(\frac{2w^i \cdot x}{\rho})$, so since $d \leq k$ part (1) of Fact 3 implies that $\|B(x)\|^2 \leq k^{O(t \log t \log 1/\rho)} (\frac{k}{\rho})^{O(t \log t \log 1/\rho)} = (\frac{k}{\rho})^{O(t \log t \log 1/\rho)}$. Simple calculations using part (1) of Fact 3 show that $\|A(x)\|^2$ and $\|p(x)\| = \|A(x)B(x)\|$ are also $(k/\rho)^{O(t \log t \log 1/\rho)}$, and we are done. □

By modifying this construction, we get a polynomial threshold function for any Boolean function of t halfspaces rather than just an intersection (at a relatively small cost in degree and PTF margin):

Theorem 5. *Let $f : \{-1,1\}^t \to \{-1,1\}$ be any Boolean function on t bits. Let X be a subset of $\mathbf{R}^k$ with $\frac{1}{2} \leq \|X\| \leq 2$ and $c : \mathbf{R}^k \to \{-1,1\}$ be the function $f(h_1, \ldots, h_t)$ where $h_1, \ldots, h_t$ are origin-centered halfspaces in $\mathbf{R}^k$. If c has margin ρ on X then there is a PTF of degree $d = O(t^2 \log \frac{1}{\rho})$ for c on X. If $d \leq k$ then this PTF has PTF margin $(\rho/k)^{O(t^2 \log 1/\rho)}$ on X.*

Proof. As before, we give a polynomial $p(x)$ of the claimed degree such that for any $z \in X$ we have $\text{sign}(p(z)) = c(z)$ and $\frac{|p(z)|}{\|p\|} \geq (k/\rho)^{O(t^2 \log 1/\rho)}$.

Again let $w^1 \cdot x = 0, \ldots, w^t \cdot x = 0$ be the hyperplanes for halfspaces $h_1, \ldots, h_t$, where each w^i is a unit vector. For each $i = 1, \ldots, t$ consider the rational function

$$Q_i(x) = P^{2^{3t}}_{\log 4/\rho}\left(2(w^i \cdot x)/\rho\right).$$

Fix any $z \in X$. As before we have that $|2(w^i \cdot z)/\rho| \in [1, \frac{4}{\rho}]$, so by Lemma 2 the value of $Q_i(z)$ differs from the ± 1 value $h_i(z) = \mathrm{sign}(w^i \cdot z)$ by at most $\frac{1}{2^{3t}}$. Since f is a Boolean function on t inputs, it is expressible as a multilinear polynomial $\tilde{f}$ of degree t, with coefficients of the form $i/2^t$ where i is an integer in $[-2^t, 2^t]$. (The polynomial $\tilde{f}$ is just the Fourier representation of f.) Multiply $\tilde{f}$ by 2^t, so now $\tilde{f} : \{+1, -1\}^t \rightarrow \{+2^t, -2^t\}$, and $\tilde{f}$ has integer coefficients which are at most 2^t in absolute value.

Now we would like to argue that $\tilde{f}(Q_1(z), \ldots, Q_t(z))$ has the same sign as $f(h_1(z), \ldots, h_t(z))$. To do this we show that the "error" of each $Q_i(z)$ relative to the ± 1 value $h_i(z)$ (which error is at most $\frac{1}{2^{3t}}$) does not cause $\tilde{f}$ to have the wrong sign. The polynomial $\tilde{f}$ has at most 2^t terms, each of which is the product of an integer coefficient of magnitude at most 2^t and up to t of the Q_i's. The product of the Q_i's incurs error at most $O(t2^{-3t})$ relative to the corresponding product of the h_i's, and thus the error of any given term (including the integer coefficient) is at most $O(t2^{-2t})$. Since we add up at most 2^t terms, the overall error is at most $O(t2^{-t})$ error, which is much less than what we could tolerate (we could tolerate error 2^t; recall that $\tilde{f}$ takes value $\pm 2^t$ on ± 1 inputs). Thus $\tilde{f}(Q_1(z), \ldots, Q_t(z))$ has the same sign as $f(h_1(z), \ldots, h_t(z))$ for all $z \in X$.

Now $\tilde{f}$ is a multilinear polynomial of degree t, and each Q_i is a rational function of degree $O(t \log w)$. We can bring $\tilde{f}(Q_1, \ldots, Q_t)$; to a common denominator (which is the product of the denominators of the Q_i's) of degree $O(t^2 \log w)$. Hence we have a single multivariate rational function $A(x)/B(x)$ which takes the right sign on z, and we can convert this rational function to a polynomial threshold function $p(x) = A(x)B(x)$ as in the proof of Theorem 4.

Now we must bound $\|p\|$. Let $Q_i(x) = \frac{a_i(x)}{b_i(x)}$. The analysis from the previous proof implies that $\|a_i(x)\|^2$ and $\|b_i(x)\|^2$ are both at most $(\frac{k}{\rho})^{O(t \log 1/\rho)}$. Now consider a monomial (in the "variables" $Q_1(x), \ldots, Q_t(x)$) in the polynomial $\tilde{f}(Q_1(x), \ldots, Q_t(x))$. Since the numerator $\alpha(x)$ of such a monomial is the product of at most t of the $a_i(x)$'s, and each $a_i(x)$ has degree at most $O(\log t \log \frac{1}{\rho})$, the fact that $d \leq k$ and part (1) of Fact 3 together give $\|\alpha(x)\|^2 \leq k^{O(t \log t \log 1/\rho)} (\frac{k}{\rho})^{O(t^2 \log 1/\rho)}$ which equals $(\frac{k}{\rho})^{O(t^2 \log 1/\rho)}$. The same holds for the denominator $\beta(x)$ of such a monomial. Since the common denomiator for $\tilde{f}(Q_1, \ldots, Q_t)$ is the product of the denominators of the Q_i's, clearing all denominators we have that $\tilde{f}(Q_1, \ldots, Q_t) = A(x)/B(x)$ with $\|A(x)\|^2$ and $\|B(x)\|^2$ both at most $(\frac{k}{\rho})^{O(t^2 \log 1/\rho)}$. We thus have $\|p(x)\|^2 = \|A(x)B(x)\|^2 = (\frac{k}{\rho})^{O(t^2 \log 1/\rho)}$ and the theorem is proved. □

4.2 Constructions Using Extremal Polynomials

The bounds from the previous section are quite strong when t is relatively small. If t is large but ρ is also quite large, then the following bounds based on Chebyshev polynomials are better.

The r-th Chebyshev polynomial of the first kind, $T_r(x)$, is a univariate degree-r polynomial with the following properties [9]:

Lemma 3. *The polynomial* $T_r(x) = \sum_{i=0}^{r} a_i x^i$ *satisfies: (i)* $|T_r(x)| \leq 1$ *for* $|x| \leq 1$ *with* $T_r(1) = 1$*; (ii)* $T_r'(x) \geq r^2$ *for* $x > 1$ *with* $T_r'(1) = r^2$*; and (iii) For* $i = 0, \ldots, r$ *each* a_i *is an integer with* $|a_i| \leq 2^r$*.*

The following theorem generalizes results in [16]:

Theorem 6. *Let* X *be a subset of* $\mathbf{R}^k$ *with* $\frac{1}{2} \leq \|X\| \leq 2$ *and let* $c : \mathbf{R}^k \to \{-1, 1\}$ *be an intersection of* t *origin-centered halfspaces* $h_1, \ldots, h_t$*. If* c *has margin* ρ *on* X *then there is a PTF of degree* $d = O(\sqrt{1/\rho} \log t)$ *for* c *on* X*. If* $d \leq k$ *then this PTF has PTF margin* $1/k^{O(\sqrt{1/\rho} \log t)}$ *on* X*.*

Proof: As in the previous proofs we must exhibit a polynomial $p(x)$ such that for any $z \in X$ we have $\text{sign}(p(z)) = c(z)$ and $\frac{|p(z)|}{\|p\|} \geq 1/k^{O(\sqrt{1/\rho} \log t)}$.

Let $w^1 \cdot x = 0, \ldots, w^t \cdot x = 0$ be the t hyperplanes for halfspaces $h_1, \ldots, h_t$ where each $\|w^i\| = 1$. Let P be the univariate polynomial $P(x) = T_r(1-x)$ where $r = \lceil \sqrt{2/\rho} \rceil$. The first part of Lemma 3 implies that $|P(x)| \leq 1$ for $x \in [0, 2]$, and the second part implies that $P(x) \geq 2$ for $x \leq \frac{-\rho}{2}$. Now consider the polynomial threshold function $\text{sign}(p(x))$ where

$$p(x) = t + \frac{1}{2} - \sum_{i=1}^{t} (P(w^i \cdot x))^{\lceil \log 2t \rceil}.$$

Since P is a polynomial of degree $r = \lceil \sqrt{2/\rho} \rceil$ and $w^i \cdot x$ is a polynomial of degree 1, this polynomial threshold function has degree $d = \lceil \sqrt{2/\rho} \rceil \cdot \lceil \log 2t \rceil$. We now show that $p(x)$ has the desired properties described above.

We first show that for any $z \in X$ the polynomial p takes the right sign and has magnitude at least $\frac{1}{2}$. Fix any $z \in X$. For each $i = 1, \ldots, t$ we have $\frac{\rho}{2} \leq \rho \|X\| \leq |w^i \cdot z| \leq \|w^i\| \cdot \|X\| \leq 2$.

- If $c(z) = 1$ then for each i we have $\frac{\rho}{2} \leq w^i \cdot z \leq 2$ and hence we have that $P(w^i \cdot z)$ (and also $P(w^i \cdot z)^{\lceil \log 2t \rceil}$) lies in $[-1, 1]$. Consequently we have that $p(z) \geq t + \frac{1}{2} - t \geq \frac{1}{2}$ so $\text{sign}(p(z)) = c(z) = 1$.
- If $c(z) = -1$ then for some i we have $w^i \cdot z \in [-2, -\frac{\rho}{2}]$, so consequently $P(w^i \cdot z) \geq 2$ and $P(w^i \cdot z)^{\lceil \log 2t \rceil} \geq 2t$. Since $P(w^j \cdot z)^{\lceil \log 2t \rceil} \geq -1$ for all j, we have $p(z) \leq t + \frac{1}{2} - 2t + (t - 1) = -\frac{1}{2}$ so $\text{sign}(p(z)) = c(z) = -1$.

To finish the proof it remains to bound $\|p\|$. Since $\|w^i \cdot x\|^2 = 1$ for all i, by part 2 of Fact 3 we have $\|1 - w^i \cdot x\|^2 \leq 4$ so by part 1 of Fact 3 we have that $\|(1 - w^i \cdot x)^j\| \leq (4k)^j$ for $j = 0, \ldots, r$. Since (by Lemma 3) $T_r(x) = \sum_{j=0}^{r} a_j x^j$ where each $|a_j| \leq 2^r$, for each $j = 0, \ldots, r$ we have $\|a_j(1 - w^i \cdot x)^j\|^2 \leq 2^{2r}(4k)^r$. By part 2 of Fact 3 we obtain $\|T_r(1 - w^i \cdot x)\|^2 \leq (r+1)^2(16k)^r$, and now part 1 implies that $(P(w^i \cdot x))^{\lceil \log 2t \rceil} = k^{O(r \log t)}$. Using part 2 again we obtain that $\|p\| \leq (t+1)^2 k^{O(r \log t)} = k^{O(r \log t)}$, and the theorem is proved. □

As Arriaga and Vempala observed in [3], DNF formulas can be viewed as unions of halfspaces. If we rescale the cube so that it is a subset of S^{k-1}, it is easy to check that a Boolean function $f : \{-1, 1\}^k \to \{-1, 1\}$ has margin ρ with respect to $X \subseteq \{-1,1\}^k$ if for every $z \in X$ we have that every Boolean string z' which differs from z in at most a $\frac{\rho^2}{4}$ fraction of bits has $f(z') = f(z)$.

Since any DNF formula with t terms can be expressed as a union of t halfspaces, we have the following corollary of Theorem 6:

Corollary 2. *Let $X \subset \{-1,1\}^k$ and let c be a t-term DNF formula on k variables. If c has margin ρ on X then there is a polynomial threshold function of degree $O(\sqrt{1/\rho}\log t)$ for c on X which has PTF margin $1/k^{O(\sqrt{1/\rho}\log t)}$ on X. If $d \leq k$ then this PTF has PTF margin $(1/k)^{O(\sqrt{1/\rho}\log t)}$ on X.*

A similar corollary for DNF formulas also follows from Theorem 4 but we are most interested in DNFs with t =poly(n) terms so we focus on Theorem 6.

5 Kernel Perceptron for learning PTFs with PTF Margin

In this section we first define a new kernel, the Complete Symmetric Kernel, which arises naturally in the context of polynomial threshold functions. We give an efficient algorithm for computing this kernel (which may be of independent interest), and indeed all results of the paper could be proved using this new kernel. To make our overall algorithm simpler, however, we ultimately use the standard polynomial kernel which we discuss later in this section.

Let $\phi_d : \mathbf{R}^k \to \mathbf{R}^{\binom{k+d}{d}}$ be a feature expansion which maps $(x_1, \ldots, x_k)$ to the vector $(1, x_1, \ldots, x_k, x_1^2, x_1x_2, \ldots)$ containing all monomials of degree up to d. Let $K_d(x,y) = \phi_d(x) \cdot \phi_d(y)$ be the kernel corresponding to ϕ_d. We refer to $K_d(x,y)$ as the *complete symmetric kernel* since as explained in Appendix B the value $K_d(x,y)$ equals the sum of certain complete symmetric polynomials.

For a data set $X \subset \mathbf{R}^k$ we write $\phi_d(X)$ to denote the expanded data set of points in $\mathbf{R}^{\binom{k+d}{d}}$. The following lemma gives a mistake bound for the Perceptron algorithm using the complete symmetric kernel:

Lemma 4. *Let $X \subset \mathbf{R}^k$ be a set of labelled examples such that there is some degree-d polynomial threshold function $p(x)$ which correctly classifies X and has PTF margin ρ over X. Then the Perceptron algorithm (run on $\phi_d(X)$ using the complete symmetric kernel K_d) makes at most $\frac{4\|\phi_d(X)\|^2}{\rho^2}$ mistakes on X.*

Proof. The vector $W \in \mathbf{R}^{\binom{k+d}{d}}$ whose coordinates are the coefficients of p has margin $\frac{\min_{z \in X}|W \cdot \phi_d(z)|}{\|W\| \cdot \|\phi_d(X)\|}$ over $\phi_d(X)$. Since $W \cdot \phi_d(z) = p(z)$ and $\|W\| = \|p\|$, the lemma follows by from the definition of the PTF margin of p and the Perceptron Convergence Theorem (Theorem 1). □

In the full version of this paper (available on either author's web page) we give a polynomial time algorithm for computing $K_d(x,y)$, but this algorithm is somewhat cumbersome. With the aim of obtaining a faster and simpler overall algorithm, we now describe an alternate approach based on the well known polynomial kernel.

As in [10], we define the degree-d polynomial kernel $K'_d : \mathbf{R}^k \times \mathbf{R}^k \to \mathbf{R}$ as $K'_d(x,y) = (1 + x \cdot y)^d$. It is clear that $K'_d(x,y)$ can be computed efficiently. Let $\phi'_d : \mathbf{R}^k \to \mathbf{R}^{\binom{k+d}{d}}$ be the feature expansion such that $K'_d(x,y) = \phi'_d(x) \cdot \phi'_d(y)$; note that $\phi'_d(x)$ differs from $\phi_d(x)$ defined above because of the coefficients that arise in the expansion of $(1 + x \cdot y)^d$.

We have the following polynomial kernel analogue of Lemma 4:

Lemma 5. *Let $X \subset \mathbf{R}^k$ be a set of labelled examples such that there is some degree-d polynomial threshold function $p(x)$ which correctly classifies X and has PTF margin ρ over X. Then the Perceptron algorithm (run on $\phi'_d(X)$ using the polynomial kernel K'_d) makes at most $\frac{4(1+\|X\|^2)^d}{\rho^2}$ mistakes on X.*

Proof. We view $\phi'_d(x)$ as a vector $(a_S x_S)$ of monomials with coefficients. By inspection of the coefficients of $(1 + x \cdot y)^d$ it is clear that each $a_S \geq 1$. Let W' be the vector in $\mathbf{R}^{\binom{k+d}{d}}$ such that $W' \cdot \phi'_d(x) = p(x)$ as a formal polynomial. For each monomial x_S in $p(x)$, the W'_S coordinate of W' equals $W_S / a_S \leq W_S$ where W is defined as in the proof of Lemma 4 so we have $\|W'\| \leq \|W\|$.

The vector W' has margin $\frac{\min_{z \in X} |W' \cdot \phi'_d(z)|}{\|W'\| \cdot \|\phi'_d(X)\|} = \frac{\min_{z \in X} |p(z)|}{\|W'\| \cdot \|\phi'_d(X)\|} \geq \frac{\min_{z \in X} |p(z)|}{\|W\| \cdot \|\phi'_d(X)\|}$ over $\phi'_d(X)$. It is easy to verify that $\|\phi'_d(X)\| \leq (1 + \|X\|^2)^{d/2}$, so W' has margin at least $\frac{\min_{z \in X} |p(z)|}{\|W\| \cdot (1+\|X\|^2)^{d/2}} = \frac{\rho}{(1+\|X\|^2)^{d/2}}$. The lemma now follows from the Perceptron Convergence Theorem. □

The output hypothesis of this kernel Perceptron is an (implicit representation of a) halfspace over $\mathbf{R}^{\binom{k+d}{d}}$ which can be viewed as a polynomial threshold function of degree d over $\mathbf{R}^k$.

6 The Main Results

In this section we give our main learning results by bounding the running time of algorithm A and proving that it outputs an accurate hypothesis.

Our first theorem gives a good bound for the case where t is relatively small:

Theorem 7. *Algorithm A learns any ρ-margin intersection of t halfspaces over $\mathbf{R}^n$ in at most $\frac{n}{\epsilon} \cdot (\frac{t}{\rho} \log \frac{1}{\delta \epsilon})^{O(t \log t \log 1/\rho)}$ time steps.*

Proof. Let c be an intersection of t origin-centered halfspaces over $\mathbf{R}^n$ which has margin ρ with respect to distribution $\mathcal{D}$ where $\text{Supp}(\mathcal{D}) \subset S^{n-1}$. Let m equal the number of examples our algorithm draws from $EX(c, \mathcal{D})$; we defer specifying m until the end of the proof. Let $k = O(\frac{1}{\rho^2} \cdot \log \frac{mt}{\delta})$, and $d = O(t \log t \log \frac{1}{\rho})$. Let X be the set of m examples in $\mathbf{R}^n$, and let $M(X)$ be the projected set of m examples in $\mathbf{R}^k$. Note that it takes nkm time steps to construct the set $M(X)$.

By Corollary 1, with probability $1 - \delta$ we have that $\frac{1}{2} \leq \|M(X)\| \leq 2$ and there is an intersection of t origin-centered halfspaces in $\mathbf{R}^k$ which has margin at least $\frac{\rho}{2}$ on $M(X)$. By Theorem 4 there is a polynomial threshold function over

$\mathbf{R}^k$ of degree $d = O(t \log t \log \frac{1}{\rho})$ which has PTF margin $(\frac{\rho}{k})^{O(d)}$ with respect to $M(X)$. By Lemma 5 the degree-d polynomial kernel Perceptron algorithm makes at most $(\frac{k}{\rho})^{O(d)}$ mistakes when run on $M(X)$, and thus once $M(X)$ is obtained the algorithm runs for at most $m \cdot (\frac{k}{\rho})^{O(d)} = (\frac{k}{\rho})^{O(d)}/\epsilon$ time steps.

Now we show that with probability $1 - \delta$ algorithm A outputs an ϵ-accurate hypothesis for c relative to $\mathcal{D}$. Since the output hypothesis $h(x) = \text{sign}(p(Mx))$ is computed by first projecting $x \in \mathbf{R}^n$ down to $\mathbf{R}^k$ via M and then evaluating the k-variable PTF p, it suffices to show that p is a good hypothesis under the distribution $M(\mathcal{D})$ obtained by projecting $\mathcal{D}$ down to $\mathbf{R}^k$ via M. It is well known (see e.g. [2]) that the VC dimension of the class of degree-d PTFs over k real variables is $\binom{k+d}{d}$. Thus by the VC theorem [8] in order to learn to accuracy ϵ and confidence δ it suffices to take $m = O(\frac{k^d}{\epsilon} \log \frac{1}{\epsilon} + \frac{1}{\epsilon} \log \frac{1}{\delta})$. It is straightforward to verify that $k = (\frac{d}{\rho} \log \frac{1}{\delta\epsilon})^{O(1)}$, $m = \frac{1}{\epsilon} \cdot (\frac{d}{\rho} \log \frac{1}{\delta\epsilon})^{O(d)}$ satisfy the above conditions on m and k. Since $d = O(t \log t \log \frac{1}{\rho})$ we have $k = (\frac{t}{\rho} \log \frac{1}{\delta\epsilon})^{O(1)}$ and $m = \frac{1}{\epsilon} \cdot (\frac{t}{\rho} \log \frac{1}{\delta\epsilon})^{O(t \log t \log 1/\rho)}$ which proves the theorem. □

Note that for a constant $t = O(1)$ number of halfspaces Algorithm A has a quasipolynomial $((\frac{1}{\rho})^{O(\log 1/\rho)})$ runtime dependence on the margin ρ, in contrast with the exponential $((\frac{1}{\rho})^{O(\log \frac{1}{\rho})/\rho^2)})$ dependence of [3].

The proof of Theorem 7 used the polynomial threshold function construction of Theorem 4. We can instead use the construction of Theorem 6 to obtain:

Theorem 8. *Algorithm A learns any ρ-margin intersection of t halfspaces over $\mathbf{R}^n$ in at most $\frac{n}{\epsilon} \cdot (\frac{\log t}{\rho} \log \frac{1}{\delta\epsilon})^{O(\sqrt{1/\rho} \log t)}$ time steps.*

For a constant $\rho = \Theta(1)$ margin Algorithm A has an almost polynomial $((t^{O(\log \log t)})$ runtime dependence on t, in contrast with the exponential $(t^{\omega(t)})$ dependence of [3]. By Corollary 2 the above bound holds for learning t-term DNF with margin ρ as well.

Finally, we can use the construction of Theorem 5 to obtain:

Theorem 9. *Algorithm A learns any Boolean function of t halfspaces with margin ρ in at most $\frac{n}{\epsilon} \cdot (\frac{t}{\rho} \log \frac{1}{\delta\epsilon})^{O(t^2 \log 1/\rho)}$ time steps.*

7 Discussion

Is Random Projection Necessary? A natural question is whether our quantitative results could be achieved simply by using kernel Perceptron (or a Support Vector Machine) without first performing random projection. Given a data set X in $\mathbf{R}^n$ classified by an intersection of $t = 2$ halfspaces with margin ρ, Theorem 4 implies the existence of a polynomial threshold function for X of degree $d = O(\log(1/\rho))$ with PTF margin $(\rho/n)^{O(\log(1/\rho))}$. Using either the degree-d polynomial kernel or the Complete Symmetric Kernel, we obtain a halfspace over $\mathbf{R}^{\binom{n+d}{d}}$ which classifies the expanded data set $\phi(X)$ with geometric margin $(\rho/n)^{O(\log(1/\rho))}$.[2] Thus it appears that without the initial projection step, the required sample complexity for either kernel Perceptron or an SVM will be $(n/\rho)^{\Omega(\log(1/\rho))}$, as opposed to the bounds in Section 6 which do not depend on n; so random projection does indeed seem to provide a gain in efficiency.

Lower Bounds on Polynomial Threshold Functions. The main result of O'Donnell and Servedio in [19], if suitably interpreted, proves that there exists a set $X \subset \mathbf{R}^2$ labelled according to the intersection of two halfspaces with margin ρ for which any PTF correctly classifying X must have degree $\Omega(\frac{\log(1/\rho)}{\log\log(1/\rho)})$. This lower bound implies that our choice of d in the proof of Theorem 7 is essentially optimal with respect to ρ. For a discussion of other lower bounds on PTF constructions see Klivans et al. [15].

Alternative Algorithms. We note that after random projection, in Step 3 of Algorithm A there are several other algorithms that could be used instead of kernel Perceptron. For example, we could run a support vector machine over $\mathbf{R}^k$ with the same degree d polynomial kernel to find the maximum margin hyperplane in $\mathbf{R}^{\binom{k+d}{d}}$; alternatively we could even explicitly expand each projected example $M(x) \in \mathbf{R}^k$ into $\phi'_d(M(x)) \in \mathbf{R}^{\binom{k+d}{d}}$ and explicitly run Perceptron (or indeed any algorithm for solving linear programs such as the Ellipsoid algorithm) to learn a single halfspace in $\mathbf{R}^{\binom{k+d}{d}}$. It can be verified that each of these approaches gives the same asymptotic runtime and sample complexity as our kernel Perceptron approach. We use kernel Perceptron both for its simplicity and for its ability to take advantage of the actual margin if it is better than the worst-case bounds presented here.

Future Work and Implications for Practice. We feel that our results give some theoretical justification for the effectiveness of the polynomial kernel in practice, as kernel Perceptron takes direct advantage of the representational power of polynomial threshold functions. We are working on experimentally assessing the algorithm's performance.

Acknowledgements. We thank Santosh Vempala for helpful discussions.

References

[1] D. Achlioptas. Database-friendly random projections: Johnson-Lindenstrauss with binary coins. *Journal of Computer and System Sciences*, 66(4):671–687, 2003.

[2] M. Anthony. Classification by polynomial surfaces. *Discrete Applied Mathematics*, 61:91–103, 1995.

[2] In Arriaga and Vempala [3] it is claimed that if the geometric margin of a degree-d PTF p in $\mathbf{R}^n$ is ρ then the margin of the corresponding halfspace in $\mathbf{R}^{\binom{n+d}{d}}$ is at least ρ^d, but this claim is in error [22]; to bound the margin of the halfspace in $\mathbf{R}^{\binom{n+d}{d}}$ one must analyze the PTF margin of p rather than its geometric margin.

[3] R. Arriaga and S. Vempala. An algorithmic theory of learning: Robust concepts and random projection. In *Proceedings of the 40th Annual Symposium on Foundations of Computer Science (FOCS)*, pages 616–623, 1999.
[4] E. Baum. A polynomial time algorithm that learns two hidden unit nets. *Neural Computation*, 2:510–522, 1991.
[5] R. Beigel. When do extra majority gates help? polylog(n) majority gates are equivalent to one. *Computational Complexity*, 4:314–324, 1994.
[6] R. Beigel, N. Reingold, and D. Spielman. PP is closed under intersection. *Journal of Computer and System Sciences*, 50(2):191–202, 1995.
[7] A. Blum and R. Kannan. Learning an intersection of a constant number of halfspaces under a uniform distribution. *Journal of Computer and System Sciences*, 54(2):371–380, 1997.
[8] A. Blumer, A. Ehrenfeucht, D. Haussler, and M. Warmuth. Learnability and the Vapnik-Chervonenkis dimension. *Journal of the ACM*, 36(4):929–965, 1989.
[9] E. Cheney. *Introduction to Approximation Theory.* McGraw-Hill, New York, New York, 1966.
[10] N. Cristianini and J. Shawe-Taylor. *An introduction to Support Vector Machines (and other kernel-based learning methods).* Cambridge University Press, 2000.
[11] Y. Freund and R. Schapire. Large margin classification using the Perceptron algorithm. In *Proceedings of the Eleventh Annual Conference on Computational Learning Theory*, pages 209–217, 1998.
[12] R. Herbrich. *Learning Kernel Classifiers.* MIT Press, 2002.
[13] W. Johnson and J. Lindenstrauss. Extensions of Lipshitz mapping into Hilbert space. *Contemporary Mathematics*, 26:189–206, 1984.
[14] R. Khardon, D. Roth, and R. Servedio. Efficiency versus Convergence of Boolean Kernels for On-Line Learning Algorithms. In T. G. Dietterich, S. Becker, and Z. Ghahramani, editors, *Advances in Neural Information Processing Systems 14*, Cambridge, MA, 2002. MIT Press.
[15] A. Klivans, R. O'Donnell, and R. Servedio. Learning intersections and thresholds of halfspaces. In *Proceedings of the Forty-Third Annual Symposium on Foundations of Computer Science*, pages 177–186, 2002.
[16] A. Klivans and R. Servedio. Learning DNF in time $2^{\tilde{O}(n^{1/3})}$. In *Proceedings of the Thirty-Third Annual Symposium on Theory of Computing*, pages 258–265, 2001.
[17] D. J. Newman. Rational approximation to $|x|$. *Michigan Mathematical Journal*, 11:11–14, 1964.
[18] R. O'Donnell and R. Servedio. Extremal properties of polynomial threshold functions. In *Proceedings of the Eighteenth Annual Conference on Computational Complexity*, pages 3–12, 2003.
[19] R. O'Donnell and R. Servedio. New degree bounds for polynomial threshold functions. In *Proceedings of the 35th ACM Symposium on Theory of Computing*, pages 325–334, 2003.
[20] M. Saks. *Slicing the hypercube*, pages 211–257. London Mathematical Society Lecture Note Series 187, 1993.
[21] S. Vempala. A random sampling based algorithm for learning the intersection of halfspaces. In *Proceedings of the 38th Annual Symposium on Foundations of Computer Science*, pages 508–513, 1997.
[22] S. Vempala. Personal communication, 2004.

A General Convergence Theorem for the Decomposition Method*

Niko List and Hans Ulrich Simon

Fakultät für Mathematik, Ruhr-Universität Bochum, 44780 Bochum, Germany
Niko.List@gmx.de, simon@lmi.rub.de

Abstract. The decomposition method is currently one of the major methods for solving the convex quadratic optimization problems being associated with support vector machines. Although there exist some versions of the method that are known to converge to an optimal solution, the general convergence properties of the method are not yet fully understood. In this paper, we present a variant of the decomposition method that basically converges for any convex quadratic optimization problem provided that the policy for working set selection satisfies three abstract conditions. We furthermore design a concrete policy that meets these requirements.

1 Introduction

Support vector machines (SVMs) introduced by Vapnik and co-workers [4,25] are a promising technique for classification, function approximation, and other key problems in statistical learning theory. In this paper, we mainly discuss the optimization problems that are induced by SVMs, which are special cases of convex quadratic optimization.[1]

Example 1. Two popular variants of SVMs lead to the optimization problems given by (1) and (2), respectively:

$$\min_x \frac{1}{2}\sum_{i=1}^{m}\sum_{j=1}^{m} Q_{i,j}x_ix_j - \sum_{i=1}^{m} x_i \text{ s.t. } \sum_{i=1}^{m} y_ix_i = 0 \ , \ \forall i=1,\ldots,m : 0 \le x_i \le C \tag{1}$$

$$\min_x \frac{1}{2}\sum_{i=1}^{m}\sum_{j=1}^{m} Q_{i,j}x_ix_j \text{ s.t. } \sum_{i=1}^{m} y_ix_i = 0, \ \sum_{i=1}^{m} x_i \ge \nu \ , \ \forall i=1,\ldots,m : 0 \le x_i \le \frac{1}{m} \tag{2}$$

* This work has been supported by the Deutsche Forschungsgemeinschaft Grant SI 498/7-1.

[1] The reader interested in more background information about SVMs is referred to [25, 6,23].

J. Shawe-Taylor and Y. Singer (Eds.): COLT 2004, LNAI 3120, pp. 363–377, 2004.

Here, $Q \in \mathbb{R}^{m \times m}$ is a positive (semi-)definite matrix, $y \in \{-1, 1\}^m$, and x is a vector of m real variables. C and ν are real constants. The first problem is related to one of the classical SVM models; the second-one is related to the so-called ν-SVM introduced by Schölkopf, Smola, Williamson, and Bartlett [24].

The difficulty of solving problems of this kind is the density of Q whose entries are typically non-zero. Thus, a prohibitive amount of memory is required to store the matrix and traditional optimization algorithms (such as Newton, for example) cannot be directly applied. Several authors have proposed (different variants of) a decomposition method to overcome this difficulty [20,11,21,22,5,13, 17,14,12,18,19,15,9,16,10]. This method keeps track of a current feasible solution which is iteratively improved. In each iteration the variable indices are split into a "working set" $I \subseteq \{1, \dots, m\}$ and its complement $J = \{1, \dots, m\} \setminus I$. Then, the subproblem with variables x_i, $i \in I$, is solved, thereby leaving the values for the remaining variables x_j, $j \in J$, unchanged. The success of the method depends in a quite sensitive manner on the policy for the selection of the working set I (whose size is typically bounded by a small constant). Ideally, the selection procedure should be computationally efficient and, at the same time, effective in the sense that the resulting sequence of feasible solutions converges (with high speed) to an optimal limit point. Clearly, these goals are conflicting in general and trade-offs are to be expected. At the time being, it seems fair to say that the issue of convergence is not fully understood (although some of the papers mentioned above certainly shed some light on this question).

We briefly note that also the random sampling technique applied in [2,1] (and being based on the Simple Sampling Lemma by Gärtner and Welzl [7]) can be viewed as a kind of decomposition method. Here, the working sets (= samples) are probabilistically selected according to a dynamic weighting scheme. The general idea is to update the weights in such a fashion that the support vectors not yet included in the sample become more and more likely to be chosen. At some point the sample will contain enough support vectors such that the solution obtained in the next iteration will be globally optimal. The efficiency of this technique seems to depend strongly on a parameter k that can be rigorously defined in mathematical terms but is unknown in practice. Parameter k is certainly bounded by m but might be much smaller under lucky circumstances. The sample size grows quadratically in k and in the dimension n of the feature space. If k and n are much smaller than m, the random sampling technique seems to produce nice results. We briefly point to the main differences between the random sampling technique and other work on the decomposition method (including ours):

- random selection of the working set
- dependence of the performance on an unknown parameter k
- comparably large working sets (samples)
- very few iterations on the average to optimum if k is small

We close the introduction by explaining the main difference between this paper and earlier work on the decomposition method. It seems that all existing papers concerned with the decomposition method perform a kind of non-uniform analysis in the sense that the results very much depend on the concrete instance of convex quadratic optimization that is induced by the specific SVM under consideration. Given the practical importance of SVM problems, this is certainly justified and may occasionally lead to methods with nice properties (concerning efficiency of working set selection and speed of convergence). On the long run, however, it bears the danger that any new variant of a SVM must be analyzed from scratch because the generality (if any) of the arguments being used so far is too much left in the dark. In this paper, we pursue the goal to establish convergence in a quite general setting. We present a variant of the decomposition method that converges for basically any convex quadratic optimization problem provided that the policy for working set selection satisfies three abstract conditions. We furthermore design a concrete policy that meets these requirements. We admittedly ignore computational issues. The analysis of the trade-off between computational efficiency, speed of convergence, and degree of generality is left as object of future research.

2 Definitions, Notations, and Basic Facts

For a matrix $A \in \mathbb{R}^{k \times m}$, $A_i \in \mathbb{R}^k$ denotes the i'th column. $A^\top \in \mathbb{R}^{m \times k}$ denotes the transpose of A. Vectors are considered as column vectors such that the transpose of a vector is a row vector. The "all-zeroes" vector is denoted as $\mathbf{0}$, where its dimension will always become clear from the context. For two vectors $w, x \in \mathbb{R}^m$, $w^\top x = \sum_{i=1}^m w_i x_i$ denotes the standard scalar product. $\|x\| := \left(\sum_{i=1}^m x_i^2\right)^{1/2}$ denotes the Euclidean norm of x. We often consider complementary sets $I \subseteq \{1, \dots, m\}$, $J = \{1, \dots, m\} \setminus I$ of indices. The notation A_I refers to the submatrix of A consisting of all column A_i such that $i \in I$. The equation $A = [A_I, A_J]$ means that A decomposes into submatrices A_I, A_J (although, strictly speaking, the equation holds only after the columns of $[A_I, A_J]$ are permuted such that they are ordered as in A). A similar convention is applied to vectors such that equations like $Ax = b$ can be expanded to

$$[A_I, A_J] \begin{pmatrix} x_I \\ x_J \end{pmatrix} = b \ .$$

Similarly, a matrix $Q \in \mathbb{R}^{m \times m}$ decomposes into four blocks $Q_{I,I}, Q_{I,J}, Q_{J,I}, Q_{J,J}$ such that an expression like $x^\top Q x$ can be expanded to

$$x^\top Q x = x_I^\top Q_{I,I} x_I + x_I^\top Q_{I,J} x_J + x_J^\top Q_{J,I} x_I + x_J^\top Q_{J,J} x_J \ .$$

If Q is symmetric (in particular, if Q is positive (semi-)definite), then $x_I^\top Q_{I,J} x_J = x_J^\top Q_{J,I} x_I$.

Let $\mathcal{P}$ denote an optimization problem that is given by a cost function $f(x)$ and a collection of constraints, where x denotes a collection of real-valued variables. As usual, a feasible solution for $\mathcal{P}$ is an assigment of values to the variables that satisfies all constraints. The feasibility region (consisting of all feasible solutions for $\mathcal{P}$) is denoted as $R(\mathcal{P})$. The smallest possible cost of a feasible solution is then given by

$$\mathrm{opt}(\mathcal{P}) = \min_{x \in R(\mathcal{P})} f(x) \ .$$

Writing "min" instead of "inf" is justified because we will deal only with problems $\mathcal{P}$ whose feasibility region is compact. In the remainder of the paper, we assume some familiarity with mathematical programming and matrix theory.

2.1 Convex Quadratic Programming Subject to Box Constraints

Throughout this paper,

$$f(x) = \frac{1}{2} x^\top Q x + w^\top x = \frac{1}{2} \sum_{i=1}^{m} \sum_{j=1}^{m} Q_{i,j} x_i x_j + \sum_{i=1}^{m} w_i x_i \tag{3}$$

denotes a convex cost function, where $Q \in \mathbb{R}^{m \times m}$ is a positive semi-definite matrix over the reals with the additional (somewhat technical) property that, for each $I \subseteq \{1, \ldots, m\}$ of size at most q, the submatrix $Q_{I,I}$ of Q is positive definite. Here, q denotes a (typically small) constant (which will later bound from above the size of the working set). Note that the technical condition for Q is satisfied if Q itself is positive definite. As the structure of the cost function has become clear by now, we move on and define our basic optimization problem $\mathcal{P}$:

$$\min_x f(x) \text{ s.t. } Ax = b, l \le x \le r \tag{4}$$

Here, $A \in \mathbb{R}^{k \times m}$, $b \in \mathbb{R}^k$, $l, r \in \mathbb{R}^m$, and $l \le x \le r$ is the short-notation for the "box constraints"

$$\forall i = 1, \ldots, m : l_i \le x_i \le r_i \ .$$

A few comments are in place:

- Any bounded[2] optimization problem with cost function $f(x)$ and linear equality- and inequality-constraints can be brought into the form (4) because we may convert the linear inequalities into linear equations by introducing non-negative slack variables. By the compactness of the feasibility region, we may also put a suitable upper bound on each slack variable such that the remaining linear inequalities take the form of box constraints.
- The technical assumption that we have put on matrix Q is slightly more restrictive than just assuming it is positive semi-definite. As far as the decomposition method and SVM applications are concerned, this assumption if often satisfied.[3]

[2] Here, "bounded" means that the feasibility region is compact (or can be made compact without changing the smallest possible cost).

[3] For some kernels like, for example, the RBF-kernel, it is certainly true; for other kernels it typically satisfied provided that q is sufficiently small. See also the discussion of this point in [17].

In order to illustrate the first comment, we convert problem (2) in a problem with box constraints by introducing the slack variable ξ:

$$\min_{x,\xi} \frac{1}{2} x^\top Qx \text{ s.t. } y^\top x = 0, \sum_{i=1}^{m} x_i - \xi = \nu, 0 \le \xi \le 1 \ , \ \forall i = 1, \dots, m : 0 \le x_i \le \frac{1}{m} \tag{5}$$

The optimal solutions for $\mathcal{P}$ can be characterized in terms of the gradient $\nabla f(x) = Qx + w$ as follows:

Lemma 1. *Let $\mathcal{P}$ denote the optimization problem that is induced by $A \in \mathbb{R}^{k \times m}$, $b \in \mathbb{R}^k$, and $l, r \in \mathbb{R}^m$ as described in (4) and let U denote the linear subspace of $\mathbb{R}^m$ that is spanned by the rows of matrix A. Then, x is optimal for $\mathcal{P}$ iff there exists $u \in U$ such that*

$$x_i \ne r_i \Rightarrow \nabla f(x)_i - u_i \ge 0 \text{ and } x_i \ne l_i \Rightarrow u_i - \nabla f(x)_i \ge 0 \ . \tag{6}$$

holds for $i = 1, \dots, m$.

Proof. It is well-known that x is optimal for $\mathcal{P}$ iff it satisfies the Karush-Kuhn-Tucker conditions. The latters are easily seen to be equivalent to the existence of $\beta \in \mathbb{R}^k$ such that the following holds for $i = 1, \dots, m$:

$$x_i \ne r_i \Rightarrow \nabla f(x)_i - A_i^\top \beta \ge 0 \text{ and } x_i \ne l_i \Rightarrow A_i^\top \beta - \nabla f(x)_i \ge 0 \ .$$

(Recall the convention that $A_i \in \mathbb{R}^k$ denotes the i'th column of A.) The lemma now follows from the observation that $A^\top \beta$ ranges over U when β ranges over $\mathbb{R}^k$. □

With each $x \in \mathbb{R}^m$, we associate the function

$$C(x) := \inf_{u \in U} \sum_{i=1}^{m} (x_i - l_i) \max\{0, \nabla f(x)_i - u_i\} + (r_i - x_i) \max\{0, u_i - \nabla f(x)_i\} \ , \tag{7}$$

whose properties are summarized in

Lemma 2. *$C(x)$ is a continuous function on $R(\mathcal{P})$. Moreover, for $x \in R(\mathcal{P})$, $C(x) \ge 0$ with equality iff x is optimal for $\mathcal{P}$.*

Proof. We first show that $C(x)$ is continuous. Obviously function

$$C(x, u) := \sum_{i=1}^{m} (x_i - l_i) \max\{0, \nabla f(x)_i - u_i\} + (r_i - x_i) \max\{0, u_i - \nabla f(x)_i\}$$

is continuous in x and u. Moreover, $C(x) = \inf_{u \in U} C(x, u)$. With each constant $B > 0$, we associate the compact region $U(B) := U \cap \{u \in \mathbb{R}^m | \ \|u\| \le B\}$. It is not hard to see that there exists a constant $B > 0$ such that $C(x) =$

$\inf_{u \in U(B)} C(x,u)$ holds for each $x \in R(\mathcal{P})$. By compactness, $C(x,u)$ is uniformly continuous on $R(\mathcal{P}) \times U(B)$. Thus, for all $x, x' \in R(\mathcal{P})$ and each $\epsilon > 0$, there exists $\delta > 0$ such that

$$\forall u \in U(B) : \|x' - x\| \le \delta \Rightarrow |C(x', u) - C(x, u)| \le \epsilon \ .$$

Since the latter statement implies that $|C(x') - C(x)| \le \epsilon$, we may conclude that $C(x)$ is continuous.
If x is a feasible solution for $\mathcal{P}$, then $l \le x \le r$, which clearly implies that $C(x) \ge 0$. Furthermore, $C(x) = 0$ iff there exists $u \in U$ such that (6) is satisfied. According to Lemma 1, this is true iff x optimally solves $\mathcal{P}$. □

The method of feasible directions by Zoutendijk [26] allows for another characterization of the optimal solutions for $\mathcal{P}$. To this end, we associate the following optimization problem $\mathcal{D}[x]$ with each $x \in R(\mathcal{P})$:

$$\min_d \nabla f(x)^\top d \text{ s.t. } Ad = \mathbf{0}, \forall i = 1, \ldots, m : -1 \le d_i \le 1 \wedge \begin{cases} x_i = l_i \Rightarrow d_i \ge 0 \\ x_i = r_i \Rightarrow d_i \le 0 \end{cases} \tag{8}$$

Intuitively, $\nabla f(x)^\top d < 0$ indicates that we can reduce the cost of the current solution x for $\mathcal{P}$ by moving it in direction d. More formally, the following holds:

Lemma 3 ([26,3]). $\mathrm{opt}(\mathcal{D}[x]) \le 0$ *with equality iff* x *is optimal for* $\mathcal{P}$.

2.2 Subproblems Induced by Working Sets

With a set $I \subseteq \{1, \ldots, m\}$, we will always associate its complement $J = \overline{I}$. Furthermore, we use the short-notation $R_I = \{x_I | \ x \in R\}$ for each $R \subseteq \mathbb{R}^m$.

For each $I \subseteq \{1, \ldots, m\}$ and each $x_J \in R(\mathcal{P})_J$, we denote by $\mathcal{P}_{I,x_J}$ the problem that results from $\mathcal{P}$ by leaving x_J unchanged and choosing x_I such as to minimize $f(x)$ subject to the constraints in $\mathcal{P}$. More formally, for cost function

$$f_{I,x_J}(x_I) = \frac{1}{2} x_I^\top Q_{I,I} x_I + (Q_{I,J} x_J + w_I)^\top x_I$$

(with gradient $\nabla f_{I,x_J}(x_I) = Q_{I,I} x_I + Q_{I,J} x_J + w_I$), problem $\mathcal{P}_{I,x_J}$ reads as follows:

$$\min_{x_I} f_{I,x_J}(x_I) \text{ s.t. } A_I x_I = b - A_J x_J, \ l_I \le x_I \le r_I$$

Note that this problem is of type (4) with $x_I, Q_{I,I}, Q_{I,J} x_J + w_I, A_I, b - A_J x_J, l_I, r_I$ substituted for x, Q, w, A, b, l, r, respectively. Note furthermore that x_I is a feasible solution for $\mathcal{P}_{I,x_J}$ iff $x \in \mathcal{P}$, i.e., iff x_I extends x_J to a feasible solution $x \in \mathcal{P}$. Recall that, according to our notational conventions, its feasibility region is written as $R(\mathcal{P}_{I,x_J})$.

2.3 The Decomposition Method

Let q be a constant that bounds from above the size of the working set. Let $(C_I(x))_{I \subseteq \{1,\dots,m\}}$ be a family of functions from $R(\mathcal{P})$ to $\mathbb{R}_0^+$. With each such family, we associate the following method for solving $\mathcal{P}$:

(1) Let x^0 be a feasible solution for $\mathcal{P}$ (arbitrarily chosen) and $s := 0$.
(2) Construct a working set $I^s \subseteq \{1,\dots,m\}$ that maximizes $c(I) := C_I(x^s)$ subject to $|I| \leq q$. If $c(I^s) = 0$, then return x^s and stop; otherwise set $J^s := \{1,\dots,m\} \setminus I^s$, find an optimal solution $x_{I^s}^{s+1}$ for $\mathcal{P}_{I^s,x_{J^s}^s}$, set

$$x_{J^s}^{s+1} := x_{J^s}^s,\ x^{s+1} := \begin{pmatrix} x_I^{s+1} \\ x_J^{s+1} \end{pmatrix},\ s := s+1$$

and goto (2).

We refer to this algorithm as the *decomposition method induced by* $(C_I(x))$. We will show in section 3 that it converges to an optimal solution for $\mathcal{P}$ if the following conditions hold:

(C1) For each $I \subseteq \{1,\dots,m\}$ such that $|I| \leq q$, $C_I(x)$ is continuous on $R(\mathcal{P})$.
(C2) If $|I| \leq q$ and x_I is an optimal solution for $\mathcal{P}_{I,x_J}$, then $C_I\begin{pmatrix} x_I \\ x_J \end{pmatrix} = 0$.
(C3) If x is not an optimal solution for $\mathcal{P}$, then there exists an $I \subseteq \{1,\dots,m\}$ such that $|I| \leq q$ and $C_I(x) > 0$.

If these conditions are satisfied, we call the family $(C_I(x))$ a *q-sparse witness of suboptimality*. In section 4, we will present such a family of functions provided that $q \geq k+1$.

A few comments are in place here. x^{s+1} is always a feasible solution for $\mathcal{P}$. Moreover, $x_{I^s}^{s+1}$ is (by construction) an optimal solution for $\mathcal{P}_{I^s,x_J^s}$. Thus,

$$C_{I^s}(x^{s+1}) = 0 \tag{9}$$

according to (C2). If x^s is (accidentally) an optimal solution for $\mathcal{P}$, then it is (à-fortiori) an optimal solution for each subproblem $\mathcal{P}_{I,x_J}$ and, again according to (C2), the decomposition method will reach the stop-condition and return x^s. If x^s is not optimal for $\mathcal{P}$, then (C3) makes sure that there exists a working set I of size at most q such that $C_I(x^s) > 0$. Thus, the working set I^s actually constructed by the decomposition method satisfies

$$C_{I^s}(x^s) > 0\ , \tag{10}$$

and the method cannot become stuck at a suboptimal solution.

We assume in the sequel that the sequence x^s evolves as described above. Note that $f(x^s)$ is decreasing with s (simply because $x_{I^s}^s$ is a feasible solution for $\mathcal{P}_{I^s,x_{J^s}^s}$). Thus, $f(x^s)$ will converge to a limit even if x^s does not converge to a limit point. However, since the feasibility region for $\mathcal{P}$ is compact, there must exist a subsequence $(x^s)_{s \in S}$ that converges to a (feasible!) limit point, say x^∞. Clearly, $f(x^\infty) = \lim_{s \to \infty} f(x^s)$. It remains to show that x^∞ is an optimal solution.

3 Analysis of the Decomposition Method

This section is devoted to the proof of convergence. The proof will proceed by assuming, for sake of contradiction, that x^∞ is not an optimal solution for $\mathcal{P}$. From condition (C3) and from a continuity argument, we will be able to conclude that x^∞ is not even optimal for subproblem $\mathcal{P}_{I^s, x^s_{J^s}}$ if $s \in S$ is chosen sufficiently large. Since x^{s+1} is an optimal solution for this subproblem (by the definition of the decomposition method), we would now be close to a contradiction if the continuity argument also applied to $s+1$. Here, however, we bomb into a difficulty since $s+1$ does not necessarily belong to S. Thus, although sequence $(x^s)_{s \in S}$ approaches x^∞ when n approaches infinity, sequence $(x^{s+1})_{s \in S}$ might perhaps behave differently? It turns out, however, that this is not the case. The main argument against this hypothetical possibility will be that the cost reduction per iteration of the decomposition method is proportional to the square of the distance between x^s and x^{s+1}. The following subsections flesh out this general idea.

3.1 Cost Reduction per Iteration

How big is the cost reduction when we pass from x^s to x^{s+1}? Here is an answer to this question:

Lemma 4. *Let $f(x)$ be the cost function of $\mathcal{P}$ as given by (3). Let*

$$\sigma := \min_{I \subseteq \{1,\ldots,m\}:|I| \leq q} \mathrm{eig}(Q_{I,I}) > 0 \ ,$$

where eig(·) *denotes the smallest eigenvalue of a matrix.*[4] *With these notations, the following holds:*

$$f(x^{s+1}) - f(x^s) \leq -\frac{\sigma}{2} \|x^{s+1} - x^s\|^2 \ .$$

Proof. Since f is a quadratic function of the form (3), Taylor-expansion around x^{s+1} yields

$$f(x^s) = f(x^{s+1}) + \nabla f(x^{s+1})^\top (x^s - x^{s+1}) + \frac{1}{2}(x^s - x^{s+1})^\top Q(x^s - x^{s+1}) \ . \tag{11}$$

Recall that x^{s+1} minimizes $f(x)$ subject to the constraints $Ax = b$, $l \leq x \leq r$, and $x^{s+1}_{J^s} = x^s_{J^s}$. Since these constraints define a convex region containing x^s and x^{s+1}, we may conclude that $f(x^{s+1}) = \min_{x \in L} f(x)$ where L denotes the line segment between x^s and x^{s+1}. Thus, the gradient at x^{s+1} in direction to x^s is ascending, i.e.,

$$\nabla f(x^{s+1})^\top (x^s - x^{s+1}) \geq 0 \ . \tag{12}$$

[4] Note that the technical property that we have put on Q in section 2.1 makes sure that σ is strictly positive.

Note furthermore that

$$(x^s - x^{s+1})^\top Q(x^s - x^{s+1}) \geq \sigma \|x^s - x^{s+1}\|^2 \tag{13}$$

is an immediate consequence of the Courant-Fischer Minimax Theorem [8]. From (11), (12), and (13), the lemma follows. □

We briefly note that Lin [17] has shown a similar lemma for the special optimization problem (1). Although our lemma is more general, the proof found in [17] is much more complicated.

3.2 Facts Being Valid Asymptotically

Lemma 5. *For each $\delta > 0$, there exists $s_0 \geq 1$ such that*

$$\|x^s - x^\infty\| \leq \frac{\delta}{2} \text{ , } \|x^{s+1} - x^s\| \leq \frac{\delta}{2} \textit{ and } \|x^{s+1} - x^\infty\| \leq \delta \text{ .}$$

holds for all $s \in S$ provided that $s \geq s_0$.[5]

Proof. Recall that $(f(x^s))_{s \geq 1}$ is a monotonously decreasing sequence that approaches $f(\alpha^\infty)$ when s tends to infinity. Thus, there exists s'_0 such that

$$0 < f(x^s) - f(x^{s+1}) \leq f(x^s) - f(x^\infty) \leq \frac{\sigma\delta^2}{8}$$

holds for all $s \geq s'_0$. According to Lemma 4,

$$\|x^{s+1} - x^s\| \leq \sqrt{\frac{2(f(x^s) - f(x^{s+1}))}{\sigma}} \text{ .}$$

Thus

$$\|x^{s+1} - x^s\| \leq \frac{\delta}{2}$$

holds for all $s \geq s'_0$. Since $(x^s)_{s \in S}$ converges to x^∞, there exists s''_0 such that

$$\|x^s - x^\infty\| \leq \frac{\delta}{2}$$

holds for all $s \in S$, $s \geq s''_0$. Setting $s_0 = \max\{s'_0, s''_0\}$, we obtain

$$\|x^{s+1} - x^s\| \leq \frac{\delta}{2} \text{ and } \|x^s - x^\infty\| \leq \frac{\delta}{2}$$

for all $s \in S$, $s \geq s_0$. This implies that $\|x^{s+1} - x^\infty\| \leq \delta$ and completes the proof of the lemma. □

[5] Inequality $\|x^{s+1} - x^\infty\| \leq \delta$, which is immediate from the preceding two inequalities, has been included for ease of later reference.

Corollary 1. *If $(C_I(x))$ satisfies condition (C1), then, for each $\epsilon > 0$, there exists $s_0 \geq 1$ such that*

$$|C_I(x^\infty) - C_I(x^s)| < \epsilon \tag{14}$$

$$|C_I(x^\infty) - C_I(x^{s+1})| < \epsilon \tag{15}$$

holds for each working set $I \subseteq \{1, \ldots, m\}$ of size at most q and for all $s \in S$ provided that $s \geq s_0$.

Proof. The corollary easily follows from Lemma 5, the fact that there are only finitely many sets $I \subseteq \{1, \ldots, m\}$ of size at most q, and condition (C1) stating that each individual function $C_I(x)$ is continuous. □

3.3 The Main Theorem

Theorem 1. *Assume that $(C_I(x))$ satisfies conditions (C1),(C2),(C3), i.e., it is a q-sparse witness of suboptimality. Let x^s be a sequence of legal solutions for $\mathcal{P}$ that is produced by the decomposition method induced by $(C_I(x))$ and let $(x^s)_{s \in S}$ be a converging subsequence. Then, the limit point x^∞ of $(x^s)_{s \in S}$ is an optimal solution for $\mathcal{P}$.*

Proof. Assume for sake of contradiction that x^∞ is not an optimal solution for $\mathcal{P}$. According to (C3), there exists a working set $I \subseteq \{1, \ldots, m\}$ such that $|I| \leq q$ and

$$\epsilon_0 := C_I(x^\infty) > 0 \ .$$

In the sequel, we will apply Corollary 1 three times with $\epsilon = \epsilon_0/3$, respectively. Assume that $s \in S$ is sufficiently large in the sense of Corollary 1 such that, according to (14), the following holds:

$$C_I(x^s) > \frac{2\epsilon_0}{3} \ .$$

Thus, the working set I^s returned by the decomposition method in iteration $s + 1$ satisfies

$$C_{I^s}(x^s) > \frac{2\epsilon_0}{3} \ .$$

Another application of (14) leads to

$$C_{I^s}(x^\infty) > \frac{\epsilon_0}{3} \ .$$

From (15), we get

$$C_{I^s}(x^{s+1}) > 0 \ .$$

Since x^{s+1} is an optimal solution for $\mathcal{P}_{I^s, x^s_J}$, we may however infer from (9) that

$$C_{I^s}(x^{s+1}) = 0 \ .$$

We arrived at a a contradiction. □

4 A Sparse Witness of Sub-optimality

In this section, we present a concrete family $(C_I(x))$ of functions that satisfies the conditions (C1),(C2),(C3) needed for our proof of convergence from section 3. We will define $C_I(x)$ such that it plays the same role for $\mathcal{P}_{I,x_J}$ that the function $C(x)$ (defined in (7)) has played for $\mathcal{P}$. More formally, let U_I denote the subspace spanned by the rows of A_I, and define $C_I(x)$ to be equal to

$$\inf_{u \in U_I} \sum_{i \in I} (x_i - l_i) \max\{0, \nabla f_{I,x_J}(x_I)_i - u_i\} + (r_i - x_i) \max\{0, u_i - \nabla f_{I,x_J}(x_I)_i\} \ .$$

In what follows, we use the notations $C_I(x)$ and $C_{I,x_J}(x_I)$ interchangeably. The former notation stresses that $C_I(x)$ is viewed as a function of all components of x, whereas the latter notation stresses the relation between this function and the subproblem $\mathcal{P}_{I,x_J}$ that is explained in Corollary 2 below.

Recall the optimization problem $\mathcal{D}[x]$ from (8). Let $\mathcal{D}_{I,x_J}[x_I]$ be the optimization problem given by

$$\min_{d_I} \nabla f_{I,x_J}(x_I)^\top d_I \text{ s.t. } A_I d_I = \mathbf{0}, \forall i \in I : -1 \le d_i \le 1 \wedge \begin{cases} x_i = l_i \Rightarrow d_i \ge 0 \\ x_i = r_i \Rightarrow d_i \le 0 \end{cases} .$$

Now, Lemmas 2 and 3 applied to the subproblem $\mathcal{P}_{I,x_J}$ induced by I and x_J read as follows:

Corollary 2. *1. $C_{I,x_J}(x_I)$ is a continuous function on $R(\mathcal{P}_{I,x_J})$. Moreover, $C_{I,x_J}(x_I) \ge 0$ with equality iff x_I is optimal for $\mathcal{P}_{I,x_J}$.*
2. $\mathrm{opt}(\mathcal{D}_{I,x_J}[x_I]) \le 0$ with equality iff x_I is optimal for $\mathcal{P}_{I,x_J}$.

The first statement in Corollary 2 can clearly be strengthened:

Remark 1. $C_I(x) = C_{I,x_J}(x_I)$ viewed as a function in $x = \begin{pmatrix} x_I \\ x_J \end{pmatrix}$ is continuous on $R(\mathcal{P})$.

This already settles conditions (C1) and (C2). Condition (C3) is settled by

Lemma 6. *If x is a feasible solution for $\mathcal{P}$ that is not optimal, then there exists a working set $I \subseteq \{1, \ldots, m\}$ such that $|I| \le k+1$ and $\mathrm{opt}(\mathcal{D}_{I,x_J}[x_I]) < 0$.*

Proof. In order to facilitate the proof, we first introduce two slight modifications of problem $\mathcal{D}[x]$. Let $\mathcal{D}'[x]$ be the problem obtained from $\mathcal{D}[x]$ by substituting the single constraint

$$\sum_{i=1}^{m} |d_i| = 1$$

for the m constraints

$$\forall i = 1, \ldots, m : -1 \le d_i \le 1 \ .$$

Problems $\mathcal{D}[x]$ and $\mathcal{D}'[x]$ exhibit the following relationship:

- If d is a feasible solution for $\mathcal{D}[x]$ of cost c, then $d/\sum_{i=1}^{m}|d_i|$ is a feasible solution for $\mathcal{D}'[x]$ of cost $c/\sum_{i=1}^{m}|d_i|$.
- Clearly, each feasible solution for $\mathcal{D}'[x]$ is also a feasible solution for $\mathcal{D}[x]$.

Thus, there is a feasible solution of negative cost for $\mathcal{D}[x]$ iff there is one for $\mathcal{D}'[x]$. We may therefore conclude that $\mathrm{opt}(\mathcal{D}'[x]) < 0$ iff $\mathrm{opt}(\mathcal{D}[x]) < 0$.
It will still be more convenient to consider another modification of $\mathcal{D}[x]$ that we denote as $\mathcal{D}''[x]$ in the sequel:

$$\min_{d^+,d^-} \begin{pmatrix} \nabla f(x) \\ -\nabla f(x) \end{pmatrix}^\top \begin{pmatrix} d^+ \\ d^- \end{pmatrix}$$

subject to

$$\forall i = 1,\ldots,m : x_i = l_i \Rightarrow d_i^- = 0 \ , \ x_i = r_i \Rightarrow d_i^+ = 0 \tag{16}$$

$$[A, -A] \begin{pmatrix} d^+ \\ d^- \end{pmatrix} = \mathbf{0} \tag{17}$$

$$\sum_{i=1}^{m} d_i^+ + d_i^- = 1 \tag{18}$$

$$d^+, d^- \geq \mathbf{0} \tag{19}$$

$\mathcal{D}'[x]$ and $\mathcal{D}''[x]$ are easily seen to be equivalent by making use of the relation $d = d^+ - d^-$. Thus, $\mathrm{opt}(\mathcal{D}''[x]) < 0$ iff $\mathrm{opt}(\mathcal{D}'[x]) < 0$. What is the advantage of dealing with $\mathcal{D}''[x]$ instead of $\mathcal{D}[x]$? The answer is that $\mathcal{D}''[x]$ is a linear program in canonical form with very few equations. To see this note first that we need not count the equations in (16) since the variables that are set to zero there can simply be eliminated (thereby passing to a lower-dimensional problem). Thus, there are only $k+1$ equations left in (17) and (18). It follows that each basic feasible solution for $\mathcal{D}''[x]$ has has at most $k+1$ non-zero components.
We are now prepared to prove the lemma. Assume that x is a feasible but suboptimal solution of $\mathcal{P}$. We may conclude from Lemma 3 that $\mathrm{opt}(\mathcal{D}[x]) < 0$ and, therefore, $\mathrm{opt}(\mathcal{D}''[x]) < 0$. If d^+, d^- represent the optimal basic feasible solution for $\mathcal{D}''[x]$ (with at most $k+1$ non-zero components and negative cost), we obtain the feasible solution $d = d^+ - d^-$ for $\mathcal{D}'[x]$ that also has at most $k+1$ non-zero components and (the same) negative cost. Consider working set $I = \{i \in \{1,\ldots,m\} | \ d_i \neq 0\}$. Clearly, d is is also a feasible solution for $\mathcal{D}_{I,x_J}[x_I]$ such that $\nabla f(x)_I^\top d_I = \nabla f(x)^\top d < 0$. Thus, $\mathrm{opt}(\mathcal{D}_{I,x_J}[x_I]) < 0$, which completes the proof. □

Combining Lemma 6 with Corollary 2, we get

Corollary 3. *If x is a feasible but non-optimal solution for $\mathcal{P}$, then there exists a working set I of size at most $k+1$ such that x is not optimal for $\mathcal{P}_{I,x_J}$ and $C_I(x) = C_{I,x_J}(x_I) > 0$.*

5 Final Remarks and Open Problems

Chang, Hsu, and Lin prove the convergence for a decomposition method that is tailored to the optimization problem (1) except that the cost function may be an arbitrary continuously differentiable function [5]. They apply techniques of "projected gradients". Although their analysis is tailored to problem (1), we would like to raise the question whether the techniques of projected gradients can be used to extend our results to a wider class of cost functions.

The function $C(x)$ defined in (7) is easily seen to bound $f(x) - f(x^\infty)$ from above. In this sense it measures (an upper bound on) the current distance from optimum. Schölkopf and Smola have proposed to select the working set I whose indices point to the (at most q) largest terms in $C(x)$ [23]. This policy for working set selection looks similar to ours (but the policies are, in general, not identical). The question whether the (somewhat simpler) policy proposed by Schölkopf and Smola makes sequence x^s converging to an optimal limit point remains open (although we cannot rule out that both policies actually coincide for the specific problems resulting from SVM applications).

The most challenging task for future research is gaining a deeper understanding of the trade-off between the following three goals:

- efficiency of working set selection
- fast convergence to optimum
- generality of the arguments

It would be nice to lift the decomposition method from SVM applications to a wider class of optimization problems without much loss of efficiency or speed of convergence.

Acknowledgments. Thanks to Dietrich Braess for pointing us to a simplification in the proof of Lemma 4. Thanks to the anonymous referees for their comments and suggestions and for drawing our attention to the random sampling technique.

References

1. José L. Balcázar, Yang Dai, and Osamu Watanabe. Provably fast trainig algorithms for support vector machines. In *Proceedings of the 1st International Conference on Data Mining*, pages 43–50, 2001.

2. José L. Balcázar, Yang Dai, and Osamu Watanabe. A random sampling technique for training support vector machines. In *Proceedings of the 12th International Conference on Algorithmic Learning Theory*, pages 119–134. Springer Verlag, 2001.
3. Mokhtar S. Bazaraa, Hanif D. Sherali, and C. M. Shetty. *Nonlinear Programming: Theory and Algorithms*. John Wiley & Sons, 1993.
4. Bernhard E. Boser, Isabelle M. Guyon, and Vladimir N. Vapnik. A training algorithm for optimal margin classifiers. In *Proceedings of the 5th Annual ACM Workshop on Computational Learning Theory*, pages 144–152. ACM Press, 1992.
5. Chih-Chung Chang, Chih-Wei Hsu, and Chih-Jen Lin. The analysis of decomposition methods for support vector machines. *IEEE Transactions on Neural Networks*, 11(4):248–250, 2000.
6. Nello Christianini and John Shawe-Taylor. *An Introduction to Support Vector Machines*. Cambridge University Press, 2000.
7. Bernd Gärtner and Emo Welzl. A simple sampling lemma: Analysis and applications in geometric optimization. *Discrete & Computational Geometry*, 25(4):569–590, 2001.
8. Gene H. Golub and Charles F. Van Loan. *Matrix Computations*. The John Hopkins University Press, third edition, 1996.
9. Chih-Wei Hsu and Chih-Jen Lin. A simple decomposition method for support vector machines. *Machine Learning*, 46(1–3):291–314, 2002.
10. Don Hush and Clint Scovel. Polynomial-time decomposition algorithms for support vector machines. *Machine Learning*, 51:51–71, 2003.
11. Thorsten Joachims. Making large scale SVM learning practical. In Bernhard Schölkopf, Christopher J. C. Burges, and Alexander J. Smola, editors, *Advances in Kernel Methods—Support Vector Learning*. MIT Press, 1998.
12. S. S. Keerthi and E. G. Gilbert. Convergence of a generalized SMO algorithm for SVM classifier design. *Machine Learning*, 46:351–360, 2002.
13. S. S. Keerthi, S. Shevade, C. Bhattacharyya, and K. Murthy. Improvements to SMO algorithm for SVM regression. *IEEE Transactions on Neural Networks*, 11(5):1188–1193, 2000.
14. S. S. Keerthi, S. Shevade, C. Bhattacharyya, and K. Murthy. Improvements to Platt's SMO algorithm for SVM classifier design. *Neural Computation*, 13:637–649, 2001.
15. P. Laskov. An improved decomposition algorithm for regression support vector machines. *Machine Learning*, 46:315–350, 2002.
16. S.-P. Liao, H.-T. Lin, and Chih-Jen Lin. A note on the decomposition methods for support vector regression. *Neural Computation*, 14:1267–1281, 2002.
17. Chih-Jen Lin. On the convergence of the decomposition method for support vector machines. *IEEE Transactions on Neural Networks*, 12:1288–1298, 2001.
18. Chih-Jen Lin. Asymptotic convergence of an SMO algorithm without any assumptions. *IEEE Transactions on Neural Networks*, 13:248–250, 2002.
19. Chih-Jen Lin. A formal analysis of stopping criteria of decomposition methods for support vector machines. *IEEE Transactions on Neural Networks*, 13:1045–1052, 2002.
20. E. Osuna, R. Freund, and F.Girosi. Training support vector machines: an application to face detection. In *Proceedings of CVPS'97*, 1997.
21. J. C. Platt. Fast training of support vector machines using sequential minimal optimization. In Bernhard Schölkopf, Christopher J. C. Burges, and Alexander J. Smola, editors, *Advances in Kernel Methods—Support Vector Learning*. MIT Press, 1998.

22. C. Saunders, M. O. Stitson, J. Weston, L. Bottou, Bernhard Schölkopf, and Alexander J. Smola. Support vector machine reference manual. Technical Report CSD-TR-98-03, Royal Holloway, University of London, Egham, UK, 1998.
23. Bernhard Schölkopf and Alexander J. Smola. *Learning with Kernels.* MIT Press, 2002.
24. Bernhard Schölkopf, Alexander J. Smola, Robert C. Williamson, and Peter L. Bartlett. New support vector algorithms. *Neural Computation*, 12:1207–1245, 2000.
25. Vladimir Vapnik. *Statistical Learning Theory.* Wiley Series on Adaptive and Learning Systems for Signal Processing, Communications, and Control. John Wiley & Sons, 1998.
26. G. Zoutendijk. *Methods of Feasible Directions.* Elsevier Publishing Company, 1960.

Oracle Bounds and Exact Algorithm for Dyadic Classification Trees

Gilles Blanchard[1*], Christin Schäfer[1**], and Yves Rozenholc[2]

[1] Fraunhofer–Institute FIRST, Kekuléstr. 7, 12489 Berlin, Germany,
{blanchar,christin}@first.fhg.de,
[2] Laboratoire de Probabilités et Modèles aléatoires,
Université Pierre et Marie Curie, BC 188, 75252 Paris Cedex 05, France,
rozen@math.jussieu.fr

Abstract. This paper introduces a new method using dyadic decision trees for estimating a classification or a regression function in a multiclass classification problem. The estimator is based on model selection by penalized empirical loss minimization. Our work consists in two complementary parts: first, a theoretical analysis of the method leads to deriving oracle-type inequalities for three different possible loss functions. Secondly, we present an algorithm able to compute the estimator in an exact way.

1 General Setup

1.1 Introduction

In this paper we introduce a new method using dyadic decision trees for estimating a classification or a regression function in a multiclass classification problem. The two main focuses of our work are a theoretical study of the statistical properties of the estimator, and an exact algorithm used to compute it.

The theoretical part (section 2) is centered around the convergence properties of piecewise constant estimators on abstract partition models (generalized histograms) for estimating either a classification function or the conditional probability distribution (cpd) $P(Y|X)$ for a classification problem. A suitable partition is selected by a penalized minimum empirical loss method and we derive oracle inequalities for different possible loss functions: for classification, we use the 0-1 loss; for cpd estimation, we consider the minus-log loss, and the square error loss. These general results are then applied to dyadic decision trees. In section 3, we present an algorithm able to compute in an exact way the solution of the minimization problem that defines the estimator in this case.

* Supported by a grant of the Humboldt Foundation.

** This research was partly supported through grants of the *Bundesministerium für Bildung und Forschung* FKZ 01–BB02A and FKZ 01–SC40A.

J. Shawe-Taylor and Y. Singer (Eds.): COLT 2004, LNAI 3120, pp. 378–392, 2004.

1.2 Related Work and Novelty of Our Approach

The oracle-style bounds presented here for generalized histograms for multiclass problems are novel up to our knowledge. Our analysis relies heavily on [1] which contains the fundamental tools used to prove Theorems 1-3. For classification, Theorem 1 presents a bound for a penalty which is *not* inverse square-root in the sample size (as is the case for example in classical VC theory for *consistent* bounds, i.e. bounds that show convergence to the Bayes classifier of a SRM procedure when sample size grows to infinity) but inverse linear, thus of strictly lower order. This holds under an identifiability assumption of the maximum class, akin to Tsybakov's condition (see [2] and [3]). For cpd estimation, result of Theorem 3 seems entirely novel in that it states an oracle inequality with the Kullback-Leibler (K-L) divergence on both sides. In contrast, related results in [4,5] for density estimation had the Hellinger distance on the left-hand side. Dyadic trees for density estimation have also been recently studied in [6] with a result for convergence in L^2.

Traditional CART-type algorithms [7] adopt a similar penalized loss approach, but do not solve exactly the minimization problem. Instead, they grow a large tree in a greedy way, and prune it afterwards. Some statistical properties of this pruning procedure have been studied in [8]. More recently, an exact algorithm for dyadic trees and related theoretical analysis for classification loss has been proposed in [9,10]. It differs fundamentally from the algorithm presented here in that the directions of the splits are fixed in advance in the latter work, so that the procedure essentially reduces to a pruning. It is also different in that the authors do not make any identifiability assumption and therefore use a square-root type penalty (see discussion in section 2.3).

On the algorithmic side, the novelty of our work resides on the fact that we are able to treat the case of arbitrary direction choice for the splits in the tree. This allows for a much increased adaptivity of the estimators to the problem as compared to a fixed-directions architecture, particularly if the target function is very anisotropic, e.g. if there are irrelevant input features.

1.3 Goals

We consider a multiclass classification problem modeled by a couple of variables $(X, Y) \in \mathcal{X} \times \mathcal{Y}$ with $\mathcal{X} = [0,1]^d$ and a finite class set $\mathcal{Y} = \{1, \ldots, t\}$. We assume that we observe a training sample $(X_i, Y_i)_{i=1,\ldots,n}$ of size n, drawn i.i.d. from some unknown probability $P(X, Y)$. We are interested in estimating either a classification function or the cpd $P(Y|X)$. Estimation of the cpd can be of practical interest of its own or can be used to form a derived classifier by "plug-in". It is generally argued that such plug-in estimates can be suboptimal and that one should directly try to estimate the classifier if it is the final aim (see [11]). However, even if classification is the goal, there is also some important added value in estimating $P(Y|X)$:

- it gives more information to the user than the classification function, allowing for a finer appreciation of ambiguous cases;

– it allows to deal with cases where the classification loss is not the same for all classes. In particular, it is more adapted when performance is measured by a ROC curve.

To qualitatively measure the fit of a function f to a data point (X, Y), a loss function $\ell(f, X, Y) \in \mathbb{R}$ is used. The goal is to be as close as possible to the function f^* minimizing the average loss:

$$f^* = \operatorname*{Arg\,Min}_{f \in \mathcal{F}} E\left[\ell(f, X, Y)\right],$$

where the minimum is taken over some suitable subset $\mathcal{F}$ of all measurable functions. We consider several possible loss functions, this will be detailed in section 1.6.

If a function $\widehat{f}$ is selected by some method using the training sample, it is coherent to measure its closeness to f^* by the means of its excess (average) loss (also called *risk*):

$$L(\ell, \widehat{f}, f^*) = E\left[\ell(\widehat{f}, X, Y)\right] - E\left[\ell(f^*, X, Y)\right];$$

our theoretical study is focused on this quantity.

1.4 Bin Estimation and Model Selection

We focus on bin estimation, i.e. the estimation of the target function using a piecewise constant function with a finite number of pieces, which can be seen as a generalized histogram. Such a piecewise constant function f is therefore characterized by a finite measurable partition $\mathcal{B}$ of the input space $\mathcal{X}$ – each piece of the partition will hereafter be called a bin – and by the values $f_{b,y}$ taken on the bins for $b \in \mathcal{B}, y \in \mathcal{Y}$:

$$f(x, y) = \sum_{b \in \mathcal{B}} \mathbb{I}_{\{x \in b\}} f_{b,y}. \tag{1}$$

Once a partition is fixed, it is natural to estimate the parameters $f_{b,y}$ using the training sample points which are present in the bin: we therefore define the following counters for all $b \in \mathcal{B}, y \in \mathcal{Y}$:

$$N_{b,y} = \sum_{i=1}^{n} \mathbb{I}_{\{X_i \in b; Y_i = y\}} \text{ and } N_b = \sum_{i=1}^{n} \mathbb{I}_{\{X_i \in b\}} = \sum_{y \in \mathcal{Y}} N_{b,y}.$$

Of course, the crucial problem here is the choice of a suitable partition, which is a problem of *model selection*. Hereafter, we identify a model with a partition: an abstract model will be denoted by m, and the associated partition by $\mathcal{B}_m$; $|m|$ denotes the number of pieces in $\mathcal{B}_m$. The set of piecewise constant real functions on bins of $\mathcal{B}_m$ (i.e. of the form (1)) will be denoted $\mathcal{G}_m$. Similarly, the set of classification functions which are piecewise constant on $\mathcal{B}_m$ will be denoted $\mathcal{C}_m$. Finally, the set of piecewise constant densities on $\mathcal{B}_m$ will be denoted $\mathcal{F}_m$:

$$\mathcal{F}_m = \left\{ f \in \mathcal{G}_m \,\middle|\, \forall x \in \mathcal{X}, \ \sum_{y} f(x, y) = 1 \right\}.$$

1.5 Dyadic Decisions Trees

Our goal is to consider specific partition models generated by dyadic decision trees. A dyadic decision tree is a binary tree structure T such that each internal node of T is "colored" with an element of $\{1, \dots, d\}$ (recall d is the dimension of $\mathcal{X} = [0,1]^d$). To each node (internal or terminal) of T is then associated a certain bin obtained by recursively splitting $[0,1]^d$ in half along the axes, according the colors at the internal nodes of T. This is defined formally in the following way:

1. To the root of T is associated $[0,1]^d$.

2. Suppose s is an interal node of T, and that a bin of the form $b(s) = \prod_{j=1}^d I_j$ is associated to s, where the (I_j) are dyadic intervals on the different axes of $\mathcal{X}$. Let k_s be the color of s, then the bins associated to the right and left children nodes r_s, ℓ_s of s are obtained by cutting $b(s)$ at its midpoint perpendicular to axis k_s; in other words, $b(r_s)$ is obtained by replacing in the product defining $b(s)$ interval I_{k_s} by its right half-interval, and correspondingly for $b(\ell_s)$.

Finally, the partition model generated by T is the set of bins attached to the terminal nodes (leaves) of T.

1.6 Loss Functions

We investigate three possible loss functions. For classification problems, we consider the set of classifier functions $\mathcal{F}_{class.} = \{f : \mathcal{X} \to \mathcal{Y}\}$ and the 0-1 loss:

$$\ell_{class.}(f, X, Y) = \mathbb{I}_{\{f(X) \neq Y\}}. \tag{2}$$

The corresponding minimizer $f^*_{class.}$ of the average loss among all functions from $\mathcal{X}$ to Y is given by the *Bayes classifier* $f^*_{class.}(x) = \operatorname*{Arg\,Max}_{y \in \mathcal{Y}} P(Y = y|X = x)$ (see e.g. [11]).

For cpd estimation, we consider the set $\mathcal{F}_{cpd}$ of functions which are conditional probabilities of Y given X, i.e. functions $\mathcal{X} \times \mathcal{Y} \to \mathbb{R}_+$ which are measurable and satisfy $\sum_{y \in \mathcal{Y}} f(x, y) = 1$ for all $x \in \mathcal{X}$. In this case we use one of two possible loss functions: the minus-log loss

$$\ell_{log}(f, X, Y) = -\log(f(X, Y)), \tag{3}$$

(which can possibly take the value $+\infty$) and the square loss

$$\ell_{sq}(f, X, Y) = (1 - f(X, Y))^2 + \sum_{j \neq Y} f(X, j)^2 = \left\| f(X, \cdot) - \overline{Y} \right\|_t^2, \tag{4}$$

where $\|\cdot\|_t$ is the standard Euclidian norm in $\mathbb{R}^t$ and $\overline{Y}$ is the Y-th canonical base vector of $\mathbb{R}^t$. It is easy to check that the function f^*_{cpd} minimizing the average losses $E\ell_{log}(f, X, Y)$ and $E\ell_{sq}(f, X, Y)$ over $\mathcal{F}_{cpd}$ is indeed $f^*_{cpd}(x, y) = P(Y = y|X = x)$. The corresponding excess losses from f to f^*_{cpd} are then given, respectively, by the average K-L divergence given X:

$$L(\ell_{log}, f, f^*_{cpd}) = E_P \left[\log \left(\frac{P(Y|X)}{f(X, Y)} \right) \right] \doteq KL(P, f|X), \tag{5}$$

and the averaged squared euclidian distance in $\mathbb{R}^t$:

$$L(\ell_{sq}, f, f^*_{cpd}) = E_{P(X)}\left[\|f(X,\cdot) - P(Y=\cdot|X)\|_t^2\right] \doteq \left\|f - f^*_{cpd}\right\|_{t,2}^2. \quad (6)$$

Finally, we will make use of the following additional notation: $\ell(f)$ is a short-cut for $\ell(f,\cdot,\cdot)$ as a function of X and Y; we denote the expectation of a function f with respect to P either by $E_P[f]$ or Pf; P_n denotes the empirical distribution associated to the sample.

2 Theoretical Results for the Bin Estimators

2.1 Fixed Model m

First let us assume that some fixed model m is chosen. We now define an estimator associated to this model and depending on the loss function used. The classical *empirical risk minimization* method consists in considering the empirical (or training) loss

$$P_n\ell(f) = \frac{1}{n}\sum_{i=1}^{n}\ell(f, X_i, Y_i), \quad (7)$$

and selecting the function attaining the minimum of this empirical loss over the set of functions $\mathcal{F}_m$ in the model. When using the classification loss, this gives rise to the classifier minimizing the training error:

$$\widetilde{f}_m(x) = \operatorname*{Arg\,Max}_{y\in Y} \sum_{b\in\mathcal{B}_m} N_{b,y}\mathbb{I}_{\{x\in b\}}; \quad (8)$$

when using the square loss or the minus-log loss (3), this gives rise to

$$\widehat{f}_m(x,y) = \sum_{b\in\mathcal{B}_m}\frac{N_{b,y}}{N_b}\mathbb{I}_{\{x\in b\}}. \quad (9)$$

In case of an undefinite ratio $0/0$ in the formula above, one can choose arbitrary values for this bin, say $1/t$ for all classes.

In the case of the minus-log loss, notice that the loss has infinite average whenever there is a bin b such that $N_{b,y} = 0$ but $P(Y = y|X \in b) \neq 0$. This motivates to consider the following slightly modified estimator which bypasses this problem:

$$\widehat{f}_m^{\rho} = (1 - t\rho)\widehat{f}_m + \rho, \quad (10)$$

where ρ is some small positive constant. Typically, we can choose ρ of order $\mathcal{O}(n^{-k})$ (see discussion after Theorem 3) for some arbitrary but fixed k (to fix ideas, say $k = 3$), so that the two functions will be very close in all cases.

2.2 Model Selection via Penalization

Now we address the problem of choosing a model m. A common approach is to use a penalized empirical loss criterion, namely selecting the model $\widehat{m}$ such that

$$\widehat{m} = \operatorname*{Arg\,Min}_{m \in \mathcal{M}} \left\{ P_n \ell(\widehat{f}_m^{\rho}) + \mathrm{pen}(m) \right\}, \tag{11}$$

where pen is a suitable penalization function. For the standard CART algorithm, the penalization is of order $\alpha|m|$. The goal of the theoretical study to come is to justify that penalties of this order with estimators defined by (11) lead to oracle-type bounds for the respective excess losses. Note that we must assume that the *exact* minimization of (11) is found, or at least with a known error margin, which typically is not the case for the greedy CART algorithm. We will show in section 3 how the minimization can be solved effectively for dyadic trees.

2.3 Oracle Inequalities for the Penalized Estimators

Classification Loss. In the case of classification loss, it has been known for some time [2,3] that the best convergence rates in classification strongly depend on the behavior of $P(Y|X)$ and in particular of the identifiability of the majority class. Without any assumption to this regard, the minimax rate of convergence for classification error is of order $\mathcal{O}(\sqrt{D/n})$ for a model of VC-dimension D (see e.g. [11]), and thus the penalty should be at least of this order. Such an analysis has been used in [9] for dyadic classification trees. Presently, we will assume instead that we are in a favorable case in which the majority class is always identifiable[1] with a fixed known "margin" η_0, which allows to use a smaller order penalty ($\mathcal{O}(|m|/n)$). Moreover, this additive (wrt. the size of the model) penalty makes the minimization problem (11) easier to solve practically. Note that the identifiability assumption is only necessary for classifier estimation in Theorem 1, not for cpd estimation in Theorems 2-3.

Theorem 1. *Assume the following identifiability condition: there exists some* $\eta_0 > 0$ *such that*

$$\forall x \in \mathcal{X}, \qquad P(Y = f^*_{class}(x)|X = x) - \max_{y \neq f^*(x)} P(Y = y|X = x) \geq \eta_0. \tag{12}$$

Let $(x_m)_{m \in \mathcal{M}}$ *be real numbers with* $\sum_{m \in \mathcal{M}} \exp(-x_m) \leq 1$. *Then for any* $K > 1$, *there exist absolute constants* C_1, C_2, C_3 *such that, if*

$$\forall m \in \mathcal{M} \qquad \mathrm{pen}(m) \geq C_1 \frac{|m| \log t}{\eta_0 n} + C_2 \frac{x_m}{\eta_0 n} \tag{13}$$

then the penalized estimator $\widetilde{f}_{\widehat{m}}$ *satisfies*

$$E\left[\mathbf{err}(\widetilde{f}_{\widehat{m}}) - \mathbf{err}(f^*_{class})\right] \leq K \inf_{\substack{m \in \mathcal{M} \\ f \in \mathcal{C}_m}} \left(\mathbf{err}(f) - \mathbf{err}(f^*_{class}) + 2\mathrm{pen}(m) + \frac{C_3}{n}\right),$$

[1] Note that this identifiability assumption (12) below is much weaker than the assumption that the Bayes error is zero, which appears in classical VC theory to justify non-square-root penalties for *consistent* bounds and SRM procedures.

where **err** *denotes the generalization error and the expectation on the left-hand side is over training sets* $(X_i, Y_i)_{i=1...n}$.

Square Loss

Theorem 2. *Let* $(x_m)_{m\in\mathcal{M}}$ *be real numbers with* $\sum_{m\in\mathcal{M}} \exp(-x_m) \leq 1$. *Then for any* $K > 1$, *there exist absolute constants* C_1, C_2, C_3 *such that, if*

$$\forall m \in \mathcal{M} \qquad \text{pen}(m) \geq C_1 \frac{t|m|}{n} + C_2 \frac{x_m}{n} \tag{14}$$

then the penalized estimator $\widehat{f}_{\widehat{m}}$ *satisfies*

$$E\left[\left\|\widehat{f}_{\widehat{m}} - f^*_{cpd}\right\|^2_{t,2}\right] \leq K \inf_{m\in\mathcal{M}} \left(\inf_{f\in\mathcal{F}_m} \left\|f - f^*_{cpd}\right\|^2_{t,2} + 2\text{pen}(m) + \frac{C_3}{n}\right).$$

Minus-log Loss

Theorem 3. *Let* $(x_m)_{m\in\mathcal{M}}$ *be real numbers with* $\sum_{m\in\mathcal{M}} \exp(-x_m) \leq 1$. *Then for any* $K > 1$, *there exist absolute constants* C_1, C_2, C_3 *such that, if*

$$\forall m \in \mathcal{M} \qquad \text{pen}(m) \geq C_1 \frac{t|m| \log \rho}{n} + C_2 \frac{x_m \log \rho}{n} \tag{15}$$

then the penalized estimator $\widehat{f}^{\rho}_{\widehat{m}}$ *satisfies*

$$E\left[KL(P, \widehat{f}^{\rho}_{\widehat{m}}|X)\right] \leq K \inf_{m\in\mathcal{M} f\in\mathcal{F}_m} \left(KL(P, f|X) + 2\text{pen}(m) + \frac{C_3}{n} - 3\log(1 - t\rho)\right).$$

Note that the typical values of ρ should be of order n^{-k} for some arbitrary $k > 0$. Assuming the number of models per dimension is at most exponential, the penalty function is then of order $t|m| \log n/n$, and the trailing term $\log(1-t\rho)$ is of order t/n^k.

Application to Dyadic Decision Trees

Corollary 1. *For dyadic decision trees in dimension* d, *Theorems 1-3 apply with the choice*

$$x_m = C|m| \log(d), \tag{16}$$

where C *is a universal constant.*

Proof. The point here is only to count the number of models of size $|m| = D$. An upper bound can be obtained the following way: the number of binary trees with $D + 1$ leaves is given by the Catalan number $Cat(D) = (D + 1)^{-1}\binom{2D}{D}$; such a tree has D internal nodes and we can therefore label these nodes in d^D different ways. It can be shown that $Cat(n) \leq C' 4^n / n^{3/2}$ for some constant C'; hence for C big enough in (16), $\sum_m \exp(-x_m) \leq 1$ is satisfied. □

3 Implementation of the Estimator

Principle and naive approach. We hereafter assume that the penalization function is on the form $\text{pen}(m) = \alpha|m|$ for some α (possibly depending on the sample size n).

In traditional CART, no exact minimization is performed. The split at each node is determined in a greedy way in order to yield the best local reduction of some empirical criterion (the entropy criterion corresponds to ℓ_{log} while the Gini criterion corresponds to ℓ_{sq}). In contrast, we introduce a method to find the global solution of (11) for dyadic decision trees by dynamic programming. This method is strongly inspired from an algorithm proposed by Donoho [12] for image compression.

We assume that there is a fixed bound k_{max} on the maximal numbers of cuts along a same dimension. Therefore, the smallest possible bins are those obtained with k_{max} cuts in every dimension, i.e. small hypercubes of edge length $2^{-k_{max}}$. We represent any achievable bin by a d-tuple $b = (L_1(b), \ldots, L_d(b))$, where for each i, $L_i(b)$ is a finite list of length $0 \leq |L_i| \leq k_{max}$, with elements in $\{r, \ell\}$. Each of these (possibly empty) lists contains the successions of cuts in the corresponding dimension needed to obtain the bin; each element of the list indicates if the left or the right child is selected after a cut, see section 1.5. Note that, while the order of the sequence of cuts along a same dimension is important, the order in which the cuts along different dimensions are performed is not relevant for the definition of the bin. Finally, we will denote $|b| = \sum_i |L_i(b)|$ and call it the depth of cell b, and $\mathcal{B}_{k_{max}}$ the set of achievable bins, i.e. such that $|L_i(b)| \leq k_{max}$ for all $1 \leq i \leq d$.

The principle of the method is simple, and is based on the additive property of the function to be optimized. If b is a bin, denote T_b a "local" dyadic tree rooted in b, i.e. a dyadic tree starting at bin b and splitting it recursively, while still satisfying the assumption that the bins attached to its leaves belong to $\mathcal{B}_{k_{max}}$. Furthermore we assume that to each terminal bin a value is associated estimated from the data, such as (10), so that T_b can be considered as a piecewise constant function on b. Denote $|T_b|$ the number of leaves of T_b and define

$$\mathcal{E}(T_b) = \sum_{i=1}^{n} \mathbb{I}_{\{X_i \in b\}} \ell(T_b, X_i, Y_i) + n\alpha|T_b|.$$

Note that when $b = [0,1]^d$, finding the minimum of $\mathcal{E}(T)$ is equivalent to the minimization problem (11). Moreover, whenever T_b is not reduced to its root (hereafter we will call such a tree *nondegenerate*), if we denote u and v the bins attached to the left and right children of the root and T_u, T_v the corresponding subtrees, then we have

$$\mathcal{E}(T_b) = \mathcal{E}(T_u) + \mathcal{E}(T_v).$$

For a bin b, let T_b^* denote the local dyadic tree minimizing $\mathcal{E}(T_b)$. Finally, let us denote by b_ℓ^i, b_r^i the left and right sub-bins obtained by splitting b in half along direction i. Then from the above observations it is straightforward that

$$\mathcal{E}(T_b^*) = \min\left(\mathcal{E}(R_b), \min\left\{\mathcal{E}(T_{b_\ell^i}^*) + \mathcal{E}(T_{b_r^i}^*)\middle| i : |L_i(B)| < k_{max}\right\}\right), \quad (17)$$

where R_b denotes the degenerate local tree $\{b\}$.

From this it is quite simple to develop the following naive bottom-up approach to solving the optimization (11): suppose we know the optimal local tree T_b^* for every bin of depth $|b| = k$, then using (17) we can compute the optimal local trees for all bins at depth $k-1$. Starting with the deepest bins (the hypercubes of side length $2^{-k_{max}}$) for which the optimal local trees are degenerate, it is possible to compute recursively optimal trees for lower depth bins, finally finding the optimal tree T^* for $[0,1]^d$.

Dictionary-based approach. The naive approach proposed above however has a significant drawback, namely its complexity; there are already $2^{dk_{max}}$ smallest bins at depth dk_{max}, and even more bins for intermediate depth values, due to the combinatorics in the choice of cuts. We therefore put forward an improved approach, based on the following observation: if $2^{dk_{max}} > n$, then some (possibly a lot) of the smallest bins are actually empty, and so are bins at intermediate depths as well. Furthermore, for an empty bin b at any depth the optimal local tree is obviously the degenerate tree $T_b^* = R_b$. Therefore, it is sufficient to keep track of the *non-empty* bins along the process. This can be done using a dictionary $\mathcal{D}_k$ of non-empty bins of depth k; the algorithm is then as follows:

Initialization: construct dictionary $\mathcal{D}_{dk_{max}}$ by finding the minimal bins (hypercubes of edge length $2^{-k_{max}}$) containing at least one datapoint, and inserting them in $\mathcal{D}_{dk_{max}}$. For each of these bins b, also store that $T_b^* = R_b$.
Loop on depth, $D = dk_{max}, \ldots, 1$:
  Initialize $\mathcal{D}_{D-1} = \emptyset$.
  Loop on elements $b \in \mathcal{D}_D$:
    Loop on dimension $k \in \{1, \ldots, d\}$ and $|L_k(b)| > 0$:
    Let b' denote the sibling of b along dimension k, i.e. the bin obtained from b by flipping the last element of $L_k(b)$. Let u denote the direct common ancestor-bin of b and b'.
    If u is already stored in $\mathcal{D}_{D-1}$ with a (provisional) T_u^*, then replace

$$T_u^* \longleftarrow \operatorname{Arg\,Min}\left(\mathcal{E}(T_u^*), \mathcal{E}(T_b^*) + \mathcal{E}(T_{b'}^*)\right).$$

    If u is not yet stored in $\mathcal{D}_{D-1}$, store it along with the provisional

$$T_u^* \longleftarrow \operatorname{Arg\,Min}\left(\mathcal{E}(R_u), \mathcal{E}(T_b^*) + \mathcal{E}(T_{b'}^*)\right).$$

    Endloop on k
  Endloop on b
Endloop on D

It is straightforward to prove that at the end of each loop over b, $\mathcal{D}_{D-1}$ contains all nonempty bins of depth $D-1$ with the corresponding optimal local trees. Therefore at the end of the procedure $\mathcal{D}_0$ contains the tree minimizing the optimization problem (11).

We now give a result about the complexity of our procedure:

Proposition 1. *For fixed training sample size $n \geq 1$, input dimension $d \geq 1$, maximum number of splits along each dimension $k_{max} \geq 1$, the complexity $\mathcal{C}(n, d, k_{max})$ of the dictionary-based algorithm satisfies*

$$\mathcal{O}\left(dk_{max}^d\right) \leq \mathcal{C}(n, d, k_{max}) \leq \mathcal{O}\left(ndk_{max}^d \log(nk_{max}^d)\right). \quad (18)$$

Proof. For a given training point (X_i, Y_i), the exact number of bins (at any depth) that contain this point is $(k_{max}+1)^d$. Namely, there is a unique bin b_0 of maximal depth dk_{max} containing (X_i, Y_i); then, any other bin b containing this point must be an "ancestor" of b_0 in the sense that for all $1 \leq k \leq d$, $L_k(b)$ must be a prefix list of $L_k(b_0)$. Bin b is uniquely determined by the length of the prefix lists $|L_k(b)|$, $1 \leq k \leq d$; for each length there are $(k_{max}+1)$ possible choices, hence the result.

Since the algorithm must loop at least through all of these bins, and makes an additional loop on dimension for each bin, this gives the lower bound. For the upper bound, we bound the total number of bins for all training points by $\mathcal{O}(nk^d)$. Note that we can implement a dictionary $\mathcal{D}$ such that search and insert operations are of complexity $\mathcal{O}(\log(|\mathcal{D}|))$ (for example an AVL tree, [13]). Coarsely upper-bounding the size of the dictionaries used by the total number of bins, we get the announced upper bound. □

Retaining nk_{max}^d as the leading factor of the upper bound, we see that the complexity of the dictionary-based algorithm is still exponential in the dimension d. To fix ideas, assume that we choose k_{max} so that the projection of the training set on any coordinate axis is totally separated by the regular grid of size $2^{-k_{max}}$. If the distribution of X has a bounded density wrt. Lebesgue measure, k_{max} should be of order $\log(n)$ and the complexity of the algorithm of order $n\log^d(n)$ (in the sense of logarithmic equivalence). Although it is much better than looping through every possible bin (which gives rise to a complexity of order $2^{d(k_{max}+1)} \overset{\log}{\approx} n^d$), it means that the algorithm will only be viable for low dimensional problems, or by imposing restrictions on k_{max} for moderate dimensional problems. Note however that other existing algorithms for dyadic decision trees [9,10,6] are all of complexity $2^{dk_{max}}$, but that the authors choose k_{max} of the order of $d^{-1}\log n$. This makes sense in [10], because the cuts are fixed in advance and the algorithm is not adaptive to anisotropy. However, in [6] the author notices that k_{max} should be chosen as large as the computational complexity permits to take full advantage of the anisotropy adaptivity.

4 Discussion and Future Directions

The two main points of our work are a theoretical study of the estimator and a practical algorithm. On the theoretical side, Theorems 1-2 are "true" oracle inequalities in the sense that the convergence rates for each of the models considered is of the order of the minimax rate (for a study of minimax rates for classification on finite VC-dimension models under the identifiability condition (12), see [3]). Theorem 3 misses the minimax rate, which is known to be of order $\mathcal{O}(|m|/n)$, by a logarithmic factor. We do not know at this point if this factor can be alleviated. Another interesting future direction is to derive from these inequalities convergence rates for anisotropic regularity function classes, similarly to what was done in [6,12].

From the algorithmic side, our algorithm is arguably only viable for low- or moderate-dimensional problems (we tested it on 10-dimensional datasets). For application to high-dimensional problems, some partly-greedy heuristic appears as an interesting strategy, for example by splitting the algorithm into several lower-dimensional problems on which we can can run the exact algorithm. We are currently investigating this direction.

Acknowledgments. The authors want to thank Lucien Birgé and Klaus-Robert Müller for valuable discussions.

References

1. Massart, P.: Some applications of concentration inequalities in statistics. Ann. Fac. Sci. Toulouse Math. **9** (2000) 245–303
2. Tsybakov, A.: Optimal aggregation of classifiers in statistical learning. Annals of Statistics **32** (2004)
3. Massart, P., Nédélec, E.: Risk bounds for statistical learning. Technical report, Laboratoire de mathématiques, Université Paris-Sud (2004)
4. Castellan, G.: Histograms selection with an Akaike type criterion. C. R. Acad. Sci., Paris, Sér. I, Math. **330** (2000) 729–732
5. Barron, A., Birgé, L., Massart, P.: Risk bounds for model selection via penalization. Probability theory and related fields **113** (1999) 301–413
6. Klemelä, J.: Multivariate histograms with data-dependent partitions. Technical report, Institut für angewandte mathematik, Universität Heidelberg (2003)
7. Breiman, L., Friedman, J., Olshen, R., Stone, C.: Classification and regression Trees. Wadsworth, Belmont, California (1984)
8. Gey, S., Nédélec, E.: Risk bounds for CART regression trees. In: Nonlinear Estimation and Classification. Volume 171 of Lecture Notes in Statistics. Springer (2003) 369–380
9. Scott, C., Nowak, R.: Dyadic classification trees via structural risk minimization. In: Proc. Neural Information Processing Systems (NIPS). (2002)
10. Scott, C., Nowak, R.: Near-minimax optimal classification with dyadic classification trees. In: Proc. Neural Information Processing Systems (NIPS). (2003)
11. Devroye, L., Györfi, L., Lugosi, G.: A probabilistic theory of pattern recognition. Volume 31 of Applications of Mathematics. Springer (1996)
12. Donoho, D.L.: CART and best ortho-basis: a connection. Annals of Statistics **25** (1997) 1870–1911
13. Adelson-Velskii, G.M., Landis, E.: An algorithm for the organization of information. Soviet Math. Doclady **3** (1962) 1259–1263

14. Blanchard, G., Bousquet, O., Massart, P.: Statistical performance of Support Vector Machines. Technical report, Laboratoire de mathématiques, Université Paris-Sud (2004)
15. Blanchard, G., Lugosi, G., Vayatis, N.: On the rate of convergence of regularized Boosting classifiers. Journal of Machine Learning Research **4** (2003) 861–894
16. Barron, A., Sheu, C.: Approximation of density functions by sequences of exponential families. Annals of Statistics **19** (1991) 1347–1369

A Proofs of Theorems 1-3

The proofs for our results are based on a general model selection theorem appearing in [14], which is a generalization of an original theorem of Massart [1]. We quote it here in a slightly modified and shortened form tailored for our needs (see also [15] for a similar form of the theorem).

Theorem 4. *Let $\ell(\cdot,\cdot)$ be a loss function defined on $\mathcal{S} \times \mathcal{X}$; denote $f^* = \operatorname{Arg\,Min}_{f \in \mathcal{S}} P\ell(f)$ and $L(f, f^*) = P\ell(f) - P\ell(f^*)$. Let $(S_m)_{m \in \mathcal{M}}$, $S_m \subset \mathcal{S}$ be a countable collection of classes of functions and assume that there exists*

- *a pseudo-distance d on $\mathcal{S}$;*
- *a sequence of sub-root [2] functions $(\phi_m), m \in \mathcal{M}$;*
- *two positive constants b and R ;*

such that

(H1) $\forall f \in \mathcal{S},\ \forall x \in \mathcal{X}, \quad |\ell(f, x)| \leq b\,;$

(H2) $\forall f, f' \in \mathcal{S}, \quad \operatorname{Var}_P[\ell(f) - \ell(f')] \leq d^2(f, f')\,;$

(H3) $\forall f \in \mathcal{S}, \quad d^2(f, f^*) \leq RL(f, f^*)\,;$

and, if r_m^* denotes the solution of $\phi_m(r) = r/R$,

(H4) $\forall m \in \mathcal{M},\ \forall f_0 \in \mathcal{F}_m,\ \forall r \geq r_m^*$

$$E\left[\sup_{\substack{f \in \mathcal{F}_m \\ d^2(f, f_0) \leq r}} (P - P_n)(\ell(f) - \ell(f_0))\right] \leq \phi_m(r).$$

Let $(x_m)_{m \in \mathcal{M}}$ be real numbers with $\sum_{m \in \mathcal{M}} e^{-x_m} \leq 1$. Let $\varepsilon \geq 0$ and $\widetilde{f}$ denote an ε-approximate penalized minimum loss estimator over the family $(\mathcal{F}_m)$ with the penalty function $\operatorname{pen}(m)$*, that is, such that there exists $\widetilde{m}$ with $\widetilde{f} \in \mathcal{F}_{\widetilde{m}}$ and*

$$P_n\ell(\widetilde{f}) + \operatorname{pen}(\widetilde{m}) \leq \inf_{m \in \mathcal{M}} \inf_{f \in \mathcal{F}_m} \left(P_n\ell(f) + \operatorname{pen}(m) + \varepsilon\right).$$

Given $K > 1$, there exist constants C_1, C_2, C_3 (depending on K only) such that, if the penalty function $\operatorname{pen}(m)$ *satisfies for each $m \in \mathcal{M}$:*

$$\operatorname{pen}(m) \geq C_1 \frac{r_m^*}{R} + C_2 \frac{(R + b)x_m}{n},$$

[2] A function ϕ on $\mathbb{R}_+$ is subroot if it is positive, nondecreasing and $\phi(r)/\sqrt{r}$ is nonincreasing for $r > 0$.

then the following inequality holds:

$$EL(\widetilde{f}, f^*) \leq K \inf_{m \in \mathcal{M}} \left(\inf_{f \in \mathcal{F}_m} L(f, f^*) + 2\text{pen}(m) + \frac{C_3}{n} + \varepsilon \right).$$

Proof outline for Theorem 1. We will apply Theorem 4 to the set of models $(\mathcal{C}_m)$. Checking for hypothesis (H1) is obvious. To check (H2)-(H3), we choose the distance $d(f,g) = E\left[(\ell_{class}(f,X,Y) - \ell_{class}(g,X,Y))^2\right]$, so that (H2) is trivially satisfied. To check (H3), denote $\eta(x,i) = P(Y = i|X = x)$ and $\eta^*(x) = \max_{i \in \mathcal{Y}} \eta(i,x)$; we then have

$$\begin{aligned} E\left[\mathbb{I}_{\{f(X) \neq Y\}} - \mathbb{I}_{\{f^*(X) \neq Y\}}\right] &= E\left[(\eta^*(X) - \eta(X, f(X)))\, \mathbb{I}_{\{f(X) \neq f^*(X)\}}\right] \\ &\geq \eta_0 E\left[\mathbb{I}_{\{f(X) \neq f^*(X)\}}\right], \end{aligned}$$

where we have used hypothesis (12). On the other hand,

$$\begin{aligned} E\left[(\mathbb{I}_{\{f(X) \neq Y\}} - \mathbb{I}_{\{f^*(X) \neq Y\}})^2\right] &= E\left[(\eta^*(X) + \eta(X, f(X)))\, \mathbb{I}_{\{f(X) \neq f^*(X)\}}\right] \\ &\leq 2E\left[\mathbb{I}_{\{f(X) \neq f^*(X)\}}\right], \end{aligned}$$

which proves that (H3) is satisfied with $R = 2/\eta_0$. Finally, for hypothesis (H4), we can follow the same reasoning as in [1], p. 294-295; in this reference the empirical shattering coefficient is taken into account, but the present case is even simpler since model $\mathcal{C}_m$ is finite with cardinality $t^{|m|}$, leading to

$$E\left[\sup_{f \in \mathcal{C}_m, d^2(f, f_0) \leq r} (P - P_n)(\ell_{class}(f) - \ell_{class}(f_0))\right] \leq C\sqrt{\frac{r|m| \log t}{n}},$$

for some universal constant C. This leads to the conclusion. □

Proof outline for Theorem 2. We apply Theorem 4 to the set of models $(\mathcal{F}_m)$. For (H1), it is easy to check that

$$\forall f \in \mathcal{F}_{cpd}, \qquad \ell_{sq}(f, X, Y) = \left\| f(X, \cdot) - \overline{Y} \right\|_t^2 = \|f(X, \cdot)\|_t^2 + 1 - 2f(X, Y) \leq 2.$$

For (H2), we note that $\ell_{sq}(f,X,Y) - \ell_{sq}(g,X,Y) = \|f(X,\cdot)\|_t^2 - \|g(X,\cdot)\|_t^2 - 2(f(X,Y) - g(X,Y))$. Using the equality $\text{Var}[F] = E[\text{Var}[F|X]] + \text{Var}[E[F|X]]$, we deduce that

$$\begin{aligned} &\text{Var}\left[\ell_{sq}(f,X,Y) - \ell_{sq}(g,X,Y)\right] \\ &\quad = E\left[\text{Var}\left[2(f(X,Y) - g(X,Y))|X\right]\right] + \text{Var}\left[\|f(X,\cdot)\|_t^2 - \|g(X,\cdot)\|_t^2\right] \\ &\quad \leq 4E\left[(f-g)^2\right] + E\left[\|f(X,\cdot) - g(X,\cdot)\|_t^2 \, \|f(X,\cdot) + g(X,\cdot)\|_t^2\right] \\ &\quad \leq 8E\left[\|f(X,\cdot) - g(X,\cdot)\|_t^2\right] \doteq d^2(f,g); \end{aligned}$$

this proves that (H2) is satisfied for the above choice of d; recalling (6), (H3) is then satisfied with $R = 1/8$. Finally, for hypothesis (H4) is is possible to show that

$$E\left[\sup_{f \in \mathcal{G}_m, d^2(f, f_0) \leq r} (P - P_n)(\ell_{sq}(f) - \ell_{sq}(f_0))\right] \leq C\sqrt{\frac{rt|m|}{n}},$$

using local Rademacher and Gaussian complexities, using a method similar to [14]. □

Proof of Theorem 3. To apply Theorem 4, we define the ambient space

$$\mathcal{S}^\rho = \{f \in \mathcal{F}_{cpd} | \forall (x,y) \in \mathcal{X} \times \mathcal{Y},\ f(x,y) \geq \rho\}$$

and the models as $\mathcal{S}^\rho_m = \mathcal{S}^\rho \cap \mathcal{F}_m$, which will insure boundedness of the loss. As a counterpart of using these restricted ambient space and models, the application of Theorem 4 will result in an inequality involving not f^*_{cpd}, but the minimizer of the average loss on $\mathcal{S}^\rho$, denoted f^*_ρ, and the model-wise minimizers of the loss on $\mathcal{S}^\rho_m$ instead of $\mathcal{F}_m$. However, it is easy to show the following inequalities:

$$\forall f \in \mathcal{F}_{cpd}, \qquad L(f, f^*_{cpd}) \leq L(f, f^*_\rho) - \log(1 - t\rho);$$

$$\forall m \in \mathcal{M}, \qquad \inf_{f \in \mathcal{S}^\rho_m} L(f, f^*_\rho) \leq \inf_{f \in \mathcal{F}_m} L(f, f^*_{cpd}) - \log(1 - t\rho);$$

finally, it can be shown that $\widehat{f^\rho_{\hat{m}}}$ is a $-\log(1-t\rho)$-approximate penalized estimator. Therefore, if Theorem 4 applies, these inequalities lead to the conclusion of Theorem 3.

We now turn to verifying the main assumptions of the abstract model selection theorem.

• Check for (H1): boundedness of the loss on the models. Obviously, we have

$$\forall f \in \mathcal{S}^\rho,\ \forall (x,y) \in \mathcal{X} \times \mathcal{Y} \qquad 0 \leq \ell_{log}(f,x,y) \leq -\log \rho$$

• Check for (H2)-(H3): distance linking the risk and its variance. We choose the distance d as the $L^2(P)$ distance between logarithms of the functions:

$$d(f,g) = E_P\left[(\ell_{log}(f,x,y) - \ell_{log}(g,x,y))^2\right] = E_P\left[\log^2 \frac{f}{g}\right].$$

Obviously we have $Var[\ell_{log}(f,x,y) - \ell_{log}(g,x,y)] \leq d(f,g)$ with this choice; the problem is then to compare $E_P\left[\log^2 \frac{P(Y|X)}{f}\right]$ to $E_P\left[\log \frac{P(Y|X)}{f}\right]$. Denoting $Z(x,i) = f(x,k)/P(Y=k|X=x)$, we therefore have to compare $E[\log^2 Z]$ to $E[-\log Z]$ with the expectation taken wrt. P, so that $E[Z] = 1$. Note that $Z \geq \rho$. Using Lemma 1 below, we deduce that

$$d(P(Y|X), f) \leq \frac{\log^2 \rho}{\rho - 1 - \log \rho} KL(P, f|X),$$

Note that typically when ρ is small the factor R in (H3) is therefore of order $-\log \rho$.

• Check for (H4): d-local risk control on models. For any $f, g \in \mathcal{S}^\rho_m$, $F = \log \frac{f}{g} \in \mathcal{G}_m$. For $A \in \mathcal{B}_m, i \in \mathcal{Y}$, denote $P_{A,i} = P[X \in A, Y = i]$ and

$$\varphi_{A,i}(x,y) = \frac{\mathbb{I}\{x \in A\}\mathbb{I}\{Y = i\}}{\sqrt{P_{A,i}}};$$

note that the family $(\varphi(A,i))_{A,i}$ is an orthonormal basis (for the $L^2(P)$ structure) of $\mathcal{G}_m$, hence any function $f \in \mathcal{G}_m$ can be written under the form

$$f = \sum_{A,i} \alpha_{A,i} \varphi_{A,i} \,,$$

with $Pf^2 = \sum \alpha_{A,i}^2$. Putting $\nu_n = (P - P_n)$, we then have for any $f \in \mathcal{S}_m^\rho$

$$E_P \left[\sup_{\substack{g \in S_m^\rho \\ d^2(f,g) \le r}} |\nu_n(\ell(f,x) - \ell(g,x))| \right] \le E_P \left[\sup_{\substack{F \in \mathcal{G}_m \\ E[F^2] \le r}} |\nu_n F| \right] = \Xi;$$

$$\begin{aligned}
\Xi = E_P \left[\sup_{\substack{(\alpha_{A,i}): \\ \sum_{A,i} \alpha_{A,i}^2 \le r}} \left| \sum_{A,i} \alpha_{A,i} \, \nu_n \phi_{A,i} \right| \right] &\le \sqrt{r} E_P \left[\left(\sum_{A,i} (\nu_n \varphi_{A,i})^2 \right)^{\frac{1}{2}} \right] \\
&\le \sqrt{r} E_P \left[\left(\sum_{A,i} (\nu_n \varphi_{A,i})^2 \right) \right]^{\frac{1}{2}} \\
&= \sqrt{r \sum_{A,i} \frac{1}{n} \frac{P_{A,i}(1 - P_{A,i})}{P_{A,i}}} \le \sqrt{\frac{rt|m|}{n}} .
\end{aligned}$$

□

The following Lemma is inspired by similar techniques appearing in [4,16].

Lemma 1. *Let Z be a real, positive random variable such that $E[Z] = 1$ and $Z \ge \eta$ a.s. Then the following inequality holds:*

$$\frac{E\left[\log^2 Z\right]}{E\left[-\log Z\right]} \le \frac{\log^2 \eta}{\eta - 1 - \log \eta} .$$

Proof. Let $u = -\log Z \le -\log \eta$; we have

$$\begin{aligned}
E[-\log Z] = E[u] = E[e^{-u} - 1 + u] &= E\left[u^2 \frac{e^{-u} - 1 + u}{u^2} \right] \\
&\ge E\left[u^2\right] \frac{\eta - 1 - \log \eta}{\log^2 \eta} ,
\end{aligned}$$

where the first line comes from the fact that $E\left[e^{-u}\right] = E\left[Z\right] = 1$, and the last inequality from the fact that the function $g(x) = x^{-2}(e^{-x} - 1 + x)$ is positive and decreasing on $\mathbb{R}$. □

An Improved VC Dimension Bound for Sparse Polynomials

Michael Schmitt

Lehrstuhl Mathematik und Informatik, Fakultät für Mathematik
Ruhr-Universität Bochum, D–44780 Bochum, Germany
http://www.ruhr-uni-bochum.de/lmi/mschmitt/
mschmitt@lmi.ruhr-uni-bochum.de

Abstract. We show that the function class consisting of k-sparse polynomials in n variables has Vapnik-Chervonenkis (VC) dimension at least $nk + 1$. This result supersedes the previously known lower bound via k-term monotone disjunctive normal form (DNF) formulas obtained by Littlestone (1988). Moreover, it implies that the VC dimension for k-sparse polynomials is strictly larger than the VC dimension for k-term monotone DNF. The new bound is achieved by introducing an exponential approach that employs Gaussian radial basis function (RBF) neural networks for obtaining classifications of points in terms of sparse polynomials.

1 Introduction

A multivariate polynomial is said to be k-sparse if it consists of at most k monomials. Sparseness is a prerequisite that has proven to be instrumental in numerous results concerning the computational aspects of polynomials. Sparse polynomials have been extensively investigated not only in the context of learning algorithms (see, e.g., Blum and Singh, 1990; Bshouty and Mansour, 1995; Fischer and Simon, 1992; Schapire and Sellie, 1996), but also with regard to interpolation and approximation tasks (see, e.g., Grigoriev et al., 1990; Huang and Rao, 1999; Murao and Fujise, 1996; Roth and Benedek, 1990).

The Vapnik-Chervonenkis (VC) dimension of a function class quantifies its classification capabilities (Vapnik and Chervonenkis, 1971): It indicates the cardinality of the largest set for which all possible binary-valued classifications are obtained using functions from the class. The VC dimension is well established as a measure for the complexity of learning (see, e.g., Anthony and Bartlett, 1999): It yields bounds for the generalization error of learning algorithms via uniform convergence results.

We establish here a new lower bound on the VC dimension of sparse multivariate polynomials: We show that the class of k-sparse polynomials in n variables has VC dimension at least $nk + 1$. The previously best known lower bound is derived from the lower bound for Boolean formulas in k-term monotone disjunctive normal form (DNF), that is, disjunctions of at most k monomials without negations. This bound has been obtained by Littlestone (1988). In particular,

J. Shawe-Taylor and Y. Singer (Eds.): COLT 2004, LNAI 3120, pp. 393–407, 2004.

Littlestone has shown that the class of k-term monotone l-DNF formulas (i.e., with monomials of size at most l) has VC dimension at least $lk\lfloor\log(n/m)\rfloor$, where $l \leq m \leq n$, and $k \leq \binom{m}{l}$. Using, for instance, $l = n/4$ and $m = n/2$, this yields the lower bound $nk/4$ for the VC dimension of k-term monotone DNF and, hence, of k-sparse polynomials, where k has to satisfy the given constraints.

The new bound that we provide here for sparse polynomials supersedes this previous bound in a threefold way:

1. It improves the bound from k-term monotone DNF in value.
2. It releases k from the constraints through n in that the bound holds for every n and k—in particular, for values of k that are larger than the number of monotone monomials.
3. The value $nk+1$ is even larger than the VC dimension of the class of k-term monotone DNF formulas itself: We show that the difference between both dimensions is larger than $k\log(k/e)+1$.

So far, a considerable number of results and techniques for VC dimension bounds have been provided in the context of real valued function classes (see, e.g., Bartlett and Maass, 2003, and the references there). For specific subclasses of sparse polynomials, tight bounds have been calculated: Karpinski and Werther (1993) have shown that k-sparse univariate polynomials have a VC dimension[1] proportional to k. Further, the VC dimension of the class of monomials over the reals is equal to n (see Ehrenfeucht et al., 1989, for the lower bound and Schmitt, 2002c, for the upper bound). There is also a VC dimension result known for n-variate d-degree polynomials (see, e.g., Ben-David and Lindenbaum, 1998): This class has VC dimension equal to $\binom{n+d}{d}$. However, as the class contains polynomials that are $\binom{n+d}{d}$-sparse and k-sparseness imposes restrictions on the number of variables in terms of k, this result entails for sparse multivariate polynomials (without constraint on the degree) a lower bound not better than the bound due to Littlestone (1988).

There has been previous work that established techniques for deriving lower bounds for quite general types of real-valued function classes. Building on results by Lee et al. (1995), Erlich et al. (1997) provide powerful means for obtaining lower bounds for parameterized function classes[2]. An essential requirement for using these techniques, however, is that the function class is "smoothly" parameterized, a fact that does not apply to the exponents of polynomials. The lower bound method of Koiran and Sontag (1997) for various types of neural networks, generalized by Bartlett et al. (1998) to neural networks with a given number of layers, cannot be employed for polynomials either. This technique

[1] Precisely, Karpinski and Werther (1993) studied a related notion, the so-called pseudo-dimension. Following their methods, it is not hard to obtain this result for the VC dimension (see also Schmitt, 2002a).

[2] A parameterized function class is given in terms of a function having two types of variables: input variables and parameter variables. The functions of the class are obtained by instantiating the parameter variables with, in general, real numbers. Neural networks are prominent examples for parameterized function classes.

is constrained to networks where each neuron computes a function with finite limits at infinity, a property monomials do not have. Further, Koiran and Sontag (1997) designed a lower bound method for networks consisting of linear and multiplication gates. However, the way these networks are constructed—with layers consisting of products of linear terms[3]—does not give rise to sparse polynomials, even when the number of layers is restricted.

We provide a completely new approach to the derivation of lower bounds on the VC dimension of sparse multivariate polynomials. First, we establish the lower bound $nk+1$ on the VC dimension of a specific type of radial basis function (RBF) neural network (see, e.g., Haykin, 1999). The networks considered here have k Gaussian units as computational elements and satisfy certain assumptions with respect to the input domain and the values taken by the parameters. The bound for these networks improves a result of Erlich et al. (1997) in combination with Lee et al. (1995) who established the lower bound $n(k-1)$ for RBF networks[4] with restrictions neither on inputs nor on parameters. Then we use our result for RBF networks to obtain the lower bound on the VC dimension of sparse multivariate polynomials. Thus, RBF networks open a new way to assess the classification capabilities of sparse multivariate polynomials. This Gaussian approach has also proven to be helpful in a different context dealing with the roots of univariate polynomials (Schmitt, 2004).

Sparse multivariate polynomials are a special case of a particular type of neural networks, the so-called product unit neural networks (Durbin and Rumelhart, 1989). It immediately follows from the bound for sparse multivariate polynomials established here that the VC dimension of product unit neural networks with n input nodes and one layer of k hidden nodes (that is, nodes that are neither input nor output nodes) is at least $nk+1$.

Concerning known upper bounds for the VC dimension of sparse multivariate polynomials, there are two relevant results: First, the bound $O(n^2k^4)$ due to Karpinski and Macintyre (1997) is the smallest upper bound known for polynomials with unlimited degree (see also Schmitt, 2002c). Second, the class of k-sparse n-variate polynomials with degree at most d has VC dimension no more than $2nk\log(9d)$ (Schmitt, 2002c). The derivation of the new lower bound not only narrows the gap between upper and lower bounds, but gives also rise to subclasses of degree-restricted polynomials for which the bound is optimal up to the factor $2\log(9d)$.

We introduce definitions and notation in Section 2. Section 3 provides geometric constructions that are required for the derivations of the main results presented in Section 4. Finally, in Section 5, we show that the new bound exceeds the VC dimension of k-term monotone DNF.

---

[3] Such a layer uses products of the form $\prod_{i=1}^{l}(x-a_i)$ where it is crucial that there is no bound on l.

[4] These results and the one presented here concern RBF networks with uniform width. (See the definition in Section 2.) Better lower bounds are known for more general types of RBF networks (Schmitt, 2002b).

2 Definitions

The class of *k-sparse polynomials in n variables* consists of the functions

$$a_0 + a_1 x_1^{b_{1,1}} \cdots x_n^{b_{1,n}} + \cdots + a_k x_1^{b_{k,1}} \cdots x_n^{b_{k,n}}$$

with real coefficients $a_0, \ldots, a_k$ and nonnegative integer exponents $b_{1,1}, \ldots, b_{k,n}$. Note that, in contrast to some other work, the notion of k-sparseness does not include the constant term a_0 in the value of k. In the derivation of the bound we associate the non-constant monomials with certain computing units of a neural network. Thus, the degree of sparseness of a polynomial coincides with the number of so-called hidden units of a neural network.

If the exponents are allowed to be arbitrary real numbers, we obtain the class of functions computed by a *product unit neural network* with k product units. In these networks, a product unit computes the term

$$x_1^{b_{i,1}} \cdots x_n^{b_{i,n}}$$

and the coefficients $a_0, \ldots, a_k$ are considered as the output weights of the network with bias a_0.

We use $\|\cdot\|$ to denote the Euclidean norm. A *radial basis function neural network* (*RBF network*, for short) computes functions that can be written as

$$w_0 + w_1 \exp\left(-\frac{\|\boldsymbol{x} - \boldsymbol{c}_1\|^2}{\sigma^2}\right) + \cdots + w_k \exp\left(-\frac{\|\boldsymbol{x} - \boldsymbol{c}_k\|^2}{\sigma^2}\right),$$

where k is the number of RBF units. This particular type of network is also known as Gaussian RBF network. Each exponential term corresponds to the function computed by a Gaussian RBF unit with center $\boldsymbol{c}_i \in \mathbb{R}^n$, where n is the number of variables, and width $\sigma \in \mathbb{R} \setminus \{0\}$. The width is a network parameter that we assume to be equal for all units, that is, we consider RBF networks with uniform width. Further, $w_0, \ldots, w_k$ are the output weights and w_0 is also referred to as the bias of the network.

The *Vapnik-Chervonenkis (VC) dimension* of a class $\mathcal{F}$ of real-valued functions is defined via the notion of shattering: A set $S \subseteq \mathbb{R}^n$ is said to be *shattered* by $\mathcal{F}$ if every dichotomy of S is induced by $\mathcal{F}$, that is, if for every pair (S^-, S^+), where $S^- \cap S^+ = \emptyset$ and $S^- \cup S^+ = S$, there is some function $f \in \mathcal{F}$ such that

$$\mathrm{sgn} \circ f(S^-) \subseteq \{0\} \text{ and } \mathrm{sgn} \circ f(S^+) \subseteq \{1\}.$$

Here $\mathrm{sgn} : \mathbb{R} \to \{0,1\}$ denotes the sign function, satisfying $\mathrm{sgn}(x) = 1$ if $x \geq 0$, and $\mathrm{sgn}(x) = 0$ otherwise. The VC dimension of $\mathcal{F}$ is then defined as the cardinality of the largest set shattered by $\mathcal{F}$. (It is said to be infinite if there is no such set.)

Finally, we make use of the geometric notions of ball and hypersphere. A *ball* in $\mathbb{R}^n$ is given in terms of a center $\boldsymbol{c} \in \mathbb{R}^n$ and a radius $\rho \in \mathbb{R}$ as the set

$$B(\boldsymbol{c}, \rho) = \{\boldsymbol{x} \in \mathbb{R}^n : \|\boldsymbol{x} - \boldsymbol{c}\| \leq \rho\}.$$

A *hypersphere* is the set of points on the surface of a ball, that is, the set

$$S(\boldsymbol{c}, \rho) = \{\boldsymbol{x} \in \mathbb{R}^n : \|\boldsymbol{x} - \boldsymbol{c}\| = \rho\}.$$

3 Geometric Constructions

In the following we provide the geometric constructions that are the basis for the main result in Section 4. The idea is to represent classifications of sets using unions of balls, where a point is classified as positive if and only if it is contained in some ball. In order for being shattered, the sets are chosen to satisfy a certain condition of independence with respect to the positions of their elements: The points are required to lie on hyperspheres such that each hypersphere is maximally determined by the set of points. In other words, removing any point increases the set of possible hyperspheres that contain the reduced set. The following definition makes this notion of independence precise.

Definition. *A set $Q \subseteq \mathbb{R}^n$ of at most $n+1$ points is* in general position for hyperspheres *if the system of equalities*

$$\|\boldsymbol{p} - \mathbf{c}\| = \eta, \qquad \text{for all } \boldsymbol{p} \in Q, \tag{1}$$

in the variables $\mathbf{c} = (c_1, \ldots, c_n)$ and η has a solution and, for every $\boldsymbol{q} \in Q$, the solution set is a proper subset of the solution set of the system

$$\|\boldsymbol{p} - \mathbf{c}\| = \eta, \qquad \text{for all } \boldsymbol{p} \in Q \setminus \{\boldsymbol{q}\}. \tag{2}$$

Given a set of points that satisfies this definition and lies on a hypersphere, we next want to find a ball such that one of the points lies outside of the ball while the other points are on its surface. We show that this can be done, provided that the set is in general position for hyperspheres. Moreover, the ball can be chosen with the center and radius as close as possible to the center and radius of the hypersphere that contains all points.

Lemma 1. *Suppose that $Q \subseteq \mathbb{R}^n$ is a set of at most $n+1$ points in general position for hyperspheres and let $\boldsymbol{q} \in Q$. Further, let $\mathbf{c} \in \mathbb{R}^n, \eta \in \mathbb{R}$ be a solution of the system*

$$\|\boldsymbol{p} - \mathbf{c}\| = \eta, \qquad \text{for all } \boldsymbol{p} \in Q. \tag{3}$$

Then, for every $\varepsilon > 0$, there exists a solution $\mathbf{c}(\varepsilon) \in \mathbb{R}^n, \eta(\varepsilon) \in \mathbb{R}$ of the system

$$\begin{aligned} \|\boldsymbol{p} - \mathbf{c}(\varepsilon)\| &= \eta(\varepsilon), \qquad \text{for all } \boldsymbol{p} \in Q \setminus \{\boldsymbol{q}\}, \\ \|\boldsymbol{q} - \mathbf{c}(\varepsilon)\| &> \eta(\varepsilon) \end{aligned}$$

satisfying

$$\begin{aligned} \|\mathbf{c} - \mathbf{c}(\varepsilon)\| &< \varepsilon, \\ |\eta - \eta(\varepsilon)| &< \varepsilon. \end{aligned}$$

Proof. Without loss of generality, we may assume that $\eta > 0$. (If $\eta = 0$ then we have $|Q| = 1$, and the statement is trivial.) Since $\boldsymbol{c}$ and η solve the system (3), $\boldsymbol{c}$ and $\vartheta = \eta^2 - \|\boldsymbol{c}\|^2$ are a solution of the system

$$\|\boldsymbol{p}\|^2 - 2\boldsymbol{pc} = \vartheta, \qquad \text{for all } \boldsymbol{p} \in Q. \tag{4}$$

Because Q is in general position for hyperspheres, the solution set of the system (4) is a proper subset of the solution set of the system

$$\|\boldsymbol{p}\|^2 - 2\boldsymbol{pc} = \vartheta, \qquad \text{for all } \boldsymbol{p} \in Q \setminus \{\boldsymbol{q}\}. \tag{5}$$

According to facts from linear algebra, there exist $\boldsymbol{a} \in \mathbb{R}^n$ and $\alpha \in \mathbb{R}$ such that for every $\lambda \neq 0$, we have with $\boldsymbol{c} + \lambda\boldsymbol{a}$ and $\vartheta + \lambda\alpha$ a solution of the system (5) that does not solve the system (4). For a given $\varepsilon > 0$, choose $\lambda(\varepsilon) \in \mathbb{R} \setminus \{0\}$ such that $|\lambda(\varepsilon)|$ is sufficiently small to satisfy the two inequalities

$$\|\lambda(\varepsilon)\boldsymbol{a}\| < \varepsilon, \tag{6}$$

$$|\sqrt{\vartheta + \|\boldsymbol{c}\|^2} - \sqrt{\vartheta + \lambda(\varepsilon)\alpha + \|\boldsymbol{c} + \lambda(\varepsilon)\boldsymbol{a}\|^2}| < \varepsilon. \tag{7}$$

It is obvious that the second inequality can be met due to the fact that the equation $\sqrt{\vartheta + \|\boldsymbol{c}\|^2} = \eta$ holds, which we get from the definition of ϑ, and the assumption $\eta > 0$. Since $\boldsymbol{c} + \lambda(\varepsilon)\boldsymbol{a}$ and $\vartheta + \lambda(\varepsilon)\alpha$ solve (5) but not (4), it follows that

$$\|\boldsymbol{q}\|^2 - 2\boldsymbol{q}(\boldsymbol{c} + \lambda(\varepsilon)\boldsymbol{a}) \neq \vartheta + \lambda(\varepsilon)\alpha,$$

which, using $\|\boldsymbol{q}\|^2 - 2\boldsymbol{qc} = \vartheta$ from (4), is equivalent to

$$-2\lambda(\varepsilon)\boldsymbol{qa} \neq \lambda(\varepsilon)\alpha.$$

Due to this inequality, we can choose the (not yet specified) sign of $\lambda(\varepsilon)$ such that

$$-2\lambda(\varepsilon)\boldsymbol{qa} > \lambda(\varepsilon)\alpha.$$

Again with $\|\boldsymbol{q}\|^2 - 2\boldsymbol{qc} = \vartheta$, it follows that

$$\|\boldsymbol{q}\|^2 - 2\boldsymbol{q}(\boldsymbol{c} + \lambda(\varepsilon)\boldsymbol{a}) > \vartheta + \lambda(\varepsilon)\alpha,$$

and, therefore,

$$\|\boldsymbol{q} - (\boldsymbol{c} + \lambda(\varepsilon)\boldsymbol{a})\|^2 > \vartheta + \lambda(\varepsilon)\alpha + \|\boldsymbol{c} + \lambda(\varepsilon)\boldsymbol{a}\|^2.$$

Hence, defining

$$\boldsymbol{c}(\varepsilon) = \boldsymbol{c} + \lambda(\varepsilon)\boldsymbol{a},$$

$$\eta(\varepsilon) = \sqrt{\vartheta + \lambda(\varepsilon)\alpha + \|\boldsymbol{c} + \lambda(\varepsilon)\boldsymbol{a}\|^2},$$

we obtain $\|\boldsymbol{q} - \boldsymbol{c}(\varepsilon)\| > \eta(\varepsilon)$. Furthermore, the inequalities (6) and (7) imply that the relations

$$\|\boldsymbol{c} - \boldsymbol{c}(\varepsilon)\| < \varepsilon,$$
$$|\eta - \eta(\varepsilon)| < \varepsilon$$

hold as claimed. □

We now apply the previous result to show that any dichotomy of a given set of points can be obtained using balls. As the set may generally be a subset of some larger set, we also ensure that the balls do not enclose any additional point. Further, we guarantee that this can be done with all centers remaining positive, a condition that will turn out to be useful in the following section. We say here that a vector is positive, if all its components are larger than zero.

Lemma 2. *Let $Q \subseteq \mathbb{R}^n$ be a set of n points in general position for hyperspheres and let $P \subseteq \mathbb{R}^n$ be a finite set with $Q \subseteq P$. Assume further that there exists a positive center $\boldsymbol{c} \in \mathbb{R}^n$ and a radius $\eta \in \mathbb{R}$ such that*

$$Q \subseteq S(\boldsymbol{c}, \eta),$$
$$P \cap B(\boldsymbol{c}, \eta) = Q.$$

Then for every $R \subseteq Q$ there exists a positive center $\boldsymbol{d} \in \mathbb{R}^n$ and a radius $\zeta \in \mathbb{R}$ such that

$$R \subseteq S(\boldsymbol{d}, \zeta),$$
$$P \cap B(\boldsymbol{d}, \zeta) = R.$$

Proof. Clearly, it is sufficient to consider sets R that are proper subsets of Q. Without loss of generality, we may assume that $|R| = |Q| - 1$. The general case then follows inductively. Suppose that $\boldsymbol{q} \in Q$ and let $R = Q \setminus \{\boldsymbol{q}\}$. According to Lemma 1, for every $\varepsilon > 0$ there exist $\boldsymbol{c}(\varepsilon), \eta(\varepsilon)$ satisfying

$$\|\boldsymbol{p} - \boldsymbol{c}(\varepsilon)\| = \eta(\varepsilon), \qquad \text{for all } \boldsymbol{p} \in Q \setminus \{\boldsymbol{q}\}, \tag{8}$$
$$\|\boldsymbol{q} - \boldsymbol{c}(\varepsilon)\| > \eta(\varepsilon), \tag{9}$$
$$\|\boldsymbol{c} - \boldsymbol{c}(\varepsilon)\| < \varepsilon, \tag{10}$$
$$|\eta - \eta(\varepsilon)| < \varepsilon. \tag{11}$$

Obviously, property (8) implies that $R \subseteq S(\boldsymbol{c}(\varepsilon), \eta(\varepsilon))$. Property (9) states that $\boldsymbol{q} \notin B(\boldsymbol{c}(\varepsilon), \eta(\varepsilon))$. Since the assumption $P \cap B(\boldsymbol{c}, \eta) = Q$ implies that for every $\boldsymbol{p}' \in P \setminus Q$ the constraint

$$\|\boldsymbol{p}' - \boldsymbol{c}\| > \eta$$

holds, properties (10) and (11) entail the condition

$$\|\boldsymbol{p}' - \boldsymbol{c}(\varepsilon)\| > \eta(\varepsilon)$$

for all sufficiently small ε. Thus, for any such ε we get the assertion

$$P \cap B(\boldsymbol{c}(\varepsilon), \eta(\varepsilon)) = R.$$

Further, as $\boldsymbol{c}$ is positive, property (10) ensures that $\boldsymbol{c}(\varepsilon)$ is positive for some sufficiently small ε. Hence, the claim follows for $\boldsymbol{d} = \boldsymbol{c}(\varepsilon)$, $\zeta = \eta(\varepsilon)$. □

4 VC Dimension Bound for Sparse Multivariate Polynomials

Before getting to the main result, we derive the lower bound $nk + 1$ for the VC dimension of a restricted type of RBF network. For more general RBF networks, results of Erlich et al. (1997) and Lee et al. (1995) yield $n(k-1)$ as lower bound. The following theorem is stronger not only in the value of the bound, but also in the assumptions that hold: The points of the shattered set all have the same distance from the origin, the centers of the RBF units are rational numbers, and the width can be chosen arbitrarily small.

Theorem 3. *Let $n \geq 2$, $k \geq 1$, and $\rho > 0$ be given. There exists a set $P \subseteq S(\mathbf{0}, \rho) \subseteq \mathbb{R}^n$ of $nk + 1$ points and a real number $\sigma_0 > 0$ so that P is shattered by the class of functions computed by the RBF network with k hidden units, positive rational centers, and any width $0 < \sigma \leq \sigma_0$.*

Proof. Suppose that $B(\boldsymbol{c}_1, \eta_1), \ldots, B(\boldsymbol{c}_k, \eta_k)$ are pairwise disjoint balls with positive centers $\boldsymbol{c}_1, \ldots, \boldsymbol{c}_k \in \mathbb{R}^n$ such that, for $i = 1, \ldots, k$, the intersection $S(\boldsymbol{c}_i, \eta_i) \cap S(\mathbf{0}, \rho)$ is non-empty and not a single point. (An example for $n = 2$ and $k = 3$ is shown in Fig. 1.) For $i = 1, \ldots, k$, let $P_i \subseteq S(\boldsymbol{c}_i, \eta_i) \cap S(\mathbf{0}, \rho)$ be a set of n points in general position for hyperspheres. (Note that P_i is constrained to lie on two different hyperspheres. This still allows to choose P_i in general position since P_i contains n (and not $n + 1$) points, so that the set of possible centers for P_i yields a line.) Further, let $\boldsymbol{s} \in S(\mathbf{0}, \rho)$ be some point such that $\boldsymbol{s} \notin B(\boldsymbol{c}_i, \eta_i)$, for $i = 1, \ldots, k$. We claim that the set $P = \{\boldsymbol{s}\} \cup P_1 \cup \cdots \cup P_k$, which has $nk + 1$ points, is shattered by the RBF network with the postulated restrictions on the parameters.

Assume that (P^-, P^+) is some arbitrary dichotomy of P where $\boldsymbol{s} \in P^-$. (We will argue at the end of the proof that the complementary case can be treated by reversing signs.) Let (P_i^-, P_i^+) denote the dichotomy induced on P_i. By construction, every P_i satisfies

$$P_i \subseteq S(\boldsymbol{c}_i, \eta_i) \text{ and } P \cap B(\boldsymbol{c}_i, \eta_i) = P_i.$$

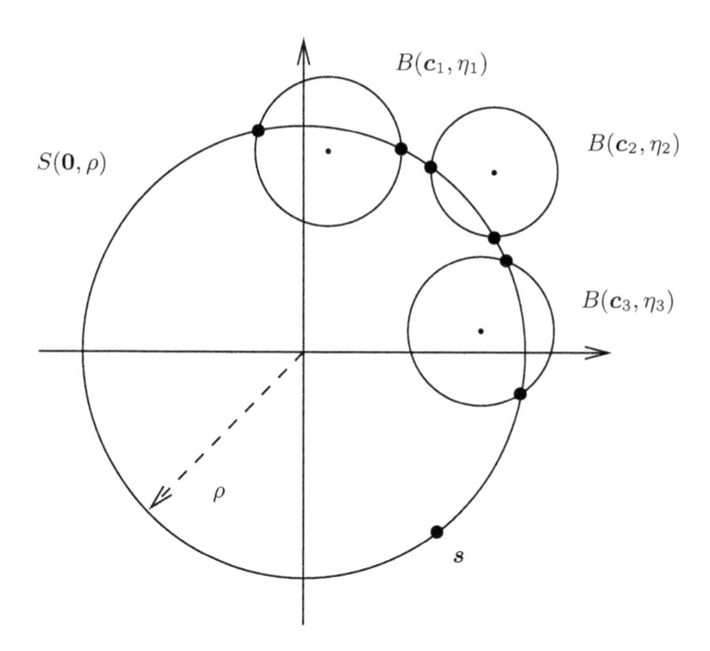

Fig. 1. The points of the shattered set are chosen from the intersections of the hypersphere $S(\mathbf{0}, \rho)$ with the surfaces of pairwise disjoint balls $B(\boldsymbol{c}_i, \eta_i)$. All balls have their centers in the positive orthant. There is one additional point $\boldsymbol{s}$ not contained in any of the balls

Hence by Lemma 2, instantiating the set Q with P_i and the set R with P_i^+, it follows that there exist positive centers $\boldsymbol{d}_i$ and radii ζ_i such that

$$P_i^+ \subseteq S(\boldsymbol{d}_i, \zeta_i) \text{ and } P \cap B(\boldsymbol{d}_i, \zeta_i) = P_i^+,$$

for $i = 1, \ldots, k$. Moreover, the centers $\boldsymbol{d}_i$ can be replaced by rational centers $\tilde{\boldsymbol{d}}_i$ that are sufficiently close to $\boldsymbol{d}_i$, such that every point of P lying outside the ball $B(\boldsymbol{d}_i, \zeta_i)$ is outside the ball $B(\tilde{\boldsymbol{d}}_i, \tilde{\zeta}_i)$ for some $\tilde{\zeta}_i \in \mathbb{R}$ close to ζ_i, and every point of P lying on the hypersphere $S(\boldsymbol{d}_i, \zeta_i)$ is contained in the ball $B(\tilde{\boldsymbol{d}}_i, \tilde{\zeta}_i)$. Thus, every $\boldsymbol{p} \in P$ satisfies

$$\boldsymbol{p} \in B(\tilde{\boldsymbol{d}}_i, \tilde{\zeta}_i) \quad \text{if and only if} \quad \boldsymbol{p} \in P_i^+, \tag{12}$$

for $i = 1, \ldots, k$. Clearly, since the centers $\boldsymbol{d}_i$ are positive, the rational centers $\tilde{\boldsymbol{d}}_i$ can be chosen to be positive as well.

The parameters of the RBF network are specified as follows: The i-th unit is associated with the ball $B(\tilde{\boldsymbol{d}}_i, \tilde{\zeta}_i)$. Assigned to it is $\tilde{\boldsymbol{d}}_i$ as the center and as output weight the value $\exp(\tilde{\zeta}_i^{\,2}/\sigma^2)$ (where σ will be determined below) so that the unit contributes the term

$$\exp\left(\frac{\tilde{\zeta}_i^2}{\sigma^2}\right)\exp\left(-\frac{\|\boldsymbol{x}-\tilde{\boldsymbol{d}}_i\|^2}{\sigma^2}\right)$$

to the computation of the network. From assertion (12) we obtain that every $\boldsymbol{p} \in P \setminus P_i^+$ satisfies the constraint

$$\|\boldsymbol{p}-\tilde{\boldsymbol{d}}_i\| > \tilde{\zeta}_i.$$

Thus, for every sufficiently small $\sigma > 0$ and every $\boldsymbol{p} \in P \setminus P_i^+$, we achieve that

$$\exp\left(-\frac{\|\boldsymbol{p}-\tilde{\boldsymbol{d}}_i\|^2-\tilde{\zeta}_i^2}{\sigma^2}\right) < \frac{1}{k} \tag{13}$$

is valid for $i = 1, \ldots, k$. On the other hand, for every $\boldsymbol{p} \in P_i^+$ condition (12) implies

$$\|\boldsymbol{p}-\tilde{\boldsymbol{d}}_i\| \leq \tilde{\zeta}_i,$$

which entails

$$\exp\left(-\frac{\|\boldsymbol{p}-\tilde{\boldsymbol{d}}_i\|^2-\tilde{\zeta}_i^2}{\sigma^2}\right) \geq 1 \tag{14}$$

for every $\sigma > 0$. Finally, we set the bias term equal to -1. It is now easy to see that the dichotomy (P^-, P^+) is induced by the parameter settings: If $\boldsymbol{p} \in P^-$ then, according to inequality (13), the weighted output values of the units and the bias sum up to a negative value. In the case $\boldsymbol{p} \in P^+$ we have $\boldsymbol{p} \in P_i^+$ for some i and, by inequality (14), the weighted unit i outputs value of at least 1, while the other units output positive values, so that the total network output is positive.

The construction for the case that classifies $\boldsymbol{s}$ as positive works similarly. We invoke Lemma 2 substituting P_i^- for R and derive the analogous version of assertion (12) with P_i^+ replaced by P_i^-. Then it is obvious that, if the weights defined above are equipped with negative signs and 1 is used as the bias, the network induces the dichotomy as claimed.

We observe that σ may have been chosen such that it depends on the particular dichotomy. To complete the proof, we require σ_0 to be small enough so that inequality (13) holds for $\sigma \leq \sigma_0$ on all points and dichotomies of P. □

We remark that one assumption of the theorem can be slightly weakened: It is not necessary to require that $\boldsymbol{s} \in S(\boldsymbol{0}, \rho)$. Instead, every point not contained in any of the balls $B(\boldsymbol{c}_i, \eta_i)$ can be selected for $\boldsymbol{s}$. However, the restriction is required for the application of the theorem in the following result, which is the main contribution of this paper. For its proof we recall the definition of a product unit neural network in Section 2.

Theorem 4. *For every $n, k \geq 1$, the VC dimension of the class of k-sparse polynomials in n variables is at least $nk + 1$.*

Proof. We first consider the case $n \geq 2$. By Theorem 3, for $\rho > 0$ let $P \subseteq \mathbb{R}^n$, $P \subseteq S(\mathbf{0}, \rho)$, be the set of cardinality $nk + 1$ that is shattered by the RBF network with k hidden units and the stated parameter settings. We show that P can be transformed into a set P' that is shattered by k-sparse polynomials. The weighted output computed by unit i in the RBF network on input $\boldsymbol{p} \in P$ can be written as

$$w_i \cdot \exp\left(-\frac{\|\boldsymbol{p} - \boldsymbol{c}_i\|^2}{\sigma^2}\right) = w_i \cdot \exp\left(-\frac{\|\boldsymbol{p}\|^2 - 2\boldsymbol{p}\boldsymbol{c}_i + \|\boldsymbol{c}_i\|^2}{\sigma^2}\right)$$

$$= w_i \cdot \exp\left(-\frac{\|\boldsymbol{p}\|^2 + \|\boldsymbol{c}_i\|^2}{\sigma^2}\right) \exp\left(\frac{2\boldsymbol{p}\boldsymbol{c}_i}{\sigma^2}\right)$$

$$= w_i \cdot \exp\left(-\frac{\rho^2 + \|\boldsymbol{c}_i\|^2}{\sigma^2}\right) \cdot \exp\left(\frac{2p_1 c_{i,1}}{\sigma^2}\right) \cdots \exp\left(\frac{2p_n c_{i,n}}{\sigma^2}\right),$$

where we have used the assumption $P \subseteq S(\mathbf{0}, \rho)$ for the last equation, and $p_j, c_{i,j}$ to denote the j-th components of the vectors $\boldsymbol{p}, \boldsymbol{c}_i$, respectively. Consider a product unit network with one hidden layer, where unit i has output weight

$$w_i' = w_i \cdot \exp\left(-\frac{\rho^2 + \|\boldsymbol{c}_i\|^2}{\sigma^2}\right)$$

and exponents $2c_{i,j}/\sigma^2$ for $j = 1, \ldots, n$. On the set

$$P' = \{(e^{p_1}, \ldots, e^{p_n}) : (p_1, \ldots, p_n) \in P\}$$

this product unit network computes the same values as the RBF network on P. Moreover, the exponents of the product units are positive rationals. According to Theorem 3, for some σ_0, any width $0 < \sigma \leq \sigma_0$ can be used. Therefore, we may choose $\sigma^2 = 1/l$ for some natural number l that is sufficiently large and a common multiple of all denominators occurring in any $c_{i,j}$, so that the exponents become integers. With these parameter settings, we have a k-sparse polynomial that computes on P' the same output values as the RBF network on P. As this can be done for every dichotomy of P, it follows that P' is shattered by k-sparse polynomials.

For the case $n = 1$, we again use the RBF technique and ideas from Schmitt (2002a,2004). Clearly, the set $M = \{0, \ldots, k\}$ can be shattered by an RBF network with $k + 1$ hidden units and zero bias: For each $i \in M$ we employ an RBF unit with center i; given a dichotomy (M^-, M^+), we let the output weight for unit i be -1 if $i \in M^-$, and 1 if $i \in M^+$. If the width σ is small enough, the output value of the network has the requested sign on every input $i \in M$. Now, let σ be the smallest width sufficient for all dichotomies of M. Then

$$w_0 \exp\left(-\frac{x^2}{\sigma^2}\right) + w_1 \exp\left(-\frac{(x-1)^2}{\sigma^2}\right) + \cdots + w_k \exp\left(-\frac{(x-k)^2}{\sigma^2}\right) \geq 0$$

is, by multiplication with $\exp(x^2/\sigma^2)$, equivalent to

$$w_0 + w_1 \exp\left(\frac{2x-1}{\sigma^2}\right) + \cdots + w_k \exp\left(\frac{2kx-k^2}{\sigma^2}\right) \geq 0.$$

The latter can be written as

$$w_0 + w_1 \exp\left(-\frac{1}{\sigma^2}\right) \exp\left(\frac{2x}{\sigma^2}\right) + \cdots + w_k \exp\left(-\frac{k^2}{\sigma^2}\right) \exp\left(\frac{2kx}{\sigma^2}\right) \geq 0.$$

Substituting $y = \exp(2x/\sigma^2)$, this holds if and only if

$$w_0 + w_1 \exp\left(-\frac{1}{\sigma^2}\right) y + \cdots + w_k \exp\left(-\frac{k^2}{\sigma^2}\right) y^k \geq 0.$$

Thus, for every dichotomy of M we obtain a dichotomy of $M' = \{e^{2i/\sigma^2} : i = 0, \ldots, k\}$ induced by a k-sparse polynomial. In other words, M' is shattered by this function class. □

5 Comparison with k-Term Monotone DNF

A Boolean formula that is a disjunction of up to k monomial terms without negations can be considered as a k-sparse polynomial restricted to Boolean inputs. The previously best known lower bound for the VC dimension of k-sparse polynomials was the bound for k-term monotone DNF due to Littlestone (1988). By deriving an upper bound for the latter class and applying Theorem 4, we show that the VC dimension for k-sparse polynomials is strictly larger than the VC dimension for k-term monotone DNF. We use "log" to denote the logarithm of base 2.

Corollary 5. *Let $n \geq 1$ and $3 \leq k \leq 2^n$. The VC dimension of the class of k-sparse n-variate polynomials exceeds the VC dimension of the class of k-term n-variate monotone DNF by more than $k \log(k/e) + 1$.*

Proof. A k-term monotone DNF formula corresponds to a collection of up to k subsets of the set of variables. For n variables, there are no more than $\sum_{i=0}^{k} \binom{2^n}{i}$ such collections. The known inequality $\sum_{i=0}^{d} \binom{m}{i} < (em/d)^d$, where $1 \leq d \leq m$, (see, e.g., Anthony and Bartlett, 1999, Theorem 3.7) yields

$$\sum_{i=0}^{k} \binom{2^n}{i} < \left(\frac{e}{k}\right)^k 2^{nk}.$$

By definition, the VC dimension of a finite function class $\mathcal{F}$ cannot be larger than $\log|\mathcal{F}|$. Hence, the VC dimension for k-term monotone DNF is less than $nk - k\log(k/e)$. Theorem 4 implies that this bound falls short of the VC dimension for k-sparse polynomials by at least $k \log(k/e) + 1$. □

It is easy to see that in the cases $k = 1, 2$, which are not covered by Corollary 5, the VC dimension of k-sparse polynomials is larger as well. First, as there are no more than 2^n Boolean monotone monomials, the VC dimension of monotone monomials is at most n. Second, the number of monotone DNF formulas with at most two terms is not larger than $2^{2n} + 1$, and $\log(2^{2n} + 1)$ is less than $2n + 1$.

6 Conclusion

We have derived a new lower bound for the VC dimension of sparse multivariate polynomials. This bound is stronger and holds for a wider class of polynomials than the previous bound via Boolean formulas in monotone DNF. Moreover, it follows that the VC dimension for k-sparse polynomials exceeds the VC dimension for k-term monotone DNF. Therefore, the techniques that use DNF formulas for deriving lower bounds on the VC dimension of sparse polynomials seem to have reached their limits.

We have introduced a method that accomplishes dichotomies of sets by polynomials via Gaussian RBF networks. At first view, the Gaussian RBF network appears to be more powerful than a polynomial, provided both have the same number of terms: Each parameter of a Gaussian RBF network may assume any real number, whereas the polynomial must have exponents that are nonnegative and integers. Nevertheless, we have shown here that RBF networks can be used to establish lower bounds on the computational capabilities of sparse multivariate polynomials. While the previous lower bound method via monotone DNF formulas gives rise to monomials with exponents not larger than 1, the approach that uses RBF networks shows that and how large exponents can be employed to shatter sets of a cardinality larger than known before. Moreover, the constructions give reason to a completely new interpretation of the exponent vectors when polynomials are used for classification tasks: They have been chosen as centers of balls. This perspective might open a new approach for the design of learning algorithms that use sparse multivariate polynomials as hypotheses.

The result of this paper narrows the gap between lower and upper bound for the VC dimension of sparse multivariate polynomials. As the bounds are not yet tight, it is to be hoped that the method presented here may lead to further insights that possibly yield additional improvements.

Acknowledgments. I thank Hans U. Simon for helpful discussions. This work was supported in part by the Deutsche Forschungsgemeinschaft (DFG).

References

Anthony, M. and Bartlett, P. L. (1999). *Neural Network Learning: Theoretical Foundations.* Cambridge University Press, Cambridge.

Bartlett, P. L. and Maass, W. (2003). Vapnik-Chervonenkis dimension of neural nets. In Arbib, M. A., editor, *The Handbook of Brain Theory and Neural Networks*, pages 1188–1192. MIT Press, Cambridge, MA, second edition.

Bartlett, P. L., Maiorov, V., and Meir, R. (1998). Almost linear VC-dimension bounds for piecewise polynomial networks. *Neural Computation*, 10:2159–2173.

Ben-David, S. and Lindenbaum, M. (1998). Localization vs. identification of semi-algebraic sets. *Machine Learning*, 32:207–224.

Blum, A. and Singh, M. (1990). Learning functions of k terms. In Fulk, M. A., editor, *Proceedings of the Third Annual Workshop on Computational Learning Theory*, pages 144–153. Morgan Kaufmann, San Mateo, CA.

Bshouty, N. H. and Mansour, Y. (1995). Simple learning algorithms for decision trees and multivariate polynomials. In *Proceedings of the 36th Annual Symposium on Foundations of Computer Science*, pages 304–311. IEEE Computer Society Press, Los Alamitos, CA.

Durbin, R. and Rumelhart, D. (1989). Product units: A computationally powerful and biologically plausible extension to backpropagation networks. *Neural Computation*, 1:133–142.

Ehrenfeucht, A., Haussler, D., Kearns, M., and Valiant, L. (1989). A general lower bound on the number of examples needed for learning. *Information and Computation*, 82:247–261.

Erlich, Y., Chazan, D., Petrack, S., and Levy, A. (1997). Lower bound on VC-dimension by local shattering. *Neural Computation*, 9:771–776.

Fischer, P. and Simon, H. U. (1992). On learning ring-sum-expansions. *SIAM Journal on Computing*, 21:181–192.

Grigoriev, D. Y., Karpinski, M., and Singer, M. F. (1990). Fast parallel algorithms for sparse multivariate polynomial interpolation over finite fields. *SIAM Journal on Computing*, 19:1059–1063.

Haykin, S. (1999). *Neural Networks: A Comprehensive Foundation.* Prentice Hall, Upper Saddle River, NJ, second edition.

Huang, M.-D. and Rao, A. J. (1999). Interpolation of sparse multivariate polynomials over large finite fields with applications. *Journal of Algorithms*, 33:204–228.

Karpinski, M. and Macintyre, A. (1997). Polynomial bounds for VC dimension of sigmoidal and general Pfaffian neural networks. *Journal of Computer and System Sciences*, 54:169–176.

Karpinski, M. and Werther, T. (1993). VC dimension and uniform learnability of sparse polynomials and rational functions. *SIAM Journal on Computing*, 22:1276–1285.

Koiran, P. and Sontag, E. D. (1997). Neural networks with quadratic VC dimension. *Journal of Computer and System Sciences*, 54:190–198.

Lee, W. S., Bartlett, P. L., and Williamson, R. C. (1995). Lower bounds on the VC dimension of smoothly parameterized function classes. *Neural Computation*, 7:1040–1053.

Littlestone, N. (1988). Learning quickly when irrelevant attributes abound: A new linear-threshold algorithm. *Machine Learning*, 2:285–318.

Murao, H. and Fujise, T. (1996). Modular algorithm for sparse multivariate polynomial interpolation and its parallel implementation. *Journal of Symbolic Computation*, 21:377–396.

Roth, R. M. and Benedek, G. M. (1990). Interpolation and approximation of sparse multivariate polynomials over GF(2). *SIAM Journal on Computing*, 20:291–314.

Schapire, R. E. and Sellie, L. (1996). Learning sparse multivariate polynomials over a field with queries and counterexamples. *Journal of Computer and System Sciences*, 52:201–213.

Schmitt, M. (2002a). Descartes' rule of signs for radial basis function neural networks. *Neural Computation*, 14:2997–3011.

Schmitt, M. (2002b). Neural networks with local receptive fields and superlinear VC dimension. *Neural Computation*, 14:919–956.

Schmitt, M. (2002c). On the complexity of computing and learning with multiplicative neural networks. *Neural Computation*, 14:241–301.

Schmitt, M. (2004). New designs for the Descartes rule of signs. *American Mathematical Monthly*, 111:159–164.

Vapnik, V. N. and Chervonenkis, A. Y. (1971). On the uniform convergence of relative frequencies of events to their probabilities. *Theory of Probability and its Applications*, 16:264–280.

A New PAC Bound for Intersection-Closed Concept Classes

Peter Auer and Ronald Ortner

Department of Mathematics and Information Technology
University of Leoben
Franz-Josef-Straße 18, A-8700 Leoben, Austria
auer@unileoben.ac.at, ronald.ortner@unileoben.ac.at

Abstract. For hyper-rectangles in $\mathbf{R}^d$ Auer et al. [1] proved a PAC bound of $O\left(\frac{1}{\varepsilon}(d+\log\frac{1}{\delta})\right)$, where ε and δ are the accuracy and confidence parameters. It is still an open question whether one can obtain the same bound for intersection-closed concept classes of VC-dimension d in general. We present a step towards a solution of this problem showing on one hand a new PAC bound of $O\left(\frac{1}{\varepsilon}(d\log d+\frac{1}{\delta})\right)$ for arbitrary intersection-closed concept classes complementing the well-known bounds $O\left(\frac{1}{\varepsilon}(\log\frac{1}{\delta}+d\log\frac{1}{\varepsilon})\right)$ and $O\left(\frac{d}{\varepsilon}\log\frac{1}{\delta}\right)$ of Blumer et al. and Haussler et al. [4,6]. Our bound is established using the *closure algorithm*, that generates as its hypothesis the smallest concept that is consistent with the positive training examples. On the other hand, we show that maximum intersection-closed concept classes meet the bound of $O\left(\frac{1}{\varepsilon}(d+\log\frac{1}{\delta})\right)$ as well. Moreover, we indicate that our new as well as the conjectured bound cannot hold for arbitrary consistent learning algorithms, giving an example of such an algorithm that needs $\Omega\left(\frac{1}{\varepsilon}(d\log\frac{1}{\varepsilon}+\log\frac{1}{\delta})\right)$ examples to learn some simple maximum intersection-closed concept class.

1 Introduction

In the PAC model a learning algorithm generalizes from given examples to a hypothesis that approximates a target concept taken from a concept class known to the learner. The learning algorithm $\mathcal{A}$ then PAC learns a concept class if for ε, δ there is an $m = m(\varepsilon, \delta)$, such that with probability at least $1-\delta$ the algorithm outputs a hypothesis with accuracy $\geq \varepsilon$ when m random examples are given to $\mathcal{A}$. Bounds on m usually depend on the VC-dimension, a combinatorial parameter of the concept class. For finite d the well-known bound of Blumer et al. [4] states that for *any* consistent learning algorithm $O\left(\frac{1}{\varepsilon}(\log\frac{1}{\delta}+d\log\frac{1}{\varepsilon})\right)$ examples suffice for PAC learning concept classes of VC-dimension d. On the other hand, for the 1-inclusion graph algorithm a bound of $O\left(\frac{d}{\varepsilon}\log\frac{1}{\delta}\right)$ was established in [6]. In this paper we give a complementing bound of $O\left(\frac{1}{\varepsilon}(d\log d+\frac{1}{\delta})\right)$ when learning intersection-closed concept classes (see e.g. [1,2,7]) with the closure algorithm. Intersection-closed concept classes include quite natural classes such as hyper-rectangles in $\mathbf{R}^d$ or the class of all subsets of some finite X with $\leq d$ elements. For these concrete intersection-closed concept classes an optimal bound

J. Shawe-Taylor and Y. Singer (Eds.): COLT 2004, LNAI 3120, pp. 408–414, 2004.

of $O\left(\frac{1}{\varepsilon}(d+\log\frac{1}{\delta})\right)$ can be shown (see [3] and Sect. 4 below, resp.). It is an open problem whether this optimal bound holds for intersection-closed concept classes in general. If so, it can be achieved only for special learning algorithms since there are consistent learning algorithms that need $\Omega\left(\frac{1}{\varepsilon}(d\log\frac{1}{\varepsilon}+\log\frac{1}{\delta})\right)$ examples to learn some intersection-closed concept classes (see Sect. 4 below).

2 Preliminaries

2.1 Intersection-Closed Concept Classes

A *concept class* over a (countable) set X is a subset $\mathcal{C} \subseteq 2^X$. For $Y \subseteq X$ we set $\mathcal{C} \cap Y := \{C \cap Y \mid C \in \mathcal{C}\}$. The *VC-dimension* of a concept class $\mathcal{C} \subseteq 2^X$ is the cardinality of a largest $Y \subseteq X$ for which $\mathcal{C} \cap Y = 2^Y$.

Definition 1. *A concept class $\mathcal{C} \subseteq 2^X$ is intersection-closed if for all $C_1, C_2 \in \mathcal{C}$: $C_1 \cap C_2 \in \mathcal{C}$.*

For any set $Y \subseteq X$ and any concept class $\mathcal{C} \subseteq 2^X$ we define the *closure of* Y (with respect to $\mathcal{C}$) as $\mathrm{clos}_{\mathcal{C}}(Y) := \bigcap_{Y \subseteq C \in \mathcal{C}} C$. If it is clear to which concept class we refer we often drop the index and write $\mathrm{clos}(Y)$. The following proposition provides an alternative definition of intersection-closed concept classes.

Proposition 2. *A concept class $\mathcal{C} \subseteq 2^X$ is intersection-closed if and only if for $Y \subseteq C \in \mathcal{C}$ one always has $\mathrm{clos}(Y) \in \mathcal{C}$.*

Proof. First, it is clear by definition that $\mathrm{clos}(Y) \in \mathcal{C}$ for intersection-closed $\mathcal{C}$. Now suppose that for $Y \subseteq C \in \mathcal{C}$ one always has $\mathrm{clos}(Y) \in \mathcal{C}$ and let $C_1, C_2 \in \mathcal{C}$. Then because of $C_1 \cap C_2 \subseteq C_1, C_2$ we have by definition of the closure, $\mathrm{clos}(C_1 \cap C_2) \subseteq C_1 \cap C_2$. On the other hand, $C_1 \cap C_2 \subseteq \mathrm{clos}(C_1 \cap C_2)$, so that $C_1 \cap C_2 = \mathrm{clos}(C_1 \cap C_2) \in \mathcal{C}$. □

Again, let $Y \subseteq X$. A *spanning set of* Y (with respect to an intersection-closed concept class) is any set $S \subseteq Y$ such that $\mathrm{clos}(S) = \mathrm{clos}(Y)$. A spanning set S of Y is called *minimal* if there is no spanning set S' of Y with $|S'| < |S|$. Finally, let $\mathrm{span}_{\mathcal{C}}(Y)$ denote the set of all minimal spanning sets of Y. Again we will often drop the index if no ambiguity can arise. The following theorem mentions a key property of intersection-closed concept classes (for a proof we refer to [7]).

Theorem 3. *All minimal spanning sets of some $Y \subseteq X$ in an intersection-closed class $\mathcal{C} \subseteq 2^X$ have size at most VC-Dim($\mathcal{C}$).*

Furthermore, we shall need the following well-known theorem.

Theorem 4 (Sauer's Lemma[9]). *Let $\mathcal{C} \subseteq 2^X$ be a concept class of VC-dimension d. Then*

$$|\mathcal{C}| \le \binom{|X|}{\le d} = \sum_{i=0}^{d} \binom{|X|}{i}.$$

2.2 Learning

Learning a concept $C \in \mathcal{C}$ means learning the characteristic function $\mathbf{1}_C$ on X. Thus the learner outputs a hypothesis $h : X \to \{0,1\}$. Given a probability distribution $\mathcal{P}$ on X the error of the hypothesis h with respect to C and $\mathcal{P}$ is defined as $\mathbf{er}_{C,\mathcal{P}}(h) := \mathcal{P}(\{x \mid h(x) \neq \mathbf{1}_C(x)\})$.

Definition 5. *A concept class $\mathcal{C} \subseteq 2^X$ is called PAC learnable if for all $\varepsilon, \delta \in (0,1)$, all probability distributions $\mathcal{P}$ on X and all $C \in \mathcal{C}$ there is an $m = m(\varepsilon, \delta)$ such that when learning C from m randomly chosen examples according to $\mathcal{P}$ and C the output hypothesis h has $\mathbf{er}_{C,\mathcal{P}}(h) > \varepsilon$ with probability $< \delta$ with respect to the m examples drawn independently according to $\mathcal{P}$.*

3 A New PAC Bound

The property mentioned in Theorem 3 can be used together with Sauer's Lemma to modify the original proof of the bound of $O\left(\frac{1}{\varepsilon}(\log\frac{1}{\delta} + d\log\frac{1}{\varepsilon})\right)$ for arbitrary concept classes by Blumer et al. [4] to obtain the following alternative bound.

Theorem 6. *Let $\mathcal{C} \subseteq 2^X$ be a well-behaved*[1] *intersection-closed concept class of VC-dimension $d \geq 10$. Then $\mathcal{C}$ is PAC learnable from*

$$m \geq \max\left\{\frac{16}{\varepsilon} d\log d,\ \frac{6}{\varepsilon}\log\frac{28}{\delta}\right\}$$

examples.

The main step of the mentioned proof is the so-called "doubling trick" (for details see [4], p.952ff): One chooses $2m$ (labelled) examples $(x_1, y_1), \ldots, (x_{2m}, y_{2m})$ and counts the number of permutations such that the hypothesis calculated from the first m examples misclassisfies at least p of the second m examples. Then choosing $p = \lceil \varepsilon m/2 \rceil$ one obtains the bound. In the following we give an improved bound for the number of permutations for intersection-closed concept classes.

Unlike in the original proof we are going to use a special learning algorithm, namely the *closure algorithm*. Given a set of labelled examples $(x_1, y_1), \ldots, (x_m, y_m)$ with labels $y_i \in \{0,1\}$ the hypothesis generated by the closure algorithm is the smallest concept $C \in \mathcal{C}$ that is consistent with the positive examples, that is, the examples with $y_i = 1$. It is easy to see that this concept is identical to the closure of $\{x_i \mid y_i = 1, 1 \leq i \leq m\}$. Thus, negative examples don't have any influence on the generated hypothesis. Moreover we have the following proposition.

Proposition 7. *The closure algorithm classifies all negative examples correctly.*

[1] The usual measurability conditions on certain sets turning up in the proof of Lemma 9 below have to be satisfied (for a detailed discussion see [4], p.952ff). However, we remark that concept classes over finite X are always well-behaved.

Proof. The algorithm returns the smallest concept that is consistent with the positive examples. Consequently, if it classified any negative example incorrectly there wouldn't be any concept in $\mathcal{C}$ that is consistent with the given examples. □

Hence, according to Proposition 7, any incorrectly classified example among $(x_{m+1}, y_{m+1}), \ldots, (x_{2m}, y_{2m})$ must be positive. Thus when counting the number of the aformentioned permutations we can confine ourselves to positive examples. Let ℓ be the number of positive examples among $(x_1, y_1), \ldots, (x_{2m}, y_{2m})$. We define recursively sets X_i and S_i for $i = 1, \ldots, \ell$, where $X_1 := \{x_i \mid y_i = 1, 1 \leq i \leq 2m\}$ is the set of positive examples. S_i is an arbitrary element of span(X_i) and for $i > 1$ we set $X_i := X_{i-1} \setminus S_{i-1}$. Now for each X_i that contains misclassified examples there must be at least one misclassified example in the corresponding spanning set S_i as well. Thus removing S_i from X_i at least one misclassified example is removed, which leads to the following proposition.

Proposition 8. *If there are k incorrectly classified examples among the $x_1, \ldots,$ x_{2m} they are in $\bigcup_{i=1}^k S_i$.*

Proof. By Proposition 7, misclassified examples must be in X_1. Now suppose there is a wrongly classified example that is not in $\bigcup_{i=1}^k S_i$. Since the S_i are disjoint it follows that there is an S_{i_0} that does not contain any misclassified example. Thus, all examples in S_{i_0} and consequently all examples in X_{i_0} are classified correctly. But this is only possible if all the k misclassified examples have been removed before, so that they have to be contained in $\bigcup_{i=1}^{i_0} S_i \subseteq \bigcup_{i=1}^k S_i$, which contradicts our assumption. □

Lemma 9. *Let $\mathcal{C} \subseteq 2^X$ be a well-behaved intersection-closed concept class of VC-dimension d, $\mathcal{P}$ be a probability distribution on X and the target concept C be a Borel set $\subseteq X$. Then for all $\varepsilon > 0$ and for all $m > 2/\varepsilon$, given m independent random examples labelled by C and drawn according to $\mathcal{P}$, the probability that the hypothesis h generated by the closure algorithm has error $\mathbf{er}_{C,\mathcal{P}}(h) > \varepsilon$ is at most*

$$2 \sum_{k=p}^{m} 2^{-k} \binom{kd}{\leq d},$$

where $p = \lceil \varepsilon m/2 \rceil$.

Proof. As mentioned before, the proof follows the main lines of [4], pp.952ff. However, our equivalent to Lemma A2.2 looks a bit different. Concerning the number of *witnesses*, i.e. the sets of wrongly classified examples, in the proof of Lemma A2.2 we need not consider $\Pi(2m)$, the number of all subsets of $\{x_1, \ldots, x_{2m}\}$ that are induced by intersections with concepts in $\mathcal{C}$. Instead, according to Proposition 8, it is sufficient to consider the corresponding subsets of $\bigcup_{i=1}^k S_i$ for $k = p, \ldots, m$. By Theorem 3, $|\bigcup_{i=1}^k S_i| \leq kd$ so that by Sauer's Lemma the number of these subsets for fixed k is at most $\binom{kd}{\leq d}$. Summing up over all $k \in \{p, \ldots, m\}$ the result follows analogously to the proofs of Lemma A2.2 and Theorem A2.1 in [4]. □

Lemma 10. *If $d \geq 10$ and*

$$m \geq \max\left\{ \frac{16}{\varepsilon} d \log d, \frac{6}{\varepsilon} \log \frac{28}{\delta} \right\} \quad \text{then} \quad 2 \sum_{k=p}^{m} 2^{-k} \binom{kd}{\leq d} < \delta ,$$

where $p = \lceil \varepsilon m/2 \rceil$.

Proof. First, we are going to use Proposition A2.1 (iii) of [4], which tells us that for $k, d \geq 1$ one has

$$\binom{kd}{\leq d} \leq (ek)^d . \tag{1}$$

It is easy to check that for $d \geq 10$ and $k \geq 8 d \log d$ it holds that

$$\frac{k}{2} > \frac{d \log(ek)}{\log 2}, \text{ or equivalently } (ek)^d < 2^{k/2} . \tag{2}$$

Hence for $k \geq 8 d \log d$ we have from (1) and (2)

$$2 \sum_{k=p}^{m} 2^{-k} \binom{kd}{\leq d} \leq 2 \sum_{k=p}^{m} 2^{-k} (ek)^d < 2 \sum_{k=p}^{m} 2^{-k/2} < 2 \cdot 2^{-p/2} \frac{2}{2 - \sqrt{2}} .$$

Setting $K := \frac{4}{2-\sqrt{2}}$ and substituting $p = \lceil \varepsilon m/2 \rceil$ it is easy to see that for $m \geq \frac{6}{\varepsilon} \log \frac{28}{\delta} > \frac{4}{\varepsilon \log 2} \log \frac{K}{\delta}$ one has $K \cdot 2^{-p/2} < \delta$, which finishes the proof. □

Proof of Theorem 6. The theorem follows immediately from Lemmata 9 and 10. □

4 Maximum Intersection-Closed Classes

A concept class $\mathcal{C}$ over finite X is called *maximum* (cf. [5]), if it meets the bound of Sauer's Lemma (Theorem 4 above), that is, if $|\mathcal{C}| = \binom{|X|}{\leq d}$. An example of a maximum (and intersection-closed) concept class of VC-dimension d is $\mathcal{C}_{X,d} := \{C \subseteq X : |C| \leq d\}$, the class of all $\leq d$-subsets of X.

This time adapting the proof of bound of $O\left(\frac{1}{\varepsilon}(d + \log \frac{1}{\delta})\right)$ for hyper-rectangles in [3] we show that the closure algorithm learns maximum intersection-closed concept classes from $O\left(\frac{1}{\varepsilon}(d + \log \frac{1}{\delta})\right)$ examples as well.

Theorem 11. *Let $\mathcal{C}$ be a maximum intersection-closed concept class of VC-dimension d over finite X. Then $\mathcal{C}$ is PAC learnable from*

$$m \geq \frac{e}{\varepsilon} \left(d + \log \frac{1}{\delta} \right)$$

examples.

For the proof of Theorem 11 we will use the following key property of maximum classes (for a proof we refer to [5]).

Theorem 12 (Welzl 1987). *Let $\mathcal{C} \subseteq 2^X$ be a maximum concept class of VC-dimension d over finite X. Then for any $x \in X$ the concept class $\mathcal{C}_x := \{C \in \mathcal{C} \mid x \in C\}$ is maximum of VC-dimension $d-1$.*

Corollary 13 (Welzl 1987). *Let $\mathcal{C} \subseteq 2^X$ be a maximum concept class of VC-dimension d over finite X. Then for any d-subset $Y \subseteq X$ the concept class $\mathcal{C}_Y := \{C \in \mathcal{C} \mid Y \subseteq C\}$ has VC-dimension 0 and hence consists of a single element.*

Proof of Theorem 11. As mentioned before we follow the main lines of the proof of Theorem 7 in [3], pp.381ff. We only have to argue that Lemma 10 of [3] holds in our case as well. This time we have to count the number of possibilities to choose m from $m+p$ examples $(x_1, y_1), \ldots, (x_{m+p}, y_{m+p})$ such that the hypothesis calculated from these m examples misclassifies the p remaining examples. Obviously, we may consider the concept class $\mathcal{C}' = \mathcal{C} \cap \{x_1, \ldots, x_{m+p}\}$ instead of $\mathcal{C}$ itself. Thus, we will show that the number of concepts in $\mathcal{C}'$ that misclassify exactly p examples among $(x_1, y_1), \ldots, (x_{m+p}, y_{m+p})$ is $\leq \binom{d+p}{p}$. Then choosing $p = \lceil \log \frac{1}{\delta} \rceil$, the theorem follows analogously to [3].

Again using the closure algorithm, only the positive examples $X_1 = \{x_i \mid y_i = 1, 1 \leq i \leq m+p\}$ are relevant for hypothesis calculation and evaluation as well. We assume that none of the positive examples occurs more than once among $(x_1, y_1), \ldots, (x_{m+p}, y_{m+p})$. Otherwise the number of partitions will be even smaller.

Now we want to encode the concepts in $\mathcal{C}'$ according to their classification of the examples in X_1. To this end we impose an arbitrary but fixed order on the elements of X_1. Each concept $C \in \mathcal{C}'$ is then encoded as a word in $\{0,1\}^{|X_1|}$ as follows: a 1 on the j-th position means that C classifies x_{i_j} correctly, while a 0 indicates that x_{i_j} is misclassified by C. Being interested only in concepts that misclassify exactly p examples of X_1 we need only consider the first $d+p$ letters of the code words. First, it is clear that there cannot occur more than p 0-entries in the code word corresponding to such a concept. On the other hand, if there are $\geq d$ 1-entries in a code word w, according to Corollary 13 there is only one concept in $\mathcal{C}$ that corresponds to w. Thus, the number of concepts is bounded above by the number of code words consisting of p 0-entries and d 1-entries. The latter is equal to $\binom{d+p}{p}$, which finishes our proof. □

The following example shows that for the new bounds in this paper, the choice of the learning algorithm is essential. Consider $\mathcal{C}_{X,d}$, the class of all $\leq d$-subsets of X, and an algorithm that chooses as its hypothesis not the smallest concept consistent with the given examples (as the closure algorithm does) but an arbitrarily chosen largest consistent concept. We claim that this algorithm needs $\Omega\left(\frac{1}{\varepsilon}(d \log \frac{1}{\varepsilon} + \log \frac{1}{\delta})\right)$ examples to learn $\mathcal{C}_{X,d}$. First we show a lower bound of $\Omega\left(\frac{d}{\varepsilon} \log \frac{1}{\varepsilon}\right)$. Let X consist of $n := \lceil \frac{d}{\varepsilon} \rceil$ elements and $\mathcal{P}$ be the uniform distribution on X. When learning the target concept $\varnothing \in \mathcal{C}_{X,d}$ the error of the algorithm's hypothesis is $< \varepsilon$ only if at least $n - (d-1)$ distinct examples appear among the training examples. The probability that a certain example is not among the m training examples is $\left(1-\frac{1}{n}\right)^m$. Let Z be a random variable denoting the number of examples in X that are not in the training set. Thus, $\mu := E(Z) = n\left(1-\frac{1}{n}\right)^m$. Note that Z is binomially distributed, so that $P(Z \geq \lfloor\mu\rfloor) \geq \frac{1}{2}$ (cf. Appendix B of [8]) . If $m = \frac{d}{\varepsilon}\log\frac{1}{\varepsilon}$ then for small $\frac{\varepsilon}{d}$ (so that $\log(1-\frac{\varepsilon}{d}) \approx -\frac{\varepsilon}{d}$) we have $\mu \approx d$. Since $P(Z \geq \lfloor\mu\rfloor) \geq \frac{1}{2}$ it follows that at least $\Omega\left(\frac{d}{\varepsilon}\log\frac{1}{\varepsilon}\right)$ examples are needed to learn $\mathcal{C}_{X,d}$. Note that for another suitable distribution on X (cf. [4] for details) one obtains the well-known lower bound of $\Omega\left(\frac{1}{\varepsilon}\log\frac{1}{\delta}\right)$, so that altogether this establishes a lower bound of $\Omega\left(\frac{1}{\varepsilon}(d\log\frac{1}{\varepsilon}+\log\frac{1}{\delta})\right)$.

5 Final Remarks

The extension of our result for maximum intersection-closed concept classes to intersection-closed concept classes in general seems to be far from trivial. For hyper-rectangles in $\mathbf{R}^d$ the given topological structure allows to obtain the conjectured bound, while for maximum intersection-closed concept classes the result of Welzl provides a similar structure that can be used. However, for arbitrary intersection-closed concept classes it seems to be hard to impose some kind of structure that is sufficient to obtain the desired bound. Our Proposition 8 is obviously not strong enough. Thus, we think that some combinatorial key result will be needed to make further progress.

Acknowledgements. We would like to thank Manfred Warmuth and Thomas Korimort for helpful discussion. This paper was partially supported by the EU-funded PASCAL network of excellency.

References

1. P. Auer: Learning Nested Differences in the Presence of Malicious Noise, *Theor. Comput. Sci.* **185**(1): 159-175 (1997).
2. P. Auer, N. Cesa-Bianchi: On-Line Learning with Malicious Noise and the Closure Algorithm, *Annals of Mathematics and Artificial Intelligence* **23**(1-2): 83-99 (1998).
3. P. Auer, P. M. Long, A. Srinivasan: Approximating Hyper-Rectangles: Learning and Pseudorandom Sets, *J. Comput. Syst. Sci.* **57**(3): 376-388 (1998).
4. A. Blumer, A. Ehrenfeucht, D. Haussler, M. Warmuth: Learnability and the Vapnik-Chervonenkis Dimension, *J. ACM* **36**(4): 929-965 (1989).
5. S. Floyd, M. Warmuth: Sample Compression, Learnability, and the Vapnik-Chervonenkis Dimension, *Machine Learning* **21**(3): 269-304 (1995).
6. D. Haussler, N. Littlestone, M. Warmuth: Predicting {0,1}-Functions on Randomly Drawn Points, *Inf. Comput.* **115**(2): 248-292 (1994).
7. D. Helmbold, R. Sloan, M. Warmuth: Learning Nested Differences of Intersection-Closed Concept Classes, *Machine Learning* **5**: 165–196 (1990).
8. F. T. Leighton, C. G. Plaxton: Hypercubic Sorting Networks, *SIAM J. Comput.* **27**(1): 1-47 (1998).
9. N. Sauer: On the Density of Families of Sets, *J. Combinatorial Theory (A)* **13**: 145–147 (1972).

A Framework for Statistical Clustering with a Constant Time Approximation Algorithms for K-Median Clustering

Shai Ben-David

Department of Computer Science
Technion, Haifa 32000, Israel
and
School of ECE**
Cornell university, Ithaca 14853, NY
shai@ece.cornell.edu

Abstract. We consider a framework in which the clustering algorithm gets as input a sample generated i.i.d by some unknown arbitrary distribution, and has to output a clustering of the full domain set, that is evaluated with respect to the underlying distribution. We provide general conditions on clustering problems that imply the existence of sampling based clusterings that approximate the optimal clustering. We show that the K-median clustering, as well as the Vector Quantization problem, satisfy these conditions. In particular our results apply to the *sampling - based approximate clustering* scenario. As a corollary, we get a sampling-based algorithm for the K-median clustering problem that finds an almost optimal set of centers in time depending only on the confidence and accuracy parameters of the approximation, but independent of the input size. Furthermore, in the Euclidean input case, the running time of our algorithm is independent of the Euclidean dimension.

1 Introduction

We consider the following fundamental problem:

> Some unknown probability distribution, over some large (possibly infinite) domain set, generates an i.i.d. sample. Upon observing such a sample, a learner wishes to generate some simple, yet meaningful, description of the underlying distribution.

The above scenario can be viewed as a high level definition of *unsupervised learning*. Many well established statistical tasks, such as Linear Regression, Principle Component Analysis and Principal Curves, can be viewed in this light. In this work, we restrict our attention to *clustering* tasks. That is, the description that the learner outputs is in the form of a finite collection of subsets (or a

** This work is supported in part by the Multidisciplinary University Research Initiative (MURI) under the Office of Naval Research Contract N00014-00-1-0564.

J. Shawe-Taylor and Y. Singer (Eds.): COLT 2004, LNAI 3120, pp. 415–426, 2004.

partition) of the domain set. As a measure of the quality of the output of the clustering algorithm, we consider objective functions defined over the underlying domain set and distribution.

This formalization is relevant to many realistic scenarios, in which it is natural to assume that the information we collect is only a sample of a larger body which is our object of interest. One such example is the problem of Quantizer Design [2] in coding theory, where one has to pick a small number of vectors, 'code words', to best represent the transmission of some unknown random source.

Results in this general framework can be applied to the worst-case model of clustering as well, and in some cases, yield significant improvements to the best previously known complexity upper bounds. We elaborate on this application in the subsection on *worst-case complexity view* below.

The paradigm that we analyze is the simplest sampling-based meta-algorithm. Namely,

1. `Draw an i.i.d random sample of the underlying probability distribution.`
2. `Find a good clustering of the sample.`
3. `Extend the clustering of the sample to a clustering of the full domain set.`

A key issue in translating the above paradigm into a concrete algorithm is the implementation of step 3; How should a clustering of a subset be extended to a clustering of a full set? For clusterings defined by a choice of a fixed number if centers, like the K median problem and vector quantization, there is a straightforward answer; namely, use the cluster centers that the algorithm found for the sample, as the cluster centers for the full set. While there are ways to extend clusterings of subsets for other types of clustering, in this paper we focus on the K-median and vector quantization problems.

The focus of this paper is an analysis of the approximation quality of sampling based clustering. We set the ground for a systematic discussion of this issue in the general context of statistical clustering, and demonstrate the usefulness of our approach by considering the concrete case of K-median clustering.

We prove that certain properties of clustering objective functions suffice to guarantee that an implicit description of an almost optimal clustering can be found in time depending on the confidence and accuracy parameters of the approximation, but independent of the input size. We show that the K-median clustering objective function, as well as the vector quantization cost, enjoy these properties. We are therefore able to demonstrate the first known constant-time approximation algorithm for the K-median problem.

The paradigm outlined above has been considered in previous work in the context of sampling based approximate clustering. Buhmann [3] describes a similar meta-algorithm under the title "Empirical Risk Approximation". Buhmann suggests to add an intermediate step of averaging over a set of empirically good clusterings, before extending the result to the full data set. Such a step helps reduce the variance of the output clustering. However, Buhmann's analysis is under the assumption that the data- generating distribution is *known* to the learner. We address the distribution free (or, worst case) scenario, where the only information available to the learner is the input sample and the underlying metric space.

Our main technical tool is a uniform convergence result that upper bounds, as a function of the sample sizes, the discrepancy between the empirical cost of certain families of clusterings to their true cost (as defined by the underlying probability distribution). Convergence results of the empirical estimates of the k-median cost of clusterings where previously obtained for the limiting behavior, as sample sizes go to infinity (see, e.g. Pollard [6]). Finite-sample convergence bounds where obtained for the k-median problem by Mishra et al [5], and for the vector quantization problem by Bartlett et al [2], which also provide a discussion of vector quantization in the context of coding theory see [2]. Smola et al [7] provide a framework for more general quantization problems, as well as convergence results for a regularized versions of these problems. However, the families of cluster centers that our method covers are much richer than the families of centers considered in these papers.

1.1 Worst-Case Complexity View

Recently there is a growing interest in sampling based algorithms for approximating NP-hard clustering problems (see, e.g, Mishra et al [5], de la Vega et al [8] and Meyerson et al [4]). In these problems, the input to an algorithm is a finite set X in a metric space, and the task is to come up with a clustering of X that minimizes some objective function. The sampling based algorithm performs this task by considering a relatively small $S \subseteq X$ that is sampled uniformly at random from X, and applying a (deterministic) clustering algorithm to S. The motivating idea behind such an algorithm is the hope that relatively small sample sizes may suffice to induce good clusterings, and thus result in computational efficiency. In these works one usually assumes that a point can be sampled uniformly at random over X in constant time. Consequently, using this approach, the running time of such algorithms is reduced to a function of the size of the sample (rather than of the full input set X) and the computational complexity analysis boils down to the statistical analysis of sufficient sample sizes.

The analysis of the model proposed here is relevant to these settings too. By taking the underlying distribution to be the uniform distribution over the input set X, results that hold for our general scenario readily apply to the sampling based approximate clustering as well.

The worst case complexity of sampling based K-median clustering is addressed in Mishra et al [5] where such an algorithm is shown to achieve a sublinear upper bound on the computational complexity for the approximate K-median problem. They prove their result by showing that with high probability, a sample of size $O\left(\left(\frac{k \log(n)}{\epsilon^2}\right)\right.$ suffices to achieve a clustering with average cost (over all the input points) of at most $2Opt + \epsilon$ (where Opt is the average cost of an optimal k clustering). By proving a stronger upper bound on sufficient sample sizes, we are able to improve these results. We prove upper bounds on the sufficient sample sizes (and consequently on the computational complexity) that are independent of the input size n.

2 The Formal Setup

We start by providing a definition of our notions of a *statistical clustering problem.* Then, in the "basic tool box' subsection, we define the central tool for this work, the notion of a *clustering description scheme*, as well as the properties of these notions that are required for the performance analysis of our algorithm. Since the generic example that this paper addresses is that of K-median clustering, we shall follow each definition with its concrete manifestation for the K-median problem.

Our definition of clustering problems is in the spirit of combinatorial optimization. That is, we consider problems in which the quality of a solution (i.e. clustering) is defined in terms of a precise objective function. One should note that often, in practical applications of clustering, there is no such well defined objective function, and many useful clustering algorithms cannot be cast in such terms.

Definition 1 (Statistical clustering problems).

- *A clustering problem is defined by a triple* $(X, \mathcal{T}, R)$, *where* X *is some domain set (possibly infinite),* $\mathcal{T}$ *is a set of legal clusterings (or partitions) of* X, *and* $R : \mathcal{P} \times \mathcal{T} \mapsto [0,1]$ *is the objective function (or risk) the clustering algorithm aims to minimize, where* $\mathcal{P}$ *is a set of probability distributions over* X [1].
- *For a finite* $S \subseteq X$, *the* empirical risk *of a clustering* T *on a sample* S, $R(S,T)$, *is the risk of the clustering* T *with respect to the uniform distribution over* S.
- For the K-median problem, the domain set X is endowed with a metric d and $\mathcal{T}$ is the set of all k-cell Voronoi diagrams over X that have points of X as centers. Clearly each $T \in \mathcal{T}$ is determined by a set $\{x_1^T, \ldots x_k^T\} \subseteq X$, consisting of the cell's centers. Finally, for a probability distribution P over X, and $T \in \mathcal{T}$, $R(P,T) = \mathrm{E}_{y \in P}\left(\min_{i \in \{1,\ldots k\}} d(y, x_i^T)\right)$. That is, the risk of a partition defined by a set of k centers is the expected distance of a P-random point from its closest center.

Note that we have restricted the range of the risk function, R to the unit interval. This corresponds to assuming that, for the K-median and vector quantization problems, the data points are all in the unit ball . This restriction allows

[1] In this paper, we shall always take $\mathcal{P}$ to be the class of all probability distributions over the domain set, therefore we do not specify it explicitly in our notation. There are cases in which one may wish to consider only a restricted set of distributions (e.g., distributions that are uniform over some finite subset of X) and such a restriction may allow for sharper sample size bounds.

simpler formulas for the convergence bounds that we derive. Alternatively, one could assume that the metric spaces are bounded by some constant and adjust the bounds accordingly. On the other extreme, if one allows unbounded metrics, then it is easy to construct examples for which, for any given sample size, the empirical estimates are arbitrarily off the true cost of a clustering.

Having defined the setting for the problems we wish to investigate, we move on to introduce the corresponding notion of desirable solution. The definition of a clustering problem being 'approximable from samples' resembles the definition of learnability for classification tasks.

Definition 2 (Approximable from samples). *A clustering problem* $(X, \mathcal{T}, R)$ *is* α - approximable from samples, *for some* $\alpha \geq 1$, *if there exist an algorithm* $\mathcal{A}$ *mapping finite subsets of* X *to clusterings in* $\mathcal{T}$, *and a function* $f : (0,1)^2 \mapsto \mathbb{N}$, *such that for every probability distribution* P *over* X *and every* ϵ, $\delta \in (0,1)$, *if a sample* S *of size* $\geq f(\epsilon, \delta)$ *is generated i.i.d. by* P *then with probability exceeding* $1 - \delta$,

$$R(P, \mathcal{A}(S)) \leq \min_{T \in \mathcal{T}} \alpha R(P, T) + \epsilon.$$

Note that formally, the above definition is trivially met for any fixed finite size domain X. We have in mind the setting where X is some infinite universal domain, and one can embed in it finite domains of interest by choosing the underlying distribution P so that it has that set of interest as its support. Alternatively, one could consider a definition in which the clustering problem is defined by a scheme $\{(X_n, \mathcal{T}_n, R_n)\}_{n \in \mathbb{N}}$ and require that the sample size function $f(\epsilon, \delta)$ is independent of n.

2.1 Our Basic Tool Box

Next, we define our notion of an implicit representation of a clustering. We call it a *clustering description scheme.* Such a scheme can be thought of as a compact representation of clusterings in terms of sets of l elements of X, and maybe some additional parameters.

Definition 3 (Clustering description scheme).
Let $(X, \mathcal{T}, R)$ *be a clustering problem. An* (l, I) clustering description scheme *for* $(X, \mathcal{T}, R)$ *is a function,* $G : X^l \times I \mapsto \mathcal{T}$, *where* l *is the number of points a description depends on, and* I *is a set of possible values for an extra parameter.*

We shall consider three properties of description schemes. The first two can, in most cases, be readily checked from the definition of a description scheme. The third property has a statistical nature, which makes it harder to check. We shall first introduce the first two properties, *completeness* and *localization*, and discuss some of their consequences. The third property, *coverage*, will be discussed in Section 3 .

Completeness: A description scheme, G, is *Complete* for a clustering problem $(X, \mathcal{T}, R)$, if for every $T \in \mathcal{T}$ there exist $x_1, \ldots x_l \in X$ and $i \in I$ such that $G(x_1, \ldots x_l, i) = T$.

Localization: A description scheme, G, is *Local* for a clustering problem $(X, \mathcal{T}, R)$, if there exist a functions $f : X^{l+1} \times I \mapsto \mathbb{R}$ such that for any probability distribution P, for all $x_1, \ldots x_l \in X$ and $i \in I$,

$$R(P, G(x_1, \ldots x_l, i)) = E_{y \in P} f(y, x_1, \ldots x_l, i)$$

Examples:

The K-median problem endowed with the natural description scheme: in this case,$l = k$ (the number of clusters), there is no extra parameter i, and $G(x_1, \ldots, x_k)$ is the clustering assigning any point $y \in X$ its closest neighbor among $\{x_1, \ldots, x_k\}$. So, given a clustering T, if $\{x_1^T, \ldots x_k^T\}$ are the centers of T's clusters, then $T = G(x_1^T, \ldots, x_k^T)$. Clearly, this is a complete and local description scheme (with $f(y, x_1 \ldots, x_k) = \min_{i \in \{1, \ldots k\}} d(y, x_i)$ and F being the identity function).

Vector Quantization: this problem arises in the context of source coding. The problem is very similar to the K-median problem. The domain X is the Euclidean space $\mathbb{R}^d$, for some d, and one is given a fixed parameter l. On an input set of d-dimensional vectors, one wishes to pick 'code points' $(x_1, \ldots x_l) \in \mathbb{R}^d$ and map each input point to one of these code points. The only difference between this and the K-median problem is the objective function that one aims to minimize. Here it is $R(P, T_{x_1, \ldots x_l}) = \mathrm{E}_{y \in P} \left[\min_{i \in \{1, \ldots l\}} d(y, x_i)^2\right]$. The natural description scheme in this case is the same one as in the K-median problem - describe a quantizer T by the set of code point (or centers) it uses. It is clear that, in this case as well, the description scheme is both complete and local.

Note, that in both the K-median clustering and the vector quantization task, once such an implicit representation of the clustering is available, the cluster to which any given domain point is assigned can be found from the description in constant time (a point y is assigned to the cluster whose index is $Argmin_{i \in \{1, \ldots k\}} d(y, x_i)$).

The next claim addresses the cost function. Let us fix a sample size m. Given a probability distribution P over our domain space, let P^m be the distribution over i.i.d. m- samples induced by P. For a random variable $f(S)$, let $E_{S \in P^m}(f)$ denote the expectation of f over this distribution.

Claim 1. *Let $(X, \mathcal{T}, R)$ be a clustering problem. For $T \in \mathcal{T}$, if there exists a function $h_T : X \mapsto \mathbb{R}^+$ such that for any probability distribution P, $R(P, T) = E_{x \in P}(h_T(x))$, then for every such P and every integer m,*

$$E_{S \in P^m}(R(S, T)) = R(P, T)$$

Corollary 2. *If a clustering problem* $(X, \mathcal{T}, R)$ *has a local and complete description scheme then, for every probability distribution* P *over* X*, every* $m \geq 1$ *and every* $T \in \mathcal{T}$*,*

$$E_{S \in P^m}(R(S,T)) = R(P,T)$$

Lemma 1. *If a clustering problem* $(X, \mathcal{T}, R)$ *has a local and complete description scheme then, for every probability distribution* P *over* X*, every* $m \geq 1$ *and every* $T \in \mathcal{T}$*,*

$$P^m\{|R(P,T) - R(S,T)| \geq \epsilon\} \leq 2e^{-2\epsilon^2 m}$$

The proof of this Lemma is a straightforward application of Hoeffding inequality to the above corollary (recall that we consider the case where the risk R is in the range $[0,1]$).

Corollary 3. *If a clustering problem* $(X, \mathcal{T}, R)$ *has a local and complete description scheme then, for every probability distribution* P *over* X*, and every clustering* $T \in \mathcal{T}$*, if a sample* $S \subseteq X$ *of size* $m \geq \frac{\ln 2/\delta}{2\epsilon^2}$ *is picked i.i.d. via* P *then, with probability* $> 1 - \delta$ *(over the choice of* S*),*

$$|R(S,T) - R(P,T)| \leq \epsilon$$

In fact, the proofs of the sample-based approximation results in this paper require only the one-sided inequality, $R(S,T) \leq R(P,T) + \epsilon$.

So far, we have not really needed description schemes. In the next theorem, claiming that the convergence of sample clustering costs to the true probability costs, we heavily rely on the finite nature of description schemes. Indeed, clustering description schemes play a role similar to that played by compression schemes in classification learning.

Theorem 4. *Let* G *be a local description scheme for a clustering problem* $(X, \mathcal{T}, R)$*. Then for every probability distribution* P *over* X*, if a sample* $S \subseteq X$ *of size* $m >> l$ *is picked i.i.d. by* P *then, with probability* $> 1 - \delta$ *(over the choice of* S*), for every* $x_1, \ldots x_l \in S$ *and every* $i \in I$*,*

$$|R(S, G(x_1, \ldots x_l, i)) - R(P, G(x_1, \ldots x_l, i))| \leq \sqrt{\frac{\ln(|I|) + l \ln m + \ln(1/\delta)}{2(m-l)}}$$

Proof. Corollary 3 implies that for every clustering of the form $G(x_1, \ldots x_l, i)$, if a large enough sample S is picked i.i.d. by P, then with high probability, the empirical risk of this clustering over S is close to its true risk. It remains to show that, with high probability, for S sampled as above, this conclusion holds simultaneously for all choices of $x_1, \ldots x_l \in S$ and all $i \in I$.

To prove this claim we employ the following uniform convergence result:

Lemma 2. *Given a family of clusterings* $\{G(x_1, \ldots x_l, i)\}_{x_1, \ldots \in X \; i \in I}$*, let* $\epsilon(m, \delta)$ *be a function such that, for every choice of* $x_1, \ldots x_l, i$ *and every choice of* m *and*

$\delta > 0$, if a sample S is picked by choosing i.i.d uniformly over X, m times, then with probability $\geq 1 - \delta$

$$|R(S, G(x_1, \ldots x_l, i)) - R(P, G(x_1, \ldots x_l, i))| < \epsilon(m, \delta)$$

then, with probability $\geq 1 - \delta$ over the choice of S,
$\forall x_1, \ldots x_l \in S \; \forall i \in I$,

$$|R(S, G(x_1, \ldots x_l, i)) - R(P, G(x_1, \ldots x_l, i))| < \epsilon(m - l, \frac{\delta}{|I| \times \binom{m}{l}})$$

One should note that the point of this lemma is the change of order of quantification. While in the assumption one first fixes $x_1, \ldots x_l, i$ and then randomly picks the samples S, in the conclusion we wish to have a claim that allows to pick S first and then guarantee that, no matter which $x_1, \ldots x_l, i$ is chosen, the S-cost of the clustering is close to its true P-cost. Since such a strong statement is too much to hope for, we invoke the sample compression idea, and restrict the choice of the x_i's by requiring that they are members of the sample S.

Proof (Sketch). The proof follows the lines of the uniform convergence results for sample compression bounds for classification learning. Given a sample S of size m, for every choice of l indices, $i_1, \ldots, i_l \in \{1, \ldots, m\}$, and $i \in I$, we use the bound of Corollary 3 to bound the difference between the empirical and true risk of the clustering $G(x_1, \ldots x_l, i)$. We then apply the union bound to 'uniformize' over all possible such choices.

In fact, the one-sided inequality,

$$R(P, G(x_1, \ldots x_l, i)) \leq R(S, G(x_1, \ldots x_l, i)) + \epsilon$$

suffices for proving the sample-based approximation results of this paper.

3 Sample Based Approximation Results for Clustering in the General Setting

Next we apply the convergence results of the previous section to obtain guarantees on the approximation quality of sample based clustering. Before we can do that, we have to address yet another component of our paradigm. The convergence results that we have so far suffice to show that the empirical risk of a description scheme clustering that is based on sample points is close to its true risk. However, there may be cases in which any such clustering fails to approximate the optimal clustering of a given input sample. To guard against such cases, we introduce our third property of clustering description schemes, the *coverage* property.

The Coverage property: We consider two versions of this property:

Multiplicative coverage: A description scheme is *α-m-covering* for a clustering problem $(X, \mathcal{T}, R)$ if for every $S \subset X$ s.t. $|S| \geq l$, there exist $\{x_1, \ldots x_l\} \subseteq S$ and $i \in I$ such that for every $T \in \mathcal{T}_X$,

$$R(S, G(x_1, \ldots x_l, i)) \leq \alpha R(S, T)$$

Namely, an optimal clustering of S can be α-approximated by applying the description scheme G to an l-tuple of members of S.

Additive coverage: A description scheme is *η-a-covering* for a clustering problem $(X, \mathcal{T}, R)$ if for every $S \subset X$ s.t. $|S| \geq l$, there exist $\{x_1, \ldots x_l\} \subseteq S$ and $i \in I$ such that for every $T \in \mathcal{T}_X$,

$$R(S, G(x_1, \ldots x_l, i)) \leq R(S, T) + \eta$$

Namely, an optimal clustering of S can be approximated to within (additive) η by applying the description scheme G to an l-tuple of members of S.

We are now ready to prove our central result. We formulate it for the case of multiplicative covering schemes. However, it is straightforward to obtain an analogous result for additive coverage.

Theorem 5. *Let $(X, \mathcal{T}, R)$ be a clustering problem that has a local and complete description scheme which is α-m-covering, for some $\alpha \geq 1$. Then $(X, \mathcal{P}, R)$ is α-approximable from samples.*

Proof. Let $m = O\left(\frac{\ln(\frac{|I|}{\delta\epsilon^l})}{\epsilon^2}\right)$. Let $T^* \in \mathcal{T}$ be a clustering of X that minimizes $R(P, T)$, and let $S \subset X$ be an i.i.d. P-random sample of size m.

Now, with probability $\geq 1 - \delta$, S satisfies the following chain of inequalities:

- By Corollary 3,
$$R(P, T^*) + \epsilon \geq R(S, T^*)$$
- Let $Opt(S)$ be a clustering of S that minimizes $R(S, T)$. Clearly,
$$R(S, T^*)) \geq R(S, (Opt(S))$$
- Since G is α covering, for some $x_1, \ldots x_l \in S$ and $i \in I$,
$$R(S, Opt(S)) \geq \frac{1}{\alpha} R(S, G(x_1, \ldots x_l, i))$$
- By Theorem 4, for the above choice of $x_1 \ldots x_l, i$,
$$R(S, G(x_1, \ldots x_l, i)) \geq R(P, G(x_1, \ldots x_l, i)) - \epsilon$$

It therefore follows that

$$R(P, G(x_1, \ldots x_l, i)) \leq \alpha(R(P, T^*) + \epsilon) + \epsilon$$

□

Theorem 6. *Let $(X, \mathcal{T}, R)$ be a clustering problem and let $G(x_1 \ldots, x_l, i)$ be a local and complete description scheme which is η-a-covering, for some $\eta \in [0, 1]$. Then for every probability distribution P over X and $m >> l$, if a sample, S, of size m is generated i.i.d by P, then with probability exceeding $1 - \delta$,*

$$\min\{R(P, G(x_1, \ldots, x_l, i)) : x_1, \ldots, x_l \in S,\ i \in I\} \leq$$

$$\min\{R(P, T) : T \in \mathcal{T}\} + \eta + \sqrt{\frac{\ln(|I|) + l \ln m + \ln(1/\delta)}{2(m - l)}}$$

The proof is similar to the proof of Theorem 5 above.

4 *K*-Median Clustering and Vector Quantization

In this section we show how to apply our general results to the specific cases of K-median clustering and vector quantization. We have already discussed the natural clustering description schemes for these cases, and argued that they are both complete and local. The only missing component is therefore the analysis of the *coverage* properties of these description schemes.

We consider two cases,

Metric K-median problem where X can be any metric space.
Euclidean K-median where X is assumed to be a Euclidean space $\mathbb{R}^d$. This is also the context for the vector quantization problem.

In the first case there is no extra structure on the underlying domain metric space, whereas in the second we assume that it is a Euclidean space (it turns out that the assumption that the domain a Hilbert space suffices for our results).

For the case of general metric spaces, we let $G(x_1, \ldots, x_k)$ be the basic description scheme that assigns each point y to the x_i closest to it. (So, in this case we do not use the extra parameter i).

It is well known, (see e.g., [5]) that for any sample S, the best clustering with center points from S is at most a factor of 2 away from the optimal clustering for S (when centers can be any points in the underlying metric space). We therefore get that is that case G is a 2-m-covering.

For the case of Euclidean, or Hilbert space domain, we can also employ a richer description scheme. For a parameter t, we wish to consider clustering centers that are the centers of mass of t-tuples of sample points (rather than just the sample points themselves). Fixing parameters t and r, let our index set I be r^{tk}, that is, the set of all vectors of length k whose entries are t-tuples of indices in $\{1, \ldots, r\}$. Let $G_t(x_1, \ldots, x_r, i) \stackrel{\triangle}{=} G(x_{i,1}, \ldots x_{i,tk})$, where $i \in r^{tk}$ indexes a sequence $(x_{i,1}, \ldots x_{i,kt})$ of points in $\{x_1, \ldots, x_r\}$, and $G(x_{i,1}, \ldots x_{i,tl})$ is the clustering defined by the set of centers $\{1/t\Sigma_{j=th+1}^{t(h+1)} x_{i,j} : h \in \{0, \ldots, k-1\}\}$. That is, we take the 'centers of mass' of t tuples of points of S, where i is the index of the sequence of kt points that defines or centers. It is easy to see that such G_t is complete iff $r \geq k$.

The following lemma of Maurey, [1], implies that, for $t \leq r$, this description scheme enjoys an η-a-coverage, for $\eta = 1/\sqrt{t}$.

Theorem 7 (Maurey, [1]). *Let F be a vector space with a scalar product $(\cdot, \cdot)$ and let $\|f\| \triangleq \sqrt{(f, f)}$ be the induced norm on F. Suppose $G \subseteq F$ and that, for some $c > 0$, $\|g\| \leq c$ for all $g \in G$. Then for all f from the convex hull of G and all $k \geq 1$ the following holds:*

$$\inf_{g_1, \ldots, g_k \in G} \left\| \frac{1}{k} \sum_{i=1}^{k} g_i - f \right\| \leq \sqrt{\frac{c^2 - \|f\|^2}{k}}.$$

Corollary 8. *Consider the K median problem over a Hilbert space, X. For every t and $r \geq \max\{k, t\}$, the clustering algorithm that, on a sample S, outputs $Argmin\{R(G_t(x_1, \ldots, x_r, i)) : x_1, \ldots, x_r \in S, \text{ and } i \leq r^{tk}\}$ produces, with probability exceeding $1 - \delta$ a clustering whose cost is no more then*

$$\frac{1}{\sqrt{t}} + \sqrt{\frac{k(t \ln r + \ln |S|) + \ln(1/\delta)}{2(|S| - r)}}$$

above the cost of the optimal k-centers clustering of the sample generating distribution (for any sample generating distribution and any $\delta > 0$).

4.1 Implications to Worst Case Complexity

As we mentioned earlier, worst case complexity models of clustering can be naturally viewed as a special case of the statistical clustering framework. The computational model in which there is access to random uniform sampling from a finite input set, can be viewed as a statistical clustering problem with P being the uniform distribution over that input set.

Let (X, d) be a metric space, $\mathcal{T}$ a set of legal clusterings of X and R an objective function. A worst case sampling-based clustering algorithm for $(X, \mathcal{T}, R)$ is an algorithm that gets as input finite subsets $Y \subseteq X$, has access to uniform random sampling over Y, and outputs a clustering of Y.

Corollary 9. *Let $(X, \mathcal{T}, R)$ be a clustering problem. If, for some $\alpha \geq 1$, there exist a clustering description scheme for $(X, \mathcal{T}, R)$ which is both complete and α-m-covering, then there exists a worst case sampling-based clustering algorithm for $(X, \mathcal{T}, R)$ that runs in constant time depending only of the approximation and confidence parameters, ϵ and δ (and independent of the input size $|Y|$) and outputs an $\alpha Opt + \epsilon$ approximations of the optimal clustering for Y, with probability exceeding $1 - \delta$.*

Note that the output of such an algorithm is an *implicit* description of a clustering of Y. It outputs the parameters from which the description scheme determines. For natural description schemes (such as describing a Voronoi diagram by listing its center points) the computation needed to figure out the cluster membership of any given $y \in Y$ requires constant time.

Acknowledgments. I would like to express warm thanks to Aharon Bar-Hillel for insightful discussions that paved the way to this research.

References

1. Martin Anthony and Peter L. Bartlett. *Neural Network Learning: Theoretical Foundations.* Cambridge University Press, 1999.
2. Peter Bartlett, Tamas Linder and gabor Lugosi "the minimax distortion Redundancy in empirical Quantizer Design" *IEEE Transactions on Information theory*, vol. 44, 1802–1813, 1998.
3. Joachim Buhmann, "Empirical Risk Approximation: An Induction Principle for Unsupervised Learning" Technical Report IAI-TR-98-3, Institut for Informatik III, Universitat Bonn. 1998.
4. Adam Meyerson, Liadan O'Callaghan, and Serge Plotkin "A k-median Algorithm with Running Time Independent of Data Size" *Journal of Machine Learning*, Special Issue on Theoretical Advances in Data Clustering (MLJ) 2004.
5. Nina Mishra, Dan Oblinger and Leonard Pitt "Sublinear Time Approximate Clustering" in *Proceedings of Syposium on Discrete Algorithms, SODA 2001* pp. 439-447.
6. D. Pollard "Quantization and the method of k-means" in *IEEE Transactions on Information theory* 28:199-205, 1982.
7. Alex J. Smola, Sebastian Mika, and Bernhard Scholkopf "Quantization Finctionals and Regularized Principal Manifolds" *NeuroCOLT Technical Report Series* NC2-TR-1998-028.
8. Fernandes de la Vega, Marek Karpinski, Calire Kenyon and Yuval Rabani "Approximation Schemes for Clustering Problems" *Proceedings of Symposium on the Theory of computation, STOC'03*, 2003.

Data Dependent Risk Bounds for Hierarchical Mixture of Experts Classifiers

Arik Azran and Ron Meir

Department of Electrical Engineering
Technion, Haifa 3200
Israel
arik@tx.technion.ac.il
rmeir@ee.technion.ac.il

Abstract. The hierarchical mixture of experts architecture provides a flexible procedure for implementing classification algorithms. The classification is obtained by a recursive soft partition of the feature space in a data-driven fashion. Such a procedure enables *local classification* where several experts are used, each of which is assigned with the task of classification over some subspace of the feature space. In this work, we provide data-dependent generalization error bounds for this class of models, which lead to effective procedures for performing model selection. Tight bounds are particularly important here, because the model is highly parameterized. The theoretical results are complemented with numerical experiments based on a randomized algorithm, which mitigates the effects of local minima which plague other approaches such as the expectation-maximization algorithm.

1 Introduction

The mixture of experts (MoE) and hierarchical mixture of experts (HMoE) architectures, proposed in [10] and extensively studied in later work, is a flexible approach to constructing complex classifiers. In contrast to many other approaches, it is based on an adaptive soft partition of the feature space into regions, to each of which is assigned a 'simple' (e.g. generalized linear model (GLIM)) classifier. This approach should be contrasted with more standard approaches which construct a complex parameterization of a classifier over the full space, and attempt to learn its parameters.

In binary pattern classification one attempts to choose a soft classifier f from some class $\mathcal{F}$, in order to classify an *observation* $x \in \mathbb{R}^k$ into one of two classes $y \in \mathcal{Y} = \{-1, +1\}$ using $\text{sgn}(f(x))$. In the case of the $0-1$ loss, the ideal classifier minimizes the *risk* $P_e(f) = \mathbf{P}\{\text{sgn}(f(X)) \neq Y\} = \mathbf{P}\{Yf(x) \leq 0\}$. If $\text{sgn}(\mathcal{F})$ consists of all possible mappings from $\mathbb{R}^k$ to $\mathcal{Y}$, then the ultimate best classifier is the Bayes classifier $f_B(X) = \text{argmax}_{y\in\mathcal{Y}} \mathbf{P}\{Y = y|X\}$. In practical situations, the selection of a classifier is based on a sample $D_N = \{(X_n, Y_n) \in \mathcal{X} \times \mathcal{Y}\}_{n=1}^N$, where each pair is assumed to be drawn i.i.d. from an unknown distribution $P(X, Y)$.

J. Shawe-Taylor and Y. Singer (Eds.): COLT 2004, LNAI 3120, pp. 427–441, 2004.

In this paper we consider the class of hierarchical mixtures of experts classifiers [10], which is based on a soft adaptive partition of the input space, and a utilization of a small number of 'expert' classifiers in each domain. Such a procedure can be thought of, on the one hand, as extending standard approaches based on mixtures, and, on the other hand, providing a soft probabilistic extension of decision trees. This architecture has been successfully applied to regression, classification, control and time series analysis. It should be noted that since the HMoE architecture is highly parameterized, it is important to obtain tight error bounds, in order to prevent overfitting. Previous results attempting to establish bounds on the estimation error of the MoE system were based on the VC dimension [9] and covering number approaches [15]. Unfortunately, such approaches are too weak to be useful in any practical setting.

2 Preliminary Results

Consider a soft classifier f, and the $0-1$ loss incurred by it, given by $I[yf(x) \leq 0]$, where $I[t \leq 0]$ is the indicator function of the event '$t \leq 0$'. While we attempt to minimize the expected value of the $0-1$ loss, it turns out to be inopportune to directly minimize functions based on this loss. First, the computational task is often intractable due to its non-smoothness. Second, minimizing the empirical $0-1$ loss may lead to severe overfitting. Many recent approaches are based on minimizing a smooth convex function $\phi(yf(x))$ which upper bounds the $0-1$ loss (e.g. [20,12,1]). Define the ϕ-risk, $E_\phi(f) = \mathbf{E}\left\{\phi(Yf(X))\right\}$, and denote the *empirical ϕ-risk* by $\hat{E}_\phi(f, D_N) = N^{-1}\sum_{n=1}^{N}\phi(y_n f(x_n))$. We assume that the loss function $\phi(t)$ satisfies $\phi(0) = 1$, $\phi(t)$ is Lipschitz with constant L_ϕ, $\phi_{\max} < \infty$ where $\phi_{\max} = \sup_{t \in \mathbb{R}} \phi(t)$ and $I[t \leq 0] \leq \phi(t)$ for all t. Using the ϕ-risk instead of the risk itself is motivated by several reasons. (i) Minimizing the ϕ-risk often leads asymptotically to the Bayes decision rule [20]. (ii) Rather tight upper bounds on the risk may be derived for finite sample sizes (e.g. [20,12,1]). (iii) Minimizing the empirical ϕ-risk instead of the empirical risk is computationally much simpler.

Data dependent error bounds are often derived using the Rademacher complexity. Let $\mathcal{F}$ be a class of real-valued functions with domain $\mathbb{R}^k$. The empirical Rademacher complexity is defined as

$$\hat{R}_N(\mathcal{F}) = \mathbf{E}_{\boldsymbol{\sigma}}\left\{\sup_{f \in \mathcal{F}} \frac{1}{N}\sum_{n=1}^{N} \sigma_n f(x_n)\right\},$$

where $\boldsymbol{\sigma} = (\sigma_1, \sigma_2, ..., \sigma_N)$ is a random vector consisting of independently distributed binary random variables with $\mathbf{P}(\sigma_n = 1) = \mathbf{P}(\sigma_n = -1) = 1/2$. The Rademacher complexity is defined as the average over all possible training sequences, $R_N(\mathcal{F}) = \mathbf{E}_{D_N}\hat{R}_N(\mathcal{F})$.

The following Theorem, adapted from [2] and [16], will serve as our starting point.

Theorem 1. *For every $\delta \in (0,1)$ and positive integer N, with probability at least $1-\delta$ over training sequences of length N, every $f \in \mathcal{F}$ satisfies*

$$P_e(f) \leq \hat{E}_\phi(f, D_N) + 2L_\phi \hat{R}_N(\mathcal{F}) + 3\phi_{max}\sqrt{\frac{\ln\frac{2}{\delta}}{2N}} .$$

This bound is proved in three steps. First McDiarmid's inequality [14] and a symmetrization argument [19] are used to bound $\sup_{f\in\mathcal{F}}(E_\phi(f) - \hat{E}_\phi(f, D_N))$ with $R_N(\phi \circ \mathcal{F})$, which is then bounded by $\hat{R}_N(\phi \circ \mathcal{F})$ using McDiarmid's inequality again. The claim is established by using the Lipschitz property of $\phi(\cdot)$ to bound $\hat{R}_N(\phi \circ \mathcal{F})$ with $L_\phi \hat{R}_N(\mathcal{F})$ (e.g. [11,16]). In the sequel we upper bound $\hat{R}_N(\mathcal{F})$ for the case where $\mathcal{F}$ is the HMoE classifier.

Remark 1. The results of the Theorem can be tightened using the entropy method [4]. This leads to improved constants in the bounds, which are of particular significance when the sample size is small. We defer discussion of this issue to the full paper.

3 Mixture of Experts Classifiers

Consider initially the simple MoE architecture defined in Figure 1, and given mathematically by

$$f(x) = \sum_{m=1}^{M} a_m(w_m, x) h_m(v_m, x). \quad (1)$$

We interpret the functions h_m as *experts*, each of which 'operates' in regions of space for which the *gating functions* a_m are nonzero. Note that assuming a_m to be independent of x leads to a standard mixture. Such a classifier can be intuitively interpreted as implementing the principle of 'divide and conquer' where instead of solving one complicated problem (over the full space), we can do better by dividing it into several regions, defined through the gating functions a_m, and using 'simple' expert h_m in each region. It is clear that some restriction needs to be imposed on the gating functions and experts, since otherwise overfitting is imminent. We formalize the assumptions regarding the experts and gating functions below. These assumptions will later be weakened.

Definition 1 (Experts). *For each $1 \leq m \leq M$, let V^m_{max} be some nonnegative scalar and v_m a vector with k elements. Then, the m-th expert is given by a mapping $h_m(v_m, x)$ where $v_m \in V_m = \left\{v \in \mathbb{R}^k : \|v\| \leq \mathrm{V}^m_{max}\right\}$. We define the collection of all functions $h_m(v_m, x)$ such that $v_m \in V_m$ as $\mathcal{H}_m$. To simplify the notation we define $\mathrm{V}_{max} = \sup_m \mathrm{V}^m_{max}$ and set $\mathcal{H} = \bigcup_{m=1}^M \mathcal{H}_m = \bigcup_{m=1}^M \{h_m(v_m, x),\ v_m \in V_m\}$.*

In the definitions below we write $\sup_{w_m, v_m}$ instead of $\sup_{w_m \in W_m, v_m \in V_m}$.

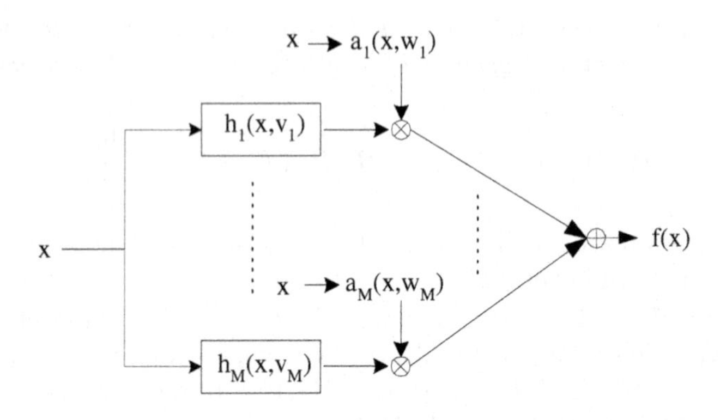

Fig. 1. MoE classifier with M experts.

Assumption 1. *The following assumptions, serving the purpose of regularization, are made for each m, $1 \leq m \leq M$. (i) To allow different types of experts, assume $h_m(v_m, x) = h_m(\tau_m(v_m, x))$ where $\tau_m(v_m, x)$ is some mapping such as $v_m^\top x$ or $\|v_m - x\|$. We assume that $h_m(\tau_m(v_m, x))$ is Lipschitz with constant L_{h_m}, i.e. $|h_m(\tau_m(v_{m_1}, x)) - h_m(\tau_m(v_{m_2}, x))| \leq L_{h_m}|\tau_m(v_{m_1}, x) - \tau_m(v_{m_2}, x)|$. (ii) $|h_m(v_m, x)|$ is bounded by some positive constant $\mathcal{M}_{\mathcal{H}_m} < \infty$. So, by defining $\mathcal{M}_{\mathcal{H}} = \max_m \mathcal{M}_{\mathcal{H}_m}$ we have that $\sup_{m,v_m} |h_m(v_m, x)| \leq \mathcal{M}_{\mathcal{H}}$. (iii) The experts are either symmetric (for regression) or antisymmetric (for classification) with respect to the parameters so that $h_m(v_m, x) = \nu h_m(-v_m, x)$ for some $\nu \in \{\pm 1\}$.*

Remark 2. Throughout our analysis we refer to x as a sample of the feature space. Yet, our results can be immediately extended to experts of the form $h_m(v_m, x) = h_m\left(v_m^\top \Phi_m(x)\right)$ where $\Phi_m(x)$ may be a high-dimensional nonlinear mapping as is used in kernel methods. Since our results are independent of the dimension of Φ_m, they can be used to obtain useful bounds for local mixtures of kernel classifiers. The use of such experts results in a powerful classifier that may select a different kernel in each region of the feature space.

The gating functions $a(\cdot, x)$ reflect the relative weights of each of the experts at a given point x. In the sequel we consider two main types of gating functions.

Definition 2 (Gating functions). *For each $1 \leq m \leq M$, let W_{max}^m be a nonnegative scalar and w_m a vector with k elements. Then, the m-th gating function is given by a mapping $a_m(w_m, x)$ where $w_m \in W_m = \{w \in \mathbb{R}^k : \|w\| \leq \mathrm{W}_{max}^m\}$. To simplify the notation we define $\mathrm{W}_{max} = \sup_m \mathrm{W}_{max}^m$ and set $\mathcal{A} = \bigcup_{m=1}^M \mathcal{A}_m = \bigcup_{m=1}^M \{a_m(w_m, x) | w_m \in W_m\}$. If $a_m(w_m, x) = a_m(w_m^\top x)$ we say that $a_m(w_m, x)$ is a* half-space gate, *and if $a_m(w_m, x) = a_m\left(\|w_m - x\|^2/2\right)$ we say that $a_m(w_m, x)$ is a* local gate.

Assumption 2. *The following assumptions are made for every* m, $1 \leq m \leq M$. *(i)* $a_m(v_m, x)$ *is Lipschitz with constant* L_{a_m}, *analogously to Assumption 1. We define* $L_a = \max_m L_{a_m}$. *(ii)* $|a_m(v_m, x)|$ *is bounded by some positive constant* $\mathcal{M}_{\mathcal{A}_m} < \infty$. *So, by defining* $\mathcal{M}_{\mathcal{A}} = \max_m \mathcal{M}_{\mathcal{A}_m}$ *we have* $\sup_{m,w_m} |a_m(w_m, x)| \leq \mathcal{M}_{\mathcal{A}}$.

In Section 6 we will remove some of the restrictions imposed on the parameters.

4 Risk Bounds for Mixture of Experts Classifiers

In this section we address the problem of bounding $\hat{R}_N(\mathcal{F})$ where $\mathcal{F}$ is the class of all MoE classifiers defined in section 3. We begin with the following Lemma, the proof of which can be found in the appendix.

Lemma 1. *Let* $\mathcal{F}_m = \{a_m(w_m, x)h_m(v_m, x) | a_m(w_m, x) \in \mathcal{A}_m, h_m(v_m, x) \in \mathcal{H}_m\}$. *Then,* $\hat{R}_N(\mathcal{F}) = \sum_{m=1}^{M} \hat{R}_N(\mathcal{F}_m)$.

Thus, it is suffices to bound $\hat{R}_N(\mathcal{F}_m)$, $m = 1, 2, \ldots, M$ in order to establish bounds for $\hat{R}_N(\mathcal{F})$. To do so, we use the following Lemma.

Lemma 2. *Let* $\mathcal{G}_1, \mathcal{G}_2$ *be two classes defined over some sets* $\mathcal{X}_1, \mathcal{X}_2$ *respectively, and define the class* $\mathcal{G}_3$ *as*

$$\mathcal{G}_3 = \{g : g(x_1, x_2) = g_1(x_1)g_2(x_2),\ g_1 \in \mathcal{G}_1, g_2 \in \mathcal{G}_2\} \ .$$

Assume further that at least one of the sets $\mathcal{X}_1$ *or* $\mathcal{X}_2$ *is closed under negation and that every function in the class defined over this set is either symmetric or antisymmetric. Then,*

$$\mathcal{Z}(\mathcal{G}_3) \leq \mathcal{M}_2 \mathcal{Z}(\mathcal{G}_1) + \mathcal{M}_1 \mathcal{Z}(\mathcal{G}_2) \ ,$$

where $\mathcal{Z}(\mathcal{G}_i) = \mathbf{E}_\sigma \left\{ \sup_{g \in \mathcal{G}_i} \sum_{n=1}^{N} \sigma_n g(x_n) \right\}$ *for* $i = 1, 2, 3$ *and* $\mathcal{M}_i = \sup_{g_i \in \mathcal{G}_i, x_i \in \mathcal{X}_i} |g_i(x_i)|$ *for* $i = 1, 2$.

The proof of Lemma 2 is given in the Appendix. Note that a simpler derivation is possible using the identity $ab = (1/4)\left((a+b)^2 - (a-b)^2\right)$. However, this approach leads to looser bound. This lemma implies the following corollary.

Corollary 1. *For every* $1 \leq m \leq M$ *define* $\mathcal{F}_m$ *as in Lemma 1. Then,*

$$\hat{R}_N(\mathcal{F}_m) \leq \mathcal{M}_{\mathcal{H}_m} \hat{R}_N(\mathcal{A}_m) + \mathcal{M}_{\mathcal{A}_m} \hat{R}_N(\mathcal{H}_m) \qquad (m = 1, 2, \ldots, M) \ .$$

We emphasize that Corollary 1 is tight. To see that, set the gating function to be a constant. In this case $\hat{R}_N(\mathcal{A}_m) = 0$ and an equality is obtained by setting the gating variable to $\mathcal{M}_{\mathcal{A}_m}$. In the sequel we use the following basic result (see [11,16] for a proof).

Lemma 3. *Assume ψ is Lipschitz with constant L_ψ and let $g : \mathbb{R}^k \times \mathcal{Y} \mapsto \mathbb{R}$ be some given function. Then, for every integer N*

$$\mathbf{E}_\sigma \left\{ \sup_{f\in\mathcal{F}} \sum_{n=1}^{N} \sigma_n \psi\left(g\left(y_n, f\left(x_n\right)\right)\right) \right\} \leq L_\psi \mathbf{E}_\sigma \left\{ \sup_{f\in\mathcal{F}} \sum_{n=1}^{N} \sigma_n g(y_n, f(x_n)) \right\} .$$

Remark 3. To minimize the technical burden, we assume the experts are generalized linear models (GLIM, see [13]), i.e. $\tau_m(v_m, x) = \tau_m(v_m^\top x)$ in Assumption 1. An extension to generalized radial basis functions (GRBF), i.e. $\tau_m(v_m, x) = \tau_m\left(\|v_m - x\|\right)$, is immediate using our analysis of local gating functions. Extensions to many other types can be achieved using similar technique.

Using the Lipschitz property of the class $\mathcal{H}_m$ along with Lemma 3 we get

$$\hat{R}_N(\mathcal{H}_m) \leq \frac{L_{h_m}}{N} \mathbf{E}_\sigma \sup_{v_m} \left\{ v_m^\top \sum_{n=1}^{N} \sigma_n x_n \right\} .$$

By the Cauchy-Schwartz and Jensen inequalities we find that

$$\hat{R}_N(\mathcal{H}_m) \leq \frac{L_{h_m}}{N} \mathbf{E}_\sigma \left\{ \mathrm{V}_{\max}^m \left\| \sum_{n=1}^{N} \sigma_n x_n \right\| \right\} \leq \frac{L_{h_m} \mathrm{V}_{\max}^m \bar{x}}{\sqrt{N}}$$

where $\bar{x} = \sqrt{N^{-1} \sum_{j=1}^{k} \sum_{n=1}^{N} x_{nj}^2}$.

For the case of half-space gating functions we have $a(w, x) = a(w^\top x)$. In this case, analogous argumentation to the one used for the experts can be used to bound $\hat{R}_N(\mathcal{A})$. For the case of local gating functions we have $a(w, x) = a\left(\|w - x\|^2/2\right)$. Similar arguments lead to the bound

$$\hat{R}_N(\mathcal{A}_m) \leq \frac{L_{a_m}}{\sqrt{N}} \left(\frac{(\mathrm{W}_{\max}^m)^2}{\sqrt{8}} + \mathrm{W}_{\max}^m \bar{x} \right) .$$

We summarize our results in the following Theorem.

Theorem 2. *Let $\mathcal{F}$ be the class of mixture of experts classifiers with M GLIM experts. Assume that gates $1, 2, \ldots, M_1$ are local and that gates $M_1 + 1, \ldots, M$ are half-space where $0 \leq M_1 \leq M$. Then,*

$$\hat{R}_N(\mathcal{F}) \leq \frac{1}{\sqrt{N}} \left[\sum_{m=1}^{M_1} c_{1,m} (\mathrm{W}_{max}^m)^2 + \sum_{m=1}^{M} c_{2,m} \mathrm{W}_{max}^m + \sum_{m=1}^{M} c_{3,m} \mathrm{V}_{max}^m \right]$$

where $c_{1,m} = \mathcal{M}_{\mathcal{H}_m} L_{a_m} / \sqrt{8}$, $c_{2,m} = \mathcal{M}_{\mathcal{H}_m} L_{a_m} \bar{x}$ and $c_{3,m} = \mathcal{M}_{\mathcal{A}_m} L_{h_m} \bar{x}$ for all $m = 1, 2, \ldots, M$.

5 Hierarchical Mixture of Experts

The MoE classifier is defined by a linear combination of M experts. An intuitive interpretation to the meaning of this combination is the division of the feature space into subspaces, in each of which the experts are combined using the weights a_m. The *Hierarchical* MoE takes this procedure one step further by recursively dividing the subspaces using a MoE classifier as the expert in each domain, as described in Figure 2.

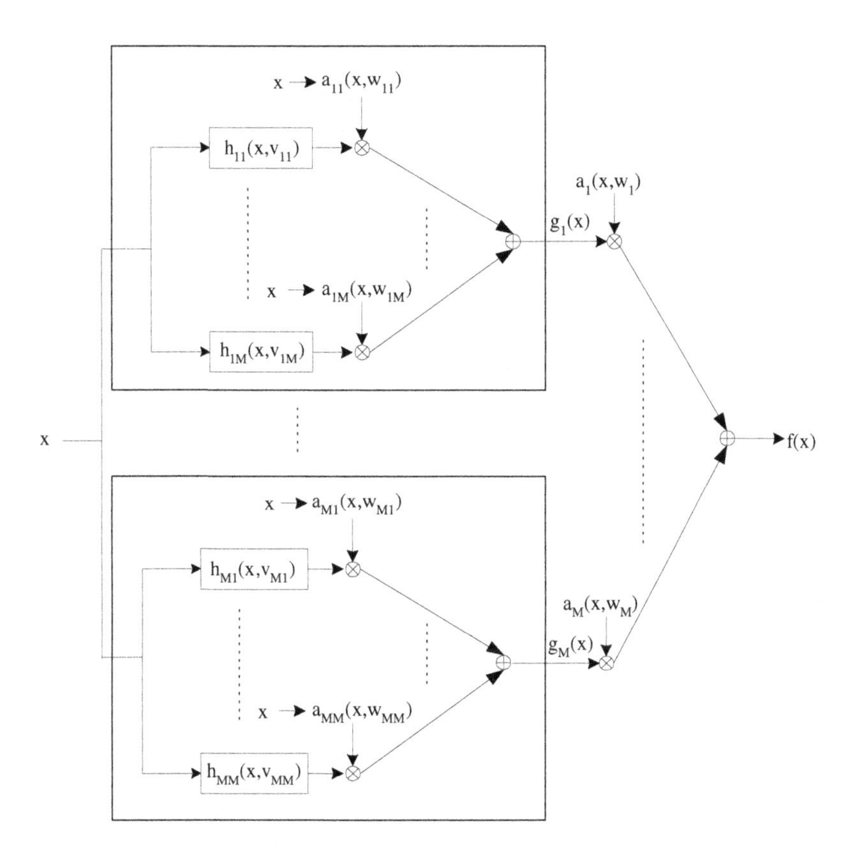

Fig. 2. Balanced 2-level HMoE classifier with M experts. Each expert in the first level is a mixture of M sub-experts.

In this section we expand the bound obtained for the MoE to the case of HMoE. We demonstrate the procedure for the case of balanced two-levels hierarchy with M experts (see Figure 2). It is easy to repeat the same procedure for any number of levels, whether the HMoE is balanced or not, using the same idea.

We begin by giving the mathematical description of the HMoE classifier. Let $f(x)$ be the output of the HMoE, and let $g_m(\theta_m, x)$ be the output of the m-th expert, $1 \leq m \leq M$. The parameter θ_m is comprised of all the parameters of the m-th first level expert, as will be detailed shortly. This is described by

$$f(x) = \sum_{m=1}^{M} a_m(w_m, x) g_m(\theta_m, x),$$

where $a_m(w_m, x)$ is the weight of the m-th expert in the first level $g_m(\theta_m, x)$, given by

$$g_m(\theta_m, x) = \sum_{j=1}^{M} a_{mj}(w_{mj}, x) h_{mj}(v_{mj}, x)$$

where $a_{mj}(w_{mj}, x)$ is the weight of $h_{mj}(v_{mj}, x)$, the j-th (sub-)expert in the m-th expert of the first level. By defining $\theta_{mj} = [w_{mj}, v_{mj}]$, we have that $\theta_m = [\theta_{m1}, \dots, \theta_{mM}]$. We also define $w = [w_1, \dots, w_M]$, the parameter vector of the gates of the first level and $\theta = [w, \theta_1, \dots, \theta_M]$, the parameter vector of the HMoE.

Recall that we are seeking to bound the Rademacher complexity for the case of HMoE. First, we use the independence of the first level gating functions to show that

$$\hat{R}_N(\mathcal{F}) = \sum_{m=1}^{M} \mathbf{E}_\sigma \left\{ \sup_{\theta_m, w_m} \frac{1}{N} \sum_{n=1}^{N} \sigma_n a_m(w_m, x_n) g_m(\theta_m, x_n) \right\} . \tag{2}$$

So, our problem boils down to bounding the summands in (2). Notice that for every $m = 1, \dots, M$ we have $\sup_{\theta_m} \{|g_m(\theta_m, x)|\} \leq M\mathcal{M}_\mathcal{H}\mathcal{M}_\mathcal{A}$. By defining $\mathcal{F}_m$ for the case of the 2-level HMoE analogously to the definition given at Lemma 1 for MoE, and using Corollary 1 recursively twice, it is easy to show that

$$\begin{aligned}
\hat{R}_N(\mathcal{F}_m) &\leq M\mathcal{M}_\mathcal{H}\mathcal{M}_\mathcal{A}\hat{R}_N(\mathcal{A}) + \mathcal{M}_\mathcal{A}\mathbf{E}_\sigma \left\{ \sup_{\theta_m} \frac{1}{N} \sum_{n=1}^{N} \sigma_n \sum_{j=1}^{M} a_{mj}(w_{mj}, x_n) h_{mj}(v_{mj}, x_n) \right\} \\
&= M\mathcal{M}_\mathcal{H}\mathcal{M}_\mathcal{A}\hat{R}_N(\mathcal{A}) + \mathcal{M}_\mathcal{A} \sum_{j=1}^{M} \mathbf{E}_\sigma \left\{ \sup_{\theta_{mj}} \frac{1}{N} \sum_{n=1}^{N} \sigma_n a_{mj}(w_{mj}, x_n) h_{mj}(v_{mj}, x_n) \right\} \\
&\leq M\mathcal{M}_\mathcal{H}\mathcal{M}_\mathcal{A}\hat{R}_N(\mathcal{A}) + M\mathcal{M}_\mathcal{A} \left(\mathcal{M}_\mathcal{H}\hat{R}_N(\mathcal{A}) + \mathcal{M}_\mathcal{A}\hat{R}_N(\mathcal{H}) \right) \\
&= M\mathcal{M}_\mathcal{A} \left[2\mathcal{M}_\mathcal{H}\hat{R}_N(\mathcal{A}) + \mathcal{M}_\mathcal{A}\hat{R}_N(\mathcal{H}) \right]
\end{aligned}$$

which, combined with Corollary 1 implies Theorem 3.

Theorem 3. *Let $\mathcal{F}$ be the class of balanced 2-level hierarchical mixture of experts classifiers with M experts in each division (see Figure 2). Then,*

$$\hat{R}_N(\mathcal{F}) \leq M^2\mathcal{M}_\mathcal{A} \left[2\mathcal{M}_\mathcal{H}\hat{R}_N(\mathcal{A}) + \mathcal{M}_\mathcal{A}\hat{R}_N(\mathcal{H}) \right] .$$

Notice that by choosing the constants more carefully, similar to Theorem 2, the bound in Theorem 3 can be tightened.

6 Fully Data Dependent Bounds

So far, the feasible set for the parameters was determined by a ball with a predefined radius ($\mathrm{W}_{\max}$ for the gates or $\mathrm{V}_{\max}$ for the experts). This predefinition is problematic as it is difficult to know in advance how to set these parameters. Notice that given the number of experts M, these predefined parameters are the only elements in the bound that do not depend on the training sequence. In this section we eliminate the dependence on these preset parameters. Even though we give bounds for the case of MoE, the same technique can be easily harnessed to derive fully data dependent bounds for the case of HMoE.

The derivation is based on the technique used in [6]. The basic idea is to consider a grid of possible values for $\mathrm{W}^m_{\max}$ and $\mathrm{V}^m_{\max}$, for each of which Theorem 2 holds. Next, we assign a probability to each of these grid points and use a variant of the union bound to establish a bound that holds for every possible parameter.

Similarly to the definition of θ in section 5, we define for the MoE classifier $\theta = [\theta_1, \theta_2, \ldots, \theta_{2M}]$ where $\theta_m = w_m$ for all $m = 1, 2, \ldots, M$ and $\theta_m = v_m$ for all $m = M+1, M+2, \ldots, 2M$. The following result provides a data dependent risk bound with no preset system parameters, and can be proved using the methods described in [16].

Theorem 4. *Let the definitions and notation of Theorem 2 hold. Let q_0 be some positive number, and assume $\|\theta_m\| \geq q_0$ for every $m = 1, \ldots, 2M$. Then, with probability at least $1 - \delta$ over training sequences of length N, every function $f \in \mathcal{F}$ satisfies*

$$P_e(f) \leq \hat{E}_\phi(f, D_N) + \frac{2}{\sqrt{N}} \left[2 \sum_{m=1}^{M_1} c_{1,m} \|\theta_m\|^2 + \sum_{m=1}^{M} c_{2,m} \|\theta_m\| + \sum_{m=M+1}^{2M} c_{3,m} \|\theta_m\| \right]$$
$$+ 3\phi_{max} \sqrt{\ln \frac{2}{\delta} + 2 \sum_{m=1}^{2M} \ln \log_2 \frac{2\|\theta_m\|}{q_0}} \, .$$

Remark 4. Theorem 4 can be generalized to hold for all θ (without the restriction $\|\theta_m\| \geq q_0$), by using the proof method in [6],[16].

7 Algorithm and Numerical Results

We demonstrate how the bound derived in Section 4 can be used to select the number of experts in the MoE model. We consider algorithms which attempt to minimize the empirical ϕ-loss $\hat{E}_\phi(f, D_N)$. It should be noted that previous methods for estimating the parameters of the MoE model were based on gradient methods for maximizing the likelihood or minimizing some risk function. Such approaches are prone to problems of local optima, which render standard gradient descent approaches of limited use. This problem also occurs for the EM algorithm discussed in [10]. Notice that even if $\phi(yf(x))$ is convex with respect to $yf(x)$, this doesn't necessarily imply that it is convex with respect to the parameters of $f(x)$. The deterministic annealing EM algorithm proposed in [17] attempts to address the local maxima problem, using a modified posterior distribution parameterized by a temperature like parameter. A modification of the EM algorithm, the split-and-merge EM algorithm proposed in [7], deals with certain types of local maxima involving an unbalanced usage of the experts over the feature space.

One possible solution to the problem of identifying the location of the global minimum of the loss is given by the *Cross-Entropy* algorithm (see [5] for a recent review, [18]). This algorithm, similarly to genetic algorithms, is based on the idea of randomly drawing samples from the parameter space and improving the way these samples are drawn from generation to generation. We observe that the algorithm below is applicable to finite dimensional problems.

To give an exact description of the algorithm used in our simulation we first introduce the following notation. We let the definition of θ from section 6 hold and denote by Θ the feasible set of values for θ. We also define a parameterized p.d.f. $\psi_\Theta(\theta;\xi)$ over Θ with ξ parameterizing the distribution.

To find a point that is likely to be in the neighborhood of the global minimum, we carry out Algorithm 1 (see box). Upon convergence, we use gradient methods with $\hat{\theta}_s^B$ (see box for definition) as the initial point to gain further accuracy in estimating the global minimum point. We denote by $\hat{\theta}^B$ the solution of the gradient minimization procedure and declare it as the final solution.

Simulation setup. We simulate a source generating data from a MoE classifier with 3 experts. The Bayes risk for this problem is 18.33%. We used a training sequence of length 300, for which we carried out Algorithm 1 followed by gradient search with respect to $\hat{E}_\phi(f, D_N)$, where $\phi(t) = 1 - \tanh(2t)$. Denoting by f_M^{CE} the classifier that was selected for each $M = 1, 2, \ldots, 5$, we denote by $\hat{E}_\phi(f_M^{CE}, D_N)$ the minimal empirical ϕ-risk obtained over the class. We evaluate the performance of each classifier by computing $\hat{P}_e(f_M^{CE}, D_{test})$ over a test sequence of 10^6 elements (D_{test}), drawn from the same source as the training sequence. This is the reported probability of error $P_e(f)$. Figure 1 describes these two measures computed over 400 different training sequences (the bars describe the standard deviation). The graph labelled as the 'complexity term' in Figure 1 is the sum of all terms on the right hand side of Theorem 2 with $\delta = 10^{-3}$, excluding $\hat{E}_\phi(f_M^{CE}, D_N)$. As for the CE parameters, we set $\psi_\Theta(.)$ to be the β distribution, $\hat{\xi}_0 = [1, 1]$ (corresponds to uniform distribution), $\rho_1 = 0.03$, $\rho_2 = 0.001$, $\rho_3 = 0.7$ and $T = 200$. The results are summarized in Figure 1.

A few observations are in place: (i) As one might expect, $\hat{E}_\phi(f_M^{CE}, D_N)$ is monotonically decreasing with respect to M. (ii) As expected, the complexity term is monotonically increasing with respect to M and (iii) $P_e(f)$ is the closest to the Bayes error (18.33%) when $M = 3$, which is the Bayes solution. We witness the phenomenon of underfitting for $M = 1, 2$ and overfitting for $M = 4, 5$, as predicted by the bound.

The Cross-Entropy Algorithm.

Input: $\psi_\Theta(.)$ and $\phi(.)$.

Output: $\hat{\theta}_s^B$, a point in the neighborhood of the global minimum of $\hat{E}(f(\theta), D_N)$.

Algorithm :

1. Pick some $\hat{\xi}_0$ (a good selection will turn $\psi_\Theta(\theta; \hat{\xi}_0)$ into a uniform distribution over Θ). Set iteration counter $s = 1$, two positive integers d, T and three parameters $0 < \rho_1, \rho_2, \rho_3 < 1$.
2. Generate an ensemble $\theta_1, \ldots, \theta_L$ where $L = 2kMT$ (k is the dimension of the feature space and M is the number of experts, thus the dimension of Θ is $2kM$), drawn i.i.d according to $\psi_\Theta(\theta; \hat{\xi}_{s-1})$.
3. Calculate $\hat{E}_\phi(f, D_N)$ for each member of the ensemble. The Elite Sample (ES) comprises the $\lfloor \rho_1 L \rfloor$ parameters that received the lowest empirical ϕ-risk. Denote the parameters that are associated with the worst and the best $\hat{E}_\phi(f, D_N)$ in the ES as $\hat{\theta}_s^W$ and $\hat{\theta}_s^B$ respectively.
4. If for some $s \geq d$
$$\max_{s-d \leq i,j \leq s} (\hat{\theta}_i^W - \hat{\theta}_j^W) \leq \rho_2$$
stop (declare $\hat{\theta}_s^B$ as the solution). Otherwise, solve the maximum likelihood estimation problem, based on the ES, to estimate the parameters of ψ_Θ (notice that it is *not* a MLE for the original empirical risk minimization problem). Denoting the solution as $\hat{\xi}_{ML}$, compute $\hat{\xi}_{s+1} = (1 - \rho_3)\hat{\xi}_s + \rho_3 \hat{\xi}_{ML}$. Set $s = s + 1$ and return to 2.

Algorithm 1: The Cross-Entropy Algorithm for estimating the location of the global minimum of the empirical ϕ-risk.

We also applied a variant of Algorithm 1, suitable for unbounded parameter feasible set (the details will be discussed in the full paper), to the real-world data sets BUPA and PIMA [3]. We considered a MoE classifier with 1 to 4 linear experts, all with local gates. The results are compared with those of linear-SVM and RBF-SVM in Table 1.

8 Discussion

We have considered the hierarchical mixture of experts architecture, and have established data dependent risk bounds for its performance. This class of architectures is very flexible and overly parameterized, and it is thus essential to establish bounds which do not depend on the number of parameters. Our bounds lead to very reasonable results on a toy problem. Also, the simulation results on real world problems are encouraging and motivate further research. Since the algorithmic issues are rather complicated for this architecture, it may be advantageous to consider some of the variational approaches proposed in recent years (e.g. [8]). We observe that the HMoE architecture can be viewed as a member of

Table 1. Real world data sets results. The results were computed using 7-fold cross-validation for BUPA and 10-fold cross-validation for PIMA. For each fold, the parameters of the classifiers were selected using cross-validation in the training sequence.

Data set	MoE (2 experts)	Linear-SVM	RBF-SVM
BUPA	0.289 ± 0.050	0.320 ± 0.084	0.317 ± 0.048
PIMA	0.241 ± 0.056	0.244 ± 0.050	0.255 ± 0.067

the large class of widely used graphical models (a.k.a. Bayesian networks). We expect that the techniques developed can be used to obtain tight risk bounds for these architectures as well.

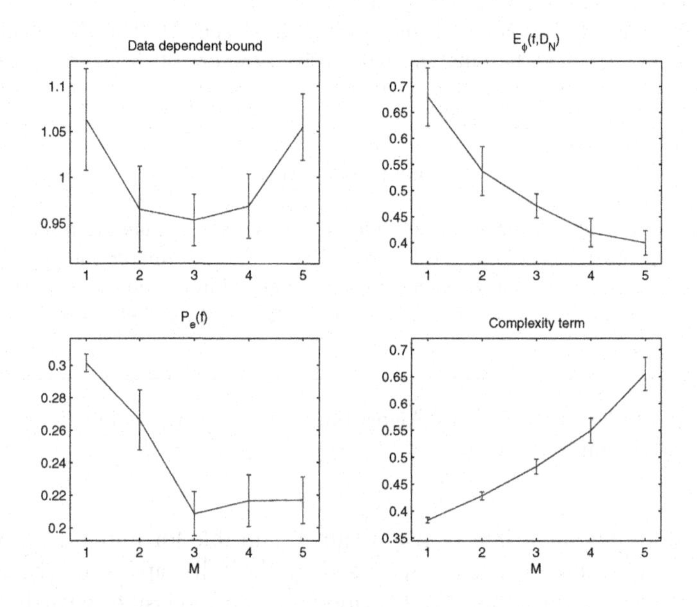

Fig. 3. A comparison between the data dependent bound of Theorem 2 and the true error, computed over 400 Monte Carlo iterations of different training sequences. The solid line describes the mean and the bars indicate the standard deviation over all training sequences. The two figures on the left demonstrates the applicability of the data dependent bound to the problem of model selection when one wishes to set the optimal number of experts. It can be observed that the optimal predicted value for M in this case is 3, which is the number of experts used to generate the data.

Acknowledgment. We are grateful to Dori Peleg for his assistance in applying the cross-entropy algorithm to our problem. The work of R.M. was partially supported by the Technion V.P.R. fund for the promotion of sponsored research. Support from the Ollendorff center of the department of Electrical Engineering at the Technion is also acknowledged.

References

1. Peter L. Bartlett, Michael I. Jordan, and Jon D. McAuliffe. Convexity, classification, and risk bounds. Technical Report 638, Department of Statistics, U.C. Berkeley, 2003.
2. P.L. Bartlett and S. Mendelson. Rademacher and Gaussian complexities: Risk bounds and structural results. *Journal of Machine Learning Research*, 3:463–482, 2002.
3. C.L. Blake and C.J. Merz. UCI repository of machine learning databases, 1998. http://www.ics.uci.edu/~mlearn/MLRepository.html.
4. S. Boucheron, G. Lugosi, and P. Massart. Concentration inequalities using the entropy method. *The Annals of Probability*, 31:1583–1614, 2003.
5. P.T. de Boer, D.P. Kroese, S. Mannor, and R.Y. Rubinstein. A tutorial on the cross-entropy method. *Annals of Operations Research*, 2004. To appear.
6. I. Desyatnikov and R. Meir. Data-dependent bounds for multi-category classification based on convex losses. In *Proc. of the sixteenth Annual Conference on Computational Learning Theory*, volume 2777 of *LNAI*. Springer, 2003.
7. Ghaharamani Z. Nakano R. Ueda N. Hinton, G.E. Smem algorithm for mixture models. *Neural Computation*, 12:2109–2128, 2000.
8. T. Jaakkola. Tutorial on variational approximation methods. In M. Opper and D. Saad, editors, *Advanced Mean Field Methods: Theory and Practice*, pages 129–159, Cambridge, MA, 2001. MIT Press.
9. W. Jiang. Complexity regularization via localized random penalties. *Neural Computation*, 12(6).
10. M.I. Jordan and R.A. Jacobs. Hierarchical mixtures of experts and the EM algorithm. *Neural Computation*, 6(2):181–214, 1994.
11. M. Ledoux and M. Talgrand. *Probability in Banach Spaces: Isoperimetry and Processes*. Springer Press, New York, 1991.
12. S. Mannor, R. Meir, and T. Zhang. Greedy algorithms for classification - consistency, convergence rates, and adaptivity. *Journal of Machine Learning Research*, 4:713–741, 2003.
13. P. McCullach and J. A. Nelder. *Generalized Linear Models*. CRC Press, 1989 (2nd edition).
14. C. McDiarmid. On the method of bounded differences. In *Surveys in Combinatorics*, pages 148–188. Cambridge University Press, 1989.
15. R. Meir, R. El-Yaniv, and S. Ben-David. Localized boosting. In N. Cesa-Bianchi and S. Goldman, editors, *Proc. Thirteenth Annual Conference on Computaional Learning Theory*, pages 190–199. Morgan Kaufman, 2000.
16. R. Meir and T. Zhang. Generalization bounds for Bayesian mixture algorithms. *Journal of Machine Learning Research*, 4:839–860, 2003.
17. R. Nakano and N. N. Ueda. Determinisic annealing em algorithm. *Neural Networks*, 11(2), 1998.
18. R.Y. Rubinstein. The cross-entropy method for combinatorial and continuous optimization. *Methodology and Computing in Applied Probability*, 1:127–190, September 1999.
19. A.W. van der Vaart and J.A. Wellner. *Weak Convergence and EmpiricalProcesses*. Springer Verlag, New York, 1996.
20. T. Zhang. Statistical behavior and consistency of classification methods based on convex risk minimization. *The Annals of Statistics*, 32(1), 2004.

A Proofs of Some of the Theorems

Proof of Lemma 1 To simplify the notation, we write $\sup_{w,v}$ instead of $\sup_{w\in W, v\in V}$. Since, by definition, the set of parameters (w_i, v_i) is independent of (w_j, v_j) for any $1 \leq i, j \leq M$, $i \neq j$ we have

$$\begin{aligned}\hat{R}_N(\mathcal{F}) &= \mathbf{E}_\sigma \left\{ \sup_{w,v} \frac{1}{N} \sum_{n=1}^{N} \sigma_n \sum_{m=1}^{M} a_m(w_m, x_n) h_m(v_m, x_n) \right\} \\ &= \frac{1}{N} \sum_{m=1}^{M} \mathbf{E}_\sigma \left\{ \sup_{w_m, v_m} \sum_{n=1}^{N} \sigma_n a_m(w_m, x_n) h_m(v_m, x_n) \right\}.\end{aligned}$$

□

Proof of Lemma 2 First, we introduce the following Lemma

Lemma 4. *For any function $C(g_1, g_2, x)$, there exist $\nu \in \{\pm 1\}$ such that*

$$\begin{aligned}&\mathbf{E}_\sigma \left\{ \sup_{g_1, g_2} \left(C(g_1, g_2, x) + \sigma g_1(x) g_2(x) \right) \right\} \\ \leq &\mathbf{E}_\sigma \left\{ \sup_{g_1, g_2} \left(C(g_1, \nu g_2, x) + \mathcal{M}_2 \sigma g_1(x) + \mathcal{M}_1 \sigma g_2(x) \right) \right\} .\end{aligned}$$

Proof. (of Lemma 4)

$$\begin{aligned}&\mathbf{E}_\sigma \left\{ \sup_{g_1, g_2} \left(C(g_1, g_2, x) + \sigma g_1(x) g_2(x) \right) \right\} \\ &= \frac{1}{2} \sup_{g_1, g_2} \left(C(g_1, g_2, x) + g_1(x) g_2(x) \right) + \frac{1}{2} \sup_{g_1, g_2} \left(C(g_1, g_2, x) - g_1(x) g_2(x) \right) \\ &= \frac{1}{2} \sup_{g_1, g_2, \tilde{g}_1, \tilde{g}_2} \left(C(g_1, g_2, x) + g_1(x) g_2(x) + C(\tilde{g}_1, \tilde{g}_2, x) - \tilde{g}_1(x) \tilde{g}_2(x) \right) \\ &\overset{(a)}{=} \frac{1}{2} \sup_{g_1, g_2, \tilde{g}_1, \tilde{g}_2} \left(C(g_1, g_2, x) + C(\tilde{g}_1, \tilde{g}_2, x) + |g_1(x) g_2(x) - \tilde{g}_1(x) \tilde{g}_2(x)| \right) \\ &\overset{(b)}{\leq} \frac{1}{2} \sup_{g_1, g_2, \tilde{g}_1, \tilde{g}_2} \left(C(g_1, g_2, x) + C(\tilde{g}_1, \tilde{g}_2, x) + \mathcal{M}_1 |g_2(x) - \tilde{g}_2(x)| + \mathcal{M}_2 |g_1(x) - \tilde{g}_1(x)| \right)\end{aligned} \tag{3}$$

where (a) is due to the symmetry of the expression over which the sepremum is taken and (b) is immediate, using the following inequality

$$\begin{aligned}|g_1(x) g_2(x) - \tilde{g}_1(x) \tilde{g}_2(x)| &= |g_1(x)(g_2(x) - \tilde{g}_2(x)) + \tilde{g}_2(x)(g_1(x) - \tilde{g}_1(x))| \\ &\leq \mathcal{M}_1 |g_2(x) - \tilde{g}_2(x)| + \mathcal{M}_2 |g_1(x) - \tilde{g}_1(x)|.\end{aligned}$$

Next, we denote by $g_1^*, g_2^*, \tilde{g}_1^*, \tilde{g}_2^*$ the functions over which the supremum in (3) is achieved and address all cases of the signum of the terms inside the absolute values at (3).

case 1: $g_2^*(x) > \tilde{g}_2^*(x)$, $g_1^*(x) > \tilde{g}_1^*(x)$

$$\begin{aligned} &\sup_{g_1,g_2,\tilde{g}_1,\tilde{g}_2} \{C(g_1,g_2,x) + C(\tilde{g}_1,\tilde{g}_2,x) + \mathcal{M}_1(g_2(x) - \tilde{g}_2(x)) + \mathcal{M}_2(g_1(x) - \tilde{g}_1(x))\} \\ &= \sup_{g_1,g_2} \{C(g_1,g_2,x) + \mathcal{M}_1 g_2(x) + \mathcal{M}_2 g_1(x)\} + \sup_{\tilde{g}_1,\tilde{g}_2} \{C(\tilde{g}_1,\tilde{g}_2,x) - \mathcal{M}_1\tilde{g}_2(x) - \mathcal{M}_2\tilde{g}_1(x)\} \\ &= 2\mathbf{E}_\sigma \sup_{g_1,g_2} \{C(g_1,g_2,x) + \mathcal{M}_1\sigma g_2(x) + \mathcal{M}_2\sigma g_1(x)\} \end{aligned}$$

case 2: $g_2^*(x) > \tilde{g}_2^*(x)$, $g_1^*(x) < \tilde{g}_1^*(x)$

$$\begin{aligned} &\sup_{g_1,g_2,\tilde{g}_1,\tilde{g}_2} \{C(g_1,g_2,x) + C(\tilde{g}_1,\tilde{g}_2,x) + \mathcal{M}_1(g_2(x) - \tilde{g}_2(x)) + \mathcal{M}_2(\tilde{g}_1(x) - g_1(x))\} \\ &\overset{(a)}{=} \sup_{g_1,g_2,\tilde{g}_1,\tilde{g}_2} \{C(g_1,-g_2,x) + C(\tilde{g}_1,-\tilde{g}_2,x) + \mathcal{M}_1(\tilde{g}_2(x) - g_2(x)) + \mathcal{M}_2(\tilde{g}_1(x) - g_1(x))\} \\ &= 2\mathbf{E}_\sigma \sup_{g_1,g_2} \{C(g_1,-g_2,x) + \mathcal{M}_1\sigma g_2(x) + \mathcal{M}_2\sigma g_1(x)\} \end{aligned}$$

where (a) is due to the assumption that $\mathcal{G}_2$ is close under negation. Notice that the cases where $g_2^*(x) < \tilde{g}_2^*(x)$, $g_1^*(x) < \tilde{g}_1^*(x)$ and $g_2^*(x) < \tilde{g}_2^*(x)$, $g_1^*(x) > \tilde{g}_1^*(x)$ are analogous to cases 1 and 2 respectively. □

We can now provide the proof of Lemma 2. By using Lemma 4 recursively with a suitable definition of $C(g_1, g_2, x)$ in each iteration, we have for every $t = 1, \ldots, N+1$

$$\begin{aligned} &\mathbf{E}_\sigma \left\{ \sup_{g_1,g_2} \sum_{n=1}^{N} \sigma_n g_1(x_n) g_2(x_n) \right\} \\ &\leq \mathbf{E}_\sigma \left\{ \sup_{g_1,g_2} \left(\sum_{n=t}^{N} \sigma_n g_1(x_n) g_2(x_n) + \mathcal{M}_2 \sum_{n=1}^{t-1} \sigma_n g_1(x_n) + \mathcal{M}_1 \sum_{n=1}^{t-1} \Gamma(n,t)\sigma_n g_2(x_n) \right) \right\} \end{aligned}$$

where

$$\Gamma(n,t) = \begin{cases} \prod_{i=n}^{t-2} \nu_i & \text{if } n \leq t-2 \\ 1 & \text{if } n = t-1 \\ \text{not defined} & \text{otherwise} \end{cases} .$$

By setting $t = N+1$ we get

$$\begin{aligned} &\mathbf{E}_\sigma \left\{ \sup_{g_1,g_2} \sum_{n=1}^{N} \sigma_n g_1(x_n) g_2(x_n) \right\} \\ &\leq \mathcal{M}_2 \mathbf{E}_\sigma \left\{ \sup_{g_1} \sum_{n=1}^{N} \sigma_n g_1(x_n) \right\} + \mathcal{M}_1 \mathbf{E}_\sigma \left\{ \sup_{g_2} \sum_{n=1}^{N} \Gamma(n,N+1)\sigma_n g_2(x_n) \right\} . \end{aligned}$$

Recall that $\nu_i \in \{\pm 1\}$ $\forall i$ and thus $\Gamma(n, N+1) \in \{\pm 1\}$ $\forall n$. So, by redefining $\sigma_n = \prod_{i=n}^{N-1} \nu_i \sigma_n$ $\forall n$ for the second term of the last inequality, we complete the proof of Theorem 2. □

Consistency in Models for Communication Constrained Distributed Learning*

J.B. Predd, S.R. Kulkarni, and H.V. Poor

Princeton University, Department of Electrical Engineering, Engineering Quadrangle, Olden Street, Princeton, NJ 08540
jpredd/kulkarni/poor@princeton.edu

Abstract. Motivated by sensor networks and other distributed settings, several models for distributed learning are presented. The models differ from classical works in statistical pattern recognition by allocating observations of an i.i.d. sampling process amongst members of a network of learning agents. The agents are limited in their ability to communicate to a fusion center; the amount of information available for classification or regression is constrained. For several simple communication models, questions of universal consistency are addressed; i.e., the asymptotics of several agent decision rules and fusion rules are considered in both binary classification and regression frameworks. These models resemble distributed environments and introduce new questions regarding universal consistency. Insofar as these models offer a useful picture of distributed scenarios, this paper considers whether the guarantees provided by Stone's Theorem in centralized environments hold in distributed settings.

1 Introduction

1.1 Models for Distributed Learning

Consider the following learning model: Suppose X and Y are $\mathbb{R}^d$-valued and $\mathcal{Y}$-valued random variables, respectively, with joint and marginal distributions denoted by $\mathbf{P}_{XY}$, $\mathbf{P}_X$, and $\mathbf{P}_Y$. Suppose $\mathcal{Y} \subseteq \mathbb{R}$ but is otherwise unspecified for now; we will consider cases where $\mathcal{Y} = \{0, 1\}$ and $\mathcal{Y} = \mathbb{R}$. Suppose further that $D_n = \{(X_i, Y_i)\}_{i=1}^n$ is an independent and identically distributed (i.i.d.) collection of training data with $(X_i, Y_i) \sim \mathbf{P}_{XY}$ for all $i \in \{1, ..., n\}$.

If D_n is provided to a single learning agent, then we have a traditional centralized setting and we can pose questions about the existence of classifiers or estimators that are universally consistent. The answers to such questions are well understood and are provided by results such as Stone's Theorem [1], [2], [3] and numerous others in the literature.

* This research was supported in part by the Army Research Office under grant DAAD19-00-1-0466, in part by Draper Laboratory under grant IR&D 6002, in part by the National Science Foundation under grant CCR-0312413, and in part by the Office of Naval Research under Grant No. N00014-03-1-0102.

J. Shawe-Taylor and Y. Singer (Eds.): COLT 2004, LNAI 3120, pp. 442–456, 2004.

Instead, suppose that for each $i \in \{1, ..., n\}$, the training datum (X_i, Y_i) is received by a distinct member of a network of n simple learning agents. At classification time, the central authority observes a new random feature vector X distributed according to $\mathbf{P}_X$ and communicates it to the network in a request for information. At this time, each agent can respond with at most one bit. That is, each learning agent chooses whether or not to respond to the central authority's request for information; if it chooses to respond, an agent sends either a 1 or a 0 based on its local decision algorithm. Upon observing the response of the network, the central authority fuses the information to create an estimate of Y.

When $\mathcal{Y} = \{0, 1\}$, we have a binary classification framework and it is natural to consider the probability of misclassification as the performance metric for the network of agents. Similarly, when $\mathcal{Y} = \mathbb{R}$, we have a natural regression framework and as is typical, we can consider the expected L^2-risk of the ensemble. A key question that arises is: given such a model, do there exist agent decision rules and a central authority fusion rule that result in a universally consistent ensemble in the limit as the number of agents increases without bound?

In what follows, we answer this question in the affirmative for both classification and regression. In the binary classification setting, we demonstrate agent decision rules and a central authority fusion rule that correspond nicely with classical kernel classifiers; the universal Bayes-risk consistency of this ensemble then follows immediately from celebrated analyses like Stone's Theorem, etc. In the regression setting, we demonstrate that under regularity, randomized agent decision rules exist such that when the central authority applies a scaled majority vote fusion of the agents' decisions, the resulting estimator is universally consistent for L^2-risk.

In this model, each agent's decision rule can be viewed as a selection of one of three states: abstain, vote and send 1, and vote and send 0. The option to abstain essentially allows the agents to convey slightly more information than the one bit that is assumed to be physically transmitted to the central authority. With this observation, these results can be interpreted as follows: $\log_2(3)$ bits per agent per classification is sufficient for universal consistency to hold for both distributed classification and regression *with abstention*.

In this view, it is natural to ask whether these $\log_2(3)$ bits are necessary. Can consistency results be proven at lower bit rates? Consider a revised model, precisely the same as above, except that in response to the central authority's request for information, each agent must respond with 1 or 0; abstention is not an option and thus, each agent responds with exactly one bit per classification. The same questions arise: are there rules for which universal consistency holds in distributed classification and regression *without abstention*?

Interestingly, we demonstrate that in the binary classification setting, randomized agent rules exist such that when a majority vote fusion rule is applied, universal Bayes-risk consistency holds. Moreover, it is clear that one bit is necessary. As an important negative result, we demonstrate that universal consistency in the L^2-risk regression framework is not possible in the one bit regime, under reasonable assumptions on the candidate decision rules.

1.2 Motivation and Background

Motivation for this problem lies in sensor networks [4]. Here, an array of sensors is distributed across a geographical terrain; using simple sensing functionality, the devices observe the environment and locally process the information for use by a central monitor. Given locally understood statistical models for the observations and the channel that the sensors use to communicate, sensors can be preprogrammed to process information optimally with respect to these models. Without such priors, can one devise distributed sensors that learn? Undoubtedly, the complexity of communication in this environment will complicate matters; how should the sensors share their data to maximize the inferential power of the network?

Similar problems exist in distributed databases. Here, there is a database of training data that is massive in both the dimension of the feature space and quantity of data. However, for political, economic or technological reasons, this database is distributed geographically or in such a way that it is infeasible for any single agent to access the entire database. Multiple agents can be deployed to make inferences from various segments of the database. How should the agents communicate in order to maximize the performance of the ensemble?

The spirit of the models presented in this paper is in line with models considered in nonparametric statistics and the study of kernel methods and other Stone-type rules. Extensive work has been done related to the consistency of Stone-type rules under various sampling processes; see [2], [3] and references therein, [5], [6], [7], [8], [9], [10], [11], [12], [13], [1], [14]. These models focus on various dependency structures within the training data and assume that a single processor has access to the entire data stream. However, in distributed scenarios, many agents have access to different data streams that differ in distribution and may depend on external parameters such as the state of a sensor network or location of a database. Moreover, agents are unable to share their data with each other or with a central authority; they may have only a few bits with which to communicate a summary.

The models presented in this paper differ from the works just cited by allocating observations of an i.i.d. sampling process to individual learning agents. By limiting the ability of the agents to communicate, we constrain the amount of information available to the ensemble and the central authority for use in classification or regression. These models more closely resemble a distributed environment and present new questions to consider with regard to universal consistency. Insofar as these models offer a useful picture of distributed scenarios, this paper considers whether the guarantees provided by Stone's Theorem in centralized environments hold in distributed settings.

Numerous other works in the literature are relevant to the research presented here. However, different points need to be made depending on whether we consider regression or classification with or without abstention. Without context, we will save such discussion for the appropriate sections in the paper.

The remainder of this paper is organized as follows. In Section II, the relevant notation and technical assumptions are introduced. In Sections III, owing to an immediate connection to Stone's Theorem, we briefly present the result for distributed classification with abstention. In Section IV, we present the results for regression with abstention. In Section V and VI, we discuss the results for the model without abstention in the binary classification and regression frameworks, respectively. In each section, we present the main results, discuss important connections to other work in nonparametrics, and then proceed to describe the basic structure of the associated proof. Technical lemmas that are readily apparent from the literature are left to the appendix in Section VII.

2 Preliminaries

As stated earlier, suppose X and Y are $\mathbb{R}^d$-valued and $\mathcal{Y}$-valued random variables, respectively, with joint and marginal distributions denoted by $\mathbf{P}_{XY}$, $\mathbf{P}_X$, and $\mathbf{P}_Y$. Assume $\mathcal{Y} \subseteq \mathbb{R}$. Suppose further that $D_n = \{(X_i, Y_i)\}_{i=1}^n$ is an independent and identically distributed (i.i.d.) collection of training data with $(X_i, Y_i) \sim \mathbf{P}_{XY}$ for all $i \in \{1, ..., n\}$.

When $\mathcal{Y} = \{0, 1\}$, $\mathbf{P}_{XY}$ specifies a binary classification problem. Let $\delta_B(x) : \mathbb{R}^d \to \mathcal{Y}$ denote the Bayes decision rule for this problem and use R^* to denote the minimum Bayes risk,

$$R^* = \mathbf{P}\{\delta_B(X) \neq Y\}. \tag{1}$$

When $\mathcal{Y} = \mathbb{R}$, $\mathbf{P}_{XY}$ specifies a regression problem and as is well known, the regression function

$$\eta(x) = \mathbf{E}\{Y \,|X = x\} \tag{2}$$

minimizes $\mathbf{E}\{|f(X) - Y|^2\}$ over all measurable functions f.

Throughout this paper, we will use $\delta_{ni}(x)$ to denote the ith learning agent's decision rule in an ensemble of n agents. For each $i \in \{1, ..., n\}$, $\delta_{ni}(x) = \delta_{ni}(x, X_i, Y_i) : \mathbb{R}^d \times \mathbb{R}^d \times \mathcal{Y} \to \mathcal{S}$ is a function of the observation X made by the central authority and (X_i, Y_i), the training data observed by the agent itself. Here $\mathcal{S}$ is the decision space for the agent; in models *with abstention* we take $\mathcal{S} = \{\text{abstain}, \text{send}\,1, \text{send}\,0\}$ and in models *without abstention* we take $\mathcal{S} = \{\text{send}\,1, \text{send}\,0\}$. In various parts of this paper, agent decision rules will be randomized; in these cases $\delta_{ni}(x) = \delta_{ni}(x, X_i, Y_i, Z_{ni})$ is dependent on an additional random variable Z_{ni}. Consistent with this notation, we assume that the agents have knowledge of n, the number of agents in the ensemble. Moreover, we assume that for each n, every agent has the same local decision rule; i.e., the ensemble is homogenous in this sense.

We use $g_n(x) = g_n(x, \{\delta_n i(x)\}_{i=1}^n) : \mathbb{R}^d \times \{0, 1\}^n \to \{0, 1\}$ to denote the fusion rule in the binary classification frameworks and similarly, we use $\hat{\eta}_n(x) = \hat{\eta}_n(x, \{\delta_n i(x)\}_{i=1}^n\}) : \mathbb{R}^d \times \{0, 1\}^n \to \mathbb{R}$ to denote the fusion rule in the regression frameworks.

3 Distributed Classification with Abstention: Stone's Theorem

In this section, we show that the universal consistency of distributed classification with abstention follows immediately from Stone's Theorem and the classical analysis of naive kernel classifiers. To start, let us briefly recap the model. Since we are in the classification framework, $\mathcal{Y} = \{0, 1\}$. Suppose that for each $i \in \{1, ..., n\}$, the training datum $(X_i, Y_i) \in D_n$ is received by a distinct member of a network of n learning agents. At classification time, the central authority observes a new random feature vector X and communicates this to the network of learning agents in a request for information. At this time, each of the learning agents can respond with at most one bit. That is, each learning agent chooses whether or not to respond to the central authority's request for information; and if an agent chooses to respond, it sends either a 1 or a 0 based on a local decision algorithm. Upon receiving the agents' responses, the central authority fuses the information to create an estimate of Y.

To answer the question of whether agent decision rules and central authority fusion rules exist that result in a universally consistent ensemble, let us construct one natural choice. With $B_{r_n}(x) = \{y \in \mathbb{R}^d : \| x - y \|_2 \leq r_n\}$, let

$$\delta_{ni}(x) = \begin{cases} Y_i, & \text{if } X_i \in B_{r_n}(x) \\ \text{abstain}, & \text{otherwise} \end{cases} \tag{3}$$

and

$$g_n(x) = \begin{cases} 1, \text{ if } \frac{\sum_{i=1}^{n} \delta_{ni}(x) 1_{\{\delta_{ni}(x) \neq \text{abstain}\}}}{\sum_{i=1}^{n} 1_{\{\delta_{ni}(x) \neq \text{abstain}\}}} \geq \frac{1}{2} \\ 0, \text{ otherwise} \end{cases}, \tag{4}$$

so that $g_n(x)$ amounts to a majority vote fusion rule. With this choice, it is straightforward to see that the net decision rule is equivalent to the plug-in kernel classifier rule with the naive kernel. Indeed,

$$g_n(x) = \begin{cases} 1, \text{ if } \frac{\sum_{i=1}^{n} Y_i 1_{B_{r_n}(x)}(X_i)}{\sum_{i=1}^{n} 1_{B_{r_n}(x)}(X_i)} \geq \frac{1}{2} \\ 0, \text{ otherwise} \end{cases}. \tag{5}$$

With this equivalence, the universal consistency of the ensemble follows from Stone's Theorem applied to naive kernel classifiers. With $R_n = \mathbf{P}\{g_n(X) \neq Y \,|D_n\}$, the probability of error of the ensemble conditioned on the random training data, we state this known result without proof as Theorem 1.

Theorem 1. *([2]) If, as $n \to \infty$, $r_n \to 0$ and $r_n n \to \infty$, then $\mathbf{E}\{R_n\} \to R^*$ for all distributions $\mathbf{P}_{XY}$.*

4 Distributed Regression with Abstention

A more interesting model to consider is in the context of regression, estimating a real-valued concept in a bandwidth starved environment. As above, the model remains the same except that $\mathcal{Y} = \mathbb{R}$; that is, Y is a $\mathbb{R}$-valued random variable and likewise, agents receive real-valued training data labels, Y_i.

With the aim of determining whether universally consistent ensembles can be constructed, let us devise candidate rules. These rules will be randomized; however they will adhere to the communication constraints of the model.

For each integer n, let $\{Z_{n,\theta}\}_{\theta \in [0,1]}$ be a family of random $\{0,1\}$-valued random variables parameterized by $[0,1]$ such that for each $\theta \in [0,1]$, $Z_{n,\theta}$ is Bernoulli with parameter θ.

Let $\{c_n\}_{n=1}^{\infty}$ and $\{r_n\}_{n=1}^{\infty}$ be arbitrary sequences of real numbers such that $c_n \to \infty$ and $r_n \to 0$ as $n \to \infty$. Let $\delta_{ni}(x)$ be defined as:

$$\delta_{ni}(x) = \begin{cases} Z_{i, \frac{1}{2c_n} Y_i + \frac{1}{2}}, & \text{if } x \in B_{r_n}(X_i) \text{ and } |Y_i| \leq c_n \\ Z_{i, \frac{1}{2}}, & \text{if } x \in B_{r_n}(X_i) \text{ and } |Y_i| > c_n \\ \text{abstain}, & \text{otherwise} \end{cases}, \tag{6}$$

for $i = 1, ..., n$. In words, the agents choose to vote if X_i is close enough to X; to vote, they flip a biased coin, with the bias determined by Y_i and the size of the ensemble, n.

Let us define the central authority fusion rule:

$$\hat{\eta}_n(x) = 2c_n \left(\frac{\sum_{i=1}^{n} \delta_{ni}(X) 1_{\{\delta_{ni}(X) \neq \text{abstain}\}}}{\sum_{i=1}^{n} 1_{\{\delta_{ni}(X) \neq \text{abstain}\}}} - \frac{1}{2} \right). \tag{7}$$

In words, the central authority shifts and scales a majority vote.

In this regression setting, it is natural to consider the L^2-risk of the ensemble. Here, we will consider $\mathbf{E}\{|\hat{\eta}_n(X) - \eta(X)|^2\}$ with the expectation taken over X, $D_n = \{(X_i, Y_i)\}_{i=1}^{n}$, and the randomness introduced in the agent decision rules.

4.1 Main Result and Comments

Assuming an ensemble using the described decision rules, Proposition 1 specifies sufficient conditions for consistency.

Proposition 1. *Suppose $\mathbf{P}_{XY}$ is such that $\mathbf{P}_X$ is compactly supported and $\mathbf{E}\{Y^2\} < \infty$. If, as $n \to \infty$,*

1. $c_n \to \infty$,
2. $r_n \to 0$, *and*
3. $\frac{c_n^2}{n r_n^d} \to 0$,

then $\mathbf{E}\{|\hat{\eta}_n(X) - \eta(X)|^2\} \to 0$.

More generally, the constraint regarding the compactness of $\mathbf{P}_X$ can be weakened. As will be observed in the proof below, $\mathbf{P}_X$ must be such that when coupled with a bounded random variable Y, there is a known convergence rate of the variance term of the naive kernel classifier (under a standard i.i.d. sampling model). $\{c_n\}_{n=1}^{\infty}$ should be chosen so that it grows at a rate slower than the rate at which the variance term decays. Notably, to select $\{c_n\}_{n=1}^{\infty}$, one does not need to understand the convergence rate of the bias term, and this is why continuity conditions are not required; the bias term will converge to zero universally as long as $c_n \to \infty$ and $r_n \to 0$ as $n \to \infty$.

Note that the divergent scaling sequence $\{c_n\}_{n=1}^{\infty}$ is required for the general case when there is no reason to assume that Y has a known bound. If, instead, $|Y| \leq B$ a.s. for some known $B > 0$, it suffices to let $c_n = B$ for all n.

Given our choice of agent decision rules, it is natural to ask whether the current model can be posed as a special case of regression with noisy labels. If so, the noise would map the label Y_i to the set $\{0, 1\}$ in a manner that would be statistically dependent on X, X_i, Y_i itself and n. Though it is possible to view the current question in this framework, to our knowledge such a highly structured noise model has not been considered in the literature.

Finally, those familiar with the classical statistical pattern recognition literature will find the style of proof very familiar; special care must be taken to demonstrate that the variance of the estimate does not decrease too slowly compared to $\{c_n\}_{n=1}^{\infty}$ and to show that the bias introduced by the "clipped" agent decision rules converges to zero.

4.2 Proof of Proposition 1

For ease of exposition, let us define a collection of independent auxiliary random variables, $\{Z_n\}_{n=1}^{\infty}$, such that $X \to Y \to Z_n$ forms a Markov chain and satisfies,

$$\mathbf{P}_{Z_n|Y} = \begin{cases} \mathbf{P}_{Z_{n,\frac{1}{c_n}Y+\frac{1}{2}}}, & |Y| \leq c_n \\ \mathbf{P}_{Z_{n,\frac{1}{2}}}, & |Y| > c_n \end{cases}.$$

for all n. $\mathbf{P}_{Z_{n,\theta}}$ is defined in the section above.

Proof. In the interest of space, we will not repeat the parts of the proof common to the analysis of other Stone-type rules; instead we highlight only the parts of the proof where differences arise.

Let $\bar{\eta}_n(x) = \mathbf{E}\{Z_n \,|X = x\}$. Proceeding in the traditional manner, note that by inequality $(a+b)^2 \leq 2a^2 + 2b^2$,

$$\begin{aligned}
\mathbf{E}\{|\hat{\eta}_n(X) - \eta(X)|^2\} \leq 2\mathbf{E}\Big\{\Big|2c_n\Big(\frac{\sum_{i=1}^n \delta_{ni}(X)1_{\{X_i \in B_{r_n}(X)\}}}{\sum_{i=1}^n 1_{\{X_i \in B_{r_n}(X)\}}} - \frac{1}{2}\Big) \\
- 2c_n\Big(\frac{\sum_{i=1}^n \bar{\eta}_n(X_i)1_{\{X_i \in B_{r_n}(X)\}}}{\sum_{i=1}^n 1_{\{X_i \in B_{r_n}(X)\}}} - \frac{1}{2}\Big)\Big|^2\Big\} \\
+ 2\mathbf{E}\Big\{\Big|2c_n\Big(\frac{\sum_{i=1}^n \bar{\eta}_n(X_i)1_{\{X_i \in B_{r_n}(X)\}}}{\sum_{i=1}^n 1_{\{X_i \in B_{r_n}(X)\}}} - \frac{1}{2}\Big) - \eta(X)\Big|^2\Big\} \\
\triangleq I_n + J_n\,.
\end{aligned}$$

Note that I_n is essentially the variance of the estimator. Using arguments typical in the study of Stone-type rules ([2]), it is straightforward to show that

$$I_n \leq 4c_n^2 \mathbf{E}\Big\{\frac{2}{n\mathbf{P}_X\{B_{r_n}(X)\}}\Big\}. \tag{8}$$

Since $\mathbf{P}_X$ is compactly supported, the expectation in (8) can be bounded by a term $O(\frac{1}{nr_n^d})$ using an argument typically used to demonstrate the consistency of kernel estimators [3]. This fact implies that,

$$I_n \leq O(\frac{c_n^2}{nr_n^d}),$$

and thus, by condition (3) of Proposition 1, $I_n \to 0$. Taking care to ensure that the multiplicative constact c_n does not cause the variance term to explode, this argument is essentially the same as showing that in traditional i.i.d. sampling process settings, the variance of naive kernel is universally bounded by a term $O(\frac{1}{nr_n^d})$ when $\mathbf{P}_X$ is compactly supported and Y is bounded [3]. This observation is consistent with the comments above.

Now, let us consider J_n. Fix $\epsilon > 0$. We will show that for all sufficiently large n, $J_n < \epsilon$. Let $\eta_\epsilon(x)$ be a bounded continuous function with bounded support such that $\mathbf{E}\{|\eta_\epsilon(X) - \eta(X)|^2\} \leq \frac{\epsilon}{12}$. Since $\mathbf{E}\{Y^2\} < \infty$ implies that $\eta(x) \in L^2(\mathbf{P}_X)$, such a function is assured to exist due to the density of such functions in $L^2(\mathbf{P}_X)$. By the inequality $(a+b+c+d)^2 \leq (4a^2+4b^2+4c^2+4d^2)$,

$$\begin{aligned} J_n \leq\ & 4\mathbf{E}\Big\{\Big|2c_n\Big(\frac{\sum_{i=1}^n \bar{\eta}_n(X_i)1_{\{X_i\in B_{r_n}(X)\}}}{\sum_{i=1}^n 1_{\{X_i\in B_{r_n}(X)\}}} - \frac{1}{2}\Big) - \frac{\sum_{i=1}^n \eta_\epsilon(X_i)1_{\{X_i\in B_{r_n}(X)\}}}{\sum_{i=1}^n 1_{\{X_i\in B_{r_n}(X)\}}}\Big|^2\Big\} \\ & + 4\mathbf{E}\Big\{\Big|\frac{\sum_{i=1}^n \eta_\epsilon(X_i)1_{\{X_i\in B_{r_n}(X)\}}}{\sum_{i=1}^n 1_{\{X_i\in B_{r_n}(X)\}}} - \frac{\sum_{i=1}^n \eta_\epsilon(X)1_{\{X_i\in B_{r_n}(X)\}}}{\sum_{i=1}^n 1_{\{X_i\in B_{r_n}(X)\}}}\Big|^2\Big\} \\ & + 4\mathbf{E}\Big\{\Big|\frac{\sum_{i=1}^n \eta_\epsilon(X)1_{\{X_i\in B_{r_n}(X)\}}}{\sum_{i=1}^n 1_{\{X_i\in B_{r_n}(X)\}}} - \eta_\epsilon(X)\Big|^2\Big\} \\ & + 4\mathbf{E}\{|\eta_\epsilon(X) - \eta(X)|^2\} \\ \triangleq\ & 4(J_{n1} + J_{n2} + J_{n3} + J_{n4}). \end{aligned}$$

One can show that for some constant c,

$$J_{n1} \leq 2c\mathbf{E}\Big\{\Big|2c_n(\bar{\eta}_n(X) - \frac{1}{2}) - \eta_\epsilon(X)\Big|^2\Big\} + 2\mathbf{E}\Big\{\frac{2c_n^2}{n\mathbf{P}_X\{B_{r_n}(X)\}}\Big\}.$$

Essentially, this follows by applying several algebraic bounds and technical Lemma 4. Continuing with the familiar inequality $(a+b)^2 \leq 2a^2 + 2b^2$,

$$J_{n1} \leq 2c\mathbf{E}\Big\{\Big|2c_n(\bar{\eta}_n(X) - \frac{1}{2}) - \eta(X)\Big|^2\Big\} + \mathbf{E}\{|\eta_\epsilon(X) - \eta(X)|^2\} + \mathbf{E}\Big\{\frac{4c_n^2}{n\mathbf{P}_X\{B_{r_n}(X)\}}\Big\}.$$

Note that $\bar{\eta}_n(x) = \mathbf{E}\{Z_n \,|X = x\} = \mathbf{E}\Big\{(\frac{1}{2c_n}Y + \frac{1}{2})1_{\{|Y|\leq c_n\}} + \frac{1}{2}1_{\{|Y|>c_n\}}\,\Big|X = x\Big\}$. Substituting this above and applying Jensen's inequality, we have

$$J_{n1} \leq 2c\mathbf{E}\{Y^2 1_{\{|Y|>c_n\}}\} + \frac{\epsilon}{12} + \mathbf{E}\Big\{\frac{4c_n^2}{n\mathbf{P}_X\{B_{r_n}(X)\}}\Big\}. \tag{9}$$

By the monotone convergence theorem, the first term in (9) converges to zero. The second term in (9) converges to zero by the same argument applied for I_n. Thus, $\lim_{n\to\infty} J_{n_1} \leq \frac{\epsilon}{12}$.

Using the uniform continuity of η_ϵ in combination with the fact that $r_n \to 0$, it is straightforward to show that $J_{n2} \leq \frac{\epsilon}{12}$ for all sufficiently large n.

Using the boundedness of η_ϵ, it is straightforward to show that

$$J_{n3} \leq \sup_x (\eta_\epsilon(x)^2) \mathbf{E}\left\{ \frac{2c_n^2}{n\mathbf{P}_X\{B_{r_n}(X)\}} \right\},$$

and thus, $J_{n3} \to 0$ by the same argument applied to I_n. Finally, $J_{n4} \leq \frac{\epsilon}{12}$ by our choice of $\eta_\epsilon(x)$. Combining each of these observations, it follows that $\lim_{n\to\infty} J_n \leq 4\left(\frac{\epsilon}{12} + \frac{\epsilon}{12} + 0 + \frac{\epsilon}{12}\right) = \epsilon$. This completes the proof. □

5 Distributed Classification Without Abstention

As noted in the introduction, given the results of the previous two sections, it is natural to ask whether the communication constraints can be tightened. Let us consider a second model in which the agents cannot choose to abstain. In effect, each agent communicates one bit per decision. First, let us consider the binary classification framework but as a technical convenience, adjust our notation so that $\mathcal{Y} = \{+1, -1\}$ instead of the usual $\{0, 1\}$; also, agents now decide between sending ± 1. We again consider whether universally Bayes-risk consistent schemes exist for the ensemble.

Let $\{Z_{n,\frac{1}{2}}\}_{n=1}^{\infty}$ be a family $\{+1, -1\}$-valued random variables such that $\mathbf{P}\{Z_{n,\frac{1}{2}} = +1\} = \frac{1}{2}$.

Consider the randomized agent decision rule specified as follows:

$$\delta_{ni}(x) = \begin{cases} Y_i, & \text{if } X_i \in B_{r_n}(x) \\ Z_{i,\frac{1}{2}}, & \text{otherwise} \end{cases} . \tag{10}$$

That is, the agents respond according to their training data if x is sufficiently close to X_i. Else, they simply "guess", flipping an unbiased coin. It is readily verified that each agent transmits one bit per decision.

A natural fusion rule for the central authority is the majority vote. That is, the central authority decides according to

$$g_n(x) = \begin{cases} 1, \text{ if } \sum_{i=1}^n \delta_{ni}(x) > 0 \\ 0, \text{ otherwise} \end{cases} . \tag{11}$$

Of course, the natural performance metric for the ensemble is the probability of misclassification. Modifying our convention slightly, let $D_n = \{(X_i, Y_i, Z_{i,\frac{1}{2}})\}_{i=1}^n$. Define

$$R_n = \mathbf{P}\{g_n(X) \neq Y \,|D_n\}. \tag{12}$$

That is, R_n is the conditional probability of error of the majority vote fusion rule conditioned on the randomness in agent training and agent decision rules.

5.1 Main Result and Comments

Assuming an ensemble using the described decision rules, Proposition 2 specifies sufficient conditions for consistency.

Proposition 2. *If, as $n \to \infty$, $r_n \to 0$ and $r_n\sqrt{n} \to \infty$, then $\mathbf{E}\{R_n\} \to R^*$.*

Yet again, the conditions of the proposition strike a similarity with consistency results for kernel classifiers using the naive kernel. Indeed, $r_n \to 0$ ensures the bias of the classifier decays to zero. However, $\{r_n\}_{n=1}^{\infty}$ must not decay too rapidly. As the number of agents in the ensemble grows large, many, indeed most, of the agents will be "guessing" for any given classification; in general, only a decaying fraction of the agents will respond with useful information. In order to ensure that these informative bits can be heard through the noise introduced by the guessing agents, $r_n\sqrt{n} \to \infty$. Note the difference between the result for naive kernel classifiers where $r_n n \to \infty$ dictates a sufficient rate of convergence for $\{r_n\}_{n=1}^{\infty}$.

Notably, to prove this result, we show directly that the expected probability of misclassification converges to the Bayes rate. This is unlike techniques commonly used to demonstrate the consistency of kernel classifiers, etc., which are so-called "plug-in" classification rules. These rules estimate the *a posteriori* probabilities $\mathbf{P}\{Y = i \,|\, X\}$, $i = \pm 1$ and construct classifiers based on thresholding the estimate. In this setting, it suffices to show that these estimates converge to the true probabilities in $L^p(\mathbf{P}_X)$. However, for this model, we cannot estimate the *a posteriori* probabilities and must resort to another proof technique; this foreshadows the negative result of Section VI.

With our choice of "coin flipping" agent decision rules, this model feels much like that presented in "Learning with an Unreliable Teacher" [15]. Several distinctions should be made. While [15] considers the asymptotic probability of error of both the 1-NN rule and "plug-in" classification rules, in our model, the resulting classifier cannot be viewed as being 1-NN nor plug-in. Thus, the results are immediately different. Even so, the noise model considered here is much different; unlike [15], the noise here is statistically dependent on X, the object to be classified, as well as dependent on n.

5.2 Proof of Proposition 2

Proof. Fix an arbitrary $\epsilon > 0$. We will show that $\mathbf{E}\{R_n\} - R^*$ is less than ϵ for all sufficiently large n. Recall from (2) that $\eta(x) = \mathbf{E}\{Y \,|\, X = x\} = \mathbf{P}\{Y = +1 \,|\, X = x\} - \mathbf{P}\{Y = -1 \,|\, X = x\}$ and define $A_\epsilon = \{x : |\eta(x)| > \frac{\epsilon}{2}\}$. Though we save the details for the sake of space, it follows from (1), (12), and a series of simple expectation manipulations that,

$$\mathbf{E}\{R_n\} - R^* \leq \mathbf{P}\Big\{g_n(X) \neq \delta_B(X) \,\Big|\, X \in A_\epsilon\Big\}\mathbf{P}\Big\{A_\epsilon\Big\} + \frac{\epsilon}{2}\,.$$

If $\mathbf{P}\{A_\epsilon\} = 0$, then the proof is complete. Proceed assuming $\mathbf{P}\{A_\epsilon\} > 0$. and define the quantities

$$m_n(x) = \mathbf{E}\{\eta(X)\delta_{ni}(X)\,|X = x\}$$
$$\sigma_n^2(x) = \mathbf{E}\{|\eta(X)\delta_{ni}(X) - m_n(X)|^2\,|X = x\},$$

with the expectation being taken over the random training data and the randomness introduced by the agent decision rules. Respectively, $m_n(x)$ and $\sigma_n^2(x)$ can be interpreted as the mean and variance of the "margin" of the agent decision rule $\delta_{ni}(X)$, conditioned on the observation X. For large positive $m_n(x)$, the agents can be expected to respond "confidently" (with large margin) according to Bayes Rule when asked to classify an object x. For large $\sigma_n^2(x)$, the central authority can expect to observe a large variance amongst the individual agent responses to x.

Fix any integer $k > 0$. Consider the sequence of sets indexed by n,

$$B_{n,k} = \{x : m_n(x)n > k\sqrt{n}\sigma_n(x)\},$$

so that $x \in B_{n,k}$ if and only if $\frac{m_n(x)\sqrt{n}}{\sigma_n(x)} > k$. We can interpret $B_{n,k}$ as the set of objects for which informed agents have a sufficiently strong signal compared with the noise of the guessing agents. One can show that,

$$\mathbf{P}\Big\{g_n(X) \neq \delta_B(X)\,\Big|X \in A_\epsilon\Big\} \leq \mathbf{P}\Big\{\eta(X)\sum_{i=1}^{n}\delta_{ni}(X) < 0\,\Big|X \in A_\epsilon \cap B_{n,k}\Big\} +$$
$$\mathbf{P}\{\bar{B}_{n,k}\,|X \in A_\epsilon\}. \tag{13}$$

Note that conditioned on X, $\eta(X)\sum_{i=1}^{n}\delta_{ni}(X)$ is a sum of independent and identically distributed random variables with mean $m_n(X)$ and variance $\sigma_n^2(X)$. Further, for $x \in B_{n,k}$, $\eta(x)\sum_{i=1}^{n}\delta_{ni}(x) < 0$ implies $|\eta(x)\sum_{i=1}^{n}\delta_{ni}(x) - m_n(x)n| > k\sqrt{n\sigma_n^2(x)}$. Thus, using Markov's inequality, one can show that,

$$\mathbf{P}\Big\{\eta(X)\sum_{i=1}^{n}\delta_{ni}(X) < 0\,\Big|X \in A_\epsilon \cap B_{n,k}\Big\} \leq \frac{1}{k^2}.$$

Thus, the first term in (13) can be made arbitrarily small. Now, let us determine specific expressions for $m_n(x)$ and $\sigma_n^2(x)$, as dictated by our choice of agent decision rules. Algebraic simplification yields,

$$m_n(x) = \eta(x)\eta_n(x)\int 1_{B_{r_n}(x)}(y)P_X(dy)$$
$$\sigma_n^2(x) = \eta^2(x)(1 - \mathbf{E}\{\delta_{ni}(X)\,|X = x\}^2),$$

with $\eta_n(x) = \mathbf{E}\{\eta(X)\,|X \in B_{r_n}(x)\}$.

Substituting these expressions into the second term of (13), it follows that

$$\mathbf{P}\{\bar{B}_{n,k}\,|X \in A_\epsilon\} = \mathbf{P}\Big\{\Big(\mathrm{sgn}(\eta(X))\eta_n(X)\Big)\Big(\frac{\sqrt{n}}{\sqrt{1 - \mathbf{E}\{\delta_{ni}(X)\,|X\}^2}}\cdot$$
$$\int 1_{B_{r_n}(X)}(y)P_X(dy)\Big) < k\Big|X \in A_\epsilon\Big\}.$$

For any $1 \geq \gamma > 0$, we have

$$\mathbf{P}\{\bar{B}_{n,k} \,|X \in A_\epsilon\} \leq \mathbf{P}\Big\{\frac{\sqrt{n}}{\sqrt{1-\mathbf{E}\{\delta_{ni}(X)\,|X\}^2}} \cdot \int 1_{B_{r_n}(X)}(y)P_X(dy) < k\Big|X \in A_\epsilon, \mathrm{sgn}(\eta(X))\eta_n(X) > \gamma\Big\} + \mathbf{P}\{\mathrm{sgn}(\eta(X))\eta_n(X) \leq \gamma\,|X \in A_\epsilon\}\,. \tag{14}$$

Set $\gamma = \frac{\epsilon}{4}$. It follows from our choice of A_ϵ that

$$\mathbf{P}\{\mathrm{sgn}(\eta(X))\eta_n(X) \leq \frac{\epsilon}{4}\,|X \in A_\epsilon\} \leq \mathbf{P}\{|\eta(X) - \eta_n(X)| > \frac{\epsilon}{4}|X \in A_\epsilon\}\,.$$

Since by Lemma 2, $\eta_n(X) \to \eta(X)$ in probability and by assumption $\mathbf{P}\{A_\epsilon\} > 0$, it follows from Lemma 1 that $\mathbf{P}\{\mathrm{sgn}(\eta(X))\eta_n(X) \leq \frac{\epsilon}{4}\,|X \in A_\epsilon\} \to 0$.

Returning to the first term of (14), note that we have just demonstrated that $\lim \mathbf{P}\{\mathrm{sgn}(\eta(X))\eta_n(X) > \frac{\epsilon}{4}\} = 1$. Thus, by Lemma 1, it suffices to show that,

$$\frac{1}{\sqrt{1-\mathbf{E}\{\delta_{ni}(X)\,|X\}^2}} \int 1_{B_{r_n}(X)}(y)P_X(dy)\sqrt{n} \to \infty \text{ i.p.} \tag{15}$$

Since $\frac{1}{\sqrt{1-\mathbf{E}\{\delta_{ni}(X)\,|X\}^2}} \geq 1$, this follows from Lemma 3 and the fact that $r_n\sqrt{n} \to \infty$. This completes the proof. □

6 Distributed Regression Without Abstention

Finally, let us consider the model presented in Section V in a regression framework. Now, $\mathcal{Y} = \mathrm{I\!R}$; agents will receive real-valued training data labels Y_i values. When asked to respond with information, they will reply with either 0 or 1. We will demonstrate that universal consistency is not achievable in this one bit regime.

Let $A = \{a : \mathrm{I\!R}^d \times \mathrm{I\!R}^d \times \mathrm{I\!R} \to [0,1]\}$. That is, A is the collection of functions mapping $\mathrm{I\!R}^d \times \mathrm{I\!R}^d \times \mathrm{I\!R}$ to $[0,1]$. For every sequence of functions $\{a_n\}_{n=1}^\infty \subseteq A$, there is a corresponding sequence of randomized agent decision rules $\{\delta_{ni}(X)\}_{n=1}^\infty$, specified by

$$\delta_{ni}(x) = Z_{i,a_n(x,X_i,Y_i)}\,, \tag{16}$$

for $i \in \{1, ..., n\}$. As before, these agent decision rules depend on n and satisfy the same constraints imposed on the decision rules in Section V.

A central authority fusion rule consists of a sequence of functions $\{\hat{\eta}_n\}_{n=1}^\infty$ mapping $\mathrm{I\!R}^d \times \{0,1\}^n$ to $\mathcal{Y} = \mathrm{I\!R}$. To proceed, we require some regularity on $\{\hat{\eta}_n\}_{n=1}^\infty$. Namely, let us consider all fusion rules for which there exists a constant C such that

$$|\hat{\eta}_n(x,b_1) - \hat{\eta}_n(x,b_2)| \leq C\Big|\frac{1}{n}\sum_{i=1}^n b_{1i} - \frac{1}{n}\sum_{i=1}^n b_{2i}\Big| \tag{17}$$

for all bit strings $b_1, b_2 \in \{0,1\}^n$, all $x \in \mathrm{I\!R}^d$, and every n. This condition essentially amounts to a type of Lipschitz continuity and implies that the fusion rule is invariant to the permutation of the bits it receives from the agents.

For any chosen agent decision rule and central authority fusion rule, the L^2-risk is the performance metric of choice. Specifically, we will consider $\mathbf{E}\{|\hat{\eta}_n(X) - \eta(X)|^2\}$. As before, the expectation is taken over X, $D_n = \{(X_i, Y_i)\}_{i=1}^n$, and any randomness introduced in the agent decision rules themselves.

6.1 Main Result

Assuming an ensemble using the decision rules satisfying the fairly natural constraints stated above, Proposition 3 specifies a negative result.

Proposition 3. *For every sequence of agent decision rules $\{\delta_n(x)\}_{n=1}^\infty$ specified according to (16) with a converging sequence of functions $\{a_n\}_{n=1}^\infty \subseteq A$, there is no combining rule $\{\hat{\eta}_n\}_{n=1}^\infty$ satisfying (17) such that*

$$\lim_{n\to\infty} \mathbf{E}\{|\hat{\eta}_n(X, \{\delta_{ni}(X)\}_{i=1}^n) - \eta(X)|^2\} = 0 \tag{18}$$

for every distribution $\mathbf{P}_{XY}$.

6.2 Proof of Proposition 3

The proof will proceed by specifying two random variables (X, Y) and (X', Y') with $\eta(x) = \mathbf{E}\{Y\,|X = x\} \neq \mathbf{E}\{Y'\,|X' = x\} = \eta'(x)$. Asymptotically, however, the central authority's estimate will be indifferent to whether the agents are trained with random data distributed according to $\mathbf{P}_{XY}$ or $\mathbf{P}_{X'Y'}$. This observation will contradict universal consistency and complete the proof.

Proof. To start, fix a convergent sequence of functions $\{a_n\}_{n=1}^\infty \subseteq A$, arbitrary $x_0, x_1 \in \mathrm{I\!R}^d$, and distinct $y_0, y_1 \in \mathrm{I\!R}$. Let us specify a distribution $\mathbf{P}_{XY}$. Let $\mathbf{P}_X\{x_0\} = q$, $\mathbf{P}_X\{x_1\} = 1 - q$, and $\mathbf{P}_{Y|X}\{Y = y_i | X = x_i\} = 1$ for $i = 0, 1$. Clearly, for this distribution $\eta(x_i) = y_i$ for $i = 0, 1$.

Suppose that the ensemble is trained with random data distributed according to (X, Y) and that the central authority wishes to classify $X = x_0$. According to the model, after broadcasting X to the agents, the central authority will observe a random sequence of n bits. For all $i \in \{1, ..., n\}$ and all n,

$$\mathbf{P}\{\delta_{ni}(X, X_i, Y_i) = 1\,|X = x_0\} = a_n(x_0, x_0, y_0)q + a_n(x_0, x_1, y_1)(1 - q)\,.$$

Define a sequence of auxiliary random variables, $\{(X'_n, Y')\}_{n=1}^\infty$, with distributions satisfying

$$\begin{aligned}
\mathbf{P}_{X'_n}\{x_1\} &= \frac{a_n(x_0, x_0, y_0)q + a_n(x_0, x_1, y_1)(1 - q) - a_n(x_0, x_1, y_1)}{a_n(x_0, x_0, y_1) - a_n(x_0, x_1, y_0)} \\
\mathbf{P}_{X'_n}\{x_0\} &= 1 - \mathbf{P}_{X'_n}\{x_1\} \\
\mathbf{P}_{Y'|X'_n}\{Y' = y_{1-i}\,|X'_n = x_i\} &= 1, \;\; i = 0, 1\,.
\end{aligned}$$

Here, $\eta'(x_i) = \mathbf{E}\{Y' \,|X'_n = x_i\} = y_{1-i}$. Note that if the ensemble were trained with random data distributed according to (X'_n, Y'), then we would have

$$\begin{aligned}
&\mathbf{P}\{\delta_{ni}(X'_n, X'_{ni}, Y'_{ni}) = 1 \,|X'_n = x_0\} \\
&= a_n(x_0, x_0, y_1)\frac{a_n(x_0, x_0, y_0)q + a_n(x_0, x_1, y_1)(1-q) - a_n(x_0, x_1, y_1)}{a_n(x_0, x_0, y_1) - a_n(x_0, x_1, y_0)} \\
&\quad + a_n(x_0, x_1, y_0)(1 - \frac{a_n(x_0, x_0, y_0)q + a_n(x_0, x_1, y_1)(1-q) - a_n(x_0, x_1, y_1)}{a_n(x_0, x_0, y_1) - a_n(x_0, x_1, y_0)}) \\
&= \mathbf{P}\{\delta_{ni}(X, X_i, Y_i) = 1 \,|X = x_0\},
\end{aligned}$$

for all n. Thus, conditioned on X and X'_n, the central authority will observe an identical stochastic process regardless of whether the ensemble was trained with data distributed according to $\mathbf{P}_{XY}$ or $\mathbf{P}_{X'_n Y'}$ for any fixed n. Note, this is true despite the fact that $\eta(x) \neq \eta'(x)$. Finally, let (X', Y') be such that

$$\begin{aligned}
\mathbf{P}_{X'}\{x_1\} &= \lim_{n\to\infty} \mathbf{P}_{X'_n}\{x_1\} \\
\mathbf{P}_{X'}\{x_0\} &= 1 - \mathbf{P}_{X'}\{x_1\} \\
\mathbf{P}_{Y'|X'}\{Y' = y_{1-i} \,|X' = x_i\} &= 1, \;\; i = 0, 1 .
\end{aligned}$$

Again, $\eta'(x_i) = \mathbf{E}\{Y' \,|X' = x_i\} = y_{1-i}$. By definition, for the ensemble to be universally consistent, both $\mathbf{E}\{|\hat{\eta}_n(X) - \eta(X)|^2\} \to 0$ and $\mathbf{E}\{|\hat{\eta}_n(X') - \eta'(X')|^2\} \to 0$. However, assuming the former holds, we can show that necessarily, $\mathbf{E}\{|\hat{\eta}_n(X') - \eta(X')|^2\} \to 0$. Since $\eta(x) \neq \eta'(x)$, this presents a contradiction and completes the proof; the details are left for the full paper. □

References

1. Stone, C.J.: Consistent nonparametric regression. Ann. Statist. **5** (1977) 595–645
2. Devroye, L., Györfi, L., Lugosi, G.: A Probabilistic Theory of Pattern Recognition. Springer, New York (1996)
3. Györfi, L., Kohler, M., Krzyzak, A., Walk, H.: A Distribution-Free Theory of Nonparametric Regression. Springer, New York (2002)
4. Akyildiz, I.F., Su, W., Sankarasubramaniam, Y., Cayirci, E.: A survey on sensor networks. IEEE Communications Magazine **40** (2002) 102–114
5. Cover, T.M.: Rates of convergence for nearest neighbor procedures. Proc. 1st Annu. Hawaii Conf. Systems Theory (1968) 413–415
6. Greblicki, W., Pawlak, M.: Necessary and sufficient conditions for bayes risk consistency of recursive kernel classification rule. IEEE Trans. Inform. Theory **IT-33** (1987) 408–412
7. Krzyżak, A.: The rates of convergence of kernel regression estimates and classification rules. IEEE Trans. Inform. Theory **IT-32** (1986) 668–679
8. Kulkarni, S.R., Posner, S.E.: Rates of convergence of nearest neighbor estimation under arbitrary sampling. IEEE Trans. Inform. Theory **41** (1995) 1028–1039
9. Kulkarni, S.R., Posner, S.E., Sandilya, S.: Data-dependent k_n-nn and kernel estimators consistent for arbitrary processes. IEEE. Trans. Inform. Theory **48** (2002) 2785–2788

10. Morvai, G., Kulkarni, S.R., Nobel, A.B.: Regression estimation from an individual stable sequence. Statistics **33** (1999) 99–119
11. Nobel, A.B.: Limits to classification and regression estimation from ergodic processes. Ann. Statist. **27** (1999) 262–273
12. Nobel, A.B., Adams, T.M.: On regression estimation from ergodic samples with additive noise. IEEE Trans. Inform. Theory **47** (2001) 2895–2902
13. Roussas, G.: Nonparametric estimation in markov processes. Ann. Inst. Statist. Math. **21** (1967) 73–87
14. Yakowitz, S.: Nearest neighbor regression estimation for null-recurrent markov time series. Stoch. Processes Appl. **48** (1993) 311–318
15. Lugosi, G.: Learning with an unreliable teacher. Pattern Recognition **25** (1992) 79–87
16. Kolmogorov, A.N., Fomin, S.V.: Introductory Real Analysis. Dover, New York (1975)

A Technical Lemmas

The following lemmas can be found in various forms in [2], [3], and [16].

Lemma 1. *Suppose* $\{X_n\}_{n=1}^{\infty}$ *is a sequence of random variables such that* $X_n \to X$ *i.p. Then, for all* $\epsilon > 0$ *and any sequence* $\{A_n\}_{n=1}^{\infty}$ *with* $\liminf \mathbf{P}\{A_n\} > 0$,

$$\mathbf{P}\{|X_n - X| > \epsilon \,|A_n\} \to 0.$$

Lemma 2. *Fix an* $\mathbb{R}^d$*-valued random variable* X *and a measurable function* f*. For an arbitrary sequence of real numbers* $\{r_n\}_{n=1}^{\infty}$*, define a sequence of functions* $f_n(x) = \mathbf{E}\{f(X)\,|X \in B_{r_n}(x)\}$*. If* $r_n \to 0$*, then* $f_n(X) \to f(X)$ *in probability.*

Lemma 3. *Suppose* X *is an* $\mathbb{R}^d$*-valued random variable and* $\{r_n\}_{n=1}^{\infty}$ *and* $\{a_n\}_{n=1}^{\infty}$ *are sequences of real numbers with* $r_n \to 0$ *and* $a_n \to \infty$*. If* $r_n a_n \to \infty$*, then*

$$a_n \int 1_{B_{r_n}(X)}(y) P_X(dy) \to \infty \text{ i.p.}$$

Lemma 4. *There is a constant* c *such that* $\forall n$ *and any measurable function* f*,*

$$\mathbf{E}\Big\{\frac{\sum_{i=1}^{n} 1_{\{X_i \in B_{r_n}(X)\}} f(X_i)}{\sum_{i=1}^{n} 1_{\{X_i \in B_{r_n}(X)\}}}\Big\} \le c\mathbf{E}\{f(X)\}$$

On the Convergence of Spectral Clustering on Random Samples: The Normalized Case

Ulrike von Luxburg[1], Olivier Bousquet[1], and Mikhail Belkin[2]

[1] Max Planck Institute for Biological Cybernetics, Tübingen, Germany
{ulrike.luxburg, olivier.bousquet}@tuebingen.mpg.de
[2] The University of Chicago, Department of Computer Science
misha@cs.uchicago.edu

Abstract. Given a set of n randomly drawn sample points, spectral clustering in its simplest form uses the second eigenvector of the graph Laplacian matrix, constructed on the similarity graph between the sample points, to obtain a partition of the sample. We are interested in the question how spectral clustering behaves for growing sample size n. In case one uses the normalized graph Laplacian, we show that spectral clustering usually converges to an intuitively appealing limit partition of the data space. We argue that in case of the unnormalized graph Laplacian, equally strong convergence results are difficult to obtain.

1 Introduction

Clustering is a widely used technique in machine learning. Given a set of data points, one is interested in partitioning the data based on a certain similarity among the data points. If we assume that the data is drawn from some underlying probability distribution, which often seems to be the natural mathematical framework, the goal becomes to partition the probability space into certain regions with high similarity among points. In this setting the problem of clustering is two-fold:

- Assuming that the underlying probability distribution is known, what is a desirable clustering of the data space?
- Given finitely many data points sampled from an unknown probability distribution, how can we reconstruct that optimal partition empirically on the finite sample?

Interestingly, while extensive literature exists on clustering and partitioning, to the best of our knowledge very few algorithms have been analyzed or shown to converge for increasing sample size. Some exceptions are the k-means algorithm (cf. Pollard, 1981), the single linkage algorithm (cf. Hartigan, 1981), and the clustering algorithm suggested by Niyogi and Karmarkar (2000). The goal of this paper is to investigate the limit behavior of a class of spectral clustering algorithms.

J. Shawe-Taylor and Y. Singer (Eds.): COLT 2004, LNAI 3120, pp. 457–471, 2004.

Spectral clustering is a popular technique going back to Donath and Hoffman (1973) and Fiedler (1973). It has been used for load balancing (Van Driessche and Roose, 1995), parallel computations (Hendrickson and Leland, 1995), and VLSI design (Hagen and Kahng, 1992). Recently, Laplacian-based clustering algorithms have found success in applications to image segmentation (cf. Shi and Malik, 2000). Methods based on graph Laplacians have also been used for other problems in machine learning, including semi-supervised learning (cf. Belkin and Niyogi, to appear; Zhu et al., 2003). While theoretical properties of spectral clustering have been studied (e.g., Guattery and Miller (1998), Weiss (1999), Kannan et al. (2000), Meila and Shi (2001), also see Chung (1997) for a comprehensive theoretical treatment of the spectral graph theory), we do not know of any results discussing the convergence of spectral clustering or the spectra of graph Laplacians for increasing sample size. However for kernel matrices, the convergence of the eigenvalues and eigenvectors has already attracted some attention (cf. Williams and Seeger, 2000; Shawe-Taylor et al., 2002; Bengio et al., 2003).

2 Background and Notations

Let $(\mathcal{X}, \text{dist})$ be a metric space, $\mathcal{B}$ the Borel σ-algebra on $\mathcal{X}$, P a probability measure on $(\mathcal{X}, \mathcal{B})$, and $L_2(P) := L_2(\mathcal{X}, \mathcal{B}, P)$ the space of square-integrable functions. Let $k : \mathcal{X} \times \mathcal{X} \to \mathbb{R}$ a measurable, symmetric, non-negative function that computes the similarity between points in $\mathcal{X}$. For given sample points $X_1, ..., X_n$ drawn iid according to the (unknown) distribution P we denote the empirical distribution by P_n. We define the similarity matrix as $K_n := (k(X_i, X_j))_{i,j=1,...,n}$ and the degree matrix D_n as the diagonal matrix with diagonal entries $d_i := \sum_{j=1}^n k(X_i, X_j)$. The unnormalized discrete Laplacian matrix is defined as $L_n := D_n - K_n$. For symmetric and non-negative k, L_n is a positive semi-definite linear operator on $\mathbb{R}^n$. Let $a = (a_1, ..., a_n)$ the second eigenvector of L_n. Here, "second eigenvector" refers to the eigenvector belonging to the second smallest eigenvalue, where the eigenvalues $\lambda_1 \leq \lambda_2 ... \leq \lambda_n$ are counted *with multiplicity*. In a nutshell, spectral clustering in its simples form partitions the sample points $(X_i)_i$ into two (or several) groups by thresholding the second eigenvector of L_n: point X_i belongs to cluster 1 if $a_i > b$, and to cluster 2 otherwise, where $b \in \mathbb{R}$ is some appropriate constant. An intuitive explanation of why this works is discussed in Section 4.
Often, spectral clustering is also performed with a normalized version of the matrix L_n. Two common ways of normalizing are $L_n' := D_n^{-1/2} L_n D_n^{-1/2}$ or $L_n'' := D_n^{-1} L_n$. The eigenvalues and eigenvectors of both matrices are closely related. Define the normalized similarity matrices $H_n' := D_n^{-1/2} K_n D_n^{-1/2}$ and $H_n'' := D_n^{-1} K_n$. It can be seen by multiplying the eigenvalue equation $L_n' v = \lambda v$ from left with $D_n^{-1/2}$ that $v \in \mathbb{R}^n$ is eigenvector of L_n' with eigenvalue λ iff $D_n^{-1/2} v$ is eigenvector of L_n'' with eigenvalue λ. Furthermore, rearranging the eigenvalue equations for L_n' and L_n'' shows that $v \in \mathbb{R}^n$ is an eigenvector of L_n' with eigenvalue λ iff v is eigenvector of H_n' with eigenvalue $(1 - \lambda)$, and that

$v \in \mathbb{R}^n$ is an eigenvector of L_n'' with eigenvalue λ iff v is eigenvector of H_n'' with eigenvalue $(1-\lambda)$. Thus, properties about the spectrum of one of the matrices L_n', L_n'', H_n', or H_n'' can be reformulated for the three other matrices as well.

In the following we want to recall some definitions and facts from perturbation theory for bounded operators. The standard reference for general perturbation theory is Kato (1966), for perturbation theory in Hilbert spaces we also recommend Birman and Solomjak (1987) and Weidmann (1980), and Bhatia (1997) for finite-dimensional perturbation theory. We denote by $\sigma(T)$ the spectrum of a linear operator T. Its essential and discrete spectra are denoted by $\sigma_{\text{ess}}(T)$ and $\sigma_{\text{d}}(T)$, respectively.

Proposition 1 (Spectral and perturbation theory).

1. **Spectrum of a compact operator:** *Let T a compact operator on a Banach space. Then $\sigma(T)$ is at most countable and has at most one limit point, namely 0. If $0 \neq \lambda \in \sigma(T)$, then λ is an isolated eigenvalue with finite multiplicity. The spectral projection corresponding to λ coincides with the projection on the corresponding eigenspace.*
2. **Spectrum of a multiplication operator:** *For a bounded function $g \in L_\infty(P)$ consider the multiplication operator $M_g : L_2(P) \to L_2(P)$, $f \mapsto gf$. M_g is a bounded linear operator whose spectrum coincides with the essential range of the multiplier g.*
3. **Perturbation of symmetric matrices:** *Let A and B be two symmetric matrices in $\mathbb{R}^{n\times n}$, and denote by $\|\cdot\|$ an operator norm on $\mathbb{R}^{n\times n}$. Then the Hausdorff distance $d(\sigma(A), \sigma(B))$ between the two spectra satisfies $d(\sigma(A), \sigma(B)) \leq \|A - B\|$. Let $\mu_1 > ... > \mu_k$ be the eigenvalues of A counted without multiplicity and $\mathrm{Pr}_1, ..., \mathrm{Pr}_k$ the projections on the corresponding eigenspaces. For $1 \leq r \leq k$ define the numbers*

$$\gamma_r(A) := \min\{|\mu_i - \mu_j|;\ 1 \leq i < j \leq r+1\}.$$

Assume that $\|B\| \leq \varepsilon$. Then for all $1 \leq l \leq r$ we have

$$\| \mathrm{Pr}_l(A+B) - \mathrm{Pr}_l(A)\| \leq 4\frac{\|B\|}{\gamma_r(A)}$$

(cf. Section VI.3 of Bhatia, 1997, Lemma A.1.(iii) of Koltchinskii, 1998, and Lemma 5.2. of Koltchinskii and Giné, 2000).
4. **Perturbation of bounded operators:** *Let $(T_n)_n$ and T be bounded operators on a Banach space E with $T_n \to T$ in operator norm, and λ an isolated eigenvalue of T with finite multiplicity. Then, for n large enough, there exist isolated eigenvalues $\lambda_n \in \sigma(T_n)$ such that $\lambda_n \to \lambda$, and the corresponding spectral projections converge in operator norm. The other way round, for a converging sequence $\lambda_n \in \sigma(T_n)$ of isolated eigenvalues with finite multiplicity, there exists an isolated eigenvalue $\lambda \in \sigma(T)$ with finite multiplicity such that $\lambda_n \to \lambda$ and the corresponding spectral projections converge in operator norm (cf. Theorems 3.16 and 2.23 in Kato, 1966).*

5. **Perturbation of the essential spectrum:** *Let A be a bounded and V a compact operator on some Banach space. Then $\sigma_{ess}(A+V) = \sigma_{ess}(A)$ (cf. Th. 5.35 in Kato, 1966, and Th. 9.1.3 in Birman and Solomjak, 1987).*

Finally we will need the following definition. A set $\mathcal{F}$ of real-valued functions on $\mathcal{X}$ is called a P-Glivenko-Cantelli class if

$$\sup_{f \in \mathcal{F}} \left| \int f dP_n - \int f dP \right| \to 0 \ P\text{-a.s.}$$

3 Convergence of the Normalized Laplacian

The goal of this section is to prove that the first eigenvectors of the normalized Laplacian converge to the eigenfunctions of some limit operator on $L_2(P)$.

3.1 Definition of the Integral Operators

Let $d(x) := \int k(x,y)dP(y)$ the "true degree function" on $\mathcal{X}$, and $d_n(x) := \int k(x,y)dP_n(y)$ the empirical degree function. To ensure that $1/d$ is a bounded function we assume that there exists some constant l such that $d(x) > l > 0$ for all $x \in \mathcal{X}$. We define the normalized similarity functions

$$h_n(x,y) := k(x,y)/\sqrt{d_n(x)d_n(y)}$$
$$h(x,y) := k(x,y)/\sqrt{d(x)d(y)} \tag{1}$$

and the operators

$$T_n : L_2(P_n) \to L_2(P_n),\ T_n f(x) = \int h(x,y)f(y)dP_n(y)$$
$$T_n' : L_2(P_n) \to L_2(P_n),\ T_n' f(x) = \int h_n(x,y)f(y)dP_n(y)$$
$$T : L_2(P) \to L_2(P),\ Tf(x) = \int h(x,y)f(y)dP(y). \tag{2}$$

If k is bounded and $d > l > 0$, then all three operators are bounded, compact integral operators. Note that the scaling factors $1/n$ which are hidden in d_n and P_n cancel. Hence, because of the isomorphism between $L_2(P_n)$ and $\mathbb{R}^n$, the eigenvalues and eigenvectors of T_n' can be identified with the ones of the empirical similarity matrix H_n', and the eigenvectors and values of T_n with those of the matrix $H_n := (h(X_i, X_j))_{ij}$.

Our goal in the following will be to show that the eigenvectors of H_n' converge to those of the integral operator T. The first step will consist in proving that the operators T_n and T_n' converge to each other in operator norm. By perturbation theory results this will allow us to conclude that their spectra also become similar. The second step is to show that the eigenvalues and eigenvectors of T_n converge to those of T. This step uses results obtained in Koltchinskii (1998). Both steps together then will show that the first eigenvectors of the normalized Laplacian matrix converge to the first eigenfunctions of the limit operator T, and hence that spectral clustering converges.

3.2 T_n and T'_n Converge to Each Other

Proposition 2 (d_n converges to d uniformly on the sample). *Let $k : \mathcal{X} \times \mathcal{X} \to \mathrm{I\!R}$ be bounded. Then $\max_{i=1,\dots,n} |d_n(X_i) - d(X_i)| \to 0$ a.s. for $n \to \infty$.*

Proof. With $M := \|k\|_\infty < \infty$ we have

$$\max_{i=1,\dots,n} |d_n(X_i) - d(X_i)| = \max_{i=1,\dots,n} |\frac{1}{n} \sum_{j=1}^{n} k(X_i, X_j) - E_X k(X_i, X)|$$
$$\leq \frac{2M}{n} + \frac{n-1}{n} \max_i |\frac{1}{n-1} \sum_{j \neq i} k(X_i, X_j) - E_X k(X_i, X)|.$$

For fixed $x \in \mathcal{X}$, the Hoeffding inequality yields

$$P\Big(|\frac{1}{n-1} \sum_{j \neq i} k(x, X_j) - E_X k(x, X)| > \varepsilon\Big) \leq \exp(-M(n-1)\varepsilon^2).$$

The same is true conditionally on X_i if we replace x by X_i, because the random variable X_i is independent of X_j for $j \neq i$. Applying the union bound and taking expectations over X_i leads to

$$P(\max_{i=1,\dots,n} |\frac{1}{n-1} \sum_{j \neq i} k(X_i, X_j) - E_X k(X_i, X)| > \varepsilon)$$
$$\leq \sum_{i=1}^{n} P\Big(|\frac{1}{n-1} \sum_{j \neq i} k(X_i, X_j) - E_X k(X_i, X)| > \varepsilon \,\Big|\, X_i\Big)$$
$$\leq n \exp(-M(n-1)\varepsilon^2).$$

This shows the convergence of $\max_{i=1,\dots,n} |d_n(X_i) - d(X_i)| \to 0$ in probability. As the deviations decrease exponentially, the Borel-Cantelli lemma shows that this convergence also holds almost surely. ☺

Proposition 3 ($\|T'_n - T_n\|_{L_2(P_n)}$ converges to 0). *Let k a bounded similarity function. Assume that there exist constants $u > l > 0$ such that $u \geq d(x) \geq l > 0$ for all $x \in \mathcal{X}$. Then $\|T_n - T'_n\|_{L_2(P_n)} \to 0$ a.s. and $\|H_n - H'_n\|_n \to 0$ a.s., where $\|\cdot\|_n$ denotes the row sum norm for $n \times n$-matrices.*

Proof. By the Cauchy-Schwartz inequality,

$$\|T_n - T'_n\|^2_{L_2(P_n)} = \sup_{\|f\|_{L_2(P_n)} \leq 1} \int \Big(\int (h_n(x,y) - h(x,y)) f(y) dP_n(y)\Big)^2 dP_n(x)$$
$$\leq \sup_{\|f\|_{L_2(P_n)} \leq 1} \int \int (h_n(x,y) - h(x,y))^2 dP_n(y) \int f^2(y) dP_n(y) \; dP_n(x)$$
$$\leq \int \int (h_n(x,y) - h(x,y))^2 dP_n(y) dP_n(x)$$
$$\leq \max_{i,j=1,\dots,n} |h_n(X_i, X_j) - h(X_i, X_j)|^2$$

By Proposition 2 we know that for each $\varepsilon > 0$ there exists some N such that for all $n > N$, $|d_n(x) - d(x)| \leq \varepsilon$ for all $x \in \{X_1, ..., X_n\}$. Then

$$|d_n(x)d_n(y) - d(x)d(y)| \leq |d_n(x)d_n(y) - d(x)d_n(y)| + |d(x)d_n(y) - d(x)d(y)| \leq 2u\varepsilon,$$

which implies that $|\sqrt{d_n(x)d_n(y)} - \sqrt{d(x)d(y)}| \leq \sqrt{2u\varepsilon}$. This finally leads to

$$\left| \frac{1}{\sqrt{d_n(x)d_n(y)}} - \frac{1}{\sqrt{d(x)d(y)}} \right| = \left| \frac{\sqrt{d_n(x)d_n(y)} - \sqrt{d(x)d(y)}}{\sqrt{d_n(x)d_n(y)}\sqrt{d(x)d(y)}} \right| \leq \frac{\sqrt{2u\varepsilon}}{l(l - 2u\varepsilon)}$$

for all $x, y \in \{X_1, ..., X_n\}$. This shows that $\|T_n - T'_n\|$ converges to 0 almost surely. The statement for $\|H_n - H'_n\|$ follows by a similar argument. ☺

3.3 Convergence of T_n to T

Now we want to deal with the convergence of T_n to T. By the law of large numbers it is clear that $T_n f(x) \to Tf(x)$ for all $x \in \mathcal{X}$ and $f \in \mathcal{F}$. But this pointwise convergence is not enough to allow any conclusion about the convergence of the eigenvalues, let alone the eigenfunctions of the involved operators. On the other hand, the best convergence statement we can possibly think of would be convergence of T_n to T in operator norm. Here we have the problem that the operators T_n and T are not defined on the same spaces. One way to handle this is to relate the operators T_n, which are currently defined on $L_2(P_n)$, to some operators S_n on the space $L_2(P)$ such that their spectra are preserved. Then we would have to prove that S_n converges to T in operator norm. We believe that such a statement cannot be true in general. Intuitively, the reason for this is the following. Convergence in operator norm means uniform convergence on the unit ball of $L_2(P)$. Independent of the exact definition of S_n, the convergence of S_n to T in operator norm is closely related to the problem

$$\sup_{\|f\| \leq 1} \| \int k(x, y)f(y)dP_n(y) - \int k(x, y)f(y)dP(y) \| \stackrel{!}{\to} 0.$$

This statement would be true if the class $\mathcal{G} := \{k(x, \cdot)f(\cdot);\ x \in \mathcal{X}, \|f\| \leq 1\}$ was a P-Glivenko-Cantelli class, which is false in general. This can be made plausible by considering the special case $k \equiv 1$. Then the condition would be that the unit ball of $L_2(P)$ is a Glivenko-Cantelli class, which is clearly not the case for large enough $\mathcal{X}$. As a consequence, we cannot hope to achieve uniform convergence over the unit ball of $L_2(P)$.

A way out of this problem might be not to consider uniform convergence on the whole unit ball, but on a smaller subset of it. Something of a similar flavor has been proved in Koltchinskii (1998). To state his results we first have to introduce some more notation. For a function $f : \mathcal{X} \to \mathbb{R}$ denote its restriction to the sample points by $\tilde{f}$. Let $h : \mathcal{X} \times \mathcal{X} \to \mathbb{R}$ a symmetric, measurable similarity function such that $E(h^2(X, Y)) < \infty$. This condition implies that the integral operator T with kernel h is a Hilbert-Schmidt operator. Let $(\lambda_i)_{i\in I}$ its eigenvalues and $(\Phi_i)_{i\in I}$ a corresponding set of orthonormal eigenfunctions. To measure the distance between two countable sets $A = (a_i)_{i\in\mathbb{N}}$, $B = (b_i)_{i\in\mathbb{N}}$, we introduce the minimal matching distance $\delta(A, B) := \inf_\pi \sum_{i=1}^{\infty} a_i - b_{\pi(i)}$, where the infimum is taken over the set of all permutations π of $\mathbb{N}$. A more general version of the following theorem has been proved in Koltchinskii (1998).

Theorem 4 (Koltchinskii). *Let $(\mathcal{X}, \mathcal{B}, P)$ an arbitrary probability space, $h : \mathcal{X}\times\mathcal{X} \to \mathbb{R}$ a symmetric, measurable function such that $E(h^2(X,Y)) < \infty$ and $E(|h(X,X)|) < \infty$, and T_n and T the integral operators as defined in equation (2). Let $(\Phi_i)_{i\in I}$ the eigenfunctions of T, and let $\lambda \neq 0$ the r-th largest eigenvalue of T (counted without multiplicity). Denote by $\Pr$ and $\Pr_n$ the projections on the eigenspaces corresponding to the r-th largest eigenvalues of T and T_n, respectively. Then:*

1. *$\delta(\sigma(T_n), \sigma(T)) \to 0$ a.s.*
2. *Suppose that $\mathcal{G}$ is a class of measurable functions on $\mathcal{X}$ with a square-integrable envelope G with $\|G\|_{L_2(P)} \leq 1$, i.e. $|g(x)| \leq G(x)$ for all $g \in \mathcal{G}$. Moreover, suppose that for all $i \in I$, the set $\mathcal{G}\Phi_i := \{g\Phi_i;\ g \in \mathcal{G}\}$ is a P-Glivenko Cantelli class. Then*

$$\sup_{f,g\in\mathcal{G}} \left| \langle \Pr_n \tilde{f}, \tilde{g} \rangle_{L_2(P_n)} - \langle \Pr f, g \rangle_{L_2(P)} \right| \to 0 \text{ a.s. for } n \to \infty.$$

Coming back to the discussion from above, we can see that this theorem also does not state convergence of the spectral projections uniformly on the whole unit ball of $L_2(P)$, but only on some subset $\mathcal{G}$ of it. The problem that the operators T_n and T are not defined on the same space has been circumvented by considering bilinear forms instead of the operators themselves.

3.4 Convergence of the Second Eigenvectors

Now we have collected all ingredients to discuss the convergence of the second largest eigenvalue and eigenvector of the normalized Laplacian. To talk about convergence of eigenvectors only makes sense if the eigenspaces of the corresponding eigenvalues are one-dimensional. Otherwise there exist many different eigenvectors for the same eigenvalue. So multiplicity one is the assumption we make in our main result. In order to compare an eigenvector of the discrete operator T_n' and the corresponding eigenfunction of T, we can only measure how distinct they are on the points of the sample, that is by the $L_2(P_n)$-distance. However, as eigenvectors are only unique up to changing their orientations we will compare them only up to a change of sign.

Theorem 5 (Convergence of normalized spectral clustering). *Let $(\mathcal{X}, \mathcal{B}, P)$ a probability space, $k : \mathcal{X}\times\mathcal{X} \to \mathbb{R}$ a symmetric, bounded, measurable function, and $(X_i)_{i\in\mathbb{N}}$ a sequence of data points drawn iid from $\mathcal{X}$ according to*

P. Assume that the degree function satisfies $d(x) > l > 0$ for all $x \in \mathcal{X}$ and some constant $l \in \mathbb{R}$. Denote by $\lambda \neq 0$ the second largest eigenvalue of T (counted with multiplicity), and assume that it has multiplicity one. Let Φ be the corresponding eigenfunction, and Pr *the projection on Φ. Let λ_n, Φ_n and Pr_n the same quantities for T_n, and λ'_n, Φ'_n and Pr'_n the same for T'_n. Then there exists a sequence of signs $(a_n)_n$ with $a_n \in \{-1, +1\}$ such that $\|a_n \Phi'_n - \tilde{\Phi}\|_{L_2(P_n)} \to 0$ almost surely.*

Proof. The boundedness of k and $d(x) > l > 0$ imply that the normalized similarity function h is bounded. Hence, the operators T, T_n and T'_n are compact operators. By Proposition 1.1, their non-zero eigenvalues are isolated in their spectra, and their spectral projections correspond to the projections on the eigenspaces. Moreover, the boundedness of h implies $E(h^2(X,Y)) < \infty$ and $E|h(X,X)| < \infty$. Theorem 4 shows $\lambda_n \to \lambda$ for $n \to \infty$, and choosing $\mathcal{F} = \{\Phi\}$ we get

$$\langle \Phi_n, \tilde{\Phi} \rangle^2 = \langle \langle \Phi_n, \tilde{\Phi} \rangle \Phi_n, \tilde{\Phi} \rangle = \langle \mathrm{Pr}_n \tilde{\Phi}, \tilde{\Phi} \rangle \to \langle \mathrm{Pr}\, \Phi, \Phi \rangle = \langle \Phi, \Phi \rangle = 1.$$

The eigenfunctions Φ and Φ_n are normalized to 1 in their respective spaces. By the law of large numbers, we also have $\|\tilde{\Phi}\|_{L_2(P_n)} \to 1$ a.s. Hence, $\langle \Phi_n, \tilde{\Phi} \rangle \to 1$ or -1 implies the $L_2(P_n)$-convergence of Φ_n to Φ up to a change of sign.

Now we have to compare λ'_n to λ_n and Φ'_n to Φ_n. In Proposition 3 we showed that $\|T'_n - T_n\| \to 0$ a.s., which according to Proposition 1.3 implies the convergence of $\lambda'_n - \lambda_n$ to zero. Theorem 4 implies the convergence of $\lambda_n - \lambda$ to zero. For the convergence of the eigenfunctions, recall the definition of γ_r in Proposition 1.3. As the eigenvalues of T are isolated we have $\gamma_2(T) > 0$, and by the convergence of the eigenvalues we also get $|\gamma_2(T'_n) - \gamma_2(T)| \to 0$. Hence, $\gamma(T'_n)$ is bounded away from 0 simultaneously for all large n. Moreover, we know by Proposition 3 that $\|T'_n - T_n\| \to 0$ a.s. Proposition 1.3 now shows the convergence of the spectral projections $\|\mathrm{Pr}'_n - \mathrm{Pr}_n\| \to 0$ a.s. This implies in particular that

$$\sup_{\|v\| \leq 1} \langle v, (\mathrm{Pr}_n - \mathrm{Pr}'_n) v \rangle \to 0 \text{ and thus } \sup_{\|v\| \leq 1} |\langle v, \Phi_n \rangle^2 - \langle v, \Phi'_n \rangle^2| \to 0.$$

Since $|a^2 - b^2| = |a-b||a+b|$, we get the convergence of Φ_n to Φ up to a change of sign on the sample, as stated in the theorem. This completes the proof. ☺

Let us briefly discuss the assumptions of Theorem 5. The symmetry of k is a standard requirement in spectral clustering as it ensures that all eigenvalues of the Laplacian are real-valued. The assumption that the degree function is bounded away from 0 prevents the normalized Laplacian from getting unbounded, which is also desirable in practice. This condition will often be trivially satisfied as the second standard assumption of spectral clustering is the non-negativity of k (as it ensures that the eigenvalues of the Laplacian are non-negative). An important assumption in Theorem 5 which is not automatically satisfied is that the second eigenvalue has multiplicity one. But note that if this assumption is not satisfied, spectral clustering will produce more or less arbitrary results anyway, as the second eigenvector is no longer unique. It then depends on the actual implementation of the algorithm which of the infinitely many eigenvectors corresponding to the second eigenvalue is picked, and the result will often be unsatisfactory. Finally, note that even though Theorem 5 is stated in terms of the second eigenvalue and eigenvector, analogous statements are true for higher eigenvalues, and also for spectral projections on finite dimensional eigenspaces with dimension larger than 1.

To summarize, all assumptions in Theorem 5 are already important for successful applications of spectral clustering on a finite sample. Theorem 5 now shows that with no additional assumptions, the convergence of normalized spectral clustering to a limit clustering on the whole data space is guaranteed.

4 Interpretation of the Limit Partition

Now we want to investigate whether the limit clustering partitions the data space $\mathcal{X}$ in a desirable way. In this section it will be more convenient to consider the normalized similarity matrix H''_n instead of H'_n as it is a stochastic matrix. Hence we consider the normalized similarity function $g(x,y) := k(x,y)/d(x)$, its empirical version $g_n(x,y) := k(x,y)/d_n(x)$, and the integral operators

$$R''_n : L_2(P_n) \to L_2(P_n),\ R''_n f(x) = \int g_n(x,y) f(y) dP_n(y)$$

$$R : L_2(P) \to L_2(P),\ Rf(x) = \int g(x,y) f(y) dP(y).$$

The spectrum of R''_n coincides with the spectrum of H''_n, and by the one-to-one relationships between the spectra of H''_n and H'_n (cf. Section 2), the convergence stated in Theorem 5 for T'_n and T holds analogously for the operators R''_n and R.

Let us take a step back and reflect what we would like to achieve with spectral clustering. The overall goal in clustering is to find a partition of $\mathcal{X}$ into two (or more) disjoint sets $\mathcal{X}_1$ and $\mathcal{X}_2$ such that the similarity between points from the same set is high while the similarity between points from different sets is low. Assuming that such a partition exists, how does the operator R look like? Let $\mathcal{X} = \mathcal{X}_1 \cup \mathcal{X}_2$ be a partition of the space $\mathcal{X}$ into two disjoint, measurable sets such that $P(\bar{\mathcal{X}}_1 \cap \bar{\mathcal{X}}_2) = 0$. As σ-algebra on $\mathcal{X}_i$ we use the restrictions $\mathcal{B}_i := \{B \cap \mathcal{X}_i;\ B \in \mathcal{B}\}$ of the Borel σ-algebra $\mathcal{B}$ on $\mathcal{X}$. Define the measures P_i as the restrictions of P to $\mathcal{B}_i$. Now we can identify the space $L_2(\mathcal{X}, \mathcal{B}, P)$ with the direct sum $L_2(\mathcal{X}_1, \mathcal{B}_1, P_1) \oplus L_2(\mathcal{X}_2, \mathcal{B}_2, P_2)$. Each function $f \in L_2(\mathcal{X})$ corresponds to a tuple $(f_1, f_2) \in L_2(\mathcal{X}_1) \oplus L_2(\mathcal{X}_2)$, where $f_i : \mathcal{X}_i \to \mathbb{R}$ is the restriction of f to $\mathcal{X}_i$. The operator R can be identified with the matrix $\begin{pmatrix} R_{11} & R_{12} \\ R_{21} & R_{22} \end{pmatrix}$ acting on $L_2(\mathcal{X}_1, \mathcal{B}_1, P_1) \oplus L_2(\mathcal{X}_2, \mathcal{B}_2, P_2)$. We denote by d_i the restriction of d to $\mathcal{X}_i$ and by g_{ij} the restriction of g to $\mathcal{X}_i \times \mathcal{X}_j$. With these notations, the operators R_{ij} for

$i, j = 1, 2$ are defined as

$$R_{ij} : L_2(\mathcal{X}_j) \to L_2(\mathcal{X}_i),\ R_{ij} f_j(x) = \int g_{ij}(x, y) f_j(y) dP_j(y).$$

Now assume that our space is ideally clustered, that is the similarity function satisfies $k(x_1, x_2) = 0$ for all $x_1 \in \mathcal{X}_1$ and $x_2 \in \mathcal{X}_2$, and $k(x_i, x_i') > 0$ for $x_i, x_i' \in \mathcal{X}_1$ or $x_i, x_i' \in \mathcal{X}_2$. Then the operator R has the form $\begin{pmatrix} R_{11} & 0 \\ 0 & R_{22} \end{pmatrix}$. It has eigenvalue 1 with multiplicity 2, and the corresponding eigenspace is spanned by the vectors $(\mathbb{1}, 0)$ and $(0, \mathbb{1})$. Hence, all eigenfunctions corresponding to eigenvalue 1 are piecewise constant on the sets $\mathcal{X}_1, \mathcal{X}_2$, and the eigenfunction orthogonal to the function $(\mathbb{1}, \mathbb{1})$ has opposite sign on both sets. Thresholding the second eigenfunction will recover the true clustering $\mathcal{X}_1 \cup \mathcal{X}_2$. When we interpret the function g as a Markov transition kernel, the operator R describes a Markov diffusion process on $\mathcal{X}$. We see that the clustering constructed by its second eigenfunction partitions the space into two sets such that diffusion takes place within the sets, but not between them.

The same reasoning also applies to the finite sample case, cf. Meila and Shi (2001), Weiss (1999), and Ng et al. (2001). We split the finite sample space $\{X_1, ..., X_n\}$ into the two sets $\mathcal{X}_{i,n} := \{X_1, ..., X_n\} \cap \mathcal{X}_i$, and define

$$R_{ij,n} : L_2(\mathcal{X}_{j,n}) \to L_2(\mathcal{X}_{i,n}),\ R_{ij,n} f_j(x) = \int g_{ij,n}(x, y) f_j(y) dP_{j,n}(y).$$

According to Meila and Shi (2001), spectral clustering tries to find a partition such that the probability of staying within the same cluster is large while the probability of going from one cluster into another one is low (Meila and Shi, 2001). So both in the finite sample case and in the limit case a similar interpretation applies. This shows in particular that the limit clustering accomplishes the goal of clustering to partition the space into sets such that the within similarity is large and the between similarity is low.

In practice, the operator R will usually be irreducible, i.e. there will exist no partition such that the operators R_{12} and R_{21} vanish. Then the goal will be to find a partition such that the norms of R_{12} and R_{21} are as small as possible, while the norms of R_{ii} should be reasonably large. If we find such a partition, then the operators $\begin{pmatrix} R_{11} & R_{12} \\ R_{21} & R_{22} \end{pmatrix}$ and $\begin{pmatrix} R_{11} & 0 \\ 0 & R_{22} \end{pmatrix}$ are close in operator norm and according to perturbation theory have a similar spectrum. Then the partition constructed by R will be approximately the same as the one constructed by $\begin{pmatrix} R_{11} & 0 \\ 0 & R_{22} \end{pmatrix}$, which is the partition $\mathcal{X}_1 \cup \mathcal{X}_2$.

The convergence results in Section 3 show that the first eigenspaces of R_n converge to the first eigenspaces of the limit operator R. This statement can be further strengthened by proving that each of the four operators $R_{ij,n}$

converges to its limit operator R_{ij} compactly, which can be done by methods from von Luxburg et al.. As a consequence, also the eigenvalues and eigenspaces of the single operators $R_{ij,n}$ converge. This statement is even sharper than the convergence statement of R_n to R. It shows that for any fixed partition of $\mathcal{X}$, the *structure* of the operator R_n is preserved when taking the limit. This means that a partition that has been constructed on the finite sample such that the diffusion between the two sets is small also keeps this property when we take the limit.

5 Convergence of the Unnormalized Laplacian

So far we always considered the *normalized* Laplacian matrix. The reason is that this case is inherently simpler to treat than the unnormalized case. In the unnormalized case, we have to study the operators

$$U_n f(x) := \int k(x,y)(f(x) - f(y))dP_n(y) = d_n(x)f(x) - \int k(x,y)f(y)dP_n(y)$$

$$Uf(x) := \int k(x,y)(f(x) - f(y))dP(y) = d(x)f(x) - \int k(x,y)f(y)dP(y).$$

It is clear that U_n is the operator corresponding to the unnormalized Laplacian $\frac{1}{n}L_n$, and U is its pointwise limit operator for $n \to \infty$. In von Luxburg et al. we show that under mild assumptions, U_n converges to U compactly. Compact convergence is a type of convergence which is a bit weaker than operator norm convergence, but still strong enough to ensure the convergence of eigenvalues and spectral projections (Chatelin, 1983). But there is a big problem related to the structure of the operators U_n and U. Both consist of a difference of two operators, a bounded multiplication operator and a compact integral operator. This is bad news, as multiplication operators are never compact. To the contrary, the spectrum of a multiplication operator consists of the whole range of the multiplier function (cf. Proposition 1.2). Hence, the spectrum of U consists of an essential spectrum which coincides with the range of the degree function, and possibly some discrete spectrum of isolated eigenvalues (cf. Proposition 1.5).

This has the consequence that although we know that U_n converges to U in a strong sense, we are not able to conclude anything about the convergence of the second eigenvectors. The reason is that perturbation theory only allows to state convergence results for *isolated* parts of the spectra. So we get that the essential spectrum of U_n converges to the essential spectrum of U. Moreover, if $\sigma(U)$ has a non-empty discrete spectrum, then we can also state convergence of the eigenvalues and eigenspaces belonging to the discrete spectrum. But unfortunately, it is impossible to conclude anything about the convergence of eigenvalues that lie *inside* the essential spectrum of U. In von Luxburg et al. we actually construct an example of a space $\mathcal{X}$ and a similarity function k such that all non-zero eigenvalues of the unnormalized Laplacian indeed lie inside the essential spectrum of U. Now we have the problem that given a finite sample, we cannot detect whether the second eigenvalue of the limit operator will lie inside or outside the essential spectrum of U, and hence we cannot guarantee that the second eigenvectors of the unnormalized Laplacian matrices converge. All together this means that although we have strong convergence results for U_n, without further knowledge we are not able to draw any useful conclusion concerning the second eigenvalues.

On the other hand, in case we can guarantee the convergence of unnormalized spectral clustering (i.e., if the second eigenvalue is not inside the essential spectrum), then the limit partition in the unnormalized case can be interpreted similarly to the normalized case by taking into account the form of the operator U on $L_2(\mathcal{X}_1, \mathcal{B}_1, P_1) \oplus L_2(\mathcal{X}_2, \mathcal{B}_2, P_2)$. Similar to above, it is composed of a matrix of four operators $(U_{ij})_{i,j=1,2}$ defined as

$$U_{ii} : L_2(\mathcal{X}_i) \to L_2(\mathcal{X}_i),\ U_{ii} f_i(x) = d_i(x) f_i(x) - \int k_{ii}(x,y) f_i(y) dP_i(y)$$

$$U_{ij} : L_2(\mathcal{X}_j) \to L_2(\mathcal{X}_i),\ U_{ij} f_j(x) = - \int k_{ij}(x,y) f_j(y) dP_j(y) \qquad (\text{ for } i \neq j).$$

We see that the off-diagonal operators U_{ij} for $i \neq j$ only consist of integral operators, whereas the multiplication operators only appear in the diagonal operators U_{ii}. Thus the operators U_{ij} for $i \neq j$ can also be seen as diffusion operators, and the same interpretation as in the normalized case is possible. If there exists a partition such that $k(x_1, x_2) = 0$ for all $x_1 \in \mathcal{X}_1$ and $x_2 \in \mathcal{X}_2$, then the second eigenfunction is constant on both parts, and thresholding this eigenfunction will recover the "true" partition. Thus, also in the unnormalized case the goal of spectral clustering is to find partitions such that the norms of the off-diagonal operators is small and the norms of the diagonal operators are large. This holds both in the discrete case and in the limit case, but only if the second eigenvalue of U is not inside the range of the degree function.

To summarize, from a technical point of view the eigenvectors of the unnormalized Laplacian are more unpleasant to deal with than the normalized ones, as the limit operator has a large essential spectrum in which the interesting eigenvalues could be contained. But if the second eigenvalue of the limit operator is isolated, some kind of diffusion interpretation is still possible. This means that if unnormalized spectral clustering converges, then it converges to a sensible limit clustering.

6 Discussion

We showed in Theorem 5 that the second eigenvector of the normalized Laplacian matrix converges to the second eigenfunction of some limit operator almost surely. The assumptions in this theorem are usually satisfied in practical applications. This allows to conclude that in the normalized case, spectral clustering converges to some limit partition of the whole space which only depends on the similarity function k and the probability distribution P. We also gave an explanation of how this partition looks like in terms of a diffusion process on the data space. Intuitively, the limit partition accomplishes the objective of clustering, namely to divide the space into sets such that the similarity within the sets is large and the similarity between the sets is low.

The methods we used to prove the convergence in case of the normalized Laplacian fail in the unnormalized case. The reason is that the limit operator in the unnormalized case is not compact and has a large essential spectrum. Convergence of the second eigenvector in the unnormalized case can be proved with different methods using collectively compact convergence of linear operators, but only under strong assumptions on the spectrum of the limit operator which are not always satisfied in practice (cf. von Luxburg et al.). However, if these assumptions are satisfied, then the limit clustering partitions the data space in a reasonable way. In practice, the fact that the unnormalized case seems much more difficult than the normalized case might serve as an indication that the normalized case of spectral clustering should be preferred.

The observations in Section 4 allow to make some more suggestions for the practical application of spectral clustering. According to the diffusion interpretation, it seems possible to to construct a criterion to evaluate the goodness of the partition achieved by spectral clustering. For a good partition, the off-diagonal operators $R_{12,n}$ and $R_{21,n}$ should have a small norm compared to the norm of the diagonal matrices $R_{11,n}$ and $R_{22,n}$, which is easy to check in practical applications. It will be a topic for future investigations to work out this idea in detail.

There are many open questions related to spectral clustering which have not been addressed in our work so far. The most obvious one is the question about the speed of convergence and the concentration of the limit results. Results in this direction would enable us to make confidence predictions about how close the clustering on the finite sample is to the "true" clustering proposed by the limit operator.

This immediately raises a second question: Which relations are there between the limit clustering and the geometry of the data space? For certain similarity functions such as the Gaussian kernel $k_t(x, y) = \exp(-\|x - y\|^2/t)$, it has been established that there is a relationship between the operator T and the Laplace operator on $\mathbb{R}^n$ (Bousquet et al., 2004) or the Laplace-Beltrami operator on manifolds (Belkin, 2003). Can this relationship also be extended to the eigenvalues and eigenfunctions of the operators?

There are also more technical questions related to our approach. The first one is the question which space of functions is the "natural" space to study spectral clustering. The space $L_2(P)$ is a large space and is likely to contain all eigenfunctions we might be interested in. On the other hand, for "nice" similarity functions the eigenfunctions are continuous or even differentiable, thus $L_2(P)$ might be too general to discuss relevant properties such as relations to continuous Laplace operators. Moreover, we want to use functions which are pointwise defined, as we are interested in the value of the function at specific data points. But of all spaces, the functions in L_p-spaces do not have this property.

Another question concerns the type of convergence results we should prove. In this work, we fixed the similarity function k and considered the limit for $n \to \infty$. As a next step, the convergence of the limit operators with respect to some kernel parameters, such as the kernel width t for the Gaussian kernel, can be studied as in the works of Bousquet et al. (2004) and Belkin (2003). But it seems more appropriate to take limits in t and n simultaneously. This might reveal other important aspects of spectral clustering, for example how the kernel width should scale with n.

References

M. Belkin. *Problems of Learning on Manifolds.* PhD thesis, University of Chicago, 2003.

M. Belkin and P. Niyogi. Semi-supervised learning on Riemannian manifolds. *Machine Learning*, to appear. Available at `http://people.cs.uchicago.edu/\char126\relaxmisha`.

Y. Bengio, P. Vincent, J.-F. Paiement, O. Delalleau, M. Ouimet, and N. Le Roux. Spectral clustering and kernel PCA are learning eigenfunctions. Technical Report TR 1239, University of Montreal, 2003.

R. Bhatia. *Matrix Analysis.* Springer, New York, 1997.

M. Birman and M. Solomjak. *Spectral theory of self-adjoint operators in Hilbert space.* Reidel Publishing Company, Dordrecht, 1987.

O. Bousquet, O. Chapelle, and M. Hein. Measure based regularization. In S. Thrun, L. Saul, and B. Schölkopf, editors, *Advances in Neural Information Processing Systems 16.* MIT Press, Cambridge, MA, 2004.

F. Chatelin. *Spectral Approximation of Linear Operators.* Academic Press, New York, 1983.

Fan R. K. Chung. *Spectral graph theory*, volume 92 of *CBMS Regional Conference Series in Mathematics.* Published for the Conference Board of the Mathematical Sciences, Washington, DC, 1997.

W. E. Donath and A. J. Hoffman. Lower bounds for the partitioning of graphs. *IBM J. Res. Develop.*, 17:420–425, 1973.

M. Fiedler. Algebraic connectivity of graphs. *Czechoslovak Math. J.*, 23:298–305, 1973.

S. Guattery and G. L. Miller. On the quality of spectral separators. *SIAM Journal of Matrix Anal. Appl.*, 19(3), 1998.

L. Hagen and A.B. Kahng. New spectral methods for ratio cut partitioning and clustering. *IEEE Trans. Computer-Aided Design*, 11(9):1074–1085, 1992.

J. Hartigan. Consistency of single linkage for high-density clusters. *JASA*, 76(374): 388–394, 1981.

B. Hendrickson and R. Leland. An improved spectral graph partitioning algorithm for mapping parallel computations. *SIAM J. on Scientific Computing*, 16:452–469, 1995.

R. Kannan, S. Vempala, and A. Vetta. On clusterings - good, bad and spectral. Technical report, Computer science Department, Yale University, 2000.

T. Kato. *Perturbation theory for linear operators.* Springer, Berlin, 1966.

V. Koltchinskii. Asymptotics of spectral projections of some random matrices approximating integral operators. *Progress in Probabilty*, 43, 1998.

V. Koltchinskii and E. Giné. Random matrix approximation of spectra of integral operators. *Bernoulli*, 6(1):113 – 167, 2000.

M. Meila and J. Shi. A random walks view of spectral segmentation. In *8th International Workshop on Artificial Intelligence and Statistics*, 2001.

A. Ng, M. Jordan, and Y. Weiss. On spectral clustering: Analysis and an algorithm. In T. Dietterich, S. Becker, and Z. Ghahramani, editors, *Advances in Neural Information Processing Systems 14*. MIT Press, 2001.

P. Niyogi and N. K. Karmarkar. An approach to data reduction and clustering with theoretical guarantees. In P. Langley, editor, *Proceedings of the Seventeenth International Conference on Machine Learning.* Morgan Kaufmann, San Francisco, 2000.

D. Pollard. Strong consistency of k-means clustering. *Annals of Statistics*, 9(1):135–140, 1981.

J. Shawe-Taylor, C. Williams, N. Cristianini, and J. Kandola. On the eigenspectrum of the Gram matrix and its relationship to the operator eigenspectrum. In N. Cesa-Bianchi, M. Numao, and R. Reischuk, editors, *Proceedings of the 13th International Conference on Algorithmic Learning Theory.* Springer, Heidelberg, 2002.

J. Shi and J. Malik. Normalized cuts and image segmentation. *IEEE Transactions on Pattern Analysis and Machine Intelligence*, 22(8):888–905, 2000.

R. Van Driessche and D. Roose. An improved spectral bisection algorithm and its application to dynamic load balancing. *Parallel Comput.*, 21(1), 1995.

U. von Luxburg, O. Bousquet, and M. Belkin. On the convergence of spectral clustering on random samples: the unnormalized case. Submitted to DAGM 2004, available at http://www.kyb.tuebingen.mpg.de/~ule.

J. Weidmann. *Linear Operators in Hilbert spaces.* Springer, New York, 1980.

Y. Weiss. Segmentation using eigenvectors: A unifying view. In *Proceedings of the International Conference on Computer Vision*, pages 975–982, 1999.

C. K. I. Williams and M. Seeger. The effect of the input density distribution on kernel-based classifiers. In P. Langley, editor, *Proceedings of the 17th International Conference on Machine Learning*, pages 1159–1166. Morgan Kaufmann, San Francisco, 2000.

X. Zhu, Z. Ghahramani, and J. Lafferty. Semi-supervised learning using Gaussian fields and harmonic functions. In T. Fawcett and N.Mishra, editors, *Proceedings of the 20th International Conference of Machine Learning.* AAAI Press, 2003.

Performance Guarantees for Regularized Maximum Entropy Density Estimation

Miroslav Dudík[1], Steven J. Phillips[2], and Robert E. Schapire[1]

[1] Princeton University, Department of Computer Science,
35 Olden Street, Princeton, NJ 08544 USA,
{mdudik,schapire}@cs.princeton.edu

[2] AT&T Labs – Research, 180 Park Avenue, Florham Park, NJ 07932 USA,
phillips@research.att.com

Abstract. We consider the problem of estimating an unknown probability distribution from samples using the principle of maximum entropy (maxent). To alleviate overfitting with a very large number of features, we propose applying the maxent principle with relaxed constraints on the expectations of the features. By convex duality, this turns out to be equivalent to finding the Gibbs distribution minimizing a regularized version of the empirical log loss. We prove non-asymptotic bounds showing that, with respect to the true underlying distribution, this relaxed version of maxent produces density estimates that are almost as good as the best possible. These bounds are in terms of the deviation of the feature empirical averages relative to their true expectations, a number that can be bounded using standard uniform-convergence techniques. In particular, this leads to bounds that drop quickly with the number of samples, and that depend very moderately on the number or complexity of the features. We also derive and prove convergence for both sequential-update and parallel-update algorithms. Finally, we briefly describe experiments on data relevant to the modeling of species geographical distributions.

1 Introduction

The maximum entropy (maxent) approach to probability density estimation was first proposed by Jaynes [9] in 1957, and has since been used in many areas of computer science and statistical learning, especially natural language processing [1,6]. In maxent, one is given a set of samples from a target distribution over some space, and a set of known constraints on the distribution. The distribution is then estimated by a distribution of maximum entropy satisfying the given constraints. The constraints are often represented using a set of *features* (real-valued functions) on the space, with the expectation of every feature being required to match its empirical average. By convex duality, this turns out to be the unique Gibbs distribution maximizing the likelihood of the samples, where a Gibbs distribution is one that is exponential in a linear combination of the features. (Maxent and its dual are described more rigorously in Section 2.)

The work in this paper was motivated by a new application of maxent to the problem of modeling the distribution of a plant or animal species, a critical problem in conservation biology. This application is explored in detail in a companion paper [13]. Input data for species distribution modeling consists of occurrence locations of a particular

J. Shawe-Taylor and Y. Singer (Eds.): COLT 2004, LNAI 3120, pp. 472–486, 2004.

species in a certain region and of environmental variables for that region. Environmental variables may include topological layers, such as elevation and aspect, meteorological layers, such as annual precipitation and average temperature, as well as categorical layers, such as vegetation and soil types. Occurrence locations are commonly derived from specimen collections in natural history museums and herbaria. In the context of maxent, the sample space is a map divided into a finite number of cells, the modeled distribution is the probability that a random specimen of the species occurs in a given cell, samples are occurrence records, and features are environmental variables or functions thereof.

It should not be surprising that maxent can severely overfit training data when the constraints on the output distribution are based on feature expectations, as described above, especially if there is a very large number of features. For instance, in our application, we sometimes consider threshold features for each environmental variable. These are binary features equal to one if an environmental variable is larger than a fixed threshold and zero otherwise. Thus, there is a continuum of features for each variable, and together they force the output distribution to be non-zero only at values achieved by the samples. The problem is that in general, the empirical averages of the features will almost never be equal to their true expectation, so that the target distribution itself does not satisfy the constraints imposed on the output distribution. On the other hand, we do expect that empirical averages will be *close* to their expectations. In addition, we often have bounds or estimates on deviations of empirical feature averages from their expectations (empirical error bounds). In this paper, we propose a relaxation of feature-based maxent constraints in which we seek the distribution of maximum entropy subject to the constraint that feature expectations be *within empirical error bounds* of their empirical averages (rather than exactly equal to them).

As was the case for the standard feature-based maxent, the convex dual of this relaxed problem has a natural interpretation. In particular, this problem turns out to be equivalent to minimizing the empirical log loss of the sample points plus an ℓ_1-style regularization term. As we demonstrate, this form of regularization has numerous advantages, enabling the proof of meaningful bounds on the deviation between the density estimate and the true underlying distribution, as well as the derivation of simple algorithms for provably minimizing this regularized loss. Beginning with the former, we prove that the regularized (empirical) loss function itself gives an upper bound on the log loss with respect to the target distribution. This provides another sensible motivation for minimizing this function. More specifically, we prove a guarantee on the log loss over the target distribution in terms of empirical error bounds on features. Thus, to get exact bounds, it suffices to bound the empirical errors. For finite sets of features, we can use Chernoff bounds with a simple union bound; for infinite sets, we can choose from an array of uniform-convergence techniques. For instance, for a set of binary features with VC-dimension d, if given m samples, the log loss of the relaxed maxent solution on the target distribution will be worse by no more than $O(\|\boldsymbol{\lambda}^*\|_1 \sqrt{d \ln(m^2/d)/m})$ compared to the log loss of *any* Gibbs distribution defined by weight vector $\boldsymbol{\lambda}^*$ with ℓ_1-norm $\|\boldsymbol{\lambda}^*\|_1$. For a finite set of bounded, but not necessarily binary features, this difference is at most $O(\|\boldsymbol{\lambda}^*\|_1 \sqrt{(\ln n)/m})$ where n is the number of features. Thus, for a moderate number of samples, our method generates a density estimate that is almost as good as the best possible, and the difference can be bounded non-asymptotically. Moreover, these bounds are very moderate in terms of the number or complexity of the features, even admitting an extremely large number of features from a class of bounded VC-dimension.

Previous work on maxent regularization justified modified loss functions as either constraint relaxations [2,10], or priors over Gibbs distributions [2,8]. Our regularized loss also admits these two interpretations. As a relaxed maxent, it has been studied by Kazama and Tsujii [10] and as a Laplace prior by Goodman [8]. These two works give experimental evidence showing benefits of ℓ_1-style regularization (Laplace prior) over ℓ_2^2-style regularization (Gaussian prior), but they do not provide any theoretical guarantees. In the context of neural nets, Laplace priors have been studied by Williams [20]. A smoothened version of ℓ_1-style regularization has been used by Dekel, Shalev-Shwartz and Singer [5].

Standard maxent algorithms such as iterative scaling [4,6], gradient descent, Newton and quasi-Newton methods [11,16] and their regularized versions [2,8,10,20] perform a sequence of feature weight updates until convergence. In each step, they update all feature weights. This is impractical when the number of features is very large. Instead, we propose a sequential update algorithm that updates only one feature weight in each iteration, along the lines of algorithms studied by Collins, Schapire and Singer [3]. This leads to a boosting-like approach permitting the selection of the best feature from a very large class. For instance, the best threshold feature associated with a single variable can be found in a single linear pass through the (pre-sorted) data, even though conceptually we are selecting from an infinite class of features. In Section 4, we describe our sequential-update algorithm and give a proof of convergence. Other boosting-like approaches to density estimation have been proposed by Welling, Zemel and Hinton [19] and Rosset and Segal [15].

For cases when the number of features is relatively small, yet we want to prevent overfitting on small sample sets, it might be more efficient to minimize the regularized log loss by parallel updates. In Section 5, we give the parallel-update version of our algorithm with a proof of convergence.

In the last section, we return to our application to species distribution modeling. We present learning curves for relaxed maxent for four species of birds with a varying number of occurrence records. We also explore the effects of regularization on the log loss over the test data. A more comprehensive set of experiments is evaluated in the companion paper [13].

2 Maximum Entropy with Relaxed Constraints

Our goal is to estimate an unknown probability distribution π over a *sample space* X which, for the purposes of this paper, we assume to be finite. We are given a set of *samples* $x_1, \ldots, x_m$ drawn independently at random according to π. The corresponding empirical distribution is denoted by $\tilde{\pi}$:

$$\tilde{\pi}(x) = \tfrac{1}{m}\big|\{1 \le i \le m : x_i = x\}\big|.$$

We also are given a set of *features* $f_1, \ldots, f_n$ where $f_j : X \to \mathbb{R}$. The vector of all n features is denoted by $\boldsymbol{f}$. For a distribution π and function f, we write $\pi[f]$ to denote the expected value of f under distribution π (and sometimes use this notation even when π is not necessarily a probability distribution):

$$\pi[f] = \sum_{x \in X} \pi(x) f(x).$$

In general, $\tilde{\pi}$ may be quite distant, under any reasonable measure, from π. On the other hand, for a given function f, we do expect $\tilde{\pi}[f]$, the empirical average of f, to be rather close to its true expectation $\pi[f]$. It is quite natural, therefore, to seek an approximation p under which f_j's expectation is equal to $\tilde{\pi}[f_j]$ for every f_j. There will typically be many distributions satisfying these constraints. The *maximum entropy principle* suggests that, from among all distributions satisfying these constraints, we choose the one of maximum entropy, i.e., the one that is closest to uniform. Here, as usual, the entropy of a distribution p on X is defined to be $\mathrm{H}(p) = -\sum_{x \in X} p(x) \ln p(x)$.

Alternatively, we can consider all *Gibbs distributions* of the form

$$q_{\boldsymbol{\lambda}}(x) = \frac{e^{\boldsymbol{\lambda} \cdot \boldsymbol{f}(x)}}{Z_{\boldsymbol{\lambda}}}$$

where $Z_{\boldsymbol{\lambda}} = \sum_{x \in X} e^{\boldsymbol{\lambda} \cdot \boldsymbol{f}(x)}$ is a normalizing constant, and $\boldsymbol{\lambda} \in \mathbb{R}^n$. Then it can be proved [6] that the maxent distribution described above is the same as the maximum likelihood Gibbs distribution, i.e., the distribution $q_{\boldsymbol{\lambda}}$ that maximizes $\prod_{i=1}^{m} q_{\boldsymbol{\lambda}}(x_i)$, or equivalently, minimizes the empirical log loss (negative normalized log likelihood)

$$\mathrm{L}_{\tilde{\pi}}(\boldsymbol{\lambda}) = -\frac{1}{m} \sum_{i=1}^{m} \ln q_{\boldsymbol{\lambda}}(x_i) = -\tilde{\pi}[\ln q_{\boldsymbol{\lambda}}] \tag{1}$$

A related measure is the relative entropy (or Kullback-Leibler divergence), defined as

$$\mathrm{RE}(\tilde{\pi} \parallel q_{\boldsymbol{\lambda}}) = \tilde{\pi}[\ln(\tilde{\pi}/q_{\boldsymbol{\lambda}})].$$

The log loss and the relative entropy differ only by the constant $\mathrm{H}(\tilde{\pi})$. We will use the two interchangeably as objective functions.

Thus, the convex programs corresponding to the two optimization problems are

$$\mathcal{P}: \quad \max_{p \in \Delta} \mathrm{H}(p) \text{ subject to} \qquad\qquad \mathcal{Q}: \quad \min_{\boldsymbol{\lambda} \in \mathbb{R}^n} \mathrm{L}_{\tilde{\pi}}(\boldsymbol{\lambda})$$
$$p[f_j] = \tilde{\pi}[f_j]$$

where Δ is the simplex of probability distributions over X.

This basic approach computes the maximum entropy distribution p for which $p[f_j] = \tilde{\pi}[f_j]$. However, we do not expect $\tilde{\pi}[f_j]$ to be *equal* to $\pi[f_j]$ but only close to it. Therefore, in keeping with the motivation above, we can soften these constraints to have the form

$$|p[f_j] - \tilde{\pi}[f_j]| \leq \beta_j \tag{2}$$

where β_j is an estimated upper bound of how close $\tilde{\pi}[f_j]$, being an empirical average, must be to its true expectation $\pi[f_j]$. Thus, the problem can be stated as follows:

$$\max_{p \in \Delta} \mathrm{H}(p) \text{ subject to}$$
$$\forall j: \left| p[f_j] - \tilde{\pi}[f_j] \right| \leq \beta_j$$

This corresponds to the convex program:

$$\mathcal{P}': \quad \max_{p\in(\mathbb{R}^+)^X} \mathrm{H}(p) \text{ subject to}$$

$$\textstyle\sum_{x\in X} p(x) = 1 \qquad (\lambda_0)$$

$$\forall j: \tilde{\pi}[f_j] - p[f_j] \le \beta_j \qquad (\lambda_j^+)$$

$$\forall j: p[f_j] - \tilde{\pi}[f_j] \le \beta_j \qquad (\lambda_j^-)$$

To compute the convex dual, we form the Lagrangian (dual variables are indicated next to constraints) to obtain the dual program

$$\min_{\substack{\lambda_0\in\mathbb{R}\\ \lambda_j^-,\lambda_j^+\in\mathbb{R}^+}} \max_{p\in(\mathbb{R}^+)^X} \Big[\mathrm{H}(p) - \lambda_0\left(\left[\textstyle\sum_{x\in X} p(x)\right] - 1\right) + \sum_j (\lambda_j^+ - \lambda_j^-)\left(p[f_j] - \tilde{\pi}[f_j]\right) + \sum_j \beta_j(\lambda_j^+ + \lambda_j^-)\Big].$$

Note that we have retained use of the notation $p[f]$ and $\mathrm{H}(p)$, with the natural definitions, even though p is no longer necessarily a probability distribution. Without loss of generality we may assume that in the solution, at most one in each pair λ_j^+, λ_j^- is nonzero. Otherwise, we could decrease them both by a positive value, decreasing the value of the third sum while not affecting the remainder of the expression. Thus, if we set $\lambda_j = \lambda_j^+ - \lambda_j^-$ then we obtain a simpler program

$$\min_{\lambda_0,\lambda_j\in\mathbb{R}} \max_{p\in(\mathbb{R}^+)^X} \Big[\mathrm{H}(p) - \lambda_0\left(\left[\textstyle\sum_{x\in X} p(x)\right] - 1\right) + \sum_j \lambda_j\left(p[f_j] - \tilde{\pi}[f_j]\right) + \sum_j \beta_j|\lambda_j|\Big].$$

The inner expression is differentiable and concave in $p(x)$. Setting partial derivatives with respect to $p(x)$ equal to zero yields that p must be a Gibbs distribution with parameters corresponding to dual variables λ_j and $\ln Z_{\boldsymbol{\lambda}} = \lambda_0 + 1$. Hence the program becomes

$$\min_{\boldsymbol{\lambda}\in\mathbb{R}^n} \Big[\mathrm{H}(q_{\boldsymbol{\lambda}}) + \boldsymbol{\lambda}\cdot(q_{\boldsymbol{\lambda}}[\boldsymbol{f}] - \tilde{\pi}[\boldsymbol{f}]) + \sum_j \beta_j|\lambda_j|\Big]. \tag{3}$$

Note that

$$\mathrm{H}(q_{\boldsymbol{\lambda}}) = -q_{\boldsymbol{\lambda}}[\ln q_{\boldsymbol{\lambda}}] = -q_{\boldsymbol{\lambda}}[\boldsymbol{\lambda}\cdot\boldsymbol{f} - \ln Z_{\boldsymbol{\lambda}}] = -\boldsymbol{\lambda}\cdot q_{\boldsymbol{\lambda}}[\boldsymbol{f}] + \ln Z_{\boldsymbol{\lambda}}.$$

Hence, the inner expression of Eq. (3) becomes

$$-\boldsymbol{\lambda}\cdot\tilde{\pi}[\boldsymbol{f}] + \ln Z_{\boldsymbol{\lambda}} + \sum_j \beta_j|\lambda_j| = \mathrm{L}_{\tilde{\pi}}(\boldsymbol{\lambda}) + \sum_j \beta_j|\lambda_j|. \tag{4}$$

(See Eq. (5) below.) Denoting this function by $\mathrm{L}_{\tilde{\pi}}^{\boldsymbol{\beta}}(\boldsymbol{\lambda})$, we obtain the final version of the dual program

$$\mathcal{Q}': \quad \min_{\boldsymbol{\lambda}} \mathrm{L}_{\tilde{\pi}}^{\boldsymbol{\beta}}(\boldsymbol{\lambda}).$$

Thus, we have shown that maxent with relaxed constraints is equivalent to minimizing $\mathrm{L}_{\tilde{\pi}}^{\boldsymbol{\beta}}(\boldsymbol{\lambda})$. This modified objective function consists of an empirical loss term $\mathrm{L}_{\tilde{\pi}}(\boldsymbol{\lambda})$ plus an additional term $\sum_j \beta_j|\lambda_j|$ that can be interpreted as a form of regularization limiting how large the weights λ_j can become.

3 Bounding the Loss on the Target Distribution

In this section, we derive bounds on the performance of relaxed maxent relative to the true distribution π. That is, we are able to bound $\mathrm{L}_\pi(\hat{\boldsymbol{\lambda}})$ in terms of $\mathrm{L}_\pi(\boldsymbol{\lambda}^*)$ when $\hat{\boldsymbol{\lambda}}$ minimizes the regularized loss and $q_{\boldsymbol{\lambda}^*}$ is an arbitrary Gibbs distribution, in particular, the Gibbs distribution minimizing the true loss. Note that $\mathrm{RE}(\pi \parallel q_{\boldsymbol{\lambda}})$ differs from $\mathrm{L}_\pi(\boldsymbol{\lambda})$ only by the constant term $\mathrm{H}(\pi)$, so analogous bounds also hold for $\mathrm{RE}(\pi \parallel q_{\hat{\boldsymbol{\lambda}}})$.

We begin with the following simple lemma on which all of the bounds in this section are based. The lemma states that the difference between the true and empirical loss of any Gibbs distribution can be bounded in terms of the magnitude of the weights λ_j and the deviation of feature averages from their means.

Lemma 1. *Let $q_{\boldsymbol{\lambda}}$ be a Gibbs distribution. Then*

$$\left|\mathrm{L}_{\tilde{\pi}}(\boldsymbol{\lambda}) - \mathrm{L}_\pi(\boldsymbol{\lambda})\right| \le \sum_{j=1}^{n} |\lambda_j| \left|\tilde{\pi}[f_j] - \pi[f_j]\right|$$

Proof. Note that

$$\mathrm{L}_{\tilde{\pi}}(\boldsymbol{\lambda}) = -\tilde{\pi}[\ln q_{\boldsymbol{\lambda}}] = -\tilde{\pi}[\boldsymbol{\lambda} \cdot \boldsymbol{f} - \ln Z_{\boldsymbol{\lambda}}] = -\boldsymbol{\lambda} \cdot \tilde{\pi}[\boldsymbol{f}] + \ln Z_{\boldsymbol{\lambda}}. \tag{5}$$

Using an analogous identity for $\mathrm{L}_\pi(\boldsymbol{\lambda})$, we obtain

$$\begin{aligned}\left|\mathrm{L}_{\tilde{\pi}}(\boldsymbol{\lambda}) - \mathrm{L}_\pi(\boldsymbol{\lambda})\right| &= \left|-\boldsymbol{\lambda} \cdot \tilde{\pi}[\boldsymbol{f}] + \ln Z_{\boldsymbol{\lambda}} + \boldsymbol{\lambda} \cdot \pi[\boldsymbol{f}] - \ln Z_{\boldsymbol{\lambda}}\right| \\ &= \left|\boldsymbol{\lambda} \cdot (\tilde{\pi}[\boldsymbol{f}] - \pi[\boldsymbol{f}])\right| \le \sum_{j=1}^{n} |\lambda_j| \left|\tilde{\pi}[f_j] - \pi[f_j]\right|\end{aligned}$$

□

This lemma yields an alternative motivation for minimizing $\mathrm{L}_{\tilde{\pi}}^{\boldsymbol{\beta}}$. For if we have bounds $\left|\tilde{\pi}[f_j] - \pi[f_j]\right| \le \beta_j$, then the lemma implies that $\mathrm{L}_\pi(\boldsymbol{\lambda}) \le \mathrm{L}_{\tilde{\pi}}^{\boldsymbol{\beta}}(\boldsymbol{\lambda})$. Thus, in minimizing $\mathrm{L}_{\tilde{\pi}}^{\boldsymbol{\beta}}(\boldsymbol{\lambda})$, we also minimize an upper bound on $\mathrm{L}_\pi(\boldsymbol{\lambda})$, the true log loss of $\boldsymbol{\lambda}$.

Next, we prove that the distribution produced using maxent cannot be much worse than the best Gibbs distribution (with bounded weight vector), assuming the empirical errors of the features are not too large.

Theorem 1. *Assume that for each j, $\left|\pi[f_j] - \tilde{\pi}[f_j]\right| \le \beta_j$. Let $\hat{\boldsymbol{\lambda}}$ minimize the regularized log loss $\mathrm{L}_{\tilde{\pi}}^{\boldsymbol{\beta}}(\boldsymbol{\lambda})$. Then for an arbitrary Gibbs distribution $q_{\boldsymbol{\lambda}^*}$*

$$\mathrm{L}_\pi(\hat{\boldsymbol{\lambda}}) \le \mathrm{L}_\pi(\boldsymbol{\lambda}^*) + 2\sum_{j=1}^{n} \beta_j |\lambda_j^*|.$$

Proof.

$$\begin{aligned}\mathrm{L}_\pi(\hat{\boldsymbol{\lambda}}) &\le \mathrm{L}_{\tilde{\pi}}(\hat{\boldsymbol{\lambda}}) + \textstyle\sum_j \beta_j |\hat{\lambda}_j| = \mathrm{L}_{\tilde{\pi}}^{\boldsymbol{\beta}}(\hat{\boldsymbol{\lambda}}) && (6)\\ &\le \mathrm{L}_{\tilde{\pi}}^{\boldsymbol{\beta}}(\boldsymbol{\lambda}^*) = \mathrm{L}_{\tilde{\pi}}(\boldsymbol{\lambda}^*) + \textstyle\sum_j \beta_j |\lambda_j^*| && (7)\\ &\le \mathrm{L}_\pi(\boldsymbol{\lambda}^*) + 2\textstyle\sum_j \beta_j |\lambda_j^*|. && (8)\end{aligned}$$

Eqs. (6) and (8) follow from Lemma 1, Eq. (7) follows from the optimality of $\hat{\boldsymbol{\lambda}}$. □

Thus, if we can bound $|\pi[f_j] - \tilde{\pi}[f_j]|$, then we can use Theorem 1 to obtain a bound on the true loss $\mathrm{L}_\pi(\hat{\boldsymbol{\lambda}})$. Fortunately, this is just a matter of bounding the difference between an empirical average and its expectation, a problem for which there exists a huge array of techniques. For instance, when the features are bounded, we can prove the following:

Corollary 1. *Assume that features $f_1, \ldots, f_n$ are bounded in $[0,1]$. Let $\delta > 0$ and let $\hat{\boldsymbol{\lambda}}$ minimize $\mathrm{L}^{\boldsymbol{\beta}}_{\tilde{\pi}}(\boldsymbol{\lambda})$ with $\beta_j = \beta = \sqrt{\ln(2n/\delta)/(2m)}$ for all j. Then with probability at least $1 - \delta$, for every Gibbs distribution $q_{\boldsymbol{\lambda}^*}$,*

$$\mathrm{L}_\pi(\hat{\boldsymbol{\lambda}}) \le \mathrm{L}_\pi(\boldsymbol{\lambda}^*) + 2\|\boldsymbol{\lambda}^*\|_1 \sqrt{\frac{\ln(2n/\delta)}{2m}}.$$

Proof. By Hoeffding's inequality, for a fixed j, the probability that $|\pi[f_j] - \tilde{\pi}[f_j]|$ exceeds β is at most $e^{-2\beta^2 m} = \delta/n$. By the union bound, the probability of this happening for any j is at most δ. The corollary now follows immediately from Theorem 1. □

Similarly, when the f_j's are selected from a possibly larger class of binary features with VC-dimension d, we can prove the following corollary. This will be the case, for instance, when using threshold features on k variables, a class with VC-dimension $O(\ln k)$.

Corollary 2. *Assume that features are binary with VC-dimension d. Let $\delta > 0$ and let $\hat{\boldsymbol{\lambda}}$ minimize $\mathrm{L}^{\boldsymbol{\beta}}_{\tilde{\pi}}(\boldsymbol{\lambda})$ with $\beta_j = \beta = \sqrt{[d\ln(em^2/d) + \ln(1/\delta) + \ln(4e^8)]/(2m)}$ for all j. Then with probability at least $1 - \delta$, for every Gibbs distribution $q_{\boldsymbol{\lambda}^*}$,*

$$\mathrm{L}_\pi(\hat{\boldsymbol{\lambda}}) \le \mathrm{L}_\pi(\boldsymbol{\lambda}^*) + 2\|\boldsymbol{\lambda}^*\|_1 \sqrt{\frac{d\ln(em^2/d) + \ln(1/\delta) + \ln(4e^8)}{2m}}.$$

Proof. In this case, a uniform-convergence result of Devroye [7], combined with Sauer's Lemma, can be used to argue that $|\pi[f_j] - \tilde{\pi}[f_j]| \le \beta$ for all f_j simultaneously, with probability at least $1 - \delta$. □

As noted in the introduction, these corollaries show that the difference in performance between the density estimate computed by minimizing $\mathrm{L}^{\boldsymbol{\beta}}_{\tilde{\pi}}$ and the best Gibbs distribution (of bounded norm), becomes small rapidly as the number of samples m increases. Moreover, the dependence of this difference on the number or complexity of the features is quite moderate.

4 A Sequential-Update Algorithm and Convergence Proof

There are a number of algorithms for finding the maxent distribution, especially iterative scaling and its variants [4,6]. In this section, we describe and prove the convergence of a sequential-update algorithm that modifies one weight λ_j at a time, as explored by Collins, Schapire and Singer [3] in a similar setting. This style of coordinate-wise descent is convenient when working with a very large (or infinite) number of features.

As explained in Section 2, the goal of the algorithm is to find $\boldsymbol{\lambda}$ minimizing the objective function $\mathrm{L}^{\boldsymbol{\beta}}_{\tilde{\pi}}(\boldsymbol{\lambda})$ given in Eq. (4). Our algorithm works by iteratively adjusting

Input: Finite domain X
features $f_1, \ldots, f_n$ where $f_j : X \to [0, 1]$
examples $x_1, \ldots, x_m \in X$
nonnegative regularization parameters $\beta_1, \ldots, \beta_n$
Output: $\boldsymbol{\lambda}_1, \boldsymbol{\lambda}_2, \ldots$ minimizing $\mathrm{L}^{\boldsymbol{\beta}}_{\tilde{\pi}}(\boldsymbol{\lambda})$
Let $\boldsymbol{\lambda}_1 = \mathbf{0}$
For $t = 1, 2, \ldots$:
– let $(j, \delta) = \arg\min_{(j,\delta)} F_j(\boldsymbol{\lambda}_t, \delta)$
where $F_j(\boldsymbol{\lambda}, \delta)$ is the expression appearing in Eq. (12)
– $\lambda_{t+1,j'} = \begin{cases} \lambda_{t,j} + \delta & \text{if } j' = j \\ \lambda_{t,j'} & \text{else} \end{cases}$

Fig. 1. A sequential-update algorithm for optimizing the regularized log loss.

the single weight λ_j that will maximize (an approximation of) the change in $\mathrm{L}^{\boldsymbol{\beta}}_{\tilde{\pi}}$. To be more precise, suppose we add δ to λ_j. Let $\boldsymbol{\lambda}'$ be the resulting vector of weights, identical to $\boldsymbol{\lambda}$ except that $\lambda'_j = \lambda_j + \delta$. Then the change in $\mathrm{L}^{\boldsymbol{\beta}}_{\tilde{\pi}}$ is

$$\begin{aligned} \mathrm{L}^{\boldsymbol{\beta}}_{\tilde{\pi}}(\boldsymbol{\lambda}') - \mathrm{L}^{\boldsymbol{\beta}}_{\tilde{\pi}}(\boldsymbol{\lambda}) &= \boldsymbol{\lambda} \cdot \tilde{\pi}[\boldsymbol{f}] - \boldsymbol{\lambda}' \cdot \tilde{\pi}[\boldsymbol{f}] + \ln Z_{\boldsymbol{\lambda}'} - \ln Z_{\boldsymbol{\lambda}} + \beta_j(|\lambda'_j| - |\lambda_j|) & (9) \\ &= -\delta\tilde{\pi}[f_j] + \ln(q_{\boldsymbol{\lambda}}[e^{\delta f_j}]) + \beta_j(|\lambda_j + \delta| - |\lambda_j|) & (10) \\ &\le -\delta\tilde{\pi}[f_j] + \ln(q_{\boldsymbol{\lambda}}[1 + (e^{\delta} - 1)f_j]) + \beta_j(|\lambda_j + \delta| - |\lambda_j|) & (11) \\ &= -\delta\tilde{\pi}[f_j] + \ln(1 + (e^{\delta} - 1)q_{\boldsymbol{\lambda}}[f_j]) + \beta_j(|\lambda_j + \delta| - |\lambda_j|). & (12) \end{aligned}$$

Eq. (9) follows from Eq. (5). Eq. (10) uses

$$Z_{\boldsymbol{\lambda}'} = \sum_{x \in X} e^{\boldsymbol{\lambda} \cdot \boldsymbol{f}(x) + \delta f_j(x)} = Z_{\boldsymbol{\lambda}} \sum_{x \in X} q_{\boldsymbol{\lambda}}(x) e^{\delta f_j(x)}. \quad (13)$$

Eq. (11) is because $e^{\delta x} \le 1 + (e^{\delta} - 1)x$ for $x \in [0, 1]$.

Let $F_j(\boldsymbol{\lambda}, \delta)$ denote the expression in Eq. (12). This function can be minimized over all choices of $\delta \in \mathbb{R}$ via a simple case analysis on the sign of $\lambda_j + \delta$. In particular, using calculus, we see that we only need consider the possibility that $\delta = -\lambda_j$ or that δ is equal to

$$\ln\left(\frac{(\tilde{\pi}[f_j] - \beta_j)(1 - q_{\boldsymbol{\lambda}}[f_j])}{(1 - \tilde{\pi}[f_j] + \beta_j)q_{\boldsymbol{\lambda}}[f_j]}\right) \quad \text{or} \quad \ln\left(\frac{(\tilde{\pi}[f_j] + \beta_j)(1 - q_{\boldsymbol{\lambda}}[f_j])}{(1 - \tilde{\pi}[f_j] - \beta_j)q_{\boldsymbol{\lambda}}[f_j]}\right)$$

where the first and second of these can be valid only if $\lambda_j + \delta \ge 0$ and $\lambda_j + \delta \le 0$, respectively.

This case analysis is repeated for all features f_j. The pair (j, δ) minimizing $F_j(\boldsymbol{\lambda}, \delta)$ is then selected and δ is added to λ_j. The complete algorithm is shown in Figure 1.

The following theorem shows that this algorithm is guaranteed to produce a sequence of $\boldsymbol{\lambda}_t$'s minimizing the objective function $\mathrm{L}^{\boldsymbol{\beta}}_{\tilde{\pi}}$ in the case of interest where all the β_j's are positive. A modified proof can be used in the unregularized case in which all the β_j's are zero.

Theorem 2. *Assume all the β_j's are strictly positive. Then the algorithm of Figure 1 produces a sequence $\boldsymbol{\lambda}_1, \boldsymbol{\lambda}_2, \ldots$ for which*

$$\lim_{t\to\infty} \mathrm{L}^{\boldsymbol{\beta}}_{\tilde{\pi}}(\boldsymbol{\lambda}_t) = \min_{\boldsymbol{\lambda}} \mathrm{L}^{\boldsymbol{\beta}}_{\tilde{\pi}}(\boldsymbol{\lambda}).$$

Proof. Let us define the vectors $\boldsymbol{\lambda}^+$ and $\boldsymbol{\lambda}^-$ in terms of $\boldsymbol{\lambda}$ as follows: for each j, if $\lambda_j \ge 0$ then $\lambda_j^+ = \lambda_j$ and $\lambda_j^- = 0$, and if $\lambda_j \le 0$ then $\lambda_j^+ = 0$ and $\lambda_j^- = -\lambda_j$. Vectors $\hat{\boldsymbol{\lambda}}^+, \hat{\boldsymbol{\lambda}}^-, \boldsymbol{\lambda}_t^+, \boldsymbol{\lambda}_t^-$, etc. are defined analogously.

We begin by rewriting the function F_j. For any λ, δ, we have that

$$|\lambda + \delta| - |\lambda| = \min\{\delta^+ + \delta^- \mid \delta^+ \ge -\lambda^+, \delta^- \ge -\lambda^-, \delta^+ - \delta^- = \delta\}. \tag{14}$$

This can be seen by a simple case analysis on the signs of λ and $\lambda + \delta$. Plugging into the definition of F_j gives

$$F_j(\boldsymbol{\lambda}, \delta) = \min\{G_j(\boldsymbol{\lambda}, \delta^+, \delta^-) \mid \delta^+ \ge -\lambda^+, \delta^- \ge -\lambda^-, \delta^+ - \delta^- = \delta\}$$

where

$$G_j(\boldsymbol{\lambda}, \delta^+, \delta^-) = (\delta^- - \delta^+)\tilde{\pi}[f_j] + \ln\left(1 + (e^{(\delta^+ - \delta^-)} - 1)q_{\boldsymbol{\lambda}}[f_j]\right) + \beta_j(\delta^+ + \delta^-).$$

Combined with Eq. (12) and our choice of j and δ, this gives that

$$\begin{aligned}\mathrm{L}^{\boldsymbol{\beta}}_{\tilde{\pi}}(\boldsymbol{\lambda}_{t+1}) - \mathrm{L}^{\boldsymbol{\beta}}_{\tilde{\pi}}(\boldsymbol{\lambda}_t) &\le \min_j \min_\delta F_j(\boldsymbol{\lambda}_t, \delta) \\ &= \min_j \min\{G_j(\boldsymbol{\lambda}_t, \delta^+, \delta^-) \mid \delta^+ \ge -\lambda^+_{t,j}, \delta^- \ge -\lambda^-_{t,j}\} \quad (15)\end{aligned}$$

Let $\min G(\boldsymbol{\lambda}_t)$ denote this last expression.

Since $G_j(\boldsymbol{\lambda}, 0, 0) = 0$, it follows that $\min G(\boldsymbol{\lambda}_t)$ is not positive and hence $\mathrm{L}^{\boldsymbol{\beta}}_{\tilde{\pi}}(\boldsymbol{\lambda}_t)$ is nonincreasing in t. Since log loss is nonnegative, this means that

$$\sum_j \beta_j |\lambda_{t,j}| \le \mathrm{L}^{\boldsymbol{\beta}}_{\tilde{\pi}}(\boldsymbol{\lambda}_1) < \infty.$$

Therefore, using our assumption that the β_j's are strictly positive, we see that the $\boldsymbol{\lambda}_t$'s must belong to a compact space.

Since $\hat{\boldsymbol{\lambda}}_t$'s come from a compact space, in Eq. (15) it suffices to consider updates δ^+ and δ^- that come from a compact space themselves. Functions G_j are uniformly continuous over these compact spaces, hence the function $\min G$ is continuous.

The fact that $\hat{\boldsymbol{\lambda}}_t$'s come from a compact space also implies that they must have a subsequence converging to some vector $\hat{\boldsymbol{\lambda}}$. Clearly, $\mathrm{L}^{\boldsymbol{\beta}}_{\tilde{\pi}}$ is nonnegative, and we already noted that $\mathrm{L}^{\boldsymbol{\beta}}_{\tilde{\pi}}(\boldsymbol{\lambda}_t)$ is nonincreasing. Therefore, $\lim_{t\to\infty} \mathrm{L}^{\boldsymbol{\beta}}_{\tilde{\pi}}(\boldsymbol{\lambda}_t)$ exists and is equal, by continuity, to $\mathrm{L}^{\boldsymbol{\beta}}_{\tilde{\pi}}(\hat{\boldsymbol{\lambda}})$. Moreover, the differences $\mathrm{L}^{\boldsymbol{\beta}}_{\tilde{\pi}}(\boldsymbol{\lambda}_{t+1}) - \mathrm{L}^{\boldsymbol{\beta}}_{\tilde{\pi}}(\boldsymbol{\lambda}_t)$ must be converging to zero, so $\min G(\lambda_t)$, which is nonpositive, also must be converging to zero by Eq. (15). By continuity, this means that $\min G(\hat{\boldsymbol{\lambda}}) = 0$. In particular, for each j, we have

$$\min\{G_j(\hat{\boldsymbol{\lambda}}, \delta^+, \delta^-) \mid \delta^+ \ge -\hat{\lambda}_j^+, \delta^- \ge -\hat{\lambda}_j^-\} = 0. \tag{16}$$

We will complete the proof by showing that this equation implies that $\hat{\boldsymbol{\lambda}}^+$ and $\hat{\boldsymbol{\lambda}}^-$ together with $q_{\boldsymbol{\lambda}}$ satisfy the KKT (Kuhn-Tucker) conditions [14] for the convex program $\mathcal{P}'$, and thus form a solution to this optimization problem as well as to its dual $\mathcal{Q}'$, the minimization of $\mathrm{L}^{\boldsymbol{\beta}}_{\tilde{\pi}}$. For $p = q_{\boldsymbol{\lambda}}$, these conditions work out to be the following for all j:

$$\hat{\lambda}^+_j \geq 0,\ \ \tilde{\pi}[f_j] - q_{\boldsymbol{\lambda}}[f_j] \leq \beta_j,\ \ \hat{\lambda}^+_j(\tilde{\pi}[f_j] - q_{\boldsymbol{\lambda}}[f_j] - \beta_j) = 0 \tag{17}$$

$$\hat{\lambda}^-_j \geq 0,\ \ q_{\boldsymbol{\lambda}}[f_j] - \tilde{\pi}[f_j] \leq \beta_j,\ \ \hat{\lambda}^-_j(q_{\boldsymbol{\lambda}}[f_j] - \tilde{\pi}[f_j] - \beta_j) = 0. \tag{18}$$

Recall that $G_j(\hat{\boldsymbol{\lambda}}, 0, 0) = 0$. Thus, by Eq. (16), if $\hat{\lambda}^+_j > 0$ then $G_j(\hat{\boldsymbol{\lambda}}, \delta^+, 0)$ is nonnegative in a neighborhood of $\delta^+ = 0$, and so has a local minimum at this point. That is,

$$0 = \left.\frac{\partial G_j(\hat{\boldsymbol{\lambda}}, \delta^+, 0)}{\partial \delta^+}\right|_{\delta^+=0} = -\tilde{\pi}[f_j] + q_{\boldsymbol{\lambda}}[f_j] + \beta_j.$$

If $\hat{\lambda}^+_j = 0$, then Eq. (16) gives that $G_j(\hat{\boldsymbol{\lambda}}, 0, 0) \geq 0$ for $\delta^+ \geq 0$. Thus, $G_j(\boldsymbol{\lambda}, \delta^+, 0)$ cannot be decreasing at $\delta^+ = 0$. Therefore, the partial derivative evaluated above must be nonnegative. Together, these arguments exactly prove Eq. (17). Eq. (18) is proved analgously.

Thus, we have proved that

$$\lim_{t\to\infty} \mathrm{L}^{\boldsymbol{\beta}}_{\tilde{\pi}}(\boldsymbol{\lambda}_t) = \mathrm{L}^{\boldsymbol{\beta}}_{\tilde{\pi}}(\hat{\boldsymbol{\lambda}}) = \min_{\boldsymbol{\lambda}} \mathrm{L}^{\boldsymbol{\beta}}_{\tilde{\pi}}(\boldsymbol{\lambda}). \qquad \square$$

5 A Parallel-Update Algorithm

Much of this paper has tried to be relevant to the case in which we are faced with a very large number of features. However, when the number of features is relatively small, it may be reasonable to minimize the regularized loss $\mathrm{L}^{\boldsymbol{\beta}}_{\tilde{\pi}}(\boldsymbol{\lambda})$ using an algorithm that updates all features simultaneously on every iteration. There are quite a few algorithms that do this for the unregularized case, such as iterative scaling [4,6], gradient descent, Newton and quasi-Newton methods [11,16].

Williams [20] outlines how to modify any gradient based search to include ℓ_1-style regularization. Kazama and Tsujii [10] use a gradient based method that imposes additional linear constraints to avoid discontinuities in the first derivative. Regularized variants of iterative scaling were proposed by Goodman [8], but without a complete proof of convergence. In this section, we describe a variant of iterative scaling with a proof of convergence. Note that the gradient based or Newton methods might be faster in practice.

Throughout this section, we make the assumption (without loss of generality) that, for all $x \in X$, $f_j(x) \geq 0$ and $\sum_j f_j(x) \leq 1$. Like the algorithm of Section 4, our parallel-update algorithm is based on an approximation of the change in the objective function $\mathrm{L}_{\tilde{\pi}}^{\boldsymbol{\beta}}$, in this case the following, where $\boldsymbol{\lambda}' = \boldsymbol{\lambda} + \boldsymbol{\delta}$:

$$\begin{aligned} \mathrm{L}_{\tilde{\pi}}^{\boldsymbol{\beta}}(\boldsymbol{\lambda}') - \mathrm{L}_{\tilde{\pi}}^{\boldsymbol{\beta}}(\boldsymbol{\lambda}) &= \boldsymbol{\lambda} \cdot \tilde{\pi}[\boldsymbol{f}] - \boldsymbol{\lambda}' \cdot \tilde{\pi}[\boldsymbol{f}] + \ln Z_{\boldsymbol{\lambda}'} - \ln Z_{\boldsymbol{\lambda}} + \sum_j \beta_j(|\lambda'_j| - |\lambda_j|) \\ &= -\boldsymbol{\delta} \cdot \tilde{\pi}[\boldsymbol{f}] + \ln q_{\boldsymbol{\lambda}}[\exp(\boldsymbol{\delta} \cdot \boldsymbol{f})] + \sum_j \beta_j(|\lambda_j + \delta_j| - |\lambda_j|) \quad (19) \\ &\le \sum_j \Big[-\delta_j \tilde{\pi}[f_j] + q_{\boldsymbol{\lambda}}[f_j](e^{\delta_j} - 1) + \beta_j(|\lambda_j + \delta_j| - |\lambda_j|) \Big]. \quad (20) \end{aligned}$$

Eq. (19) uses Eq. (13). For Eq. (20), note first that, if $x_j \in \mathbb{R}$ and $p_j \ge 0$ with $\sum_j p_j \le 1$ then

$$\exp\left(\textstyle\sum_j p_j x_j\right) - 1 \le \sum_j p_j(e^{x_j} - 1).$$

(See Collins, Schapire and Singer [3] for a proof.) Thus,

$$\begin{aligned} \ln q_{\boldsymbol{\lambda}}\left[\exp\left(\textstyle\sum_j \delta_j f_j\right)\right] &\le \ln q_{\boldsymbol{\lambda}}\left[1 + \textstyle\sum_j f_j(e^{\delta_j} - 1)\right] \\ &= \ln\left(1 + \textstyle\sum_j q_{\boldsymbol{\lambda}}[f_j](e^{\delta_j} - 1)\right) \\ &\le \sum_j q_{\boldsymbol{\lambda}}[f_j](e^{\delta_j} - 1) \end{aligned}$$

since $\ln(1 + x) \le x$ for all $x > -1$.

Our algorithm, on each iteration, minimizes Eq. (20) over all choices of the δ_j's. With a case analysis on the sign of $\lambda_j + \delta_j$, and some calculus, we see that the minimizing δ_j must occur when $\delta_j = -\lambda_j$, or when δ_j is either

$$\ln\left(\frac{\tilde{\pi}[f_j] - \beta_j}{q_{\boldsymbol{\lambda}}[f_j]}\right) \quad \text{or} \quad \ln\left(\frac{\tilde{\pi}[f_j] + \beta_j}{q_{\boldsymbol{\lambda}}[f_j]}\right)$$

where the first and second of these can be valid only if $\lambda_j + \delta_j \ge 0$ and $\lambda_j + \delta_j \le 0$, respectively. The full algorithm is shown in Figure 2. As before, we can prove the convergence of this algorithm when the β_j's are strictly positive.

Theorem 3. *Assume all the β_j's are strictly positive. Then the algorithm of Figure 2 produces a sequence $\boldsymbol{\lambda}_1, \boldsymbol{\lambda}_2, \ldots$ for which*

$$\lim_{t \to \infty} \mathrm{L}_{\tilde{\pi}}^{\boldsymbol{\beta}}(\boldsymbol{\lambda}_t) = \min_{\boldsymbol{\lambda}} \mathrm{L}_{\tilde{\pi}}^{\boldsymbol{\beta}}(\boldsymbol{\lambda}).$$

Proof. The proof mostly follows the same lines as for Theorem 2. Here we sketch the main differences.

Let us redefine F_j and G_j as follows:

$$F_j(\boldsymbol{\lambda}, \delta) = -\delta\tilde{\pi}[f_j] + q_{\boldsymbol{\lambda}}[f_j](e^{\delta} - 1) + \beta_j(|\lambda_j + \delta| - |\lambda_j|)$$

and

$$G_j(\boldsymbol{\lambda}, \delta^+, \delta^-) = (\delta^- - \delta^+)\tilde{\pi}[f_j] + q_{\boldsymbol{\lambda}}[f_j](e^{\delta^+ - \delta^-} - 1) + \beta_j(\delta^+ + \delta^-).$$

Input: Finite domain X
features $f_1, \ldots, f_n$ where $f_j : X \to [0,1]$
and $\sum_j f_j(x) \le 1$ for all $x \in X$
examples $x_1, \ldots, x_m \in X$
nonnegative regularization parameters $\beta_1, \ldots, \beta_n$
Output: $\boldsymbol{\lambda}_1, \boldsymbol{\lambda}_2, \ldots$ minimizing $\mathrm{L}^{\boldsymbol{\beta}}_{\tilde{\pi}}(\boldsymbol{\lambda})$
Let $\boldsymbol{\lambda}_1 = \mathbf{0}$
For $t = 1, 2, \ldots$:
- for each j, let $\delta_j = \arg\min_{\delta} \left(-\delta\tilde{\pi}[f_j] + q_{\boldsymbol{\lambda}}[f_j](e^{\delta} - 1) + \beta_j(|\lambda_j + \delta| - |\lambda_j|)\right)$
- update $\boldsymbol{\lambda}_{t+1} = \boldsymbol{\lambda}_t + \boldsymbol{\delta}$

Fig. 2. A parallel-update algorithm for optimizing the regularized log loss.

Then by Eq. (14),

$$F_j(\boldsymbol{\lambda}, \delta) = \min\{G_j(\boldsymbol{\lambda}, \delta^+, \delta^-) \mid \delta^+ \ge -\lambda_j^+, \delta^- \ge -\lambda_j^-, \delta = \delta^+ - \delta^-\}.$$

So, by Eq. (20),

$$\begin{aligned}
\mathrm{L}^{\boldsymbol{\beta}}_{\tilde{\pi}}(\boldsymbol{\lambda}_{t+1}) - \mathrm{L}^{\boldsymbol{\beta}}_{\tilde{\pi}}(\boldsymbol{\lambda}_t) &\le \min_{\boldsymbol{\delta}} \textstyle\sum_j F_j(\boldsymbol{\lambda}_t, \delta_j) \\
&= \textstyle\sum_j \min_{\delta_j} F_j(\boldsymbol{\lambda}_t, \delta_j) \\
&= \textstyle\sum_j \min\{G_j(\boldsymbol{\lambda}_t, \delta_j^+, \delta_j^-) \mid \delta_j^+ \ge -\lambda_j^+, \delta_j^- \ge -\lambda_j^-\}.
\end{aligned}$$

Note that $G_j(\boldsymbol{\lambda}, 0, 0) = 0$, so none of the terms in this sum can be positive. As in the proof of Theorem 2, the $\boldsymbol{\lambda}_t$'s have a convergent subsequence converging to some $\hat{\boldsymbol{\lambda}}$ for which

$$\textstyle\sum_j \min\{G_j(\hat{\boldsymbol{\lambda}}, \delta_j^+, \delta_j^-) \mid \delta_j^+ \ge -\lambda_j^+, \delta_j^- \ge -\lambda_j^-\} = 0.$$

This fact, in turn, implies that $\hat{\boldsymbol{\lambda}}^+$, $\hat{\boldsymbol{\lambda}}^-$ and $q_{\hat{\boldsymbol{\lambda}}}$ satisfy the KKT conditions for convex program $\mathcal{P}'$. This follows using the same arguments on the derivatives of G_j as in Theorem 2. □

6 Experiments

In order to evaluate the effect of regularization on real data, we used maxent to model the distribution of some bird species, based on occurrence records in the North American Breeding Bird Survey [17]. Experiments described in this section overlap with the (much more extensive) experiments given in the companion paper [13].

We selected four species with a varying number of occurrence records: Hutton's Vireo (198 occurrences), Blue-headed Vireo (973 occurrences), Yellow-throated Vireo (1611 occurrences) and Loggerhead Shrike (1850 occurrences). The occurrence data of each species was divided into ten random partitions: in each partition, 50% of the occurrence localities were randomly selected for the training set, while the remaining 50% were set

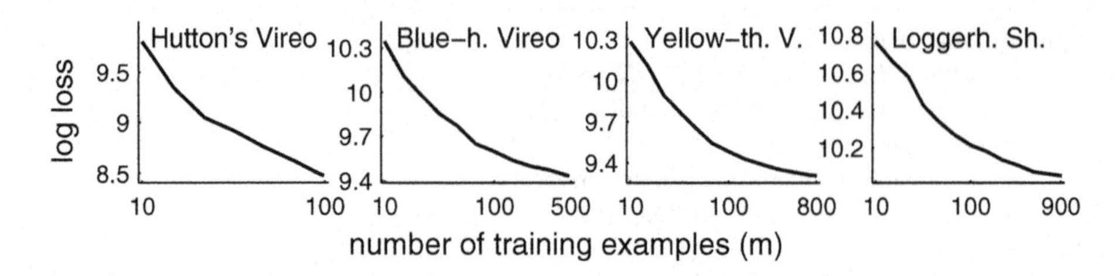

Fig. 3. *Learning curves.* Log loss averaged over 10 partitions as a function of the number of training examples. Numbers of training examples are plotted on a logarithmic scale.

aside for testing. The environmental variables (coverages) use a North American grid with 0.2 degree square cells. We used seven coverages: elevation, aspect, slope, annual precipitation, number of wet days, average daily temperature and temperature range. The first three derive from a digital elevation model for North America [18], and the remaing four were interpolated from weather station readings [12]. Each coverage is defined over a 386 × 286 grid, of which 58,065 points have data for all coverages.

In our experiments, we used threshold features derived from all environmental variables. We reduced the β_j to a single regularization parameter β as follows. We expect $|\pi[f_j] - \tilde{\pi}[f_j]| \approx \sigma[f_j]/\sqrt{m}$, where $\sigma[f_j]$ is the standard deviation of f_j under π. We therefore approximated $\sigma[f_j]$ by the sample deviation $\tilde{\sigma}[f_j]$ and used $\beta_j = \beta\tilde{\sigma}[f_j]/\sqrt{m}$. We believe that this method is more practical than the uniform convergence bounds from section 3, because it allows differentiation between features depending on empirical error estimates computed from the sample data. In order to analyze this method, we could, for instance, bound errors in standard deviation estimates using uniform convergence results.

We ran two types of experiments. First, we ran maxent on increasing subsets of the training data and evaluated log loss on the test data. We took an average over ten partitions and plotted the log loss as a function of the number of training examples. These plots are referred to as learning curves. Second, we also varied the regularization parameter β and plotted the log loss for fixed numbers of training examples as functions of β. These curves are referred to as sensitivity curves. In addition to these curves, we give examples of Gibbs distributions returned by maxent with and without regularization.

Fig. 3 shows learning curves for the four studied species. In all our runs we set $\beta = 1.0$. This choice is justified by the sensitivity curve experiments described below. In the absence of regularization, maxent would exactly fit the training data with delta functions around sample values of the environmental variables. This would result in severe overfitting even when the number of examples is large. As the learning curves show, the regularized maxent does not exhibit this behavior, and finds better and better distributions as the number of training examples increases.

In order to see how regularization facilitates learning, we examine the resulting distributions. In Fig. 4, we show Gibbs distributions returned by a regularized and an insufficently regularized run of maxent on the first partition of the Yellow-throated Vireo. To represent Gibbs distributions, we use feature profiles. For each environmental variable, we plot the contribution to the exponent by all the derived threshold features as

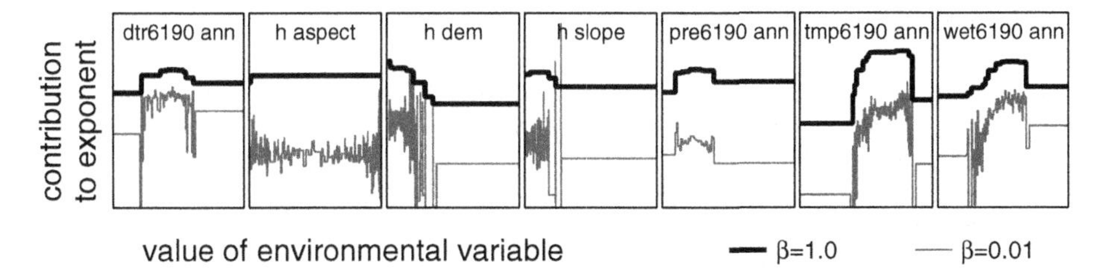

Fig. 4. *Feature profiles learned on the first partition of the Yellow-throated Vireo.* For every environmental variable, its additive contribution to the exponent of the Gibbs distribution is given as a function of its value. Profiles for the two values of β have been shifted for clarity — this corresponds to adding a constant in the exponent; it has, however, no effect on the resulting model since constants in the exponent cancel out with the normalization factor.

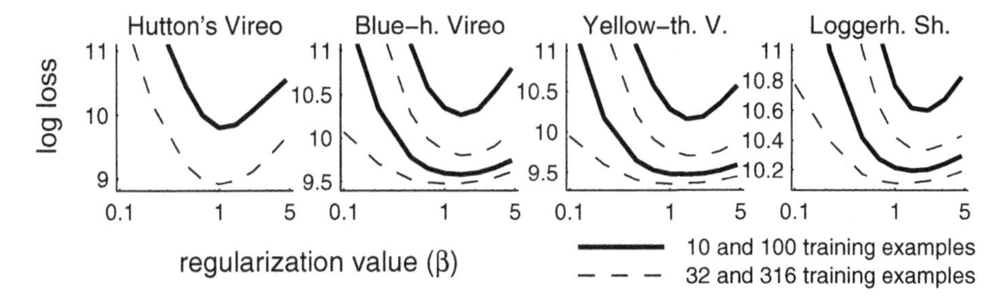

Fig. 5. *Sensitivity curves.* Log loss averaged over 10 partitions as a function of β for a varying number of training examples. For a fixed value of β, maxent finds better solutions (with smaller log loss) as the number of examples grows. We ran maxent with 10, 32, 100 and 316 training examples. Curves from top down correspond to these numbers; curves for higher numbers are missing where fewer training examples were available. Values of β are plotted on a log scale.

a function of the value of the environmental variable. This contribution is just the sum of step functions corresponding to threshold features weighted by the corresponding lambdas. As we can see, the value of $\beta = 0.01$ only prevents components of $\boldsymbol{\lambda}$ from becoming arbitrarily large, but it does little to prevent heavy overfitting with many peaks capturing single training examples. Raising β to 1.0 completely eliminates these peaks.

Fig. 5 shows the sensitivity of maxent to the regularization value β. Note that the minimum log loss is achieved consistently around $\beta = 1.0$ for all studied species. This suggests that for the purposes of maxent regularization, $\tilde{\sigma}[f_j]$ are good estimates of $|\tilde{\pi}[f_j] - \pi[f_j]|$ and that the maxent criterion models the underlying distribution well, at least for threshold features. Log loss minima for other feature types may be less consistent accross different species [13].

Acknowledgements. R. Schapire and M. Dudík received support through NSF grant CCR-0325463. M. Dudík was also partially supported by a Gordon Wu fellowship.

References

1. Adam L. Berger, Stephen A. Della Pietra, and Vincent J. Della Pietra. A maximum entropy approach to natural language processing. *Computational Linguistics*, 22(1):39–71, 1996.
2. S. F. Chen and R. Rosenfeld. A survey of smoothing techniques for ME models. *IEEE Transactions on Speech and Audio Processing*, 8(1):37–50, January 2000.
3. Michael Collins, Robert E. Schapire, and Yoram Singer. Logistic regression, AdaBoost and Bregman distances. *Machine Learning*, 48(1):253–285, 2002.
4. J. N. Darroch and D. Ratcliff. Generalized iterative scaling for log-linear models. *The Annals of Mathematical Statistics*, 43(5):1470–1480, 1972.
5. Ofer Dekel, Shai Shalev-Shwartz, and Yoram Singer. Smooth ϵ-insensitive regression by loss symmetrization. In *Proceedings of the Sixteenth Annual Conference on Computational Learning Theory*, pages 433–447. Springer, 2003.
6. Stephen Della Pietra, Vincent Della Pietra, and John Lafferty. Inducing features of random fields. *IEEE Transactions on Pattern Analysis and Machine Intelligence*, 19(4):1–13, April 1997.
7. Luc Devroye. Bounds for the uniform deviation of empirical measures. *Journal of Multivariate Analysis*, 12:72–79, 1982.
8. Joshua Goodman. Exponential priors for maximum entropy models. Technical report, Microsoft Research, 2003. (Available from http://research.microsoft.com/~joshuago/longexponentialprior.ps).
9. E. T. Jaynes. Information theory and statistical mechanics. *Physics Reviews*, 106:620–630, 1957.
10. Jun'ichi Kazama and Jun'ichi Tsujii. Evaluation and extension of maximum entropy models with inequality constraints. In *Conference on Empirical Methods in Natural Language Processing*, pages 137–144, 2003.
11. Robert Malouf. A comparison of algorithms for maximum entropy parameter estimation. In *Proceedings of the Sixth Conference on Natural Language Learning*, pages 49–55, 2002.
12. Mark New, Mike Hulme, and Phil Jones. Representing twentieth-century space-time climate variability. Part 1: Development of a 1961-90 mean monthly terrestrial climatology. *Journal of Climate*, 12:829–856, 1999.
13. Steven J. Phillips, Miroslav Dudík, and Robert E. Schapire. A maximum entropy approach to species distribution modeling. In *Proceedings of the Twenty-First International Conference on Machine Learning*, 2004.
14. R. Tyrrell Rockafellar. *Convex Analysis*. Princeton University Press, 1970.
15. Saharon Rosset and Eran Segal. Boosting density estimation. In *Advances in Neural Information Processing Systems 15*, pages 641–648. MIT Press, 2003.
16. Ruslan Salakhutdinov, Sam T. Roweis, and Zoubin Ghahramani. On the convergence of bound optimization algorithms. In *Uncertainty in Artificial Intelligence 19*, pages 509–516, 2003.
17. J. R. Sauer, J. E. Hines, and J. Fallon. The North American breeding bird survey, results and analysis 1966–2000, Version 2001.2. http://www.mbr-pwrc.usgs.gov/bbs/bbs.html, 2001. USGS Patuxent Wildlife Research Center, Laurel, MD.
18. USGS. HYDRO 1k, elevation derivative database. Available at http://edcdaac.usgs.gov/gtopo30/hydro/, 2001. United States Geological Survey, Sioux Falls, South Dakota.
19. Max Welling, Richard S. Zemel, and Geoffrey E. Hinton. Self supervised boosting. In *Advances in Neural Information Processing Systems 15*, pages 665–672. MIT Press, 2003.
20. Peter M. Williams. Bayesian regularization and pruning using a Laplace prior. *Neural Computation*, 7(1):117–143, 1995.

Learning Monotonic Linear Functions

Adam Kalai

TTI-Chicago
kalai@tti-c.org

Abstract. Learning *probabilities* (p-concepts [13]) and other real-valued concepts (regression) is an important role of machine learning. For example, a doctor may need to predict the probability of getting a disease $P[y|x]$, which depends on a number of risk factors.
Generalized additive models [9] are a well-studied nonparametric model in the statistics literature, usually with monotonic link functions. However, no known efficient algorithms exist for learning such a general class. We show that regression graphs *efficiently* learn such real-valued concepts, while regression trees *inefficiently* learn them. One corollary is that any function $E[y|x] = u(w \cdot x)$ for u *monotonic* can be learned to arbitrarily small squared error ϵ in time polynomial in $1/\epsilon$, $|w|_1$, and the Lipschitz constant of u (analogous to a margin). The model includes, as special cases, linear and logistic regression, as well as learning a noisy half-space with a margin [5,4].
Kearns, Mansour, and McAllester [12,15], analyzed decision trees and decision graphs as boosting algorithms for classification accuracy. We extend their analysis and the boosting analogy to the case of real-valued predictors, where a small positive *correlation coefficient* can be boosted to arbitrary accuracy. Viewed as a noisy boosting algorithm [3,10], the algorithm learns both the target function and the asymmetric noise.

1 Introduction

One aim of machine learning is predicting probabilities (such as p-concepts [13]) or general real values (regression). For example, Figure 1 illustrates the standard prediction of relapse probability for non-Hodgkin's lymphoma, given a vector of patient features. In this application and many others, probabilities and real-valued estimates are more useful than simple classification.

A powerful statistical model for regression is that of generalized *linear* models [16], where the expected value of the dependent variable y can be written as $E[y|x] = u(w \cdot x)$, an arbitrary *link function* $u : \mathbb{R} \to \mathbb{R}$ of a linear function of the feature vector $x \in \mathbb{R}^n$. Our results apply to *mono-linear functions*, where u is monotonic and Lipschitz continuous.[1]

Linear and logistic regression both learn mono-linear functions. The model also captures (noisy) linear threshold functions with a margin [5,4].[2]

[1] A function u is Lipschitz continuous with constant L if $|u(a) - u(b)| \le L|a - b|$ for all $a, b \in \mathbb{R}$. (For differentiable u, $|u'(a)| \le L$.)

[2] For a linear threshold function, $L = 1/\text{margin}$.

J. Shawe-Taylor and Y. Singer (Eds.): COLT 2004, LNAI 3120, pp. 487–501, 2004.

# Risk Factors	complete response rate	relapse-free 2-year survival	relapse-free 5-year survival	2-year survival	5-year survival
0,1	87%	79%	70%	84%	73%
2	67%	66%	50%	66%	51%
3	55%	59%	49%	54%	43%
4,5	44%	58%	40%	34%	26%

Risk Factors: $x_1 \geq 60, x_2 \geq 2, x_3 \geq 2, x_4 \geq$ normal, and $x_5 \geq 3$.
($x_1 =$ age, $x_2 =$ # extranodal sites, $x_3 =$ performance status, $x_4 =$ LDH, $x_5 =$ stage.)

Fig. 1. Non-Hodgkin's lymphoma International Prognostic Index probabilities [21]. Each probability (column) can be written in the form $u(I(x_1 \geq 60) + \ldots + I(x_5 \geq 3))$ for monotonic u, but does not fit a linear or logistic (or threshold) model.

In fact, our results apply to the more general *generalized additive models.* Random examples are seen from a distribution $\mathcal{D}$ over $\mathcal{X} \times \mathcal{Y}$, where $\mathcal{X} = \mathbb{R}^n$ and $\mathcal{Y} \subset \mathbb{R}$. ($Y = \{0,1\}$ corresponds to probability learning [13].) The assumption is that $f(x) = E[y|x] = u(\sum_i v_i(x_i))$, where u is a continuous monotonic *link function* and each $v_i : \mathbb{R} \to \mathbb{R}$ is an arbitrary function of bounded total variation[3].

A *regression tree* is simply a decision tree with real (rather than binary) predictions in the leaves. A *decision graph* (also called branching program, DAG, or binary decision diagram) is a decision tree where internal nodes may be merged. We suggest the natural *regression graph*, which is a decision graph with real-valued predictions in the leaves (eq. a regression graph with merging). We give an algorithm for learning these functions that is derivative of Mansour and McAllester [15]. We show that, for error of h defined as $\epsilon(h) = E_{\mathcal{D}}[(h(x) - f(x))^2]$, the error of regression graphs decreases quickly, while regression trees suffer from the "curse of dimensionality."

Theorem 1. *Let $\mathcal{D}$ be a distribution on $\mathcal{X} \times \mathcal{Y}$, where $\mathcal{X} \subseteq \mathbb{R}^n$ and $\mathcal{Y} \subseteq [0,1]$. Suppose $f(x) = E[y|x] = u(\sum v_i(x_i))$, where u is monotonic (nondecreasing or nonincreasing). Let L be the Lipschitz constant of u and $V = \sum V_{v_i}$ is the sum of the total variations of v_i.*
1. Natural top-down regression graph learning, with exact values of leaf weights and leaf means, achieves $\epsilon(R) \leq \epsilon$ with size$(R) \leq L^3V^3/(10\epsilon^4)$.
2. For regression trees *with exact values, $\epsilon(R) \leq \epsilon$ with size$(R) \leq 2(1.04)^{L^2V^2/\epsilon^3}$.*

While the above assumes knowing the exact values of parameters, standard tools extend the analysis to the case of estimation, as described in Section 5.3. Also, notice the Winnow-like dependence on V. In the case where each $v_i(x_i) = w_i x_i$ and $\mathcal{X} = [0,1]^n$, $V = W = \sum |w_i|$. If $f(x)$ is a linear threshold function of boolean $\mathcal{X} = \{0,1\}$, and $w_i \in \mathbb{Z}$, then $V = W$ and u can be chosen with $L = 1$, since the increase from $u(z) = 0$ to $u(z) = 1$ happens between integer z's. Since the sample complexity depends only logarithmically on the n, if there are only a

[3] The total variation of v is how much "up and down" it goes. For differentiable functions, it's $\int_{-\infty}^{\infty} |v'(a)|da$. For monotonic functions it's $\sup_a v(a) - \inf_a v(a)$.

few relevant dimensions (with small W) then the algorithm will be very attribute efficient.

1.1 Real-Valued Boosting

In learning a regression graph or tree, one naturally searches for binary splits of the form $x_i \geq \theta$. We first show that there always exists such a split with positive *correlation coefficient.* We then show that a positive correlation leads to a reduction in error.

This is clearly similar to boosting, and we extend the analyses of Kearns, Mansour, and McAllester, who showed that decision trees and more efficiently decision graphs can perform a type of boosting [20]. Rather than a weakly accurate hypothesis (one with accuracy $P[h(x) = f(x)] \geq 1/2$), we use weakly correlated hypotheses that have correlation bounded from 0. This is similar to the "okay" learners [10] designed for noisy classification.[4]

2 Related Work

While generalized additive models have been studied extensively in statistics [9], often with monotonic link functions, to the best of our knowledge no existing algorithm can efficiently guarantee $\epsilon(h) < \epsilon$ for arbitrarily small ϵ, even though such guarantees exist for much simpler single-variable problems.

For example, an algorithm for efficiently learning a monotonic function of a *single variable* $x \in \mathbb{R}$, $f(x) = E[y|x]$ was given by Kearns and Schapire [13]. Statisticians also have efficient learning algorithms for this *scatterplot smoothing* problem.

For the important special case of learning a linear threshold function with classification noise, Bylander showed that Perceptron-like algorithms are efficient in terms of a margin [5]. This would correspond to $u = \eta$ for negative examples, $u = 1 - \eta$ for positive examples, and linearly increasing at a slope of $(1 - 2\eta)/\text{margin}$ in between, where η is the noise rate. Blum et. al. removed the dependence on the margin [4]. Bylander also proved efficient *classification* in the case with a margin and random noise that monotonically and *symmetrically* decreased in the margin. It would be very interesting if one could extend these techniques to a non-symmetric noise rate, as symmetric techniques for other problems, such as learning the intersection of half-spaces with a symmetric density [1], have not been extended.

[4] As observed in [10], correlation is arguably a more popular and natural measure of weak association between two random variables than accuracy, e.g. the boolean indicators $f(x) =$"person x lives in Chicago" and $h(x) =$"person x lives in Texas" are negatively correlated, but have high accuracy $P[h(x) = f(x)]$.

3 Definitions

We use the Kearns and Schapire's definition of efficient learnability in a real-valued setting [13]. There is a distribution $\mathcal{D}$ over $\mathcal{X} \times \mathcal{Y}$. Kearns and Schapire take binary labels $\mathcal{Y} = \{0, 1\}$ in the spirit of learning probabilities and PAC learning [22]. In the spirit of regression, we include real labels $\mathcal{Y} \subseteq \mathbb{R}$, though the theory is unchanged. The target function is $f(x) = E[y|x]$.

An algorithm A *learns* concept class $\mathcal{C}$ of real-valued functions from $\mathcal{X}$, if, for every $\epsilon, \delta > 0$ and every distribution $\mathcal{D}$ over $\mathcal{X} \times \mathcal{Y}$ such that $E_{\mathcal{D}}[y|x] = f(x) \in \mathcal{C}$, given access to random labelled examples from $\mathcal{D}$, with probability $1 - \delta$, A outputs hypothesis h with error,

$$\epsilon(h) = E_{\mathcal{D}}[(h(x) - f(x))^2] \leq \epsilon.$$

It *efficiently learns* if it runs in time polynomial in $1/\epsilon, 1/\delta$, and size(f).[5]

While $\epsilon(h)$ cannot directly be estimated, $E[(h(x)-y)^2]$ can be and is related:

$$E_{\mathcal{D}}[(h(x) - y)^2] = E_{\mathcal{D}}[(f(x) - y)^2] + E_{\mathcal{D}}[(h(x) - f(x))^2].$$

Let the indicator function $I(P) = 1$ if predicate P holds and 0 otherwise. Recall various statistical definitions for random variables $u, v \in \mathbb{R}$.

$$\begin{aligned}
\mu_u &= E[u] \\
\mathrm{cov}(u, v) &= E[(u - \mu_u)(v - \mu_v)] = E[uv] - \mu_u \mu_v \\
\mathrm{var}(u) &= \sigma_u^2 = \mathrm{cov}(u, u) = E[(u - \mu_u)^2] = E[u^2] - \mu_u^2 \\
\sigma_u &= \sqrt{\mathrm{var}(u)} \\
\mathrm{cor}(u, v) &= \rho_{uv} = \frac{\mathrm{cov}(u, v)}{\sigma_u \sigma_v}
\end{aligned}$$

In most of the analysis, the random variables $f, h : \mathcal{X} \to \mathbb{R}$ can either be thought of as functions or the induced random variables for x from $\mathcal{D}$. We use ρ_{fh} or $\rho_{f(x)h(x)}$, as is convenient. We will use a few properties of covariance. It is shift invariant, i.e. $\mathrm{cov}(u + c, v) = \mathrm{cov}(u, v)$ for a constant c. It is symmetric and *bilinear*, i.e.

$$\mathrm{cov}(c_1 u_1 + c_2 u_2, v) = c_1 \mathrm{cov}(u_1, v) + c_2 \mathrm{cov}(u_2, v),$$

for constants c_1, c_2.

The (possibly infinite) *Lipschitz constant* of a function $u : \mathbb{R} \to \mathbb{R}$ is,

$$L = \sup_{a \neq b} \frac{|u(a) - u(b)|}{|a - b|}.$$

Let V_g be the *total variation* of a function $g : \mathbb{R} \longrightarrow \mathbb{R}$, which can be defined as the following maximum over all increasing sequences of $a_i \in \mathbb{R}$.

$$V_g = \sup_{k \in \mathbb{Z}} \sup_{a_1 < a_2 < \ldots < a_k} \sum_{i=1}^{k-1} |g(a_{i+1}) - g(a_i)|.$$

[5] In our example size$(f) = LV$, where L is a Lipschitz constant and V is total variation.

4 Top-Down Regression Graph Learning

For our purposes, a *regression tree* R is a binary tree with boolean split predicates, functions from $\mathcal{X}$ to $\{0,1\}$, at each internal node. The leaves are annotated with real numbers. A *regression graph* R is just a regression tree with merges. More specifically, it's a directed acyclic graph where each internal node again has a boolean split predicate and two labelled outgoing edges, but children may be shared across many parents. The internal nodes determine a partition of $\mathcal{X}$ into the leaves. The weight of a leaf is $w_\ell = P[x \in \ell]$. The value of a leaf ℓ is $q_\ell = E[y|x \in \ell]$. We define the prediction $R(x)$ to be the value of the leaf that x falls into. (These quantities are exact; estimation is discussed in the next section.) This enables us to discuss the correlation coefficient and other quantities relating to R. We also define the distribution $\mathcal{D}_\ell$, which is the distribution $\mathcal{D}$ restricted to the leaf ℓ.

It is straightforward to verify that $\mu_y = \mu_f = \mu_R = \sum_\ell w_\ell q_\ell$. Most decision tree algorithms work with a potential function, such as $\epsilon(R) = E[\big(R(x)-f(x)\big)^2]$, and make each local choice based on which one decreases the potential most. In Appendix C, we show that all of the following potential functions yield the same ordering on graphs:

$$\epsilon(R),\ -\sum w_\ell q_\ell^2,\ -\rho_{Rf},\ -\sigma_R^2,\ -\sum_\ell w_\ell\big(a(q_\ell - b)\big)^2,\ \sum_\ell w_\ell 4 q_\ell(1-q_\ell)$$

We use the second one, $G(R) \stackrel{\text{def}}{=} -\sum_\ell w_\ell q_\ell^2$, because it is succ. in terms of w_ℓ, q_ℓ. However, the (a,b) formulation (for $a \neq 0, b \in \mathbb{R}$) illustrates that minimizing $G(R)$ is scale-invariant (and shift-invariant), which mean that the algorithm can be run as-is even if Y is larger than $[0,1]$ (and the guarantees scale accordingly). Also, the last quantity shows that it is equivalent to the Gini splitting criterion used by CART [6].

A natural top-down regression graph learning algorithm with stopping parameter $\Delta_{\min}$ is as follows. We start with a single leaf ℓ_1 and repeat:

1. Sort leaves so that $q_{\ell_1} \leq q_{\ell_2} \leq \ldots \leq q_{\ell_N}$. ($N = \#$ of leaves.)
2. Merge leaves $\ell_a, \ell_{a+1}, \ldots, \ell_b$ into a single internal node. Split this node into two leaves with a split of the form $(x_i \leq \theta)$. Choose $\theta \in \mathbb{R}$, $i \in \mathbb{Z}$, and $1 \leq a \leq b \leq L$ that minimize $G(R)$.
3. Repeat until the change in $G(R)$ is less than $\Delta_{\min}$.

Every author seems to have their own suggestion about which nodes to merge. Our merging rule above is in the spirit of decision trees. Several rules have been proposed [15,14,18,7,2,19], including some that are bottom-up. Mansour and McAllester's algorithm [15] is more computationally efficient than ours, has the same sample complexity guarantees, but requires fixed-width buckets of leaves. The *regression tree* learner is the same without merges, i.e. $a = b$. The size(R) is defined to be the number of nodes.

The following lemma serves the same purpose as Lemma 5 of [12] (using correlation rather than classification error).

Lemma 1. *Let $h : \mathcal{X} \to \{0,1\}$ be a binary function. The split of ℓ into leaves $\ell_0 = \{x \in \ell | h(x) = 0\}$ and $\ell_1 = \{x \in \ell | h(x) = 1\}$ has score (reduction in $G(R)$) of $w_{\ell_0} w_{\ell_1} (q_{\ell_0} - q_{\ell_1})^2 / w_\ell = w_\ell (cor_{\mathcal{D}_\ell}(f,h))^2 var_{\mathcal{D}_\ell}(f)$.*

The proof is in Appendix A. We move the buckets of Mansour and McAllester [15] into our analysis, like [10].

Lemma 2. *The merger of leaves $\ell_a, \ell_{a+1}, \ldots, \ell_b$ with $q_{\ell_a} \leq \ldots \leq q_{\ell_b}$ into a single leaf can increase $G(R)$ by at most $(w_{\ell_{a+1}} + w_{\ell_{a+2}} + \ldots + w_{\ell_b})(q_{\ell_b} - q_{\ell_a})^2$.*

Proof. Proof by induction on b. The case $b = a$ is trivial. Let $\ell_{<b} = \ell_a \cup \ldots \cup \ell_{b-1}$ be the merger of all leaves except b. Then clearly $q_{\ell_a} \leq q_{\ell_{<b}} \leq q_{\ell_b}$. In terms of change in $G(R)$, the merger of ℓ_b and $\ell_{<b}$ is exactly the opposite of a split, and thus by Lemma 1, it increases $G(R)$ by an additional,

$$\frac{w_{\ell_b} w_{\ell_{<b}}}{w_{\ell_b} + w_{\ell_{<b}}} (q_{\ell_b} - q_{\ell_{<b}})^2 \leq w_{\ell_b} (q_{\ell_b} - q_{\ell_a})^2.$$

5 Mono-linear and Mono-additive Learning

Lemma 4 will show that for any mono-linear or mono-additive function, there is a threshold of a single attribute that has sufficiently large covariance with the target function. Then, using Lemmas 1 and 1 above, Lemma 5 shows that $\epsilon(R)$ will become arbitrarily small.

5.1 Existence of a Correlated Split

Lemma 3. *Let $u : \mathbb{R} \to \mathbb{R}$ be a monotonically nondecreasing L-Lipschitz function. Then for any distribution over $z \in \mathbb{R}$, $cov(u(z), z) \geq \sigma_u^2 / L$.*

Proof. By the bilinearity of covariance, and since $\sigma_u^2 = \text{cov}(u,u)$, the statement of the lemma can be rewritten as $\text{cov}(u,t) \geq 0$ for $t(z) = z - u(z)/L$. Note that $t(z)$ is nondecreasing as well. To see this, $t(z) - t(z') = z - z' - (u(z) - u(z'))/L$ which is nonnegative for $z > z'$, by definition of L-Lipschitz.

Now imagine picking $\hat{z}$ independently from the same distribution as z. Then, since $\text{sign}\big(u(z) - u(\hat{z})\big) = \text{sign}\big(t(z) - t(\hat{z})\big)$ always,

$$\begin{aligned} E[\big(u(z) - u(\hat{z})\big)\big(t(z) - t(\hat{z})\big)] &\geq 0 \\ E[u(z)t(z)] + E[u(\hat{z})t(\hat{z})] - E[u(z)t(\hat{z})] - E[u(\hat{z})t(z)] &\geq 0 \\ 2E[u(z)t(z)] - 2E[u(z)]E[t(z)] &\geq 0 \end{aligned}$$

The last line follows from independence and is equivalent to $\text{cov}(u,t) \geq 0$. □

Lemma 4. *Let $f : \mathbb{R}^n \to \mathbb{R}$ be of the form $f(x) = u(\sum_{i=1}^n v_i(x_i))$, where u is monotonic and L-Liptschitz, each $v_i : \mathbb{R} \to \mathbb{R}$ is a function of bounded variation V_{v_i}, and $V = \sum V_{v_i}$. Then there exists $i \in \{1,2,\ldots,n\}$, $\diamond \in \{<,>,\leq,\geq\}$, and $\theta \in \mathbb{R}$, such that*

$$cov(I(x_i \diamond \theta), f) \geq \frac{\sigma_f^2}{LV}.$$

Proof. WLOG u is monotonically nondecreasing. A theorem from real analysis states that every function v of bounded variation V_v can be written as the sum of a monotonically nondecreasing function v_1 and a monotonically nonincreasing function v_2 with $V_v = V_{v_1} + V_{v_2}$ [17]. Thus, we can write,

$$\sum_{i=1}^{n} v_i(x_i) = \sum_{i=1}^{n} v_{i1}(x_i) + v_{i2}(x_i),$$

for *monotonic* v_{ij}, and $V = \sum_{j=1}^{j=2} \sum_{i=1}^{i=n} V_{v_{ij}}$. Let $c_{ij} = \inf_{x_i} v_{ij}(x_i)$ (so $v_{ij} : \mathbb{R} \to [c_{ij}, c_{ij} + V_{v_{ij}}]$).

Now we argue that a random threshold function of a random attribute will have large covariance. Observe that for any $z \in [0,1]$, $E_{\alpha \in [0,1]}[I(z \geq \alpha)] = z$, where α is uniform over $[0,1]$. Then, since $(v_{ij}(x_i) - c_{ij})/V_{v_{ij}} \in [0,1]$,

$$\frac{v_{ij}(x_i) - c_{ij}}{V_{v_{ij}}} = E_{\alpha \in [0,1]}\left[I(\frac{v_{ij}(x_i) - c_{ij}}{V_{v_{ij}}} \geq \alpha)\right]$$

$$v_{ij}(x_i) - c_{ij} = V_{v_{ij}} E_{\alpha \in [0,1]}\left[I(v_{ij}(x_i) \geq c_{ij} + \alpha V_{v_{ij}})\right].$$

Choose i, j from the distribution $P(i,j) = V_{ij}/V$. Then,

$$\begin{aligned} E_{i,j \leftarrow P, \alpha \in [0,1]}[I(v_{ij}(x_i) \geq c_{ij} + \alpha V_{ij})] &= \sum_{j=1}^{2} \sum_{i=1}^{n} \frac{V_{v_{ij}}}{V} E_\alpha[I(v_{ij}(x_i) \geq c_{ij} + \alpha V_{ij})] \\ &= \sum_{j=1}^{2} \sum_{i=1}^{n} \frac{v_{ij}(x_i) - c_{ij}}{V} \\ &= \frac{1}{V} \sum_{i=1}^{n} v_i(x_i) - c, \end{aligned}$$

for some constant $c \in \mathbb{R}$. By the bilinearity of covariance, the above, and the fact that covariance is immune to shifts,

$$\begin{aligned} E_{i,j,\alpha}\left[\mathrm{cov}(f, I(v_{ij}(x_i) \geq c_{ij} + \alpha V_{ij}))\right] &= \mathrm{cov}(f, E_{i,j,\alpha}[I(v_{ij}(x_i) \geq c_{ij} + \alpha V_{ij})]) \\ &= \mathrm{cov}(f, \frac{1}{V} \sum v_i(x_i) - c) \\ &= \frac{\mathrm{cov}(f, \sum v_i(x_i))}{V} \end{aligned}$$

From the previous lemma, the last quantity is at least $\sigma_f^2/(LV)$. Since the above holds in expectation, there must be an i, j, and α for which it holds instantaneously. Finally, since v_{ij} is monotonic, $I(v_{ij}(x_i) \geq c_{ij} + \alpha V_{v_{ij}}) \equiv I(x_i \diamond \theta)$ for some $\diamond \in \{<, >, \leq, \geq\}$ and $\theta \in \mathbb{R}$. □

The dependence on σ_f in the above lemma is necessary. If $\sigma_f = 0$, then $\mathrm{cov}(h, f)$ must also be 0. But the lemma does gives us the following guarantee on correlation in terms of σ_f,

$$\rho_{hf} = \frac{\mathrm{cov}(h,f)}{\sigma_h \sigma_f} \geq \frac{\sigma_f}{\sigma_h LV} \geq \frac{4\sigma_f}{LV}. \tag{1}$$

5.2 The Implications for $\epsilon(R)$

Anticipating some kind of correlation boosting, we state the following lemma in terms of a guaranteed correlation $\rho(\sigma_f^2)$. In the above case $\rho(z) = 4\sqrt{z}/LV$.

Lemma 5. *Suppose $\rho : \mathbb{R} \to \mathbb{R}_+$ is a nondecreasing guarantee function such that, for each leaf ℓ, there exists a split predicate $h : \mathcal{X} \to \{0,1\}$ of correlation $cor_{\mathcal{D}_\ell}(h, f) \geq \rho(var_{\mathcal{D}_\ell}(f))$. Suppose $E[y|x] \in [0,1]$. Then with the regression graph learner with $\Delta_{min} = \epsilon^{2.5}\big(\rho(\epsilon/2)\big)^3/4$, error $\epsilon(R) \leq \epsilon$ with at most $\epsilon^{-2.5}(\rho(\frac{\epsilon}{2}))^{-3}$ splits. For the regression tree learner, after $\exp(1/(4(\rho(\frac{\epsilon}{2}))^2\epsilon^2))$ splits, $\epsilon(R) \leq \epsilon$.*

Proof. By definition of leaf variance $\mathrm{var}_{\mathcal{D}_\ell}(f)$ and error $\epsilon(R)$,

$$\epsilon(R) = E_{\mathcal{D}}[\big(R(x) - f(x)\big)^2] = \sum_\ell w_\ell E_{\mathcal{D}_\ell}[(q_\ell - f(x))^2] = \sum_\ell w_\ell \mathrm{var}_{\mathcal{D}_\ell}(f).$$

Let N be the current number of leaves. As long as $\epsilon(R) > \epsilon$, there must be some leaf ℓ with both $w_\ell \geq 2\epsilon/N$ and $\mathrm{var}_{\mathcal{D}_\ell}(f) \geq \epsilon/2$. Otherwise, the contribution to $\epsilon(R)$ from leaves with $\mathrm{var}_{\mathcal{D}_\ell}(f) < \epsilon/2$ would be $< \epsilon/2$ and from the rest of leaves would be at most $N(2\epsilon/N)(1/4) = \epsilon/2$, since $\mathrm{var}_{\mathcal{D}_\ell}(f) \leq 1/4$ (since $f(x) \in [0,1]$).

By Lemma 1, using $\mathrm{cor}_{\mathcal{D}_\ell}(f, h) \geq \rho(\epsilon/2)$ correlation, splitting this leaf ℓ gives a reduction in $G(R)$ of at least,

$$\Delta G \geq w_\ell\big(\rho(\epsilon/2)\big)^2 \mathrm{var}_{\mathcal{D}_\ell}(f) \geq \big(\rho(\epsilon/2)\big)^2 \epsilon^2/N.$$

Now $\epsilon(R) = \sigma_f^2$ at the start and decreases in each step, but never goes below 0. Also, the change in $G(R)$ is equal to the change in $\epsilon(R)$ since $\epsilon(R) = G(R) + E_{\mathcal{D}}[f(x)^2]$. Thus the total change in $G(R)$ is at most $\sigma_f^2 \leq 1/4$. In the case of regression trees, where we do splits and no merges, each split increases the number of leaves by 1. Thus, after T splits,

$$\sum_{N=1}^{T} \frac{\big(\rho(\epsilon/2)\big)^2 \epsilon^2}{N} \leq \frac{1}{4}.$$

Since $\sum_1^T 1/N \geq \ln(T)$, we get the regression tree half of the lemma.

For regression graphs, say at some point there are N leaves with values $q_\ell \in [0,1]$. Now bucket the leaves by value of q_ℓ into $1/s$ intervals of width $s = \rho(\epsilon/2)\sqrt{\epsilon}/2$. For the moment, imagine merging all leaves in every bucket. Then there would be at most $1/s$ leaves, and by the above reasoning, there must be one of these merged leaves $\ell = \ell_a \cup \ell_{a+1} \cup \ldots \cup \ell_b$ with $w_\ell \geq 2\epsilon s$ and $\mathrm{var}_{\mathcal{D}_\ell}(f) \geq \epsilon/2$ (the error $\epsilon(R)$ can only have increased due to the merger). Now imagine merging *only* the leaves in this bucket and not any of the others. By Lemma 2, the increase in $G(R)$ due to the merger at most $w_\ell(q_{\ell_b} - q_{\ell_a})^2 \leq w_\ell s^2$. Using Lemma 1 as well, the total decrease in $G(R)$ is at least

$$\Delta G \geq w_\ell\big(\rho(\epsilon/2)\big)^2 \mathrm{var}_{\mathcal{D}_\ell}(f) - w_\ell s^2$$

$$\geq w_\ell\big(\rho(\epsilon/2)\big)^2\epsilon/2 - w_\ell\big(\rho(\epsilon/2)\big)^2\epsilon/4$$
$$\geq (2\epsilon s)\big(\rho(\epsilon/2)\big)^2\epsilon/4$$
$$= \epsilon^{2.5}\big(\rho(\epsilon/2)\big)^3/4$$

Thus there exists a merge-split that reduces $G(R)$ by at least $\epsilon^{2.5}\big(\rho(\epsilon/2)\big)^3/4$ as long as $\epsilon(R) \geq \epsilon$, and by choice of $\Delta_{\min}$ we will not stop prematurely. Using that the total reduction in $G(R)$ is at most $1/4$, completes the lemma. □

We are now ready to prove the main theorem.

Proof (of Theorem 1). For part 1, we run the regression graph learning algorithm (getting exact values of p_ℓ and q_ℓ). By (1), we have $\rho(z) = 4\sqrt{z}/LV$. Since size(R) increases at most 2 per split, by Lemma 5, $\epsilon(R) \leq \epsilon$ with

$$\text{size}(R) \leq 2\epsilon^{-2.5}\left(\frac{4\sqrt{\epsilon/2}}{LV}\right)^{-3} = \epsilon^{-4}(LV)^3/8\sqrt{2} \leq \epsilon^{-4}(LV)^3/10.$$

We use $\Delta_{\min} = 4\sqrt{2}\epsilon^4/(LV)^3$ to guarantee we get this far and don't run too long. Similarly, for regression trees in part 2, by Lemma 5, since $\rho(\epsilon/2)^2 = 8\epsilon/(LV)^2$, size$(R) \leq 2\exp((LV)^2/\epsilon^3/32)$. Finally, $e^{1/32} < 1.04$.

5.3 Estimations Via Sampling

Of course, we don't have exact values of $g_\ell = w_\ell q_\ell^2$ for each leaf, so one must use estimates. For simplicity of analysis, we use fresh samples to estimate this quantity (the only quantity necessary) for each leaf. (Though a more sophisticated argument could be used, since the VC dimension of splits is small, to argue that one large sample is enough.) It is not difficult to argue that if each estimate of g_ℓ, for each potential leaf ℓ encountered, is accurate to within, say $\tau = \Delta_{\min}/10$, the algorithm will still have the same asymptotic guarantees.

While it is straightforward to estimate w_ℓ to within fixed additive tolerance, estimating q_ℓ to within fixed additive tolerance is not necessarily easy when w_ℓ is small. However, if w_ℓ is very small, then g_ℓ is also small. More precisely, if $\hat{w}_\ell < \tau/2$ and the estimate is accurate to within tolerance $\tau/10$, then we can safely estimate $\hat{g}_\ell = 0$ and still be accurate to within τ. On the other hand, if $w_\ell > \tau$, then it takes only $1/\tau$ samples to get one from leaf w_ℓ, and we can estimate q_ℓ to additive accuracy $\tau/10$ and thus g_ℓ to additive accuracy τ.

To have failure probability $1/\delta$, the number of samples required depends polynomially on $1/\epsilon, \log(n/\delta)$, and size$(R)$. The $poly - \log(n)$ dependence on n can be good in situations where there are only a few relevant attributes and LV is small.

6 Correlation Boosting

Lemma 5 is clearly hiding a statement about boosting. Recall that in classification boosting, a weak learner, is basically an algorithm that output a boolean hypothesis h with accuracy $P[h(x) = f(x)] \geq 1/2 + \gamma$ (for any distribution), where $1/\gamma$ is polynomial in size(f). Then the result was that the accuracy could be "boosted" to $1 - \epsilon$ in time $poly(1/\epsilon, \text{size}(f))$. We follow the same path, replacing accuracy with correlation. We define a *weak correlator*, also similar to an "okay" learner [10].

Definition 1. *Let $\rho : [0,1] \rightarrow [0,1]$ be a nondecreasing function. An efficient ρ weak correlator for concept $\mathcal{C}$ is an algorithm (that takes inputs δ and samples from $\mathcal{D}$) such that, for any $\delta > 0$, any distribution $\mathcal{D}$ over $\mathcal{X} \times \mathcal{Y}$ with $\mathcal{Y} = [0,1]$ and $f(x) = E[y|x] \in \mathcal{C}$, with probability $1 - \delta$ it outputs a hypothesis $h : \mathcal{X} \rightarrow \mathbb{R}$ with $\rho_{fh} \geq \rho(\sigma_f^2)$. It must run in time polynomial in $1/\delta, 1/\sigma_f^2$, and size(f), and $1/\rho$ must be polynomial in $1/\sigma_f^2$, and size(f).*

The algorithm is very similar. We start with a single leaf ℓ. Repeat:

1. Sort leaves so that $q_{\ell_1} \leq q_{\ell_2} \leq \ldots \leq q_{\ell_N}$. ($N = \#$ of leaves.)
2. For each $\ell_a, \ell_{a+1}, \ldots, \ell_b$, run the weak correlator (for a maximum of T time) on the distribution $\mathcal{D}_{\ell_{ab}}$ where ℓ_{ab} would be the merger of $\ell_a \ldots \ell_b$. If it terminates, the output will be some predictor $h_{ab} : \mathcal{X} \rightarrow \mathbb{R}$. Choose $1 \leq a \leq b \leq N$ and θ such that the merge-split of $\ell_a \ldots \ell_b$ with split $(h_{ab}(x) \geq \theta)$ gives the smallest $G(R)$.
3. Repeat until the change in $G(R)$ is less than $\Delta_{\min}$.

The point is that such a weak correlator can be used to get an arbitrarily accurate regression graph R with $\epsilon(R) \leq \epsilon$ for any $\epsilon > 0$ (efficiently in $1/\epsilon$). Appendix C shows,

$$\rho_{Rf} = \sqrt{1 - \frac{\epsilon(R)}{\sigma_f^2}} \geq 1 - \frac{\epsilon(R)}{\sigma_f^2}.$$

Thus, reducing $\epsilon(R)$ to arbitrary inversely polynomial ϵ is equivalent to "boosting" correlation from inversely polynomial to $1 - \epsilon/\sigma_f^2$. Appendix C also shows $\rho_{Ry} = \rho_{Rf}\rho_{fy}$. Thus ρ_{Ry}, the correlation coefficient reported in so many statistical studies, also becomes arbitrarily close to ρ_{fy}, the optimal correlation coefficient.

Theorem 2. *Given a ρ weak correlator, with probability $1-\delta$, the learned regression graph R has $\epsilon(R) \leq \epsilon$, with runtime polynomial in $1/\epsilon, 1/\delta$, and $1/\rho(\epsilon/2)$.*

Proof (sketch). The proof follows that of Lemma 5. There are three differences.

First, we must have a maximum time restriction on our weak correlators. If a leaf has tiny $\text{var}_{\mathcal{D}_\ell}(f)$, then the weak correlator will have to run for a very long time, e.g. if in one leaf there are only two types of x, one with $f(x) = 0.5$ and the other with $f(x) = 0.49999$, then it could easily take the weak correlator a long time to correlate with them. However, as seen in the proof of Lemma 5, we can safely ignore all leaves with $\text{var}_{\mathcal{D}_\ell}(f) < \epsilon/2$. Since we can't identify them, we simply stop each one after a certain amount of time running, for if we've gone longer than T time (which depends on the runtime guarantees of the weak correlator, but is polynomial in $1/\epsilon$ and size(f)), then we know that leaf has low variance anyway.

Second, we estimate weights and values for each different leaf with fresh samples. This makes the analysis simple.

Third, h_{ab} is not necessarily a boolean attribute. Fortunately, there is some threshold so that $I(h_{ab}(x) \geq \theta)$ also has large correlation. The arguments of Lemma 5 show there exists an h_{ab} with $\rho_{h_{ab}f} \geq \rho(\epsilon/2)$ and $\sigma_f^2 \geq \epsilon/2$, which are polynomial in $1/\epsilon$ and size(f) by definition of weak correlator. Lemma 6 in Appendix B implies that there will be some such threshold indicator h with,

$$\rho_{hf} > \frac{\rho_{h_{ab}f}}{2 + 2\sqrt{2\log(2/(\rho_{h_{ab}f}\sigma_f))}},$$

where quantities are measured over $\mathcal{D}_{\ell_{ab}}$. This is nearly $\rho_{h_{ab}f}/2$ and its reciprocal is certainly inverse polynomial in $1/\epsilon$ and size(f). □

7 Conclusions

While generalized additive models have been studied extensively in statistics, we have proven the first efficient learning guarantee, namely that regression graphs efficiently learn a generalized additive model (with a monotonic link function) to within arbitrary accuracy.

In the case of classification boosting, most boosting algorithms are parametric and maintain a linear combination of weak hypotheses. In fact, if a function is boostable, then it is writable as a linear threshold of weak hypotheses (just imagine running AdaBoost sufficiently long). We have shown that the class of boostable functions in the real valued setting is much richer. It includes at least the mono-linear functions of base hypotheses.

It would be especially nice to remove the dependence on the Lipschitz constant. (The bounded variation condition does not seem too restrictive.) For the related problem of learning a linear threshold function with uniform classification noise, Blum et. al. [4] were able to remove the dependence on a margin that was in Bylander's original work [5].

It would be nice to relax the assumption that $f(x) = E[y|x]$ is exactly distributed according to a mono-additive function. While it seems difficult to provably get as far as one can get in linear regression, i.e. find the best fit linear predictor, it may be possible to do something in between. For any given distribution there are often several mono-additive functions $f(x)$ that are *calibrated* with the distribution, i.e. $f(x) = E[y|f(x)]$. For example, the historical probability of white winning in a game of chess is almost certainly monotonic in the quantity $w_1 \cdot x =$ (#white pieces)−(#black pieces). But it should also be monotonic in terms of something like $w_2 \cdot x =$ (#white pawns + ... + 3#white bishops) − (#black pawns+...+3#black bishops). Can one do as well as the best calibrated mono-additive function without assumptions on $\mathcal{D}$?

Acknowledgments. I would like to thank Marc Coram for identifying the model as a generalized additive model (before it was too late), Ehud Kalai for suggesting the use of a Lipschitz condition, David McAllester and Rob Schapire for insightful discussions, and the anonymous referees for pointing out the disorganization.

References

1. E. Baum. A polynomial time algorithm that learns two hidden unit nets. *Neural Computation* 2:510-522, 1991.
2. L. Bahl, P. Brown, P. deSouze, and R. Mercer. A Tree-based statistical language model for natural language speech recognition. *IEEE Transactions on Acoustics, Speec, and Signal Processing,* 37:1001-1008, 1989.
3. J. Aslam and S. Decatur. Specification and simulation of statistical query algorithms for efficiency and noise tolerance. *Journal of Computer and System Sciences,* 56:191–208, 1998.
4. A. Blum, A. Frieze, R. Kannan, and S. Vempala. A polynomial time algorithm for learning noisy linear threshold functions. *Algorithmica,* 22(1/2):35–52, 1997.
5. T. Bylander. Polynomial learnability of linear threshold approximations. In *Proceedings of the Sixth Annual ACM Conference on Computational Learning,* 297–302, 1993.
6. L. Breiman, J. Friedman, R. Olshen, and C. Stone. *Classification and Regression Trees.* Wadsworth International Group, 1984.
7. P. Chou. *Applications of Infromation Theory to Pattern Recognition and the Design of Decision Trees and Trellises.* PhD thesis, Department of Electrical Engineering, Stanford University, June 1988.
8. J. Friedman, T. Hastie, and R. Tibshirani. Additive logistic regression: A statistical view of boosting. The Annals of Statistics, 28:337 – 374, 2000.
9. T. Hastie and R. Tibshirani. *Generalized Additive Models.* London: Chapman and Hall, 1990.
10. A. Kalai and R. Servedio. Boosting in the presence of Noise. *Proceedings of the thirty-fifth ACM symposium on theory of computing,* pages 195–205, 2003.
11. M. Kearns. Efficient noise-tolerant learning from statistical queries. *Journal of the ACM,* 45(6):983–1006, 1998.
12. M. Kearns and Y. Mansour. On the boosting ability of top-down decision tree learning algorithms. *Journal of Computer and System Sciences,* 58(1):109–128, 1999.
13. M. Kearns and R. Schapire. Efficient distribution-free learning of probabilistic concepts. *Journal of Computer and Systems Sciences,* 48:464-497, 1994.
14. R. Kohavi. Wrappers for Performance Enhancement and Oblivious Decision Graphs. Ph.D. dissertation, Comput. Sci. Depart., Stanford Univ., Stanford, CA, 1995.
15. Y. Mansour and D. McAllester. Boosting using branching programs. *Journal of Computer and System Sciences,* 64(1):103–112, 2002.
16. P. McCullagh and J. Nelder. *Generalized Linear Models,* Chapman and Hall, London, 1989.
17. H. Royden. *Real Analysis,* 3rd edition. Macmillan, New York, 1988.
18. J. Oliver. Decision graphs – an extension of decision trees. In *Proceedings of the Fourth International Workshop on Artificial Intelligence and Statistics,* pp. 334-350, 1993.

19. J. Oliver, D. Dowe, and C. Wallace. Inferring decision graphs using the minimum message length principle. In *Proceedings of the 5th Austrailian Conference on Artificial Intelligence*, pp. 361-367, 1992.
20. R. Schapire. The strength of weak learnability. *Machine Learning*, 5(2):197–227, 1990.
21. M. Shipp, D. Harrington, J. Anderson, J. Armitage, G. Bonadonna, G. Brittinger, et al. A predictive model for aggressive non-Hodgkin's lymphoma. The International Non-Hodgkin's Lymphoma Prognostic Factors Project. *New England Journal of Medicine* 329(14):987-94, 1993.
22. L. Valiant. A theory of the learnable. *Communications of the ACM*, 27(11):1134-1142, 1984.
23. B. Zadrony and C. Elkan. Obtaining calibrated probability estimates from decision trees and naive Bayesian classifiers. In *Proceedings of the Eighteenth International Conference on Machine Learning*, pages 609–616, 2001.

A Proof of Lemma 1

Using the facts that $w_\ell = w_{\ell_0} + w_{\ell_1}$ and $q_\ell = (w_{\ell_0} q_{\ell_0} + w_{\ell_1} q_{\ell_1})/w_\ell$, the change in G is,

$$\begin{aligned}\Delta G &= w_{\ell_0} q_{\ell_0}^2 + w_{\ell_1} q_{\ell_1}^2 - w_\ell \left(\frac{w_{\ell_0} q_{\ell_0} + w_{\ell_1} q_{\ell_1}}{w_\ell}\right)^2 \\ &= \frac{(w_{\ell_0} + w_{\ell_1})(w_{\ell_0} q_{\ell_0}^2 + w_{\ell_1} q_{\ell_1}^2) - (w_{\ell_0} q_{\ell_0} + w_{\ell_1} q_{\ell_1})^2}{w_\ell} \\ &= \frac{w_{\ell_0} w_{\ell_1} (q_{\ell_0} - q_{\ell_1})^2}{w_\ell}.\end{aligned}$$

Next,

$$\begin{aligned}\mathrm{cov}_{\mathcal{D}_\ell}(f,h) &= E_{\mathcal{D}_\ell}[f(x)h(x)] - E_{\mathcal{D}_\ell}[f(x)]E_{\mathcal{D}_\ell}[h(x)] \\ &= \frac{w_{\ell_1}}{w_\ell} q_{\ell_1} - \frac{w_{\ell_0} q_{\ell_0} + w_{\ell_1} q_{\ell_1}}{w_\ell} \frac{w_{\ell_1}}{w_\ell} \\ &= \frac{(w_{\ell_0} + w_{\ell_1}) w_{\ell_1} q_{\ell_1} - (w_{\ell_0} q_{\ell_0} + w_{\ell_1} q_{\ell_1}) w_{\ell_1}}{w_\ell^2} \\ &= \frac{w_{\ell_0} w_{\ell_1} (q_{\ell_1} - q_{\ell_0})}{w_\ell^2}.\end{aligned}$$

Meanwhile, since h is boolean,

$$\mathrm{var}_{D_\ell}(h) = P_{\mathcal{D}_\ell}[h(x)=0] P_{\mathcal{D}_\ell}[h(x)=1] = \frac{w_{\ell_0}}{w_\ell}\frac{w_{\ell_1}}{w_\ell} = \frac{w_{\ell_0} w_{\ell_1}}{w_\ell^2}$$

Finally, $\Delta G = w_\ell \mathrm{cov}_{D_\ell}(f,h)^2 / \mathrm{var}_{D_\ell}(h) = w_\ell \mathrm{cor}_{D_\ell}(f,h)^2 \mathrm{var}_{D_\ell}(f)$. □

B Thresholds

Lemma 6. *Let $u \in [0,1]$ be a random variable and $v \in \mathbb{R}$ be a positively correlated random variable. Then there exists some threshold $t \in \mathbb{R}$ such that the indicator random variable $v_t = I(v \geq t)$ has correlation near $\rho_{uv} > 0$,*

$$\rho_{uv_t} > \frac{\rho_{uv}}{2 + 2\sqrt{2\log(2/(\rho_{uv}\sigma_u))}}.$$

Proof. WLOG let v be a standard random variable, i.e. $\mu_v = 0$ and $\sigma_v = 1$. The main idea is to argue, for $\tau = 2/\sigma_{uv}$, that

$$\int_{-\tau}^{\tau} \sigma_{uv_t} dt > \frac{\sigma_{uv}}{2 + 2\sqrt{2\log(1/\tau)}} \int_{-\tau}^{\tau} \sigma_{v_t} dt. \tag{2}$$

This implies that there exists a $t \in [-\tau, \tau]$ for which the above holds instantaneously, i.e.,

$$\sigma_{uv_t} > \frac{\sigma_{uv}}{2 + 2\sqrt{2\log(1/\tau)}} \sigma_{v_t}$$
$$\frac{\sigma_{uv_t}}{\sigma_u \sigma_{v_t}} > \frac{\sigma_{uv}}{\sigma_u(2 + 2\sqrt{2\log(1/\tau)})}$$

The above is equivalent to the lemma for $\tau = 2/\sigma_{uv} = 2/(\rho_{uv}\sigma_u)$. Thus it suffices to show (2).

First, a simple translation can bring $\mu_u = 0$. This will not change any correlation, so WLOG let us assume that $\mu_u = 0$ and that $u \in (-1,1)$. This makes calculations easier because now $\sigma_{uv_t} = E[uv_t] - \mu_u \mu_{v_t} = E[uv_t]$ for all t. Define the random variable w by,

$$w = \int_{-\tau}^{\tau} v_t dt - \tau = \begin{cases} \tau & \text{if } v \geq \tau \\ v & \text{if } v \in (-\tau, \tau) \\ -\tau & \text{if } v \leq -\tau \end{cases}$$

Then we have, by linearity of expectation,

$$\int_{-\tau}^{\tau} \sigma_{uv_t} dt = \int_{-\tau}^{\tau} E[uv_t] dt = E\left[u \int_{-\tau}^{\tau} v_t dt\right] = E[u(w + \tau)] = E[uw].$$

Next, notice that $|v - w| \leq |v|$ and, if $v - w \neq 0$ then $|v| \geq \tau$. This means that $|v - w| \leq v^2/\tau$. Consequently, $E[u(v-w)] < E[|v-w|] \leq E[v^2/\tau] = 1/\tau$, so,

$$\int_{-\tau}^{\tau} \sigma_{uv_t} dt = E[uw] = E[uv] - E[u(v-w)] > E[uv] - \frac{1}{\tau} = \frac{\sigma_{uv}}{2}. \tag{3}$$

For the second part, by the Cauchy-Schwartz inequality,

$$\int_1^{\tau} \sigma_{v_t} dt = \int_1^{\tau} \sigma_{v_t} \sqrt{t} \cdot \frac{1}{\sqrt{t}} dt \leq \sqrt{\int_1^{\tau} \sigma_{v_t}^2 t dt \int_1^{\tau} \frac{1}{t} dt}.$$

Now, $\sigma_{v_t}^2 = E[v_t^2] - E[v_t]^2 = P[v \geq t]P[v < t]$. The above is at most:

$$\sqrt{\int_1^\tau P[v \geq t]tdt \cdot \log(1/\tau)} = \sqrt{\int_1^{\tau^2} P[v \geq \sqrt{y}]\frac{1}{2}dy \cdot \log(1/\tau)}.$$

For a nonnegative random variable A, $E[A] = \int_0^\infty P[A \geq y]dy$. Thus

$$\int_1^{\tau^2} P[v \geq \sqrt{y}]dy \leq \int_0^\infty P[v^2 \geq y]dy = E[v^2] = 1.$$

By symmetry, we get

$$\int_{-\tau}^{\tau} \sigma_{v_t}dt \leq \int_{-1}^{1} \sigma_{v_t}dt + 2\sqrt{\frac{\log(1/\tau)}{2}} \leq 1 + \sqrt{2\log(1/\tau)}. \quad (4)$$

Equations (4) and (3) imply (2), and we are done. □

C Facts About Regression Graphs

It is easy to see that $\mu_y = \mu_f = \mu_R = \sum_\ell w_\ell q_\ell$. Also,

$$\begin{aligned}
\epsilon(R) &= E[f(x)^2] + E[R(x)^2] - 2E[f(x)R(x)] \\
&= E[f(x)^2] - E[R(x)^2] = \sigma_f^2 - \sigma_R^2 \\
&= E[f(x)^2] - \sum_\ell w_\ell(q_\ell^2 - 2q_\ell^2) \\
&= \sigma_f^2 + \mu_f^2 - \sum_\ell w_\ell q_\ell^2.
\end{aligned}$$

Since $\sum w_\ell = 1$, we have $\sum aw_\ell + bw_\ell q_\ell$ is constant across graphs. So $\sum aw_\ell + bw_\ell q_\ell - cw_\ell q_\ell^2$ for $c > 0$ as an objective function is equivalent to using $-\sum w_\ell q_\ell^2$. Finally, $\mathrm{cov}(R, f) = \sigma_R^2 = \sum w_\ell q_\ell^2 - \mu_R^2 = \sum w_\ell q_\ell^2 - \mu_f^2$, implying that $\rho_{rf} = \sigma_R/\sigma_f = \sqrt{\sum w_\ell q_\ell^2 - \mu_f^2}/\sigma_f = \sqrt{1 - \epsilon(R)/\sigma_f^2}$

Boosting Based on a Smooth Margin*

Cynthia Rudin[1], Robert E. Schapire[2], and Ingrid Daubechies[1]

[1] Princeton University, Program in Applied and Computational Mathematics
Fine Hall, Washington Road, Princeton, NJ 08544-1000
{crudin,ingrid}@math.princeton.edu
[2] Princeton University, Department of Computer Science
35 Olden St., Princeton, NJ 08544
schapire@cs.princeton.edu

Abstract. We study two boosting algorithms, *Coordinate Ascent Boosting* and *Approximate Coordinate Ascent Boosting*, which are explicitly designed to produce maximum margins. To derive these algorithms, we introduce a smooth approximation of the margin that one can maximize in order to produce a maximum margin classifier. Our first algorithm is simply coordinate ascent on this function, involving a line search at each step. We then make a simple approximation of this line search to reveal our second algorithm. These algorithms are proven to asymptotically achieve maximum margins, and we provide two convergence rate calculations. The second calculation yields a faster rate of convergence than the first, although the first gives a more explicit (still fast) rate. These algorithms are very similar to AdaBoost in that they are based on coordinate ascent, easy to implement, and empirically tend to converge faster than other boosting algorithms. Finally, we attempt to understand AdaBoost in terms of our smooth margin, focusing on cases where AdaBoost exhibits cyclic behavior.

1 Introduction

Boosting is currently a popular and successful technique for classification. The first practical boosting algorithm was AdaBoost, developed by Freund and Schapire [4]. The goal of boosting is to construct a "strong" classifier using only a training set and a "weak" learning algorithm. A weak learning algorithm produces "weak" classifiers, which are only required to classify somewhat better than a random guess. For an introduction, see the review paper of Schapire [13].

In practice, AdaBoost often tends not to overfit (only slightly in the limit [5]), and performs remarkably well on test data. The leading explanation for AdaBoost's ability to generalize is the *margin theory*. According to this theory, the margin can be viewed as a confidence measure of a classifier's predictive ability. This theory is based on (loose) generalization bounds, e.g., the bounds of Schapire et al. [14] and Koltchinskii and Panchenko [6]. Although the empirical

* This research was partially supported by NSF Grants IIS-0325500, DMS-9810783, and ANI-0085984.

J. Shawe-Taylor and Y. Singer (Eds.): COLT 2004, LNAI 3120, pp. 502–517, 2004.

success of a boosting algorithm depends on many factors (e.g., the type of data and how noisy it is, the capacity of the weak learning algorithm, the number of boosting iterations before stopping, other means of regularization, entire margin distribution), the margin theory does provide a reasonable qualitative explanation (though not a complete explanation) of AdaBoost's success, both empirically and theoretically. However, AdaBoost has not been shown to achieve the largest possible margin. In fact, the opposite has been recently proved, namely that AdaBoost may converge to a solution with margin significantly below the maximum value [11]. This was proved for specific cases where AdaBoost exhibits cyclic behavior; such behavior is common when there are very few "support vectors".

Since AdaBoost's performance is not well understood, a number of other boosting algorithms have emerged that directly aim to maximize the margin. Many of these algorithms are not as easy to implement as AdaBoost, or require a significant amount of calculation at each step, e.g., the solution of a linear program (LP-AdaBoost [5]), an optimization over a non-convex function (DOOM [7]) or a huge number of very small steps (ϵ-boosting, where convergence to a maximum margin solution has not been proven, even as the step size vanishes [10]). These extra calculations may slow down the convergence rate dramatically. Thus, we compare our new algorithms with arc-gv [2] and AdaBoost* [9]; these algorithms are as simple to program as AdaBoost and have convergence guarantees with respect to the margin. Our new algorithms are more aggressive than both arc-gv and AdaBoost*, providing an explanation for their empirically faster convergence rate.

In terms of theoretical rate guarantees, our new algorithms converge to a maximum margin solution with a polynomial convergence rate. Namely, within $poly(1/\epsilon)$ iterations, they produce a classifier whose margin is within ϵ of the maximum possible margin. Arc-gv is proven to converge to a maximum margin solution asymptotically [2,8], but we are not aware of any proven convergence rate. AdaBoost* [9] converges to a solution within ϵ of the maximum margin in $2(\log_2 m)/\epsilon^2$ steps (where the user specifies a fixed value of ϵ); there is a tradeoff between user-determined accuracy and convergence rate for this algorithm. In practice, AdaBoost* converges very slowly since it is not aggressive; it takes small steps (though it has the nice convergence rate guarantee stated above). In fact, if the weak learner always finds a weak classifier with a large edge (i.e., if the weak learning algorithm performs well on the weighted training data), the convergence of AdaBoost* can be especially slow.

The two new boosting algorithms we introduce (which are presented in [12] without analysis) are based on coordinate ascent. For AdaBoost, the fact that it is a minimization algorithm based on coordinate descent does not imply convergence to a maximum margin solution. For our new algorithms, we can directly use the fact that they are coordinate ascent algorithms to help show convergence to a maximum margin solution, since they make progress towards increasing a differentiable approximation of the margin (a "smooth margin function") at every iteration.

To summarize, the advantages of our new algorithms, *Coordinate Ascent Boosting* and *Approximate Coordinate Ascent Boosting* are as follows:

- They empirically tend to converge faster than both arc-gv and AdaBoost*.
- They provably converge to a maximum margin solution asymptotically. This convergence is robust, in that we do not require the weak learning algorithm to produce the best possible classifier at every iteration; only a sufficiently good classifier is required.
- They have convergence rate guarantees that are polynomial in $1/\epsilon$.
- They are as easy to implement as AdaBoost, arc-gv, and AdaBoost*.
- These algorithms have theoretical and intuitive justification: they make progress with respect to a smooth version of the margin, and operate via coordinate ascent.

Finally, we use our smooth margin function to analyze AdaBoost. Since AdaBoost's good generalization properties are not completely explained by the margin theory, and still remain somewhat mysterious, we study properties of AdaBoost via our smooth margin function, focusing on cases where cyclic behavior occurs. "Cyclic behavior for AdaBoost" means the weak learning algorithm repeatedly chooses the same sequence of weak classifiers, and the weight vectors repeat with a given period. This has been proven to occur in special cases, and occurs often in low dimensions (i.e., when there are few "support vectors") [11].

Our results concerning AdaBoost and our smooth margin are as follows: first, the value of the smooth margin increases if and only if AdaBoost takes a large enough step. Second, the value of the smooth margin must decrease for at least one iteration of a cycle unless all edge values are identical. Third, if all edges in a cycle are identical, then support vectors are misclassified by the same number of weak classifiers during the cycle.

Here is the outline: in Section 2, we introduce our notation and the AdaBoost algorithm. In Section 3, we describe the smooth margin function that our algorithms are based on. In Section 4, we describe Coordinate Ascent Boosting (Algorithm 1) and Approximate Coordinate Ascent Boosting (Algorithm 2), and in Section 5, the convergence of these algorithms is discussed. Experimental trials on artificial data are presented in Section 6 to illustrate the comparison with other algorithms. In Section 7, we show connections between AdaBoost and our smooth margin function.

2 Notation and Introduction to AdaBoost

The training set consists of examples with labels $\{(\mathbf{x}_i, y_i)\}_{i=1,...,m}$, where $(\mathbf{x}_i, y_i) \in \mathcal{X} \times \{-1, 1\}$. The space $\mathcal{X}$ never appears explicitly in our calculations. Let $\mathcal{H} = \{h_1, ..., h_n\}$ be the set of *all possible* weak classifiers that can be produced by the weak learning algorithm, where $h_j : \mathcal{X} \to \{1, -1\}$. We assume that if h_j appears in $\mathcal{H}$, then $-h_j$ also appears in $\mathcal{H}$ (i.e., $\mathcal{H}$ is symmetric). Since our classifiers are binary, and since we restrict our attention to their behavior on a finite training set, we can assume that n is finite. We think of n as being large, $m \ll n$, so a gradient descent calculation over an n dimensional space is impractical; hence AdaBoost uses coordinate descent instead, where only one weak classifier is chosen at each iteration.

We define an $m \times n$ matrix $\mathbf{M}$ where $M_{ij} = y_i h_j(\mathbf{x}_i)$, i.e., $M_{ij} = +1$ if training example i is classified correctly by weak classifier h_j, and -1 otherwise. We assume that no column of $\mathbf{M}$ has all $+1$'s, that is, no weak classifier can classify all the training examples correctly. (Otherwise the learning problem is trivial.) Although $\mathbf{M}$ is too large to be explicitly constructed in practice, mathematically, it acts as the only "input" to AdaBoost, containing all the necessary information about the weak learner and training examples.

AdaBoost computes a set of coefficients over the weak classifiers. The (unnormalized) coefficient vector at iteration t is denoted $\boldsymbol{\lambda}_t$. Since the algorithms we describe all have positive increments, we take $\boldsymbol{\lambda} \in \mathbb{R}_+^n$. We define a seminorm by $|||\boldsymbol{\lambda}||| := \min_{\boldsymbol{\lambda}'}\{\|\boldsymbol{\lambda}'\|_1$ such that $\forall j : \lambda_j - \lambda_{\tilde{j}} = \lambda'_j - \lambda'_{\tilde{j}}\}$ where $\tilde{j}$ is the index for $-h_j$, and define $s(\boldsymbol{\lambda}) := \sum_{j=1}^n \lambda_j$, noting $s(\boldsymbol{\lambda}) \geq |||\boldsymbol{\lambda}|||$. For the (non-negative) vectors $\boldsymbol{\lambda}_t$ generated by AdaBoost, we will denote $s_t := s(\boldsymbol{\lambda}_t)$. The final combined classifier that AdaBoost outputs is $f_{Ada} = \sum_{j=1}^n (\lambda_{t_{max},j}/|||\boldsymbol{\lambda}_{t_{max}}|||)h_j$. The *margin of training example* i is defined to be $y_i f_{Ada}(\mathbf{x}_i)$, or equivalently, $(\mathbf{M}\boldsymbol{\lambda})_i/|||\boldsymbol{\lambda}|||$.

A boosting algorithm maintains a distribution, or set of weights, over the training examples that is updated at each iteration, which is denoted $\mathbf{d}_t \in \Delta_m$, and $\mathbf{d}_t^T$ is its transpose. Here, Δ_m denotes the simplex of m-dimensional vectors with non-negative entries that sum to 1. At each iteration t, a weak classifier h_{j_t} is selected by the weak learning algorithm. The *probability of error* of h_{j_t} at time t on the weighted training examples is $d_- := \sum_{\{i:M_{ij_t}=-1\}} d_{t,i}$. Also, denote $d_+ := 1 - d_-$, and define $\mathcal{I}_+ := \{i : M_{ij_t} = +1\}$ and $\mathcal{I}_- := \{i : M_{ij_t} = -1\}$. Note that $d_+, d_-, \mathcal{I}_+$, and $\mathcal{I}_-$ depend on t; the iteration number will be clear from the context. The *edge* of weak classifier j_t at time t is $r_t := (\mathbf{d}_t^T\mathbf{M})_{j_t}$, which can be written as $r_t = (\mathbf{d}_t^T\mathbf{M})_{j_t} = \sum_{i\in\mathcal{I}_+} d_{t,i} - \sum_{i\in\mathcal{I}_-} d_{t,i} = d_+ - d_- = 1 - 2d_-$. Thus, a smaller edge indicates a higher probability of error. Note that $d_+ = (1 + r_t)/2$ and $d_- = (1 - r_t)/2$. Also define $\gamma_t := \tanh^{-1} r_t$.

We wish our learning algorithms to have robust convergence, so we will not require the weak learning algorithm to produce the weak classifier with the largest possible edge value at each iteration. Rather, we only require a weak classifier whose edge exceeds ρ, where ρ is the largest possible margin that can be attained for $\mathbf{M}$, i.e., we use the "non-optimal" case for our analysis. AdaBoost in the "optimal case" means $j_t \in \text{argmax}_j(\mathbf{d}_t^T\mathbf{M})_j$, and AdaBoost in the "non-optimal" case means $j_t \in \{j : (\mathbf{d}_t^T\mathbf{M})_j \geq \rho\}$.

To achieve the best indication of a small probability of error (for margin-based bounds), our goal is to find a $\tilde{\boldsymbol{\lambda}} \in \Delta_n$ that maximizes the minimum margin over training examples, $\min_i (\mathbf{M}\tilde{\boldsymbol{\lambda}})_i$ (or equivalently $\min_i y_i f_{Ada}(\mathbf{x}_i)$), i.e., we wish to find a vector $\tilde{\boldsymbol{\lambda}} \in \text{argmax}_{\bar{\boldsymbol{\lambda}}\in\Delta_n} \min_i(\mathbf{M}\bar{\boldsymbol{\lambda}})_i = \text{argmax}_{\boldsymbol{\lambda}\in\mathbb{R}^n} \min_i(\mathbf{M}\boldsymbol{\lambda})_i/|||\boldsymbol{\lambda}|||$. We call the minimum margin over training examples (i.e., $\min_i(\mathbf{M}\boldsymbol{\lambda})_i/|||\boldsymbol{\lambda}|||$) the *margin* of classifier $\boldsymbol{\lambda}$, denoted $\mu(\boldsymbol{\lambda})$. Any training example that achieves this minimum margin is a *support vector*. Due to the von Neumann Min-Max

Theorem, $\min_{\mathbf{d}\in\Delta_m}\max_j(\mathbf{d}^T\mathbf{M})_j = \max_{\bar{\boldsymbol{\lambda}}\in\Delta_n}\min_i(\mathbf{M}\bar{\boldsymbol{\lambda}})_i$. We denote this value by ρ.

Figure 1 shows pseudocode for AdaBoost. At each iteration, the distribution $\mathbf{d}_t$ is updated and renormalized (Step 3a), classifier j_t with sufficiently large edge is selected (Step 3b), and the weight of that classifier is updated (Step 3e).

1. **Input:** Matrix $\mathbf{M}$, No. of iterations t_{max}
2. **Initialize:** $\lambda_{1,j} = 0$ for $j = 1, ..., n$
3. **Loop for** $t = 1, ..., t_{max}$
   a) $d_{t,i} = e^{-(\mathbf{M}\boldsymbol{\lambda}_t)_i} / \sum_{\tilde{i}=1}^m e^{-(\mathbf{M}\boldsymbol{\lambda}_t)_{\tilde{i}}}$ for $i = 1, ..., m$
   b) $\begin{cases} j_t \in \text{argmax}_j(\mathbf{d}_t^T\mathbf{M})_j & \text{“optimal” case} \\ j_t \in \{j : (\mathbf{d}_t^T\mathbf{M})_j > \rho\} & \text{“non-optimal” case} \end{cases}$
   c) $r_t = (\mathbf{d}_t^T\mathbf{M})_{j_t}$
   d) $\alpha_t = \frac{1}{2}\ln\left(\frac{1+r_t}{1-r_t}\right)$
   e) $\boldsymbol{\lambda}_{t+1} = \boldsymbol{\lambda}_t + \alpha_t\mathbf{e}_{j_t}$, where $\mathbf{e}_{j_t}$ is 1 in position j_t and 0 elsewhere.
4. **Output:** $\boldsymbol{\lambda}_{t_{max}}/|||\boldsymbol{\lambda}_{t_{max}}|||$

Fig. 1. Pseudocode for the AdaBoost algorithm.

AdaBoost is known to be a coordinate descent algorithm for minimizing $F(\boldsymbol{\lambda}) := \sum_{i=1}^m e^{-(\mathbf{M}\boldsymbol{\lambda})_i}$ [1]. The proof (for the optimal case) is that the choice of weak classifier j_t is given by: $j_t \in \text{argmax}_j \left[-dF(\boldsymbol{\lambda}_t + \alpha\mathbf{e}_j)/d\alpha\Big|_{\alpha=0}\right] = \text{argmax}_j(\mathbf{d}_t^T\mathbf{M})_j$, and the step size AdaBoost chooses at iteration t is α_t, where α_t satisfies the equation for the line search along direction j_t: $0 = -dF(\boldsymbol{\lambda}_t + \alpha_t\mathbf{e}_{j_t})/d\alpha_t$. Convergence in the non-separable case is fully understood [3]. In the separable case ($\rho > 0$), the minimum value of F is 0 and occurs as $|||\boldsymbol{\lambda}||| \to \infty$; this tells us nothing about the value of the margin, i.e., an algorithm which simply minimizes F can achieve an arbitrarily bad margin. So it must be the *process* of coordinate descent which awards AdaBoost its ability to increase margins, not simply AdaBoost's ability to minimize F.

3 The Smooth Margin Function $G(\boldsymbol{\lambda})$

We wish to consider a function that, unlike F, actually tells us about the value of the margin. Our new function G is defined for $\boldsymbol{\lambda} \in \mathbb{R}_+^n$, $s(\boldsymbol{\lambda}) > 1$ by:

$$G(\boldsymbol{\lambda}) := \frac{-\ln F(\boldsymbol{\lambda})}{s(\boldsymbol{\lambda})} = \frac{-\ln\left(\sum_{i=1}^m e^{-(\mathbf{M}\boldsymbol{\lambda})_i}\right)}{\sum_j \lambda_j}. \tag{1}$$

One can think of G as a smooth approximation of the margin, since it depends on the entire margin distribution when $s(\boldsymbol{\lambda})$ is finite, and weights training examples with small margins much more highly than examples with larger margins. The function G also bears a resemblance to the objective implicitly used for ϵ-boosting [10]. Note that since $s(\lambda) \geq |||\boldsymbol{\lambda}|||$, we have $G(\boldsymbol{\lambda}) \leq -(\ln F(\boldsymbol{\lambda}))/|||\boldsymbol{\lambda}|||$. Lemma 1 (parts of which appear in [12]) shows that G has many nice properties.

Lemma 1.

1. *$G(\boldsymbol{\lambda})$ is a concave function (but not necessarily strictly concave) in each "shell" where $s(\boldsymbol{\lambda})$ is fixed. In addition, $G(\boldsymbol{\lambda})$ becomes concave when $s(\boldsymbol{\lambda})$ becomes large.*
2. *$G(\boldsymbol{\lambda})$ becomes concave when $|||\boldsymbol{\lambda}|||$ becomes large.*
3. *As $|||\boldsymbol{\lambda}||| \to \infty$, $-(\ln F(\boldsymbol{\lambda}))/|||\boldsymbol{\lambda}||| \to \mu(\boldsymbol{\lambda})$.*
4. *The value of $G(\boldsymbol{\lambda})$ increases radially, i.e., $dG(\boldsymbol{\lambda}(1+a))/da\Big|_{a=0} > 0$*

It follows from 3 and 4 that the maximum value of G is the maximum value of the margin, since for each $\boldsymbol{\lambda}$, we may construct a $\boldsymbol{\lambda}'$ such that $G(\boldsymbol{\lambda}') = -\ln F(\boldsymbol{\lambda})/|||\boldsymbol{\lambda}|||$. We omit the proofs of 1 and 4. Note that if $|||\boldsymbol{\lambda}|||$ is large, $s(\boldsymbol{\lambda})$ is large since $|||\boldsymbol{\lambda}||| \leq s(\boldsymbol{\lambda})$. Thus, 2 follows from 1.

Proof. (of property 3)

$$me^{-\mu(\boldsymbol{\lambda})|||\boldsymbol{\lambda}|||} = \sum_{i=1}^{m} e^{-\min_\ell (\mathbf{M}\boldsymbol{\lambda})_\ell} \geq \sum_{i=1}^{m} e^{-(\mathbf{M}\boldsymbol{\lambda})_i} > e^{-\min_i (\mathbf{M}\boldsymbol{\lambda})_i} = e^{-\mu(\boldsymbol{\lambda})|||\boldsymbol{\lambda}|||},$$

$$\text{hence,} \quad -(\ln m)/|||\boldsymbol{\lambda}||| + \mu(\boldsymbol{\lambda}) \leq -(\ln F(\boldsymbol{\lambda}))/|||\boldsymbol{\lambda}||| < \mu(\boldsymbol{\lambda}). \tag{2}$$

□

The properties of G shown in Lemma 1 outline the reasons why we choose to maximize G using coordinate ascent; namely, maximizing G leads to a maximum margin solution, and the region where G is near its maximum value is concave.

4 Derivation of Algorithms

We now suggest two boosting algorithms (derived without analysis in [12]) that aim to maximize the margin explicitly (like arc-gv and AdaBoost*) and are based on coordinate ascent (like AdaBoost). Our new algorithms choose the direction of ascent (value of j_t) using the same formula as AdaBoost, arc-gv, and AdaBoost*, i.e., $j_t \in \text{argmax}_j(\mathbf{d}_t^T\mathbf{M})_j$. Thus, our new algorithms require exactly the same type of weak learning algorithm.

To help with the analysis later, we will write recursive equations for F and G. The recursive equation for F (derived only using the definition) is:

$$F(\boldsymbol{\lambda}_t + \alpha \mathbf{e}_{j_t}) = \frac{\cosh(\gamma_t - \alpha)}{\cosh \gamma_t} F(\boldsymbol{\lambda}_t). \tag{3}$$

By definition of G, we know $-\ln F(\boldsymbol{\lambda}_t) = s_t G(\boldsymbol{\lambda}_t)$ and $-\ln F(\boldsymbol{\lambda}_t + \alpha \mathbf{e}_{j_t}) = (s_t + \alpha) G(\boldsymbol{\lambda}_t + \alpha \mathbf{e}_{j_t})$. From (3), we find a recursive equation for G:

$$(s_t + \alpha) G(\boldsymbol{\lambda}_t + \alpha \mathbf{e}_{j_t}) = -\ln F(\boldsymbol{\lambda}_t) - \ln\left(\frac{\cosh(\gamma_t - \alpha)}{\cosh \gamma_t}\right) = s_t G(\boldsymbol{\lambda}_t) + \int_{\gamma_t - \alpha}^{\gamma_t} \tanh u \, du. \tag{4}$$

We shall look at two different algorithms; in the first, we assign to α_t the value α that maximizes $G(\boldsymbol{\lambda}_t+\alpha\mathbf{e}_{j_t})$, which requires solving an implicit equation. In the second algorithm, inspired by the first, we pick a value for α_t that can be computed in a straightforward way, even though it is not a maximizer of $G(\boldsymbol{\lambda}_t+\alpha\mathbf{e}_{j_t})$. In both cases, the algorithm starts by simply running AdaBoost until $G(\boldsymbol{\lambda})$ becomes positive, which must happen (in the separable case) since:

Lemma 2. *In the separable case (where $\rho > 0$), AdaBoost achieves a positive value for $G(\boldsymbol{\lambda}_t)$ in at most $\lceil -2\ln F(\boldsymbol{\lambda}_1)/\ln(1-\rho^2)\rceil + 1$ iterations.*

The proof of Lemma 2 (which is omitted) uses (3). Denote $\boldsymbol{\lambda}_1^{[1]}, ..., \boldsymbol{\lambda}_t^{[1]}$ to be a sequence of coefficient vectors generated by Algorithm 1, and $\boldsymbol{\lambda}_1^{[2]}, ..., \boldsymbol{\lambda}_t^{[2]}$ to be generated by Algorithm 2. Similarly, we distinguish sequences $\alpha_t^{[1]}$ and $\alpha_t^{[2]}$, $g_t^{[1]} := G(\boldsymbol{\lambda}_t^{[1]})$, $g_t^{[2]} := G(\boldsymbol{\lambda}_t^{[2]})$, $s_t^{[1]}$, and $s_t^{[2]}$. Sometimes we compare the behavior of Algorithms 1 and 2 based on one iteration (from t to $t+1$) as if they had started from the same coefficient vector at iteration t; we denote this vector by $\boldsymbol{\lambda}_t$. When both Algorithms 1 and 2 satisfy a set of equations, we will remove the superscripts $^{[1]}$ and $^{[2]}$. Although sequences such as j_t, r_t, γ_t, and d_t are also different for Algorithms 1 and 2, we leave the notation without the superscript.

4.1 Algorithm 1: Coordinate Ascent Boosting

Rather than considering coordinate descent on F as in AdaBoost, let us consider coordinate ascent on G. In what follows, we will use only positive values of G, as we have justified above. The choice of direction j_t at iteration t (in the optimal case) obeys: $j_t \in \operatorname{argmax}_j dG(\boldsymbol{\lambda}_t^{[1]}+\alpha\mathbf{e}_j)/d\alpha\Big|_{\alpha=0}$, that is,

$$j_t \in \operatorname*{argmax}_j \left[\frac{\sum_{i=1}^m e^{-(\mathbf{M}\boldsymbol{\lambda}_t^{[1]})_i} M_{ij}}{F(\boldsymbol{\lambda}_t^{[1]})}\right] \frac{1}{s_t^{[1]}} + \frac{\ln(F(\boldsymbol{\lambda}_t^{[1]}))}{\left(s_t^{[1]}\right)^2}.$$

Of these two terms on the right, the second term does not depend on j, and the first term is simply a constant times $(\mathbf{d}_t^T\mathbf{M})_j$. Thus the same direction will be chosen here as for AdaBoost. The "non-optimal" setting we define for this algorithm will be the same as AdaBoost's, so Step 3b of this new algorithm will be the same as AdaBoost's.

To determine the step size, ideally we would like to maximize $G(\boldsymbol{\lambda}_t^{[1]}+\alpha\mathbf{e}_{j_t})$ with respect to α, i.e., we will define $\alpha_t^{[1]}$ to obey $dG(\boldsymbol{\lambda}_t^{[1]}+\alpha\mathbf{e}_{j_t})/d\alpha = 0$ for $\alpha = \alpha_t^{[1]}$. Differentiating (4) with respect to α (while incorporating $dG(\boldsymbol{\lambda}_t^{[1]}+\alpha\mathbf{e}_{j_t})/d\alpha = 0$) gives the following condition for $\alpha_t^{[1]}$:

$$G(\boldsymbol{\lambda}_{t+1}^{[1]}) = G(\boldsymbol{\lambda}_t^{[1]}+\alpha_t^{[1]}\mathbf{e}_{j_t}) = \tanh(\gamma_t - \alpha_t^{[1]}). \qquad (5)$$

There is not a nice analytical solution for $\alpha_t^{[1]}$, but minimization of $G(\boldsymbol{\lambda}_t^{[1]}+\alpha\mathbf{e}_{j_t})$ is 1-dimensional so it can be performed quickly. Hence we have defined the first of our new boosting algorithms: coordinate ascent on G, implementing a line search at each iteration. To clarify the line search step at iteration t using (5) and (4), we use $G(\boldsymbol{\lambda}_t^{[1]})$, γ_t, and $s_t^{[1]}$ to solve for $\alpha_t^{[1]}$ that satisfies:

$$s_t^{[1]} G(\boldsymbol{\lambda}_t^{[1]}) + \ln\left(\frac{\cosh \gamma_t}{\cosh(\gamma_t - \alpha_t^{[1]})}\right) = (s_t^{[1]} + \alpha_t^{[1]}) \tanh(\gamma_t - \alpha_t^{[1]}). \tag{6}$$

Summarizing, we define Algorithm 1 as follows:

- First, use AdaBoost (Figure 1) until $G(\boldsymbol{\lambda}_t^{[1]})$ defined by (1) is positive. At this point, replace Step 3d of AdaBoost as prescribed: $\alpha_t^{[1]}$ equals the (unique) solution of (6). Proceed, using this modified iterative procedure.

Let us rearrange the equation slightly. Using the notation $g_{t+1}^{[1]} := G(\boldsymbol{\lambda}_{t+1}^{[1]})$ in (5), we find that $\alpha_t^{[1]}$ satisfies the following (implicitly):

$$\alpha_t^{[1]} = \gamma_t - \tanh^{-1}(g_{t+1}^{[1]}) = \tanh^{-1} r_t - \tanh^{-1}(g_{t+1}^{[1]}) = \frac{1}{2} \ln\left[\frac{1+r_t}{1-r_t} \frac{1-g_{t+1}^{[1]}}{1+g_{t+1}^{[1]}}\right]. \tag{7}$$

For any $\boldsymbol{\lambda} \in \mathbb{R}_+^n$, from (2) and since $|||\boldsymbol{\lambda}||| \leq s(\boldsymbol{\lambda})$, we have $G(\boldsymbol{\lambda}) < \rho$. Consequently, $g_{t+1}^{[1]} < \rho \leq r_t$, so $\alpha_t^{[1]}$ is strictly positive. On the other hand, since $G(\boldsymbol{\lambda}_{t+1}^{[1]}) \geq G(\boldsymbol{\lambda}_t^{[1]})$, we again have $G(\boldsymbol{\lambda}_{t+1}^{[1]}) > 0$, and thus $\alpha_t^{[1]} \leq \gamma_t$.

4.2 Algorithm 2: Approximate Coordinate Ascent Boosting

The second of our two new boosting algorithms avoids the line search of Algorithm 1, and is even slightly more aggressive. It performs very similarly to Algorithm 1 in our experiments. To define this algorithm, we consider the following approximate solution to the maximization problem (5):

$$G(\boldsymbol{\lambda}_t^{[2]}) = \tanh(\gamma_t - \alpha_t^{[2]}), \quad \text{or more explicitly,} \tag{8}$$

$$\alpha_t^{[2]} = \gamma_t - \tanh^{-1}(g_t^{[2]}) = \tanh^{-1} r_t - \tanh^{-1}(g_t^{[2]}) = \frac{1}{2} \ln\left[\frac{1+r_t}{1-r_t} \frac{1-g_t^{[2]}}{1+g_t^{[2]}}\right]. \tag{9}$$

This update still yields an increase in G. (This can be shown using (4) and the monotonicity of tanh.) Summarizing, we define Algorithm 2 as the iterative procedure of AdaBoost (Figure 1) with one change:

- Replace Step 3d of AdaBoost as follows:

$$\alpha_t^{[2]} = \frac{1}{2} \ln\left(\frac{1+r_t}{1-r_t} \frac{1-g_t^{[2]}}{1+g_t^{[2]}}\right), g_t^{[2]} := \max\{0, G(\boldsymbol{\lambda}_t^{[2]})\},$$

where G is defined in (1). (Note that we could also have written the procedure in the same way as for Algorithm 1. As long as $G(\boldsymbol{\lambda}_t^{[2]}) \leq 0$, this update is the same as in AdaBoost.)

Algorithm 2 is slightly more aggressive than Algorithm 1, in the sense that it picks a larger relative step size α_t, albeit not as large as the step size defined by AdaBoost itself. If Algorithm 1 and Algorithm 2 were started at the same position $\boldsymbol{\lambda}_t$, with $g_t := G(\boldsymbol{\lambda}_t)$, then Algorithm 2 would always take a slightly larger step than Algorithm 1; since $g_{t+1}^{[1]} > g_t$, we can see from (7) and (9) that $\alpha_t^{[1]} < \alpha_t^{[2]}$.

As a remark, if we use the updates of Algorithms 1 or 2 from the start, they would also reach a positive margin quickly. In fact, after at most $\ulcorner 2 \ln F(\boldsymbol{\lambda}_1)/[-\ln\,(1-\rho^2) + \ln(1-G(\boldsymbol{\lambda}_1))]\urcorner + 1$ iterations, $G(\boldsymbol{\lambda}_t)$ would have a positive value.

5 Convergence of Algorithms

We will show convergence of Algorithms 1 and 2 to a maximum margin solution. Although there are many papers describing the convergence of specific classes of coordinate descent/ascent algorithms (e.g., [15]), this problem did not fit into any of the existing categories. The proofs below account for both the optimal and non-optimal cases, and for both algorithms.

One of the main results of this analysis is that both algorithms make significant progress at each iteration. In the next lemma, we only consider one increment, so we fix $\boldsymbol{\lambda}_t$ at iteration t and let $g_t := G(\boldsymbol{\lambda}_t)$, $s_t := \sum_j \lambda_{t,j}$. Then, denote $g_{t+1}^{[1]} := G(\boldsymbol{\lambda}_t + \alpha_t^{[1]})$, $g_{t+1}^{[2]} := G(\boldsymbol{\lambda}_t + \alpha_t^{[2]})$, $s_{t+1}^{[1]} := s_t + \alpha_t^{[1]}$, and $s_{t+1}^{[2]} := s_t + \alpha_t^{[2]}$.

Lemma 3.

$$g_{t+1}^{[1]} - g_t \geq \frac{\alpha_t^{[1]}(r_t - g_t)}{2s_{t+1}^{[1]}}, \quad \textit{and} \quad g_{t+1}^{[2]} - g_t \geq \frac{\alpha_t^{[2]}(r_t - g_t)}{2s_{t+1}^{[2]}}.$$

Proof. We start with Algorithm 2. First, we note that since tanh is concave on $\mathbb{R}_+$, we can lower bound tanh on an interval $(a,b) \subset (0,\infty)$ by the line connecting the points $(a, \tanh(a))$ and $(b, \tanh(b))$. Thus,

$$\int_{\gamma_t - \alpha_t^{[2]}}^{\gamma_t} \tanh u \, du \geq \frac{1}{2}\alpha_t^{[2]} \left[\tanh \gamma_t + \tanh(\gamma_t - \alpha_t^{[2]})\right] = \frac{1}{2}\alpha_t^{[2]}(r_t + g_t), \qquad (10)$$

where the last equality is from (8). Combining (10) with (4) yields:

$$s_{t+1}^{[2]} g_{t+1}^{[2]} \geq s_t g_t + \frac{1}{2}\alpha_t^{[2]}(r_t + g_t), \text{ thus } s_{t+1}^{[2]}(g_{t+1}^{[2]} - g_t) + \alpha_t^{[2]} g_t \geq \frac{1}{2}\alpha_t^{[2]}(r_t + g_t),$$

and the statement of the lemma follows (for Algorithm 2). By definition, $g_{t+1}^{[1]}$ is the maximum value of $G(\boldsymbol{\lambda}_t + \alpha \mathbf{e}_{j_t})$, so $g_{t+1}^{[1]} \geq g_{t+1}^{[2]}$. Because $\alpha/(s+\alpha) = 1 - s/(\alpha + s)$ increases with α and since $\alpha_t^{[1]} \leq \alpha_t^{[2]}$,

$$g_{t+1}^{[1]} - g_t \geq g_{t+1}^{[2]} - g_t \geq \left(\frac{\alpha_t^{[2]}}{s_{t+1}^{[2]}} \right) \frac{(r_t - g_t)}{2} \geq \left(\frac{\alpha_t^{[1]}}{s_{t+1}^{[1]}} \right) \frac{(r_t - g_t)}{2}. \qquad \square$$

Another important ingredient for our convergence proofs is that the step size does not increase too quickly; this is the main content of the next lemma. We now remove superscripts since each step holds for both algorithms.

Lemma 4. $\lim_{t\to\infty} \alpha_t / s_{t+1} \to 0$ *for both Algorithms 1 and 2.*

If $\lim_{t\to\infty} s_t$ is finite, the statement can be proved directly. If $\lim_{t\to\infty} s_t = \infty$, our proof (which is omitted) uses (4), (5) and (8).

At this point, it is possible to use Lemma 3 and Lemma 4, to show asymptotic convergence of both Algorithms 1 and 2 to a maximum margin solution; we defer this calculation to the longer version. In what follows, we shall prove two different results about the convergence rate. The first theorem gives an explicit a priori upper bound on the number of iterations needed to guarantee that $g_t^{[1]}$ or $g_t^{[2]}$ is within $\epsilon > 0$ of the maximum margin ρ. As is often the case for uniformly valid upper bounds, the convergence rate provided by this theorem is not optimal, in the sense that faster decay of $\rho - g_t$ can be proved for large t if one does not insist on explicit constants. The second convergence rate theorem provides such a result, stating that $\rho - g_t = \mathcal{O}\left(t^{-1/(3+\delta)}\right)$, or equivalently $\rho - g_t \leq \epsilon$ after $\mathcal{O}(\epsilon^{-(3+\delta)})$ iterations, where $\delta > 0$ can be arbitrarily small.

Both convergence rate theorems rely on estimates limiting the growth rate of α_t. Lemma 4 is one such estimate; because it is only an asymptotic estimate, our first convergence rate theorem requires the following uniformly valid lemma.

Lemma 5.

$$\alpha_t^{[1]} \leq c_1 + c_2 s_t^{[1]} \text{ and } \alpha_t^{[2]} \leq c_1 + c_2 s_t^{[2]}, \text{ where } c_1 = \frac{\ln 2}{1-\rho} \text{ and } c_2 = \frac{\rho}{1-\rho}. \tag{11}$$

Proof. Consider Algorithm 2. From (4),

$$s_{t+1}^{[2]} g_{t+1}^{[2]} - s_t^{[2]} g_t^{[2]} = \ln\cosh\gamma_t - \ln\cosh(\gamma_t - \alpha_t^{[2]}).$$

Because $\frac{1}{2}e^{\xi} \leq \frac{1}{2}\left(e^{\xi} + e^{-\xi}\right) = \cosh\xi \leq e^{\xi}$ for $\xi > 0$, we have $\xi - \ln 2 \leq \ln\cosh\xi \leq \xi$. Now,

$$s_{t+1}^{[2]} g_{t+1}^{[2]} - s_t^{[2]} g_t^{[2]} \geq \gamma_t - \ln 2 - (\gamma_t - \alpha_t^{[2]}), \text{ so}$$
$$\alpha_t^{[2]}(1-\rho) \leq \alpha_t^{[2]}(1 - g_{t+1}^{[2]}) \leq \ln 2 + s_t^{[2]}\left(g_{t+1}^{[2]} - g_t^{[2]}\right) \leq \ln 2 + \rho s_t^{[2]}.$$

Thus we directly find the statement of the lemma for Algorithm 2. A slight extension of this argument proves the statement for Algorithm 1. $\square$

Theorem 1. *(first convergence rate theorem) Suppose $R < 1$ is known to be an upper bound for ρ. Let $\tilde{1}$ be the iteration at which G becomes positive. Then both the margin $\mu(\boldsymbol{\lambda}_t)$ and the value of $G(\boldsymbol{\lambda}_t)$ will be within ϵ of the maximum margin ρ within at most*

$\tilde{1} + 1 + \ulcorner(s_{\tilde{1}} + \ln 2)\,\epsilon^{-(3-R)/(1-R)}\urcorner$ *iterations, for both Algorithms 1 and 2.*

Proof. Define $\Delta G(\boldsymbol{\lambda}) := \rho - G(\boldsymbol{\lambda})$. Since (2) tells us that $0 \le \rho - \mu(\boldsymbol{\lambda}_t) \le \rho - G(\boldsymbol{\lambda}_t) = \Delta G(\boldsymbol{\lambda}_t)$, we need only to control how fast $\Delta G(\boldsymbol{\lambda}_t) \to 0$ as $t \to \infty$. That is, if $G(\boldsymbol{\lambda}_t)$ is within ϵ of the maximum margin ρ, so is the margin $\mu(\boldsymbol{\lambda}_t)$.

Starting from Lemma 3,

$$\rho - g_{t+1} \le \rho - g_t - \frac{\alpha_t}{2s_{t+1}}(r_t - \rho + \rho - g_t), \quad \text{thus}$$

$$\Delta G(\boldsymbol{\lambda}_{t+1}) \le \Delta G(\boldsymbol{\lambda}_t)\left[1 - \frac{\alpha_t}{2s_{t+1}}\right] - \frac{\alpha_t(r_t - \rho)}{2s_{t+1}} \le \Delta G(\boldsymbol{\lambda}_{\tilde{1}}) \prod_{\ell=\tilde{1}}^{t}\left[1 - \frac{\alpha_\ell}{2s_{\ell+1}}\right]. \quad (12)$$

We stop the recursion at $\boldsymbol{\lambda}_{\tilde{1}}$, where $\boldsymbol{\lambda}_{\tilde{1}}$ is the coefficient vector at the first iteration where G is positive. We upper bound the product in (12) using Lemma 5.

$$\prod_{\ell=\tilde{1}}^{t}\left[1 - \frac{\alpha_\ell}{2s_{\ell+1}}\right] = \prod_{\ell=\tilde{1}}^{t}\left[1 - \frac{1}{2}\frac{s_{\ell+1} - s_\ell}{s_{\ell+1}}\right] \le \exp\left[-\frac{1}{2}\sum_{\ell=\tilde{1}}^{t}\frac{s_{\ell+1} - s_\ell}{s_{\ell+1}}\right]$$

$$\le \exp\left[-\frac{1}{2}\sum_{\ell=\tilde{1}}^{t}\frac{s_{\ell+1} - s_\ell}{s_\ell + \frac{\rho}{1-\rho}s_\ell + \frac{\ln 2}{1-\rho}}\right] = \exp\left[-\frac{1-\rho}{2}\sum_{\ell=\tilde{1}}^{t}\frac{s_{\ell+1} - s_\ell}{s_\ell + \ln 2}\right]$$

$$\le \exp\left[-\frac{1-\rho}{2}\int_{s_{\tilde{1}}}^{s_{t+1}}\frac{dv}{v + \ln 2}\right] = \left[\frac{s_{\tilde{1}} + \ln 2}{s_{t+1} + \ln 2}\right]^{(1-\rho)/2}. \quad (13)$$

It follows from (12) and (13) that

$$s_t \le s_t + \ln 2 \le (s_{\tilde{1}} + \ln 2)\left[\frac{\Delta G(\boldsymbol{\lambda}_{\tilde{1}})}{\Delta G(\boldsymbol{\lambda}_t)}\right]^{2/(1-\rho)}. \quad (14)$$

On the other hand, using some trickery one can show that for all t, for both algorithms, $\alpha_t \ge (\Delta G(\boldsymbol{\lambda}_{t+1}))/(1 - \rho g_{\tilde{1}})$, which implies:

$$s_t \ge s_{\tilde{1}} + (t - \tilde{1})\frac{\Delta G(\boldsymbol{\lambda}_t)}{1 - \rho g_{\tilde{1}}}. \quad (15)$$

Combining (14) with (15) leads to:

$$t - \tilde{1} \le \frac{(1 - \rho g_{\tilde{1}})s_t}{\Delta G(\boldsymbol{\lambda}_t)} \le \frac{(1 - \rho g_{\tilde{1}})(s_{\tilde{1}} + \ln 2)\,[\Delta G(\boldsymbol{\lambda}_{\tilde{1}})]^{2/(1-\rho)}}{[\Delta G(\boldsymbol{\lambda}_t)]^{1+[2/(1-\rho)]}}, \quad (16)$$

which means $\Delta G(\boldsymbol{\lambda}_t) \ge \epsilon$ is possible only if $t \le \tilde{1} + (s_{\tilde{1}} + \ln 2)\epsilon^{-(3-\rho)/(1-\rho)}$. Therefore, $\Delta(G(\boldsymbol{\lambda}_t) < \epsilon$ whenever t exceeds

$$\tilde{1} + 1 + (s_{\tilde{1}} + \ln 2)\epsilon^{-(3-R)/(1-R)} \ge \tilde{1} + 1 + (s_{\tilde{1}} + \ln 2)\epsilon^{-(3-\rho)/(1-\rho)}. \qquad \square$$

In order to apply the proof of Theorem 1, one has to have an upper bound for ρ, which we have denoted by R. This we may obtain in practice via the minimum achieved edge $R = \min_{\ell \leq t} r_\ell < 1$.

An important remark is that the technique of proof of Theorem 1 is much more widely applicable. In fact, this proof used only two main ingredients: Lemma 3 and Lemma 5. Inspection of the proof shows that the exact values of the constants occurring in these estimates are immaterial. Hence, Theorem 1 may be used to obtain convergence rates for other algorithms.

The convergence rate provided by Theorem 1 is not tight; our algorithms perform at a much faster rate in practice. The fact that the step-size bound in Lemma 5 holds for all t allowed us to find an upper bound on the number of iterations; however, we can find faster convergence rates in the asymptotic regime by using Lemma 4 instead. The following lemma holds for both Algorithms 1 and 2. The proof, which is omitted, follows from Lemma 3 and Lemma 4.

Lemma 6. *For any $0 < \nu < 1/2$, there exists a constant C_ν such that for all $t \geq \tilde{1}$ (i.e., all iterations where G is positive), $\rho - g_t \leq C_\nu s_t^{-\nu}$.*

Theorem 2. *(second convergence rate theorem) For both Algorithms 1 and 2, and for any $\delta > 0$, a margin within ϵ of optimal is obtained after at most $\mathcal{O}(\epsilon^{-(3+\delta)})$ iterations from the iteration $\tilde{1}$ where G becomes positive.*

Proof. By (15), we have $t - \tilde{1} \leq (1 - \rho g_{\tilde{1}})(\rho - g_t)^{-1}(s_t - s_{\tilde{1}})$. Combining this with Lemma 6 leads to $t - \tilde{1} \leq (1 - \rho g_{\tilde{1}}) C_\nu^{1/\nu} (\rho - g_t)^{-(1+1/\nu)}$. For $\delta > 0$, we pick $\nu = \nu_\delta := 1/(2 + \delta) < 1/2$, and we can rewrite the last inequality as: $(\rho - g_t)^{3+\delta} \leq (1 - \rho g_{\tilde{1}}) C_{\nu_\delta}^{2+\delta} (t - \tilde{1})^{-1}$, or $\rho - g_t \leq C'_\delta (t - \tilde{1})^{-1/(3+\delta)}$, with $C'_\delta = (1 - \rho g_{\tilde{1}})^{1/(3+\delta)} C_{\nu_\delta}^{(2+\delta)/(3+\delta)}$. It follows that $\rho - \mu(\boldsymbol{\lambda}_t) \leq \rho - g_t < \epsilon$ whenever $t - \tilde{1} > (C'_\delta \epsilon^{-1})^{(3+\delta)}$, which completes the proof of Theorem 2. □

Although Theorem 2 gives a better convergence rate than Theorem 1 since $3 < 1 + 2/(1 - \rho)$, there is an unknown constant C'_δ, so that this estimate cannot be translated into an a priori upper bound on the number of iterations after which $\rho - g_t < \epsilon$ is guaranteed, unlike Theorem 1.

6 Simulation Experiments

The updates of Algorithm 2 are less aggressive than AdaBoost's, but slightly more aggressive than the updates of arc-gv, and AdaBoost*. Algorithm 1 seems to perform very similarly to Algorithm 2 in practice, so we use Algorithm 2. This section is designed to illustrate our analysis as well as the differences between the various coordinate boosting algorithms; in order to do this, we give each algorithm the same random input, and examine convergence of all algorithms with respect to the margin. Experiments on real data are in our future plans.

Artificial test data for Figure 2 was designed as follows: 50 examples were constructed randomly such that each $\mathbf{x}_i$ lies on a corner of the hypercube $\{-1, 1\}^{100}$.

We set $y_i = \text{sign}(\sum_{k=1}^{11} \mathbf{x}_i(k))$, where $\mathbf{x}_i(k)$ indicates the kth component of $\mathbf{x}_i$. The jth weak learner is $h_j(\mathbf{x}) = \mathbf{x}(j)$, thus $M_{ij} = y_i \mathbf{x}_i(j)$. To implement the "non-optimal" case, we chose a random classifier from the set of sufficiently good classifiers at each iteration.

We use the definitions of arc-gv and AdaBoost* found in Meir and Rätsch's survey [8]. AdaBoost, arc-gv, Algorithm 1 and Algorithm 2 have initially large updates, based on a conservative estimate of the margin. AdaBoost*'s updates are initially small based on an overestimate of the margin.

AdaBoost's updates remain consistently large, causing $\boldsymbol{\lambda}_t$ to grow quickly and causing fast convergence with respect to G. AdaBoost seems to converge to the maximum margin in (a); however, it does not seem to in (b), (d) or (e). Algorithm 2 converges fairly quickly and dependably; arc-gv and AdaBoost* are slower here. We could provide a larger value of ν in AdaBoost* to encourage faster convergence, but we would sacrifice a guarantee on accuracy. The more "optimal" we choose the weak learners, the better the larger step-size algorithms (AdaBoost and Algorithm 2) perform, relative to AdaBoost*; this is because AdaBoost*'s update uses the minimum achieved edge, which translates into smaller steps while the weak learning algorithm is doing well.

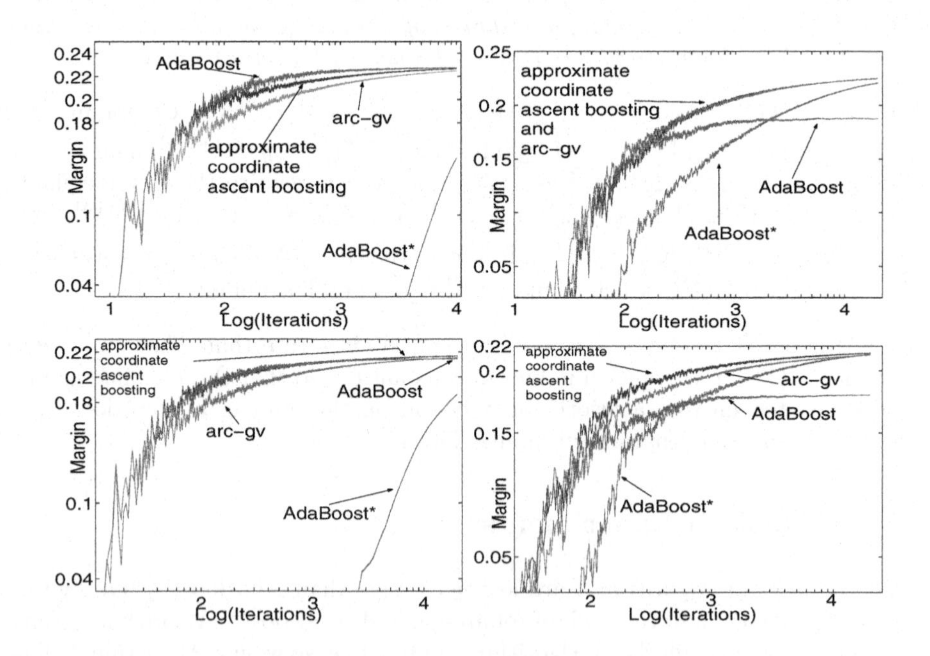

Fig. 2. AdaBoost, AdaBoost* (parameter ν set to .001), arc-gv, and Algorithm 2 on synthetic data. (a-Top Left) Optimal case. (b-Top Right) Non-optimal case, using the same 50×100 matrix $\mathbf{M}$ as in (a). (c-Bottom Left) Optimal case, using a different matrix. (d-Bottom Right) Non-optimal case, using the same matrix as (c).

7 A New Way to Measure AdaBoost's Progress

AdaBoost is still a mysterious algorithm. Even in the optimal case it may converge to a solution with margin significantly below the maximum [11]. Thus, the margin theory only provides a significant piece of the puzzle of AdaBoost's strong generalization properties; it is not the whole story [5,2,11]. Hence, we give some connections between our new algorithms and AdaBoost, to help us understand how AdaBoost makes progress. In this section, we measure the progress of AdaBoost according to something other than the margin, namely, our smooth margin function G. First, we show that whenever AdaBoost takes a large step, it makes progress according to G. We use the superscript $^{[A]}$ for AdaBoost.

Theorem 3. $G(\boldsymbol{\lambda}_{t+1}^{[A]}) \geq G(\boldsymbol{\lambda}_t^{[A]}) \iff \Upsilon(r_t) \geq G(\boldsymbol{\lambda}_t^{[A]})$, *where* $\Upsilon : (0,1) \to (0,\infty)$ *is a monotonically increasing function.*

In other words, $G(\boldsymbol{\lambda}_{t+1}^{[A]}) \geq G(\boldsymbol{\lambda}_t^{[A]})$ if and only if the edge r_t is sufficiently large.

Proof. Using AdaBoost's update $\alpha_t^{[A]} = \gamma_t$, $G(\boldsymbol{\lambda}_t^{[A]}) \leq G(\boldsymbol{\lambda}_{t+1}^{[A]})$ if and only if:

$$(s_t^{[A]} + \alpha_t^{[A]})G(\boldsymbol{\lambda}_t^{[A]}) \leq (s_t^{[A]} + \alpha_t^{[A]})G(\boldsymbol{\lambda}_{t+1}^{[A]}) = s_t^{[A]}G(\boldsymbol{\lambda}_t^{[A]}) + \int_0^{\alpha_t^{[A]}} \tanh u \, du,$$

$$\text{i.e.,} \quad G(\boldsymbol{\lambda}_t^{[A]}) \leq \frac{1}{\alpha_t^{[A]}} \int_0^{\alpha_t^{[A]}} \tanh u \, du,$$

where we have used (4). We denote the expression on the right hand side by $\Upsilon(r_t)$, which can be rewritten as: $\Upsilon(r_t) := -\ln\left(1 - r_t^2\right) \Big/ \ln\left(\frac{1+r_t}{1-r_t}\right)$. Since $\Upsilon(r)$ is monotonically increasing in r, our statement is proved. □

Hence, AdaBoost makes progress (measured by G) if and only if it takes a big enough step. Figure 3, which shows the evolution of the edge values, illustrates this. Whenever G increased from the current iteration to the following iteration, a small dot was plotted. Whenever G decreased, a large dot was plotted. The fact that the larger dots are below the smaller dots is a direct result of Theorem 3. In fact, one can visually track the progress of G using the boundary between the larger and smaller dots.

AdaBoost's weight vectors often converge to a periodic cycle when there are few support vectors [11]. Where Algorithms 1 and 2 make progress with respect to G at every iteration, the opposite is true for cyclic AdaBoost, namely that AdaBoost cannot increase G at every iteration, by the following:

Theorem 4. *If AdaBoost's weight vectors converge to a cycle of length T iterations, the cycle must obey one of the following conditions:*

1. *the value of G decreases for at least one iteration within the cycle, or*
2. *the value of G is constant at every iteration, and the edge values in the cycle $r_{t,1}^{(cyc)}, \ldots, r_{t,T}^{(cyc)}$ are equal.*

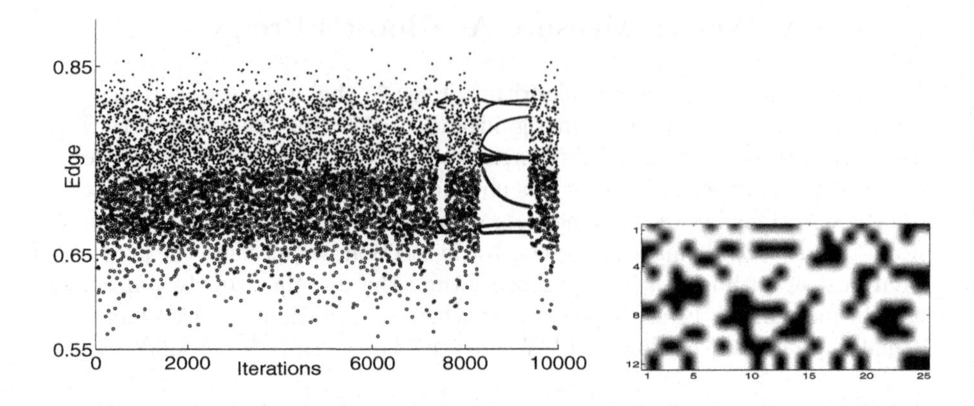

Fig. 3. Value of the edge at each iteration t, for a run of AdaBoost using the 12×25 matrix $\mathbf{M}$ shown (black is -1, white is +1). AdaBoost alternates between chaotic and cyclic behavior. For further explanation of the interesting dynamics in this plot, see [11].

In other words, the value of G cannot be strictly increasing within a cycle. The main ingredients for the proof (which is omitted) are Theorem 3 and (4). For specific cases that have been studied [11], the value of G is non-decreasing, and the value of r_t is the same at every iteration of the cycle. In such cases, a stronger equivalence between support vectors exists here; they are all "viewed" similarly by the weak learning algorithm, in that they are misclassified the same proportion of the time. (This is surprising since weak classifiers may appear more than once per cycle.)

Theorem 5. *Assume AdaBoost cycles. If all edges are the same, then all support vectors are misclassified by the same number of weak classifiers per cycle.*

Proof. Let $r_t =: r$ which is constant. Consider support vectors i and i'. All support vectors obey the cycle condition [11], namely: $\prod_{t=1}^{T}(1 + M_{ij_t}r) = \prod_{t=1}^{T}(1 + M_{i'j_t}r) = 1$. Define $\tau_i := |\{t : M_{ij_t} = 1\}|$, the number of times example i is correctly classified during one cycle of length T. Now, $1 = \prod_{t=1}^{T}(1 + M_{ij_t}r) = (1+r)^{\tau_i}(1-r)^{T-\tau_i} = (1+r)^{\tau_{i'}}(1-r)^{T-\tau_{i'}}$. Hence, $\tau_i = \tau_{i'}$. Thus, example i is misclassified the same number of times that i' is misclassified. Since the choice of i and i' were arbitrary, this holds for all support vectors. □

References

[1] Leo Breiman. Arcing the edge. Technical Report 486, Statistics Department, University of California at Berkeley, 1997.

[2] Leo Breiman. Prediction games and arcing algorithms. *Neural Computation*, 11(7):1493–1517, 1999.

[3] Michael Collins, Robert E. Schapire, and Yoram Singer. Logistic regression, AdaBoost and Bregman distances. *Machine Learning*, 48(1/2/3), 2002.

[4] Yoav Freund and Robert E. Schapire. A decision-theoretic generalization of on-line learning and an application to boosting. *Journal of Computer and System Sciences*, 55(1):119–139, August 1997.
[5] Adam J. Grove and Dale Schuurmans. Boosting in the limit: Maximizing the margin of learned ensembles. In *Proceedings of the Fifteenth National Conference on Artificial Intelligence*, 1998.
[6] V. Koltchinskii and D. Panchenko. Empirical margin distributions and bounding the generalization error of combined classifiers. *The Annals of Statistics*, 30(1), February 2002.
[7] Llew Mason, Peter Bartlett, and Jonathan Baxter. Direct optimization of margins improves generalization in combined classifiers. In *Advances in Neural Information Processing Systems 12*, 2000.
[8] R. Meir and G. Rätsch. An introduction to boosting and leveraging. In S. Mendelson and A. Smola, editors, *Advanced Lectures on Machine Learning*, pages 119–184. Springer, 2003.
[9] Gunnar Rätsch and Manfred Warmuth. Efficient margin maximizing with boosting. Submitted, 2002.
[10] Saharon Rosset, Ji Zhu, and Trevor Hastie. Boosting as a regularized path to a maximum margin classifier. Technical report, Department of Statistics, Stanford University, 2003.
[11] Cynthia Rudin, Ingrid Daubechies, and Robert E. Schapire. The dynamics of AdaBoost: Cyclic behavior and convergence of margins. Submitted, 2004.
[12] Cynthia Rudin, Ingrid Daubechies, and Robert E. Schapire. On the dynamics of boosting. In *Advances in Neural Information Processing Systems 16*, 2004.
[13] Robert E. Schapire. The boosting approach to machine learning: An overview. In *MSRI Workshop on Nonlinear Estimation and Classification*, 2002.
[14] Robert E. Schapire, Yoav Freund, Peter Bartlett, and Wee Sun Lee. Boosting the margin: A new explanation for the effectiveness of voting methods. *The Annals of Statistics*, 26(5):1651–1686, October 1998.
[15] Tong Zhang and Bin Yu. Boosting with early stopping: convergence and consistency. Technical Report 635, Department of Statistics, UC Berkeley, 2003.

Bayesian Networks and Inner Product Spaces*

Atsuyoshi Nakamura[1], Michael Schmitt[2],
Niels Schmitt[2], and Hans Ulrich Simon[2]

[1] Graduate School of Engineering, Hokkaido University, Sapporo 060-8628, Japan
atsu@main.eng.hokudai.ac.jp
[2] Fakultät für Mathematik, Ruhr-Universität Bochum, 44780 Bochum, Germany
{mschmitt,nschmitt,simon}@lmi.ruhr-uni-bochum.de

Abstract. In connection with two-label classification tasks over the Boolean domain, we consider the possibility to combine the key advantages of Bayesian networks and of kernel-based learning systems. This leads us to the basic question whether the class of decision functions induced by a given Bayesian network can be represented within a low-dimensional inner product space. For Bayesian networks with an explicitly given (full or reduced) parameter collection, we show that the "natural" inner product space has the smallest possible dimension up to factor 2 (even up to an additive term 1 in many cases). For a slight modification of the so-called logistic autoregressive Bayesian network with n nodes, we show that every sufficiently expressive inner product space has dimension at least $2^{n/4}$. The main technical contribution of our work consists in uncovering combinatorial and algebraic structures within Bayesian networks such that known techniques for proving lower bounds on the dimension of inner product spaces can be brought into play.

1 Introduction

During the last decade, there has been a lot of interest in learning systems whose hypotheses can be written as inner products in an appropriate feature space, trained with a learning algorithm that performs a kind of empirical or structural risk minimization. The inner product operation is often not carried out explicitly, but reduced to the evaluation of a so-called kernel-function that operates on instances of the original data space, which offers the opportunity to handle high-dimensional feature spaces in an efficient manner. This learning strategy introduced by Vapnik and co-workers [4,33] in connection with the so-called Support Vector Machine is a theoretically well founded and very powerful method that, in the years since its introduction, has already outperformed most other systems in a wide variety of applications.

Bayesian networks have a long history in statistics, and in the first half of the 1980s they were introduced to the field of expert systems through work by Pearl [25] and Spiegelhalter and Knill-Jones [29]. They are much different from

* This work has been supported in part by the Deutsche Forschungsgemeinschaft Grant SI 498/7-1.

J. Shawe-Taylor and Y. Singer (Eds.): COLT 2004, LNAI 3120, pp. 518–533, 2004.

kernel-based learning systems and offer some complementary advantages. They graphically model conditional independence relationships between random variables. There exist quite elaborated methods for choosing an appropriate network, for performing probabilistic inference (inferring missing data from existing ones), and for solving pattern classification tasks or unsupervised learning problems. Like other probabilistic models, Bayesian networks can be used to represent inhomogeneous training samples with possibly overlapping features and missing data in a uniform manner.

Quite recently, several research groups considered the possibility to combine the key advantages of probabilistic models and kernel-based learning systems. For this purpose, several kernels (like the Fisher-kernel, for instance) were studied extensively [17,18,24,27,31,32,30]. Altun, Tsochantaridis, and Hofmann [1] proposed (and experimented with) a kernel related to the Hidden Markov Model.

In this paper, we focus on two-label classification tasks over the Boolean domain and on probabilistic models that can be represented as Bayesian networks. Intuitively, we aim at finding the "simplest" inner product space that is able to express the class of decision functions (briefly called "concept class" in what follows) induced by a given Bayesian network. We restrict ourselves to Euclidean spaces equipped with the standard scalar product.[1] Furthermore, we use the Euclidean dimension of the space as our measure of simplicity.[2] Our main results are as follows:

1) For Bayesian networks with an explicitly given (full or reduced) parameter collection, the "natural" inner product space (obtained from the probabilistic model by fairly straightforward algebraic manipulations) has the smallest possible dimension up to factor 2 (even up to an additive term 1 in many cases). The (almost) matching lower bounds on the smallest possible dimension are found by analyzing the VC-dimension of the concept class associated with a Bayesian network.

2) We present a quadratic lower bound and the upper bound $O(n^6)$ on the VC-dimension of the concept class associated with the so-called "logistic autoregressive Bayesian network" (also known as "sigmoid belief network")[3], where n denotes the number of nodes.

3) For a slight modification of the logistic autoregressive Bayesian network with $n+2$ nodes, we show that every sufficiently expressive inner product space has dimension at least $2^{n/4}$. The proof of this lower bound proceeds by showing that

---

[1] This is no loss of generality (except for the infinite-dimensional case) since any finite-dimensional reproducing kernel Hilbert space is isometric with $\mathbb{R}^d$ for some d.

[2] This is well motivated by the fact that most generalization error bounds for linear classifiers are given in terms of either the Euclidean dimension or in terms of the geometrical margin between the data points and the separating hyperplanes. Applying random projection techniques from [19,14,2], it can be shown that any arrangement with a large margin can be converted into a low-dimensional arrangement. Thus, a large lower bound on the smallest possible dimension rules out the possibility of a large margin classifier.

[3] originally proposed by Mc-Cullagh and Nelder [7] and studied systematically, for instance, by Neal [23] and by Saul, Jaakkola, and Jordan [26]

the concept class induced by such a network contains exponentially many decision functions that are pairwise orthogonal on an exponentially large subdomain. Since the VC-dimension of this concept class has the same order of magnitude, $O(n^6)$, as the original (unmodified) network, VC-dimension considerations would be insufficient to reveal the exponential lower bound.

While (as mentioned above) there exist already some papers that investigate the connection between probabilistic models and inner product spaces, it seems that this work is the first one which addresses explicitly the question of finding a smallest-dimensional sufficiently expressive inner product space. It should be mentioned however that there exist a couple of papers [10,11,3,13,12,20,21] (not concerned with probabilistic models) considering the related question of finding an embedding of a given concept class into a system of half-spaces. The main technical contribution of our work can be seen in uncovering combinatorial and algebraic structures within Bayesian networks such that techniques known from these papers can be brought into play.

2 Preliminaries

In this section, we present formal definitions for the basic notions in this paper. Subsection 2.1 is concerned with notions from learning theory. In Subsection 2.2, we formally introduce Bayesian networks and the distributions and concept classes induced by them. The notion of a linear arrangement for a concept class is presented in Subsection 2.3.

2.1 Concept Classes and VC-Dimension

A *concept class* $\mathcal{C}$ over domain $\mathcal{X}$ is a family of functions of the form $f : \mathcal{X} \to \{-1, +1\}$. Each $f \in \mathcal{C}$ is then called a *concept.* A set $S = \{s_1, \ldots, s_m\} \subseteq \mathcal{X}$ of size m is said to be *shattered* by $\mathcal{C}$ if

$$\forall b \in \{-1, +1\}^m, \exists f \in \mathcal{C}, \forall i = 1, \ldots, m : f(s_i) = b_i \ .$$

The *VC-dimension* of $\mathcal{C}$ is given by

$$\mathrm{VCdim}(\mathcal{C}) = \sup\{m | \exists S \subseteq \mathcal{X} : |S| = m \text{ and } S \text{ is shattered by } \mathcal{C}\} \ .$$

For every $z \in \mathbb{R}$, let $\mathrm{sign}(z) = +1$ if $z \geq 0$ and $\mathrm{sign}(z) = -1$ otherwise. In the context of concept classes, the sign-function is sometimes used for mapping real-valued functions f to ± 1-valued functions $\mathrm{sign} \circ f$.

We write $\mathcal{C} \leq \mathcal{C}'$ for concept classes $\mathcal{C}$ over domain $\mathcal{X}$ and $\mathcal{C}'$ over domain $\mathcal{X}'$ if there exist mappings

$$\mathcal{C} \ni f \mapsto f' \in \mathcal{C}', \mathcal{X} \ni x \mapsto x' \in \mathcal{X}'$$

such that $f(x) = f'(x')$ for every $f \in \mathcal{C}$ and every $x \in \mathcal{X}$. Note that $\mathcal{C} \leq \mathcal{C}'$ implies that $\mathrm{VCdim}(\mathcal{C}) \leq \mathrm{VCdim}(\mathcal{C}')$ because the following holds: if $S \subseteq \mathcal{X}$ is a set of size m that is shattered by $\mathcal{C}$ then $S' = \{s' | s \in S\} \subseteq \mathcal{X}'$ is a set of size m that is shattered by $\mathcal{C}'$.

2.2 Bayesian Networks

Definition 1. *A* Bayesian network $\mathcal{N}$ *consists of the following components:*

1. *a directed acyclic graph* $\mathcal{G} = (V, E)$,
2. *a collection* $(p_{i,\alpha})_{i \in V, \alpha \in \{0,1\}^{m_i}}$ *of programmable parameters with values in the open intervall* $]0,1[$, *where* m_i *denotes the number of* $j \in V$ *such that* $(j,i) \in E$,
3. *constraints that describe which assignments of values from* $]0,1[$ *to the parameters of the collection are allowed.*

If the constraints are empty, we speak of an unconstrained *network. Otherwise, we say the network is* constrained.

Conventions: We will identify the $n = |V|$ nodes of $\mathcal{N}$ with the numbers from 1 to n and assume that every edge $(j,i) \in E$ satisfies $j < i$ (topological ordering). If $(j,i) \in E$, then j is called a parent of i. P_i denotes the set of parents of node i and $m_i = |P_i|$ denotes the number of parents. $\mathcal{N}$ is said to be *fully connected* if $P_i = 1, \ldots, i-1$ for every node i. We will associate with every node i a Boolean variable x_i with values in $\{0,1\}$. We say x_j is a parent-variable of x_i if j is a parent of i. Each $\alpha \in \{0,1\}^{m_i}$ is called a possible bit-pattern for the parent-variables of x_i. $M_{i,\alpha}(x)$ denotes the polynomial that indicates whether the parent variables of x_i exhibit bit-pattern α. More formally, $M_{i,\alpha}(x) = \prod_{j \in P_i} x_j^{\alpha_j}$, where $x_j^0 = 1 - x_j$ and $x_j^1 = x_j$.

An unconstrained network with a dense graph has an exponentially growing number of parameters. In a constrained network, the number of parameters can be kept reasonably small even in case of a dense topology. The following two definitions exemplify this approach. Definition 2 contains (as a special case) the networks that were proposed in [5]. (See Example 2 below.) Definition 3 deals with so-called logistic autoregressive Bayesian networks that, given their simplicity, perform surprisingly well on some problems. (See the discussion of these networks in [15].)

Definition 2. *A Bayesian network with a* reduced parameter collection *is a Bayesian network whose constraints can be described as follows. For every* $i \in \{1, \ldots, n\}$, *there exists a surjective function* $R_i : \{0,1\}^{m_i} \to \{1, \ldots, d_i\}$ *such that the parameters of* $\mathcal{N}$ *satisfy*

$$\forall i = 1, \ldots, n, \forall \alpha, \alpha' \in \{0,1\}^{m_i} : R_i(\alpha) = R_i(\alpha') \implies p_{i,\alpha} = p_{i,\alpha'} \ .$$

We denote the network as $\mathcal{N}^R$ *for* $R = (R_1, \ldots, R_n)$. *Obviously,* $\mathcal{N}^R$ *is completely described by the reduced parameter collection* $(p_{i,c})_{1 \le i \le n, 1 \le c \le d_i}$.

Definition 3. *The* logistic autoregressive *Bayesian network* $\mathcal{N}_\sigma$ *is the fully connected Bayesian network with the following constraints on the parameter collection:*

$$\forall i = 1, \ldots, n, \exists (w_{i,j})_{1 \le j \le i-1} \in \mathbb{R}^{i-1}, \forall \alpha \in \{0,1\}^{i-1} : p_{i,\alpha} = \sigma\left(\sum_{j=1}^{i-1} w_{i,j}\alpha_j\right) ,$$

where $\sigma(y) = 1/(1 + e^{-y})$ denotes the standard sigmoid function. Obviously, $\mathcal{N}_\sigma$ is completely described by the parameter collection $(w_{i,j})_{1 \le i \le n, 1 \le j \le i-1}$.

In the introduction, we mentioned that Bayesian networks graphically model conditional independence relationships. This general idea is captured in the following

Definition 4. *Let $\mathcal{N}$ be a Bayesian network with nodes $1, \ldots, n$. The class of distributions induced by $\mathcal{N}$, denoted as $\mathcal{D}_\mathcal{N}$, consists of all distributions on $\{0,1\}^n$ of the form*

$$P(x) = \prod_{i=1}^{n} \prod_{\alpha \in \{0,1\}^{m_i}} p_{i,\alpha}^{x_i M_{i,\alpha}(x)} (1 - p_{i,\alpha})^{(1-x_i) M_{i,\alpha}(x)} . \tag{1}$$

For every assignment of values from $]0,1[$ to the parameters of $\mathcal{N}$, we obtain a concrete distribution from $\mathcal{D}_\mathcal{N}$. Recall that not each assignment is allowed if $\mathcal{N}$ is constrained.

The polynomial representation of $\log P(x)$ resulting from (1) is called *Chow expansion* in the pattern classification literature [9]. Parameter $p_{i,\alpha}$ represents the conditional probability for $x_i = 1$ given that the parent variables of x_i exhibit bit-pattern α. Formula (1) expresses $P(x)$ as a product of conditional probabilities (chain-expansion).

Example 1 (k-order Markov chain). For $k \ge 0$, $\mathcal{N}_k$ denotes the unconstrained Bayesian network with $P_i = \{i-1, \ldots, i-k\}$ for $i = 1, \ldots, n$ (with the convention that numbers smaller than 1 are ignored such that $m_i = |P_i| = \min\{i-1, k\}$). The total number of parameters equals $2^k(n-k) + 2^{k-1} + \cdots + 2 + 1 = 2^k(n - k + 1) - 1$.

We briefly explain that, for a Bayesian network with a reduced parameter set, distribution $P(x)$ from Definition 4 can be written in a simpler fashion. Let $R_{i,c}(x)$ denote the $0,1$-valued function that indicates for every $x \in \{0,1\}^n$ whether the projection of x to the parent-variables of x_i is mapped to c by R_i. Then, the following holds:

$$P(x) = \prod_{i=1}^{n} \prod_{c=1}^{d_i} p_{i,c}^{x_i R_{i,c}(x)} (1 - p_{i,c})^{(1-x_i) R_{i,c}(x)} . \tag{2}$$

Example 2. Chickering, Heckerman, and Meek [5] proposed Bayesian networks "with local structure". They used a decision tree T_i (or, alternatively, a decision graph G_i) over the parent-variables of x_i for every $i \in \{1, \ldots, n\}$. The conditional probability for $x_i = 1$ given the bit-pattern of the variables from P_i is attached to the corresponding leaf in T_i (or sink in G_i, respectively). This fits nicely into our framework of networks with a reduced parameter collection. Here, d_i denotes the number of leaves in T_i (or sinks of G_i, respectively), and $R_i(\alpha) = c \in \{1, \ldots, d_i\}$ if α is routed to leaf c in T_i (or to sink c in G_i, respectively).

In a two-label classification task, functions $P(x), Q(x) \in \mathcal{D}_{\mathcal{N}}$ are used as discriminant functions, where $P(x)$ and $Q(x)$ represent the distributions of x conditioned to label $+1$ and -1, respectively. The corresponding decision function assigns label $+1$ to x if $P(x) \geq Q(x)$ and -1 otherwise. The obvious connection to concept classes in learning theory is made explicit in the following

Definition 5. *Let $\mathcal{N}$ be a Bayesian network with nodes $1, \dots, n$ and $\mathcal{D}_{\mathcal{N}}$ the corresponding class of distributions. The class of concepts induced by $\mathcal{N}$, denoted as $\mathcal{C}_{\mathcal{N}}$, consists of all ± 1-valued functions on $\{0,1\}^n$ of the form* $\mathrm{sign}(\log(P(x)/Q(x)))$ *for $P, Q \in \mathcal{D}_{\mathcal{N}}$. Note that this function attains value $+1$ if $P(x) \geq Q(x)$ and value -1 otherwise.*

The VC-dimension of $\mathcal{C}_{\mathcal{N}}$ is simply denoted as $\mathrm{VCdim}(\mathcal{N})$ throughout the paper.

2.3 Linear Arrangements in Inner Product Spaces

As explained in the introduction, we restrict ourselves to finite-dimensional Euclidean spaces and the standard scalar product $u^\top v = \sum_{i=1}^d u_i v_i$, where $u^\top$ denotes the transpose of u.

Definition 6. *A d-dimensional* linear arrangement *for a concept class $\mathcal{C}$ over domain $\mathcal{X}$ is given by collections $(u_f)_{f \in \mathcal{C}}$ and $(v_x)_{x \in \mathcal{X}}$ of vectors in $\mathbb{R}^d$ such that*

$$\forall f \in \mathcal{C}, x \in \mathcal{X} : f(x) = \mathrm{sign}(u_f^\top v_x) \ .$$

The smallest d such that there exists a d-dimensional linear arrangement for $\mathcal{C}$ (possibly ∞ if there is no finite-dimensional arrangement) is denoted as $\mathrm{Edim}(\mathcal{C})$.
[4]

If $\mathcal{C}_{\mathcal{N}}$ is the concept class induced by a Bayesian network $\mathcal{N}$, we simply write $\mathrm{Edim}(\mathcal{N})$ instead of $\mathrm{Edim}(\mathcal{C}_{\mathcal{N}})$. Note that $\mathrm{Edim}(\mathcal{C}) \leq \mathrm{Edim}(\mathcal{C}')$ if $\mathcal{C} \leq \mathcal{C}'$.

It is easy to see that $\mathrm{Edim}(\mathcal{C}) \leq \min\{|\mathcal{C}|, |\mathcal{X}|\}$ for finite classes. Less trivial upper bounds are usually obtained constructively, by presenting an appropriate arrangement. As for lower bounds, the following is known:

Lemma 1. $\mathrm{Edim}(\mathcal{C}) \geq \mathrm{VCdim}(\mathcal{C})$.

Lemma 2 ([10]). *Let $f_1, \dots, f_m \in \mathcal{C}$, $x_1, \dots, x_n \in \mathcal{X}$, and $M \in \{-1,+1\}^{m \times n}$ be the matrix given by $M_{i,j} = f_i(x_j)$. Then,* $\mathrm{Edim}(\mathcal{C}) \geq \sqrt{mn}/\|M\|$, *where $\|M\| = \sup_{z \in \mathbb{R}^n : \|z\|_2 = 1} \|Mz\|_2$ denotes the spectral norm of M.*

Lemma 1 easily follows from a result by Cover [6] which states that $\mathrm{VCdim}(\{\mathrm{sign} \circ f | f \in \mathcal{F}\}) = d$ for every d-dimensional vector space $\mathcal{F}$ consisting of real-valued functions. Lemma 2 (proven in [10]) is highly non-trivial.

Let PARITY_n denote the concept class $\{h_a | a \in \{0,1\}^n\}$ on the Boolean domain given by $h_a(x) = (-1)^{a^\top x}$. Let $H_n \in \{-1,+1\}^{2^n \times 2^n}$ denote the matrix with entry $h_a(x)$ in row a and column x (Hadamard-matrix). From Lemma 2 and the well-known fact that $\|H_n\| = 2^{n/2}$ (which holds for any orthogonal matrix from $\{-1,+1\}^{2^n \times 2^n}$), one gets

Corollary 1 ([10]). $\mathrm{Edim}(\mathrm{PARITY}_n) \geq 2^n/\|H_n\| = 2^{n/2}$.

[4] Edim stands for Euclidean dimension.

3 Linear Arrangements for Bayesian Networks

In this section, we present concrete linear arrangements for several types of Bayesian networks, which leads to upper bounds on $\mathrm{Edim}(\mathcal{N})$. We sketch the proofs only.

For a set M, 2^M denotes its power set.

Theorem 1. *For every unconstrained Bayesian network, the following holds:*

$$\mathrm{Edim}(\mathcal{N}) \leq \left| \bigcup_{i=1}^{n} 2^{P_i \cup \{i\}} \right| \leq 2 \cdot \sum_{i=1}^{n} 2^{m_i} .$$

Proof. From the expansion of P in (1) and the corresponding expansion of Q (with parameters $q_{i,\alpha}$ in the role of $p_{i,\alpha}$), we get

$$\log \frac{P(x)}{Q(x)} = \sum_{i=1}^{n} \sum_{\alpha \in \{0,1\}^{m_i}} x_i M_{i,\alpha}(x) \log \frac{p_{i,\alpha}}{q_{i,\alpha}} + (1 - x_i) M_{i,\alpha}(x) \log \frac{1 - p_{i,\alpha}}{1 - q_{i,\alpha}} . \quad (3)$$

On the right-hand side of (3), we find the polynomials $M_{i,\alpha}(x)$ and $x_i M_{i,\alpha}(x)$. Note that $| \cup_{i=1}^{n} 2^{P_i \cup \{i\}}|$ equals the number of monomials that occur when we express these polynomials as sums of monomials by successive applications of the distributive law. A linear arrangement of the appropriate dimension is now obtained in the obvious fashion by introducing one coordinate per monomial. □

Corollary 2. *Let $\mathcal{N}_k$ denote the Bayesian network from Example 1. Then:*

$$\mathrm{Edim}(\mathcal{N}_k) \leq (n - k + 1)2^k .$$

Proof. Apply Theorem 1 and observe that

$$\bigcup_{i=1}^{n} 2^{P_i \cup \{i\}} = \bigcup_{i=k+1}^{n} \{J_i \cup \{i\} | J_i \subseteq \{i-1, \ldots, i-k\}\} \cup \{J | J \subseteq \{1, \ldots, k\}\} . \quad \square$$

Theorem 2. *Let $\mathcal{N}^R$ be a Bayesian network with a reduced parameter set $(p_{i,c})_{1 \leq i \leq n, 1 \leq c \leq d_i}$ in the sense of Definition 2. Then:*

$$\mathrm{Edim}(\mathcal{N}^R) \leq 2 \cdot \sum_{i=1}^{n} d_i .$$

Proof. Recall that the distributions from $\mathcal{D}_{\mathcal{N}^R}$ can be written in the form (2). We make use of the following obvious equation:

$$\log \frac{P(x)}{Q(x)} = \sum_{i=1}^{n} \sum_{c=1}^{d_i} x_i R_{i,c}(x) \log \frac{p_{i,c}}{q_{i,c}} + (1 - x_i) R_{i,c}(x) \log \frac{1 - p_{i,c}}{1 - q_{i,c}} \quad (4)$$

A linear arrangement of the appropriate dimension is now obtained in the obvious fashion by introducing two coordinates per pair (i,c): if x is mapped to v_x in this arrangement, then the projection of v_x to the two coordinates corresponding to (i,c) is $(R_{i,c}(x), x_i R_{i,c}(x))$; the appropriate mapping $(P,Q) \mapsto u_{P,Q}$ in this arrangement is easily derived from (4). □

Theorem 3. *Let $\mathcal{N}_\sigma$ denote the logistic autoregressive Bayesian network from Definition 3. Then,* $\mathrm{VCdim}(\mathcal{N}_\sigma) = O(n^6)$.

The proof of this theorem is found in the full paper.

Remark 1. The linear arrangements for unconstrained Bayesian networks or for Bayesian networks with a reduced parameter set were easy to find. This is no accident: a similar remark is valid for every class of distributions (or densities) from the *exponential family* because (as pointed out in [8] for example) the corresponding Bayes-rule takes the form of a so-called *generalized linear rule* from which a linear arrangement is evident.[5] See the full paper for more details.

4 Lower Bounds on the Dimension of an Arrangement

In this section, we derive lower bounds on $\mathrm{Edim}(\mathcal{N})$ that match the upper bounds from Section 3 up to a small gap. Before we move on to the main results in Subsections 4.1 and 4.2, we briefly mention (without proof) some specific Bayesian networks where upper and lower bound match. The proofs are found in the full paper.

Theorem 4. $\mathrm{VCdim}(\mathcal{N}_0) = \mathrm{Edim}(\mathcal{N}_0) = n+1$ *if $\mathcal{N}_0$ has $n \geq 2$ nodes and* $\mathrm{VCdim}(\mathcal{N}_0) = \mathrm{Edim}(\mathcal{N}_0) = 1$ *if $\mathcal{N}_0$ has 1 node.*

Theorem 5. *For $k \geq 0$, let $\mathcal{N}'_k$ denote the unconstrained network with $P_i = \{1,\ldots,k\}$ for $i = k+1,\ldots,n$ and $P_i = \emptyset$ for $i = 1,\ldots,k$. Then,* $\mathrm{VCdim}(\mathcal{N}'_k) = \mathrm{Edim}(\mathcal{N}'_k) = 2^k(n-k+1)$

4.1 Lower Bounds Based on VC-Dimension Considerations

Since $\mathrm{VCdim}(\mathcal{C}) \leq \mathrm{VCdim}(\mathcal{C}')$ if $\mathcal{C} \leq \mathcal{C}'$, a lower bound on $\mathrm{VCdim}(\mathcal{C}')$ can be obtained from classes $\mathcal{C} \leq \mathcal{C}'$ whose VC-dimension is known or easy to determine. We first define concept classes that will fit this purpose.

Definition 7. *Let $\mathcal{N}$ be a Bayesian network. For every $i \in \{1,\ldots,n\}$, let $\mathcal{F}_i$ be a family of ± 1-valued functions on the domain $\{0,1\}^{m_i}$ and $\mathcal{F} = \mathcal{F}_1 \times \cdots \times \mathcal{F}_n$.*

[5] The bound given in Theorem 1 is slightly stronger than the bound obtained from the general approach for members of the exponential family.

We define $\mathcal{C}_{\mathcal{N},\mathcal{F}}$ as the concept class over domain $\{0,1\}^n \setminus \{\bar{0}\}$ consisting of all functions of the form

$$L_{\mathcal{N},f} := [(x_n, f_n), \ldots, (x_1, f_1)] \ ,$$

where $f = (f_1, \ldots, f_n) \in \mathcal{F}$. The right-hand side of this equation is understood as a decision list, where $L_{\mathcal{N},f}(x)$ for $x \neq \bar{0}$ is determined as follows:

1. *Find the largest i such that $x_i = 1$.*
2. *Apply f_i to the projection of x to the parent-variables of x_i and output the result.*

Lemma 3. $\mathrm{VCdim}(\mathcal{C}_{\mathcal{N},\mathcal{F}}) = \sum_{i=1}^{n} \mathrm{VCdim}(\mathcal{F}_i)$.

Proof. We prove that $\mathrm{VCdim}(\mathcal{C}_{\mathcal{N},\mathcal{F}}) \geq \sum_{i=1}^{n} \mathrm{VCdim}(\mathcal{F}_i)$. (The proof for the other direction is similar.) For every i, we embed the vectors from $\{0,1\}^{m_i}$ into $\{0,1\}^n$ according to $\tau_i(a) := (a', 1, 0, \ldots, 0)$, where $a' \in \{0,1\}^{i-1}$ is chosen such that its projection to the parent-variables of x_i coincides with a and the remaining components are projected to 0. Note that $\tau_i(a)$ is absorbed in item (x_i, f_i) of the decision list $L_{\mathcal{N},f}$. It is easy to see that the following holds. If, for $i = 1, \ldots, n$, S_i is a set that is shattered by $\mathcal{F}_i$, then $\cup_{i=1}^{n} \tau_i(S_i)$ is shattered by $\mathcal{C}_{\mathcal{N},\mathcal{F}}$. Thus, $\mathrm{VCdim}(\mathcal{C}_{\mathcal{N},\mathcal{F}}) \geq \sum_{i=1}^{n} \mathrm{VCdim}(\mathcal{F}_i)$. □

The first application of Lemma 3 concerns unconstrained networks.

Theorem 6. *Let $\mathcal{N}$ be an unconstrained Bayesian network and let $\mathcal{F}_i^*$ denote the set of all ± 1-valued functions on domain $\{0,1\}^{m_i}$ and $\mathcal{F}^* = \mathcal{F}_1^* \times \cdots \times \mathcal{F}_n^*$. Then, $\mathcal{C}_{\mathcal{N},\mathcal{F}^*} \leq \mathcal{C}_{\mathcal{N}}$.*

Proof. We have to show that, for every $f = (f_1, \ldots, f_n)$, we find a pair (P, Q) of distributions from $\mathcal{D}_{\mathcal{N}}$ such that, for every $x \in \{0,1\}^n$, $L_{\mathcal{N},f}(x) = \mathrm{sign}(\log(P(x)/Q(x)))$. To this end, we define the parameters for the distributions P and Q as follows:

$$p_{i,\alpha} = \begin{cases} \frac{1}{2} 2^{-2^{i-1} n} & \text{if } f_i(\alpha) = -1 \\ \frac{1}{2} & \text{if } f_i(\alpha) = +1 \end{cases} \quad \text{and } q_{i,\alpha} = \begin{cases} \frac{1}{2} & \text{if } f_i(\alpha) = -1 \\ \frac{1}{2} 2^{-2^{i-1} n} & \text{if } f_i(\alpha) = +1 \end{cases}$$

An easy calculation now shows that

$$\log\left(\frac{p_{i,\alpha}}{q_{i,\alpha}}\right) = f_i(\alpha) 2^{i-1} n \text{ and } \left|\log \frac{1 - p_{i,\alpha}}{1 - q_{i,\alpha}}\right| < 1 \ . \tag{5}$$

Fix an arbitrary $x \in \{0,1\}^n \setminus \{\bar{0}\}$. Choose i_* maximal such that $x_{i_*} = 1$ and let α_* denote the projection of x to the parent-variables of x_{i_*}. Then, $L_{\mathcal{N},f}(x) = f_{i_*}(\alpha_*)$. Thus, $L_{\mathcal{N},f}(x) = \mathrm{sign}(\log(P(x)/Q(x)))$ would follow immediately from

$$\mathrm{sign}\left(\log \frac{P(x)}{Q(x)}\right) = \mathrm{sign}\left(\log \frac{p_{i_*,\alpha_*}}{q_{i_*,\alpha_*}}\right) = f_{i_*}(\alpha_*) \ . \tag{6}$$

The second equation in (6) is evident from (5). As for the first equation in (6), we argue as follows. By the choice of i_*, $x_i = 0$ for every $i > i_*$. In combination with (3) and (5), we get

$$\log \frac{P(x)}{Q(x)} = \log \frac{p_{i_*,\alpha_*}}{q_{i_*,\alpha_*}} + \sum_{i=1}^{i_*-1} \sum_{\alpha \in \{0,1\}^{m_i}} x_i M_{i,\alpha}(x) \log \frac{p_{i,\alpha}}{q_{i,\alpha}}$$
$$+ \sum_{i \in I} \sum_{\alpha \in \{0,1\}^{m_i}} (1 - x_i) M_{i,\alpha}(x) \log \frac{1 - p_{i,\alpha}}{1 - q_{i,\alpha}} ,$$

where $I = \{1, \ldots, n\} \setminus \{i_*\}$. The sign of the right-hand side of this equation is determined by $\log(p_{i_*,\alpha_*}/q_{i_*,\alpha_*})$ since this term is of absolute value $2^{i_*-1}n$ and $2^{i_*-1}n - \sum_{j=1}^{i_*-1} 2^{j-1}n - (n-1) \geq 1$. This concludes the proof. □

The next two results are straightforward applications of Lemma 3 combined with Theorems 6, 1, and Corollary 2.

Corollary 3. *For every unconstrained Bayesian network $\mathcal{N}$, the following holds:*

$$\sum_{i=1}^{n} 2^{m_i} \leq \mathrm{VCdim}(\mathcal{N}) \leq \mathrm{Edim}(\mathcal{N}) \leq \left| \bigcup_{i=1}^{n} 2^{P_i \cup \{i\}} \right| \leq 2 \cdot \sum_{i=1}^{n} 2^{m_i}$$

Corollary 4. *Let $\mathcal{N}_k$ denote the Bayesian network from Example 1. Then:*

$$(n-k+1)2^k - 1 \leq \mathrm{VCdim}(\mathcal{N}_k) \leq \mathrm{Edim}(\mathcal{N}_k) \leq (n-k+1)2^k .$$

We now show that Lemma 3 can be applied in a similar fashion to the more general case of networks with a reduced parameter collection.

Theorem 7. *Let $\mathcal{N}^R$ be a Bayesian network with a reduced parameter collection $(p_{i,c})_{1 \leq i \leq n, 1 \leq c \leq d_i}$ in the sense of Definition 2. Let $\mathcal{F}_i^{R_i}$ denote the set of all ± 1-valued functions on domain $\{0,1\}^{m_i}$ that depend on $\alpha \in \{0,1\}^{m_i}$ only through $R_i(\alpha)$. In other words, $f \in \mathcal{F}_i^{R_i}$ iff there exists a ± 1-valued function g on domain $\{1, \ldots, d_i\}$ such that $f(\alpha) = g(R_i(\alpha))$ for every $\alpha \in \{0,1\}^{m_i}$. Finally, let $\mathcal{F}^R = \mathcal{F}_1^{R_1} \times \cdots \times \mathcal{F}_n^{R_n}$. Then, $\mathcal{C}_{\mathcal{N}^R, \mathcal{F}^R} \leq \mathcal{C}_{\mathcal{N}^R}$.*

Proof. We focus on the differences to the proof of Theorem 6. First, the decision list $L_{\mathcal{N}^R,f}$ uses a function $f = (f_1, \ldots, f_n)$ of the form $f_i(x) = g_i(R_i(x))$ for some function $g_i : \{1, \ldots, d_i\} \to \{-1, +1\}$. Second, the distributions P, Q that satisfy $L_{\mathcal{N},f}(x) = \mathrm{sign}(\log(P(x)/Q(x)))$ for every $x \in \{0,1\}^n$ have to be defined over the reduced parameter collection. Compare with (4). An appropriate choice is as follows:

$$p_{i,c} = \begin{cases} \frac{1}{2} 2^{-2^{i-1}n} & \text{if } g_i(c) = -1 \\ \frac{1}{2} & \text{if } g_i(c) = +1 \end{cases} \quad \text{and } q_{i,c} = \begin{cases} \frac{1}{2} & \text{if } g_i(c) = -1 \\ \frac{1}{2} 2^{-2^{i-1}n} & \text{if } g_i(c) = +1 \end{cases}$$

The rest of the proof is completely analogous to the proof of Theorem 6. □

From Lemma 3 and Theorems 7 and 2, we get

Corollary 5. *Let $\mathcal{N}^R$ be a Bayesian network with a reduced parameter collection $(p_{i,c})_{1\le i\le n, 1\le c\le d_i}$ in the sense of Definition 2. Then:*

$$\sum_{i=1}^{n} d_i \le \mathrm{VCdim}(\mathcal{N}^R) \le \mathrm{Edim}(\mathcal{N}^R) \le 2 \cdot \sum_{i=1}^{n} d_i \ .$$

Lemma 3 does not seem to apply to constrained networks. However, some of these networks allow for a similar reasoning as in the proof of Theorem 6. More precisely, the following holds:

Theorem 8. *Let $\mathcal{N}$ be a constrained Bayesian network. Assume there exists, for every $i \in \{1,\ldots,n\}$, a collection of pairwise different bit-patterns $\alpha_{i,1},\ldots,\alpha_{i,d_i} \in \{0,1\}^{m_i}$ such that the constraints of $\mathcal{N}$ allow for the following independent decisions: for every pair (i,c), where i ranges from 1 to n and c from 1 to d_i, parameter $p_{i,\alpha_{i,c}}$ is set either to value $2^{-2^{i-1}n}/2$ or to value $1/2$. Then:*

$$\mathrm{VCdim}(\mathcal{N}) \ge \sum_{i=1}^{n} d_i \ .$$

Proof. For every pair (i,c), let $x_{i,c} \in \{0,1\}^n$ be the vector that has bit 1 in coordinate i, bit-pattern $\alpha_{i,c}$ in the coordinates corresponding to the parents of i, and zeros in the remaining coordinates (including positions $i+1,\ldots,n$). Following the train of thoughts in the proof of Theorem 6, it is easy to see that the vectors $x_{i,c}$ are shattered by $\mathcal{C}_{\mathcal{N}}$. □

Corollary 6. *Let $\mathcal{N}_\sigma$ denote the logistic autoregressive Bayesian network from Definition 3. Then:*

$$\mathrm{VCdim}(\mathcal{N}_\sigma) \ge \frac{1}{2}(n-1)n \ .$$

Proof. We aim at applying Theorem 8 with $d_i = i-1$ for $i = 1,\ldots,n$. For $c = 1,\ldots,i-1$, let $\alpha_{i,c} \in \{0,1\}^{i-1}$ be the pattern with bit 1 in position c and zeros elsewhere. It follows now from Definition 3 that $p_{i,\alpha_{i,c}} = \sigma(w_{i,c})$. Since $\sigma(\mathbb{R}) =]0,1[$, the parameters $p_{i,\alpha_{i,c}}$ can independently be set to any value of our choice in $]0,1[$. Thus, Theorem 8 applies. □

4.2 Lower Bounds Based on Spectral Norm Considerations

We would like to show an exponential lower bound on $\mathrm{Edim}(\mathcal{N}_\sigma)$. However, at the time being, we get such a bound for a slight modification of this network only:

Definition 8. *The* modified logistic autoregressive *Bayesian network* $\mathcal{N}'_\sigma$ *is the fully connected Bayesian network with nodes* $0, 1, \ldots, n+1$ *and the following constraints on the parameter collection:*

$$\forall i = 0, \ldots, n, \exists (w_{i,j})_{0 \le j \le i-1} \in \mathbb{R}^i, \forall \alpha \in \{0,1\}^i : p_{i,\alpha} = \sigma\left(\sum_{j=0}^{i-1} w_{i,j}\alpha_j\right)$$

and

$$\exists (w_i)_{0 \le i \le n}, \forall \alpha \in \{0,1\}^{n+1} : p_{n+1,\alpha} = \sigma\left(\sum_{i=0}^{n} w_i \sigma\left(\sum_{j=0}^{i-1} w_{i,j}\alpha_j\right)\right) .$$

Obviously, $\mathcal{N}_\sigma$ *is completely described by the parameter collections* $(w_{i,j})_{0 \le i \le n, 0 \le j \le i-1}$ *and* $(w_i)_{0 \le i \le n}$.

The crucial difference between $\mathcal{N}'_\sigma$ and $\mathcal{N}_\sigma$ is the node $n+1$ whose sigmoidal function gets the outputs of the other sigmoidal functions as input. Roughly speaking, $\mathcal{N}_\sigma$ is a "one-layer" network whereas $\mathcal{N}'_\sigma$ has an extra node at a "second layer".

Theorem 9. *Let* $\mathcal{N}'_\sigma$ *denote the modified logistic autoregressive Bayesian network with* $n+2$ *nodes, where we assume (for sake of simplicity only) that* n *is a multiple of* 4. *Then,* $\mathrm{PARITY}_{n/2} \le \mathcal{N}'_\sigma$ *even if we restrict the "weights" in the parameter collection of* $\mathcal{N}'_\sigma$ *to integers of size* $O(\log n)$.

Proof. The mapping

$$\{0,1\}^{n/2} \ni x = (x_1, \ldots, x_{n/2}) \mapsto (\overbrace{1, x_1, \ldots, x_{n/2}, 1, \ldots, 1}^{\alpha}, 1) = x' \in \{0,1\}^{n+2} , \tag{7}$$

embeds $\{0,1\}^{n/2}$ into $\{0,1\}^{n+2}$. Note that α, as indicated in (7), equals the bit-pattern of the parent-variables of x'_{n+1} (which are actually all other variables). We claim that the following holds. For every $a \in \{0,1\}^{n/2}$, there exists a pair (P, Q) of distributions from $\mathcal{D}_{\mathcal{N}'_\sigma}$ such that, for every $x \in \{0,1\}^{n/2}$,

$$(-1)^{a^\top x} = \mathrm{sign}\left(\log \frac{P(x')}{Q(x')}\right) . \tag{8}$$

(Clearly the theorem follows once the claim is settled.) The proof of the claim makes use of the following facts:

Fact 1. For every $a \in \{0,1\}^{n/2}$, function $(-1)^{a^\top x}$ can be computed by a 2-layer (unit weights) threshold circuit with $n/2$ threshold units at the first layer (and, of course, one output threshold unit at the second layer).

Fact 2. Each 2-layer threshold circuit C with polynomially bounded integer weights can be simulated by a 2-layer sigmoidal circuit C' with polynomially bounded integer weights, the same number of units, and the following output convention: $C(x) = 1 \implies C'(x) \ge 2/3$ and $C(x) = 0 \implies C'(x) \le 1/3$. The same remark holds when we replace "polynomially bounded" by "logarithmically bounded".

Fact 3. $\mathcal{N}'_\sigma$ contains (as a "substructure") a 2-layer sigmoidal circuit C' with $n/2$ input nodes, $n/2$ sigmoidal units at the first layer, and one sigmoidal unit at the second layer.

Fact 1 (even its generalization to arbitrary symmetric Boolean functions) is well known [16]. Fact 2 follows from a more general result by Maass, Schnitger, and Sontag. (See Theorem 4.3 in [22].) The third fact needs some explanation. (The following discussion should be compared with Definition 8.) We would like the term $p_{n+1,\alpha}$ to satisfy $p_{n+1,\alpha} = C'(\alpha_1, \dots, \alpha_{n/2})$, where C' denotes an arbitrary 2-layer sigmoidal circuit as described in Fact 3. To this end, we set $w_{i,j} = 0$ if $1 \le i \le n/2$ or if $i, j \ge n/2 + 1$. We set $w_i = 0$ if $1 \le i \le n/2$. The parameters which have been set to zero are referred to as *redundant* parameters in what follows. Recall from (7) that $\alpha_0 = \alpha_{n/2+1} = \cdots = \alpha_n = 1$. From these settings (and from $\sigma(0) = 1/2$), we get

$$p_{n+1,\alpha} = \sigma\left(\frac{1}{2}w_0 + \sum_{i=n/2+1}^{n} w_i \sigma\left(w_{i,0} + \sum_{j=1}^{n/2} w_{i,j}\alpha_j\right)\right) .$$

This is the output of a 2-layer sigmoidal circuit C' on input $(\alpha_1, \dots, \alpha_{n/2})$, indeed.

We are now in the position to describe the choice of distributions P and Q. Let C' be the sigmoidal circuit that computes $(-1)^{a^\top x}$ for some fixed $a \in \{0,1\}^{n/2}$ according to Facts 1 and 2. Let P be the distribution obtained by setting the redundant parameters to zero (as described above) and the remaining parameters as in C'. Thus, $p_{n+1,\alpha} = C'(\alpha_1, \dots, \alpha_{n/2})$. Let Q be the distribution with the same parameters as P except for replacing w_i by $-w_i$. Thus, by symmetry of σ, $q_{n+1,\alpha} = 1 - C'(\alpha_1, \dots, \alpha_{n/2})$. Since $x'_{n+1} = 1$ and since all but one factor in $P(x')/Q(x')$ cancel each other, we arrive at

$$\frac{P(x')}{Q(x')} = \frac{p_{n+1,\alpha}}{q_{n+1,\alpha}} = \frac{C'(\alpha_1, \dots, \alpha_{n/2})}{1 - C'(\alpha_1, \dots, \alpha_{n/2})} .$$

Since C' computes $(-1)^{a^\top x}$ (with the output convention from Fact 3), we get $P(x')/Q(x') \ge 2$ if $(-1)^{a^\top x} = 1$, and $P(x')/Q(x') \le 1/2$ otherwise, which implies (8) and concludes the proof of the claim. □

From Corollary 1 and Theorem 9, we get

Corollary 7. $\mathrm{Edim}(\mathcal{N}'_\sigma) \ge 2^{n/4}$.

We mentioned in the introduction (see the remarks about random projections) that a large lower bound on $\mathrm{Edim}(\mathcal{C})$ rules out the possibility of a large margin classifier. For the class PARITY_n, this can be made more precise. It was shown in [10,13] that every linear arrangement for PARITY_n has an average geometric margin of at most $2^{-n/2}$. Thus there can be no linear arrangement with an average margin exceeding $2^{-n/4}$ for $\mathcal{C}_{\mathcal{N}'_\sigma}$ even if we restrict the weight parameters in $\mathcal{N}'_\sigma$ to logarithmically bounded integers.

Open Problems 1) Determine Edim for the (unmodified) logistic autoregressive Bayesian network.
2) Determine Edim for other popular classes of distributions or densities (where, in the light of Remark 1, those from the exponential family look like a good thing to start with).

Acknowledgements. Thanks to the anonymous referees for valuable comments and suggestions.

References

1. Yasemin Altun, Ioannis Tsochantaridis, and Thomas Hofmann. Hidden Markov support vector machines. In *Proceedings of the 20th International Conference on Machine Learning*, pages 3–10. AAAI Press, 2003.
2. Rosa I. Arriaga and Santosh Vempala. An algorithmic theory of learning: Robust concepts and random projection. In *Proceedings of the 40'th Annual Symposium on the Foundations of Computer Science*, pages 616–623, 1999.
3. Shai Ben-David, Nadav Eiron, and Hans Ulrich Simon. Limitations of learning via embeddings in euclidean half-spaces. *Journal of Machine Learning Research*, 3:441–461, 2002. An extended abstract of this paper appeared in the Proceedings of the 14th Annual Conference on Computational Learning Theory (COLT 2001).
4. Bernhard E. Boser, Isabelle M. Guyon, and Vladimir N. Vapnik. A training algorithm for optimal margin classifiers. In *Proceedings of the 5th Annual ACM Workshop on Computational Learning Theory*, pages 144–152. ACM Press, 1992.
5. David Maxwell Chickering, David Heckerman, and Christopher Meek. A Bayesian approach to learning Bayesian networks with local structure. In *Proceedings of the Thirteenth Conference on Uncertainty in Artificial Intelligence*, pages 80–89. Morgan Kaufman, 1997.
6. Thomas M. Cover. Geometrical and statistical properties of systems of linear inequalities with applications in pattern recognition. *IEEE Transactions on Electronic Computers*, 14:326–334, 1965.
7. P. Mc Cullagh and J. A. Nelder. *Generalized Linear Models.* Chapman and Hall, 1983.
8. Luc Devroye, László Györfi, and Gábor Lugosi. *A Probabilistic Theory of Pattern Recognition.* Springer Verlag, 1996.
9. Richard O. Duda and Peter E. Hart. *Pattern Classification and Scene Analysis.* Wiley–Interscience. John Wiley & Sons, New York, 1973.
10. Jürgen Forster. A linear lower bound on the unbounded error communication complexity. *Journal of Computer and System Sciences*, 65(4):612–625, 2002. An extended abstract of this paper appeared in the Proceedings of the 16th Annual Conference on Computational Complexity (CCC 2001).
11. Jürgen Forster, Matthias Krause, Satyanarayana V. Lokam, Rustam Mubarakzjanov, Niels Schmitt, and Hans Ulrich Simon. Relations between communication complexity, linear arrangements, and computational complexity. In *Proceedings of the 21'st Annual Conference on the Foundations of Software Technology and Theoretical Computer Science*, pages 171–182, 2001.

12. Jürgen Forster, Niels Schmitt, Hans Ulrich Simon, and Thorsten Suttorp. Estimating the optimal margins of embeddings in euclidean half spaces. *Machine Learning*, 51(3):263–281, 2003. An extended abstract of this paper appeared in the Proceedings of the 14th Annual Conference on Computational Learning Theory (COLT 2001).
13. Jürgen Forster and Hans Ulrich Simon. On the smallest possible dimension and the largest possible margin of linear arrangements representing given concept classes. In *Proceedings of the 13th International Workshop on Algorithmic Learning Theory*, pages 128–138, 2002.
14. P. Frankl and H. Maehara. The Johnson-Lindenstrauss lemma and the sphericity of some graphs. *Journal of Combinatorial Theory (B)*, 44:355–362, 1988.
15. Brendan J. Frey. *Graphical Models for Machine Learning and Digital Communication.* MIT Press, 1998.
16. Andras Hajnal, Wolfgang Maass, Pavel Pudlák, Mario Szegedy, and György Turán. Threshold circuits of bounded depth. *Journal of Computer and System Sciences*, 46:129–1154, 1993.
17. Tommi S. Jaakkola and David Haussler. Exploiting generative models in discriminative classifiers. In *Advances in Neural Information Processing Systems 11*, pages 487–493. MIT Press, 1998.
18. Tommi S. Jaakkola and David Haussler. Probabilistic kernel regression models. In *Proceedings of the 7th International Workshop on AI and Statistics.* Morgan Kaufman, 1999.
19. W. B. Johnson and J. Lindenstrauss. Extensions of Lipshitz mapping into Hilbert spaces. *Contemp. Math.*, 26:189–206, 1984.
20. Eike Kiltz. On the representation of boolean predicates of the Diffie-Hellman function. In *Proceedings of 20th International Symposium on Theoretical Aspects of Computer Science*, pages 223–233, 2003.
21. Eike Kiltz and Hans Ulrich Simon. Complexity theoretic aspects of some cryptographic functions. In *Proceedings of the 9th International Conference on Computing and Combinatorics*, pages 294–303, 2003.
22. Wolfgang Maass, Georg Schnitger, and Eduardo D. Sontag. A comparison of the computational power of sigmoid and Boolean theshold circuits. In Vwani Roychowdhury, Kai-Yeung Siu, and Alon Orlitsky, editors, *Theoretical Advances in Neural Computation and Learning*, pages 127–151. Kluwer Academic Publishers, 1994.
23. Radford M. Neal. Connectionist learning of belief networks. *Artificial Intelligence*, 56:71–113, 1992.
24. Nuria Oliver, Bernhard Schölkopf, and Alexander J. Smola. Natural regularization from generative models. In Alexander J. Smola, Peter L. Bartlett, Bernhard Schölkopf, and Dale Schuurmans, editors, *Advances in Large Margin Classifiers*, pages 51–60. MIT Press, 2000.
25. Judea Pearl. Reverend Bayes on inference engines: A distributed hierarchical approach. In *Proceedings of the National Conference on Artificial Intelligence*, pages 133–136. AAAI Press, 1982.
26. Laurence K. Saul, Tommi Jaakkola, and Michael I. Jordan. Mean field theory for sigmoid belief networks. *Journal of Artificial Intelligence Research*, 4:61–76, 1996.
27. Craig Saunders, John Shawe-Taylor, and Alexei Vinokourov. String kernels, Fisher kernels and finite state automata. In *Advances in Neural Information Processing Systems 15.* MIT Press, 2002.
28. Michael Schmitt. On the complexity of computing and learning with multiplicative neural networks. *Neural Computation*, 14:241–301, 2002.

29. D. J. Spiegelhalter and R. P. Knill-Jones. Statistical and knowledge-based approaches to clinical decision support systems. *Journal of the Royal Statistical Society*, pages 35–77, 1984.
30. Koji Tsuda, Shotaro Akaho, Motoaki Kawanabe, and Klaus-Robert Müller. Asymptotic properties of the Fisher kernel. *Neural Computation*, 2003. To appear.
31. Koji Tsuda and Motoaki Kawanabe. The leave-one-out kernel. In *Proceedings of the International Conference on Artificial Neural Networks*, pages 727–732. Springer, 2002.
32. Koji Tsuda, Motoaki Kawanabe, Gunnar Rätsch, Sören Sonnenburg, and Klaus-Robert Müller. A new discriminative kernel from probabilistic models. *Neural Computation*, 14(10):2397–2414, 2002.
33. Vladimir Vapnik. *Statistical Learning Theory*. Wiley Series on Adaptive and Learning Systems for Signal Processing, Communications, and Control. John Wiley & Sons, 1998.

An Inequality for Nearly Log-Concave Distributions with Applications to Learning

Constantine Caramanis* and Shie Mannor

Laboratory for Information and Decision Systems
Massachusetts Institute of Technology, Cambridge, MA 02139
{cmcaram,shie}@mit.edu

Abstract. We prove that given a nearly log-concave density, in any partition of the space to two well separated sets, the measure of the points that do not belong to these sets is large. We apply this isoperimetric inequality to derive lower bounds on the generalization error in learning. We also show that when the data are sampled from a nearly log-concave distribution, the margin cannot be large in a strong probabilistic sense. We further consider regression problems and show that if the inputs and outputs are sampled from a nearly log-concave distribution, the measure of points for which the prediction is wrong by more than ϵ_0 and less than ϵ_1 is (roughly) linear in $\epsilon_1 - \epsilon_0$.

1 Introduction

Large margin classifiers (e.g., [CS00,SBSS00] to name but a few recent books) have become an almost ubiquitous approach in supervised machine learning. The plethora of algorithms that maximize the margin, and their impressive success (e.g., [SS02] and references therein) may lead one to believe that obtaining a large margin is synonymous with successful generalization and classification. In this paper we directly consider the question of how much weight the margin must carry. We show that essentially if the margin between two classes is large, then the weight of the "no-man's land" between the two classes must be large as well. Our probabilistic assumption is that the data are sampled from a nearly log-concave distribution. Under this assumption, we prove that for any partition of the space into two sets such that the distance between those two sets is t, the measure of the "no man's land" outside the two sets is lower bounded by t times the minimum of the measure of the two sets times a dimension-free constant. The direct implication of this result is that a large margin is unlikely when sampling data from such a distribution.

Our modelling assumption is that the underlying distribution has a β-log-concave density. While this assumption may appear restrictive, we note that many "reasonable" functions belong to this family. We discuss this assumption in Section 2, and point out some interesting properties of β-log-concave functions.

* C. Caramanis is eligible for the Best student paper award.

J. Shawe-Taylor and Y. Singer (Eds.): COLT 2004, LNAI 3120, pp. 534–548, 2004.

In Section 3 we prove an inequality stating that the measure (under a β-log-concave distribution) of the "no-man's" land is large if the sets are well separated. This result relies essentially on the Prékopa-Leindler inequality which is a generalization of the Brunn-Minkowski inequality (we refer the reader to the excellent survey [Gar02]). We note that Theorem 2 was stated in [LS90] for volumes, and in [AK91] for β-log-concave distributions, in the context of efficient sampling from convex bodies. However, there are steps in the proof which we were unable to follow. Specifically, the reduction in [AK91] to what they call the "needle-like" case is based on an argument used in [LS90], which uses the Ham-Sandwich Theorem to guarantee not only bisection, but also some orthogonality properties of the bisecting hyperplane. It is not clear to us how one may obtain such guarantees from the Ham-Sandwich Theorem. Furthermore, the solution of the needle-like case in [AK91] relies on a uniformity assumption on the modulation of the distribution, which does not appear evident from the assumptions on the distribution. We provide a complete proof of the result using the Ham-Sandwich Theorem (as in [LS90]) and a different reduction argument. We further point out a few natural extensions.

In Section 4 we specialize the isoperimetric inequality to two different setups. First, we provide lower bounds for the generalization error in classification under the assumption that the classifier will be tested using a β-log-concave distribution, which did not necessarily generate the data. While this assumption is not in line with the standard PAC learning formulation, it is applicable to the setup where data are sampled from one distribution and performance is judged by another. Suppose, for instance, that the generating distribution evolves over time, while the true classifier remains fixed. We may have access to a training set generated by a distribution quite different from the one we use to test our classifier. We show that if there is a large (in a geometric sense) family of classifiers that agree with the training points, then for any choice of classifier there exists another classifier compared to which the generalization error is relatively large. Second, we consider the typical statistical machine learning setup, and show that for any classifier the probability of a large margin (with respect to that classifier) decreases exponentially fast to 0 with the number of samples, if the data are sampled from a β-log-concave distribution. It is important to note that the β-log-concave assumption applies to the input space. If we use a Mercer kernel, the induced distribution in the feature space may not be β-log-concave. If the kernel map is Lipschitz continuous with constant L, then we can relate the "functional" margin in the feature space to the "geometric" margin in the input space, and our results carry over directly. If the kernel map is not Lipschitz, then our results do not directly apply.

In Section 5 we briefly touch on the issue of regression. We show that if we have a regressor, then the measure of a tube around its prediction with inner radius ϵ_0 and outer radius ϵ_1 is bounded from below by $\epsilon_1 - \epsilon_0$ times a constant (as long as ϵ_1 is not too large). The direct implication of this inequality is that the margins of the tube carry a significant portion of the measure.

Some recent results [BES02,Men04] argue that the success of large margin classifiers is remarkable since most classes cannot have a useful embedding in some Hilbert space. Our results provide a different angle, as we show that having a large margin is unlikely to start with. Moreover, if there happens to be a large margin, it may well result in a large error (which is proportional to the margin). A notable feature of our bounds is that they are dimension-free and are therefore immune to the curse of dimensionality (this is essentially due to the β-log-concave assumption). We note the different flavor of our results from the "classical" lower bounds (e.g., [AB99,Vap98]) that are mostly concerned with the PAC setup and where the sample complexity is the main object of interest. We do not address the sample complexity directly in this work.

2 Nearly Log-Concave Functions

We assume throughout the paper that generalization error is measured using a nearly log-concave distribution. In this section we define such distributions and highlight some of their properties. While we are mostly interested in distributions, it is useful to write the following definitions in terms of a general function on $\mathbb{R}^n$.

Definition 1. *A function $f : \mathbb{R}^n \to \mathbb{R}$ is* β-log-concave *for some $\beta \geq 0$ if for any $\lambda \in (0,1)$, $x_1 \in \mathbb{R}^n$, $x_2 \in \mathbb{R}^n$, we have that:*

$$f(\lambda x_1 + (1-\lambda)x_2) \geq e^{-\beta} f(x_1)^{\lambda} f(x_2)^{1-\lambda}. \tag{2.1}$$

A function f is log-concave *if it is 0-log-concave.*

The class of log-concave distributions itself is rather rich. For example, it includes Gaussian, Uniform, Logistic, and Exponential distributions. We refer the reader to [BB89] for an extensive list of such distributions, sufficient conditions for a distribution to be log-concave, and ways to "produce" log-concave distributions from other log-concave distributions. The class of β-log-concave distributions is considerably richer since we allow a factor of $e^{-\beta}$ in Eq. (2.1). For example, unlike log-concave distributions, β-log-concave distributions need not be continuous. We now provide some results that are useful in the sequel. We start from the following observation.

Lemma 1. *The support of a β-log-concave function is a convex set. Also, β-log-concave functions are bounded on bounded sets.*

Distributions that are β-log-concave are not necessarily unimodal, but possess a unimodal quality, in the sense of Lemma 2 below. This simple lemma captures the properties of β-log-concavity that are central to our main results and subsequent applications. It implies that if we have a β-log-concave distribution on an interval, there cannot be any big "holes" or "valleys" in the mass distribution. Thus if we divide the interval into three intervals, if the middle interval is large, it must also carry a lot of the weight. In higher dimensions, essentially this says that if we divide our set into two sets, if the distance between the sets is large, the mass of the "no-man's land" will also be large. This is essentially the content of Theorem 2 below.

Lemma 2. *Suppose that $f(x)$ is β-log-concave on an interval $[u_1, u_2]$. Let $u_1 < x_1 < x_2 < u_2$. Then for any $x \in [x_1, x_2]$, at least one of the following holds:*

$$f(x) \geq f(y) \cdot e^{-\beta}, \quad \text{for all } y \in [u_1, x_1],$$

or

$$f(x) \geq f(y) \cdot e^{-\beta}, \quad \text{for all } y \in [x_2, u_2].$$

Proof. Fix $\epsilon > 0$. There is some $x^* \in [u_1, u_2]$ such that $\sup_{x \in [u_1, u_2]} f(x) < f(x^*) + \epsilon$. Suppose $x^* \in [u_1, x_1]$. Then for any $x \in [x_1, x_2]$ and $y \in [x_2, u_2]$, and for some $\lambda \in (0,1)$ we have $x = \lambda x^* + (1-\lambda)y$, and by the β-log-concavity of f, we have

$$f(x) \geq f(x^*)^\lambda f(y)^{1-\lambda} e^{-\beta} \geq (f(y) - \epsilon)^\lambda f(y)^{1-\lambda} e^{-\beta}. \tag{2.2}$$

Similarly, if $x^* \in [x_2, u_2]$, then for every $x \in [x_1, x_2]$ and $y \in [u_1, x_1]$, Eq. (2.2) holds. Finally, if $x^* \in [x_1, x_2]$, then for any $x \in [x_1, x^*]$, Eq. (2.2) holds for $y \in [u_1, x_1]$, and for $x \in [x^*, x_2]$, Eq. (2.2) holds for any $y \in [x_2, u_2]$. Take a sequence $\epsilon_i \searrow 0$. We know that for every ϵ_i Eq. (2.2) holds for all $x \in [x_1, x_2]$ and all $y \in [u_1, x_1]$ or all $y \in [x_2, u_2]$. It follows that there exists a sequence $\epsilon_i \searrow 0$ such that for all $x \in [x_1, x_2]$, Eq. (2.2) holds for all $y \in [u_1, x_1]$ or for all $y \in [x_2, u_2]$. Since ϵ_i converges to 0, $f(x) \geq f(y)e^{-\beta}$ in at least one of those domains. □

The following inequality has many uses in geometry, statistics, and analysis (see [Gar02]). Note that it is stated with respect to a specific $\lambda \in (0,1)$ and not to all λ.

Theorem 1 (Prékopa-Leindler Inequality). *Let $0 < \lambda < 1$, and h, g_1, g_2 be nonnegative integrable functions on $\mathbb{R}^n$, such that $h((1-\lambda)x + \lambda y) \geq g_1(x)^{1-\lambda} g_2(y)^\lambda$, for every $x, y \in \mathbb{R}^n$. Then*

$$\int_{\mathbb{R}^n} h(x)\, dx \geq \left(\int_{\mathbb{R}^n} g_1(x)\, dx \right)^{1-\lambda} \left(\int_{\mathbb{R}^n} g_2(x)\, dx \right)^{\lambda}.$$

The following lemma plays a key part in the reduction technique we use below. Recall that the orthogonal projection of a set $K \subseteq \mathbb{R}^{n+m}$ onto $\mathbb{R}^n$ is defined as $K|_{\mathbb{R}^n} \triangleq \{x \in \mathbb{R}^n : \exists y \in \mathbb{R}^m \text{ s.t. } (x,y) \in K\}$.

Lemma 3. *Let $f(x,y)$ be a β-log-concave distribution on a convex set $K \subseteq \mathbb{R}^{n+m}$. For every x in $K|_{\mathbb{R}^n}$ consider the section $K(x) \triangleq \{(x,y) \in \mathbb{R}^{n+m} : (x,y) \in K\}$. Then the distribution $F(x) \triangleq \int_{K(x)} f(x,y)\, dy$ is β-log-concave on $K(x)$.*

Proof. This is a consequence of the Prékopa-Leindler inequality as in [Gar02], Section 9, for log-concave distributions. Adapting the proof for β-log-concave distributions is straightforward. □

There are quite a few interesting properties of β-log-concave distributions. For example, the convolution of a β_1-log-concave and a β_2-log-concave distribution is $(\beta_1+\beta_2)$-log-concave; Gaussian mixtures are β-log-concave; and mixtures of distributions with bounded Radon-Nikodym derivative are also β-log-concave. These properties will be provided elsewhere.

3 Isoperimetric Inequalities

In this section we prove our main result concerning β-log-concave distributions. We show that if two sets are well separated, then the "no man's land" between them has large measure relative to the measure of the two sets. We first prove the result for bounded sets and then provide two immediate corollaries. Let $d(x, y)$ denote the Euclidean distance in $\mathbb{R}^n$. We define the distance between two sets K_1 and K_2 as $d(K_1, K_2) \triangleq \inf_{x\in K_1, y\in K_2} d(x, y)$ and the diameter of a set K as $\operatorname{diam}(K) \triangleq \sup_{x,y\in K} d(x, y)$. Given a distribution f we say that $\mu(K) = \int_K f(x)\,dx$ is the induced measure. A decomposition of a closed set $K \subseteq \mathbb{R}^n$ to a collection of closed sets $K_1, K_2, \ldots, K_\ell$ satisfies that: $\bigcup_{i=1}^{\ell} K_i = K$ and $\nu(K_i \cap K_j) = 0$ for all $i \neq j$ where ν is the Lebesgue measure on $\mathbb{R}^n$.

Theorem 2. *Let K be a closed and bounded convex set with non-zero diameter in $\mathbb{R}^n$ with a decomposition $K = K_1 \cup B \cup K_2$. For any β-log-concave distribution $f(x)$, the induced measure μ satisfies that*

$$\mu(B) \geq e^{-\beta}\frac{d(K_1, K_2)}{\operatorname{diam}(K)} \min\{\mu(K_1), \mu(K_2)\}.$$

We remark that this bound is dimension-free. The ratio $d(K_1, K_2)/\operatorname{diam}(K)$ is necessary, as essentially it adjusts for any scaling of the problem. We further note that the minimum $\min\{\mu(K_1), \mu(K_2)\}$ might be quite small, however, this appears to be unavoidable (e.g., consider the tail of a Gaussian, which is log-concave). The proof proceeds by induction on the dimension n, with base case $n = 1$. To prove the inductive step, first we show that it is enough to consider an "ϵ-flat" set K, i.e., a set that is contained in an ellipse whose smallest axis is smaller than some $\epsilon > 0$. Next, we show that for an ϵ-flat set K, we can project onto $n-1$ dimensions where the theorem holds by induction. By properly performing the projection, we show that if the result holds for the projection, it holds for the original set. We abbreviate $t = d(K_1, K_2)$. The theorem trivially holds if $t = 0$, so we can assume that $t > 0$. From Lemma 1 above, we know that the support of $f(x)$ is convex. Thus, we can assume without loss of generality, that since K is compact, $f(x)$ is strictly positive on the interior of K.

Lemma 4. *Theorem 2 holds for $n = 1$.*

Proof. If $n = 1$, then K is some interval, $K = [u_1, u_2]$, with $\text{diam}(K) = |u_2 - u_1|$. Since $t = d(K_1, K_2) > 0$, no point of K_1 is within a distance t from any point of K_2. Furthermore, there must be at least one interval $(b_1, b_2) \subseteq B$ such that $|b_2 - b_1| \geq t$, and such that $(b_1, b_2) \cap (K_1 \cup K_2) = \emptyset$. Fix some $\epsilon > 0$, with $\epsilon < t/2$. Define the ϵ-expansion sets $\hat{K}_1 \triangleq \{x \in K : d(x, K_1) \leq \epsilon\}$, and $\hat{K}_2 \triangleq \{x \in K : d(x, K_2) \leq \epsilon\}$. Define $\hat{B}$ to be the closure of the complement in K of $\hat{K}_1 \cup \hat{K}_2$. Each set is a union of a finite number of closed intervals, and thus we have the decomposition $[u_1, u_2] = \bigcup_{i=1}^{m} [r_{i-1}, r_i]$, where each interval $[r_{i-1}, r_i]$ is either a $\hat{K}_1$-interval, a $\hat{K}_2$-interval, or a $\hat{B}$-interval. We modify the sets so that if the $\hat{B}$-interval $[r_{i-1}, r_i]$ is sandwiched by two $\hat{K}_i$-intervals $(i = 1, 2)$ then we add that interval to $\hat{K}_i$. If the $\hat{B}$-interval is either the first interval $[r_0, r_1]$, or the last interval, $[r_{m-1}, r_m]$, then we add it to whichever set $\hat{K}_i$ is to its right, or left, respectively.

The three resulting sets $\hat{K}_1, \hat{K}_2$, and $\hat{B}$ are closed, intersect at most at a finite number of points, and thus are a decomposition of K. Each set is a union of a finite number of closed intervals. Furthermore, $\hat{t} = d(\hat{K}_1, \hat{K}_2) \geq t - 2\epsilon$, and $\hat{K}_1 \supseteq K_1$, $\hat{K}_2 \supseteq K_2$, and $\hat{B} \subseteq B$. By our modifications above, each $\hat{B}$-interval must have length at least $\hat{t}$.

Consider any $\hat{B}$-interval $[r_{i-1}, r_i]$. Let x^* be a maximizer[1] of $f(x)$ on $[u_1, u_2]$, and $x_{\min}$ a minimizer of $f(x)$ on $[r_{i-1}, r_i]$. Suppose that $x^* \geq x_{\min}$. Then by Lemma 2, for any $y \leq r_{i-1}$, we must have $f(x_{\min}) \geq f(y)e^{-\beta}$. Therefore,

$$\begin{aligned} e^{-\beta}\mu([u_1, r_{i-1}]) &= e^{-\beta} \int_{u_1}^{r_{i-1}} f(x)\, dx \leq (r_{i-1} - u_1) f(x_{\min}) \\ &\leq \text{diam}(K) \cdot f(x_{\min}) \leq \frac{\text{diam}(K)}{(r_i - r_{i-1})} \int_{r_{i-1}}^{r_i} f(x)\, dx \\ &\leq \frac{\text{diam}(K)}{\hat{t}} \mu([r_{i-1}, r_i]). \end{aligned}$$

If instead we have $x^* \leq x_{\min}$, then in a similar manner we obtain the inequality

$$e^{-\beta}\mu([r_i, u_2]) \leq \frac{\text{diam}(K)}{\hat{t}} \mu([r_{i-1}, r_i]).$$

Therefore, in general, for any $\hat{B}$-interval (r_{i-1}, r_i),

$$\mu([r_{i-1}, r_i]) \geq e^{-\beta} \frac{\hat{t}}{\text{diam}(K)} \min\{\mu([u_1, r_{i-1}]), \mu([r_i, u_2])\}.$$

Suppose, without loss of generality, that $[r_0, r_1]$ is a K_1-interval. Consider the first $\hat{B}$-interval $[r_1, r_2]$. If $\mu([r_1, r_2]) \geq e^{-\beta}(\hat{t}/\text{diam}(K))\mu([r_2, u_2])$,

[1] As in Lemma 2, f may not be continuous, so we may only be able to find a point x^* ($x_{\min}$) that is infinitesimally close to the supremum (infimum) of f. For convenience of exposition, we assume f is continuous. This assumption can be removed with an argument exactly parallel to that given in Lemma 2.

then $\mu(\hat{B}) \geq e^{-\beta}(\hat{t}/\operatorname{diam}(K))\mu(\hat{K_2})$ and we are done. So let us assume that $\mu([r_1, r_2]) \geq e^{-\beta}(\hat{t}/\operatorname{diam}(K))\mu([u_1, r_1])$. Similarly, for the last $\hat{B}$-interval (r_{m-2}, r_{m-1}), we can assume that $\mu([r_{m-2}, r_{m-1}]) \geq e^{-\beta}(\hat{t}/\operatorname{diam}(K))\mu([r_{m-1}, u_2])$ otherwise the result immediately follows. This implies that there must be two consecutive $\hat{B}$-intervals, say (r_{j-1}, r_j) and (r_{j+1}, r_{j+2}) such that $\mu([r_{j-1}, r_j]) \geq e^{-\beta}(\hat{t}/\operatorname{diam}(K))\mu([u_1, r_{j-1}])$ and $\mu([r_{j+1}, r_{j+2}]) \geq e^{-\beta}(\hat{t}/\operatorname{diam}(K))\mu([r_{j+2}, u_2])$. Since $[u_1, r_{j-1}] \cup [r_{j+2}, u_2]$ contains either all of $\hat{K}_1$ or $\hat{K}_2$, combining these two inequalities, and using the fact that $\hat{K}_i \supseteq K_i$, and $\hat{B} \subseteq B$, we obtain

$$\begin{aligned}
\mu(B) \geq \mu(\hat{B}) &\geq \mu([r_{j-1}, r_j] \cup [r_{j+1}, r_{j+2}]) \\
&\geq e^{-\beta} \frac{\hat{t}}{\operatorname{diam}(K)} (\mu([u_1, r_{j-1}]) + \mu([r_{j+2}, u_2])) \\
&\geq e^{-\beta} \frac{\hat{t}}{\operatorname{diam}(K)} \min\{\mu(\hat{K}_1), \mu(\hat{K}_2)\} \\
&\geq e^{-\beta} \frac{t - 2\epsilon}{\operatorname{diam}(K)} \min\{\mu(K_1), \mu(K_2)\}.
\end{aligned}$$

Since this holds for every $\epsilon > 0$, the result follows. □

We now prove the n-dimensional case. The first part of our inductive step is to show that it is enough to consider an "ϵ-flat" set K. To make this precise, we use the *Löwner-John Ellipsoid* of a set K. This is the minimum volume ellipsoid E containing K (see, e.g. [GLS93]). This ellipsoid is unique. The key property we use is that if we shrink E from its center by a factor of n, then it is contained in K. We define an ϵ-flat set to be such that the smallest axis of its Löwner-John Ellipsoid has length no more than ϵ.

Lemma 5. *Suppose the theorem* fails by δ *on K, for some $\delta > 0$, i.e.*

$$(1 + \delta)\mu(B) \leq e^{-\beta} \frac{t}{\operatorname{diam}(K)} \min\{\mu(K_1), \mu(K_2)\}. \tag{3.3}$$

Then for any $\epsilon > 0$, there exists some ϵ-flat set $\tilde{K} \subseteq K$ with decomposition $\tilde{K} = \tilde{K}_1 \cup \tilde{B} \cup \tilde{K}_2$, such that $\tilde{K}_i \subseteq K_i$, $\tilde{B} \subseteq B$, $d(\tilde{K}_1, \tilde{K}_2) \geq t$, and $\operatorname{diam}(\tilde{K}) \leq d$, and such that the theorem fails by δ, i.e., Eq. (3.3) holds for $\tilde{K}, \tilde{K}_1, \tilde{K}_2, \tilde{B}$.

Proof. Let K, K_1, K_2, B and δ be as in the statement above. Pick some $\epsilon > 0$ much smaller than t. Suppose that all axes of the Löwner-John ellipsoid of K are greater than ϵ. A powerful consequence of the Borsuk-Ulam Theorem, the so-called Ham-Sandwich Theorem (see, e.g., [Mat02]) says that in $\mathbb{R}^n$, given n Borel measures $\mu_k, k = 1, \ldots, n$, such that the weight of any hyperplane under each measure is zero, there exists a hyperplane H that bisects each measure, i.e., $\mu_k(H^+) = \mu_k(H^-) = \frac{1}{2}\mu_k(\mathbb{R}^n)$ for each k, where H^+, H^- denote the two half-spaces defined by H. Now, since we have $n \geq 2$, the Ham-Sandwich Theorem guarantees that there exists some hyperplane H that bisects (in terms of the measure μ) both K_1 and K_2. Let K' and K'' be the two parts of K defined by H (K and B are not necessarily bisected), and similarly define K_1', K_1'', K_2', K_2'', and B', B''. The minimum distance cannot decrease, i.e., $d(K_1', K_2') \geq t$, and $d(K_1'', K_2'') \geq t$, and the diameter of K cannot be smaller than either the diameter of K' or K''. Consequently, if the theorem holds, or fails by less than δ, for both K' and K'', then

$$
\begin{aligned}
(1+\delta)\mu(B) &= (1+\delta)\mu(B') + (1+\delta)\mu(B'') \\
&\geq e^{-\beta}\frac{t}{\operatorname{diam}(K)}\left(\min\left\{\frac{1}{2}\mu(K_1'), \frac{1}{2}\mu(K_2')\right\} + \min\left\{\frac{1}{2}\mu(K_1''), \frac{1}{2}\mu(K_2'')\right\}\right) \\
&= e^{-\beta}\frac{t}{\operatorname{diam}(K)}\min\{\mu(K_1), \mu(K_2)\}.
\end{aligned}
$$

Therefore the theorem must fail by δ for either K' or K''. We note that this is the *same* δ as above. Call the set for which the theorem does not hold $K^{(1)}$, and similarly define $K_1^{(1)}, K_2^{(1)}$ and $B^{(1)}$. We continue bisecting $K^{(j)}$ in this way, always focusing on the side for which the theorem fails by δ, thus obtaining a sequence of nested sets $K \supseteq K^{(1)} \supseteq \cdots \supseteq K^{(j)} \supseteq \cdots$.

We claim that eventually the smallest axis of the Löwner-John ellipsoid will be smaller than ϵ. If this is not the case, then the set K always contains a ball of radius ϵ/n. This follows from the properties of the Löwner-John ellipsoid. Therefore, letting $B_{\epsilon/n}(x_0)$ denote the ball of radius ϵ/n centered at x_0, we have

$$
\mu(K^{(j)}) = \int_{K^{(j)}} f(x)\,dx \geq \inf_{B_{\epsilon/n}(x_0)\subseteq K}\left(\int_{B_{\epsilon/n}(x_0)} f(x)\,dx\right) \geq \eta > 0,
$$

for some $\eta > 0$, independent of j. We know that $\eta > 0$ by our initial assumption that $f(x)$ is non-zero on K.

However, by our choice of hyperplanes, the sets $K_1^{(j)}, K_2^{(j)}$ are bisected with respect to the measure μ. Thus $\mu(K_1^{(j)}) = 2^{-j}\mu(K_1)$, and $\mu(K_2^{(j)}) = 2^{-j}\mu(K_2)$, and the measure of each set $K_1^{(j)}, K_2^{(j)}$ becomes arbitrarily small as j increases. Since the measure of $K^{(j)}$ does not also become arbitrarily small, the measure of $B^{(j)}$ must also be bounded away from zero. In particular, $\mu(B^{(j)}) \geq \eta - 2^{-j}(\mu(K_1) + \mu(K_2))$, and thus for $j \geq \log_2(2(\mu(K_1) + \mu(K_2))/\eta)$, $\mu(B^{(j)}) \geq \eta/2 \geq \min\{\mu(K_1^{(j)}), \mu(K_2^{(j)})\}$. This contradicts our assumption that the theorem fails on all elements of our nested chain of sets. The contradiction completes the proof of the lemma. □

Proof of Theorem 2: The proof is by induction on the number of dimensions. By Lemma 4 above, the statement holds for $n = 1$. Assume that the result holds for n dimensions. Suppose we have $K \subseteq \mathbb{R}^{n+1}$, with the decomposition $K = K_1 \cup B \cup K_2$, satisfying the assumptions of the theorem. We show that for every $\delta > 0$:

$$
(1+\delta)\mu(B) \geq e^{-\beta}\frac{t}{\operatorname{diam}(K)}\min\{\mu(K_1), \mu(K_2)\}.
$$

Taking δ to zero yields our result. Let E be the Löwner-John ellipsoid of K. By Lemma 5 above, we can assume that the Löwner-John ellipsoid of K has at least one axis of length no more than ϵ. Figure 1 illustrates the bisecting process of Lemma 5, and also the essential reason why the bisection allows us to project to one fewer dimensions. We take ϵ smaller than $t/2$, and also such

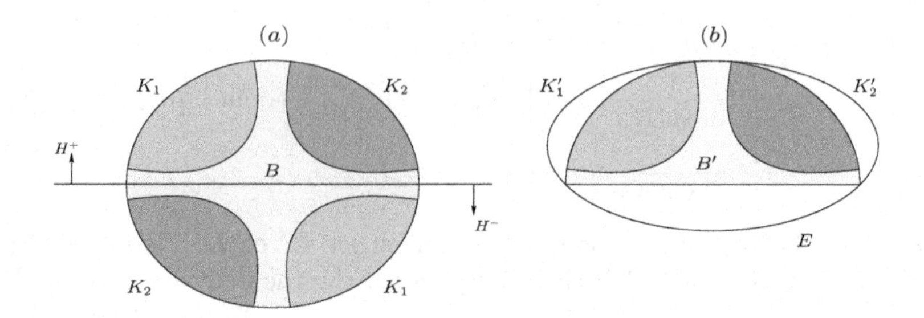

Fig. 1. The inductive step works by projecting K onto one less dimension. In (a) above, a projection on the horizontal axis would yield a distance of zero between the projected K_1 and K_2. Once we bisect to obtain (b), we see that a projection onto the horizontal axis would not affect the minimum distance between K_1 and K_2.

that $\sqrt{t^2 - 4\epsilon^2} > t/(1+\delta)$. Assume that the $(n+1)^{st}$ coordinate direction is parallel to the shortest axis of the ellipsoid, and the first n coordinate directions span the same plane as the other n axes of the ellipse (changing coordinates if necessary). Call the last coordinate y, so that we refer to points in $\mathbb{R}^{n+1}$ as (x, y), for $x \in \mathbb{R}^n$, and $y \in \mathbb{R}$. Let Π denote the plane spanned by the other n axes, and let $K_\Pi = \pi(K)$ denote the projection of K onto Π. Since $\epsilon < t/2$, no point in K_Π is the image of points in both K_1 and K_2, otherwise the two pre-images would be at most $2\epsilon < t$ apart. This allows us to define the sets

$$\begin{aligned}
\hat{K}_1 &\triangleq \{(x,y) \in K \,:\, \pi(x,y) \in \pi(K_1)\}, \\
\hat{K}_2 &\triangleq \{(x,y) \in K \,:\, \pi(x,y) \in \pi(K_2)\}, \\
\hat{B} &\triangleq \{(x,y) \in K \,:\, \pi(x,y) \notin \pi(K_1) \cup \pi(K_2)\}.
\end{aligned}$$

Note that $\mu(\hat{K}_i) \geq \mu(K_i)$, $i = 1, 2$, and $\mu(\hat{B}) \leq \mu(B)$. Again we have a decomposition $K = \hat{K}_1 \cup \hat{B} \cup \hat{K}_2$. On K_Π, we also have a decomposition: $K_\Pi = \pi(\hat{K}_1) \cup \pi(\hat{B}) \cup \pi(\hat{K}_2)$. Since we project with respect to the L^2 norm, by the Pythagorean Theorem, $d(\pi(\hat{K}_1), \pi(\hat{K}_2)) \geq \sqrt{t^2 - 4\epsilon^2}$. In addition, $\text{diam}(K_\pi) \leq \text{diam}(K)$.

For $x \in K_\Pi$, define the section $K(x) = \{(x,y) \in \mathbb{R}^{n+1} \,:\, (x,y) \in K\}$. We define a function on $K_\Pi \subseteq \mathbb{R}^n$: $F(x) \triangleq \int_{K(x)} f(x,y)\, dy$, where $f(x,y)$ is our β-log-concave function on $\mathbb{R}^{n+1}$. We have

$$\int_{\pi(\hat{K}_i)} F(x)\, dx = \int_{\hat{K}_i} f(x,y)\, dx\, dy = \mu(\hat{K}_i), \quad i = 1, 2,$$

and similarly for $\hat{B}$. By Lemma 3, $F(x)$ is β-log-concave. Therefore, by the inductive hypothesis, we have that

$$\begin{aligned}
\mu(B) \geq \mu(\hat{B}) &= \int_{\hat{B}} f(x,y)\,dx\,dy = \int_{\pi(\hat{B})} F(x)\,dx \\
&\geq e^{-\beta} \frac{\sqrt{t^2 - 4\epsilon^2}}{\operatorname{diam}(K_\pi)} \min\left\{ \int_{\pi(\hat{K}_1)} F(x)\,dx, \int_{\pi(\hat{K}_2)} F(x)\,dx \right\} \\
&= e^{-\beta} \frac{\sqrt{t^2 - 4\epsilon^2}}{\operatorname{diam}(K_\pi)} \min\left\{ \int_{\hat{K}_1} f(x,y)\,dx\,dy, \int_{\hat{K}_2} f(x,y)\,dx\,dy \right\} \\
&> e^{-\beta} \frac{t/(1+\delta)}{\operatorname{diam}(K)} \min\{\mu(\hat{K}_1), \mu(\hat{K}_2)\},
\end{aligned}$$

and thus $(1+\delta)\mu(B) \geq (t/\operatorname{diam}(K)) \min(\mu(K_1), \mu(K_2))$. Since this holds for every $\delta > 0$, the result follows. □

Corollaries 1 and 2 below offer some flexibility for obtaining a tighter lower bound on $\mu(B)$.

Corollary 1. *Let K be a closed and bounded convex set with a decomposition $K = K_1 \cup B \cup K_2$ as in Theorem 2 above. Let $f(x)$ be any distribution that is bounded away from zero on K, say $f(x) > \eta$ for $x \in K$. Then the induced measure μ satisfies*

$$\mu(B) \geq \eta \cdot \frac{d(K_1, K_2)}{\operatorname{diam}(K)} \min\{\nu(K_1), \nu(K_2)\}.$$

where ν denotes Lebesgue measure.

Proof. Consider the uniform distribution on K. Since it is log-concave, Theorem 2 applies with $\beta = 0$. Since the Lebesgue measure ν is just a scaled uniform distribution, $\nu(B) \geq (d(K_1, K_2)/\operatorname{diam}(K)) \min\{\nu(K_1), \nu(K_2)\}$. The corollary follows since $\mu(B) \geq \eta\nu(B)$. □

Corollary 2. *Fix $\epsilon > 0$. Let K be a closed, convex, but not necessarily bounded set. Let $K = K_1 \cup B \cup K_2$ be a decomposition of K. Let f be a β-log-concave distribution with induced measure μ, such that there exists $d(\epsilon)$ for which $(1-\epsilon)\mu(K_1) \leq \mu(K_1 \cap B_{d(\epsilon)})$, $(1-\epsilon)\mu(K_2) \leq \mu(K_2 \cap B_{d(\epsilon)})$, and $(1-\epsilon)\mu(B) \leq \mu(B \cap B_{d(\epsilon)})$, where $B_{d(\epsilon)}$ is a ball with radius $d(\epsilon)$ around the origin. Then*

$$\mu(B) \geq e^{-\beta}(1-\epsilon)^2 \frac{d(K_1, K_2)}{d(\epsilon)} \min\{\mu(K_1), \mu(K_2)\}.$$

Proof. We have that $\mu(K \cap B_{d(\epsilon)}) \geq (1-\epsilon)\mu(K)$. Let $P = \mu(K \cap B_{d(\epsilon)})$, and note that $P \geq 1-\epsilon$. Consider the measure $\hat{\mu}$ defined on $K \cap B_{d(\epsilon)}$ by the distribution $\hat{f}(x) = f(x)/P$. It follows that $\hat{f}$ is β-log-concave. We now apply Theorem 2 on $\hat{f}$ to obtain that: $\hat{\mu}(B \cap B_{d(\epsilon)}) \geq e^{-\beta}(t/d(\epsilon)) \min\{\hat{\mu}(K_1 \cap B_{d(\epsilon)}), \hat{\mu}(K_2 \cap B_{d(\epsilon)})\}$, where $t \geq d(K_1, K_2)$. It follows that $\hat{\mu}(K_1 \cap B_{d(\epsilon)}) \geq (1-\epsilon)\mu(K_1)$, and similarly for K_2, and $\mu(B)/(1-\epsilon) \geq \mu(B)/P \geq \hat{\mu}(B \cap B_{d(\epsilon)})$. The result follows by some algebra. □

4 Lower Bounds for Classification and the Size of the Margin

Lower bounds on the generalization error in classification require a careful definition of the probabilistic setup. In this section we consider a generic setup where proper learning is possible. We first consider the standard classification problem where data points $x \in \mathbb{R}^n$ and labels $y \in \{-1, 1\}$ are given, and not necessarily generated according to any particular distribution. We assume that we are given a set of classifiers $\mathcal{H}$ which are functions from $\mathbb{R}^n$ to $\{-1, 1\}$. Suppose that the performance of the classifier is measured using some β-log-concave distribution f (and associated measure μ). We note that this model deviates from the "classical" statistical machine learning setup. Given a distribution f, the disagreement of a classifier $h \in \mathcal{H}$ with another classifier h' is defined as:

$$\Delta(h; h') \triangleq \int_{\mathbb{R}^n} \frac{1}{2}(1 - h(x)h'(x))f(x)dx = \mu\{x \in \mathbb{R}^n : h(x) \neq h'(x)\},$$

where μ is the probability measure induced by f. If there exists a true classifier h^{true} (not necessarily in $\mathcal{H}$) such that $y = h^{true}(x)$ then the error of h is $\Delta(h; h^{true})$. For a classifier h, let $K^+(h) \triangleq \{x \in K : h(x) = 1\}$, and similarly $K^- \triangleq \{x \in K : h(x) = -1\}$. Given a pair of classifiers h_1 and h_2 we define the distance between them as

$$\text{dist}(h_1, h_2) \triangleq \max\left\{d\left(K^+(h_1), K^-(h_2)\right), d\left(K^-(h_1), K^+(h_2)\right)\right\}.$$

We note that $\text{dist}(h_1, h_2)$ may equal zero even if the classifiers are rather different. However, in some cases, $\text{dist}(h_1, h_2)$ provides a useful measure of difference; see Proposition 1 below.

Suppose we have to choose a classifier from a set $\mathcal{H}$. This may occur if, for example, we are given sample data points and there are several classifiers that classify the data correctly. The following theorem states that if the set of classifiers we choose from is too large, then the error might be large as well. Note that we have to scale the error lower bound by the minimal weight of the positively/negatively labelled region.

Theorem 3. *Suppose that f is β-log-concave defined on a bounded set K. Then for every $h \in \mathcal{H}$ there exists $h' \in \mathcal{H}$ such that*

$$\Delta(h; h') \geq \frac{e^{-\beta} P_0}{2\,\text{diam}(K)} \sup_{h_1, h_2 \in \mathcal{H}} \text{dist}(h_1, h_2),$$

where $P_0 = \inf_{\tilde{h} \in \mathcal{H}} \min\{\mu(K^+(\tilde{h})), \mu(K^-(\tilde{h}))\}$.

Proof. If $\sup_{h_1, h_2 \in \mathcal{H}} \text{dist}(h_1, h_2) = 0$, the result follows, so we can assume this is not the case. For every $\epsilon > 0$ we can choose $h_1 \in \mathcal{H}$ and $h_2 \in \mathcal{H}$ such that $\text{dist}(h_1, h_2) \geq \sup_{h_1, h_2 \in \mathcal{H}} \text{dist}(h_1, h_2) - \epsilon$. We consider the case where $\text{dist}(h_1, h_2) = d(K^+(h_1), K^-(h_2))$; the other case where $d(K^-(h_1), K^+(h_2)) =$

$\mathrm{dist}(h_1, h_2)$ follows in a symmetric manner. Let $B = K \setminus (K^+(h_1) \cup K^-(h_2))$. It follows by Theorem 2 that

$$\mu(B) \geq e^{-\beta} \frac{\mathrm{dist}(h_1, h_2)}{\mathrm{diam}(K)} \min\left\{\mu(K^+(h_1)), \mu(K^-(h_2))\right\}. \tag{4.4}$$

Now, $\Delta(h; h_1) \geq \int_B \chi_{\{h(x) \neq h_1(x)\}} f(x)dx$ and $\Delta(h; h_2) \geq \int_B \chi_{\{h(x) \neq h_2(x)\}} f(x)dx$. Since $h_1(x) \neq h_2(x)$ on B, then either $\Delta(h; h_1) \geq \mu(B)/2$ or $\Delta(h; h_2) \geq \mu(B)/2$. Since $P_0 \leq \mu(K^+(h_1))$ and $P_0 \leq \mu(K^-(h_2))$, and by substituting in Eq. (4.4) we obtain that $\Delta(h, h_i) \geq e^{-\beta}\, \mathrm{dist}(h_1, h_2) P_0/(2\, \mathrm{diam}(K))$ for $i = 1$ or $i = 2$. The result follows by taking ϵ to 0. □

The following example demonstrates the power of Theorem 3 in the context of linear classification. Consider an input-output sequence $\{(x_1, y_1), \ldots, (x_N, y_N)\}$ arising from some unknown source (not necessarily β-log-concave) as in the classical binary classification problem. Define $X_N^+ = \{x_i : y_i = 1\}$ and $X_N^- = \{x_i : y_i = -1\}$. Suppose that the true error is measured according to a β-log-concave distribution, and that X_N^+ and X_N^- are linearly separable. Recall that a linear classifier h is a function given by $h(x) = \mathrm{sign}(\langle x, u\rangle + b)$, where 'sign' is the sign function and '$\langle\cdot,\cdot\rangle$' is the standard inner product in $\mathbb{R}^n$. The following proposition provides a lower bound on the true error. We state it for generic sets of vectors, so the data are not assumed to be sampled from any concrete source. The lower bound concerns the case where we are faced with a choice from a set of classifiers, all of which agree with the data (i.e., zero training error). If we commit to any specific classifier, then there exists another classifier (whose training error is zero as well) such that the true error of the classifier we committed to is relatively large if the other classifier happens to equal h^{true}.

Proposition 1. *Suppose that we are given two sets of linearly separable vectors X^+ and X^- and let $t = d(\mathrm{conv}(X^+), \mathrm{conv}(X^-))$. Then for every linear classifier h that separates X^+ and X^-, and any β-log-concave distribution f and induced measure μ defined on a bounded set K, there exists another linear classifier h' that separates the X^+ and X^- as well, such that $\Delta(h; h') \geq e^{-\beta} P_0 t/(2\, \mathrm{diam}(K))$, where $P_0 = \min\{\mu(\{x : \langle x, u\rangle \geq \langle x^+, u\rangle\}), \mu(\{x : \langle x, u\rangle \leq \langle x^-, u\rangle\})\}$ for some $x^\pm \in \mathrm{conv}(X^\pm)$ such that $d(x^+, x^-) = t$ and $u = (x^+ - x^-)/2$.*

Proof. Let $\mathcal{H}$ be the set of all hyperplanes that separate X^+ from X^-. It follows by a standard linear programming argument (see [BB00]) that $\sup_{h_1, h_2 \in \mathcal{H}} \mathrm{dist}(h_1, h_2) = t$. This is attained for $h_1(x) = \mathrm{sign}(\langle x, u\rangle - \langle x^+, u\rangle)$ and $h_2(x) = \mathrm{sign}(\langle x, u\rangle - \langle x^-, u\rangle)$. We now apply Theorem 3 to obtain the desired result. Note that P_0 in the declaration of the proposition is tighter than P_0 in Theorem 3. This is the result of calculating $\mu(K^+(h_1))$ and $\mu(K^-(h_2))$ directly (instead of taking the infimum as in Theorem 3). □

We now consider the standard machine learning setup, and assume that the data are sampled from a β-log-concave distribution. We examine the geometric margin as opposed to the "functional" margin which is often defined with respect to a real valued function g. In that case classification is performed by considering

$h(x) = \mathrm{sign}(g(x))$ and the margin of g at $(x, y) \in \mathbb{R}^n \times \{-1, 1\}$ is defined as $g(x)y$. If such a function g is Lipschitz with a constant L, then for $x \in K^+(h)$ the event that $\{d(x, K^-(h)) < \gamma\}$ is contained in the event that $\{g(x) < \gamma L\}$ (and for $x \in K^-(h)$ if $d(x, K^-(h)) < \gamma$ then $-g(x) < \gamma L$). Consequently, results on the geometric margin can be easily converted to results on the "functional" margin as long as the Lipschitz assumption holds.

Suppose now that we have a classifier h, and we ask the following question: what is the probability that if we sample N vectors $\boldsymbol{X}_N = \boldsymbol{x}_1, \dots \boldsymbol{x}_N$ from f, they are far away from the boundary between $K^+(h)$ and $K^-(h)$. More precisely, we want to bound the probability of the event $\left\{\min_{i:\boldsymbol{x}_i \in K^+(h)} d(\boldsymbol{x}_i, K^-(h)) > \gamma\right\}$, and similarly for negatively labelled samples. We next show that the probability that the distance of a sampled point from the boundary is almost linear in this distance to the boundary. An immediate consequence is an exponential concentration inequality.

Proposition 2. *Suppose we are given a classifier h defined on a bounded set K. Fix some $\gamma > 0$ and consider the set $B = \{x \in K^-(h) : d(x, K^+(h)) < \gamma\}$. Let f be a β-log-concave distribution on K with induced measure μ. Then*

$$\mu(B) \geq \gamma \frac{e^{-\beta}}{\mathrm{diam}(K)} \min\left\{\mu(K^+(h)), \frac{\mu(K^-(h))}{1 + \gamma e^{-\beta}/\mathrm{diam}(K)}\right\}.$$

Proof. Consider the decomposition of K to $K_1 = K^+(h)$, B, and $K_2 = K^-(h) \setminus B$. By Theorem 2 we know that $\mu(B) \geq \gamma e^{-\beta} \min\{\mu(K_1), \mu(K_2)\}/\mathrm{diam}(K)$. We also know that $\mu(B) = \mu(K^-(h)) - \mu(K_2)$. So that

$$\mu(B) \geq \max\{\gamma e^{-\beta} \min\{\mu(K_1), s\}/\mathrm{diam}(K), \mu(K^-(h)) - s\}, \qquad (4.5)$$

where $s = \mu(K_2)$. Minimizing over s in the interval $[0, \mu(K^-(h))]$, it is seen that the minimizer s is either at the point where $\mu(K^-(h)) - s = \gamma e^{-\beta}\mu(K_1)/\mathrm{diam}(K)$ or at the point where $\mu(K^-(h)) - s = s\gamma e^{-\beta}/\mathrm{diam}(K)$. Substituting those s in Eq. (4.5) and some algebra gives the desired result. □

A similar result holds by interchanging K^+ and K^- throughout Proposition 2. The following corollary is an immediate application of the above.

Corollary 3. *Suppose that N samples $\boldsymbol{X}_N = \{\boldsymbol{x}_1, \dots, \boldsymbol{x}_N\}$ are drawn independently from a β-log-concave distribution f defined on a bounded set K. Let h be a classifier. Then for every $\gamma > 0$:*

$$\Pr\left(\min_{\{i\,:\,\boldsymbol{x}_i \in K^-(h)\}} d(\boldsymbol{x}_i, K^+(h)) > \gamma\right) \leq \exp\left(-N\gamma C \min\left\{\mu(K^+(h)), \frac{\mu(K^-(h))}{1 + \gamma C}\right\}\right),$$

where Pr *is the probability measure of drawing N samples from f and $C = e^{-\beta}/\mathrm{diam}(K)$.*

Proof. The proof follows from Proposition 2 and the inequality $(1 - a)^N \leq \exp(-aN)$ for $a \in [0, 1]$ and $N \geq 0$. □

Corollary 3 is a dimension-free inequality. It implies that when sampling from a β-log-concave distribution, for any specific classifier, we cannot hope to have a large margin. It does not claim, however, that the empirical margin is small. Specifically, for $\boldsymbol{X}_N = \{\boldsymbol{x}_1, \ldots, \boldsymbol{x}_N\}$ one can consider the probabilistic behavior of the following empirical gap between the classes: $\text{gap}(\boldsymbol{X}_N; h) = \min_{i,j:h(\boldsymbol{x}_i)\neq h(\boldsymbol{x}_j)} d(\boldsymbol{x}_i, \boldsymbol{x}_j)$. The probability that this quantity is larger than γ cannot be bounded in a dimension-free manner. The reason is that as the number of dimensions grows to infinity the distance between the samples may become bounded away from zero. To see that, consider uniformly distributed samples on the unit ball in $\mathbb{R}^n$. If n is much bigger than N it is not hard to prove that all the sampled vectors will be (with high probability) equally far apart from each other. So $\text{gap}(\boldsymbol{X}_N; h)$ does not converge to 0 (for every non trivial h) in the regime where n increases fast enough with N. For every fixed n one can bound the probability that $\text{gap}(\boldsymbol{X}_N; h)$ is large using covering number arguments, as in [SC99], but such a bound must be dimension-dependent.

We finally note that a uniform bound in the spirit of Corollary 3 is of interest. Specifically, let the empirical margin of a classifier h on sample points $\boldsymbol{X}_N$ be denoted by:

$$\text{margin}(\boldsymbol{X}_N; h) \triangleq \min\{d\left((\boldsymbol{X}_N \cap K^-(h)), K^+(h)\right), d\left((\boldsymbol{X}_N \cap K^+(h)), K^-(h)\right)\}.$$

It is of interest to bound $\Pr\left(\sup_{h\in\mathcal{H}} \text{margin}(\boldsymbol{X}_N; h) \geq \gamma\right)$. We leave the issue of efficiently bounding the empirical margin to future research.

5 Regression Tubes

Consider a function k from $\mathbb{R}^n$ to $\mathbb{R}^m$. In this section we provide a result of a different flavor that concerns the weight of tubes around k. The probabilistic setup is as follows. We have a probability measure f on $\mathbb{R}^{n+m}$ that prescribes the probability of getting a pair $(x, y) \in \mathbb{R}^n \times \mathbb{R}^m$. For a function $k : \mathbb{R}^n \to \mathbb{R}^m$ we consider the set

$$T_{\epsilon_0,\epsilon_1}(k) \triangleq \{(x, y) : \epsilon_0 \leq \|k(x) - y\| \leq \epsilon_1\}.$$

This set represents all the pairs where the prediction of k is off by more than ϵ_0 and less then ϵ_1, or alternatively, the set of pairs whose prediction is converted to zero error when changing the ϵ in an ϵ-insensitive error criterion from ϵ_0 to ϵ_1.

Corollary 4. *Suppose that f is β-log-concave on a bounded set $K \subseteq \mathbb{R}^{n+m}$, with induced measure μ. Assume that k is Lipschitz continuous with constant L. Then for every $\epsilon_1 > \epsilon_0 > 0$*

$$\mu(T_{\epsilon_0,\epsilon_1}(k)) \geq \frac{(\epsilon_1 - \epsilon_0)e^{-\beta}}{L\,\text{diam}(K)} \min\left\{\mu(T_{0,\epsilon_0}(k)), \mu(T_{\epsilon_1,\text{diam}(K)}(k))\right\}.$$

Proof. We use Theorem 2 with the decomposition $K_1 = T_{0,\epsilon_0}(k)$, $B = T_{\epsilon_0,\epsilon_1}(k)$ and $K_2 = T_{\epsilon_1,\text{diam}(K)}(k)$. Note that $d(T_{0,\epsilon_0}, T_{\epsilon_1,\text{diam}(K)}) \geq (\epsilon_1 - \epsilon_0)/L$, since k is Lipschitz with constant L. □

A result where f is conditionally β-log-concave (i.e., given that x was sampled, the conditional probability of y is β-log-concave) is desirable. This requires some additional continuity assumptions on f, and is left for future research.

Acknowledgements. We thank three anonymous reviewers for thoughtful and detailed comments. Shie Mannor was partially supported by the National Science Foundation under grant ECS-0312921.

References

[AB99] M. Anthony and P.L. Bartlett. *Neural Network Learning: Theoretical Foundations.* Cambridge University Press, 1999.

[AK91] D. Applegate and R. Kannan. Sampling and integration of near log-concave functions. In *Proc. 23th ACM STOC*, pages 156–163, 1991.

[BB89] M. Bagnoli and T. Bergstrom. Log–concave probability and its applications. Available from `citeseer.nj.nec.com/bagnoli89logconcave.html`, 1989.

[BB00] K. Bennett and E. Bredensteiner. Duality and geometry in SVM classifiers. In *Proc. 17th Int. Conf. on Machine Learning*, pages 57–64, 2000.

[BES02] S. Ben-David, N. Eiron, and H.U. Simon. Limitations of learning via embeddings in Euclidean half spaces. *Journal of Machine Learning Research*, 3:441–461, 2002.

[CS00] N. Cristianini and J. Shawe-Taylor. *An Introduction to Support Vector Machines and Other Kernel-Based Learning Methods.* Cambridge University Press, Cambridge, England, 2000.

[Gar02] R. J. Gardner. The Brunn-Minkowski inequality. *Bull. Amer. Math. Soc.*, 39:355–405, 2002.

[GLS93] M. Grötschel, L. Lovász, and A. Schrijver. *Geometric Algorithms and Combinatorial Optimization.* Springer Verlag, New Jersey, 1993.

[LS90] L. Lovász and M. Simonovits. Mixing rate of Markov chains, an isoperimetric inequality, and computing the volume. In *Proc. 31st Annual Symp. on Found. of Computer Science*, pages 346–355, 1990.

[Mat02] J. Matoušek. *Using the Borsuk-Ulam Theorem.* Springer Verlag, Berlin, 2002.

[Men04] S. Mendelson. Lipschitz embeddings of function classes. Available from `http://web.rsise.anu.edu.au/~shahar/`, 2004.

[SBSS00] A.J. Smola, P. Bartlett, B. Schölkopf, and C. Schuurmans, editors. *Advances in Large Margin Classifiers.* MIT Press,, 2000.

[SC99] J. Shawe-Taylor and N. Cristianini. Further results on the margin distribution. In *Computational Learing Theory*, pages 278–285, 1999.

[SS02] B. Schölkopf and A. J. Smola. *Learning with Kernels.* MIT Press, Cambridge, MA, 2002.

[Vap98] V. N. Vapnik. *Statistical Learning Theory.* Wiley Interscience, New York, 1998.

Bayes and Tukey Meet at the Center Point

Ran Gilad-Bachrach[1], Amir Navot[2], and Naftali Tishby[2]

[1] School of Computer Science and Engineering
ranb@cs.huji.ac.il
[2] Interdisciplinary Center for Neural Computation
The Hebrew University, Jerusalem, Israel
{anavot,tishby}@cs.huji.ac.il

Abstract. The Bayes classifier achieves the minimal error rate by constructing a weighted majority over all concepts in the concept class. The *Bayes Point* [1] uses the single concept in the class which has the minimal error. This way, the *Bayes Point* avoids some of the deficiencies of the Bayes classifier. We prove a bound on the generalization error for *Bayes Point Machines* when learning linear classifiers, and show that it is at most ~ 1.71 times the generalization error of the Bayes classifier, independent of the input dimension and length of training. We show that when learning linear classifiers, the *Bayes Point* is almost identical to the *Tukey Median* [2] and *Center Point* [3]. We extend these definitions beyond linear classifiers and define the *Bayes Depth* of a classifier. We prove generalization bound in terms of this new definition. Finally we provide a new concentration of measure inequality for multivariate random variables to the *Tukey Median.*

1 Introduction

In this paper we deal with supervised concept learning in a Bayesian framework. The task is to learn a concept c from a concept class $\mathcal{C}$. We assume that the target c is randomly chosen from $\mathcal{C}$ according to a known probability distribution ν. The Bayes classifier is known to be optimal in this setting, i.e. it achieves the minimal possible expected loss. However the Bayes classifier suffers from two major deficiencies. First, it is usually computationally infeasible, since each prediction requires voting over all parameters. The second problem is the possible inconsistency of the Bayes classifier [4], as it is often outside of the target class. Consider for example the following scenario: Alice, Bob and Eve would like to vote on the linear order of three items $\mathcal{A}, \mathcal{B}$ and $\mathcal{C}$. Alice suggests $\mathcal{A} < \mathcal{B} < \mathcal{C}$, Bob suggests $\mathcal{C} < \mathcal{A} < \mathcal{B}$, and Eve suggests $\mathcal{B} < \mathcal{C} < \mathcal{A}$. Voting among the three, as the Bayes classifier does, will lead to $\mathcal{A} < \mathcal{B}$, $\mathcal{B} < \mathcal{C}$ and $\mathcal{C} < \mathcal{A}$ which does not form a linear order.

The computational infeasibility and possible inconsistency of the Bayes optimal classifier are both due to the fact that it is not a single classifier from the given concept class but rather a weighted majority among concepts in the class. These drawbacks can be resolved if one selects a single classifier in the proper

J. Shawe-Taylor and Y. Singer (Eds.): COLT 2004, LNAI 3120, pp. 549–563, 2004.

class (or a proper ordering in the previous example). Indeed, once the single concept is selected, its predictions are usually both efficient and consistent. It is, however, no longer Bayes optimal. Our problem is to find the single member of the concept class which best approximates the optimal Bayes classifier.

Herbrich, Graepel and Campbell [1] have recently studied this problem. They called the single concept which minimizes the expected error the *Bayes Point.* Specifically for the case of linear classifiers, they designed the *Bayes Point Machine* (BPM), which employs the center of gravity of the version space (which is convex in this case) as the candidate classifier. This method has been applied successfully to various domains, achieving comparable results to those obtained by Support Vector Machines [5].

1.1 The Results of This Paper

Theorem 1 provides a generalization bound for *Bayes Point Machines.* We show that the expected generalization error of BPM is greater than the expected generalization error of the Bayes classifier by a factor of at most $(e-1) \simeq 1.71$. Since the Bayes classifier obtains the minimal expected generalization error we conclude that BPM is "almost" optimal. Note that this bound is independent of the input dimension and it holds for any size of the training sequence. These two factors, i.e. input dimension and training set size, affect the error of BPM only through the error of the optimal Bayes classifier. The error of *Bayes Point Machines* can also be bounded in the online mistake bound model. In theorem 2 we prove that the mistake bound of BPM is at most $\frac{n}{-\log(1-1/e)} \log \frac{2R}{r}$, where n is the input dimension, R is a bound on the norm of the input data points, and r is a margin term. This bound is different from Novikoff's well known mistake bound for the perceptron algorithm [6] of R^2/r^2. In our new bound, the dependency on the ratio R/r is logarithmic, whereas Novikoff's bound is dimension independent.

The proofs of theorems 1 and 2 follow from a definition of the proximity of a classifier to the Bayes optimal classifier. In the setting of linear classifier the proximity measure is a simple modification of the *Tukey Depth* [2]. The *Tukey Depth* measures the *centrality* of a point in $\mathbb{R}^n$. For a Borell probability measure ν over $\mathbb{R}^n$ the *Tukey Depth* (or halfspace depth) of $x \in \mathbb{R}^n$ is defined as

$$D(x) = \inf \{\nu(H) \text{ s.t. H is half space and } x \in H\} \ , \tag{1}$$

i.e. the depth of x is the minimal probability of an half space which contains x. Using this definition Donoho and Gasko [7] defined the *Tukey Median* as the point x which maximizes the depth function $D(x)$ (some authors refer to this median as the *Center Point* [3]).

Donoho and Gasko [7] studied the properties of the *Tukey Median.* They showed that the median always exists but need not be unique. They also showed that for any measure ν over $\mathbb{R}^n$, the depth of the *Tukey Median* is at least $\frac{1}{n+1}$. Caplin and Nalebuff [4] proved the *Mean Voter Theorem.* This theorem (using different motivations and notations) states that if the measure ν is log-concave then the center of gravity of ν has a depth of at least $1/e$. ν is log-concave if it conforms with

$$\nu(\lambda A + (1-\lambda) B) \geq \nu(A)^{\lambda} \nu(B)^{1-\lambda} .$$

For example, uniform distributions over convex bodies are log-concave, normal and chi-square distributions are log-concave as well. See [8] for a discussion and examples of log-concave measures (a less detailed discussion can be found in appendix A).

The lower bound of $1/e$ for the depth of the center of gravity for log-concave measures is the key to our proofs of the bounds for BPM. The intuition behind the proofs is that any "deep" point must generalize well. This can be extended beyond linear classifiers to general concept classes. We define the *Bayes Depth* of a hypothesis and show in theorem 3 that the expected generalization error of any classifier can be bounded in terms of its *Bayes Depth.* This bound holds for any concept class, including multi-class classifiers.

Finally we provide a new concentration of measure inequality for multivariate random variables to their *Tukey Median.* This is an extension of the well known concentration result of scalar random variables to the median [9].

This paper is organized as follows. In section 2 the *Bayes Point Machine* is introduced and the generalization bounds are derived. In section 3 we extend the discussion beyond linear classifiers. We define the *Bayes Depth* and prove generalization bounds for the general concept class setting. A concentration of measure inequality for multivariate random variables to their *Tukey Median* is provided in section 4. Further discussion of the results is provided in section 5. Some background information regarding concave measures can be found in appendix A. The statement of the Mean Voter Theorem is given in appendix B.

1.2 Preliminaries and Notation

Throughout this paper we study the problem of concept learning with Bayesian prior knowledge. The task is to approximate a concept $c \in \mathcal{C}$ which was chosen randomly using a probability measure ν. The Bayes classifier (denoted by $h_{\texttt{opt}}$) assigns the instance x to the class with minimal expected loss:

$$h_{\texttt{opt}}(x) = \arg\min_{y} E_{c\sim\nu}\left[l(y, c(x))\right] \tag{2}$$

where l is some loss function $l : \mathcal{Y}\times\mathcal{Y} \to \mathrm{I\!R}$. The Bayes classifier is optimal among all possible classifiers since it minimizes the expected generalization error:

$$\text{error}(h) = E_x\left[E_{c\sim\nu}\left[l(h(x), c(x))\right]\right] \tag{3}$$

The Bayes classifier achieves the minimal possible error on each individual instance x and thus also when averaging over x. If a labeled sample is available the Bayes classifier uses the posterior induced by the sample, and likewise the expected error is calculated with respect to the same posterior. If the concepts in $\mathcal{C}$ are stochastic then the loss in (2) and (3) should be averaged over the internal randomness of the concepts.

2 Bayes Point Machine

Herbrich, Graepel and Campbell [1] introduced the *Bayes Point Machine* as a tool for learning classifiers. They defined the Bayes Point as follows:

Definition 1. *Given a concept class $\mathcal{C}$, a loss function $l : \mathcal{Y} \times \mathcal{Y} \to \mathbb{R}$ and a posterior ν over $\mathcal{C}$, the* Bayes Point *is:*

$$\arg\min_{h \in \mathcal{C}} E_x \left[E_{c \sim \nu} \left[l \left(h(x), c(x) \right) \right] \right]$$

Note that $E_x \left[E_{c \sim \nu} \left[l \left(h(x), c(x) \right) \right] \right]$ is the average error of the classifier h, as defined in (3), and thus the *Bayes Point*, as defined in definition 1, is simply the classifier in $\mathcal{C}$ which minimizes the average error, while the Bayes optimal rule minimizes the same term without the restriction of choosing h from $\mathcal{C}$.

When applying to linear classifiers with the zero-one loss function[1], [1] assumed a uniform distribution over the class of linear classifiers. Furthermore they suggested that the center of gravity is a good approximation of the *Bayes Point*. In theorem 1 we show that this is indeed the case. The center of gravity is indeed a good approximation of the *Bayes Point*.

We will consider the case of linear classifiers through the origin. In this case the sample space is $\mathbb{R}^n$ and a classifier is half-space through the origin. Formally, any vector $\theta \in \mathbb{R}^n$ represents a classifier. Given an instance $x \in \mathbb{R}^n$ the corresponding label is $+1$ if $\theta \cdot x > 0$ and -1 otherwise. Note that if $\lambda > 0$ then the vector θ and the vector $\lambda\theta$ represent the same classifier; hence we may assume that θ is in the unit ball.

Given a sample of labeled instances, the *Version Space* is defined as the set of classifiers consistent with the sample:

$$\text{Version-Space} = \{\theta \; : \; \|\theta\| \leq 1 \;\text{ and }\; y_i \theta \cdot x_i > 0 \;\;\text{forall } 1 \leq i \leq m\}$$

This version space is the intersection of the unit ball with a set of linear constraints imposed by the observed instances and hence it is convex. The posterior is the restriction of the original prior to the version space. Herbrich et al. [1] suggested using the center of gravity of the version space as the hypothesis of the learning algorithm which they named the *Bayes Point Machine*. They suggested a few algorithms which are based on random walks in the version space to approximate the center of gravity.

2.1 Generalization Bounds for Bayes Point Machines

Our main result is a generalization bound for the Bayes Point Machine learning algorithm.

[1] The zero-one loss function is zero whenever the predicted class and the true class are the same. Otherwise, the loss is one.

Theorem 1. *Let ν be a continuous log-concave measure*[2] *over the unit ball in $\mathbb{R}^n$ (the prior) and assume that the target concept is chosen according to ν. Let BPM be a learning algorithm such that after seeing a batch of labeled instances S returns the center of gravity of ν restricted to the version space as a hypothesis $h_{\mathtt{bpm}}$. Let $h_{\mathtt{opt}}(\cdot)$ be the Bayes optimal classifier. For any $x \in \mathbb{R}^n$ and any sample S*

$$\Pr_c\left[h_{\mathtt{bpm}}(x) \neq c(x)\,|S\right] \leq (e-1)\Pr_c\left[h_{\mathtt{opt}}(x) \neq c(x)\,|S\right]$$

Theorem 1 proves that the generalization error of $h_{\mathtt{bpm}}$ is at most $(e-1) \sim 1.7$ times larger than the best possible. Note that this bound is dimension free. There is no assumption on the size of the training sample S or the way it was collected. However, the size of S, the dimension and maybe other properties influence the error of $h_{\mathtt{opt}}$ and thus affect the performance of BPM.

Proof. If ν is log-concave, then any restriction of ν to a convex set is log-concave as well. Since the version space is convex, the posterior induced by S is log-concave. Let $x \in \mathbb{R}^n$ be an instance for which the prediction is unknown. Let H be the set of linear classifiers which predict that the label of x is $+1$, therefore

$$H = \{\theta : \theta \cdot x \geq 0\}$$

and hence H is a half-space. Algorithm $h_{\mathtt{opt}}$ will predict that the label of x is $+1$ iff $\nu(H|S) \geq 1/2$. W.l.o.g. assume that $\nu(H|S) \geq 1/2$. We consider two cases.

First assume that $\nu(H|S) > 1 - 1/e$. From theorem 6 and the definition of the depth function (1) it follows that any half space with measure $> 1 - 1/e$ must contain the center of gravity. Hence the prediction made by $h_{\mathtt{bpm}}$ is the same as the prediction made by $h_{\mathtt{opt}}$.

The second case is when $1/2 \leq \nu(H|S) \leq 1 - 1/e$. If BPM predicts that the label is $+1$, then it suffers from the same error as $h_{\mathtt{opt}}$. If $h_{\mathtt{bpm}}$ predicts that the label of x is -1 then:

$$\frac{\Pr_c\left[h_{\mathtt{bpm}}(x) \neq c(x)\,|S\right]}{\Pr_c\left[h_{\mathtt{opt}}(x) \neq c(x)\,|S\right]} = \frac{\nu(H|S)}{1-\nu(H|S)} \leq \frac{1-1/e}{1/e} = e - 1$$

Note that if $\nu(H|S) < 1/2$ the prediction of $h_{\mathtt{opt}}$ will be that the label of x is -1 and we can apply the same proof to

$$\bar{H} = \{\theta : \theta \cdot x \leq 0\}$$

□

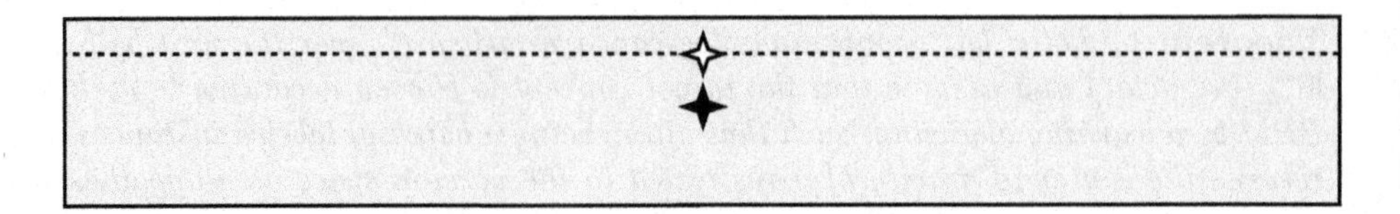

Fig. 1. Although the white point is close (distance wise) to the *Tukey Median* (in black), it does not have large depth, as demonstrated by the dotted line.

2.2 Computational Complexity

Theorem 1 provides a justification for the choice of the center of gravity in the *Bayes Point Machine* [1]. Herbrich et al. [1] suggested algorithms for approximating the center of gravity. In order for our bounds to follow for the approximation, it is necessary to have some lower bound on the *Tukey Depth* of the approximating point. For this purpose, Euclidean proximity is not good enough (see figure 1). Bertsimas and Vempala [10] have suggested a solution for this problem. The algorithm they suggest requires $O^*(n^4)$ operations where n is the input dimension. However it is impractical due to large constants. Nevertheless, the research in this field is active and faster solutions may emerge.

2.3 Mistake Bound

The On-line Mistake-Bound model is another common framework in statistical learning. In this setting the learning is an iterative process, such that at iteration i, the student receives an instance x_i and has to predict the label y_i. After making this prediction, the correct label is revealed. The goal of the student is to minimize the number of wrong predictions in the process.

The following theorem proves that when learning linear classifiers in the online model, if the student makes its predictions using the center of gravity of the current version space, then the number of predictions mistakes is at most $\frac{n}{-\log(1-1/e)} \log \frac{2R}{r}$ where R is a radius of a ball containing all the instances and r is a margin term. Note that the algorithm of the perceptron has a bound of R^2/r^2 in the same setting [6]. Hence the new bound is better when the dimension n is finite (i.e. small).

Theorem 2. *Let $\{(x_i, y_i)\}_{i=1}^{\infty} \subset \mathbb{R}^n \times \{-1, 1\}$ be a sequence such that $\|x_i\|_2 \leq R$ and there exists $r > 0$ and a unit vector $\theta \in \mathbb{R}^n$ such that $y_i x_i \cdot \theta \geq r$ for any i. Let BPM be an algorithm that predicts the label of the next instance x_{m+1} to be the label assigned by the center of gravity of the intersection of the version space induced by $\{(x_i, y_i)\}_{i=1}^{m}$ and the unit ball. The number of prediction mistakes that BPM makes is at most $\frac{n}{-\log(1-1/e)} \log \frac{2R}{r}$.*

[2] See appendix A for discussion and definitions of concave measures. Note however, that the uniform distribution over the version space is always log-concave.

Proof. Recall that the version space is the set of all linear classifiers (inside the unit ball) which correctly classifies all instances seen so far. The proof track is as follows: first we will show that the volume of the version space is bounded from below. Second, we will show that whenever a mistake occurs, the volume of the version space reduces by a constant factor. Combining these two together, we conclude that the number of mistakes is bounded.

Let θ be a unit vector such that $y_i x_i \cdot \theta \geq r$. Note that if $\|\theta' - \theta\|_2 < r/R$ then $y_i x_i \cdot \theta' > 0$. Therefore, there exists a ball of radius $r/2R$ inside the unit ball of $\mathbb{R}^n$ such that all θ' in this ball correctly classify all x_i's. Hence, the volume of the version space is at least $(r/2R)^n V_n$ where V_n is the volume of the n-dimensional unit ball.

Assume that BPM made a mistake while predicting the label of x_i. W.l.o.g. assume that BPM predicted that the label is $+1$. Let $H = \{\theta : \theta \cdot x_i \geq 0\}$, since the center of gravity is in H, and the *Tukey Depth* of the center of gravity $\geq 1/e$, the volume of H is at least $1/e$ of the volume of the version space. This is true since the version space is convex and the uniform measure over convex bodies is log-concave.

Therefore, whenever BPM makes a wrong prediction, the volume of the version space reduces by a factor of $(1 - 1/e)$ at least. Assume that BPM made k wrong predictions while processing the sequence $\{(x_i, y_i)\}_{i=1}^m$ then we have that the volume of the version space is at most $V_n\left(1 - \frac{1}{e}\right)^k$ and at least $V_n\left(\frac{r}{2R}\right)^n$ and thus we conclude that

$$k \leq \frac{n}{-\log\left(1 - \frac{1}{e}\right)} \log \frac{2R}{r}$$

□

3 The Bayes Depth

As we saw in the previous section the *Tukey Depth* plays a key role in bounding the error of *Bayes Point Machine* when learning linear classifiers. We would like to extend these results beyond linear classifiers; thus we need to extend the notion of depth. Recall that the *Tukey Depth* (1) measures the centrality of a point with respect to a probability measure. We say that a point $x \in \mathbb{R}^n$ has depth $D = D(x)$ if when standing at x and looking in any direction, the points you will see have a probability measure of D at least. The question is thus how can we extend this definition to other classes? How should we deal with multi-class partitions of the data, relative to the binary partitions in the linear case? For this purpose we define *Bayes Depth*:

Definition 2. *Let $\mathcal{C}$ be a concept class such that $c \in \mathcal{C}$ is a function $c : \mathcal{X} \to \mathcal{Y}$. Let $l : \mathcal{Y} \times \mathcal{Y} \to \mathbb{R}$ be a loss function, and let ν be a probability measure over $\mathcal{C}$. The* Bayes Depth *of a hypothesis h is*

$$D_{Bayes}(h) = \inf_x \frac{\min_{y \in \mathcal{Y}} E_{c \sim \nu}\left[l\left(y, c\left(x\right)\right)\right]}{E_{c \sim \nu}\left[l\left(h\left(x\right), c\left(x\right)\right)\right]} \tag{4}$$

The denominator in (4) is the expected loss of h when predicting the class of x, while the numerator is the minimal possible expected loss, i.e. the loss of the Bayes classifier. Note that the hypothesis h need not be a member of the concept class $\mathcal{C}$. Furthermore, it need not be a deterministic function; if h is stochastic then the loss of h should be averaged over its internal randomness.

An alternative definition of depth is provided implicitly in definition 1. Recall that Herbrich et al. [1] defined the *Bayes Point* h as the point which minimizes the term

$$E_x \left[E_{c \sim \nu} \left[l \left(h(x), c(x) \right) \right] \right] \tag{5}$$

when l is some loss function. Indeed the concept which minimizes the term in (5) is the concept with minimal average loss, and thus this is a good candidate for a depth function. However, evaluating this term requires full knowledge of the distribution of the sample points. This is usually unknown and in some cases it does not exist since the sample point might be chosen by an adversary.

3.1 Examples

Before going any further we would like to look at a few examples which demonstrate the definition of *Bayes Depth.*

Example 1. Bayesian prediction rule

Let h be the Bayesian prediction rule, i.e. $h(x) = \min_{y \in \mathcal{Y}} E_{c' \sim \nu} \left[l \left(y, c'(x) \right) \right]$. It follows from the definition of depth that $D_{\text{Bayes}}(h) = 1$. Note that any prediction rule cannot have a depth greater than 1.

Example 2. MAP on finite concept classes

Let $\mathcal{C}$ be a finite concept class of binary classifiers and let l be the zero-one loss function. Let $h = \arg\max_{c \in \mathcal{C}} \nu(\mathcal{C})$, i.e. h is the Maximum A-Posteriori. Since $\mathcal{C}$ is finite we obtain $\nu(h) \geq 1/|\mathcal{C}|$. Simple algebra yields $D_{\text{Bayes}}(h) \geq \frac{1}{|\mathcal{C}|-1}$.

Example 3. Center of Gravity

In this example we go back to linear classifiers. The sample space consists of tuples (x, b) such that $x \in \mathbb{R}^n$ and $b \in \mathbb{R}$. A classifier is a vector $w \in \mathbb{R}^n$ such that the label w assigns to (x, b) is $\text{sign}(w \cdot x + b)$. The loss is the zero-one loss as before. Unlike the standard setting of linear classifiers the offset b is part of the sample space and not part of the classifier. This setting has already been used in [11]. In this case the *Bayes Depth* is a normalized version of the *Tukey Depth*:

$$D_{\text{Bayes}}(w) = \frac{D(w)}{1 - D(w)}$$

Example 4. Gibbs Sampling

Our last example uses the Gibbs prediction rule which is a stochastic rule. This rule selects at random $c \in \mathcal{C}$ according to ν and uses it to predict the label of x. Note that Haussler et al. [12] already analyzed this special case using different notation. Let h be the Gibbs stochastic prediction rule such that $\Pr[h(x) = y] = \nu\{c : c(x) = y\}$. Let l be the zero-one loss function Assume that $\mathcal{Y} = \{-1, +1\}$, and denote by $p = \nu\{c : c(x) = +1\}$. We obtain $D_{\text{Bayes}}(h) \geq \inf_{p\in(0,1)} \frac{\min(p,1-p)}{2p(1-p)} = 0.5$.

3.2 Generalization Bounds

Theorems 1 and 2 are special cases of a general principle. In this section we show that a "deep" classifier, i.e. a classifier with large *Bayes Depth*, generalizes well. We will see that both the generalization error, in the batch framework, and the mistake bound, in the online framework, can be bounded in terms of the *Bayes Depth*.

Theorem 3. *Let $\mathcal{C}$ be a parameter space and let ν be a probability measure (prior or posterior) over $\mathcal{C}$ and l be a loss function. Let h be a classifier then for any probability measure over $\mathcal{X}$*

$$E_{c\sim\nu}E_x\left[l\left(h\left(x\right), c\left(x\right)\right)\right] \leq \frac{1}{D_{Bayes}(h)} E_{c\sim\nu}E_x\left[l\left(h_{\text{opt}}\left(x\right), c\left(x\right)\right)\right] \tag{6}$$

where $h_{\text{opt}}(\cdot)$ is the optimal predictor, i.e. the Bayes prediction rule.

The generalization bound presented in (6) differs from the common PAC bounds (e.g. [13,14, ...]). The common bounds provide a bound on the generalization error based on the empirical error. (6) gives a multiplicative bound on the ratio between the generalization error and the best possible generalization error. A similar approach was used by Haussler et al. [12]. They proved that the generalization error of the Gibbs sampler is at most twice as large as the best possible.

Proof. Let $x \in X$ and let $D = D_{\text{Bayes}}(h)$ be the depth of h. Thus ,

$$D \leq \frac{\min_{y\in\mathcal{Y}} E_{c'\sim\nu}\left[l\left(y, c'\left(x\right)\right)\right]}{E_{c'\sim\nu}\left[l\left(h\left(x\right), c'\left(x\right)\right)\right]}$$

Therefore,

$$\begin{aligned} E_{c'\sim\nu}\left[l\left(h\left(x\right), c'\left(x\right)\right)\right] &\leq \frac{1}{D}\min_{y\in\mathcal{Y}} E_{c'\sim\nu}\left[l\left(y, c'\left(x\right)\right)\right] \\ &= \frac{1}{D}E_{c'\sim\nu}\left[l\left(h_{\text{opt}}\left(x\right), c'\left(x\right)\right)\right] \end{aligned} \tag{7}$$

Averaging (7) over x we obtain the stated result. □

We now turn to prove the extended version of theorem 2, which deals with the online setting. This analysis resembles the analysis of the *Halving* algorithm [15]. However, the algorithm presented avoids the computational deficiencies of the *Halving* algorithm.

Theorem 4. *Let $\{(x_i, y_i)\}_{i=1}^{\infty}$ be a sequence of labeled instances where $x_i \in \mathcal{X}$ and $y_i \in \{\pm 1\}$. Assume that there exists a probability measure ν over a concept class $\mathcal{C}$ such that $\nu\{c \in \mathcal{C} : \forall i\ c(x_i) = y_i\} \geq \gamma > 0$. Let L be a learning algorithm such that given a training set $S = \{(x_i, y_i)\}_{i=1}^{m}$, L returns a hypothesis h which is consistent with S and such that $D_{Bayes}(h) \geq D_0 > 0$ (with respect to the measure ν restricted to the version-space and the zero-one loss). Then the algorithm which predicts the label of a new instance using the hypothesis returned by L on the data seen so far will make at most*

$$\frac{\log 1/\gamma}{\log(1 + D_0)}$$

mistakes.

Proof. Assume that the algorithm presented made a mistake in predicting the label of x_m. Denote by V_{m-1} the version space at this stage; then

$$V_{m-1} = \{c \in \mathcal{C} : \forall 1 \leq i < m,\ c(x_i) = y_i\}$$

from the definition of the version space and the assumptions of this theorem we have that $\nu(V_{m-1}) \geq \gamma$. We will consider two cases. One is when the majority of the classifiers are misclassifies x_m, and the second is when only the minority misclassifies. If the majority made a mistake then $\nu(V_m) \leq \frac{1}{2}\nu(V_{m-1})$.

However if the minority made a mistake, the hypothesis h returned by L is in the minority, but since $D_{\text{Bayes}}(h) \geq D_0$ we obtain

$$D_0 \geq \frac{\nu\{c \in V_{m-1} : c(x_m) = -y_m\}}{\nu\{c \in V_{m-1} : c(x_m) = y_m\}} \tag{8}$$

Note that the denominator in (8) is merely $\nu(V_m)$ while the numerator is $\nu(V_{m-1}) - \nu(V_m)$. Thus

$$D_0 \leq \frac{\nu(V_{m-1}) - \nu(V_m)}{\nu(V_m)} = \frac{\nu(V_{m-1})}{\nu(V_m)} - 1$$

and thus $\nu(V_m) \leq \frac{1}{1+D_0}\nu(V_{m-1})$.

If there were k wrong predictions on the labels of $x_1, \ldots, x_m$ then

$$\nu(V_m) \leq \max\left(\frac{1}{2}, \frac{1}{1 + D_0}\right)^k$$

while $\gamma \leq \nu(V_m)$ and thus, since D_0 is upper bounded by 1, we conclude

$$k \leq \frac{\log \gamma}{\log \frac{1}{1+D_0}}$$

□

4 Concentration of Measure for Multivariate Random Variables to the Tukey Median

In previous sections we have seen the significance of the *Tukey Depth* [2] in proving generalization bounds. Inspired by this definition we also used the extended *Bayes Depth* to prove generalization bounds on general concept classes and loss functions. However, the *Tukey Depth* has many other interesting properties. For example, Donoho and Gasko [7] defined the *Tukey Median* as the point which achieves the best *Tukey Depth.* They showed that such a point always exists, but it need not be unique. The *Tukey Median* has high breakdown point [7] which means that it is resistant to outliers, much like the univariate median.

In this section we use *Tukey Depth* to provide a novel concentration of measure inequality for multivariate random variables. The theorem states that any Lipschitz[3] function from a product space to $\mathbb{R}^n$ is concentrated around its *Tukey Median.*

Theorem 5. *Let $\Omega_1, \ldots, \Omega_d$ be measurable spaces and let $\mathcal{X} = \Omega_1 \times \ldots \times \Omega_d$ be the product space with P being a product measure. Let $F : \mathcal{X} \longrightarrow \mathbb{R}^n$ be a multivariate random variable such that F is a Lipschitz function in the sense that for any $x \in \mathcal{X}$ there exists $a = a(x) \in \mathbb{R}^d_+$ with $\|a\|_2 = 1$ such that for every $y \in \mathcal{X}$*

$$\|F(x) - F(y)\|_2 \leq \sum_{i \,:\, x_i \neq y_i} a_i \tag{9}$$

Assume furthermore that F is bounded such that $\|F(x) - F(y)\| \leq M$.

Let $z \in \mathbb{R}^n$ then for any $r > 0$

$$P_x \left[\|F(x) - z\| \geq r\right] \leq \left(\frac{4M}{r}\right)^n \frac{1}{D(z)} e^{-r^2/16} \tag{10}$$

where $D(z)$ is the Tukey Depth *of z with respect to the push forward measure induced by F.*

Proof. Let $w \in \mathbb{R}^n$ be in the unit ball. From (9), it follows that if $a = a(x)$ then for any $y \in \mathbb{R}^n$

$$F(x) \cdot w - F(y) \cdot w = (F(x) - F(y)) \cdot w \leq \|F(x) - F(y)\| \, \|w\| \leq \sum_{i \,:\, x_i \neq y_i} a_i$$

which means that the functional $x \rightarrow F(x) \cdot w$ is Lipschitz. Let $z \in \mathbb{R}^n$ then $\Pr_{x \sim P}\left[F(x) \cdot w \leq z \cdot w\right] \geq D(z)$. Using Talagrand's theorem [16] we conclude that

$$\Pr_{x \sim P}\left[F(x) \cdot w \geq z \cdot w + r/2\right] \leq \frac{1}{D(z)} e^{-r^2/16}$$

clearly this will hold for any vector w such that $\|w\| \leq 1$.

[3] Lipschitz is in Talagrand's sense. See e.g [9, pg 72-79].

Let W be a minimal $r/2M$ covering of the unit sphere in $\mathbb{R}^n$, i.e. for any unit vector u there exists $w \in W$ such that $\|u - w\| \leq r/2M$. W.l.o.g. W is a subset of the unit ball, otherwise project all the points in W onto the unit ball. Since W is minimal then $|W| \leq (4M/r)^n$. Using the union bound over all $w \in W$ it follows that

$$\Pr_{x \sim P}\left[\exists w \in W,\ \ F(x) \cdot w \geq z \cdot w + r/2\right] \leq \left(\frac{4M}{r}\right)^n \frac{1}{D(z)} e^{-r^2/16}$$

Finally we claim that if x is such that $\|F(x) - z\| \geq r$ then there exists $w \in W$ such that $F(x) \cdot w \geq z \cdot w + r/2$. For this purpose we assume that $z \in \mathrm{conv}(F(X))$ otherwise the statement is trivial since $D(z) = 0$. Let

$$u = \frac{F(x) - z}{\|F(x) - z\|}$$

then u is a unit vector and

$$F(x) \cdot u - z \cdot u = (F(x) - z) \cdot u = \|F(x) - z\| \geq r$$

Since w is a cover of the unit sphere and u is a unit vector, there exist $w \in W$ such that $\|w - u\| \leq r/2M$.

$$\begin{aligned} F(x) \cdot w - z \cdot w &= (F(x) - z) \cdot w \\ &= (F(x) - z) \cdot u + (F(x) - z) \cdot (w - u) \\ &\geq r - \|F(x) - z\| \, \|w - u\| \\ &\geq r - (M)\,(r/2M) \\ &= r/2 \end{aligned}$$

and thus $F(x) \cdot w \geq z \cdot w + r/2$. Hence,

$$\begin{aligned} \Pr_x\left[\|F(x) - z\| \geq r\right] &\leq \Pr_x\left[\exists w \in W,\ \ F(x) \cdot w \geq z \cdot w + r/2\right] \\ &\leq \left(\frac{4M}{r}\right)^n \frac{1}{D(z)} e^{-r^2/16} \end{aligned}$$

□

Corollary 1. *In the setting of theorem 5, if m_F is the* Tukey Median *of F, i.e. the* Tukey Median *of the push-forward measure induced by F then for any $r > 0$*

$$P_x\left[\|F(x) - m_F\| \geq r\right] \leq \left(\frac{4M}{r}\right)^n (n+1)\, e^{-r^2/16}$$

Proof. From Helly's theorem [3] it follows that $D(m_F) \geq 1/(n+1)$ for any measure on $\mathbb{R}^n$. Substitute this in (10) to obtain the stated result. □

Note also that any Lipschitz function is bounded since

$$\|F(x) - F(y)\| \leq \sum_{i: x_i \neq y_i} a_i \leq \sqrt{d}$$

hence M in the above results is bounded by $\sqrt{d}$.

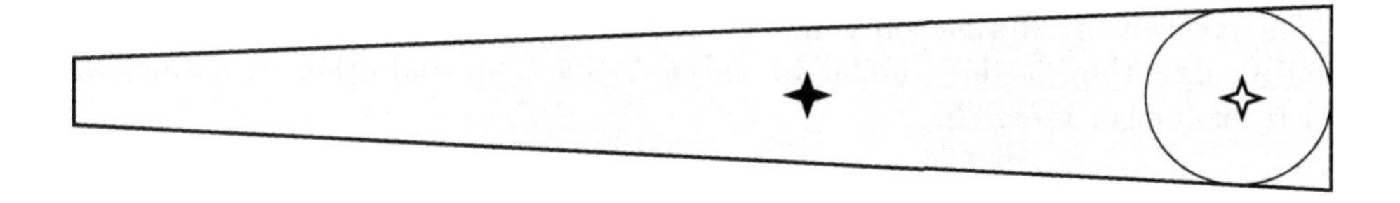

Fig. 2. A comparison of the *Tukey Median* (in black) and the maximal margin point (in white). In this case, the maximal margin point has small *Tukey Depth*

5 Summary and Discussion

In this paper we present new generalization bounds for *Bayes Point Machines* [1]. These bounds apply the mean voter theorem [4] to show that the generalization error of *Bayes Point Machines* is greater than the minimal possible error by at most a factor of $(e-1) \sim 1.71$. We also provide a new on-line mistake bound of $\frac{n}{-\log(1-1/e)} \log(2R/r) \sim 2.18n \ln(2R/r)$ for this algorithm.

The notion of *Bayes Point* is extended beyond linear classifiers to a general concept class. We defined the *Bayes Depth* in the general supervised learning context, as an extension of the familiar *Tukey Depth.* We give examples for calculating the *Bayes Depth* and provide a generalization bound which is applicable to this more general setting. Our bounds hold for multi-class problems and for any loss function.

Finally we provide a concentration of measure inequality for multivariate random variables to their *Tukey Median.* This inequality suggests that the center of gravity is indeed a good approximation to the *Bayes Point.* This provides additional evidence for the fitness of the *Tukey Median* as the multivariate generalization of the scalar median (see also [17] for a discussion on this issue).

The nature of the generalization bounds presented in this paper is different from the more standard bounds in machine learning. Here we bound the multiplicative difference between the learned classifier and the optimal Bayes classifier. This multiplicative factor is a measure of the efficiency of the learning algorithm to exploit the available information. On the other hand, the more standard PAC-like bounds [13,14, ...], provide an additive bound, on the difference between the training error and the generalization error, with high confidence. The advantage of additive bounds is in their performance guaranty. Nevertheless, empirically it is known that PAC bounds are very loose due to their worst case distributional assumptions. The multiplicative bounds are tighter than the additive ones in these cases.

The bounds for linear *Bayes Point Machines* and the use of *Tukey Depth* can provide another explanation for the success of *Support Vector Machines* [5]. Although the depth of the maximal margin classifier can be arbitrarily small (see figure 2), if the version space is "round" the maximal margin point is close to the *Tukey Median.* We argue that in many cases this is indeed the case.

There seems to be a deep relationship between *Tukey Depth* and *Active Learning*, especially through the *Query By Committee* (QBC) algorithm [11].

The concept of information gain, as used by Freund et al. [11] to analyze the QBC algorithm, is very similar to *Tukey Depth*. This and other extensions are left for further research.

Acknowledgments. We thank Ran El-Yaniv, Amir Globerson and Nati Linial for useful comments. RGB is supported by the Clore foundation. AN is supported by the Horowitz foundation.

References

1. Herbrich, R., Graepel, T., Campbell, C.: Bayes point machines. Journal of Machine Learning Research (2001)
2. Tukey, J.: mathematics and picturing data. In: proceeding international congress of mathematics. Number 2 (1975) 523–531
3. Matoušek, J.: Lectures on discrete geometry. Springer-Verlag (2002)
4. Caplin, A., Nalebuff, B.: Aggregation and social choice: A mean voter theorem. Exonometrica **59** (1991) 1–23
5. Vapnik, V.: Statistical Learning Theory. Wiley (1998)
6. Novikoff, A.B.J.: On convergence proofs on perceptrons. In: Proceedings of the Symposium on the Mathematical Theory of Automata. Volume 12. (1962) 615–622
7. Donoho, D., Gasko, M.: Breakdown properties of location estimates based on halfspace depth and projected outlyingness. Annals of Statistics **20** (1992) 1803–1827
8. Bagnoli, M., Bergstrom, T.: Log-concave probability and its applications. http://www.econ.ucsb.edu/~tedb/Theory/logconc.ps (1989)
9. Ledoux, M.: The Concentration of Measure Phenomenon. American Mathematical Society (2001)
10. Bertsimas, D., Vempala, S.: Solving convex programs by random walks. In: STOC. (2002) 109–115
11. Freund, Y., Seung, H., Shamir, E., Tishby, N.: Selective sampling using the query by committee algorithm. Macine Learning **28** (1997) 133–168
12. Haussler, D., Kearns, M., Schapie, R.E.: Bounds on the sample complexity of bayesian learning using information theory and the vc dimension. Machine Learning **14** (1994) 83–113
13. Vapnik, V., Chervonenkis, A.Y.: On the uniform covergence of relative frequencies of events to their probabilities. Theory of Probability and its Applications **16** (1971) 264–280
14. Bartlett, P., Mendelson, S.: Rademacher and gaussian complexities: risk bounds and structural results. Journal of Machine Learning Research **3** (2002) 463–482
15. Littlestone, N.: Learning quickly when irrelevant attributes abound: A new linear-threshold algorithm. In: In 28th Annual Symposium on Foundations of Computer Science. (1987) 68–77
16. Talagrand, M.: Concentration of measure and isoperimetric inequalities in product space. Publ. Math. I.H.E.S. **81** (1995) 73–205
17. Zuo, Y., Serfling, R.: General notions of statistical depth function. The Annals of Statistics **28** (2000) 461–482
18. Prekopa, A.: Logarithmic concave measures with applications to stochastic programming. Acta Sci. Math. (Szeged) **32** (1971) 301–315
19. Borell, C.: Convex set functions in *d*-space. Periodica Mathematica Hungarica **6** (1975) 111–136

A Concave Measures

We provide a brief introduction to concave measures. See [8,4,18,19] for more information about log-concavity and log-concave measures.

Definition 3. *A probability measure ν over $\mathbb{R}^n$ is said to be* log-concave *if for any measurable sets A and B and every $0 \leq \lambda \leq 1$ the following holds:*

$$\nu\left(\lambda A + (1-\lambda) B\right) \geq \nu\left(A\right)^{\lambda} \nu\left(B\right)^{1-\lambda}$$

Note that many common probability measures are log-concave, for example uniform measures over compact convex sets, normal distributions, chi-square and more. Moreover the restriction of any log-concave measure to a convex set is a log-concave measure.

In some cases, there is a need to quantify concavity. The following definition provides such a quantifier.

Definition 4. *A probability measure ν over $\mathbb{R}^n$ is said to be* ρ-concave *if for any measurable sets A and B and every $0 \leq \lambda \leq 1$ the following holds:*

$$\nu\left(\lambda A + (1-\lambda) B\right) \geq \left[\lambda \nu\left(A\right)^{\rho} + (1-\lambda)\nu\left(B\right)^{\rho}\right]^{1/\rho}$$

A few facts about ρ-concave measures:

- If ν is ρ-concave with $\rho = \infty$ then $\nu(\lambda A + (1-\lambda)B) \geq \max(\nu(A), \nu(B))$.
- If ν is ρ-concave with $\rho = -\infty$ then $\nu(\lambda A + (1-\lambda)B) \geq \min(\nu(A), \nu(B))$.
- If ν is ρ-concave with $\rho = 0$ then $\nu(\lambda A + (1-\lambda)B) \geq \nu(A)^{\lambda}\nu(B)^{1-\lambda}$, in this case ν is called log-concave.

B Mean Voter Theorem

Caplin and Nalebuff [4] proved the Mean Voter Theorem in the context of the voting problem. They did not phrase their theorem using *Tukey Depth* but the translation is trivial. Hence, we provide here (without proof) a rephrased version of their theorem.

Theorem 6. *(Caplin and Nalebuff) Let ν be a ρ-concave measure over $\mathbb{R}^n$ with $\rho \geq -1/(n+1)$. Let z be the center of gravity of ν, i.e. $z = E_{x \sim \nu}[x]$. Then*

$$D(z) \geq \left(\frac{n + 1/\rho}{n + 1 + 1/\rho}\right)^{n+1/\rho} \tag{11}$$

where $D(\cdot)$ is the Tukey Depth.

First note that when $\rho \to 0$ the bound in (11) approches $1/e$; hence for log-concave measures $D(z) \geq 1/e$. However, this bound is better than $1/e$ in many cases, i.e. when $\rho > 0$. This fact can be used to obtain an improved version of theorems 1 and 2.

Sparseness Versus Estimating Conditional Probabilities: Some Asymptotic Results

Peter L. Bartlett[1] and Ambuj Tewari[2]

[1] Division of Computer Science and Department of Statistics
University of California, Berkeley
bartlett@cs.berkeley.edu
[2] Division of Computer Science
University of California, Berkeley
ambuj@cs.berkeley.edu

Abstract. One of the nice properties of kernel classifiers such as SVMs is that they often produce sparse solutions. However, the decision functions of these classifiers cannot always be used to estimate the conditional probability of the class label. We investigate the relationship between these two properties and show that these are intimately related: sparseness does not occur when the conditional probabilities can be unambiguously estimated. We consider a family of convex loss functions and derive sharp asymptotic bounds for the number of support vectors. This enables us to characterize the exact trade-off between sparseness and the ability to estimate conditional probabilities for these loss functions.

1 Introduction

Consider the following familiar setting of a binary classification problem. A sequence $T = ((x_1, y_1), \ldots, (x_n, y_n))$ of i.i.d. pairs is drawn from a probability distribution over $\mathcal{X} \times \mathcal{Y}$ where $\mathcal{X} \subseteq \mathbb{R}^d$ and $\mathcal{Y}$ is the set of labels (which we assume is $\{+1, -1\}$ for convenience). The goal is to use the training set T to predict the label of a new observation $x \in \mathcal{X}$. A common way to approach the problem is to use the training set to construct a decision function $f_T : \mathcal{X} \to \mathbb{R}$ and output $\mathrm{sign}(f_T(x))$ as the predicted label of x.

In this paper, we consider classifiers based on an optimization problem of the form:

$$f_{T,\lambda} = \arg\min_{f \in H} \lambda \|f\|_H^2 + \frac{1}{n}\sum_{i=1}^{n} \phi(y_i f(x_i)) \tag{1}$$

Here, H is a reproducing kernel Hilbert space (RKHS) of some kernel k, $\lambda > 0$ is a regularization parameter and $\phi : \mathbb{R} \to [0, \infty)$ is a convex loss function. Since optimization problems based on the non-convex function 0-1 loss $t \mapsto I_{(t \le 0)}$ (where $I_{(\cdot)}$ is the indicator function) are computationally intractable, use of convex loss functions is often seen as using upper bounds on the 0-1 loss to make the problem computationally easier. Although computational tractability is one of the goals we have in mind while designing classifiers, it is not the only one.

J. Shawe-Taylor and Y. Singer (Eds.): COLT 2004, LNAI 3120, pp. 564–578, 2004.

We would like to compare different convex loss functions based on their statistical and other useful properties. Conditions ensuring Bayes-risk consistency of classifiers using convex loss functions have already been established [2,4,9,12]. It has been observed that different cost functions have different properties and it is important to choose a loss function judiciously (see, for example, [10]). In order to understand the relative merits of different loss functions, it is important to consider these properties and investigate the extent to which different loss functions exhibit them. It may turn out (as it does below) that different properties are in conflict with each other. In that case, knowing the trade-off allows one to make an informed choice while choosing a loss function for the classification task at hand.

One of the properties we focus on is the ability to estimate the conditional probability of the class label $\eta(x) = P(Y = +1|X = x)$. Under some conditions on the loss function and the sequence of regularization parameters λ_n, the solutions of (1) converge (in probability) to a function $F^*_\phi(\eta(x))$ which is set valued in general [7]. As long as we can uniquely identify $\eta(x)$ based on a value in $F^*_\phi(\eta(x))$, we can hope to estimate conditional probabilities using $f_{T,\lambda_n}(x)$, at least asymptotically. Choice of the loss function is crucial to this property. For example, the L2-SVM (which uses the loss function $t \mapsto (\max\{0, 1-t\})^2$) is much better than L1-SVM (which uses $t \mapsto \max\{0, 1-t\}$) in terms of asymptotically estimating conditional probabilities.

Another criterion is the sparseness of solutions of (1). It is well known that any solution $f_{T,\lambda}$ of (1) can be represented as

$$f_{T,\lambda}(x) = \sum_{i=1}^{n} \alpha_i^* k(x, x_i) \ . \tag{2}$$

The observations x_i for which the coefficients α_i^* are non-zero are called support vectors. The rest of the observations have no effect on the value of the decision function. Having fewer support vectors leads to faster evaluation of the decision function. Bounds on the number of support vectors are therefore useful to know. Steinwart's recent work [8] has shown that for the L1-SVM and a suitable kernel, the asymptotic fraction of support vectors is twice the Bayes-risk. Thus, L1-SVMs can be expected to produce sparse solutions. It was also shown that L2-SVMs will typically not produce sparse solutions.

We are interested in how sparseness relates to the ability to estimate conditional probabilities. What we mentioned about L1 and L2-SVMs leads to several questions. Do we always lose sparseness by being able to estimate conditional probabilities? Is it possible to characterize the exact trade-off between the asymptotic fraction of support vectors and the ability to estimate conditional probabilities? If sparseness is indeed lost when we are able to fully estimate conditional probabilities, we may want to estimate conditional probabilities only in an interval, say $(0.05, 0.95)$, if that helps recover sparseness. Estimating η for x's that have $\eta(x) \geq 0.95$ may not be too crucial for our prediction task. How can we design loss functions which enable us to estimate probabilities in sub-intervals of $[0, 1]$ while preserving as much sparseness as possible?

This paper attempts to answer these questions. We show that if one wants to estimate conditional probabilities in an interval $(\gamma, 1-\gamma)$ for some $\gamma \in (0, 1/2)$, then sparseness is lost on that interval in the sense that the asymptotic fraction of data that become support vectors is lower bounded by $\mathbb{E}_x G(\eta(x))$ where $G(\eta) = 1$ throughout the interval $(\gamma, 1-\gamma)$. Moreover, one cannot recover sparseness by giving up the ability to estimate conditional probabilities in some sub-interval of $(\gamma, 1-\gamma)$. The only way to do that is to increase γ thereby shortening the interval $(\gamma, 1-\gamma)$. We also derive sharp bounds on the asymptotic number of support vectors for a family of loss functions of the form:

$$\phi(t) = h((t_0 - t)_+),\ t_0 > 0$$

where t_+ denotes $\max\{0, t\}$ and h is a continuously differentiable convex function such that $h'(0) \geq 0$. Each loss function in the family allows one to estimate probabilities in the interval $(\gamma, 1-\gamma)$ for some value of γ. The asymptotic fraction of support vectors is then $\mathbb{E}_x G(\eta(x))$, where $G(\eta)$ is a function that increases linearly from 0 to 1 as η goes from 0 to γ. For example, if $\phi(t) = \frac{1}{3}((1-t)_+)^2 + \frac{2}{3}(1-t)_+$ then conditional probabilities can be estimated in $(1/4, 3/4)$ and $G(\eta) = 1$ for $\eta \in (1/4, 3/4)$ (see Fig. 1).

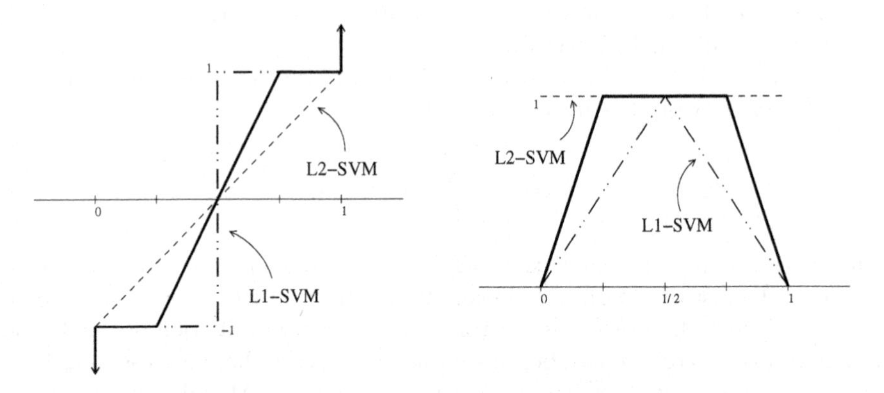

Fig. 1. Plots of $F_\phi^*(\eta)$ (left) and $G(\eta)$ (right) for a loss function which is a convex combination of the L1 and L2-SVM loss functions. Dashed lines represent the corresponding plots for the original loss functions.

2 Notation and Known Results

Let P be the probability distribution over $\mathcal{X} \times \mathcal{Y}$ and let $T \in (\mathcal{X} \times \mathcal{Y})^n$ be a training set. Let $\mathbb{E}_P(\cdot)$ denote expectations taken with respect to the distribution P. Similarly, let $\mathbb{E}_x(\cdot)$ denote expectations taken with respect to the marginal distribution on $\mathcal{X}$. Let $\eta(x)$ be $P(Y = +1|X = x)$. For a decision function $f : \mathcal{X} \to \mathbb{R}$, define its risk as

$$R_P(f) = \mathbb{E}_P I_{(yf(x) \leq 0)} \cdot$$

The Bayes-risk $R_P = \inf\{R_P(f) : f \text{ measurable}\}$ is the least possible risk. Given a loss function ϕ, define the ϕ-risk of f by

$$R_{\phi,P}(f) = \mathbb{E}_P \phi(yf(x)) \ .$$

The optimal ϕ-risk $R_{\phi,P} = \inf\{R_{\phi,P}(f) : f \text{ measurable}\}$ is the least achievable ϕ-risk. When the expectations in the definitions of $R_P(f)$ and $R_{\phi,P}(f)$ are taken with respect to the empirical measure corresponding to T, we get the empirical risk $R_T(f)$ and the empirical ϕ-risk $R_{\phi,T}(f)$ respectively. Conditioning on x, we can write the ϕ-risk as

$$\begin{aligned} R_{\phi,P}(f) &= E_x[E(\phi(yf(x)|x)] \\ &= E_x[\eta(x)\phi(f(x)) + (1-\eta(x))\phi(-f(x))] \\ &= E_x[C(\eta(x), f(x))] \ . \end{aligned}$$

Here, we have defined $C(\eta, t) = \eta\phi(t) + (1-\eta)\phi(-t)$. To minimize the ϕ-risk, we have to minimize $C(\eta, \cdot)$ for each $\eta \in [0,1]$. So, define the set valued function $F_\phi^*(\eta)$ by

$$F_\phi^*(\eta) = \{t : C(\eta, t) = \min_{s \in \bar{\mathbb{R}}} C(\eta, s)\}$$

where $\bar{\mathbb{R}}$ is the set of extended reals $\mathbb{R} \cup \{-\infty, \infty\}$. Any measurable selection f^* of F_ϕ^* actually minimizes the ϕ-risk. The function F_ϕ^* is plotted for three choices of ϕ in Fig. 1. From the definitions of $C(\eta, t)$ and $F_\phi^*(\eta)$, it is easy to see that $F_\phi^*(\eta) = -F_\phi^*(1-\eta)$. Steinwart [7] also proves that $\eta \mapsto F_\phi^*(\eta)$ is a monotone operator. This means that if $\eta_1 > \eta_2$, $t_1 \in F_\phi^*(\eta_1)$ and $t_2 \in F_\phi^*(\eta_2)$ then $t_1 \geq t_2$.

A convex loss function is called classification calibrated if the following two conditions hold:

$$\eta < \frac{1}{2} \Rightarrow F_\phi^*(\eta) \subset [-\infty, 0) \text{ and } \eta > \frac{1}{2} \Rightarrow F_\phi^*(\eta) \subset (0, +\infty] \ .$$

A necessary and sufficient condition for a convex ϕ to be classification calibrated is that $\phi'(0)$ exists and is negative [2]. If ϕ is classification calibrated then it is guaranteed that for any sequence f_n such that $R_{\phi,P}(f_n) \to R_{\phi,P}$, we have $R_P(f_n) \to R_P$. Thus, classification calibrated loss functions are good in the sense that minimizing the ϕ-risk leads to classifiers that have risks approaching the Bayes-risk. Note, however, that in the optimization problem (1), we are minimizing the regularized ϕ-risk

$$R_{\phi,T,\lambda}^{reg} = \lambda \|f\|_H^2 + R_{\phi,T} \ .$$

Steinwart [9] has shown that if one uses an classification calibrated convex loss function, a universal kernel (one whose RKHS is dense in the space of continuous functions over $\mathcal{X}$) and a sequence of regularization parameters such that $\lambda_n \to 0$ sufficiently slowly, then $R_{\phi,P}(f_{T,\lambda_n}) \to R_{\phi,P}$. In another paper [7], he proves that this is sufficient to ensure the convergence in probability of f_{T,λ_n} to $F_\phi^*(\eta(\cdot))$. That is, for all $\epsilon > 0$

$$P_x(\{x \in \mathcal{X} : \rho(f_{T,\lambda_n}(x), F_\phi^*(\eta(x))) \geq \epsilon\}) \to 0 \tag{3}$$

The function $\rho(t, B)$ is just the distance from t to the point in B which is closest to t. The definition given by Steinwart [7] is more complicated because one has to handle the case when $B \cap \mathbb{R} = \emptyset$. We will ensure in our proofs that F_ϕ^* is not a singleton set just containing $+\infty$ or $-\infty$.

Since f_{T,λ_n} converges to $F_\phi^*(\eta(\cdot))$, the plots in Fig. 1 suggest that the L2-SVM decision function can be used to estimate conditional probabilities in the whole range $[0, 1]$ while it not possible to use the L1-SVM decision function to estimate conditional probabilities in any interval. However, the L1-SVM is better if one considers the asymptotic fraction of support vectors. Under some conditions on the kernel and the regularization sequence, Steinwart proved that the fraction is $\mathbb{E}_x[2\min(\eta(x), 1 - \eta(x))]$, which also happens to be the optimal ϕ-risk for the hinge loss function. For L2-SVM, he showed that the asymptotic fraction is $P_x(\{x \in \mathcal{X} : 0 < \eta(x) < 1\})$, which is the probability of the set where noise occurs. Observe that we can write the fraction of support vectors as $\mathbb{E}_x[G(\eta(x))]$ where $G(\eta) = 2\min\{\eta, 1 - \eta)\}$ for the hinge loss and $G(\eta) = I_{(\eta \notin \{0,1\})}$ for the squared hinge loss. We will see below that these two are extreme cases. In general, there are loss functions which allow one to estimate probabilities in an interval centered at $1/2$ and for which $G(\eta) = 1$ only on that interval.

Steinwart [7] also derived a general lower bound on the asymptotic number of support vectors in terms of the probability of the set

$$S = \{(x, y) \in \mathcal{X}_{cont} \times \mathcal{Y} : 0 \notin \partial\phi(yF_\phi^*(\eta(x)))\} .$$

Here, $\mathcal{X}_{cont} = \{x \in \mathcal{X} : P_x(\{x\}) = 0\}$ and $\partial\phi$ denotes the subdifferential of ϕ. In the simple case of a function of one variable $\partial\phi(x) = [\phi'_-(x), \phi'_+(x)]$, where ϕ'_- and ϕ'_+ are the left and right hand derivatives of ϕ (which always exist for convex functions). If $\mathcal{X}_{cont} = \mathcal{X}$, one can write $P(S)$ as

$$\begin{aligned} P(S) &= \mathbb{E}_P[I_{(0 \notin \partial\phi(yF_\phi^*(\eta(x))))}] \\ &= \mathbb{E}_x[\eta(x) I_{(0 \notin \partial\phi(F_\phi^*(\eta(x)))))} + (1 - \eta(x) I_{(0 \notin \partial\phi(-F_\phi^*(\eta(x)))))}] \\ &= \mathbb{E}_x G(\eta(x)) . \end{aligned}$$

For the last step, we simply defined

$$G(\eta) = \eta I_{(0 \notin \partial\phi(F_\phi^*(\eta)))} + (1 - \eta) I_{(0 \notin \partial\phi(-F_\phi^*(\eta)))} . \tag{4}$$

3 Preliminary Results

We will consider only classification calibrated convex loss functions. Since ϕ is classification calibrated we know that $\phi'(0) < 0$. Define t_0 as

$$t_0 = \inf\{t : 0 \in \partial\phi(t)\}$$

with the convention that $\inf \emptyset = \infty$. Because $\phi'(0) < 0$ and subdifferentials of a convex function are monotonically decreasing, we must have $t_0 > 0$. However, it may be that $t_0 = \infty$. The following lemma says that sparse solutions cannot be expected if that is the case.

Lemma 1. *If $t_0 = \infty$, then $G(\eta) = 1$ on $[0, 1]$.*

Proof. $t_0 = \infty$ implies that for all t, $0 \notin \partial\phi(t)$. Using (4), we get $G(\eta) = \eta.1 + (1 - \eta).1 = 1$. □

Therefore, let us assume that $t_0 < \infty$. The next lemma tell us about the signs of $\phi'_-(t_0)$ and $\phi'_+(t_0)$.

Lemma 2. *If $t_0 < \infty$, then $\phi'_-(t_0) \leq 0$ and $\phi'_+(t_0) \geq 0$.*

Proof. Suppose $\phi'_-(t_0) > 0$. This implies $\partial\phi(t_0) > 0$. Since subdifferential is a monotone operator, we have $\partial\phi(t) > 0$ for all $t > t_0$. By definition of t_0, $0 \notin \partial\phi(t)$ for $t < t_0$. Thus, $\{t : 0 \in \partial\phi(t)\} = \emptyset$, which contradicts the fact that $t < \infty$. Now, suppose that $\phi'_+(t_0) = -\epsilon$, such that $\epsilon > 0$. Since $\lim_{t' \downarrow t} \phi'_-(t') = \phi'_+(t_0)$ (see [6], Theorem 24.1), we can find a $t' > t_0$ sufficiently close to t_0 such that $\phi'_-(t') \leq -\epsilon/2$. Therefore, by monotonicity of the subdifferential, $\partial\phi(t) < 0$, for all $t < t'$. This implies $t' \leq \inf\{t : 0 \in \partial\phi(t)\}$, which is a contradiction since $t' > t_0$. □

The following lemma describes the function $F^*_\phi(\eta)$ near 0 and 1. Note that we have $\phi'_-(-t_0) \leq \phi'_+(-t_0) \leq \phi'(0) < 0$. Also $\phi'(0) \leq \phi'_-(t_0) \leq 0$.

Lemma 3. *$t_0 \in F^*_\phi(\eta)$ iff $\eta \in [1 - \gamma, 1]$, where γ is defined as*

$$\gamma = \frac{\phi'_-(t_0)}{\phi'_-(t_0) + \phi'_+(-t_0)} .$$

Moreover, $F^*_\phi(\eta)$ is the singleton set $\{t_0\}$ for $\eta \in (1 - \gamma, 1)$.

Proof. $t_0 \in F^*_\phi(\eta) \Leftrightarrow t_0$ minimizes $C(\eta, \cdot) \Leftrightarrow 0 \in \partial_2 C(\eta, t_0)$, where ∂_2 denotes that the subdifferential is with respect to the second variable. This is because $C(\eta, \cdot)$, being a linear combination of convex functions, is convex. Thus, a necessary and sufficient condition for a point to be a minimum is that the subdifferential there should contain zero. Now, using the linearity of the subdifferential operator and the chain rule, we get

$$\begin{aligned} \partial_2 C(\eta, t_0) &= \eta\partial\phi(t_0) - (1 - \eta)\partial\phi(-t_0) \\ &= [\eta\phi'_-(t_0) - (1 - \eta)\phi'_+(-t_0), \eta\phi'_+(t_0) - (1 - \eta)\phi'_-(-t_0)] . \end{aligned}$$

Hence, $0 \in \partial_2 C(\eta, t_0)$ iff the following two conditions hold.

$$\eta\phi'_-(t_0) - (1 - \eta)\phi'_+(-t_0) \leq 0 \tag{5}$$

$$\eta\phi'_+(t_0) - (1 - \eta)\phi'_-(-t_0) \geq 0 \tag{6}$$

The inequality (6) holds for all $\eta \in [0, 1]$ since $\phi'_+(t_0) \geq 0$ and $\phi'_-(-t_0) < 0$. The other inequality is equivalent to

$$\eta \geq \frac{-\phi'_+(-t_0)}{-\phi'_-(t_0) - \phi'_+(-t_0)} .$$

Moreover, the inequalities are strict when $\eta \in (1 - \gamma, 1)$. Therefore, t_0 is the unique minimizer of $C(\eta, \cdot)$ for these values of η. □

Corollary 4. *$-t_0 \in F_\phi^*(\eta)$ iff $\eta \in [0, \gamma]$. Moreover, $F_\phi^*(\eta)$ is the singleton set $\{-t_0\}$ for $\eta \in (0, \gamma)$.*

Proof. Straightforward once we observe that $F_\phi^*(1-\eta) = -F_\phi^*(\eta)$. □

The next lemma states that if $F_\phi^*(\eta_1)$ and $F_\phi^*(\eta_2)$ intersect for $\eta_1 \neq \eta_2$ then ϕ must have points of non-differentiability. This means that differentiability of the loss function ensures that one can uniquely identify η via any element in $F_\phi^*(\eta)$.

Lemma 5. *Suppose $\eta_1 \neq \eta_2$ and $\eta_1, \eta_2 \in (\gamma, 1-\gamma)$. Then $F_\phi^*(\eta_1) \cap F_\phi^*(\eta_2) \neq \emptyset$ implies that*

- *$F_\phi^*(\eta_1) \cap F_\phi^*(\eta_2)$ is a singleton set (= $\{t\}$ say).*
- *ϕ is not differentiable at one of the points $t, -t$.*

Proof. Without loss of generality assume $\eta_1 > \eta_2$. Suppose $t > t'$ and $t, t' \in F_\phi^*(\eta_1) \cap F_\phi^*(\eta_2)$. This contradicts the fact that F_ϕ^* is monotonic since $t' \in F_\phi^*(\eta_1)$, $t \in F_\phi^*(\eta_2)$ and $t' < t$. This establishes the first claim. To prove the second claim, suppose $F_\phi^*(\eta_1) \cap F_\phi^*(\eta_2) = \{t\}$ and assume, for sake of contradiction, that ϕ is differentiable at t and $-t$. Since $\eta_1, \eta_2 \in (\gamma, 1-\gamma)$, Lemma 3 and Corollary 4 imply that $t \neq \pm t_0$. Therefore, $t \in (-t_0, t_0)$ and $\phi'(t), \phi'(-t) > 0$. Also, $t \in F_\phi^*(\eta_1) \cap F_\phi^*(\eta_2)$ implies that

$$\eta_1 \phi'(t) - (1-\eta_1)\phi'(-t) = 0$$

$$\eta_2 \phi'(t) - (1-\eta_2)\phi'(-t) = 0 \ .$$

Subtracting and rearranging, we get

$$(\phi'(t) + \phi'(-t))(\eta_1 - \eta_2) = 0$$

which is absurd since $\eta_1 > \eta_2$ and $\phi'(t), \phi'(-t) > 0$. □

Theorem 6. *Let ϕ be an classification calibrated convex loss function such that $t_0 = \inf\{t : 0 \in \partial\phi(t)\} < \infty$. Then, for $G(\eta)$ as defined in (4), we have*

$$G(\eta) = \begin{cases} 1 & \eta \in (\gamma, 1-\gamma) \\ \min\{\eta, 1-\eta\} & \eta \in [0, \gamma] \cup [1-\gamma, 1] \end{cases} \tag{7}$$

where $\gamma = \phi'_-(t_0)/(\phi'_-(t_0) + \phi'_+(-t_0))$.

Proof. Using Lemmas 2 and 3, we have $0 \in \partial\phi(F_\phi^*(\eta))$ for $\eta \in [1-\gamma, 1]$. If $\eta < 1-\gamma$, Lemma 3 tells us that $t_0 \notin F_\phi^*(\eta)$. Since F_ϕ^* is monotonic, $F_\phi^*(\eta) < t_0$. Since $t_0 = \inf\{t : 0 \in \partial\phi(t)\}$, $0 \notin \partial\phi(F_\phi^*(\eta))$ for $\eta \in [0, 1-\gamma)$. Thus, we can write $I_{(0 \notin \partial\phi(F_\phi^*(\eta)))}$ as $I_{(\eta \notin [1-\gamma, 1])}$. Also $I_{(0 \notin \partial\phi(-F_\phi^*(\eta))} = I_{(0 \notin \partial\phi(F_\phi^*(1-\eta))}$. Plugging this in (4), we get

$$\begin{aligned} G(\eta) &= \eta I_{(\eta \notin [1-\gamma, 1])} + (1-\eta) I_{(1-\eta \notin [1-\gamma, 1])} \\ &= \eta I_{(\eta \notin [1-\gamma, 1])} + (1-\eta) I_{(\eta \notin [0, \gamma])} \ . \end{aligned}$$

Since $\gamma \leq 1/2$, we can write $G(\eta)$ in the form given above. □

Corollary 7. *If* $\eta_1 \in [0,1]$ *is such that* $F_\phi^*(\eta_1) \cap F_\phi^*(\eta) = \emptyset$ *for* $\eta \neq \eta_1$, *then* $G(\eta) = 1$ *on* $[\min\{\eta_1, 1-\eta_1\}, \max\{\eta_1, 1-\eta_1\}]$.

Proof. Lemma 3 and Corollary 4 tell us that $\eta_1 \in (\gamma, 1-\gamma)$. Rest follows from Theorem 6. □

The preceding theorem and corollary have important implications. First, we can hope to have sparseness only for values of $\eta \in [0,\gamma] \cup [1-\gamma, 1]$. Second, we cannot estimate conditional probabilities in these two intervals because $F_\phi^*(\cdot)$ is not invertible there. Third, any loss function for which $F_\phi^*(\cdot)$ is invertible, say at $\eta_1 < 1/2$, will necessarily not have sparseness on the interval $[\eta_1, 1-\eta_1]$.

Note that for the case of L1 and L2-SVM, γ is $1/2$ and 0 respectively. For these two classifiers, the lower bounds $\mathbb{E}_x G(\eta(x))$ obtained after plugging in γ in (7) are the ones proved initially [7]. For the L1-SVM, the bound was later significantly improved [8]. This suggests that $\mathbb{E}_x G(\eta(x))$ might be a loose lower bound in general. In the next section we will show, by deriving sharp improved bounds, that the bound is indeed loose for a family of loss functions.

4 Improved Bounds

We will consider convex loss functions of the form

$$\phi(t) = h((t_0 - t)_+) \tag{8}$$

The function h is assumed to be continuously differentiable and convex. We also assume $h'(0) > 0$. The convexity of ϕ requires that $h'(0)$ be non-negative. Since we are not interested in everywhere differentiable loss functions we want a strict inequality. In other words the loss function is constant for all $t \geq t_0$ and is continuously differentiable before that. Further, the only discontinuity in the derivative is at t_0. Without loss of generality, we may assume that $h(0) = 0$ because the solutions to (1) do not change if we add or subtract a constant from ϕ. Note that we obtain the hinge loss if we set $h(t) = t$. We now derive the dual of (1) for our choice of the loss function.

4.1 Dual Formulation

For a convex loss function $\phi(t) = h((t_0 - t)_+)$, consider the optimization problem:

$$\arg\min_w \lambda \|w\|^2 + \frac{1}{n} \sum_{i=1}^{n} \phi(y_i w^T x_i) \; . \tag{9}$$

Make the substitution $\xi_i = t_0 - y_i w^T x_i$ to get

$$\arg\min_w \lambda \|w\|^2 + \frac{1}{n} \sum_{i=1}^{n} \phi(t_0 - \xi_i) \tag{10}$$

$$\text{subject to } \xi_i = t_0 - y_i w^T x_i \text{ for all } i \; . \tag{11}$$

Introducing Lagrange multipliers, we get the Lagrangian:

$$\mathrm{L}(w, \xi, \alpha) = \lambda \|w\|^2 + \frac{1}{n} \sum_{i=1}^{n} \phi(t_0 - \xi_i) + \sum_{i=1}^{n} \alpha_i (t_0 - y_i w^T x_i - \xi_i) .$$

Minimizing this with respect to the primal variables w and ξ_i's, gives us

$$w = \frac{1}{2\lambda} \sum_{i=1}^{n} \alpha_i y_i x_i \tag{12}$$

$$\alpha_i \in -\partial\phi(t_0 - \xi_i)/n . \tag{13}$$

For the specific form of ϕ that we are working with, we have

$$-\partial\phi(t_0 - \xi_i)/n = \begin{cases} \{h'(\xi_i)/n\} & \xi_i > 0 \\ [0, h'(0)/n] & \xi_i = 0 \\ \{0\} & \xi_i < 0 . \end{cases} \tag{14}$$

Let (w^*, ξ_i^*) be a solution of (10). Then we have

$$\begin{aligned} \lambda \|w^*\|^2 &= \lambda (w^*)^T \left(\frac{1}{2\lambda} \sum_{i=1}^{n} \alpha_i^* y_i x_i \right) \\ &= \frac{1}{2} \sum_{i=1}^{n} \alpha_i^* y_i (w^*)^T x_i = \frac{1}{2} \sum_{i=1}^{n} \alpha_i^* (t_0 - \xi_i^*) . \end{aligned} \tag{15}$$

4.2 Asymptotic Fraction of Support Vectors

Recall that a kernel is called universal if its RKHS is dense in the space of continuous functions over $\mathcal{X}$. Suppose the kernel k is universal and analytic. This ensures that any function in the RKHS H of k is analytic. Following Steinwart [8], we call a probability distribution P non-trivial (with respect to ϕ) if

$$R_{\phi,P} < \inf_{b \in \mathbb{R}} R_{\phi,P}(b) .$$

We also define the P-version of the optimization problem (1):

$$f_{P,\lambda} = \arg\min_{f \in H} \lambda \|f\|_H^2 + E_P \phi(y f(x)) .$$

Further, suppose that $K = \sup\{\sqrt{k(x,x)} : x \in \mathcal{X}\}$ is finite. Fix a loss function of the form (8). Define $G(\eta)$ as

$$G(\eta) = \begin{cases} \eta/\gamma & 0 \leq \eta \leq \gamma \\ 1 & \gamma < \eta < 1 - \gamma \\ (1-\eta)/\gamma & 1 - \gamma \leq \eta \leq 1 \end{cases}$$

where $\gamma = h'(0)/(h'(0)+h'(2t_0))$. Since ϕ is differentiable on $(-t_0, t_0)$, Lemma 5 implies that F_ϕ^* is invertible on $(\gamma, 1-\gamma)$. Thus, one can estimate conditional probabilities in the interval $(\gamma, 1-\gamma)$. Let $\#SV(f_{T,\lambda})$ denote the number of support vectors in the solution (2):

$$\#SV(f_{T,\lambda}) = |\{i : \alpha_i^* \neq 0\}| \ .$$

The next theorem says that the fraction of support vectors converges to the expectation $\mathbb{E}_x G(\eta(x))$ in probability.

Theorem 8. *Let H be the RKHS of an analytic and universal kernel on $\mathbb{R}^d$. Further, let $\mathcal{X} \subset \mathbb{R}^d$ be a closed ball and P be a probability measure on $\mathcal{X} \times \{\pm 1\}$ such that P_x has a density with respect to the Lebesgue measure on X and P is non-trivial. Suppose $\sup\{\sqrt{k(x,x)} : x \in \mathcal{X}\} < \infty$. Then for a classifier based on (1), which uses a loss function of the form (8), and a regularization sequence which tends to 0 sufficiently slowly, we have*

$$\frac{\#SV(f_{T,\lambda_n})}{n} \to \mathbb{E}_x G(\eta(x))$$

in probability.

Proof. Let us fix an $\epsilon > 0$. The proof will proceed in four steps of which the last two simply involve relating empirical averages to expectations.

Step 1. In this step we show that $f_{P,\lambda_n}(x)$ is not too close to $\pm t_0$ for most values of x. We also ensure that $f_{T,\lambda_n}(x)$ is sufficiently close to $f_{P,\lambda_n}(x)$ provided $\lambda_n \to 0$ slowly. Since $f_{P,\lambda}$ is an analytic function, for any constant c, we have

$$P_x(\{x \in X : f_{P,\lambda}(x) = c\}) > 0 \Rightarrow f(x) = c \ P_x\text{-a.s.} \tag{16}$$

Assume that $P_x(\{x \in \mathcal{X} : f_{P,\lambda}(x) = t_0\}) > 0$. By (16), we get $P_x(\{x \in \mathcal{X} : f_{P,\lambda}(x) = t_0\}) = 1$. But for small enough λ, $f_{P,\lambda} \neq t_0$ since $R_{\phi,P}(f_{P,\lambda}) \to R_{\phi,P}$ and $R(t_0) \neq R_{\phi,P}$ by the non-triviality of P. Therefore, assume that for all sufficiently large n, we have

$$P_x(\{x \in \mathcal{X} : f_{P,\lambda_n}(x) = t_0\}) = 0 \ .$$

Repeating the reasoning for $-t_0$ gives us

$$P_x(\{x \in \mathcal{X} : |f_{P,\lambda_n}(x) - t_0| \leq \delta\}) \downarrow 0 \text{ as } \delta \downarrow 0$$

$$P_x(\{x \in \mathcal{X} : |f_{P,\lambda_n}(x) + t_0| \leq \delta\}) \downarrow 0 \text{ as } \delta \downarrow 0 \ .$$

Define the set $A_\delta(\lambda) = \{x \in \mathcal{X} : |f_{P,\lambda}(x) - t_0| \leq \delta \text{ or } |f_{P,\lambda}(x) + t_0| \leq \delta\}$. For small enough λ and for all $\epsilon > 0$, there exists $\delta > 0$ such that $P_x(A_\delta(\lambda)) \leq \epsilon$. Therefore, we can define

$$\delta(\lambda) = \frac{1}{2} \sup\{\delta > 0 : P_x(A_\delta(\lambda)) \leq \epsilon\} \ .$$

Let $m(\lambda) = \inf\{\delta(\lambda') : \lambda' \geq \lambda\}$ be a decreasing version of $\delta(\lambda)$. Using Proposition 33 from [7] with $\epsilon = m(\lambda_n)$, we conclude that for a sequence $\lambda_n \to 0$ sufficiently slowly, the probability of a training set T such that

$$\|f_{T,\lambda_n} - f_{P,\lambda_n}\| < m(\lambda_n)/K \tag{17}$$

converges to 1 as $n \to \infty$. It is important to note that we can draw this conclusion because $m(\lambda) > 0$ for $\lambda > 0$ (See proof of Theorem 3.5 in [8]). We now relate the 2-norm of an f to its ∞-norm.

$$\begin{aligned} f(x) &= \langle k(x,\cdot), f(\cdot)\rangle \leq \|k(x,\cdot)\| \, \|f\| \\ &= \sqrt{\langle k(x,\cdot), k(x,\cdot)\rangle}\|f\| \\ &= k(x,x)\|f\| \leq K\|f\| \end{aligned} \tag{18}$$

Thus, (17) gives us

$$\|f_{T,\lambda_n} - f_{P,\lambda_n}\|_\infty < m(\lambda_n) \ . \tag{19}$$

Step 2. In the second step, we relate the fraction of support vectors to an empirical average. Suppose that, in addition to (19), our training set T satisfies

$$\lambda_n \|f_{T,\lambda_n}\|^2 + R_{\phi,P}(f_{T,\lambda_n}) \leq R_{\phi,P} + \epsilon \tag{20}$$

$$\left|\{i : x_i \in A_{\delta(\lambda_n)}\}\right| \leq 2\epsilon n \ . \tag{21}$$

The probability of such a T also converges to 1. For (20), see the proof of Theorem III.6 in [9]. Since $P_x(A_{\delta(\lambda_n)}) \leq \epsilon$, (21) follows from Hoeffding's inequality. By definition of $R_{\phi,P}$, we have $R_{\phi,P} \leq R_{\phi,P}(f_{T,\lambda_n})$. Thus, (20) gives us $\lambda_n \|f_{T,\lambda_n}\|^2 \leq \epsilon$. Now we use (15) to get

$$\left|\sum_{i=1}^n \alpha_i^* t_0 - \sum_{i=1}^n \alpha_i^* \xi_i^*\right| \leq 2\epsilon \ . \tag{22}$$

Define three disjoint sets: $A = \{i : \xi_i^* < 0\}$, $B = \{i : \xi_i^* = 0\}$ and $C = \{i : \xi_i^* > 0\}$. We now show that B contains few elements. If x_i is such that $i \in B$ then $\xi_i^* = 0$ and we have $y_i f_{T,\lambda_n}(x_i) = t_0 \Rightarrow f_{T,\lambda_n}(x_i) = \pm t_0$. On the other hand, if $x_i \notin A_{\delta(\lambda_n)}$ then $\min\{|f_{P,\lambda_n}(x_i) - t_0|, |f_{P,\lambda_n}(x_i) + t_0|\} > \delta(\lambda_n) \geq m(\lambda_n)$, and hence, by (19), $f_{T,\lambda_n}(x_i) \neq \pm t_0$. Thus we can have at most $2\epsilon n$ elements in the set B by (21). Equation (14) gives us a bound on α_i^* for $i \in B$ and therefore

$$\left|\sum_{i \in B} \alpha_i^* t_0\right| \leq 2\epsilon n \times h'(0) t_0 / n = 2h'(0) t_0 \epsilon \ . \tag{23}$$

Using (14), we get $\alpha_i = 0$ for $i \in A$. By definition of B, $\xi_i^* = 0$ for $i \in B$. Therefore, (22) and (23) give us

$$\left|\sum_{i \in C} \alpha_i^* t_0 - \sum_{i \in C} \alpha_i^* \xi_i^*\right| \leq 2(1 + h'(0)t_0)\epsilon = c_1 \epsilon \ .$$

where $c_1 = 2(1 + h'(0)t_0)$ is just a constant. We use (14) once again to write α_i^* as $h'(\xi_i^*)/n$ for $i \in C$:

$$\left| \frac{1}{n} \sum_{i \in C} h'(\xi_i^*) t_0 - \frac{1}{n} \sum_{i \in C} h'(\xi_i^*) \xi_i^* \right| < c_1 \epsilon \ . \tag{24}$$

Denote the cardinality of the sets B and C by N_B and N_C respectively. Then we have $N_C \leq \#SV(f_{T,\lambda_n}) \leq N_C + N_B$. But we showed that $N_B \leq 2\epsilon n$ and therefore

$$\frac{N_C}{n} \leq \frac{\#SV(f_{T,\lambda_n})}{n} \leq \frac{N_C}{n} + 2\epsilon \ . \tag{25}$$

Observe that $(\xi_i^*)_+ = 0$ for $i \in A \cup B$ and $(\xi_i^*)_+ = \xi_i^*$ for $i \in C$. Thus, we can extend the sums in (24) to the whole training set.

$$\left| \frac{1}{n} \sum_{i=1}^{n} h'((\xi_i^*)_+) t_0 - (n - N_C) \frac{h'(0) t_0}{n} - \frac{1}{n} \sum_{i=1}^{n} h'((\xi_i^*)_+)(\xi_i^*)_+ \right| < c_1 \epsilon$$

Now let $c_2 = c_1 / h'(0) t_0$ and rearrange the above sum to get

$$\left| \frac{N_C}{n} - \frac{1}{n} \sum_{i=1}^{n} \left(1 - \frac{h'((\xi_i^*)_+) t_0 - h'((\xi_i^*)_+)(\xi_i^*)_+}{h'(0) t_0} \right) \right| \leq c_2 \epsilon \ . \tag{26}$$

Define $g(t)$ as

$$g(t) = 1 - \frac{h'((t_0 - t)_+) t_0 - h'((t_0 - t)_+)(t_0 - t)_+}{h'(0) t_0} \ .$$

Now (26) can be written as

$$\left| \frac{N_C}{n} - \mathbb{E}_T g(y f_{T,\lambda_n}(x)) \right| \leq c_2 \epsilon \ . \tag{27}$$

Step 3. We will now show that the empirical average of $g(y f_{T,\lambda_n}(x))$ is close to its expectation. We can bound the norm of f_{T,λ_n} as follows. The optimum value for the objective function in (1) is upper bounded by the value it attains at $f = 0$. Therefore,

$$\lambda_n \|f_{T,\lambda_n}\|^2 + R_{\phi,T}(f_{T,\lambda_n}) \leq \lambda_n . 0^2 + R_{\phi,T}(0) = \phi(0) = h(t_0)$$

which, together with (18), implies that

$$\|f_{T,\lambda_n}\| \leq \sqrt{\frac{h(t_0)}{\lambda_n}} \tag{28}$$

$$\|f_{T,\lambda_n}\|_\infty \leq K \sqrt{\frac{h(t_0)}{\lambda_n}} \ . \tag{29}$$

Let $\mathcal{F}_{\lambda_n}$ be the class of functions with norm bounded by $\sqrt{h(t_0)/\lambda_n}$. The covering number in 2-norm of the class satisfies (see, for example, Definition 1 and Corollary 3 in [11]):

$$\mathcal{N}_2(\mathcal{F}_{\lambda_n}, \epsilon, n) \le e^{\frac{Kh(t_0)}{\lambda_n \epsilon^2} \log(2n+1)} . \tag{30}$$

Define $L_g(\lambda_n)$ as

$$L_g(\lambda_n) = \sup \left\{ \frac{|g(t) - g(t')|}{|t - t'|} : t, t' \in \left[-K\sqrt{\frac{h(t_0)}{\lambda_n}}, +K\sqrt{\frac{h(t_0)}{\lambda_n}} \right], t \ne t' \right\} \tag{31}$$

Let $\mathcal{G}_{\lambda_n} = \{(x, y) \mapsto g(yf(x)) : f \in \mathcal{F}_{\lambda_n}\}$. We can express the covering numbers of this class in terms of those of $\mathcal{F}_{\lambda_n}$ (see, for example, Lemma 14.13 on p. 206 in [1]):

$$\mathcal{N}_2(\mathcal{G}_{\lambda_n}, \epsilon, n) \le \mathcal{N}_2(\mathcal{F}_{\lambda_n}, \epsilon/L_g(\lambda_n), n) . \tag{32}$$

Now, using a result of Pollard (see Section II.6 on p. 30 in [5]) and the fact that 1-norm covering numbers are bounded above by 2-norm covering numbers, we get

$$P^n \left(T \in (\mathcal{X} \times \mathcal{Y})^n : \sup_{\tilde{g} \in \mathcal{G}_{\lambda_n}} |\mathbb{E}_T \tilde{g}(x, y) - \mathbb{E}_P \tilde{g}(x, y)| > \epsilon \right)$$
$$\le 8\mathcal{N}_2(\mathcal{G}_{\lambda_n}, \epsilon/8, n) e^{-n\epsilon^2 \lambda_n / 512 L_g^2(\lambda_n) K^2 h(t_0)} . \tag{33}$$

The estimates (30) and (32) imply that if

$$\frac{n\lambda_n^2}{L_g^4(\lambda_n) \log(2n+1)} \to \infty \text{ as } n \to \infty$$

then the probability of a training set which satisfies

$$|\mathbb{E}_T g(yf_{T,\lambda_n}(x)) - \mathbb{E}_P g(yf_{T,\lambda_n}(x))| \le \epsilon \tag{34}$$

tends to 1 as $n \to \infty$.

Step 4. The last step in the proof is to show that $\mathbb{E}_P g(yf_{T,\lambda_n}(x))$ is close to $E_x G(\eta(x))$ for large enough n. Write $\mathbb{E}_P g(yf_{T,\lambda_n}(x))$ as

$$\mathbb{E}_P g(yf_{T,\lambda_n}(x)) = \mathbb{E}_x[\eta(x) g(f_{T,\lambda_n}(x)) + (1 - \eta(x)) g(-f_{T,\lambda_n}(x))] .$$

Note that if $t^* \in F_\phi^*(\eta)$ then

$$\eta g(t^*) + (1 - \eta) g(-t^*) = G(\eta) . \tag{35}$$

This is easily verified for $\eta \in [0, \gamma] \cup [1 - \gamma, 1]$ since $g(t) = 0$ for $t \ge t_0$ and $g(-t_0) = 1/\gamma$. For $\eta \in (\gamma, 1 - \gamma)$ we have

$$\eta g(t^*) + (1 - \eta) g(-t^*) = 1 - \frac{t^*}{t_0 h'(0)} (\eta h'(t_0 - t^*) - (1 - \eta) h'(t_0 + t^*)) .$$

Since t^* minimizes $\eta h(t_0 - t) + (1-\eta)h(t_0 + t)$ and h is differentiable, we have $\eta h'(t_0 - t^*) - (1-\eta)h'(t_0 + t^*) = 0$. Thus, we have verified (35) for all $\eta \in [0,1]$. Define the sets $E_n = \{x \in \mathcal{X} : \rho(f_{T,\lambda_n}(x), F_\phi^*(\eta(x)) \geq \epsilon\}$. We have $P_x(E_n) \to 0$ by (3). We now bound the difference between the two quantities of interest.

$$\begin{aligned} &|\,\mathbb{E}_P g(y f_{T,\lambda_n}(x)) - \mathbb{E}_x G(\eta(x))\,| \\ &= |\,\mathbb{E}_x[\eta(x)g(f_{T,\lambda_n}(x)) + (1-\eta(x))g(-f_{T,\lambda_n}(x))] - \mathbb{E}_x G(\eta(x))\,| \\ &\leq \mathbb{E}_x\,|\,\eta(x)g(f_{T,\lambda_n}(x)) + (1-\eta(x))g(-f_{T,\lambda_n}(x)) - G(\eta(x))\,| \\ &= I_1 + I_2 \leq |I_1| + |I_2| \end{aligned} \tag{36}$$

where the integrals I_1 and I_2 are

$$I_1 = \int_{E_n} \eta(x)g(f_{T,\lambda_n}(x)) + (1-\eta(x))g(-f_{T,\lambda_n}(x)) - G(\eta(x))\,dP_x \tag{37}$$

$$I_2 = \int_{\mathcal{X}\setminus E_n} \eta(x)g(f_{T,\lambda_n}(x)) + (1-\eta(x))g(-f_{T,\lambda_n}(x)) - G(\eta(x))\,dP_x\,. \tag{38}$$

Using (29) and (31) we bound $|g(\pm f_{T,\lambda_n}(x))|$ by $g(0) + L_g(\lambda_n)K\sqrt{h'(t_0)/\lambda_n}$. Since $g(0) = 1$ and $|G(\eta)| \leq 1$, we have

$$|I_1| \leq \left(1 + g(0) + L_g(\lambda_n)K\sqrt{\frac{h'(t_0)}{\lambda_n}}\right) P_x(E_n)\,.$$

If $\lambda_n \to 0$ slowly enough so that $L_g(\lambda_n)P_x(E_n)/\sqrt{\lambda_n} \to 0$, then for large n, $|I_1| \leq \epsilon$. To bound $|I_2|$, observe that for $x \in \mathcal{X}\setminus E_n$, we can find a $t^* \in F_\phi^*(\eta(x))$, such that $|f_{T,\lambda_n}(x) - t^*| \leq \epsilon$. Therefore

$$\begin{aligned} &\eta(x)g(f_{T,\lambda_n}(x)) + (1-\eta(x))g(-f_{T,\lambda_n}(x)) \\ &\qquad = \eta(x)g(t^*) + (1-\eta(x)g(-t^*) + \Delta\,. \end{aligned} \tag{39}$$

where $|\Delta| \leq c_3\epsilon$ and the constant c_3 does not depend on λ_n. Using (35), we can now bound $|I_2|$:

$$|I_2| \leq c_3\epsilon(1 - P_x(E_n)) \leq c_3\epsilon\,.$$

We now use (36) to get

$$|\,\mathbb{E}_P g(y f_{T,\lambda_n}(x)) - \mathbb{E}_x G(\eta(x))\,| \leq (c_3 + 1)\epsilon\,. \tag{40}$$

Finally, combining (25), (27), (34) and (40) proves the theorem. □

5 Conclusion

We saw that the decision functions obtained using minimization of regularized empirical ϕ-risk approach $F_\phi^*(\eta(\cdot))$. It is not possible to preserve sparseness on intervals where $F_\phi^*(\cdot)$ is invertible. For the regions outside that interval, sparseness is maintained to some extent. For many convex loss functions, the general lower bounds known previously turned out to be quite loose.

But that leaves open the possibility that the previously known lower bounds are actually achievable by some loss function lying outside the class of loss functions we considered. However, we conjecture that it is not possible. Note that the bound of Theorem 8 only depends on the left derivative of the loss function at t_0 and the right derivative at $-t_0$. The derivatives at other points do not affect the asymptotic number of support vectors. This suggests that the assumption of the differentiability of ϕ before the point where it attains its minimum can be relaxed. It may be that results on the continuity of solution sets of convex optimization problems can be applied here (see, for example, [3]).

Acknowledgements. Thanks to Grace Wahba and Laurent El Ghaoui for helpful discussions.

References

1. Anthony, M. and Bartlett, P. L.: *Neural network learning: Theoretical foundations.* Cambridge University Press, Cambridge (1999)
2. Bartlett, P. L., Jordan, M.I. and McAuliffe, J.D.: Large Margin Classifiers: convex loss, low noise and convergence rates. In *Advances in Neural Information Processing Systems* **16**. MIT Press, Cambridge, MA (2004)
3. Fiacco, A. V.: *Introduction to sensitivity and stability ananlysis in nonlinear programming.* Academic Press, New York (1983)
4. Lugosi, G. and Vayatis, N.: On the Bayes-risk consistency of regularized boosting methods. *Annals of Statistics* **32**:1 (2004) 30–55
5. Pollard, D.: *Convergence of stochastic processes.* Springer-Verlag, New York (1984)
6. Rockafellar, R. T.: *Convex analysis.* Princeton University Press, Princeton (1970)
7. Steinwart, I.: Sparseness of support vector machines. *Journal of Machine Learning Research* **4** (2003) 1071–1105
8. Steinwart, I.: Sparseness of support vector machines – some asymptotically sharp bounds. In *Advances in Neural Information Processing Systems* **16**. MIT Press, Cambridge, MA (2004)
9. Steinwart, I.: Consistency of support vector machines and other regularized kernel classifiers. *IEEE Transactions on Information Theory*, to appear
10. Wahba, G.: Soft and hard classification by reproducing kernel Hilbert space methods. *Proceedings of the National Academy of Sciences USA* **99**:26 (2002) 16524–16530
11. Zhang, T.: Covering number bounds of certain regularized linear function classes. *Journal of Machine Learning Research* **2** (2002) 527–550
12. Zhang, T.: Statistical behavior and consistency of classification methods based on convex risk minimization. *Annals of Statistics* **32**:1 (2004) 56–85

A Statistical Mechanics Analysis of Gram Matrix Eigenvalue Spectra

David C. Hoyle[1] and Magnus Rattray[2]

[1] Dept. Computer Science, University of Exeter, Harrison Building, North Park Road, Exeter, EX4 4QF, UK.
D.C.Hoyle@exeter.ac.uk
http://www.dcs.ex.ac.uk/$\sim$dch201

[2] Dept. Computer Science, University of Manchester, Kilburn Building, Oxford Rd., Manchester, M13 9PL,UK.
magnus@cs.man.ac.uk
http://www.cs.man.ac.uk/$\sim$magnus

Abstract. The Gram matrix plays a central role in many kernel methods. Knowledge about the distribution of eigenvalues of the Gram matrix is useful for developing appropriate model selection methods for kernel PCA. We use methods adapted from the statistical physics of classical fluids in order to study the averaged spectrum of the Gram matrix. We focus in particular on a variational mean-field theory and related diagrammatic approach. We show that the mean-field theory correctly reproduces previously obtained asymptotic results for standard PCA. Comparison with simulations for data distributed uniformly on the sphere shows that the method provides a good qualitative approximation to the averaged spectrum for kernel PCA with a Gaussian Radial Basis Function kernel. We also develop an analytical approximation to the spectral density that agrees closely with the numerical solution and provides insight into the number of samples required to resolve the corresponding process eigenvalues of a given order.

1 Introduction

The application of the techniques of statistical physics to the study of learning problems has been an active and productive area of research [1]. In this contribution we use the methods of statistical physics to study the eigenvalue spectrum of the Gram matrix, which plays an important role in kernel methods such as Support Vector Machines, Gaussian Processes and kernel Principal Component Analysis (kernel PCA) [2]. We focus mainly on kernel PCA, in which data is projected into a high-dimensional (possibly infinite-dimensional) feature space and PCA is carried out in the feature space. The eigensystem of the sample covariance of feature vectors can be obtained by a trivial linear transformation of the Gram matrix eigensystem. Kernel PCA has been shown to be closely related to a number of clustering and manifold learning algorithms, including spectral clustering, Laplacian eigenmaps and multi-dimensional scaling (see e.g. [3]).

J. Shawe-Taylor and Y. Singer (Eds.): COLT 2004, LNAI 3120, pp. 579–593, 2004.

The eigenvalue spectrum of the Gram matrix is of particular importance in kernel PCA. In order to find a low-dimensional representation of the data, only the eigenvectors corresponding to the largest few eigenvalues are used. Model selection methods are required in order to determine how many eigenvectors to retain. For standard PCA it is instructive to study the eigenvalues of the sample covariance for idealised distributions, such as the Gaussian Orthogonal Ensemble (GOE), in order to construct appropriate model selection criteria [4]. For kernel PCA it would also be instructive to understand how the eigenvalues of the Gram matrix behave for idealised distributions, but this is expected to be significantly more difficult than for standard PCA. In this paper we present some preliminary results from an analysis of Gram matrix eigenvalue spectra using methods from statistical mechanics.

In a recent paper we studied the case of PCA with non-isotropic data and kernel PCA with a polynomial kernel function [5]. In the case of a polynomial kernel, kernel PCA is equivalent to PCA in a finite-dimensional feature space and the analysis can be carried out explicitly in the feature space. We presented numerical evidence that an asymptotic theory for standard PCA can be adapted to kernel PCA in that case. In contrast, here we consider the more general case in which the feature space may be infinite dimensional, as it is for the popular Gaussian Radial Basis Function (RBF) kernel. In this case it is more useful to carry out the analysis of the Gram matrix directly. We review some different approaches that have been developed in the physics literature for the analysis of the spectra of matrices formed from the positions of particles randomly distributed in a Euclidean space (Euclidean Random Matrices), which are related to the instantaneous normal modes of a classical fluid. We focus in particular on a variational mean-field approach and a closely related diagrammatic expansion approach. The theory is shown to reproduce the correct asymptotic result for the special case of standard PCA. For kernel PCA the theory provides a set of self-consistent equations and we solve these equations numerically for the case of data uniformly distributed on the sphere, which can be considered a simple null distribution. We also provide an analytical approximation that is shown to agree closely with the numerical results. Our results provide insight into how many samples are required to accurately estimate the eigenvalues of the associated continuous eigenproblem. We provide simulation evidence showing that the theory provides a good qualitative approximation to the average spectrum for a range of parameter values.

The Gram matrix eigenvalue spectrum has previously been studied by Shawe-Taylor *et. al.* who have derived rigorous bounds on the difference between the eigenvalues of the Gram matrix and those of the related continuous eigenproblem [6]. The statistical mechanics approach is less rigorous, but provides insight into regimes where the rigorous bounds are not tight. For example, in the study of PCA one can take the asymptotic limit of large sample size for fixed data dimension, and in this regime the bounds developed by Shawe-Taylor *et. al.* can be expected to become asymptotically tight [7]. However, other asymptotic results for PCA have been developed in which the ratio of the sample size to data dimension is held fixed while the sample size is increased (eg. [8,9]). Our results reduce to the exact asymptotics of standard PCA in this latter regime, and we therefore expect that our methods will provide an alternative but complementary approach to the problem.

The paper is organised as follows. In the next section we introduce some results from random matrix theory for the eigenvalues of a sample covariance matrix. These results are relevant to the analysis of PCA. We introduce kernel PCA and define the class of centred kernels used there. In section 3 we discuss different theoretical methods for determining the average Gram matrix spectrum and derive general results from the variational mean-field method and a related diagrammatic approach. We then derive an analytical approximation to the spectrum that is shown to agree closely with numerical solution of the mean-field theory. In section 4 we compare the theoretical results with simulations and in section 5 we conclude with a brief summary and discussion.

2 Background

2.1 Limiting Eigenvalue Spectrum for PCA

Consider a data set of p-dimensional data vectors $\boldsymbol{x}_i, i = 1, \ldots, N$, with mean $\bar{\boldsymbol{x}}$. A number of results for the asymptotic form of the sample covariance matrix, $\hat{\boldsymbol{C}} = p^{-1}\sum_i(\boldsymbol{x}_i - \bar{\boldsymbol{x}})(\boldsymbol{x}_i - \bar{\boldsymbol{x}})^T$, have been derived in the limit of large p with the ratio $\alpha = N/p$ held fixed[1]. We will see later that these results are closely related to our approximate expressions for kernel PCA.

We denote the eigenvalues of the sample covariance matrix $\hat{\boldsymbol{C}}$ as $\hat{\lambda}_i$, $i = 1, \ldots, p$. The eigenvalue density $\rho(\hat{\lambda})$ can be written in terms of the trace of the sample covariance resolvent,

$$R_{\hat{\boldsymbol{C}}}(z) = N^{-1}\mathrm{Tr}(z\boldsymbol{I} - \hat{\boldsymbol{C}})^{-1} = \frac{1}{N}\sum_{i=1}^{p}\frac{1}{z - \hat{\lambda}_i} . \quad (1)$$

The eigenvalue density is obtained from the identity

$$\alpha^{-1}\rho(\hat{\lambda}) = \lim_{\epsilon\to 0^+}\frac{1}{\pi}\mathrm{Im}\, R_{\hat{\boldsymbol{C}}}(\hat{\lambda} - i\epsilon) . \quad (2)$$

This is the starting point for a number of studies in the physics and statistics literature (e.g. [8,10]) and the function $-R_{\hat{\boldsymbol{C}}}(z)$ is also known as the Stieltjes transform of the eigenvalue distribution. As $N, p \to \infty$ the density $\rho(\hat{\lambda})$ is self-averaging and approaches a well defined limit. It has been shown, with relatively weak conditions on the data distribution, that as $N \to \infty$ with α fixed [8,9]

$$z = \frac{1}{R_{\hat{\boldsymbol{C}}}(z)} + \frac{1}{N}\sum_i \frac{1}{\lambda_i^{-1} - R_{\hat{\boldsymbol{C}}}(z)} , \quad (3)$$

[1] The notation differs from our previous work [5,12] since N is more often used for the number of data points in the machine learning literature.

where λ_i are the eigenvalues of the population covariance, or equivalently they are the eigenvalues of the sample covariance in the limit of infinite data, i.e. $\hat{\lambda}_i \to \lambda_i$ as $\alpha \to \infty$. For non-Gaussian data vectors with *i.i.d.* components this result has been shown to hold so long as the second moments of the covariance exist [9], while other results have been derived with different conditions on the data (e.g. [8]). An equivalent result has also been derived using the replica trick from statistical physics [10], although this was limited to Gaussian data.

The solution of the Stieltjes transform relationship in eq.(3) provides insight into the behaviour of PCA. Given the eigenvalues of the population covariance, eq.(3) can be solved in order to determine the observed distribution of eigenvalues for the sample covariance. For finite values of α, the observed eigenvalues are dispersed about the true population eigenvalues and significantly biased. One can observe phase-transition like behaviour, where the distribution splits into distinct regions with finite support as the parameter α is increased, corresponding to signal and noise [5,11]. One can therefore determine how much data is required in order to successfully identify structure in the data. We have shown that the asymptotic result can be accurate even when $N \ll p$, which may often be the case in very high-dimensional data sets [12]. It is also possible to study the overlap between the eigenvectors of the sample and population covariance within the statistical mechanics framework (see [13] and other references in [1]) but here we will limit our attention to the eigenvalue spectrum.

2.2 Kernel PCA

By construction, PCA only finds features that are linear combinations of the data vector components. Often one constructs higher dimensional non-linear features $\boldsymbol{\chi}(\boldsymbol{x})$ from an input vector $\boldsymbol{x}$ in order to gain improved performance. In this case PCA can then be performed on the new high-dimensional feature vectors $\boldsymbol{\chi}$. Given a data set $\boldsymbol{x}_i, i = 1, \ldots, N$, the feature space covariance matrix is $\boldsymbol{C}_{\boldsymbol{\chi}} = N^{-1} \sum_i \boldsymbol{\chi}(\boldsymbol{x}_i) \boldsymbol{\chi}^T(\boldsymbol{x}_i)$. We have initially taken the sample mean vector in feature space, $\bar{\boldsymbol{\chi}}$, to be zero. Decomposition of $\boldsymbol{C}_{\boldsymbol{\chi}}$ can be done entirely in terms of the decomposition of the Gram matrix $\boldsymbol{K}$, with elements $K_{ij} = \boldsymbol{\chi}(\boldsymbol{x}_i) \cdot \boldsymbol{\chi}(\boldsymbol{x}_j)$. The "kernel trick" tells us that a suitably chosen kernel function $k(\boldsymbol{x}, \boldsymbol{y})$ represents the inner product, $\boldsymbol{\chi}(\boldsymbol{x}) \cdot \boldsymbol{\chi}(\boldsymbol{y})$, in a particular (possibly unknown) feature space. Thus PCA in the feature space can be performed by specifying only a kernel function $k(\boldsymbol{x}, \boldsymbol{y})$, without ever having to determine the corresponding mapping into feature space. This is kernel PCA [2].

For the kernel to represent an inner product in some feature space it must be symmetric, i.e. $k(\boldsymbol{x}, \boldsymbol{y}) = k(\boldsymbol{y}, \boldsymbol{x})$. Popular choices of kernel for fixed length vectors mostly fall into one of two categories: Dot-product kernels $k(\boldsymbol{x}, \boldsymbol{y}) = k(\boldsymbol{x} \cdot \boldsymbol{y})$ and translationally invariant kernels $k(\boldsymbol{x}, \boldsymbol{y}) = k(||\boldsymbol{x} - \boldsymbol{y}||)$. A common and important choice for $k(t)$ in this latter case is the Gaussian Radial Basis Function (RBF) kernel $k(t) = \exp(-t^2/2b^2)$. It should be noted that for data constrained to the surface of a sphere, a kernel of the form $k(\boldsymbol{x}, \boldsymbol{y}) = k(||\boldsymbol{x} - \boldsymbol{y}||^2)$ is equivalent to a dot-product kernel. Standard PCA corresponds to a linear dot-product kernel $k(\boldsymbol{x}, \boldsymbol{y}) = \boldsymbol{x} \cdot \boldsymbol{y}$.

In reality, the kernels above will not result in $\bar{\chi} = 0$ for most data sets. In this case the sample covariance in feature space corresponds to $N^{-1}\sum_i(\chi(\boldsymbol{x}_i) - \bar{\chi})(\chi(\boldsymbol{x}_i) - \bar{\chi})^T$. The Gram matrix can be centred to produce a new matrix $\boldsymbol{F}$ with elements

$$F_{ij} = K_{ij} - \frac{1}{N}\sum_j K_{ij} - \frac{1}{N}\sum_i K_{ij} + \frac{1}{N^2}\sum_{ij} K_{ij} \,. \tag{4}$$

This is equivalent to transforming the feature vectors to have zero mean, but again $\boldsymbol{F}$ can be calculated with knowledge only of the kernel function $k(\boldsymbol{x}, \boldsymbol{y})$. It should be noted that $\sum_i F_{ij} = \sum_j F_{ij} = 0$, and so $\boldsymbol{F}$ always has a zero eigenvalue with corresponding eigenvector $(1, 1, \ldots, 1)$. If the pattern vectors $\boldsymbol{x}_i$ are drawn from some distribution $\rho_{\boldsymbol{x}}(\boldsymbol{x})$ then as $N \to \infty$ the matrix elements F_{ij} can be considered a random sample produced by a kernel function,

$$f(\boldsymbol{x},\boldsymbol{y}) = k(\boldsymbol{x},\boldsymbol{y}) - \int d\mu(\boldsymbol{y})\, k(\boldsymbol{x},\boldsymbol{y}) - \int d\mu(\boldsymbol{x})\, k(\boldsymbol{x},\boldsymbol{y}) + \int d\mu(\boldsymbol{x}) \int d\mu(\boldsymbol{y})\, k(\boldsymbol{x},\boldsymbol{y}) \,, \tag{5}$$

by sampling N pattern vectors $\boldsymbol{x}_i$ drawn from $\rho_{\boldsymbol{x}}(\boldsymbol{x})$ (where the measure $d\mu(\boldsymbol{x})$ denotes $d\boldsymbol{x}\rho_{\boldsymbol{x}}(\boldsymbol{x})$). Clearly $\int d\mu(\boldsymbol{x}) f(\boldsymbol{x},\boldsymbol{y}) = \int d\mu(\boldsymbol{y}) f(\boldsymbol{x},\boldsymbol{y}) = 0$.

3 Statistical Mechanics Theory

We now use $R_{\boldsymbol{F}}(z)$ to represent the ensemble averaged trace of the centred Gram matrix resolvent, i.e.,

$$R_{\boldsymbol{F}}(z) = N^{-1}\overline{\mathrm{Tr}(z\boldsymbol{I} - \boldsymbol{F})^{-1}} = N^{-1}\overline{\frac{\partial}{\partial z}\log\det(z\boldsymbol{I} - \boldsymbol{F})} \,, \tag{6}$$

where the bar denotes an ensemble average over data sets. The *expected* eigenvalue density can then be obtained from $R_{\boldsymbol{F}}(z)$ as in eq.(2). The replica trick of using the representation $\log x = \lim_{n\to 0} n^{-1}(x^n - 1)$ is used to facilitate the evaluation of the expectation of the log of the determinant in (6). Following Mézard *et. al.* [14] we define $\Xi_N = \overline{\det(z\boldsymbol{I} - \boldsymbol{F})^{-n/2}}$ and then take the replica limit $n \to 0$. Using a Gaussian integral representation of the square root of the determinant one finds,

$$\Xi_N = \int \prod_{i=1}^{N} d\mu(\boldsymbol{x}_i) \int \prod_{i=1}^{N}\prod_{a=1}^{n} d\phi_i^a \exp\left(-\frac{z}{2}\sum_{i,a}(\phi_i^a)^2 + \frac{1}{2}\sum_{i,j,a} f(\boldsymbol{x}_i,\boldsymbol{x}_j)\phi_i^a\phi_j^a \right) , \tag{7}$$

where $f(\boldsymbol{x},\boldsymbol{y})$ is the kernel function. We introduce the field $\psi_a(\boldsymbol{x}) = \sum_{i=1}^N \phi_i^a \delta(\boldsymbol{x} - \boldsymbol{x}_i)$ and its conjugate $\widehat{\psi}_a(\boldsymbol{x})$ which serves as a Lagrange multiplier. Moving to the grand canonical partition function $\mathcal{Z}(\omega) = \sum_N^\infty \Xi_N \omega^N/N!$, we find (after some straightforward algebra and Gaussian integrations),

$$\mathcal{Z}(\omega) = \int \prod_a \mathcal{D}\widehat{\psi}_a \exp\left(\omega A - \frac{n}{2}\mathrm{Tr}\log f + \frac{1}{2}\sum_a \int d\boldsymbol{x}d\boldsymbol{y}\, \widehat{\psi}_a(\boldsymbol{x}) f^{-1}(\boldsymbol{x},\boldsymbol{y}) \widehat{\psi}_a(\boldsymbol{y}) \right)$$

$$= \int \prod_a \mathcal{D}\widehat{\psi}_a \exp\left(S[\widehat{\psi}]\right) , \tag{8}$$

where f is considered an operator and we have introduced,

$$A = \left(\frac{2\pi}{z}\right)^{\frac{n}{2}} \int d\mu(\boldsymbol{x}) \exp\left(-\frac{1}{2z}\sum_a \widehat{\psi}_a^2(\boldsymbol{x})\right) . \tag{9}$$

With $\omega\langle A\rangle = \omega\partial \log \mathcal{Z}(\omega)/\partial\omega = N$ and $\langle A\rangle \to 1$ as $n \to 0$ we take $\omega = N$ in the limit $n \to 0$. Having obtained a formal expression for the grand canonical partition function we have a number of avenues available to us,

- Asymptotically expanding $\mathcal{Z}(\omega)$ using ω as either a small or large parameter (low & high density expansions).
- Variational approximation, such as the Random Phase Approximation (RPA) used by Mézard *et. al.* [14], to provide a non-asymptotic approximation to the expected eigenvalue density.
- Formal diagrammatic expansion of $\mathcal{Z}(\omega)$ to elucidate the nature of the various other approximations.
- Density functional approaches, appropriate for approximating the behaviour of the expected spectra when the input density is inhomogeneous, i.e. not uniform over the sphere or some other analytically convenient distribution.

In this paper we shall focus on the second and third approaches. The results in [14] suggest that the variational approach will reduce to the low and high density expansions in the appropriate limits. We leave the fourth approach for future study.

3.1 Variational Approximation

We now make a variational approximation to the grand canonical free energy, $F = -\log \mathcal{Z}(\omega)$, by introducing the quadratic action,

$$S_{RPA} = -\frac{1}{2}\sum_{a,b}\int d\boldsymbol{x}\, d\boldsymbol{y}\, \widehat{\psi}_a(\boldsymbol{x}) G_{ab}^{-1}(\boldsymbol{x},\boldsymbol{y})\widehat{\psi}_b(\boldsymbol{y}) , \tag{10}$$

with corresponding partition function,

$$\mathcal{Z}_{RPA} = \int \prod_a \mathcal{D}\widehat{\psi}_a \exp\left(S_{RPA}[\widehat{\psi}]\right) . \tag{11}$$

The grand canonical free energy satisfies the Bogoliubov inequality,

$$F \le F_{var} \equiv \langle S - S_{RPA}\rangle - \log \mathcal{Z}_{RPA} , \tag{12}$$

where the brackets denote an integral with respect to $\widehat{\psi}$. We then proceed by minimising this upper bound.

Define eigenfunctions of the kernel f with respect to the measure $\mu(\boldsymbol{x})$,

$$\int d\mu(\boldsymbol{x})\, f(\boldsymbol{x},\boldsymbol{y}) q_m(\boldsymbol{x}) \;=\; \lambda_m q_m(\boldsymbol{y}) \,. \tag{13}$$

We can represent both f and its inverse f^{-1} over $\mathbb{R}^p$ in terms of the eigenfunctions $q_m(\boldsymbol{x})$,

$$f(\boldsymbol{x},\boldsymbol{y}) \;=\; \sum_m \lambda_m q_m^*(\boldsymbol{x}) q_m(\boldsymbol{y}) \,,\; f^{-1}(\boldsymbol{x},\boldsymbol{y}) \;=\; \sum_m \rho_{\boldsymbol{x}}(\boldsymbol{x}) q_m^*(\boldsymbol{x}) q_m(\boldsymbol{y}) \rho_{\boldsymbol{x}}(\boldsymbol{y})/\lambda_m \,. \tag{14}$$

Writing the variational free energy solely in terms of the propagator G (and dropping irrelevant constant terms) we obtain,

$$\begin{aligned} F_{var} = \frac{1}{2}\sum_a \int d\boldsymbol{x} \int d\boldsymbol{y}\, f^{-1}(\boldsymbol{x},\boldsymbol{y}) G_{aa}(\boldsymbol{y},\boldsymbol{x}) \;-\; \frac{1}{2}\mathrm{Tr}\log \boldsymbol{G} \\ -\,\omega\left(\frac{2\pi}{z}\right)^{\frac{n}{2}} \int d\mu(\boldsymbol{x}) \exp\left(-\tfrac{1}{2}\mathrm{Tr_n}\log\left(\boldsymbol{I} - z^{-1}\boldsymbol{G}(\boldsymbol{x},\boldsymbol{x})\right)\right) \,. \end{aligned} \tag{15}$$

Here Tr represents a trace over both $\mathbb{R}^p$ and replicas, whilst $\mathrm{Tr_n}$ represents a trace only over replicas. The variational free energy is minimized by setting,

$$\begin{aligned} 0 \;=\; \frac{\delta F_{var}}{\delta G_{ab}(\boldsymbol{x},\boldsymbol{y})} = \frac{1}{2}\,\delta_{ab} f^{-1}(\boldsymbol{y},\boldsymbol{x}) \;-\; \frac{1}{2}(\boldsymbol{G})^{-1}_{ba}(\boldsymbol{y},\boldsymbol{x}) \;- \\ \left[\omega\left(\frac{2\pi}{z}\right)^{\frac{n}{2}} \delta(\boldsymbol{x}-\boldsymbol{y})\rho_{\boldsymbol{x}}(\boldsymbol{x}) \exp\left(-\tfrac{1}{2}\mathrm{Tr_n}\log\left(\boldsymbol{I} - z^{-1}\boldsymbol{G}(\boldsymbol{x},\boldsymbol{x})\right)\right) \right. \\ \left. \times\, \frac{1}{2z}\left(\boldsymbol{I} - z^{-1}\boldsymbol{G}(\boldsymbol{x},\boldsymbol{x})\right)^{-1}_{ba}\right] \,. \end{aligned} \tag{16}$$

Looking for a solution of the form $G_{ab}(\boldsymbol{x},\boldsymbol{y}) = \delta_{ab}\widetilde{G}(\boldsymbol{x},\boldsymbol{y})$ and taking $n \to 0$ we find

$$f^{-1}(\boldsymbol{x},\boldsymbol{y}) \;-\; N\delta(\boldsymbol{x}-\boldsymbol{y})\rho_{\boldsymbol{x}}(\boldsymbol{x})\frac{1}{z - \widetilde{G}(\boldsymbol{x},\boldsymbol{x})} \;-\; \widetilde{G}^{-1}(\boldsymbol{x},\boldsymbol{y}) \;=\; 0 \,, \tag{17}$$

with the resolvent given as,

$$R_{\boldsymbol{F}}(z) \;=\; \int d\mu(\boldsymbol{x}) \frac{1}{z - \widetilde{G}(\boldsymbol{x},\boldsymbol{x})} \,. \tag{18}$$

If we write $\widetilde{G}^{-1}(\boldsymbol{x},\boldsymbol{y}) = f^{-1}(\boldsymbol{x},\boldsymbol{y}) - \delta(\boldsymbol{x}-\boldsymbol{y})\rho_{\boldsymbol{x}}(\boldsymbol{x})h(\boldsymbol{x})$ then we have,

$$R_{\boldsymbol{F}}(z) \;=\; N^{-1}\int d\boldsymbol{x}\, \rho_{\boldsymbol{x}}(\boldsymbol{x})\, h(\boldsymbol{x}) \quad \text{with} \quad h(\boldsymbol{x}) \;=\; \frac{N}{z - \widetilde{G}(\boldsymbol{x},\boldsymbol{x})} \,. \tag{19}$$

Closed form solution of these self-consistent equations is not possible in general and they would have to be solved numerically.

A useful approximation is obtained by replacing $\widetilde{G}(\boldsymbol{x},\boldsymbol{x})$ in $h(\boldsymbol{x})$ by its average $\overline{G} = \int d\boldsymbol{x}\, \rho_{\boldsymbol{x}}(\boldsymbol{x})\widetilde{G}(\boldsymbol{x},\boldsymbol{x})$, from which we find $\overline{G} = \sum_m \lambda_m[1 - NR_{\boldsymbol{F}}(z)\lambda_m]^{-1}$. Using this approximation and substituting into $h(\boldsymbol{x})$ we obtain the Stieltjes transform relationship in eq.(3) for $R_{\boldsymbol{C}_{\boldsymbol{\chi}}}$ - the trace of the resolvent of the feature space covariance matrix $\boldsymbol{C}_{\boldsymbol{\chi}}$. This result can also be obtained by expanding $G_{ab}(\boldsymbol{x},\boldsymbol{y})$ in terms of the eigenfunctions $q_m(\boldsymbol{x})$ and assuming replica symmetry, i.e. writing $G_{ab}(\boldsymbol{x},\boldsymbol{y}) = \sum_m \eta_m q_m(\boldsymbol{x})q_m(\boldsymbol{y})$. Minimizing the variational free energy with respect to the coefficients η_m and using Jensen's inequality one again obtains the relationship in eq.(3). This was the approach taken by Mézard *et. al.* [14]. They considered the case where the kernel is translationally invariant and the input density $\rho_{\boldsymbol{x}}(\boldsymbol{x})$ is uniform, and in this case the Stieltjes transform relationship (3) represents an exact solution to the variational problem. In the simulation results in section 4 we consider a dot-product kernel with data distributed uniformly on the sphere, and in this case eq.(3) again represents an exact solution to the variational problem. However, our derivation above shows that eq.(3) is actually also an approximate solution to a more general variational approach. We will see that this more general variational result can also be derived from the diagrammatic approach in the next section. In section 3.3 we show how to solve the relationship in eq.(3) for the specific case of data uniformly distributed on the sphere.

3.2 Diagrammatic Expansion

The partition function $\mathcal{Z}(\omega)$ in eq.(8) can be expanded in powers of ωA. The exponential form for each occurrence of A (see eq.(9)) can also be expanded to yield a set of Gaussian integrations. These can be represented in standard diagrammatic form and so we do not give the full details here but merely quote the final results. The free energy $\log \mathcal{Z}(\omega)$ only contains connected diagrams [15]. Thus we find,

$\log \mathcal{Z}(\omega) = \bullet + \ldots + \ldots + \ldots$

$+ \ldots + \ldots + \ldots + \ldots + \ldots + \ldots$

A node $\bullet$ represents integration with weight $\omega(\frac{2\pi}{z})^n \rho_{\boldsymbol{x}}(\boldsymbol{x})$. The connecting lines correspond to a propagator $z^{-1}f(\boldsymbol{x},\boldsymbol{y})$ and all diagrams have an additional weight n.

From this expansion of $\log \mathcal{Z}(\omega)$ a diagrammatic representation of the resolvent $R_{\boldsymbol{F}}(z)$ can easily be obtained on making the replacement $\omega = N$. Diagrams with articulation points can be removed by re-writing $R_{\boldsymbol{F}}(z) = N^{-1}\int d\mu(\boldsymbol{x})h(\boldsymbol{x})$ and $h(\boldsymbol{x}) = N/[z - \widetilde{G}(\boldsymbol{x},\boldsymbol{x})]$, where $\widetilde{G}(\boldsymbol{x},\boldsymbol{x})$ is given by

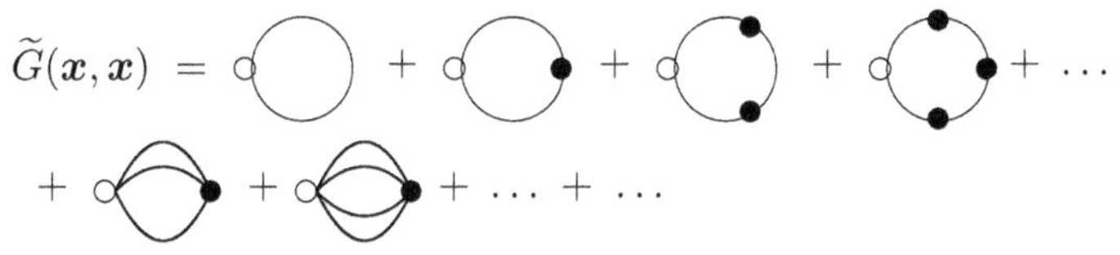

$$\widetilde{G}(\boldsymbol{x},\boldsymbol{x}) \; = \; \dots + \dots + \dots + \dots + \dots$$
$$+ \dots + \dots + \dots + \dots$$

where in all diagrams for $\widetilde{G}(\boldsymbol{x},\boldsymbol{x})$ a connecting line now represents a propagator $f(\boldsymbol{x},\boldsymbol{y})$ and a node $\bullet$ represents an integration with weight $\rho_{\boldsymbol{x}}(\boldsymbol{x})h(\boldsymbol{x})$. If we re-sum only those diagrams in $\widetilde{G}(\boldsymbol{x},\boldsymbol{x})$ consisting of simple loops we recover the RPA and the relationships given by eqs. (17) and (19).

3.3 Solution of the Stieltjes Transform Relationship

From the variational approximation described in section 3.1 we obtained the Stieltjes transform relationship given by eq.(3). Solving the relationship requires knowledge of the eigenvalues of the centred kernel. In this section we develop an approximate analytical solution to eq.(3) and illustrate it for the special case of data uniformly distributed on the sphere, which is a useful null distribution for kernel PCA.

For illustrative purposes we will restrict ourselves to dot-product kernels, in which case we have a centred kernel,

$$f(\boldsymbol{x}\cdot\boldsymbol{y}) \; = k(\boldsymbol{x}\cdot\boldsymbol{y}) \; - \; C \, , \tag{20}$$

where $C = \int_{-1}^{1} dt(1-t^2)^{(p-3)/2}k(t)$. The Hecke-Funk theorem tells us that the eigenfunctions $q_n(\boldsymbol{x})$ of $k(t)$ are Spherical Harmonics [16]. The nth (non-zero) eigenvalue has degeneracy $N(p,n)$ and is found to be,

$$\lambda_n \; = \; \frac{1}{\sqrt{\pi}}\left(\frac{1}{2}\right)^n \frac{\Gamma(p/2)}{\Gamma((2n+p-1)/2)} \int_{-1}^{1} dt\,(1-t^2)^{(2n+p-3)/2}\left(\frac{d}{dt}\right)^n k(t)\, , \tag{21}$$

$$N(p,n) \; = \; \frac{2n+p-2}{n}\binom{n+p-3}{n-1} \, . \tag{22}$$

For the Gaussian RBF kernel we have,

$$k(\boldsymbol{x},\boldsymbol{y}) \; = \; \exp\left(-\frac{1}{2b^2}||\boldsymbol{x}-\boldsymbol{y}||^2\right) \; = \; \exp\left(-\frac{1}{b^2}\right)\exp\left(\frac{\boldsymbol{x}\cdot\boldsymbol{y}}{b^2}\right) \, , \tag{23}$$

for $\boldsymbol{x},\boldsymbol{y}$ on the unit sphere. The centred kernel is easily found to be, $f(\boldsymbol{x},\boldsymbol{y}) = k(\boldsymbol{x},\boldsymbol{y}) - C$, $C = \exp(-b^{-2})\Gamma(\frac{p}{2})(2b^2)^{\frac{p}{2}-1}I_{\frac{p}{2}-1}(b^{-2})$, where $I_\nu(x)$ is the modified Bessel function of the first kind, of order ν [17]. The nth eigenvalue is given by,

$$\lambda_n \; = \; \Gamma\left(\frac{p}{2}\right)\exp\left(-\frac{1}{b^2}\right)\left(2b^2\right)^{\frac{1}{2}(p-2)} I_{n+\frac{p}{2}-1}\left(\frac{1}{b^2}\right) \, . \tag{24}$$

For $p=2$ we have two-fold degenerate eigenvalues $\lambda_n = \exp(-b^{-2})I_n(b^{-2})$, in agreement with Twining and Taylor [18].

The density of observed eigenvalues is given by eq.(2) and is obtained from the imaginary part of the function $R_{\mathbf{C_x}}(z)$ which solves eq.(3),

$$z = \frac{1}{R_{\mathbf{C_x}}} + \frac{1}{N}\sum_{n=1} \frac{N(p,n)\lambda_n}{1-\lambda_n R_{\mathbf{C_x}}} \, , \quad z = \mathrm{Re}\, z - i\epsilon \, , \tag{25}$$

in the limit $\epsilon \to 0^+$. Here λ_n and $N(p,n)$ would be given by (24) and (22) for the RBF kernel. We can solve this equation numerically and results of the numerical solution for some specific examples are given in section 4. However, it is also instructive to obtain an analytical approximation for limiting cases as this provides us with greater insight. The approximate expression derived here appears to provide a good approximation to the numerical results in many cases. The expansion is perturbative in nature, and we recover the exact results for standard PCA in the limit of large N with $\alpha = N/p$ held fixed [8]. However, our simulations also show that the approximation works well for small values of p.

In general as N increases (for fixed p) we would expect to recover the process eigenvalues λ_n from the eigenvalues of the Gram matrix. We will see below that larger values of N are required in order to resolve the smaller eigenvalues. As $N \to \infty$ we expect $R_{\mathbf{C_x}}(z)$ to be become localized around each λ_k^{-1}. If we put $R_{\mathbf{C_x}} = \lambda_k^{-1}(1+\delta_k)$ and expand, we have

$$z = \lambda_k(1-\delta_k) - \frac{\lambda_k N(p,k)}{N\delta_k} + \Sigma_1 + \delta_k\lambda_k^{-1}\Sigma_2 + \mathcal{O}(\delta_k^2) \, , \tag{26}$$

where Σ_1 and Σ_2 are given by,

$$\Sigma_1 = \frac{1}{N}\sum_{n\neq k}\frac{N(p,n)}{\Delta_{nk}} \, , \quad \Sigma_2 = \frac{1}{N}\sum_{n\neq k}\frac{N(p,n)}{\Delta_{nk}^2} \, , \tag{27}$$

and $\Delta_{nk} = \lambda_n^{-1} - \lambda_k^{-1}$. Dropping the higher order terms and solving for δ_k gives,

$$\delta_k = \frac{-(\lambda_k + \Sigma_1 - z) \pm \sqrt{(\lambda_k+\Sigma_1-z)^2 + 4N(p,k)\lambda_k(\lambda_k^{-1}\Sigma_2 - \lambda_k)/N}}{2(\lambda_k^{-1}\Sigma_2 - \lambda_k)} \, . \tag{28}$$

From (28) we can see that provided $\lambda_k^2 > \Sigma_2$, δ_k will give a contribution to the Gram matrix eigenvalue density of,

$$\frac{1}{2\pi}\frac{\sqrt{(\hat{\lambda}-\lambda_{min,k})(\lambda_{max,k}-\hat{\lambda})}}{\lambda_k - \lambda_k^{-1}\Sigma_2} \times \Theta(\hat{\lambda};\lambda_{min,k};\lambda_{max,k}) \, , \tag{29}$$

where,

$$\begin{aligned}\lambda_{\{max,min\},k} &= \lambda_k + \Sigma_1 \pm \sqrt{4N(p,k)\lambda_k^2(1-\lambda_k^{-2}\Sigma_2)/N} \\ &= \lambda_k \pm 2\lambda_k\left(\frac{N(p,k)}{N}\right)^{\frac{1}{2}} + \mathcal{O}(N^{-1}) \, ,\end{aligned} \tag{30}$$

and we have defined $\Theta(\lambda; \lambda_{min}; \lambda_{max}) = \Theta(\lambda_{max} - \lambda)\Theta(\lambda - \lambda_{min})$ with $\Theta(x)$ being the usual Heaviside step function. If we take $\lambda_{max,1}$ as our estimate of the expectation of the largest observed eigenvalue then we can see that the fractional bias is $2\sqrt{N(p,1)/N} + \mathcal{O}(N^{-1})$. Thus for dot-product kernel with an input distribution that is uniform on the sphere the RPA estimates the fractional bias in the largest eigenvalue to be $2\sqrt{p/N} + \mathcal{O}(N^{-1})$ and so is the same for *all* dot-product kernels.

The inequality $\lambda_k^2 > \Sigma_2$ can always be satisfied for sufficiently large N, and therefore the kth population eigenvalue can be resolved provided N is large enough. It is easily verified that for the standard PCA case by taking population eigenvalues $\lambda_1 = \sigma^2(1+A), \lambda_n = \sigma^2$, $n = 2, \ldots, p$, the known condition $\alpha = N/p > A^{-2}$ is recovered [13]. Unsurprisingly, the dispersion of $\rho(\hat{\lambda})$ about λ_k decreases as $N \to \infty$.

The validity of the expansion in (26) depends upon the neglected terms in the expansion being considerably smaller in magnitude than those retained. Thus we require,

$$|\delta_k| \ll 1 \ , \ |\delta_k| \ll \lambda_k |\Delta_{nk}| \, \forall n \neq k \ . \tag{31}$$

It is the second of these relations which is important and utilising the solution (28) for δ_k we find,

$$N|\delta_k|^2 = \frac{N(p,k)}{1 - \lambda_k^{-2}\Sigma_2} \ . \tag{32}$$

For large p we have,

$$N(p,n) = \frac{p^n}{n!}\left(1 + \mathcal{O}(p^{-1})\right) \ , \tag{33}$$

and for the RBF kernel,

$$\lambda_n = \exp\left(-b^{-2}\right)\exp\left(\frac{b^{-4}p^{-1}}{2}\right)\left(\frac{1}{b^2 p}\right)^n \left(1 + \mathcal{O}(p^{-1})\right) \ , \tag{34}$$

from which we find,

$$\max_{n \neq k} \lambda_k |\Delta_{nk}| \to 1 \ , \ \ |\delta_k|^2 = \frac{p^k}{Nk!} \times \left(1 + \mathcal{O}(p^{-1})\right) \quad \text{as } p \to \infty \ . \tag{35}$$

The localized contribution to the Gram matrix eigenvalue density given by (29) is then valid provided $p^k/Nk! \ll 1$ which suggests that as p becomes large, $N = \mathcal{O}(p^k)$ pattern vectors are required in order to resolve the kth population eigenvalue as a separate peak within the observed spectra of the Gram matrix.

Let $k_0(N)$ denote the number of peaks that can be resolved for a given number of data points N. For the RBF kernel $k_0 \sim p^{-1} \ln N \times \mathcal{O}(1)$. For some $k > k_0$, dropping higher order terms in the expansion (26) is not valid. To obtain an approximation to the expected spectrum in the range $\lambda < \lambda_{k_0}$ consider that since $\lambda_k \to 0^+$ as $k \to \infty$ then for sufficiently large k the kernel eigenvalue λ_k

will be smaller than $|R_{\mathbf{C_x}}|$. Thus for some integer k_c we expand,

$$\sum_{k=1}^{\infty} \frac{N(p,k)}{\lambda_k^{-1} - R_{\mathbf{C_x}}} = \sum_{k=1}^{k_c} \frac{N(p,k)}{R_{\mathbf{C_x}}} \left(\frac{1}{\lambda_k R_{\mathbf{C_x}}} - 1 \right)^{-1} + \sum_{k=k_c+1}^{\infty} \lambda_k N(p,k) \left(1 - R_{\mathbf{C_x}} \lambda_k \right)^{-1} . \tag{36}$$

Binomially expanding the two sums on the right-hand side of (36), retaining only the first term in the first sum and the first two terms in the second sum, and solving the resulting approximation for $R_{\mathbf{C_x}}(z)$ yields a single bulk-like contribution (denoted by subscript B) to the density,

$$\frac{1}{2\pi\Delta}\sqrt{(\hat{\lambda} - \lambda_{min,B})(\lambda_{max,B} - \hat{\lambda})} \times \Theta(\hat{\lambda}; \lambda_{min,B}; \lambda_{max,B}) \ , \tag{37}$$

with $\lambda_{\{max,min\},B} = \gamma \pm 2\sqrt{\Delta\Omega}$ and,

$$\gamma = \frac{1}{N} \sum_{k=k_c+1}^{\infty} N(p,k)\lambda_k \ , \ \Delta = \frac{1}{N} \sum_{k=k_c+1}^{\infty} N(p,k)\lambda_k^2 \ , \ \Omega = 1 - \frac{1}{N}\sum_{k=1}^{k_c} N(p,k) \ . \tag{38}$$

Combining (37) and (29) we obtain the approximation,

$$\begin{aligned} \rho(\hat{\lambda}) \simeq & \frac{1}{2\pi} \sum_{k=1}^{k_0} \frac{\sqrt{(\hat{\lambda} - \lambda_{min,k})(\lambda_{max,k} - \hat{\lambda})}}{\lambda_k - \lambda_k^{-1} N^{-1} \Sigma_2} \times \Theta(\hat{\lambda}; \lambda_{min,k}; \lambda_{max,k}) \\ & + \frac{1}{2\pi\Delta}\sqrt{(\hat{\lambda} - \lambda_{min,B})(\lambda_{max,B} - \hat{\lambda})} \times \Theta(\hat{\lambda}; \lambda_{min,B}; \lambda_{max,B}) \ . \end{aligned} \tag{39}$$

It is easily confirmed that if $k_c = k_0$ then the approximate density given by (39) is correctly normalized to leading order in N^{-1}, i.e. $\int d\hat{\lambda}\, \rho(\hat{\lambda}) = 1 + \mathcal{O}(N^{-1})$.

We note that the above approximation (39) is not restricted to dot-product kernels. It can be applied to other kernels and data distributions for which the process eigenvalues and their degeneracy are known, but it obviously limited by the validity of the starting Stieltjes transform relationship (3).

4 Simulation Results

In this section we compare the theory with simulation results. We consider a Gaussian RBF kernel with data uniformly distributed on the sphere. In figure 1 we show the spectrum averaged over 1000 simulations for N data points of dimension $p = 10$ with kernel width parameter $b^2 = 1$. For figure 1(a) with $N = 50$ only two peaks are discernable and the eigenvalues are greatly dispersed from their limiting values, whilst for figure 1(b), with $N = 100$, more structure is discernable. These are examples of a regime where the bounds developed by Shawe-Taylor *et. al.* would not be tight [6], since the sample and process eigenvalues are not close. The numerical solution of the RPA result in eq.(25), shown

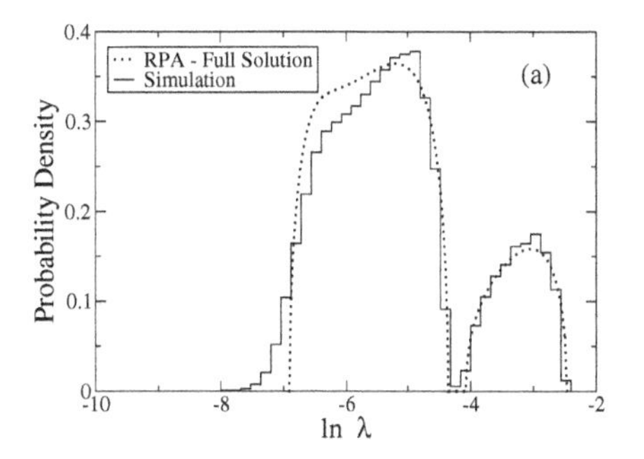

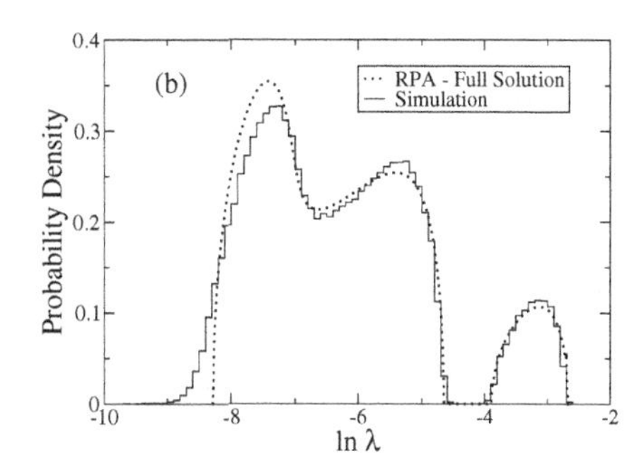

Fig. 1. We show the Gram matrix eigenvalue spectrum averaged over 1000 simulations (solid line) compared to the variational mean-field theory (dashed line) obtained by numerically solving eq.(25). Each data set was created by sampling N points uniformly from a $p = 10$ dimensional sphere and a Gaussian RBF kernel with $b^2 = 1$. a)$N = 50$. b)$N = 100$.

by the dotted line in both figure 1(a) and figure 1(b), provides an impressive fit to the simulation results in this case.

We might expect the statistical mechanics theory to work well for high dimensional data, but we would also like to test the theory for lower dimensionality. In figure 2 we consider the case of $p = 2$ dimensional data. This is far removed from typical case of high-dimensional data often considered in statistical mechanics studies of learning. In figure 2(a) we show results of simulations with $N = 50$ data points. Other parameters are as in figure 1. In this case several separate peaks are clearly visible. There is also an agglomeration of remaining eigenvalues around $\ln \lambda \simeq -40$ (not shown) corresponding approximately to the limit of machine and algorithmic precision in the simulations. The dashed line shows the approximate solution in eq.(39) of the RPA relationship in eq.(25). We have set $k_0 = 14$ in accordance with the number of resolved peaks which can be visually distinguished in the simulation results. In fact the approximate solution (39) yields a real density for $k_0 \leq 25$. The dotted line shows the full numerical solution of eq.(25), which is almost indistinguishable from the approximate solution. For the largest eigenvalues the qualitative agreement between the RPA and simulations is good.

In figure 2(b) we show the averaged spectrum for a smaller data set of $N = 25$ points. All other parameters are as for figure 2(a). Clearly fewer resolved peaks are observable in this case and the remaining bulk is considerably more dispersed than in figure 2(a), as expected for smaller N. The validity of the perturbative approximate RPA solution in eq.(39) is more questionable in this case and the discrepancy between the full and approximate solutions (dashed and dotted lines respectively) to the RPA is more discernable.

In order to use these results for model selection it would be useful to estimate the expectation value of the top eigenvalue. Figure 3(a) shows the convergence of the top eigenvalue to its asymptotic value as the number of data points N increases. We have plotted the log of the fractional error (between the top eigen-

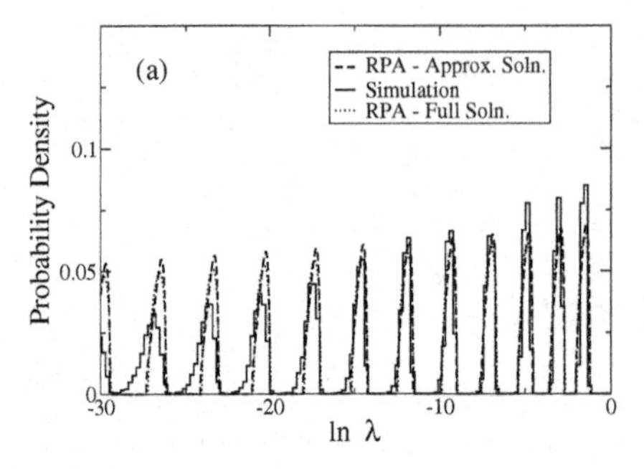

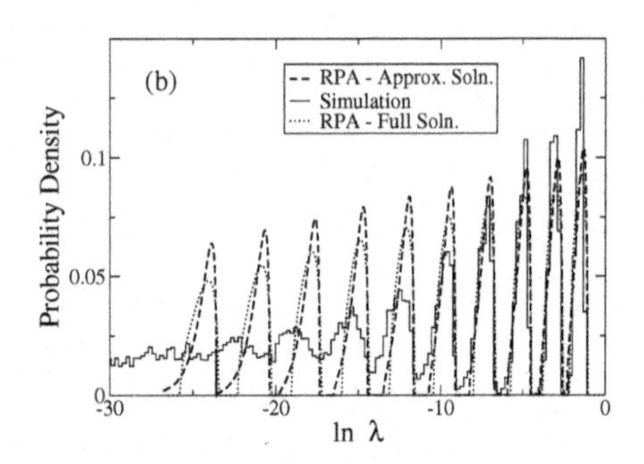

Fig. 2. We show the Gram matrix eigenvalue density averaged over 1000 simulations (solid line) for (a) $N = 50$ and (b) $N = 25$ data points distributed uniformly from a $p = 2$ dimensional sphere and Gaussian RBF with $b^2 = 1$. The dotted line shows the full numerical solution to eq.(25), over the range $\ln \lambda \in [-26, 0]$, and the dashed line shows the approximate analytical solution given by eq.(39).

value and its asymptotic value, i.e. $(\langle \hat{\lambda}_1 \rangle / \lambda_1) - 1)$ against $\ln N$. As in figure 2 we have chosen $p = 2$ and a Gaussian RBF kernel with $b^2 = 1$. The solid circles show simulation results averaged over 1000 Gram matrices (error bars are of the order of the size of the plotted symbols). Also plotted is the theoretical estimate from eq.(30) obtained from the approximate solution of the RPA. Clearly from the simulation results the top observed eigenvalue has an expectation value that converges as $N^{-\frac{1}{2}}$ to its asymptotic value. In figure 3(b) we observe that as the dimensionality p increases, the discrepancy between the theoretical estimate in eq.(30) and simulation decreases and then increases again. This is ultimately because the simulation results indicate that the fractional error scales as $p^{3/4}$ at large N, rather than $\sqrt{p}$ as suggested by eq.(30). To test the idea, suggested by eq.(30), that this convergence is universal for all dot-product kernels with an input distribution that is uniform on the sphere, we have also simulated the kernel $k(\boldsymbol{x} \cdot \boldsymbol{y}) = \cosh(a + \boldsymbol{x} \cdot \boldsymbol{y})$. The constant $a > 0$ is to ensure that the first eigenvalue of this even kernel function is non-vanishing for $p = 2$ and we have chosen $a = 0.5$. The similarity between the simulation results for the two different kernels is apparent and although not exact, the two sets of simulation results appear to converge at large N.

5 Discussion

We studied the averaged spectrum of the Gram matrix in kernel PCA using methods adapted from statistical physics. We mainly focussed on a mean-field variational approximation, the Random Phase Approximation (RPA). The RPA was shown to reduce to an identity for the Stieltjes transform of the spectral density that is known to be the correct asymptotic solution for PCA. We developed an approximate analytical solution to the theory that was shown to agree well with a numerical solution of this identity and the theory was shown to give a good qualitative match to simulation results. The theory correctly described the

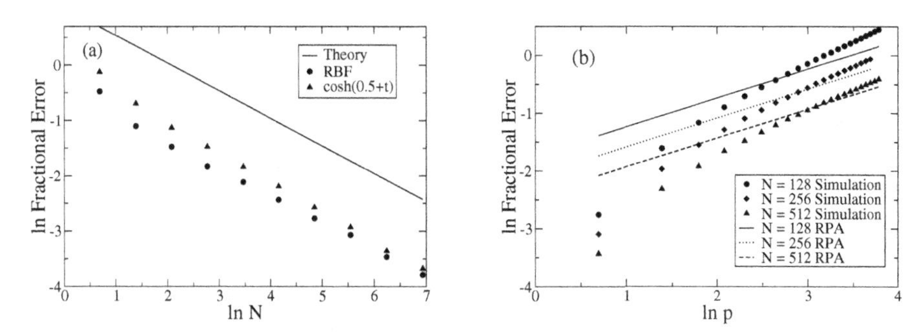

Fig. 3. a) Log-log plot of fractional error of the top eigenvalue of the centred Gram matrix with N. Plotted are simulation results for $p = 2$: Gaussian RBF kernel with $b^2 = 1$ (solid circles), a $\cosh(\frac{1}{2} + \boldsymbol{x} \cdot \boldsymbol{y})$ dot-product kernel (solid triangles ▲) and theoretical estimate given by eq.(30) (solid line). b) Log-log plot of the fractional error of the top eigenvalue of the centred Gram matrix with increasing dimensionality p and three values of $N = 128, 256$ & 512. Also plotted are the theoretical estimates.

scaling of the top eigenvalue with sample size but there were systematic errors because the scaling with dimension was not correctly predicted and further work is required to develop a better approximation for the top eigenvalue.

References

1. Engel, A. and Van den Broeck, C. *Statistical Mechanics of Learning* CUP, Cambridge 2001.
2. Scholköpf, B., Smola, A., Müller, K.-R. Neural Computation **10** (1998) 1299.
3. Bengio, Y., Paiement, J.-F., Vincent P., Delalleau O., Le Roux, N., Ouimet, M. Advances in Neural Information Processing Systems **16** (2003).
4. Johnstone, I.M. Ann Stat. **29** (2001) 295.
5. Hoyle, D.C., Rattray, M. Advances in Neural Information Processing Systems **16** (2003).
6. Shawe-Taylor, J., Williams, C.K.I., Cristiannini, N., Kandola, J. Proc. of Algorithmic Learning Theory (2002) 23.
7. Anderson, T.W. Ann. Math. Stat. **34** (1963) 122.
8. Marčenko, V.A., Pastur, L.A. Math. USSR-Sb **1** (1967) 507.
9. Bai, Z.D. Statistica Sinica **9** (1999) 611.
10. Sengupta, A.M., Mitra, P.P. Phys. Rev. E **60** (1999) 3389.
11. Silverstein, J.W., Combettes, P.L. IEEE Trans. Sig. Proc. **40** (1992) 2100.
12. Hoyle, D.C., Rattray, M. Europhys. Lett. **62** (2003) 117-123.
13. Reimann, P., Van den Broeck, C., Bex, G.J. J. Phys A **29** (1996), 3521.
14. Mézard, M., Parisi, G., Zee, A. Nucl. Phys. B[FS] **599** (1999) 689.
15. Hansen, J.-P., McDonald, I.R. *Theory of Simple Liquids* (2nd. Ed.), Academic Press, London, 1986.
16. Hochstadt, H. *The Functions of Mathematical Physics*, Dover, New York, 1986.
17. Abramowitz, M., Stegun, I. A. *Handbook of Mathematical Functions*, Dover, New York, 1957.
18. Twining, C.J., Taylor, C.J. Pattern Recognition **36** (2003), 217.

Statistical Properties of Kernel Principal Component Analysis

Laurent Zwald[1], Olivier Bousquet[2], and Gilles Blanchard[3]*

[1] Département de Mathématiques,
Université Paris-Sud, Bat. 425, F-91405 Orsay, France
Laurent.Zwald@math.u-psud.fr
[2] Max Planck Institute for Biological Cybernetics,
[3] Spemannstr. 38, D-72076 Tübingen, Germany
olvier.bousquet@tuebingen.mpg.de
[4] Fraunhofer First,
Kékuléstr. 7, D-12489 Berlin, Germany
blanchar@first.fhg.de

Abstract. We study the properties of the eigenvalues of Gram matrices in a non-asymptotic setting. Using local Rademacher averages, we provide data-dependent and tight bounds for their convergence towards eigenvalues of the corresponding kernel operator. We perform these computations in a functional analytic framework which allows to deal implicitly with reproducing kernel Hilbert spaces of infinite dimension. This can have applications to various kernel algorithms, such as Support Vector Machines (SVM). We focus on Kernel Principal Component Analysis (KPCA) and, using such techniques, we obtain sharp excess risk bounds for the reconstruction error. In these bounds, the dependence on the decay of the spectrum and on the closeness of successive eigenvalues is made explicit.

1 Introduction

Due to their versatility, kernel methods are currently very popular as data-analysis tools. In such algorithms, the key object is the so-called kernel matrix (the Gram matrix built on the data sample) and it turns out that its spectrum can be related to the performance of the algorithm. This has been shown in particular in the case of Support Vector Machines [19]. Studying the behavior of eigenvalues of kernel matrices, their stability and how they relate to the eigenvalues of the corresponding kernel integral operator is thus crucial for understanding the statistical properties of kernel-based algorithms.
Principal Component Analysis (PCA), and its non-linear variant, kernel-PCA are widely used algorithms in data analysis. They extract from the vector space where the data lie, a basis which is, in some sense, adapted to the data by looking for directions where the variance is maximized. Their applications are very

* Supported by a grant of the Humboldt Foundation

J. Shawe-Taylor and Y. Singer (Eds.): COLT 2004, LNAI 3120, pp. 594–608, 2004.

diverse, ranging from dimensionality reduction, to denoising. Applying PCA to a space of functions rather than to a space of vectors was first proposed by Besse [5] (see also [15] for a survey). Kernel-PCA [16] is an instance of such a method which has boosted the interest in PCA as it allows to overcome the limitations of linear PCA in a very elegant manner.
Despite being a relatively old and commonly used technique, little has been done on analyzing the statistical performance of PCA. Most of the previous work has focused on the asymptotic behavior of empirical covariance matrices of Gaussian vectors (see e.g. [1]). In the non-linear setting where one uses positive definite kernels, there is a tight connection between the covariance and the kernel matrix of the data. This is actually at the heart of the kernel-PCA algorithm, but it also indicates that the properties of the kernel matrix, in particular its spectrum, play a role in the properties of the kernel-PCA algorithm.
Recently, J. Shawe-Taylor, C. Williams, N. Cristianini and J. Kandola [17] have undertaken an investigation of the properties of the eigenvalues of kernel matrices and related it to the statistical performance of kernel-PCA.
In this work, we mainly extend the results of [17]. In particular we treat the infinite dimensional case with more care and we refine the bounds using recent tools from empirical processes theory. We obtain significant improvements and more explicit bounds.
The fact that some of the most interesting positive definite kernels (e.g. the Gaussian RBF kernel), generate an infinite dimensional reproducing kernel Hilbert space (the "feature space" into which the data is mapped), raises a technical difficulty. We propose to tackle this difficulty by using the framework of Hilbert-Schmidt operators and of random vectors in Hilbert spaces. Under some reasonable assumptions (like separability of the RKHS and boundedness of the kernel), things work nicely but some background in functional analysis is needed which is introduced below.
Our approach builds on ideas pioneered by Massart [13], on the fact that Talagrand's concentration inequality can be used to obtain sharp oracle inequalities for empirical risk minimization on a collection of function classes when the variance of the relative error can be related to the expected relative error itself. This idea has been exploited further in [2].

The paper is organized as follows. Section 2 introduces the necessary background on functional analysis and the basic assumptions. We then present, in Section 3 bounds on the difference between sums of eigenvalues of the kernel matrix and of the associated kernel operator. Finally, Section 4 gives our main results on kernel-PCA.

2 Preliminaries

In order to make the paper self-contained, we introduce some background, and give the notations for the rest of the paper.

2.1 Background Material on Functional Analysis

Let $\mathcal{H}$ be a separable Hilbert space. A linear operator L from $\mathcal{H}$ to $\mathcal{H}$ is called Hilbert-Schmidt if $\sum_{i\geq 1} \|Le_i\|^2_{\mathcal{H}} < \infty$, where $(e_i)_{i\geq 1}$ is an orthonormal basis of $\mathcal{H}$. This sum is independent of the chosen orthonormal basis and is the squared of the Hilbert-Schmidt norm of L when it is finite. The set of all Hilbert-Schmidt operators on $\mathcal{H}$ is denoted by $\mathrm{HS}(\mathcal{H})$. Endowed with the following inner product $\langle L, N\rangle_{\mathrm{HS}(\mathcal{H})} = \sum_{i,j\geq 1}\langle Le_i, e_j\rangle\langle Ne_i, e_j\rangle$, it is a separable Hilbert space.

A Hilbert-Schmidt operator is compact, it has a countable spectrum and an eigenspace associated to a non-zero eigenvalue is of finite dimension. A compact, self-adjoint operator on a Hilbert space can be diagonalized i.e. there exists an orthonormal basis of $\mathcal{H}$ made of eigenfunctions of this operator. If L is a compact, positive self-adjoint operator $\lambda(L)$ denotes its spectrum sorted in non-increasing order, repeated according to their multiplicities $(\lambda_1(A) \geq \lambda_2(A) \geq \ldots)$. An operator L is called trace-class if $\sum_{i\geq 1}\langle e_i, Le_i\rangle$ is a convergent series. In fact, this series is independent of the chosen orthonormal basis and is called the trace of L, denoted by $\operatorname{tr} L$. By Lidskii's theorem $\operatorname{tr} L = \sum_{i\geq 1} \lambda_i(L)$.

We will keep switching from $\mathcal{H}$ to $\mathrm{HS}(\mathcal{H})$ and treat their elements as vectors or as operators depending on the context, so we will need the following identities. Denoting, for $f, g \in \mathcal{H}$, by $f \otimes g$ the rank one operator defined as $f \otimes g(h) = \langle g, h\rangle f$, it easily follows from the above definitions that $\|f \otimes g\|_{\mathrm{HS}(\mathcal{H})} = \|f\|_{\mathcal{H}} \|g\|_{\mathcal{H}}$, and for $A \in \mathrm{HS}(\mathcal{H})$,

$$\langle f \otimes g, A\rangle_{\mathrm{HS}(\mathcal{H})} = \langle Ag, f\rangle_{\mathcal{H}} \,. \tag{1}$$

We recall that an orthogonal projector in $\mathcal{H}$ is an operator U such that $U^2 = U$ and $U = U^*$ (hence positive). In particular one has $\|U(h)\|^2_{\mathcal{H}} = \langle h, Uh\rangle_{\mathcal{H}}$. U has rank $d < \infty$ (i.e. it is a projection on a finite dimensional subspace), if and only if it is Hilbert-Schmidt with $\|U\|_{\mathrm{HS}(\mathcal{H})} = \sqrt{d}$ and $\operatorname{tr} U = d$. In that case it can be decomposed as $U = \sum_{i=1}^d \phi_i \otimes \phi_i$ where $(\phi_i)_{i=1}^d$ is an orthonormal basis of the image of U.

If V denotes a closed subspaces of $\mathcal{H}$, we denote by Π_V the unique orthogonal projector such that $\operatorname{ran} \Pi_V = V$ and $\ker \Pi_V = V^\perp$. When V is of finite dimension, $\Pi_{V^\perp}$ is not Hilbert-Schmidt, but we will denote, for a trace-class operator A, $\langle \Pi_{V^\perp}, A\rangle = \operatorname{tr} A - \langle \Pi_V, A\rangle_{\mathrm{HS}(\mathcal{H})}$ with some abuse of notation.

2.2 Kernel and Covariance Operators

We recall basic facts about random elements in Hilbert spaces. A random element Z in a separable Hilbert space has an expectation $e \in \mathcal{H}$ when $\mathbb{E}\|Z\| < \infty$ and e is the unique vector satisfying $\langle e, f\rangle_{\mathcal{H}} = \mathbb{E}\langle Z, f\rangle_{\mathcal{H}}$, $\forall f \in \mathcal{H}$. Moreover, when $\mathbb{E}\|Z\|^2 < \infty$, there exists a unique operator $C : \mathcal{H} \to \mathcal{H}$ such that $\langle f, Cg\rangle_{\mathcal{H}} = \mathbb{E}\left[\langle f, Z\rangle_{\mathcal{H}}\langle g, Z\rangle_{\mathcal{H}}\right]$, $\forall f, g \in \mathcal{H}$. C is called the covariance operator of Z and is self-adjoint, positive, trace-class operator, with $\operatorname{tr} C = \mathbb{E}\|Z\|^2$ (see e.g. [4]).

The core property of kernel operators that we will use is its intimate relationship with a covariance operator and it is summarized in next theorem. This property was first used in a similar but more restrictive context (finite dimensional) by Shawe-Taylor, Williams, Cristianini and Kandola [17].

Theorem 1. *Let $(\mathcal{X}, P)$ be a probability space, $\mathcal{H}$ be a separable Hilbert space and Φ be a map from $\mathcal{X}$ to $\mathcal{H}$ such that for all $h \in \mathcal{H}$, $\langle h, \Phi(.)\rangle_H$ is measurable and $\mathbb{E}\|\Phi(X)\|^2 < \infty$. Let C be the covariance operator associated to $\Phi(X)$ and $K : L_2(P) \to L_2(P)$ be the integral operator defined as*

$$(Kf)(x) = \int f(y) \langle \Phi(x), \Phi(y)\rangle_{\mathcal{H}} \, dP(y) \, .$$

Then $\lambda(K) = \lambda(C)$.
In particular, K is a positive self-adjoint trace-class operator and $\operatorname{tr}(K) = \mathbb{E}\|\Phi(X)\|^2 = \sum_{i\geq 1} \lambda_i(K)$.

2.3 Eigenvalues Formula

We denote by $\mathcal{V}_d$ the set of subspaces of dimension d of $\mathcal{H}$. The following theorem whose proof can be found in [18] gives a useful formula to compute sums of eigenvalues.

Theorem 2 (Fan). *Let C a compact self-adjoint operator on $\mathcal{H}$, then*

$$\sum_{i=1}^{d} \lambda_i(C) = \max_{V \in \mathcal{V}_d} \langle \Pi_V, C\rangle_{HS(\mathcal{H})} \, ,$$

and the maximum is reached when V is the space spanned by the first d eigenvectors of C.

We will also need the following formula for single eigenvalues.

Theorem 3 (Courant-Fischer-Weyl, see e.g. [9]). *Let C a compact self-adjoint operator on $\mathcal{H}$, then for all $d \geq 1$,*

$$\lambda_d(C) = \min_{V \in \mathcal{V}_{d-1}} \max_{f \perp V} \frac{\langle f, Cf\rangle}{\|f\|^2} \, ,$$

where the minimum is attained when V is the span of the first $d-1$ eigenvectors of C.

2.4 Assumptions and Basic Facts

Let $\mathcal{X}$ denote the input space (an arbitrary measurable space) and P denote a distribution on $\mathcal{X}$ according to which the data is sampled i.i.d.
We will denote by P_n the empirical measure associated to a sample $X_1, \ldots, X_n$ from P, i.e. $P_n = \frac{1}{n}\sum \delta_{X_i}$. With some abuse of notation, for a function $f : \mathcal{X} \to \mathbb{R}$, we may use the notation $Pf := \mathbb{E}[f(X)]$ and $P_n f := \frac{1}{n}\sum_{i=1}^n f(X_i)$. Also, $\varepsilon_1, \ldots, \varepsilon_n$ will denote a sequence of Rademacher random variables (i.e.

independent with value +1 or −1 with probability 1/2).
Let k be a positive definite function on $\mathcal{X}$ and $\mathcal{H}_k$ the associated reproducing kernel Hilbert space. They are related by the reproducing property: $\forall f \in \mathcal{H}_k, \forall x \in \mathcal{X}, \langle f, k(x,.)\rangle_{\mathcal{H}_k} = f(x)$. We denote by $\mathcal{V}_d$ the set of all vector subspaces of dimension d of $\mathcal{H}_k$.
We will always work with the following assumption.

Assumption 1. *We assume that*

- *For all $x \in \mathcal{X}$, $k(x,.)$ is P-measurable.*
- *There exists $M > 0$ such that $k(X,X) \leq M$ P-almost surely.*
- *$\mathcal{H}_k$ is separable.*

For $x \in \mathcal{X}$, we denote $\varphi_x = k(x,.)$ understood as an element of $\mathcal{H}_k$.
Let C_x the operator defined on $\mathcal{H}_k$ by

$$\langle f, C_x g\rangle_{\mathcal{H}_k} = f(x)g(x) .$$

It is easy to see that $C_x = \varphi_x \otimes \varphi_x$ and C_x is trace-class with $\operatorname{tr} C_x = k(x,x)$ and $\|C_x\|^2_{\mathrm{HS}(\mathcal{H}_k)} = k(x,x)^2$.
Also, from the definitions and by (1) we have for example $\langle C_x, C_y\rangle_{\mathrm{HS}(\mathcal{H}_k)} = k^2(x,y)$ and , for any projector U, $\|U\varphi_x\|^2_{\mathcal{H}_k} = \langle U, C_x\rangle_{HS(\mathcal{H}_k)}$.
We will denote by $C_1 : \mathcal{H}_k \to \mathcal{H}_k$ (resp. $C_2 : \mathrm{HS}(\mathcal{H}_k) \to \mathrm{HS}(\mathcal{H}_k)$) the covariance operator associated to the random element φ_X in $\mathcal{H}_k$ (resp. C_X in $\mathrm{HS}(\mathcal{H}_k)$). Also, let K_1 (resp. K_2) be the integral operator with kernel $k(x,y)$ (resp. $k(x,y)^2$).

Lemma 1. *Under Assumption 1 the operators C_1, C_2, K_1, K_2 defined above are trace-class with $\operatorname{tr} C_1 = \mathbb{E}[k(X,X)]$, $\operatorname{tr} C_2 = \mathbb{E}\left[k^2(X,X)\right]$. They satisfy the following properties*

(i) $\lambda(C_1) = \lambda(K_1)$ *and* $\lambda(C_2) = \lambda(K_2)$.
(ii) C_1 *is the expectation in* $\mathrm{HS}(\mathcal{H}_k)$ *of* C_X.
(iii) C_2 *is the expectation in* $\mathrm{HS}(\mathrm{HS}(\mathcal{H}_k))$ *of* $C_X \otimes C_X$.

Proof. (i) To begin with, we prove that $\operatorname{tr} C_1 = \mathbb{E}k(X,X)$ and $\lambda(C_1) = \lambda(K_1)$ by applying Theorem 1 with $\Phi(x) = \varphi_x$: since $k(x,\cdot)$ is measurable, all linear combinations and pointwise limits of such combinations are measurable, so that all the functions in $\mathcal{H}_k$ are measurable. Hence measurability, for $h \in \mathcal{H}_k$ of $x \mapsto \langle \Phi_x, h\rangle_{\mathcal{H}_k}$ follows and we have $\mathbb{E}\|\Phi_X\|^2 = \mathbb{E}k(X,X) < \infty$.
Then, we prove that $\operatorname{tr} C_2 = \mathbb{E}k^2(X,X)$ and $\lambda(C_2) = \lambda(K_2)$ by applying Theorem 1 with $\Phi(x) = C_x$: for $h \in \mathrm{HS}(\mathcal{H}_k)$ with finite rank (i.e. $h = \sum_{i=1}^n \phi_i \otimes \psi_i$ for an orthonormal set ϕ_i and $\psi_i = h^*\phi_i$), the function $x \mapsto \langle C_x, h\rangle_{\mathrm{HS}(\mathcal{H}_k)} = \sum_{i=1}^n \phi_i(x)\psi_i(x)$ is measurable (since ϕ_i and ψ_i are measurable as elements of $\mathcal{H}_k$). Moreover, since the finite rank operators are dense in $\mathrm{HS}(\mathcal{H}_k)$ and $h \mapsto \langle C_x, h\rangle_{\mathrm{HS}(\mathcal{H}_k)}$ is continuous, we have measurability for all $h \in \mathrm{HS}(\mathcal{H}_k)$. Finally, we have $\mathbb{E}\|C_X\|^2_{\mathrm{HS}(\mathcal{H}_k)} = \mathbb{E}k^2(X,X) < \infty$.
(ii) Since $\mathbb{E}\|C_X\|_{\mathrm{HS}(\mathcal{H}_k)} = \mathbb{E}k(X,X) < \infty$ the expectation of C_X is well defined in $\mathrm{HS}(\mathcal{H}_k)$. Moreover for all $f, g \in \mathcal{H}_k$, $\langle \mathbb{E}C_X f, g\rangle = \langle \mathbb{E}C_X, g \otimes f\rangle :=$

$\mathbb{E}\langle C_X, g \otimes f\rangle = \mathbb{E}\langle C_X f, g\rangle = \mathbb{E}f(X)g(X) = \langle C_1 f, g\rangle$
(iii) Using $\|C_X \otimes C_X\|_{\mathrm{HS}(\mathrm{HS}(\mathcal{H}_k))} = \|C_X\|^2_{\mathrm{HS}(\mathcal{H}_k)} = k(X,X)^2$ and a similar argument gives the last statement. □

The generality of the above results implies that we can replace the distribution P by the empirical measure P_n associated to an i.i.d. sample $X_1, \dots, X_n$ without any changes. If we do so, the associated operators are denoted by $K_{1,n}$ (which is identified [12] with the normalized kernel matrix of size $n \times n$, $K_{1,n} \equiv (k(X_i, X_j)/n)_{i,j=1,\dots,n}$) and $C_{1,n}$ which is the empirical covariance operator (i.e. $\langle f, C_{1,n} g\rangle = \frac{1}{n}\sum_{i=1}^n f(X_i)g(X_i)$). We can also define $K_{2,n}$ and $C_{2,n}$ similarly. In particular, Theorem 1 implies that $\lambda(K_{1,n}) = \lambda(C_{1,n})$ and $\lambda(K_{2,n}) = \lambda(C_{2,n})$ and $\operatorname{tr} K_{1,n} = \operatorname{tr} C_{1,n} = \frac{1}{n}\sum_{i=1}^n k(X_i, X_i)$ while $\operatorname{tr} K_{2,n} = \operatorname{tr} C_{2,n} = \frac{1}{n}\sum_{i=1}^n k^2(X_i, X_i)$.

3 General Results on Eigenvalues of Gram Matrices

We first relate sums of eigenvalues to a class of functions of type $x \mapsto \langle \Pi_V, C_x\rangle$. This will allow us to introduce classical tools of Empirical Processes Theory to study the relationship between eigenvalues of the empirical Gram matrix and of the corresponding integral operator.

Corollary 1. *Under Assumption 1, we have*

$$\sum_{k=1}^d \lambda_k(K_1) = \max_{V \in \mathcal{V}_d} \mathbb{E}\left[\langle \Pi_V, C_X\rangle\right] \quad \textit{and} \quad \sum_{k \geq d+1} \lambda_k(K_1) = \min_{V \in \mathcal{V}_d} \mathbb{E}\left[\langle \Pi_{V^\perp}, C_X\rangle\right].$$

Proof. The result for the sums of the largest eigenvalues follows from Theorem 2 applied to C_1 and Lemma 1. For the smallest ones, we use the fact that $\operatorname{tr} C_1 = \mathbb{E} \operatorname{tr} C_X = \sum_{k \geq 1} \lambda_k(C_1)$, and $\langle \Pi_V, C_X\rangle + \langle \Pi_{V^\perp}, C_X\rangle = \operatorname{tr} C_X$. □

Notice that similar results hold for the empirical versions (replacing P by P_n).

3.1 Global Approach

In this section, we obtain concentration result of the sum of the largest eigenvalues and of the sum of the lowest towards eigenvalues of the integral operator. We start with an upper bound on the Rademacher averages of the corresponding classes of functions.

Lemma 2.

$$\mathbb{E}_\varepsilon\left[\frac{1}{n}\sup_{V \in \mathcal{V}_d} \sum_{j=1}^n \varepsilon_j \langle \Pi_{V^\perp}, C_{X_j}\rangle\right] = \mathbb{E}_\varepsilon\left[\frac{1}{n}\sup_{V \in \mathcal{V}_d} \sum_{j=1}^n \varepsilon_j \langle \Pi_V, C_{X_j}\rangle\right] \leq \sqrt{\frac{d}{n}\operatorname{tr} K_{2,n}}$$

Proof. We use the symmetry of ε_i, Theorem 8 with $r \to \infty$ and $h = 0$, and Lemma 1. □

We now give the main result of this section, which consists in data-dependent upper and lower bounds for the largest and smallest eigenvalues.

Theorem 4. *Under Assumption 1, with probability at least* $1 - 3e^{-\xi}$,

$$-M\sqrt{\frac{\xi}{2n}} \leq \sum_{i=1}^{d} \lambda_i(K_{1,n}) - \sum_{i=1}^{d} \lambda_i(K_1) \leq 2\sqrt{\frac{d}{n} \operatorname{tr} K_{2,n}} + 3M\sqrt{\frac{\xi}{2n}} . \quad (2)$$

Also, with probability at least $1 - 3e^{-\xi}$,

$$-M\sqrt{\frac{\xi}{2n}} \leq \sum_{i \geq d+1} \lambda_i(K_1) - \sum_{i \geq d+1} \lambda_i(K_{1,n}) \leq 2\sqrt{\frac{d}{n} \operatorname{tr} K_{2,n}} + 3M\sqrt{\frac{\xi}{2n}} . \quad (3)$$

Proof. We start with the first statement. Recall that

$$\sum_{i=1}^{d} \lambda_i(K_{1,n}) - \sum_{i=1}^{d} \lambda_i(K_1) = \max_{V \in \mathcal{V}_d} \langle \Pi_V, C_{1,n} \rangle - \max_{V \in \mathcal{V}_d} \langle \Pi_V, C_1 \rangle .$$

This gives, denoting by V_d the subspace attaining the second maximum,

$$(P_n - P) \langle \Pi_{V_d}, C_X \rangle \leq \sum_{i=1}^{d} \lambda_i(K_{1,n}) - \sum_{i=1}^{d} \lambda_i(K_1) \leq \sup_{V \in \mathcal{V}_d} (P_n - P) \langle \Pi_V, C_X \rangle .$$

To prove the upper bound, we use McDiarmid's inequality and symmetrization as in [3] along with the fact that, for a projector U, $\langle U, C_x \rangle \leq \|\varphi_x\|^2 \leq M$. We conclude the proof by using Lemma 2. The lower bound is a simple consequence of Hoeffding's inequality [10]. The second statement can be proved via similar arguments. □

It is important to notice that the upper and lower bounds are different. To explain this, following the approach of [17] where McDiarmid's inequality is applied to $\sum_{i=1}^{d} \lambda_i(K_{1,n})$ directly[1], we have with probability at least $1 - e^{-\xi}$,

$$-M\sqrt{\frac{\xi}{2n}} \leq \sum_{i=1}^{d} \lambda_i(K_{1,n}) - \mathbb{E}\left[\sum_{i=1}^{d} \lambda_i(K_{1,n})\right] \leq M\sqrt{\frac{\xi}{2n}} .$$

Then by Jensen's inequality, symmetrization and Lemma 2 we get

$$0 \leq \mathbb{E}\left[\sum_{i=1}^{d} \lambda_i(K_{1,n})\right] - \sum_{i=1}^{d} \lambda_i(K_1) \leq \mathbb{E}\left[\sup_{V \in \mathcal{V}_d} (P_n - P) \langle \Pi_V, C_X \rangle\right] \leq 2\sqrt{\frac{d}{n} \operatorname{tr} K_2} .$$

We see that the empirical eigenvalues are biased estimators of the population ones whence the difference between upper and lower bound in (2). Note that applying McDiarmid's inequality again would have given precisely (2), but we prefer to use the approach of the proof of Theorem 4 as it can be further refined (see next section).

[1] Note that one could actually apply the inequality of [7] to this quantity to obtain a sharper bound. This is in the spirit of next section.

3.2 Local Approach

We now use recent work based on Talagrand's inequality (see e.g. [13,2]) to obtain better concentration for the large eigenvalues of the Gram matrix. We obtain a better rate of convergence, but at the price of comparing the sums of eigenvalues up to a constant factor.

Theorem 5. *Under Assumption 1, for all $\alpha > 0$ and $\xi > 0$, with probability at least $1 - e^{-\xi}$,*

$$\sum_{k=1}^{d} \lambda_k(K_{1,n}) - (1+\alpha)\sum_{k=1}^{d} \lambda_k(K_1) \leq 704(1+\alpha^{-1})r_d^* + \frac{M\xi(11(1+\alpha)+26(1+\alpha^{-1}))}{n} \quad (4)$$

where

$$r_d^* \leq \inf_{h\geq 0}\left\{\frac{Mh}{n} + 2\sqrt{\frac{d}{n}\sum_{j>h}\lambda_j(K_2)}\right\}.$$

Moreover, with probability at least $1 - e^{-\xi}$, for all $\alpha \in (0,1)$,

$$\sum_{k=1}^{d} \lambda_k(K_{1,n}) - (1-\alpha)\sum_{k=1}^{d} \lambda_k(K_1) \geq \frac{-M\xi}{n}(\frac{1}{3} + \frac{1}{2\alpha}). \quad (5)$$

Notice that the complexity term obtained here is always better than the one of (2) (take $h = 0$). As an example of how this bound differs from (2), assume that $\lambda_j(K_2) = O(j^{-\alpha})$ with $\alpha > 1$, then (2) gives a bound of order $\sqrt{d/n}$, while the above Theorem gives a bound of order $d^{1/(1+\alpha)}/n^{\alpha/(1+\alpha)}$ which is better. In the case of an exponential decay ($\lambda_j(K_2) = O(e^{-\gamma j})$ with $\gamma > 0$), the rate even drops to $\log(nd)/n$.

4 Application to Kernel-PCA

We wish to find the linear space of dimension d that conserves the maximal variance, i.e. which minimizes the error of approximating the data by their projections.

$$V_n = \underset{V\in\mathcal{V}_d}{\operatorname{argmin}} \frac{1}{n}\sum_{j=1}^{n} \|\varphi_{X_j} - \Pi_V(\varphi_{X_j})\|^2 .$$

V_n is the vector space spanned by the first d eigenfunctions of $C_{1,n}$. Analogously, we denote by V_d the space spanned by the first d eigenfunctions of C_1. We will adopt the following notation:

$$R_n(V) = \frac{1}{n}\sum_{j=1}^{n} \|\varphi_{X_j} - \Pi_V(\varphi_{X_j})\|^2 = P_n \langle \Pi_{V^\perp}, C_X\rangle .$$

$$R(V) = \mathbb{E}\left[\|\varphi_X - \Pi_V\varphi_X\|^2\right] = P\langle \Pi_{V^\perp}, C_X\rangle .$$

One has $R_n(V_n) = \sum_{i>d} \lambda_i(K_{1,n})$ and $R(V_d) = \sum_{i>d} \lambda_i(K_1)$.

4.1 Bound on the Reconstruction Error

We give a data dependent bound for the reconstruction error.

Theorem 6. *Under Assumption 1, with probability at least* $1 - 2e^{-\xi}$,

$$R(V_n) \leq \sum_{i=d+1}^{n} \lambda_i(K_{1,n}) + 2\sqrt{\frac{d}{n} \operatorname{tr} K_{2,n}} + 3M\sqrt{\frac{\xi}{2n}} .$$

Proof. We have

$$R(V_n) - R_n(V_n) = (P - P_n)\left\langle \Pi_{V_n^\perp}, C_X \right\rangle \leq \sup_{V \in \mathcal{V}_d} (P - P_n)\left\langle \Pi_{V^\perp}, C_X \right\rangle .$$

We have already treated this quantity in the proof of Theorem 4. □

In order to compare the global and the local approach, we give a theoretical bound on the reconstruction error. By definition of V_n, we have $R(V_n) - R(V_d) \leq 2\sup_{V \in \mathcal{V}_d}(R - R_n)(V_n)$ so that from the proof of Theorem 4 one gets

$$R(V_n) - R(V_d) \leq 4\sqrt{\frac{d}{n} tr(K_2)} + 2M\sqrt{\frac{\xi}{2n}} .$$

4.2 Relative Bound

We now show that when the eigenvalues of the kernel operator are well separated, estimation becomes easier in the sense that the excess error of the best empirical d-dimensional subspace over the error of the best d-dimensional subspace can decay at a much faster rate.
The following lemma captures the key property which allows this rate improvement.

Lemma 3. *For any subspace* $V \subset \mathcal{H}_k$,

$$\operatorname{Var}\left[\langle \Pi_{V^\perp}, C_X\rangle - \left\langle \Pi_{V_d^\perp}, C_X \right\rangle\right] \leq \mathbb{E}\left[\left\langle \Pi_{V^\perp} - \Pi_{V_d^\perp}, C_X \right\rangle^2\right] ,$$

and for all $V \in \mathcal{V}_d$, *with* $\lambda_d(C_1) > \lambda_{d+1}(C_1)$,

$$\mathbb{E}\left[\left\langle \Pi_{V^\perp} - \Pi_{V_d^\perp}, C_X \right\rangle^2\right] \leq \frac{2\sqrt{\mathbb{E}k^4(X,X')}}{\lambda_d(C_1) - \lambda_{d+1}(C_1)} \mathbb{E}\left[\left\langle \Pi_{V^\perp} - \Pi_{V_d^\perp}, C_X \right\rangle\right] , \quad (6)$$

where X' *is an independent copy of* X.

Here is the main result of the section.

Theorem 7. *Under Assumption 1, for all* d *such that* $\lambda_d(C_1) > \lambda_{d+1}(C_1)$, *for all* $\xi > 0$, *with probability at least* $1 - e^{-\xi}$

$$R(V_n) - R(V_d) \leq 705 \inf_{h \geq 0} \left\{ \frac{B_d h}{n} + 4\sqrt{\frac{d}{n} \sum_{j \geq h+1} \lambda_j(K_2)} \right\} + \frac{\xi(22M + 27B_d)}{n} ,$$

where $B_d = 2\sqrt{\mathbb{E}k^4(X,X')}/(\lambda_d(C_1) - \lambda_{d+1}(C_1))$.

It is easy to see that the term $\sqrt{\mathbb{E}k^4(X,X')}$ is upper bounded by $\mathbb{E}k^2(X,X)$. Similarly to the observation after Theorem 5, the complexity term obtained here will decay faster than the one of Theorem 6, at a rate which will depend on the rate of decay of the eigenvalues.

5 Discussion

Dauxois and Pousse [8] studied asymptotic convergence of PCA and proved almost sure convergence in operator norm of the empirical covariance operator to the population one. These results were further extended to PCA in a Hilbert space by [6]. However, no finite sample bounds were presented.
Compared to the work of [12] and [11], we are interested in non-asymptotic (i.e. finite sample sizes) results. Also, as we are only interested in the case where $k(x, y)$ is a positive definite function, we have the nice property of Theorem 1 which allows to consider the empirical operator and its limit as acting on the same space (since we can use covariance operators on the RKHS). This is crucial in our analysis and makes precise non-asymptotic computations possible unlike in the general case studied in [12,11].
Comparing with [17], we overcome the difficulties coming from infinite dimensional feature spaces as well as those of dealing with kernel operators (of infinite rank). Moreover their approach for eigenvalues is based on the concentration around the mean of the empirical eigenvalues and on the relationship between the expectation of the empirical eigenvalues and the operator eigenvalues. But they do not provide two-sided inequalities and they do not introduce Rademacher averages which are natural to measure such a difference. Here we use a direct approach and provide two-sided inequalities with empirical complexity terms and even get refinements. Also, when they provide bounds for KPCA, they use a very rough estimate based on the fact that the functional is linear in the feature space associated to k^2. Here we provide more explicit and tighter bounds with a global approach. Moreover, when comparing the expected residual of the empirical minimizer and the ideal one, we exploit a subtle property to get tighter results when the gap between eigenvalues is non-zero.

6 Conclusion

We have obtained sharp bounds on the behavior of sums of eigenvalues of Gram matrices and shown how this entails excess risk bounds for kernel-PCA. In particular our bounds exhibit a fast rate behavior in the case where the spectrum of the kernel operator decays fast and contains a gap. These results significantly improve previous results of [17]. The formalism of Hilbert-Schmidt operator spaces over a RKHS turns out to be very well suited to a mathematically rigorous treatment of the problem, also providing compact proofs of the results. We plan to investigate further the application of the techniques introduced here to the study of other properties of kernel matrices, such as the behavior of single eigenvalues instead of sums, or eigenfunctions. This would provide a non-asymptotic version of results like those of [1] and of [6].

Acknowledgements. The authors are extremely grateful to Stéphane Boucheron for invaluable comments and ideas, as well as for motivating this work.

References

1. T. W. Anderson. Asymptotic theory for principal component analysis. *Ann. Math. Stat.*, 34:122–148, 1963.
2. P. Bartlett, O. Bousquet, and S. Mendelson. Localized Rademacher complexities, 2003. Submitted, available at `http://www.kyb.mpg.de/publications/pss/ps2000.ps`.
3. P.L. Bartlett and S. Mendelson. Rademacher and Gaussian complexities: risk bounds and structural results. *Journal of Machine Learning Research*, 3:463–482, 2002.
4. P. Baxendale. Gaussian measures on function spaces. *Amer. J. Math.*, 98:891–952, 1976.
5. P. Besse. *Etude descriptive d'un pocessus; approximation, interpolation.* PhD thesis, Université de Toulouse, 1979.
6. P. Besse. Approximation spline de l'analyse en composantes principales d'une variable aléatoire hilbertienne. *Ann. Fac. Sci. Toulouse (Math.)*, 12(5):329–349, 1991.
7. S. Boucheron, G. Lugosi, and P. Massart. A sharp concentration inequality with applications. *Random Structures and Algorithms*, 16:277–292, 2000.
8. J. Dauxois and A. Pousse. *Les analyses factorielles en calcul des probabilités et en statistique: essai d'étude synthétique.* PhD thesis.
9. N. Dunford and J. T. Schwartz. *Linear Operators Part II: Spectral Theory, Self Adjoint Operators in Hilbert Space.* Number VII in Pure and Applied Mathematics. John Wiley & Sons, New York, 1963.
10. W. Hoeffding. Probability inequalities for sums of bounded random variables. *Journal of the American Statistical Association*, 58:13–30, 1963.
11. V. Koltchinskii. Asymptotics of spectral projections of some random matrices approximating integral operators. *Progress in Probability*, 43:191–227, 1998.
12. V. Koltchinskii and E. Giné. Random matrix approximation of spectra of integral operators. *Bernoulli*, 6(1):113–167, 2000.
13. P. Massart. Some applications of concentration inequalities to statistics. *Annales de la Faculté des Sciencies de Toulouse*, IX:245–303, 2000.
14. S. Mendelson. Estimating the performance of kernel classes. *Journal of Machine Learning Research*, 4:759–771, 2003.
15. J. O. Ramsay and C. J. Dalzell. Some tools for functional data analysis. *Journal of the Royal Statistical Society, Series B*, 53(3):539–572, 1991.
16. B. Schölkopf, A. J. Smola, and K.-R. Müller. Kernel principal component analysis. In B. Schölkopf, C. J. C. Burges, and A. J. Smola, editors, *Advances in Kernel Methods - Support Vector Learning*, pages 327–352. MIT Press, Cambridge, MA, 1999. Short version appeared in *Neural Computation* 10:1299–1319, 1998.
17. J. Shawe-Taylor, C. Williams, N. Cristianini, and J. Kandola. Eigenspectrum of the gram matrix and its relationship to the operator eigenspectrum. In *Algorithmic Learning Theory : 13th International Conference, ALT 2002*, volume 2533 of *Lecture Notes in Computer Science*, pages 23–40. Springer-Verlag, 2002. Extended version available at `http://www.support-vector.net/papers/eigenspectrum.pdf`.

18. M. Torki. Etude de la sensibilité de toutes les valeurs propres non nulles d'un opérateur compact autoadjoint. Technical Report LAO97-05, Université Paul Sabatier, 1997. Available at http://mip.ups-tlse.fr/publi/rappLAO/97.05.ps.gz.
19. R. C. Williamson, J. Shawe-Taylor, B. Schölkopf, and A. J. Smola. Sample-based generalization bounds. *IEEE Transactions on Information Theory*, 1999. Submitted. Also: NeuroCOLT Technical Report NC-TR-99-055.

A Localized Rademacher Averages on Ellipsoids

We give a bound on Rademacher averages of ellipsoids intersected with balls using a method introduced by Dudley.

Theorem 8. *Let $\mathcal{H}$ be a separable Hilbert space and Z be a random variable with values in $\mathcal{H}$. Assume $\mathbb{E}\left[\|Z\|^2\right] \leq \infty$, and let C be the covariance operator of Z. For an i.i.d. sample*[2] *$Z_1, \ldots, Z_n$, denote by C_n the associated empirical covariance operator. Let $B_\alpha = \{\|v\| \leq \alpha\}$, $\mathcal{E}_r = \{\langle v, Cv\rangle \leq r\}$ and $\mathcal{E}_{n,r} = \{\langle v, C_n v\rangle \leq r\}$. We have*

$$\mathbb{E}_\varepsilon\left[\sup_{v\in B_\alpha\cap\mathcal{E}_{n,r}} \frac{1}{n}\sum_{i=1}^n \varepsilon_i\langle v, Z_i\rangle\right] \leq \frac{1}{\sqrt{n}} \inf_{0\leq h\leq n}\left\{\sqrt{hr} + \alpha\sqrt{\sum_{j=h+1}^n \lambda_j(C_n)}\right\}, \quad (7)$$

and

$$\mathbb{E}\left[\sup_{v\in B_\alpha\cap\mathcal{E}_r} \frac{1}{n}\sum_{i=1}^n \varepsilon_i\langle v, Z_i\rangle\right] \leq \frac{1}{\sqrt{n}} \inf_{h\geq 0}\left\{\sqrt{hr} + \alpha\sqrt{\sum_{j\geq h+1} \lambda_j(C)}\right\}. \quad (8)$$

Proof. We will only prove (8), the same argument gives (7). Let $(\Phi_i)_{i\geq 1}$ be an orthonormal basis of $\mathcal{H}$ of eigenvectors of C. Define $p = \min\{\mathrm{i} : \lambda_\mathrm{i}(\mathrm{C}) = 0\}$. If we prove the result for $h < p$ we are done, so we assume $h < p$. For $v \in B_\alpha \cap \mathcal{E}_r$, we have

$$\begin{aligned}\sum_{i=1}^n \varepsilon_i\langle v, Z_i\rangle &= \left\langle \sum_{j=1}^h \langle v, \Phi_j\rangle \Phi_j, \sum_{i=1}^n \varepsilon_i Z_i\right\rangle + \left\langle v, \sum_{j>h}\left\langle \sum_{i=1}^n \varepsilon_i Z_i, \Phi_j\right\rangle \Phi_j\right\rangle \\ &\leq \sqrt{r\sum_{i=1}^h \frac{1}{\lambda_i(C)}\langle\sum_{j=1}^n \varepsilon_j Z_j, \Phi_i\rangle^2} + \alpha\sqrt{\sum_{i\geq h+1}\langle\sum_{j=1}^n \varepsilon_j Z_j, \Phi_i\rangle^2},\end{aligned}$$

where we used Cauchy-Schwarz inequality and $\langle v, Cv\rangle = \sum_{i\geq 1}\lambda_i(C)\langle v, \Phi_i\rangle^2$. Moreover

$$\frac{1}{n}\mathbb{E}\langle\sum_{j=1}^n \varepsilon_j Z_j, \Phi_i\rangle^2 = \mathbb{E}\left[\langle Z, \Phi_i\rangle^2\right] = \langle\Phi_i, C\Phi_i\rangle = \lambda_i(C).$$

We finally obtain (8) by Jensen's inequality. □

[2] The result also holds if the Z_i are not independent but have the same distribution.

Notice that Mendelson [14] shows that these upper bounds cannot be improved. We also need the following lemma. Recall that a sub-root function [2] is a non-decreasing non-negative function on $[0, \infty)$ such that $\psi(x)/\sqrt{(x)}$ is non-increasing.

Lemma 4. *Under the conditions of Theorem 8, denoting by ψ the function*

$$\psi(r) := \frac{1}{\sqrt{n}} \inf_{h \geq 0} \left\{ \sqrt{hr} + \alpha \sqrt{\sum_{j \geq h+1} \lambda_j(C)} \right\},$$

we have that ψ is a sub-root function and the unique positive solution r^* of $\psi(r) = r/c$ where $c > 0$ satisfies

$$r^* \leq \inf_{h \geq 0} \left\{ \frac{c^2 h}{n} + \frac{2c\alpha}{\sqrt{n}} \sqrt{\sum_{j \geq h+1} \lambda_j(C)} \right\}$$

Proof. It is easy to see that the minimum of two sub-root functions is sub-root, hence ψ as the minimum of a collection of sub-root function is sub-root. Existence and uniqueness of a solution is proved in [2]. To compute it, we use the fact that $x \leq A\sqrt{x} + B$ implies $x \leq A^2 + 2B$.

We finish this section with two corollaries of Theorem 8 and Lemma 4.

Corollary 2. *Define* $\mathcal{W}_d = \left\{ V \in \mathcal{V}_d : \mathbb{E} \left\langle \Pi_{V^\perp} - \Pi_{V_d^\perp}, C_X \right\rangle^2 \leq r \right\}$, *then*

$$\mathbb{E}\left[\sup_{V \in \mathcal{W}_d} \frac{1}{n} \sum_{i=1}^{n} \varepsilon_i \left\langle \Pi_{V^\perp} - \Pi_{V_d^\perp}, C_{X_i} \right\rangle \right] \leq \sqrt{\frac{1}{n}} \inf_{h \geq 0} \left\{ \sqrt{rh} + 2\sqrt{d \sum_{j > h} \lambda_j(K_2)} \right\}$$

Proof. This is a consequence of Theorem 8 since $\|\Pi_V - \Pi_{V_d}\|^2_{\mathrm{HS}(\mathcal{H}_k)} \leq 4d$, so that for $V \in \mathcal{W}_d$, $P_V \in B_{4d} \cap \mathcal{E}_r$ with $\mathcal{E}_r = \{v \in \mathrm{HS}(\mathcal{H}_k), \langle v, C_2 v\rangle_{\mathrm{HS}(\mathcal{H}_k)} \leq r\}$. □

Corollary 3. *Define* $\widetilde{\mathcal{W}_d} = \left\{ V \in \mathcal{V}_d : \mathbb{E} \left\langle P_V, C_X \right\rangle^2 \leq r \right\}$ *then,*

$$\mathbb{E}\left[\sup_{V \in \widetilde{\mathcal{W}_d}} \frac{1}{n} \sum_{i=1}^{n} \varepsilon_i \left\langle \Pi_V, C_{X_i} \right\rangle \right] \leq \sqrt{\frac{1}{n}} \inf_{h \geq 0} \left(\sqrt{rh} + \sqrt{d \sum_{k \geq h+1} \lambda_k(K_2)} \right).$$

Proof. Use the same proof as in Corollary 2. □

B Proofs

Proof (of Theorem 1). Then $\Phi(X)$ is a random element of $\mathcal{H}$. By assumption, each element $h \in \mathcal{H}$ can be identified to a measurable function $x \mapsto \langle f, \Phi(x) \rangle$.

Also, if $\mathbb{E}[\|\Phi(X)\|] < \infty$, $\Phi(X)$ has an expectation which we denote by $\mathbb{E}[\Phi(X)] \in \mathcal{H}$. Consider the linear operator $T : \mathcal{H} \to L_2(P)$ defined as $(Th)(x) = \langle h, \Phi(x)\rangle_{\mathcal{H}}$. By Cauchy-Schwarz inequality, $\mathbb{E}\langle h, \Phi(X)\rangle^2 \leq \|h\|^2 \mathbb{E}\|\Phi(X)\|^2$. Thus, T is well-defined and continuous, thus it has a continuous adjoint T^*. Let $f \in L_2(P)$, then $(\mathbb{E}\|f(X)\Phi(X)\|)^2 \leq \|f\|^2 \mathbb{E}\|\Phi(X)\|^2$. So, the expectation of $f(X)\Phi(X) \in \mathcal{H}$ can be defined. But for all $g \in \mathcal{H}$, $\langle T^* f, g\rangle_{\mathcal{H}} = \langle f, Tg\rangle_{L_2(P)} = \mathbb{E}[\langle g, f(X)\Phi(X)\rangle_{\mathcal{H}}]$ which shows that $T^*(f) = \mathbb{E}[\Phi(X)f(X)]$.
We now prove that $C = T^*T$ and $K = TT^*$. By the definition of the expectation, for all $h, h' \in \mathcal{H}$, $\langle h, T^*T(h')\rangle = \langle h, \mathbb{E}[\Phi(X)\langle \Phi(X), h'\rangle]\rangle = \mathbb{E}[\langle h, \Phi(X)\rangle \langle h', \Phi(X)\rangle]$. Thus, by the uniqueness of a covariance operator, we get $C = T^*T$. Similarly $(TT^*f)(x) = \langle T^*f, \Phi(x)\rangle = \mathbb{E}[\langle f(X)\Phi(X), \Phi(x)\rangle] = \int f(y)\langle \Phi(y), \Phi(x)\rangle dP(y)$ so that $K = TT^*$. By singular value decomposition, it is easy to see that $\lambda(C) = \lambda(K)$ if T is a compact operator. Actually, T is Hilbert-Schimdt. Indeed, $\|T\|^2_{\mathrm{HS}(\mathcal{H})} = \sum_{i\geq 1}\|Te_i\|^2 = \sum_{i\geq 1}\mathbb{E}\left[\langle e_i, \Phi(X)\rangle^2\right] = \mathbb{E}\left[\|\Phi(X)\|^2\right]$. Hence, T is compact, C is trace-class ($\operatorname{tr} C = \|T\|^2_{\mathrm{HS}(\mathcal{H})}$) and since $\operatorname{tr} TT^* = \operatorname{tr} T^*T$, K is trace-class too. □

Proof (of Theorem 5). As in the proof of Theorem 4, we have to bound $\sup_{V\in\mathcal{V}_d}(P_n - P)\langle \Pi_V, C_X\rangle$. We will use a slight modification of Theorem 3.3 of [2]. It is easy to see that applying Lemma 3.4 of [2] to the class of functions $\{f' = -f; f \in \mathcal{F}\}$, with the assumption $T(f') \leq -BPf'$, one obtains (with the notations of this lemma),

$$Pf' \leq \frac{K}{K+1}P_n f' + \frac{r}{\lambda BK},$$

so that under the assumptions of Theorem 3.3, one can obtain the following version of the result

$$Pf' \leq \frac{K}{K+1}P_n f' + \frac{704K}{B}r^* + \frac{\xi(11(b-a) + 26BK)}{n},$$

which shows (for the initial class) that

$$P_n f \leq \frac{K+1}{K}Pf + \frac{704(K+1)}{B}r^* + \frac{\xi(11(b-a)(K+1)/K + 26B(K+1))}{n}.$$

We apply this result to the class of functions $x \mapsto \langle \Pi_V, C_x\rangle$ for $V \in \mathcal{V}_d$, which satisfies $P\langle \Pi_V, C_x\rangle^2 \leq MP\langle \Pi_V, C_x\rangle$, and $\langle \Pi_V, C_x\rangle \in [0, M]$, and use Lemma 4. We obtain that for all $\alpha > 0$ and $\xi > 0$, with probability at least $1 - e^{-\xi}$, every $V \in \mathcal{V}_d$ satisfies

$$P_n\langle \Pi_V, C_X\rangle \leq (1+\alpha)P\langle \Pi_V, C_X\rangle + 704(1+\alpha^{-1})r_d^* + \frac{M\xi(11(1+\alpha) + 26(1+\alpha^{-1}))}{n}.$$

where $r_d^* = \frac{r^*}{M}$ and $M\Psi_d(r^*) = r^*$. $\Psi_d(r)$ is the sub-root function that appeared in Corollary 3 This concludes the proof. Inequality (5) is a simple consequence of Bernstein's inequality. □

Proof (of Lemma 3). The first inequality is clear. For the second we start with

$$\mathbb{E}\left[\left\langle \Pi_{V^\perp} - \Pi_{V_d^\perp}, C_X \right\rangle^2\right] = \langle \Pi_{V_d} - \Pi_V, C_2 \Pi_{V_d} - \Pi_V \rangle_{\mathrm{HS}(\mathcal{H})}$$
$$\leq \|C_2\| \|\Pi_{V_d} - \Pi_V\|^2_{\mathrm{HS}(\mathcal{H})}$$
$$= 2\|C_2\| (d - \langle \Pi_V, \Pi_{V_d} \rangle_{\mathrm{HS}(\mathcal{H})}) . \quad (9)$$

By Lemma 1, $\mathbb{E}\left[\left\langle \Pi_{V^\perp} - \Pi_{V_d^\perp}, C_X \right\rangle\right] = \langle \Pi_{V_d} - \Pi_V, C_1 \rangle$. We now introduce an orthonormal basis $(f_i)_{i=1,\dots,d}$ of V and the orthonormal basis $(\phi_i)_{i=1,\dots,d}$ of the first d eigenvectors of C_1.
Moreover, we have

$$\langle \Pi_{V_d} - \Pi_V, C_1 \rangle = \sum_{i=1}^{d} \lambda_i(C_1) - \sum_{i=1}^{d} \langle f_i, C_1 f_i \rangle .$$

We decompose $f_i = \sum_{j=1}^{d} \langle f_i, \phi_j \rangle \phi_j + g_i$, where $g_i \in \mathrm{span}(\phi_1, \dots, \phi_d)^\perp$ so that

$$\langle f_i, C_1 f_i \rangle = \sum_{j=1}^{d} \lambda_j(C_1) \langle f_i, \phi_j \rangle^2 + \langle g_i, C_1 g_i \rangle ,$$

Theorem 3, implies $\langle g_i, C_1 g_i \rangle \leq \lambda_{d+1}(C_1)(1 - \sum_{j=1}^{d} \langle f_i, \phi_j \rangle^2)$, hence we get

$$\langle \Pi_{V_d} - \Pi_V, C_1 \rangle \geq \sum_{i=1}^{d} \lambda_i(C_1)(1 - \sum_{j=1}^{d} \langle f_j, \phi_i \rangle^2) - \lambda_{d+1}(C_1)(d - \sum_{i,j=1}^{d} \langle f_i, \phi_j \rangle^2) .$$

Using $1 - \sum_{j=1}^{d} \langle f_j, \phi_i \rangle^2 = \|\Pi_{V^\perp}(\phi_i)\|^2 \geq 0$, and the fact that the eigenvalues of C_1 are in a non-decreasing order we finally obtain

$$\langle \Pi_{V_d} - \Pi_V, C_1 \rangle \geq (\lambda_d(C_1) - \lambda_{d+1}(C_1))(d - \sum_{i,j=1}^{d} \langle f_i, \phi_j \rangle^2) . \quad (10)$$

Also we notice that $\|C_2\| \leq \|C_2\|_{\mathrm{HS}(\mathrm{HS}(\mathcal{H}_k))} = \|K_2\|_{\mathrm{HS}(L_2(P))}$ (by Lemma 1) and since K_2 is an integral operator with kernel $k^2(x,y)$, $\|K_2\|^2_{\mathrm{HS}(\mathrm{HS}(\mathcal{H}_k))} = \int k^4(x,y) dP(x) dP(y)$. Now, Equation (1) gives $\langle \Pi_V, \Pi_{V_d} \rangle_{\mathrm{HS}(\mathcal{H})} = \sum_{i,j=1}^{d} \langle f_i, \phi_j \rangle^2_{\mathcal{H}}$. Combining this with Inequalities (9) and (10) we get the result. □

Proof (of Theorem 7). We will apply Theorem 3.3 of [2] to the class of functions $f_V : x \mapsto \left\langle \Pi_{V^\perp} - \Pi_{V_d^\perp}, C_x \right\rangle$ for $V \in \mathcal{V}_d$ and taking $V = V_n$ will give the result. With the notations of [2], we set $T(f_V) = \mathbb{E}\left[f_V(X)^2\right]$ and by Lemma 3 we have $T(f_V) \leq B_d \mathbb{E}\left[f_V(X)\right]$. Also, $f_V(x) \in [-M, M]$. Moreover, we can upper bound the localized Rademacher averages of the class f_V using Corollary 2, which combined with Lemma 4 gives the result. □

Kernelizing Sorting, Permutation, and Alignment for Minimum Volume PCA

Tony Jebara

Columbia University, New York, NY 10027, USA
jebara@cs.columbia.edu

Abstract. We propose an algorithm for permuting or sorting multiple sets (or bags) of objects such that they can ultimately be represented efficiently using kernel principal component analysis. This framework generalizes sorting from scalars to arbitrary inputs since all computations involve inner products which can be done in Hilbert space and kernelized. The cost function on the permutations or orderings emerges from a maximum likelihood Gaussian solution which approximately minimizes the volume data occupies in Hilbert space. This ensures that few kernel principal components are necessary to capture the variation of the sets or bags. Both global and almost-global iterative solutions are provided in terms of iterative algorithms by interleaving variational bounding (on quadratic assignment problems) with a Kuhn-Munkres algorithm (for solving linear assignment problems).

1 Introduction

Sorting or ordering a set of objects is a useful task in practical unsupervised learning as well as in general computation. For instance, we may have a set of unordered words describing an individual's characteristics in paragraph form and we may wish to sort them in a consistent manner into fields such that the first field or word describes the individual's eye color, the second word describes his profession, the third word describes his gender, and so forth. Alternatively, as in Figure 1, we may want to sort or order dot-drawings of face images such that the first dot is consistently the tip of the nose, the second dot is the left eye, the third dot is the right eye and so forth. However, finding a meaningful way to sort or order sets of objects is awkward when the objects are not scalars (scalars can always be sorted using, e.g. quick-sort). We instead propose sorting many bags or sets of objects such that the resulting sorted versions of the bags are easily representable using a small number of kernel principal components. In other words, we will find the sorting or ordering of many bags of objects such that the manifold formed by these sorted bags of objects will have low dimensionality.

In this article, we refer to sorting or ordering in the relative sense of the word and seek the relative ordering between objects in two or more unordered sets. This is equivalent to finding the correspondence between multiple sets of objects. A classical incarnation of the correspondence task (also referred to as

J. Shawe-Taylor and Y. Singer (Eds.): COLT 2004, LNAI 3120, pp. 609–623, 2004.

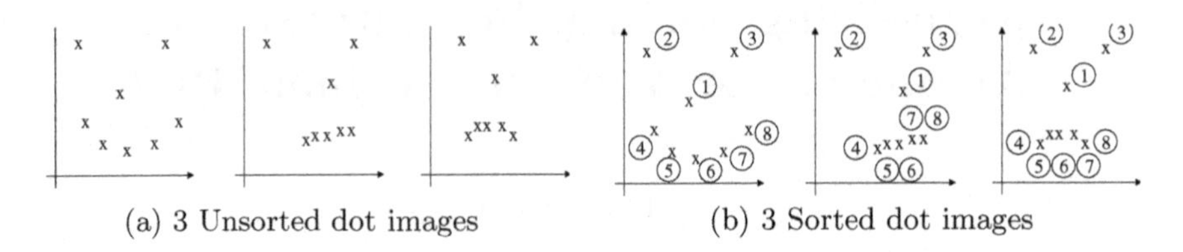

(a) 3 Unsorted dot images (b) 3 Sorted dot images

Fig. 1. Sorting or matching of 3 bags of 8 (x, y) coordinates representing faces.

matching, permutation or ordering between sets) is the so-called linear assignment problem (LAP). A familiar example of LAP is in an auction or garage-sale where N goods are available and N consumers each attribute a value to each good. This solution to LAP is the the best pairing of each consumer to a single good such that the total value obtained is maximal. This is solvable using the classical Kuhn-Munkres algorithm in $O(N^3)$ time. Kuhn-Munkres provides a permutation matrix capturing the relative ordering between the two sets (goods and consumers).

Recent efficient variants of Kuhn-Munkres make it practical to apply to bags of thousands of objects [3]. Alternatively, relaxations of LAP have been proposed including the so-called invisible hand algorithm [8]. These tools have been used for finding correspondence and aligning images of, for instance, digits [2,14] to obtain better models (such as morphable or corresponded models). In fact, handling permutable or unordered sets is relevant for learning and image classification as well. For example, permutable images and other objects have been handled via permutationally invariant kernels for support vector machine classifiers [7] or permutationally invariant expectation-maximization frameworks [6]. It is known that removing invariant aspects of input data (such as permutation) can improve a learning method [13]. Another approach is to explicitly estimate the ordering or permutation by minimizing the number of principal components needed to linearly model the variation of many sets or bags of objects [5,4].

In this paper, we build up a novel algorithm starting from the Kuhn-Munkres algorithm. Kuhn-Munkres sorts only a pair of bags or sets containing N vector-objects such that we minimize their squared norm. Our novel algorithm upgrades the search for an ordering from two bags to many simultaneous bags of objects by iterating the Kuhn-Munkres algorithm with variational bounds. The iterations either minimize the squared norm from all sorted bags to a common "mean bag" or minimize the dimensionality of the resulting manifold of sorted bags. These two criteria correspond to a generalization of the linear assignment problem and to the quadratic assignment problem, respectively. Both are handled via iterative solutions of the Kuhn-Munkres algorithm (or fast variants). We also kernelize the Kuhn-Munkres algorithm such that non-vectorial objects [11] can also be ordered or sorted.

2 Permuting Several Sets

Consider a dataset $\mathcal{D}$ of T sets or bags $\mathcal{D} = \{\chi_t\}_{t=1}^T$. Each of these bags is merely a collection of N unordered objects $\chi_t = \{\gamma_{t,n}\}_{n=1}^N$. We wish to find an ordering for objects in these bags that makes sense according to some fairly general criterion. However, in the general case of bags over unusual objects (vectors, strings, graphs, etc.) it is not clear that a natural notion of ordering exists a priori. We will exploit kernels since they have been shown to handle a diverse range of input spaces. If our sorting algorithms leverage these by exclusively using generalized inner products within sorting computations we would be able to sort a variety of non-scalar objects. We therefore propose another criterion for sorting that finds orderings. The criterion is that the resulting ordered bags can be *efficiently* encoded using principal components analysis (PCA) or kernel principal component analysis (kPCA) [12]. Essentially, we want kPCA to capture the variation seen in the dataset with as few dimensions as possible.

We will eventually deal with non-vectorial objects but for simplicity, we could assume that all bags simply contain N vectors of dimensionality D. Thus, we assume each $\gamma_{t,n} \in \mathbb{R}^D$ and we can rewrite each bag χ_t in an $N \times D$ matrix form as X_t. Our dataset of many bags can then be stored as T matrices and consists of $\{X_t\}_{t=1}^T$. To reorder each of these bags, we consider endowing each matrix X_t with an unknown $N \times N$ permutation matrix A_t which re-sorts its N row entries. Therefore, we augment our dataset with matrices that re-sort it as follows $\{A_t X_t\}_{t=1}^T$. In the more general case where we are not dealing with vectors for each $\gamma_{t,n}$, we will take the permutation matrices A_t to be a general permutation p_t of the set $\{1, \ldots, N\}$ which defines an ordering of the bag as follows $p_t \otimes \chi_t = \left(\gamma_{t,p_t(n)}\right)_{n=1}^N$. This gives us an ordered version of the dataset for a specific configuration of orderings denoted P which we write as follows $\mathcal{D}_P = \{p_t \otimes \chi_t\}_{t=1}^T$.

Given the original dataset, we want to find a *good* permutation configuration by optimizing the matrices $\{A_t\}_{t=1}^T$ or the permutation configurations $\{p_t\}_{t=1}^T$. To make the notion of goodness of permutation configurations concrete, we will argue that good permutations will reveal a compact low-dimensional representation of the data. For instance, the data may lie on a low dimensional manifold that is much smaller than the embedding space of size ND or $N|\gamma_{t,n}|$, where $|\gamma_{t,n}|$ is the dimensionality of the objects being permuted (if and when such a quantity makes sense). We now elaborate how to approximately measure the dimensionality of the potentially nonlinear manifold spanning the data. This is done by observing the eigenvalue spectrum of kernel PCA which approximates the volume data occupies in Hilbert space. Clearly, a low volume suggests that we are dealing with a low dimensional manifold in Hilbert space.

2.1 Kernel PCA and Gaussians in Hilbert Space

We subscribe to the perspective that PCA finds a subspace from data by modeling it as a degenerate Gaussian since only first and second order statistics of a dataset $\{x_t\}_{t=1}^T$ are computed [7]. Similarly, kernel PCA finds a subspace in

Hilbert space by only looking at first and second order statistics of the feature vectors $\{\phi(x_t)\}_{t=1}^T$ instead[1]. In fact, we are also restricted to second order statistics since we wish to use kernel methods and can thus only interact with data in Hilbert space via inner-products $k(x_t, x_{t'}) = \langle \phi(x_t), \phi(x_{t'}) \rangle$.

One way to evaluate the quality of a subspace discovered by kernel PCA is by estimating the volume occupied by the data. In cases where the volume of the data in Hilbert space is low, we anticipate that only a few kernel principal components will be necessary to span and reconstruct the dataset. Since kernel PCA hinges on Gaussian statistics, we will only use a second order estimator of the volume of our dataset. Consider computing the mean and covariance of a Gaussian from the dataset in Hilbert space. In kernel PCA [12], recall that the top eigenvalues of the covariance matrix $\Sigma = \frac{1}{T}\sum_t \phi(x_t)\phi(x_t)^T$ of the data are related to the top eigenvalues of the $T \times T$ Gram matrix K of the data which is defined element-wise as $[K]_{t,t'} = k(x_t, x_{t'})$. The eigenvalues λ and eigenvectors $\boldsymbol{\alpha}$ of the Gram matrix are given by the solution to the problem:

$$\begin{bmatrix} \langle k_{x_1}, k_{x_1} \rangle & \cdots & \langle k_{x_1}, k_{x_T} \rangle \\ \vdots & & \vdots \\ \langle k_{x_T}, k_{x_1} \rangle & \cdots & \langle k_{x_T}, k_{x_T} \rangle \end{bmatrix} \begin{bmatrix} \alpha_1 \\ \vdots \\ \alpha_T \end{bmatrix} = T\lambda \begin{bmatrix} \alpha_1 \\ \vdots \\ \alpha_T \end{bmatrix}.$$

From the above, we find the top J eigenvectors $\boldsymbol{\alpha}^j$ which produce the highest J eigenvalues and approximate the dataset with a J-dimensional nonlinear manifold. The eigenfunctions $v^j(x)$ of the covariance matrix describe axes of variation on the manifold and are unit-norm functions approximated by:

$$v^j(x) \propto \sum_{t=1}^T \alpha_t^j k(x, x_t).$$

These are normalized such that $\langle v^j, v^j \rangle = 1$. The spectrum of eigenvalues describes the overall shape of a Gaussian model of the data in Hilbert space while the eigenvectors of the covariance matrix capture the Gaussian's orientation. The volume of the data can then be approximated by the determinant of the covariance matrix which equals the product of its eigenvalues λ^j.

$$\text{Volume} \approx |\Sigma| = \prod_j \lambda^j.$$

If we are dealing with a truly low-dimensional subspace, only a few eigenvalues (corresponding to eigenvectors spanning the manifold) will be large. The many remaining eigenvalues corresponding to noise off of the manifold will be small and the volume we ultimately estimate by multiplying all these eigenvalues will be

[1] While this Hilbert space could potentially be infinite dimensional and Gaussians and kernel PCA should be handled more formally (i.e. using Gaussian processes with white noise and appropriate operators) in this paper and for our purposes we will assume we are manipulating only finite-dimensional Hilbert spaces. Formalising the extensions to infinite Hilbert space is straightforward.

low[2]. Thus, a kernel PCA manifold that is low-dimensional should typically have low volume. It is well known that kernel PCA can also be (implicitly) centered by estimating and removing the mean of the data yet we will not elaborate this straightforward issue (refer instead to [12]). Before applying PCA, recall that we perform maximum likelihood estimation to obtain the mean $\hat{\mu}$ and the covariance $\hat{\Sigma}$. The volume of the dataset is related to its log-likelihood under the maximum likelihood estimate of a Gaussian model as shown in [4]:

$$\begin{aligned} l(\mu, \Sigma) &= \sum_t \log \mathcal{N}(x_t|\mu, \Sigma) \\ &= -\frac{TD}{2}\log(2\pi) - \frac{T}{2}\log|\Sigma| - \frac{1}{2}\sum_t (x_t-\mu)^T \Sigma^{-1}(x_t-\mu). \end{aligned}$$

Log-likelihood simplifies as follows when we use the maximum likelihood setting for the mean $\hat{\mu} = \frac{1}{T}\sum_t x_t$ and covariance $\hat{\Sigma} = \frac{1}{T}\sum_t (x_t - \hat{\mu})(x_t - \hat{\mu})^T$.

$$l(\hat{\mu}, \hat{\Sigma}) = -\frac{TD}{2}\log(2\pi) - \frac{T}{2}\log|\hat{\Sigma}| - \frac{TD}{2}.$$

Therefore, we can see that a kernel PCA solution which has high log-likelihood according to the Gaussian mean and covariance will also have low volume low $\log|\hat{\Sigma}|$ and produce a compact low-dimensional manifold requiring few principal axis to span the data.

2.2 Permutations That Maximize Likelihood and Minimize Volume

We saw that we are solving a maximum likelihood problem to perform kernel PCA and higher likelihoods indicate lower volume and a better subspace. However, the above formulation assumes we have vectors or can readily compute kernels or inner products between kPCA's T Hilbert-space vectors $\{\phi(x_t)\}_{t=1}^T$. This is not trivial when each x_t is actually an unordered bag of tuples as we had when we were previously dealing with χ_t. However, given an ordering of each via A_t matrices or p_t permutations, we can consider computing a kernel on the sorted bags as follows:

$$k(p_t \otimes \chi_t, p_t \otimes \chi_{t'}) = \sum_{i=1}^N \langle \phi(\gamma_{t,p_t(i)}), \phi(\gamma_{t',p_{t'}(i)}) \rangle = \sum_{i=1}^N \kappa(\gamma_{t,p_t(i)}, \gamma_{t',p_{t'}(i)})$$

assuming we have defined a base kernel $\kappa(.,.)$ between the actual objects $\gamma_{t,n}$ in our bags. Another potentially clearer view of the above is to instead assume we have bags of Hilbert-space vectors where our dataset $\mathcal{D}$ has T of these sets or bags $\mathcal{D} = \{\Phi_t\}_{t=1}^T$. Each of these bags is merely a collection of N unordered objects in Hilbert space $\Phi_t = \{\phi(\gamma_{t,n})\}_{n=1}^N$. Applying the ordering p_t to this

[2] Here we are assuming that we do not obtain any zero-valued eigenvalues which produce a degenerate estimate of volume. We will regularize eigenvalues in the subsequent sections to avoid this problem.

unordered bag of Hilbert space vectors provides an ordered set as follows $p_t \otimes \Phi_t = \left(\phi(\gamma_{t,p_t(n)})\right)_{n=1}^{N}$. Inner products between two ordered bags are again given in terms of the base kernel $\kappa(.,.)$ as follows:

$$\langle p_t \otimes \Phi_t, p_t' \otimes \Phi_t' \rangle = \sum_{i=1}^{N} \langle \phi(\gamma_{t,p_t(i)}), \phi(\gamma_{t',p_{t'}(i)}) \rangle = \sum_{i=1}^{N} \kappa(\gamma_{t,p_t(i)}, \gamma_{t',p_{t'}(i)}).$$

As in [4] we will find settings of A_t or p_t that maximize likelihood under a Gaussian model to minimize volume. However, instead of directly minimizing the volume by assuming we always have updated the mean and covariance with their maximum likelihood setting, we will treat the problem as an iterative likelihood maximization scheme. We have the following log-likelihood problem which we argued measures the volume of the data at the maximum likelihood estimate of μ and Σ:

$$l(p_1, \ldots, p_T, \mu, \Sigma) = \sum_t l_t(p_t, \mu, \Sigma) = \sum_t \log \mathcal{N}(p_t \otimes \Phi_t | \mu, \Sigma).$$

Further increasing likelihood by adjusting $p_1, \ldots, p_T$ will also further decrease volume as we interleave updates of μ and Σ. Thus, the above is an objective function on permutations and maximizing it should produce an ordering of our bags that keeps kernel PCA efficient. Here, we are assuming we have a Gaussian in Hilbert space yet it is not immediately clear how to maximize or evaluate the above objective function and obtain permutation configurations that give low-volume kernel PCA manifolds. We will next elaborate this and show that all computations are straightforward to perform in Hilbert space.

We will maximize likelihood over $p_1, \ldots, p_T$, μ and Σ iteratively in an axis-parallel manner. This is done by locking all parameters of the log-likelihood and modifying a single one at a time. Note, first, that it is straightforward, given a current setting of $(p_1, \ldots, p_T)$ to compute the maximum likelihood μ and Σ as the mean and covariance in Hilbert space. Now, assume we have locked μ and Σ at a current setting and we wish to only increase likelihood by adjusting the permutation p_t of a single bag Φ_t. We investigate two separate cases. In the first case, we assume the covariance matrix Σ is locked at a scalar times identity and we find the optimal update for a given p_t by solving a linear assignment problem. We will then consider the more general case where the current Σ covariance matrix in Hilbert space is an arbitrary positive semi-definite matrix and updating the current p_t will involve solving a quadratic assignment problem.

3 Kernelized Sorting Via LAP and Mean Alignment

Given μ, $p_1, \ldots, p_T$ and $\Sigma = \sigma I$ we wish to find a setting of p_t which maximizes the likelihood of an isotropic Gaussian. This clearly involves only maximizing the following contribution of bag t to the total log-likelihood:

$$l_t(p_t, \mu, \Sigma) = \log \mathcal{N}(p_t \otimes \Phi_t | \mu, \sigma I).$$

We can simplify the above as follows:

$$l_t(p_t, \mu, \Sigma) = \text{const} - \frac{1}{2\sigma} \left(\langle p_t \otimes \Phi_t, p_t \otimes \Phi_t \rangle - 2 \langle p_t \otimes \Phi_t, \mu \rangle + \langle \mu, \mu \rangle \right).$$

Since $\langle p_t \otimes \Phi_t, p_t \otimes \Phi_t \rangle$ is constant despite our choice of p_t, maximizing the above over p_t is equivalent to minimizing the following cost function:

$$\hat{p}_t = \arg\min_{p_t} \langle p_t \otimes \Phi_t, \mu \rangle .$$

Assume we have the current maximum likelihood mean which is computed from the locked permutation configurations from the previous iteration $\hat{p}_1, \ldots, \hat{p}_T$. The above then simplifies into:

$$\hat{p}_t = \arg\min_{p_t} \left\langle p_t \otimes \Phi_t, \frac{1}{T} \sum_{t'=1}^{T} \hat{p}_{t'} \otimes \Phi_{t'} \right\rangle = \arg\min_{p_t} \sum_{i=1}^{N} \sum_{t'=1}^{T} \kappa \left(\gamma_{t,p_t(i)}, \gamma_{t',\hat{p}_{t'}(i)} \right).$$

The above problem is an instance of the linear assignment problem (LAP) and can directly be solved producing the optimal p_t in $O(N^3)$ via the Kuhn-Munkres algorithm (or more efficient variants such as QuickMatch [10], auction algorithms or the cost scaling algorithm). Essentially, we find the permutation matrix A_t which is analogous to p_t by solving the assignment problem on the $N \times N$ matrix D_t via a simple call to the (standard) function KuhnMunkres($-D_t$) where D_t is an $N \times N$ matrix giving the value of kernel evaluations between items in the current bag and the mean bag. We define the D_t matrix element-wise as:

$$[D_t]_{i,i'} = \sum_{t'=1}^{T} \kappa \left(\gamma_{t,i}, \gamma_{t',\hat{p}_{t'}(i')} \right).$$

Iterating the update of each p_t in this way for $t = 1 \ldots T$ and updating the mean μ repeatedly by its maximum likelihood estimate will converge to a maximum of the log-likelihood. While a formal proof is deferred in this paper, this maximum may actually be global since the above problem is analogous to the generalized Procrustes problem [1]. In the general Procrustes setting, we can mimic the problem of aligning or permuting many bags towards a common mean by instead computing the alignments or permutations between all possible pairs of bags. For instance, it is possible to find permutations $p_{t,t'}$ or matrices $A_{t,t'}$ that align each bag χ_t to any other bag $\chi_{t'}$ via $[D_{t,t'}]_{i,i'} = \kappa(\gamma_{t,i}, \gamma_{t',i'})$. These then give a consistent set of permutations to align the data towards a common mean prior to kernel PCA. This provides us with the ordering $\hat{p}_1, \ldots, \hat{p}_T$ of the data which now becomes a dataset of ordered bags $\{\hat{p}_t \otimes \Phi_t\}_{t=1}^{T}$. Subsequently, we perform kernel PCA on the data in $O(T^3)$ using singular value decomposition on the $T \times T$ centered Gram matrix. This gives the eigenvectors, eigenvalues and eigenfunctions that span the nonlinear manifold representation of the ordered data. This will have a higher likelihood and potentially use fewer principal components to achieve the same reconstruction accuracy than immediate application of kernel PCA on the dataset $\mathcal{D}$. Of course, this argument only holds if the dataset itself truly has a natural permutation invariance or was a collection of sets or bags.

We now turn to the more general case where the Gaussian covariance is arbitrary and is not artificially locked at a spherical configuration. However, in this setting, global convergence claims are even more elusive.

4 Kernelized Sorting Via QAP and Covariance Alignment

In the case where we consider anisotropic Gaussians, the covariance matrix is an arbitrary positive semi-definite matrix and we have a more involved procedure for updating a given p_t. However, this is more closely matched to the full problem of minimizing the volume of the data and should produce more valuable orderings that further reduce the number of kernel principal components we need to represent the ordered bags. Here, we are updating a single p_t again yet the covariance matrix Σ is not a scaled identity. We therefore have the following contribution of bag t to the log-likelihood objective function:

$$l_t(p_t, \mu, \Sigma) = \log \mathcal{N}(p_t \otimes \Phi_t | \mu, \Sigma).$$

Due to the presence of the Σ, this will no longer reduce to a simple linear assignment problem that is directly solvable for A_t or $\hat{p}_t$ using a polynomial time algorithm. In fact, this objective will produce an NP-Complete quadratic assignment problem [9]. Instead we will describe an iterative technique for maximizing the likelihood over p_t by using a variational upper bound on the objective function.

Define the inverse matrix $M = \Sigma^{-1}$ which we will assume has actually been regularized as follows $M = (\Sigma + \epsilon_1 I)^{-1} + \epsilon_2 I$ where ϵ_1 and ϵ_2 are small scalars (the intuition for this regularization is given in [5]). Recall kernel PCA (with abuse of notation) gives the matrix Σ as follows $\Sigma = \sum_j \lambda^j v^j (v^j)^T$. Meanwhile, the matrix M can also be expressed with abuse of notation in terms of its eigenvalues $\tilde{\lambda}_k$ and eigenfunctions v^j from as follows $M = \sum_{j=1}^{J} \tilde{\lambda}^j v^j (v^j)^T + \sigma I$. We can assume we pick a finite J that is sufficiently large to have a faithful approximation to M. Recall that, as in kernel PCA, the (unnormalized) eigenfunctions are given by the previous estimate of the inverse covariance at the previous (locked) estimates of the permutations $\hat{p}_t$:

$$\left\langle v^j, p \otimes \Phi \right\rangle = \sum_{t=1}^{T} \alpha_t^j \left\langle p \otimes \Phi, \hat{p}_t \otimes \Phi_t \right\rangle$$

where the normalization such that $\left\langle v^j, v^j \right\rangle = 1$ is absorbed into the $\tilde{\lambda}^j$ for brevity. We can now rewrite the (slightly regularized) log-likelihood more succinctly by noting that μ and Σ are locked (thus some terms become mere constants):

$$\begin{aligned} l_t(p_t) &= \text{const} - \frac{1}{2}(p_t \otimes \Phi_t - \mu)^T M (p_t \otimes \Phi_t - \mu) \\ &= \text{const} - \frac{1}{2}(p_t \otimes \Phi_t)^T M (p_t \otimes \Phi_t) + (p_t \otimes \Phi_t)^T M \mu \\ &= \text{const} - \frac{1}{2}(p_t \otimes \Phi_t)^T \sum_{j=1}^{J} \tilde{\lambda}^j v^j (v^j)^T (p_t \otimes \Phi_t) + (p_t \otimes \Phi_t)^T M \mu \end{aligned}$$

where we have used the expanded definition of the M matrix yet its isotropic contribution σI as before has no effect on the quadratic term involving p_t. However, the anisotropic contribution remains and we have a QAP problem which we continue simplifying by writing the eigenvectors as linear combinations of Hilbert space vectors or kernel functions:

$$l_t(p_t) = \text{const} - \frac{1}{2}\sum_{j=1}^{J}\tilde{\lambda}^j\left(\sum_{m=1}^{T}\alpha_m^j\left\langle p_t\otimes\Phi_t,\hat{p}_m\otimes\Phi_m\right\rangle\right)^2$$

$$+\sum_{j=1}^{J}\tilde{\lambda}^j\sum_{m=1}^{T}\alpha_m^j\left\langle p_t\otimes\Phi_t,\hat{p}_m\otimes\Phi_m\right\rangle\sum_{n=1}^{T}\alpha_n^j\left\langle\mu,\hat{p}_n\otimes\Phi_n\right\rangle+\sigma\left\langle p_t\otimes\Phi_t,\mu\right\rangle.$$

For notational convenience, exchange the p_t notation and start using the permutation matrix notation A_t by noting the following relationship:

$$\left\langle p_t\otimes\Phi_t,\hat{p}_{t'}\otimes\Phi_{t'}\right\rangle=\sum_{i=1}^{N}\sum_{i'=1}^{N}[A_t]_{i,i'}\kappa(\gamma_{t,i},\gamma_{t',\hat{p}_{t'}(i')}).$$

We can now rewrite the (negated) log-likelihood term as a cost function $C(A_t)\equiv -l(A_t)$ over the space of permutation matrices A_t. This cost function is as follows after we drop some trivial constant terms:

$$C(A_t)=\sum_{j=1}^{J}\frac{\tilde{\lambda}^j}{2}\left(\sum_{i=1}^{N}\sum_{i'=1}^{N}[A_t]_{i,i'}\sum_{m=1}^{T}\alpha_m^j\kappa(\gamma_{t,i},\gamma_{m,\hat{p}_m(i')})\right)^2-\sum_{i=1}^{N}\sum_{i'=1}^{N}[A_t]_{i,i'}[D_t]_{i,i'}$$

where we have defined the readily computable $N\times N$ matrix D_t element-wise as follows for brevity:

$$[D_t]_{i,i'}=\sum_{j=1}^{J}\tilde{\lambda}^j\sum_{m=1}^{T}\alpha_m^j\kappa(\gamma_{t,i},\gamma_{m,\hat{p}_m(i')})\left(\sum_{n=1}^{T}\alpha_n^j\left\langle\mu,\hat{p}_n\otimes\Phi_n\right\rangle\right)$$

$$+\frac{\sigma}{T}\sum_{t'=1}^{T}\kappa(\gamma_{t,i},\gamma_{t',\hat{p}'_t(i')}).$$

This matrix degenerates to the previous isotropic case if all anisotropic Lagrange multipliers go to zero leaving only the σI contribution. Note, we can fill in the terms in the parentheses as follows:

$$\left\langle\mu,\hat{p}_n\otimes\Phi_n\right\rangle=\frac{1}{T}\sum_{t'=1}^{T}\left\langle\hat{p}_{t'}\otimes\Phi_{t'},\hat{p}_n\otimes\Phi_n\right\rangle=\frac{1}{T}\sum_{t'=1}^{T}\sum_{i=1}^{N}\kappa(\gamma_{n,\hat{p}_n(i)},\gamma_{t',\hat{p}_{t'}(i)})$$

which lets us numerically compute the D_t matrix's $N\times N$ entries.

Clearly the first term in $C(A_t)$ is quadratic in the permutation matrix A_t while the second term in $C(A_t)$ is linear in the permutation matrix. Therefore, the second LAP term could be optimized using a Kuhn-Munkres algorithm however, the full cost function is a quadratic assignment problem. To address this issue, we will upper bound the first quadratic cost term with a linear term such that we can minimize $C(A_t)$ iteratively using repeated applications of Kuhn-Munkres. This approach to solving QAP iteratively via bounding and LAP is similar in spirit to the well-known Gilmore-Lawler bound method as well as other techniques in the literature [9].

First, we construct an upper bound on the cost by introducing two $J \times N$ matrices called Q and $\tilde{Q}$. The entries of both Q and $\tilde{Q}$ are non-negative and have the property that summing across their columns gives unity as follows:

$$\sum_i [Q]_{j,i} = 1 \quad \text{and} \quad \sum_{i'} [\tilde{Q}]_{j,i'} = 1.$$

We insert the ratio of a convex combination of these two matrices (weighted by a positive scalar $\delta^j \in [0,1]$) into our cost such that $C(A_t) =$

$$\sum_{j=1}^{J} \frac{\tilde{\lambda}^j}{2} \left(\sum_{i=1}^{N} \sum_{i'=1}^{N} [A_t]_{i,i'} \frac{\delta^j [Q]_{j,i} + (1-\delta^j)[\tilde{Q}]_{j,i'}}{\delta^j [Q]_{j,i} + (1-\delta^j)[\tilde{Q}]_{j,i'}} \sum_{m=1}^{T} \alpha_m^j \kappa(\gamma_{t,i}, \gamma_{m,\hat{p}_m(i')}) \right)^2 - \sum_{i=1}^{N} \sum_{i'=1}^{N} [A_t]_{i,i'} [D_t]_{i,i'}.$$

Note that this in no way changes the cost function, we are merely multiplying each entry of the matrix A_t by unity. Next recall that the squaring function $f(x) = x^2$ is convex and we can therefore apply Jensen's inequality to pull terms out of it. We first recognize that we have a convex combination within the squaring since:

$$\sum_{i=1}^{N} \sum_{i'=1}^{N} [A_t]_{i,i'} \left(\delta^j [Q]_{j,i} + (1-\delta^j)[\tilde{Q}]_{j,i'} \right) = \delta^j + (1-\delta^j) = 1 \quad \forall\, j.$$

Therefore, we can proceed with Jensen to obtain the upper bound on cost as follows, $C(A_t) \leq$

$$\sum_{j=1}^{J} \frac{\tilde{\lambda}^j}{2} \sum_{i=1}^{N} \sum_{i'=1}^{N} [A_t]_{i,i'} \left(\delta^j [Q]_{j,i} + (1-\delta^j)[\tilde{Q}]_{j,i'} \right) \left(\frac{\sum_{m=1}^{T} \alpha_m^j \kappa(\gamma_{t,i}, \gamma_{m,\hat{p}_m(i')})}{\delta^j [Q]_{j,i} + (1-\delta^j)[\tilde{Q}]_{j,i'}} \right)^2 - \sum_{i=1}^{N} \sum_{i'=1}^{N} [A_t]_{i,i'} [D_t]_{i,i'}.$$

The above bound is actually just a linear assignment problem (LAP) which we write succinctly as follows:

$$C(A_t) \leq \sum_{i=1}^{N} \sum_{i'=1}^{N} [A_t]_{i,i'} \left[\sum_{j=1}^{J} \frac{\tilde{\lambda}^j}{2} \frac{\left(\sum_{m=1}^{T} \alpha_m^j \kappa(\gamma_{t,i}, \gamma_{m,\hat{p}_m(i')}) \right)^2}{\delta^j [Q]_{j,i} + (1-\delta^j)[\tilde{Q}]_{j,i'}} - [D_t]_{i,i'} \right].$$

The above upper bound can immediately be minimized over permutation matrices and gives A_t via a Kuhn-Munkres computation or some variant. However, we would need to actually specify Q, $\tilde{Q}$ and all the δ^j for this computation. In fact, the right hand side is a variational LAP bound over our original QAP with the (augmented parameters) over Q, $\tilde{Q}$, $\boldsymbol{\delta} = (\delta^1, \ldots, \delta^J)$ and A_t which can each be iteratively minimized. Thus, we anticipate repeatedly minimizing over A_t using Kuhn-Munkres operations followed by updates of the remaining bound parameters given a current setting of A_t. Note, the left term in the square bracket is constant if all eigenvalues $\tilde{\lambda}_j$ are equal (in which case the log-likelihood term overall is merely an LAP). Thus, we can see that the variance in the eigenvalues is likely to have some effect as we depart from a pure LAP setting to a more *severe* QAP setting. This variance in eigenvalue spectrum can give us some indication about the convergence of the iterative procedure.

We next minimizing the bound on the right hand size over Q and $\tilde{Q}$ which is written more succinctly as follows:

$$\min_{Q} \min_{\tilde{Q}} \sum_{i=1}^{N} \sum_{i'=1}^{N} \sum_{j=1}^{J} \frac{[P^j]_{i,i'}}{\delta^j [Q]_{j,i} + (1-\delta^j)[\tilde{Q}]_{j,i'}}$$

where we have defined each matrix P^j element-wise using the formula at the current setting of A_t

$$[P^j]_{i,i'} = [A_t]_{i,i'} \tilde{\lambda}^j \left(\sum_{m=1}^{T} \alpha_m^j \kappa(\gamma_{t,i}, \gamma_{m,\hat{p}_m(i')}) \right)^2 .$$

This is still not directly solvable as is. Therefore we consider another variational bounding step (which leads to more iterations) by applying Jensen on the convex function $f(x) = 1/x$ (this is true only when x is non-negative which is the case here). This produces the following inequality:

$$\sum_{i=1}^{N} \sum_{i'=1}^{N} \sum_{j=1}^{J} \frac{[P^j]_{i,i'}}{\delta^j [Q]_{j,i} + (1-\delta^j)[\tilde{Q}]_{j,i'}} \leq \sum_{i=1}^{N} \sum_{i'=1}^{N} \sum_{j=1}^{J} \delta^j \frac{[P^j]_{i,i'}}{[Q]_{j,i}} + (1-\delta^j) \frac{[P^j]_{i,i'}}{[\tilde{Q}]_{j,i'}}$$

Clearly, once we have invoked the second application of Jensen's inequality on this function, we get an easy update rule for Q by taking derivatives and setting to zero. In addition, we introduce the Lagrangian constraint that enforces the summation to unity $\sum_i [Q]_{j,i} = 1$. Ultimately, we obtain this update rule:

$$[Q]_{j,i} = \frac{\sum_{i'} \sqrt{[P^j]_{i,i'}}}{\sum_{i,i'} \sqrt{[P^j]_{i,i'}}}.$$

Similarly, $\tilde{Q}$ is updated as follows:

$$[\tilde{Q}]_{j,i'} = \frac{\sum_{i} \sqrt{[P^j]_{i,i'}}}{\sum_{i,i'} \sqrt{[P^j]_{i,i'}}}.$$

The remaining update rule for the δ^j values is then given as follows:

$$\min_{\boldsymbol{\delta}} \sum_{i=1}^{N} \sum_{i'=1}^{N} \sum_{j=1}^{J} \frac{[P^j]_{i,i'}}{\delta^j [Q]_{j,i} + (1-\delta^j)[\tilde{Q}]_{j,i'}}$$

The terms for each single δ^j are independent and yield the following:

$$\min_{\delta^j} \sum_{i=1}^{N} \sum_{i'=1}^{N} \frac{[P^j]_{i,i'}}{\delta^j [Q]_{j,i} + (1-\delta^j)[\tilde{Q}]_{j,i'}}$$

One straightforward manner to minimize the above extremely simple cost over a scalar $\delta^j \in [0,1]$ is to use brute force techniques or bisection/Brent's search.

Thus, we can iterate updates of Q, $\tilde{Q}$, and the $\boldsymbol{\delta}$ with updates of A_t to iteratively minimize the upper bound on $C(A_t)$ and maximize likelihood. Updating A_t is straightforward via a Kuhn Munkres algorithm (or faster heuristic algorithms such as QuickMatch [10]) on the terms in the square bracket multiplying the entries of the A_t matrix (in other words, iterate a linear assignment problem, LAP). Convergence of this iterative scheme is reasonable and improves the likelihood as we update A_t. But, it may have local minima[3]. We are working on even tighter bounds that seem promising and should further improve convergence and alleviate the local minima problem. Once the iterative scheme converges for a given bag Φ_t, we obtain the A_t matrix which directly gives the permutation configuration p_t.

We continue updating the p_t for each bag in our data set while also updating the mean and the covariance (or, equivalently, the eigenvalues, eigenvectors and eigenfunctions for kernel PCA). This iteratively maximizes the log-likelihood (and minimizes the volume of the data) until we reach a local maximum and converge to a final ordering of our dataset of bags $\{\hat{p}_t \otimes \Phi_t\}_{t=1}^{T}$.

5 Implementation Details

We now discuss some particular implementation details of applying the method in practice. First, we are not bound to assuming that there must be exactly N objects in each bag. Assume we are given $t = 1 \ldots T$ bags with a variable number N_t of objects in each bag. We first pick a constant N (typically $N = \max_t N_t$) and then randomly replicate (or sample without replacement for small N) the objects in each bag such that each bag has N objects. Another consideration is that we generally hold the permutation of one bag fixed since permutations are relative. Therefore, the permutation p_1 for bag Φ_1 is locked (i.e. for a permutation matrix we would set $A_1 = I$) and only the remaining permutations need to be optimized. We then iterate through the data randomly updating each p_t at a time from the permutations $p_2, \ldots, p_T$. We first start by using the mean estimator (LAP) and update its estimate for each p_t until it longer reduces the volume (as measured by the regularized product of kPCA's eigenvalues). We then iterate the update rule for the covariance QAP estimator until it no longer reduces volume. Finally, once converged, we perform kernel PCA on the sorted bags with the final setting of $p_2, \ldots, p_T$.

[3] This is not surprising since QAP is NP-Complete.

6 Experiments

In a preliminary experiment, we obtained a dataset of $T = 100$ digits of 9's and 3's as shown in Figure 2(a). Each digit is actually a bag or a set of $N = 70$ total (x, y) coordinates which form our $\gamma_{t,n} \in \mathbb{R}^2$. We computed the optimal permutations p_t for each digit using the minimum volume criterion (i.e. maximum likelihood with the anisotropic Gaussian case). Figure 2(b) shows the eigenvalue spectrum for PCA before ordering (i.e. assuming the given pseudo-random ordering in the raw input dataset) as well as the eigenvalue spectrum after optimizing the ordering. Note that lower eigenvalues indicate a smaller subspace and that there are few true dimensions of variability in the data once we sort the bags.

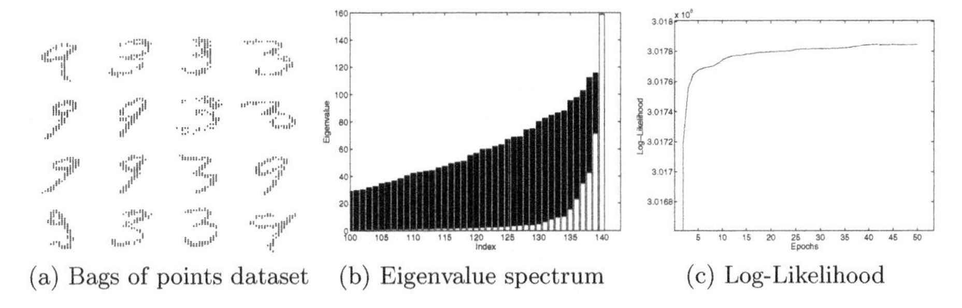

(a) Bags of points dataset (b) Eigenvalue spectrum (c) Log-Likelihood

Fig. 2. Ordering figits as bags of permutable point-clouds prior to PCA. In (a) we see a sample of the original training set of 100 digits while in (b) we see the original PCA eigenvalue spectrum (darker bars) with the initial pseudo-random ordering in the data. In (b) we see the eigenvalue spectrum (lighter bars) after optimizing the ordering to minimize the volume of the subspace (or maximize likelihood under an anisotropic Gaussian). In (c), note the increasing log-likelihood as we optimize each $\hat{p}_t$.

To visualize the resulting orderings, we computed linear interpolations between the sorted bags for different pairs of digits in the input dataset. Figure 3 depicts the morphing as we mix the coordinates of each dot in each digit with another. Note in (a), these 'bags of coordinates' are unordered. Therefore, blending their coordinates results in a meaningless cloud of points during the transition. However, in (b), we note that the points in each bag or cloud are corresponded and ordered so morphing or linearly interpolating their coordinates for two different digits results in a meaningful smooth movement and bending of the digit. Note that in (b) morphs from 3 to another 3, 9 to another 9 or a 3 to a 9 maintain meaningful structure at the half-way point as we blend between one digit and another. This indicates a more meaningful ordering has emerged unlike the initial random one which, when blending between two digit shapes, always generates a random cloud of (x, y) coordinates (see Figure 3(a)). For this dataset, results were similar for the mean vs. covariance estimator as well as linear vs. quadratic choices for the base kernel $\kappa(.,.)$.

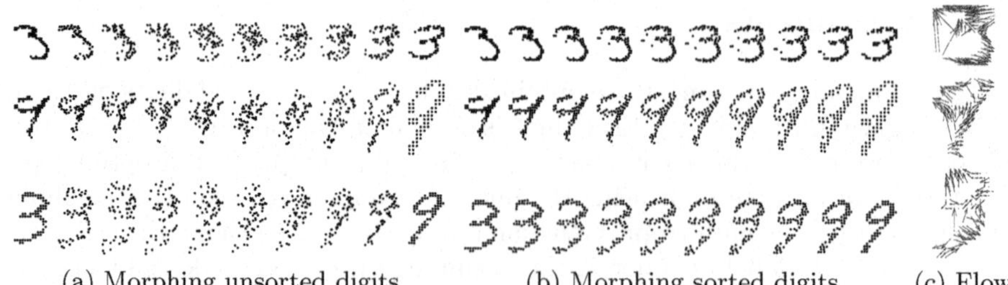

(a) Morphing unsorted digits (b) Morphing sorted digits (c) Flow

Fig. 3. Linear interpolation from left to right (morphing) of the point-clouds with and without sorting. In (a) we see the linear morphing between unordered point clouds which results in poor intermediate morphs that are not meaningful. Meanwhile in (b) where we have recovered good orderings p_t for each digit by minimizing the Gaussian's volume, we note that the digits preserve the correspondence between different parts and induce a smooth and natural morph between the two initial digit configurations. In (c) we show the two digits with arrows indicating the flow or correspondence.

7 Conclusions

We have proposed an algorithm for finding orderings or sortings of multiple sets of objects. These sets or bags need not contain scalars or vectors but rather contain N arbitrary objects. Interacting with these objects is done solely via kernel functions on pairs of them leading to a general notion of sorting in Hilbert space. The ordering or sorting we propose is such that we form a low-dimensional kernel PCA approximation with as few eigenfunctions as possible to reconstruct the manifold on which these bags exist. This is done by finding the permutations of the bags such that we move them towards a common mean in Hilbert space or a low-volume Gaussian configuration in Hilbert space. In this article, this criterion suggested two maximum likelihood objective functions: one which is a linear assignment problem and the other a quadratic assignment problem. Both can be iteratively minimized by using a Kuhn Munkres algorithm along with variational bounding. This permits us to sort or order sets in a general way in Hilbert space using kernel methods and to ultimately obtain a compact representation of the data. We are currently investigating ambitious applications of the method with various kernels and additional results available at:

`http://www.cs.columbia.edu/~jebara/bags/`

In future work, we plan on investigating discriminative variations of the sorting/ordering problem to build classifiers based on support vector machines or kernelized Fisher discriminants that sort data prior to classification (see [4] which elaborates a quadratic cost function for the Fisher discriminant).

Acknowledgments. Thanks to R. Dovgard, R. Kondor and the reviewers for suggestions. T. Jebara is supported in part by NSF grants CCR-0312690 and IIS-0347499.

References

1. Ian L. Dryden and Kanti V. Mardia. *Statistical Shape Analysis.* John Wiley and Sons, 1998.
2. S. Gold, C.P. Lu, A. Rangarajan, S. Pappu, and E. Mjolsness. New algorithms for 2D and 3D point matching: Pose estimation and correspondence. In *NIPS 7*, 1995.
3. A.V. Goldberg and R. Kennedy. An efficient cost scaling algorithm for the assignment problem. *Mathematical Programming*, 71(2):153–178, 1995.
4. T. Jebara. Convex invariance learning. In *9th International Workshop on Artificial Intelligence and Statistics*, 2003.
5. T. Jebara. Images as bags of pixels. In *International Conference on Computer Vision*, 2003.
6. S. Kirshner, S. Parise, and P. Smyth. Unsupervised learning with permuted data. In *Machine Learning: Tenth International Conference, ICML*, 2003.
7. R. Kondor and T. Jebara. A kernel between sets of vectors. In *Machine Learning: Tenth International Conference, ICML*, 2003.
8. J. Kosowsky and A. Yuille. The invisible hand algorithm: Solving the assignment problem with statistical physics. *Neural Networks*, 7:477–490, 1994.
9. Y. Li, P. M. Pardalos, K. G. Ramakrishnan, and M. G. C. Resende. Lower bounds for the quadratic assignment problem. *Annals of Operations Research*, 50:387–411, 1994.
10. J.B. Orlin and Y. Lee. Quickmatch: A very fast algorithm for the assignment problem. Technical Report WP# 3547-93, Sloan School of Management, Massachusetts Institute of Technology, March 1993.
11. Bernhard Schölkopf and Alexander J. Smola. *Learning with Kernels: Support Vector Machines, Regularization, Optimization and Beyond.* MIT Press, 2001.
12. Bernhard Schölkopf, Alexander J. Smola, and K.-R. Müller. Nonlinear principal component analysis as a kernel eigenvalue problem. *Neural Computation*, 10:1299–1319, 1998.
13. P. Y. Simard, Y. LeCun, J. S. Denker, and B. Victorri. Transformation invariance in pattern recognition – tangent distance and tangent propagation. *International Journal of Imaging Systems and Technology*, 11(3), 2000.
14. J.B. Tenenbaum and W.T. Freeman. Separating style and content with bilinear models. *Neural Computation*, 12(6), 1999.

Regularization and Semi-supervised Learning on Large Graphs

Mikhail Belkin, Irina Matveeva, and Partha Niyogi

The University of Chicago, Department of Computer Science
{misha, matveeva, niyogi}@cs.uchicago.edu

Abstract. We consider the problem of labeling a partially labeled graph. This setting may arise in a number of situations from survey sampling to information retrieval to pattern recognition in manifold settings. It is also of potential practical importance, when the data is abundant, but labeling is expensive or requires human assistance.
Our approach develops a framework for regularization on such graphs. The algorithms are very simple and involve solving a single, usually sparse, system of linear equations. Using the notion of algorithmic stability, we derive bounds on the generalization error and relate it to structural invariants of the graph. Some experimental results testing the performance of the regularization algorithm and the usefulness of the generalization bound are presented.

1 Introduction

In pattern recognition problems, there is a probability distribution P according to which labeled and possibly unlabeled examples are drawn and presented to a learner. This P is usually far from uniform and therefore might have some non-trivial geometric structure. We are interested in the design and analysis of learning algorithms that exploit this geometric structure. For example, P may have support on or close to a manifold. In a discrete setting, it may have support on a graph. In this paper we consider the problem of predicting the labels on vertices of a partially labeled graph. Our goal is to design algorithms that are adapted to the structure of the graph. Our analysis shows that the generalization ability of such algorithms is controlled by geometric invariants of the graph.

Consider a weighted graph $G = (V, E)$ where $V = \{\mathbf{x}_1, \ldots, \mathbf{x}_n\}$ is the vertex set and E is the edge set. Associated with each edge $e_{ij} \in E$ is a weight W_{ij}. If there is no edge present between $\mathbf{x}_i$ and $\mathbf{x}_j$, $W_{ij} = 0$. Imagine a situation where a subset of these vertices are labeled with values $y_i \in \mathbb{R}$. We wish to predict the values of the rest of the vertices. In doing so, we would like to exploit the structure of the graph. In particular, in our approach we will assume that the weights are indications of the affinity of nodes with respect to each other and consequently are related to the potential similarity of the y values these nodes are likely to have. Ultimately we propose an algorithm for regularization on graphs.

J. Shawe-Taylor and Y. Singer (Eds.): COLT 2004, LNAI 3120, pp. 624–638, 2004.

This general problem arises in a number of different settings. For example, in survey sampling, one has a database of individuals along with their preference profiles that determines a graph structure based on similarity of preferences. One wishes to estimate a survey variable (e.g. hours of TV watched, amount of cheese consumed, etc.). Rather than survey the entire set of individuals every time, which might be impractical, one may sample a subset of the individuals and then attempt to infer the survey variable for the rest of the individuals. In Internet and information retrieval applications, one is often in possession of a database of objects that have a natural graph structure (or more generally affinity matrix). One may wish to categorize the objects into various classes but only a few (object, class) pairs may be obtained by access to a supervised oracle. In the Finite Element Method for solving PDEs, one sometimes evaluates the solution at some of the points of the finite element mesh and one needs to estimate the value of the solution at all other points. A final example arises when data is obtained by sampling an underlying manifold embedded in a high dimensional space. In recent approaches to dimensionality reduction, clustering and classification in this setting, a graph approximation to the underlying manifold is computed. Semi-supervised learning in this manifold setting reduces to a partially labeled classification problem of the graph. This last example is an instantiation of transductive learning where other approaches include the Naive Bayes for text classification in [12], transductive SVM [15,9], the graph mincut approach in [2], and the random walk on the adjacency graph in [14]. We also note the closely related work [11], which uses kernels and in particular diffusion kernels on graphs for classification.

In the manifold setting the graph is easily seen to be an empirical object. It is worthwhile to note that in all applications of interest, even those unrelated to the manifold setting, the graph reflects pairwise relationships on the data, and hence is an empirical object whenever the data consists of random samples.

We consider this problem in some generality and introduce a framework for regularization on graphs. Two algorithms are derived within this framework. The resulting optima have simple analytical expressions. If the graph is sparse, the algorithms are fast and, in particular, do not require the computation of multiple eigenvectors as is common in many spectral methods (including our previous approach [1]). Another advantage of the current framework is that it is possible to provide theoretical guarantees for generalization error. Using techniques from algorithmic stability we show that generalization error is bounded in terms of the smallest nontrivial eigenvalue (Fiedler number) of the graph. Interestingly, it suggests that generalization performance depends on the geometry of the graph rather than on its size. Finally some experimental evaluation is conducted suggesting that this approach to partially labeled classification is competitive.

Several groups of researchers have been investigating related ideas. In particular, [13] also proposed algorithms for graph regularization. In [17] the authors propose the Label Propagation algorithm for semi-supervised learning, which is similar to our Interpolated Regularization when $S = L$. In [16] a somewhat different regularizer together with the normalized Laplacian is used for semi-supervised learning. The ideas of spectral clustering motivated the authors of [4] to introduce Cluster Kernels for semi-supervised learning. The authors suggest explicitly manipulating eigenvalues of the kernel matrix. We also note closely related work on metric labeling [10].

2 Regression on Graphs

2.1 Regularization and Regression on Graphs

To approximate a function on a graph G, with the weight matrix W_{ij} we need a notion of a "good" function. One way to think about such a function is that is that it does not make too many "jumps". We formalize that notion (see also our earlier paper [1]), by the smoothness functional

$$\mathcal{S}(f) = \sum_{i \sim j} W_{ij}(f_i - f_j)^2$$

where the sum is taken over the adjacent vertices of G. For "good" functions f the functional $\mathcal{S}$ takes small values.

It is important to observe that

$$\sum_{i \sim j} W_{ij}(f_i - f_j)^2 = \mathbf{f}^T L \mathbf{f}$$

where L is the Laplacian $L = D - W$, $D = \mathrm{diag}(\sum_i W_{1i}, \dots, \sum_i W_{ni})$. This is a basic identity in the spectral graph theory and provides some intuition for the remarkable properties of the graph Laplacian L.

Other smoothness matrices, such as L^p, $p \in \mathbb{N}$, $\exp(-tL)$, $t \in \mathbb{R}$ are also possible. In particular, L^2 often seems to work well in practice.

2.2 Algorithms for Regression on Graphs

Let $G = (V, E)$ be a graph with n vertices and the weight matrix W_{ij}. For the purposes of this paper we will assume that G is connected and that the vertices of the graph are numbered. We would like to regress a function $f : V \to \mathbb{R}$. f is defined on vertices of G, however we have only partial information, say for the first k vertices. That is $f(\mathbf{x}_i) = y_i$, $1 \leq i \leq k$. The labels can potentially be noisy. We also allow data points to have multiplicities, i.e. each vertex of the graph may appear more than once with same or different y value.

We precondition the data by mean subtracting first. That is we take

$$\tilde{\mathbf{y}} = (y_1 - \bar{y}, \dots, y_k - \bar{y})$$

where $\bar{y} = \frac{1}{k} \sum y_i$. This is needed for stability of the algorithms as will be seen in the theoretical discussion.

Algorithm 1: Tikhonov regularization (parameter $\gamma \in \mathbb{R}$). The objective is to minimize the square loss function plus the smoothness penalty.

$$\tilde{\mathbf{f}} = \underset{\substack{\mathbf{f}=(f_1,\ldots,f_n) \\ \sum f_i = 0}}{\operatorname{argmin}} \frac{1}{k} \sum_i (f_i - \tilde{y}_i)^2 + \gamma \mathbf{f}^t S \mathbf{f}^t$$

S here is a smoothness matrix, e.g. $S = L$ or $S = L^p$, $p \in \mathbb{N}$. The condition $\sum f_i = 0$ is needed to make the algorithm stable. It can be seen by following the proof of Theorem 1 that necessary stability and the corresponding generalization bound cannot be obtained unless the regularization problem is constrained to functions with mean 0.

Without the loss of generality we can assume that the first l points on the graph are labeled. l might be different from the number of sample points k, since we allow vertices to have different labels (or the same label several times).

The solution to the quadratic problem above is not hard to obtain by standard linear algebra considerations. If we denote by $\mathbf{1} = (1, 1, \ldots, 1)$ the vector of all ones, the solution can be given in the form

$$\tilde{\mathbf{f}} = (k\gamma S + I_k)^{-1}(\tilde{\mathbf{y}} + \mu \mathbf{1})$$

Here $\tilde{\mathbf{y}}$ is the n-vector $\mathbf{y} = (\sum_i y_{1i}, \sum_i y_{2i}, \ldots, \sum_i y_{mi}, 0, \ldots, 0)$, where we sum the labels corresponding to the same vertex on the graph.

I_k is a diagonal matrix of multiplicities

$$I_k = diag\,(n_1, n_2, \ldots, n_l, 0, \ldots, 0)$$

where n_i is the number of occurrences of vertex i among the labeled point in the sample. μ is chosen so that the resulting vector $\mathbf{f}$ is orthogonal to $\mathbf{1}$. Denote by $s(\mathbf{f})$ the functional

$$s : \mathbf{f} \to \sum_i f_i$$

Since s is linear, we obtain $0 = s(\tilde{\mathbf{f}}) = s\left((k\gamma S + I_k)^{-1}\tilde{\mathbf{y}}\right) + s\left((k\gamma S + I_k)^{-1}\mathbf{1}\right)$. Therefore we can write

$$\mu = -\frac{s\left((k\gamma S + I_k)^{-1}\tilde{\mathbf{y}}\right)}{s\left((k\gamma S + I_k)^{-1}\mathbf{1}\right)}$$

Note that dropping the condition $\mathbf{f} \perp \mathbf{1}$ is equivalent to putting $\mu = 0$.

Algorithm 2: Interpolated Regularization (no parameters).
Here we assume that the values $y_1, \ldots, y_k$ have no noise. Thus the optimization problem is to find a function of maximum smoothness satisfying $f(\mathbf{x}_i) = \tilde{y}_i$, $1 \le i \le k$:

$$\tilde{\mathbf{f}} = \underset{\substack{\mathbf{f}=(\tilde{y}_1,\ldots,\tilde{y}_k,f_{k+1},\ldots,f_n) \\ \sum f_i = 0}}{\operatorname{argmin}} \mathbf{f}^t S \mathbf{f}$$

As before S is a smoothness matrix, e.g. L or L^2. However, here we are not allowing multiple vertices in the sample. We partition S as

$$S = \begin{pmatrix} S_1 & S_2 \\ S_2^T & S_3 \end{pmatrix}$$

where S_1 is a $k \times k$ matrix, S_2 is $k \times n-k$ and S_3 is $(n-k) \times (n-k)$. Let $\tilde{f}$ be the values of f, where the function is unknown, $\tilde{f} = (f_{k+1}, \dots, f_n)$.

Straightforward linear algebra yields the solution:

$$\tilde{f} = S_3^{-1} S_2^T ((\tilde{y_1}, \dots, \tilde{y_k})^T + \mu \mathbf{1})$$

$$\mu = -\frac{s\,(S_3^{-1}\, S_2^T\, \tilde{\mathbf{y}})}{s\,(S_3^{-1}\, S_2^T\, \mathbf{1})}$$

The regression formula is very simple and has no free parameters. However, the quality of the results depends on whether S_3 is well conditioned.

It can be shown that Interpolated Regularization is the limit case of Tikhonov regularization when γ tends to 0. That is, given a function f, and denoting by $\mathcal{R}eg_\gamma$ and $\mathcal{R}eg_{int}$, Tikhonov regularization and Interpolated regularization, respectively, we have

$$\lim_{\gamma \to 0} \mathcal{R}eg_\gamma(f) = \mathcal{R}eg_{int}(f)$$

That correspondence suggests using the condition $f \perp \mathbf{1}$ for interpolated regularization as well, even though no stability-based bounds are available in that case.

It is interesting to note that this condition, imposed for purely theoretical reasons, seems similar to class mass normalization step in [17].

3 Theoretical Analysis

In this section we investigate some theoretical guarantees for the generalization error of regularization on graphs. We use the notion of algorithmic stability, first introduced by Devroye and Wagner in [6] and later used by Bousquet and Elisseeff in [3] to prove generalization bounds for regularization networks.

The goal of a learning algorithm is to learn a function on some space V from examples. Given a set of examples T the learning algorithm produces a function $f_T : V \to \mathbb{R}$. Therefore a learning rule is a map from data sets into functions on V. We will be interested in the case where V is a graph.

The empirical risk $R_k(f)$ (with the square loss function) is a measure of how well we do on the training set:

$$R_k(f) = \frac{1}{k} \sum_{1}^{k} (f(\mathbf{x}_i) - y_i)^2$$

The generalization error $R(f)$ is the expectation of how well we do on all points, labeled or unlabeled.

$$R(f) = E_\mu \left(f(\mathbf{x}) - y(\mathbf{x})\right)^2$$

where the expectation is taken over an underlying distribution μ on $V \times \mathbb{R}$ according to which the labeled examples are drawn.

As before denote the smallest nontrivial eigenvalue of the smoothness matrix S by λ_1. If S is the Laplacian of the graph, this value,first introduced by Fiedler in [7] as algebraic connectivity and is sometimes known as the Fiedler constant, plays a key role in spectral graph theory. One interpretation of λ_1 is that it gives an estimate of how well V can be partitioned. We expect λ_1 to be relatively large, say $\lambda_1 > O\left(\frac{1}{n^r}\right)$, $0 \leq r \ll 1$. For example for an n-dimensional hypercube $\lambda_1 = 2$. If λ_1 is very small, a sensible possibility would be to cut the graph in two, using the eigenvector corresponding to λ_1 and proceed with regularization separately for the two parts.

The theorem below states that as long as k is large and the values of the solution to the regularization problem are bounded, we get good generalization results. We note that the constant K can be bounded using the properties of the graph. See the propositions below for the details. We did not make these estimates a part of the Theorem 1 as it would make the formulas even more cumbersome.

Theorem 1 (Generalization Performance of Graph Regularization). *Let γ be the regularization parameter, T be a set of $k \geq 4$ vertices $\mathbf{x}_1, \ldots, \mathbf{x}_k$, where each vertex occurs no more than t times, together with values $y_1, \ldots, y_k$, $|y_i| \leq M$. Let f_T be the regularization solution using the smoothness functional S with the second smallest eigenvalue λ_1. Assuming that $\forall \mathbf{x} |f_T(\mathbf{x})| \leq K$ we have with probability $1 - \delta$ (conditional on the multiplicity being no greater than t):*

$$|R_k(f_T) - R(f_T)| \leq \beta + \sqrt{\frac{2\log(2/\delta)}{k}} \left(k\beta + (K+M)^2\right)$$

where

$$\beta = \frac{3M\sqrt{tk}}{(k\gamma\lambda_1 - t)^2} + \frac{4M}{k\gamma\lambda_1 - t}$$

Proof. The theorem is obtained by rewriting the formula in the Theorem 4 in terms of k and then applying the Theorem 5.

We see that as usual in the estimates of the generalization error it decreases at a rate $\frac{1}{\sqrt{k}}$. It is important to note that the estimate is nearly independent of the total number of vertices n in the graph. We say "nearly" since the probability of having multiple points increases as k becomes close to n and since the value of λ_1 may (or may not) implicitly depend on the number of vertices.

The only thing that is missing is an estimate for K. Below we give two such estimates, one for the case of general S and the other, possibly sharper, when the smoothness matrix is the Laplacian $S = L$.

Proposition 1. *With λ_1, M and γ as above we have the following inequality:*

$$\|f\|_\infty \leq \frac{M}{\sqrt{\lambda_1 \gamma}}$$

Proof. Let's first denote the quantity we are trying to minimize by $P(\mathbf{f})$:

$$P(\mathbf{f}) = \frac{1}{k} \sum_i (f_i - y_i)^2 + \gamma \mathbf{f}^t L \mathbf{f}^t$$

The first observation we make is that when $\mathbf{f} = 0$, $P(\mathbf{f}) = \frac{1}{k} \sum_i y_i^2 \leq M^2$. Thus, if $\tilde{\mathbf{f}}$ minimizes $P(\mathbf{f})$, we have $0 \leq \gamma \tilde{\mathbf{f}}^t L \tilde{\mathbf{f}} \leq M^2$. Recall that $f \in H$, where H is the linear space of vectors with mean 0 and that the smallest eigenvalue of S restricted to H is λ_1. Therefore, recalling that $\|f\|_2 \geq \|f\|_\infty$, we obtain

$$\tilde{\mathbf{f}}^t L \tilde{\mathbf{f}} \geq \lambda_1 \|f\|^2 \geq \lambda_1 \|f\|_\infty^2$$

Thus

$$\|f\|_\infty \leq \sqrt{\frac{\tilde{\mathbf{f}}^t L \tilde{\mathbf{f}}}{\lambda_1}} \leq \frac{M}{\sqrt{\lambda_1 \gamma}}$$

A different inequality can be obtained when $S = L$. Note the the diameter of the graph is typically far smaller than the number of vertices. For example, when G is a n-cube, the number of vertices is 2^n, while the diameter is n.

Proposition 2. *Let $W = \min_{i \sim j} w_{ij}$ be the smallest nonzero weight of the graph G. Assume G is connected. Let D be the unweighted diameter of the graph, i.e. the maximum length of the shortest path between two points on the graph. Then the maximum entry K of the solution to the γ-regularization problem with y's bounded by M satisfies the following inequality:*

$$K \leq M \sqrt{\frac{D}{\gamma W}}$$

A useful special case is

Corollary 2. *If all weights of G are either 0 or 1, then*

$$K \leq M \sqrt{\frac{D}{\gamma}}$$

Proof. Using the same notation as above, we see by substituting the 0 vector that if $\tilde{\mathbf{f}}$ minimizes $P(\mathbf{f})$, then $P\tilde{\mathbf{f}} \leq M^2$.

Let K be the biggest entry of $\mathbf{f}$ with the corresponding vertex v_1. Take any vertex v_2 for which there is a $y \leq 0$. Such vertex exists, since the data has mean 0. Now let $e_1, e_2, \ldots, e_m$ be a sequence of edges on the graph connecting the vertices v_1 and v_2. We put $w_1, \ldots, w_m$ to be the corresponding weights and let $g_0, g_1, \ldots, g_m$ be the values of $\tilde{\mathbf{f}}$ corresponding to the consecutive vertices of that sequence. Now let $h_i = g_i - g_{i-1}$ be the differences of values of $\tilde{\mathbf{f}}$ along that path. We have $\sum_i h_i = g_m - g_0 \geq K$.

Consider the minimum value Z of $\sum_i w_i h_i^2$, given that $\sum_i h_i \geq K$. Using Lagrangian multipliers, we see that the solution is given by $h_i = \frac{\alpha}{w_i}$. We find α using the condition $\sum_i h_i = \alpha \sum_i \frac{1}{w_i} = K$. Therefore

$$\sum_i w_i h_i^2 = \sum_i \frac{\alpha^2}{w_i} = \frac{K^2}{\sum_i \frac{1}{w_i}}$$

Recall that $\frac{m}{\sum_{i=1}^m \frac{1}{w_i}}$ is the harmonic mean of numbers w_i and is therefore greater than $\min(w_1, \dots, w_m)$. Thus we obtain

$$\sum_i w_i h_i^2 \geq \frac{K^2}{m} \min(w_1, \dots, w_m)$$

On the other hand, we see that

$$\tilde{\mathbf{f}}^t L \tilde{\mathbf{f}}^t = \sum_{i<j,\ i\sim j} w_{ij} (\tilde{f}_i - \tilde{f}_j)^2 \geq \sum_i w_i h_i^2$$

since the right-hand sight of the inequality is a partial sum of the terms of the left-hand side.

Hence

$$P(\tilde{\mathbf{f}}) \geq \frac{K^2}{m} \min(w_1, \dots, w_m)$$

Recalling that $P(\tilde{\mathbf{f}}) \leq M^2$, we finally obtain:

$$K \leq \frac{M\sqrt{m}}{\sqrt{\gamma \min(w_1, \dots, w_m)}}$$

Since the path between those points can be chosen arbitrarily, we can chose it so that the length of the path m does not exceed the unweighted diameter D of the graph, which proves the theorem.

In particular, if all weights of G are either zero or one, we have:

$$K \leq \frac{M\sqrt{D}}{\sqrt{\gamma}}$$

assuming, of course, that G is connected.

To prove the main theorem we will use a result of Bousquet and Elisseeff ([3]). First we need the following

Definition 3. *A learning algorithm is said to be uniformly (or algorithmically) β-stable, if for any two training sets T_1, T_2 different at no more than one point,*

$$\forall \mathbf{x} \qquad |f_{T_1}(\mathbf{x}) - f_{T_2}(\mathbf{x})| \leq \beta$$

The stability condition can be thought of as the Lipschitz property for maps from the set of training samples endowed with the Hamming distance into $L^\infty(V)$.

Theorem 4 (Bousquet, Elisseeff). *For a β-stable algorithm $T \to f_T$ we have:*

$$\forall \epsilon > 0 \qquad \mathrm{Prob}\left(|R_k(f_T) - R(f_T)| > \epsilon + \beta\right) \le 2\exp\left(-\frac{k\epsilon^2}{2(k\beta + (K+M))^2}\right)$$

The above theorem[1] together with the appropriate stability of graph regularization algorithm yields Theorem 1. We now proceed to show that regularization on graphs using the smoothness functional S is β-stable, with β as in Theorem 1.

Theorem 5 (Stability of Regularization on Graphs). *For data samples of size $k \ge 4$ with multiplicity of at most t, γ-regularization using the smoothness functional S is a $\left(\frac{3M\sqrt{tk}}{(k\gamma\lambda_1 - t)^2} + \frac{4M}{k\gamma\lambda_1 - t}\right)$-stable algorithm, assuming that the denominator $k\gamma\lambda_1 - t$ is positive.*

Proof. Let H be the hyperplane orthogonal to the vector $\mathbf{1} = (1, \dots, 1)$. We will denote by P_H the operator corresponding to the orthogonal projection on H. Recall that the solution to the regularization problem is given by

$$(k\gamma S + I_k)\mathbf{f} = \tilde{\mathbf{y}} + \mu\mathbf{1}$$

where μ is chosen so that $\mathbf{f}$ belongs to H. We order the graph so that the labeled points come first Then the diagonal matrix I_k can be written as

$$I_k = \mathrm{diag}(n_1, \dots, n_l, 0, \dots, 0)$$

where l is the number of distinct labeled vertices of the graph and $n_i \le t$ is the multiplicity of the ith data point. The spectral radius of I_k is $\max(n_1, \dots, n_l)$ and is therefore no greater than t. Note that $l \le k$.

On the other hand, the smallest eigenvalue of S restricted to H is λ_1. Noticing that H is invariant under S and that for any vector $\mathbf{v}$, $\|P_H(\mathbf{v})\| \le \|\mathbf{v}\|$, since P_H is an orthogonal projection operator, and using the triangle inequality, we immediately obtain that for any $\mathbf{f} \in H$

$$\|P_H(k\gamma S + I_k)\mathbf{f}\| \ge \|P_H k\gamma S\mathbf{f}\| - \|P_H I_k \mathbf{f}\| \ge (\lambda_1\gamma k - t)\|\mathbf{f}\|$$

It follows that the spectral radius of the inverse operator $(P_H(k\gamma S + I_k))^{-1}$ does not exceed $\frac{1}{\lambda_1\gamma k - t}$, when restricted to H (of course, the inverse is not even defined outside of H).

To demonstrate stability we need to show that the output of the algorithm does not change much when we change the input at exactly one data point. Suppose that $\mathbf{y}$, $\mathbf{y}'$ are the data vectors different in at most one entry. We can

[1] Which is, actually, a special case of the original theorem, when the cost function is quadratic.

assume that $\mathbf{y}'$ contains a new point. The other case, when only the multiplicities differ, follows easily from the same considerations. Thus we write:

$$\mathbf{y} = (\sum_i y_{i1}, \sum_i y_{i2}, \dots, \sum_i y_{il}, 0, \dots, 0)$$

$$\mathbf{y}' = (\sum_i y_{i1}, \sum_i y_{i2}, \dots, \sum_i{}' y_{il}, y_{l+1}, 0 \dots, 0)$$

The sums are taken over all values of y corresponding to a node on a graph. The last sum $\sum'$ contains one fewer term than the corresponding sum for $\mathbf{y}$.

Put $\bar{y}$, $\bar{y}'$ to be the averages for $\mathbf{y}, \mathbf{y}'$ respectively. We note that $|\bar{y} - \bar{y}'| \leq \frac{2M}{k}$ and that the entries of $\tilde{\mathbf{y}}, \tilde{\mathbf{y}}'$ differ by no more than that except for the last two entries, which differ by at most $2M + \frac{2M}{k}$. Of course, the last $n - l - 1$ entries of both vectors are equal to zero. Therefore

$$\|\tilde{\mathbf{y}} - \tilde{\mathbf{y}}'\| \leq \sqrt{2\left(2M + \frac{2M}{k}\right)^2 + k\left(\frac{2M}{k}\right)^2} < 4M$$

assuming that $k \geq 4$.

The solutions to the regularization problem $\mathbf{f}$, $\mathbf{f}'$ are given by the equations

$$\mathbf{f} = (P_H(\gamma k S + I_k))^{-1}\, \tilde{\mathbf{y}}$$

$$\mathbf{f}' = (P_H(\gamma k S + I_k'))^{-1} \tilde{\mathbf{y}}'$$

where I_k and I_k' are $n \times n$ diagonal matrices, $I_k = \mathrm{diag}(n_1, n_2, \dots, n_l, 0, \dots, 0)$, $I_k' = \mathrm{diag}(n_1, n_2, \dots, n_l - 1, 1, 0, \dots, 0)$ and the operators are restricted to the hyperplane H.

In order to ascertain stability, we need to estimate the maximum difference between the entries of $\mathbf{f}$ and $\mathbf{f}'$, $\|\mathbf{f} - \mathbf{f}'\|_\infty$. We will use the fact that $\| \;\|_\infty \leq \| \;\|$.

Put $A = P_H(\gamma k S + I_k)$, $B = P_H(\gamma k S + I_k')$ restricted to the hyperplane H. We have

$$\mathbf{f} - \mathbf{f}' = A^{-1}\tilde{\mathbf{y}} - B^{-1}\tilde{\mathbf{y}}' = A^{-1}(\tilde{\mathbf{y}} - \tilde{\mathbf{y}}') + A^{-1}\tilde{\mathbf{y}}' - B^{-1}\tilde{\mathbf{y}}'$$

Therefore

$$\|\mathbf{f} - \mathbf{f}'\|_\infty \leq \|\mathbf{f} - \mathbf{f}'\| \leq \|A^{-1}(\tilde{\mathbf{y}} - \tilde{\mathbf{y}}')\| + \|A^{-1}\tilde{\mathbf{y}}' - B^{-1}\tilde{\mathbf{y}}'\|$$

Since the spectral radius of A^{-1} and B^{-1} is at most $\frac{1}{k\gamma\lambda_1 - t}$ and $\|\tilde{\mathbf{y}} - \tilde{\mathbf{y}}'\| \leq 4M$,

$$\|A^{-1}(\tilde{\mathbf{y}} - \tilde{\mathbf{y}}')\| \leq \frac{4M}{k\gamma\lambda_1 - t}$$

On the other hand, it can be checked that $\|\tilde{\mathbf{y}}'\| \leq 2\sqrt{tk}M$. Indeed, it can be easily seen that the length is maximized, when the multiplicity of each point is exactly t. Noticing that the spectral radius of $P_H(I_k - I_k')$ cannot exceed $\sqrt{2} < 1.5$, we obtain:

$$\|A^{-1}\tilde{\mathbf{y}}' - B^{-1}\tilde{\mathbf{y}}'\| = \|B^{-1}(B - A)A^{-1}\tilde{\mathbf{y}}'\| = \|B^{-1}P_H(I_k - I_k')A^{-1}\tilde{\mathbf{y}}')\| \leq$$

$$\leq \frac{3M\sqrt{tk}}{(k\gamma\lambda_1 - t)^2}$$

Putting it all together

$$\|\mathbf{f} - \mathbf{f}'\|_\infty \leq \frac{3M\sqrt{tk}}{(k\gamma\lambda_1 - t)^2} + \frac{4M}{k\gamma\lambda_1 - t}$$

Of course, we would typically expect $\frac{2M\sqrt{tk}}{(k\gamma\lambda_1 - t)^2} \ll \frac{4M}{k\gamma\lambda_1 - t}$.

However one issue still remains unresolved. Just how likely are we to have multiple points in a sample. Having high multiplicities is quite unlikely as long as $k \ll n$ and the distribution is reasonably close to the uniform.

We make a step in the direction with the following simple combinatorial estimate to show that for the uniform distribution on the graph, data samples, where point occur with high multiplicities (and, in fact, with any multiplicity greater than 1) are unlikely as long as k is relatively small compared to n.

It would be easy to give a similar estimate for a more general distribution, where probability of each point is bounded from below by, say, $\frac{\alpha}{n}$, $0 < \alpha \leq 1$.

Proposition 3. *Assuming the uniform distribution on the graph, the probability P of a sample that contains some data point with multiplicity more than t can be estimated as follows:*

$$P < \frac{2n}{(t+1)!} \left(\frac{k}{n}\right)^{t+1}$$

Proof. Let us first estimate the probability P_l that the lth point will occur more than t times, when choosing k points at random from a dataset of n points with replacement.

$$P_l = \sum_{i=t+1}^{k} \binom{k}{i} \frac{1}{n^i} \left(1 - \frac{1}{n}\right)^{k-i} < \sum_{i=t+1}^{k} \binom{k}{i} \frac{1}{n^i}$$

Writing out the binomial coefficients and using an estimate via the sum of a geometric progression yields:

$$\sum_{i=t+1}^{k} \binom{k}{i} \frac{1}{n^i} < \frac{1}{(t+1)!} \sum_{i=t+1} \left(\frac{k}{n}\right)^i = \frac{1}{(t+1)!} \left(\frac{k}{n}\right)^{t+1} \frac{1}{1 - \frac{k}{n}}$$

Assuming that $k \leq \frac{n}{2}$, we finally obtain

$$P_l < \frac{2}{(t+1)!} \left(\frac{k}{n}\right)^{t+1}$$

Applying the union bound, we see that the probability P of some point being chosen more than t times is bounded as follows:

$$P \leq \sum_{i=1}^{n} P_i < \frac{2n}{(t+1)!} \left(\frac{k}{n}\right)^{t+1}$$

By rewriting k in terms of the probability, we immediately obtain the following

Corollary 6. *With probability at least* $1-\epsilon$ *the multiplicity of the sample does not exceed* t, *given that* $k \leq \sqrt[t+1]{\epsilon \frac{(t+1)!}{2}} \; n^{t-\frac{1}{t+1}}$. *In particular, the multiplicity of the sample is exactly* 1 *with probability at least* $1-\epsilon$, *as long as* $k \leq \sqrt{\epsilon n}$.

4 Experiments and Discussion

An interesting aspect of the generalization bound derived in the previous section is that it depends on certain geometric aspects of the graph. The size of the graph seems relatively unimportant. For example consider the edge graph of a d-dimensional hypercube. Such a graph has $n = 2^d$ vertices. However, the spectral gap is always $\lambda_1 = 2$. Thus the generalization bound on such graphs is *independent* of the size n. For other kinds of graphs, it may be the case that λ_1 depends weakly on n. For such graphs, we may hope for good generalization from a small number of labeled examples relative to the size of the graph.

To evaluate the performance of our regularization algorithms and the insights from our theoretical analysis, we conducted a number of experiments. For example, our experimental results indicate that both Tikhonov and interpolated regularization schemes are generally competitive and often better than other semi-supervised algorithms. However, in this paper we do not discuss these performance comparisons. Instead, we focus on the performance of our algorithm and the usefulness of our bounds.

We present results on two data sets of different sizes.

4.1 Ionosphere Data Set

The Ionosphere data set has 351 examples of two classes in a 34 dimensional space. A graph is made by connecting nearby (6) points to each other. This graph therefore has 351 vertices. We computed the value of the spectral gap of this graph and the corresponding bound using different values of γ for different numbers of labeled points (see table 4). We also computed the training error (see table 2), the test error (see table 1), and the generalization gap (see table 3), to compare it with the value of the bound.

For $\gamma \geq 1$, the value of the bound is reasonable and the difference between the training and the test error is small, as can be seen in the last columns of these tables. However, both the training and the test error for $\gamma = 1$ were high. In regimes where training and test errors were smaller, we find that our bound becomes vacuous.

4.2 Mnist Data Set

We also tested the performance of the regularization algorithm on the MNIST data set. We used a training set with 11,800 examples corresponding to a two class problem with digits 8 and 9.

Table 1. Ionosphere data set. Classification error rates on the test set. #L is the number of labeled examples.

#L	γ=0.001	γ=0.01	γ=0.1	γ=1
10	0.36	0.40	0.38	0.36
20	0.29	0.35	0.38	0.36
40	0.22	0.36	0.37	0.36
60	0.20	0.36	0.36	0.36
80	0.17	0.35	0.39	0.36
100	0.18	0.30	0.36	0.36
200	0.20	0.36	0.35	0.36
300	0.13	0.40	0.36	0.34

Table 2. Ionosphere data set. Classification error rates on the training set. #L is the number of labeled examples.

#L	γ=0.001	γ=0.01	γ=0.1	γ=1
10	0.00	0.09	0.26	0.30
20	0.01	0.22	0.29	0.33
40	0.01	0.25	0.31	0.35
60	0.08	0.28	0.36	0.34
80	0.09	0.30	0.35	0.36
100	0.10	0.31	0.36	0.37
200	0.14	0.35	0.36	0.36
300	0.15	0.35	0.36	0.36

Table 3. Ionosphere data set. Difference between error rates on the test set and on the training set.

#L	γ=0.001	γ=0.01	γ=0.1	γ=1
10	0.36	0.31	0.12	0.06
20	0.28	0.13	0.09	0.03
40	0.21	0.11	0.06	0.01
60	0.12	0.08	0.00	0.02
80	0.08	0.05	0.04	0.00
100	0.08	0.01	0.00	0.01
200	0.06	0.01	0.01	0.00
300	0.02	0.05	0.00	0.02

Table 4. Ionosphere data set, $\lambda_1 = 34.9907$. Generalization bound for confidence $(1-\delta)$, $\delta = 0.1$.

#L	γ=0.001	γ=0.01	γ=0.1	γ=1
10	173.59	32.87	2.92	1.16
20	1641.55	16.38	2.02	0.82
40	2138.57	9.73	1.40	0.58
60	469.07	7.44	1.14	0.47
80	251.67	6.22	0.98	0.41
100	173.02	5.43	0.87	0.36
200	72.72	3.64	0.61	0.26
300	48.97	2.90	0.50	0.21

We computed the training and the test error as well as the bound for this two-class problem. We report the results for the digits 8 and 9, averaged over 10 random splits. Table 5 and table 6 show the error on the test and on the training set, respectively. The regularization algorithm achieves a very low error rate on this data set even with a small number of labeled points. The difference between the training and the test error is shown in table 7 and can be compared to the value of the bound in table 8.

Here again, we observe that the value of the bound is reasonable for $\gamma = 0.1$ and $\gamma = 1$ but the test and training errors for these values of γ are rather high. Note, however, that with 2000 labeled points, the error rate for $\gamma = 0.1$ is very similar to the error rates achieved with smaller values of γ.

Interestingly, the regularization algorithm has very similar gaps between the training and the test error for these two data sets although the number of points in their graphs is very different (351 for the Ionosphere and 11,800 for the MNIST two-class problem). The value of the smallest non-zero eigenvalue for these two graphs is, however, similar. Therefore the similarity in the generalization gaps is consistent with our analysis.

Table 5. Mnist data set, two-class classification problem for digits 8 and 9. Classification error rates on the test set.

#L	γ=0.001	γ=0.01	γ=0.1	γ=1
20	0.04	0.03	0.45	0.50
40	0.02	0.03	0.42	0.40
100	0.02	0.03	0.37	0.40
200	0.02	0.02	0.28	0.41
400	0.02	0.02	0.09	0.46
800	0.02	0.02	0.11	0.44
2000	0.02	0.02	0.03	0.41

Table 6. Mnist data set, two-class classification problem for digits 8 and 9. Classification error rates on the training set.

#L	γ=0.001	γ=0.01	γ=0.1	γ=1
20	0.00	0.01	0.33	0.40
40	0.00	0.01	0.36	0.36
100	0.01	0.02	0.32	0.38
200	0.02	0.02	0.24	0.39
400	0.02	0.02	0.09	0.45
800	0.02	0.02	0.10	0.42
2000	0.02	0.02	0.03	0.40

Table 7. Mnist data set, two-class classification problem for digits 8 and 9. Difference between error rates on the test set and the on the training set.

#L	γ=0.001	γ=0.01	γ=0.1	γ=1
20	0.04	0.02	0.12	0.10
40	0.02	0.02	0.06	0.04
100	0.01	0.01	0.05	0.02
200	0.00	0.00	0.04	0.02
400	0.00	0.00	0.00	0.01
800	0.00	0.00	0.01	0.02
2000	0.00	0.00	0.00	0.01

Table 8. Mnist data set, two-class classification problem for digits 8 and 9, λ_1=35.5460. Generalization bound for confidence (1-δ), δ=0.1.

#L	γ=0.001	γ=0.01	γ=0.1	γ=1
20	1774.43	16.04	2.00	0.81
40	1928.94	9.55	1.39	0.57
100	166.74	5.34	0.87	0.36
200	70.69	3.58	0.61	0.26
400	37.13	2.44	0.43	0.18
800	21.60	1.69	0.30	0.13
2000	11.50	1.04	0.19	0.08

5 Conclusions

In a number of different settings, the need arises to fill in the labels (values) of a partially labeled graph. We have provided a principled framework within which one can meaningfully formulate regularization for regression and classification on such graphs. Two different algorithms were then derived within this framework and have been shown to perform well on different data sets.

The regularization framework offers several advantages.

1. It eliminates the need for computing multiple eigenvectors or complicated graph invariants (min cut, max flow etc.). Unlike some previously proposed algorithms, we obtain a simple closed form solution for the optimal regressor. The problem is reduced to a single, usually sparse, linear system of equations whose solution can be computed efficiently. One of the algorithms proposed (interpolated regularization) is extremely simple with no free parameters.
2. We are able to bound the generalization error and relate it to properties of the underlying graph using arguments from algorithmic stability.
3. If the graph arises from the local connectivity of data obtained from sampling an underlying manifold, then the approach has natural connections to regularization on that manifold.

The experimental results presented here suggest that the approach has empirical promise. Our future plans include more extensive experimental comparisons and investigating potential applications to survey sampling and other areas.

Acknowledgments. We would like to thank Dengyoung Zhou, Olivier Chapelle and Bernard Schoelkopf for numerous conversations and, in particular, for pointing out that Interpolated Regularization is the limit case of Tikhonov regularization, which motivated us to modify the Interpolated Regularization algorithm by introducing $f \perp \mathbf{1}$ condition.

References

1. M. Belkin, P. Niyogi, *Using Manifold Structure for Partially Labeled Classification* Advances in Neural Information Processing Systems 15, MIT Press, 2003,
2. A. Blum, S. Chawla, *Learning from Labeled and Unlabeled Data using Graph Mincuts*, ICML, 2001,
3. Bousquet, O., A. Elisseeff, *Algorithmic Stability and Generalization Performance.* Advances in Neural Information Processing Systems 13, 196-202, MIT Press, 2001,
4. Chapelle, O., J. Weston and B. Scholkopf,*Cluster Kernels for Semi-Supervised Learning*, Advances in Neural Information Processing Systems 15. (Eds.) S. Becker, S. Thrun and K. Obermayer,
5. Fan R. K. Chung, *Spectral Graph Theory,* Regional Conference Series in Mathematics, number 92, 1997
6. L.P. Devroye, T. J. Wagner, *Distribution-free Performance Bounds for Potential Function Rules*, IEEE Trans. on Information Theory, 25(5): 202-207, 1979.
7. M. Fiedler, *Algebraic connectibity of graphs*, Czechoslovak Mathematical Journal, 23(98):298–305, 1973.
8. D. Harville, *Matrix Algebra From A Statisticinan's Perspective*, Springer, 1997.
9. T. Joachims, *Transductive Inference for Text Classification using Support Vector Machines*,Proceedings of ICML-99, pps 200–209, 1999.
10. Jon M. Kleinberg, Éva Tardos, *Approximation algorithms for classification problems with pairwise relationships: metric labeling and Markov random fields*, J. ACM 49(5): 616-639, 2002.
11. I.R. Kondor, J. Lafferty, *Diffusion Kernels on Graphs and Other Discrete Input Spaces*, Proceedings of ICML, 2002.
12. K. Nigam, A.K. McCallum, S. Thrun, T. Mitchell, *Text Classification from Labeled in Unlabeled Data*, Machine Learning 39(2/3), 2000.
13. A. Smola and R. Kondor, *Kernels and Regularization on Graphs*, COLT/KW 2003.
14. Martin Szummer, Tommi Jaakkola, *Partially labeled classification with Markov random walks*, Neural Information Processing Systems (NIPS) 2001, vol 14.,.
15. V. Vapnik, *Statistical Learning Theory*, Wiley, 1998.
16. D. Zhou, O. Bousquet, T.N. Lal, J. Weston and B. Schoelkopf, *Learning with Local and Global Consistency*, Max Planck Institute for Biological Cybernetics Technical Report, June 2003.
17. X. Zhu, J. Lafferty and Z. Ghahramani, *Semi-supervised learning using Gaussian fields and harmonic functions*, Machine Learning: Proceedings of the Twentieth International Conference, 2003.

Perceptron-Like Performance for Intersections of Halfspaces

Adam R. Klivans[1] and Rocco A. Servedio[2]

[1] Harvard University
[2] Columbia University

Given a set of examples on the unit ball in $\mathbf{R}^n$ which are labelled by a halfspace h which has margin ρ (minimum Euclidean distance from any point to the separating hyperplane), the well known Perceptron algorithm finds a separating hyperplane. The Perceptron Convergence Theorem (see e.g. [2]) states that at most $4/\rho^2$ iterations of the Perceptron update rule are required, and thus the algorithm runs in time $O(\frac{n}{\rho^2})$.

Our question is the following: is it possible to give an algorithm which has Perceptron-like performance, i.e. poly$(n, \frac{1}{\rho})$ runtime, for learning the intersection of two halfspaces with margin ρ? We say that a concept c has margin ρ with respect to a set of points $X \subset \mathbf{R}^n$ if

$$\rho = \min\{\|z - y\| : z \in X, y \in \mathbf{R}^n, c(z) \neq c(y)\}/\|X\|.$$

Here $\|X\|$ denotes $\max_{z \in X} \|z\|$. Note that for the case of a single halfspace where all examples lie on the unit ball, this definition of margin is simply the minimum Euclidean distance from any example to the separating hyperplane as stated above.

The desired learning algorithm need not output an intersection of halfspaces as its hypothesis; any reasonable hypothesis class (which gives an online or PAC algorithm with the stated runtime) is fine.

Motivation: This is a natural restricted version of the more general problem of learning an intersection of two arbitrary halfspaces with no condition on the margin, which is a longstanding open question that seems quite hard (for this more general problem no learning algorithm is known which runs in time less than $2^{O(n)}$). Given the ubiquity of margin-based approaches for learning a single halfspace, it is likely that a solution to the proposed problem would be of significant practical as well as theoretical interest. As described below it seems plausible that a solution may be within reach.

Current status: The first work on this question is by Arriaga and Vempala [1] who gave an algorithm that runs in time $n \cdot \text{poly}\left(\frac{1}{\rho}\right) + \left(\frac{1}{\rho}\right)^{\tilde{O}(1/\rho^2)}$, i.e. polynomial in n but exponential in $1/\rho$. Their algorithm randomly projects the examples to a low-dimensional space and uses brute-force search to find a consistent intersection of halfspaces. Recently we gave an algorithm [3] that runs

J. Shawe-Taylor and Y. Singer (Eds.): COLT 2004, LNAI 3120, pp. 639–640, 2004.

in time $n\left(\frac{1}{\rho}\right)^{O(\log(1/\rho))}$, i.e. polynomial in n and quasipolynomial in $\frac{1}{\rho}$. Our algorithm also uses random projection as a first step, but then runs the kernel Perceptron algorithm with the polynomial kernel to find a consistent hypothesis as opposed to using brute-force search. We show that low degree *polynomial threshold functions* can correctly computing intersections of halfspaces with a margin (in a certain technical sense — see [3] for details); this implies that the degree of the polynomial kernel can be taken to be logarithmic in $1/\rho$, which yields our quasipolynomial runtime dependence on ρ. Can this quasipolynomial dependence on the margin ρ be reduced to a polynomial?

References

[1] R. Arriaga and S. Vempala. An algorithmic theory of learning: Robust concepts and random projection. In *Proceedings of the 40th Annual Symposium on Foundations of Computer Science (FOCS)*, pages 616–623, 1999.

[2] N. Cristianini and J. Shawe-Taylor. *An introduction to Support Vector Machines (and other kernel-based learning methods)*. Cambridge University Press, 2000.

[3] A. Klivans and R. Servedio. Learning intersections of halfspaces with a margin. In Proceedings of COLT 2004.

The Optimal PAC Algorithm

Manfred K. Warmuth

UC Santa Cruz

Assume we are trying to learn a concept class C of VC dimension d with respect to an arbitrary distribution. There is PAC sample size bound that holds for any algorithm that always predicts with some consistent concept in the class C (BEHW89): $O(\frac{1}{\epsilon}(d \log \frac{1}{\epsilon} + \log \frac{1}{\epsilon}))$, where ϵ and δ are the accuracy and confidence parameters. Thus after drawing this many examples (consistent with any concept in C), then with probability at least $1 - \delta$, the error of the produced concept is at most ϵ. Here the examples are drawn with respect to an arbitrary but fixed distribution D, and the accuracy is measured with respect to the same distribution. There is also a lower bound that holds for any algorithm (EHKV89): $\Omega(\frac{1}{\epsilon}(d + \log \frac{1}{\delta}))$. It means that at least this many examples are required for any algorithm to achieve error at most ϵ with probability at least $1 - \delta$. The lower bound is realized by distributions on a fixed shattered set of size d.

Conjecture: The one-inclusion graph algorithm of HLW94 always achieves the lower bound. That is after receiving $O(\frac{1}{\epsilon}(d + \log \frac{1}{\epsilon}))$ examples, its error is at most ϵ with probability at least $1 - \delta$.

The one-inclusion graph for a set of $t+1$ unlabeled examples uses the following subset of the $(t+1)$-dimensional hypercube as its vertex set: all bit patterns in $\{0,1\}^{t+1}$ produced by labeling the $t+1$ examples with a concept in C. There is an edge between two patterns if they are adjacent in the hypercube (i.e. Hamming distance one).

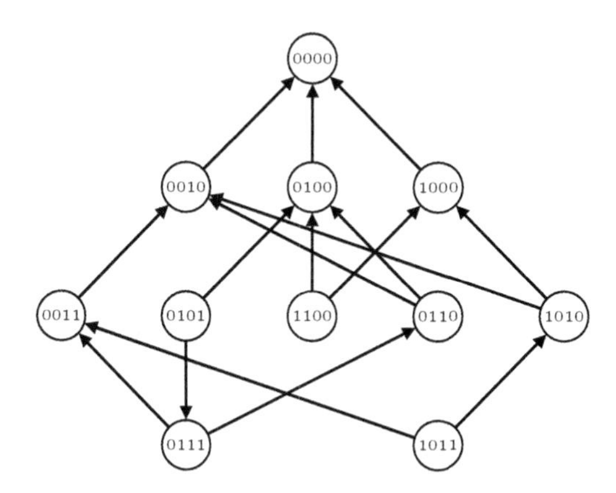

An orientation of a one-inclusion graph is an orientation of its edges so that the maximum out-degree of all the vertices is minimized. In HLW94 it is shown how to do this using a network flow argument. The minimum maximum out-degree can be shown to be at most at most d, the VC dimension of C.

J. Shawe-Taylor and Y. Singer (Eds.): COLT 2004, LNAI 3120, pp. 641–642, 2004.

The one-inclusion graph algorithm is formulated as a prediction algorithm: When given t examples labeled with a concept in C and one more unlabeled example, the algorithm produces a binary prediction on the unlabeled example.[1] How does this algorithm predict? It creates and orients the one-inclusion graph for all $t+1$ examples. If there is a unique extension of the t labeled examples to a labeling of the last example, then the one-inclusion graph algorithm predicts with that labeling. However, if there are two labels possible for the unlabeled example (i.e. the unlabeled example corresponds to an edge), then the algorithm predicts with the label of the bit pattern at the head of the oriented edge.

The expected error[2] of the one-inclusion graph algorithm is at most $\frac{d}{t+1}$ (HLW94), and it has been shown that this bound is within a factor of $1 + o(1)$ of optimal (LLS02). On the other hand, predicting with an arbitrary consistent hypothesis, can lead to an expected error of $\Omega(\frac{d \log n}{t} \log \frac{t}{d})$ (HLW94). So in this open problem we conjecture that the one-inclusion algorithm is also optimal in the PAC model.

For special cases of intersection closed concept classes, the *closure algorithm* has been shown to have the optimum $O(\frac{1}{\epsilon}(d + \log \frac{1}{\delta}))$ bound (AO04). This algorithm is can be seen as an instantiation of the one-inclusion graph algorithm (the closure algorithm predicts with an orientation of the one-inclusion graph with maximum out-degree at most d). There are cases that show that the upper bound of $O(\frac{1}{\epsilon}(d \log \frac{1}{\epsilon} + \log \frac{1}{\delta}))$ that holds for any algorithm that predicts with a consistent hypothesis cannot be improved (e.g. AO04). However all such cases that we are aware of seem to predict with orientations of the one-inclusion graph that have unnecessarily high out-degree.

References

P. Auer and R. Ortner. A new PAC bound for intersection-closed concept classes. Appearing concurrently in this COLT 2004 proceedings.

A. Blumer, A. Ehrenfeucht, D. Haussler, and M. K. Warmuth. Learnability and the Vapnik-Chervonenkis dimension. *J. ACM*, 36(4):929–965, 1989.

A. Ehrenfeucht, D. Haussler, M. Kearns, and L. G. Valiant. A general lower bound on the number of examples needed for learning. *Information and Computation*, 82:247–261, 1989.

D. Haussler, N. Littlestone, and M. K. Warmuth. Predicting $\{0,1\}$ functions on randomly drawn points. *Information and Computation*, 115(2):284–293, 1994. Was in FOCS88, COLT88, and Univ. of California at Santa Cruz TR UCSC-CRL-90-54.

Y. Li, P. M. Long, and A. Srinivasan. The one-inclusion graph algorithm is near optimal for the prediction model of learning. *Transaction on Information Theory*, 47(3):1257–1261, 2002.

---

[1] Prediction algorithms implicitly represent hypotheses. For any fixed set of t labeled examples, the predictions on the next unlabeled example define a hypothesis. However, as for the algorithm discussed here, this hypothesis is typically not in C.

[2] This is the same as the probability of predicting wrong on the unlabeled example.

The Budgeted Multi-armed Bandit Problem

Omid Madani[1], Daniel J. Lizotte[2], and Russell Greiner[2]

[1] Yahoo! Research Labs, 74 N. Pasadena Ave, Pasadena, CA 91101
omid.madani@overture.com
[2] Dept. of Computing Science, University of Alberta, Edmonton, T6J 2E8
{dlizotte|greiner}@cs.ualberta.ca

The following *coins problem* is a version of a multi-armed bandit problem where one has to select from among a set of objects, say classifiers, after an experimentation phase that is constrained by a time or cost budget. The question is how to spend the budget. The problem involves pure exploration only, differentiating it from typical multi-armed bandit problems involving an exploration/exploitation tradeoff [BF85]. It is an abstraction of the following scenarios: choosing from among a set of alternative treatments after a fixed number of clinical trials, determining the best parameter settings for a program given a deadline that only allows a fixed number of runs; or choosing a life partner in the bachelor/bachelorette TV show where time is limited. We are interested in the computational complexity of the coins problem and/or efficient algorithms with approximation guarantees.

1 The Coins Problem

We are given:

- A collection of n independent coins, indexed by the set $\mathcal{I}$, where each coin is specified by a probability density function (prior) over its head probability. The priors of the different coins are independent, and they can be different for different coins.
- A budget b on the total number of coin flips.

We assume the tail and the head outcomes correspond to receiving no reward and a fixed reward (1 unit) respectively. We are allowed a trial/learning period, constrained by the budget, for the sole purpose of experimenting with the coins, *i.e.*, we do not collect rewards in this period. At the end of the period, we are allowed to pick only a single coin for all our future flips (reward collection).

Let the actual head probability of coin i be θ_i. We define the *regret* from picking coin i to be $\theta^* - \theta_i$, where $\theta^* = \max_{j \in \mathcal{I}} \theta_j$. As we have the densities only, we basically seek to make coin flip decisions and a final choice that lead to minimizing our *expected* regret. It is easy to verify that when the budget is 0, the choice of coin that minimizes expected regret is one with maximum expected head probability over all the coins, *i.e.*, $\max_i E(\Theta_i)$, where Θ_i denotes the random variable corresponding to head probability of coin i, and the expectation $E(\Theta_i)$ is taken over the density for coin i.

J. Shawe-Taylor and Y. Singer (Eds.): COLT 2004, LNAI 3120, pp. 643–645, 2004.

A strategy is a prescription of which coin to flip given all the coins' flip outcomes so far. A strategy may be viewed as a finite directed rooted tree, where each node indicates a coin to flip, each edge indicates an outcome (heads or tails), and the leaves indicate the coin to choose [MLG04]. No path length from root to leaf exceeds the budget. Thus the set S of such strategies is finite. Associated with each leaf node j is the (expected) regret r_j, computed using the densities (one for each coin) at that node. Let p_j be the probability of "reaching" leaf j: p_j is the product of the probabilities of coin flip outcomes along the path from root to that leaf. We define the *regret* of a strategy to be the expected regret, where the expectation is taken over the coins' densities and the possible flip outcomes: $Regret(s) = \sum_{j \in \text{Tree Leafs of } s} p_j r_j$. The optimal regret r^* is then the minimum achievable (expected) regret and an *optimal strategy* s^* is one achieving it[1]

$$r^* = \min_{s \in S} Regret(s), \quad s^* = \arg\min_{s \in S} Regret(s). \tag{1}$$

We assume the budget is no larger than a polynomial in n, and that we can represent the densities and update them (when the corresponding coin yields a heads or tails outcome), and compute their expectation efficiently (*e.g.*, the family of beta densities). With these assumptions, the problem is in PSPACE [MLG04].

Open Problem 1. *Is computing the first action of an optimal strategy NP-hard?*

2 Discussion and Related Work

We explore *budgeted learning* in [MLG04,LMG03]. We show that the coins problem is NP-hard under non-identical coin flip costs and non-identical priors, by reduction from the Knapsack problem. We present some evidence that the problem remains difficult even under identical costs. We explore constant-ratio approximability for strategies and algorithms[2]: an algorithm is a constant ratio approximation algorithm if its regret does not go above a constant multiple of the minimum regret. We show that a number of algorithms such as round-robin and greedy cannot be approximation algorithms. In the special case of identical priors (and coin costs), we observe empirically that a simple algorithm we refer to as *biased-robin* beats the other algorithms tested, and furthermore, its regret is very close to the optimal regret on the limited range of problems for which we could compute the optimal. Biased-robin sets $i = 1$, and continues flipping coin i until the outcome is tails, at which time it sets i to $(i \bmod n) + 1$, and repeats until the budget is exhausted. Note that biased-robin doesn't take the budget into account except for stopping! An interesting open problem is then:

Open Problem 2. *Is biased-robin a constant-ratio approximation algorithm, for identical priors and budget of $b = O(n)$?*

---

[1] No randomized strategy has regret lower than the optimal deterministic strategy [MLG04].

[2] An algorithm defines a strategy (for each problem instance) implicitly, by indicating the next coin to flip [MLG04].

References

[BF85] D. Berry and B. Fristedt. *Bandit Problems: Sequential Allocation of Experiments*. Chapman and Hall, New York, NY, 1985.

[LMG03] D. Lizotte, O. Madani, and R. Greiner. Budgeted learning of Naive Bayes classifiers. In *UAI-2003*, 2003.

[MLG04] O. Madani, D. Lizotte, and R. Greiner. Active model selection (submitted). Technical report, University of Alberta and AICML, 2004. http://www.cs.ualberta.ca/~madani/budget.html.

Author Index

Lecture Notes in Artificial Intelligence (LNAI)

Vol. 3120: J. Shawe-Taylor, Y. Singer (Eds.), Learning Theory. X, 648 pages. 2004.

Vol. 3097: D. Basin, M. Rusinowitch (Eds.), Automated Reasoning. XII, 493 pages. 2004.

Vol. 3070: L. Rutkowski, J. Siekmann, R. Tadeusiewicz, L.A. Zadeh (Eds.), Artificial Intelligence and Soft Computing - ICAISC 2004. XXV, 1208 pages. 2004.

Vol. 3068: E. André, L. Dybkj{\}ae r, W. Minker, P. Heisterkamp (Eds.), Affective Dialogue Systems. XII, 324 pages. 2004.

Vol. 3067: M. Dastani, J. Dix, A. El Fallah-Seghrouchni (Eds.), Programming Multi-Agent Systems. X, 221 pages. 2004.

Vol. 3066: S. Tsumoto, R. Słowiński, J. Komorowski, J.W. Grzymala-Busse (Eds.), Rough Sets and Current Trends in Computing. XX, 853 pages. 2004.

Vol. 3065: A. Lomuscio, D. Nute (Eds.), Deontic Logic in Computer Science. X, 275 pages. 2004.

Vol. 3060: A.Y. Tawfik, S.D. Goodwin (Eds.), Advances in Artificial Intelligence. XIII, 582 pages. 2004.

Vol. 3056: H. Dai, R. Srikant, C. Zhang (Eds.), Advances in Knowledge Discovery and Data Mining. XIX, 713 pages. 2004.

Vol. 3055: H. Christiansen, M.-S. Hacid, T. Andreasen, H.L. Larsen (Eds.), Flexible Query Answering Systems. X, 500 pages. 2004.

Vol. 3040: R. Conejo, M. Urretavizcaya, J.-L. Pérez-de-la-Cruz (Eds.), Current Topics in Artificial Intelligence. XIV, 689 pages. 2004.

Vol. 3035: M.A. Wimmer (Ed.), Knowledge Management in Electronic Government. XII, 326 pages. 2004.

Vol. 3034: J. Favela, E. Menasalvas, E. Chávez (Eds.), Advances in Web Intelligence. XIII, 227 pages. 2004.

Vol. 3030: P. Giorgini, B. Henderson-Sellers, M. Winikoff (Eds.), Agent-Oriented Information Systems. XIV, 207 pages. 2004.

Vol. 3029: B. Orchard, C. Yang, M. Ali (Eds.), Innovations in Applied Artificial Intelligence. XXI, 1272 pages. 2004.

Vol. 3025: G.A. Vouros, T. Panayiotopoulos (Eds.), Methods and Applications of Artificial Intelligence. XV, 546 pages. 2004.

Vol. 3012: K. Kurumatani, S.-H. Chen, A. Ohuchi (Eds.), Multi-Agnets for Mass User Support. X, 217 pages. 2004.

Vol. 3010: K.R. Apt, F. Fages, F. Rossi, P. Szeredi, J. Váncza (Eds.), Recent Advances in Constraints. VIII, 285 pages. 2004.

Vol. 2990: J. Leite, A. Omicini, L. Sterling, P. Torroni (Eds.), Declarative Agent Languages and Technologies. XII, 281 pages. 2004.

Vol. 2980: A. Blackwell, K. Marriott, A. Shimojima (Eds.), Diagrammatic Representation and Inference. XV, 448 pages. 2004.

Vol. 2977: G. Di Marzo Serugendo, A. Karageorgos, O.F. Rana, F. Zambonelli (Eds.), Engineering Self-Organising Systems. X, 299 pages. 2004.

Vol. 2972: R. Monroy, G. Arroyo-Figueroa, L.E. Sucar, H. Sossa (Eds.), MICAI 2004: Advances in Artificial Intelligence. XVII, 923 pages. 2004.

Vol. 2961: P. Eklund (Ed.), Concept Lattices. IX, 411 pages. 2004.

Vol. 2953: K. Konrad, Model Generation for Natural Language Interpretation and Analysis. XIII, 166 pages. 2004.

Vol. 2934: G. Lindemann, D. Moldt, M. Paolucci (Eds.), Regulated Agent-Based Social Systems. X, 301 pages. 2004.

Vol. 2930: F. Winkler (Ed.), Automated Deduction in Geometry. VII, 231 pages. 2004.

Vol. 2926: L. van Elst, V. Dignum, A. Abecker (Eds.), Agent-Mediated Knowledge Management. XI, 428 pages. 2004.

Vol. 2923: V. Lifschitz, I. Niemelä (Eds.), Logic Programming and Nonmonotonic Reasoning. IX, 365 pages. 2004.

Vol. 2915: A. Camurri, G. Volpe (Eds.), Gesture-Based Communication in Human-Computer Interaction. XIII, 558 pages. 2004.

Vol. 2913: T.M. Pinkston, V.K. Prasanna (Eds.), High Performance Computing - HiPC 2003. XX, 512 pages. 2003.

Vol. 2903: T.D. Gedeon, L.C.C. Fung (Eds.), AI 2003: Advances in Artificial Intelligence. XVI, 1075 pages. 2003.

Vol. 2902: F.M. Pires, S.P. Abreu (Eds.), Progress in Artificial Intelligence. XV, 504 pages. 2003.

Vol. 2892: F. Dau, The Logic System of Concept Graphs with Negation. XI, 213 pages. 2003.

Vol. 2891: J. Lee, M. Barley (Eds.), Intelligent Agents and Multi-Agent Systems. X, 215 pages. 2003.

Vol. 2882: D. Veit, Matchmaking in Electronic Markets. XV, 180 pages. 2003.

Vol. 2871: N. Zhong, Z.W. Raś, S. Tsumoto, E. Suzuki (Eds.), Foundations of Intelligent Systems. XV, 697 pages. 2003.

Vol. 2854: J. Hoffmann, Utilizing Problem Structure in Planing. XIII, 251 pages. 2003.

Vol. 2843: G. Grieser, Y. Tanaka, A. Yamamoto (Eds.), Discovery Science. XII, 504 pages. 2003.

Vol. 2842: R. Gavaldá, K.P. Jantke, E. Takimoto (Eds.), Algorithmic Learning Theory. XI, 313 pages. 2003.

Vol. 2838: N. Lavrač, D. Gamberger, L. Todorovski, H. Blockeel (Eds.), Knowledge Discovery in Databases: PKDD 2003. XVI, 508 pages. 2003.

Vol. 2837: N. Lavrač, D. Gamberger, L. Todorovski, H. Blockeel (Eds.), Machine Learning: ECML 2003. XVI, 504 pages. 2003.

Vol. 2835: T. Horváth, A. Yamamoto (Eds.), Inductive Logic Programming. X, 401 pages. 2003.

Vol. 2821: A. Günter, R. Kruse, B. Neumann (Eds.), KI 2003: Advances in Artificial Intelligence. XII, 662 pages. 2003.

Vol. 2807: V. Matoušek, P. Mautner (Eds.), Text, Speech and Dialogue. XIII, 426 pages. 2003.

Vol. 2801: W. Banzhaf, J. Ziegler, T. Christaller, P. Dittrich, J.T. Kim (Eds.), Advances in Artificial Life. XVI, 905 pages. 2003.

Vol. 2797: O.R. Zaïane, S.J. Simoff, C. Djeraba (Eds.), Mining Multimedia and Complex Data. XII, 281 pages. 2003.

Vol. 2792: T. Rist, R.S. Aylett, D. Ballin, J. Rickel (Eds.), Intelligent Virtual Agents. XV, 364 pages. 2003.

Vol. 2782: M. Klusch, A. Omicini, S. Ossowski, H. Laamanen (Eds.), Cooperative Information Agents VII. XI, 345 pages. 2003.

Vol. 2780: M. Dojat, E. Keravnou, P. Barahona (Eds.), Artificial Intelligence in Medicine. XIII, 388 pages. 2003.

Vol. 2777: B. Schölkopf, M.K. Warmuth (Eds.), Learning Theory and Kernel Machines. XIV, 746 pages. 2003.

Vol. 2752: G.A. Kaminka, P.U. Lima, R. Rojas (Eds.), RoboCup 2002: Robot Soccer World Cup VI. XVI, 498 pages. 2003.

Vol. 2741: F. Baader (Ed.), Automated Deduction – CADE-19. XII, 503 pages. 2003.

Vol. 2705: S. Renals, G. Grefenstette (Eds.), Text- and Speech-Triggered Information Access. VII, 197 pages. 2003.

Vol. 2703: O.R. Zaïane, J. Srivastava, M. Spiliopoulou, B. Masand (Eds.), WEBKDD 2002 - MiningWeb Data for Discovering Usage Patterns and Profiles. IX, 181 pages. 2003.

Vol. 2700: M.T. Pazienza (Ed.), Extraction in the Web Era. XIII, 163 pages. 2003.

Vol. 2699: M.G. Hinchey, J.L. Rash, W.F. Truszkowski, C.A. Rouff, D.F. Gordon-Spears (Eds.), Formal Approaches to Agent-Based Systems. IX, 297 pages. 2002.

Vol. 2691: V. Mařík, J.P. Müller, M. Pechoucek (Eds.), Multi-Agent Systems and Applications III. XIV, 660 pages. 2003.

Vol. 2684: M.V. Butz, O. Sigaud, P. Gérard (Eds.), Anticipatory Behavior in Adaptive Learning Systems. X, 303 pages. 2003.

Vol. 2671: Y. Xiang, B. Chaib-draa (Eds.), Advances in Artificial Intelligence. XIV, 642 pages. 2003.

Vol. 2663: E. Menasalvas, J. Segovia, P.S. Szczepaniak (Eds.), Advances in Web Intelligence. XII, 350 pages. 2003.

Vol. 2661: P.L. Lanzi, W. Stolzmann, S.W. Wilson (Eds.), Learning Classifier Systems. VII, 231 pages. 2003.

Vol. 2654: U. Schmid, Inductive Synthesis of Functional Programs. XXII, 398 pages. 2003.

Vol. 2650: M.-P. Huget (Ed.), Communications in Multiagent Systems. VIII, 323 pages. 2003.

Vol. 2645: M.A. Wimmer (Ed.), Knowledge Management in Electronic Government. XI, 320 pages. 2003.

Vol. 2639: G. Wang, Q. Liu, Y. Yao, A. Skowron (Eds.), Rough Sets, Fuzzy Sets, Data Mining, and Granular Computing. XVII, 741 pages. 2003.

Vol. 2637: K.-Y. Whang, J. Jeon, K. Shim, J. Srivastava, Advances in Knowledge Discovery and Data Mining. XVIII, 610 pages. 2003.

Vol. 2636: E. Alonso, D. Kudenko, D. Kazakov (Eds.), Adaptive Agents and Multi-Agent Systems. XIV, 323 pages. 2003.

Vol. 2627: B. O'Sullivan (Ed.), Recent Advances in Constraints. X, 201 pages. 2003.

Vol. 2600: S. Mendelson, A.J. Smola (Eds.), Advanced Lectures on Machine Learning. IX, 259 pages. 2003.

Vol. 2592: R. Kowalczyk, J.P. Müller, H. Tianfield, R. Unland (Eds.), Agent Technologies, Infrastructures, Tools, and Applications for E-Services. XVII, 371 pages. 2003.

Vol. 2586: M. Klusch, S. Bergamaschi, P. Edwards, P. Petta (Eds.), Intelligent Information Agents. VI, 275 pages. 2003.

Vol. 2583: S. Matwin, C. Sammut (Eds.), Inductive Logic Programming. X, 351 pages. 2003.

Vol. 2581: J.S. Sichman, F. Bousquet, P. Davidsson (Eds.), Multi-Agent-Based Simulation. X, 195 pages. 2003.

Vol. 2577: P. Petta, R. Tolksdorf, F. Zambonelli (Eds.), Engineering Societies in the Agents World III. X, 285 pages. 2003.

Vol. 2569: D. Karagiannis, U. Reimer (Eds.), Practical Aspects of Knowledge Management. XIII, 648 pages. 2002.

Vol. 2560: S. Goronzy, Robust Adaptation to Non-Native Accents in Automatic Speech Recognition. XI, 144 pages. 2002.

Vol. 2557: B. McKay, J. Slaney (Eds.), AI 2002: Advances in Artificial Intelligence. XV, 730 pages. 2002.

Vol. 2554: M. Beetz, Plan-Based Control of Robotic Agents. XI, 191 pages. 2002.

Vol. 2543: O. Bartenstein, U. Geske, M. Hannebauer, O. Yoshie (Eds.), Web Knowledge Management and Decision Support. X, 307 pages. 2003.

Vol. 2541: T. Barkowsky, Mental Representation and Processing of Geographic Knowledge. X, 174 pages. 2002.

Vol. 2533: N. Cesa-Bianchi, M. Numao, R. Reischuk (Eds.), Algorithmic Learning Theory. XI, 415 pages. 2002.

Vol. 2531: J. Padget, O. Shehory, D. Parkes, N.M. Sadeh, W.E. Walsh (Eds.), Agent-Mediated Electronic Commerce IV. Designing Mechanisms and Systems. XVII, 341 pages. 2002.

Vol. 2527: F.J. Garijo, J.-C. Riquelme, M. Toro (Eds.), Advances in Artificial Intelligence - IBERAMIA 2002. XVIII, 955 pages. 2002.

Vol. 2522: T. Andreasen, A. Motro, H. Christiansen, H.L. Larsen (Eds.), Flexible Query Answering Systems. X, 383 pages. 2002.